The Total Spectrum of Technology

Personal Trainer®

Eliminate Grading Homework!

Instructors consistently cite reading the text and completing graded homework assignments as a key to student success in management accounting; however, finding time to grade homework is difficult. Personal Trainer solves this time problem by allowing professors to assign textbook exercises and problems. Personal Trainer will grade the homework and then post the grade into a full-blown gradebook, all real time! Personal Trainer is an Internet-based homework tutor where students can complete the textbook homework assignments, receive hints, submit their answers and then receive immediate feedback on their answers. Access certificates for WebTutor™ Advantage with Personal Trainer® can be bundled with the textbook or sold separately. For more information, including a demo, visit http://webtutor.swlearning.com.

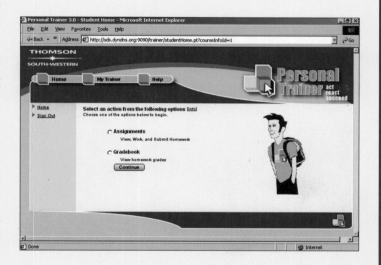

Xtra!

This online resource provides lecture enhancement resources and access to games and quizzes so that students can test their understanding of the content. Packaged FREE with a new text, students receive an online access code to receive Xtra! reinforcement in management accounting!

Management Accounting

Monte R. Swain
PhD, CPA, CMA
Brigham Young University

W. Steve Albrecht
PhD, CPA, CIA, CFE
Brigham Young University

James D. Stice
PhD
Brigham Young University

Earl K. Stice
PhD
Brigham Young University

edition 3

THOMSON

SOUTH-WESTERN

Australia · Canada · Mexico · Singapore · Spain · United Kingdom · United States

Management Accounting, 3e

Monte R. Swain, W. Steve Albrecht, James D. Stice, and Earl K. Stice

VP/Editorial Director:
Jack W. Calhoun

VP/Editor-in-Chief:
George Werthman

Executive Editor:
Sharon Oblinger

Developmental Editor:
Carol Bennett

Marketing Manager:
Heather MacMaster

Senior Production Editor:
Kara ZumBahlen

Media Developmental Editor:
Sally Nieman

Media Production Editor:
Kelly Reid

Manufacturing Coordinator:
Doug Wilke

Production House/Composition:
Litten Editing and Production, Inc. and
GGS Information Services

Printer:
RR Donnelley

Senior Design Project Manager:
Michelle Kunkler

Cover and Internal Designer:
Imbue Design/Kim Torbeck
Cincinnati, OH

Cover Image:
© Farida Zaman/Stock Illustration Source

Photo Researcher:
Stuart Kunkler

For permission to use material from this
text or product, contact us by
Tel (800) 730-2214
Fax (800) 730-2215
http://www.thomsonrights.com

For more information
contact South-Western,
5191 Natorp Boulevard,
Mason, Ohio 45040.
Or you can visit our Internet site at:
http://www.swlearning.com

Monte R. Swain

Dr. Swain received his PhD in managerial accounting and information systems from Michigan State University. His dissertation, which examined the impact of information load on capital budgeting decision processes, was awarded an Institute of Management Accountants Dissertation Grant. At BYU, Dr. Swain has received the Teaching Excellence Award for Management Skills in 1994, 1995, and 1997; the Marriott School of Management Outstanding Teacher in 1999; and was selected as the Deloitte & Touche Research Fellow in 2001. His research area includes the development and use of computer programs that capture and analyze the interaction of human decision processes and computerized information systems. Additionally, he uses the events-driven business solutions to study the incorporation of activity-based costing, the Balanced Scorecard, and the Theory of Constraints in management information systems. He has published numerous papers in leading academic and practitioner journals, sits on the editorial board for two academic journals, and is a coauthor on a management accounting textbook. Dr. Swain has spent significant time working with or researching organizations such as IBM, Clorox, Deere and Company, the Church of Jesus Christ of Latter-Day Saints, and Habitat for Humanity. He is a Certified Public Accountant and a Certified Management Accountant. Dr. Swain took an academic leave from BYU from July 1999 to July 2000 to serve as the Chief Financial Officer for Authorize.Net (payment-processing service for e-commerce), a wholly owned subsidiary of InfoSpace, Inc. He currently serves as the Associate Director of the School of Accountancy and Information Systems where he is the Deloitte & Touche Professor of Accounting. He and his wife, Shannon, have seven children.

W. Steve Albrecht

W. Steve Albrecht is the Associate Dean of the Marriott School of Management and Arthur Andersen Professor at Brigham Young University. Dr. Albrecht, a certified public accountant, certified internal auditor, and certified fraud examiner, came to BYU in 1977 after teaching at Stanford and at the University of Illinois. Earlier, he worked as a staff accountant for Deloitte & Touche. Prior to becoming associate dean of the Marriott School, Dr. Albrecht served for eight years as the director of the School of Accountancy and Information Systems at BYU. During that time, BYU's undergraduate and graduate accounting programs were ranked 2nd and 3rd in the United States.

Dr. Albrecht received a bachelor's degree in accounting from Brigham Young University and his MBA and PhD degrees from the University of Wisconsin at Madison. He is past President of the American Accounting Association and the Association of Certified Fraud Examiners. He was a former member of the Board of Regents of the Institute of Internal Auditors and the Board of Directors of the Utah Association of CPAs. He was also president of the Accounting Program Leadership Group (chairs of accounting departments and programs) and served on the task force of the American Institute of CPAs that wrote the fraud auditing standard. He was a member of the Committee of Sponsoring Organizations (COSO) from 1997-2000 and is past president of Beta Alpha Psi, the national accounting honors fraternity. He is also a member of the AICPA Council and chairs their Pre-Certification Executive Education Committee.

Dr. Albrecht has done extensive research on business fraud. His research has resulted in the publication of over eighty articles in professional journals. He is the author or co-author of over 20 books or monographs, several of which are on fraud. His financial and principles of accounting textbooks are in their 9th editions. In 2000, he completed a major study (Accounting Education: Charting the Course through a Perilous Future) on the future of accounting education in the United States. He is a frequent speaker on the topics of fraud examination, accounting education, and personal financial planning.

Dr. Albrecht has received numerous awards and honors, including BYU's highest faculty honor, the Karl G. Maeser Distinguished Faculty Lecturer Award for superior scholarship and teaching. He has also received the BYU School of Management's Outstanding Faculty Award, the BYU Outstanding Researcher Award, and was recognized, as part of Utah's Centennial Celebration, as one of 131 Utahans who have made outstanding contributions or brought unusual recognition to the state. He has been recognized by Beta Alpha Psi, the Federation of Schools of Accountancy, and the AICPA as Educator of the Year. He has also received awards for outstanding teaching at Stanford University, the University of Illinois, and the

University of Wisconsin. In 1997, 2001, and 2002, he was chosen as one of the 100 most influential accounting professionals in the United States by *Accounting Today* magazine. In 1998, he received the *Cressey Award* from the Association of Certified Fraud Examiners, the highest award given for a lifetime of achievement in fraud detection and deterrence. (Past winners were Jane Bryant Quinn of *Newsweek* magazine and Rudolph Giuliani, past United States Attorney for the Southern District of New York and mayor of New York City.) In 2002, in honor of his contribution in fighting fraud, the Association of Certified Fraud Examiners named one of the buildings at their headquarters after Dr. Albrecht. And in 2001, in recognition of his contributions to BYU and to academia, an anonymous donor endowed the W. Steve Albrecht Professorship in Accounting.

Dr. Albrecht has consulted with numerous organizations, including a variety of Fortune 500 companies, major financial institutions, the United Nations, FBI, and other organizations, and he has been an expert witness in some of the largest fraud cases in America. He currently serves on the audit committees and boards of directors of three public and two private companies.

Dr. Albrecht is married to the former LeAnn Christiansen, and they have six children and six grandchildren.

James D. Stice

James D. Stice is the Distinguished Teaching Professor in the Marriott School of Management at Brigham Young University. He is currently the Director of the Marriott School's MBA Program. He holds bachelor's and master's degrees from BYU and a PhD from the University of Washington, all in accounting. Professor Stice has been on the faculty at BYU since 1988. During that time, he has been selected by graduating accounting students as "Teacher of the Year" on numerous occasions, he was selected by his peers in the Marriott School at BYU to receive the "Outstanding Teaching Award" in 1995, and in 1999 he was selected by the University to receive its highest teaching award, the Maeser Excellence in Teaching Award. Professor Stice is also a visiting professor for INSEAD's MBA Program in France. Professor Stice has published articles in *The Journal of Accounting Research, The Accounting Review, Decision Sciences, Issues in Accounting Education, The CPA Journal*, and other academic and professional journals. In addition to this textbook, he has published two other textbooks: *Financial Accounting: Reporting and Analysis*, and *Intermediate Accounting*. In addition to his teaching and research, Dr. Stice has been involved in executive education for such companies as IBM, Bank of America, and Ernst & Young and currently serves on the board of directors of Nutraceutical Corporation. Dr. Stice and his wife, Kaye, have seven children: Crystal, J.D., Ashley, Whitney, Kara, Skyler, and Cierra.

Earl K. Stice

Earl K. Stice is the PricewaterhouseCoopers Professor of Accounting in the School of Accountancy and Information Systems at Brigham Young University where he has been on the faculty since 1998. He holds bachelor's and master's degrees from Brigham Young University and a PhD from Cornell University. Dr. Stice has taught at Rice University, the University of Arizona, Cornell University, and the Hong Kong University of Science and Technology (HKUST). He won the Phi Beta Kappa teaching award at Rice University and was twice selected at HKUST as one of the ten best lecturers on campus. Dr. Stice has also taught in a variety of executive education and corporate training programs in the United States, Hong Kong, China, and South Africa, and he is currently on the executive MBA faculty of the China Europe International Business School in Shanghai. He has published papers in the *Journal of Financial and Quantitative Analysis, The Accounting Review, Review of Accounting Studies*, and *Issues in Accounting Education*, and his research on stock splits has been cited in *Business Week, Money*, and *Forbes*. Dr. Stice has presented his research results at seminars in the United States, Finland, Taiwan, Australia, and Hong Kong. He is co-author of *Intermediate Accounting, 15th edition* and *Financial Accounting: Reporting and Analysis, 6th Edition*. Dr. Stice and his wife, Ramona, are the parents of seven children: Derrald, Han, Ryan Marie, Lorien, Lily, Taraz, and Kamila.

Contents

Appendices

Indexes

Thank you for adopting *Management Accounting, 3e*. Our newest edition provides a perfect balance of procedural and conceptual coverage which gives students a realistic view of how accounting is used by leading companies across the nation. We understand students enter the introductory accounting course with a variety of career goals and learning styles. Balancing the needs of the accounting major and non-accounting major has become increasingly difficult. Our unique text organization, student-oriented pedagogy and innovative technology are designed to better address every student's needs regardless of their career ambitions. We continue to make the text more flexible with each edition; splitting the chapters into basic and expanded material and making it easier for you to select a perfect balance of material essential to your course objectives.

We are confident that *Management Accounting, 3e* will better prepare your students to make more informed business decisions regardless of their chosen career path.

Monte R. Swain
W. Steve Albrecht
James D. Stice
Earl K. Stice

new features

If you're one of our many loyal adopters, we suggest you review the NEW features we've added to this edition.

If this is the first time you've used this text, you'll want to review everything that makes your decision worthwhile.

New to the Third Edition

▶ **MANAGING INVENTORY AND SERVICE COSTS – Chapter 7**
This NEW chapter introduces techniques such as just-in-time (JIT) and other inventory systems that are used to manage inventory in manufacturing, service, and merchandising organizations.

▶ **SIGNIFICANT RESTRUCTURING** – A number of chapters have been restructured, making the text more approachable for students.

▶ **FIXED OVERHEAD VARIANCE ANALYSIS AND RECONCILIATION OF ABSORPTION COSTING** – These two traditional topics have been returned to the text as expanded material.

▶ **SUNBIRD BOAT COMPANY** – This new comprehensive case presents and integrates operating budgets and variance analysis.

▶ **THE SARBANES-OXLEY ACT OF 2002** has been incorporated throughout the text and the end-of-chapter material. Real-world discussions of companies, such as ARTHUR ANDERSEN, ENRON, WORLDCOM, and TYCO provide the background and reasons for this congressional act and how it impacts financial reporting.

▶ **PRACTICE EXERCISES** – Approximately 20 brief exercises per chapter have been added, perfect for in-class coverage or as an assignment.

▶ **JUDGMENT CALLS** –You Decide! These new and unique end-of-chapter exercises make the student the decision-maker, reinforcing critical thinking and analytical skills.

▶ **PERSONAL TRAINER® 3.0** – Students can complete exercises and problems online and receive immediate feedback with Personal Trainer. Students' results flow directly into your gradebook.

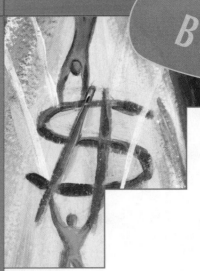

Meeting Individual Student Abilities and Learning Styles

Tailor Material to Your Students
Expanded Material found at the end of most chapters gives you the flexibility to tailor the text to meet the needs and abilities of all students.

Visual Learners
WebTutor™ Advantage for WebCT™ and Blackboard®, Xtra!, and the textbook Web site provide interactive and media reinforcement for all students, especially visual learners.

Learning Levels
End-of-Chapter Materials offer a large number of easy, medium, and difficult problems. Your best students can move on to more difficult problems while struggling learners get plenty of opportunity to build confidence before attacking more challenging problems.

Problem-Solving Help
Now you can give students who need extra problem-solving help valuable guidance without providing the answers. Each chapter includes a review problem with a fully illustrated solution. Check Figures for selected problems are included in the text.

Comprehensive Problems
Three comprehensive problems, integrating multiple issues and methods, are found throughout the text. These problems provide an opportunity to challenge students and bring their knowledge full circle.

Head Start
NEW! Approximately 20 brief practice exercises per chapter are perfect to use for starting class or as a pre-lecture assignment.

IS A BALANCING ACT...

S atisfying Different Student Majors

Preparing Future CEOs with CEO
Competency **E**nhancement **O**pportunities are found at the end of all chapters and include problems that develop analysis, communication, and decision-making—skills encouraged by the AICPA and the Accounting Education Change Commission. International Cases, Ethics Cases, Writing Assignments, Debates, Cumulative Spreadsheets, and Internet Search exercises provide interesting, unique and challenging assignments.

Appealing to All Students
Each chapter is written to simplify difficult concepts and promote understanding. *Management Accounting, 3e* holds their interest by focusing on current real-world situations and actual companies.

Organized Around Business Activities
The organization of the text, consistent with business activities and cycles, gives students a more accurate framework for understanding accounting and business.

B alancing Work vs. Time

Eliminate Grading Homework!
Personal Trainer® 3.0 lets students complete their assigned homework from the text. The results instantaneously flow into your online gradebook. This tool frees up your time by taking away the important, but time consuming chore of grading homework from you!

Personal Tutoring Tools for Students
Our WebTutor™ Advantage for Blackboard® or WebCT™ contains many tools that act as a tutor to your student when you can't be there to help them. Some of these include an illustrative Exercise Demo, an animation with audio of all steps to solving a problem, and visual E-Lectures with audio review of more difficult concepts of the chapter. WebTutor Advantage also automatically includes Personal Trainer (described above). Best of all, these tools are all textbook specific and already created for you!

TECHNOLOGY AND

WebTutor™ Advantage on WebCT™ with Personal Trainer® 3.0
WebTutor™ Advantage on Blackboard® with Personal Trainer® 3.0

WebTutor™ Advantage provides you with the most robust and pedagogically advanced content for either the WebCT™ or Blackboard® course management platform.

WebTutor Advantage includes engaging videos and E-Lectures, plus fascinating quizzes, games, and more.

▶ **NEW Video Cases** Each two- to five-minute video covers a key accounting concept as it is played out in a real-world company or situation. Accompanying the video is a summary and some suggested critical-thinking questions for students to answer.
▶ **E-Lectures** Each chapter includes one or two visual lectures with audio presentations that review major topics.
▶ **Exercise Demos** These step-by-step Flash presentations walk the student through an illustrative problem.

▶ **Quizzes** Students make great strides with continuous reinforcement, now they can select from a variety of quizzes per chapter: pretests, multiple choice and true-false.
▶ **QuizBowl** Popular with students, this engaging Jeopardy®-like game with sound effects allows them to review key accounting concepts.
▶ **Test Your Knowledge** game provides additional reinforcement of accounting concepts and key terms in a fun, interactive format.
▶ **Accounting Cycle Review** Students get a firm grasp on the key concepts of the accounting cycle by applying what they've learned to realistic situations and problems.
▶ **Spanish Dictionary** This timely resource defines common accounting terms in Spanish.

Personal Trainer® 3.0

Specifically designed to ease the time-consuming task of grading homework, Personal Trainer lets students complete their assigned homework from the text or practice on unassigned homework online. The results are instantaneously entered into your online gradebook.

Features of New 3.0 Personal Trainer:

▶ **Enhanced Questions** The latest version now includes exercises and problems. Students get help entering their answers in the proper format and they can spell check their answers.
▶ **Enhanced Instructor Capabilities** The flexible gradebook can display and download any combination of student work, chapters, or activities. Capture grades on demand or set a particular time for grades to be automatically captured. Assign questions as "required" or "excluded," so students cannot access selected questions.

▶ **Enhanced Hints** Students get up to three hints from the text, PowerPoint slides, exhibits, spreadsheets, images and more for each problem. Plus instructors can add an additional hint.
▶ **Enhanced Look-and-Feel** Fast, reliable, dependable and even easier to use, Version 3.0 sports a fresh, new graphic design.

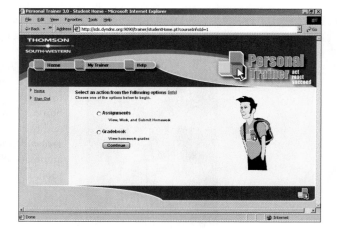

ELECTRONIC SOLUTIONS

Xtra!

Available as an optional, free bundle item with a new textbook, Xtra! gives students FREE access to the following set of online learning tools:

▶ **E-Lectures** Brief E-Lectures review more difficult concepts from the chapter.
▶ **Topical Quizzes** Measure a student's "test readiness" on the concepts in the chapter.
▶ **Multiple Choice Quizzing** Additional quizzes help students review chapter concepts and prepare for exams.

▶ **Crosswords** The Crossword Puzzles are a fun way students can review their understanding of key terms and concepts.
▶ **Business Environment articles** Real world vignettes, adapted from financial newspapers and business publications, which illustrate concepts in the chapter.

P.A.S.S.

Our best-selling comput-erized accounting soft-ware, prepared by Dale Klooster and Warren Allen, *Power Accounting System Software* (formerly General Ledger Software) shows students the effects that accounting entries have on financial

statements. P.A.S.S. is also available with our selection of comprehensive practice sets.

▶ **Text Icon** Each problem that can be completed with P.A.S.S. is marked with an icon in the text.

Excel Spreadsheet Templates

Excel templates are provided for solving selected end-of-chapter exercises and problems, which are identified with the spreadsheet icon.

Spreadsheet

Product Support Web Site — http://swain.swlearning.com

The Swain/Albrecht/Stice/Stice web site provides a variety of instructor and student resources. You'll find text-specific and other related resources organized by chapter and topic.

The Product Support Site includes a wide variety of materials for extra studying and review.

▶ **Learning Objectives**
▶ **PowerPoint® Presentations** Reviews each chapter's major topics.
▶ **Check Figures** Enables students to see if their entries are correct.
▶ **Internet Applications** These activities from the text allow students to apply chapter concepts and improve their online research skills.
▶ **Crosswords** This fun, interactive tool gives students a great way to review and understand the key terms from each chapter.
▶ **Quizzes** Interactive quizzes in both true-false and multiple-choice formats provide students with immediate feedback after submitting their answers.

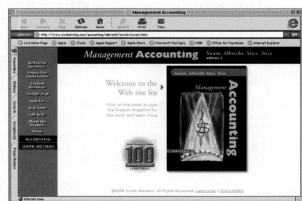

▶ **Instructor Resources** Available to download are the Instructor's Manual, Solutions Manual, PowerPoint Presentations, Excel Spreadsheets with Solutions, Business Environment Articles, and Check Figures.

Instructor Supplements

When it comes to supporting instructors, South-Western is unsurpassed. *Management Accounting, 3e,* continues the tradition with powerful printed materials along with the latest integrated classroom technology!

- **WebTutor Advantage with Personal Trainer** Robust content for online course management systems on WebCT and Blackboard.
- **Solutions Manual** This manual provides the answers to all end-of-chapter materials in the text, suggested answers to Stop and Think included.
- **Instructor's Manual** Contains a wide range of writing exercises, group learning activities, demonstration problems, and accounting scenarios.
- **Instructor's Resource CD-ROM** This convenient resource includes PowerPoint® Presentations, Instructor's Manual, Test Bank, ExamView, Solutions Manual, Excel Application Templates and Solutions, all on one CD-ROM.
- **Test Bank** Includes more than 700 true-false questions, multiple-choice questions, and problems, plus multiple-choice quizzes for each chapter. The Test Bank is also included in the ExamView Pro® Testing Software on the instructor's CD-ROM.

- **ExamView Pro® Testing Software** Lets you easily customize exams, practice tests, and tutorials and deliver them over a network, on the Internet, or in printed form.
- **Instructor PowerPoint® Presentations** Each presentation found at the Web site enhances lectures and simplifies class preparation.
- **Instructor Spreadsheet Template Solutions** Provide the completed solution for the exercises and problems marked with an icon in the text. These are available to download at **http://swain.swlearning.com**.
- **Solutions Transparencies** Acetate transparencies of exercise and problem solutions.
- **Teaching Transparencies** Acetates of the PowerPoint® Presentation Slides.
- **Product Support Web Site (http://swain.swlearning.com)** Our text-specific web site provides a variety of instructor resources that are password protected. You'll find text-specific and other related resources organized by chapter and topic. Many are also available on the Instructor's Resource CD-ROM.

Student Supplements

Management Accounting, 3e, offers a broad range of supplements in both printed form and in easy-to-use, affordable technologies. We've designed our entire supplement package around the comments instructors have provided, making this supplement package the best in the business!

- **Study Guide** Prepared by the authors, the study guide includes learning objectives, detailed chapter summaries, discussions of topics that typically cause problems for the students and suggestions for overcoming those problems and tests for self-assessment.
- **Working Papers for Exercises and Problems** Forms for solving end-of-chapter problems are perforated for easy removal and use.
- **Personal Trainer 3.0** Students can complete textbook end-of-chapter exercises and problems online and receive immediate feedback with Personal Trainer! Additionally, student results instantaneously flow into your gradebook!

- **Spreadsheet Templates** Each spreadsheet template problem is marked with an icon in the text. Templates are available at **http://swain.swlearning.com**.
- **Xtra!** Gives students free access to E-Lectures, Topical Quizzes, Crosswords, and quizzing.
- **Product Support Web Site (http://swain.swlearning.com)** Our Web site provides a variety of student resources, including quizzing and lecture reviews. You'll find text-specific content and other related resources organized by chapter and topic.

Acknowledgements

The third edition of *Management Accounting* reflects many comments from colleagues and students, all of which are deeply appreciated. In particular we wish to thank the following:

Survey Participants:

Afshad J. Irani
University of New Hampshire

Mack Tennyson
College of Charleston

Alexandra L. Anna
Colorado College

Robert W. Rouse
College of Charleston

Robert L. Vogel
College of Eastern Utah

Cindy M. Navaroli
Chaffey College

John C. Corless
CSU-Sacramento

Constance M. Cooper
University of Cincinnati

Jacqueline C. Richards
Mesa College

Paul Buck
Plymouth State College

Jeffery R. Cowan
Fullerton College

Rosalie C. Hallbauer
Florida International University

Roger A. Gee
San Diego Mesa College

Robert I. Sanner
Central Community College-Grand Island

Jill E. Whitley
University of Sioux Falls

Willaim H. Svihla
ISU School of Business

Cathy L. Miller
University of Michigan-Flint

Larry P. Hegstad
Pacific Lutheran University

Paul Buck
Plymouth State College

Hal Ranck
Franklin & Marshall College

Reviewers:

Susan Anders
St. Bonaventure University

Becky Kerr
University of South Carolina

Susan Hamlen
University of Buffalo

Progyan Basu
University of Georgia

In addition, we would like to thank the following content providers and verifiers for their professional services and consideration in providing a more concise, higher-quality product.

Content Providers:

Michael Blue
Bloomburg University

Joseph E. Dowd
Eastern Washington University

Sharie Dow
Dow Publishing

Jason Fink
University of Phoenix

Peggy Hussey
Colorado Springs, CO

Marcella Combs
Summerfield, FL

Jeff Ritter
St. Norberts College

David Cottrell
Brigham Young University

Verifiers:

Jason Fink
University of Phoenix

James Emig
Villanova University

Samuel L. Tiras
University of Buffalo

Dave O'Dell
McPherson College

Special Consideration and thanks from the Authors:

John Gammon
Brigham Young University

Cameron Pratt
Brigham Young University

Brad Tingey
Brigham Young University

Monte R. Swain   James D. Stice
W. Steve Albrecht   Earl K. Stice

Part

1

Foundations

chapter

1

Introduction to Management Accounting

After studying this chapter, you should be able to:

Learning Objectives

1 Understand the essential differences between management accounting and financial accounting.

2 Understand that successfully managing a company requires good information that supports effective planning, controlling, and evaluating processes.

3 Describe how the concepts of fixed and variable costs are used in C-V-P analysis in the management planning process.

4 Realize how the product cost classifications of direct materials, direct labor, and overhead are used in the management controlling process.

5 Understand the concepts of direct, indirect, and opportunity costs in the management evaluating process.

6 Understand that management accounting still continues to evolve.

7 Discuss the need for ethics in management accounting and describe the Standards of Ethical Conduct that apply to this profession.

You may not have heard of E. I. DU PONT DE NEMOURS AND COMPANY, but you may be familiar with its more common name, DUPONT. Some of this company's best-known brands are Teflon® (cookware), Coolmax® (athletic clothing), Lycra® (stretch fabric), Stainmaster® (carpet), Hollofil® (sleeping bags), Kevlar® (protective covering), Corian® (countertops), and Mylar® (packaging). With revenues of over $24 billion in 2002, DuPont ranks number 70 in the Fortune 500 list. DuPont operates in more than 70 countries worldwide with roughly 135 manufacturing and processing facilities. Working in these facilities are 79,000 employees; approximately one-half of them work outside the United States. In addition to its manufacturing and processing facilities, DuPont has more than 40 research and development and customer service labs in the United States and more than 35 labs in 11 other countries. This is a big company!

The DuPont company was established in 1802 near Wilmington, Delaware, by a French immigrant, Eleuthére Irénée du Pont de Nemours, to produce black blasting powder. During the 1800s, the company grew into a major family corporation. However, the start of the twentieth century brought increased competition from other companies, and DuPont fell on hard times. To deal with the crisis, three of E. I. du Pont's great-grandsons, Alfred, Coleman, and Pierre, borrowed a lot of money and purchased the firm's assets from the family in 1902. With all of this debt hanging over them, the three cousins felt great pressure to make the company profitable very quickly. In a bold and risky move, they decided to make the company even bigger by borrowing more money to purchase many of the company's suppliers of raw mate-

rials (such as charcoal, sodium nitrate, and crude glycerin) used in DuPont's explosive products. In addition, instead of wholesaling the products through traditional retailers, DuPont's new managers decided to create their own network of branch sales offices scattered across the United States. As a result of expanding the company's manufacturing operations to include mining, transportation, and retailing, most of the profits usually earned by outside companies (either by selling DuPont products to customers or by selling raw materials to DuPont) were now being earned by DuPont itself.

Diversified companies are quite common today, but DuPont's diversification was unusual at the turn of the twentieth century when most companies focused on just one business activity. Although Alfred, Coleman, and Pierre were confident that their new way of doing business was going to make them a lot of money (and they were right!), they had created a serious challenge for themselves. They knew how to run a manufacturing business, but now they were in the mining, shipping, and sales business as well. They were now operating in four different industries, each with its own way of communicating results and measuring success. The three cousins had a limited amount of time and resources to invest in developing their company. How were they going to be able to effectively plan schedules, control operations, and evaluate the profitability of each division? Essentially, Alfred, Coleman, and Pierre had an accounting problem. What would you have done if you were in their shoes in 1903? As you'll see in a moment, the cousins handled this multi-million dollar challenge with some simple arithmetic.[1]

Setting the Stage

---

1 Historical sources: A. D. Chandler, *The Invisible Hand* (Boston: HBS Press, 1977); H. T. Johnson and R. S. Kaplan, *Relevance Lost* (Boston: HBS Press, 1987); the DuPont Heritage Web site at **http://heritage.dupont.com/**.

t his chapter introduces management accounting and distinguishes it from financial accounting. The key purpose of management accounting is fulfilling the competitive needs of the company. DuPont had a competitive need to manage a very large and diverse organization and so invented new accounting measurements to serve as important management tools. A company's management accounting system is used to support the management processes of planning, controlling, and evaluating. In this chapter we will use cost-volume-profit analysis to introduce the planning process, product cost classifications to introduce the controlling process, and segment analysis to introduce the evaluating process. These topics are merely introduced in this chapter; more detailed coverage is given in subsequent chapters.

Business professionals who are in a position to use management accounting data to make impor-tant decisions must take care to make the best decisions possible on behalf of the organization, its owners, its employees, the surrounding community, and the public at large. As a result, it is critical that these decision makers understand the ethics of good business and are committed to perform ethically.

In summary, this chapter has four purposes.

1. To distinguish management accounting from financial accounting.
2. To introduce the management processes of planning, controlling, and evaluating.
3. To introduce management accounting terminology in the context of several key management tools.
4. To present the need for business ethics in management accounting and describe the Institute of Management Accountant's Standards of Ethical Conduct.

Management Accounting and Financial Accounting

▮ Understand the essential differences between management accounting and financial accounting.

The differences between management accounting and financial accounting can be summarized as follows:

Source:
- Management accounting *evolves* from the best practices of managers working within their companies.
- Financial accounting is *legislated and governed* by regulatory agencies and professional institutions.

Purpose:
- Management accounting exists to serve the *competitive needs* of organizations that must constantly plan, control, and evaluate operations.
- Financial accounting exists to serve the need for organizations to *periodically report* results to outside investors and lenders.

Outcome:
- Management accounting results in both *financial and nonfinancial data* that are *proprietary* (i.e., guarded from becoming available to competitors and the general public).
- Financial accounting results in *only financial data* that are *public* and reported to investors and creditors.

Knowing a little of the history of management accounting is very useful in understanding the differences between management accounting and financial accounting. Hence, as you read further about the history of the DUPONT company, be sure to see that the "rules" of management accounting are not governed by anything other than by market forces.

Example of a Management Accounting Technique: Return on Investment (ROI)

By the time Alfred, Coleman, and Pierre du Pont had finished buying out suppliers and establishing sales offices throughout the country, they had created a giant organization. The fact that their company was big, however, is not what makes their situation interesting. There were a lot of big companies in America at that time. However, most companies at the turn of the twentieth century focused on doing *one thing well* such as making cloth, moving railway cars, producing steel, or selling goods. The du Ponts, on the other hand, were trying to combine within one company many different types of businesses: mining and shipping, raw materials and finished goods manufacturing, and retail distribution and sales.

DuPont had many employees and a complicated management organization, production processes that were expensive and complicated, divisions spread all over North and South America, and high levels of expensive inventory that needed to be manufactured and sold quickly. Each of these divisions required constant attention and additional investments in order to grow and flourish. The du Ponts knew they could make or lose money in any part of their monstrous new company. Obviously, neither they (nor their money) could be everywhere at once. They needed to make trade-off decisions. The problem was, with very diverse divisions, how could they decide which divisions should receive additional investments of time and money? They couldn't really compare the cost reports of retail stores in Denver with a black powder manufacturing factory in Delaware or with a sodium nitrate processing plant in Chile. Having all these unique business activities also made it quite difficult to relate various measures of efficiency directly to overall company profit.

The first thing the new DuPont management team did was develop extensive budgets to coordinate the flow of resources from raw materials to the final customer. Notice that the development of these budgets was not mandated by a government regulatory agency or by an accounting standard-setting body. Instead, DuPont's management team decided that they could improve their business through better budgeting, so they did it. As mentioned above, this is a key characteristic of management accounting—management accounting practices are intended to fill a company's competitive business needs.

But improved budgets alone were not enough to satisfy DuPont's need for better measurements with which to plan, control, and evaluate their far-flung operations. The company still needed a measure for comparing performance in its separate divisions with performance of the whole company. Enter the management accountant, Donaldson Brown (DuPont's chief financial officer or CFO). Mr. Brown, along with other executives at DuPont, realized that every division required an investment in assets in order to be in business. The overall goal of every business should be to effectively use its assets to make a profit. For example, an explosives plant using assets worth $10 million and earning $500,000 in profit is not performing as well as a major sales division that also creates a $500,000 profit but only requires $5 million in assets. If you had an additional $1 million to invest, which division should receive your money? The sales division is earning a 10% return ($500,000 ÷ $5,000,000) on the DuPont investment in inventory, equipment, and buildings. The explosives plant is earning only a 5% return on investment ($500,000 ÷ $10,000,000). Obviously, additional investment would first go to the sales division in order to earn a 10% return rather than a mere 5% return.

Although this simple formula was not really new to American business in the first part of the twentieth century, Brown took the idea of **return on investment (ROI)** and began expanding it from a simple formula into a more complex management technique that could be used in the process of managing any kind of business operation at DuPont. He demonstrated how ROI can be decomposed and used to *separately* measure how well assets are being used and how well profit is being created. Use of ROI in evaluating diverse business divisions within a company

return on investment (ROI) A measure of operating performance and efficiency in utilizing assets; computed in its simplest form by dividing net income by average total assets. This measure is also known as ROA (return on assets).

FYI:

Donaldson Brown took the ROI approach with him when he followed Pierre du Pont to help rescue a little company in the midst of an inventory crisis in 1920. The name of the company was GENERAL MOTORS. The evidence that the DuPont technique was successful at General Motors can be seen today in any parking lot in America.

Caution

Don't think management accounting is not important just because it is not defined as precisely as financial accounting. Management accounting is critical to the success of businesses throughout the world.

STOP & THINK

We have described some differences in financial and management accounting. Why is it important for an accounting system to provide both types of accounting information?

is explained in detail in a later chapter on monitoring performance. The ROI tool allowed the du Pont cousins to be hugely successful in managing the country's first integrated company by combining cost management with asset management and raising it to an art form! It's likely that few management accounting techniques have had as great an impact on business management as the DuPont ROI formula.

Management Accounting and Financial Accounting

The DuPont story is an example of how management accounting evolves within organizations that have a particular need for good information. This development pattern has been playing out across companies for a long time. Since the first days of the Industrial Revolution, business owners and managers have generally adopted the best accounting ideas available from other companies and then created their own new accounting system that provided a competitive edge in terms of good management information. Over time, management accounting has, quite literally, evolved within and migrated between organizations and industries in the process of satisfying individual information needs in a competitive world. In fact, a company often regards a good management accounting system as a valuable company secret—and rarely discloses its details to the public.

In contrast, financial accounting has effectively developed in the United States to provide a *common reporting platform* to the public. The purpose of financial accounting, as defined by generally accepted accounting principles (GAAP), is to satisfy the needs of outside investors, creditors, and regulators for fair and consistent reports of operations. Accordingly, all companies are required to apply the same general financial accounting rules so that outsiders can compare financial reports coming from many different companies. These financial accounting rules are established by the Financial Accounting Standards Board (FASB) and are enforced by the Securities and Exchange Commission (SEC). However, no government regulator or auditor is going to insist that a company implement a good management accounting system; the choice of how to collect and use information within a company is part of a company's competitive strategy. For example, no one forced the du Pont cousins to use the ROI formula to better manage their business; however, because the ROI evaluation framework worked well for DuPont, it was subsequently mimicked by many (but not all) of DuPont's competitors. Remember, the only reason a company does management accounting is to satisfy a competitive need, and competitive need often dictates that one organization's management accounting system will not look like another's!

TO SUMMARIZE: A good management accounting system is the product of many years of business owners and managers experimenting with methods for capturing and using information about their organization that will give them a unique competitive edge. Organizations and managers are motivated to be innovative in developing and effective in deploying these new accounting tools by the need to compete in a growing economy. In contrast, financial accounting rules are established by an authoritative body in order to enhance company-to-company comparability of financial accounting reports.

The Management Process and Management Accounting Terminology

2 Understand that successfully managing a company requires good information that supports effective planning, controlling, and evaluating processes.

Critical to the success experienced by great companies such as DUPONT is intelligent decision making by individuals supported by competitive management accounting information. Managers will always need to make choices. What should be produced? What should be sold? How should the service be delivered? What does this client need? Which supplier should be used? Who should be promoted? How should financing be obtained? Hence, as you prepare yourself to participate in the management process of an organization, you need to think carefully about how good decisions are made and how you're going to make them! Exhibit 1 illustrates the central role that decision making plays in the general management process.

Notice that the decision-making circle intersects three other circles, each representing a major management function. This intersection is meant to show that each of these functions requires decision making. The three management functions of planning, controlling, and evaluating generally follow a natural order—at least in theory. In practice, managers are often required to work with processes, customers, and employees requiring all three decision-making functions at once. For example, the manager of a campus copy center must simultaneously plan the week's work flow, control the production process by balancing the needs of student customers and faculty copy requests, and evaluate the performance of both the employees and the copy machines.

Planning

planning Outlining the activities that need to be performed for an organization to achieve its objectives.

Management **planning** involves a process of identifying problems or opportunities, identifying alternatives, evaluating alternatives, then choosing and implementing the best alternative(s). There are two basic types of planning:

1. Long-run planning, which includes:
   a. Strategic planning
   b. Capital budgeting
2. Short-run planning, which includes:
   a. Production and process prioritizing
   b. Operational budgeting (profit planning)

strategic planning Broad, long-range planning usually conducted by top management.

Long-run planning involves making decisions with effects that extend several years into the future—usually three to five years, but sometimes longer. This includes broad-based decisions about products, markets, productive facilities, and financial resources. Long-run planning is often called strategic planning. **Strategic planning**, likely the most critical decision-making process that takes place at the executive level in any organization today, usually involves identifying an organization's mission, the goals flowing from that mission, and strategies and action steps to accomplish those goals. Successful executives, such as Bill Gates (MICROSOFT) or Warren Buffett (BERKSHIRE HATHAWAY), have always displayed great skill in studying the market, identifying customer needs, evaluating competitors' strengths and weaknesses, and defining the right investments and processes their organization needs for success. Good management accounting supports good strategic planning by providing the internal information needed by executives to evaluate and adjust their strategic plans.

capital budgeting Systematic planning for long-term investments in operating assets.

With strategic planning in place (or in process), the company can then plan for the purchase and use of major assets such as buildings or equipment to help the company meet its long-range goals. For example, if part of a university's long-run strategic plan is to increase the competitive level of its football team, then the university probably should consider replacing its existing football stadium and practice facility. This type of long-run planning of the acquisition of assets is called **capital budgeting**. We will cover capital budgeting in detail in a later chapter.

Short-run planning is divided into two categories. Once the organization has made long-term resource commitments (e.g., land, buildings, equipment,

FYI:

Colleges and universities often conduct "capital" campaigns. These are fundraising campaigns targeted at generating funds for the construction of long-term assets such as academic buildings and athletic facilities.

Exhibit 1: The Management Process

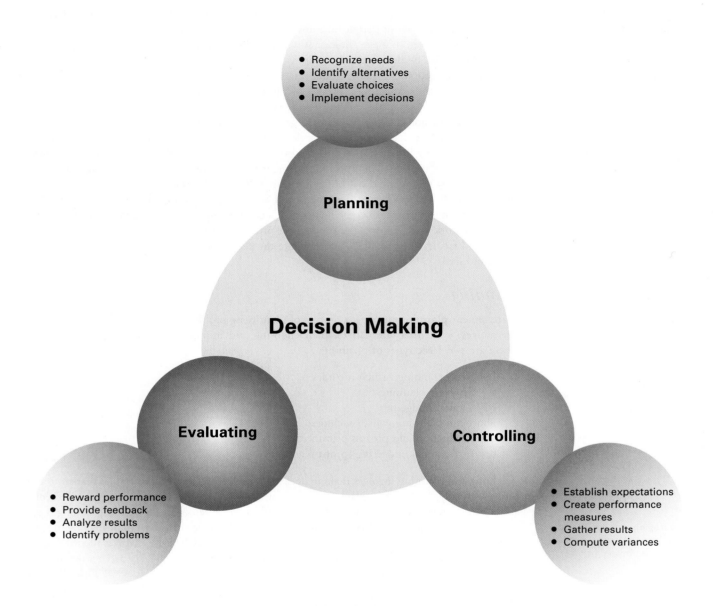

- Recognize needs
- Identify alternatives
- Evaluate choices
- Implement decisions

Planning

Decision Making

Evaluating

Controlling

- Reward performance
- Provide feedback
- Analyze results
- Identify problems

- Establish expectations
- Create performance measures
- Gather results
- Compute variances

production prioritizing
Management's continual evaluation of the profitability of the various product lines and divisions within an organization so that products or divisions that are performing below expectations can be analyzed to identify problems and potential solutions.

management personnel, etc.), then managers need to determine how to best use those committed resources to maximize the return on their capital investments—a process often referred to as **production prioritizing**.[2] Did you catch the phrase "return on capital investment" in the last sentence? Sound familiar? The DuPont ROI concept is one way to establish priorities on products, service processes, or divisions that make the largest contributions to the goals of the organization. For example, you can view your study of accounting as a production process; production prioritizing involves analysis to determine how you should best spend your time in preparing for the next exam—reading the chapters, doing homework problems, studying in a group, or catching up on your sleep.

2 Production prioritizing includes the process of prioritizing what *services* will be created and delivered to the marketplace (e.g., airlines, consulting, and banking).

FYI:

In the next section, we'll introduce another popular method of prioritizing the production potential of an organization—cost-volume-profit analysis.

operational budgeting
Managerial planning decisions regarding current operations and those of the immediate future (typically one year or less) that are characterized by regularity and frequency.

controlling Implementing management plans and identifying how plans compare with actual performance.

Once the organization has determined what to provide to the marketplace in order to maximize its goals, then managers are ready to go on to the next phase of short-run planning—**operational budgeting**. Sometimes known as profit plans, operational budgets are used by managers to establish and communicate daily, weekly, and monthly goals (also known as "standards") for the organization. Many individuals—young, middle-aged, and old—face severe personal financial problems because they fail to use even the most basic techniques of regular operational budgeting. We will discuss operational budgets in a later chapter.

Controlling

Controlling involves a process of tracking actual performance in terms of measuring costs, quality, and timeliness. These data are then used subsequently in the evaluating process to compare against the budgets previously prepared in the planning process to measure deviations from the original goals or standards. Controlling also involves the real-time, day-to-day management of all of a company's business processes. A good example of a control device is the radar gun used by major league baseball teams to measure the speed the pitcher is throwing his pitches. These measurements can be used at the end of the season in evaluating which pitchers are most valuable to the team. But these measurements can also be used by the manager during the course of a game to indicate when a pitcher is getting tired and should be replaced. The radar gun measurements are useful for evaluating individual performance after the fact but are also useful in effectively managing the team.

Evaluating

evaluating Analyzing results, rewarding performance, and identifying problems.

Evaluating involves analyzing results, providing feedback to managers and other employees, rewarding performance, and identifying problems. Evaluating is typically a process of comparing actual performance against expected inputs of costs, expected outputs of quality, and expected timelines. This comparison typically results in information called *variances*, which tell management how well the organization is achieving its plans. If performance is in accordance with the plan, the variances signal that operations are in control and no unusual management action is necessary. If performance is substantially different from the plan, management needs to decide how to alter operations in order to improve future performance. For example, most students in college classes are asked to evaluate their instructors near the end of the term. These evaluation results can be used by conscientious faculty members who are trying to improve their teaching, and the results can also be used by department heads in deciding which teachers should be retained or replaced.

Evaluating products and processes also takes place regularly. Managers need to assess the performance of their products or services, as well as the processes that have been put into place to create products and services. Such evaluation naturally leads to decisions that will affect future operations, including whether to enter or exit a market for a particular service or product, whether to make or buy a component, whether to sell a product before or after additional processing, and what prices to charge for services and products. The process of making these types of decisions is discussed in a later chapter on activity-based costing.

This third function in the management process, evaluating, brings us back to the point where we started, planning. The information gained through the evaluating function is used in planning for the following period. Remember that as managers *evaluate* performance in the last period, they may also be making *planning* decisions to improve operations for the next period while gathering and receiving results to *control* the current period.

TO SUMMARIZE: The essential purpose of management accounting is to support decision making that adds value to the organization. Effective decision making is the key to the management process, and it is central to the management functions of planning, controlling, and evaluating. Planning is the process of making decisions about future products and services, operations, and investments. Controlling involves tracking actual costs, quality, and timing performance within the organization. Evaluating is a process of analyzing results, computing variances, and providing feedback to assess personnel, divisions, products, and processes. The natural end result of evaluating is the identification of problems and opportunities, and from there, the next stage of planning begins.

Introduction to Cost-Volume-Profit Analysis

3 Describe how the concepts of fixed and variable costs are used in C-V-P analysis in the management planning process.

cost-volume-profit (C-V-P) analysis Techniques for determining how changes in revenues, costs, and level of activity affect the profitability of an organization.

variable costs Costs that change in total in direct proportion to changes in activity level.

This section introduces **cost-volume-profit (C-V-P) analysis**, which is a management tool primarily used in the planning process. The basic objective of C-V-P analysis is determining the volume of products or services that will be required to generate a desired profit. For example, before opening a new Thai restaurant, the would-be restaurateur should calculate how many customers a day, on average, must be served in order to pay the rent and generate a reasonable profit. If the necessary number of customers to "break even" seems unreasonably high, the business plan must be revised or abandoned. This sounds like an obvious planning exercise, but too many small business owners neglect doing even this basic analysis.

To use C-V-P analysis successfully, a manager must categorize costs as either fixed or variable costs. The concept of fixed and variable costs is fairly simple. Total **variable costs** change in *direct proportion* to changes in some particular activity level, such as production or sales volumes. One example of a variable cost is the costs of materials (such as bolts of cloth in a clothing factory), which vary proportionately with the number of units produced. Sales commissions, which vary proportionately with sales volume, are another example of a variable cost. Another way to think of a variable cost is that the cost is a set amount per unit—$3.50 per meal or $2,000 per car or $12 per book. The more meals or cars or books that are sold, the higher the total variable cost.

The cost of bolts of cloth used in a clothing factory is classified as a variable cost because it varies proportionately by the number of units produced. The more cloth used in production, the more the total amount of this cost.

fixed costs Costs that remain constant in total, regardless of activity level, at least over a certain range of activity.

C a u t i o n

In theory, distinguishing between variable and fixed costs sounds simple. If the activity, such as production volume or sales volume, increases and the cost in question increases, then it must be a variable cost. Otherwise, it is a fixed cost. In reality, however, identifying and managing variable and fixed costs can involve many complexities. Subsequent chapters, particularly the next chapter, will focus more on identifying and using variable and fixed costs in the planning process.

In contrast, **fixed costs** remain constant in total, regardless of activity level, at least over a certain range of activity. Examples of fixed costs are rent, insurance, equipment depreciation, and supervisors' salaries. Regardless of changes in sales or production output, these costs typically remain constant. For example, think back on the Thai restaurant example mentioned earlier. The rent on the restaurant location is a fixed cost because, no matter how many customers are attracted to the restaurant during the month, the monthly rent is typically still the same amount.

To demonstrate C-V-P analysis in the planning process, let's use an example involving two DUPONT products, Teflon and Kevlar. Let's assume that you as a DuPont executive need to work through which product line to prioritize for the next year. It's not simply a matter of which product line is more profitable or which is expected to return the higher ROI. The decision also involves an assessment of the risk of these two products—in this case, the risk that either or both of these products will generate a loss instead of a profit. C-V-P analysis is used to assess this risk. The fundamental question addressed by C-V-P analysis is as follows: At what sales volume will the company "break even" (i.e., profit is exactly zero) in the Kevlar product line and in the Teflon product line? Answering this question requires that you use the concept of fixed and variable costs. Assume the following estimated price and cost data for the Kevlar and Teflon product lines for the upcoming year:

	Kevlar Product Line	Teflon Product Line
Sales price	$50.00 per pound	$140.00 per gallon
Variable cost	$18.00 per pound	$65.00 per gallon
Total monthly fixed costs	$5,600,000	$9,600,000

Introduction to Teflon® and Kevlar®

To better understand the nature of planning, controlling, and evaluating, we work through in this chapter some typical decisions that managers at DuPont may, in fact, be working on at the moment. We will focus on two product lines at DuPont—Teflon® resins and Kevlar® fiber. These flagship products at DuPont are actually quite amazing. You may already be familiar with them. Teflon is considered the most slippery material in existence. It begins as a mixture of chemicals that are then manipulated by DuPont's engineers to produce a product that has become a familiar household name through its use as a nonstick liner for pots and pans and as a soil and stain repellant for fabrics and clothing. One of Teflon's many less-known uses is as a coating for fiberglass fabrics used in permanent structures such as the Pontiac Silverdome in Detroit, Michigan, and the Carrier Dome at Syracuse University in Syracuse, New York. Currently, Teflon has an average sales price of approximately $140 per gallon.

Kevlar is an even more interesting product. It is a specialty fabric that is extremely strong and tough—so tough that ordinary scissors will not cut through a piece of the fabric! Kevlar starts in a liquid form, is then spun to the point where the Kevlar fibers come together, and finally is heated to complete the process. It is used for boat hulls, bullet-resistant vests, cut-resistant gloves, fiber-optic cables, tennis rackets, and skis. For example, a bullet-resistant vest that is made of seven layers of Kevlar weighs only 2.5 pounds, but can stop a .38-caliber bullet shot from only 10 feet away. The average sales price for Kevlar is approximately $50 per pound. This is expensive fabric! Usually, DuPont ships Kevlar as a staple fiber (similar to cotton balls), continuous filament (essentially, a yarn), or chopped fiber.

FYI:

C-V-P analysis is often referred to as break-even analysis.

STOP & THINK

Refer back to the fixed and variable cost data for the Teflon product line. For some C-V-P analysis practice, compute the number of gallons of Teflon that DuPont must sell each month in order to break even.

Typical variable costs are the costs of the raw chemicals used to produce Kevlar and Teflon and the labor costs of the workers involved in the manufacturing process. These costs are variable because the more Kevlar or Teflon produced, the more the total amount of these costs increases. Typical fixed costs are the cost of insurance on a chemical plant, the cost of plant supervisors, and the property taxes paid on a chemical facility. These costs are fixed because, within certain limits, they are the same no matter how much Kevlar or Teflon is produced.

As you examine the assumed cost numbers for Kevlar, you can see that DuPont sells a pound of Kevlar for $32.00 more than the *variable* costs associated with making the product ($50.00 sales price per pound − $18.00 variable cost per pound). A basic objective of C-V-P analysis is to determine how many pounds of Kevlar must be sold each month to generate enough profit to pay the $5,600,000 in fixed costs associated with manufacturing that product. The computation of this "break-even" amount is as follows:

$$\frac{\$5,600,000 \text{ fixed cost}}{\$50 \text{ sales price per pound} - \$18 \text{ variable cost per pound}} = 175,000 \text{ pounds}$$

This computation means that DuPont must sell 175,000 pounds of Kevlar each month, generating a profit of $32.00 on each pound, in order to be able to pay for its fixed costs of $5,600,000 per month. If DuPont sells fewer than 175,000 pounds in a month, then the fixed costs will not be covered, and the Kevlar product line will report a loss. Remember that the fixed costs of $5,600,000 will be there no matter how many pounds of Kevlar are sold!

You can use the information from this simple C-V-P analysis to make production plans with respect to Kevlar. For example, if current production plans, in conjunction with an assessment of the market demand, indicate that DuPont will consistently sell fewer than 175,000 pounds of Kevlar per month, you will almost certainly wish to change the plans. Costs must be squeezed, new markets need to be sought, perhaps prices should be raised—in short, something has to change because the C-V-P analysis suggests that sales of less than 175,000 pounds per month will not result in profits. We will study C-V-P analysis in detail in the next chapter.

TO SUMMARIZE: By defining costs as either fixed or variable, managers can add cost-volume-profit (C-V-P) analysis to the set of tools available in the management process of planning. Fixed costs are defined as those costs that will not change in relationship to a particular activity level such as sales volume. Conversely, variable costs are those costs that change in direct proportion to sales volume. Organizations can use C-V-P analysis to determine the sales volume necessary to break even (i.e., profit equals zero). Insights gained from C-V-P computations are extremely useful in the process of planning how and which product lines to emphasize for the future.

Product and Period Costs

4 Realize how the product cost classifications of direct materials, direct labor, and overhead are used in the management controlling process.

product costs Costs associated with products or services offered.

Imagine a trip to your favorite fast-food restaurant. Now consider all of the costs incurred by that entire fast-food organization, from the president's salary down to the cost of the lettuce for the sandwiches. For management accounting purposes, we can divide these costs into two groups, product costs and period costs. Costs closely associated with the products or services offered are called **product costs**. Examples in a fast-food setting are the cost of the food, the wages of the food preparers, the salary of the store manager, and the rent on the store location. As you sit there, ready to bite into your sandwich, you can look around and see all of these costs. In this sense, they are closely associated with the product (the sandwich) and are classified as product costs. In a manufacturing company such as DUPONT, for example, product

The Steely-Eyed Business Tycoon In the nineteenth century and much of the twentieth century, management accounting, known then as cost accounting, focused strictly on cost measurement and cost management. Business owners were making a great deal of money using this information to build and expand large companies. And no one understood cost information quite like Andrew Carnegie, who controlled about 25% of the American iron and steel production in 1899. Carnegie was obsessed with costs. One of his favorite sayings was "Watch the costs and the profits will take care of themselves." Was Carnegie's management accounting focus successful? In 1901 he sold his company, CARNEGIE STEEL, to the UNITED STATES STEEL CORPORATION for $250 million and retired. During his lifetime he gave more than $350 million to various educational, cultural, and peace institutions, many of which bear his name. Not bad for an immigrant with no formal education.

STOP & THINK

A major difference between Kelly Services and manufacturers or merchandisers is inventory. Kelly sells services. Can we put service labor into inventory? Think about this question; we'll discuss it later in the chapter on product cost flows.

period costs Costs not directly related to a product, service, or asset. These costs are charged as expenses to the income statement in the period in which they are incurred.

costs (often referred to as manufacturing costs) are all costs necessary to create finished goods ready for sale. They include all costs related to production: the factory manager's salary, depreciation and taxes on the factory building, wages of the factory workers, and the materials that go into the product. In a merchandising company such as MACY'S or SEARS, product costs are the costs incurred to purchase goods and get them ready for resale to customers. In a service company such as the UNION PACIFIC RAILROAD or KELLY SERVICES (which provides temporary employees), product costs (sometimes called cost of services) involve labor, supplies, and other costs directly related to providing services to customers.

Period costs are all costs incurred that are not closely associated with a specific product or service. In the fast-food setting we considered earlier, examples of period costs are the president's salary, advertising, and office costs incurred in the corporate headquarters. These are costs that are not associated with the sandwich that you are eating or the environment in which you are eating it. In general, the most common period costs are selling and administrative costs. Examples of selling costs are sales salaries, advertising, and delivery costs. Examples of administrative costs are salaries of the president and controller, depreciation or rent on office buildings, taxes on assets used in administration, and other office expenditures such as postage, supplies, and utilities.

The labels "product" and "period" stem from the procedure followed in reporting these costs as expenses on the income statement. For product costs, these costs are associated with specific products or services and are expensed when those products are sold. For example, if Sears sells two-thirds of the inventory it purchased during November, only the cost of the inventory sold (i.e., Cost of Goods Sold) becomes an expense on that month's income statement. The other third of the inventory cost remains an asset (i.e., Inventory) on the balance sheet. In contrast, period costs are reported as an expense *immediately* in the period in which they are incurred. So, regardless of how many products are sold during the month, the president's entire salary for November is recognized as an expense on the November monthly income statement. Thus, these costs are called period costs because they are always expensed in the period (e.g., month) in which they are incurred.

Types of Product Costs

Now let's consider how you might measure and control product and period costs in a variety of organizations. How would you measure product costs for a merchandiser? Actually, that is

Watch Your Language in Management Accounting! As good business professionals work to compete in the marketplace, a set of common management accounting terms has evolved. Remember, this is not financial accounting—it is important to understand that no official regulatory body of professionals has defined these terms. As you work in various organizations later in your career, you may find that these definitions can become a little unclear. Depending on the decision context, a particular cost can have several names. You need to understand this fact and recognize that allowing these definitions to "shift about" can be completely appropriate!

To illustrate, if you like playing card games such as bridge or canasta, you understand that it is often very important in the game to distinguish between cards of different suits—hearts, spades, clubs, or diamonds. On the other hand, for some decisions in the card game it may be more useful to concentrate on the value of the card—ace, 10, deuce, and so on. Thus, sometimes you care about the ace of hearts because of its "heartness," and at other times you are really more interested in its "aceness." Similarly, a product cost may also be a variable cost. Depending on the management setting, you may choose to categorize costs as fixed or variable versus product or period or direct or indirect.

So, in business conversations (discussions concerning costs, for example), never assume you are talking about the same concept as another individual. You always need to be sure that everyone is using the same definition of a management accounting term or concept before you let the conversation get too far.

a fairly easy question. The resources Macy's spends to acquire store inventory for resale to customers clearly are product costs. As products are sold, these inventory costs become an expense on the income statement. What about the wages and salaries of Macy's store clerks and managers? Macy's will likely categorize these costs as part of its selling and administrative expenses and treat them as a period cost on the income statement. That's not too difficult.

Now consider the same question for ERNST & YOUNG LLP, one of the largest certified public accounting (CPA) firms in the world. What are the products sold by this service firm? Ernst & Young sells the time of its tax accountants, auditors, and consultants. The salaries of these professionals represent the costs of its "product." These costs are reported as the expense "cost of services sold" in the same period in which Ernst & Young reports the corresponding service revenue. Thus, if the consulting revenue from a specific job is reported in January 2006, any product costs associated with that job which were incurred in 2005 are not expensed until January 2006. As of the end of 2005, these costs are given a label such as "consulting projects in progress" or "unbilled services" and reported as inventory on the December 2005 balance sheet. Ernst & Young also employs many other people (such as clerks, secretaries, and office managers) to support the professionals and to administer office needs. The costs of these people are not closely associated with specific consulting jobs. Accordingly, the wages and salaries of these clerks and office managers, along with costs of office rent, desk supplies, and computers, are likely treated as period costs and recognized as selling and administrative expenses on the income statement in the period in which they are incurred.

When identifying product costs for control purposes, the most challenging organization to analyze is a manufacturing business. Does DuPont purchase inventory for resale? Actually, it does purchase some inventory, such as basic chemicals. But it doesn't simply turn around and resell these basic chemicals to customers. Significant processing has to take place before these raw materials become a finished product ready for sale. DuPont must employ laborers to work with these chemicals. In addition, DuPont builds factory buildings and purchases manufactur-

direct materials Materials that become part of the product and are traceable to it.

indirect materials Materials that are necessary to a manufacturing or service business but are not directly included in or are not a significant part of the actual product.

direct labor Wages that are paid to those who physically work on direct materials to transform them into a finished product and are traceable to specific products.

indirect labor Labor that is necessary to a manufacturing or service business but is not directly related to the actual production of the manufactured or service product.

manufacturing overhead All costs incurred in the manufacturing process other than direct materials and direct labor.

ing equipment. DuPont must also employ managers and other support personnel (such as engineers and custodians) to support the line workers' efforts to convert basic chemicals into finished products. These are all product costs. Basically, any cost required to get the product manufactured and ready for sale is a product cost.

To help management analyze the manufacturing cost of its products, product costs are divided into three components: (1) direct materials, (2) direct labor, and (3) manufacturing overhead. **Direct materials** are materials that become part of the product and are traceable to it. Some materials, however, such as the glue and nails in a finished piece of furniture, are so minor and their use so difficult to trace to a specific product that they are not considered direct materials, but rather **indirect materials**. Indirect materials also include the materials and supplies used in nonproduction activities such as maintenance and custodial processes. **Direct labor** consists of the wages that are paid to those who physically work on the direct materials to transform them into a finished product. Conversely, wages and salaries paid to factory supervisors and management, maintenance staff, and factory security guards are treated as **indirect labor**. **Manufacturing overhead** includes all other costs incurred in the manufacturing process not specifically identified as direct materials or direct labor. Both indirect materials and indirect labor are included in manufacturing overhead. Exhibit 2 summarizes the relationship between product costs and period costs in various types of organizations.

Computing the Cost of Manufactured Products: How Low Can You Go?

Imagine that another company has recently introduced a new product on the market that competes directly with DuPont's Kevlar. Soon the intense competition between DuPont and the other company for customer orders starts to force down the market price of Kevlar. Now you and the rest of the DuPont management team have a problem. How low can you let the price of Kevlar drop before the company starts losing money? Answering this question requires that DuPont's accountants do a good job of measuring the costs of creating Kevlar. The following simple numbers illustrate how difficult it is to answer the straightforward question: How much does it cost to make a pound of Kevlar?

Direct materials	$16.00 per pound
Direct labor	$0.60 per pound
Manufacturing overhead:	
Variable	$1.40 per pound
Fixed	$1,500,000 per month
General corporate sales and administrative costs	$4,100,000 per month

Exhibit 2: Product Costs and Period Costs in Business Organizations

Type of Company	Product Costs	Period Costs
Service company	Costs of providing services	Selling costs Administrative costs
Merchandising company (wholesale or retail)	Costs incurred in purchasing goods from suppliers	Selling costs Administrative costs
Manufacturing company	All manufacturing costs including direct materials, direct labor, and manufacturing overhead	Selling costs Administrative costs

Caution

Even though the general corporate sales and administrative costs would not be included in computing the cost to make a pound of Kevlar, the sales price of a pound of Kevlar must cover both the direct product costs and the period costs, and provide a reasonable profit as well. Proper pricing is discussed in a later chapter on making decisions.

The $4,100,000 per month in general corporate sales and administrative costs is a period cost and, therefore, would not be included in computing the cost to make a pound of Kevlar.

The variable manufacturing overhead costs might include some utility costs (e.g., power to run the equipment) and repairs and maintenance costs that change based on production volumes (similar to the way maintenance costs of your car increase the more you drive it). From the data in the cost table above, it is clear that the variable product cost to make a pound of Kevlar is $18.00 ($16.00 + $0.60 + $1.40), as mentioned earlier in our discussion of fixed and variable costs. But it clearly isn't correct to state that a pound of Kevlar "costs" $18.00 because the Kevlar manufacturing process includes fixed manufacturing overhead costs as well. These fixed costs include factory rent, depreciation, production supervisor salaries, and so forth. So, the cost of a pound of Kevlar is at least $18.00, plus some addition for the fixed manufacturing overhead costs.

Determining the proper amount of fixed manufacturing overhead that should be assigned to, or allocated to, each unit of production is one of the most difficult tasks in the field of management accounting. For one thing, the amount of fixed manufacturing overhead per pound of Kevlar produced depends on the number of pounds that are actually produced in a month. Remember that, by definition, the fixed overhead amount of $1,500,000 per month is the same whether one pound or one million pounds are produced. If one pound is produced, the fixed overhead per unit is $1,500,000; if one million pounds are produced, the fixed overhead per pound is $1.50. With these numbers, we see that we can compute a cost per pound of Kevlar of anywhere from $19.50 ($18.00 variable + $1.50 fixed allocation) to $1,500,018 ($18.00 variable + $1,500,000 fixed allocation). Obviously, this ridiculously wide range of cost estimates is useless in helping to determine what price DuPont should charge for a pound of Kevlar. The company needs accurate, reliable estimates of production volume in order to generate useful cost computations. Assuming that DuPont expects to produce on average 300,000 pounds of Kevlar each month, the fixed manufacturing overhead cost per pound can be allocated as follows:

$$\$1,500,000 \div 300,000 \text{ pounds} = \$5.00 \text{ per pound}$$

Adding together the fixed and variable manufacturing costs per batch, the expected total manufacturing cost is $23.00 per pound of Kevlar ($18.00 variable manufacturing costs + $5.00 fixed manufacturing overhead). Assuming that this method of allocating manufacturing overhead costs to Kevlar is appropriate, you can use this measure as a benchmark to track actual production costs as they come in throughout the year.

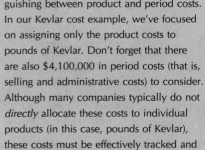

Caution

Remember that this section began by distinguishing between product and period costs. In our Kevlar cost example, we've focused on assigning only the product costs to pounds of Kevlar. Don't forget that there are also $4,100,000 in period costs (that is, selling and administrative costs) to consider. Although many companies typically do not *directly* allocate these costs to individual products (in this case, pounds of Kevlar), these costs must be effectively tracked and considered in the management process of controlling (as well as planning and evaluating) specific products and services.

You've probably already wondered if this simple spreading of the fixed manufacturing overhead costs evenly across the units produced might ignore some important realities in manufacturing. Some products simply require more overhead costs than do others. For example, producing a pound of Kevlar involves hazardous chemicals and careful inspection by chemical engineers trained in quality control. The existence of these hazardous chemicals necessitates the use of special handling equipment and extra insurance, and the quality control inspectors must be paid a salary commensurate with their skills. Accordingly, the production of Kevlar requires additional overhead costs that would not be required by the production of, say, Lycra® fabric. Proper management accounting involves the identification of specific activities (often called cost drivers) that create a need to spend money on fixed manufacturing overhead. A good managerial accounting system assigns a higher cost to those products that create more fixed manufacturing overhead. The computation of product costs, and the procedures involved in the allocation of fixed manufacturing overhead costs to different products, are discussed later in two chapters on product cost flows and activity-based costing, respectively.

TO SUMMARIZE: Costs are initially categorized as either product or period costs. Many period costs are classified as sales and administrative overhead and are, generally, quite difficult to associate with any of the particular products or services that the company provides to the marketplace. Examples of period costs include salaries of selling and advertising personnel and rent or depreciation costs on administrative office buildings. On the other hand, product costs are closely related to the actual process of providing specific goods and services to customers. Because the management process of controlling costs involves the effort to classify and track costs of providing specific goods and services, product costs are typically assigned to specific products or services in an effort to effectively control these costs. Product costs for manufacturing companies such as DuPont are traditionally divided into costs of direct materials, direct labor, and manufacturing overhead. Direct materials are those items that become part of the final product and are easily traceable to it. Direct labor costs are the wages of workers who are "hands on" involved in the production of the final product. Manufacturing overhead costs are essentially defined as all costs essential to the production of goods or services that cannot be categorized as direct materials and direct labor and *directly* assigned to specific goods and services. Perhaps the most challenging aspect of controlling costs for accountants is the process of *indirectly* assigning (i.e., allocating) overhead costs to specific products.

Segment Analysis

5 Understand the concepts of direct, indirect, and opportunity costs in the management evaluating process.

Managers and executives are typically paid well to make hard decisions. You may find in your future business career as a manager that the process of evaluating the performance of divisions, personnel, processes, and products is complicated as markets for particular products change based on developments in technology, new fads and trends in consumer taste, and increased pressure from new and existing competitors. Occasionally, the situation requires a serious look at the potential need to exit from a particular market or to drop a specific product line. Sometimes these decisions are motivated by the opportunity to enter a new market or add a new product line. For example, airlines are constantly evaluating whether to cut service on less-traveled routes, to increase or cut back the number of first-class seats, and so forth. The decision to drop a product line is critical because subsequently reversing the decision can be difficult or impossible. Good management accounting can do much to facilitate the process of evaluating divisions, personnel, processes, and products. Conversely, a poor understanding of some critical management accounting concepts can lead to painful, if not potentially lethal, company problems. To illustrate how accounting supports this evaluation process, we need to extend your vocabulary of key management accounting terms.

Direct and Indirect Costs

So far we have identified fixed and variable costs as a method of cost classification that provides good support to the planning process. We've also defined product and period costs and used those classifications to demonstrate the management controlling process. Now we introduce some new ways to classify costs that are useful for evaluating performance. One of these classifications is direct costs and indirect costs. **Direct costs** are costs that can be obviously and physically traced to a business unit or segment being analyzed. The unit may be a sales territory, product line, division, plant, or any other subdivision for which performance needs to be analyzed. Direct costs are often described as those costs that could be saved if the segment were to be discontinued. Typically, many types of direct costs are variable, but some direct costs are fixed. For example, if the business segment being considered is a branch sales office, the cost of inventory and labor to run the store would be direct costs that are variable, while the cost to rent the building would be a direct cost that is fixed.

Indirect costs—sometimes referred to as common costs or joint costs—are costs that are normally incurred for the benefit of several segments. Indirect costs can also be either fixed or

direct costs Costs that are specifically traceable to a unit of business or segment being analyzed.

indirect costs Costs normally incurred for the benefit of several segments within the organization; sometimes called common costs or joint costs.

variable, although these costs are nearly always fixed. Sometimes these costs are allocated in order to be assigned to a segment. For example, consider a sales manager's salary. If a segment is defined as a branch sales office and a sales manager supervises only one segment, the manager's salary is likely a direct cost of that sales office. If the manager is responsible for several segments, however, the salary would then be an indirect cost to any one of the sales offices. Total indirect costs, such as the manager's salary, normally do not change if one or more of the segments (in this case, the sales offices) are discontinued. Another example of an indirect cost may be manufacturing overhead. In most large organizations, many (but not all) types of manufacturing overhead costs are not directly identifiable with a specific product or product line. Hence, manufacturing overhead costs are typically classified as indirect costs to these products or product lines because they are incurred as a consequence of general or overall operating activities.

Costs are designated as either direct or indirect so that a business segment such as a division or product line can be evaluated on the basis of only those costs *directly* traceable or chargeable to it. Although companies sometimes allocate indirect costs among segments, such allocations often confuse the analysis of the segment's operations. By focusing only on direct costs, management can both identify segments where performance needs to be improved and recognize segments where performance is outstanding and should be rewarded.

FYI:

Activity-based costing (ABC) is a relatively new method of cost assignment that we will fully discuss in a later chapter on activity-based costing. A major emphasis of ABC is to connect costs directly with certain activities. One result of ABC is an increase in the number of costs that can be classified as direct costs.

Differential Costs and Sunk Costs

The difference between direct costs and indirect costs is similar to the difference between another set of cost terms—differential costs and sunk costs. The **differential costs** of a decision—sometimes called avoidable costs, incremental costs, or relevant costs—are the future costs that change as a result of that decision. In the context of making a decision as to whether to drop a product line, there is likely little difference between the terms *differential cost* and *direct cost.* (The term *differential* is also commonly applied to future *revenues* that will be affected by the decision.) **Sunk costs**, on the other hand, are past costs that cannot be changed as the result of a future decision. You should note that the definition of sunk costs is not quite the same as that of indirect costs. Indirect costs are those costs that are not affected by a *particular* decision. For example, whether DUPONT decides to continue or discontinue its Kevlar product line will likely not affect its general and administrative costs. These costs are indirect to the Kevlar product line. This does not mean that management cannot change any of DuPont's general and administrative costs. It just means that a different management decision process is required to change these costs than the process used in evaluating the feasibility of the Kevlar product line. If this sounds as though a cost could be indirect to one evaluation situation or focus and direct to another, you're right! Defining a cost as direct or indirect depends on the object of the decision. On the other hand, sunk costs are not dependent at all on any decision object. A sunk cost is exactly what it sounds like—sunk! There is nothing a company can reasonably do to change a sunk cost.

differential costs Future costs that change as a result of a decision; also called incremental or relevant costs.

sunk costs Costs, such as depreciation, that are past costs and do not change as a result of a future decision.

As an example of sunk costs, the costs that DuPont may have spent last year upgrading its Teflon manufacturing facilities are not relevant to the decision this year as to whether it should continue to compete in the market for performance coatings. Yet many individuals and companies make poor decisions because they fail to correctly distinguish between differential costs and sunk costs. As a personal example, assume you have season tickets to a school's basketball game. On the night of a game, a friend asks you to go to a movie with her. You have wanted to see the movie for a long time. If you decline because you have already purchased the basketball tickets and believe you must therefore go to the game, you may have made the wrong decision. The cost of the basketball tickets is a sunk cost. The only costs that are relevant to your decision are the costs associated with going to the movie, such as the ticket price and popcorn and other goodies you might buy, as well as any out-of-pocket costs you might spend at the basketball game.

Out-of-Pocket Costs and Opportunity Costs

out-of-pocket costs Costs that require an outlay of cash or other resources.

opportunity costs The benefits lost or forfeited as a result of selecting one alternative course of action over another.

At the most general level, costs can be separated into out-of-pocket costs and opportunity costs. **Out-of-pocket costs** require an outlay of cash or other resources. Many of the costs discussed thus far in this chapter could be called out-of-pocket costs (though sunk costs are never considered an out-of-pocket cost). If a company is deciding whether to accept a special order, the costs of materials needed to produce that order are out-of-pocket costs. If a fast-food restaurant is considering installing a drive-up window, the cost of construction is an out-of-pocket cost. Naïve individuals and organizations usually consider only out-of-pocket costs when making decisions. For example, an individual deciding whether to attend a movie might consider only the $9 cost of the ticket required to gain admittance. On the other hand, opportunity costs do not require an outlay of resources. Nevertheless, they are as important as out-of-pocket costs to good management decision making. **Opportunity costs** are the benefits lost or forfeited as a result of selecting one alternative course of action over another. For example, choosing to go to a movie instead of working two hours at $8 per hour has an opportunity cost of $16, as well as an out-of-pocket cost of $9 for the ticket. Installing a drive-up window at a fast-food outlet may have several opportunity costs, such as lost seating or lost parking available to customers.

STOP & THINK

Which of the following costs are typically recorded in a traditional accounting system: product costs, fixed costs, indirect costs, out-of-pocket costs, sunk costs, opportunity costs?

Segment Analysis at DuPont

Let's return once more to DuPont and have you apply these new cost concepts in the process of evaluating the Kevlar and Teflon product lines to determine if the company can continue to

b u s i n e s s   e n v i r o n m e n t

Accounting and the "Shaq Impact" Opportunity costs are important in all organizations but are especially critical in situations where there are defined limits on available resources. Professional basketball teams, for example, have league-imposed salary caps that dictate the maximum total amount of salaries they can pay to team members. In the 2002/2003 season, the salary cap was $40.3 million per team. When an exceptional player, such as Shaquille O'Neal (Shaq) of the LOS ANGELES LAKERS, comes up for salary negotiations, the team's management must consider both out-of-pocket and opportunity costs when deciding whether to pay the salary requested. For example, Shaq's salary in the 2002/2003

season with the Los Angeles Lakers was close to $24 million. Before agreeing to this contract, the Lakers management had to decide whether ticket sales and TV revenues would be sufficient to meet the out-of-pocket cost of $24 million. Management also had to consider what other player(s) it could sign for $24 million per year and whether, based on the existence of the salary cap, it would be able to pay other current and prospective players enough. For example, the Lakers paid Kobe Bryant approximately $12 million for the 2002/2003 season. Paying $36 million per year to Shaq and Kobe makes it nearly impossible for the Lakers to pay other players that much money and thus is a high opportunity cost for a professional basketball team. (*Note:* The Lakers' total team salary payout for 2002/2003 was nearly $63 million. The NBA penalizes teams going over the salary cap with a hefty salary "luxury tax.")

profitably offer both products to the public. Assume that the following data represent the results of operations this last month for these two products:

Operating Statements	Kevlar	Teflon	Total
Sales revenue	$15,000,000	$14,000,000	$ 29,000,000
Variable manufacturing costs	(5,400,000)	(6,500,000)	(11,900,000)
Fixed manufacturing overhead	(1,500,000)	(3,200,000)	(4,700,000)
Sales and administrative costs	(4,100,000)	(6,400,000)	(10,500,000)
Operating profit	**$ 4,000,000**	**$ (2,100,000)**	**$ 1,900,000**

It looks as though DuPont had a tough month with the Teflon product. In fact, let's assume that the past several months show similar losses on the Teflon product line. In evaluating these results, perhaps you should consider the possibility of dropping this product line. Doing so would certainly improve overall profits for the organization, wouldn't it? Actually, we need to be careful with this analysis. The operating statements above categorize the costs in terms of product costs and period costs. Is that the right way to view these costs for this particular decision? What are the *direct* costs in this decision? Stated another way, what are the *differential* (or *avoidable*) costs of producing Teflon? If you choose to exit from the market for Teflon products, can all of the variable manufacturing costs be avoided in the future? With some effort, yes. How about fixed manufacturing overhead? These costs are going to be more difficult to handle. Fixed manufacturing overhead includes items such as supervisors' salaries and depreciation on equipment and plant facilities. Can you avoid some of these costs? Actually, perhaps some of these costs can be avoided, but many of these costs are usually unavoidable. For example, let's assume that both Kevlar and Teflon are manufactured in the same building. The depreciation on this building, a fixed manufacturing cost, is allocated to both product lines (a classic example of an indirect cost). In this case, if you choose to drop a product line, the cost related to building depreciation is simply reassigned to the remaining products. Sales and administrative costs assigned to the Teflon product line are even less likely to be avoided by a decision to exit this market. These costs often remain within the company and are the responsibility of all of the product lines.

To better support a decision process involving the possibility of dropping Teflon from DuPont's mix of products, you really need to reclassify the product and period costs above as either direct or indirect to the product line. In making this new classification, we'll assume that approximately 30% of the fixed manufacturing overhead can be avoided if Teflon is dropped (e.g., 30% of the fixed manufacturing overhead costs are salaries of personnel that can be dismissed or reassigned to other product lines). This means that 30% of the fixed manufacturing overhead is a *direct* cost to the segment.

Operating Statements	Kevlar	Teflon	Total
Sales revenue	$15,000,000	$14,000,000	$ 29,000,000
Direct costs:			
Variable manufacturing costs	(5,400,000)	(6,500,000)	(11,900,000)
Fixed manufacturing overhead (30%)	(450,000)	(960,000)	(1,410,000)
Segment profit	**$ 9,150,000**	**$ 6,540,000**	**$ 15,690,000**
Indirect costs:			
Fixed manufacturing overhead (70%)	(1,050,000)	(2,240,000)	(3,290,000)
Sales and administrative costs	(4,100,000)	(6,400,000)	(10,500,000)
Operating profit	**$ 4,000,000**	**$ (2,100,000)**	**$ 1,900,000**

What do you learn from this new analysis? Those costs that can be removed from the system by discontinuing the Teflon business segment are direct costs to the segment, and these are the only costs relevant to this decision. All other costs are actually indirect costs (also called common costs) that have been assigned by the accounting system to the Teflon segment. Should you choose to exit the market for Teflon products, these costs will remain in the company and will likely be reallocated to the remaining business segments. So what will be the financial impact of dropping the Teflon product line? The "true" performance of Teflon last month was *not* a loss, but a $6,540,000 contribution to overall company profits.

Finally, in your analysis of the profitability of these two products lines, you also need to think about the opportunity costs of producing Teflon. In other words, if you choose to leave the Teflon business, can DuPont use the Teflon assets to produce and sell another product? Whatever value that alternative product might contribute to overall company profits is an opportunity cost of producing Teflon. This is an important cost that doesn't get formally reported in most accounting systems, yet a good business manager (like you!) will need to consider these very relevant costs in some decisions. We'll talk more about opportunity cost and segment analysis in a later chapter on making decisions.

> ⚠ **Caution**
>
> It is important to understand that opportunity costs are very important costs that are not formally tracked in the company's accounting system.

TO SUMMARIZE: Different terms are used to describe costs depending on the aspect of the management process involved—planning, controlling, or evaluating. In the evaluation of segments such as product lines or business divisions, managers need to be clear about the difference between direct and indirect costs. Direct costs are costs that are specifically traceable to a segment. Sometimes direct costs are referred to as differential costs, avoidable costs, incremental costs, or relevant costs. The direct costs of a particular segment will change based on future decisions affecting the segment. On the other hand, indirect costs, also known as common costs, are costs that are normally incurred for the benefit of several segments. Although indirect costs can be changed by some high-level management processes, decisions that specifically affect any one of the segments will not affect indirect costs that are common across all the segments. On the other hand, sunk costs are costs that cannot be changed based on *any* decisions made by management. These are costs that have already been spent (such as depreciation on a purchased building) or costs that cannot be realistically avoided (such as the property tax on the administration building). Finally, opportunity costs are measured as the benefits lost by choosing one alternative over another. Opportunity costs, though not recorded formally in most companies' accounting systems, are relevant to most decisions. These cost terms are particularly useful in the management process of evaluating the contribution of product lines or departments in an organization.

Expanding Management Accounting: Cost, Quality, and Time

6 Understand that management accounting still continues to evolve.

just-in-time (JIT) A management philosophy that emphasizes removing all waste of effort, time, and inventory costs from the organization. One obvious result of JIT is the reduction or removal of needless inventory in a production process.

The DUPONT ROI (return on investment) formula is a terrific tool for managing most kinds of organizations. You realize, though, that ROI has been with us now for nearly a century. Most educated managers are fully aware of ROI and how to apply it within their particular organization. Remember that the development of management accounting is a function of the need for information and tools that provide a competitive edge. Would you expect then that the use of ROI provides managers a significant competitive edge in *today's* economy? The truth of the matter is that, in most industries, effective use of ROI and other traditional management accounting tools is still necessary, but using only these tools is probably not sufficient to successfully plan, control, and evaluate a business process. In order to be competitive, today's managers constantly need more and better information. In fact, beginning with the Japanese innovation of **just-in-time (JIT)** in the mid-twentieth century, accountants and other information providers have moved beyond just providing data on costs to include innovative methods of measuring the *quality* and the *timeliness* of products and production processes, as well as service and distribution systems. As an example, businesses today create a competitive advantage by delivering more

cycle time The total time a product spends moving through a particular process or cycle within the organization, such as the product design cycle, the production cycle, or the order and delivery cycle.

value to customers in less **cycle time** than competitors. As a firm creates and exploits a competitive advantage in cost, quality, and time, it creates increased shareholder value. In other words, if you make your customers happy, you create more profitable financial outcomes and, in the process, make the owners (shareholders) of the business happy! As a result, new performance measures related to cost, quality, and time are being created, tracked, and monitored by firms in many modern industries and have become a hot topic for research among managers and accountants. Some examples of the new performance measures being tracked by managers

business environment

One Company's Experience with Cost, Quality, and Time Developing measures of cost, quality, and time is a highly proprietary strategic activity. Many organizations are very reluctant to disclose the specifics of their efforts to develop competitive information in these three areas. One company (a medium-sized aerospace corporation in the Pacific Northwest that chooses to remain anonymous) provides a good illustration of the process of creating cost, quality, and time strategic measures. In 1989, the executive team started work to develop new competitive information for this company. It first conducted a survey of key customers, asking about product design, quality, and reliability; the company's ability to meet delivery schedules and other commitments; pricing and perceived value; service and the capability to recover from mistakes; and the overall ease of doing business with the company.

The results were surprising. Contrary to expectations, customers weren't concerned with the company's technological innovations that management had been proud of for years. Instead, customers were concerned with cost, quality, and delivery performance. To their dismay, the executives discovered that customers were dissatisfied with the company's performance in these three areas. Some said they continued to buy from the company only because it was easy to do business with and resolved problems quickly. Clearly, the company was at risk of losing its customers to a competitor unless some changes were made!

To refocus the company on the needs of its customers, an executive staff team was formed to meet weekly to develop a new performance measurement system. The meetings turned into prolonged debates over the number and kind of measures to use. Hours of brainstorming eventually led to the following list:

Cost Measures
- Engineering cost performance
- Production efficiency
- Rework and scrap costs

Quality Measures
- Quality of supplier's products
- Manufacturing first-pass yield
- Warranty returns

Time Measures
- New-product development cycle time
- Master schedule stability
- Manufacturing cycle time
- On-time delivery

The executive team assigned the company's controller to collect performance data for each of these 10 measures and issue a monthly report. Graphs of the results were posted for employees and customers to see and became a critical part of any meeting in which management reviewed performance. Some adjustments to these measures were made based on feedback from employees and customers. Eventually, this new approach to performance measures played a crucial role in the company's overall efforts to increase its competitive position. By 1993, it achieved the following performance improvements:

- Customer-quoted delivery times were cut by 50%.
- On-time shipments rose 89%.
- Product-development cycle time fell 35%.
- Manufacturing costs as a percentage of manufacturing sales fell 10%.

Source: K. V. Ramanathan and D. S. Schaffer, "How Am I Doing?" *Journal of Accountancy*, May 1995, pp. 79–82.

in the strategic areas of cost, quality, and time are displayed in Exhibit 3. We'll discuss many of these performance measures in later chapters.

The idea of extending beyond cost to also compete on quality and time is having a major impact in industries across the world. These developments present a real opportunity for today's accountants to jump in and be a part of the competitive management process! However, some accountants are frankly not paying attention to this recent shift in management information needs. These accountants continue to focus on providing cost data only. Apparently, they haven't learned their history lesson. Success and profits flow to the business that creates new views of information it can use to gain a competitive edge in the marketplace. On the other hand, some farsighted managers and accountants see this trend and are currently bringing together "balanced scorecards" that combine cost, quality, and time data to support decision making that can literally redefine customer and client service. We'll talk more about balanced scorecards and other recent innovations in management accounting in the final chapter on continuous improvement.

Exhibit 3: New Measures of Cost, Quality, and Time

Cost Measures	Quality Measures	Time Measures
Engineering cost performance	Manufacturing first-pass yield	On-time delivery
Rework and scrap costs	Warranty returns	Master schedule stability
Cost versus features/benefits delivered	Vendor supply quality	New-product development cycle time
Costs of quality	Service and support events	Manufacturing cycle time
Life cycle costs	Successful availability events	Recovery-response time
Target costs	Alignment with customer expectations	Time to market
Learning costs	Six sigma error rate	Order fulfillment cycle time
Activity costs	Waste, scrap, and rework rates	Rework and other non-value-added time

TO SUMMARIZE: In the twenty-first century, strategic performance measures of cost, quality, and time have continued to support and improve decisions that build organizations both in the profit and the not-for-profit sectors of our society. Accountants working inside of companies, if they expect to have jobs as key decision-support professionals in the twenty-first century, must provide data that encompass all three of these strategic imperatives.

The Role of Ethics in Management Accounting

7 Discuss the need for ethics in management accounting and describe the Standards of Ethical Conduct that apply to this profession.

The function of management accounting in the organization is to support competitive decision making by collecting, processing, and communicating information that helps managers plan, control, and evaluate business processes and company strategy. The top accountant in most large organizations is usually called the controller. In most organizations, professionals responsible for accounting systems and other critical decision-support data report to the controller. The controller usually reports to a vice president of finance or perhaps the chief finance officer (CFO). This individual, in turn, reports to the organization's president or chief executive officer (CEO). As the chief accounting officer, the controller is ultimately responsible for what information is created to manage the organization, as well as how that information is used. This individual, as well as all others who work with him or her, are in a position of significant power. Those who manage the management accounting process have access to the organization's most important and sensitive competitive information used to make operational and strategic decisions. Hence, it is absolutely critical that these individuals conduct their work professionally and with utmost integrity. Otherwise, the consequences of unethical behavior in the practice of management accounting can ruin (and, on occasion, has ruined) individuals, companies, and communities.

Unfortunately, ethical dilemmas in both large and small organizations are not rare. As white-collar crime continues to rise, those who work in management accounting are often confronted with ethical issues on the job and need to be prepared to deal with them on a rational basis. A sampling of some of the ethical dilemmas that business professionals may be exposed to are listed in Exhibit 4. If your career path leads you to the position that involves management accounting (and most management positions in an organization do somehow involve management accounting processes), you will find that dealing with these types of ethical indiscretions is often not easy. The situation is often complicated by the fact that violators are frequently people you know and work with. Further, your role as a member of the management team requires that as far as possible you work to handle questions of ethics *within* the organization. However, some occasions may require you to involve outside authorities. The Institute of Management Accountants (IMA) is the leading professional organization in North America devoted exclusively to management accounting. Its goals are to help those working in management accounting to develop both personally and professionally, by means of education, certification, and association with other business professionals. As a respected leader within the global financial community, the IMA's ethical standards provide guidance to practitioners for maintaining the highest levels of ethical conduct. Essentially, the IMA notes that its members are ethically required to (1) be competent in their profession, (2) not disclose confidential information, (3) act with both actual and apparent integrity in all situations, and (4) maintain objectivity when communicating information to decision makers. If confronted with situations that may involve ethical conflicts, the business professional should consider the following courses of action:

Exhibit 4: Ethical Dilemmas Faced by Management Accountants

> ***Ethical internal dilemmas***
> - Padding expense accounts
> - Theft in the workplace
> - Inflating profits on financial reports
> - Violating a firm's purchasing policies
> - Understating or postponing recognition of costs to achieve higher bonuses or make the financial statements look better
> - Using company assets for personal use
>
> ***Ethical issues involving third-party transactions***
> - Bid rigging to give business to favored suppliers
> - Taking kickbacks on purchase contracts
> - Adjusting inspection reports to reflect higher quality of product
> - Withholding unfavorable information

(1) Discuss the problem with the immediate supervisor (only when the supervisor is involved should higher management levels be involved). (2) Confidentially use an objective advisor to help clarify the issues. (3) Resign from the organization and submit an informative report to an appropriate representative of the organization (after exhausting all levels of internal communication).[3]

Although the IMA has a formal code of ethics, there really isn't a perfect set of rules you can follow to help you resolve every conflict. Therefore, you need to be developing values and skills right now in order to prepare for future challenges. To help you, we have included at the end of each chapter at least one ethics case. Perhaps more than anything else you do, developing a commitment to and an understanding of good ethics will develop you into a great business professional and will help improve our society.

> **TO SUMMARIZE:** Management accounting plays a key role in organizations today. The chief accountant in most organizations is the controller. This person is ultimately responsible for the quality of the management accounting used in the organization. The fact that management accounting provides a wide variety of information critical to many decisions means that those involved with creating this information will occasionally confront ethical issues inside the organization. Hence, these business professionals need to anticipate and be prepared to deal with various ethical dilemmas. The Institute of Management Accountants provides standards of ethical conduct to help guide professionals involved in management accounting processes.

In Conclusion—The Management Process

We have focused this chapter around DUPONT and the way this company uses management accounting to provide managers with information that has competitive value. To accomplish this, however, those who use management accounting must understand the types of decisions being made and how these decisions affect management of a successful organization. In particular, we've introduced a number of important accounting terms in the context of the management process of planning, controlling, and evaluating. Throughout the remainder of this text, we'll continue to organize management accounting topics around this management process.

review of learning objectives

1 Understand the essential differences between management accounting and financial accounting. Management accounting as we know it today is a product of managers and owners reacting to competitive forces. At the turn of the twentieth century, the DUPONT CORPORATION combined many management accounting innovations into a new performance evaluation model based on the return on investment (ROI) measure. Hence, the development trend of management accounting is in contrast to the legislative and regulatory forces that define financial accounting.

2 Understand that successfully managing a company requires good information that supports effective planning, controlling, and evaluating processes. Planning involves both long-term planning such as strategic planning and capital budgeting and short-term planning involving

---

3 A more complete description of the IMA's "Standards of Ethical Conduct" can be viewed at the following URL: **http://www.imanet.org/ima/sec.asp?TRACKID=&CID=191&DID=323**

production and process prioritizing as well as operational budgeting. Effective control of costs in the organization requires good tracking of actual performance. Evaluating involves analyzing results, providing feedback to managers and other employees, rewarding performance, and identifying problems. Evaluating naturally leads management back to the planning process, illustrating the interrelationship of the management process.

3 **Describe how the concepts of fixed and variable costs are used in C-V-P analysis in the management planning process.** It is important to understand how accounting terminology must change to support specific management settings. In the context of cost-volume-profit (C-V-P) analysis, costs are classified as variable costs or fixed costs. Using this classification, C-V-P analysis then follows a formula approach to determine the sales volumes necessary to achieve a specified profit level.

4 **Realize how the product cost classifications of direct materials, direct labor, and overhead are used in the management controlling process.** For manufacturing firms, product costs include direct materials, direct labor, and manufacturing overhead. In a merchandising company, product costs are costs incurred to purchase goods and get them ready for resale. For service firms, product costs are costs of providing services to customers. These costs are used to determine both asset values on the balance sheet and costs of goods sold on the income statement. In contrast to product costs, period costs are used strictly to compute the selling and general administrative expenses on the income statement. The process of identifying, tracking, and controlling product costs requires an intelligent method of allocating overhead costs to goods and services.

5 **Understand the concepts of direct, indirect, and opportunity costs in the management evaluating process.** Costs can be distinguished as being direct or indirect depending on their relationship to a particular segment being evaluated. Essentially, all costs that would be eliminated if the business discontinued the segment are considered the direct costs of that particular segment. Other costs currently allocated to the segment being considered for removal that would essentially shift to other segments are indirect costs. Sunk costs are those costs in the organization that no reasonable decision of any kind can avoid. These costs are essentially irrelevant to any decisions in the organization. On the other hand, opportunity costs, which are rarely tracked in the formal accounting system, are nearly always relevant to decisions.

6 **Understand that management accounting still continues to evolve.** As competition has increased and markets have become more sophisticated, management accounting today is expanding beyond cost management to include performance measures of quality and timeliness.

7 **Discuss the need for ethics in management accounting and describe the Standards of Ethical Conduct that apply to this profession.** The process of management accounting is critical in most organizations. Therefore, those involved in this process must conduct themselves professionally at all times and be prepared to deal with ethical dilemmas. The Institute of Management Accountants (IMA) has a code of ethical conduct that establishes an expectation of competence, confidentiality, integrity, and objectivity.

k ey terms & concepts

capital budgeting, 7
controlling, 9
cost-volume-profit (C-V-P) analysis, 10
cycle time, 22
differential costs, 18
direct costs, 17
direct labor, 15
direct materials, 15

evaluating, 9
fixed costs, 11
indirect costs, 17
indirect labor, 15
indirect materials, 15
just-in-time (JIT), 21
manufacturing overhead, 15
operational budgeting, 9
opportunity costs, 19

out-of-pocket costs, 19
period costs, 13
planning, 7
product costs, 12
production prioritizing, 8
return on investment (ROI), 5
strategic planning, 7
sunk costs, 18
variable costs, 10

discussion questions

1. The chapter states that the focus of management accounting is to create information to fill a competitive need. Explain how management accounting can provide a competitive edge in business.
2. How can management accounting information help companies to be competitive and profitable?
3. What exactly did Donaldson Brown, the accountant for DuPont, develop, and why was it so revolutionary?
4. Management accounting and financial accounting provide different information for different purposes. Explain what this means and provide an example that illustrates the differences between management and financial accounting.
5. Managers need not be concerned about external financial statements. Do you agree or disagree with this statement? Explain.
6. Why is GAAP so important for external financial reporting but not for internal management reporting?
7. Identify the three management functions relating to the decision-making process. Briefly define each function.
8. How is strategic planning related to capital budgeting?
9. How do variable costs and fixed costs differ? Give an example of each.
10. Analyze your personal expenses on a variable and fixed basis. What are some of your personal fixed costs and variable costs? What would cause them to change?
11. What is C-V-P analysis used for? In the process of using C-V-P analysis, what does it mean to "break even"?
12. Explain the difference between a product cost and a period cost.
13. What are the three components of manufacturing costs? Briefly describe them.
14. How do nonmanufacturing costs and indirect costs differ?
15. What classification determines whether materials used in the production of a product are direct materials or indirect materials? Is the classification always simple to determine? What are some examples of direct materials and indirect materials used in the production of a chair?
16. What are some of the major challenges in tracking and controlling manufacturing overhead costs?
17. What is the difference between a direct cost and an indirect cost? Give an example of each in the context of teaching an accounting class at your school.
18. What is the difference between sunk costs and differential costs? Give an example of each.
19. How can out-of-pocket costs and opportunity costs be applied to your personal financial decisions?

practice exercises

Practice 1-1

Management Accounting and Financial Accounting
Which one of the following is correct?

a. Management accounting reports are usually available to the public.
b. Management accounting is legislated and governed by regulatory agencies.
c. Financial accounting focuses primarily on qualitative company data.
d. Financial accounting exists to serve the competitive needs of an organization.
e. Management accounting evolves from the best practices of managers working within their companies.

Practice 1-2

DuPont's Development of ROI (Return on Investment)
Which one of the following statements best describes the reason DuPont developed return on investment (ROI) into an important management technique?

a. A bankruptcy court trustee required DuPont to improve its management practices.
b. Antitrust legislation passed at the turn of the twentieth century required all corporations to adopt ROI.
c. DuPont was concerned about competition from low-cost foreign imports.

(continued)

    d.   DuPont needed a technique for comparing the operating performance of its different business divisions.

    e.   DuPont needed a technique for evaluating the performance of its stock market investment portfolio.

Practice 1-3

Management Accounting and Financial Accounting

Which one of the following is incorrect?

a.   Management accounting is not as important as financial accounting for the competitive success of a company.

b.   Governments do not require a company to implement a good management accounting system.

c.   Management accounting systems evolve over time to adapt to the needs of a company.

d.   Financial accounting provides a common reporting platform to the public.

e.   A company often regards a good management accounting system as a valuable company secret.

Practice 1-4

Primary Management Functions

The three primary management functions are:

a.   Planning, surveying, and competing.

b.   Planning, evaluating, and aerating.

c.   Planning, controlling, and evaluating.

d.   Planning, controlling, and competing.

e.   Planning, competing, and evaluating.

Practice 1-5

Planning

Which one of the following is correct?

a.   Short-run planning includes capital budgeting and operational budgeting.

b.   Long-run planning includes production and process prioritizing.

c.   Long-run planning includes strategic planning and capital budgeting.

d.   Short-run planning includes strategic planning, and production and process prioritizing.

e.   Long-run planning includes capital budgeting and operational budgeting.

Practice 1-6

Controlling

Which one of the following is a correct description of "controlling" in a management accounting context?

a.   Deciding on the acquisition of long-term assets

b.   The real-time, day-to-day management of a company's business processes

c.   Identifying a company's mission and the goals flowing from that mission

d.   Prioritizing the production potential of an organization through cost-volume-profit analysis

e.   Communicating daily, weekly, and monthly goals

Practice 1-7

Evaluating

Which of the following is *not* an example of evaluating?

a.   Comparing actual costs and budgeted costs

b.   Budgeting costs between various departments

c.   Assessing the performance of products and services

d.   Analyzing profitability of different products

e.   Identifying problems in the production process

Practice 1-8

Fixed Costs and Variable Costs

Which of the following is an example of a variable cost?

a.   Insurance premium for fire insurance on the factory building

    b.   The salary of the company president
    c.   Wood used to make custom tables
    d.   Rent for use of a storage warehouse
    e.   Depreciation on the factory building

Practice 1-9

Computing the Break-Even Point
Using the following data, compute the company's break-even point in terms of the number of units.

Sales price per unit	$ 240
Variable cost per unit	165
Total monthly fixed costs	187,500

Practice 1-10

Product and Period Costs
Which one of the following is an example of a product cost for a manufacturing company?

    a.   Office supplies at corporate headquarters
    b.   Wages paid to office staff
    c.   Wages paid to factory workers
    d.   Fire insurance premium on office building
    e.   Commissions paid to salespeople

Practice 1-11

Types of Product Costs
Which one of the following statements is incorrect?

    a.   Manufacturing overhead includes all direct material and direct labor costs.
    b.   Indirect materials include those materials that become part of the product but cannot be traced to specific products.
    c.   Direct labor includes the wages paid to factory workers who do the actual assembly of a product.
    d.   Direct materials include those materials that become part of the product and can be traced to specific products.
    e.   Indirect labor includes the salaries of manufacturing supervisors.

Practice 1-12

Computing the Cost of a Manufactured Product
The company manufactures filing cabinets. The company's costs are as follows:

Direct materials	$22.30 per unit
Direct labor	$46.25 per unit
Variable manufacturing overhead	$9.34 per unit
Fixed manufacturing overhead	$1,000,000 per year
Administrative costs	$750,000 per year

In an average year, the company manufactures 40,000 units.
    What is the variable cost to manufacture each filing cabinet?

Practice 1-13

Direct and Indirect Costs
Which one of the following statements best explains why companies want to distinguish between direct and indirect costs?

    a.   To evaluate business segments on the basis of only those costs directly traceable to each segment
    b.   To better determine whether a company is a large organization or a small organization
    c.   To determine the sales prices necessary to break even
    d.   To better distinguish between variable and fixed costs for each product
    e.   To better distinguish between materials costs and labor costs

Practice 1-14

Differential Costs and Sunk Costs

Which one of the following statements is incorrect?

a. Sunk costs should be irrelevant in decision making.
b. Differential costs are the costs a company considers when making decisions.
c. Differential costs cannot be reasonably changed by a company.
d. Sunk costs are costs made in the past that do not pertain to future decisions.
e. Differential costs are sometimes called avoidable costs.

Practice 1-15

Out-of-Pocket Costs and Opportunity Costs

Which one of the following is an example of an opportunity cost?

a. Revenue lost from sale of cakes by deciding to sell only cookies
b. Wages paid to construction workers
c. Materials used to assemble computers
d. Ordering costs related to a customer's special order of guitar strings
e. Rent paid for the use of a factory building

Practice 1-16

Expanding Management Accounting

Which one of the following statements is incorrect?

a. Management accountants can add value to an organization by giving insights related to the strategic performance measures of cost, quality, and time.
b. In today's business environment, accountants should not focus only on cost issues.
c. Management accounting is constantly evolving, so accountants need to show innovation to keep up with the many changes.
d. Although it is an old technique, the use of return on investment (ROI) analysis is still sufficient to give most companies a competitive edge over their competitors.
e. Balanced scorecards combine cost, quality, and time data.

Practice 1-17

Ethics in Management Accounting

Which one of the following statements is correct?

a. The Institute of Management Accountants has implemented a perfect set of rules to resolve every conflict.
b. The top accountant in most large organizations is usually called the controller.
c. Upon discovering an ethical dilemma in an organization, a management accountant's first responsibility is to notify outside authorities and government officials.
d. Ethical dilemmas in both large and small organizations are rare.
e. The chief executive officer (CEO) in a company typically reports to the company's chief financial officer (CFO).

 # **e** x e r c i s e s

Exercise 1-1

Changes in Business Affecting Management Accounting

You are at the student union having lunch with a friend who is attending law school. In the course of your conversation, you tell your friend that, in contrast to financial accounting or tax accounting, management accounting has "competitive value" and is highly proprietary. Further, management accounting is more important in business today than ever before, and only those organizations that best control costs and improve quality are competitive. Your friend asks you two questions:

1. What do you mean by "competitive value"?
2. Why is it more important for accountants to provide useful information to management today than it was before?

Exercise 1-2

Characteristics of Accounting Reports

Indicate whether each of the following is characteristic of financial accounting reports, management accounting reports, or both:

1. They are used primarily by creditors and investors.
2. They aid management in identifying problems.
3. They are based on generally accepted accounting principles.
4. They are standardized across companies.
5. They provide information for decision making by management.
6. They measure performance and isolate differences between planned and actual results.
7. They are created based on competitive needs that are unique to the organization.

Exercise 1-3

Financial and Management Accounting

A friend who is thinking about majoring in accounting has asked you to distinguish between the work of financial accounting and management accounting. What is your response?

Exercise 1-4

Period Costs and Product Costs

Bright, Inc., a producer of educational toys for children, incurs the following types of costs:

a. Depreciation on the production plant
b. Depreciation on the corporate offices
c. Paper, toner, and miscellaneous supplies for the office copy machines
d. Wages of production-line employees
e. Raw materials used in the production of toys
f. Wages of the corporate headquarters' secretarial staff
g. Maintenance costs on the production equipment
h. Advertising costs
i. Shipping costs for products sold
j. Salaries of plant supervisors
k. Interest on bank loans
l. Property tax on the production plant
m. Property tax on the corporate offices
n. Commissions paid to sales personnel
o. Administrative salaries of corporate executives

Classify each cost as a period cost or a product cost. For each item classified as a product cost, indicate whether it would usually be included in direct materials, direct labor, or manufacturing overhead.

Exercise 1-5

Spreadsheet

Manufacturing Costs

Jordan Industries is a manufacturing company that produces solid oak office furniture. During the year, the following costs were incurred. The building depreciation and the utilities are allocated three-fourths to production and one-fourth to administration. The cost of furniture parts can be traced to specific production runs.

Oak wood	$ 50,000
Miscellaneous supplies (glue, saw blades, varnish, etc.)	10,000
Furniture parts (wheels, locks, etc.)	5,500
Payroll—plant manager's salary	25,000
Payroll—administrative salaries	100,000
Payroll—production-line employees' wages	45,500
Building depreciation	28,000
Maintenance—plant and equipment	5,000
Utilities	16,000
Income taxes	8,500

(continued)

1. Classify the costs into the following four categories: direct materials, direct labor, manufacturing overhead, and period costs.
2. Calculate the total amount of cost for each category.

Exercise 1-6

Manufacturing and Nonmanufacturing Costs

The Benson Manufacturing Company produces rides for amusement parks. Parts for the rides are purchased from other suppliers. Rides are then assembled in various company plants.

Recently, Benson Manufacturing hired two new employees. One will be working in an assembly plant, and the other will be working in the marketing division of the corporate offices as a sales representative.

The assembly plant employee will be paid an annual salary of $34,000, or $17.00 per hour. Her time will be charged to the individual rides that she assembles. The marketing division employee will receive an annual salary of $30,000 plus commission. He will be responsible for both advertising and selling. His salary is for advertising responsibilities, and he will be paid a commission on sales of amusement rides.

1. Should the salary of the assembly plant employee be classified as a manufacturing or a nonmanufacturing cost? Should the salary of the marketing division employee be classified as a manufacturing or a nonmanufacturing cost? How is this classification made?
2. After classifying the salaries as manufacturing or nonmanufacturing costs, determine how the salary costs will affect the cost of assembling the amusement rides. Classify the employee costs as direct, indirect, fixed, variable, product, or period. (Each cost can be classified in more than one way.)

Exercise 1-7

Performance Measurement

The president of Radkline Corporation, Karen Pinkus, has asked you, the company's controller, to advise her on whether Radkline should develop a new inventory management system. Is the decision facing Karen Pinkus an example of a strategic planning decision, a capital budgeting decision, a production prioritization decision, or an operational budgeting decision? Be sure to defend your answer.

Exercise 1-8

Cost Classifications

The following are costs associated with manufacturing firms, merchandising firms, or service firms:

a. Miscellaneous materials used in production
b. Salesperson's commission in a real estate firm
c. Administrators' salaries for a furniture wholesaler
d. Administrators' salaries for a furniture manufacturer
e. Freight costs associated with acquiring inventories for a grocery store
f. Office manager's salary in a doctor's office
g. Utilities for the corporate offices of a toy manufacturer
h. Line supervisor's salary for a clothing manufacturing firm
i. Training seminar for sales staff of a service firm
j. Fuel used in a trucking firm
k. Paper used at a printing business
l. Oil for machinery at a plastics manufacturing firm
m. Food used at a restaurant
n. Windshields used for a car manufacturer

Classify the costs as (1) product or period; (2) variable or fixed; and (3) for those that are product costs, as direct materials, direct labor, or manufacturing overhead. Write "not applicable (N/A)" if a category doesn't apply.

Exercise 1-9

Cost Classifications

The following are costs associated with manufacturing firms, merchandising firms, or service firms:

a. Legal services for an accounting firm
b. Car leases for company management
c. Oil used to service manufacturing equipment
d. Office supplies for a grocery store
e. Entertainment expense for clients
f. Travel expenses for doctors in a medical firm
g. Plastic used in making computers
h. Collection costs of accounts receivable
i. Electricity to run saws at a lumber yard
j. Food for a company banquet
k. Advertising expense
l. Continuing education for a doctor
m. Commissions paid to salespersons
n. Depreciation on sports equipment by a professional football team
o. Calculators used by office employees
p. Fuel used in baggage transporters at an airport
q. Toll charges incurred because of business travel
r. Fuel used in manufacturing equipment

Classify the costs as (1) product or period; (2) variable or fixed; and (3) for those that are product costs, as direct materials, direct labor, or manufacturing overhead. Write "not applicable (N/A)" if a category doesn't apply.

Exercise 1-10

C-V-P Analysis

Tyrell, Inc., located in Sacramento, California, manufactures high-end baby chairs. The firm's cost accountant, Lisa, has been assigned by the CEO to determine how many baby chairs Tyrell, Inc., needs to make to break even. She is given the following data:

Baby chair sales price	$ 15
Variable cost per baby chair	7
Production worker salary	1,600

Determine how many baby chairs Tyrell, Inc., needs to make to break even.

Exercise 1-11

Spreadsheet

C-V-P Analysis

The DALLAS MAVERICKS basketball team has hired you as its new accountant. On your first day on the job, Mavericks' owner, Mark Cuban, comes to you and asks, "How many tickets must we sell to pay for Michael Finley's salary?" He then hands you a sheet of paper with the following information:

Michael Finley's salary	$12,000,000
Average ticket price	80
Printing cost of one ticket	1

1. Prepare your response to Mark's question.
2. How many tickets would the Mavericks have to sell to pay for the entire Mavericks team if the total team salary (including Finley) is $80,000,000?

Exercise 1-12

C-V-P Analysis

In the text you used accounting data on DUPONT's Kevlar product line to compute the number of pounds sold of Kevlar in order for DuPont to break even on this product line. Similar data on DuPont's Teflon product line are provided on the following page.

(continued)

Wholesale price	$145.00 per gallon
Variable cost	$60.30 per gallon
Total monthly fixed costs	$9,630,000

1. How many gallons of Teflon does DuPont need to sell each month in order to break even?
2. Assume that DuPont is considering a significant change to the Teflon production process. As a result of this change, variable costs would increase to $64.60, but monthly fixed costs would be reduced to $8,100,000. Recompute the number of gallons that need to be sold each month in order to break even if these changes are made. What would you recommend to DuPont?

Exercise 1-13

Spreadsheet

Product Costing

In the text you used accounting data on DuPont's Kevlar product line to determine the total manufacturing cost to produce a pound of Kevlar. Similar data on DuPont's Teflon product line are provided below.

Direct materials	$60.00 per gallon
Direct labor	$1.80 per gallon
Manufacturing overhead:	
Variable	$3.20 per gallon
Fixed	$3,200,000 per month
General corporate sales and administrative costs	$6,400,000 per month

Following the same costing procedure as was used with the Kevlar product line, and assuming that DuPont expects to produce 100,000 gallons in the next month, what appears to be the total manufacturing cost per gallon of Teflon?

Exercise 1-14

Product Costing

BatsRUs, Inc., has created a unique line of aluminum baseball bats that, while illegal for league use, are designed to nearly double the average length of a batted ball. They are a great "hit" in the personal and family use market. Recently, a new competitor, Awesome Bats, Inc., has introduced a competing bat to the market. Suddenly, BatsRUs is experiencing severe market pressure to significantly lower its normal market price of $175. The problem is that management is not very confident about the actual production cost per bat. With some effort, the following data have been developed for management to use in setting a new market price and, more importantly, beginning an effort to better control costs.

Standard Variable Costs to Produce One Batch of 10 Bats (600 batches are typically produced each week)

	Average Cost per Pound	Average Pounds per Batch	Total Costs
Direct materials	$ 3	16	$ 48
	Average Rate per Hour	**Average Hours per Batch**	
Direct labor	$15	2	30
Variable manufacturing overhead	20	2	40
Total variable costs			$118

Standard Weekly Fixed Costs

Manufacturing overhead	$240,000
Sales and administrative costs	180,000
Total fixed costs	$420,000

1. What appears to be the average cost for BatsRUs to manufacture a single baseball bat?
2. Do you have any questions or concerns about how the data are being used to determine the cost of manufacturing a baseball bat at BatsRUs?

Exercise 1-15

Product Costing and C-V-P Analysis

Wakefield, Inc., offers a CPA review course in cities throughout the eastern United States. Wakefield hires local CPAs to do the teaching. Each instructor is paid $120 an hour to teach the course; a course consists of 12 weeks of instruction with sessions taking place four evenings a week for two hours at each session. The other instruction costs to Wakefield are to pay for hotel conference rooms to host the course. Generally, Wakefield pays the hotel $625 per evening to rent a conference room. Also, tuition for the course includes all course materials, which cost the company $180 for each student.

1. What is the product cost of providing one evening of instruction for all students?
2. What is the product cost of training a student over the entire course (there are 75 students in this particular course)?
3. Assuming that Wakefield charges each student $1,200 for the course, how many students would be required to break even on this course?

Exercise 1-16

Spreadsheet

Segment Analysis

You are the accountant for the largest manufacturer of sheet steel. The company's hottest product is the RX-6, which provides most of the firm's revenue. Management is considering dropping the RX-5 product line, which hasn't turned a profit for two consecutive years. The CFO comes to you and asks what you would do given the following data:

Operating Statements	RX-6	RX-5	Total
Batches produced and sold	200	240	
Sales revenue	$30,000	$ 43,200	$ 73,200
Direct materials	(2,000)	(8,400)	(10,400)
Direct labor	(4,000)	(7,680)	(11,680)
Variable manufacturing overhead	(1,000)	(4,800)	(5,800)
Fixed manufacturing overhead	(2,000)	(17,400)	(19,400)
Sales and administrative costs	(2,000)	(6,000)	(8,000)
Operating profit	$19,000	$ (1,080)	$ 17,920

Note: Approximately 20% of the fixed manufacturing overhead is directly related to (i.e., created within) each segment.

1. Distinguish between direct and indirect costs and find the segment profit for each product.
2. Determine the gain or loss that the firm would incur if it dropped the RX-5 product line. What figure would you provide the CFO?
3. Explain your recommendation to continue or discontinue product line RX-5.

Exercise 1-17

Opportunity Costs

Dave is employed by a company that currently pays him $65,000 per year. He owns a new car that he bought for cash of $32,500. Dave is thinking about returning to school to obtain a law degree. Tuition for the school he wants to attend is $28,000 per year, books average $1,350 per year, and room and board average $12,550 per year.

Determine the total sunk cost and the total opportunity cost for Dave if he decides to go back to law school for three years.

Exercise 1-18

Segment Analysis and Opportunity Costs

The text used accounting data to perform a segment analysis of DUPONT's Teflon product line. Assume that sales of Kevlar have dropped significantly. DuPont reported the following

(continued)

results for this product line for the past month and expects this sales pattern to continue into the future.

Operating Statements	Kevlar
Sales revenue	$ 7,500,000
Variable manufacturing costs	(2,700,000)
Fixed manufacturing overhead	(1,500,000)
Sales and administrative costs	(4,100,000)
Operating profit	$ (800,000)

1. Assume that approximately 30% of the fixed manufacturing overhead can be avoided if Kevlar is dropped. In order to determine the "true performance" of the Kevlar product line, what is its incremental segment profit or loss?
2. If DuPont were to drop the Kevlar product line and use the available resources to produce another product that provided an incremental profit of $3,500,000, what is the economic profit or loss of the Kevlar product line?

d i s c u s s i o n   c a s e s

Case 1-1

Developing Management Accounting Information (DuPont)

The story of E. I. DU PONT DE NEMOURS AND COMPANY detailed at the beginning of this chapter provides key insights into the development of management accounting. In particular, we see how the structure of a business affects the kinds of information required for planning, controlling, and evaluating purposes. Consider the decision to expand and diversify the company by acquiring its suppliers and creating its own network of sales offices. What were the potential risks to DUPONT of this decision? What accounting information would have been required to determine if the decision to diversify was successful? Does the traditional accounting system designed to produce external financial reports provide the required information in an easily obtainable fashion?

Case 1-2

Supporting the Management Process (IBM)

INTERNATIONAL BUSINESS MACHINES CORPORATION (IBM) has faced challenges this last decade due to increased competition in the home-consumer segment of the personal computer (PC) market. When IBM introduced the PC in the early 1980s, it was a huge success. Over time, however, the PC market grew immensely, and competition began to rise.

Although the PC was initially marketed toward businesses, a home-consumer market emerged as well. In 1995, IBM, under the direction of then-CEO Louis Gerstner, set up a home-consumer PC division to augment its business PC division. IBM hoped that with the two divisions, each employing its own design, manufacturing, and marketing personnel, it could better focus on the needs of its various customers and increase total sales.

IBM's consumer division quickly developed PCs that had high customer appeal. In early 1996, the division released its "Aptiva" PC in a sleek, dark gray color. The model was equipped with many high-tech features. Also, IBM's reputation for quality allowed the consumer division to charge a higher price for the PCs. (In December 1996, IBM PCs sold for an average of $1,880, whereas other companies charged as little as $1,300 to $1,400.)

Initially, the manufacturing department in IBM's consumer division could not keep up with consumer demand. Soon, however, IBM began losing market share to companies such as DELL, COMPAQ, and GATEWAY. These companies discovered that consumers prefer low price to the extra "frills" that IBM offers in its computers. Furthermore, IBM found that many consumers were no longer willing to pay higher prices for IBM's reputation. IBM, the company that originally created and dominated the PC market, began losing market share in the PC business very fast. IBM's PC division lost almost $1 billion in 1998. In 1999, IBM reduced its PC workforce from 10,000 to approximately 9,000 employees and cut its losses down to $360 million. In early 2000, IBM unveiled a new line of sleek, stylish machines that it branded as the NetVista line of products. With these and a number of other changes in place, business finally began growing in the second half of 2000. By the fourth quarter of 2000, IBM regained enough market share to be listed as No. 5 for PC shipments in the United States.

1. Did IBM make a good decision in setting up its consumer division? How so?
2. Analyze IBM's decisions and actions involving the consumer division. Try to categorize these decisions and actions following the threefold management process of planning, controlling, and evaluating.

3. Based on the threefold management process of planning, controlling, and evaluating, where do you think IBM was weakest in its decision-making practice with respect to the consumer division? Where do you think it was strongest?
4. If you were Sam Palmisano (IBM's current CEO), what information would you want from your accountants in order to effectively plan, control, and evaluate the decision to either shut down or continue to operate a division?

Source: Raju Narisetti, "IBM to Revamp Struggling Home-PC Business," *The Wall Street Journal*, October 14, 1997; Lisa Smith, "IBM's Personal Computer Unit Makes Turnaround," *The Herald-Sun*, March 22, 2001.

 j u d g m e n t   c a l l s

Judgment 1-1

You Decide: When allocating costs, if you don't know where costs should be allocated, should you take time to figure out if the costs relate to materials or labor, or should you allocate all the costs as manufacturing overhead?

It is your first day on the job at a bicycle manufacturing company. Your first job is to determine the cost of a new line of bikes. After reviewing all the cost information, your boss says, "If you don't know how to allocate a cost, just put it in manufacturing overhead. Whether it is a direct or indirect material, it will end up in the same place." Do you agree with your boss? Why or why not?

Judgment 1-2

You Decide: Should sunk costs be considered in a planning decision or ignored?

You currently work part time at a flower shop. You split your time between keeping the books and making deliveries. The van you use to make these deliveries has been in and out of the repair shop over the past two months. In addition to the engine, the transmission was just replaced. The mechanic said that the van is old enough to require constant repair. Your boss isn't too happy about all this repair work and was heard saying, "I would like to get a new van, but I can't afford it. I have invested too much money in the one we have now!" What should you tell your boss?

C o m p e t e n c y   E n h a n c e m e n t   O p p o r t u n i t i e s

▶ **Analyzing Real Company Information**
▶ **International Case**
▶ **Ethics Case**
▶ **Writing Assignment**

▶ **The Debate**
▶ **Internet Search**

The following additional assignments provide opportunities for students to develop critical thinking, ethical perspectives, oral and written communication skills, experience with electronic research, and teamwork through group and business activities.

▷ *Analyzing Real Company Information*

Analyzing 1-1 (Microsoft)

1. Bill Gates is the chairman of the Board for MICROSOFT, and Steve Ballmer is the CEO. Together, they are committed to investing heavily in the future. In 2002, Microsoft spent $4.3 billion on research and development for the products of tomorrow, probably more than any company in the world. Since 1997, Microsoft has increased its R&D spending by nearly 225%! R&D is currently more than 27% of its current operating expenses. Microsoft clearly spends a lot of money on R&D. What are the potential advantages and disadvantages of this cost commitment to R&D?

2. A large part of Microsoft's R&D expenditures is for outside software developers who contract with Microsoft to work on specific projects. What factors does Microsoft need to consider in deciding to assign a research project to an outside contractor rather than to its internal software development staff?

Analyzing 1-2 (DuPont)

As described in the chapter, the challenge facing DUPONT in the early twentieth century was how to manage the diverse set of businesses operating under the control of the DuPont management team. This diversity still exists today. In its 2002 annual report, DuPont notes that its strategic business units (operating segments) are organized by product line. For purposes of financial reporting, these have been aggregated into eight reportable segments: Agriculture & Nutrition, Coatings & Color Technologies, Electronic & Communication Technologies, Performance Materials, Pharmaceuticals, Safety & Protection, Textiles & Interiors, and Other.

Summary segment results for 2002 for six of these eight segments are as follows (dollars in millions):

	Agriculture & Nutrition	Coatings & Color Technologies	Electronic & Communication Technologies	Performance Materials	Safety & Protection	Textiles & Interiors
Total revenue	$4,510	$5,026	$2,540	$4,868	$3,438	$6,279
After-tax operating income	443	483	217	476	490	72
Identifiable assets at December 31, 2002	5,963	3,235	2,190	3,254	1,942	5,598

1. Which segment has the highest return on investment? The lowest?
2. How could the segment with the lowest return on investment improve its financial performance?

▷ *International Case*

International

Toyota

TOYOTA MOTOR CORPORATION was the company that originally defined and implemented the just-in-time (JIT) management technique mentioned in this chapter. Toyota was started in 1918 by Sakichi Toyoda as the TOYOTA SPINNING AND WEAVING COMPANY; in fact, a subsidiary of Toyota still makes spinning and weaving equipment today. By 1995, Toyota was the third-largest motor vehicle producer in the world, manufacturing 4,512,076 vehicles (behind GENERAL MOTORS at 7,997,794 and FORD at 6,401,495). In January 1997, Toyota made its 100 millionth vehicle. Despite a difficult world economy since 2000, Toyota has continued to prosper. In 2002, consolidated net income rose 29%, to 1,094 billion yen ($8,207 million). In the 2002 annual report, Fujio Cho, president of Toyota, noted three main factors behind his company's strong financial performance in 2002. First, Toyota sold more vehicles than ever in North America, reaching 1.78 million units. Second, efforts to reduce costs through partnership with suppliers began to generate tangible results. Finally, a favorable foreign exchange rate contributed to financial performance.

1. Toyota attributes its 29% increase in net income to three factors: growth in sales volume, cost savings, and the weakening of the yen (which makes its cars cheaper in North America). Consider conducting a performance evaluation on the following people, and decide which of the three factors should be considered in the evaluation of:
   a. an assembly-line worker
   b. a factory manager
   c. a sales manager
   d. the company president
2. In relation to its cost savings, Toyota reports that the savings stem from improvements in engineering design, improvements in manufacturing processes, and improved logistics. Consider conducting a performance evaluation on the following people, and decide which (and why!) of the three cost savings factors should be considered in the evaluation of:
   a. an assembly-line worker
   b. a factory manager
   c. a purchasing manager
   d. the company president

▶ Ethics Case

Whom to Tell about Medicare Overbilling

Professor Mary Allen is sitting in her office one day when Mark Sullivan, an accounting graduate from five years ago, knocks on her door. Mark had been an exceptionally good student and had started with the CPA firm Peat & Price upon graduation. After three years with that firm, he joined MiniCare Health Company as the chief accountant and is now serving as its controller. Mark asks if he can talk with Professor Allen in confidence and then tells her that he has a problem: "Two years ago, I started working for MiniCare. Not long after I was promoted to controller, I noticed that the officers of the company were doing things that I didn't think were right. They have overbilled Medicare on several occasions, and senior management executives are misusing their positions by taking company perks that are against the company code of ethics. I have talked to my superior, the financial vice president, and he has, in essence, told me to mind my own business—that accountants are to report results and assist management, not question them."

Mark informs Professor Allen that he is making $110,000 a year, far more than he could earn in another company at this stage in his career. He asks for her advice. What should Professor Allen recommend that he do? Should Mark quit his job? Should he talk to someone else? If so, who? Should he go public with his information?

▶ Writing Assignment

Sunk Costs: They May Be Sunk, but They Aren't Forgotten

You are the manager of the tire manufacturing subdivision of Uniyear Diversified Products. Last year, you were successful in convincing corporate executives that your division needed to purchase a new warehouse facility costing $40 million to house raw materials. You argued at the time that you could be much more productive if delays in getting materials from suppliers could be eliminated.

During the past 18 months, your company has worked hard to adopt JIT inventory and total quality control. You have successfully placed online terminals at key supplier locations, and the lag time in getting the raw materials you need has dropped from an average of four weeks to six hours.

Your problem now is that you no longer need the $40 million warehouse. It is a sunk cost. However, you are afraid that if you reveal that fact to the corporate executives, they will penalize or even fire you for being so shortsighted.

Draft a one-page memo to the president of Uniyear Diversified Products that explains why the $40 million warehouse is no longer needed. Remember that the memo has two purposes: to inform the president that the warehouse is no longer needed and to do so in a way that doesn't cost you your job.

▷ *The Debate*

When Should You Surrender?

You are a partner in a CPA firm. For over 15 years, you conducted the audit of XYZ Corporation. Three years ago, however, the company went bankrupt. To your surprise, a class-action lawsuit was filed against your firm for $5 million, alleging that you failed to warn stockholders that the company was in financial difficulty. Your audit fee for XYZ Corporation was only $15,000 per year. Thus far you have spent $957,000 on legal fees and expert witness costs. Your attorney has worked out a settlement that would involve you paying the plaintiffs $750,000. You believe your defense is excellent, that the quality of your audits of XYZ Corporation was high, and that you will win the lawsuit. However, you also believe that it will cost another $900,000 in legal fees to successfully defend the case. Should you settle?

Divide your group into two teams.

- One team represents the "Fight to the Death" group. Prepare a two-minute oral presentation supporting the notion that you should not pay a penny to settle the lawsuit when you know that you did nothing wrong. You believe that the best long-run business strategy is to vigorously fight every lawsuit in order to discourage future suits.
- The other team represents the "Cut Our Losses" group. Prepare a two-minute oral presentation arguing that the past litigation costs are sunk and that the only reasonable comparison is between the cost of settling now and the cost of continuing the lawsuit.

▷ *Internet Search*

DuPont

Access DUPONT's Web site at **http://www.dupont.com**. Sometimes Web addresses change, so if this DuPont address doesn't work, access the Web site for this textbook (**http://swain .swlearning.com**) for an updated link to DuPont.

Once you've gained access to DuPont's Web site, answer the following questions:

1. Click on the "DuPont Overview" tab. Who is the current chief executive officer (CEO) of DuPont? How long has he or she been with the company? What is his or her background (e.g., legal, accounting, engineering, etc.)?
2. As mentioned in the chapter, the DuPont organization includes many diverse types of businesses. DuPont also has a strong commitment to diversity among its employees, including

the members of its Board of Directors. Click on the "DuPont Overview" tab. What is the current state of diversity within DuPont's outside directors?

3. The history of DuPont, and some of its well-known products, is summarized in the chapter. DuPont's Web site offers further information. Click on the "Consumer Solutions" tab. How does CoolMax® work? How does Kevlar® compare to steel?

4. DuPont reports a corporate commitment to community outreach. Click on the "Social Commitment" tab. What are the three focus areas of DuPont's community outreach?

c h a p t e r

2

Analyzing Cost-Volume-Profit Relationships

After studying this chapter, you should be able to:

Learning Objectives

1 Understand the key factors involved in cost-volume-profit (C-V-P) analysis and why it is such an important tool in management decision making.

2 Explain and analyze the basic cost behavior patterns—variable, fixed, stepped, and mixed.

3 Analyze mixed costs using the scattergraph and high-low methods.

4 Perform C-V-P analyses, and describe the effects potential changes in C-V-P variables have on company profitability.

5 Visualize C-V-P relationships using graphs.

6 Identify the limiting assumptions of C-V-P analysis, and explain the issues of quality and time relative to C-V-P analysis decisions.

eXpanded *Material*

7 Analyze mixed costs using the least squares method.

8 Explain the effects of sales mix on profitability.

9 Describe how fixed and variable costs differ in manufacturing, service, merchandising, and e-commerce organizations, and illustrate these differences with the operating leverage concept.

chapter 2

If you've ever watched an international-caliber soccer match, you know that goals are scarce. Each goal requires extensive work, patient play, and many attempts. This same approach seems to apply to the business of professional soccer in the United States where MAJOR LEAGUE SOCCER (MLS) completed its seventh season in the United States in 2002. The year 2002 was a banner year for U.S. soccer with the men's national soccer team reaching new heights by finally cracking the Top 10 of the FIFA World Rankings and competing in the quarter-finals of the World Cup in Korea/Japan (after taking last place at the previous World Cup tournament). This followed on the momentum generated by the U.S. women's team, which won the World Cup in 1999 and placed third in the world in 2003. Nevertheless, MLS has so far been unable to score financially in America where sports fans continue to prefer attending basketball, football, and even baseball games to watching the most popular sport in the (rest of the) world.

Professional soccer has been launched several times in the United States amid much fanfare, but so far each attempt has failed. The last failure, that of the NORTH AMERICAN SOCCER LEAGUE (NASL)—which brought Pelé, Cruyff, Best, and Beckenbauer to the United States in the early 1970s—was especially painful because, with the big names, professional soccer looked so promising. One of the major reasons previous efforts failed is that fixed costs were too high for the small number of fans and meager TV revenues. Each attempt ended up with the team owners losing money. To better manage player salaries, which are a significant part of the fixed costs of running a soccer team, the MLS set up an unusual single-entity structure in 1996, under which the league owns all the teams as well as all player contracts, and investors buy operating rights rather than setting up franchises. The purpose of this structure is to eliminate the financial disparities between large and small markets and to control player salaries and other fixed costs. This approach has successfully kept players' salaries low; so low in fact that a number of players have filed class action lawsuits arguing the MLS structure is holding down salaries in violation of U.S. antitrust laws.

Despite these efforts to contain the fixed cost of players' salaries, MLS teams continue to lose millions of dollars, largely due to their inability to generate enough revenue from ticket sales alone to cover another signif-icant fixed cost, the cost of the leases on the stadiums in which they play their games. And while the cost of these lease payments is high, the larger problem is that soccer teams forced to rent their facilities are only able to keep the revenue from ticket sales and are generally cut off from the all-important ancillary revenue that accompanies each game—revenue from concessions, parking, merchandise, stadium signage and naming rights, and luxury boxes.

The situation faced currently by Nick Sakiewicz, general manager of the METROSTARS in New Jersey, is pretty typical of the rest of the league. New Jersey has long been a hotbed of soccer in America, from producing three of the greatest American players of all-time (Tab Ramos, John Harkes, and Tony Meola) to being home to the winningest high school soccer coach in U.S. history (Gene Chyzowych of Columbia High School). Nonetheless, the MetroStars can't seem to break even financially. Part of this shortfall stems from the $1.5 million annual rent the MetroStars must pay to use Giants Stadium at the Meadowlands. Worse, the Meadowlands stadium is also used by two NFL teams (the GIANTS and the JETS), the New Jersey State Fair, and multiple concerts, which means that the MetroStars can only play one or two home games each month in June and July. With most of the home games being played in April and May, average attendance is not as high as it could be (attendance in 2002 averaged just 19,000 per game). Hence, the team loses millions of dollars every year.

General Manager Nick Sakiewicz is convinced that a new stadium is crucial to the MetroStars' financial success. At an estimated cost of $152 million, Sakiewicz wants to build a roofed, 25,000-seat stadium in Harrison City (also in New Jersey) to be located in a vast complex that would include residential housing, retail space, and a shopping center. And although he believes that more people would buy a ticket to come see the MetroStars play in their own stadium, what makes the construction proposal most attractive is the ancillary revenue that would finally belong to the team because it would own the stadium. It is estimated that a crowd of 20,000 can generate an extra $100,000 in profit from concessions, parking, and so forth. Sakiewicz believes strongly that those kinds of numbers will move his soccer team beyond the break-even point and into profitability.[1]

1 John McLaughlin, *Sky*, October 1997, pp. 27-32; Ridge Mahoney, "Homes of Their Own," July 30, 2001, **http://www.si.com**; Chris Isidore, "New Homes Get Old Quickly," July 27, 2001, **http://www.cnnmoney.com**; and the homepage for the MetroStars, **http://www.metrostars.com**.

n the previous chapter, we discussed different ways to categorize costs, and we briefly illustrated how you can use these cost categories to make management decisions. We also emphasized the fact that management accounting is defined as all accounting information that is useful in planning, controlling, and evaluating an organization. Some costs, such as direct materials and direct labor costs in a manufacturing firm, increase in direct proportion to the number of products or services produced. These are called variable costs. Other costs, such as factory rent, remain the same no matter what the level of production is. These are called fixed costs. We used these definitions of variable costs and fixed costs in the previous chapter to introduce you to **cost-volume-profit (C-V-P) analysis**, a critical tool in the management process. C-V-P analysis is used to make important planning decisions concerning appropriate levels of production and spending. C-V-P analysis allows a manager to answer the very important question: How much do I need to sell in order to earn a profit?

In this chapter, you will further explore the C-V-P analysis tool to analyze relationships between variable costs, fixed costs, and revenues. You will learn that successful managers must think carefully about **cost behavior**—how costs change in relation to changes in activity levels, such as the number of patients in a hospital or the pounds of ore processed in a copper smelter. An understanding of how costs behave in relation to levels of activity helps managers predict the effects of their plans on future performance. In addition, because the C-V-P analysis technique is applicable to all types of firms, we will discuss the behavior of costs in manufacturing, merchandising, service, and e-commerce firms.

You will also use the knowledge of cost behavior patterns to analyze the kinds of problems facing organizations such as the MetroStars' lack of profitability as described in the opening scenario. As you work through this chapter making calculations that will determine how profits will change in relation to changes in sales volume, fixed costs, and variable costs, be sure to think about how these calculations reflect the process of managing actual organizations. For instance, because of decreased air travel in the wake of the 9/11 attacks, the airline industry has struggled to be profitable in light of the heavy fixed costs of owning and operating commercial aircraft. Many owners of retail outlets in a mall breathe a sigh of relief each month on the day when enough profit has been generated to allow them to pay the monthly fixed cost of the lease payment to the mall. The owner of a baseball team will look out over a half-filled stadium on game day and worry that the ticket sales may not have been enough to cover the costs of paying the players and running the stadium. Every business owner must carefully plan how he or she is going to generate enough money to cover the fixed costs of the business. Those who have a clear idea of exactly how many airline seats, or pairs of pants, or hot dogs must be sold to break even will be in a better position to create and maintain profitability in the organization.

We believe that the best way to appreciate the importance of good management information is to begin by using that data to make significant management planning decisions. Accordingly, this chapter will give you lots of opportunities to practice. Also note that although we will focus primarily on examining the financial implications of cost-volume-profit analysis decisions, we will also pay attention to the effects these decisions have on quality and time issues as well.

cost-volume-profit (C-V-P) analysis Techniques for determining how changes in revenues, costs, and level of activity affect the profitability of an organization.

cost behavior The way a cost is affected by changes in activity levels.

Understanding Why C-V-P Analysis Is Important

I Understand the key factors involved in cost-volume-profit (C-V-P) analysis and why it is such an important tool in management decision making.

Management must make many critical operating decisions that affect a firm's profitability. With respect to planning, management is often interested in the impact a particular action will have on profitability. C-V-P analysis can help managers assess that impact. The following are examples of questions that can be answered with C-V-P analysis:

• When planning whether or not to open a scuba shop in the mall, how many customers will need to be served each month in order to break even and be able to pay the monthly store rental fee?

- How will the profits of a bookstore be affected if the store raises its prices by 10%, resulting in a reduction of 2% in the number of books sold?
- How many carpets must a fledgling entrepreneur clean in a month in order to generate a net profit of $3,000 each month?
- By how much will the profits of a discount electronics store change if a $100,000 advertising campaign increases the number of computers sold by 13%?
- How will the profits of a fast-food restaurant change if the restaurant stops selling milk shakes and instead focuses on raising the volume of soft drink sales by 25%?

It should be clear to you from these examples that C-V-P analysis involves studying the interrelationships among revenues, costs, levels of activity, and profits. However, quality of products and services and speed of production and delivery must also be considered as managers use C-V-P analysis to determine product prices, the mix of products, market strategy, appropriate sales commissions, advertising budgets, production schedules, and a host of other important planning decisions. Although C-V-P analysis is most useful for planning, it can also be used to assist with controlling decisions (e.g., are the costs too high for the level of sales?) and evaluating decisions (e.g., should we reward employees for holding costs down or be concerned that sales growth has slowed?). In fact, a lot of what is done in management accounting involves some aspect of C-V-P analysis because of the tremendous potential it has to help management increase the profitability and effectiveness of an organization. For this reason, as you use this chapter to learn the mechanics of C-V-P analysis, be sure to see how important it is to be able to understand and manage costs. As you study C-V-P analysis, you will gain a better understanding of basic cost behavior patterns. And once you understand these cost behavior patterns and how to work with them, you can use them to make effective planning, controlling, and evaluating decisions.

TO SUMMARIZE: C-V-P analysis is a very important concept in management accounting. Key factors involved in C-V-P analysis include (1) the revenues derived from the sales prices charged for goods and services, (2) the fixed and variable costs, (3) the sales volume, (4) the mix of products, (5) the speed and quality of production, and (6) the resulting profits. Understanding the interrelationships of the key variables in C-V-P analysis can assist you in planning and in making critical control and evaluation decisions.

Basic Cost Behavior Patterns

2 Explain and analyze the basic cost behavior patterns—variable, fixed, stepped, and mixed.

The two basic cost behavior patterns—variable and fixed—were introduced in the previous chapter. Other cost behavior patterns, such as mixed costs, are variations of these two. Mixed costs exhibit characteristics of both variable and fixed costs. In this section, we will review both variable and fixed costs and examine the reality of how these costs often look in many organizations. We will also introduce stepped costs and mixed costs.

A quick example of what we're talking about may be helpful before we dive into all the details of working with cost behavior. A cost may be classified as either fixed or variable by the way it reacts to changes in level of activity. Think of a doughnut shop such as KRISPY KREME or WINCHELL'S. Activity in the shop may be measured in terms of the volume of doughnuts sold, the number of customers served, the number of hours the shop is open, the number of employees, or the total square feet of the serving area, and so forth. Get the point? There are a lot of ways to measure activity in this organization. There are also a lot of different kinds of costs. The first task is to identify the costs and activities where we intend to focus our management effort. Let's say that we are initially interested in understanding how the number of doughnuts sold impacts costs and profits. Which costs will change, and which costs will not change, as we expect to sell more or less doughnuts? This is the starting point of C-V-P analysis. It seems logical that as more doughnuts are sold, the cost of doughnut ingredients will increase. This is a variable cost. On the other hand, we probably wouldn't expect the cost of property taxes to increase as more doughnuts are sold. This is a fixed cost. However, there are costs that have both variable and fixed components. For instance, the electricity costs to run the doughnut shop will increase as we sell more doughnuts because of the cost of the power to make the additional doughnuts. However, even if we don't sell any doughnuts, we will have to pay the utility costs of just keeping the shop open. Utility costs are a mixed cost. The cost of a supervisor's salary isn't normally going to increase as we sell more doughnuts *until* we have so many customers that we need to hire an additional supervisor to help with the higher volume. At this point, the fixed cost of salaries will *jump* to a new level. This is an example of a stepped cost.

Overall, once we have defined the activity, measurements of changes in activity level can be used to determine cost behavior patterns.

Measuring Level of Activity

Before we can manage an organization, we need to identify exactly what it is that we intend to manage. In other words, what is the activity upon which we intend to focus our planning, controlling, and evaluating efforts? In the doughnut shop example, it makes sense for management to focus on increasing the number of doughnuts sold; management efforts can reasonably be expected to influence the number of doughnuts sold. Activity is often measured in terms of output, input, or a combination of the two. Some of the most common activity bases used are number of units sold and number of units produced in manufacturing firms, number of units sold in merchandising firms, and number of contract hours paid for or billed in service firms. We will generally use production volume or sales volume as the activity basis in this chapter to demonstrate the use of C-V-P analysis.

Note that just because a cost doesn't vary with a particular activity base (e.g., total units sold) does not mean it could never be considered as a variable cost. For example, the total cost of wages for a doughnut shop may not vary with the amount of sales volume (the clerks get paid the same whether they sell a lot of doughnuts or just a few), but total wages would vary based on the number of hours per week that the store is open. So, if another type of activity other than sales volume is more relevant in determining changes in the variable costs being planned, the C-V-P analysis should be based on that activity. It all comes down to an issue of "focus." Where do you believe you can best focus your management attention in order to plan for and control costs and profits—on store hours, doughnuts sold, or customers served? There is some subjectivity in this focus decision. Nevertheless, managers must be careful to understand the various activity bases within their company so that they can properly plan for and control costs. We will discuss a number of alternative activity bases in a later chapter on managing inventory.

Manufacturing and merchandising companies with a single product generally measure volume of activity in terms of output, for example, number of cars, television sets, or desks produced. However, many companies produce or sell several different products (refrigerators, toasters, and irons, for example), and a simple total of all the products manufactured or sold during a given period may not provide a good measure of activity. This is particularly true for manufacturing firms. For example, GENERAL ELECTRIC manufactures a wide variety of products, ranging from light bulbs to locomotives. It obviously takes more effort (and consequently costs more) to produce a locomotive than a light bulb; accordingly, it wouldn't make any sense to state that total production for a given day was 1,000,001—1,000,000 light bulbs and 1 locomotive. In multiproduct situations, these manufacturing firms usually use input measures, such as direct labor hours worked, machine time used, or the time needed to set up a job, as the activity base. Such specific input measures are often more useful than general output measures.

Variable Costs

variable costs Costs that change in total in direct proportion to changes in activity level.

Total **variable costs** change in direct proportion to changes in activity level. Examples are costs of direct materials, which vary proportionately with the number of units produced, and sales commissions, which vary proportionately with the sales volume. For instance, as an automobile manufacturer, you might define the activity of focus as the number of cars produced. If engines, tires, axles, and steering wheels are purchased from suppliers, the related costs would be variable because the total cost of steering wheels, for example, would vary proportionately with the number of cars produced. If no cars are produced, there are no steering wheel costs; if 1,000 cars are manufactured during a period, the total cost for steering wheels and other purchased parts is 1,000 times the unit cost of each item. As more cars are produced, the total cost of each item increases. The unit cost, however, remains constant. For example, if an auto company pays $150 per steering wheel, the total cost of steering wheels for 200 cars is $30,000; for 500 cars, it is $75,000. At both levels of activity, however, the unit cost is still $150. This relationship between variable costs and level of activity is shown graphically in Exhibit 1, which relates the number of cars produced to the total cost of the steering wheels used in production.

STOP & THINK

In a manufacturing plant, are direct labor costs variable or fixed? Does your answer change if the direct labor employees belong to a powerful union?

In addition to sales commissions and materials, many other costs (such as labor) have a variable cost behavior pattern. For example, if it takes four hours of labor to assemble a frame and each hour costs $25, a unit labor cost of $100 per frame is a variable cost; the total labor cost would be $100 times the number of frames produced.

curvilinear costs Variable costs that do not vary in direct proportion to changes in activity level but vary at decreasing or increasing rates due to economies of scale, productivity changes, and so on.

Curvilinear Variable Costs

Our definition of the variable cost behavior pattern specifies that variable costs have a linear relationship to the level of activity; that is, when the level of activity increases, total variable costs rise at a directly proportional rate. For example, if the level of activity doubles, the total variable costs will also double; this is called a linear relationship. The reality is that, in practice, a truly linear relationship usually does not exist. Overall, many variable costs are actually **curvilinear costs** when considered over many activity levels. That is, these curvilinear costs actually vary at increasing or decreasing rates across large changes in the activity level. To illustrate, think about a manufacturer that makes a very specialized "premium natural" ice cream that is handmade. Now consider Exhibit 2. The top diagram is a graph that shows the cost of raw materials (for example, milk, sugar, and other ingredients) purchased from suppliers to make ice cream. Because the ice cream maker gets a bigger price discount as it purchases higher volumes of raw materials, the variable cost of these materials is not linear but curvilinear. That is, the cost increases at a decreasing rate.

FYI:

If you've had an introductory class in economics, you have likely been introduced to the term *economies of scale*. The cost of milk that becomes cheaper as production volume increases (top graph in Exhibit 2) is a cost that displays economies of scale. On the other hand, the direct labor costs to produce ice cream that become more costly as production increases (bottom graph in Exhibit 2) represent costs with *diseconomies of scale*.

On the other hand, the manager of the ice cream production process faces an understandable labor challenge—it is difficult to find people who can make ice cream efficiently. Plans to increase the production volume of the operation mean that the manager will have to hire more individuals for the ice cream production crew. As the manager scrambles to satisfy her labor needs, she will

Exhibit 1: An Example of Variable Costs

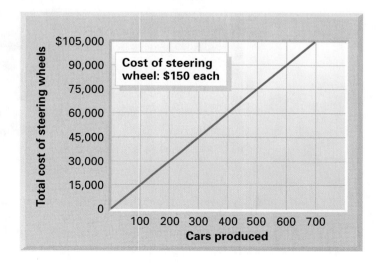

Exhibit 2: Curvilinear Variable Costs

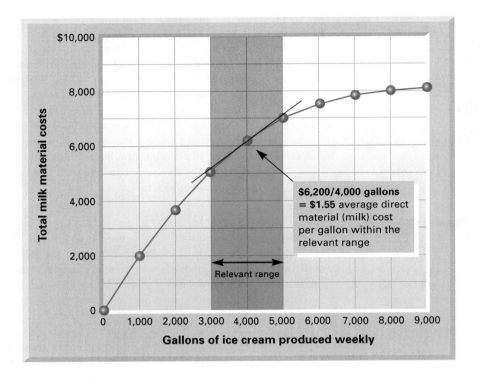

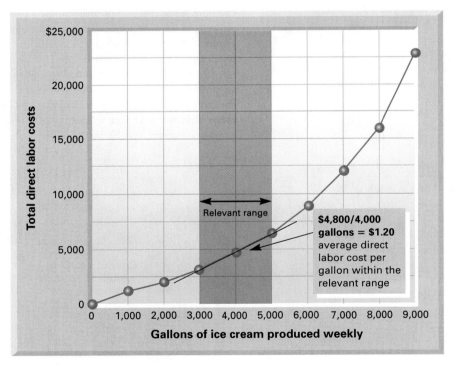

probably have to increase the wages she offers in order to attract more employees. As a result, the direct labor cost of each gallon of ice cream will increase as planned production volumes go up because the wage rate of the workers goes up. Thus, this curvilinear variable cost increases at an *increasing* rate, as depicted in the bottom graph in Exhibit 2. If you've ever had a class in economics, then this concept of curvilinear costs is familiar to you. The fact that most variable costs are curved instead of linear is an economic fact of most organizations. However, when doing C-V-P analysis, we assume that costs are *linear*. This is a potentially limiting assumption of C-V-P work; but, as you'll see in the next section, it is an appropriate assumption for most managers.

Relevant Range and the Linearity of Variable Costs

relevant range The range of operating level, or volume of activity, over which the relationship between total costs (variable plus fixed) and activity level is approximately linear.

While this is never exactly true, it is usually safe to assume that variable costs are *approximately* linear within a certain range of production, called the **relevant range**. To illustrate the relevant range concept, let's return to our ice cream manufacturing business. Realistically, the production manager does not expect to vary weekly production volume outside the range of 3,000 to 5,000 gallons of ice cream. As displayed in Exhibit 2 for both milk material cost and direct labor cost, a linear segment within the relevant range of weekly production can effectively approximate the curvilinear cost relationship of producing between 3,000 and 5,000 gallons of ice cream. By assuming a linear (rather than a curvilinear) relationship, the variable costs of milk and direct labor are estimated at $1.55 and $1.20, respectively, per gallon of ice cream using the costs in the midpoint of the relevant range (weekly production of 4,000 gallons of ice cream).

Relevant range is an important concept. If activity increases or decreases significantly, cost relationships will probably change. If production volume soars, for example, such factors as overtime work and bulk-purchase discounts may cause direct labor and materials costs per unit to change. That is why we say that the definition of variable costs—costs that are constant per unit of activity—is applicable only within relevant ranges. The important point to remember is that whenever we define a particular variable cost, we are assuming that the cost is within the relevant range of activity.

Caution

The relevant range concept is particularly difficult to apply when using C-V-P analysis in companies in very high growth situations, such as high-tech start-ups. If a company's sales are increasing by 60% each quarter, for example, it is unlikely to remain in the same "relevant range" from quarter to quarter; so careful analysis of variable and fixed costs must be repeated on a regular basis.

Fixed Costs

fixed costs Costs that remain constant in total, regardless of activity level, at least over a certain range of activity.

Fixed costs remain constant in total, regardless of activity level, at least within the relevant range of activity. Examples include property taxes, insurance, executives' salaries, plant depreciation, and rent. Because total fixed costs remain constant as activity increases, the fixed cost per unit (total fixed cost ÷ level of activity) decreases. Similarly, as the level of activity decreases, the fixed cost per unit increases. This is in contrast to variable costs, where the costs per unit are assumed to remain constant through changes in the level of activity within the relevant range.

Before we go any further, it is a good idea for us to remind ourselves why identifying fixed and variable costs is important. Remember that this chapter is about managing the relationships among costs, volume, and profit. In the previous chapter, we briefly introduced the concept of C-V-P and break-even analysis. In the C-V-P formula below (which we introduced in the previous chapter), you can see that calculating what a company needs to do to "break even" and start making a profit requires a clear measure of total fixed costs and variable costs per unit:

Caution

While total variable costs increase as production increases, the per-unit variable cost is constant across activity levels within the relevant range. In contrast, while total fixed costs are constant over the relevant range, the per-unit fixed cost changes with increases or decreases in production. Many introductory students of management accounting become confused and forget that per-unit variable costs are *fixed* and per-unit fixed cost will *vary* over the relevant range!

$$\frac{\text{Total fixed costs}}{(\text{Sales price per unit} - \text{Variable cost per unit})} = \text{Break-even sales (in units)}$$

In an actual company, the fixed and variable costs are very challenging to identify. That is why it is important that you understand the nature of cost behavior and how to classify costs as either fixed or variable. Once we've completed our discussion of cost behavior, we'll be ready to spend some time on this very useful C-V-P formula later in this chapter.

Fixed Costs Are Shifting Over the past few decades, fixed costs have increased as a percentage of total costs for many manufacturing companies, primarily due to the increase in factory automation. As a machine replaces each manual job, costs change from variable labor costs to fixed depreciation or rental charges. It is important to note that many service companies have much higher ratios of fixed-to-variable costs than do manufacturing companies. The costs of providing services in companies such as banks, consulting agencies, and airlines typically do not vary much depending on the volume of banking transactions, consulting hours, or passengers carried. Perhaps more significantly, e-commerce organizations often have even fewer variable costs than service organizations do! Once the technology has been put in place to run an e-commerce business, there is typically very little additional cost of technology based on usage (within the relevant range). Personnel costs in e-commerce organizations, such as engineering personnel, marketing teams, and executive personnel, also do not change much based on the volume of customer use of the organization's technology.

As fixed costs in manufacturing organizations increase, and the economy continues to shift more and more to service and e-commerce organizations, this fixed cost emphasis has a significant effect on the decision-making process. When costs are fixed, management's ability to influence costs with activity-level decisions is limited. With variable costs, management has more flexibility to change activity levels and thereby increase or decrease total operating cost structures. This trend of replacing variable costs with fixed costs has an important impact on the cost structure of an organization that is captured in the concept of operating leverage, which is discussed in the expanded material section of this chapter.

stepped costs Costs that change in total in a stair-step fashion (in large amounts) with changes in volume of activity.

Stepped Fixed Costs

Let's continue with our example of the ice cream manufacturer. The top graph in Exhibit 3 shows the relationship between the production line supervisor cost and the total number of gallons of ice cream produced. In this case, until weekly ice cream production reaches 1,000 gallons a week, the manufacturing manager is able to oversee all line workers. At 1,000 gallons a week production, however, the manager expects to hire a production line supervisor at $500 per week to provide more supervision of the workers. Further, the manager expects that she'll need to hire an additional supervisor each time weekly production is increased another 2,000 gallons. Although the production line supervisor cost is changing as the scale of ice cream production changes, we still consider this cost to be fixed *within the relevant range.* Hence, as shown in the top graph in Exhibit 3, within a relevant range of activity of between 3,000 and 5,000 gallons of ice cream, the total fixed manufacturing supervisor cost of $1,000 does not change. On the other hand, the per-unit supervisor cost will drop considerably as production increases. For example, when the fixed supervisor cost is $1,000 and 3,000 gallons of ice cream are being produced, the supervisor cost per gallon of ice cream is $0.33 ($1,000 ÷ 3,000 gallons). With production of 4,000 gallons, however, this fixed cost is only $0.25 ($1,000 ÷ 4,000 gallons) per gallon.

As you can see in Exhibit 3, the fixed cost of the production line supervision "steps up" as the volume of ice cream production increases. **Stepped costs** are costs that change in total in a stair-step fashion with changes in volume of activity. Another example of a stepped cost might be the labor charges for the maintenance of the tools and machinery in a small manufacturing plant. One maintenance worker can handle the upkeep of all the equipment during normal

Exhibit 3: Stepped Fixed Costs

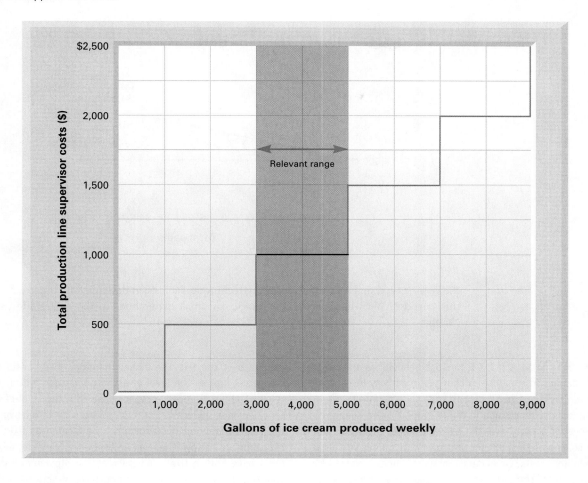

mixed costs Costs that contain both variable and fixed cost components.

levels of activity. However, when there is a significant increase in activity, a second worker must be hired, and the maintenance cost approximately doubles.

Mixed Costs

Mixed costs, like curvilinear costs and stepped costs, are variations of the basic fixed and variable cost behavior patterns. Specifically, mixed costs are costs that contain both variable and fixed components. An example is rent that is based on a fixed fee plus a percentage of total sales. Thus, the rental terms for an automobile dealer's showroom might include a flat payment of $4,000 per month plus 1% of each month's sales. The 1% of sales is the variable portion, and the $4,000 is the fixed cost. The total rent, therefore, would be considered a mixed cost and could be diagrammed as shown in Exhibit 4. As this exhibit shows, the cost of renting the showroom increases as sales increase. The total rent is $4,000 when there are no sales; $6,000 when sales are $200,000 [$4,000 + (0.01 × $200,000)]; and $8,000 when sales are $400,000 [$4,000 + (0.01 × $400,000)]. This increase is directly due to the variable cost element, which increases in total as activity level (car sales) increases.

One of the important challenges in using C-V-P analysis in the planning process is the need to effectively separate mixed costs into their fixed and variable cost components. Over

Exhibit 4: An Example of a Mixed Cost

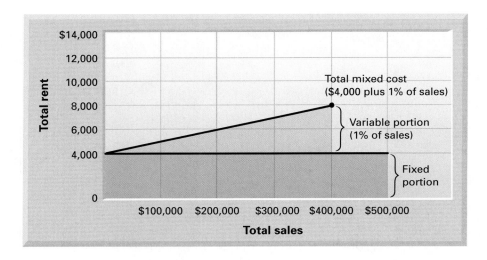

the years several management accounting techniques have been developed by organizations for this purpose. We will explore these mixed cost analysis methods in the next section of this chapter.

TO SUMMARIZE: Cost behavior is the way a cost changes in response to changes in activity level. There are two basic cost behavior patterns, variable and fixed. Total variable costs change in direct proportion to changes in the level of activity over the relevant range; therefore, variable costs are constant per unit over this range. In analyzing variable costs, we generally assume a linear relationship between total costs and the level of activity within the relevant range; outside of this range, variable costs are usually curvilinear. On the other hand, total fixed costs do not change over the relevant range; therefore, fixed costs decrease per unit as the level of activity increases within the relevant range. Stepped costs increase with the level of activity but not smoothly. If the steps are wide in relation to the relevant range, these costs can be treated as fixed; if the steps are narrow, they can be treated as variable. Mixed costs have both a fixed and a variable component. An increase in a mixed cost with a rising level of activity is due entirely to the variable cost element.

Analysis of Mixed Costs

3 Analyze mixed costs using the scattergraph and high-low methods.

With an understanding of the different types of cost behavior, we can discuss how to identify and separate mixed costs into variable and fixed components. This separation is essential because we have to clearly classify all costs as fixed or variable before doing C-V-P analysis. When it comes to mixed costs, remember that the fixed portion represents the cost necessary to maintain a service (such as a telephone) or a facility (such as a building), and the variable portion covers actual use. Recall the example of the automobile showroom's rental cost, part of which was a flat monthly fee and part a percentage of sales. Other common mixed costs are such overhead costs as electricity and repairs.

The most accurate way to separate the actual fixed and variable components of mixed costs is to analyze each invoice. An electricity bill, for example, may include a flat monthly service charge that would be classified as a fixed cost. Additional variable costs are those based on the amount of electricity actually used during the month. This approach could be very time consuming, however, and may not be cost effective (that is, it would cost more to do the analysis than the detailed information is worth). An alternative approach is to analyze the historical trend in past costs as the level of activity has changed as the basis for classifying costs as fixed or variable. There are several methods of doing this. In this section, we will introduce you to two methods: the scattergraph method and the high-low method. In the expanded material, we introduce least squares analysis, a more sophisticated method for analyzing mixed costs.

scattergraph (visual-fit) method A method of segregating the fixed and variable components of a mixed cost by plotting on a graph total costs at several activity levels and drawing a regression line through the points.

regression line On a scattergraph, the straight line that most closely expresses the relationship between the variables.

variable cost rate The change in cost divided by the change in activity; the slope of the regression line.

The Scattergraph, or Visual-Fit, Method

Probably the simplest method of separating mixed costs into their variable and fixed components is the **scattergraph** (or **visual-fit**) **method**. Essentially, we're talking here about simply *looking* at a trend of mixed cost points over time and learning how to "see" the fixed and variable cost components. To do this, the total mixed cost for each level of activity is plotted on a graph, and a straight line (called the **regression line**) is visually fitted through the points. The idea is to position the line through the set of plotted data points in a way that minimizes the average distance between all the data points and the fitted regression line. With the regression line inserted into the graph, the fixed portion of the mixed cost is estimated to be the amount on the cost (vertical) axis at the point where it is intercepted by the regression line. The variable cost per unit (referred to as the **variable cost rate**) is equal to the slope of the regression line, which is simply the change in cost divided by the change in activity.

Caution

When making these cost graphs, remember that the dollars go on the vertical axis and the level of activity goes on the horizontal axis.

To illustrate the scattergraph method, let's use the example of electricity costs for an automobile manufacturer. In the analysis and calculations that follow, all costs are assumed to fall within the relevant range of activity. In this example, we use direct labor hours as a measure of the activity level.

Exhibit 5 shows a scattergraph on which electricity costs and direct labor hours have been plotted. The regression line has been visually fitted to minimize the distance between data points. It appears that the total fixed portion of electricity cost is about $40,000 per month, which is where the regression line intersects the cost axis. The variable cost rate is approximately $4.29 per direct labor hour, which is the slope of the regression line. To calculate the slope, we use the following formula and the data points of zero and 7,000 direct labor hours, respectively.

Caution

Once the regression line has been fitted through the data points, the scattergraph method does not depend any longer on the *data points* to estimate fixed and variable costs. Cost estimations are entirely based on *points along the regression line*. For instance, notice that in this case we used the points 0 and 7,000 along the visually fitted regression line. However, we could have used any two points on the regression line (such as 2,000 direct labor hours and 10,000 direct labor hours) to calculate the variable costs per direct labor hour.

$$\text{Variable cost rate} = \frac{\text{Change in (electricity) cost}}{\text{Change in activity (direct labor hours)}}$$

$$X = \frac{\$70,000 - \$40,000}{7,000 - 0}$$

$$X = \frac{\$30,000}{7,000}$$

$$X = \$4.29 \text{ (rounded)}$$

Obviously, the scattergraph method has some limitations as a cost estimation tool. Perhaps the most critical limitation is that how the user fits the regression line through the data points is entirely subjective. Consider Exhibit 5 once more. If you were the one fitting the regression line to these data points, would you have set the line exactly where it is in this graph? Hopefully, your line would have been quite close to the current line. Still, it probably wouldn't have been exactly the same, resulting in some small differences in your own estimations of fixed and variable costs. Hence, the scattergraph method is a classic "quick and dirty" management accounting technique. Yet, although the scattergraph

Exhibit 5: Total Electricity Costs

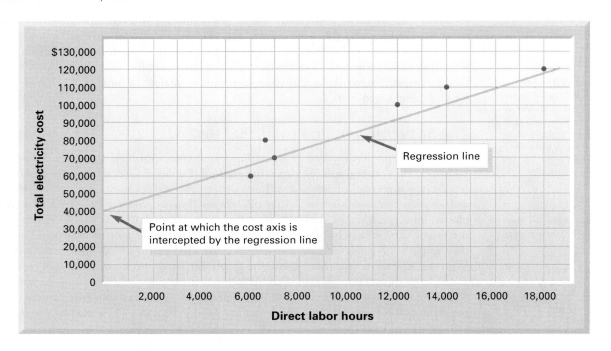

provides only subjective estimates of the fixed and variable portions of mixed costs, it can be an extremely useful tool to describe and discuss cost behavior in the planning process. It is also useful for thinking about how to control operating costs. For instance, it shows at a glance any trends and abrupt changes in cost behavior patterns. As such, it can be used as a preliminary step before using more sophisticated methods of cost evaluation.

The High-Low Method

high-low method A method of segregating the fixed and variable components of a mixed cost by analyzing the costs at the highest and the lowest activity levels within a relevant range.

A second approach to identifying fixed and variables costs is the **high-low method**, which analyzes mixed costs on the basis of total costs incurred at both the highest and the lowest levels of activity. To illustrate this method, we refer again to the electricity costs of the automobile manufacturer. This time, however, we will focus on the following table of reported electricity costs and direct labor hours worked. (The numbers in this table correspond exactly to the points plotted in the scattergragh in Exhibit 5.)

Month	Direct Labor Hours Worked	Total Electricity Cost
January	7,000	$ 70,000
February	6,000	60,000
March	12,000	100,000
April	6,600	80,000
May	18,000	120,000
June	14,000	110,000

Although these two columns of figures do not visually show trends as clearly as the scattergraph does, they do suggest that as the activity level (direct labor hours) increases, total electricity costs increase. Given this relationship, the high-low method can be used to determine the fixed and variable portions of the electricity cost as follows:

1. Identify the highest and lowest activity levels (18,000 hours in May and 6,000 hours in February). As you can see, these two months also represent the highest and lowest levels of electricity costs, or $120,000 and $60,000, respectively (although this may not always be the case).
2. Determine the differences between the high and low points.

	Total Electricity Cost	Direct Labor Hours
High point (May)	$120,000	18,000
Low point (February)	60,000	6,000
Difference	$ 60,000	12,000

3. Calculate the variable cost rate (variable cost per unit). The formula is the same as the one used to compute the slope of the regression line in the scattergraph method. The results are different, of course, because the scattergraph method is based on a regression line that is plotted, as much as possible, using all the data points, whereas the high-low method uses only the highest and lowest data points.

$$\text{Variable cost rate} = \frac{\text{Change in costs}}{\text{Change in activity}}$$

$$= \frac{\$60,000}{12,000}$$

$$= \$5 \text{ per direct labor hour}$$

4. Determine fixed costs based on the variable cost rate ($5 in this case). The formula for this computation is:

$$\text{Fixed costs} = \text{Total costs} - \text{Variable costs}$$

At the high level of activity, the calculation is as follows:

$$X = \$120,000 - (18,000 \times \$5)$$
$$X = \$120,000 - \$90,000$$
$$X = \$30,000$$

You get the same result if you calculate fixed costs at the low level of activity as follows:

$$X = \$60,000 - (6,000 \times \$5)$$
$$X = \$60,000 - \$30,000$$
$$X = \$30,000$$

Caution

Once you have selected the high and low activity levels to use in the high-low method, don't use any other activity levels or costs than these two data points to calculate the fixed costs.

In summary, using the high-low method of analyzing mixed costs, the variable portion of the total electricity cost is estimated to be $5 per direct labor hour, and the fixed portion is $30,000 per month. This means that $30,000 appears to be the amount the company pays each month just to have electricity available, and $5 is the average additional electricity cost for each hour of direct labor worked.

FYI:

What if the highest and lowest levels of activity do *not* correspond to the highest and lowest levels of costs? This could easily (and often does) happen in real-life companies. Remember that the high-low method is a method that determines *approximately* the fixed and variable costs. Hence, companies must then choose to base the estimate on either the highest and lowest activities or the highest and lowest costs. For simplicity, this textbook will always present data such that the highest and lowest levels of activity do correspond to the highest and lowest levels of costs.

A Comparison of the Scattergraph and High-Low Methods

As we have illustrated, the scattergraph and high-low methods may produce different results.

Method	Variable Cost Rate	Fixed Cost
Scattergraph	$4.29	$40,000
High-low	5.00	30,000

Both methods are useful for a quick approximation. The scattergraph method takes all the data into account. Therefore, this method tends to be more accurate, although it is somewhat subjective and inconsistent because different people might draw the line through the points differently. On the other hand, anyone using the high-low method will consistently get the same results. However, because only two data points are used, the high-low method may not be representative of the costs incurred at all levels of activity. It is important that you realize that the math used in the high-low method essentially plots the regression line through the two most extreme points in a scattergraph. To understand what we mean, look at the scattergraph of the electricity cost data in Exhibit 5. Notice that the low point lies below the scattergraph regression line and the high point lies above the scattergraph regression line. Now, if you were to draw a straight line through the high and low points, that line would not be the same line created using the scattergraph (visual-fit) method, and may not necessarily represent all six data points plotted. Nevertheless, you can use either method or both methods to predict future costs. If, for example, management wants to know how much electricity will cost next month with 10,000 direct labor hours budgeted, the following calculations would be made:

Method	Formula	Estimated Cost
Scattergraph	$40,000 + 10,000($4.29) =	$82,900
High-low	$30,000 + 10,000($5.00) =	$80,000

As you can see, the total estimated costs resulting from these two methods, in this case, are reasonably close to each other (although this may not necessarily be the case with sets of actual cost and activity data in some real-life companies).

TO SUMMARIZE: Two common techniques for analyzing mixed costs are the scattergraph and high-low methods. The scattergraph method involves visually fitting a straight line (the regression line) through data points plotted on a graph, then noting where the line intercepts the cost axis (the fixed cost) and calculating the slope of the line (the variable cost rate). With the high-low method, the high and the low levels of activity are used to calculate first the variable cost rate and then the fixed cost component.

Methods of C-V-P Analysis

4 Perform C-V-P analyses, and describe the effects potential changes in C-V-P variables have on company profitability.

Now that you have a better understanding of cost behaviors and can separate mixed costs into their fixed and variable cost elements, you are ready to use your knowledge of cost behaviors to make planning decisions. The previous chapter provided a quick introduction to C-V-P analysis in the process of planning and analyzing decisions to prioritize Kevlar versus Teflon products at DUPONT. However, in order to effectively use this valuable tool, we need a more detailed discussion and lots of practice.

If you haven't done so already, now is a good time to think of an actual business organization that is familiar to you, perhaps one by which you've been employed or are now employed. Think about the product or service this organization creates and the costs and processes it uses. Now, as you study the C-V-P analysis method below, be sure to consider how this tool

business environment

Managing an Airline in the Post-9/11 Economy Is Not Easy. Prior to the terrorist tragedies in 2001, CONTINENTAL AIRLINES was posting an incredible string of consecutive profitable quarters. Since filing for bankruptcy protection in 1995, Continental reported 24 straight quarters of profit, even when most of the other major U.S. airlines reported losses. This all changed, of course, on September 11, 2001. Since then, Continental, the fifth largest airline in the United States, has struggled very hard just to stay alive. Both 2001 and 2002 resulted in significant operating losses for Continental, as was the case with many of its competitors. Continental, however, appears to be weathering the storm better than most other airlines. In 2002, three of the top seven U.S.-based international carriers filed bankruptcy. By the end of the first quarter in 2003, TWA no longer existed, and UNITED and US AIRWAYS were still struggling in bankruptcy. In contrast, Continental Airlines again earned a coveted spot on Fortune's list of the 100 Best Companies to Work For—the only airline to do so and the fifth consecutive year for it to make the list. More importantly, in March 2002, Continental posted its first profitable month since 9/11, and Gordon Bethune, chairman and CEO, predicted that his company would be able to break even in 2004. This progress is significant in that the Air Transport Association (ATA) forecasts that the overall airline industry will lose $7 billion in 2003.

How has Continental's management team carried this company through a disastrous period of time for the airline industry? For one thing, Continental Airlines' management carefully analyzed its costs, divided those costs into fixed and variable components, and made several decisions to reduce fixed costs. For example, Continental grounded planes and slashed excess capacity. The airline eliminated 12,000 jobs in 2002 and planned to cut another 1,200 jobs, including 25% of top management, in 2003. All of this helped reduce Continental's jet cost per available seat mile by 3.8%, which is a significant percentage in an industry defined by extremely thin profit margins.

With better control of its fixed costs, Continental Airlines is again becoming profitable, and becoming profitable more quickly than most of its competitors. Because of these cut costs, Continental Airlines' passengers pay lower fares than on other airlines and receive better service. These lower fares and better service enable Continental to fill more seats than its competitors. Because its costs are low, it is profitable. Fixed costs are now a smaller percentage of total costs at Continental Airlines than at almost all other airlines.

Sources: Adapted from PR Newswire, "Continental Airlines Reports First Quarter Loss; Carrier Profitable for Month of March, the First Profitable Month Since 9/11," April 15, 2002; Continental Airlines 2002 Annual Report; "Continental Air CEO Now Sees Break-Even Results for 2004," *The Wall Street Journal*, March 19, 2003.

would be used in your own organization to plan and manage costs and activities in order to obtain desired results.

Contribution Margin

contribution margin The difference between total sales and variable costs; the portion of sales revenue available to cover fixed costs and provide a profit.

In order to effectively use C-V-P analysis, we first need to spend some time working with the concept of contribution margin. **Contribution margin** is equal to sales revenue less variable costs; it is the amount of revenue that remains to cover fixed costs and provide a profit for an organization. For example, the contribution margin from the sale of one order of French fries by a fast-food restaurant is the selling price less the variables costs (potatoes, salt, container, cooking oil, wages of the cook) of producing the fries. Any contribution margin generated by the sale of an order of French fries can be used to pay the fixed costs of the fast-food outlet, such as the monthly rent, the insurance, the supervisor's salary, and so forth. Contribution margin is one of the most important management accounting concepts you will learn because many operating decisions are made on the basis of how contribution margin will be affected. A company may decide, for example, to advertise one product more than others because that product has a higher contribution margin.

© 2003 Getty Images

The contribution margin generated by the sale of an order of French fries can be used to pay fixed costs such as rent, insurance, and salaries. Now you know why you often hear that ever popular question "Would you like fries with that?" at fast-food restaurants.

The Contribution Margin Income Statement

To illustrate the concept of contribution margin, let's use the following format of a contribution margin income statement. The statement data for Jewels Corporation, a producer of high-quality baseball gloves, follow.[2]

Jewels Corporation
Contribution Margin Income Statement
For the Month Ended November 30, 2006

	Total	Per Unit
Sales revenue (1,000 gloves)	$200,000	$200
Less variable costs	110,000	110
Contribution margin	$ 90,000	$ 90
Less fixed costs	63,000	
Profit*	$ 27,000	

*In this chapter, "profit" means pretax income; the terms *income* and *profit* are interchangeable.

per-unit contribution margin The excess of the sales price of one unit over its variable costs.

As this income statement shows, for internal decision-making purposes, Jewels Corporation computes its contribution margin on a per-unit (glove) and total-dollar basis. During November, Jewels' **per-unit contribution margin** is $90; the total contribution margin at a sales volume of 1,000 baseball gloves is $90,000.

The per-unit contribution margin tells us that $90 is available from each glove sold to cover fixed costs and provide a profit. By showing the $63,000 of fixed costs separately, this income statement also tells us that Jewels must generate sufficient contribution margin to cover these costs before a profit can be earned. With $200,000 of sales revenue, the contribution margin ($90,000) is sufficient to cover the fixed costs and provide a profit of $27,000.

2 In this example, we assume that there is only one model of baseball glove, which sells for $200.

This type of contribution margin income statement is particularly useful as a planning tool. The statement helps a company to project profits at any level of activity within the relevant range. For example, if Jewels Corporation forecasts sales of 1,200 baseball gloves next month, the company can prepare a forecasted (or pro-forma) income statement (in contribution margin format) as follows:

Jewels Corporation
Pro-Forma Contribution Margin Income Statement
For the Month Ended December 31, 2006

Sales revenue (1,200 gloves × $200)	$240,000
Less variable costs (1,200 gloves × $110)	132,000
Contribution margin	$108,000
Less fixed costs	63,000
Profit	$ 45,000

Notice that with an increase in sales of 200 baseball gloves, the contribution margin increases $18,000 ($108,000 − $90,000). You can confirm this by multiplying the per-unit contribution margin by the increase in volume ($90 per unit × 200 gloves = $18,000). Because we assume that the increase in volume is still within the relevant range of activity (which is a *very* important assumption!), the fixed costs remain at $63,000, and profit increases by the $18,000 increase in contribution margin. The critical thing you should see here is that once the fixed costs are covered, each subsequent dollar in contribution margin goes straight to profit! In other words, when Jewels Corporation hits its break-even point (which is the point where all fixed costs are covered), each additional glove sold will generate $90 in profit.

Notice the importance of accurately determining cost behavior when forecasting profit levels. If one ignores cost behavior, then the $27,000 profit generated by November sales of 1,000 gloves may lead to the conclusion that each glove creates $27 ($27,000 profit/1,000 gloves) in profit. With this *incorrect* information, the forecasted level of profit for December sales of 1,200 gloves is $32,400 ($27 per glove × 1,200 gloves). This forecast differs significantly from the $45,000 profit forecast above that stems from a *correct* consideration of the behavior (fixed or variable) of Jewels Corporation's costs.

The Contribution Margin Ratio

contribution margin ratio
The percentage of net sales revenue left after variable costs are deducted; the contribution margin divided by net sales revenue.

Knowing the **contribution margin ratio**, which is the percentage of sales revenue left after variable costs are deducted, will help you compare the profitability of various products. For example, if product A has a 60% contribution margin ratio and the contribution margin ratio of product B is only 20%, the company should emphasize product A, assuming that other factors are equal. As a concrete example, in a supermarket the prepared foods (baked goods, squeezed juices, ready-to-eat barbecued chicken) have high contribution margin ratios whereas the staples such as milk and eggs have lower contribution margin ratios.

To illustrate the calculation of contribution margin ratios, let's look again at the initial Jewels Corporation example. The ratio is computed as follows:

	Total	Per Unit	Ratio (Percentage)
Sales revenue (1,000 gloves)	$200,000	$200	100%
Less variable costs	110,000	110	55
Contribution margin	$ 90,000	$ 90	45%
Less fixed costs	63,000		
Profit	$ 27,000		

The contribution margin ratio is 45% of sales revenue ($90 ÷ $200), which means that for every $1.00 increase in sales revenue, the contribution margin increases by $0.45 (45% of $1.00). If fixed costs are already covered, profit will also increase by $0.45 for every $1.00 increase in sales. As you can see, there is another ratio presented in these calculations—the variable cost ratio. These two ratios are complements of each other. Hence, the variable cost ratio ($110 ÷ $200 = 55%) plus the contribution margin ratio (45%) will always equal 100%. This is important because whether we're describing contribution margin ratios or variable cost ratios, we are really talking about the same basic issue—the relationship of variable costs to sales revenue.

With contribution margin or variable cost ratios, it is easy to analyze the impact of changes in sales on the contribution margin. For example, if you estimate that Jewels' sales will increase by $20,000, you can apply the contribution margin ratio of 45% or the variable cost ratio of 55% and estimate that the contribution margin will increase by $9,000, which is equal to $20,000 × 0.45 or $20,000 × (1 − 0.55). The higher the contribution margin ratio, the larger the share of each additional dollar of sales that goes toward covering fixed costs and increasing profit.

The C-V-P Equation

As you can see, contribution margin calculations will be very useful to you when analyzing cost-volume-profit relationships in the management planning process. Doing C-V-P analysis using contribution margin calculations is a straightforward process. C-V-P analysis does require some simple algebra; here is where you reap the benefits of paying attention during your eighth grade math class.

We began this chapter with the assumption that all costs can be described as either fixed or variable. To highlight the important idea that C-V-P analysis depends on dividing costs into fixed and variable behavior patterns, we will develop the C-V-P equation as follows:[3]

1. Because all costs can be classified as either variable or fixed, we can express the calculation of profit with the following basic formula:

   Sales revenue − Variable costs − Fixed costs = Profit

2. We can specify the formula more precisely by expressing the equation in units:

   (Sales price × Units) − (Variable cost × Units) − Fixed costs = Profit

3. Or, we can express the equation using ratios:

   Sales revenue − (Variable cost ratio × Sales revenue) − Fixed costs = Profit

These equations are quick and useful methods for examining the financial aspects of C-V-P analysis problems. To illustrate, see if you can use the C-V-P equation based on units and the data from the Jewels Corporation example to determine profit assuming that sales of 1,200 baseball gloves are expected.

(Sales price × Units) − (Variable cost × Units) − Fixed costs = Profit
($200 × 1,200) − ($110 × 1,200) − $63,000 = Profit
$240,000 − $132,000 − $63,000 = Profit
$45,000 = Profit

Alternatively, you could calculate Jewels' profits using the equation based on ratios.

---

3 Granted, fixed and variable costs often get "mixed together" and can be difficult (and sometimes impossible) to separate. The fact that C-V-P analysis is based on an assumption that all costs can be divided clearly into fixed and variable is one of the limitations of this technique.

$$\text{Sales revenue} - (\text{Variable cost ratio} \times \text{Sales revenue}) - \text{Fixed costs} = \text{Profit}$$
$$\$240{,}000 - [(\$110 \div \$200) \times \$240{,}000] - \$63{,}000 = \text{Profit}$$
$$\$240{,}000 - (0.55 \times \$240{,}000) - \$63{,}000 = \text{Profit}$$
$$\$240{,}000 - \$132{,}000 - \$63{,}000 = \text{Profit}$$
$$\$45{,}000 = \text{Profit}$$

Note that we calculated the same profit of $45,000 using both formula approaches. This result is no surprise because these are simply alternative routes to the same destination. Both methods are commonly used in business, depending on the data available for the analysis. So, although there may appear to be many alternative ways to write the C-V-P formula, there is really only one formula, and it is not hard to remember:

$$\text{Sales revenue} - \text{Variable costs} - \text{Fixed costs} = \text{Profit}$$

Once you understand this fact, C-V-P analysis using the equation approach is basic math; you merely insert the known elements into the formula and solve for the one unknown element.

Break-Even Point

break-even point The amount of sales at which total costs of the number of units sold equal total revenues; the point at which there is no profit or loss.

In many cases, as a manager you will want to know how many units need to be sold to break even. The **break-even point** is defined as the volume of activity at which total revenues equal total costs, or where profit is zero. The break-even point may also be thought of as the volume of activity at which the contribution margin equals the fixed costs.

Although the goal of business planning is to make a profit, not just to break even, knowing the break-even point can be useful in assessing the risk of selling a new product, setting sales goals and commission rates, deciding on marketing and advertising strategies, and other similar operating decisions. Because the break-even point is, by definition, that activity level at which no profit or loss is earned, the basic C-V-P equation can be modified to calculate the break-even point as follows:

$$\text{Sales revenue} - \text{Variable costs} - \text{Fixed costs} = \$0$$

As you can see, to compute the break-even point, all that you need to do is simply set income equal to zero and then solve for the unknown—such as the number of units to be sold or the total revenues to be achieved.

Let's again use the Jewels Corporation example. How many units must Jewels sell to break even? (Note that we will use "X" to represent the unknown element, in this case, the number of baseball gloves.)

$$(\text{Sales price} \times \text{Units}) - (\text{Variable cost} \times \text{Units}) - \text{Fixed costs} = \$0$$
$$[\text{Sales price} \times (X)] - [\text{Variable cost} \times (X)] - \text{Fixed costs} = \$0$$
$$\$200X - \$110X - \$63{,}000 = \$0$$
$$\$90X = \$63{,}000$$
$$X = \$63{,}000 \div \$90 = 700 \text{ units (baseball gloves)}$$

In this case, if Jewels sells 700 baseball gloves, the company will generate enough revenues to cover its variable and fixed costs, earning zero profit [($200 × 700) − ($110 × 700) − $63,000 = $0]. Once you understand the basic C-V-P formula, you just set it up and solve for whatever unknown you're interested in planning. Think you've got it? Then try this one as a check on yourself: Assuming that Jewels can sell only 600 baseball gloves, what price per glove would the company have to use in order to break even?[4]

---

4 $(\text{Sales price} \times \text{Units}) - (\text{Variable cost} \times \text{Units}) - \text{Fixed costs} = \$0$
$[(X) \times \text{Units}] - (\text{Variable cost} \times \text{Units}) - \text{Fixed costs} = \$0$
$[(X) \times 600] - (\$110 \times 600) - \$63{,}000 = \$0$
$600X - \$66{,}000 - \$63{,}000 = \$0$
$600X = \$129{,}000$
$X = \$215 \text{ (new baseball glove price)}$

Determining Sales Volume to Achieve Target Income

Another way we can use C-V-P analysis in the planning process is to determine what level of activity is necessary to reach a target level of income. Instead of setting profit at $0 to do a break-even analysis, we can just as easily set income in the formula at the targeted level and then use the formula to plan or predict what fixed costs, variable costs, sales prices, and sales volumes are needed to achieve the target level of income. **Target income** is usually defined as the amount of income that will enable management to reach its objectives—paying dividends, meeting analysts' predictions, purchasing a new plant and equipment, or paying off existing loans. Target income can be expressed as either a percentage of revenues or as a fixed amount.

> **target income** A profit level desired by management.

To illustrate target income, suppose that we want to know how many baseball gloves must be sold by Jewels Corporation to achieve a target income of $36,000, assuming no changes in per-unit variable costs or total fixed costs. The calculation is as follows:

$$\text{(Sales price} \times \text{Units)} - \text{(Variable cost} \times \text{Units)} - \text{Fixed costs} = \text{Target income}$$
$$\$200X - \$110X - \$63,000 = \$36,000$$
$$\$90X = \$99,000$$
$$X = 1,100 \text{ units (baseball gloves)}$$

Thus, we can see that if Jewels sells 1,100 baseball gloves at a contribution margin of $90 each, and assuming that fixed costs are $63,000, the company will earn a pretax profit of $36,000 [($90 × 1,100 units) − $63,000 = $36,000].

A fixed dollar amount of income, such as the $36,000 that would be earned by selling 1,100 baseball gloves, is probably the most typical way of expressing a target income goal for many companies. However, because investors often evaluate companies partially on the basis of the **return on sales revenue** (or simply "return on sales"), management may want to state its goal as a percentage return as opposed to a fixed amount of income. For example, if Jewels Corporation set a target income of a 20% return on sales, the computation would be:

> **return on sales revenue** A measure of operating performance; computed by dividing net income by total sales revenue. Similar to profit margin.

$$\text{Sales revenue} - \text{Variable costs} - \text{Fixed costs} = 0.20 \times \text{Sales revenue}$$
$$\$200X - \$110X - \$63,000 = 0.2(\$200X)$$
$$\$200X - \$110X - \$63,000 = \$40X$$
$$\$200X - \$110X - \$40X = \$63,000$$
$$\$50X = \$63,000$$
$$X = \$63,000 \div \$50 = 1,260 \text{ gloves}$$

As we can see in this calculation, Jewels Corporation can earn a 20% return on sales by selling 1,260 baseball gloves.

Short-Cut Formulas for C-V-P Analysis

Notice that in the C-V-P analysis examples that we've worked through so far, the basic C-V-P equation remains constant. That's what makes this formula so powerful. Once you're comfortable with it, you can use it to manage any number of factors in planning for profits. However, you may remember from your brief introduction to C-V-P analysis in the previous chapter and from our C-V-P formula example on page 49 that we calculated break-even sales in units directly using the following formula.

$$\frac{\text{Total fixed costs}}{\text{(Sales price per unit} - \text{Variable cost per unit)}} = \text{Break-even sales (in units)}$$

This formula is a "short-cut" version of the C-V-P formulas above. You can see that it is simply the last step in the C-V-P calculation above for Jewels' break-even point of 700 baseball gloves. So, if you understand the basic C-V-P equation, you can simply skip to the last step of the calculation. There are short cuts for computing the level of sales for both break-even volume and target income volume. The short-cut formula for both the break-even volume and the target income volume in units is:

$$\frac{\text{Fixed costs} + \text{Target income}}{\text{Contribution margin per unit}^5}$$

Note that if you use this formula to determine the break-even volume, then you will assume that target income is $0, giving you:

$$\frac{\text{Fixed costs}}{\text{Contribution margin per unit}}$$

Plugging in the numbers for Jewels Corporation, the results are the same as shown earlier. As you can see, the short-cut calculation for both the break-even volume and the target income volume is really the same formula. For target sales:

$$\frac{\$63,000 + \$36,000}{\$90} = 1,100 \text{ units}$$

For the break-even volume:

$$\frac{\$63,000 + \$0}{\$90} = 700 \text{ units}$$

Always remember, though, that short cuts are useful, but they should not be applied until you fully understand the basic C-V-P relationships. In addition, managing some aspects of the C-V-P relationships can be tricky when you use short cuts. So if you ever get confused in solving a C-V-P analysis problem, just put the problem back in the original C-V-P equation:

$$\text{Sales revenue} - \text{Variable costs} - \text{Fixed costs} = \text{Target income}$$

Computation in Dollar Amounts versus Units

Before we finish with C-V-P equations, you should note that a variable cost ratio is sometimes used instead of a per-unit variable cost. In such cases, the basic C-V-P equation is modified as follows:

$$\text{Sales revenue} - (\text{Variable cost ratio} \times \text{Sales}) - \text{Fixed costs} = \text{Profit}$$

Because the variable costs are stated as a percentage of sales dollars rather than on a per-unit basis, this approach expresses activity in terms of sales dollars, not units. This is still the same basic C-V-P equation, but setting up the equation using the variable cost ratio will result in a break-even point in dollars instead of units. For example, the break-even point for Jewels Corporation would then be expressed as $140,000 in sales revenue ($200 per unit × 700 units) instead of 700 units as previously illustrated. This may be verified using the preceding equation and a 55% variable cost ratio as follows:

$$\text{Sales revenue} - (0.55)\text{Sales revenue} - \$63,000 = \$0$$
$$(0.45)\text{Sales revenue} = \$63,000$$
$$\text{Sales revenue} = \$140,000$$

The short-cut formula for break-even volume and target income volume in sales dollars is:

$$\frac{\text{Fixed costs} + \text{Target income}}{\text{Contribution margin ratio}}$$

(Remember the following: Contribution margin ratio = 1 − Variable cost ratio.)

---

5 Remember that per-unit contribution margin is the sales price per unit less the variable cost per unit.

IBM Gets on the Internet Wave In 1998, if you wanted an IBM desktop personal computer (PC), you had to walk into a store to make the purchase. In hindsight, this was a strange way to sell computers for a company that believed itself to be at the forefront of the e-business revolution. And in hindsight, this sales approach, being both slow and expensive, clearly didn't work. The PC division for IBM lost $986 million in 1998 and was bracing itself for similar losses in 1999. Market analysts were pushing IBM to sell its PC division based in Research Triangle Park in North Carolina. Finally, in the last quarter of 1999, IBM officials announced that it would yank its entire line of home desktop PCs from retail stores in the United States and sell the machines almost exclusively over the Internet. IBM also launched a $20 million advertising campaign (TV and direct mail flyers) to back up the move.

IBM's decision to sell over the Internet was driven largely by cut-throat pricing of components and systems by its major competitors and suppliers, the overhead costs of selling through dealers, and the inability to distinguish its product from dozens of competitor PCs sitting next to it on the retail shelf. In 2000, IBM followed the Internet decision by cutting $1.1 billion in annual manufacturing and distribution expenses. These cost savings were achieved largely by three means. First, IBM changed the way the PCs are built and redesigned the PC product to use as many industry standard parts as possible. Second, by building PCs to order (i.e., only building PCs when an order was placed), IBM was able to significantly reduce the amount of inventory it had to keep on hand. Third, IBM told its suppliers that it wanted 95% of its components ready on demand in well-stocked mini-warehouses near IBM manufacturing facilities. "The whole object is to not own the parts for very long," said Adalio Sanchez, general manager of manufacturing and operations for the PC division.

The change to IBM's PC business started to pay off as costs were reduced and shipments increased using the new ShopIBM Web site. Losses in the PC division were cut to $360 million in 1999 and $148 million in 2000. In 2001, after four straight years of losing money, the PC division was back in the black with a pretax profit of $99 million by the middle of the year. In a business today where prices on desktop PCs are typically in the $800 range, if IBM is $10 or $20 higher than the price of a DELL or COMPAQ PC, it can lose the sale. Clearly, controlling costs and managing sales is becoming more and more important in the very competitive PC market.

Sources: Ed Scannell, "IBM to Go Online with Home PC Sales," *InfoWorld Daily News*, October 19, 1999; Lisa Smith, "IBM's Personal Computer Unit Makes Turnaround," *The Herald-Sun*, March 22, 2001.

Caution

If you want to use C-V-P analysis to calculate the necessary sales volume in terms of *dollars*, the per-unit variable cost is *not* used. Rather, use the variable cost *ratio* times sales to determine total variable costs. Many students make the mistake of multiplying the per-unit variable cost times sales instead of the variable cost ratio times sales to get total variable costs.

Measuring the Effect of Potential Changes in C-V-P Variables

The basic techniques of C-V-P analysis that you have worked with in this chapter are used almost daily by organizations in the management processes of planning, controlling, and evaluating. As a result of understanding C-V-P analysis, you will be adept at evaluating the effects on profitability of the following common changes in C-V-P variables: (1) the amount of fixed costs, (2) the variable cost rate, (3) the sales price, (4) the sales volume or the number of units sold, and (5) combinations of these variables.

Changes in Fixed Costs

Many factors, such as an increase in property taxes or an increase in management's salaries, for example, will cause an increase in fixed costs. (Recall also from the opening scenario for this chapter that building a new facility such as a stadium can also increase fixed costs.) If all other factors remain constant, an increase in fixed costs always increases the number of units needed to break even. Obviously, the number of units needed to reach a target income will also increase. To illustrate, let's return again to the Jewels Corporation and assume that we need to analyze the effect on profits if fixed costs increase from $63,000 to $81,000. How many more baseball gloves must be sold to maintain Jewels' income goal of $36,000?

$$\text{Sales revenue} - \text{Variable costs} - \text{Fixed costs} = \text{Target income}$$
$$\$200X - \$110X - \$81,000 = \$36,000$$
$$\$90X = \$117,000$$
$$X = 1,300 \text{ gloves}$$

Because of the added fixed costs, Jewels must now sell 1,300 baseball gloves, instead of 1,100, to earn a target income of $36,000. The computations are quite simple. In fact, you may have found them unnecessary, realizing that if fixed costs increase by $18,000 ($81,000 − $63,000), and if the unit contribution margin remains $90 per glove, 200 additional gloves ($18,000 ÷ $90) will have to be sold in order to reach the $36,000 target income (1,100 + 200 = 1,300 gloves).

Changes in the Variable Cost Rate

Like an increase in fixed costs, an increase in the variable cost rate also increases the number of units needed to break even or to reach target income levels, when all other factors remain constant. Suppose that the variable cost rate increased from $110 per baseball glove to $130 per glove because of higher wages for factory personnel, increased costs of direct materials, or other factors. How does this cost increase affect the number of gloves needed to reach the target income, assuming that fixed costs are again $63,000?

$$\text{Sales revenue} - \text{Variable costs} - \text{Fixed costs} = \text{Target income}$$
$$\$200X - \$130X - \$63,000 = \$36,000$$
$$\$70X = \$99,000$$
$$X = 1,415 \text{ gloves*}$$

*Technically, if the C-V-P analysis results in a fractional answer, you should always round the answer *up* to the next digit. In this case, if you round the calculated answer of 1,414.29 to 1,414 gloves, you won't quite achieve the target income of $36,000.

The increase in the variable cost rate reduces the unit contribution margin (from $90 to $70), which means that more gloves must be sold to maintain the same target income. With a unit contribution margin of $90, the company would make a $36,000 target income by selling 1,100 baseball gloves; with a unit contribution margin of only $70, an additional 315 (1,415 − 1,100) gloves must be sold to earn at least a $36,000 target income.

Changes in Sales Price

If all other variables remain constant, an increase in the sales price decreases the sales volume needed to reach a target income. This is because an increase in sales price increases the contribution margin per baseball glove, thereby decreasing the number of gloves that must be sold to earn the same amount of target income.

To illustrate, assume that the demand for baseball gloves is overwhelming and that Jewels cannot produce gloves fast enough. Hence, we make a decision to increase the price from $200 to $230 per glove. As a result of the price increase, the number of gloves that must be sold to reach the target income of $36,000 decreases:

$$\text{Sales revenue} - \text{Variable costs} - \text{Fixed costs} = \text{Target income}$$
$$\$230X - \$110X - \$63,000 = \$36,000$$
$$\$120X = \$99,000$$
$$X = 825 \text{ gloves}$$

With the sales price increase of $30 per glove, the contribution margin also increases $30 per glove to $120; and with a $120 contribution margin per glove, only 825 gloves need to be sold to reach the $36,000 target income. Obviously, a decrease in the sales price would have the opposite effect; it would increase the number of units needed to reach the target income.

Changes in Sales Volume

As you have seen, the sales volume (the number of gloves to be sold) for the target income has varied with each change in one of the other variables. When other variables remain constant, an increase in the sales volume will result in an increase in income. Very simply, the more gloves sold, the higher the income (as long as the contribution margin is positive!). The degree of change in profits resulting from volume change depends on the size of the unit contribution margin. To be specific, the change in income will be equal to the change in sales volume units multiplied by the contribution margin per unit. So, when the unit contribution margin is high, a slight change in volume results in a dramatic change in profit. With a lower unit contribution margin, the change in profit is less.

Simultaneous Changes in Several Variables

Thus far, we have examined changes in only one variable at a time. However, in your work in actual business organizations, you will find that individual changes are quite rare. More often, a decision will affect several variables, all at the same time. For example, should Jewels Corporation increase fixed advertising costs by $20,000 and reduce the sales price by 10% if the result would be to increase sales volume by 500 units? The impact on the target income from these proposed changes is as follows:

	Initial Data	Proposed Changes
Sales price per glove	$200	$180 ($200 × 90%)
Variable costs per glove	$110	$110
Fixed costs	$63,000	$83,000 ($63,000 + $20,000)
Target income	$36,000	X
Sales volume	1,100 gloves	1,600 gloves (1,100 + 500)

Computations and Result:

$$\text{Sales revenue} - \text{Variable costs} - \text{Fixed costs} = \text{Target income}$$
$$(\$180 \times 1,600) - (\$110 \times 1,600) - \$83,000 = X$$
$$\$288,000 - \$176,000 - \$83,000 = X$$
$$\$29,000 = X \text{ (target income)}$$

The analysis shows that target income would drop by $7,000 ($36,000 − $29,000) as a result of these changes. So, our decision should be to *not* implement the proposed changes.

Consider another possible decision: Should Jewels automate part of its production, thereby reducing (by $10) variable costs to $100 per unit and increasing (by $5,000) fixed costs to $68,000? The computation is as follows:

$$\text{Sales revenue} - \text{Variable costs} - \text{Fixed costs} = \text{Target income}$$
$$(\$200 \times 1,100) - (\$100 \times 1,100) - \$68,000 = X$$
$$\$220,000 - \$110,000 - \$68,000 = X$$
$$\$42,000 = X \text{ (target income)}$$

This analysis shows that implementing these proposed changes would be beneficial because they would increase target income by $6,000 ($42,000 − $36,000). Obviously, this is true only if the assumptions can be relied on—that is, if fixed costs will rise by no more than $5,000 and unit variable costs will decrease by a full $10.

Consider another example. Suppose Jewels Corporation could use part of the excess capacity of its operating facilities to make baseball bats. These bats would sell for $90 per unit, increase fixed costs by $40,000, and have a variable cost per unit of $45. Jewels wants to add this new product line only if it can increase income by $25,000. How many baseball bats must Jewels sell to reach this target income? The computation follows:

Caution

Remember, any change that affects the number of units sold changes both the total sales revenue *and* total variable costs.

$$\text{Sales revenue} - \text{Variable costs} - \text{Fixed costs} = \text{Target income}$$
$$\$90X - \$45X - \$40,000 = \$25,000$$
$$\$45X = \$65,000$$
$$X = 1,445 \text{ baseball bats (rounded up)}$$

Now that we have completed the C-V-P calculations, we must determine whether the company can produce and sell 1,445 baseball bats. If that sales goal seems attainable, the facilities should be used to make the bats. Don't forget that making C-V-P calculations is the easy part of managing an organization. It takes an excellent manager to successfully implement the results of a C-V-P analysis into a real business process.

business environment

Breaking Even in the Hotel Industry An international hotel chain undertook a project to increase the effectiveness of decision making of its properties in Europe, the Middle East, and Africa. In 1996, company executives wanted to improve the financial planning and control decisions of the hotel management teams. The Europe, Middle East, Africa division was responsible at that time for approximately 240 hotels. Essentially, the executives aimed to encourage a greater use of basic managerial accounting techniques such as budgeting models and C-V-P analysis in order to improve the profitability of individual hotels.

It was clear to the company that understanding how hotel costs behaved is absolutely key to making good decisions that affect market share analysis, annual budget preparation and monitoring of results, sales volume and business mix decisions, pricing policies, and cost management. In order to identify the fixed and variable costs in the hotels, the company first worked with individual hotel management teams within its organization who were intimately familiar with how costs behaved based on changes in sales volumes (i.e., hotel rooms rented). Initially, the company had these individuals determine from their own experience which costs were fixed, variable, or semi-variable (i.e., mixed) costs with respect to changes in sales volume. Scattergraph and statistical analyses were then used to estimate the fixed and variable proportions of the mixed costs—again related to sales volume—and allocate these costs to the main fixed and variable groups.

Computer spreadsheets were then used to assess key "what if" questions. For instance, "What is the likely effect on profit of a 3% shortfall in room revenue?". . . or . . . "How will profit change if a 5% growth in total sales volume occurs?" This alerts managers to the critical areas of profitability and indicates which revenue and cost areas require greater attention for a given decision. It also enables management to gain an overall indication of "profit stability" or "profit instability'" in relation to changes in revenue and cost of particular hotel properties. Knowledge of break-even levels and profit-and-loss implications of different business scenarios are relevant if managers are to make informed decisions which ensure survival, optimize profits, and limit risk, giving rise to a feeling of "being more in control" when making decisions.

In 1995, the year before the new management focus on C-V-P analysis commenced, the average operating profit margin in the Europe, Middle East, Africa division was 35%. In 1998, the average operating profit margin was 39%. Although the hotel executives do not believe that the new focus on C-V-P tools is the only reason for this improvement, it has played a positive role in significantly adding to shareholder value.

Source: Ian C. Graham and Peter J. Harris, "Development of a Profit Planning Framework in an International Hotel Chain: A Case Study," *International Journal of Contemporary Hospitality Management,* 1999 (Issue 5), pp. 198–204.

TO SUMMARIZE: The contribution margin is sales revenue less variable costs and is the amount of revenue left to cover fixed costs and provide a profit. The contribution margin can be expressed in total dollars, on a per-unit basis, or on a percentage basis. Because fixed costs remain constant within a relevant range, once fixed costs have been covered, income increases by the amount of the per-unit contribution margin for every additional unit sold. This relationship is used in C-V-P analysis. The basic C-V-P equation is:

Sales revenue − Variable costs − Fixed costs = Target income

Using this equation, you as a manager can work to plan, control, and evaluate the costs, prices, and sales output of the organization. The effects of changes in costs, prices, and volume on profitability may be determined by C-V-P analysis. Changes in individual variables or simultaneous changes in several variables can be analyzed with this technique.

Using Graphs to "See" C-V-P Relationships

5 Visualize C-V-P relationships using graphs.

Earlier in this chapter, we talked about using scattergraph methods as a way to analyze cost behavior. Recall that once we have plotted the history of costs on a graph and visually fitted a regression line through the data, we can then essentially "see" how the cost can be separated into its fixed and variable cost components. Now, by simply adding a line to the cost chart to represent revenue, we can graphically work with cost-volume-profit relationships. In fact, using graphs may be the most effective way to manage and communicate C-V-P information. This graphical approach allows you to visually examine cost and revenue data over a range of activity rather than at a single volume. Sometimes, though, reading precise information from a graph can be difficult. Hence, when analyzing specific proposals in the future, you will typically combine the C-V-P equations discussed in the preceding section with the graphs discussed in this section.

On a C-V-P graph, volume or activity level usually is shown on the horizontal axis, and total dollars of sales and costs are shown on the vertical axis. Lines are then drawn to represent total fixed costs, total costs, and total revenues. Exhibit 6 shows a C-V-P graph for Jewels Corporation.

Remember that fixed and variable cost relationships are valid only for the relevant range of activity (the screened area on the graph in Exhibit 6). In this case, fixed costs are $63,000, and variable costs are $110 per glove over the range of activity between 400 and 1,200 gloves sold. Total costs are $118,000 at 500 gloves [$63,000 + ($110 × 500 gloves)], $129,000 at 600 gloves [$63,000 + ($110 × 600 gloves)], and so on. Similarly, total revenues are $100,000 at 500 gloves ($200 × 500 gloves), $120,000 at 600 gloves, and so forth. The break-even point, the point at which total revenues equal total costs, is 700 gloves, or $140,000 in sales.

As shown in Exhibit 7, we can use the graphic format to isolate such items of interest as total variable costs, total fixed costs, the area in which losses occur, the area in which profits will be realized, and the break-even point. Because C-V-P graphs illustrate a wide range of activity, this tool can help in quickly determining approximately how much profit or loss will be realized at various levels of sales.

The Profit Graph

profit graph A graph that shows how profits vary with changes in volume.

With a few adjustments to a standard C-V-P graph, we can create what is called a **profit graph**, which plots only profits and losses and omits costs and revenues. A profit graph is another useful way to visualize how decisions regarding costs and revenues will impact profit. Exhibit 8 shows a profit graph for Jewels Corporation based on the same underlying data used in Exhibit 6.

Exhibit 6: A Cost-Volume-Profit Graph

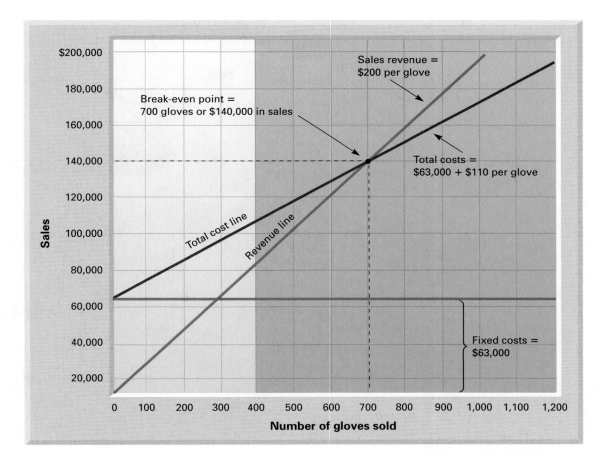

Notice that, though the horizontal axis of the profit graph is the same as those of the previous graphs, the vertical axis represents only profits and losses. As long as the contribution margin is positive, the maximum amount of losses that can occur is at a zero level of sales. With no sales, total losses will be the amount of the fixed costs. With the axes properly labeled, we can draw the profit line as follows:

1. Locate the loss for zero sales volume on the vertical axis. This is the total fixed cost, or negative $63,000 in this case.
2. Locate the profit or loss at another sales volume. For example, at sales of 700 gloves, profits are zero [$140,000 − ($63,000 + $77,000)], or at sales of 1,000 gloves, profits are $27,000 [$200,000 − ($63,000 + $110,000)].
3. After the two profit or loss points have been identified, draw a line through them back to the vertical axis.

Because of how simple it is to create, the profit graph is widely used for comparing competing projects. It has the disadvantage, however, of not showing specifically how revenues and costs vary with changes in sales volume.

A Comparison of C-V-P Graphs with C-V-P Equations

C-V-P graphs are very useful in understanding contribution margin income statements and C-V-P equations. To illustrate this point, let's again explore the question of what volume of

Exhibit 7: Cost-Volume-Profit Graphs

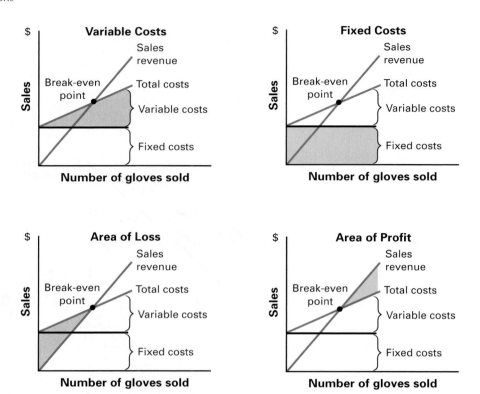

Exhibit 8: Profit Graph for Jewels Corporation

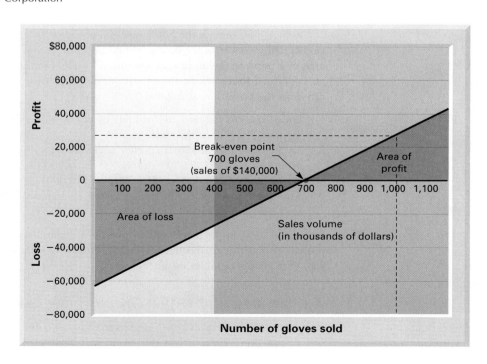

STOP & THINK

When analyzing costs, volume, and profit, do you think most managers would prefer to use graphs or equations?

activity Jewels Corporation needs to reach a target income of $36,000. This was illustrated earlier with the equation approach, but it is repeated here to show that the graph approach will produce the same quantitative results. As you can see in Exhibit 9, Jewels Corporation must sell 1,100 baseball gloves to reach a target income of $36,000.

Exhibit 9: Comparison of C-V-P Equation with C-V-P Graph

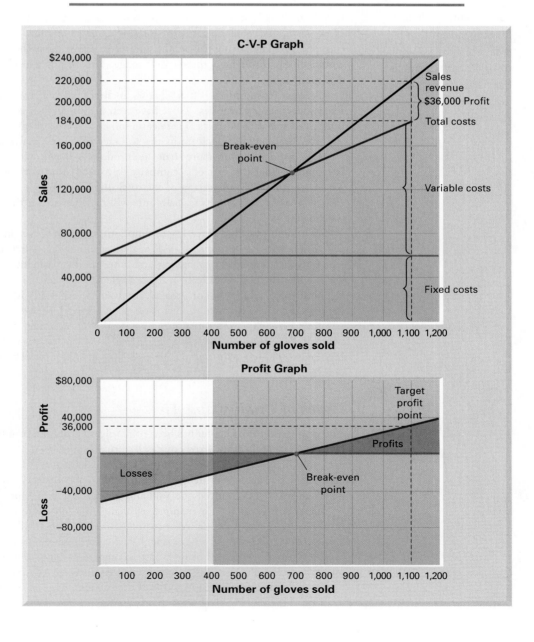

C-V-P Equation

(Sales price × Units) − (Variable costs × Units) − Fixed costs = Profit

$$\$200X - \$110X - \$63,000 = \$36,000$$
$$\$90X = \$99,000$$
$$X = 1,100 \text{ gloves}$$

TO SUMMARIZE: The financial effects on cost-volume-profit decisions can be examined by using either equations or graphs. These methods of analysis can be used to calculate the break-even point, which occurs at the point where total revenues equal total fixed costs plus total variable costs. These methods can also be used to project a target profit level, with profit being equal to the excess of revenues over total costs. The graphic approaches are useful because they highlight cost-volume-profit relationships over wide ranges of activity. The most common graphic approach involves plotting fixed costs as a horizontal line with variable costs representing the distance between the fixed costs and total costs line. A profit graph, which shows only profit or loss and volume, is much simpler, but it does not show how costs vary with changes in sales volume. Regardless of the approach, all variations of C-V-P analysis are based on the same calculations and on the same underlying concept of fixed and variable costs.

Limiting Assumptions of C-V-P Analysis

6 Identify the limiting assumptions of C-V-P analysis, and explain the issues of quality and time relative to C-V-P analysis decisions.

C-V-P analysis is an extremely useful tool to assist in making short-term operating decisions. However, C-V-P analysis has some limiting assumptions that must not be overlooked.

The first key assumption underlying C-V-P analysis is that the behavior of revenues and costs is linear throughout the relevant range. This means that C-V-P analysis is valid only for a relevant range.

A second assumption is that all costs, including mixed costs, can be accurately divided into fixed and variable categories. As we have seen in this chapter, some costs have characteristics of both fixed and variable costs. These costs sometimes are not easily classified into their fixed and variable components, which limits the accuracy of C-V-P analysis.

For companies with more than one product, a third major assumption in C-V-P analysis is required—that the mix of a company's products does not change over the relevant range. The sales mix is the proportion of the total units sold (or the total dollar sales) represented by each of a company's products. Sales mix will be discussed in the expanded material section of this chapter.

In addition to these three key assumptions, there are other limiting assumptions implicit in C-V-P analysis. For example, C-V-P analysis assumes that efficiency and productivity are held constant, that the prices of materials and other product components are constant, and that revenues and costs can be analyzed using a single activity base, such as volume. A related and very significant assumption, and one that clearly is not always valid, is that volume is the only, or even the primary, driver of costs. As discussed below, delivery time and quality can also impact costs.

Because of the limiting assumptions just described, a manager must use reasonable caution when making decisions using C-V-P analysis. Nevertheless, C-V-P analysis does provide a good model for predicting future operating results when specific relationships are defined and recognized.

Issues of Quality and Time

The emphasis in this chapter has been primarily on costs and profits and how they change when changes in variable costs, fixed costs, sales prices, and sales volume are made. Remember, however, that financial results are just one of several elements of performance that a manager must consider. Good managers are equally interested in how these changes will affect the quality of goods and services produced and sold and the speed at which products and services can be delivered to customers. If, for example, reducing fixed costs means that goods will be produced more slowly or that the quality of manufactured products will be reduced, then a decision to reduce fixed costs may be a poor one. On the other hand, if a company can automate a function using robotics instead of high-cost workers, for example, it may be possible to simultaneously reduce total costs, increase quality and consistency, and improve speed of production. To determine whether quality and speed of production are good or bad, a management team may need to compare its results with those of other firms, a process called *benchmarking*, which will be introduced in a later chapter.

TO SUMMARIZE: C-V-P analysis is based on three critical and limiting assumptions: (1) that the behavior of revenues and costs is linear throughout the relevant range, (2) that all costs can be categorized as either fixed or variable, and (3) that the sales mix does not change. When considering how changes in variable costs, fixed costs, sales prices, sales volume, and sales mix will affect profits, it is important to also consider how these changes will affect the quality of goods and services and the speed at which products and services can be delivered to customers. Decisions that increase quality, reduce costs, and speed up production are valuable changes and should be made; decisions that have a negative effect on one or more of these variables must be carefully analyzed and trade-offs considered.

Thus far, we have covered various types of costs, simple methods of analyzing mixed costs, and the basics of C-V-P analysis. In this expanded section, we cover an additional, more advanced method of analyzing mixed costs—least squares analysis. We also cover the effect of the sales mix on profitability and use the concept of operating leverage to explore differences in cost structures among manufacturing, merchandising, service, and e-commerce organizations.

Analysis of Mixed Costs—The Least Squares Method

7 Analyze mixed costs using the least squares method.

least squares method A method of segregating the fixed and variable portions of a mixed cost; the regression line, a line of averages, is statistically fitted through all cost points.

Earlier, we described two common methods for analyzing mixed costs: the scattergraph and high-low methods. These methods are relatively easy to use and provide useful estimates of the fixed and variable components of mixed costs. A more sophisticated method for analyzing mixed costs is the **least squares method**, which is the most accurate method of using a specific set of data to determine the fixed and variable portions of a mixed cost. Like the scattergraph, the least squares method fits a straight line through all points on a graph. However, instead of visually fitting the regression line through the cost points, it uses statistical analysis to guarantee that the line is the best possible fit for the applicable costs. As a result, the least squares method provides a better analysis because it isn't based on a subjective regression line like scattergraphs and because it uses all the cost data points rather than just the high and low data points as with the high-low method.

The formula for the least squares method is based on the equation for a straight line:

$$Y = a + bX$$

You probably recognize this classic equation from previous math classes you may have had. When this equation is used to do cost analysis, Y represents the total predicted cost; a represents the intercept and the fixed cost (if in the relevant range); b represents the variable cost rate or the slope of the line; and X represents the activity level being considered. Using cost and activity level data, this method involves the use of simultaneous equations to find the values of a and b. Once computed, these values can be combined with the projected activity level X to predict or estimate the total future cost Y. For example, if the values of a and b are computed to be $200 and $5, respectively, then for an estimated activity level of 100 direct labor hours, we can predict that:

$$Y \text{ (total predicted cost)} = \$200 + \$5(100 \text{ hours})$$
$$Y = \$200 + \$500$$
$$Y = \$700$$

You should understand that the regression line is basically a line of averages. Therefore, the *actual* total cost for 100 direct labor hours might be somewhat different from the *predicted* cost of $700. The method of least squares, however, attempts to minimize the differences between predicted and actual costs. Once a regression line has been fitted to historical data, the fixed and variable costs represented by the line can be used to predict the level of future costs.

Calculating the estimates of *a* (the intercept, or the total fixed cost) and *b* (the slope, or variable cost rate) requires solving the following two simultaneous equations:

1. $\Sigma XY = a\Sigma X + b\Sigma X^2$
2. $\Sigma Y = na + b\Sigma X$

where

a = fixed cost
b = variable cost rate
n = number of observations
Σ = summation sign (which means the sum of all historical data indicated by the sign)
X = activity level, or independent variable
Y = total (predicted) mixed cost, or dependent variable

Actually, solving these equations is easy with a calculator or computer, but difficult and tedious by hand. Initially solving these equations by hand may be useful to you in learning exactly how these equations work. However, as a manager working with cost estimations, you are going to have computers available to analyze large amounts of data very quickly. Hence, we will focus on describing and interpreting the typical output from a computerized application of least squares analysis. We will leave it to math classes to illustrate the manual calculations of the least squares method.

To illustrate the concept of least squares, let's return once more to the electricity cost data used earlier in this chapter to work with the scattergraph and high-low methods. Note that the historical data that we are using for this example are given for only six months; thus, the resulting regression equation will likely be less accurate than it would be with more data (say, 12 or 18 months of data).

Month	Direct Labor Hours Worked	Total Electricity Cost
January	7,000	$ 70,000
February	6,000	60,000
March	12,000	100,000
April	6,600	80,000
May	18,000	120,000
June	14,000	110,000

Using these data, the following output, shown in Exhibit 10, can be generated in just a matter of minutes using the "data analysis" tool in Excel®, a Microsoft database software program.[6] Now compare the least squares output with the results from our earlier work using the scattergraph and high-low methods:

	Fixed Costs	Variable Cost per Direct Labor Hour
Scattergraph method	$40,000 per month	$4.29 per direct labor hour
High-low method	30,000 per month	5.00 per direct labor hour
Least squares analysis	40,402 per month	4.68 per direct labor hour

6 There are literally hundreds of software programs that can be used to run regressions or least squares analysis.

Exhibit 10: Output of Least Squares Analysis Application

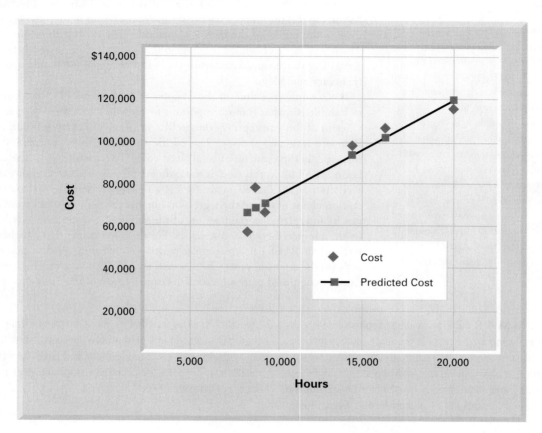

Month	Hours	Cost
January	7,000	$ 70,000
February	6,000	60,000
March	12,000	100,000
April	6,600	80,000
May	18,000	120,000
June	14,000	110,000

Summary Output	
Regression Statistics	
Multiple R	0.962
R square	0.926
Adjusted R square	0.907
Standard error	7207.705
Observations	6

	Coefficients	Standard Error	t Stat	P-value	Lower 95%	Upper 95%
Intercept	$40,402.03	$7,613.10	$5.31	0.0061	$19,264.63	$61,539.43
Hours	$ 4.68	$ 0.66	$7.05	0.0021	$ 2.84	$ 6.52

FYI:

An R^2 of more than 0.9 is actually not very common in practice. It is often quite rare to identify a *single* cost driver that explains most of the variance of important costs in an organization. Typically, organizations find that there are many things that affect a particular cost (e.g., headcount, floor space, operating hours, etc.), which requires that cost analysis be based on multiple cost drivers. The least squares analysis method we have discussed here is also known as simple or single linear regression. *Multiple* linear regression, a technique you may have learned about in a statistics class, uses a similar approach to identify the impact of several activities on changes in a specific cost.

You can see that the least squares analysis results in fixed costs estimated at $40,402 and the variable cost rate estimated to be $4.68 per direct labor hour. As you can see, the results are more similar to the results of the scattergraph method than to the results of the high-low method. Why do you think this is the case? The reason is that both the scattergraph and least squares methods are essentially using all of the historical data while the high-low method uses only two data points (February and May).

We won't take time in this chapter to understand all of the output shown in Exhibit 10; what is most important is that you know three things: (1) the coefficient of the intercept, (2) the coefficient of the direct labor hours, and (3) the R square summary statistic. The coefficient of the intercept, or $40,402.03 in this case, is the estimate of total fixed costs. The coefficient of the direct labor hours, or $4.68 in this case, is the estimate of the variable electricity cost per direct labor hour. The R square (R^2) is a descriptive statistic that provides information about how well the regression line fits the data; in other words, R square can be interpreted as the fraction of the variability in the data that is explained by the computed regression statistics. For now, remember that a higher R^2 is better, and an R^2 of 1.0 represents a perfect fit (meaning all data points were exactly on the regression line). In this case, an R^2 of 0.926 is very high and suggests that the computed regression statistics explain most of the variability in the data.[7]

TO SUMMARIZE: A more sophisticated technique for analyzing mixed costs is the least squares method. The least squares method is essentially equivalent to simple regression analysis, using the equation for a straight line ($Y = a + bX$) and simultaneous equations to calculate the fixed and variable portions of a mixed cost. Even though the least squares method is more mathematically correct than the scattergraph or high-low methods, it still should be used with caution in analyzing mixed costs. Least squares results can be quickly calculated using computer programs such as Microsoft's Excel®.

Sales Mix

8 Explain the effects of sales mix on profitability.

sales mix The relative proportion of total units sold (or total sales dollars) that is represented by each of a company's products.

Earlier in this chapter, we described some important limiting assumptions of C-V-P analysis. As a manager using C-V-P, you need to be aware of what this tool can and cannot do. One important issue is that C-V-P analysis must be adjusted when a company starts changing the mix of products that it sells. **Sales mix** is the proportion of the total units represented by each of a company's products. To keep our discussions simple, in previous sections of the chapter we used examples of companies with only one product. Many companies have more than one product, however, so you need to understand how sales mix issues are resolved. To illustrate how a change in sales mix can affect a company's C-V-P relationships, let's assume that Multi-Product, Inc., sells three different products. Following are the monthly revenues and costs for each type of product:

	Product A		Product B		Product C		Total	
	Amount	Percent	Amount	Percent	Amount	Percent	Amount	Percent
Sales revenue	$25,000	100%	$45,000	100.00%	$30,000	100%	$100,000	100%
Less variable costs	20,000	80	30,000	66.67	21,000	70	71,000	71
Contribution margin	$ 5,000	20%	$15,000	33.33%	$ 9,000	30%	$ 29,000	29%
Sales mix		25%		45%		30%		100%

7 The adjusted R^2 of 0.907 is a more conservative estimate of the variance explained in the data and is preferred to the R^2 statistic in some circumstances.

FYI:

A computer can make sales mix and other C-V-P analysis computations easier to do. Using simulation or other programs, you can quickly calculate the financial effects of changes in the sales of one product or simultaneous changes in sales of several products.

Total sales are $100,000, which in this example includes $25,000 in sales of Product A, $45,000 of Product B, and $30,000 of Product C. Therefore, the sales mix is 25% Product A ($25,000 ÷ $100,000), 45% Product B ($45,000 ÷ $100,000), and 30% Product C ($30,000 ÷ $100,000). With this sales mix, the average variable cost ratio is 71%, which is determined by dividing total variable costs of $71,000 by total sales of $100,000. If Multi-Product, Inc., had fixed costs of $17,400 and desired a target income of $40,000, the necessary sales volume (in dollars) would be:

$$\text{Sales revenue} - (0.71)\text{Sales revenue} - \$17,400 = \$40,000$$
$$(0.29)\text{Sales revenue} = \$57,400$$
$$\text{Sales revenue} = \$57,400 \div 0.29$$
$$\text{Sales revenue} = \$197,932 \text{ (rounded up)}$$

Alternatively, you could calculate the average contribution margin ratio by subtracting the total variable costs from total sales and dividing the result (total contribution margin of $29,000) by total sales of $100,000. The company could then divide the average contribution margin ratio (29%) into fixed costs plus target income ($17,400 + $40,000). This revised, more compact formula is simply a restatement of the preceding equation.

$$\frac{\text{Fixed costs} + \text{Target income}}{\text{Average contribution margin ratio}} = \frac{\$57,400}{0.29} = \$197,932 \text{ (rounded up)}$$

Remember, though, that $197,932 in sales will achieve the target income only if the average variable cost and contribution margin ratios, and therefore the sales mix, do not change. In order for you to better understand this fact, assume that the total sales revenue and the sales price of each product remain the same but that the sales mix changes as follows:

	Product A		Product B		Product C		Total	
	Amount	**Percent**	**Amount**	**Percent**	**Amount**	**Percent**	**Amount**	**Percent**
Sales revenue	$50,000	100%	$30,000	100.00%	$20,000	100%	$100,000	100%
Less variable costs	40,000	80	20,000	66.67	14,000	70	74,000	74
Contribution margin	$10,000	20%	$10,000	33.33%	$ 6,000	30%	$ 26,000	26%
Sales mix	50%		30%		20%		100%	

As you can see in this example, the variable cost and contribution margin ratios for each product remain the same, but the sales mix changes. Product A now comprises 50% of total sales instead of 25%. Because Product A has a lower contribution margin ratio than Products B and C, the average contribution margin ratio decreases from 29 to 26% (stated another way, the average variable cost ratio increases from 71% to 74%). Now think about how this change in the sales mix would affect profit and the volume of sales revenue needed to break even. Would you expect the necessary sales volume to increase or decrease?

Let's use the more compact formula based on the average contribution margin ratio to calculate the new sales volume. When we run the new C-V-P calculation, the sales volume needed to generate $40,000 of target income increases to $220,770, computed as follows:

STOP & THINK

Before moving on, can you calculate the necessary sales volume of $220,770 in the second sales mix example using the familiar C-V-P equation: Sales revenue − Variable costs − Fixed costs = Target income?

$$\frac{\text{Fixed costs} + \text{Target income}}{\text{Average contribution margin ratio}} = \frac{\$57,400}{0.26} = \$220,770 \text{ (rounded up)}$$

The important thing that we've learned from these sales mix calculations is that one sensible profit-maximizing strategy for management would be to maintain as large a contribution margin as possible on all products and then

STOP & THINK

Would maximizing the sales of the highest contribution margin products still be the best profit-maximizing strategy if the company experienced production constraints such that producing more of the highest contribution margin products severely limited the quality or production speed of other products?

to emphasize those products with the largest individual contribution margins. In the remaining chapters of this text, we discuss procedures that management can use to control costs and, hence, maintain high contribution margins. The second part of this strategy—emphasizing the products with the highest contribution margin ratios—is a marketing function. Multi-Product, Inc., for example, should promote Product B more aggressively than Product A. With other factors being equal, a company should spend more advertising dollars and pay higher sales commissions on its products with higher contribution margin ratios. In fact, instead of paying commissions based on total sales, a good strategy would be to base sales commissions on the total contribution margin generated. This way, the mix of products that maximizes the sales staff's commissions will be the mix that provides the company with the greatest overall profit.

TO SUMMARIZE: Sales mix is the proportion of the total units sold represented by each of a company's products. Changes in sales mix can affect profits because not all products have the same contribution margin. Other things being equal, to maximize profits, management should put greater emphasis on the sale of products with higher contribution margin ratios.

Cost Structure in Different Types of Organizations

9 Describe how fixed and variable costs differ in manufacturing, service, merchandising, and e-commerce organizations, and illustrate these differences with the operating leverage concept.

operating leverage The extent to which fixed costs are part of a company's cost structure; the higher the proportion of fixed costs to variable costs, the faster income increases or decreases with changes in sales volume.

Now that we have nearly completed this chapter, we have developed a lot of insight into how to think about and manage costs in the process of making profit-planning decisions. This chapter is actually a lot about the strategy—the strategy of how a company works with its specific types of costs and activities to create a profit. Overall, we now basically understand how cost-volume-profit relationships and contribution margins highlight the different effects that variable and fixed costs have on profitability. As we close this chapter, an important management issue to be understood has to do with the amount of fixed costs a company has in its cost structure. The amount of fixed costs an organization commits itself to often has a lot to do with its type of business, e.g., merchandising, manufacturing, or service. In addition, the arrival of e-commerce into the economy is having an impact on cost structures of organizations. We'll talk more about differences between merchandising, manufacturing, service, and e-commerce companies throughout the remaining chapters in this textbook. For now, we'll simply illustrate the differences among these organizations by applying the concept of **operating leverage** to illustrate how a company can manage risk (in terms of profits) by the way it organizes its cost structure—in other words, how much the company is committed to using fixed costs versus variable costs to do business.

Imagine that you have worked with two of your college friends to design a new computer software game that you expect to market to college campuses across the nation. You and your partners have identified three ways to approach the market. First, you can take on the role of the merchant by contracting with a software manufacturing company to handle all the production of the packaged software. You can then concentrate on the sales and marketing of their new game. This approach won't require an expensive production facility, but the reality is that you will have to pay a high price per unit to the company that handles the production of the packaged software. In the second approach, you can take on the role of manufacturer by setting up your own production facilities. In this case, because all of your effort will be dedicated to producing the game, you will need to wholesale the software product to another merchant company that will then resell the product to the actual customers. Finally, you can "virtually" sell the game to other college students by contracting with an e-commerce company that will host your software download site for a significant fixed fee per month. In any case, regardless of whether you and your partners will wholesale the game to another merchant or retail the game directly to the college student market, you have determined that you can sell the game for $100. The costs of each of these methods of structuring your business are as follows:

Business Structure	Variable Cost per Unit to Manufacture or to Purchase from a Manufacturer	Fixed Cost per Year for the Merchandising, Manufacturing, or E-Commerce Facility
Traditional retail merchant	$80	$100,000
Manufacturer	25	375,000
E-commerce merchant	0	500,000

Caution

Don't confuse the concept of operating leverage with the concept of financial leverage, though there is a lot of similarity in these concepts. While both concepts focus on risk and the sensitivity of profit to changes in sales volume, financial leverage has to do with the use of debt versus equity to provide financing for a company. In general, the financial leverage (and risk) of a company increases as management chooses to use debt, rather than equity, to raise funds for the company. Similarly, the operating leverage (and risk) of a company increases as management chooses to emphasize fixed cost, rather than variable cost, to create or obtain the product for sale to the marketplace.

STOP & THINK

Think about the level of operating leverage you would expect to find in a service organization such as a consulting company or a law firm. Would these kinds of organizations typically have high or low levels of operating leverage?

As you can see, one of the issues that you must decide when selecting your company's business structure is whether you and your partners want to commit to high fixed costs in order to have low variable costs, or vice versa. This trade-off of fixed versus variable costs is what we mean when we talk about operating leverage. As total fixed costs increase and variable costs per unit decrease, the operating leverage of the organization increases. In the example above, the operating leverage of your company will be very high if you choose to structure your company as an e-commerce merchant. So, the question you should be asking yourself is whether it is good or bad to have high operating leverage? The answer is that it depends on whether the company is operating above or below the break-even point.

The C-V-P graphs in Exhibit 11 show us the impact of operating leverage for these three types of companies. The break-even point (which is the same for all three companies) is at a sales volume of 5,000 games sold each year. At this point, all three companies would generate the same level of profit—nothing. As sales move above or below the break-even point, however, there are significant differences in profit (i.e., the distance between the revenue line and the total costs line) between the company structures. If sales are below the break-even point, then structuring the company as an e-commerce merchant will generate a lot of losses. If the company can sell more than 5,000 games per year, however, then the e-commerce merchant structure will generate the most profit per year. Essentially, operating leverage is a measure of risk. With high levels of operating leverage, the company is at risk of losing a lot of money if sales go down. But business risk often has an upside. In the case of operating leverage, the risk of loss is balanced by the potential for large gains in income as sales go up. So your decision on how to structure your company partly depends on the impact on operating leverage and on how much risk you are willing to accept.

TO SUMMARIZE: The relationship between fixed and variable costs differs across different types of organizations. Generally, traditional merchandising companies have relatively low levels of fixed costs and high levels of variable costs. On the other hand, manufacturing companies often have higher levels of fixed costs and lower levels of variable costs. The emergence of e-commerce in this economy has resulted in some companies that are even more extremely committed to fixed costs with little or no variable product costs. These cost structure differences are important and are illustrated in the concept of operating leverage. Operating leverage relates to the amount of fixed costs a company has in its cost structure. When sales are expected to increase, high operating leverage results in higher income, and vice versa.

Exhibit 11: "Seeing" Operating Leverages

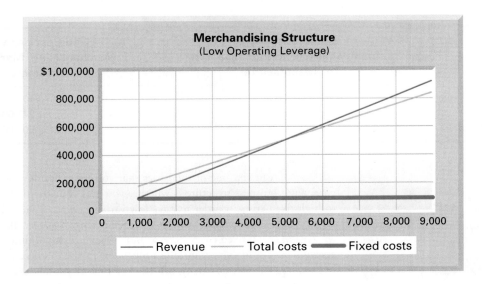

		Sales in Units	Revenue	Total Variable Costs	Contribution Margin	Total Fixed Costs	Operating Income
Price per unit	$ 100	3,000	$300,000	$(240,000)	$ 60,000	$(100,000)	$(40,000)
Variable cost per unit	80	5,000	500,000	(400,000)	100,000	(100,000)	—
Total fixed costs	100,000	7,000	700,000	(560,000)	140,000	(100,000)	40,000

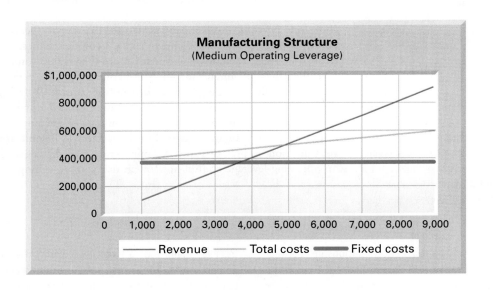

		Sales in Units	Revenue	Total Variable Costs	Contribution Margin	Total Fixed Costs	Operating Income
Price per unit	$ 100	3,000	$300,000	$ (75,000)	$225,000	$(375,000)	$(150,000)
Variable cost per unit	25	5,000	500,000	(125,000)	375,000	(375,000)	—
Total fixed costs	375,000	7,000	700,000	(175,000)	525,000	(375,000)	150,000

Exhibit 11: (Concluded)

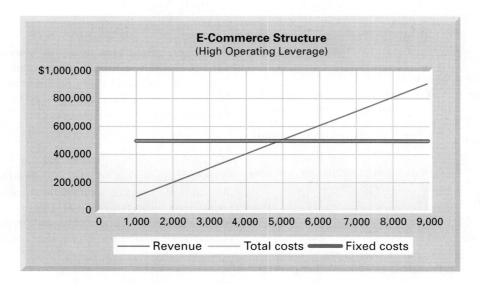

		Sales in Units	Revenue	Total Variable Costs	Contribution Margin	Total Fixed Costs	Operating Income
Price per unit	$ 100	3,000	$300,000	$ —	$300,000	$(500,000)	$(200,000)
Variable cost per unit	0	5,000	500,000	—	500,000	(500,000)	—
Total fixed costs	500,000	7,000	700,000	—	700,000	(500,000)	200,000

review of learning objectives

1 **Understand the key factors involved in cost-volume-profit (C-V-P) analysis and why it is such an important tool in management decision making.** C-V-P analysis is a very important management concept. It is a technique you will use as a manager to understand how profits may be expected to vary in relation to changes in key variables: sales price and volume, variable costs, fixed costs, and mix of products. C-V-P analysis is a particularly useful tool for planning and making operating decisions. It can provide data to stimulate increased sales efforts or cost reduction programs; assist in production scheduling or marketing strategy; and help establish company policies, for example, the appropriate product mix or the fixed cost structure of a company. In order to be effective as a manager, you will need a comprehensive understanding and ability to use C-V-P analysis.

2 **Explain and analyze the basic cost behavior patterns—variable, fixed, mixed, and stepped.** Understanding cost behavior patterns can assist you in making key operating decisions. The two basic cost behavior patterns are variable and

fixed. Costs that vary in total in direct proportion to changes in the level of activity are variable costs. Therefore, per-unit variable costs remain constant. Generally, we assume that there is a linear relationship between variable costs and level of activity within the relevant range; for other ranges, variable costs are curvilinear. Costs that do not change in total with changes in activity level (within the relevant range) are fixed costs; thus, per-unit fixed costs decrease as level of activity increases. Costs that contain both fixed and variable components are mixed costs. Stepped costs increase in total in a stair-step fashion with the level of activity. If the steps are wide, the cost is treated as a fixed cost for analysis purposes; if the steps are narrow, the cost is approximated as a variable cost.

3 **Analyze mixed costs using the scattergraph and high-low methods.** Before mixed costs can be analyzed and used in decision making, they must be divided into their fixed and variable components. The scattergraph and high-low methods are commonly used to analyze mixed costs. The scattergraph method involves visually plotting a straight line (the regression line) through points on a graph of cost data at various activity levels. With the high-low method, the highest and lowest levels of activity and their associated costs are used to calculate the variable cost rate and the total fixed costs.

4 **Perform C-V-P analyses, and describe the effects potential changes in C-V-P variables have on company profitability.** C-V-P analysis is based on the computation of contribution margin, which is sales revenue less variable costs. Contribution margin is the amount available to cover fixed costs and then provide a profit. C-V-P analysis is commonly used to assess break-even points (where contribution margin equals fixed costs) and to compute target income levels. The basic C-V-P equation is:

Sales revenue − Variable costs − Fixed costs = Profit

The C-V-P equation will be especially useful to you as a manager in assessing how profits can be expected to change when costs or sales revenue change. Increases in fixed or variable costs result in a larger number of sales being required to break even and reach target income levels. Increases in sales price result in a decreased number of sales being required to break even and reach target income levels.

5 **Visualize C-V-P relationships using graphs.** C-V-P graphs and profit graphs are effective methods for visualizing the effect of impacts on key variables in the C-V-P equation. In addition, the graphic approach effectively allows managers to simultaneously analyze several different activity levels.

6 **Identify the limiting assumptions of C-V-P analysis, and explain the issues of quality and time relative to C-V-P analysis decisions.** C-V-P analysis has several limiting assumptions, including the following: (1) cost and revenue behavior patterns are linear and remain constant over the relevant range, (2) all costs can be categorized as either fixed or variable, and (3) the sales mix of products is constant over the relevant range. When making changes in costs, revenues, and volume, remember to consider the impact on the quality of products or services and the speed at which those products and services can be delivered to customers. Changes that result in decreased costs that also decrease product or service quality or that slow down the delivery of products or services may not be good decisions.

7 **Analyze mixed costs using the least squares method.** The least squares method uses a simple regression analysis to identify the variable and fixed portions of mixed costs. The formula for the least squares method is based on the following equation for a straight line:

$$Y = a + bX$$

where a is total fixed cost and b is per-unit variable cost. Least square calculations can be easily performed using basic computer software programs or programmed calculators. One output of least square analysis calculations is the R^2 statistic, which measures the amount of variance in the cost that is explained by changes in the activity level (depicted by X in the equation above).

8 **Explain the effects of sales mix on profitability.** Sales mix is the proportion of total units sold represented by each of a company's products. Because all products do not have the same contribution margin ratios, changes in the sales mix of products sold can significantly affect total profits. When you are working as a manager to maximize profits, it is best to maintain as large a contribution margin as possible on all products and then emphasize those products with the largest individual contribution margin ratios.

9 **Describe how fixed and variable costs differ in manufacturing, service, merchandising, and e-commerce organizations, and illustrate these differences with the operating leverage concept.** The trade-off between fixed costs and variable costs is often related to whether a company is structured as a manufacturing, merchandising, or service firm. The advent of e-commerce has created the potential for companies to have very high levels of fixed costs and very low levels of variable costs. The impact of the fixed cost/variable cost relationship on profits is captured in the concept of operating leverage. Operating leverage is a measure of the extent to which a company's costs are fixed rather than variable. Companies with higher fixed costs and lower per-unit variable costs will experience higher operating leverage and, therefore, a tendency for profits to increase at a faster rate when sales increase. Hence, a company with high operating leverage will be more profitable in good times but have higher losses in bad times.

k **ey terms & concepts**

review problems

Variable and Fixed Costs Analyses

Blade Corporation manufactures two types of inline skates—a basic model and a racing model. During the year 2006, Blade accumulated the following summary information about its two products:

	Racing Model	Basic Model
Selling price	$130	$65
Number of units manufactured and sold	14,000	9,000

	Racing Model		Basic Model	
	Units	Costs	Units	Costs
January	1,200	$ 112,000	800	$ 39,600
February	900	91,000	600	30,000
March	800	76,400	450	25,800
April	1,400	124,800	900	36,900
May	950	92,650	1,000	47,000
June	1,600	146,800	1,200	57,300
July	1,400	134,600	1,300	60,600
August	1,700	154,500	650	32,195
September	1,550	140,200	850	44,250
October	1,500	134,500	500	27,000
November	600	62,500	350	20,700
December	400	44,000	400	22,000
Totals	14,000	$1,313,950	9,000	$443,345

Required:

1. Use the high-low method to estimate the variable and fixed production costs of both the racing model and the basic model skates.

2. All selling costs are fixed, and they total $200,000 for the racing model and $80,000 for the basic model. Prepare a contribution margin income statement for each model at sales of 10,000 racing and 10,000 basic skates.

Solution

1. Variable and Fixed Costs

The high-low method involves finding the variable and fixed costs at the high and low levels of production. In this case:

	Racing Model	Basic Model
High-production month	1,700 (Aug.)	1,300 (July)
Low-production month	400 (Dec.)	350 (Nov.)
Difference	1,300	950
Total production costs of high month	$154,500	$60,600
Total production costs of low month	44,000	20,700
Difference	$110,500	$39,900

Once the differences are known, the change in units (production) is divided into the change in costs to determine the variable cost rate.

$$\frac{\text{Change in costs}}{\text{Change in units}} = \text{Variable cost rate}$$

$$\text{Racing model: } \frac{\$110,500}{1,300} = \$85$$

$$\text{Basic model: } \frac{\$39,900}{950} = \$42$$

Because total variable costs equal unit variable cost times number of units produced, and total costs equal total variable costs plus total fixed costs, fixed costs can now be calculated.

$$\text{Total costs} - (\text{Variable cost per unit} \times \text{Number of units}) = \text{Total fixed costs}$$

	Racing Model	Basic Model
High production level (X) =	$154,500 − $85(1,700)	$60,600 − $42(1,300)
	X = $154,500 − $144,500	X = $60,600 − $54,600
	X = $10,000	X = $6,000
Low production level (X) =	$44,000 − $85(400)	$20,700 − $42(350)
	X = $44,000 − $34,000	X = $20,700 − $14,700
	X = $10,000	X = $6,000

Thus, we have the following:

	Racing Model	Basic Model
Variable cost rate	$ 85	$ 42
Total fixed costs	10,000	6,000

2. Contribution Margin Income Statements

Blade Corporation
Contribution Margin Income Statements
For the Year Ended December 31, 2006

	Racing Model	Basic Model
Sales revenue (at 10,000 units)	$1,300,000	$ 650,000
Less variable cost of goods sold*	(850,000)	(420,000)
Contribution margin	$ 450,000	$ 230,000
Less fixed cost of goods sold	(10,000)	(6,000)
Less fixed selling costs	(200,000)	(80,000)
Income	$ 240,000	$ 144,000

*$85 per unit for racing model; $42 per unit for basic model.

Assessing the Effects of Changes in Costs, Prices, and Volume on Profitability

K&D Company plans the following for the coming year:

Sales volume	100,000 units
Sales price	$2.50 per unit
Variable costs	$1.30 per unit
Fixed costs	$60,000

Required:
1. Determine K&D's target income.
2. Compute what the target income would be under each of the following independent assumptions:
   a. The sales volume increases 20%.
   b. The sales price decreases 20%.
   c. Variable costs increase 20%.
   d. Fixed costs decrease 20%.

Solution
1. Target Income
Basic C-V-P equation: Sales revenue − Variable costs − Fixed costs = Target income

$$\text{(Units sold} \times \text{Sales price)} - \text{(Units sold} \times \text{Variable unit cost)} - \text{Fixed costs} = \text{Target income}$$
$$(100{,}000 \times \$2.50) - (100{,}000 \times \$1.30) - \$60{,}000 = X$$
$$\$250{,}000 - \$130{,}000 - \$60{,}000 = X$$
$$\$60{,}000 = X$$

This answer can be validated by dividing fixed costs by the per-unit contribution margin to find the break-even point and then multiplying the excess units to be sold above the break-even point by the per-unit contribution margin of $1.20 ($2.50 − $1.30).

$$\frac{\text{Fixed costs}}{\text{Per-unit contribution margin}} = \text{Break-even point}$$

$$\frac{\$60{,}000}{\$1.20} = 50{,}000 \text{ units}$$

Units sold	100,000
Less break-even point (units)	50,000
Excess	50,000
Per-unit contribution margin	× $1.20
Target income	$60,000

2a. The sales volume increases 20%.

$$(100{,}000 \times 1.2 \times \$2.50) - (100{,}000 \times 1.2 \times \$1.30) - \$60{,}000 = X$$
$$\$300{,}000 - \$156{,}000 - \$60{,}000 = X$$
$$\$84{,}000 = X$$

In this case, the contribution margin does not change. Therefore, the answer can be validated by multiplying the units to be sold in excess of the break-even point by the per-unit contribution margin of $1.20 to find the target income.

Units sold	120,000
Less break-even point (units)	50,000
Excess	70,000
Per-unit contribution margin	× $1.20
Target income	$84,000

2b. The sales price decreases 20%.

$$(100,000 \times \$2.50 \times 0.8) - (100,000 \times \$1.30) - \$60,000 = X$$
$$\$200,000 - \$130,000 - \$60,000 = X$$
$$\$10,000 = X$$

In this case, the contribution margin changes. Therefore, the answer can be validated by dividing fixed costs by the new per-unit contribution margin of $0.70 ($2.00 − $1.30) to find the new break-even point and then multiplying the units to be sold in excess of the break-even point by the new per-unit contribution margin.

$$\frac{\$60,000 \text{ (fixed costs)}}{\$0.70 \text{ (new per-unit contribution margin)}} = 85,715 \text{ units (new break-even point, rounded up)}$$

Units sold	100,000
Less break-even point (units)	85,715
Excess	14,285
Per-unit contribution margin	× $0.70
Target income	$10,000 (rounded)

2c. Variable costs increase 20%.

$$(100,000 \times \$2.50) - (100,000 \times \$1.30 \times 1.2) - \$60,000 = X$$
$$\$250,000 - \$156,000 - \$60,000 = X$$
$$\$34,000 = X$$

In this case, the contribution margin changes. Therefore, the answer can be validated by dividing fixed costs by the new per-unit contribution margin of $0.94 ($2.50 − $1.56) to find the new break-even point and then multiplying the units to be sold in excess of the break-even point by the new per-unit contribution margin.

$$\frac{\$60,000 \text{ (fixed costs)}}{\$0.94 \text{ (new per-unit contribution margin)}} = 63,830 \text{ units (new break-even point, rounded up)}$$

Units sold	100,000
Less break-even point (units)	63,830
Excess	36,170
Per-unit contribution margin	× $0.94
Target income	$34,000 (rounded)

2d. Fixed costs decrease 20%.

$$(100,000 \times \$2.50) - (100,000 \times \$1.30) - (\$60,000 \times 0.8) = X$$
$$\$250,000 - \$130,000 - \$48,000 = X$$
$$\$72,000 = X$$

In this case, the contribution margin does not change, but fixed costs, and hence the break-even point, do. Therefore, the answer can be validated by dividing the per-unit contribution margin of $1.20 into the new fixed costs to find the break-even point and then multiplying the units to be sold in excess of the break-even point by the per-unit contribution margin.

$$\frac{\$48,000 \text{ (new fixed costs)}}{\$1.20 \text{ (per-unit contribution margin)}} = 40,000 \text{ units (new break-even point)}$$

Units sold	100,000
Less break-even point (units)	40,000
Excess	60,000
Per-unit contribution margin	× $1.20
Target income	$72,000

discussion questions

1. Explain how understanding cost behavior patterns can assist management.
2. Discuss how level of activity is measured in manufacturing, merchandising, and service firms.
3. What is meant by the linearity assumption, and why is it made? Relate this assumption to the relevant-range concept.
4. What factors in the current economy seem to have caused the shift from variable to fixed cost patterns?
5. How should stepped costs be treated in the planning process?
6. Why must all mixed costs be segregated into their fixed and variable components?
7. What is the major weakness of the scattergraph, or visual-fit, method of analyzing mixed costs?
8. What is the major limitation of the high-low method of analyzing mixed costs?
9. What is the basic C-V-P equation? What is a more detailed version of this equation?
10. What is the contribution margin, and why is it important for managers to know the contribution margins of their products?
11. How much will profits increase for every unit sold over the break-even point?
12. What is the major advantage of using C-V-P graphs?
13. When other factors are constant, what is the effect on profits of an increase in fixed costs? Of a decrease in variable costs?
14. What are the limiting assumptions of C-V-P analysis?
15. How do the issues of quality and time relate to C-V-P analysis decisions?

16. How does the method of least squares differ from the scattergraph method?
17. What effect is a change in the sales mix likely to have on a firm's overall contribution margin ratio?

practice exercises

Practice 2-1

Measuring Level of Activity
Which one of the following is *not* an activity base used by a company?

a. Number of defects per hour in an assembly plant
b. Number of units sold for a merchandising firm
c. Number of units produced for a manufacturing firm
d. Number of client hours billed for an accounting firm
e. Number of hours a retail store is open

Practice 2-2

Variable Costs
Which one of the following would *not* be a variable cost for a construction company?

a. Cost of trusses used to construct a roof for a house
b. Cost of windows to be installed in a house
c. Salary paid to overall project supervisor
d. Cost of drywall to be installed in house
e. Cost of exterior house paint

Practice 2-3

Linearity of Variable Costs within the Relevant Range
The company has assembled the following data about its variable costs:

(continued)

Level of Activity	Total Variable Cost
1,000 units	$ 25,000
2,000 units	46,000
3,000 units	69,000
4,000 units	92,000
5,000 units	100,000

The company is currently producing 3,300 units. According to these data, what is the relevant range over which the company can assume that the variable cost per unit is constant?

Practice 2-4

Fixed Costs

If the level of activity increases during the month, does the fixed cost per unit increase, decrease, or remain constant?

Practice 2-5

Break-Even Computation

The company reports the following items.

Direct materials per unit	$ 2.50
Direct labor per unit	4.60
Variable overhead per unit	2.10
Monthly rent	1,900.00
Monthly depreciation	650.00
Other monthly fixed costs	2,680.00
Sales price per unit	14.25

Using the above information, compute the company's monthly break-even point (in units).

Practice 2-6

Stepped Fixed Costs

The company pays $3,000 per month to each of its four production supervisors. Each supervisor can handle the workload associated with up to 2,400 units of production per month; the current level of production is 9,000 units. If the company increases its level of production to 12,800 units per month, how much will the company pay, in total, for the salaries of the necessary production supervisors?

Practice 2-7

Mixed Costs

The company's president receives a $100,000 base salary and a bonus of 0.5% of sales for the year. How much will the president earn at a sales level of $2,750,000 for the year?

Practice 2-8

Scattergraph Method

Which one of the following statements is incorrect?

a. The scattergraph method can be somewhat subjective depending on where one visually places the regression line.
b. The scattergraph method is the most accurate method of analyzing mixed costs.
c. When graphing mixed costs, the dollars go on the vertical axis, and the level of activity goes on the horizontal axis.
d. Regression lines attempt to minimize the average distance between all the data points and the fitted regression line.
e. The slope of the regression line is equal to the variable cost per unit of activity.

Practice 2-9

Using the High-Low Method to Estimate the Variable Cost Rate

The company reports the following utility costs for different levels of activity during the first half of the year:

Month	Machine Hours	Total Utility Costs
January	470	$14,000
February	410	12,500
March	520	14,400
April	500	14,450
May	550	15,350
June	535	15,100

Using the high-low method, estimate the variable cost rate.

Practice 2-10

Using the High-Low Method to Estimate Fixed Costs
Refer to the data in Practice 2-9. Using the high-low method, estimate the fixed costs per month based on the variable cost rate (computed in Practice 2-9).

Practice 2-11

Contribution Margin Income Statement
The company sells desks for $550 each. The variable cost per desk is $385. The company's monthly fixed costs are $72,000. Prepare a contribution margin income statement for a month in which the company sells 500 desks.

Practice 2-12

Contribution Margin Ratio and Variable Cost Ratio
Refer to the data in Practice 2-11. Compute the contribution margin ratio and the variable cost ratio.

Practice 2-13

The C-V-P Equation
The company sells lawnmowers for $895 each. The variable cost per lawnmower is $520. The company's monthly fixed costs are $84,500. Using the C-V-P equation, compute the amount of profit the company will have for a month in which the company sells 375 lawnmowers.

Practice 2-14

Break-Even Units
The company sells shovels for $27.75 each. The variable cost per shovel is $14.25. The company's monthly fixed costs are $2,538. Compute the number of shovels the company must sell to break even.

Practice 2-15

Determining Sales Volume to Achieve Target Income
Refer to the data in Practice 2-14. How many shovels must the company sell to achieve a profit of $10,000?

Practice 2-16

Determining Sales Volume to Achieve Target Return on Sales
The company sells pianos for $7,000 each. The variable cost per piano is $5,500. The company has fixed costs per month of $45,000. Compute the number of units the company must sell in a month to achieve a 15% return on sales.

Practice 2-17

Break-Even Sales Revenue
The company has a variable cost ratio of 65% and monthly fixed costs of $91,000. What is the company's break-even point in terms of sales dollars?

Practice 2-18

C-V-P Analysis with Simultaneous Changes in Several Variables
The company currently sells 50,000 feet of cable each month for $3.50 per foot. The variable cost of the cable is $1.10 per foot, and monthly fixed costs are $75,000. The company is considering whether to raise the sales price for the cable to $4.00 per foot. The marketing team has determined that such an increase in sales price will discourage some customers from purchasing

(continued)

the cable, so the company will be able to sell only 40,000 feet of cable per month. Calculate the profit for the company under both of the following scenarios:

1.   50,000 feet of cable at $3.50 per foot.
2.   40,000 feet of cable at $4.00 per foot.

In terms of profit maximization, should the company raise the price per foot?

Practice 2-19

C-V-P Analysis with Simultaneous Changes in Several Variables
Refer to the data in Practice 2-18. The company is considering whether to change its production process to reduce the variable cost per foot to $0.90 by raising fixed costs per month to $83,000. This change will have no impact on selling price ($3.50) or sales volume (50,000 feet). In terms of profit maximization, should the company change its production process?

Practice 2-20

Interpreting a C-V-P Graph

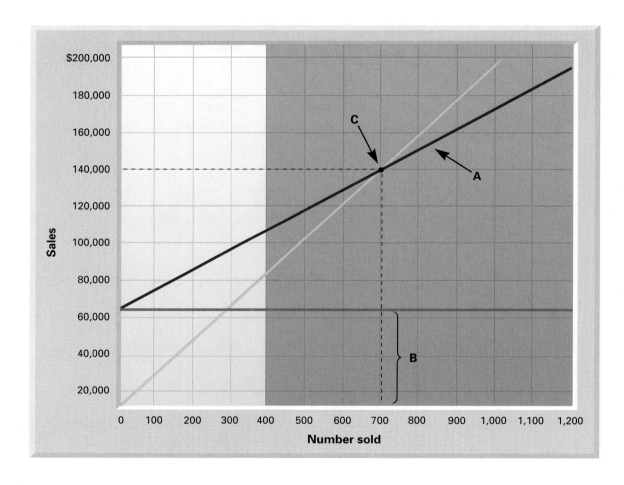

Look at the given C-V-P graph. Which one of the following sets of labels correctly labels items A, B, and C in the C-V-P graph?

a.   A: Total cost line; B: Fixed costs; C: Break-even point
b.   A: Revenue line; B: Variable costs; C: Fixed costs
c.   A: Fixed cost line; B: Break-even point; C: Fixed costs
d.   A: Revenue line; B: Break-even point; C: Fixed costs
e.   A: Total cost line; B: Break-even point; C: Fixed costs

Practice 2-21   **Interpreting a Profit Graph**

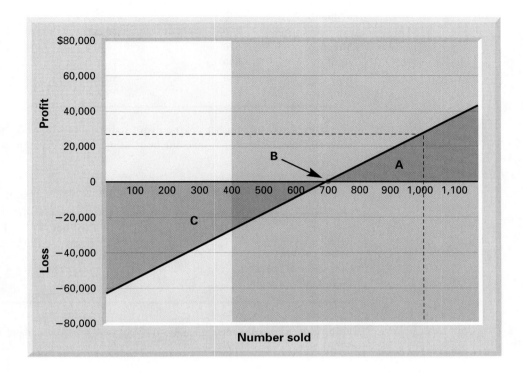

Look at the given profit graph. Which one of the following sets of labels correctly labels items A, B, and C in the profit graph?

a.   A: Area of loss; B: Break-even point; C: Area of profit
b.   A: Area of loss; B: Area of profit; C: Break-even point
c.   A: Break-even point; B: Area of loss; C: Area of profit
d.   A: Area of profit; B: Break-even point; C: Area of loss
e.   A: Area of profit; B: Area of loss; C: Break-even point

Practice 2-22   **Limiting Assumptions of C-V-P Analysis**
Which one of the following is *not* an assumption of C-V-P analysis?

a.   Fixed costs are always greater than variable costs.
b.   All costs can be divided into fixed and variable categories.
c.   C-V-P analysis is valid only for a relevant range.
d.   The mix of a company's products does not change over the relevant range.

Practice 2-23   **Least-Squares Method**
The company reports the following costs at different levels of activity for the first half of the year.

(continued)

Month	Machine Hours	Total Utility Costs
January	470	$14,000
February	410	12,500
March	520	14,400
April	500	14,450
May	550	15,350
June	535	15,700

Using Excel (or another program with statistical capabilities), estimate the company's fixed costs and variable costs per machine hour using the least-squares method.

Practice 2-24

Sales Mix

The company has fixed costs of $21,500 and the following sales mix.

	Product A	Product B	Product C
Sales revenue	$35,000	$70,000	$45,000
Less variable costs	20,000	50,000	36,000
Contribution margin	$15,000	$20,000	$ 9,000

Using this same sales mix, calculate the required sales (in dollars) to earn a target income of $25,000.

Practice 2-25

Cost Structure

If you experience much higher sales than expected this year, which kind of operating leverage would you like to have in your company for profit maximization?

a. High operating leverage
b. Low operating leverage
c. Medium operating leverage
d. Operating leverage does not affect profitability.

e x e r c i s e s

Exercise 2-1

Variable and Fixed Costs Over the Relevant Range

Cook Corporation manufactures plastic garbage cans. In a typical year, the firm produces between 40,000 and 50,000 cans. At this level of production, fixed costs are $10,000 and variable costs are $2 per can.

1. Graph the cost of producing cans, with cost as the vertical axis and production output as the horizontal axis.
2. Indicate on the graph the relevant range of the $10,000 in fixed costs, and explain the significance of the relevant range.
3. What would total production costs be if 46,000 cans were produced?

Exercise 2-2

Fixed Costs—The Relevant Range

Sabrina Company manufactures large leisure boats. The following schedule shows total fixed costs at various levels of boat production:

Units Produced	Total Fixed Costs
0–100	$150,000
101–400	250,000
401–900	400,000

1. What is the fixed cost per unit when 75 boats are produced?
2. What is the fixed cost per unit when 300 boats are produced?
3. What is the fixed cost per unit when 750 boats are produced?
4. Plot total fixed costs on a graph similar to that shown in Exhibit 3.

Exercise 2-3

Scattergraph Method of Analyzing Mixed Costs

Wyoming Company makes windmills. The company has the following total costs at the given levels of windmill production:

Units Produced	Total Costs
20	$16,000
30	22,000
40	20,000
50	28,000

1. Use the scattergraph method to estimate the fixed and variable elements of Wyoming's total costs.
2. Compute the total cost of making 44 windmills, assuming that total fixed costs are $10,000 and that the variable cost rate computed in part (1) does not change.

Exercise 2-4

Scattergraph Method of Analyzing Mixed Costs

Given the following mixed costs at various levels of production, complete the requirements.

Month	Units Produced	Mixed Costs
January	2	$24.00
February	3	28.00
March	1	21.00
April	5	30.00
May	4	25.00

1. Plot the data on a scattergraph, and visually fit a straight line through the points.
2. Based on your graph, estimate the monthly fixed cost and the variable cost per unit produced.
3. Compute the total cost of producing eight units in a month, assuming that the same relevant range applies.
4. **Interpretive Question:** Why is it so important to be able to determine the components of a mixed cost?

Exercise 2-5

Scattergraph Method and High-Low Method of Analyzing Mixed Costs

Sailmaster makes boats and has the following costs and production levels for the last eight quarters:

(continued)

Quarter	Boats Produced	Total Costs
1	108	$101,250
2	128	168,750
3	185	189,000
4	245	200,145
5	311	276,200
6	352	255,250
7	389	305,700
8	428	376,500

1. Plot the data on a scattergraph, and visually fit a straight line through the points.
2. Based on your graph, estimate the quarterly fixed cost and the variable cost per unit produced.
3. Use the high-low method to compute the variable and fixed elements of Sailmaster's total costs, and then draw a straight line through the high and low data points on the scattergraph.
4. Compute the total cost of making 500 boats using first the scattergraph results and then using the high-low method results.
5. Comment on the differences between these two methods. Which method appears to most accurately represent the actual variable and fixed costs for Sailmaster?

Exercise 2-6

High-Low Method of Analyzing Mixed Costs

The *Stamford Times* has determined that the annual printing of 750,000 newspapers costs 11 cents per copy. If production were to be increased to 1,000,000 copies per year, the per-unit cost would drop to 9 cents per copy.

1. Using the high-low method, determine the total fixed and variable costs of printing 750,000 newspapers.
2. Using the fixed and variable costs you determined in part (1), what would be the total cost of producing 900,000 copies?

Exercise 2-7

Contribution Margin Calculations

Jerry Stone owns and operates a small beach shop in a mall on Sanibel Island, Florida. For the last six months, Jerry has had a display of sunglasses in the front window. Largely because of the display, Jerry has sold 100 pairs of sunglasses per month at an average cost of $26 and selling price of $50. The sales volume has doubled since the display was put in the window. One-fourth of Jerry's storage space is occupied by 190 ice coolers. The coolers have not been selling as well as Jerry hoped, but he is convinced that a front window display of coolers would increase sales by 50%. The coolers cost Jerry a total of $2,280 and have been selling at a rate of 100 per month at $28 each.

1. Assuming that cost of goods sold is the only variable cost, compute the contribution margin per unit for sunglasses and ice coolers.
2. Compute the total contribution margins for both sunglasses and ice coolers assuming window displays and no window displays for both items.
3. What are the economic costs associated with keeping the sunglass display in the store window?
4. What are the economic costs associated with replacing the sunglass display with an ice cooler display?

Exercise 2-8

Spreadsheet

Contribution Margin Income Statement

The following data apply to Gordon Company for 2006:

Sales revenue (10 units at $25 each)	$250
Variable selling expenses	45
Variable administrative expenses	25
Fixed selling expenses	30

Fixed administrative expenses	$ 15
Direct labor	50
Direct materials	60
Fixed manufacturing overhead	5
Variable manufacturing overhead	3

1. Prepare a contribution margin income statement. Assume there were no beginning or ending inventories in 2006.
2. How much would Gordon Company have lost if only five units had been sold during 2006?

Exercise 2-9

Analysis of a Contribution Margin Income Statement

Fill in the missing amounts for the following three cases:

	Case I	Case II	Case III
Sales revenue	$50,000	$60,000	$ (7)
Variable cost of goods sold:			
Direct materials	$12,500	$ (4)	$20,000
Direct labor	(1)	15,000	20,000
Variable selling and administrative costs	3,500	(5)	10,000
Contribution margin	$ (2)	$20,000	$ (8)
Gross margin	20,000	30,000	40,000
Fixed selling and administrative costs*	5,500	10,000	(9)
Rent expense on office building	(3)	5,000	2,000
Depreciation expense on delivery trucks	5,000	2,500	8,000
Profit	$ 4,000	$ (6)	$ 0

*Except rent and depreciation.

Exercise 2-10

Analysis of the Contribution Margin

Dr. Hughes and Dr. Hawkins, owners of the Spanish Fork Care Clinic, have $150,000 of fixed costs per year. They receive 20,000 patient visits in a year, charging each patient an average of $20 per visit; variable costs average $2 per visit (needles, medicines, and so on).

1. What is the contribution margin per patient visit?
2. What is the total contribution margin per year?
3. What is the total pretax profit for a year?
4. Drs. Hughes and Hawkins can bring in another doctor at a salary of $100,000 per year. If this new doctor can handle 5,000 patient visits per year, should the new doctor be hired? (Assume no additional fixed costs will be incurred.)

Exercise 2-11

Contribution Margin Analysis

Compute the missing amounts for the following independent cases. (Assume zero beginning and ending inventories.)

	Case I	Case II	Case III
Sales volume (units)	24,000	(5)	16,000
Sales price per unit	$10	$8	(9)
Variable costs (total)	(1)	$200,000	$100,000
Contribution margin (total)	(2)	(6)	$60,000
Contribution margin per unit (rounded)	$4	$3	(10)
Fixed costs (total)	(3)	(7)	(11)
Fixed costs per unit (rounded)	(4)	$2	(12)
Profit	$20,000	(8)	$40,000

Exercise 2-12

Spreadsheet

Break-Even Point and Target Income

Detienne Company manufactures and sells one product for $20 per unit. The unit contribution margin is 40% of the sales price, and fixed costs total $80,000.

1. Using the equation approach, compute:
    a. The break-even point in sales dollars and units.
    b. The sales volume (in units) needed to generate a profit of $40,000.
    c. The break-even point (in units) if variable costs increase to 80% of the sales price and fixed costs increase to $100,000.
2. See if you can recompute the solutions to 1(a), 1(b), and 1(c) in *one equation step* using either the contribution margin ratio or the contribution margin dollars per unit.

Exercise 2-13

Break-Even Point and Target Income

Steven Newman, Inc., estimates 2006 costs to be as follows:

Direct materials	$5 per unit
Direct labor	$8 per unit
Variable manufacturing overhead	$3 per unit
Variable selling and administrative expenses	$2 per unit
Fixed expenses	$80,000

1. Assuming that Newman will sell 55,000 units, what sales price per unit will be needed to achieve a $75,000 profit?
2. Assuming that Newman decides to sell its product for $23 per unit, determine the break-even sales volume in dollars and units.
3. Assuming that Newman decides to sell its product for $23 per unit, determine the number of units it must sell to generate a $100,000 profit.

Exercise 2-14

Break-Even Point—Graphic Analysis

Using the graph below, answer the following questions:

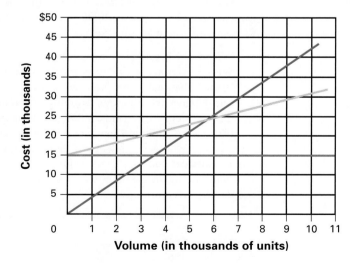

1. Copy the graph and identify (label) fixed costs, variable costs, total revenues, the total cost line, and the break-even point.
2. Determine the break-even point in both sales dollars and volume.
3. Suppose that as a manager you forecast sales volume at 7,000 units. At this level of sales, what would be your total fixed costs, approximate variable costs, and profit (or loss)?
4. At a sales volume of 3,000 units, what would be the level of fixed costs, variable costs, and approximate profit (or loss)?

Exercise 2-15

The Profit Graph

Using the graph below, answer the following questions:

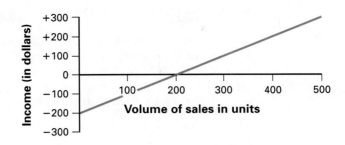

1. What is the break-even point in sales volume (in units)?
2. Approximately what volume of sales (in units) must this company have to generate an income of $300?
3. How much are the fixed costs?

Exercise 2-16

Graphing Revenues and Costs

Montana Company manufactures chocolate candy. Its manufacturing costs are as follows:

Annual fixed costs $15,000
Variable costs . . . . $2 per box of candy

1. Plot variable costs, fixed costs, and total costs on a graph for activity levels of 0 to 30,000 boxes of candy.
2. Plot a revenue line on the graph, assuming that Montana sells the chocolates for $5 a box.

Exercise 2-17

C-V-P Analysis

The Last Outpost is a tourist stop in a western resort community. Kerry Yost, the owner of the shop, sells hand-woven blankets for an average price of $30 per blanket. Kerry buys the blankets from weavers at an average cost of $21. In addition, he has selling expenses of $3 per blanket. Kerry rents the building for $300 per month and pays one employee a fixed salary of $500 per month.

1. Determine the number of blankets Kerry must sell to break even.
2. Determine the number of blankets Kerry must sell to generate a profit of $1,000 per month.
3. Assume that Kerry can produce and sell his own blankets at a total variable cost of $16 per blanket, but that he would need to hire one additional employee at a monthly salary of $600.
   a. Determine the number of blankets Kerry must sell to break even.
   b. Determine the number of blankets Kerry must sell to generate a profit of $1,000 per month.

Exercise 2-18

C-V-P Analysis—Changes in Variables

Tracy, Inc., estimates that next year's results will be:

Sales revenue (75,000 units) . . . . $ 900,000
Less variable costs . . . .   (375,000)
Less fixed costs . . . .   (300,000)
Profit . . . . $ 225,000

Recompute profit, assuming each of the following independent conditions:

1. A 9% increase in the contribution margin.
2. An 8% increase in the sales volume.
3. A 4% decrease in the sales volume.

(continued)

4. A 6% increase in variable costs per unit.
5. A 5% decrease in fixed costs.
6. A 5% increase in fixed costs.
7. A 12% increase in the sales volume and a 6% increase in fixed costs.

Exercise 2-19

C-V-P Analysis—Changes in Variables

Modern Fun Corporation sells electronic games. Its three salespersons are currently being paid fixed salaries of $30,000 each; however, the sales manager has suggested that it might be more profitable to pay the salespersons on a straight commission basis. He has suggested a commission of 15% of sales. Current data for Modern Fun Corporation are as follows:

Sales volume	15,000 units
Sales price	$40 per unit
Variable costs	$29 per unit
Fixed costs	$140,000

1. Assuming that Modern Fun Corporation has a target income of $50,000 for next year, which alternative is more attractive?
2. The sales manager believes that by switching to a commission basis, sales will increase 20%. If that is the case, which alternative is more attractive? (Assume that sales are expected to remain at 15,000 units under the fixed salary alternative.)

Exercise 2-20

Mixed Costs—Least Squares Analysis

Given the following mixed costs at various levels of production, complete the requirements.

Month	Units Produced	Mixed Costs
January	8	$30
February	12	36
March	4	22
April	20	44
May	8	26

1. Using the least squares method (either the equation approach or a software package), calculate the monthly fixed and variable components of the mixed costs.
2. Using the estimates from part (1), compute the total cost of producing 16 units in a month.
3. Describe a major advantage and a major disadvantage of the least squares method.

Exercise 2-21

Sales Mix

Klein Brothers sells products X and Y. Because of the nature of the products, Klein sells two units of product X for each unit of product Y. Relevant information about the products is as follows:

	X	Y
Sales price per unit	$10	$30
Variable cost per unit	8	18

1. Assuming that Klein's fixed costs total $140,000, compute Klein's break-even point in sales dollars.

2. Assuming that Klein sells one unit of product X for each unit of product Y, and fixed costs remain at $140,000, compute Klein's break-even point in sales dollars.
3. Explain any differences in your answers to parts (1) and (2).

Exercise 2-22

C-V-P Analysis

Mower Manufacturing's income statement for January 2006 is given below.

Sales (25,000 units × $25)	$625,000
Less variable costs	468,750
Contribution margin	$156,250
Less fixed costs	125,000
Profit	$ 31,250

1. Calculate the company's break-even point in sales dollars and units.
2. The company is contemplating the purchase of new production equipment that would reduce variable costs per unit to $16.25. However, fixed costs would increase to $175,000 per month. Assuming sales of 26,000 units next month, prepare an income statement for both the current and the proposed production methods. Calculate the break-even point (in dollars and units) for the new production method.
3. Comment on the difference (if any) in the break-even point for the new production method. What explains the difference in income at sales of 26,000 units between the two production methods?

Exercise 2-23

Operating Leverage

Ludlam Company and Kassandra Company both make school desks. They have the same production capacity, but Ludlam is more automated than Kassandra. At an output of 2,500 desks per year, the two companies have the following costs:

	Ludlam	Kassandra
Fixed costs	$137,500	$ 37,500
Variable costs at $20 per desk	50,000	
Variable costs at $60 per desk		150,000
Total cost	$187,500	$187,500
Unit cost (2,500 desks)	$ 75	$ 75

Assuming that both companies sell desks for $100 each and that there are no other costs or expenses for the two firms, complete the following:

1. Which company will lose the least money if production and sales fall to 1,000 desks per year?
2. What would be each company's profit or loss at production and sales levels of 1,000 desks per year?
3. What would be each company's profit or loss at production and sales levels of 4,000 desks per year?

problems

Problem 2-1

Graphing Revenues and Costs

Cloward and Hawkins, CPAs, took in $350,000 of gross revenues this year. Besides themselves, they have two professional staff (one manager and one senior) and a full-time secretary. Fixed operating expenses for the office were $50,000 last year. This year the volume of activity is up

5%, and fixed operating expenses are still $50,000. Total variable operating costs, except for bonuses, average $5 per billable hour. The billable time for all professionals is as follows:

Partners:	3,000 hours at $75/hour
Manager:	1,800 hours at $40/hour
Senior:	2,120 hours at $25/hour

Salaries for the professional staff are $40,000 and $28,000, respectively; the secretary is paid $18,000. The partners each draw salaries of $60,000; plus they share a 5% bonus based on gross revenues. The manager is given a 2% bonus, also based on gross revenues.

Required:
1. Plot the data on a graph clearly showing (a) fixed costs, (b) variable costs, (c) total costs, and (d) total revenues.
2. How much profit did the CPA firm make this year (after partners' salaries)?

Problem 2-2

High-Low and Scattergraph Methods of Analysis
Woodfield Company makes bed linens. During the first six months of 2006, Woodfield had the following production costs:

Month	Units Produced	Total Costs
January	10,000	$ 68,000
February	20,000	100,000
March	15,000	90,000
April	8,000	52,000
May	17,000	94,000
June	12,000	74,000

Required:
1. Use the high-low method to compute the monthly fixed cost and the variable cost rate.
2. Plot the costs on a scattergraph.
3. **Interpretive Question:** Based on your scattergraph, do you think the fixed costs and the variable cost rate determined in part (1) are accurate? Why?

Problem 2-3

Contribution Margin Income Statement
Early in 2007, Lili H Company (a retailing firm) sent the following income statement to its stockholders:

Lili H Company
Income Statement
For the Year Ended December 31, 2006

Sales revenue (2,000 units)	$240,000	
Less cost of goods sold (variable)	160,000	
Gross margin		$80,000
Operating expenses:		
Selling	$ 24,000	
Administrative	16,000	
Depreciation (fixed)	4,000	
Insurance (fixed)	200	
Utilities ($80 fixed and $120 variable)	200	44,400
Profit		$35,600

Required:

1. Prepare a contribution margin income statement. (Assume that the fixed components of the selling and administrative expenses are $12,000 and $8,000, respectively.)
2. **Interpretive Question:** Why is a contribution margin income statement helpful to management?
3. **Interpretive Question:** How would the analysis in part (1) be different if the depreciation expense was considered a stepped cost with wide steps compared to the relevant range?

Problem 2-4

Contribution Margin Income Statement

Susan Young is an attorney for a small law firm in Arizona. She is also a part-time inventor and an avid golfer. One day Susan's golf foursome included a man named Henry Jones, a manufacturer of Christmas ornaments. Henry explained to Susan that he manufactures an ornament everyone loves, but stores will not carry the ornaments because they are very fragile and often break during shipping. Susan told Henry about a plastic box she had developed recently that would protect such fragile items during shipping. After crash testing the plastic box, Henry offered Susan a contract to purchase 100,000 of the boxes for $2.20 each. Susan is convinced that the box has many applications and that she can obtain future orders. Production of the plastic boxes will take one year. Estimated costs for the first year are as follows:

Lease payments on building	$800 per month
Lease payments on machine	$2,200 per month
Cost to retool machine	$10,000
Depreciation on machine	$9,600
Direct materials	$0.70 per box
Direct labor	$0.30 per box
Indirect materials and other manufacturing overhead	$10,000
Interest on loan	$2,500
Administrative salaries	$15,000

Required:

1. Using the information provided, determine Susan's contribution margin and projected profit at a sales level of 100,000 boxes.
2. If Susan's salary as an attorney is $44,500, determine how many boxes Susan must sell to earn profits equal to her salary.

Problem 2-5

Functional and Contribution Margin Income Statements

Bassically Jammin', Inc. (BJI) is a retail outlet for customized bass guitars. The average cost of a bass guitar to the company is $1,000. BJI includes a markup of 50% of cost in the sales price. In 2006, BJI sold 380 bass guitars and finished the year with the same amount of inventory it had at the beginning of the year. Additional operating costs for the year were as follows:

Selling expenses:

Advertising (fixed)	$ 700 per month
Commissions (mixed)	3,000 per month plus 2% of sales
Depreciation (fixed)	400 per month
Utilities (fixed)	125 per month
Freight on delivery (variable)	20 per bass guitar

Administrative expenses:

Salaries (fixed)	$4,200 per month
Depreciation (fixed)	330 per month
Utilities (fixed)	200 per month
Clerical (variable)	12 per sale

Required:

1. Prepare a traditional income statement using the functional approach.
2. Prepare an income statement using the contribution margin format.
3. **Interpretive Question:** Which statement is more useful for decision making? Why?

Problem 2-6

Contribution Margin and Functional Income Statements
The following information is available for Dabney Company for 2006:

Sales revenue (at $20 per unit)	$151,200
Fixed manufacturing costs	24,000
Variable manufacturing costs (at $8 per unit)	60,480
Fixed selling expenses	70,000
Variable selling expenses (at $2 per unit)	15,120

Required:
1. Prepare a contribution margin income statement.
2. Prepare a functional income statement.
3. Calculate the number of units sold.
4. Calculate the contribution margin per unit.
5. **Interpretive Question:** Why is a knowledge of the contribution margin more useful than a knowledge of the markup per unit when management has to make a decision about profitability?

Problem 2-7

Unifying Concepts: High-Low Method, Contribution Margins, and Analysis
Press Publishing Corporation has two major magazines: *Star Life* and *Weekly News*. During 2006, *Star Life* sold 3 million copies at $1.00 each, and *Weekly News* sold 2.1 million copies at $1.10 each. Press Publishing accumulated the following cost information:

	Star Life		Weekly News	
Month	**Copies Produced**	**Manufacturing Cost**	**Copies Produced**	**Manufacturing Cost**
January	400,000	$170,000	300,000	$170,000
February	300,000	150,000	150,000	105,000
March	400,000	180,000	130,000	100,000
April	200,000	120,000	120,000	90,000
May	250,000	140,000	200,000	130,000
June	200,000	125,000	250,000	150,000
July	240,000	130,000	150,000	110,000
August	200,000	130,000	200,000	135,000
September	180,000	110,000	150,000	105,000
October	230,000	130,000	150,000	108,000
November	200,000	125,000	150,000	115,000
December	200,000	126,000	150,000	112,500

Required:
1. Use the high-low method to estimate the per-unit variable and total fixed manufacturing costs of each magazine. (Round the variable cost rate to three decimal places.)
2. If all selling expenses are fixed and they total $500,000 for *Star Life* and $400,000 for *Weekly News*, prepare contribution margin income statements for the two magazines at sales of 3 million copies each.
3. Which magazine is more profitable at sales of 2 million copies?
4. **Interpretive Question:** If the same total dollar amount spent on either magazine will result in the same number of new subscriptions, which magazine should be advertised?

Problem 2-8

Contribution Margin Analysis
Clearview Company is a manufacturer of glass vases. The following information pertains to Clearview's 2006 sales:

Sales price per unit	. . . .	$ 32
Variable costs per unit	. . . .	24
Total fixed costs	. . . .	500,000

Required:
1. Determine Clearview Company's per-unit contribution margin and contribution margin ratio.
2. Using the per-unit contribution margin and the contribution margin ratio, compute:
   a. The break-even point in sales dollars and units.
   b. The sales volume (in dollars and units) needed to generate a target income of $75,000.
3. Using the equation approach of C-V-P analysis, compute:
   a. The break-even point in sales dollars and units.
   b. The sales volume (in dollars and units) needed to generate a 15% return on sales.

Problem 2-9

Break-Even Analysis

Jane Tamlyn paid $225 to rent a carnival booth for four days. She has to decide whether to sell doughnuts or popcorn. Doughnuts cost $1.80 per dozen and can be sold for $3.60 per dozen. Popcorn will require a $113 rental fee for the popcorn maker and $0.08 per bag of popcorn for the popcorn, butter, salt, and bags; a bag of popcorn could sell for $0.45.

Required:
1. Compute the break-even point in dozens of doughnuts if Jane decides to sell doughnuts exclusively and the break-even point in bags of popcorn if she decides to sell popcorn exclusively.
2. Jane estimates that she can sell either 75 doughnuts or 45 bags of popcorn every hour the carnival is open (10 hours a day for four days). Which product should she sell?
3. Jane can sell back to the baker at half cost any doughnuts she fails to sell at the carnival. Unused popcorn must be thrown away. If Jane sells only 70% of her original estimate, which product should she sell? (Assume that she bought or produced just enough to satisfy the demands she originally estimated.)

Problem 2-10

C-V-P Graphic Analysis

Using the graph below, complete the requirements.

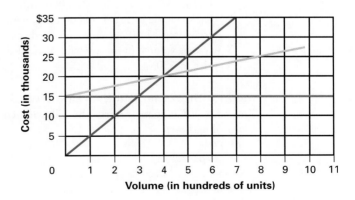

Required:
1. Determine the following:
   a. The break-even point in sales dollars and volume.
   b. The sales price per unit.
   c. Total fixed costs.
   d. Total variable costs at the break-even point.
   e. The variable cost per unit.
   f. The unit contribution margin.
2. What volume of sales must the company generate to reach a target income of $7,500?

Problem 2-11

Spreadsheet

Contribution Margin Analysis—Changes in Variables

SMC, Inc., is a producer of hand-held electronic games. Its 2006 income statement was as follows:

SMC, Inc.
Contribution Margin Income Statement
For the Year Ended December 31, 2006

	Total	Per Unit
Sales revenue (150,000 games)	$5,250,000	$35
Less variable costs	3,750,000	25
Contribution margin	$1,500,000	$10
Less fixed costs	900,000	
Profit	$ 600,000	

In preparing its budget for 2007, SMC is evaluating the effects of changes in costs, prices, and volume on profit.

Required:
1. Evaluate the following independent cases, and determine SMC's 2007 budgeted profit or loss in each case. (Assume that 2006 figures apply unless stated otherwise.)
   a. Fixed costs increase $150,000.
   b. Fixed costs decrease $100,000.
   c. Variable costs increase $3 per unit.
   d. Variable costs decrease $4 per unit.
   e. Sales price increases $5 per unit.
   f. Sales price decreases $5 per unit.
   g. Sales volume increases 25,000 units.
   h. Sales volume decreases 15,000 units.
   i. Sales price decreases $4 per unit, sales volume increases 40,000 units, and variable costs decrease by $2.50 per unit.
   j. Fixed costs decrease by $100,000, and variable costs increase $4 per unit.
   k. Sales volume increases 30,000 units, with a decrease in sales price of $2 per unit. Variable costs drop $1.50 per unit, and fixed costs increase $50,000.
2. What sales volume in units would be needed to realize $1,000,000 in profit if SMC reduces its price to $30?

Problem 2-12

Income Statement and Break-Even Analysis

Zimmerman Company records the following costs associated with the production and sale of a steel slingshot:

Selling expenses:

Fixed	$6,500
Variable	$0.50 per unit sold

Administrative expenses:

Fixed	$4,500
Variable	$0.25 per unit sold

Manufacturing costs:

Fixed	$15,500
Variable	$7.50 per unit produced

Required:
Assume that in 2006 the beginning and ending inventories were the same. Also assume that 2006 sales were 11,000 units at $11.50 per slingshot.

1. Prepare a contribution margin income statement.
2. Determine the break-even point in sales dollars.
3. **Interpretive Question:** Zimmerman believes that sales volume could be improved 20% if an additional commission of $0.50 per unit were paid to the salespeople. Zimmerman also believes, however, that the same percentage increase could be achieved through an increase of $3,000 in annual advertising expense. Which action, if either, should Zimmerman take? Why?

Problem 2-13

C-V-P Analysis—Changes in Variables

Wonder T Manufacturing Company produces lanterns. The firm has not been as profitable as expected in the past three years. As a result, it has excess capacity that could be used to produce an additional 20,000 lanterns per year. However, any production above that amount would require a capital investment of $100,000. Operating results for the previous year are shown here. Assume that there is never any ending inventory.

Sales revenue (31,250 lanterns × $40)		$1,250,000
Variable costs (31,250 lanterns × $25)	$781,250	
Fixed costs	400,000	1,181,250
Profit		$ 68,750

Required:

Respond to the following independent proposals, and support your recommendations:

1. The production manager believes that profits could be increased through the purchase of more automated production machinery, which would increase fixed costs by $100,000 and reduce the variable costs by $2.00 per lantern. Is she correct if sales are to remain at 31,250 lanterns annually?
2. The sales manager believes that a 10% discount on the sales price would increase the sales volume to 40,000 units annually. If he is correct, would this action increase or decrease profits?
3. Would the implementation of both proposals be worthwhile?
4. The sales manager believes that an increase in sales commissions could improve the sales volume. In particular, he suggests that an increase of $2.50 per lantern would increase the sales volume 30%. If he is correct, would this action increase profits?
5. The accountant suggests another alternative: Reduce administrative salaries by $15,000 so that prices can be reduced by $0.50 per unit. She believes that this action would increase the volume to 35,000 units annually. If she is correct, would this action increase profits?
6. The corporate executives finally decide to spend an additional $42,000 on advertising to bring the sales volume up to 34,050 units. If the increased advertising can bring in these extra sales, is this a good decision?

Problem 2-14

C-V-P Analysis—Return on Sales

The federal government recently placed a ceiling on the selling price of sheet metal produced by MOB Company. In 2006, MOB was limited to charging a price that would earn a 20% return on gross sales. On the basis of this restriction, MOB had the following results for 2006:

Sales revenue (1,150,000 feet at $2.00 per foot)		$2,300,000
Variable costs (1,150,000 feet × $1.40)	$1,610,000	
Fixed costs	230,000	1,840,000
Profit		$ 460,000

In 2007, MOB predicted that the sales volume would decrease to 900,000 feet of sheet metal. With this level of sales, however, the company anticipated no changes in the levels of fixed and variable costs.

Required:

1. Determine MOB's profit for 2007 if all forecasts are realized. Compute both the dollar amount of profit and the percentage return on sales.

(continued)

2. MOB plans to petition the government for a price increase so that the 2006 rate of return on sales (20%) can be maintained. What sales price should the company request, based on 2007 projections? (Round to the nearest cent.)
3. How much profit (in dollars) will MOB earn in 2007 if this sales price, as determined in part (2), is approved?
4. **Interpretive Question:** What other factors must be considered by MOB and the government?

Problem 2-15

Unifying Concepts: C-V-P Analysis and Changes in Variables

The 2006 pro-forma income statement for Grover Company is as follows (ignore taxes):

Grover Company
Pro-Forma Income Statement
For the Year Ended December 31, 2006

Sales (50,000 units)		$450,000
Cost of goods sold:		
Direct materials	$ 35,000	
Direct labor	60,000	
Variable manufacturing overhead	14,000	
Fixed manufacturing overhead	5,000	
Total cost of goods sold		114,000
Gross margin		$336,000
Selling expenses:		
Variable	$ 45,000	
Fixed	102,000	
Administrative expenses:		
Variable	15,000	
Fixed	75,000	
Total selling and administrative expenses		237,000
Profit		$ 99,000

Required:
1. Compute how many units must be sold to break even.
2. Compute the increase (decrease) in profit under the following independent situations:
   a. Sales increase 25%.
   b. Fixed selling and administrative expenses decrease 5%.
   c. Contribution margin decreases 20%.
3. Compute sales in units and dollars at the break-even point if fixed costs increase from $182,000 to $224,800.
4. Compute the number of units that must be sold if expected profit is $1 million.

Problem 2-16

Least Squares Methods

This problem uses the same data for Press Publishing Corporation as displayed in Problem 2-7.

Required:
Use the least squares method to estimate the per-unit variable and total fixed manufacturing costs of the *Star Life* and *Weekly News* magazines. (Round the variable cost rate to three decimal places.)

Problem 2-17

Spreadsheet

Unifying Concepts: High-Low, Scattergraph, and Least Squares Methods

You have been hired as a consultant for Jones Inc. The company manufactures high-density compact disks and sells them to a wide variety of business clients. Management is eager to learn more about the company's cost behavior. You have been provided the following data. Assume all production falls within the relevant range.

Month	Machine Hours	Utility Costs
January	290	$10,700
February	280	10,400
March	320	11,600
April	340	12,100
May	350	12,400
June	290	10,750
July	300	10,800
August	300	10,900
September	310	11,200
October	340	12,200
November	290	10,600
December	310	11,000

Required:
1. Using the high-low method, compute the variable and fixed elements of Jones' utility costs.
2. Plot the information on a scattergraph. Based on your graph, determine the unit variable cost and monthly fixed costs.
3. Using the least squares method (either the equation approach or a software package), calculate the variable and fixed cost components. Determine the cost formula.
4. **Interpretive Question:** Why are the variable cost per unit and fixed costs different for each of these methods of analysis? Which method is the most accurate for determining variable and fixed cost components?

Problem 2-18

Sales Mix

Mike's Ice Cream Company produces and sells ice cream in three sizes: quart, half-gallon, and gallon. Relevant information for each of the sizes is as follows:

	Quart	Half-Gallon	Gallon
Average sales price	$1.00	$1.85	$3.60
Less variable cost	0.80	1.40	2.40
Unit contribution margin	$0.20	$0.45	$1.20
Sales mix (% of sales)	15%	60%	25%

Mike anticipates sales of $500,000 and fixed costs of $120,000 in 2006.

Required:
1. Determine the break-even sales volume in units and dollars for 2006.
2. Determine Mike's 2006 projected profit.
3. Assume that Mike's sales mix changes to 10% quarts, 40% half-gallons, and 50% gallons. Determine Mike's break-even sales volume in units and dollars.

Problem 2-19

Unifying Concepts: Break-Even Point and Operating Leverage

The summary data are provided on the following page for Spencer Mercantile Corporation and James Service, Inc. During the year for which these data are reported, Spencer sold 50,000 units and James sold 100,000 units.

(continued)

(000's omitted)	Spencer Mercantile Corporation	James Service, Inc.
Sales revenue	$1,040	$2,100
Less variable costs	520	630
Contribution margin	$ 520	$1,470
Less fixed costs	200	600
Income	$ 320	$ 870

Required:
1. Determine the break-even point for Spencer and James in both sales dollars and units.
2. **Interpretive Question:** Which company has a higher operating leverage? Why?
3. **Interpretive Question:** Based on your analysis of the cost structures of Spencer and James, which company's cost structure is better? What factors are important to consider in answering such a question?

d iscussion cases

Case 2-1

Colorado Outdoors Federation

The Colorado Outdoors Federation sponsors an annual banquet. This year the guest speaker is a noted wildlife photographer and lecturer. In planning for the event, the group's treasurer has determined the following costs:

Rental of meeting facility	$250
Honorarium for speaker	800
Tickets and advertising	300
Cost of dinner (per person)	20
Door prizes	500

Last year, tickets were sold at $20 per person, and 350 people attended the banquet. This year the planning committee is hoping for an attendance of 450 at a price of $25 each.

1. a. At $25 per person, how many people must attend the banquet for the Federation to break even?
   b. How much profit (loss) will occur if 450 people attend?
2. Should the Federation increase its advertising costs by $200 and its door prizes by $300 if it can expect 550 people to attend the banquet?
3. If the Federation maintains its original expected costs but reduces the price per ticket from $25 to $22, it can expect 500 people to attend the banquet. Should the Federation reduce the price of its tickets to $22 per person?

Case 2-2

Entertainment Enterprises

Entertainment Enterprises, a firm that sells magazine subscriptions, is experiencing increased competition from a number of companies. The president, Betty Kincher, has asked you, the controller, to prepare an income statement that will highlight the fixed and variable costs; this will provide more useful information for planning and control purposes. Sales revenues are $25 per subscription. An analysis of company costs for the past six months reveals the following:

Administrative salaries	$10,000 per month
Advertising expense	$2,000 per month
Cost of goods sold	$12.50 per subscription
Rent expense	$5,000 per month
Sales commissions	15% of sales

In addition, the company makes most sales contacts through an extensive telephone network. Consequently, the telephone expense is significant and has both fixed and variable components. Relevant data concerning the telephone expense for the past six months follow:

Month	Unit Sales	Telephone Expense
July	4,000	$10,200
August	5,000	12,300
September	3,500	9,150
October	4,500	11,250
November	5,200	12,720
December	5,500	13,350

Prepare a management report for the president that:

1. Computes the fixed and variable portions of the telephone expense using the high-low method. (*Note:* A scattergraph may be used to visually check your answer.)

2. Presents a budgeted (pro-forma) contribution margin income statement for Entertainment Enterprises for the next six months (January through June), assuming that it expects to sell 30,000 subscriptions at a price of $25 each.

3. Explains how the information provided in part (2) might help the president make better management decisions.

 judgment calls

Judgment 2-1

You Decide: Should the management of a company consider fixed costs in the decision-making process, or should they ignore fixed costs and base their decision on what makes the most business sense?

Recently, the board of directors for a television manufacturing company was considering a change in products from TVs to computers. The board claims, after performing a C-V-P analysis of a new computer manufacturing plant facility, that the computer industry is more profitable and would increase the bottom line immediately. However, just six months earlier, the company built a state-of-the-art television manufacturing plant. The overhead costs on the television plant represent a sizable portion of the company's fixed costs. If the board voted to begin computer manufacturing, a new plant would need to be constructed. What should the board do?

Judgment 2-2

You Decide: Should companies have large amounts of inventory on hand for customers, or should companies keep inventory at a minimum to free up cash for other parts of the business?

Your uncle, Tim, started a very successful "home improvement" business 10 years ago. He wanted to create a place where people could go to get anything they needed to complete their "do-it-yourself" home building projects. Coupled with excellent service, Tim believes that he can gain and retain customers by having a large assortment of inventory from which to choose. In addition, he can obtain significant purchase discounts by buying the inventory in large bulk. You argue that maintaining amounts of inventory requires significant commitments to fixed warehousing and other costs that could be avoided by setting up an e-commerce Web site and taking customer orders that are then acquired and delivered one customer at a time. Although this approach will increase the overall variable costs as a result of not receiving bulk discounts on the smaller individual orders, you are able to demonstrate with C-V-P analysis that there is less risk in your approach to selling home improvement products. Your uncle strongly argues that, "Having the inventory on hand for your customers is the key to success. If I don't have what they are looking for, they will just go down the street to HOME DEPOT! I have got to have inventory in the stores. There is no other way!"

Competency Enhancement Opportunities

▶ **Analyzing Real Company Information**
▶ **International Case**
▶ **Ethics Case**
▶ **Writing Assignment**

▶ **The Debate**
▶ **Internet Search**

The following additional assignments provide opportunities for students to develop critical thinking, ethical perspectives, oral and written communication skills, experience with electronic research, and teamwork through group and business activities.

▷ *Analyzing Real Company Information*

Analyzing 2-1 (Microsoft)

Annual revenues, as well as sales and marketing expenses, for the 1991–2002 years are provided below for MICROSOFT CORPORATION:

	Microsoft Corporation (millions)	
Year	Sales and Marketing Expenses	Annual Revenue
1991	$ 490	$ 1,847
1992	758	2,777
1993	1,086	3,786
1994	1,135	4,714
1995	1,564	6,075
1996	2,185	9,050
1997	2,411	11,936
1998	2,887	15,262
1999	3,238	19,747
2000	4,126	22,956
2001	4,885	25,296
2002	5,407	28,365

1. Operating output data, such as the number of software products sold each year, are not provided in Microsoft's Form 10-K. However, while it is a little odd to use revenues to predict marketing expense (instead of the other way around), it seems sensible that changes in revenues can serve as an approximate measure of changes in the number of products sold by Microsoft. Use the high-low method to analyze the data above to determine if there is a relationship between revenues and sales and marketing expenses. (*Hint:* Don't round off the value you calculate for variable costs per revenue dollar.) What appears to be the amount of fixed costs in these expenses? Does this fixed cost amount make sense? (*Note:* Remember that the data are in millions of dollars!)

2. Using your calculator (or some computer software program such as Microsoft Excel®), compute a regression analysis on the data above. What do you learn from the analysis? The Management's Discussion in Microsoft's 2002 Form 10-K generally uses the following language to describe changes to sales and marketing expenses: "Sales and marketing expenses increased due to higher relative headcount-related costs, higher marketing and sales expenses associated with MSN (Microsoft's popular portal destination on the Web), the Microsoft Agility advertising campaign, and other new sales initiatives." Does this statement provide any help in understanding the analysis? (*Hint:* When setting up to perform the regression, remember that the revenue is the *X* variable and the sales and marketing expense is the *Y* variable.)

Analyzing 2-2 (Star Video)

It is likely that a number of grocery stores in your town have video rental departments. Generally, however, grocery stores do not focus much management attention on their small video rental businesses. The main purpose of having a video department is to encourage more customers to come into the store and purchase groceries! Nevertheless, a grocery store cannot simply buy a large selection of videotapes, corner off a section of floor space, and start renting tapes. Successfully managing a rental business requires being aware of an unimaginably large number of video titles. Obviously, new movies are constantly being released, while old movies gradually lose their appeal and are eventually scrapped. Further, large-scale video rental chains such as BLOCKBUSTER constantly track shifting consumer tastes for certain titles and movie categories. These consumer preferences differ based on demographic data like geographic location, average age, ethnicity, average income, etc. A grocery store really can't manage all these data without losing focus on its main business. Hence, most grocery stores contract out their video rental business to a large-scale video management company. These management companies can purchase huge quantities of tapes, maintain large distribution warehouses, and track demographic data that allow them to manage and move specific inventories to the appropriate grocery store locations. In 1992, one such video management company, Star Video (not its real name), was managing 86 stores representing three supermarket chains in five states—Arizona, California, Montana, Washington, and Wyoming. Total revenue in 1992 for Star Video was $3.6 million. Star Video made all the inventory investments and handled all management activities involved in providing video rentals at each of the 86 stores. Video rental revenue was then split between Star Video and each grocery store, with Star Video keeping the lion's share. Stores liked this arrangement because they made most of their money on grocery sales to customers who came to rent videotapes. Star Video needed to carefully manage revenue and costs at each store in order to stay profitable. Following are the data for six stores located in Washington:

Store Name	Monthly Revenue	Monthly Operating Expenses
Moses Lake	$ 6,408	$ 3,295
W. Kennewick	4,264	2,289
Pasco	4,038	2,270
S. Kennewick	3,692	2,142
E. Wenatchee	1,395	1,316
Richland	2,104	1,516
Total	$21,901	$12,828

Use the high-low method to analyze the operating expenses at these six stores. Determine if operating expenses are related to store revenue. What appear to be the fixed costs of operating each store? Create a graph and plot these costs using revenue on the horizontal axis and operating expenses on the vertical axis. Does the scattergraph agree or disagree with the results of your high-low analysis?

▶ *International Case*

International

The Paper Company

The GHANATA GROUP OF COMPANIES (GGC) is a locally owned and controlled company in Ghana, West Africa. One of its principal operating divisions, THE PAPER COMPANY, is one of Africa's most modern and largest manufacturers/distributors of paper products. For both operating and reporting purposes, The Paper Company is organized into product lines: scholastic, envelope, and stationery. During the 1980s, the economy in Ghana was stagnant. The country faced severe economic problems as a result of unfavorable trade terms with other countries. The official exchange rate of U.S. $1.00 to the local currency, the *cedi*, was about 39.00 as of the end of 1984. (The unofficial rate, e.g., the black market rate, was at least five times worse!) As a result of the economy, it became very difficult for GGC to secure direct materials for its divisions. If a division could secure direct materials, it could sell almost everything it produced. Hence, in terms of being able to predict sales volumes, there was a great deal of risk for GGC divisions. The 1985 budgeted operating data for the three departments in The Paper Company were as follows:

The Paper Company
1985 Budgeted Operations Data
(*Cedi* 000's)

	Scholastic	Envelope	Stationery
Budgeted sales	$ 1,785,000	$ 984,000	$ 3,334,050
Budgeted variable costs	(410,550)	(442,800)	(2,200,473)
Contribution margin	$ 1,374,450	$ 541,200	$ 1,133,577
Budgeted fixed costs	(1,267,350)	(482,160)	(933,534)
Income	$ 107,100	$ 59,040	$ 200,043

Using these operating data, create C-V-P graphs for each department. (*Note:* Since you don't have per-unit prices and costs, you may assume that the product sales price for each department is $1 per unit, and then plot your graphs at 0, 2 million, and 4 million units.) Given the high-risk business environment in Ghana at this time, which department presents the highest risk to GGC? The lowest risk? Be sure to explain your answer in terms of operating leverage. You may also want to consider each department's break-even point compared to budgeted (expected) operations.

Source: A. Oppong, "The Paper Company," *The Journal of Accounting Case Research*, Vol. 3, No. 2 (1996), pp. 80–88. Permission to use has been granted by Captus Press, Inc. and the Accounting Education Resource Centre of The University of Lethbridge. [Journal Subscription: Captus Press, Inc., York University Campus, 4700 Keele Street, North York, Ontario, M3J 1P3, by calling (416) 736-5537, or by fax at (416) 736-5793, E-mail: info@captus.com, Internet: **http://www.captus.com**]

▷ *Ethics Case*

Pickmore International

Joan Hildabrand is analyzing some cost data for her boss, Ross Cumings. The data relate to a special sales order that Pickmore International is considering from a large customer in Singapore. The following data are applicable to the product being ordered:

Normal unit sales price	$49.95
Variable unit manufacturing costs	10.50
Variable unit selling and administrative expenses	18.25

The customer is requesting that the sales order be accepted on the following terms:

a. The unit sales price would equal the unit contribution margin plus 10%.
b. Freight would be paid by the customer.
c. Pickmore International would pay a $5,000 "facilitating payment" to a "friend of the customer" to get the product through customs more quickly.

In considering the order, Ross has indicated to Joan that this is a very important customer. Furthermore, this work would help some employees earn a little extra Christmas money with overtime.

1. What are the accounting and ethical issues involved in this case?
2. Should Joan recommend acceptance of the sales terms proposed for this special order?

▶ *Writing Assignment*

Issues of Quality and Time on C-V-P Analysis Decisions

This chapter described how to analyze whether the difference between sales price and variable costs, as well as the volume of sales, is sufficient to pay for all fixed costs in an organization and provide a sufficient profit. A number of methods have been presented for analyzing these costs, volume, and price relationships. These methods all focus on *quantitative* issues that affect how a company manages its resources to maximize overall profits. However, there are a number of *qualitative* issues involving quality and time that should also affect decisions about what sales prices to set, how to manage fixed and variable costs, and which products should be emphasized within the organization. One way to trade off fixed costs for variable costs is to consider making large fixed cost investments in technology that result in automated production, merchandising, and service processes. These kinds of investments allow some variable costs, such as direct labor, to be reduced. Managing this cost trade-off often has strong implications on the quality of the product or service, as well as the timeliness with which it can be delivered. Both of these qualitative issues eventually affect the quantitative issues of costs, volume, and price. Go to your library and find an article describing one organization's effort to invest in automation or other technologies in order to reduce costs. Determine what quality and time issues are affected by the investment. Write a one- to two-page memo describing what you found.

▶ *The Debate*

Which Cost Analysis Method Is Better?

Many costs within an organization are mixed costs, combining elements of both fixed and variable costs. Separating these types of costs into their fixed and variable cost components is necessary before C-V-P analysis work can be done. Two potential cost analysis methods are the scattergraph (visual-fit) approach and the high-low approach. Each of these methods has both disadvantages and advantages compared to the other.

Divide your group into two teams and prepare a two-minute oral argument supporting your assigned position.

- One team represents "The scattergraph (visual-fit) method is superior!" Explain why this method should be used for determining the variable and fixed cost components in a mixed cost.
- The other team represents "High-low; the way to go!" Explain why this method should be used for determining the variable and fixed cost components in a mixed cost.

▶ *Internet Search*

Applied Ethics Resources on WWW

We have discussed ethical issues for accountants in this text and have included an ethics case at the end of each chapter. Obviously, ethical issues are of concern to accountants and all other business professionals. There are a number of good resources on the Internet for those interested in further exploring ethical issues in business (hopefully, we're all interested in this topic!). One of the better sites is Applied Ethics Resources on WWW Centre at **http://www .ethicsweb.ca/resources/**. Sometimes Web addresses change, so if this address doesn't work, access the Web site for this textbook (**http://swain.swlearning.com**) for an updated link.

Go to this site and explore the materials regarding applied ethics resources on the World Wide Web. Find a publication that discusses either business or professional ethics. Write a short paragraph that describes exactly where you found the article and give a brief summary.

chapter

3

Product Cost Flows and Business Organizations

Learning Objectives

After studying this chapter, you should be able to:

1 Understand the difficulty, yet importance, of having accurate product cost information.

2 Explain the flow of goods and services in a manufacturing organization and follow the corresponding accumulation of product costs in the accounting system.

3 Understand the process of accounting for overhead.

4 Create a Cost of Goods Manufactured schedule and understand how it is used to calculate cost of goods sold.

5 Explain the flow of goods and services in a merchandising organization and follow the corresponding accumulation of product costs in the accounting system.

6 Explain the flow of goods and services in a service organization and follow the corresponding accumulation of product costs in the accounting system.

7 Understand the impact of e-business on product costing.

8 Use the FIFO method to do process costing.

Before 1810, American business was basically made up of a loose collection of independent contractors, each focused on doing just one thing.[1] As you can imagine, the wheels of commerce turned rather slowly. However, these small businesses were fairly easy to manage. They had few employees and simple processes. Cost accounting, if it existed at all, was not a difficult procedure. For example, if the wainwright wanted to know how much it cost to build a wagon for a customer, he simply added up the costs of buying lumber products from the sawmill, leather products from the tanner, and iron products from the blacksmith. He then set the price of the wagon high enough to compensate him for the time he spent assembling the materials.

The Industrial Revolution came to the United States with the mechanized, integrated cotton textile factories of New England. In 1814, at a cotton mill established by the American industrialist Francis Cabot Lowell in Waltham, Massachusetts, all the steps of an industrial process were combined under one roof for the first time. Instead of contracting with a dozen different little family-owned businesses to card, spin, and sew raw material into cloth, Lowell brought raw cotton fiber into a heavily equipped factory staffed with workers who were organized by specialty. In one massive facility, Lowell could take raw materials and create a finished product ready for sale. This was "big business," and like all business innovations before and since, Lowell's integrated production facility substantially complicated the accounting process. In order to run this textile mill, Lowell and his managers needed a reporting system that would provide the information to plan, control, and evaluate work they themselves could not personally oversee. History shows that the managers of these early textile mills developed a remarkably good accounting system that tracked inventory, payroll, and production work.

Shortly after the textile manufacturing industry was launched, the advent of railroads presented some of the most complex administrative problems of the nineteenth century. On May 10, 1869, the UNION PACIFIC RAILROAD from the East and the CENTRAL PACIFIC RAILROAD from the West were joined at Promontory Point, Utah. Railroad companies soon grew to sizes that dwarfed the scale of the largest textile factories, and the names of railroad tycoons like J. P. Morgan and Edward Henry Harriman became famous (or infamous, depending on your perspective). Managing these huge administrative entities required special record-keeping systems that captured enormous numbers of daily transactions and summarized essential information for frequent internal reports to management. The challenge for railroads was that employees and processes were literally spread all over the map! Senior managers needed some means of assessing the performance of station managers at terminals and yards across the country. Management accounting expanded as "costs per ton-mile" (the average cost to move a ton of material one mile) and "operating ratio" (a ratio of operating expenses to revenues) began providing competitive information to indicate how the performance of various station managers would affect the railroad's total financial performance. These performance measures were used to delegate responsibilities and to control and evaluate the business from a distance, facilitating the spread of the railroads.

The last quarter of the nineteenth century brought an incredible outpouring of inexpensive, mass-produced goods and services for consumers, leading to the emergence of the mass merchandising industry composed of wholesalers and retailers. In addition to making many diverse items available for purchase from a single source, these wholesalers and retailers provided other critical services, including distribution, delivery, and extension of credit. Companies such as R. H. MACY & COMPANY, INC., in New York City and SEARS, ROEBUCK & COMPANY in Chicago were achieving tremendous financial success by focusing on a very important idea: move the inventory! The success of the mass merchant hinged on **inventory turnover**, called "**stockturns**." By selling goods faster than smaller local merchants, large-scale wholesalers and retailers could charge lower prices and still realize tremendous profit. Up to this point, big business in America had focused almost exclusively on costs. But wholesalers and retailers introduced a new concept to management accounting. By controlling and evaluating the use of assets (in this case, inventory), merchandisers helped management accounting grow to include the process management technique of asset management (also known as capital management). As is described in the opening scenario for the chapter on managing inventory, this is a strategy that has been perfected in our day by WAL-MART.

inventory turnover (stockturns) The number of times the inventory in an organization "turns over" during a period of time. It is often easier to think of inventory turnover as the number of times a dollar invested in inventory is sold during a period of time. Inventory turnover is computed as cost of goods sold divided by average inventory value.

1 Historical sources: A. D. Chandler, *The Invisible Hand* (Boston: HBS Press, 1977); H. T. Johnson and R. S. Kaplan, *Relevance Lost* (Boston: HBS Press, 1987).

management accounting is the result of the efforts of many individuals and organizations to create information that has a competitive value in the marketplace. To really understand management accounting, you need to grasp how **manufacturing, merchandising,** and **service organizations** do business. Management accounting historically began with a focus on planning, controlling, and evaluating costs. Cost accounting continues to be a central facet of management accounting. In fact, understanding cost flows is a useful way to understand how a business is structured or organized. And although accurately determining the costs of products and services is difficult, it is one of the most important aspects of management accounting and provides one of the most useful pieces of information for business decision makers. Without accurate cost information, it is difficult to set appropriate prices, evaluate performance, reward employees, or make production decisions. It is even difficult to know whether a company should be competing in a specific market.

In this chapter, you will learn how goods and services flow in manufacturing, merchandising, and service companies and how product costs incurred in these organizations are tracked and accumulated. In subsequent chapters you will learn how to use product costs to manage and control manufacturing, merchandising, and service companies.

manufacturing organizations Organizations that focus on using labor and/or machinery to convert raw materials into marketable products.

merchandising organizations Organizations that focus on procuring tangible products, then distributing them to customers. These customers may include individuals or other business organizations such as manufacturing organizations.

service organizations Organizations that focus on delivery of marketable services, such as legal advice or education, to individuals or other organizations.

Why Having Accurate Product Costs Is so Difficult, Yet Important

1 Understand the difficulty, yet importance, of having accurate product cost information.

Managers need accurate product cost information to plan for the future, to control current operations, and to evaluate past performance. They also need accurate product cost information so that they can deliver high-quality products to customers at the lowest price and at the fastest speed. For most companies, accurately determining product costs is a surprisingly difficult challenge. Regardless of the difficulty, however, having accurate product cost information is critical for a business. Without knowledge of accurate product costs, managers could easily over- or underprice products and make other poor decisions.

What if, for example, TOYOTA sells its 2003 Camry SE V-6 for $23,265 (its intended sales price), but the actual cost of producing the car is $26,000? How long could Toyota stay in business losing $2,735 ($26,000 − $23,265) per car? In this case, buyers will probably rush to buy Camrys because they will likely be priced much lower than other comparable cars (assuming Toyota's competitors have more accurate cost information and have priced their cars to cover their total manufacturing costs). Not only will Toyota lose money on every car it sells, but the more cars Toyota sells, the greater its losses will be.

On the other hand, what if Toyota attempts to sell its Camry SE for $23,265, not realizing that its cost of making the car is actually only $15,000? If the accurate cost is only $15,000, other manufacturers, such as FORD, may sell their cars for much less than Toyota (assuming Ford has a better cost accounting system); sales of Camrys will dwindle. If Toyota mistakenly believes its costs are higher than $15,000, say, $22,500, it will not lower prices to the point where the company can compete with Ford and other manufacturers. The competitors that better understand their own costs will probably reduce prices, leaving Toyota behind in the market. With lower sales, Toyota may again lose money because it can't sell enough cars to cover its fixed operating expenses. As you can see, having accurate product cost information helps managers in many ways, including making planning, controlling, and evaluating decisions such as the following:

network exercises

Toyota

Access TOYOTA's Web site at **http://www.toyota.com**. The base price for the 2003 Camry SE V-6 4 cylinder is $23,265.

Net Work:

1. How much does the price increase if options package #1, a CD autochanger, a simulated maple dash, and a V.I.P. Plus security system are added?

2. How do these features affect Toyota's manufacturing costs?

1. As part of the *planning* process, a company can determine whether it can or should compete in certain markets. It is possible that prices of competitors in some markets are already lower than the manufacturing costs would be for a new company trying to enter the market. For example, before starting a new airline, you should calculate whether the prevailing prices on the routes you intend to serve are high enough to cover the costs of the aircraft, air crew, ground crew, airport gate rental charges, regulatory approvals, ticketing system, and so forth.

2. When *controlling* operations, a company can analyze the relationship between production levels and costs and determine whether to increase, decrease, or stop production of certain products. For example, some MAJOR LEAGUE BASEBALL teams (the OAKLAND ATHLETICS are the prime example) have determined that some types of players (big-time free agents, glamorous closing relief pitchers, and highly-touted high school players are some examples) just cost too much to allow the team to make a profit with such players on the payroll.[2]

3. In the *evaluation* process, a company can compare actual costs against budgeted costs (a management accounting process known as variance analysis that we'll discuss later in a chapter on making decisions) and identify both progress and problems for subsequent management action. For example, when President Reagan initially proposed the construction of the International Space Station in 1984, the estimated cost was $8 billion. Recent estimates on the ultimate total cost of the project run as high as $90 billion, prompting some rather unfavorable "evaluation" of NASA.

Having accurate product cost information also allows a company to identify and eliminate costly, complicated processes so that higher-quality, lower-priced products and services can be delivered to customers in increasingly shorter **cycle times**. Accurate cost information allows management to determine the appropriate level at which to operate, to assess the long-term profitability of various products, and to manage the costs of production activities.

Overhead: The Problem in Determining Accurate Product Costs

You have learned in a previous chapter that costs of manufacturing products can be broken down into three elements: (1) direct materials, (2) direct labor, and (3) manufacturing overhead. Direct materials include the cost of raw materials that are used directly in the manufacture of products. Direct materials are kept in the raw materials warehouse until used and include such things as rubber used in making tires, steel used to make cars, wood used to make tables, and plastic used to make eyeglasses. Direct labor includes the wages and other payroll-related expenses of factory employees who work directly on products. Direct labor includes the cost of wages and benefits for assembly-line workers, but it does not include the wages and benefits of the factory custodians or the factory controller because, even though they work in the factory, they don't work directly on making products. Manufacturing overhead includes all manufacturing costs that are not classified as direct materials or direct labor. This includes miscellaneous materials used in production, such as glue or nails; wages for the factory supervisor, controller, and custodians who work in the factory, but not directly on products; and other manufacturing costs such as utilities, depreciation of manufacturing facilities, insurance, and property taxes.

Although it is usually easy to assign direct materials and direct labor costs to specific products, it is extremely difficult to assign manufacturing costs, such as rent or the custodian's salary, to specific manufactured products. Most manufacturing overhead costs are not related to the flow of production. For example, think about the cost of driving your car (if you have one) from your house or apartment to the nearest supermarket and back. It is unlikely that your tires will

cycle times The total time a product spends moving through a particular process or cycle within the organization, such as the product design cycle, the production cycle, or the order and delivery cycle.

Caution

Product costs are only one element management must consider when establishing prices for its products. Pricing is a complex issue, and management usually looks to its own strategy and to the market to set prices (also considering competitors' prices, market's ability to pay, and so forth). It would be wrong to assume that management uses only its product cost information to set prices.

2 M. Lewis, *Moneyball* (New York: W. W. Norton & Company, 2003).

The Commercialization of the Internet Who invented the Internet? The Internet began at the U.S. Department of Defense in the late 1950s at the direction of President Dwight D. Eisenhower. At the time of the Cold War and the Soviet Union's successful launch of *Sputnik*, the Eisenhower administration felt the need for a network of computers between major U.S. cities so that the Department of Defense could easily connect with them. Soon major universities began to tap into the network. The timeline below shows the network's origins and growth.

Fifteen servers

First cross-country connection installed by AT&T.

Four servers

Number of Internet users estimated to be 2,000.

First e-mail management program written.

Domain Name System (DNS) introduced; 1,000 servers.

10,000 servers

Domain name "business.com" is sold for $7.5 million. Originally purchased for $150,000 in 1997.

Over 80,000 Internet security incidents (less than 4,000 in 1998)

| 1954 | | | | | 1973 | | 1983 | | | 1991 | 1992 | | 2000 | |
| 1965 | 1970 | 1971 | 1972 | | 1973 | | 1984 | 1987 | | | 1999 | | 2002 |

USSR launches *Sputnik*, first artificial earth satellite. In response, the following year, the United States forms the Advanced Research Projects Agency (ARPA) within the Department of Defense to establish U.S. lead in science and technology applicable to the military.

Desktop workstations come into being; 113 servers.

1 million servers

1 billion searchable Web pages

Commercialization of the Internet begins.

First international connection made between United States and England.

Source: Robert Hobbes, *Hobbes' Internet Timeline.* http:// www.zakon.org/robert/internet/timeline/.

wear out or that you will need an engine overhaul or an oil change on this short trip. However, over the life of the car, you will spend substantial amounts of money on maintenance and repair costs. An extremely difficult accounting issue is computing how much of the overhead maintenance and repair cost should be included in the calculation of the cost of your short trip to the store and back. And this cost information is essential as you decide whether it is better to use your car or sell your car and ride a bicycle.

Companies face the same problem. They have insurance and tax bills that are part of manufacturing overhead costs that must be paid only once or twice a year. Utility costs, like heating and air conditioning in the plant, vary from month to month, sometimes significantly. The oc-

As early as 1988, pressure to commercialize the Internet began when businesses saw its potential as a means of communication and a way to create new marketplaces. Before the Internet could become commercial property, however, Congress had to enact new laws. A few years passed before the Internet was successfully commercialized. Then businesses jumped onto the "backbone" that the government had established and have since created a World Wide Web that enables businesses and consumers to enjoy the technology of the Internet that has been termed the "Technological Revolution" in business.

Like the Industrial Revolution, the Technological Revolution started with individuals who had a unique vision that eventually profited millions of people. For example, Barry Shein, a college dropout, created the first ISP (Internet service provider) in 1989. Barry's idea stemmed from the "withdrawal" he felt when he no longer had Internet access after leaving his university. Soon after, giants such as AMERICA ONLINE (AOL), PRODIGY, and COMPUSERVE began reaping the benefits of Barry's "withdrawal" symptoms. E-commerce on the Internet as we know it today is the result of the vision and efforts of many individuals such as Barry Shein. Without them, the explosive growth in e-commerce shown in the following graph would not have occurred. As a result, managers need to clearly understand the impact of e-commerce on business and accounting.

Source: John Thomson, Jr., *Privatization of the New Communication Channel: Computer Networks and the Internet*, © 2000. **http://www.sit.wisc.edu/%7Ejcthomsonjr/j561/.**

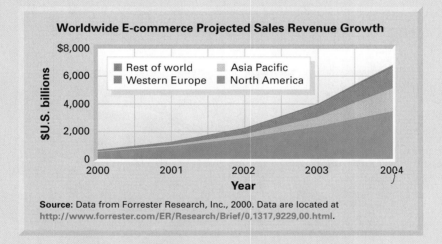

Worldwide E-commerce Projected Sales Revenue Growth

■ Rest of world ▨ Asia Pacific
■ Western Europe ■ North America

Source: Data from Forrester Research, Inc., 2000. Data are located at http://www.forrester.com/ER/Research/Brief/0,1317,9229,00.html.

casional repairs and maintenance on equipment are difficult to predict and to budget for accurately. Nevertheless, most management accountants are required by their organizations to relate these "lumpy" costs back to the volume of production output. In addition, accurate product costing is even more difficult because the actual amount of all manufacturing overhead costs isn't known until the end of the period, long after some products have been completed and even sold.

Management accountants must find some artificial (but hopefully logical) and fair way to assign or "allocate" manufacturing overhead costs to products produced. This "artificial allocation," if done poorly, can result in inaccurate product costs and can lead to serious problems when making planning, controlling, and evaluating decisions.

activity-based costing (ABC) A method of attributing costs to products based on first assigning costs of resources to activities and then costs of activities to products or other cost objects.

New Methods of Cost Accumulation

Many researchers and manufacturers have spent more time trying to determine ways to provide accurate product cost information than they have spent on any other management accounting topic. The result has been the introduction of several new product costing methods including **activity-based costing (ABC)**. Advocates maintain that ABC can provide management with a more accurate assignment of overhead to products and, therefore, a better understanding of profitability. Because of these changes in management accounting and cost accumulation systems, many business organizations are currently in a state of transition. Companies such as DELUXE CORPORATION (the world's largest printer of bank checks as well as a provider of electronic products and services to financial institutions) have completely restructured strategies and operations based on new cost accounting systems.[3] Other companies have been slower to change and still use conventional cost accumulation systems. As a result, some companies struggle to compete effectively in their markets.

In view of the transitional state of accounting for product costs, we will cover both conventional product costing systems (in this chapter) and new cost accumulation systems (in later chapters). You need to understand both types of systems in order to facilitate organizational transitions to more competitive costing systems during your career. In the remainder of this chapter, we describe the conventional accumulation of product costs. The ABC concept will be defined and discussed in a later chapter.

By integrating technology such as robotics into the production process, companies can reduce costs, improve quality, and increase productivity. However, technology also leads to significant changes in the types of costs companies must now manage.

© Romilly Lockyer/2003 Getty Images

TO SUMMARIZE: While it is difficult to exactly measure a product's true cost, having accurate product cost information is extremely important. Without accurate costs, management can easily overprice or underprice products and make bad business decisions. Although it is usually easy to allocate direct material and direct labor costs to specific products, manufacturing overhead costs make accurate product costing difficult. New methods of cost accumulation, though challenging to implement, offer significant potential benefits to manufacturing, merchandising, and service companies. Hence, in order to be competitive in today's economy, management needs accurate product cost information in order to plan for the future, control current operations, and evaluate past performance.

3 P. B. B. Turney, *Deluxe Corporation: A Strategic Need for Activity-Based Costing* (Charlottesville, Va.: University of Virginia Darden School Foundation, 1999).

The Flow of Goods and Costs in a Manufacturing Firm

2 Explain the flow of goods and services in a manufacturing organization and follow the corresponding accumulation of product costs in the accounting system.

It should be clear to you at this point that management accounting provides information with competitive value that supports management efforts to plan, control, and evaluate the organization's performance in providing goods and services to the world. In addition, you know that organizations compete on the basis of costs, quality, and timeliness, and that management accounting needs to provide information regarding all three of these performance characteristics. As you read in the opening of this chapter, however, management accounting had its beginnings in tracking and reporting costs. Today, one of the best ways to understand how an organization works to provide goods and services is to "follow the money"; in other words, observe how costs flow through the organization. We'll use cost flows to introduce you to manufacturing, merchandising, and service organizations. For a long time, manufacturing was the basis of the U.S. economy. Today, relative to other industries, manufacturing is much smaller. Nevertheless, management accounting systems were originally built to support the manufacturing process, so we'll start there.

Consider the layout for a simple, hypothetical manufacturing company shown in Exhibit 1. This floor plan is for a manufacturer of furniture, Broyman Furniture Company. The floor plan

Exhibit 1: Broyman Furniture Company (A Manufacturing Firm's Layout)

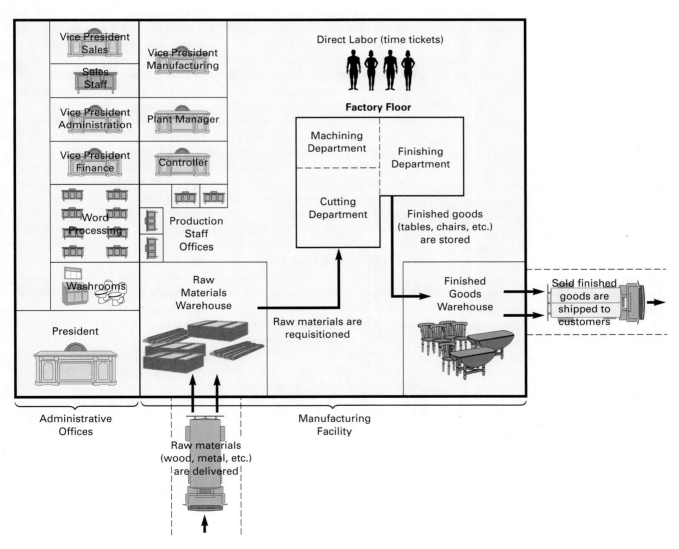

shows a building that is partitioned into two sections. The administrative offices include office space for various vice presidents, the sales staff, the president, and the word-processing staff. The manufacturing facility encompasses the offices of the vice president of manufacturing, the plant manager, and the controller; the raw materials and finished goods warehouses; and the factory floor, where production takes place.

The manufacturing process for Broyman is quite straightforward. When purchased, raw materials are delivered to the **raw materials inventory** warehouse where they are stored until requisitioned for production. When requisitioned, raw materials are moved out onto the factory floor for the actual manufacturing process; there all material is referred to as **work-in-process inventory** until the process is completed. The factory floor includes three different manufacturing departments: cutting, machining, and finishing. Whereas some furniture products require work in all three areas, others may require work in only one or two areas. On the factory floor, factory employees combine materials with their labor to produce finished products. The finished products are then moved into the **finished goods inventory** warehouse and stored until sold.

Although the movement of goods through this simple factory is straightforward, tracking the costs of goods manufactured (the product costs) is not always so simple. You remember from the chapter that introduced management accounting that product costs include all costs necessary to create the product: essentially, the costs of all people and processes within Broyman's manufacturing facility. On the other hand, the costs of people and processes in Broyman's administrative offices, which are not associated with the production of furniture, are period costs. The basic idea that defines product costs is that these are the costs that can be associated with specific products. Certainly, the costs of the raw materials and the wages of factory employees who work on the factory floor are manufacturing costs that can be traced to specific products. But what about the salaries of the vice president of manufacturing, the plant manager, and the individuals working in the administrative offices? Should any part of their salaries be included in product costs? What about the utility bills to heat and light the building, the depreciation or rent on the building, the cost of the parking lot, the cost of paper towels for the washrooms, and other miscellaneous expenditures? Should any part of these expenses be included in manufacturing costs?

Because the individuals working in the administrative offices perform administrative and selling duties, rather than manufacturing functions, their salaries should probably not be classified as product costs. Likewise, the costs to pay for electricity, heat, and other expenses for the administrative offices are probably not manufacturing costs. However, the vice president of manufacturing and the plant manager perform functions related to manufacturing, so their salaries should probably be included as product costs. Although these employees perform administrative functions within the manufacturing facility, the work they perform cannot easily be identified with or assigned to specific products, unlike the factory employees who work directly on the products. Similarly, the heat, power, and depreciation related to the manufacturing facility should be included as manufacturing costs but cannot be easily traced to specific products. What about the costs of delivering purchased raw materials to the plant or the delivery of finished goods to customers? Should these delivery costs be classified as manufacturing, administrative, or selling expenses?

As you can see, accurately determining the costs of manufactured products can be challenging, even in a simple firm with one product and one location. When the "real world" introduces the complexities of multiple products being produced, changing prices and labor rates, multiple manufacturing locations (perhaps some international locations), and individuals performing multiple functions, etc., it becomes very challenging to accurately determine product costs. Essentially, in order to accurately measure product costs, management accountants must be able to:

1. Determine which costs relate to manufacturing and which relate to administrative and selling functions.

---

raw materials inventory
The inventory of raw materials that have not yet begun the production process.

work-in-process inventory
Inventory that is partly completed in the production process, but not yet ready for sale to customers.

finished goods inventory
Inventory that has completed the production process and is ready for sale to customers.

FYI:

In 2001, U.S. domestic companies created $8.7 trillion in products and services (known as gross domestic product or GDP). When we break this number down by industries, manufacturers (including mining and construction) created $2 trillion, merchandisers created another $1.6 trillion, and service companies (including transportation and finance companies) created $5.1 trillion. As you can see, service industries created more output than the other two industries combined! Perhaps more importantly, service industries grew nearly 90% during the prior 10-year period, while manufacturers and merchandisers grew approximately 60% during the same time.

Source: U.S. Department of Commerce, Bureau of Economic Analysis, 2002, **http://www.bea.gov**.

2. Accurately identify and measure all costs associated with manufacturing.
3. Determine appropriate ways to assign costs incurred to the individual products manufactured.

These issues are discussed in the following section.

The Product Costing System

Most accounting systems that track costs of producing and providing goods and services are based on a few key procedures.

- First, identify the product or project that needs cost measurement and track this project through the production process.[4]
- Second, specifically trace the direct costs (costs of direct materials and direct labor) to each product or project.
- Finally, allocate an appropriate amount of overhead costs to each product or project.

job order costing A method of product costing whereby each job, product, or batch of products is costed separately.

This accounting approach is traditionally called **job order costing**. As we discuss the mechanics of this product costing system, keep in mind the overall procedure—identify the product or service (the "job"), trace the direct costs, and allocate the overhead. Also be sure to remember the big picture. In other words, why are we doing this? Product and service cost information is used to plan future operations (e.g., at what level of production should we operate?), to control current operations (e.g., are our costs too high?), and to evaluate performance (e.g., were our costs and performance last period good or bad?). This information is used by management to support continuous decisions about costs, quality, and time.

In our example, we will track product costs as we follow an order for a mahogany table that is manufactured by Broyman Furniture Company. The production of the table is a custom job requiring two operations: machining (preparing the mahogany) and finishing (assembling, staining, and packaging the table). (You will recall that there were three manufacturing areas in Exhibit 1. This table does not require work in the cutting department.)

Exhibit 2 shows that the mahogany table costs $393.50 to make. This amount includes $135 of direct materials, $134 of direct labor, and $124.50 of manufacturing overhead (which includes supervisor and production staff salaries, insurance, utilities, depreciation on plant and machinery, and so on). Looking at the cost summary in Exhibit 2, we can see that the hourly wage rate for direct labor is $10 per hour in machining and $12 per hour in finishing; the manufacturing overhead rate is $11 per machine hour in machining and $13 per direct labor hour in finishing. The **manufacturing overhead rate** is an estimate of the overhead that will be incurred for each unit (in this case, allocated on the basis of machine and direct labor hours). In this example, the company incurs an average of $11 of overhead for every hour the machine is run in the machining department. Thus, each table that requires the use of the machine is allocated a portion of the overhead costs. The use of different manufacturing overhead rates is common. Each department will allocate manufacturing overhead to products on the basis of the most meaningful activity in that department. (Remember the challenge discussed earlier of accurately estimating and allocating manufacturing overhead to products.) The machining department is more automated, so activity is tied more closely to machine hours; the finishing department requires more handwork, so activity is tied more closely to direct labor hours. With these "finished costs" in mind, let's talk about how Broyman Furniture Company actually created these data on the mahogany table. But first, take a brief look at Exhibit 3 on page 125. In this rather complicated-looking exhibit you can literally "see" how the costs follow the

manufacturing overhead rate The rate at which manufacturing overhead is assigned to products; equals estimated manufacturing overhead for the period divided by the number of units of the activity base being used.

---

4 In some organizations, it is not reasonable or possible to specifically track the product being produced. For example, a lumber mill that continuously processes timber into planks may not specifically track individual products. Instead, the mill would track the total production costs expended for a particular period of time (e.g., a day), then assign those costs to the total amount of timber processed during that same period of time. This management accounting approach is called process costing and will be discussed in the expanded material section of this chapter.

Exhibit 2: Total Product Costs for One Mahogany Table

Machining Department Costs

Direct Materials	Direct Labor			Manufacturing Overhead (based on machine hours)		
Requisitioned	Hours	Wage Rate	Amount	Hours	Overhead Rate	Amount
$100	8	$10	$80	6	$11	$66

Finishing Department Costs

Direct Materials	Direct Labor			Manufacturing Overhead (based on direct labor hours)		
Requisitioned	Hours	Wage Rate	Amount	Hours	Overhead Rate	Amount
$30.00	3	$12.00	$36.00	3	$13.00	$39.00
5.00	1.5	$12.00	18.00	1.5	$13.00	19.50
$35.00			$54.00			$58.50

Final Product Cost for Mahogany Table

	Machining	Finishing	Total
Direct materials	$100.00	$ 35.00	$135.00
Direct labor	80.00	54.00	134.00
Manufacturing overhead	66.00	58.50	124.50
Total cost	$246.00	$147.50	$393.50

production process and flow through the accounting system. We'll work through the details of Exhibit 3 below. (*Note:* Don't worry if you are still a little confused about how Broyman creates and uses manufacturing overhead rates. We're going to discuss these concepts in detail later in this chapter.)

Direct Materials Costs

To illustrate the accounting for direct materials costs, we will assume that Broyman purchased a supply of mahogany and placed it in a materials storeroom. The entry to record this purchase is:[5]

Raw Materials Inventory	50,000	
Accounts Payable (or Cash)		50,000
Purchased 25,000 board feet of mahogany at $2 per foot.		

When raw materials are needed (such as for the manufacture of the table), the machining department sends a request (i.e., a requisition) to the storeroom (usually via computer) identifying the quantity and type of materials needed. When the raw materials warehouse fills the requisition, it records the transfer of goods to the factory floor by making an entry (usually by

---

5 In this chapter, we will use an *actual* cost accounting system. We will discuss standard cost accounting systems later in the chapter on making decisions.

Exhibit 3: Flow of Product Costs in Broyman Company Job Order Cost Accounting System

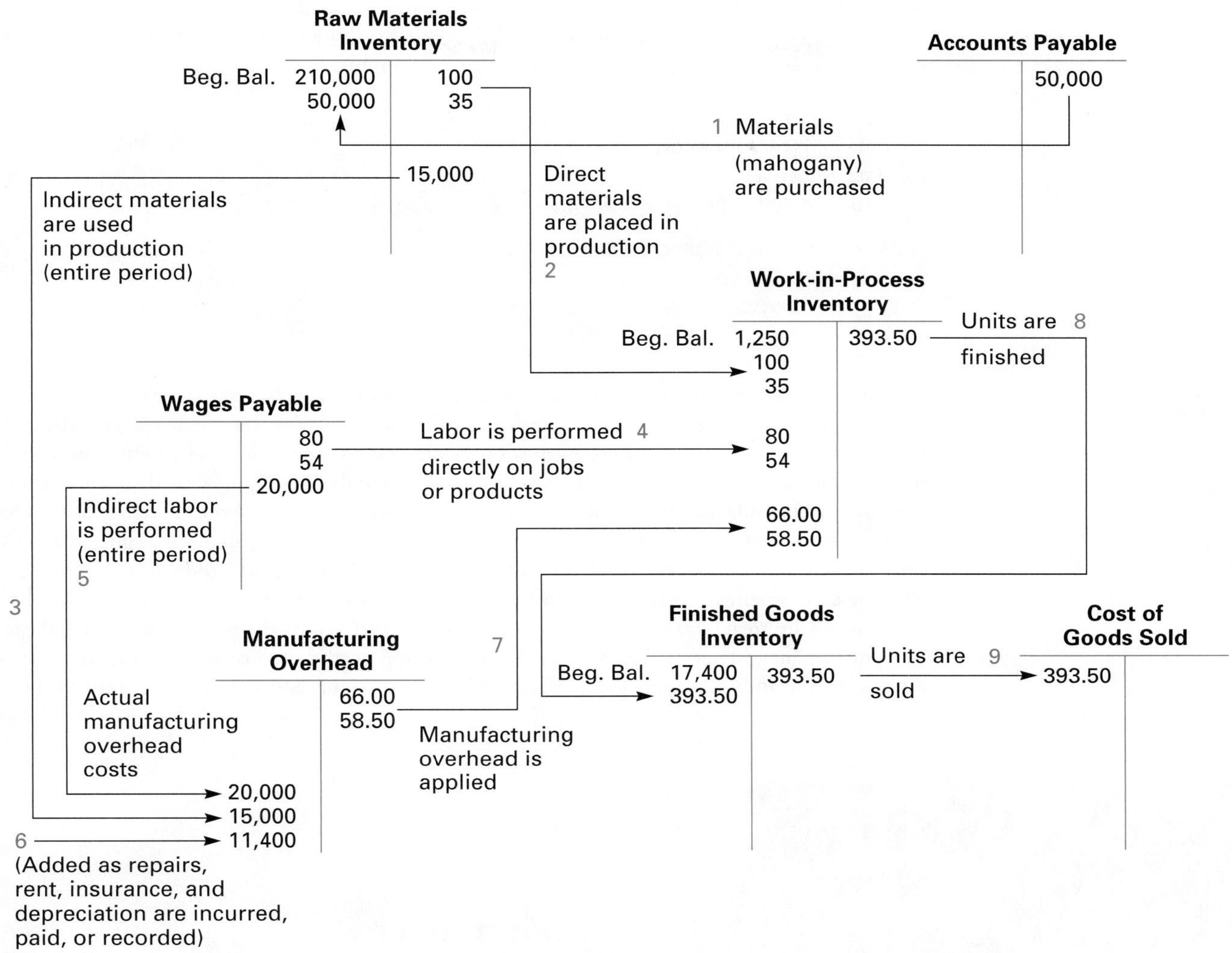

Journal Entries for Manufacturing Firms:

1 Raw Materials Inventory	50,000	
Accounts Payable (or Cash)		50,000
Purchased raw materials.		
2 Work-in-Process Inventory	100	
Raw Materials Inventory		100
Work-in-Process Inventory	35	
Raw Materials Inventory		35
Used direct materials in production		
(includes materials used in both the		
machining and finishing departments).		
3 Manufacturing Overhead	15,000	
Raw Materials Inventory		15,000
Used indirect materials in production		
(amount used during entire period).		
4 Work-in-Process Inventory	80	
Wages Payable.		80
Work-in-Process Inventory	54	
Wages Payable.		54
Incurred direct labor costs in the		
machining and finishing departments.		
5 Manufacturing Overhead	20,000	
Wages Payable		20,000
Incurred indirect labor costs (includes		
indirect labor costs for entire period).		

6 Manufacturing Overhead	11,400	
Accounts Payable		1,200
Rent Payable		6,450
Prepaid Insurance		850
Accumulated Depreciation		2,900
Incurred manufacturing overhead		
costs (includes amounts for entire		
period).		
7 Work-in-Process Inventory	66.00	
Manufacturing Overhead		66.00
Work-in-Process Inventory	58.50	
Manufacturing Overhead		58.50
Applied manufacturing overhead		
from the machining and finishing		
departments to production.		
8 Finished Goods Inventory	393.50	
Work-in-Process Inventory		393.50
Completed production.		
9 Cost of Goods Sold	393.50	
Finished Goods Inventory		393.50
Sold finished goods.		

computer) that serves as the basis for the accounting records. The storeroom manager sends the requisition information to the accounting department, where the unit cost is entered and the total cost calculated. The accounting entry made to record the transfer of mahogany from storage to machining is provided below. In addition, the finishing department requisitioned some packaging material to prepare mahogany tables for shipping.

Work-in-Process Inventory	100	
Raw Materials Inventory		100
Issued 50 board feet of mahogany to production at $2 per foot.		
Work-in-Process Inventory	35	
Raw Materials Inventory		35
Issued packaging material to production.		

The mahogany and packaging material were used directly in the production and shipping preparation of the table; the cost is assigned as direct materials for this particular job. Because the amount of direct materials used varies proportionately with the level of production, direct materials are almost always variable costs. Indirect materials and supplies used in production (classified as manufacturing overhead costs), such as glue, nails, and varnish, are ordered from the storeroom in the same manner. Although some inexpensive materials, such as glue, are used directly in the manufactured products and others are used to support production, it is generally not cost-beneficial to trace such miscellaneous items to a particular job. These miscellaneous items are treated as indirect materials costs and recorded in the manufacturing overhead account (explained later in the chapter). Manufacturing overhead consists of numerous expenditures such as indirect labor, indirect materials, utilities, rent, and the like. The sum of these

business environment

Costs and the Medical Profession Have you ever gone to the doctor's office, spent 20 minutes in the waiting room, then another 20 minutes in the examination room before the doctor comes in? When she finally comes in, she examines you for 10 minutes and then sends you on your way, charging you $85 for the visit. No wonder medical doctors make so much money—or do they? Does the doctor put your $85 right in her pocket?

What costs must your $85 cover? Unfortunately, you must help the doctor pay for office medical supplies, rent on the office, utilities, salaries of nurses and office personnel,

fees charged by hospitals to use their facilities, and costs of training seminars to remain current in her field. While these costs are expensive, perhaps the most rapidly rising cost is for malpractice insurance. As an example, in many communities in the United States, the cost of obstetrical malpractice insurance is so high that some doctors will no longer deliver babies.

Where does the doctor get the money to cover these costs? By charging you $85 for your visit. Medicine is a business. The doctor is pricing patient visits to cover all costs incurred in providing that service. Costs must be covered and we, the consumers, must pay for them. The next time you visit the doctor, take a look around the waiting room, enjoy those pictures, and read those magazines. After all, you paid for them!

various expenditures provides the balance in the manufacturing overhead account. The following entry records the sum of all the requisitions for indirect materials for the period:

Manufacturing Overhead (indirect materials)	15,000	
Raw Materials Inventory		15,000
Issued miscellaneous materials and supplies to the production floor.		

At the end of a period, the amount of materials and supplies that remain on hand in the raw materials warehouse is shown on the balance sheet as Raw Materials Inventory.

Direct Labor Costs

The method of charging direct labor costs to production jobs is similar to that for direct materials costs. Most factories have a time clock where employees punch in and record their hourly activities. These time clocks often allow workers to identify specific jobs worked on. When the time clocks do not capture specific job information, the information is noted by making entries in the computer or on manual time tickets. The product costs, shown in Exhibit 2, reveal that machining employees worked on the mahogany table for 8 hours. Because the wage rate was $10 per hour in machining, the total direct labor cost in machining was $80 ($10 per hour × 8 hours). Similar calculations provide the entry to record the direct labor costs in the finishing department. The entries to record all the direct labor costs (ignoring payroll taxes and benefits) for the mahogany table are:

Work-in-Process Inventory	80	
Wages Payable		80
To record the machining department's direct labor costs.		
Work-in-Process Inventory	54	
Wages Payable		54
To record the finishing department's direct labor costs.		

Remember that within certain limits, direct labor costs vary proportionately with the number of products made and, thus, are typically considered variable costs.

Like materials, labor costs can be either direct or indirect. Indirect labor costs include the wages of employees who perform functions not related to a specific job, such as maintenance and custodial. Usually, these employees still punch time clocks, but their wages become part of the indirect labor costs that are included in manufacturing overhead, as discussed in the next section. The following entry records the sum of all indirect labor for the period:

Manufacturing Overhead (indirect labor)	20,000	
Wages Payable		20,000
To record indirect labor costs.		

Manufacturing Overhead Costs

In contrast to direct materials and direct labor, manufacturing overhead (the third type of product cost) involves more complex accounting procedures and estimation problems. As we've discussed earlier, usually direct materials and direct labor can be readily assigned to specific jobs or products. However, manufacturing overhead costs are difficult to trace directly to the production of a single item and must often be estimated in advance of their incurrence. By definition, most manufacturing overhead costs benefit all products made in a department or a company during a period. The depreciation on equipment and the wages paid for maintenance in the machining department, for example, ensure the smooth operation of the entire department for the period; however, these costs cannot be traced directly to individual items produced during the period. Some manufacturing overhead costs, such as property taxes and repairs, are not known until the end of an accounting period. However, managers need current product cost information (for pricing similar jobs, estimating costs for next year, and so forth), so each job is assigned a share of *estimated* (i.e., budgeted) manufacturing overhead costs. In accounting terminology, manufacturing overhead costs are applied to (or absorbed by) jobs or products. Overall, knowing how to set up and handle the accounting for overhead costs at Broyman Company is a tricky business, which we'll talk further about later in this chapter.

> **STOP & THINK**
>
> In our example, the company makes a mahogany table using two operations: machining and finishing. When making a real table, how many separate operations do you think would be necessary? Can you envision how complicated it is to track product costs in a "real-world" production setting?

For now, as *actual* manufacturing overhead costs for Broyman are incurred, the management accounting system needs to recognize and record the costs. During the current production period, these costs include $1,200 for repairs to equipment, $6,450 for monthly rent allocated to the production facility, $850 for liability insurance, and $2,900 in depreciation of manufacturing equipment. The total of these costs is debited to Manufacturing Overhead, and the individual amounts are credited to their respective accounts, as shown here.

Manufacturing Overhead	11,400	
Accounts Payable		1,200
Rent Payable		6,450
Prepaid Insurance		850
Accumulated Depreciation		2,900
To record actual manufacturing overhead costs.		

Caution

Many students will make the mistake of debiting manufacturing overhead costs to an expense account. Although these costs eventually do become an expense, first they are debited to Manufacturing Overhead, then allocated to Work-in-Process Inventory, then transferred to Finished Goods Inventory, and finally expensed in Cost of Goods Sold.

predetermined overhead rate A rate at which estimated manufacturing overhead costs are assigned to products throughout the year; equals total estimated manufacturing overhead costs divided by a suitable allocation base, such as number of units produced, direct labor hours, direct materials used, or direct labor costs.

In addition to recording the actual costs of manufacturing overhead, Broyman's accountants need to allocate overhead costs to the mahogany table in production. As you can see in Exhibit 2, the Broyman management accountants follow a traditional approach of assigning manufacturing overhead costs by taking the expected annual costs of overhead for each department and dividing this estimated amount by the selected activity base (in this case, machine hours for the machining department and direct labor hours for the finishing department). Estimated overhead costs typically come from the company's annual budgets. Selection of the activity base is the result of experience and analysis. The result is an allocation rate for each department that is used to uniformly assign a "fair share" of manufacturing overhead costs to production volume throughout the year. This allocation rate is called the **predetermined overhead rate**. In this case, Broyman's accountants allocate to the mahogany table $66 based on activity in the machining department ($11 predetermined overhead rate × 6 machine hours) and $58.50 based on activity in the finishing department ($13 rate × 4.5 direct labor hours). The entries to record these allocations are:

Work-in-Process Inventory	66.00	
Manufacturing Overhead		66.00
To apply manufacturing overhead from the machining department.		
Work-in-Process Inventory	58.50	
Manufacturing Overhead		58.50
To apply manufacturing overhead from the finishing department.		

Notice in Exhibit 3 that as *actual* overhead costs are incurred (as with indirect materials and indirect labor), the manufacturing overhead account is debited. As overhead costs are *applied* to products, the manufacturing overhead account is credited. This relationship is better illustrated and discussed later in this chapter.

Transferring the Costs of Completed Jobs and Computing Unit Costs

While a job is in process, the costs of direct materials, direct labor, and manufacturing overhead are accounted for separately. When the job is completed, however, these costs (in total) are transferred from Work-in-Process Inventory to Finished Goods Inventory. In the Broyman Furniture Company example, the total cost assigned to the mahogany table is $393.50, as illustrated in Exhibit 2. The entry to transfer the completed cost of the table to Finished Goods Inventory is:

Finished Goods Inventory	393.50	
Work-in-Process Inventory		393.50
To record the completion of the mahogany table.		

It's important that you now take a moment to compare Exhibits 1 and 3. Can you see that how the flow of costs through the accounts in Exhibit 3 closely resembles how the product is created and moves through the manufacturing facility in Exhibit 1? The product costs assigned to the table literally follow that table as it moves through the factory floor (and through the work-in-process inventory account) until the table is completed and moves into the finished goods warehouse (and into the finished goods inventory account). Once completed, cost data for the mahogany table are used in pricing similar jobs, estimating costs for the next year, and measuring income. Note that this process would be no different if, instead of a single table, Broyman were to identify and cost an entire batch of mahogany tables. In this case, at the completion of the job, the unit cost of each table is computed by adding the direct materials, direct labor, and manufacturing overhead costs for the batch and dividing the total by the number of tables produced in the batch (i.e., the job).

Transferring the Costs of Products That Are Sold

When a product is sold, the costs assigned to it are transferred to Cost of Goods Sold. For example, when the mahogany table, which cost $393.50 to make, is shipped to a customer, the table is loaded from the warehouse onto the truck, and the cost of the table is transferred from Finished Goods Inventory to Cost of Goods Sold, using the following entry:

Cost of Goods Sold	393.50	
Finished Goods Inventory		393.50
To record the cost of goods sold for the mahogany table.		

STOP & THINK

Compare Exhibit 1 with Exhibit 3. Try to identify the physical location (from Exhibit 1) with each type of accounting cost in Exhibit 3.

With this entry, costs have been traced all the way through the production cycle and expensed onto the income statement. Once again, inspect Exhibit 3 and be sure that you can clearly see how all the costs flow through the manufacturing process for Broyman. Note that direct labor, when incurred, and raw materials, when used, are debited directly to Work-in-Process Inventory. Actual manufacturing overhead costs, on the other hand, are entered first as debits to Manufacturing Overhead and then are allocated to Work-in-Process Inventory by crediting Manufacturing Overhead. Be careful to note that in Exhibit 3, entry 1 is for mahogany that will be used on several jobs; entries 3, 5, and 6 are actual manufacturing costs incurred for the entire accounting period in which the table was manufactured. Entries 2, 4, 7, 8, and 9 are entries specifically associated with the mahogany table in our example. At the end of the period, the company will usually have three inventory balances: Raw Materials Inventory, Work-in-Process Inventory, and Finished Goods Inventory.

> **TO SUMMARIZE:** In traditional job order cost accounting systems for manufacturing organizations where a specific product can be identified, all direct labor, direct materials, and manufacturing overhead costs are accumulated for each unit or batch (generally referred to as a job). Because the exact amount of manufacturing overhead cannot be determined until the accounting period is completed, an estimated amount of manufacturing overhead is applied to jobs. To estimate the amount of manufacturing overhead to be applied to a job, a predetermined overhead rate is calculated for each department involved in production, using an appropriate measure of activity. This rate is multiplied by the actual quantity of the activity used to complete the job. Total costs for completed jobs are then transferred from Work-in-Process Inventory to Finished Goods Inventory. When manufactured goods are sold, costs are transferred from Finished Goods Inventory to Cost of Goods Sold.

Accounting For Overhead

3 Understand the process of accounting for overhead.

In the Broyman Company example of producing a mahogany table and tracking its production costs, you can see that accounting for manufacturing overhead costs is not the same process as accounting for direct materials and direct labor costs. Because manufacturing overhead costs generally do not coincide with the flow of production, a few extra steps are required to handle the accounting. These steps are:

1. Before the year begins, budget the *estimated* manufacturing overhead, estimate the allocation activity, and establish the predetermined overhead rate.
2. During the year, as costs are incurred, record *actual* manufacturing overhead as debits to the manufacturing overhead account.
3. During the year, as activity takes place, record *applied* manufacturing overhead as credits to the manufacturing overhead account and debits to the work-in-process account.
4. At the end of the year, compare *actual* and *applied* overhead balances and close out the difference in the manufacturing overhead account.

Estimated Manufacturing Overhead

estimated manufacturing overhead Budgeted manufacturing overhead costs that are used to establish the predetermined overhead rate.

As you can see, the list above includes three difference classifications of manufacturing overhead costs—estimated, actual, and applied. It is *critical* that you understand the differences among these numbers. **Estimated manufacturing overhead** is the amount of overhead costs that management has budgeted for the upcoming production period. The predetermined overhead rate is created by dividing estimated manufacturing overhead by the estimate of the expected level of activity (e.g., direct labor hours) to be used to allocate overhead during the year.

To illustrate the use of estimated manufacturing overhead to create the predetermined overhead rate for the machining department at Broyman Company, assume that at the beginning of the year the accountants and production personnel estimated that 24,500 machine hours would be used on the factory floor. Budgeted (estimated) overhead costs for the machining department are shown below. Note that these costs have been separated into fixed and variable components.

Variable manufacturing overhead:

Indirect labor	$ 45,000	
Indirect materials	15,000	
Repairs	7,500	$ 67,500

Fixed manufacturing overhead:

Rent	$105,000	
Depreciation	85,000	
Insurance	12,000	202,000
Total expected manufacturing overhead cost		
for the year (machining department)		$269,500

Using these data, the accountants then computed the predetermined overhead rate in the machining department to be $11 per machine hour, as follows:

$$\frac{\text{Total estimated manufacturing overhead cost for the year}}{\text{Total estimated machine hours}} = \frac{\$269,500}{24,500} = \$11 \text{ per machine hour in machining department}$$

FYI:

One useful way to think about the manufacturing overhead account is to consider it to be simply a temporary holding tank for overhead costs that we don't immediately know how to assign to production. By the end of the period, however, we will have sorted out how much was actually spent on overhead and how much actual production took place. At that point, we can clear out the "holding tank" and start over the process of tracking and applying overhead costs in the next period.

Similar calculations were used to calculate the predetermined overhead rate of $13 per direct labor hour in the finishing department.

Actual Manufacturing Overhead

After studying financial accounting, some students have a difficult time with the accounting for actual manufacturing overhead. For example, in financial accounting, we accounted for salaries by debiting Salaries Expense and crediting Salaries Payable, which is the correct entry when the salaries are for sales or other nonmanufacturing personnel. However, as you saw in tracking production costs for Broyman's mahogany table, when the wages are related to manufacturing, the debit is to Work-in-Process Inventory for direct labor and to Manufacturing Overhead for indirect labor. Thus, in management accounting, it is important to determine first whether salaries are for manufacturing or for nonmanufacturing personnel. Then, for manufacturing personnel, it must be determined whether the individuals worked directly on the product (Work-in-Process Inventory) or indirectly on the product (Manufacturing Overhead). The same is true for other costs such as depreciation and rent. If these costs relate to manufacturing, they are debited to Manufacturing Overhead; costs not related to manufacturing are debited to Depreciation Expense, Rent Expense, and so forth. The manufacturing costs will eventually become expenses when the products are sold (Cost of Goods Sold).

Applied Manufacturing Overhead

It is important to understand that the debit side of the manufacturing overhead account is used to record actual overhead expenses. Conversely, the credit side of this account is used to record applied manufacturing overhead that is simultaneously debited to the work-in-process inventory account, as illustrated in Exhibit 4. In essence, this entry transfers the overhead cost from the temporary holding account called Manufacturing Overhead to the asset account called Work-in-Process Inventory.

Actual costs, including actual manufacturing overhead costs, are needed for accurate reporting of annual income and for computing a company's income tax liability at the end of the

Exhibit 4: Recording Costs in the Manufacturing Overhead Account

Manufacturing Overhead

Actual manufacturing overhead costs are entered as debits on a regular basis as they are incurred.	Applied overhead costs are entered as credits as production takes place; costs are applied to Work-in-Process on the basis of a predetermined overhead rate.

year. However, the management process of controlling and evaluating costs and setting prices cannot wait until the end of the year. Hence, while both actual and applied manufacturing overhead costs are accounted for constantly throughout the year, actual overhead costs are too sporadic to be effectively used for pricing and costing decisions that take place continuously. For this reason, predetermined overhead rates are used to apply overhead throughout the year.

Disposition of Over- and Underapplied Manufacturing Overhead

If the beginning-of-the-year estimates of both manufacturing overhead costs *and* the activity basis (e.g., machine hours) are perfect, then at the end of the year the accountants at the Broyman Company will have applied as much overhead to Work-in-Process as was actually incurred, and the ending balance in the manufacturing overhead account will be $0 (this rarely happens). Typically, though, the ending balance in the manufacturing overhead account is not very large. Nevertheless, the manufacturing overhead account is a temporary account that must be closed out at the end of the year. Handling any balance left in Manufacturing Overhead is the process of disposing of over- and underapplied manufacturing overhead.

Note in Exhibit 3 that a total of $46,400 in actual costs have been debited to the manufacturing overhead account. To illustrate the accounting for the difference between actual and applied manufacturing overhead costs, we will assume that these costs represent the total actual manufacturing overhead for March 2006. Further, including the work done on the mahogany table in our example, the machining department at Broyman used a total of 1,600 machine hours and applied $17,600 to Work-in-Process Inventory, and the finishing department employed 1,250 direct labor hours and applied $16,250. Finally, the cutting department (using a similar overhead allocation procedure) applied $11,800. At the end of March, the manufacturing overhead account would appear as follows.

Manufacturing Overhead

(Actual costs)	(Applied costs)
20,000	17,600 applied in machining department
15,000	16,250 applied in finishing department
11,400	11,800 applied in cutting department
46,400	45,650
750 balance (underapplied)	

STOP & THINK

What would it mean if the debit (actual overhead) and credit (applied overhead) amounts in the manufacturing overhead account were vastly different?

overapplied manufacturing overhead The excess of applied manufacturing overhead (based on a predetermined application rate) over the actual manufacturing overhead costs for a period.

underapplied manufacturing overhead The excess of actual manufacturing overhead costs over the applied overhead costs for a period (based on a predetermined application rate).

A comparison of the debit and credit sides of the manufacturing overhead account shows that actual manufacturing overhead costs incurred were $750 higher than applied costs (which indicates that overhead was underapplied for the month). This difference is usually ignored until year-end because management is concerned with immediate decisions, for which current estimates are adequate. At year-end, however, this difference must be accounted for, not only to balance the books, but also to show actual costs in measuring income.

If, at the end of the year, total actual manufacturing overhead is less than the amount applied, the account will have a credit balance. This result is referred to as **overapplied manufacturing overhead**. Conversely, if applied manufacturing overhead is less than actual costs, the account will have a debit balance representing **underapplied manufacturing overhead**.

Which is better to have at the end of the year—under- or overapplied overhead? If overhead is underapplied, then the total cost of jobs will be understated. If a company were to price its products in the future based on this understated cost, the company could lose money because it might not cover its actual manufacturing overhead costs. On the other hand, overapplied manufacturing overhead indicates that jobs were overcharged for overhead and costs were overstated. If future pricing decisions were made based on these overstated costs, the company would soon find customers looking elsewhere for more reasonably priced products. Neither under- nor overapplied overhead is desirable. A company's objective is to attempt to anticipate overhead costs and accurately charge those costs to the various jobs.

There are two methods of treating over- and underapplied manufacturing overhead in the accounting system:

1. Close over- or underapplied manufacturing overhead directly to Cost of Goods Sold.
2. Allocate over- or underapplied manufacturing overhead to Work-in-Process Inventory, Finished Goods Inventory, and Costs of Goods Sold on the basis of the ending balances in these three accounts.

The first method is easier and more commonly used, especially if the over- or underapplied amount is small, because it requires only a single entry to correct the amount of manufacturing overhead applied. Let's assume that at year-end, when total actual and applied manufacturing overhead have been recorded, manufacturing overhead for Broyman was overapplied by $1,900. The entry to assign this overapplied manufacturing overhead to Cost of Goods Sold would be:

| Manufacturing Overhead | 1,900 | |
| Cost of Goods Sold | | 1,900 |

    To recognize the excess of applied manufacturing overhead costs over actual manufacturing overhead.

*Note: The entries for *underapplied* manufacturing overhead would be opposite from what is shown above—debit Cost of Goods Sold and credit Manufacturing Overhead.

This entry will decrease the cost of goods sold account for the year by $1,900 and will close out the manufacturing overhead account. Companies that have very small or zero inventory balances would normally charge any over- or underapplied overhead to Cost of Goods Sold.

The second method is more accurate because, theoretically, any difference between applied and actual manufacturing overhead should be allocated proportionately to all items in production during the period. The items in production include those produced and sold (Cost of Goods Sold), those produced and not sold (Finished Goods Inventory), and those still being produced (Work-in-Process Inventory). If the estimate had been accurate, manufacturing overhead costs would have been allocated proportionately to all products. Therefore, those products actually sold should not be burdened with, or relieved of, the entire amount of the estimation error. This alternative is more complicated, however, and requires detailed calculations and several journal entries, so it will not be illustrated here. When differences between actual and applied overhead are small, this more accurate method is usually not worth the extra effort.

TO SUMMARIZE: Actual manufacturing overhead costs are accumulated and debited to Manufacturing Overhead throughout the year. Applied (or estimated) manufacturing overhead costs are assigned to jobs on the basis of a predetermined overhead rate. These costs are credited to Manufacturing Overhead and debited to Work-in-Process Inventory. Any difference between actual and applied manufacturing overhead at the end of the period must be accounted for in order to properly measure income. When total actual manufacturing overhead exceeds total applied overhead, the excess is referred to as underapplied manufacturing overhead. When total applied overhead exceeds total actual overhead, the excess is referred to as overapplied manufacturing overhead. The easiest and most commonly used method of eliminating over- or underapplied manufacturing overhead is to transfer it directly to Cost of Goods Sold. In some cases, the over- or underapplied manufacturing overhead is allocated among Work-in-Process Inventory, Finished Goods Inventory, and Cost of Goods Sold to arrive at a more accurate assignment of costs.

The Cost of Goods Manufactured Schedule

4 Create a Cost of Goods Manufactured schedule and understand how it is used to calculate cost of goods sold.

Cost of Goods Manufactured schedule A schedule supporting the income statement that summarizes the total cost of goods manufactured and transferred out of the work-in-process inventory account during a period. These costs include direct materials, direct labor, and applied manufacturing overhead.

In this section we will examine a single report, the Cost of Goods Manufactured schedule, that summarizes the cost flows in a manufacturing organization during a given period. We will also see how this cost information is used to then compute cost of goods sold.

Be sure that you review Exhibit 3 and see again how manufacturing costs (materials, labor, and overhead) are accumulated in the work-in-process inventory account, then flow to Finished Goods Inventory, and finally to the cost of goods sold account. These cost flows are summarized on a **Cost of Goods Manufactured schedule**, which supports the cost of goods sold calculation on the income statement.

The purpose of the Cost of Goods Manufactured schedule is to report the total costs that have been incurred to manufacture goods during a period. In our example, Exhibit 5 shows the Cost of Goods Manufactured schedule for Broyman Furniture Company. You will note that the numbers used in Exhibit 5 cannot be specifically traced back to Exhibit 3. This is because the costs flowing through the accounts in Exhibit 3 are focused on the cost associated with the manufacture of a single table. Conversely, the costs in Exhibit 5 are for an entire year. The important thing for you to focus on in Exhibit 5 is the format for summarizing and reporting manufacturing cost flows. Note how the calculation for raw materials used in production is actually based on using the raw materials inventory account to calculate (or "plug") the number that flows into the work-in-process account as shown below.

Raw Materials Inventory

Beginning Balance	50,000		
Purchases	270,000	*290,000*	Transferred to Work-in-Process
Ending Balance	30,000		

Plug this

Exhibit 5: Cost of Goods Manufactured Schedule

Broyman Furniture Company
Cost of Goods Manufactured Schedule
For the Year Ended December 31, 2006

Raw materials:		
Beginning raw materials inventory	$ 50,000	
Add: Raw materials purchased	270,000	
Total raw materials available	$320,000	
Less: Ending raw materials inventory	30,000	
Raw materials used in production		$290,000
Direct labor		300,000
Manufacturing overhead:		
Indirect labor	$ 20,000	
Utilities	7,000	
Rent	72,000	
Depreciation	30,000	
Indirect materials	15,000	
Insurance	24,000	
Total actual manufacturing overhead	$168,000	
Add: Overapplied manufacturing overhead	6,000	
Applied manufacturing overhead		174,000
Total manufacturing costs		$764,000
Add: Beginning work-in-process inventory		90,000
Less: Ending work-in-process inventory		(80,000)
Cost of goods manufactured		$774,000

The Cost of Goods Manufactured schedule provides the calculations that support the flow of costs for a manufacturing firm. In our example, the schedule shows that materials costing $290,000 were combined with direct labor costs of $300,000 and *applied* manufacturing overhead costs of $174,000 to transfer $764,000 of manufacturing costs to Work-in-Process Inventory. This $764,000 amount of total manufacturing costs represents the new manufacturing costs incurred during the period and is a good representation of the level of production activity carried out during the period. The $764,000 was then adjusted for the beginning and ending work-in-process inventories to determine the $774,000 cost of goods manufactured for the period. The amount of cost of goods manufactured represents the total cost of items for which production was completed during the period; this cost includes some costs incurred in prior periods (from beginning work-in-process inventory) and most costs incurred during this period. Effectively, cost of goods manufactured represents the flow of costs out of the work-in-process account as shown below.

Work-in-Process Inventory

Beginning Balance	90,000		
Direct Materials Costs	290,000		
Direct Labor Costs	300,000		
Applied Manuf. Overhead Costs	174,000	*774,000*	Transferred to Finished Goods
Ending Balance	80,000		

Plug this

Note that the cost of goods manufactured number of $774,000 is based on *applied* manufacturing overhead costs (not actual overhead costs). However, the actual manufacturing overhead costs are reported in the Cost of Goods Manufactured schedule in Exhibit 5. The reason for this is to provide useful information for purposes of management planning, control, and evaluation. Overapplied manufacturing overhead is then *added* to the actual overhead costs in order to adjust these costs to applied manufacturing overhead for the calculation of cost of goods manufactured.

Knowing the total cost of goods manufactured makes it easy to determine the total cost of goods sold. The cost of goods manufactured amount is added to beginning finished goods inventory (assume $60,000) and adjusted for any over- or underapplied manufacturing overhead (assume $6,000 overapplied) to arrive at cost of goods available for sale of $828,000. The ending finished goods inventory (assume $40,000) is then subtracted to determine the cost of goods sold ($788,000). This calculation of cost of goods sold is shown below.

Cost of Goods Sold

Beginning finished goods inventory	$ 60,000
Add: Cost of goods manufactured	774,000
Cost of goods available for sale	$834,000
Less: Ending finished goods inventory	(40,000)
Unadjusted cost of goods sold	$794,000
Less: Overapplied manufacturing overhead	(6,000)
Adjusted cost of goods sold	$788,000

This calculation can also be shown using the finished goods inventory and cost of goods sold accounts as shown below.

Finished Goods Inventory

Beginning Balance	60,000		
Cost of Goods Manufactured	774,000	*794,000*	Transferred to Cost of Goods Sold
Ending Balance	40,000		

Plug this

Cost of Goods Sold

Unadjusted Cost of Goods Sold	794,000*	6,000	Overapplied Manuf. Overhead Costs
Adjusted Cost of Goods Sold	788,000		

Caution

Remember that over- or underapplied overhead is usually charged to the cost of goods sold account. Thus, in the cost of goods sold calculation, underapplied overhead is added to, and overapplied overhead is subtracted from, the costs transferred from the finished goods inventory account. However, when actual overhead costs are reported in the Cost of Goods Manufactured schedule, the underapplied overhead is *subtracted* from, and overapplied overhead is *added* to, the actual overhead costs in order to adjust these costs to *applied* overhead for the calculation of cost of goods manufactured.

*Cost of Goods Sold	794,000
Finished Goods Inventory	794,000

Sale of inventory valued using the applied manufacturing overhead rate.

Total cost of goods manufactured should include only those costs that have gone through the work-in-process inventory account during the period. Thus, as shown both in Exhibit 3 and Exhibit 5, applied (rather than actual) overhead costs are included in the Cost of Goods Manufactured schedule. As illustrated, the cost of goods sold account is then adjusted for the amount of over- or underapplied overhead. Cost of goods sold, while an important number for reporting on the income statement for investors and creditors, is not particularly useful for management purposes. Much more detailed information that is useful for planning, controlling, and evaluating manufacturing activities is provided in the Cost of Goods Manufactured schedule.

TO SUMMARIZE: The costs of direct materials, direct labor, and applied overhead used during the period are summarized on a Cost of Goods Manufactured schedule in order to provide information useful for planning, controlling, and evaluating these costs. The cost of goods manufactured is added to the beginning finished goods inventory to determine cost of goods available for sale. Ending finished goods inventory is then subtracted from this number to compute unadjusted cost of goods sold. Cost of goods sold is then adjusted for over- or underapplied manufacturing overhead costs. Cost of goods sold is a summary number that is audited and used in the financial statements, but is not very useful for internal management decision making. For decision making, managers examine more detailed manufacturing costs in the Cost of Goods Manufactured schedule.

The Flow of Goods and Costs in a Merchandising Firm

5 Explain the flow of goods and services in a merchandising organization and follow the corresponding accumulation of product costs in the accounting system.

channel The distribution line that a product travels from the original manufacturer to the eventual end-user customer. The channel is typically composed of a manufacturer, a wholesaler, a retailer, and the end-user customer.

Retailing is the most visible component of our economic system. Nevertheless, we probably fail to appreciate that what happens over that last three feet of counter in the store is the culmination of the efforts of a great industrial machine and the related mass distribution system. Similar to the concept of an ecosystem in nature, manufacturers, wholesalers, and retailers are linked together in an economic system called a **channel**. If retailers cannot move goods and services the last three feet into the hands of those who will use them, the whole distribution system of manufacturing, wholesaling, and retailing falls apart.

The Distribution Channel

Exhibit 6 illustrates the channel system that typically interrelates manufacturers, wholesalers, and retailers. We've discussed manufacturing operations (the starting point of the channel) and the related management accounting systems. In order to understand the full cycle of business, we now discuss the process of distributing goods to customers. As you can see in Exhibit 6, the existence of wholesale middlemen in the distribution channel does not prevent retailers from occasionally dealing directly with manufacturers. For example, WAL-MART is noted for its

Exhibit 6: A Typical Channel of Distribution

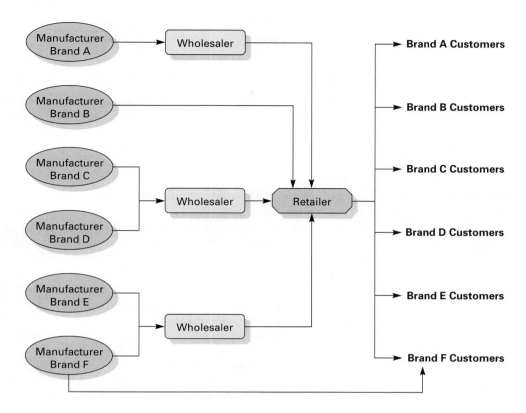

ability to use technology to make direct contact with manufacturers to obtain a significant number of its inventory items. Similarly, some manufacturers may handle some (or even all) of their distribution to retailers. HONDA and FORD, as an example, work directly with their car dealerships and bypass the wholesalers to distribute their products directly to retailers. Finally, a limited number of manufacturers, particularly small manufacturers, have direct relationships with the ultimate end-user customers of their products. They do this by setting up the well-known factory outlet store or by allowing customers to order directly from them; these direct sales are increasingly being done through the Web. A good example of this particular distribution approach is DELL COMPUTER CORPORATION. Dell is one of several large personal computer manufacturers in the United States that take orders directly from end-user customers, build computers to customer specifications, and then ship the finished computers directly to the customers.

Some people argue that the presence of middlemen simply adds to the cost of getting products from manufacturers to consumers. In some cases, this is true. The furniture store probably adds to the consumer's cost of buying a rocking chair from our example manufacturer, the Broyman Furniture Company. But the reality is that most customers cannot buy directly from furniture manufacturers. Further, Broyman may not be interested in (nor equipped for) dealing directly with its many customers! Similarly, many retailers (such as your local grocery store) are not in a position to deal directly with the manufacturers of the items they sell to the public. In addition, wholesalers may be able to provide the retailer such things as next-day delivery, unlimited returns, expert advice on merchandise selection, and customized product mix. If the cost of using a wholesaler is less than the cost to the retailers of providing these services for themselves, then the use of a middleman makes good economic sense. Hence, in providing important options, services, and convenience, wholesalers and retailers can actually add to the efficiency of the distribution system and decrease costs for the ultimate consumer. Management accountants help merchandising companies carefully manage the costs of obtaining and distributing inventory. If costs become too high, then the merchant's customers may either go to a competitor to obtain the goods or skip over the middleman to negotiate directly with the supplier.

Inventory Flow in the Distribution Channel

Spend a few minutes studying Exhibit 7. This exhibit shows the basic layout of a typical wholesaler's operation and a retailer's operation. Although the layouts of operations vary for both retailers and wholesalers, this exhibit will help us visualize the process of moving inventory from manufacturers into the hands of the ultimate end-user.

Wholesalers

Let's begin with wholesalers. **Wholesalers** generally work within a particular industry (e.g., vegetable produce, running shoes, or calculators) to secure distribution contracts with a few key manufacturers. They receive goods in huge bulk shipments that they then break down for smaller shipments to retailers. This is a lot of inventory to manage, and a lot of money is at risk. Obviously, wholesalers will not make a profit unless there is a difference between the price at which they buy goods from manufacturers and the price at which they sell goods to retailers. However, the wholesaling process is much more involved than simply managing the cost of buying and selling goods. Quality and timeliness are also important performance measures that are critical to successful wholesale management. Not only must wholesalers negotiate profitable contracts with manufacturers, but they must then handle the **logistics** of transporting those goods long distances to multiple retail locations. This requires wholesalers to work closely with large transportation companies to both receive and ship out goods as quickly and inexpensively as possible. To help control transportation costs and make the process as timely as possible, wholesalers often locate their distribution centers near large transit hubs such as train yards, shipping docks, airports, and major freeways. Usually, these distribution centers are very large buildings with little advertisement of their business to passersby. If you happen to live or travel near a large transit hub, see if you can spot these giant distribution warehouses, typically surrounded by lots of trucks, trains, or ships.

Retailers

The business process for retailers is probably quite familiar to you. Most **retailers** place orders with and receive shipments from wholesalers. As shown in the floor plan in Exhibit 7, many retailers have a receiving dock and a breakdown area used to prepare goods for display on their sales floor. Some retailers also keep a stock room for holding excess inventory. However, the cost of holding inventory in today's competitive environment is causing retailers to demand that wholesalers provide smaller and more frequent shipments. As a result, many retailers are able to avoid having a stock room. Inventory in these companies can then be moved directly from the breakdown area onto the sales floor.

Like wholesalers, retailers invest a lot of money in their inventory. Also similar to wholesalers, the big risk in the retailing business is having money tied up in inventory that is not selling. Obviously, having inventory is important to a retailer's business, but holding on to inventory for too long usually results in a significant opportunity cost. For example, as long as a shoe retailer has its money currently invested in a large inventory of running shoes, it is unable to use that money to purchase basketball shoes. These opportunity costs become particularly painful when the retailer is unable to sell its inventory of running shoes during the running season and, as a result, lacks the money to purchase basketball shoe inventory in time for the basketball season. This is why management accountants in the merchandising business are so focused on measuring stockturns. The faster you can turn your stock (i.e., sell your inventory), the sooner you have the money available to purchase more inventory to sell. Obviously, retailers are just as concerned as wholesalers with the cost and timeliness involved in managing inventory. Further, given the demanding nature of today's informed consumer, management accountants must

wholesalers Top-tier merchants who typically deal directly with the original manufacturers to distribute products to retailers.

logistics The management process involved in obtaining, managing, and transporting inventory and other assets in organizations.

retailers Second-tier merchants who typically purchase products from wholesalers to distribute to end-user customers. Many large retailers, however, often bypass wholesalers to purchase products directly from the original manufacturers.

Exhibit 7: A Comparison of the Floor Plans for a Wholesaler and a Retailer

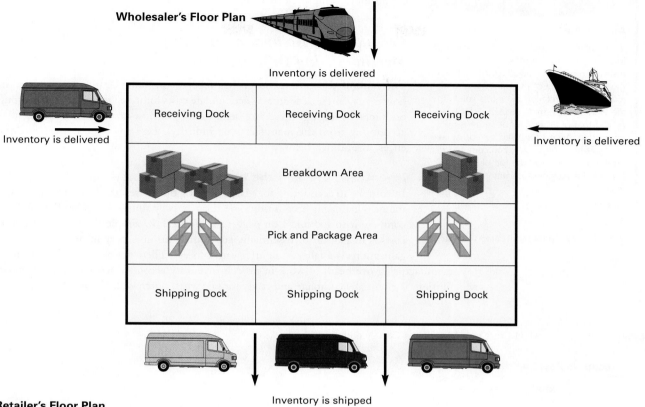

Wholesaler's Floor Plan

Inventory is delivered

Inventory is delivered

Inventory is delivered

Receiving Dock	Receiving Dock	Receiving Dock
	Breakdown Area	
	Pick and Package Area	
Shipping Dock	Shipping Dock	Shipping Dock

Inventory is shipped

Retailer's Floor Plan

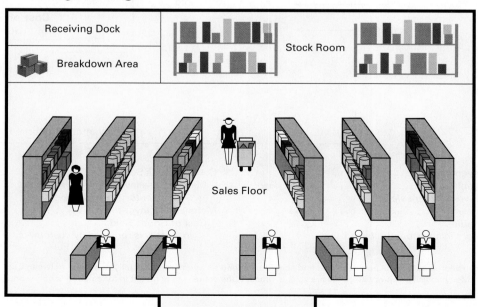

Inventory is delivered

Receiving Dock

Breakdown Area

Stock Room

Sales Floor

Store Entrance

also provide retail managers with information on inventory quality. We'll talk more about the opportunity costs of holding inventory too long in a later chapter on monitoring performance.

Product Cost Accumulation in Merchandising Organizations

The bulk of this chapter so far has focused on manufacturing companies and how management accountants accumulate costs for these organizations. Although both merchandising and service organizations borrow much of their management accounting from the manufacturing industry, there are some important differences, as outlined below.

Inventory Flow and the Income Statement

In contrast to accounting for manufacturing businesses, the flow of costs through the merchandising accounting system is relatively simple. Examine Exhibit 8 and compare it to Exhibit 3 on page 125. Notice how simple the flow of inventory costs is in Exhibit 8. Essentially, accounting for inventory in merchandising organizations is a fairly straightforward process. There are no raw materials inventory, manufacturing overhead, or work-in-process inventory accounts. Merchandise inventory, by definition, is essentially complete and ready for sale when purchased. Hence, the cost of pur-

Exhibit 8: Flow of Product Costs in a Merchant's Cost Accounting System

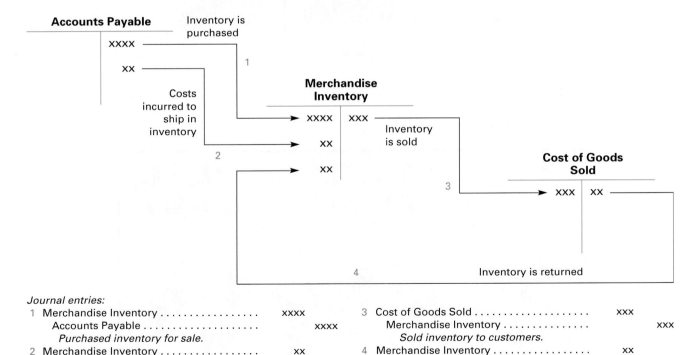

Journal entries:

1 Merchandise Inventory xxxx
    Accounts Payable xxxx
    Purchased inventory for sale.

2 Merchandise Inventory xx
    Accounts Payable xx
    Incurred freight in costs on purchased inventory.*

3 Cost of Goods Sold xxx
    Merchandise Inventory xxx
    Sold inventory to customers.

4 Merchandise Inventory xx
    Cost of Goods Sold xx
    Inventory is returned by customers.

*Note: Freight in is considered part of the purchase cost and should be added to inventory, eventually to be split between Cost of Goods Sold and the ending balance in Merchandise Inventory as goods are sold. In practice, the entire cost of freight in for a period is often simply debited directly to Cost of Goods Sold.

chased inventory is debited to Merchandise Inventory throughout the year as it is acquired.[6] Conceptually, the inventory costs for a merchant should also include all costs required to purchase the inventory, transport it to the merchant's place of business, and prepare it for sale (unpacking, displaying, etc.). Hence, the inventory cost should include the purchase price, shipping costs (freight in), insurance while in transit, administrative costs incurred by the merchant related to purchasing and handling activities, and storage costs prior to sale. In practice, though, most of these overhead-related costs, other than freight in costs, are difficult to allocate to specific inventory items. As a result, overhead costs related to merchandise inventory are often expensed as a period cost and included in Selling and General Administrative Expenses.

As inventory is sold, the cost of inventory is credited from Merchandise Inventory and debited to Cost of Goods Sold. When customers return merchandise that can be resold, Cost of Goods Sold is credited and the inventory account is debited (if the returned merchandise cannot be resold, then nothing happens in either of these particular accounts).

Tracking inventory costs in a merchant's accounting system may appear to be a fairly easy conceptual process. However, developing useful information on merchandise inventory for managers who need to plan, control, and evaluate inventory and inventory costs is a bit more involved. Managing merchandise inventory is a significant topic we'll reserve for a later chapter.

TO SUMMARIZE: Merchants are interconnected with manufacturers in a distribution channel that basically involves manufacturers selling to large-scale wholesalers, who then sell to retailers, who then sell to the end-user customer. Managing the movement (i.e., logistics) of inventory across the distribution channel is a critical business activity. Because wholesalers and retailers generally do not have to deal with raw materials or work in process, the process of accounting for inventory in a merchandising business is not nearly as complicated as it is in a manufacturing business. However, *managing* inventory costs (discussed in a later chapter on managing inventory) is both complicated and critical for a merchant.

The Flow of Services and Costs in Service Companies

6 Explain the flow of goods and services in a service organization and follow the corresponding accumulation of product costs in the accounting system.

So far in this chapter we have defined and discussed the nature of manufacturing and merchandising businesses and identified examples of companies in each type of business. The third type of business is service. What is a service business? Frankly, this is a rather difficult question. Simply stated, the service industry in the United States generally comprises all businesses that cannot be classified as merchandising or manufacturing (this assumes that we classify organizations that convert natural resources into useful products, such as farming or mining, as manufacturers). This is obviously a simple definition, but it is not very useful for us. It is important to more precisely define the service industry because nonmerchandising/nonmanufacturing businesses are the largest and fastest-growing sector in our economy. Hence, it is more likely that your career will involve working with service businesses than any other business type. For our purposes, we'll define a service business as follows:

A service business is any organization whose main economic activity involves producing a nonphysical product that provides value to a customer.

6 Recall that this method of continuously debiting and crediting Merchandise Inventory as inventory is purchased and sold (and debiting Cost of Goods Sold as inventory is sold) is called the *perpetual* inventory method of accounting. The alternative to the perpetual method is the *periodic* inventory method. There are several more accounts involved with the periodic inventory method, including Purchases, Purchase Discounts, and Purchase Returns. A significant difference between the perpetual and periodic inventory methods is that the periodic inventory method adjusts Merchandise Inventory *only at the end* of each period when cost of goods sold is calculated for the income statement.

The definition sounds pretty academic, but it needs to cover a lot of conceptual ground. As you'll see in the list in Exhibit 9, there is a lot of variety in the specific types of organizations that are neither merchandising nor manufacturing. As you study Exhibit 9, try to apply our definition of a service business to each of these categories and see if the definition fits.

Caution

When trying to decide whether a company is in the service business, consider the following old joke:

A plumber is called out to fix a clogged pipe. The plumber examines the situation for a few seconds, then pulls out a hammer and taps on the offending pipe. The problem is solved. However, the customer is a bit upset upon receiving the bill for $100.17. "All you did was tap on the pipe. I demand an itemized bill!" the customer complains. So, the plumber sends the following itemized bill:

Tapping on pipe	$ 0.17
Knowing where to tap	100.00
Total	$100.17

Remember that expertise is a significant component of most service companies.

Comparing Service and Manufacturing Business Activities

Service companies actually share more similarities with manufacturing companies than with merchandising companies. In this section, we will discuss the similarities of and the differences between service and manufacturing firms.

Similarities between Service and Manufacturing Firms

As you now understand, merchants purchase goods from manufacturers in finished condition. As a result, inventory in merchandising companies requires little, if any, conversion cost before being sold to customers. Inventory costs used to determine cost of goods sold on the merchant's income statement are relatively easy to determine. On the other hand, like manufacturers, most service companies perform a significant number of activities to prepare their service products for sale and delivery to their customers. Typically, a lot of direct labor and overhead is involved in a service business. Hence, the management process in service organizations shares a number of similarities with the process of managing a manufacturing business.

Most service companies engage in a very real production activity. However, what they provide is not nearly as tangible as the product provided by manufacturers. Yes, an architect or engineer does provide a tangible set of drawings or blueprints. But what is really being sold is the knowledge and customized advice that is represented by the drawings.

Service companies essentially build a product (the service) and deliver it to the customer (versus a merchant that resells a product built by another company). Consider the organizational effort required for a CPA firm to provide an audit service to a client. This organization is depicted in Exhibit 10. As you can see, there is direct labor (the auditing staff) involved in this audit that is supported by a complex system of supervisors, supplies, equipment, capital as-

Exhibit 9: Categories of Service Businesses

- Accounting/legal
- Architectural/engineering
- Communications (e.g., television, radio, etc.)
- Banking/financial (including insurance, investment brokers, consulting, etc.)
- Health care
- Software/systems integration (e.g., programming, installation, service, consulting, etc.)
- Marketing/advertising
- Public utilities
- Research and development
- Transportation
- Entertainment
- Education and training (not including state-owned schools and universities)

Source: Adapted from O. B. Martinson, *Cost Accounting in the Service Industry: A Critical Assessment* (Montvale, N.J.: Institute of Management Accountants, 1989).

Exhibit 10: The Service Process at a CPA Firm

sets, computer network and databases, and so forth. This support system essentially forms the overhead costs of the audit product, and these overhead costs will need to be appropriately allocated as part of the product cost of the audit. You can see, then, that there are many similarities between the process of manufacturing and service companies.

Differences between Service and Manufacturing Firms

Some service organizations do sound as though they are really in the manufacturing business. Notwithstanding, there are some important differences between most service and manufacturing businesses that affect the information provided by management accountants. Whereas manufacturers are dependent on merchants to distribute their products to the final customers, most service businesses deal directly with the end-user customer. Also, there is probably a lot more customization in the service process than in the manufacturing process. Hence, most service businesses use a job order approach rather than a process approach to cost accounting. Additionally, very little raw material is involved in the process of converting labor or capital equipment into a service product. Note, though, that items such as paper and syringes are sometimes included as part of the delivered service, but these items are not the main focus of what the customer is paying to receive. As a result, raw material inventories are typically insignificant or nonexistent in a service business. Similarly, it is often difficult to store a finished service in anticipation of a later sale to customers, making finished goods inventories insignificant or nonexistent. At the close of a reporting period, however, most service companies will be in the process of completing a service for delivery to a customer. This indicates that work-in-process inventories exist and may be significant for many service organizations. (We will discuss work-in-process inventories further below.)

Product Cost Accumulation in Service Organizations

As you now understand, there are a number of accounting similarities between manufacturing and service organizations. One important similarity is that both manufacturing and service organizations use a significant amount of direct labor in producing their products. In addition, large amounts of overhead costs typically are allocated to individual products. Similar to many manufacturers, service businesses often allocate overhead on the basis of direct labor hours. One important difference is that manufacturers must also manage large amounts of raw materials costs, while the materials included in the services sold by service companies are typically limited to insignificant amounts of supplies used in the service process.

FYI:

Over the past 100 years, costs for raw materials in manufacturing firms have averaged nearly 50% of total product costs.

"Inventory" Flow and the Income Statement in Service Companies

Exhibit 11 summarizes the flow of costs for a service company. Comparing Exhibit 11 to Exhibits 3 and 8 illustrates that accounting for service cost flows can be more complicated than accounting for merchandise inventory cost flows, but is quite similar to accounting for manufacturing cost flows. Materials (e.g., supplies), labor, and overhead costs are all involved in, and should be assigned to, the process of creating and delivering a service product to the customer.

The overhead for service firms can involve nearly any kind of management costs—service firms generally do not distinguish between manufacturing and administrative overhead costs. Allocating overhead to service activities generally involves factoring an overhead rate into the billing rate used to charge customers. Think about all the services you buy and use. Often, some type of a billing rate per hour or per event is used to determine the price you pay for the service. For example, accountants, lawyers, consultants, computer programmers, and automotive repair shops often charge by the hour. When you get the bill, you understand that the huge rate per hour does not represent solely the wage or salary of the professional who provided the service to you. This rate has been enhanced (sometimes significantly!) in order to cover all the overhead and supplies costs necessary to support the work done by the service professional. Similarly, doctors, trainers, entertainers, and transportation companies usually charge by event. You understand that the doctor isn't paid the full $175 charge when he or she gives you a physical exam. Much of that amount goes to pay for the costs of staff, equipment, and building occupancy necessary to support the actual service provided by your doctor.

Assigning overhead costs to a service event follows a pattern very similar to that for manufacturing firms. Total overhead for the service organization is estimated for a period of time, generally a year. This estimated overhead is then divided by an appropriate activity measure. For an accountant, this activity measure may be billable hours. The measure for a bank could be the number of teller transactions or number of accounts. For a cable TV company, it could be the average number of accounts expected for the year or the total billable months of service. The activity measure for an electric company might be the expected number of kilowatts produced during the next year. Other examples of possible overhead rate calculations for several types of service companies are shown below.

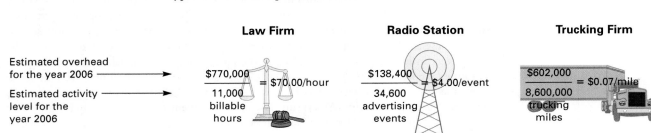

Exhibit 11: Summary of Service Cost Flows

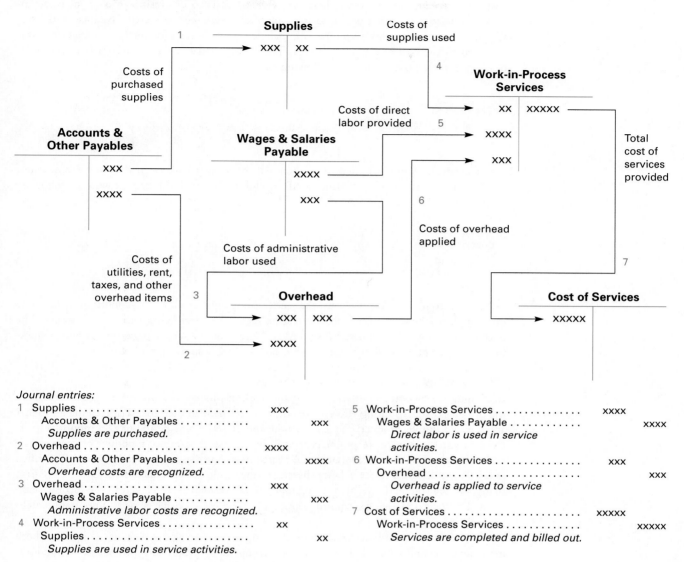

Journal entries:

1 Supplies xxx
  Accounts & Other Payables   xxx
  Supplies are purchased.
2 Overhead xxxx
  Accounts & Other Payables   xxxx
  Overhead costs are recognized.
3 Overhead xxx
  Wages & Salaries Payable xxx
  Administrative labor costs are recognized.
4 Work-in-Process Services xx
  Supplies xx
  Supplies are used in service activities.

5 Work-in-Process Services xxxx
  Wages & Salaries Payable   xxxx
  Direct labor is used in service
  activities.
6 Work-in-Process Services xxx
  Overhead   xxx
  Overhead is applied to service
  activities.
7 Cost of Services xxxxx
  Work-in-Process Services   xxxxx
  Services are completed and billed out.

STOP & THINK

The selection of the activity base that is used to allocate overhead is a very important management decision because any particular activity base could have a significant impact on how much cost is assigned to one product versus another. For example, suppose that the academic advisement center at your college is trying to determine what it costs to provide advisement services to a specific student each semester. What are some possible activity bases this department might use to allocate the costs of the office equipment, supervisor salary, and other overhead items? Would your choice of a base have an effect on which students are then identified as "high-cost-to-serve" students?

With a predetermined overhead rate, service companies are able to allocate overhead costs to service events as they occur. This method of allocating overhead helps managers control overhead costs, establish prices for services provided, and measure profit on each service event or contract. The overhead account for a service company is used in much the same manner as in a manufacturing firm. As actual overhead costs are incurred, they are debited to the overhead account rather than being debited to an expense account. Then, as the appropriate overhead activities actually take place (e.g., consulting hours, teller transactions, and kilowatts), overhead costs are allocated to Work-in-Process Services (more about this account in the next section). As services are actually billed, these overhead costs are combined with the direct labor costs of the service professionals (if any) and any incidental costs of supplies are debited to Cost of Services (an account very similar to the cost of goods sold account used by manufacturers and merchants). At the end of the year (or any other time period relevant to the company), the total actual overhead costs are compared to the total allocated overhead costs to determine an over- or underapplied overhead amount. If overhead is overapplied, there will be a credit balance in the service company's overhead account. This balance means that too much overhead cost was allocated to the cost of service activities. The overapplied costs are removed (and the overhead account is closed) with the following entry:

Overhead	xxx	
Cost of Services		xxx

If overhead is underapplied, then there will be a debit balance in the overhead account, and Cost of Services is adjusted (increased) by closing the overhead account with the following entry:

Cost of Services	xxx	
Overhead		xxx

Similar to manufacturing firms, the service company may choose to apportion the over- or underapplied overhead amount between Cost of Services and Work-in-Process Services. The question you might be asking at this point is, "Why would a service organization have a work-in-process inventory account?" Good question! We'll talk about this account next.

Who Has Work-in-Process Inventory?

In manufacturing companies, accounting for work-in-process inventory is a significant part of the product cost accounting effort. Costs of resources used in the process of creating a product are attached to that product. Typically, at the end of an income period (e.g., a month, a quarter, or a year), a number of products are still in process. A significant amount of costs can be tied up in these in-process products. GAAP requires that these costs be capitalized (identified as assets) and assigned to the balance sheet until the products are actually sold. Only at the time that goods are sold and revenue is recognized are the related costs charged to the income statement. The basic underlying accounting concept behind this approach is the all-important matching principle.

The logic for identifying work-in-process inventory as a balance sheet asset applies to both manufacturing and service businesses. Service companies typically earn revenue as the service is provided to the customer. At the end of an accounting period, however, significant effort and resources may have been invested in a service product that is not yet completed for the customer. As a result, revenue is not yet earned, and the costs invested at this point should not be recognized as expenses. In other words, until they actually complete the project and bill it to the client, service companies have work in process.

The following are some examples of work in process that are likely to exist at the end of an accounting period for various types of service companies:[7]

- Accounting/legal—An audit that will take three months to complete is in its initial stage.
- Architectural/engineering—The blueprints for a large construction project are only partially completed.
- Banking/financial—The fieldwork has been completed and the lending documents are being finalized for a large loan that will be closed next month.

---

7 O. B. Martinson, *Cost Accounting in the Service Industry: A Critical Assessment* (Montvale, N.J.: Institute of Management Accountants, 1989), pp. 47–48.

- Marketing/advertising—Three weeks of effort have been expended on the development of a new advertising campaign that will not be ready for presentation to the client for another three weeks.
- Transportation—A large shipment of coal is being held in a midwestern freight yard en route to its shipping point on the East Coast.

In each of these examples, resources have been invested in creating a service that the customer has not yet received. As a result, work in process exists and should be recognized on the balance sheet. As you can see in Exhibit 11, as supplies and labor costs are directly invested in the process of creating a service for customers, these amounts are debited to Work-in-Process Services. As overhead costs such as utilities, rent, taxes, and support staff salaries are incurred, these costs are debited to the overhead account and are subsequently allocated to Work-in-Process Services using an overhead rate. When the service is completed and delivered to the customer, then the revenue earning process is complete and the service costs are transferred out of Work-in-Process Services and into Cost of Services.[8]

TO SUMMARIZE: Essentially, a service business is any organization whose main economic activity involves producing a nonphysical product that provides value to a customer. Because service companies generally create the service they provide, they have some similarities with manufacturing companies in both the management and the accounting processes, including the need to manage and account for work in process. A major difference between service and manufacturing operations is that raw materials typically are not a significant component of a service company's product. Costs flow through a service firm in a manner very similar to a manufacturing firm. Costs of supplies (usually insignificant in size) and direct labor (usually significant in size) accumulate in an account called Work-in-Process Services. This account performs much the same function as a work-in-process inventory account in a manufacturing firm. In addition, overhead must often be applied to Work-in-Process Services as service activities take place. The process of applying overhead is typically done using a predetermined overhead application rate.

The Effect of E-Business

7 Understand the impact of e-business on product costing.

Before we conclude the main part of this chapter, we should say a little about the impact of e-business on business organizations and the product costing process.[9] First of all, it is important to understand that e-business is not a separate new industry like manufacturing, merchandising, or service. Rather, e-business provides new platforms for conducting business *within* the current industries in the economy.

You have probably had some experience in shopping on the Internet. Most organizations today have an Internet site. Often all you have to do is open your Internet browser and add a ".com" to the end of the name of your favorite company, and you can be doing business with that company in no time. Obviously, a lot of business is being transacted on the Internet. However, the lion's share of Internet business is *not* taking place with individual consumers like most of us. To help you understand this point, we need to distinguish between two kinds of e-business. One kind is conducted between companies and consumers (or end-users). This sort of business is often referred to as business-to-consumer (or "B2C"). When you shop at WALMART.COM or NORDSTROMS.COM, you're engaged in B2C e-business. B2C e-business in the United

8 Some fairly large long-term service contracts are sometimes designed to allow the provider to bill and receive partial payments as the contract is completed. In these cases, as the revenue process is partially completed, some service costs can be transferred out of Work-in-Process Services and into Cost of Services. Learning about this type of accounting, called percentage-of-completion accounting, is reserved for more advanced accounting courses.

9 Some of the material in this section is based on information presented in S. M. Glover, S. W. Liddle, and D. F. Prawitt, *eBusiness: Principles & Strategies for Accountants*, 2nd ed. (Upper Saddle River, N.J.: Prentice Hall, 2002).

The Birth of an e-Business
Jeffrey P. Bezos quit his lucrative job with a New York investment firm and moved his family to Seattle, Washington, to start a new company in a new industry. A short time later, on July 16, 1995, AMAZON.COM, the largest e-tailer in the world in 2001, opened its Web doors. After having 300 of his friends and family members test the site, Jeff asked them to tell everyone they knew about Amazon.com. Within 30 days, with no press or traditional advertising, Amazon.com had sold books in all 50 states and 45 countries—an instant Web success! How did this all begin?

Amazon.com began as a bookseller over the Internet that offered competitive prices, accessibility, and extreme convenience. It was readily apparent to Bezos, as his book-selling Web site grew exceptionally fast, that Amazon.com could become the "Earth's Biggest Store." In 1998, Amazon.com offered its first product other than books—music CDs. From there, Amazon.com has expanded into videos, DVD movies, toys, hardware, greeting cards, electronics, software, home improvement products, auctions, and more. How does Amazon.com manage this huge distribution channel?

With more than 2 million unique visitors a month currently, Amazon.com has established a highly automated system that prides itself on discovering and satisfying customer needs. In addition, the Amazon system must maintain a critical relationship with manufacturers and suppliers. One glitch in the system could spell disaster for the company and its end-users (us!). The life of an order begins well before a customer hits the "Buy it" button on the site. Management must forecast consumer needs, arrange to be able to ship merchandise from suppliers on demand, maintain a precise calculation of inventory available from its suppliers, and meet customer demands quickly and effectively. One of the original strengths of Amazon's business model was that it rarely held inventory (recently, Amazon expanded its business operations significantly by building some large distribution warehouses that do hold inventory). Instead, in many cases Amazon has direct connections to its suppliers that allow customer orders to be shipped directly from supplier to customer. Computers track most of this complicated distribution channel, but it is the knowledge of management that ultimately provides the success that Amazon.com enjoys.

Source: J. C. Ramo, "1999 Person of the Year," *Time*, December 27, 1999.

FYI:

Many people originally predicted that the Internet would significantly change how goods and services are sold. The reality is that, in the first quarter of 2003, only 1.5% of consumer retail sales takes place on the Internet. In other words, the Internet is not creating a lot of new sales. Nevertheless, 1.5% of retail sales in the first quarter of 2003 represents nearly $14 billion! More importantly, the percentage of Internet retail sales has doubled since the first quarter of 2001.

Source: U.S. Department of Commerce News, May 23, 2003.

States amounted to 71 billion in 2001 and is expected to continue growing at a significant rate in the future. In addition, business also takes place between businesses, such as the purchase of raw materials, consulting, outsourcing of services, and important partnerships or joint ventures where companies work together to provide goods and services to the public. When this work is managed with Internet-type technology, it is referred to as a business-to-business process (or "B2B"). This aspect of e-business is, frankly, huge. B2B e-business amounted to $995 billion in 2001 and is growing very fast![10]

As manufacturers, merchants, and service providers move more and more of their business onto the Internet, they expect to enjoy a number of significant benefits, including expanded sales opportunities; improved communications, customer service, and loyalty; and better management of human resources and supply channels. Perhaps most relevant to this chapter is the fact that companies expect to lower their costs of business using Internet technology. For example, bank transactions involving a teller cost an average of $1.07 per transaction. On the other hand, ATM transactions cost just $0.39. However, when you log on to your bank at its ".com" Internet site, an online banking transaction costs only $0.01! As another example, IBM bought $13 billion worth of goods and services

---

10 U.S. Census Bureau, 2001 E-commerce Multi-Sector Report (March 19, 2003).

over the Internet in 1999, saving more than $270 million in procurement costs. Further, SOUTHWEST AIRLINES saved $80 million in 2000 in commissions and reservation-system fees by Web-enabling its reservation and ticketing processes. E-billing, the delivery of routine bills online, can save as much as 60% per bill in handling costs. Hence, cost savings in running a billing process at a large utility could be as much as $50 million per year when an e-billing process is implemented. WAL-MART has achieved tremendous improvements in the costs, quality, and timing of goods purchased from wholesalers through the use of inventory management systems that have direct Internet-based connections to its suppliers. Even hiring costs can be reduced, as evidenced by the fact that IBM has installed Internet software that has cut the cost of hiring temporary workers by $3 million annually.

E-business can have tremendous impacts on product costs. Specifically, costs of raw materials are reduced as organizations use the Internet to find and demand better pricing and save significant costs in the process of ordering and managing raw material inventories. Costs of direct labor can also be better managed by using the Internet to identify, hire, and train the organization's workforce. In some cases, direct service labor, such as bank tellers, are redeployed to new assignments in the organization as Internet technology becomes the means of interacting with clients and customers. Perhaps most significantly, companies are making significant changes in the structure of their organizations, which can greatly affect the costs of overhead. At many companies, overhead costs are much higher than the costs of raw materials/supplies and direct labor combined, so finding new ways to handle the management and logistics of a company can have immediate and important impacts on costs. The example of IBM using the Internet to change the way it obtains goods and services (and temporary employees) demonstrates the savings that can result.

FYI:

Car manufacturers are rushing to become "the Dell of automobile manufacturing." DELL COMPUTERS has made an important name for itself by its ability to use the Internet to deliver custom-built computers to individual customers in a matter of days. Harold Kutner, a GM executive, is one example of a business professional who is focused on using the Internet (as well as a complete redesign of the GM design and production process) to deliver custom-built cars in 4 to 11 days (down from the normal 3 to 8 weeks).

Source: G. L. White, "Heavy Tech: Big U.S. Car Makers May Take Internet to the Next Level," *The Wall Street Journal*, December 3, 1999.

TO SUMMARIZE: E-business and Internet technology are dramatically changing all types of business organizations, including manufacturing, merchandising, and service organizations. As these companies make adjustments in both their organizational structure and in the way they connect to and do business with suppliers and customers within their distribution channel, there have been (and will continue to be) significant changes and improvements in the costs, quality, and timeliness of goods and services. These changes are affecting the process of both business-to-consumer (B2C) and business-to-business (B2B) operations.

In the first part of the chapter we illustrated product costing using the job order costing method. This method is commonly used in both manufacturing and service organizations. In this expanded material section, we discuss how companies, predominantly manufacturers, use process costing when it is difficult to specifically identify unique products or jobs during the manufacturing process.

The Process Costing System

8 Use the FIFO method to do process costing.

All the product costing methods described so far in this chapter assume that the accountant is able to specifically identify the job (i.e., the product or service) being produced for customers.

By identifying each specific job, the accountant is then able to specifically track a job as it moves through the work-in-process inventory and into the finished goods inventory. While it is in the production process, the accountant assigns the actual direct materials and direct labor costs, as well as allocates a specific amount of overhead costs, that are required to produce a particular job. This cost accounting method is often referred to as job order costing. Some manufacturing companies cannot use job order costing because they cannot specifically identify each job (product) being produced. Examples of such companies include manufacturers of bricks, lumber, paint, soft drinks, and newspapers and most food processing plants. These companies manufacture large volumes of product using a series of uniform processes. For these companies, **process costing** is the appropriate product cost accounting method. Because these companies can't focus on costing a particular job, they focus on costing the amount of work done for a particular *period of time*. We'll talk more about this concept of work done in a particular time period below. For now, remember that for process costing to be appropriate, two general conditions typically exist:

1. The activities performed in each process center are identical for all units.
2. The units produced as a result of passing through the process centers are basically the same.

Steps in Process Costing

A firm whose products and processes meet the preceding conditions would employ process costing using five steps:

1. Identify units that went into the process and identify where those units are at the end of the processing time. Determine the amount of "work done" (equivalent units of production) during the processing time period.
2. Determine the amount of production costs that went into the process and compute the product costs per unit for the processing time period.
3. Compute the total cost of units completed and transferred out (cost of goods manufactured) during the processing time period.
4. Compute the total cost of units remaining in process (ending work-in-process inventory) at the end of the processing time period.
5. Prepare the production cost report.

Step 1. Compute Equivalent Units of Production

The first step in process costing is to track the flow of units and compute the **equivalent units of production**. The concept of equivalent units of production essentially means to calculate the amount of work actually done during any particular period of time in terms of units of output. It's really a very simple concept. For example, let's assume that you are being paid by the hour to hand paint porcelain figurines for a small local art shop. It's an arduous process, taking several hours to paint a single figurine. On average, you can do only three or four figurines per day. At the end of your first day on the job, you have painted three figurines and have another one nearly complete. If your boss were to ask you how much work you did for the day, are you going to reply that you painted only three figurines? Of course not! Instead, you'll likely tell her that you completely painted three figurines and that you have another one nearly done (let's say it is 90% done). So, did you paint four figurines? Not really. The amount of work done on your first day is 3.9 figurines (three whole units plus 90% of a fourth unit), right? In other words, you did 3.9 equivalent units of production. The work that you have done includes one unit in ending work-in-process inventory (the figurine that is 90% done).

The more interesting measure of equivalent units of production is what happens on your second day on the job. When you come back to the shop the next day, the first thing you will do is work on that day's beginning work-in-process inventory, which is the figurine that is 90% done from the day before.[11] Let's assume that you then start and complete three more figurines.

---

process costing A method of product costing whereby costs are accumulated by process or work centers and averaged over all products manufactured in a center or department during a particular production period. There are two methods of process costing: The FIFO method separately tracks the costs of beginning work-in-process units and the costs of units started in the current production period. The weighted-average method (not discussed in this text) averages together the costs of beginning work-in-process units and the costs of units started in the current production period.

equivalent units of production A method used in a process costing system to measure the production output during a period. Equivalent units of production essentially measures the "work done" by the center or department in terms of units of output.

---

11 This is the reason we call this particular method of process costing the FIFO (first in, first out) method. It is based on the assumption that all beginning work-in-process inventory is completed before any new units are started.

Before it's time to go home, you are able to start one more figurine and get it about 30% done. Now how do you answer the boss's question about how much work was done on your second day? You completed a total of four figurines (the figurine that was work-in-process when you came to work plus three more that were both started and completed this same day), but to say that you did the work of four figurines isn't quite accurate, is it? To be accurate, you completed 10% of one figurine, 100% of three figurines, and 30% of a final figurine that is still work-in-process. In other words, the work done for the day was 3.4 figurines, computed as follows:

	Physical Units	Percent Completed (i.e., "work done")	Equivalent Units of Production
Beginning work-in-process	1	× 10%	= 0.1
Started and completed	3	× 100%	= 3.0
Ending work-in-process	1	× 30%	= 0.3
Total equivalent units of production			3.4

With this example of equivalent units of production in mind, let's now use an example that's more representative of manufacturers that follow the process costing approach to accounting for product costs. Exhibit 12 shows how products and costs move through the two process centers (mixing and bagging) of the Allied Cement Company. For now, we will focus on the process costing for the mixing center at Allied Cement. Production units at Allied are measured in pounds of finished cement. When the mixing machines are shut down at the end of a production period (let's assume a production period at Allied is one month), not all pounds of cement started the last day of the month in the mixing center will have been completed. In fact, as at most manufacturers, units are usually in process at both the beginning and the end of a period. Were it not for these beginning and ending work-in-process inventories, the number of units actually produced in the mixing center for the period could be determined merely by counting all pounds of cement that were transferred out of the mixing center and into the bagging center. However, as you saw in our earlier example of hand painting figurines, the amount of work actually done in the mixing center for the period also includes how much work was done in the beginning and ending work-in-process inventories.

With this in mind, look at the report below on equivalent units of production for the mixing center.

Step 1: Compute equivalent units of production.

	Physical Units (pounds)	Direct Materials Costs		Conversion Costs	
		Percent Done	Equivalent Units	Percent Done	Equivalent Units
Beginning work-in-process	4,000	× 0%	= 0	× 80%	= 3,200
Started and completed	44,000	× 100%	= 44,000	× 100%	= 44,000
Ending work-in-process	2,000	× 100%	= 2,000	× 60%	= 1,200
Equivalent units of production			46,000		48,400
Transferred out (to Bagging)	48,000				

The "Physical Units" column reports that the mixing center had 4,000 pounds of cement in beginning work-in-process when the month started. The department finished mixing these 4,000 pounds and mixed an additional 44,000 pounds before the end of the month, allowing the mixing center to transfer a total of 48,000 pounds to the bagging center. At the end of the month, 2,000 pounds of cement remained in ending work-in-process.

Exhibit 12: The Flow of Products and Costs through Process Centers

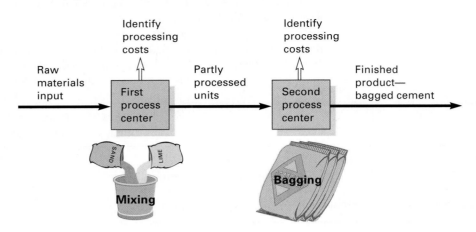

FYI:

In the FIFO approach to process costing, the total *physical* units "started" always equal total units "started and completed" plus total units in "ending work-in-process." Similarly, the total *physical* units "transferred out" always equal total units "started and completed" plus total units in "beginning work-in-process."

conversion costs The costs of converting raw materials to finished products; include direct labor and manufacturing overhead costs.

Now look at the "Equivalent Units" column for the Direct Materials Costs. In this case, all of the materials necessary to mix a pound of cement are put in place at the beginning of the mixing process. In other words, when the month began, the 4,000 pounds of cement in beginning work-in-process were already 100% complete in terms of materials. Similarly, at the end of the month, the 2,000 pounds of cement in ending work-in-process were 100% complete in terms of materials. As a result, the equivalent units of production (i.e., "work done") to be used when accounting for costs of direct materials for Allied is simply the number of pounds of cement *started* into production during the production period, or 100% of units started and completed plus 100% of units in ending work-in-process (and 0% of units in beginning work-in-process).[12]

Finally, look at the "Equivalent Units" column under "Conversion Costs." **Conversion costs** is the term we use to describe all product costs necessary to "convert" raw materials into finished goods. Hence, conversion costs include all costs of direct labor and manufacturing overhead.[13] In this example, at the beginning of the month, the beginning work-in-process inventory was 20% complete in terms of costs of direct labor and manufacturing overhead. As a result, the first work done in the mixing center for the current production period was to finish the remaining 80% of the effort required to complete these 4,000 pounds of cement. In other words, the mixing center did 3,200 equivalent units of production (4,000 × 80%) on beginning work-in-process. At the end of the month, there were 2,000 pounds in ending work-in-process that were 60% complete in terms of direct labor and manufacturing overhead costs, which means that the mixing center did 1,200 equivalent units of production (2,000 × 60%) on ending work-in-process. When combined with the work done on units started and completed, the mixing center's "work done" in terms of direct labor and manufacturing overhead was 48,400 equivalent units (3,200 + 44,000 + 1,200).

Step 2. Compute the Product Costs per Unit

With Step 1 completed, we know how much work was done in terms of production output for the mixing center. Now, to compute the product cost per unit, we need to determine how

---

12 When computing equivalent units in this chapter, we will always assume that direct materials are all added at the beginning of the process. However, this assumption is not always the case in actual companies.

13 Because we assume in this example that costs of manufacturing overhead are being allocated on the basis of direct labor, we can combine the equivalent units calculation for direct labor and for manufacturing overhead costs into one calculation for conversion costs. This is the assumption that we will follow for all subsequent equivalent units calculations in this chapter.

much was spent on production. For the mixing center, we will assume that the beginning work-in-process of 4,000 pounds includes $800 in direct materials and $1,200 in direct labor and manufacturing overhead (i.e., conversion costs). Further, Allied spent $9,660 for direct materials and $70,180 for conversion costs in the current production period. Computing the product costs per unit (pound) for the mixing department is then a simple matter of dividing the product costs by the appropriate equivalent units of production, reported as follows:

Step 2: Compute the product costs per unit.

	Total Costs	Equivalent Units	Cost per Unit
Beginning work-in-process			
Direct materials costs	$ 800	× 4,000	= $0.20
Conversion costs	1,200	× 800	= 1.50
Total	$ 2,000		**$1.70**
Current period			
Direct materials costs	$ 9,660	× 46,000	= $0.21
Conversion costs	70,180	× 48,400	= 1.45
Total	$79,840		**$1.66**

Caution

When using beginning work-in-process in the calculation of equivalent units of production for the current production period, remember to use the percentage *yet to be done*. In other words, the "work done" in the current period on *beginning* work-in-process is:

$$\text{Number of physical units in inventory} \times (1 - \text{Percent completed})$$

The "work done" on *ending* work-in-process for the current period is:

$$\text{Number of physical units in inventory} \times \text{Percent completed}$$

As you can see in the report above on product costs per unit, Allied spent $0.21 per pound for direct materials in the mixing center in the current production period. This cost is based on dividing the total equivalent units of 46,000 for work done on direct materials into the total direct materials costs of $9,660. Bearing in mind that beginning work-in-process came from the previous production period, Allied can compare the current direct materials cost to the direct materials cost in the previous production period, which was $0.20 per pound. This cost is obtained by dividing the costs of direct materials in beginning work-in-process by the equivalent units in beginning work-in-process (remember that when the day begins, all 4,000 pounds in inventory are 100% done with respect to direct materials). The current-period conversion cost per unit is $1.45, based on dividing the total equivalent units of 48,400 for work done in terms of direct labor and manufacturing overhead into the total conversion costs of $70,180. Again, Allied's management can check their efforts to control conversion costs by comparing the current-period costs with the previous period's cost of $1.50 per pound, which is calculated by dividing conversion costs in beginning work-in-process by the work already done in beginning work-in-process when the month begins (800 equivalent pounds = 4,000 physical pounds × 20% "work done").

Step 3. Compute the Costs Transferred Out

Allied has spent a total of $79,840 in the current production period in the mixing center. In addition, when the production period began, there was work-in-process inventory in the mixing center that had a total value of $2,000. Hence, as you can see in the report above on product costs per unit, the mixing center needs to account for $81,840. Assuming that there has been no waste or pilferage in the mixing process, at the end of the production period all costs have either been transferred out to the bagging center or remain in ending work-in-process. To compute the costs transferred out to the bagging center, the mixing center needs to account for the costs of completing the cement in beginning work-in-process, as well as the cement that was started and completed in the current period. The following report shows the costs transferred out:

Step 3: Compute the costs transferred out.

	Cost per Unit	Equivalent Units	
Beginning work-in-process			
Initial direct materials costs			$ 800
Initial conversion costs			1,200
Costs to complete materials	$0.21	× 0	= 0
Costs to complete conversion	$1.45	× 3,200	= 4,640
Total			$ 6,640
Started and completed	$1.66	× 44,000	= 73,040
Total costs transferred out			**$79,680**

As you can see in the above report, the mixing center did not need to add any more direct materials costs to complete the beginning work-in-process. However, there were 3,200 equivalent units of work in terms of direct labor and manufacturing overhead that needed to be completed in the current period before the 4,000 pounds of cement in beginning work-in-process could be transferred out to the bagging center. Hence, the mixing department spent $4,640 in conversion costs ($1.45 per unit × 3,200 equivalent units) to complete the mixing on beginning work-in-process. When added to the initial beginning work-in-process costs of $2,000 ($800 + $1,200), the first 4,000 pounds of cement transferred to the bagging center carried total production costs of $6,640.

Of the total 48,000 pounds transferred to the bagging center, 44,000 pounds were started and completed in the current production period. At a total cost per unit of $1.66 ($0.21 per unit for direct materials + $1.45 per unit for direct labor and manufacturing overhead), the mixing department spent $73,040 to mix the remaining units transferred out of its operations in the current production period.

Step 4. Compute Costs of Ending Work-in-Process Inventory

The fourth step in the mixing center's process costing effort is to determine the costs of the 2,000 pounds of cement remaining in work-in-process inventory at the end of the current production period. These calculations are reported below.

Step 4: Compute costs of ending work-in-process inventory.

	Cost per Unit	Equivalent Units	
Costs for direct materials	$0.21	× 2,000	= $ 420
Conversion costs	$1.45	× 1,200	= 1,740
Cost of ending work-in-process			**$2,160**

Because all 2,000 pounds are 100% complete in terms of direct materials, this inventory represents $420 ($0.21 per unit × 2,000 pounds × 100%) in direct materials costs. On the other hand, because these 2,000 pounds are only 60% complete in terms of direct labor and manufacturing overhead, there are $1,740 ($1.45 per unit × 2,000 pounds × 60%) in conversion costs residing in ending work-in-process inventory. In total, ending work-in-process contains $2,160 ($420 + $1,740) in product costs.

Step 5. Prepare the Production Cost Report

All the data calculated so far are combined into the **production cost report** for the mixing center. This report is shown in Exhibit 13. As you can see, this report includes a large number of calculations. However, we've carefully worked through all the calculations in this report together, so you should feel fairly comfortable understanding how it all fits together. (You'll feel

production cost report A document that compiles all the costs of a manufacturing center for a particular production period. The information on this report is used to control and evaluate production costs, as well as transfer costs and units of output from one manufacturing center to another.

Exhibit 13: A Production Cost Report

Allied Cement Company
Mixing Center
Production Cost Report
For the Month of October 2006

Equivalent Units of Production

	Physical Units (pounds)	Direct Materials Costs		Conversion Costs	
		Percent Done	Equivalent Units	Percent Done	Equivalent Units
Beginning work-in-process	4,000	× 0%	= 0	× 80%	= 3,200
Started and completed	44,000	× 100%	= 44,000	× 100%	= 44,000
Ending work-in-process	2,000	× 100%	= 2,000	× 60%	= 1,200
Equivalent units of production			**46,000**		**48,400**
Transferred out.	48,000				

Product Costs Per Unit

	Total Costs	Equivalent Units	Cost per Unit
Beginning work-in-process			
Direct materials costs.	$ 800	÷ 4,000	= $0.20
Conversion costs	1,200	÷ 800	= 1.50
Total	$ 2,000		**$1.70**
Current period			
Direct materials costs.	$ 9,660	÷ 46,000	= $0.21
Conversion costs	70,180	÷ 48,400	= 1.45
Total	$79,840		**$1.66**
TOTAL DOLLARS IN	**$81,840**		

Costs Transferred Out

	Cost per Unit	Equivalent Units	
Beginning work-in-process			
Initial direct materials costs			$ 800
Initial conversion costs.			1,200
Costs to complete materials	$0.21	× 0	= 0
Costs to complete conversion.	$1.45	× 3,200	= 4,640
Total			$ 6,640
Started and completed	$1.66	× 44,000	= 73,040
Total costs transferred out			**$79,680**

Costs of Ending Work-in-Process

	Cost per Unit	Equivalent Units	
Costs for direct materials.	$0.21	× 2,000	= $ 420
Conversion costs.	$1.45	× 1,200	= 1,740
Cost of ending work-in-process.			**$ 2,160**
TOTAL DOLLARS OUT.			**$81,840**

more comfortable once you've worked through the review problem at the end of this chapter and a few homework problems!) Remember that the report is composed of four overall steps, each of which should make sense to you.

When a lot of calculations are involved, as in the production cost report in Exhibit 13, a good check figure can be a wonderful tool! Notice in Exhibit 13 that the arrows point to a very good check figure—$81,840. This amount represents the total dollars that have gone into the mixing center in the current period ($2,000 in beginning work-in-process + $79,840 in current production costs), as well as the total dollars that have come out of the mixing process ($79,680 transferred out + $2,160 in ending work-in-process). If the production cost report can balance out to this check figure, you have good (though not perfect) assurance that the calculations have been done correctly.

TO SUMMARIZE: Process costing involves five steps: (1) determine the amount of "work done" (equivalents units of production) during the processing time period, (2) compute the product costs per unit by dividing total costs by "work done," (3) compute the total cost of units completed and transferred out, (4) compute the total cost of units in ending work-in-process inventory, and (5)

prepare the production cost report. With process costing, both units and costs must be transferred from one process center to the next until the final unit cost is accumulated at the end of the total production process. The production cost report provides a method of accounting for the flow of units and costs between process centers.

review of learning objectives

Understand the difficulty, yet importance, of having accurate product cost information. It is usually easy to associate direct materials and direct labor costs with specific products. However, it is very difficult, and often even arbitrary, to assign overhead costs to specific products. Hence, it is difficult to accurately determine the cost of products because overhead costs have to be estimated before being incurred; they often cannot be easily assigned to units produced; and they are often "lumpy"—that is, overhead costs typically do not follow the same even flow pattern of production and service output as followed by direct materials and direct labor. Regardless of the difficulty, however, having accurate product cost information is critical for management to make good planning, controlling, and evaluation decisions.

2 Explain the flow of goods and services in a manufacturing organization and follow the corresponding accumulation of product costs in the accounting system. In a manufacturing firm, employees work with raw materials to make finished goods to be sold to customers. When purchased, raw materials are stored in a raw materials warehouse as raw materials inventory; as they are manufactured, goods move through the factory floor as work-in-process inventory; when completed, goods are stored in a finished goods warehouse as finished goods inventory. The costs of direct materials and direct labor (factory employees who work directly in

production) are combined with manufacturing overhead costs as goods are being produced to make up the cost of finished goods. The process of tracing manufacturing costs to specific goods typically follows an accounting method traditionally known as job order costing. When a manufacturing firm purchases materials, the costs are recorded in a raw materials inventory account. As direct materials are used, costs are removed from this account and debited to Work-in-Process Inventory. Direct labor and manufacturing overhead costs are also debited to Work-in-Process Inventory. As units are completed, the costs in Work-in-Process Inventory are transferred to Finished Goods Inventory. When the units are sold, the costs are transferred to Cost of Goods Sold. Whereas direct materials and direct labor costs assigned to products are actual costs, manufacturing overhead is transferred to Work-in-Process Inventory and assigned to products on the basis of some predetermined overhead rate.

3 Understand the process of accounting for overhead. *Estimated* manufacturing overhead costs for a period are determined at the beginning of the period and combined with an estimated level of activity (such as direct labor hours) to create the predetermined overhead rate that is used to allocate overhead costs to products as they are produced. As *actual* manufacturing overhead costs are incurred, they are debited to Manufacturing Overhead. This account is credited (and

Work-in-Process Inventory is debited) as overhead costs are applied to specific jobs on the basis of the predetermined rate. At the end of the period, if total *applied* manufacturing overhead costs are larger (smaller) than total *actual* manufacturing overhead costs, the manufacturing overhead account will have a credit (debit) balance, indicating that manufacturing overhead costs were overapplied (underapplied). The debit or credit balance in the manufacturing overhead account is either closed directly to Cost of Goods Sold or allocated among Cost of Goods Sold, Finished Goods Inventory, and Work-in-Process Inventory.

4 Create a Cost of Goods Manufactured schedule and understand how it is used to calculate cost of goods sold. The computation of cost of goods sold can be quite complex for manufacturing organizations because the computation involves combining information about materials, labor, and overhead costs, as well as adjusting for beginning and ending inventory balances in raw materials, work-in-process, and finished goods. The Cost of Goods Manufactured schedule is used as an important input into the calculation of cost of goods sold. More importantly, the Cost of Goods Manufactured schedule is used as an important management tool for planning, controlling, and evaluating manufacturing costs.

5 Explain the flow of goods and services in a merchandising organization and follow the corresponding accumulation of product costs in the accounting system. Manufacturers sell to large-scale wholesalers, who then sell to retailers, who then sell to the end-user customers. These interconnected business relationships are called a distribution channel. Within this system, wholesalers and retailers are the merchants who are most concerned with effectively managing the costs involved in the inventory movement along the distribution channel. Because merchants basically purchase inventory in a finished state, the process of accounting for inventory in a merchandising business is not nearly as complicated as it is in a manufacturing business. As inventory is purchased, it is essentially ready for resale. Although there is often some effort expended to make some final preparations of the inventory for the customer, merchants will rarely assign additional costs of materials, labor, and overhead to specific products. Hence, inventory is debited to the merchandise inventory account as it is purchased. These costs are then directly transferred to the cost of goods sold account as merchandise is sold. In contrast to manufacturing (and service) organizations, there is little need for merchants to involve the complexities of tracking labor and overhead costs into a work-in-process account.

6 Explain the flow of goods and services in a service organization and follow the corresponding accumulation of product costs in the accounting system. Essentially, a service business is any organization whose main economic activity involves producing a nonphysical product that provides value to a customer. As service industries have deregulated in the last few decades, increased competition has forced these companies to develop better cost management systems. There are a number of similarities between accounting for service organizations and accounting for manufacturing organizations. Although most service firms do not need to manage large investments in raw materials, some firms do have large investments in partially completed service projects and contracts. Partially completed service jobs require management accounting that is very similar to the process of accounting for work-in-process in manufacturing firms. Supplies, direct labor, and overhead costs accumulate in an account called Work-in-Process Services. This account performs much the same function as Work-in-Process Inventory in a manufacturing firm. In addition, as service activities take place, overhead is applied to Work-in-Process Services using a predetermined overhead application rate. When the firm has completed and delivered the contracted service, the relevant costs are transferred from Work-in-Process Services to Cost of Services (an account similar to the cost of goods sold account used by manufacturing and merchandising firms).

7 Understand the impact of e-business on product costing. As a result of the growth of e-business being conducted on the Internet, accountants and managers are experiencing tremendous change in the way business is conducted across all types of organizations (manufacturing, merchandising, and service). These changes in business processes are also dramatically changing the size of (and the process of managing) all three types of product costs, i.e., direct materials, direct labor, and overhead.

8 Use the FIFO method to do process costing. Process costing involves five steps: (1) Identify units that went into the process and identify where those units are at the end of the processing time. Determine the amount of "work done" (equivalent units of production) during the processing time period. (2) Determine the amount of production costs that went into the process and compute the product costs per unit for the processing time period. (3) Compute the total cost of units completed and transferred out (cost of goods manufactured) during the processing time period. (4) Compute the total cost of units that remain in process (ending work-in-process inventory) at the end of the processing time period. (5) Prepare the production cost report. The production cost report provides unit cost data that are used to cost inventory as it transfers from one process center to the next and to cost the ending work-in-process inventory of each process center.

key terms & concepts

activity-based costing (ABC), 120
channel, 136
Cost of Goods Manufactured
    schedule, 134
cycle times, 117
estimated manufacturing overhead,
    130
finished goods inventory, 122
inventory turnover (stockturns), 115
job order costing, 123
logistics, 138

manufacturing organizations, 116
manufacturing overhead rate, 123
merchandising organizations, 116
overapplied manufacturing overhead,
    132
predetermined overhead rate, 128
raw materials inventory, 122
retailers, 138
service organizations, 116
underapplied manufacturing overhead,
    132

wholesalers, 138
work-in-process inventory, 122

conversion costs, 152
equivalent units of production, 150
process costing, 150
production cost report, 154

review problems

Job Order Costing

Salem Manufacturing Company applies manufacturing overhead costs on the basis of direct materials costs. The year 2006 estimates are:

Direct materials costs	$300,000
Manufacturing overhead	180,000

For every dollar of direct materials costs, 60 cents of overhead is applied ($180,000 ÷ $300,000 = $0.60).

    Following are the Salem Manufacturing Company transactions for 2006 (entries rounded to the nearest dollar):

a.   Purchased materials for cash, $500,000.
b.   Issued $400,000 of materials to production (80% direct, 20% indirect).
c.   Incurred direct labor costs of $250,000.
d.   Incurred indirect labor costs of $70,000.
e.   Incurred costs for administrative and sales salaries of $70,000 and $60,000, respectively.
f.   Incurred manufacturing overhead costs: property taxes on manufacturing plant, $6,000; plant utilities, $14,000; insurance on plant and equipment, $3,000. (Assume these expenses have not yet been paid.)
g.   Recorded depreciation on manufacturing plant and equipment of $18,000 and $6,000, respectively.
h.   Applied manufacturing overhead.
i.   Transferred 65% of Work-in-Process Inventory to Finished Goods Inventory. Beginning Work-in-Process Inventory was $13,000.
j.   Sold 90% of finished goods on account at a markup of 60% of cost. There was no beginning inventory of finished goods.
k.   Closed the balance in Manufacturing Overhead to Cost of Goods Sold.

Required:
Prepare a journal entry for each transaction.

Solution

a.	Raw Materials Inventory	500,000	
	Cash		500,000
	Purchased raw materials.		

b. Manufacturing Overhead 80,000

    Work-in-Process Inventory 320,000

        Raw Materials Inventory   400,000

        Issued materials to production.

c. Work-in-Process Inventory 250,000

    Wages Payable (or Cash)   250,000

        Incurred direct labor costs.

d. Manufacturing Overhead 70,000

    Wages Payable (or Cash)   70,000

        Incurred indirect labor costs.

e. Salaries Expense, Administrative 70,000

    Salaries Expense, Sales 60,000

        Salaries Payable (or Cash)   130,000

        Incurred sales and administrative salaries expense.

f. Manufacturing Overhead 23,000

    Property Taxes Payable   6,000

    Utilities Payable   14,000

    Insurance Payable   3,000

        Incurred manufacturing overhead costs.

g. Manufacturing Overhead 24,000

    Accumulated Depreciation—Plant   18,000

    Accumulated Depreciation—Equipment   6,000

        Recorded depreciation on plant and equipment.

h. Work-in-Process Inventory 192,000

    Manufacturing Overhead 192,000*

        Applied manufacturing overhead to Work-in-Process Inventory.

*The predetermined overhead rate is equal to estimated total manufacturing overhead divided by estimated direct materials costs ($180,000 ÷ $300,000), or 60% of direct materials costs. In this case, $192,000 ($320,000 × 0.60) is applied because direct materials costs were $320,000 ($400,000 × 0.80).

i. Finished Goods Inventory 503,750

    Work-in-Process Inventory 503,750*

        Transferred Work-in-Process Inventory to

        Finished Goods Inventory (0.65 × $775,000).

*The amount transferred is determined as follows:

Work-in-Process Inventory

Beginning Balance	13,000		
(b)	320,000		
(c)	250,000		
(h)	192,000		
	775,000	(i)	503,750
Ending Balance	271,250		

j. Accounts Receivable 725,400

    Sales 725,400*

Cost of Goods Sold 453,375*

    Finished Goods Inventory   453,375

        Sold 90% of Finished Goods Inventory.

*Because Finished Goods Inventory is $503,750 (i), Cost of Goods Sold is $453,375 ($503,750 × 0.90). Because Finished Goods Inventory is marked up 60%, Sales are $725,400 ($453,375 × 1.6).

k. Cost of Goods Sold   5,000

   Manufacturing Overhead 5,000*

   Closed underapplied manufacturing overhead.

*The amount of underapplied manufacturing overhead is determined as follows:

Manufacturing Overhead

Actual Overhead	(b)	80,000	(h)	192,000	} Applied Overhead
	(d)	70,000			
	(f)	23,000			
	(g)	24,000			
	Balance	5,000			

Accounting for Overhead in a Service Business

Columbus & Hercules, a public accounting firm, is computing the overhead rates to use when billing customers and bidding on jobs. Columbus & Hercules provides the following estimates relating to overhead costs for the year 2006:

Utilities	$ 12,000
Rent	30,000
Equipment depreciation	22,000
Office supplies	20,000
Support staff salaries	120,000
Total estimated overhead costs	$204,000

In addition, Columbus & Hercules offers the following annual estimates (based on a 50-week work year) regarding the salaries and estimated hours associated with the professionals employed by the firm:

Position	Total Estimated Salaries	Total Estimated Billable Hours
Partners (2 × $100,000)	$200,000	4,400
Managers (3 × $70,000)	210,000	6,600
Seniors (6 × $50,000)	300,000	13,200
Staff auditors (10 × $25,000)	250,000	22,000

Columbus & Hercules computes a chargeable hourly rate for each position that is the sum of the following: (1) each position's hourly rate (based on salary), (2) an overhead rate, and (3) a markup of 20% of (1) and (2). The overhead rate allocates estimated overhead costs to each position, then relates the allocated costs to the hours expected to be worked by each position. Travel and materials costs are directly traceable and billed to each job.

   Columbus & Hercules has no client projects in process on January 1, 2006. During January of 2006, Columbus & Hercules worked on several auditing and accounting jobs and incurred the following costs:

Jan. 1 Paid rent for January, $2,500.

   4   Purchased office supplies on account, $1,200.

   9   Paid $4,500 for payables from last year.

   15 Paid office support salaries, $5,000.

   15 Paid biweekly salaries of professionals: partners, $8,000; managers, $8,400; seniors, $12,000; staff, $10,000.

   15 Applied overhead costs based on billable hours: partners, 170 hours; managers, 270 hours; seniors, 500 hours; staff, 900 hours.

   18 Used office supplies totaling $800 to prepare client materials.

Jan. 21   Purchased office supplies on account, $1,100.
  25   Received and paid invoice from office supply store for purchase on January 4.
  27   Billed clients for the following jobs using the computed hourly rate for each position:

	Job #1	Job #2
Partner	90 hours	80 hours
Manager	150 hours	140 hours
Senior	320 hours	200 hours
Staff	560 hours	400 hours

  27   Transferred costs from Work-in-Process Services to Cost of Services based on information from January 27.
  31   Estimated utility costs for the month of January to be $1,000.
  31   Paid office support salaries, $5,400.
  31   Recognized depreciation of office equipment, $1,900.
  31   Paid biweekly salaries of professionals: partners, $8,000; managers, $8,400; seniors, $12,000; staff, $10,000.
  31   Applied overhead costs based on billable hours: partners, 180 hours; managers, 280 hours; seniors, 525 hours; staff, 950 hours.

Required:
1.   Compute the billing rate to be used for each position.
2.   Provide the journal entries made by Columbus & Hercules for January.
3.   Compute the ending balance in Work-in-Process Services.
4.   Compute the ending balance in Overhead.

Solution
1. Billing rate
Overhead allocation rate: $204,000 \div $960,000 = $0.2125 per dollar of salary.

Position	Estimated Salaries	Preliminary Rate	Allocated Overhead	Billable Hours	Overhead Rate per Hour
Partner	$200,000	$0.2125	$ 42,500	4,400	$9.66
Manager	210,000	0.2125	44,625	6,600	6.76
Senior	300,000	0.2125	63,750	13,200	4.83
Staff	250,000	0.2125	53,125	22,000	2.41
Total	$960,000		$204,000		

		Billable Rate for Each Position		
Position	Hourly Rate (1)	Overhead Rate (2)	Markup [(1) + (2)] × 0.20 = (3)	Billable Rate (1) + (2) + (3)
Partner	$45.45[1]	$9.66	$11.02	$66.13
Manager	31.82[2]	6.76	7.72	46.30
Senior	22.73[3]	4.83	5.51	33.07
Staff	11.36[4]	2.41	2.75	16.52

[1]$200,000 \div 4,400 hours = $45.45 per hour
[2]$210,000 \div 6,600 hours = $31.82 per hour
[3]$300,000 \div 13,200 hours = $22.73 per hour
[4]$250,000 \div 22,000 hours = $11.36 per hour

2. Journal entries

Jan. 1	Overhead	2,500	
	Cash		2,500
	Paid rent for the month of January.		

4	Office Supplies	1,200	
	Accounts Payable		1,200
	Purchased office supplies on account.		

9	Accounts Payable	4,500	
	Cash		4,500
	Paid accounts payable from prior period.		

15	Overhead	5,000	
	Cash		5,000
	Paid office support salaries.		

15	Work-in-Process Services	38,400	
	Cash		38,400
	Paid salaries of professionals.		

Partners	$ 8,000
Managers	8,400
Seniors	12,000
Staff	10,000
Total	$38,400

15	Work-in-Process Services	8,051	
	Overhead		8,051
	Allocated overhead based on billable hours.		

Partners—170 hours × $9.66	$1,642
Managers—270 hours × $6.76	1,825
Seniors—500 hours × $4.83	2,415
Staff—900 hours × $2.41	2,169
Total	$8,051

18	Work-in-Process Services	800	
	Office Supplies		800
	Used office supplies on behalf of clients.		

21	Office Supplies	1,100	
	Accounts Payable		1,100
	Purchased office supplies on account.		

25	Accounts Payable	1,200	
	Cash		1,200
	Paid for supplies purchased on January 4.		

27	Accounts Receivable	57,724	
	Service Revenue		57,724
	Billed clients for Jobs #1 and #2.		

Partners—170 hours × $66.13	$11,242
Managers—290 hours × $46.30	13,427
Seniors—520 hours × $33.07	17,196
Staff—960 hours × $16.52	15,859
Total	$57,724

27	Cost of Services	48,107	
	Work-in-Process Services		48,107
	Transferred completed work in process to cost of services;		
	comprised of each position's hourly rate and overhead rate.		

Partners—170 hours × ($45.45 + $9.66)	$ 9,369
Managers—290 hours × ($31.82 + $6.76)	11,188
Seniors—520 hours × ($22.73 + $4.83)	14,331
Staff—960 hours × ($11.36 + $2.41)	13,219
Total	$48,107

Jan. 31	Overhead	1,000	
	Utilities Payable		1,000
	To record estimated utilities expense for the month.		
31	Overhead	5,400	
	Cash		5,400
	Paid office support salaries.		
31	Overhead	1,900	
	Accumulated Depreciation—		
	Office Equipment		1,900
	To record depreciation expense for the month.		
31	Work-in-Process Services	38,400	
	Cash		38,400
	Paid salaries of professionals.		

Partners	$ 8,000	
Managers	8,400	
Seniors	12,000	
Staff	10,000	
Total	$38,400	

31	Work-in-Process Services	8,458	
	Overhead		8,458
	Allocated overhead based on billable hours.		

Partners—180 hours × $9.66	$1,739	
Managers—280 hours × $6.76	1,893	
Seniors—525 hours × $4.83	2,536	
Staff—950 hours × $2.41	2,290	
Total	$8,458	

3. Ending balance in Work-in-Process Services

Work-in-Process Services

1/15	38,400	1/27	48,107
1/15	8,051		
1/18	800		
1/31	38,400		
1/31	8,458		
End. bal.	46,002		

4. Ending balance in Overhead

Overhead

1/1	2,500	1/15	8,051
1/15	5,000	1/31	8,458
1/31	1,000		
1/31	5,400		
1/31	1,900		
		End. bal.	709
		(overapplied)	

eXpanded *Material*

Process Costing

Cleveland Enterprises produces flour in a continuous manufacturing process. The flour is mixed in one step and transferred to the finished goods department. At the beginning of September,

Cleveland had 1,600 bags of flour in process (100% complete as to materials and 20% complete as to processing) that held $2,800 in costs of direct materials and $800 in conversion costs. During September, 20,000 bags of flour were placed into production, and by the end of the month, only 2,000 bags of flour remained in process (100% complete as to materials and 30% complete as to processing). Production costs for September are as follows:

Direct materials	$36,000
Conversion costs	47,712

Required:
1. Prepare the production cost report for September.
2. Prepare the journal entries required to record the production of flour and the transfer of the finished bags to finished goods inventory. Assume that the processing costs are 75% direct labor and 25% manufacturing overhead.

Solution
1. Production cost report

Cleveland Enterprises
Production Cost Report
For the Month of September

EQUIVALENT UNITS OF PRODUCTION

	Physical Units	Direct Materials Costs		Conversion Costs	
		Percent Done	Equivalent Units	Percent Done	Equivalent Units
Beginning work-in-process	1,600	0%	0	80%	1,280
Started and completed	18,000	100%	18,000	100%	18,000
Ending work-in-process	2,000	100%	2,000	30%	600
Equivalent units of production . .			**20,000**		**19,880**
Transferred out	19,600				

PRODUCT COSTS PER UNIT

	Total Costs	Equivalent Units	Cost per Unit
Beginning work-in-process			
Direct materials costs	$ 2,800	1,600	$1.75
Conversion costs	800	320	2.50
Total	$ 3,600		**$4.25**
Current period			
Direct materials costs	$36,000	20,000	$1.80
Conversion costs	47,712	19,880	2.40
Total	$83,712		**$4.20**
TOTAL DOLLARS IN	**$87,312**		

COSTS TRANSFERRED OUT

	Cost per Unit	Equivalent Units	
Beginning work-in-process			
Initial direct materials costs			$ 2,800
Initial conversion costs			800
Costs to complete materials	$1.80	0	0
Costs to complete conversion	$2.40	1,280	3,072
Total			$ 6,672
Started and completed	$4.20	18,000	75,600
Total costs transferred out			**$82,272**

COSTS OF ENDING WORK-IN-PROCESS

	Cost per Unit	Equivalent Units	
Costs for direct materials	$1.80	2,000	$ 3,600
Conversion costs	$2.40	600	1,440
Cost of ending work-in-process			**$ 5,040**
TOTAL DOLLARS OUT			**$87,312**

2. Journal entries

Work-in-Process Inventory	36,000	
Direct Materials Inventory		36,000

Transferred direct materials to work-in-process inventory.

Work-in-Process Inventory	47,712	
Wages Payable		35,784
Manufacturing Overhead		11,928

To record the department's payroll costs and applied manufacturing overhead ($47,712 × 75% = $35,784; $47,712 × 25% = $11,928).

Finished Goods Inventory	82,272	
Work-in-Process Inventory		82,272

Transferred finished goods to the finished goods inventory.

discussion questions

1. Why do managers need accurate product cost information?
2. For financial reporting, which costs are usually included as product costs in a manufacturing company?
3. Why should a firm know how much it costs to produce its goods and services?
4. Describe some possible resources that organizations can use to help in the effort to improve quality while also reducing product costs.
5. Why is it difficult to track the costs of manufactured products?
6. What is the difference in the accounting treatment for direct materials and indirect materials?
7. Why are actual manufacturing overhead costs not assigned directly to products as they are incurred?
8. What is the normal flow of costs in a job order costing system?
9. What are some common bases for applying manufacturing overhead costs to products?
10. Why might Manufacturing Overhead be referred to as a "clearing account"?
11. How does a firm dispose of over- or underapplied overhead costs?
12. Cost of goods manufactured represents the costs being transferred out of the work-in-process account into the finished goods inventory account. Does the cost of goods manufactured calculation include actual manufacturing overhead costs or applied manufacturing overhead costs? Why does the Cost of Goods Manufactured schedule include both actual and applied manufacturing overhead costs?
13. What is the difference between a manufacturing company and a merchandising company? Between a merchandising company and a service company?
14. What does a distribution channel consist of?
15. What is a service organization?
16. Name three ways in which the service industry differs from the manufacturing industry.
17. What is the principal "product cost" for a service company?
18. Which three costs go into the work-in-process services account for a service company? How does this account differ between service and manufacturing firms?
19. What similarities and differences exist among the costs of merchandising, manufacturing, and service firms?
20. Should managers concentrate only on the costs of production (e.g., the cost of goods sold), or should they also consider other costs and factors?

21. What is the major difference between job order costing and process costing?
22. What two conditions generally exist for process costing to be appropriate?

23. What are the five steps involved in employing process costing?

24. What is meant by the term "equivalent units of production"?

 practice exercises

Practice 3-1

Importance of Accurately Identifying Product Costs
Which one of the following statements is *false*?

a. A company wishing to enter a new market may decide not to enter the market because the prices charged by potential competitors are too low to allow the company to cover its costs.
b. Because gathering accurate cost data is so difficult, the benefits rarely outweigh the costs.
c. Having accurate cost information helps companies identify and eliminate costly processes or products.
d. Comparing budgeted costs with actual costs helps companies identify progress and problems of current projects.

Practice 3-2

Manufacturing Overhead Components
Which one of the following is *not* an example of manufacturing overhead?

a. Tires used in the assembly of cars
b. Production supervisor's salary
c. Utilities for production plant
d. Staples used in assembling furniture
e. Insurance on assembly equipment

Practice 3-3

Cost Flow Sequence
Which one of the following sequences is the *correct* sequence for the flow of costs through a production process?

a. Raw materials inventory, work-in-process inventory, cost of goods sold, finished goods inventory
b. Raw materials inventory, cost of goods sold, work-in-process inventory, finished goods inventory
c. Raw materials inventory, work-in-process inventory, finished goods inventory, cost of goods sold
d. Cost of goods sold, raw materials inventory, work-in-process inventory, finished goods inventory
e. Raw materials inventory, finished goods inventory, cost of goods sold, work-in-process inventory

Practice 3-4

Purchasing Raw Materials
The company purchased plastic costing $20,000 and sheet metal costing $75,000. The company paid cash. Both of these materials are used in the production process. Make the necessary journal entry or entries to record these transactions.

Practice 3-5

Direct Materials
The company transferred plastic costing $4,000 and sheet metal costing $22,000 to the factory floor to be used as direct materials in production. Make the necessary journal entry or entries to record these transactions.

Practice 3-6

Indirect Materials
The company transferred plastic costing $1,400 and sheet metal costing $3,000 to the factory floor to be used in general maintenance projects. Because these materials will not be used in the production process itself, they are classified as indirect materials. Make the necessary journal entry or entries to record these transactions.

Practice 3-7

Direct Labor

Two workers worked six hours each to build a custom entertainment center. Each worker earns $12 per hour. Make the necessary journal entry to record this transaction. *Note:* The wages have not yet been paid in cash.

Practice 3-8

Indirect Labor

The company paid $4,500 to its production supervisor for her April salary. Make the necessary journal entry to record this transaction.

Practice 3-9

Recording Actual Manufacturing Overhead

The cost of certain overhead items for the month was as follows:

Rent for production facility	$3,900
Insurance premium for the month	2,250
Monthly depreciation on equipment	4,750
Repairs on equipment	5,200

Payment for these items was as follows:

a. The company is required to pay for one year's rent in advance. The total for one year is $46,800; this amount was paid three months ago. The $3,900 amount represents the rent applicable for this month.

b. The company is required to pay for six months' insurance in advance. The total for six months is $13,500; this amount was paid two months ago. The $2,250 amount represents the insurance applicable for this month.

c. Depreciation is recognized on a straight-line basis.

d. The repairs were performed in the current month. The company will pay for the repairs next month.

Make the necessary journal entries to record these items.

Practice 3-10

Applying Manufacturing Overhead

The company used 150 direct labor hours to complete a certain job. The company applies manufacturing overhead based on direct labor hours at a rate of $5.75 per hour. Make the necessary journal entry to record the application of manufacturing overhead to this job.

Practice 3-11

Transferring the Cost of Completed Jobs

The total cost allocated to a job was $563. The company transferred this job to its finished goods warehouse. Make the necessary journal entry to record this transaction.

Practice 3-12

Transferring the Costs of Products That Are Sold

Refer to the data in Practice 3-11. The company sold for $1,000 the inventory produced in this job. Make the journal entry to record this transaction. The sale was on account. The company uses a perpetual inventory system.

Practice 3-13

Calculating Predetermined Overhead Rates

The company reports the following information from the budget for the coming year:

Estimated total amount of manufacturing overhead	$1,600,000
Average wage for production employees	$13.50
Estimated direct labors hours	250,000
Estimated machine hours	145,000

The company allocates manufacturing overhead based on direct labor hours. Compute the company's predetermined overhead rate.

Practice 3-14

Over- and Underapplied Manufacturing Overhead
The company incurred $32,056 in manufacturing overhead and applied $32,537. The company uses the most common and simple method of handling differences between actual and applied overhead. Make the necessary journal entry to dispose of the difference.

Practice 3-15

Computing Cost of Goods Manufactured
Using the following information, compute cost of goods manufactured, which is the cost of inventory transferred to Finished Goods Inventory.

Work-in-process inventory, beginning balance	$124,500
Work-in-process inventory, ending balance	130,240
Direct materials costs	340,700
Direct labor costs	369,080
Actual manufacturing overhead costs	284,200
Applied manufacturing overhead costs	284,200

Practice 3-16

Cost of Goods Manufactured Schedule
Using the following information, prepare a cost of goods manufactured schedule.

Work-in-process inventory, beginning balance	$160,000
Work-in-process inventory, ending balance	180,000
Raw materials inventory, beginning balance	100,000
Raw materials inventory, ending balance	60,000
Raw materials purchased	540,000
Direct labor cost	600,000
Depreciation on factory building	100,000
Indirect labor	150,000
Other manufacturing overhead costs	86,000
Applied manufacturing overhead costs	330,000

Practice 3-17

Computing Cost of Goods Sold
Using the following information, compute cost of goods sold. Make sure to consider all necessary adjustments.

Finished goods inventory, beginning balance	$120,000
Finished goods inventory, ending balance	130,000
Cost of goods manufactured	340,000
Actual manufacturing overhead costs	160,000
Applied manufacturing overhead costs	175,000

Note: The $340,000 amount of cost of goods manufactured includes the $175,000 in applied manufacturing overhead.

Practice 3-18

The Flow of Goods and Costs in Merchandising Companies
Which one of the following is *not* an example of a way in which middlemen, such as wholesalers, add value?

a. Some manufacturers are not set up to deal with a large number of retail customers.
b. Wholesalers can provide retailers with inventory management services such as fast delivery, easy returns, and enhanced product mix.
c. Wholesalers are given special tax incentives by most state and local governments.
d. Wholesalers can efficiently break down large manufacturer product shipments into the small amounts needed by individual retailers.
e. Customers benefit from the diversity of products available in one retail location rather than going directly to a manufacturer for each product.

Practice 3-19

The Flow of Services and Costs in Service Companies
Which one of the following statements is *false*?

a. Service companies use predetermined overhead rates.
b. Service firms generally do not distinguish between manufacturing and administrative overhead costs.
c. Regarding the accounting for cost of "goods" sold, service companies are more similar to merchants than to manufacturers.
d. Service companies use work-in-process inventory accounts to accumulate costs such as direct labor and manufacturing overhead.
e. A service business is any organization whose main economic activity involves producing a nonphysical product.

Practice 3-20

Units Started and Completed
At the beginning of the month, the company had 35 units that were 45% complete in inventory. At the end of the month, the company had 50 units that were 80% complete in inventory. During the month, the company completed and transferred 1,200 units out of inventory. Compute the number of units started and completed during the month.

Practice 3-21

Equivalent Units of Production
Given the following information, compute the equivalent units of production.

	Physical Units	Percent Complete
Beginning work-in-process	25	20%
Started and completed	430	100
Ending work-in-process	35	40

Practice 3-22

Product Costs per Unit
Using the following information, compute the total product costs per unit for both beginning work-in-process inventory and for current period production.

	Total Costs	Equivalent Units
Beginning work-in-process direct materials costs	$ 2,840	5,400
Current period direct materials costs	7,400	13,300
Beginning work-in-process conversion costs	3,200	2,100
Current period conversion costs	21,700	14,000

Practice 3-23

Costs Transferred out of Work-in-Process Inventory
The company spent a total of $102,340 in the current period in one of its production centers. In addition, when the production period began, there was work-in-process inventory in the production center that had a total value of $3,820. If the costs of the inventory at the end of the period are $4,190, what are the total costs of the inventory transferred out of the production center?

Practice 3-24

Costs of Ending Work-in-Process Inventory
The company spent a total of $309,203 in the current period in one of its production centers. In addition, when the production period began, there was work-in-process inventory in

the production center that had a total value of $18,802. If the total costs of the inventory transferred out of the production center are $311,214, what are the costs of the inventory at the end of the period?

e x e r c i s e s

Exercise 3-1

Manufacturing Costs

Springville Manufacturing Company uses a job order costing system. For Job #151, the production manager requisitioned $1,200 of direct materials and used 40 hours of direct labor at $18 per hour. Manufacturing overhead is applied on the basis of direct labor hours, using a predetermined overhead rate. At the beginning of the year, $800,000 of manufacturing overhead costs were estimated based on a forecast of 200,000 direct labor hours. Prepare a summary of the costs for Job #151. (*Note:* You have to calculate the predetermined overhead rate.)

Exercise 3-2

Manufacturing Costs

The Make-It-Right Company manufactures special wheelchairs for handicapped athletes. The company uses a job order costing system. Partial data for a particular job include:

Direct materials	$450
Direct labor	375
Manufacturing overhead	?
Total cost	$?

The company allocates manufacturing overhead on the basis of direct labor hours. The estimated total manufacturing costs for the year are $750,000, and the total estimated direct labor hours are 150,000. Factory workers are paid $15 per hour.

1. Compute the predetermined manufacturing overhead rate.
2. What is the allocated manufacturing overhead cost and the total cost of the above referenced job?

Exercise 3-3

Predetermined Manufacturing Overhead Rates

Memphis Corporation uses a job order costing system. Thus, management must establish a predetermined overhead rate for applying manufacturing overhead. During the past three years, the following data have been accumulated:

	2004	2005	2006
Direct labor hours	40,000	52,000	65,000
Machine hours	80,000	65,000	45,000
Direct materials costs	$400,000	$250,000	$390,000
Total budgeted manufacturing overhead	$80,000	$65,000	$45,000

1. What would the predetermined overhead rate be for each of the three years, if based on (a) direct labor hours, (b) machine hours, and (c) direct materials costs?
2. **Interpretive Question:** Which allocation basis would you recommend be used in the future for applying manufacturing overhead? Why?

Exercise 3-4

Predetermined Manufacturing Overhead Rates

East Lake Corporation uses a job order costing system and applies manufacturing overhead using a predetermined overhead rate. The following data are available for the past two years.

	2005	2006
Direct labor hours	104,000	130,000
Direct materials costs	$500,000	$780,000
Machine hours	100,000	70,000
Total budgeted manufacturing overhead	$130,000	$90,000

1. Compute the predetermined overhead rate for each of the two years, based on (a) direct labor hours, (b) direct materials costs, and (c) machine hours.
2. **Interpretive Question:** Which allocation basis would you recommend for applying manufacturing overhead? Why?

Exercise 3-5

Work-in-Process Analysis in a Manufacturing Organization

Matt Jones, a recently hired internal auditor, is currently auditing the work-in-process inventory account. Matt has forgotten some basic cost accounting concepts and asks for your assistance. Identify the four types of transactions or events that affect the work-in-process inventory account in a manufacturing organization. Prepare and explain a sample journal entry for each type of transaction.

Exercise 3-6

Flow of Manufacturing Costs

Post the following cost data to the appropriate T-accounts to trace the flow of costs from the time they are incurred until the product is completed and sold. (Assume that purchases and expenses are credited to Cash or Accounts Payable.)

a.	Direct materials purchased	$ 60,000
b.	Direct materials used	50,000
c.	Indirect materials purchased	9,000
d.	Indirect materials used	7,000
e.	Wages payable, direct	60,000
f.	Wages payable, indirect	12,000
g.	Selling and administrative expenses	32,000
h.	Actual manufacturing overhead costs other than	
	indirect materials and indirect labor	25,000
i.	Manufacturing overhead applied	40,000
j.	Work-in-process completed	120,000
k.	Finished goods sold	135,000

Exercise 3-7

Applying Manufacturing Overhead

Keith Company has four manufacturing subsidiaries: W, X, Y, and Z. Each subsidiary keeps a separate set of accounting records. Manufacturing cost forecasts for 2006 for each subsidiary are:

(continued)

	Subsidiaries			
	W	**X**	**Y**	**Z**
Materials to be used (lbs.)	40,000	40,000	30,000	26,250
Direct labor hours	15,000	20,000	12,500	20,000
Direct labor costs	$6,000	$5,000	$1,875	$3,500
Machine hours	12,500	7,500	4,750	20,000
Manufacturing overhead	$30,000	$25,000	$10,000	$50,000

The predetermined overhead rates for each subsidiary are based on the following:

Subsidiary W: Machine hours
Subsidiary X: Direct labor costs
Subsidiary Y: Materials to be used
Subsidiary Z: Direct labor hours

1. Compute the predetermined overhead rate to be used in 2006 by each subsidiary.
2. If Subsidiary X actually had $4,000 of direct labor costs and $18,750 of manufacturing overhead, will overhead be over- or underapplied and by how much?
3. If Subsidiary Y used 33,000 pounds of materials in 2006, what will be the applied manufacturing overhead?
4. **Interpretive Question:** Identify the two most commonly used methods to dispose of under- or overapplied manufacturing overhead. What is the major advantage of each method?

Exercise 3-8

Applying Manufacturing Overhead
Valtec Company has three manufacturing divisions: A, B, and C. Each division has its own job order costing system and forecasts the following manufacturing costs for the year 2006:

	Division		
	A	**B**	**C**
Materials to be used (lbs.)	120,000	100,000	80,000
Direct labor hours	45,000	60,000	25,000
Machine hours	40,000	25,000	15,000
Total budgeted manufacturing overhead	$50,000	$70,000	$45,000

The predetermined overhead rates for each division are based on the following:

Division A: Machine hours
Division B: Materials to be used
Division C: Direct labor hours

1. Compute the predetermined overhead rate to be used in 2006 by each division.
2. If Division A actually had 37,000 machine hours and $49,000 of manufacturing overhead, will overhead be over- or underapplied and by how much?
3. If Division B used 95,000 pounds of materials in 2006, what will be the applied manufacturing overhead?
4. **Interpretive Question:** Of the two commonly used methods to dispose of over- or underapplied manufacturing overhead, which method would you recommend and why?

Exercise 3-9

Assigning Manufacturing Costs to Jobs
Farrer Manufacturing Company uses a job order costing system. All relevant information for Jobs #203 and #204, which were completed during May, is provided here. No other jobs were in process during the month of May.

Spreadsheet

	Job #203	Job #204
Direct materials cost	$10,000	$13,000
Direct labor cost	$7,800	$10,800
Direct labor hours on job	800	1,400
Units produced	1,000	1,750

A predetermined overhead rate of $12 per direct labor hour is used to apply manufacturing overhead costs to jobs. Actual manufacturing overhead for the month of May totaled $25,000. All completed products are delivered to customers immediately after completion, so costs are transferred directly to Cost of Goods Sold without going through Finished Goods Inventory.

1. How much manufacturing overhead will be assigned to each job completed during May?
2. Compute the total cost of each job.
3. Compute the unit cost for each job.
4. Compute the over- or underapplied manufacturing overhead for May.
5. Prepare the journal entries to transfer the cost of direct materials, direct labor, and manufacturing overhead to Work-in-Process Inventory and to transfer the cost of completed jobs to Cost of Goods Sold. (Omit explanations.)
6. **Interpretive Question:** How would the company have computed its predetermined overhead rate of $12 per direct labor hour? Explain.

Exercise 3-10

Assigning Manufacturing Costs to Jobs

Remington Company uses predetermined overhead rates in assigning manufacturing overhead costs to jobs. The rates are based on machine hours in the machining department and on direct labor hours in the assembly department. Estimated costs, machine hours, and direct labor hours for the year in each department are:

	Machining	Assembly
Direct labor cost	$64,000	$100,000
Manufacturing overhead	$90,000	$50,000
Direct labor hours	12,000	32,000
Machine hours	18,000	2,500

During the month of April, Job #402X had the following data for 50 completed units of product:

	Machining	Assembly
Direct materials cost	$400	$700
Direct labor cost	$650	$2,300
Direct labor hours	120	740
Machine hours	900	80

1. What predetermined overhead rates would be used by the company in assigning manufacturing overhead costs to Job #402X in machining and in assembly? (*Note:* You should round all rates you calculate to two decimal places.)
2. Using the overhead rates you calculated in part (1), how much manufacturing overhead is applied to Job #402X?
3. What is the unit cost for Job #402X? (Round the unit cost to two decimal places.)

Exercise 3-11

Analyzing Manufacturing Costs

The following T-accounts represent inventory costs as of December 31, 2006:

(continued)

Raw Materials Inventory		
Bal. 12/31/05	70,000	200,000
	175,000	
Bal. 12/31/06	45,000	

Finished Goods Inventory		
Bal. 12/31/05	39,500	336,500
	350,000	
Bal. 12/31/06	53,000	

Work-in-Process Inventory		
Bal. 12/31/05	12,500	350,000
	200,000	
	124,500	
	86,000	
Bal. 12/31/06	73,000	

Manufacturing Overhead		
	24,500	124,500
	26,000	
	30,000	
	36,000	

1. Determine the direct labor costs for 2006.
2. Determine the cost of goods manufactured for 2006.
3. Determine the cost of goods sold for 2006.
4. Compute over- or underapplied manufacturing overhead for 2006.
5. Determine actual indirect manufacturing costs for 2006.

Exercise 3-12

Total Manufacturing Costs and Cost of Goods Manufactured
The following information is for Kiev Derrald Company:

Manufacturing overhead (actual)	$100,000
Ending raw materials inventory	12,000
Manufacturing overhead (applied)	95,000
Beginning work-in-process inventory	55,000
Ending work-in-process inventory	47,000
Beginning raw materials inventory	10,000
Direct labor costs	60,000
Raw materials purchases	40,000

1. Compute total manufacturing costs.
2. Compute cost of goods manufactured.

Exercise 3-13

**Total Manufacturing Costs, Cost of Goods Manufactured,
and Cost of Goods Sold**
The following information is for MTC Harry Company:

Beginning raw materials inventory	$ 25,000
Raw materials *used* in production as direct materials	110,000
Ending raw materials inventory	40,000
Manufacturing overhead (actual)	300,000
Beginning work-in-process inventory	150,000
Ending work-in-process inventory	180,000
Direct labor costs	95,000
Beginning finished goods inventory	71,000
Ending finished goods inventory	86,000
Underapplied manufacturing overhead	19,000

1. Compute total manufacturing costs.
2. Compute cost of goods manufactured.
3. Compute cost of goods sold.

Exercise 3-14

Service Cost Flows

Xavier & Associates Law Firm estimated its total overhead costs for 2006 to be $1.8 million. It allocates overhead based on direct labor hours. Xavier employs a total of 11 attorneys, each working an average of 2,000 hours per year. The average annual salary for Xavier attorneys is $140,000, or approximately $70 per hour. Xavier attorneys worked a total of 23 hours and used $150 of supplies in doing work for Mr. Bailey, one of Xavier's clients.

1. What is Xavier's overhead rate?
2. Prepare the journal entry to record the overhead for the Bailey job.
3. Prepare the journal entry to record the cost of supplies for the Bailey job.
4. Prepare the journal entry to record the cost of labor for the Bailey job.

Exercise 3-15

Service Cost Flows

Pierce Engineers incurred (but has not yet paid) the following costs in 2006:

Use of supplies for clients	$ 3,500
Utilities	8,000
Property taxes	12,000
Engineers' salaries	100,000
Support staff salaries	35,000
Applied overhead	50,000

Prepare the journal entries to account for the costs given. Close the overhead account to Cost of Services.

Exercise 3-16

Predetermined Service Overhead Rates

The following data are available for Haul-It-Away Truckers:

	2005	2006
Budgeted direct labor hours	135,000	140,000
Planned number of moving jobs	300	310
Total miles to be driven	450,000	597,000
Total budgeted overhead	$900,000	$1,200,000

1. Compute the predetermined overhead rate for each of the two years, if based on (a) direct labor hours, (b) number of moving jobs, and (c) total miles driven.
2. **Interpretive Question:** Which allocation basis would you recommend for applying overhead? Why?

Exercise 3-17

Applying Overhead

Gammonomics Schools teaches private accounting courses. It applies overhead based on instructor hours. The following information was forecasted for 2006:

Direct labor	$270,000
Property tax on equipment	$2,700
Supplies	$9,000
Rent	$18,000
Support staff salaries	$120,000
Instructor hours	16,000

1. Calculate the predetermined overhead rate for 2006.
2. If Gammonomics actually had 18,000 instructor hours and spent $150,000 on overhead, will overhead be under- or overapplied for 2006? By how much?

Exercise 3-18

Service Costs
The following information is available for a particular consulting contract performed by Newland Business Consultants in 2006:

Consulting labor costs	$4,000
Supplies	500
Overhead	?
Total cost	$?

Newland applies overhead on the basis of client consulting hours. The estimated total overhead costs for 2006 are $6.2 million, and the estimated total consulting hours are 150,000. Newland pays its consultants $40 per hour.

1. Compute the predetermined overhead rate.
2. What are the allocated overhead cost and the total cost of this particular contract?

Exercise 3-19

Equivalent Units—Process Costing
Assume that you are the owner and sole employee of a lube, oil, and filter service business that you run out of your home. Currently, you are running a spring special on a "super maintenance service" on cars. The maintenance service you offer is quite comprehensive and includes (among other things) changing the oil, rotating the tires, topping off all fluids, and washing and waxing each car. It takes about one to two hours to complete a car. With the great price you're offering on this service, you immediately find yourself with about five days of customer order backlog. To catch up, you decide to spend the next week working solely on the "super maintenance service." Further, you want to track your output to see if you can improve the amount of maintenance work you do each of the next five days.

When you come to work the following Monday, you have one car that is about 70% complete. At the end of the week, the results are as follows:

	Total Cars Completed Each Day	End-of-Day Car in Process
Monday	5	50% complete
Tuesday	5	80% complete
Wednesday	7	10% complete
Thursday	6	80% complete
Friday	7	10% complete

How much work did you get done each day? In other words, how many equivalent units of production did you have each day?

Exercise 3-20

Equivalent Units and Unit Costs—Process Costing
A large factory that manufactures wooden furniture has several assembly lines. One of the assembly lines is dedicated to assembly of wooden kitchen chairs. All raw materials necessary to complete each chair are requisitioned from the raw materials warehouse at the time each chair starts production on the assembly line. The following data relate to one week of production:

Beginning Work-in-Process
40 chairs; 80% complete; $350 in direct materials costs; $320 in conversion costs

Ending Work-in-Process
60 chairs; 40% complete

Current Week
550 chairs started and completed; $4,880 requisitioned from raw materials warehouse, $5,820 incurred in conversion costs

1. Compute the equivalent units of production for both direct materials and conversion costs for the week.
2. Compute the total production cost per chair for the week on the assembly line.
3. How does this week's production cost on the assembly line compare to last week's production cost?

Exercise 3-21

Spreadsheet

Equivalent Units and Unit Costs—Process Costing

Heidi Corporation began producing quick-drying paper cement in June 2006 (i.e., there was no beginning work-in-process inventory on June 1). The manufacturing process involves only one step. In June, the costs were $4,000 for direct materials and $3,108 for conversion costs. During the month, 3,200 pounds of direct materials were placed in production. At the end of June, 600 pounds of direct materials were still being processed and were 40% complete. Assume that all direct materials are added at the beginning of production.

1. Compute the number of equivalent units of output in terms of materials costs and labor and overhead (conversion) costs for June, assuming FIFO cost flow.
2. Determine the total cost of goods transferred to Finished Goods Inventory and the total cost of Work-in-Process Inventory at the end of June.

p roblems

Problem 3-1

Job Order Costing in a Manufacturing Organization—Journal Entries

Following are transactions for Montigo Manufacturing Company. Assume that the company has no beginning work-in-process inventory.

1. Montigo purchased $600,000 of raw materials, paying 10% down, with the remainder to be paid in 10 days.
2. The production manager requisitioned $260,000 of materials (90% for direct use and the remainder for indirect purposes).
3. The liability incurred in (1) was paid in full.
4. 24,000 hours of direct labor and 2,000 hours of indirect labor were incurred. (Assume an average hourly wage rate of $9 for both direct and indirect labor.)
5. The following salaries were paid:

Factory supervisor (a product cost)	$80,000
Administrative executives	70,000
Sales personnel	90,000

6. Rent and utilities for the building of $30,000 and $7,000, respectively, were paid. Three-fourths of these expenses are applicable to manufacturing and the remainder to administration.
7. Depreciation on factory equipment was $15,000.
8. Advertising costs for the year totaled $15,000.
9. Manufacturing overhead is applied at a rate of $6.90 per direct labor hour.
10. All but $35,000 of Work-in-Process Inventory was completed and transferred to Finished Goods Inventory.

(continued)

11. The sales price of finished goods that were sold was 130% of manufacturing costs. Assume a perpetual inventory system and that all finished goods were sold.
12. Close over- or underapplied overhead directly to cost of goods sold.

Required:
Prepare journal entries for the transactions.

Problem 3-2

Accounting For Manufacturing Transactions—Journal Entries
Payson Company uses a job order costing system. The following is a *partial* list of the company's accounts. (*Note:* Additional accounts may be needed.)

Cash
Manufacturing Overhead
Sales
Cost of Goods Sold
Sales Commissions Expense
Administrative Expenses
Accounts Receivable
Commissions Payable

Required:
1. Prepare journal entries for each of the following transactions (omit explanations).
2. Prepare T-accounts and post the journal entries to the T-accounts. Transaction (a) has been completed as an example.
   a. Raw materials previously purchased on account were paid for in cash, $700.

Cash			**Accounts Payable**		
	(a)	700	(a)	700	

   b. Raw materials were purchased for $1,500 on account.
   c. Direct labor costs of $3,000 were recorded.
   d. Direct materials costing $1,100 were issued directly to production.
   e. Depreciation of $1,500 on manufacturing equipment was recorded. (Assume this is a product cost.)
   f. Property taxes payable of $2,600 were recorded, half to manufacturing and half to administration.
   g. Manufacturing overhead costs of $400 were applied to a job in process.
   h. Materials previously purchased on account were paid for in cash, $1,500.
   i. Sales commissions of $240 were recorded.
   j. Goods costing $2,700 were transferred from Work-in-Process Inventory to Finished Goods Inventory.
   k. Finished goods costing $2,300 were sold for $3,200 on credit, and the cost of goods sold was recorded.

Problem 3-3

Manufacturing Cost Flows
Lehi Corporation uses a job order costing system in its manufacturing operation. For the year 2006, Lehi's predetermined overhead rate was 75% of direct labor costs. For September 2006, the company incurred the following costs:

Purchased raw materials on account	$ 70,000
Issued raw materials to manufacturing process	65,000
Incurred direct labor costs ($10 per hour $\times$ 7,500 hrs.)	75,000
Actual manufacturing overhead costs	52,300
Cost of goods completed and sold	211,250

The company's inventories at the beginning of September 2006 were as follows:

Raw materials	. . . .	$12,000
Work-in-process	. . . .	57,500

The costs of all completed orders are transferred directly from Work-in-Process Inventory to Cost of Goods Sold.

Required:
1. Compute the following amounts.
   a. Work-in-Process Inventory balance at the end of September 2006.
   b. Over- or underapplied manufacturing overhead for the month of September.
2. Prepare journal entries to reflect the flow of costs into and out of Work-in-Process Inventory during September (omit explanations).

Problem 3-4

Using T-Accounts: Cost Flows in a Job Order Manufacturing Organization

High Country Furniture Company manufactures custom furniture only and uses a job order costing system to accumulate costs. Actual direct materials and direct labor costs are accumulated for each job, but a predetermined overhead rate is used to apply manufacturing overhead costs to individual jobs. Manufacturing overhead is applied on the basis of direct labor hours. In computing a predetermined overhead rate, the controller estimated that manufacturing overhead costs for 2006 would be $80,000 and direct labor hours would be 20,000. The following information is available for the year 2006:

a. Direct materials purchased, $22,000.
b. Direct materials used in production, $19,500.
c. Wages and salaries paid for the year: direct labor (18,000 hours), $117,000; indirect labor, $12,000; sales and administrative salaries, $21,000.
d. Depreciation on machinery and equipment, $9,000.
e. Rent and utilities for building (75% factory), $16,000.
f. Miscellaneous manufacturing overhead, $51,500.
g. Advertising costs, $12,000.
h. Manufacturing overhead is applied to Work-in-Process Inventory.
i. Eighty percent of Work-in-Process Inventory was completed and transferred to Finished Goods Inventory.

Required:
1. Compute the predetermined overhead rate at which manufacturing overhead costs will be applied to jobs.
2. Set up T-accounts and post the transactions.
3. Compute the under- or overapplied manufacturing overhead. Prepare a journal entry to close Manufacturing Overhead and transfer the balance to Cost of Goods Sold.

Problem 3-5

Applying Manufacturing Overhead

Swenson Corporation has four independent manufacturing divisions. The following data apply to the divisions for the year ended December 31, 2006:

	A	B	C	D
Direct materials costs	$240,000	$280,000	$160,000	$130,000
Direct labor hours	80,000	60,000	48,000	28,000
Direct labor costs	$220,000	$130,000	$140,000	$84,000
Actual manufacturing overhead	$146,900	$205,400	$140,000	$33,000
Machine hours worked	40,000	12,000	28,000	16,000
Number of units produced	200,000	4,000	30,000	10,000
Predetermined overhead rate	80% of direct labor costs	65% of direct materials costs	$3.30 per direct labor hour	$2.10 per machine hour

(continued)

Required:
1. For each of the four divisions, calculate:
   a. Applied manufacturing overhead.
   b. Over- or underapplied manufacturing overhead.
   c. Cost of goods manufactured, assuming no work-in-process inventories.
   d. Average cost per unit produced.
2. **Interpretive Question:** How would you recommend that the over- or underapplied manufacturing overhead be disposed of in each division? Why?

Problem 3-6

Applying Manufacturing Overhead

Openshaw Manufacturing Company made the following estimates at the beginning of the year:

	Department G	Department H
Direct labor costs	$219,000	$166,980
Manufacturing overhead	$86,700	$153,340
Machine hours	17,000	12,500
Direct labor hours	30,000	22,000

Manufacturing overhead is applied on the basis of machine hours in Department G and on the basis of direct labor hours in Department H. During the year, the following two jobs were completed (there were no jobs in process at the beginning or end of the year):

Job #29

	Department G	Department H
Direct materials used	$16,000	$9,200
Direct labor costs	$18,250	$14,420
Direct labor hours	2,500	1,900
Machine hours	1,410	1,080

Job #30

	Department G	Department H
Direct materials used	$17,500	$8,100
Direct labor costs	$19,710	$13,920
Direct labor hours	2,700	1,800
Machine hours	1,530	1,020

Required:
1. Compute the predetermined overhead rate for each department.
2. Determine the amount of manufacturing overhead to be applied to each job.
3. Determine the total cost of each job.
4. Given that the actual manufacturing overhead costs for the year in Departments G and H were $88,200 and $152,500, respectively; that the actual machine hours in Department G were 18,100; and that the direct labor hours in Department H were 21,600; compute the amount of over- or underapplied manufacturing overhead.
5. **Interpretive Question:** Why is the predetermined overhead rate based on estimated rather than actual information?

Problem 3-7

Unifying Concepts: Job Order Costing, Cost Flows, Journal Entries, and Predetermined Overhead Rates

Brooks Manufacturing Company applies manufacturing overhead on the basis of direct materials costs. The estimates for 2006 were:

Direct materials costs $250,000
Manufacturing overhead 75,000

Following are the transactions of Brooks Manufacturing Company for 2006:

a. Raw materials purchased on account, $275,000 (80% for direct use and 20% for indirect use).
b. Raw materials issued to production, 80% for direct use and 20% for indirect use, for a total of $175,000.
c. Direct labor costs, $250,000.
d. Indirect labor costs, $25,000.
e. Administrative and sales salaries, $70,000 and $45,000, respectively.
f. Utilities, $10,500; plant depreciation, $20,000; maintenance, $7,500; miscellaneous administrative expenses, $2,000. (These costs are allocated on the basis of plant floor space—administrative facilities, 1,000 square feet; manufacturing, 5,000 square feet; sales facilities, 2,000 square feet.)
g. Manufacturing equipment depreciation, $6,000.
h. Additional raw materials issued to production for direct use, $125,000.
i. Manufacturing overhead is applied.
j. Recorded factory foreman's salary, $27,000.
k. Ninety percent of existing Work-in-Process Inventory is transferred to Finished Goods Inventory. (Work-in-Process beginning inventory was $15,000.)
l. All finished goods are sold. (Assume no beginning inventory. Sales are marked up 40% of cost.)
m. Over- or underapplied manufacturing overhead is closed to Cost of Goods Sold.

Required:
1. Prepare a journal entry for each of the transactions and show the T-accounts for Manufacturing Overhead and Work-in-Process Inventory.
2. What is the ending balance in the cost of goods sold account?
3. **Interpretive Question:** Comparing actual manufacturing overhead with estimates for 2006, what would you recommend that Brooks Manufacturing Company estimate for manufacturing overhead costs in 2007?

Problem 3-8

Unifying Concepts: Job Order Costing

Jones Custom Furniture Manufacturing, Inc., made the following estimates at the beginning of the year, 2006:

Budgeted direct labor costs $300,000
Budgeted direct labor hours 20,000
Budgeted manufacturing overhead $520,000

Jones applies manufacturing overhead to specific job orders on the basis of direct labor hours.

During the month of January, the following transactions occurred for Job #345, an order for 10 custom oak chairs, manufactured in the first week of January 2006:

Jan. 3   Requisitioned direct materials (lumber, fabric, paint), $876; put into production on Job #345.

(continued)

Jan. 3 Requisitioned indirect materials (glue, staples, sandpaper, and equipment grease), $154, for use in manufacturing the 10 chairs for Job #345, as well as other subsequent jobs.

7 Processed time card for Employee #214; 25 direct labor hours attributed to Job #345 at wage rate of $15 per hour.

7 Applied manufacturing overhead at the predetermined rate to Job #345, based on the actual direct labor hours.

7 Processed the manufacturing supervisor's weekly salary of $1,000. (This salary is considered indirect labor because the supervisor oversees all jobs in process and does not account for her time on a job-by-job basis.)

7 Job #345 was completed and transferred to the finished goods warehouse to await shipment to the customer.

9 The 10 oak chairs (Job #345) were shipped to the customer. The sales invoice reflects a sales price of $3,000 on account.

In addition to Job #345, Jones completed 47 other job orders in January and had 7 others in process at month-end. The following information summarizes additional manufacturing transactions for Jones for the month of January (not relating to Job #345):

a. Raw materials purchased on account, $102,675.

b. Requisitioned raw materials to specific job orders, $90,430; 80% direct materials and the remainder indirect materials not directly attributable to any one specific job.

c. Incurred and paid direct labor wages totaled, $24,600; an average of $15 per hour for 1,640 total direct labor hours for January.

d. Applied manufacturing overhead at the predetermined rate to all jobs in progress on the basis of the actual direct labor hours incurred by job.

e. Incurred and paid supervisor salaries and other indirect manufacturing labor (e.g., maintenance labor) totaled $7,000.

f. Incurred and paid the following costs associated with the manufacturing process and facility:

Factory rent	$ 7,600
Factory utilities	2,700
Insurance	1,200
Miscellaneous	1,900
	$13,400

g. Recorded depreciation of manufacturing equipment for the month, $5,500.

h. The cost of the 47 jobs completed during the month totaled $125,446.

i. Shipped all completed jobs to customers by month-end at a total sales price of $200,714 on account.

j. Incurred and paid selling and administrative costs (e.g., administrative salaries, sales commissions, office supplies, office rent, etc.), $46,514.

Required:
1. a. Calculate Jones' predetermined overhead rate for the year 2006.
   b. Prepare journal entries for the first seven transactions (relating to Job #345). Omit explanations.
   c. Determine the total cost of manufacturing each of the 10 oak chairs.
   d. Determine the total gross margin earned on all 10 oak chairs.
2. Prepare the journal entries for transactions (a)–(j). Omit explanations.
3. Close Manufacturing Overhead to Cost of Goods Sold (include all transactions noted for Job #345).
4. Calculate Jones' total gross margin for January, including Job #345.
5. Calculate Jones' total operating income for January.
6. Determine the ending January balances in Raw Materials Inventory, Work-in-Process Inventory, and Finished Goods Inventory (assume no beginning balances).

Problem 3-9

Cost of Goods Manufactured

The following data apply to Newton Company and Alexander Company (two independent companies):

	Newton Company	Alexander Company
Raw materials inventory, January 1, 2006	$ 1	$ 4,000
Raw materials purchased	21,000	4
Raw materials inventory, December 31, 2006	6,000	3,000
Manufacturing overhead (actual)	8,000	5
Manufacturing overhead (applied)	2	16,000
Selling and administrative expenses	14,000	25,000
Work-in-process inventory, January 1, 2006	3	20,000
Work-in-process inventory, December 31, 2006	16,000	22,000
Direct (raw) materials used in production	15,000	6
Direct labor costs	25,000	30,000
Cost of goods manufactured	49,000	55,000
Overapplied (or underapplied) manufacturing overhead	(2,000)	4,000

Required:

Fill in the unknowns for the two cases. (*Hint:* Indirect materials are not used in either company.)

Problem 3-10

Cost of Goods Manufactured Schedule

(*Note:* This problem is a continuation of Problem 3-7.) Brooks Manufacturing Company's journal entries and T-accounts for Manufacturing Overhead and Work-in-Process Inventory were completed in Problem 3-7. Assume that Brooks had the following beginning inventory amounts:

Raw materials inventory	$80,000
Work-in-process inventory	15,000
Finished goods inventory	0

Required:

Prepare a Cost of Goods Manufactured schedule for 2006 for Brooks Manufacturing Company. Assume all beginning and ending raw materials amounts include only direct materials.

Problem 3-11

Cost of Goods Manufactured Schedule

Delta Manufacturing Company applies manufacturing overhead to jobs on the basis of machine hours. The 2006 estimates of manufacturing overhead and machine hours were:

Manufacturing overhead	$1,825,000
Machine hours	365,000

Delta had the following transactions for October 2006:

a. Raw materials of $420,000 were purchased on account.
b. Raw materials of $400,000 were issued to production; 90% were direct materials, and the balance was indirect materials.
c. Direct labor costs incurred, $300,000.
d. Indirect labor costs incurred, $55,000.
e. Selling, general, and administrative expenses incurred, $150,000.
f. Manufacturing overhead costs incurred:

(continued)

Plant depreciation (factory)	$25,000
Equipment depreciation (factory)	14,000
Utilities (factory)	7,000
Factory maintenance	9,000
Factory taxes and insurance	5,000
Miscellaneous manufacturing overhead	6,000

g. Machine hours for the month, 30,400.

h. Eighty-five percent of Work-in-Process Inventory was transferred to Finished Goods Inventory. Assume that beginning Work-in-Process Inventory amounted to $95,000.

i. *All* finished goods are sold for cash at a 20% markup over costs of production. (There is no beginning or ending finished goods inventory.)

j. Over- or underapplied manufacturing overhead is charged to Cost of Goods Sold, and the overhead account is closed.

Required:

1. Prepare journal entries to reflect the flow of costs incurred during October.

2. Assuming that beginning raw materials inventory was $16,000 and beginning work-in-process inventory was $95,000, prepare a Cost of Goods Manufactured schedule for October 2006.

Problem 3-12

Analysis of Manufacturing Cost Flows

The following T-accounts represent manufacturing cost flows for Kanton Manufacturing Company for the year 2006.

Direct Materials Inventory

1/1	70,000		250,000
	210,000		
12/31	30,000		

Work-in-Process Inventory

1/1	80,000		700,000
	250,000		
	310,000		
	140,000		
12/31	80,000		

Finished Goods Inventory

1/1	90,000		740,000
	700,000		
12/31	50,000		

Manufacturing Overhead

30,000		140,000
22,000		
16,000		
38,000		
40,000		

Required:

1. Compute the following amounts for 2006:
   a. Direct labor cost.
   b. Cost of goods manufactured.
   c. Cost of goods sold.
   d. Actual manufacturing overhead costs.
2. Prepare a Cost of Goods Manufactured schedule for 2006.
3. Prepare a cost of goods sold schedule for 2006.
4. **Interpretive Question:** Explain how the over- or underapplied manufacturing overhead is usually accounted for.

Problem 3-13

Computing Overhead Rates and Client Billing in a Service Firm

Sutherland Estimating Company employs three professional estimators, each having a different specialty. John Spencer specializes in structural estimating; Steve Ray, electrical estimating; and

Dave Eugene, mechanical estimating. The firm expects to incur the following operating costs for 2006; travel and materials costs are billed separately to clients.

Office salaries and wages	$ 54,000
Office supplies	30,000
Utilities and telephone	23,100
Depreciation	24,300
Taxes and insurance	15,450
Miscellaneous expenses	3,150
Total estimated costs for 2006	$150,000

The salaries and billable hours of the three estimators are expected to be as follows:

	Expected Salary	Expected Hours
Spencer	$ 90,000	1,900
Ray	72,000	2,000
Eugene	63,000	1,850
Total	$225,000	5,750

Required:
1. Compute the overhead cost rate that should be used for each of the estimators (based on the expected hours to be billed, with overhead cost rates varying in proportion to each estimator's compensation) to ensure that the total expected operating costs for 2006 will be recovered from clients. (*Hint:* Allocate total estimated overhead costs to each estimator based on relative salaries, then relate the allocated costs to the hours expected to be worked by each estimator.)
2. Using the overhead cost rates determined in part (1), determine the costs associated with the firm's work for Landslide Company with the following estimating services and related costs: Spencer, 150 hours; Ray, 60 hours; Eugene, 15 hours; transportation and supplies costs, $2,400.

Problem 3-14

Service Costing—Journal Entries
Following are transactions for Andersen Custodial, Inc. Assume the company's beginning work-in-process services account balance is zero.

a. Purchased supplies costing $5,000 for cash.
b. Received and immediately paid a utility bill, $800.
c. Used supplies costing $3,000 in doing work for a customer.
d. Incurred and paid 3,000 hours of direct labor and 1,500 hours of indirect labor. The average hourly wage rate for both direct and indirect labor is $7.
e. Made monthly rent payment, $2,000.
f. Applied overhead at $4.50 per direct labor hour.
g. Andersen bills its customers at a rate of $20 per direct labor hour. All work in process was moved to Cost of Services.
h. Closed all under- or overapplied overhead to Cost of Services.

Required:
Prepare the journal entries for the above transactions.

Problem 3-15

Service Costing—Journal Entries
Blake Accounting Services has the following transactions. Its beginning work-in-process services account balance is zero.

a. Purchased supplies costing $11,000 on account.
b. Paid property tax, $20,000.

(continued)

c. Paid rent, $2,000; and utilities, $700.
d. Paid support staff salaries, $35,000.
e. Used supplies costing $9,000.
f. Paid direct labor salaries, $50,000. Average rate was $10 per hour.
g. Applied overhead at $11.50 per direct labor hour.
h. Transferred $100,000 from Work-in-Process to Cost of Services and billed customers for 4,500 hours of work. Blake bills its customers $40 per direct labor hour.
i. Closed under- or overapplied overhead to Cost of Services.

Required:
1. Prepare the journal entries for the above transactions.
2. Determine the ending balance in the work-in-process services account.

Problem 3-16

Service Cost Flows

Allee Company had the following balances at the beginning of 2006:

	Debit	Credit
Accounts receivable	$44,000	
Supplies	10,000	
Work-in-process services	30,000	
Accounts payable (related to supplies)		$ 7,000
Salaries and wages payable		70,000
Utilities payable		2,400
Rent payable		3,000

Allee estimates that its total 2006 overhead will amount to $400,000. It allocates overhead based on direct labor hours. Allee estimates that its total 2006 direct labor hours will be 100,000 hours. Because it produces monthly financial statements, Allee makes adjusting entries at the end of each month. However, over- or underapplied overhead is not closed to Cost of Services until the end of the year.

During January 2006, Allee had the following transactions:

Jan. 1 Paid rent. Allee has a three-year, $162,000 lease. Rent is payable on the first of each month.
    3 Paid for all supplies purchased in 2005.
    4 Paid all utilities payable from 2005.
    7 Purchased supplies, $1,200.
   10 Paid all salaries and wages payable from 2005. $46,000 was for direct labor; $24,000 was for indirect labor.
   12 Used supplies, $900.
   19 Collected $30,000 from a customer for services performed and billed in December 2005.
   27 Used supplies, $2,600.
   31 Paid all employees for January labor. Total direct labor costs for the month of January were $50,000, direct labor hours, 8,000. Indirect labor costs were $30,000.
   31 Applied overhead for the month.
   31 Estimated its January utility expenses to be $2,000.
   31 Completed and billed jobs costing $80,000. The company billed customers $140,000.

Required:
1. Prepare all journal entries necessary for the month of January.
2. What is the balance in the work-in-process services account at the end of January?
3. Compute the balance in the overhead account on January 31.

Problem 3-17

FIFO Cost Flow—Process Costing

The cleaning division of Rulon Corn Company had the following data for January 2006:

	Tons	Percentage Completed	Direct Materials Costs	Conversion Costs
Beginning work-in-process inventory . .	600	80%	$ 12,750	$ 1,800
Units started in production	39,900	—		
Costs added this month			897,750	189,072
Ending work-in-process inventory	900	30%		
Units completed during month and transferred to packing	39,600	—		

Required:
1. Using the FIFO cost flow method, compute the per-ton cost of corn processed by the cleaning division in this period (all materials are in place at the beginning of the process).
2. Compute the cost of the 39,000 tons of corn that were started and completed during January.
3. Compute the cost of the ending work-in-process inventory.

Problem 3-18

FIFO Cost Flow—Process Costing

Western Oil Company has three process centers: drilling, processing, and distributing. During September 2006, the processing department had the following operating data:

	Barrels	Percentage Completed	Direct Materials Costs	Conversion Costs
Beginning work-in-process inventory	4,000	60%	$ 2,200	$ 4,200
Units started and completed this month . .	36,000	—		
Costs added this month			33,150	88,410
Ending work-in-process inventory	15,000	30%		
Units completed during month and transferred to distributing	40,000	—		

Required:
All raw materials are put in place at the beginning of the operation in the processing department. Assuming a FIFO flow of costs, compute:

1. The "work done" for September (in equivalent units of production) for direct materials and for conversion costs.
2. The September cost per barrel of oil in the processing department.
3. The cost of all oil transferred to distributing.
4. The cost of ending work-in-process inventory in the processing department.

Problem 3-19

FIFO Cost Flow—Process Costing

The assembly department of Charles Manufacturing Company reported the following data for the month of August 2006:

(continued)

	Units	Costs
Beginning inventory (75% complete)	3,000	
Units transferred from prior department	22,500	
Ending inventory (50% complete)	4,500	
Cost of beginning inventory (prior department $18,300; assembly materials $11,250; assembly conversion $12,375)		$ 41,925
Cost transferred in from prior department		135,000
Cost of materials used in assembly department		67,500
Conversion costs for August in assembly department		117,600
Total cost		$362,025

(*Note:* Materials used in the assembly department are added at the beginning of the assembly process.)

Required:
Prepare the production cost report for the assembly department. (*Note:* The prior department's manufacturing costs should be included in this department's production cost report.)

Problem 3-20

Spreadsheet

Equivalent Units and FIFO Cost Flow—Process Costing
Midtown Manufacturing Company has two process centers—manufacturing and assembly. The data that follow show the production and cost results for the manufacturing center for the month of July 2006:

Production data:	
Units in process, July 1 (materials 50% complete, conversion 40% complete)	500
Units started in production	2,500
Units in process, July 31 (materials 100% complete, conversion 60% complete)	700

Cost data:	
Units in process, July 1:	
Direct materials	$ 3,000
Conversion costs	6,400
Direct materials used in July	27,500
Conversion costs for July	73,080
Total	$109,980

(*Note:* In this problem, materials are *not* added at the beginning of the manufacturing process.)

Required:
Prepare the production cost report for the manufacturing center.

d iscussion cases

Case 3-1

Packard, Inc.
Packard, Inc., produces and sells mousetraps. The cost of a mousetrap can be broken down as follows:

Direct materials	$0.23
Direct labor	0.09
Manufacturing overhead	0.12
Cost per trap	$0.44

The traps are then sold for 120% of cost, or $0.53 each. The manufacturing overhead is applied based on direct labor costs and was computed at the beginning of the year using the following estimates:

Estimated manufacturing overhead for the period	$540,000
Estimated direct labor costs	405,000
Predetermined overhead rate (per direct labor dollar)	1.33

For the first six months of the year, overhead costs of $272,000 were actually incurred. For that same time period, actual direct labor costs were $204,000. However, during the year several changes in the production process were made. As a result, by the midpoint of the year, expected manufacturing overhead costs have been significantly reduced below the original estimate of $540,000. Hence, for the last six months of the year, overhead costs are expected to be $225,000, and direct labor costs are expected to be $202,500.

1. What changes (if any) should be made in the predetermined manufacturing overhead rate for Packard, Inc.?
2. Assuming that per-unit direct materials and direct labor costs will remain the same for the last six months of the year, determine the new cost of a single mousetrap.
3. Because the cost of producing mousetraps dropped during the second half of the year, Packard can reduce the price of its traps and still earn its 20% markup on cost. Should the company reduce the price of its mousetraps? What factors would affect your decision?

Case 3-2

US MacDonald Corporation

You work for US MacDonald Corporation (USMC), an airplane manufacturer. USMC makes airplanes for commercial airlines, such as UNITED, AMERICAN, and DELTA, and for the U.S. AIR FORCE. Many parts are common to all planes made by USMC. The market for commercial planes is extremely competitive with GENERAL DYNAMICS, LOCKHEED, and European manufacturer AIRBUS often bidding lower than USMC. However, USMC's contract with the Air Force allows it to bill them at cost plus a 9% profit.

Times have been tough lately for USMC. In fact, if you can't find a way to increase profits, the company may have to lay off 5,000 employees.

A colleague has just presented you with an idea that he believes will increase profits. He suggests that instead of using direct labor hours to allocate overhead costs among airplanes, you should allocate costs on the basis of the number of each type of airplane made. Because you make far more, smaller, less expensive planes for the Air Force, more of the overhead costs will be allocated to those planes. This action will not only decrease your cost per unit on commercial planes (allowing you to be competitive in that market), but will also increase your profits on Air Force planes because the cost per plane will be higher.

You are not sure about your colleague's suggested action. You do know that your allocation base of direct labor hours is quite arbitrary and probably does not correspond well to the way overhead costs are consumed.

1. What is an appropriate allocation basis? Would adopting the suggestion be ethical?
2. Would you change your mind if you learned that competitors were allocating overhead on the basis of number of each type of plane made?
3. Is your action appropriate, from both a business and an ethical point of view, if direct labor hours is not an accurate allocation base?

Case 3-3

The Distribution Channel

You have just been hired as a branch manager for Perkins Retailers, a chain of office-supply stores in the Midwest. Perkins often purchases inventory items from Walker Wholesalers, a local distributor. However, Perkins also has the option of purchasing directly from various manufacturers, all of whom ensure prompt delivery. A comparative price list is as follows:

Lined paper:	
Gates Paper Manufacturers	$ 0.25
Walker Wholesalers	0.35
Steno chairs:	
Sturdychairs Manufacturers	$27.80
Walker Wholesalers	30.00
Desk lamps:	
Illumination Manufacturers	$ 7.60
Walker Wholesalers	11.25
Day planners:	
Olsen Manufacturers	$12.50
Walker Wholesalers	15.40

While examining past purchase invoices, you are perplexed to discover that despite the significantly higher prices, the previous branch manager had made most of his purchases from Walker Wholesalers.

1. Why might the previous branch manager have purchased from Walker Wholesalers when purchasing directly from the manufacturers is less expensive?
2. Why do wholesalers need to charge higher prices than manufacturers? Are they justified from the customers' point of view?
3. Will you, the new branch manager, always purchase from the manufacturers? Why or why not?

Case 3-4

Service Cost Flows

The CPA firm you work for has just been hired by Phillips Attorneys at Law to perform an audit. In the process of the audit, you notice that Phillips' accountant has been inconsistent in accounting for the company president's salary. You notice that sometimes he has accounted for the company president's salary as follows:

Overhead	20,000	
Salaries and Wages Payable		20,000
To record the company president's salary.		

Other times, the accountant has debited Salaries and Wages Expense instead of Overhead. When you confront the accountant about the inconsistency, he gets somewhat defensive and says that it doesn't matter which method is used because both methods result in an expense, and net income will be the same either way.

1. Assuming that the company president's tasks are exclusively administrative, do you agree with the accountant? Why or why not?
2. Which journal entry is correct? Why?

 j u d g m e n t   c a l l s

Judgment 3-1

You Decide: With advancements in the Internet and e-commerce, will retailers be important to the future success of businesses, or will their services be eliminated in order to decrease costs?

Companies such as AMAZON.COM and EBAY eliminated retailers altogether and have changed the way their customers shop. Amazon.com and Ebay have no physical store locations. Customers order their products over the Internet and pay shipping to have goods delivered to any location they choose. Amazon.com and Ebay are able to pass the extra savings on to the consumer in the form of lower prices. Will retailers be completely eliminated in 15 years? What do you think?

Judgment 3-2

You Decide: Should the costs associated with an uncompleted consulting project be classified as a work-in-process asset on the balance sheet, or should the cost be expensed on the income statement as a part of doing business?

Your marketing company has been working on a consulting project for a client. Your team has worked on the project for two months, and it is now year-end. The project will be completed by February of the next year, and the client has not yet been billed. For the financial statements, how should the project be classified?

C o m p e t e n c y   E n h a n c e m e n t   O p p o r t u n i t i e s

▶ **Analyzing Real Company Information**   ▶ **The Debate**
▶ **International Case**   ▶ **Internet Search**
▶ **Ethics Case**
▶ **Writing Assignment**

The following additional assignments provide opportunities for students to develop critical thinking, ethical perspectives, oral and written communication skills, experience with electronic research, and teamwork through group and business activities.

▶ *Analyzing Real Company Information*

Analyzing 3-1 (Microsoft)

1. Is MICROSOFT a service business, a manufacturing business, or a merchandising business? Explain.

2. Microsoft's 2002 income statement (Appendix A) lists research and development expense of $4,379 billion for the year. The notes to the financial statements say that "research and development costs are expensed as incurred" in accordance with generally accepted accounting principles. Do you think that Microsoft treats R&D costs any differently in its internal accounting reports? Explain.

3. In its management's discussion and analysis (Appendix A), Microsoft describes four primary segments that it uses to categorize its product revenue. What are these segments, and what are some of the familiar products or services within these revenue segments?

Analyzing 3-2 (Pump, Inc.)

Acquiring management accounting data on real companies can be a challenge because this information is generally highly proprietary and of significant competitive value. The cost data below are for a medium-size family-owned pump manufacturing business located in the Midwest. (This business chooses to remain anonymous in order to keep its competitors from using these data to compete against it.) We'll refer to this company simply as Pump, Inc.

Pump, Inc., had reorganized much of its production into manufacturing "cells": self-supervising work centers that produce complete products. The cell program was initiated because of a strategic decision (with no management accounting data to support it) to improve customer service. The financial impact of the program was unclear; the operational causes and the financial effects were murky. As a result, the management team at Pump, Inc., was having a difficult time evaluating the effects of its strategic decision to change *most* of the company to manufacturing cells. (Some of the production process continued to be organized as a typical production line, similar to what is demonstrated in the chapter.) The current year's cost data are presented below in the standard format typically used by the management accountant for Pump, Inc.

Typical Cost Data Format		
Cost Category	**Cost**	**Percent of Cost**
Direct materials	$433,966	54.55%
Direct labor	96,990	12.19
Manufacturing overhead	264,583	33.26
Total costs	$795,539	100.00%

The management team, however, had a difficult time using the cost data in the typical format to effectively control and evaluate its reorganization decision. The management accountant was asked to reformat the data to make them more useful for the management team. After some analysis, the accountant decided to provide more detail by breaking down Manufacturing Overhead into subcategories organized by function: Indirect Materials, Indirect Labor, Factory Support, Occupancy Costs, and Non-Factory Support. The accountant also realized that she could divide all costs into two additional categories: People Costs (represent costs for wages and salaries) and Purchased Costs (represent costs for materials, supplies, and services acquired from outside agencies). The new report format is presented on the following page.

(continued)

Cost Category	People Costs	Purchased Costs	Total Cost
New Cost Data Format			
Direct materials		$433,966	$433,966
Indirect materials		9,460	9,460
Direct labor	$ 96,990		96,990
Indirect labor (production line supervision)	29,100		29,100
Factory support (material handling, equipment depreciation, utilities, expediting, engineering, etc.) . . .	80,953	71,310	152,263
Occupancy costs (rents, taxes, maintenance, etc.)	15,180	32,550	47,730
Non-factory support (cost accounting, personnel, etc.) ..	23,390	2,640	26,030
Total costs	**$245,613**	**$549,926**	**$795,539**

Source: Adapted from J. S. McGroarty and C. T. Horngren, "Functional Costing for Better Teamwork and Decision Support," *Journal of Cost Management*, Winter 1993, pp. 24–36. Reprinted with permission.

Consider the two reports on cost data for Pump, Inc.

1. Do you think the new report format provides any additional information value for controlling and evaluating the decision to change most of the production process into manufacturing cells?
2. What costs do you think the management team at Pump, Inc., should pay careful attention to in its effort to better control costs in the production plant?
3. Most importantly, if you were on the management team at Pump, Inc., what *additional* data would you like to see the management accountant provide?

▷ *International Case*

International

Management Accounting in France

France has a well-developed set of financial accounting rules, as embodied in the *Plan Comptable Général (PCG)*. The French PCG is comparable to U.S. GAAP. You may not have realized it, but the cost accounting for manufacturers we have studied in this chapter has a very clear connection to the way financial accounting is reported. Exhibit 1 in the text visibly demonstrates the difference between the production process and the administration process in a manufacturing organization. U.S. cost accounting makes a clear functional distinction between costs related to the production process (e.g., direct materials, direct labor, and manufacturing overhead) versus the administration process (e.g., selling costs and general administration costs). Further, Exhibit 3 demonstrates that the flow of direct materials costs and direct labor costs through the accounting system, as well as the allocation of manufacturing overhead costs, allows U.S. companies to determine product costs and easily compute cost of goods sold for financial reporting purposes. However, cost accounting (*comptabilité analytique*) in France is explicitly decoupled from financial accounting, as defined by the PCG. What this means is that the chart of accounts French companies use for cost accounting is completely different from the chart of accounts used for financial accounting. The reason is not necessarily because French companies perform cost accounting differently from U.S. companies, but that the nature of French financial accounting is quite different from financial accounting in the United States. The PCG requires financial accounting reports in France to organize and report costs by their inherent nature (materials, labor, depreciation, etc.). Costs are not assigned to products or to departments. Hence, one wouldn't expect to see a French company report Cost of Goods Sold or Selling and General Administrative Expense.

Think about this for a moment. If costs are not being assigned to products, departments, or operations within the organization, how does the organization perform the management processes of planning, controlling, and evaluating? Actually, French companies do not have a tradition of using costs to manage their companies. In fact, the traditional phrase used in France to describe the techniques and practices of planning, control, and evaluation has been *contrôle de gestion*, literally, "management control." The absence of the word *comptabilité* (accounting) in this phrase is significant: it indicates that accounting numbers play a limited role in managerial reporting systems in France. Only very recently has the phrase *comptabilité de gestion* become more common. French business has had a long tradition of being led by engineers, not by accountants and financiers. Even today some 50% of managing directors in France are engineers by profession or training.

Costs are not being used as the main tool for managing companies in France. Given that a large number of the management executives of French companies have engineering backgrounds, how do French companies handle the management processes of planning, controlling, and evaluating (e.g., what kinds of numbers and reports might you expect to find in a French company)? Would you expect that French companies reconcile their *comptabilité analytique* systems with their financial accounting systems, as U.S. companies typically do?

Source: Reprinted from A. Roberts, "Management Accounting in France," *Management Accounting (UK)*, March 1995, pp. 44–46, by permission of the publisher Academic Press Limited, London.

▶ *Ethics Case*

State Home Builders Inc.

You have recently been hired as an accountant for the largest residential construction company in the state. Your primary responsibility is to track costs for each home being constructed. Tracking the costs for direct materials and direct labor is relatively straightforward. Materials requisitioned for each home site are carefully tracked, and the construction workers are very careful about assigning their time to the homes they work on.

Accounting for manufacturing overhead costs, on the other hand, presents quite a problem. In the past, overhead has been allocated on the basis of direct labor hours. As a result, because larger houses require more workers, those houses have been allocated a larger share of the overhead.

Your company was recently selected by the state to build a number of low-income housing complexes. The state has agreed to an arrangement whereby it will pay your costs plus a 10% profit. Construction of these low-income housing units will be relatively simple and will not require a great deal of materials or labor, compared to the average house the company builds.

At a meeting following the granting of the construction contract by the state, the production foreman proposes the following idea:

> Since the state has agreed to pay our costs plus 10%, the higher the costs on the project, the more money we make. What we need to do is to funnel as much of our costs as possible to this low-income housing project. Now I don't want anyone to think I am proposing something unethical. I am not saying that we should charge the state for fictitious costs. What I am saying is that we should allocate as much overhead as possible to the low-income project. Therefore, I propose that we allocate overhead on a per-house basis with each house, regardless of size, being allocated the same amount of overhead.

(continued)

You have analyzed the activities that drive overhead costs and have found that bigger houses, in addition to requiring more direct materials and direct labor, require more inspections, more supervision, etc. You can see that most in attendance at the meeting are being persuaded by the production foreman's idea. You slowly raise your hand. It takes about 10 seconds before all the voices quiet. You look around the table and see 10 of your colleagues staring at you. You open your mouth and. . .

1. What would you do in this situation? Is the overhead allocation method being proposed by the production foreman illegal? Is it unethical?
2. Suppose you argue that overhead should continue to be allocated on the basis of direct labor hours. After hearing your points, the group votes to go with the production foreman and allocate the overhead on a per-house basis. What would you do next?

▶ *Writing Assignment*

Trends in Product Cost Relationships
The ratios among the three types of product costs have changed quite a bit over the last 150 years of business. Generally, costs of direct materials have consistently formed approximately 50% of total product costs for manufacturing firms. However, the ratio of direct labor costs has been decreasing with an offsetting increase in the ratio of manufacturing overhead costs. What kinds of costing challenges does this shift from direct costs to manufacturing overhead costs pose for a manufacturing company? What factors do you think have contributed to this trend? Do you think that the advent of e-business will significantly affect the amount or ratio of direct labor costs in manufacturing products? If so, how? Write a one- to two-page paper on this topic.

▶ *The Debate*

When Does a Direct Materials Cost Turn into an Indirect Cost (e.g., Manufacturing Overhead)?
Consider your automobile. What costs would be considered direct materials? What costs would be considered indirect materials? Are the fender panels direct or indirect materials? Are the rivets that connect the fender to the frame direct or indirect materials? Are the headlights direct or indirect materials? Are the screws that hold the headlights in place direct or indirect materials? In light of the intense price competition that takes place in the automobile industry, these are important cost questions: direct materials are assigned to a specific automobile (or automobile model), while indirect materials are gathered together in the pool of manufacturing overhead costs and generally allocated across all types of automobiles in the manufacturing plant.

Divide your group into two teams.

- One team represents: "Rivets and screws should be treated as direct costs." Prepare a two-minute oral argument supporting this view. Be careful that you don't make too many quick assumptions. Tracking direct materials costs to specific product units or product lines can be a very expensive process in a complex manufacturing organization.
- The other team represents: "Rivets and screws should be treated as indirect costs." Prepare a two-minute oral argument supporting this view. You must be careful that you don't make too many quick assumptions. Before you say that rivets and screws are indirect because their costs are small, consider that the bigger automakers spend tens of millions of dollars each year on rivets and screws.

▶ *Internet Search*

Wal-Mart

Access WAL-MART's customer Web site at **http://www.walmart.com**. Sometimes Web addresses change, so if this address doesn't work, access the Web site for this textbook (**http://swain .swlearning.com**) for an updated link.

Once you've gained access to the site, answer the following questions.

1. Use Wal-Mart's Store Finder to find the store nearest you (look at the bottom of its homepage).
2. What is the current price on a hardback version of J. K. Rowling's *Harry Potter and the Order of the Phoenix* (a popular children's book)?

Now access Wal-Mart's corporate Web site at **http://www.walmartstores.com** (you could also click on the "Wal-Mart Stores Info" link at the bottom of the customer Web site). Again, if this Web address should change, access the Web site for this textbook (**http://swain .swlearning.com**) for an updated link.

Once you've gained access to this site, answer the following questions:

3. In order to be a Wal-Mart supplier you would need to adhere to certain "Supplier Standards." Although these standards are very detailed, what are the seven general areas of supplier standards?
4. Wal-Mart's first non-U.S. store opened in December 1991. Where? How many Wal-Mart stores are operating outside of the United States? Which countries, other than the United States, now have Wal-Mart stores?

Part

2

Planning

Capital Investment Decisions

After studying this chapter, you should be able to:

FEDERAL EXPRESS CORPORATION (FEDEX) is the largest air-freight company in the world. Fred Smith, founder of Federal Express, came up with his initial overnight-delivery idea as he was writing a term paper in 1965 as a Yale undergraduate. Smith's Yale professor was unimpressed with the idea and gave the paper a "C" grade. After serving two tours of duty in Vietnam as a Marine, Smith returned to the United States and began assembling the pieces to implement his idea. In 1971, Smith was optimistic about obtaining the contract to ship canceled checks around the country; he named his company "Federal Express" because the contract would have been with the Federal Reserve System. That contract never came to be, and Smith focused his attention on shipping small, time-sensitive packages through his hub-and-spoke air system centered in Memphis, Tennessee. The inaugural night of service was March 12, 1973, but only six packages arrived at the 10,000-per-hour package handling system in Memphis. After further marketing in an expanded set of cities, a second start was attempted on April 17, 1973. That night, Federal Express handled 186 packages, and daily volume has climbed steadily ever since. In 2003, FedEx Corporation delivered 5.3 million shipments per day.

For FedEx and other firms in the air-freight industry, the most important investment is the airplanes that haul the freight. Indeed, making good airplane acquisition decisions is critical to the success of FedEx and its competitors. Although FedEx is profitable and expanding, questions have been raised about whether the company has made the right kind of airplane investment decisions. In early 1998, the Federal Aviation Administration (FAA) began public hearings to question the structural safety of scores of FedEx's aircraft. The FAA contended that the maximum allowed weight limit of these 727s should be cut from 8,000 pounds per modu-

lar cargo container to 3,000 pounds, which would significantly increase the per-pound cost of shipping cargo and reduce FedEx's profitability.

For years, the air-freight industry has relied heavily on the practice of converting retired passenger planes into cargo freighters. The safety questions raised by the FAA involve how cargo doors were installed and other structural changes made when the aircraft were modified. Safety concerns range from the stability of cargo doors to the ability of aircraft to survive a strong downward gust. FAA research has shown that under combinations of certain extreme conditions, the floor beams of 727s might fail, causing the aircraft to suddenly break apart in a massive midair convulsion. [Those who have seen the Tom Hanks movie *Cast Away* are familiar with this scenario.]

FedEx countered that the probability of the combination of conditions that would cause such an accident is highly remote. The FAA said it didn't want to wait until after an accident had occurred to raise safety issues about the 727s. In the end, the FAA compromised and only required FedEx to reduce its modular cargo container weights to 4,800 pounds in the 120 FedEx BOEING 727s in question. While FedEx was fighting the FAA claims and allegations, the company must have wondered if it made the right kind of investment decision by acquiring and converting the 727s. At a minimum, the questions raised about the safety of FedEx's operations represented a public relations nightmare for FedEx.

Sources: Douglas A. Blackmon, "FedEx Faults Claims by FAA over Aircraft," *The Wall Street Journal*, Wednesday, February 18, 1998, p. A3; Paul Richfield, "FAA Issues Final Ruling on 727 Freighters," *The Wall Street Journal*, January 11, 1999, p. B2; Robert A. Sigafoos, *Absolutely Positively Overnight!: The Unofficial History of Federal Express* (Memphis: St. Lukes Press, 1988).

Setting the Stage

how do FedEx and other companies decide which types of equipment to buy and what other capital investments to make? In this chapter, we examine that part of planning called **capital budgeting,** the systematic planning for long-term investments in operating assets (primarily property, plant, equipment, intangible assets, and natural resources). Capital budgeting techniques are also important in planning for a company's investments in people and information. For example, the most important decisions a university makes are not

about where or when to build buildings but instead are about whom to hire for the university's faculty.

Capital budgeting differs from the types of planning already discussed in that it is more permanent and less retractable. A decision to increase inventory levels, for example, can be reversed within a relatively short time by cutting back on future purchases or by lowering prices to increase sales. Even

capital budgeting Systematic planning for long-term investments in operating assets.

a nonroutine decision to purchase, rather than make or deliver internally, a component or service can generally be changed without too much disruption to operations. On the other hand, a capital investment decision to purchase 120 Model 727 freight aircraft at several million dollars each requires a long-term commitment of resources, a commitment that will probably be difficult and very expensive to change at a later date. Because of its long-term consequences, capital budgeting is an important part of a company's strategic plan. Strategic planning involves establishing the overall direction of a company's activities. Strategic planning is discussed in the next chapter.

Because capital budgeting involves long-range planning, the time value of money must be consid-

> **FYI:**
>
> FedEx, along with most airlines, leases many of the airplanes it uses. Technically, these leases, which are often for long terms and are not cancelable, are not equivalent to the purchase of the airplanes. However, the same capital budgeting analysis used to evaluate a purchase is used to evaluate a long-term lease.

ered. But before we begin to explain how capital budgeting provides management with information for evaluating long-term investments in operating assets, we must introduce some basic concepts.

Conceptual Basis of Capital Budgeting

1 Understand the importance of capital budgeting and the concepts underlying strategic and capital investment decisions.

The primary objective of a business is to generate a profit for its owners. Profitable businesses can be based on a low-cost strategy (such as WAL-MART), a customer service strategy (such as FEDEX), a product-branding strategy (such as COCA-COLA), and a variety of other business strategies. No matter what a company's underlying strategy, it must make long-term investment decisions in buildings, equipment, information technology, personnel, and so forth. Capital budgeting is the process of determining whether the future sales, cost savings, quality improvements, and other future benefits stemming from these strategic investment decisions are sufficient to justify the significant up-front costs associated with those decisions. In short, capital budgeting involves a comparison of the magnitude of up-front costs to the magnitude of estimated future multi-year benefits.

capital The total amount of money or other resources owned or used to acquire future income or benefits.

The term **capital** may be defined broadly as any form of material wealth. As used in business, it is more specifically defined as the total amount of money or other resources owned or used by an individual or a company to acquire future income or benefits.

Thus, capital is something to be invested with the expectation that it will be recovered along with a profit, and capital budgeting is the planning for that investment. From a quantitative viewpoint, the success of an investment depends on the amount of net future cash inflows (or future cash savings) in relation to the cost (current cash outlays) of the investment. Ignoring the time value of money for the moment, if a company invests $10,000 and receives only $10,000 in the future, there has been only a return of the investment but no profit. However, if $15,000 is received in the future, there is not only a return of the original investment but also an additional return, or profit, of $5,000. Other things being equal, investors obviously wish to receive the greatest future benefits for the least investment cost.

Importance of Capital Investment Decisions in Planning

Three aspects of capital investment decisions are critical to long-run profitability:

1. *Large initial outlay.* Decisions to invest in assets such as land, buildings, and equipment usually require large outlays of capital. Unless a reasonable return is received on such significant investments, the overall profitability of a firm will suffer.
2. *Potential long-term impact on earnings.* Long-term investments, by definition, extend over several years. Thus, poor capital budgeting, resulting in bad investment decisions, is likely to have an adverse effect on earnings over a long period.

3. *Difficult to reverse course.* Long-term investments in land, buildings, and specialized equipment are much less liquid than other investments. Investments in stocks and bonds, for example, can usually be terminated by sale through regularly established markets at almost any time; operating assets may not be so readily disposed of.

Each of these three factors can be seen in the FedEx scenario described at the beginning of the chapter. FedEx had expended millions of dollars on the 120 BOEING 727s that the FAA was concerned about. The efficient, or inefficient, use of this portion of FedEx's fleet would have implications for FedEx's reported earnings for many years; many 727s have now been in use for over 30 years. Finally, once FedEx had committed itself to using these converted 727 freighters, it was extremely costly to overhaul or retire the planes in response to the FAA concerns.

Uses of Capital Budgeting: Screening and Ranking

Clearly, all long-term investment decisions are important. The larger the investment, however, the more critical is the need to budget for that expenditure. And the longer the time period, the more difficult it is to assess future outcomes and to plan accordingly. Following are some typical business situations that lend themselves to analysis with capital budgeting techniques:

1. A machine breaks down. Should the manager have the machine repaired or replaced?
2. Should a pharmaceutical company hire a renowned research scientist and commit to supporting this scientist and her staff for the next 10 years?
3. Should a company add to its manufacturing facility or build a new, larger factory?
4. Should a professional sports team sign a long-term guaranteed contract for $252 million with a key player?
5. Should Company A purchase Company B and, if so, on what terms?

Situations such as these require careful consideration of all factors, qualitative as well as quantitative, and it is just as important for nonprofit organizations to make sound strategic and capital investment decisions as for-profit organizations. Thus, the concepts and techniques discussed in this chapter are applicable to all types of organizations—companies, governmental agencies, school districts, hospitals, city governments, and so forth.

Capital budgeting analysis can help by answering two basic questions. First, does the investment make sense? That is, does it meet a minimum standard of financial acceptability? This is the **screening** function of capital budgeting. Second, is an investment the best among available acceptable alternatives? We determine this by ranking the alternatives. Before we discuss the screening and **ranking** of investment alternatives, we will briefly review the time value of money concept.

The Time Value of Money

Like other commodities, money has value because it is a scarce resource. Therefore, a payment is generally required for its use. This payment is called **interest**. Because the time value of money is widely recognized, few people would consider hiding money under a mattress or otherwise keeping large amounts of idle cash; they realize that there is a significant opportunity cost in doing so. Money left idle will not earn interest, nor will it earn the potentially higher returns that can be obtained from investments in corporate stocks and bonds or real estate, for example.

Because money has value over time, the timing of expected cash flows is important in investment decisions. This is the essence of capital budgeting—comparing the cost of an investment with the expected future net cash inflows to decide whether, given the risks and available alternatives, the project should be undertaken. An investment made today will not generate cash inflows until the future, either periodically over a number of years or in a lump sum several

screening Determining whether a capital investment meets a minimum standard of financial acceptability.

ranking The ordering of acceptable investment alternatives from most to least desirable.

interest The payment (cost) for the use of money.

years hence. Thus, for the comparison of cash flows to be accurate, all amounts should be stated at their value at one point in time, generally the present; this means that all future cash flows should be stated in terms of their present values. This mathematical process of adjusting future cash flows to their present values is called discounting.

The choice of the correct interest rate, or discount rate, to use in doing time value of money computations is extremely important. In fact, this is one of the topics emphasized in the field of finance. Generally speaking, managers use relatively high discount rates when evaluating projects or investments that involve a high degree of risk; an expectation of a high rate of return is necessary to entice a rational manager into undertaking a very risky project. In addition, a manager must consider what it will cost to obtain the funds to finance the project. We will return later to the problem of selecting a discount rate for making capital investment decisions.

In the remainder of this chapter and in the end-of-chapter exercises and problems, we will assume that you understand the concepts of present value and the underlying notion of the time value of money. If you do not, or if you want to refresh your memory, you might want to review the appendix to this chapter.

Caution

If you are using a business calculator, you might note that a more precise calculation of the present value of $100,000 to be received one year from now, if the interest rate is 10%, is $90,909.09. The $90,910 amount results from using present value tables. In this chapter, calculations using both present value tables and business calculators will be illustrated.

Discounting Cash Flows

Because of the time value of money, a difference in the timing of cash flows can make one investment more attractive than another, even if both involve the same total amount of money. To illustrate, we assume that project A will produce $100,000 at the end of one year and that project B will return $50,000 at the end of each year for two years. Both projects will generate a total of $100,000. However, by using present value computations (reviewed in the chapter appendix) and assuming a discount (interest) rate of 10% per year, you will see that the discounted cash flows from project A are $90,910 and from project B are $86,775. In other words, if the appropriate discount rate is 10%, receiving $90,910 right now is the same as receiving $100,000 one year from now. Similarly, receiving

Project A

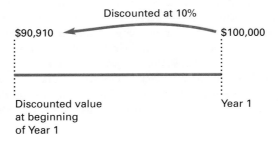

Project B

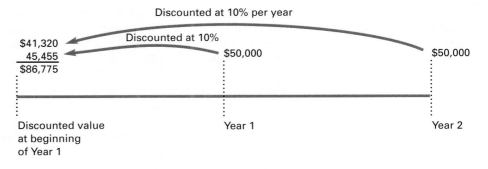

$86,775 right now is the same as receiving $50,000 at the end of each year for the next two years. The difference in the present values of these two projects with the same total cash flows arises because with project A, the cash is received sooner. Cash received sooner is worth more because it can be put to productive use—invested, used to pay off loans, and so forth. If all other factors—that is, any qualitative considerations—are the same, an investor would be $4,135 (in today's dollars) better off by investing in project A.

As the analysis on the previous page shows, discounted cash flows reflect the time value of money and should be considered in capital budgeting. The determination of net income in accordance with GAAP is based, as you know, on accrual concepts that recognize income when it is earned, not when cash is actually received. Thus, accounting net income doesn't necessarily coincide with cash flows. For short-term investments, this approach does not significantly affect the results. Ignoring the time value of money can be misleading, however, for evaluating long-term projects.

To be able to compare cash outflows and inflows, you need a solid understanding of the discounting of cash flows. In the following paragraphs, we provide some definitions and examples.

Cash Outflows

cash outflows The initial cost and other expected outlays associated with an investment.

Cash outflows include the initial cost of an investment plus any other expected future cash outlays associated with the investment. For example, suppose that a company purchases a drill press for $8,000 cash less a trade-in allowance of $500 for its old press. With maintenance expenses of $400 at the end of each year for the 5-year life of the press, and assuming a 12% discount rate, the present value of the cash outflows for the investment is computed as follows:

	Time Period	Cash Outflows	Present Value Factor	Present Value of Cash Outflows
Initial cash outlay	Today	$7,500	1.0000	$7,500
Future cash outlays	Years 1–5	400	3.6048*	1,442
Total present value of cash outflows				$8,942

*From Table II, 5 years at 12%.

The $7,500 is invested immediately, so it is already stated at its present value. The $400 series of equal payments (an annuity) is to be extended over five years, so it must be discounted to its present value equivalent.

Maintenance expense is only one category of future cash outflows. Another is manufacturing overhead costs—such as heat, electricity, and rent—that may be incurred as a consequence of an investment. In addition, income taxes are expenses that must be considered in almost all capital budgeting decisions made by businesses. For simplicity, income taxes are ignored in the first part of this chapter; the impact of income taxes on capital budgeting decisions is explained in the expanded material section of the chapter. In brief, all current or expected cash outlays (expressed in terms of present values) should be considered as cash outflows in evaluating investments.

Note that some expenses, although deducted from revenues in arriving at accounting net income, do not involve actual cash disbursements and so should not be considered outflows in capital budgeting. It would obviously be wrong, for example, to include depreciation expense as an outflow, since no cash flow is directly involved.

Cash Inflows

Cash inflows include all current and expected future revenues or savings directly associated with an investment. For example, rent receipts, installment payments, and other revenues represent cash inflows. Returning to our earlier example, we now assume that the drill press is expected to generate annual revenues of $2,500 for five years, after which it can be sold as scrap for $750. The present value of the cash inflows for the investment is computed as follows:

	Time Period	Cash Outflows	Present Value Factor	Present Value of Cash Outflows
Revenues	Years 1–5	$2,500	3.6048*	$9,012
Salvage value	Year 5	750	0.5674**	426
Total present value of cash inflows				$9,438

*From Table II, 5 years at 12%.
**From Table I, 5 years at 12%.

These revenues may be shown "net"—that is, reduced by any direct expenses, such as those for maintenance or materials and supplies. Thus, the net annual cash inflows from the drill press would be $2,100 per year ($2,500 − $400 maintenance expense).

Less obvious cash inflows are represented by the present value of the savings to be derived from an investment that reduces costs. In brief, the present value of all cash that is likely to be received or saved as a result of an investment should be included as cash inflows.

> **TO SUMMARIZE:** Certain long-term investment decisions require significant capital outlays. Proper planning for these decisions is critical to long-run profitability. Capital budgeting techniques are designed to help in analyzing the quantitative factors relating to these decisions. Essentially, capital budgeting involves a comparison of the current and expected cash outflows and inflows in order to decide whether, given the risks and available alternatives, an investment should be made. To make comparisons more meaningful, all future cash flows should be discounted to the present.

Nondiscounted Capital Budgeting Techniques

2 Describe and use two nondiscounted capital budgeting techniques: the payback method and the unadjusted rate of return method.

The four most commonly used capital budgeting techniques are (1) the payback method, (2) the unadjusted rate of return method, (3) the net present value method, and (4) the internal rate of return method. We will discuss the first two methods in this section and the latter two in the next section.

We have chosen the sequence of our discussion to parallel the pattern of most companies as they grow larger and become more sophisticated in the way that they make investment decisions. That is, companies generally first use the payback method or the unadjusted rate of return method because these techniques are relatively simple. Both of these techniques have a serious weakness, however, in that they ignore the time value of money. As a result, most companies eventually turn to either the net present value method or the internal rate of return method, both of which are more theoretically correct approaches to capital budgeting. The last two techniques are referred to as **discounted cash flow methods** because they use a discount rate in comparing the cash flows of investments.

Payback Method

payback method A capital budgeting technique that determines the amount of time it takes the net cash inflows of an investment to repay the investment cost.

The **payback method** is widely used in business because it is simple to apply and it provides a preliminary screening of investment opportunities. It can also be used as a crude measure of a project's risk. Basically, this method is used to determine the length of time it will take the net cash inflows of an investment to equal the cash outlay. The payback period may be a particularly important consideration for companies in a tight credit position. Assuming that the payback period is to be computed in years (any time frame can be applied) and that equal cash flows are generated for each period, the formula for a project's payback period is:

$$\frac{\text{Investment cost}}{\text{Annual net cash inflows}} = \text{Payback period}$$

To illustrate the payback method, we will consider Kristi Felt's decision to purchase a personal computer, printer, and software for typing and printing essays and term papers for other students. A reasonably good PC, printer, and appropriate software will cost Kristi a total of $1,500. She can borrow the $1,500 from her parents, who require no interest but need to be repaid at the end of 18 months. Kristi expects to make $100 per month after paying for supplies and other related expenses. The payback period (in months) may be computed as follows:

$$\frac{\$1,500}{\$100} = 15 \text{ months}$$

Since Kristi would generate sufficient cash to recover the investment in 15 months, she could repay her parents within the agreed period of time (assuming she spends none of the money).

This is one of the strengths of the payback method: It can be used to determine whether an investment fits within an acceptable period for the use of funds. For example, a company's cash position may lead it to establish a rule of thumb that no investment with a payback period exceeding three years will be accepted. In such a situation, a manager may be obliged to select an investment alternative with a slightly lower rate of return but a shorter payback period.

The payback method has several weaknesses, however. One is that it measures the time needed to recover the initial outlay but does not consider the investment's profitability. Investments obviously are made in order to earn an acceptable return, not just to recover their costs. In our example, Kristi is not solely interested in recovering the $1,500 in the shortest time possible. Her purpose in buying the equipment is to earn some extra money. Assuming that the equipment will last for more than 15 months, Kristi not only will recover her initial investment, but will also generate subsequent earnings (at least $100 per month). Although the payback method may provide some clues about the advisability of investments, it does not directly measure profitability.

To clarify this last point and show why the payback method must be used with care, consider a manager's decision to purchase one of two machines. Machine A costs $5,500 and is expected to generate $1,000 of net cash inflows annually. Machine B costs $3,500 and will produce $800 of net cash inflows annually. The payback period for machine A is 5.5 years ($5,500 ÷ $1,000); for machine B, the payback period is 4.4 years ($3,500 ÷ $800). Other things being equal, the payback method would indicate that the manager should purchase machine B because it would result in a shorter payback period. That is, its original cost would be recovered in a shorter time. However, if machine B were expected to last less than 4.4 years, such an investment would be unwise. The machine would not last long enough to recover its original cost, let alone generate any earnings.

Now suppose that both machines were estimated to have a 7-year life. Which machine would be the better investment? What if the estimated lifetimes of both machines were more than 10 years? To answer these questions, we would have to use one of the discounted cash flow methods (to be discussed later) in conjunction with the payback period.

This example highlights the other major weakness of the payback method: It does not take into account the time value of money. As a result, incorrect investment decisions may result unless the payback period is relatively short.

Unadjusted Rate of Return Method

Another commonly used capital budgeting technique is the **unadjusted rate of return method**. Also referred to as the simple rate of return method or the accounting rate of return method, the unadjusted rate of return is computed as follows:

$$\frac{\text{Increase in future average net income}}{\text{Initial investment cost}} = \text{Unadjusted rate of return}$$

unadjusted rate of return method A capital budgeting technique in which a rate of return is calculated by dividing the increase in the average annual net income a project will generate by the initial investment cost.

To illustrate the unadjusted rate of return method, consider the following situation. Seal Right Company manufactures cans for fruits, vegetables, and other farm produce. Management wants to add a new, larger can size to the product line in order to take advantage of a potential demand for food storage items in the western states. This new can is expected to increase the company's annual revenues by an average of $51,500 a year for 10 years. The additional machinery needed to manufacture the can will cost $215,000. Assuming that there are no other expenses, the new can will increase annual net income by $30,000 each year; this $30,000 is computed as the difference between the $51,500 increase in revenues and the $21,500 ($215,000 ÷ 10 years) increase in annual depreciation. The unadjusted rate of return (or accounting rate of return) on the investment is $30,000 ÷ $215,000 = 14% (rounded).

Unlike the payback method, the unadjusted rate of return method attempts to measure the profitability of an investment. A company compares the unadjusted rate of return with a preselected rate that it considers acceptable. Management invests only in projects with accounting rates of return that are equal to or greater than the established standard. Thus, if Seal Right's standard acceptance rate is less than or equal to 14%, the project would be acceptable. In the business world, any investment that provides a positive return (increases net income and EPS) is said to be **accretive**.

The main weakness of the unadjusted rate of return method is that, like the payback method, it does not consider the time value of money. The computation uses average future net income rather than expected future earnings discounted to the present. A second problem is that this method counts the initial investment cost twice. This occurs because depreciation is a component in the computation of the average net income added by a project.

The problem of double counting can be eliminated by using refined models of the unadjusted rate of return method. The more serious problem—the omission of the time value of money—cannot be corrected. And because this omission can produce misleading results and incorrect long-term investment decisions, the unadjusted rate of return method must be used with extreme care.

TO SUMMARIZE: The payback method measures the time required to recover the initial cost of an investment from future net cash inflows (investment cost divided by annual net cash inflows). It may be useful as a preliminary screen of investment projects. The unadjusted rate of return method provides a measure of the profitability of an investment (increases in future average annual net income divided by the cost of the investment). If the resulting return is greater than the company's minimum standard of acceptability, the project is acceptable quantitatively. Because the payback and the unadjusted rate of return methods do not consider the time value of money, they should be used only in conjunction with one of the discounted cash flow methods.

Discounted Capital Budgeting Techniques

3 Describe and use two discounted capital budgeting techniques: the net present value method and the internal rate of return method.

Two widely used capital budgeting techniques recognize the time value of money—the net present value method and the internal rate of return method. Both methods apply discounted cash flow principles in determining the acceptability of an investment. The net present value method uses a standard discount rate to restate all cash flows in terms of present values and then makes comparisons. The internal rate of return method calculates the investment's "true" discounted rate of return and compares it with the firm's "hurdle" rate. Thus, an appropriate discount rate is extremely important in capital budgeting. Before explaining each of the two methods, we first discuss how to select an appropriate discount rate.

Selecting a Discount Rate

cost of capital The average cost of a firm's debt and equity capital; equals the rate of return that a company must earn in order to satisfy the demands of its owners and creditors.

An excellent starting point for computing the correct discount rate is a company's cost of capital. The **cost of capital** is basically an average cost of a firm's debt (primarily bank loans and bonds) and its equity (primarily common and preferred stock and retained earnings). These costs are measured in terms of effective interest rates on bank loans and bonds and the rate of return expected to be earned by the company's stockholders. In essence, then, the cost of capital is the rate a company must earn in order to satisfy its owners and creditors.

The computation of the cost of capital is complex and beyond the scope of this book. However, the following example should help you understand the concept. Assume that 30% of a company's total capital is debt, 20% is equity from the issuance of stock, and 50% is equity from retained earnings. Upon analysis, the company has determined that the cost of its debt capital is 10%, and the cost of its equity capital is 22% from stock and 16% from retained earnings. (*Note:* The cost of equity capital from the issuance of new shares is considered to be higher because of the commissions, registration fees, and so forth, associated with the issuance of new shares.) The firm's cost of capital would be determined as follows:

Type	Cost of Capital	×	Weight	=	Average Cost of Capital
Debt (bonds)	10%	×	30%	=	3.0%
Equity (stocks)	22	×	20	=	4.4
Equity (retained earnings)	16	×	50	=	8.0
Total cost of capital			100%		15.4%

STOP & THINK

Assume you were trying to decide whether to purchase or lease an automobile and you wanted to use the net present value method to determine which alternative to choose. What factors would you consider in determining the rate at which to discount the future cash outflows (i.e., what factors would determine your personal cost of capital)?

The weighting procedure may seem fairly simple. As you will learn in more advanced courses, however, it is not always easy to calculate the costs of the different types of capital. This is because the necessary information is often not readily available or absolutely verifiable. For example, debt costs must be adjusted to an after-tax basis, and equity costs include some subjective elements, such as the opportunity cost of retained earnings. Although you now have a general understanding of the cost of capital, you will need further study in finance courses in order to be able to confidently use this concept.

As mentioned above, the cost of capital is a starting point in identifying an appropriate discount rate. The riskiness of a project should also be considered in choosing the appropriate discount rate. For example, the cost of capital computed earlier is 15.4%. If the company were considering a very risky project, a higher discount rate would be used because high-risk projects must yield higher-than-average returns in order to compensate for the increased probability of no returns at all. The techniques of correctly computing risk-adjusted discount rates are beyond the scope of this text; however, remember that the selection of the right discount rate is critical in the execution of a useful capital budgeting analysis.

Net Present Value Method

net present value method
A capital budgeting technique that uses discounted cash flows to compare the present values of an investment's expected cash inflows and outflows.

The **net present value method** compares all expected cash inflows associated with an investment with the current and future cash outflows. All cash flows are discounted to their present values, giving recognition to the time value of money. For this reason, the net present value method is superior to both the payback method and the unadjusted rate of return method.

In general, the net present value method involves the following five steps:

1. *Estimate* the amount and timing of all cash flows associated with the investment.
2. *Evaluate* the riskiness of the cash flows in order to determine the appropriate discount rate to use in the present value calculations.
3. *Compute* the present values of all the expected cash inflows and outflows of the investment. (Note that most present value calculations assume end-of-year inflows and outflows.)
4. *Subtract* the total present value of the cash outflows from the total present value of the cash inflows. The difference is the investment's net present value.
5. *Decide* whether to undertake the investment. If the net present value of the investment is positive, or at least zero, the project is acceptable from a financial standpoint.

Steps 1 and 2, the estimation of the amount and timing of the cash flows and the selection of an appropriate discount rate, are the most difficult steps in evaluating a long-term investment. These steps are where business judgment, experience, and careful analysis of details separate companies that make good long-term investment decisions from those that make bad long-term investment decisions. Implementation of steps 1 and 2 is a topic for more advanced finance and accounting courses as well as being the object of much on-the-job training for young managers. For the illustrations in this chapter, the cash flows and the discount rate will be given so that we can focus on the calculations and decision process in steps 3, 4, and 5.

The following case illustrates the net present value method. The fleet manager of MBK Company is thinking of replacing an old truck before it begins to need major repairs. Because the company has limited funds and cannot spend more than $18,000, the manager is considering a small, fuel-efficient pickup truck that is presently selling for that amount. The truck would save the company $5,625 a year in gas and other expenses. The truck's estimated useful life is four years, and the expected salvage value is $1,800. The company uses a 10% discount rate. What is this investment's net present value? Should the truck be purchased?

Because the cash flows and the discount rate are given, we are assuming that steps 1 and 2 have already been completed. Step 3 of the net present value method is to use the predetermined discount rate to state all cash flows at their present values (rounded to the nearest dollar in this example).

Cash inflows:

	Annual cash savings	×	Discount factor	=	Present value
	$5,625	×	3.1699*	=	$17,831
	Salvage value	×	Discount factor	=	Present value
	$1,800	×	0.6830**	=	$1,229

Cash outflows:

	Initial cost	×	Discount factor	=	Present value
	$18,000	×	1.0000	=	$18,000

*From Table II, 4 years at 10%.
**From Table I, 4 years at 10%.

net present value The difference between the present values of an investment's expected cash inflows and outflows.

Step 4 is to compute the **net present value**, that is, the difference between the present values of cash inflows and outflows.

Present value of inflows:

Cash savings	$17,831
Salvage value	1,229
Total	$19,060

Less present value of outflows:

Cost of truck	18,000
Net present value	$ 1,060

FYI:

Another way to think of the $1,060 net present value is that on the day the company decides to buy the truck, the market value of the company immediately increases by $1,060. This increase stems from the fact that the company has embarked on a course that involves exchanging cash flows with a present value of $18,000 for cash flows with a present value of $19,060. When viewed this way, it is obvious that a company should want to engage in as many positive net present value projects as possible.

The analysis in step 4 shows that investing in the truck would produce a positive net present value. In other words, after adjusting for the time value of money, purchasing the truck is like paying $18,000 in exchange for a stream of cash flows that is worth $19,060. Clearly, this is something that you would want to do. Thus, from a quantitative standpoint, it seems that the truck should be purchased. Exhibit 1 illustrates the process just described.

A common misinterpretation of the $1,060 net present value is that the acquisition of the truck will generate a net profit of just $1,060. Actually, because a 10% discount rate was used in evaluating the truck, the $1,060 net present value means that the investment in the truck will yield a net value gain of $1,060 OVER AND ABOVE the 10% minimum required rate of return. Similarly, a computed net present value of $0 does not mean that an investment just barely breaks even; instead, a $0 net present value means that the investment yields a return exactly equal to the discount rate used in evaluating the investment.

Before the company decides whether to purchase the truck, however, management must consider other factors. For example, a policy of support for U.S. car manufacturers or a lack of certain safety features on the pickup might dictate a particular course of action. Qualitative factors are discussed in greater detail later in the chapter.

Exhibit 1: Computing Net Present Value

	Present Time	Year 1	Year 2	Year 3	Year 4
Cost	$18,000				
Savings		$5,625	$5,625	$5,625	$5,625
Salvage value					1,800

	Time Period	Cash Flows	Present Value Factor	Present Value of Cash Flows
Present value of cash inflows:				
Savings	Years 1–4	$ 5,625	3.1699*	$17,831
Salvage value	Year 4	1,800	0.6830**	1,229
				$19,060
Present value of cash outflows:				
Cost	Today	(18,000)	1.0000	18,000
Net present value				$ 1,060

*From Table II, 4 years at 10%.
**From Table I, 4 years at 10%.

© 2003 Getty Images

Managers must sometimes make least-cost decisions to fulfill certain imposed requirements at the lowest possible cost. For example, government regulations may require a company to purchase pollution-control equipment.

least-cost decision A decision to undertake the project with the smallest negative net present value.

FYI:

This pollution control example is somewhat misleading. Many companies have found that the effort to control emissions or reduce waste actually improves overall efficiency, turning environmental initiatives into positive net present value business projects.

Source: Martha Hamilton, "Generating Profit from the Waste Up," *The Washington Post*, April 12, 1995, p. F01.

Least-Cost Decisions

The net present value method generally assumes that an investment must be justified by cash savings or increased revenues. Sometimes, however, funds must be used to purchase assets regardless of whether they can be justified financially. Such situations arise, for example, when (1) government regulations require a firm to purchase safety or pollution-control equipment, (2) personnel contracts stipulate the establishment of retirement funds, or (3) a company is required to invest in cafeteria or recreational facilities, either to comply with a labor union contract or because management is persuaded that morale considerations warrant it.

Such situations may seem to be beyond help from capital budgeting. However, the net present value method may assist managers in making a **least-cost decision**—a decision that satisfies certain requirements at the lowest possible cost to the firm. The two major differences between least-cost decisions and all other capital budgeting decisions are:

1. Least-cost decisions are limited to alternatives that fulfill certain imposed requirements.
2. None of the alternatives may produce a positive net present value.

To illustrate, we will assume that New England Steel Company has been told by the Environmental Protection Agency to install a pollution-control device. One alternative would cost $1,000,000 immediately but would not add to operating costs. It would last for 10 years. A second alternative is a device that costs $200,000 immediately but would add $125,000 to annual operating costs. Like the first device, it would last 10 years. Which device should be purchased? The firm uses a 12% discount rate.

The first alternative involves no future cash inflows or outflows. Its outlay cost in net present value terms is its initial cash outlay of $1,000,000. The second alternative has an initial cost of $200,000 plus future cash outflows of $125,000 per year for the next 10 years. Therefore, its outlay cost in net present value terms would be:

Annual cash outflows	×	Discount factor	=	Present value
$125,000	×	5.6502*	=	$706,275

Initial cost	200,000
Outlay cost at net present value	$906,275

*From Table II, 10 years at 12%.

If the company had a choice between installing and not installing, neither alternative would be acceptable because both net present values are negative. However, one of the alternatives must be accepted. Because a cost of $906,275 is less than a cost of $1,000,000, the second alternative should be chosen to minimize costs.

Internal Rate of Return Method

The **internal rate of return method**, also known as the time-adjusted rate of return method or the discounted rate of return method, is similar to the net present value approach in that it emphasizes the profitability of investments and takes into account the time value of money. As a discounted cash flow method, it is superior to either the payback method or the unadjusted rate of return method. Some managers consider the internal rate of return method more diffi-

Investing for a Cleaner World

Businesses have traditionally used capital budgeting to guide them on making wise investments in property, plant, and equipment that will earn a return. However, in recent years, investments in environmental cleanup activities have become extremely common. Companies today face a climate with increasingly significant environmental concerns. Environmental costs have soared, in some cases to billion of dollars each year. Fines and penalties for violation of environmental regulations are substantial. And, due to new sentencing guidelines, strict liability for environmental losses has been imposed on directors and officers of companies. There is currently a myriad of environmental laws forcing companies to spend huge amounts of money to comply with these laws and to clean up environmental damage. Some of the most costly laws are the Clean Air Act, the Clean Water Act, the Resource Conservation and Recovery Act of 1976, the Comprehensive Environmental Response, the Compensation and Liability Act of 1980 (known as Superfund), and the Superfund Amendments Reauthorization Act of 1986 (SARA). The impact of these laws on capital investment decisions can be substantial. For example, under SARA, purchasers of real property are usually financially liable for environmental cleanup costs even if the property was contaminated before it was purchased.

Environmental concerns impact several stages of the capital budgeting decision. First, capital budgeting decision makers must expand traditional company boundaries to consider all entities affected by environmental degradation. Even though a project may be profitable from the firm's perspective, if it pollutes the environment, cleanup liability may make the investment a real loser. Second, environmental laws, current conditions, and trends can significantly affect the feasibility of an investment. Third, in deciding whether an investment is profitable, environmental costs and benefits, as well as environmental risk, must be considered. Finally, once an investment in a capital asset is made, attention must be given to environmental events such as accidents or increased regulation, which might affect the continued viability of the investment.

Source: Devaun Kite, "Capital Budgeting: Integrating Environmental Impact," *Journal of Cost Management*, Summer 1995, Vol. 9, No. 2, pp. 11–14.

---

internal rate of return method A capital budgeting technique that uses discounted cash flows to find the "true" discount rate of an investment; this true rate produces a net present value of zero.

internal rate of return The "true" discount rate that will produce a net present value of zero when applied to the cash flows of investment inventory goods held for resale.

cult than the net present value method because the computations can be challenging. Some managers, however, prefer to analyze investment alternatives in terms of comparative rates of return rather than net present values.

The **internal rate of return** is defined as the "true" discount rate that an investment yields. For example, assume that your parents have $100,000 that they are considering investing in one of two ways—in a mutual fund containing the stocks of large U.S. companies or in your college education. They learn that the mutual fund investment will yield an average return of 12%. They estimate the increased value of your lifetime annual earnings stemming from your college education and calculate that, after adjusting for the time value of money, the investment in your college education will yield an average return of, say, 20% per year. The 20% number is the internal rate of return generated by an investment in your education; because this return is higher than the return your parents can earn on a mutual fund, they would naturally invest the $100,000 in your future.

Mathematically, the internal rate of return is the discount rate that yields a net present value of zero when applied to the cash flows of an investment—both inflows and outflows.

When using present value tables, the internal rate of return method involves three steps.

1. Calculate the present value factor by dividing the investment cost by the annual net cash inflows.
2. Using applicable present value tables and the life of the investment, find the present value factor closest to the number derived in step 1.
3. Using interpolation, if necessary, find the exact internal rate of return represented by the present value factor in step 1.

Caution

Of course, as mentioned earlier, there may be QUALITATIVE considerations that would cause your parents to invest in your education even if the MONETARY return were expected to be lower than what they could earn in the stock market.

To help you understand this concept, we will again refer to MBK Company's plan to purchase a new truck. For the purpose of this explanation, however, we will ignore the truck's salvage value; later, we will show how to incorporate salvage value into the calculation. The calculations for the MBK example are as follows:

1. Calculate the present value factor with the following formula:

$$\frac{\text{Investment cost}}{\text{Annual net cash inflows}} = \text{Present value factor}$$

$$\frac{\$18,000}{\$5,625} = 3.2000$$

(Note that this is also the formula for calculating the payback period.)

2. In Present Value Table II, find the applicable row for the life of the investment. By moving across the table, you can find the present value factor closest to the number derived in step 1. In our example, the investment's life is known to be 4 years, so find row 4 and move across the row until you come to the factor 3.2397. This is the factor for 9%. The next factor, 3.1699, represents 10%. Since the factor is between these two numbers, the truck purchase yields between a 9 and 10% return.

interpolation A method of determining the internal rate of return when the factor for that rate lies between the factors given in the present value table.

3. If necessary, use **interpolation** to find the exact internal rate of return. Interpolation is most easily visualized by setting up a table as follows:

		Present Value Factors	
	Rate of Return (Discount Rate)	High and True Factors	High and Low Factors
High factor*	9%	3.2397	3.2397
True factor		3.2000	
Low factor	10		3.1699
Differences	1%	0.0397	0.0698

*Note that the high factor is associated with the low rate and that the low factor is associated with the high rate.

The number 0.0397 is the difference between the high factor and the true factor determined in step 1. The number 0.0698 is the difference between the high factor and the low factor. One percent is the difference between the discount rates for the high and the low factors. To find the approximate rate of return in this example, you would make the following calculation:

$$\text{Internal rate of return} = 0.09 + \left(0.01 \times \frac{0.0397}{0.0698}\right) = 0.0957 \text{ or } 9.6\% \text{ (rounded)}$$

What we are doing is adding the proportion $0.0397 \div 0.0698$ of the 1% difference to the low rate to get the true rate. The result, 9.6%, means that if the annual savings of $5,625 were discounted at 9.6%, the net present value of the investment would be zero. (Note that there may be slight differences due to rounding.)

The purpose of interpolation is to determine the "true" rate of interest indicated by the present value factor. Although the factor's true rate of interest is fairly easy to roughly estimate, interpolation produces a more precise estimate.

Computation of internal rates of return is one area in which knowledge of how to use a standard business calculator really pays off. For example, the internal rate of return in the MBK example could be computed using the following keystrokes with a Hewlett-Packard business calculator:

Caution

For you mathematicians, it is necessary to note that this interpolation process only approximates the internal rate of return. This is because the formulas generating the present value factors are nonlinear.

Hewlett-Packard Keystrokes:

1. −18,000: Press **PV** (you must enter the cash outflow as a NEGATIVE number)
2. 5,625: Press **PMT** (this is the annual cash inflow)
3. 4: Press **N** (number of years)
4. Press **I/YR** for the answer = 9.5642274%

Using the Internal Rate of Return

hurdle rate The minimum rate of return that an investment must provide in order to be acceptable.

To determine the value of an investment, management must compare the project's internal rate of return with the company's usual discount rate, often called the **hurdle rate**, or the rate that must be cleared for a project to be acceptable. If the internal rate is higher than or equal to the company's hurdle rate, the project is acceptable. If the internal rate is lower than the hurdle rate, the project is usually rejected. As with any of the capital budgeting techniques, even if the investment is acceptable from an internal rate of return standpoint, qualitative factors must still be considered before a final decision can be made.

FYI:

A calculator actually computes the internal rate of return using a repeated interpolation process; most business calculators take a couple of seconds to come up with the final answer.

The Problem of Uneven Cash Flows

In the truck example, annual cash flows were the same because salvage value was ignored. However, when salvage value is considered, the investment will have uneven cash flows. When this occurs, an annuity table cannot be used. Each cash flow has to be discounted back at an assumed discount rate until the net present value of all the cash flows discounted at this rate approximates zero. The rate that results after a trial-and-error process is the internal rate of return. A simplified example of this method is shown on page 215. Although this can be a tedious procedure, it is facilitated by using a business calculator. For example, computing the internal rate of return of the MBK truck purchase, including consideration of the $1,800 salvage value cash inflow at the end of four years, would be done as follows using a Hewlett-Packard business calculator:

Hewlett-Packard Keystrokes:

1. −18,000: Press **PV**
2. 5,625: Press **PMT**
3. 4: Press **N** (number of years)
4. 1,800: Press **FV** (this is a single amount occurring at the end of the period of time indicated in step 3)
5. Press **I/YR** for the answer = 12.5774719%

Note that the internal rate of return is higher (12.6% vs. 9.6%) when the additional cash inflow from the salvage value is considered.

In addition to using present value tables and business calculators, net present values and internal rates of return can also be calculated using Excel spreadsheet functions. These calculations are illustrated in the appendix to this chapter.

TO SUMMARIZE: The net present value method is a capital budgeting technique that takes into consideration the time value of money by discounting future cash flows to their present values. By comparing the discounted net cash inflows and outflows, this method derives a net present value figure. If the net present value is zero or positive, the project is acceptable from a quantitative stand-point. The discount rate used is the minimum rate of interest that a company will accept. The net present value method also may be used in making least-cost decisions. The internal rate of return is a capital budgeting technique that utilizes discounted cash flows. It derives the "true" rate of return for an investment by comparing the cost of the project with the amounts to be returned. This produces a present value factor that is associated with the internal rate of return for the project. Often, the rate must be derived by interpolation and, if uneven cash flows are involved, by trial and error or business calculator.

Comparative Example of Capital Budgeting Techniques

To solidify your understanding of the capital budgeting techniques introduced thus far in this chapter, we present the example of Will's Pit Stop, a small service station that sells gasoline on a self-service basis as its only source of revenue. Because one wall of the enclosed station area is vacant, the manager has decided to install one or two food vending machines. A sales representative has suggested that a freezer for ice cream and other dairy items would do well. The freezer would cost $42,045. It has an estimated useful life of 10 years, with an expected salvage value of $4,000. The sales representative is confident that the freezer will generate revenues of $15,000 a year on goods that cost $7,600. The freezer will need $8,000 of servicing during its fifth year of operation. The increase in Will's average yearly net income if the freezer is purchased is estimated to be $3,500. Note that the difference between annual net cash inflows of $7,400 ($15,000 − $7,600) and the estimated average net income of $3,500 is due to noncash expenses, such as depreciation, which are deducted on the income statement.

The manager of the station has come to you for advice, indicating that the firm's hurdle rate is 12%—Will's estimated cost of capital. Compute the payback period, the unadjusted rate of return, the net present value, and the internal rate of return of the project. Then give your recommendations. Note that companies generally do not analyze an investment with all these techniques. They are all used here for illustrative purposes.

1. *Payback period:*

$$\frac{\$50,045 \text{ (investment cost)}^*}{\$7,400 \text{ (annual net cash inflows)}} = 6.76 \text{ years}$$

*$42,045 initial investment + $8,000 servicing cost after 5 years.

Note that the salvage value is not considered here because it is received in the tenth year.

2. *Unadjusted rate of return:*

$$\frac{\$3,500 \text{ (increase in future average annual net income)}}{\$42,045 \text{ (initial investment cost)}} = 8.3\%$$

3. *Net present value:*

	Time Period	Cash Flows	Present Value Factor	Present Value of Cash Flows
Present value of cash inflows:				
Net revenues ($15,000 − $7,600) . .	Years 1–10	$ 7,400	5.6502*	$41,811
Salvage value	Year 10	4,000	0.3220**	1,288
Total cash inflows				$43,099
Present value of cash outflows:				
Initial cost	Today	$42,045	1.0000	$42,045
Servicing cost	Year 5	8,000	0.5674***	4,539
Total cash outflows				$46,584
Net present value				$ (3,485)

*From Table II, 10 years at 12%.
**From Table I, 10 years at 12%.
***From Table I, 5 years at 12%.

4. *Internal rate of return:*

Since the cash flows are uneven due to the servicing cost and the salvage value, a trial-and-error process is required in computing the internal rate of return. From the net present value method, we can see that the 12% rate is too high. A 10% rate is selected for trial, and the net present value at that rate is calculated.

	Time Period	Cash Flows	Present Value Factor	Present Value of Cash Flows
Present value of cash inflows:				
Net revenues ($15,000 − $7,600) ..	Years 1–10	$ 7,400	6.1446*	$45,470
Salvage value	Year 10	4,000	0.3855**	1,542
Total cash inflows				$47,012
Present value of cash outflows:				
Initial cost	Today	$42,045	1.0000	$42,045
Servicing cost	Year 5	8,000	0.6209***	4,967
Total cash outflows				$47,012
Net present value				$ 0

  *From Table II, 10 years at 10%.
 **From Table I, 10 years at 10%.
***From Table I, 5 years at 10%.

At 10%, the net present value is zero. Therefore, 10% is the internal rate of return.

On the basis of the foregoing information, you should recommend rejection. The payback period is well within the life of the investment; however, it is not short enough to warrant any special consideration. The unadjusted rate of return is only 8.3%, and the internal, or adjusted, rate of return of 10% is well under Will's hurdle rate, which means that the project's net present value is negative. Therefore, on the basis of the quantitative results, the manager should look for an opportunity that is more attractive financially. However, if the 10% rate is close enough to the 12% hurdle rate, perhaps qualitative factors, such as the probability that the additional customers attracted by the freezer items will also buy gas, might make the project acceptable.

Qualitative Factors in Strategic and Capital Investment Decisions

4 Understand the need for evaluating qualitative factors in strategic and capital investment decisions.

In explaining the fundamental concepts of capital budgeting, we have focused on the financial (quantitative) aspects of analyzing investment alternatives. However, a discussion of capital budgeting is incomplete without mentioning factors that cannot be reduced to numbers. These qualitative factors are often of overriding importance in strategic and capital investment decisions. Here, we consider three types of qualitative factors: (1) an investment's effect on the *quality* of products and services offered, (2) an investment's effect on the *time* with which products and services can be produced and delivered to customers, and (3) other qualitative factors. Thus far in the chapter, we have made the determination of whether a capital investment decision is a good one solely on the basis of its financial return, computed using one of four methods. If the financial return was positive, our conclusion was to invest; if the financial return was negative, we recommended that the project not be undertaken. However, throughout the management accounting chapters of this book, we have focused on three aspects of decision making: cost, quality, and time.

Quality and time considerations can sometimes dictate that a capital investment should be made even if the financial returns don't justify the expenditure. For example, if buying a new machine will help the company produce higher quality products or deliver those products to its customers faster, the machine may be a good investment. Companies know that their competitors are doing everything possible to speed up delivery and increase quality. Thus, even if a company has a cost of capital of 12%, and an investment will return only 8%, if buying a machine will allow the company to deliver products or services faster than competitors, the purchase may be a good one. Likewise, if buying a machine will mean fewer defects, higher quality, and more satisfied customers, the purchase may be a good one. Companies must always be continuously improving in order to keep up with or surpass their competition. Unfortunately, capital investments often are long-term decisions that make continuous improvement difficult. Thus, even if a company has not completely recovered its investment in a capital project, recognizing that competitors have better or more efficient equipment may motivate a company to abandon an investment (a machine that works fine, for example) and make a costlier new investment that will allow the company to remain competitive. The impact of quality and time on capital budgeting decisions cannot be underestimated. In fact, because of the need to continuously improve, companies are always looking for shorter and shorter capital investment opportunities so that they are more flexible, such as leasing or renting equipment and other operating assets where possible.

In addition to quality and time, there are a number of other qualitative factors that must be considered when making capital budgeting decisions. Consider, for example, consumer safety. In one lawsuit, a major U.S. automobile manufacturer was cited for producing cars that were not as safe as they should have been. The company was essentially accused of comparing the present value of the legal and other costs that might result from the unsafe condition of the cars with the cash savings from manufacturing the cars more cheaply, and of choosing the less expensive route. The question was then posed: What is the value of a life? This situation provides a dramatic illustration of the need to include qualitative factors in capital investment decisions.

Other qualitative factors include such matters as (1) government regulations, (2) pollution control and environmental protection, (3) worker safety, (4) company image and prestige,

business environment

Ethics in Capital Investment Decisions In 1990, after making substantial investments in two plants in Thailand and one in China, HUNTSMAN CHEMICAL CORPORATION (HCC) abruptly sold out its business interests when unethical practices were encountered. After winning a major bid in competition with worldwide firms, HCC was virtually guaranteed a significant profit on a $40 million investment. It became clear, however, that business practices involving bribes, payoffs, inflated invoices, and the like were going to be a part of the deal. As soon as Jon Huntsman, founder, chairman, and CEO of HCC, became aware of these unethical prac-

tices, he called his managers home and refused to participate further in the projects. HCC sold all its interests and walked away from the deal. When asked about this situation, Mr. Huntsman was quoted as saying, "We simply refuse to carry out negotiations based on factors other than competitiveness, quality, and productivity."

Although the quantitative factors led HCC to become involved in a major capital investment project, other factors caused the company to withdraw. As noted in the text, qualitative factors often override purely quantitative results.

Source: Adapted from "The Heart of the Deal," *Wharton Alumni Magazine* (Summer 1991), pp. 8–14.

(5) preferences of owners and management, and (6) the general welfare of the community in which the company operates. The business environment on the previous page provides a specific example of one company that combined strategic objectives with humanitarian motives in making a major capital investment decision. Many more examples could be mentioned, but the point is that numbers alone do not control the investment decisions of a good manager. Quality, time, and other qualitative, as well as quantitative, factors should all be considered in reaching long-term investment decisions.

TO SUMMARIZE: In making capital budgeting decisions, the effects of a decision on the quality of and the time with which products can be delivered to customers must be considered. In addition, other qualitative factors such as litigation effects, government regulations, environmental impact, worker safety, company image, preferences of owners, and welfare of community must also be considered.

In the previous sections of the chapter, we have explained the importance of capital budgeting and the concepts underlying strategic and capital investment decisions, including the time value of money. We have also described and illustrated the four most commonly used capital budgeting techniques. Finally, we have discussed briefly the need for evaluating qualitative factors in any investment decision. In the expanded material, we explain how to use sensitivity analysis in dealing with uncertainty in capital budgeting decisions and the concept of "capital rationing," which is the process of ranking capital investment projects. We also discuss the impact of taxes on capital budgeting decisions.

Dealing with Uncertainty in Strategic and Capital Investment Decisions

5 Use sensitivity analysis to assess the potential effects of uncertainty in capital budgeting.

sensitivity analysis A method of assessing the reasonableness of a decision that was based upon estimates; involves calculating how far reality can differ from an estimate without invalidating the decision.

Throughout this chapter, we have applied capital budgeting techniques as though the future were certain. That is, we have assumed perfect knowledge of expected cash flows, the useful lives of assets, salvage values, and so forth. Actually, the future is almost always uncertain, and the applicable numbers are estimates. By using "sensitivity analysis," we can evaluate, at least to some extent, the degree to which an error in a particular estimate is likely to invalidate the decision reached. Essentially, **sensitivity analysis** is a method of examining the effect of changes in an estimate on the results of the calculations. We use sensitivity analysis to determine whether the conclusions still seem reasonable under modified circumstances.

To illustrate this approach, we will consider the following situation. An asset can be purchased for $100,000; it is expected to provide $20,000 of annual net cash inflows. It has a 10-year life and an expected salvage value of $10,000. The hurdle rate is 8%. We can use either of the discounted cash flow techniques to assess this investment opportunity. For illustrative purposes, we use both.

Net present value method:

Discounted expected cash inflows ($20,000 × 6.7101*)	$134,202
Discounted disposal value ($10,000 × 0.4632**)	4,632
Net cash inflows	$138,834
Net cash outflows	100,000
Net present value	$ 38,834

*From Table II, 10 years at 8%.
**From Table I, 10 years at 8%.

Internal rate of return method:

$$\frac{\text{Investment cost } (\$100,000 - \$4,632)}{\text{Annual net cash inflows}} = \frac{\$95,368}{\$20,000} = 4.7684 \text{ present value factor}$$

For 10 years, the internal rate of return is between 16 and 18%.

The net present value is greater than zero, and the internal rate of return is considerably more than the minimum acceptable rate of 8%. Therefore, from a quantitative standpoint, we should accept this investment opportunity. But what about the uncertainties? What if $20,000 is not received each year? What if the asset does not last 10 years? What if the disposal value is less than $10,000? Sensitivity analysis enables us to evaluate the potential effect of each of these uncertainties.

If Expected Cash Flows Are Uncertain

To assess the amount of error we can tolerate in expected cash flows, we need to determine the break-even amount of net cash flow—that is, the annual cash flow that would earn the minimum rate of 8%. We accomplish this by determining the discounted net cost of the investment and dividing that amount by the present value factor for the minimum acceptable interest rate (8%) for 10 years.

Computations:

Initial cost	$100,000
Discounted disposal value	4,632
Net cost of investment	$ 95,368

$95,368 ÷ 6.7101 (present value factor of 8%) = $14,213 cash flow return in order to break even.

We could then assess how likely it is that this project will generate annual cash flows of at least $14,213. Any amount above that, of course, would be acceptable with an 8% hurdle rate.

If Useful Life Is Uncertain

To assess the amount of error we can tolerate in the estimate that the asset will have a useful life of 10 years, we take the discounted net cost of the investment and divide it by the expected cash flows. This produces a present value factor of 4.7684. Looking under 8% interest in Table II, we find that this factor falls between 6 and 7 years. Thus, assuming that the $20,000 estimate of cash inflows is reliable, the asset does not have to last a full 10 years for the investment to be acceptable. In fact, only 7 years are necessary.

Computations:

$$\frac{\text{Net cost of investment}}{\text{Annual net cash inflows}} = \frac{\$95,368}{\$20,000} = 4.7684 \text{ at } 8\%$$

= Between 6 and 7 years of useful
life in order to break even

If Disposal Value Is Uncertain

Usually, the disposal value is an insignificant factor in the investment decision. However, to see if it would make a difference in the acceptability of a project, we can assume it is zero. In our example, if the asset has a zero disposal value, the investment cost of $100,000 divided by $20,000 annual net cash inflows equals a 5.0 present value factor. For an assumed 10-year life, the return is between 15 and 16%, which is clearly acceptable according to our 8% hurdle rate.[1]

---

1 In this example, we looked at the uncertainty of each variable separately. Using computer simulation, uncertainty in all variables could have been examined simultaneously.

Computations:

$$\frac{\text{Initial investment cost}}{\text{Annual net cash inflows}} = \frac{\$100,000}{\$20,000} = 5.0 \text{ for 10 years}$$

$$= 15 \text{ to } 16\% \text{ return}$$

> **TO SUMMARIZE:** Capital budgeting decisions always involve estimates of future amounts, and estimates involve uncertainty. To evaluate the potential effect of this uncertainty, we can use sensitivity analysis, which shows how far reality can deviate from the estimate without invalidating an investment decision.

Capital Rationing

6 Explain how to use capital budgeting techniques in ranking capital investment projects.

Thus far, we have dealt exclusively with the screening function of capital budgeting—that is, determining whether an investment meets a minimum standard of acceptability. In many cases, however, a company has not one but several investment opportunities, all of which offer returns in excess of the company's hurdle rate. Since a company's resources are limited, some projects should be given priority. The ranking function of capital budgeting enables management to select the most profitable investments first. Projects should not be ranked, however, until the screening process is completed.

Another factor to consider in ranking projects is whether particular projects are compatible, complementary, or mutually exclusive. We assume mutually exclusive projects in this section on ranking, that is, that each project is independent and adds neither an advantage nor a disadvantage to other projects. Certainly, there are situations where the acceptance of one project adds value, directly or indirectly, to another project and might therefore alter a ranking consideration. These factors, like the qualitative factors that we discussed earlier, may significantly influence the strategy involved in a capital investment decision.

capital rationing Allocating limited resources among ranked acceptable investments.

The objective of ranking is to help a company use limited resources to the best advantage by investing only in the projects that offer the highest return. The process of allocating limited resources based on the ranking of projects is called **capital rationing**. Either the internal rate of return method or the net present value method may be used in ranking investments.

Ranking by the Internal Rate of Return Method

If the internal rate of return method is used, investments that pass the screening test are ranked in the order of their internal rate of return, from highest to lowest. This method is simple, requires no additional computations, and is widely used.

To illustrate the process, we will assume the following situation. Sundance Enterprises is considering six capital investment projects. Management requires a minimum return of 15% on its investments. The six projects are first screened, then ranked by their internal rates of return, as shown below.

Project	Expected Rate of Return	Screening Decision	Ranking Decision
A	10%	Reject	—
B	18	Accept	3
C	12	Reject	—
D	22	Accept	1
E	20	Accept	2
F	16	Accept	4

From a quantitative standpoint, Sundance should invest in all four of the projects that passed the screening test. If resources are limited, however, capital must be rationed. In this situation, the ranking process indicates that limited resources would be allocated to project D first, then to projects E, B, and F, respectively. This conclusion ignores the additional complications of the investments having different lives. It also does not consider differences in the size of the initial investment.

Ranking by the Net Present Value Method

If the net present value method is used for ranking investments, additional computations are necessary because the net present value of one investment usually cannot be directly compared with that of another. Only projects that require the same amount of investment are comparable. For example, you cannot readily compare an investment of $10,000 that produces a $2,000 net present value (project A) with a $20,000 investment that also results in a $2,000 net present value (project B), although project A certainly seems more desirable. To rank such projects, we need to compute a **profitability index**.

profitability index The present value of net cash inflows divided by the cost of an investment.

$$\frac{\text{Present value of net cash inflows}}{\text{Investment cost}} = \text{Profitability index}$$

Projects can then be ranked from highest to lowest in terms of their respective profitability indexes. The project with the highest profitability index should obviously be undertaken first; other projects will be undertaken according to the amount of resources available for investment.

To illustrate the ranking of projects using the net present value method, we will use the example in the preceding paragraph. The amount of the investment and its net present value are added to arrive at the present value of net cash inflows. Then, present value is divided by the investment cost to calculate a profitability index and respective ranking.

	Project A	Project B
Present value of net cash inflows	$12,000 (a)	$22,000 (a)
Investment cost	10,000 (b)	20,000 (b)
Net present value	$ 2,000	$ 2,000
Profitability index (a ÷ b)	1.20	1.10
Rank	1	2

Note that the profitability index must be 1.0 or greater for a project to be acceptable; this means that the net present value is at least zero.

Exhibit 2 summarizes the rules for making screening and ranking decisions using the net present value (with a profitability index) and the internal rate of return methods. Note that each technique leads management to the same screening decision. However, the methods may produce different rankings. In selecting between the two for the purposes of ranking, the profitability index is preferred because it considers directly the amount invested in each project, which results in the selection of the most profitable alternative.

TO SUMMARIZE: The screening function determines if projects are acceptable; the ranking function enables management to select the most profitable investment first and thus use limited resources to the best advantage. Ranking may be accomplished by the internal rate of return or by the net present value method.

Exhibit 2: Capital Budgeting Decision Rules

Selected Capital Budgeting Techniques	Decision Rules	
	Screening	Ranking
Net present value method (NPV) using the profitability index (PI)	If PI > 1, invest If PI = 1, indifferent If PI < 1, don't invest	For two projects, a and b; If PI$_a$ > PI$_b$, pick a, etc.
Internal rate of return (IRR)	If IRR > CC*, invest If IRR = CC, indifferent If IRR < CC, don't invest	For two projects, a and b; If IRR$_a$ > IRR$_b$, pick a, etc.
*CC = cost of capital, or hurdle rate.		

Income Tax Considerations in Capital Budgeting Decisions

7 Explain how income taxes affect capital budgeting decisions.

To keep the concepts simple, when considering capital budgeting decisions thus far in the chapter, we ignored the effects of income taxes on capital budgeting decisions. Unfortunately, ignoring tax effects is not very realistic because capital budgeting decisions can be significantly affected by tax considerations. As an example of the income tax effects, the net cash inflows from the profits stemming from a project are reduced because those profits are taxed. On the other hand, any losses stemming from a project will generate tax savings. And the depreciation of the cost of an investment also generates tax deductions, leading to cash savings. Such tax effects can be so significant that the net present value of the cash flows changes from positive to negative, or vice versa.

To illustrate these income tax effects, we will use the Will's Pit Stop example discussed earlier. Recall that the gas station owner was considering installing a freezer for ice cream and other dairy products. The cost of the freezer was $42,045. It was expected to have a salvage value of $4,000 at the end of its 10-year useful life and to generate revenues of $15,000 per year on goods that cost $7,600. Thus, the cash flow was expected to be $7,400 ($15,000 − $7,600). At the end of the fifth year, the freezer would need $8,000 of repairs and servicing. Based on this information, the management of Will's Pit Stop decided not to buy the freezer because, at a hurdle rate of 12%, the net present value was negative. Furthermore, the internal rate of return was only 10%.

In making this decision, management neglected to consider the income tax effects. Here, we will incorporate the tax effects of the investment, based on the following initial assumptions: (1) Will's Pit Stop is a corporation with an effective tax rate of 25%, and (2) the hurdle rate of 12% is an after-tax rate. Assumption (2) means that the calculation of the cost of capital reflects the after-tax cost of interest expense, which is a deduction in computing a corporation's tax liability.

To compute the present values of the cash inflows and outflows, we must first convert them to after-tax amounts. This conversion is accomplished as follows:

1. Income on the freezer before taxes was $7,400 ($15,000 revenues − $7,600 cost of goods sold). This $7,400 represents the before-tax net cash inflow from the freezer. At a 25% tax rate, the after-tax net cash inflow is $5,550 ($7,400 × 0.25 = $1,850; $7,400 − $1,850 = $5,550). In other words, the company keeps 75% (1.00 less the tax rate of 25%) of the before-tax net cash inflow from the freezer ($7,400 × 0.75 = $5,550).
2. The U.S. income tax regulations allow a company to reduce its income tax liability by expensing some of the cost of tangible personal property immediately in the year of

acquisition. The tax people call this the "Section 179 expensing election." If Will's Pit Stop elects to expense $10,000 of the cost of the freezer, this amount is deducted from the original cost in computing the depreciation base. The tax savings from taking this deduction in the year of acquisition is $2,500 ($10,000 × 0.25 tax rate).

3. Although the freezer has an estimated useful life of 10 years, the modified accelerated cost recovery system (MACRS), which is the depreciation method used for income tax purposes in the United States, would allow Will's Pit Stop to write the freezer off over a 7-year period on an accelerated basis (using the double-declining-balance method). Accordingly, under MACRS Will's Pit Stop will use the 7-year period to deduct the $32,045 ($42,045 − $10,000) in cost that remains after the Section 179 election discussed in item 2. The depreciation deduction for each year will be as follows:

Year	Pretax Depreciation Deduction
1	$ 4,578 ($32,045 on a double-declining-balance basis for 1/2 year)
2	7,848 [($32,045 − $4,578) ÷ 7 × 2]
3	5,605 [($27,467 − $7,848) ÷ 7 × 2]
4	4,004 [($19,619 − $5,605) ÷ 7 × 2]
5	2,860 [($14,014 − $4,004) ÷ 7 × 2]
6	2,860 [straight-line: ($10,010 − $2,860) ÷ 2 1/2 years]
7	2,860 (straight-line)
8	1,430 (straight-line for 1/2 year)
	$32,045

Caution

Under MACRS, a half year of depreciation is deducted in the first and last year of the asset's life. In addition, estimated salvage values are ignored in the computations.

Note that the company shifts to the straight-line method in Year 6 in order to deduct as much depreciation as possible in that year and thereafter. As shown in Exhibit 3, at a 25% tax rate, the MACRS deduction will save the company $1,145 in taxes in the first year in addition to the $2,500 saved by expensing the first $10,000 of the freezer's cost under Section 179.

4. Under MACRS, the entire cost of the freezer will have been written off in the first eight years of its life. If the freezer is sold at the end of 10 years at its $4,000 estimated salvage value, there will be a $4,000 gain on the sale. This gain will be taxable as ordinary income at 25% (assuming no change in tax rates), so the after-tax cash inflow will be only $3,000 ($4,000 × 0.75).

5. The estimated repairs and servicing cost of $8,000 at the end of Year 5 is an expense deduction from the company's income for that year. Therefore, the net cost of this expense to the company is only $6,000 ($8,000 × 0.75).

These adjusted cash flows can now be used to compute the net present value of the cash inflows and outflows that would result if the freezer were purchased. The present values of these cash flows are presented in Exhibit 3 at three different hurdle rates: 8, 10, and 12%.

Three different rates are used to illustrate that the net present value decreases as the hurdle rate increases from 8 to 12%. In other words, as the rate of return increases, the present value of the cash inflows decreases in relation to the present value of the cash outflows, eventually changing the net present value from positive to negative. The point at which the present values of the inflows and outflows are equal reflects the expected internal rate of return. If the expected return is less than the company's hurdle rate, it is unlikely that the company will acquire the asset unless there are compensating qualitative factors.

Exhibit 3 shows that the tax effects on cash inflows and outflows, given a tax rate of 25%, reduce the rate of return on Will's Pit Stop's proposed freezer from a pretax 10% calculated earlier in the chapter to just over 8%. This occurs because taxes reduce the present value of the

Exhibit 3: Income Tax Effects of Capital Budgeting

Will's Pit Stop
Net Present Value of Cash Inflows and Outflows (25% Tax Rate)

Type of Cash Flow	Period	After-Tax Cash Flow	8% Present Value	8% Amount*	10% Present Value	10% Amount*	12% Present Value	12% Amount*
Inflows:								
Revenue less cost of goods sold (net of tax): ($15,000 − $7,600) × 0.75	Years 1–10	$ 5,550	6.7101	$37,241	6.1446	$34,103	5.6502	$31,359
MACRS expensing ($10,000 × 0.25)	Year 1	2,500	0.9259**	2,315	0.9091	2,273	0.8929	2,232
MACRS [($42,045 − $10,000): $32,045 at 7-year, 200%]:								
$4,578 × 0.25	Year 1	$ 1,145	0.9259	$ 1,060	0.9091	$ 1,041	0.8929	$ 1,022
7,848 × 0.25	2	1,962	0.8573	1,682	0.8264	1,621	0.7972	1,564
5,605 × 0.25	3	1,401	0.7938	1,112	0.7513	1,053	0.7118	997
4,004 × 0.25	4	1,001	0.7350	736	0.6830	684	0.6355	636
2,860 × 0.25	5	715	0.6806	487	0.6209	444	0.5674	406
2,860 × 0.25	6	715	0.6302	451	0.5645	404	0.5066	362
2,860 × 0.25	7	715	0.5835	417	0.5132	367	0.4523	323
1,430 × 0.25	8	357	0.5403	193	0.4665	167	0.4039	144
				$ 6,138		$ 5,781		$ 5,454
Salvage value ($4,000 × 0.75)	End of Year 10	3,000	0.4632	$ 1,390	0.3855	$ 1,157	0.3220	$ 966
Total cash inflows				$47,084		$43,314		$40,011
Outflows:								
Initial freezer cost	Today	42,045	1.0000	$42,045	1.0000	$42,045	1.0000	$42,045
Repairs and servicing cost ($8,000 × 0.75)	End of Year 5	6,000	0.6806	4,084	0.6209	3,725	0.5674	3,404
Total cash outflows				$46,129		$45,770		$45,449
Excess cash inflow (outflow)				$ 955		$(2,456)		$(5,438)

*After-tax cash flow × present value.
**Note that this is the present value of the cash flow discounted for 1 year.

cash inflows more than they reduce the present value of the cash outflows. (Remember the initial cost is already at its present value.) If the tax rate were at the U.S. federal corporate rate of 35%, which is the rate that would be applicable to almost all large U.S. corporations, the internal rate of return would decrease even further. This is because the negative effect of the increased tax expense on gross margin is greater than the positive effect of the increased tax savings from expensing the first $10,000 of the freezer's cost and from the tax effects of the annual depreciation deduction and the deduction for repairs. In general, income taxes reduce the internal rate of return—and the higher the tax rate, the greater the reduction.

For the company to justify purchasing the freezer in the face of a 12% hurdle rate, the company would have to increase its gross margin significantly (increase sales volume with the same freezer capacity). You should also keep in mind that when the net present value at a selected hurdle rate is at or near zero, important qualitative factors not incorporated into the calculations of net present value will be the primary determinants of whether the asset is acquired.

> **TO SUMMARIZE:** The cash inflows and outflows of capital budgeting decisions must be converted to after-tax amounts before the present values are computed in order to obtain a realistic measure of net present value. Income taxes cause after-tax amounts of both cash revenues and cash expenses to be less than their before-tax amounts. Depreciation is a noncash expense, but because depreciation can be deducted in the computation of taxable income, depreciation results in a cash inflow in the form of income tax savings.

Appendix: The Time Value of Money

Present Value and Future Value Concepts

The concepts of present value and future value are used to measure the effect of time on the value of money. To illustrate, if you are to receive $100 one year from today, is it worth $100 today? Obviously not, because if you had the $100 today you could either use it now or invest it and earn interest. If the $100 isn't to be received for one year, those options are not available. The present value of $1 is the value today of $1 to be received or paid in the future, given a specified interest rate. To determine the value today of money to be received or paid in the future, we must "discount" the future amount (reduce the amount to its present value) by an appropriate interest rate. For example, if money can earn 10% per year, $100 to be received one year from now is approximately equal to $90.91 received today.

Putting it another way, if $90.91 is invested today in an account that earns 10% interest for one year, the interest earned will be $9.09 ($90.91 × 10% × 1 year = $9.09). The sum of the $90.91 principal plus $9.09 interest would equal $100 at the end of one year. Thus, the present value of $100 to be received (or paid) in one year with 10% interest is $90.91. This present value relationship can be diagramed as follows:

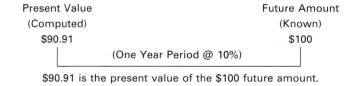

Present Value (Computed) $90.91 — (One Year Period @ 10%) — Future Amount (Known) $100

$90.91 is the present value of the $100 future amount.

The relationships in this diagram can be described in two ways. We have just looked at the relationship by recognizing that the $90.91 is the present value of $100 to be received one year from now when interest is 10%. In this example, the $100 to be received one year from now is known, and the present value of $90.91 must be computed. We are computing a present value amount from a known future value amount.

Another way to look at the relationship is on a future value basis. Future values apply when the amount today ($90.91) is known, and the future amount must be calculated. Future values are exactly the opposite of present values. Thinking in terms of future values, $100 is the future amount we can expect to receive in one year, given a present known amount of $90.91 when the interest rate is 10%. We can diagram this relationship as follows:

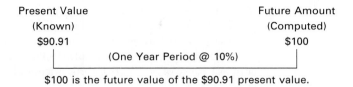

Present Value		Future Amount
(Known)		(Computed)
$90.91		$100
	(One Year Period @ 10%)	

$100 is the future value of the $90.91 present value.

Present and future values can be calculated using formulas. However, if more than one period is involved, the calculations become rather complicated. Therefore, it is more convenient to use either a present value table or a calculator that gives the present value of $1 for various numbers of periods and interest rates (see Table I, page 231) or a future value table that gives the future value of $1 for various numbers of periods and interest rates (see Table III, page 233). We will illustrate the use of both a present value table and a future value table.

Present Value Table

To use a present value table, you simply locate the appropriate number of periods in the left-most column and the interest rate in the row at the top of the table. The intersection of the row and column is the factor representing the present value of $1 for the number of periods and the relevant interest rate. To find the present value of an amount other than $1, multiply the factor in the table by that amount.

To illustrate the use of a present value table (Table I) to find the present value of a known future amount, assume that $10,000 is to be paid four years from today when the interest rate is 10%. What is the present value of the $10,000 payment?

Amount of payment $10,000
Present value factor of $1 to be paid in 4 periods
   at 10% interest (from Table I) . . . . ×0.6830
Present value of payment . . . . $ 6,830

This present value amount, $6,830, is the amount that could be paid today to satisfy the obligation that is due four years from now. As indicated, this procedure is sometimes referred to as "discounting." Thus, we say that $10,000 discounted for four years at 10% is $6,830. Stated another way, if $6,830 is invested today in an account that pays 10% interest, in four years the balance in that account would be $10,000.

The same present value computed in the previous example can be obtained using a business calculator. The necessary keystrokes are illustrated below. *Note:* The exact sequences of keystrokes illustrated are for a Hewlett-Packard business calculator; the keystrokes for other business calculators are similar if not exactly the same.

Hewlett-Packard Keystrokes for Present Value of a Single Payment:

1. 10,000: Press **FV** (this is the amount of the future payment)
2. 4: Press **N** (number of years)
3. 10: Press **I** (interest rate)
4. Press **PV** for the answer = $6,830.13455 = $6,830 (rounded)

Future Value Table

To find the future value of an amount that is known today, you use a future value table. When using a future value table, you simply locate the appropriate number of periods in the leftmost column and the interest rate in the row at the top of the table. The intersection of the row and column is the factor representing the future value of $1 for the number of periods and the relevant interest rate. To find the future value of an amount other than $1, multiply the factor in the table by that amount.

To illustrate the use of a future value table (Table III), we will use the same information that was presented before, except that we will now assume that the present value of $6,830 is known, not the future amount of $10,000. Assume that we have a savings account with a current balance of $6,830 that earns interest of 10%. What will be the balance in that account in four years?

Present value in savings account	$ 6,830
Future value factor of $1 in 4 periods	
at 10% interest (from Table III)	×1.4641
Future value	$10,000*

*Rounded

Hewlett-Packard Keystrokes for Future Value of a Single Payment:

1. 6,830: Press **PV** (this is the amount of the current payment)
2. 4: Press **N** (number of years)
3. 10: Press **I** (interest rate)
4. Press **FV** for the answer = $9,999.80300 = $10,000 (rounded)

When computing future values, we often use the term *compounding* to mean the frequency with which interest is added to the principal. Thus, we say that interest of 10% has been compounded once a year (annually) to arrive at a future value at the end of four years of $10,000. If the interest is added more or less frequently than once a year, the future amount will be different.

The preceding example assumed an annual compounding period for interest. If the 10% interest had been compounded semiannually (twice a year) for four years, the calculation would have involved using a 5% (one-half of the 10%) rate for 8 periods (4 years × 2 periods per year) instead of 10% for 4 periods. To illustrate, what is the present value of $10,000 to be paid in four years if interest of 10% is compounded semiannually?

Amount of payment	$10,000
Present value factor of $1 to be paid in 8 periods	
at 5% interest (from Table I)	×0.6768
Present value of payment	$ 6,768

Thus, the present value of $10,000 to be paid in four years is $6,768 if interest is compounded semiannually. Likewise, if semiannual compounding is used to determine the future value of $6,768 in four years at 10% compounded semiannually, the result is as follows:

Present value in savings account	$ 6,768
Future value factor of $1 in 8 periods	
at 5% interest (from Table III)	×1.4775
Future value	$10,000*

*Rounded

Note that the present value ($6,768) is lower with semiannual compounding than with annual compounding ($6,830). The more frequently interest is compounded, the greater the total amount of interest deducted (in computing present values) or added (in computing future values).

Hewlett-Packard Keystrokes for Present Value of a Single Payment:

1. 10,000: Press **FV** (this is the amount of the future payment)
2. 8: Press **N** (number of semiannual periods)
3. 5: Press **I** (interest rate per semiannual period)
4. Press **PV** for the answer = $6,768.39362 = $6,768 (rounded)

Hewlett-Packard Keystrokes for Future Value of a Single Payment:

1. 6,768: Press **PV** (this is the amount of the current payment)
2. 8: Press **N** (number of semiannual periods)
3. 5: Press **I** (interest rate per semiannual period)
4. Press **FV** for the answer = $9,999.41844 = $10,000 (rounded)

Since interest may also be compounded quarterly, monthly, daily, or for some other period, you should learn the relationship of interest to the compounding period. Semiannual interest means that you double the interest periods and halve the annual interest rate; with quarterly interest you quadruple the periods and take one-fourth of the annual interest rate. The formula for interest rate is:

$$\frac{\text{Yearly interest rate}}{\text{Compounding periods per year}} = \text{Interest rate per compounding period}$$

The number of interest periods is simply the number of periods per year times the number of years. That formula is:

$$\frac{\text{Compounding}}{\text{periods per year}} \times \frac{\text{Number}}{\text{of years}} = \frac{\text{Number of}}{\text{interest periods}}$$

The Present Value of an Annuity

In discussing present values and future values, we have assumed only a single present value or future value with one of the amounts known and the other to be computed. With liabilities, we generally know the future amount that must be paid and would like to compute the present value of that future payment.

Many long-term liabilities involve a series of payments rather than one lump-sum payment. For example, a company might purchase equipment under an installment agreement requiring payments of $5,000 each year for five years. Determining the value today (present value) of a series of equally spaced, equal amount payments (called annuities) is more complicated than determining the present value of a single future payment. If you were to try to calculate the present value of an annuity by hand, you would have to discount the first payment for one period, the second payment for two periods, and so on, and then add all the present values together. Because such calculations are time-consuming, a table is generally used (see Table II, page 232). The factors in the table are the sums of the individual present values of all future payments. Based on the present value of an annuity of $1, the table provides factors for various interest rates and payments.

To illustrate the use of a present value of an annuity table (Table II), we will assume that $10,000 is to be paid at the end of each of the next 10 years. If the interest rate is 12% compounded annually, Table II shows a present value factor of 5.6502. This factor means that the present value of $1 paid each year for 10 years discounted at 12% is approximately $5.65. Applying this factor to payments of $10,000 results in the following:

Amount of the annual payment	$10,000
Present value factor of an annuity of $1 discounted for 10 payments at 12%	×5.6502
Present value	$56,502

This amount, $56,502, is the amount (present value) that could be paid today to satisfy the obligation if interest is 12%.

Hewlett-Packard Keystrokes for Present Value of an Annuity:

1. 10,000: Press **PMT** (this is the amount of the annual payments)
2. 10: Press **N** (number of payments)
3. 12: Press **I** (interest rate)
4. Press **PV** for the answer = $56,502.23028 = $56,502 (rounded)

Using Excel Spreadsheets for Time Value of Money Calculations

Because of the widespread use of laptop computers, many people now use functions available in Excel spreadsheets to do time value of money calculations. Three of those functions—PV, NPV, and IRR—are introduced in this section.

The following example will be used to illustrate the use of all three Excel functions.

Initial cost of machine	$10,000
Net annual cash inflows from the machine	$3,000
Salvage value at the end of the machine's useful life	$1,000
Useful life	5 years
Appropriate discount rate	12%

For simplicity, income taxes will be ignored.

PV Excel Function

If you push the "Insert Function," or f_x button, in Excel, you can scan the menu of "Financial" functions and find the PV function. The function arguments for the PV function are as follows:

Rate   The discount rate, which is 12% in this example.

Nper   The number of periods, which is five years in this example.

Pmt   The regular annuity (or periodic, equal cash flow) amount. In this case, the annuity is $3,000.

Fv   The amount of any single cash flow to occur in the future. In this case, the salvage value is a single cash flow at the end of five years of $1,000.

Type   Indication of whether the cash flows occur at the beginning or the end of the periods. In the examples shown in this chapter, we have always assumed that cash flows occur at the end of the periods; this is indicated by leaving this field blank or by inserting a zero. If the cash flows occur at the beginning of the period, this is indicated by entering a one in this field. In this case, we will enter a zero to indicate that the cash flows occur at the end of the periods.

The completed set of Excel function arguments appears as follows:

Rate	.12
Nper	5
Pmt	3000
Fv	1000
Type	0

With these inputs, the value of the function is ($11,381.76). Note that Excel is designed such that the function returns a negative number. This can easily be remedied by placing a minus sign in front of the function. This calculation indicates that the net present value, or NPV, of this project is positive because the initial cost of the machine is just $10,000. Thus, the NPV is $1,381.76 ($11,381.76 − $10,000.00). This computation will be confirmed in an alternate way using the NPV Excel function.

NPV Excel Function

The annual cash flow information regarding the machine can be entered into a spreadsheet in the following format:

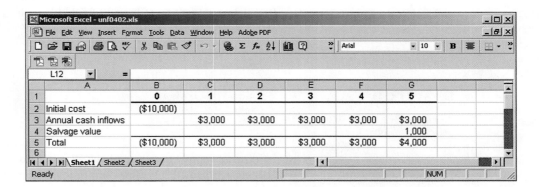

This format, rather than emphasizing the cash flows that come from each source (initial cost, annual cash inflows, or salvage value), instead emphasizes the net annual cash inflow or outflow from all sources. An advantage of presenting the cash flows in this fashion is that it allows for the use of the NPV function in Excel. If you push the "Insert Function," or f_x button, in Excel, you can scan the menu of "Financial" functions and find the NPV function. The function arguments for the NPV function are as follows:

Rate   The discount rate, which is 12% in this example.

Value1   The range of spreadsheet cells containing the net annual cash flows. In this case, that range is C5:G5. This function requires that all cash flows occur at the end of the periods. Note that the initial outflow of $10,000 is not included in the C5:G5 range of cells because that outflow occurs at the beginning, not the end, of the first year.

The completed set of Excel function arguments appears as follows:

Rate	.12
Value1	C5:G5

With these inputs, the value of the function is $11,381.76. Computation of the NPV of the project requires subtracting the initial cost of $10,000 from the present value of these net annual cash flows. Again, as computed previously, the NPV is $1,381.76.

IRR Excel Function

Another advantage of presenting the total net cash flows by year as shown in the preceding section is that it allows for the use of the IRR function in Excel. If you push the "Insert Function," or f_x button, in Excel, you can scan the menu of "Financial" functions and find the IRR function. The function arguments for the IRR function are as follows:

Values   The range of spreadsheet cells containing the net annual cash flows. In this case, that range is B5:G5. In contrast to the NPV function, the IRR function requires that the first cash flow included in the function occur immediately.

Guess   An initial estimate of the IRR. Because the IRR calculation involves an iterative interpolation process, the mathematical algorithm has to have a starting place. It is almost always safe to leave this field blank; if the field is blank, Excel uses 10% as the initial estimate.

The completed set of Excel function arguments appears as follows:

Caution

The NPV function assumes that the first cash flow included in the function occurs at the end of the first year. The IRR function assumes that the first cash flow occurs immediately.

Values	B5:G5
Guess	.10

With these inputs, the value of the IRR function is 17.23%. We expected an IRR greater than 12% because our previous computations demonstrated that the NPV (using a 12% discount rate) is greater than zero.

Table I: The Present Value of $1 Due in *n* Periods*

Period	1%	2%	3%	4%	5%	6%	7%	8%	9%	10%	12%	14%	15%	16%	18%	20%
1	.9901	.9804	.9709	.9615	.9524	.9434	.9346	.9259	.9174	.9091	.8929	.8772	.8696	.8621	.8475	.8333
2	.9803	.9612	.9426	.9246	.9070	.8900	.8734	.8573	.8417	.8264	.7972	.7695	.7561	.7432	.7182	.6944
3	.9706	.9423	.9151	.8890	.8638	.8396	.8163	.7938	.7722	.7513	.7118	.6750	.6575	.6407	.6086	.5787
4	.9610	.9238	.8885	.8548	.8227	.7921	.7629	.7350	.7084	.6830	.6355	.5921	.5718	.5523	.5158	.4823
5	.9515	.9057	.8626	.8219	.7835	.7473	.7130	.6806	.6499	.6209	.5674	.5194	.4972	.4761	.4371	.4019
6	.9420	.8880	.8375	.7903	.7462	.7050	.6663	.6302	.5963	.5645	.5066	.4556	.4323	.4104	.3704	.3349
7	.9327	.8706	.8131	.7599	.7107	.6651	.6227	.5835	.5470	.5132	.4523	.3996	.3759	.3538	.3139	.2791
8	.9235	.8535	.7894	.7307	.6768	.6274	.5820	.5403	.5019	.4665	.4039	.3506	.3269	.3050	.2660	.2326
9	.9143	.8368	.7664	.7026	.6446	.5919	.5439	.5002	.4604	.4241	.3606	.3075	.2843	.2630	.2255	.1938
10	.9053	.8203	.7441	.6756	.6139	.5584	.5083	.4632	.4224	.3855	.3220	.2697	.2472	.2267	.1911	.1615
11	.8963	.8043	.7224	.6496	.5847	.5268	.4751	.4289	.3875	.3503	.2875	.2366	.2149	.1954	.1619	.1346
12	.8874	.7885	.7014	.6246	.5568	.4970	.4440	.3971	.3555	.3186	.2567	.2076	.1869	.1685	.1372	.1122
13	.8787	.7730	.6810	.6006	.5303	.4688	.4150	.3677	.3262	.2897	.2292	.1821	.1625	.1452	.1163	.0935
14	.8700	.7579	.6611	.5775	.5051	.4423	.3878	.3405	.2992	.2633	.2046	.1597	.1413	.1252	.0985	.0779
15	.8613	.7430	.6419	.5553	.4810	.4173	.3624	.3152	.2745	.2394	.1827	.1401	.1229	.1079	.0835	.0649
16	.8528	.7284	.6232	.5339	.4581	.3936	.3387	.2919	.2519	.2176	.1631	.1229	.1069	.0930	.0708	.0541
17	.8444	.7142	.6050	.5134	.4363	.3714	.3166	.2703	.2311	.1978	.1456	.1078	.0929	.0802	.0600	.0451
18	.8360	.7002	.5874	.4936	.4155	.3503	.2959	.2502	.2120	.1799	.1300	.0946	.0808	.0691	.0508	.0376
19	.8277	.6864	.5703	.4746	.3957	.3305	.2765	.2317	.1945	.1635	.1161	.0829	.0703	.0596	.0431	.0313
20	.8195	.6730	.5537	.4564	.3769	.3118	.2584	.2145	.1784	.1486	.1037	.0728	.0611	.0514	.0365	.0261
25	.7798	.6095	.4776	.3751	.2953	.2330	.1842	.1460	.1160	.0923	.0588	.0378	.0304	.0245	.0160	.0105
30	.7419	.5521	.4120	.3083	.2314	.1741	.1314	.0994	.0754	.0573	.0334	.0196	.0151	.0116	.0070	.0042
40	.6717	.4529	.3066	.2083	.1420	.0972	.0668	.0460	.0318	.0221	.0107	.0053	.0037	.0026	.0013	.0007
50	.6080	.3715	.2281	.1407	.0872	.0543	.0339	.0213	.0134	.0085	.0035	.0014	.0009	.0006	.0003	.0001
60	.5504	.3048	.1697	.0951	.0535	.0303	.0173	.0099	.0057	.0033	.0011	.0004	.0002	.0001	†	†

*The formula used to derive the values in this table was $PV = F \dfrac{1}{(1+i)^n}$ where PV = present value, F = future amount to be discounted, i = interest rate, and n = number of periods.
†The value of 0 to four decimal places.

Table II: The Present Value of an Annuity of $1 per Number of Payments*

Number of Payments	1%	2%	3%	4%	5%	6%	7%	8%	9%	10%	12%	14%	15%	16%	18%	20%
1	0.9901	0.9804	0.9709	0.9615	0.9524	0.9434	0.9346	0.9259	0.9174	0.9091	0.8929	0.8772	0.8596	0.8621	0.8475	0.8333
2	1.9704	1.9416	1.9135	1.8861	1.8594	1.8334	1.8080	1.7833	1.7591	1.7355	1.6901	1.6467	1.6257	1.6052	1.5656	1.5278
3	2.9410	2.8839	2.8286	2.7751	2.7232	2.6730	2.6243	2.5771	2.5313	2.4869	2.4018	2.3216	2.2832	2.2459	2.1743	2.1065
4	3.9820	3.8077	3.7171	3.6299	3.5460	3.4651	3.3872	3.3121	3.2397	3.1699	3.0373	2.9137	2.8550	2.7982	2.6901	2.5887
5	4.8884	4.7135	4.5797	4.4518	4.3295	4.2124	4.1002	3.9927	3.8897	3.7908	3.6048	3.4331	3.3522	3.2743	3.1272	2.9906
6	5.7985	5.6014	5.4172	5.2421	5.0757	4.9173	4.7665	4.6229	4.4859	4.3553	4.1114	3.8887	3.7845	3.6847	3.4976	3.3255
7	6.7282	6.4720	6.2303	6.0021	5.7864	5.5824	5.3893	5.2064	5.0330	4.8684	4.5638	4.2883	4.1604	4.0386	3.8115	3.6046
8	7.6517	7.3255	7.0197	6.7327	6.4632	6.2098	5.9713	5.7466	5.5348	5.3349	4.9676	4.6389	4.4873	4.3436	4.0776	3.8372
9	8.5660	8.1622	7.7861	7.4353	7.1078	6.8017	6.5152	6.2469	5.9952	5.7590	5.3282	4.9464	4.7716	4.6065	4.3030	4.0310
10	9.4713	8.9826	8.5302	8.1109	7.7217	7.3601	7.0236	6.7101	6.4177	6.1446	5.6502	5.2161	5.0188	4.8332	4.4941	4.1925
11	10.3676	9.7868	9.2526	8.7605	8.3064	7.8869	7.4987	7.1390	6.8052	6.4951	5.9377	5.4527	5.2337	5.0286	4.6560	4.3271
12	11.2551	10.5733	9.9540	9.3851	8.8633	8.3838	7.9427	7.5361	7.1607	6.8137	6.1944	5.6603	5.4206	5.1971	4.7932	4.4392
13	12.1337	11.3484	10.6350	9.9856	9.3936	8.8527	8.3577	7.9038	7.4869	7.1034	6.4235	5.8424	5.5831	5.3423	4.9095	4.5327
14	13.0037	12.1062	11.2961	10.5631	9.8986	9.2950	8.7455	8.2442	7.7862	7.3667	6.6282	6.0021	5.7245	5.4675	5.0081	4.6106
15	13.8651	12.8493	11.9379	11.1184	10.3797	9.7122	9.1079	8.5595	8.0607	7.6061	6.8109	6.1422	5.8474	5.5755	5.0916	4.6755
16	14.7179	13.5777	12.5611	11.6523	10.8378	10.1059	9.4466	8.8514	8.3126	7.8237	6.9740	6.2651	5.9542	5.6685	5.1624	4.7296
17	15.5623	14.2919	13.1661	12.1657	11.2741	10.4773	9.7632	9.1216	8.5436	8.0216	7.1196	6.3729	6.0472	5.7487	5.2223	4.7746
18	16.3983	14.9920	13.7535	12.6593	11.6896	10.8276	10.0591	9.3719	8.7556	8.2014	7.2497	6.4674	6.1280	5.8178	5.2732	4.8122
19	17.2260	15.6785	14.3238	13.1339	12.0853	11.1581	10.3356	9.6036	8.9501	8.3649	7.3658	6.5504	6.1982	5.8775	5.3162	4.8435
20	18.0456	16.3514	14.8775	13.5903	12.4622	11.4699	10.5940	9.8181	9.1285	8.5136	7.4694	6.6231	6.2593	5.9288	5.3527	4.8696
25	22.0232	19.5235	17.4131	15.6221	14.0939	12.7834	11.6536	10.6748	9.8226	9.0770	7.8431	6.8729	6.4641	6.0971	5.4669	4.9476
30	25.8077	22.3965	19.6004	17.2920	15.3725	13.7648	12.4090	11.2578	10.2737	9.4269	8.0552	7.0027	6.5660	6.1772	5.5168	4.9789
40	32.8347	27.3555	23.1148	19.7928	17.1591	15.0463	13.3317	11.9246	10.7574	9.7791	8.2438	7.1050	6.6418	6.2335	5.5482	4.9966
50	39.1961	31.4236	25.7298	21.4822	18.2559	15.7619	13.8007	12.2335	10.9617	9.9148	8.3045	7.1327	6.6605	6.2463	5.5641	4.9995
60	44.9550	34.7609	27.6756	22.6235	18.9293	16.1614	14.0392	12.3766	11.0480	9.9672	8.3240	7.1401	6.6651	6.2482	5.5553	4.9999

*The formula used to derive the values in this table was $PV = F\left(\dfrac{1 - \dfrac{1}{(1+i)^n}}{i}\right)$ where PV = present value, F = periodic payment to be discounted, i = interest rate, and n = number of payments.

Table III: Amount of $1 Due in *n* Periods

Period	1%	2%	3%	4%	5%	6%	7%	8%	9%	10%	12%	14%	15%	16%	18%	20%
1	1.0100	1.0200	1.0300	1.0400	1.0500	1.0600	1.0700	1.0800	1.0900	1.1000	1.1200	1.1400	1.1500	1.1600	1.1800	1.2000
2	1.0201	1.0404	1.0609	1.0816	1.1025	1.1236	1.1449	1.1664	1.1881	1.2100	1.2544	1.2996	1.3225	1.3456	1.3924	1.4400
3	1.0303	1.0612	1.0927	1.1249	1.1576	1.1910	1.2250	1.2597	1.2950	1.3310	1.4049	1.4815	1.5209	1.5609	1.6430	1.7280
4	1.0406	1.0824	1.1255	1.1699	1.2155	1.2625	1.3108	1.3605	1.4116	1.4641	1.5735	1.6890	1.7490	1.8106	1.9388	2.0736
5	1.0510	1.1041	1.1593	1.2167	1.2763	1.3382	1.4026	1.4693	1.5386	1.6105	1.7623	1.9254	2.0114	2.1003	2.2878	2.4883
6	1.0615	1.1262	1.1941	1.2653	1.3401	1.4185	1.5007	1.5869	1.6771	1.7716	1.9738	2.1950	2.3131	2.4364	2.6996	2.9860
7	1.0721	1.1487	1.2299	1.3159	1.4071	1.5036	1.6058	1.7138	1.8280	1.9487	2.2107	2.5023	2.6600	2.8262	3.1855	3.5832
8	1.0829	1.1717	1.2668	1.3686	1.4775	1.5938	1.7182	1.8509	1.9926	2.1436	2.4760	2.8526	3.0590	3.2784	3.7589	4.2998
9	1.0937	1.1951	1.3048	1.4233	1.5513	1.6895	1.8385	1.9990	2.1719	2.3579	2.7731	3.2519	3.5179	3.8030	4.4355	5.1598
10	1.1046	1.2190	1.3439	1.4802	1.6289	1.7908	1.9672	2.1589	2.3674	2.5937	3.1058	3.7072	4.0456	4.4114	5.2338	6.1917
11	1.1157	1.2434	1.3842	1.5395	1.7103	1.8983	2.1049	2.3316	2.5804	2.8531	3.4785	4.2262	4.6524	5.1173	6.1759	7.4031
12	1.1268	1.2682	1.4258	1.6010	1.7959	2.0122	2.2522	2.5182	2.8127	3.1384	3.8960	4.8179	5.3502	5.9360	7.2876	8.9161
13	1.1381	1.2936	1.4685	1.6651	1.8856	2.1329	2.4098	2.7196	3.0658	3.4523	4.3635	5.4924	6.1528	6.8858	8.5994	10.699
14	1.1495	1.3195	1.5126	1.7317	1.9799	2.2609	2.5785	2.9372	3.3417	3.7975	4.8871	6.2613	7.0757	7.9875	10.147	12.839
15	1.1610	1.3459	1.5580	1.8009	2.0789	2.3966	2.7590	3.1722	3.6425	4.1772	5.4736	7.1379	8.1371	9.2655	11.973	15.407
16	1.1726	1.3728	1.6047	1.8730	2.1829	2.5404	2.9522	3.4259	3.9703	4.5950	6.1304	8.1372	9.3576	10.748	14.129	18.488
17	1.1843	1.4002	1.6528	1.9479	2.2920	2.6928	3.1588	3.7000	4.3276	5.0545	6.8660	9.2765	10.761	12.467	16.672	22.186
18	1.1961	1.4282	1.7024	2.0258	2.4066	2.8543	3.3799	3.9960	4.7171	5.5599	7.6900	10.575	12.375	14.462	19.673	26.623
19	1.2081	1.4568	1.7535	2.1068	2.5270	3.0256	3.6165	4.3157	5.1417	6.1159	8.6128	12.055	14.231	16.776	23.214	31.948
20	1.2202	1.4859	1.8061	2.1911	2.6533	3.2071	3.8697	4.6610	5.6044	6.7275	9.6463	13.743	16.366	19.460	27.393	38.337
30	1.3478	1.8114	2.4273	3.2434	4.3219	5.7435	7.6123	10.062	13.267	17.449	29.959	50.950	66.211	85.849	143.37	237.37
40	1.4889	2.2080	3.2620	4.8010	7.0400	10.285	14.974	21.724	31.409	45.259	93.050	188.88	267.86	378.72	750.37	1469.7
50	1.6446	2.6916	4.3839	7.1067	11.467	18.420	29.457	46.901	74.357	117.39	289.00	700.23	1083.6	1670.7	3927.3	9100.4
60	1.8167	3.2810	5.8916	10.519	18.679	32.987	57.946	101.25	176.03	304.48	897.59	2595.9	4383.9	7370.1	20555.	56347.

Table IV: Amount of an Annuity of $1 per Number of Payments

Number of Payments	1%	2%	3%	4%	5%	6%	7%	8%	9%	10%	12%	14%	15%	16%	18%	20%
1	1.0000	1.0000	1.0000	1.0000	1.0000	1.0000	1.0000	1.0000	1.0000	1.0000	1.0000	1.0000	1.0000	1.0000	1.0000	1.0000
2	2.0100	2.0200	2.0300	2.0400	2.0500	2.0600	2.0700	2.0800	2.0900	2.1000	2.1200	2.1400	2.1500	2.1600	2.1800	2.2000
3	3.0301	3.0604	3.0909	3.1216	3.1525	3.1836	3.2149	3.2464	3.2781	3.3100	3.3744	3.4396	3.4725	3.5056	3.5724	3.6400
4	4.0604	4.1216	4.1836	4.2465	4.3101	4.3746	4.4399	4.5061	4.5731	4.6410	4.7793	4.9211	4.9934	5.0665	5.2154	5.3680
5	5.1010	5.2040	5.3091	5.4163	5.5256	5.6371	5.7507	5.8666	5.9847	6.1051	6.3528	6.6101	6.7424	6.8771	7.1542	7.4416
6	6.1520	6.3081	6.4684	6.6330	6.8019	6.9753	7.1533	7.3359	7.5233	7.7156	8.1152	8.5355	8.7537	8.9775	9.4420	9.9299
7	7.2135	7.4343	7.6625	7.8983	8.1420	8.3938	8.6540	8.9228	9.2004	9.4872	10.8090	10.7305	11.0668	11.4139	12.1415	12.9159
8	8.2857	8.5830	8.8923	9.2142	9.5491	9.8975	10.2598	10.6366	11.0285	11.4359	12.2997	13.2328	13.7268	14.2401	15.3270	16.4991
9	9.3685	9.7546	10.1591	10.5828	11.0266	11.4913	11.9780	12.4876	13.0210	13.5795	14.7757	16.0853	16.7858	17.5185	19.0859	20.7989
10	10.4622	10.9497	11.4639	12.0061	12.5779	13.1808	13.8164	14.4866	15.1929	15.9374	17.5487	19.3373	20.3037	21.3215	23.5213	25.9587
11	11.5668	12.1687	12.8078	13.4864	14.2068	14.9716	15.7836	16.6455	17.5603	18.5312	20.6546	23.0445	24.3493	25.7329	28.7551	32.1504
12	12.6825	13.4121	14.1920	15.0258	15.9171	16.8699	17.8885	18.9771	20.1407	21.3843	24.1331	27.2707	29.0017	30.8502	34.9311	39.5805
13	13.8093	14.6803	15.6178	16.6268	17.7130	18.8821	20.1406	21.4953	22.9534	24.5227	28.0291	32.0887	34.3519	36.7862	42.2187	48.4966
14	14.9474	15.9739	17.0863	18.2919	19.5986	21.0151	22.5505	24.2149	26.0192	27.9750	32.3926	37.5811	40.5047	43.6720	50.8180	59.1959
15	16.0969	17.2934	18.5989	20.0236	21.5786	23.2760	25.1290	27.1521	29.3609	31.7725	37.2797	43.8424	47.5804	51.6595	60.9653	72.0351
16	17.2579	18.6393	20.1569	21.8245	23.6575	25.6725	27.8881	30.3243	33.0034	35.9497	42.7535	50.9804	55.7178	60.9250	72.9390	87.4421
17	18.4304	20.0121	21.7616	23.6975	25.8404	28.2129	30.8402	33.7502	36.9737	40.5447	48.8837	59.1176	65.0751	71.6730	87.0680	105.9306
18	19.6147	21.4123	23.4144	25.6454	28.1324	30.9057	33.9990	37.4502	41.3013	45.5992	55.7497	68.3941	75.8364	84.1407	103.7403	128.1167
19	20.8190	22.8406	25.1169	27.6712	30.5390	33.7600	37.3790	41.4463	46.0185	51.1591	63.4397	78.9692	88.2118	98.6032	123.4135	154.7400
20	22.0190	24.2974	26.8704	29.7781	33.0660	36.7856	40.9955	45.7620	51.1601	57.2750	72.0524	91.0249	102.4436	115.3797	146.6280	186.6880
30	34.7849	40.5681	47.5754	56.0849	66.4388	79.0582	94.4608	113.2832	136.3075	164.4940	241.3327	356.7868	434.7451	530.3117	790.9480	1181.8816
40	48.8864	60.4020	75.4013	95.0255	120.7998	154.7620	199.6351	259.0565	337.8824	442.5926	767.0914	1342.0251	1779.0903	2360.7572	4163.2130	7343.8578
50	64.4632	84.5794	112.7969	152.6671	209.3480	290.3359	406.5289	573.7702	815.0836	1163.9085	2400.0182	4994.5213	7217.7163	10435.6488	21813.0937	45497.1908
60	81.6697	114.0515	163.0534	237.9907	353.5837	533.1282	813.5204	1253.2133	1944.7921	3034.8164	7471.6411	18535.1333	29219.9916	46057.5085	114189.6665	281732.5718

review of learning objectives

1 **Understand the importance of capital budgeting and the concepts underlying strategic and capital investment decisions.** Strategic planning, especially as related to capital investment decisions, is critical to the success of organizations. The systematic planning for long-term investments in operating assets is known as capital budgeting. Long-term investments are usually large and represent commitments that are difficult to change, so capital budgeting is crucial to the long-run profitability of a company.

2 **Describe and use two nondiscounted capital budgeting techniques: the payback method and the unadjusted rate of return method.** Several capital budgeting techniques have been developed to assist in the decision-making process. The payback and unadjusted rate of return methods are commonly used in business because they are simple to apply. However, they generally should be used together with the discounted cash flow methods—net present value and internal rate of return—which are theoretically more correct because they consider the time value of money.

3 **Describe and use two discounted capital budgeting techniques: the net present value method and the internal rate of return method.** The net present value method uses a predetermined discount rate to state all the cash flows of an investment in present value terms. This rate is a company's cost of capital. The discounted cash inflows and outflows are then compared, and if the result is positive, or at least zero, the project is acceptable from a quantitative standpoint.

The internal rate of return method determines the "true" rate of return on an investment. This is the discount rate at which a project would have a net present value of zero. The internal rate is compared with the company's hurdle rate. If the internal rate is higher than or equal to the hurdle rate, the project is acceptable from a quantitative standpoint.

4 **Understand the need for evaluating qualitative factors in strategic and capital investment decisions.** Qualitative factors—such as the effect of an investment on quality and time, consumer and worker safety, and environmental and civic responsibility—are important considerations in capital investment decisions and may override the conclusions suggested by quantitative data.

5 **Use sensitivity analysis to assess the potential effects of uncertainty in capital budgeting.** Sensitivity analysis is used to assess the potential effect of uncertainty with regard to capital budgeting. It enables management to examine how the results of the calculations would vary if certain estimates were to change and thereby to gauge how reasonable the decision is.

6 **Explain how to use capital budgeting techniques in ranking capital investment projects.** Capital budgeting deals with both the screening and the ranking of projects. Investments must first be screened to determine which are acceptable. They must then be ranked to ensure that a company's limited funds are invested in the projects that will earn the greatest rate of return and otherwise accomplish the company's overall objectives.

7 **Explain how income taxes affect capital budgeting decisions.** The cash inflows and outflows of capital budgeting decisions must be converted to after-tax amounts before the present values are computed in order to obtain realistic measures of net present values. Cash inflows and outflows are converted to after-tax amounts by taking into account such tax provisions as expense deductions for repairs and depreciation, the estimated gain on disposal of the asset at the end of its useful life, and annual operating revenues and expenses.

key terms & concepts

review problem

Capital Budgeting

High Flying Company has an opportunity to make an investment that will yield $1,000 net cash inflow per year for the next 10 years. The investment will cost $6,000 and will have no salvage value. After cost reductions and depreciation related to the new investment, the future average annual net income will increase $800.

Required:

Compute the following:

1. The payback period.
2. The unadjusted rate of return.
3. The net present value. (Use a 10% discount rate.)
4. The internal rate of return. (The hurdle rate is 10%.)

Solution

1. The Payback Period

To compute the payback period, divide the investment cost by the annual net cash inflows.

$$\frac{\text{Investment cost}}{\text{Annual net cash inflows}} = \frac{\$6,000}{\$1,000} = 6 \text{ years}$$

2. The Unadjusted Rate of Return

To compute the unadjusted rate of return, divide the increase in future average annual net income by the initial investment cost.

$$\frac{\text{Increase in future average annual net income}}{\text{Initial investment cost}} = \frac{\$800}{\$6,000} = 13.3\%$$

3. The Net Present Value

To compute the net present value, first state in present value terms all expected cash outflows and inflows.

Present value of 10 annual payments of $1,000 discounted at 10%	$6,145
Present value of payment of $6,000 now	6,000
Net present value of project (present value of cash inflows minus present value of cash outflow)	$ 145

Since this investment's net present value is greater than zero, it is acceptable from a quantitative standpoint.

4. The Internal Rate of Return

To compute the internal rate of return, first compute the present value factor, as follows:

$$\frac{\text{Investment cost}}{\text{Annual net cash inflows}} = \frac{\$6,000}{\$1,000} = 6.0000$$

Next, use this present value factor to find the investment's internal rate of return in a present value table. Using Table II, find the row for 10 years, the life of the investment. Move across the row until you find the present value factor closest to 6.0000, which is 6.1446. This is the factor for 10%. Since 6.0000 is between 6.1446 and 5.6502, the investment's internal rate of return is between 10 and 12%. Next, use interpolation to find a more exact internal rate of return.

	Rate of Return	Present Value Factors	
High factor	10%	6.1446	6.1446
True factor		6.0000	0.0000
Low factor	12		5.6502
Differences	2%	0.1446	0.4944

The number 0.1446 is the difference between the high factor and the true factor. The number 0.4944 is the difference between the high factor and the low factor. The difference between the high rate and the low rate is 2%. The proportion 0.1446 ÷ 0.4944 of this 2% difference must be added to the low rate to give the true internal rate of return.

$$\text{True internal rate of return} = 0.10 + \left(0.02 \times \frac{0.1446}{0.4944}\right) = 10.58\%$$

The internal rate of return could also be computed using the following keystrokes with a Hewlett-Packard business calculator:

Hewlett-Packard Keystrokes:

1. −6,000: Press **PV** (you must enter the cash outflow as a NEGATIVE number)
2. 1,000: Press **PMT** (this is the annual cash inflow)
3. 10: Press **N** (number of years)
4. Press **I/YR** for the answer = 10.56%

Note that the answer obtained using table interpolation (10.58%) is very close to the actual internal rate of return of 10.56%.

Next, this internal rate of return is compared with the hurdle rate. Since it is greater, the investment is acceptable quantitatively. Note that this is the same decision reached by calculating the net present value.

d iscussion questions

1. Define *capital budgeting*. Give two examples of long-term investment decisions that require capital budgeting.
2. Why do long-term capital investment decisions often have a significant effect on a company's profitability?
3. Why is the time value of money so important in capital budgeting decisions?
4. If the time value of money is so important, why isn't the timing of cash flows emphasized in the accounting cycle?
5. How is depreciation expense treated when the discounted cash flow methods are used? Why?
6. How are cost savings and increased revenues related in capital budgeting?
7. Identify four capital budgeting methods, and explain why some are considered better than others.
8. Why is the payback method inferior to the discounted cash flow methods? When is the payback method helpful?

9. What is the major weakness of the unadjusted rate of return method?
10. Does a net present value of zero indicate that a project should be rejected? Explain.
11. As the desired rate of return increases, does the net present value of a project increase? Explain.
12. Under what circumstances might a project with a negative net present value be accepted?
13. What discount rate yields a net present value of zero? How is it determined?
14. What is a company's hurdle rate? How is it used?
15. How do quality and time considerations affect capital budgeting decisions?
16. Identify several qualitative factors, other than quality and time considerations, that may affect strategic and capital investment decisions. Why are qualitative factors important?

17. How can we deal with uncertainties involved in capital budgeting?

18. Distinguish between the screening and ranking functions of capital budgeting.
19. Of what value is a profitability index in capital budgeting?
20. How do income taxes influence capital budgeting decisions?

practice exercises

Practice 4-1

Capital Investment Decisions in Planning

Which one of the following is *not* a reason why a company should carefully plan its capital investment decisions?

a. Capital investments usually require a large initial outlay of capital.
b. Capital investments are usually tied to management bonus plans.
c. Capital investment decisions affect earnings over a long period of time.
d. Capital investments are less liquid, so poor investment decisions are difficult to reverse.

Practice 4-2

Screening, Ranking, and Discounting

Which one of the following statements is correct?

a. Screening is the process of finding the best among available acceptable alternatives.
b. Ranking is the process of determining whether an investment meets a minimum standard of financial acceptability.
c. For the comparison of cash flows to be accurate, all amounts should be stated at their value at the point in time when the cash flow occurs.
d. Cash received sooner is worth more than cash received later.
e. Generally speaking, managers use relatively low discount rates when evaluating investments that involve a high degree of risk.

Practice 4-3

Discounting Cash Outflows

The company is deciding whether to invest in a certain capital investment. The investment requires an initial outlay of $65,000 and annual payments of $7,500 made at the end of the year for four years. The company's discount rate is 14%. What is the present value of cash outflows related to this investment?

Practice 4-4

Discounting Cash Inflows

Refer to the data in Practice 4-3. The company expects the new investment will generate revenues of $22,500 per year for the four years of the investment's life. At the end of the four years, the company expects the investment to have a salvage value of $20,750. What is the present value of cash inflows related to this investment? Should the company make this investment?

Practice 4-5

Payback Method

The company paid $50,000 cash for a capital investment. The company expects the investment to generate net cash inflows of $8,400 per year. What is the payback period of this investment?

Practice 4-6

Unadjusted Rate of Return Method

Refer to the data in Practice 4-5. What is the unadjusted rate of return on the investment? *Note:* The investment is expected to have a useful life of 10 years, and the company uses straight-line depreciation with zero salvage value.

Practice 4-7

Cost of Capital

Twenty percent of a company's total capital is debt, 35% is from the issuance of stock, and 45% is equity from retained earnings. The company has determined that the cost of its debt capital is 8% and the cost of its equity capital is 20% from stock and 15% from retained earnings. Compute the company's average cost of capital.

Practice 4-8

Net Present Value Method

Which one of the following investment opportunities would be rejected by a company that accepts all projects with net present values greater than zero?

a. Present value of inflows = $35,740; present value of outflows = $32,023.
b. Present value of inflows = $452,800; present value of outflows = $450,020.
c. Present value of inflows = $1,003,840; present value of outflows = $1,003,810.
d. Present value of inflows = $125,114; present value of outflows = $125,843.
e. Present value of inflows = $85,084; present value of outflows = $82,000.

Practice 4-9

Least-Cost Decisions

The company is required to install a new piece of safety equipment. The company has two alternatives for the equipment. One alternative would cost $260,000 immediately but would not add to operating costs over the 5-year life of the equipment. The second alternative costs $75,000 immediately but would add $45,000 to annual operating costs for five years. The company uses an 8% discount rate. Which alternative should the company purchase?

Practice 4-10

Calculating Internal Rate of Return

The company is considering a 7-year investment. The initial cost of the investment is $45,638. The investment will yield net cash inflows of $10,000 per year. What is the internal rate of return for this investment?

Practice 4-11

Internal Rate of Return Interpolation

The company is considering whether to invest in a project with an initial cost of $538,000 that will provide annual net cash inflows of $82,500 for 10 years. Use interpolation to estimate the internal rate of return.

Practice 4-12

Uneven Cash Flows and Internal Rate of Return

The company is considering whether to invest in a piece of equipment that requires an investment of $250,000 today. The project will provide net cash flows of $50,000 per year for eight years, and it will have a salvage value of $51,509 at the end of eight years. Calculate the internal rate of return. (*Hint:* The IRR is greater than 10%.)

Practice 4-13

Qualitative Factors in Strategic and Capital Investment Decisions

Which one of the following is an important qualitative factor to consider when making strategic and capital investment decisions?

a. Company image and prestige.
b. Pollution control and environmental protection.
c. Government regulation.
d. Worker safety.
e. All of the above are examples of important qualitative factors.

Practice 4-14

Uncertain Expected Cash Flows

The company is considering an investment that costs $785,000 today and has a salvage value in 10 years of $137,714, but the company is not sure how much net annual cash inflow will be provided by the investment. The company has a discount rate of 7%. Compute the net amount of annual cash inflow required to break even.

Practice 4-15

Uncertain Useful Life

The company is considering an investment that costs $430,000 today and will provide $72,000 each year in net cash inflow, but the company is not sure how long the investment will last. The company has a discount rate of 10%. Compute the number of years of useful life required for this investment to break even.

Practice 4-16

Ranking by the Internal Rate of Return Method

The company is considering eight capital investment projects. The company has a minimum required internal rate of return of 13%. Screen and rank the eight capital investment projects using the internal rate of return.

Project	Expected Rate of Return
S	14%
T	24
U	20
V	10
W	17
X	9
Y	12
Z	18

Practice 4-17

Profitability Index

The company is considering a project with a present value of net cash inflows of $1,340,000 and an initial investment cost of $973,000. What is the profitability index of this investment?

Practice 4-18

Ranking Using the Profitability Index

Screen and rank the following projects using the profitability index.

	Project J	Project K	Project L	Project M
Present value of net cash inflows ...	$1,000,000	$500,000	$1,250,000	$250,000
Investment cost	950,000	430,000	1,280,000	205,000

Practice 4-19

Income Tax Considerations in Capital Budgeting Decisions

The company has decided to invest in some equipment that costs $50,000 today and will generate cash inflows of $20,000 per year for the 5-year life of the equipment. At the end of the five years, the equipment will have no salvage value. The company will depreciate the equipment using straight-line depreciation. The company's tax rate is 30%, and its discount rate is 10%. Compute the net present value of this investment.

Practice 4-20

Capital Budgeting, MACRS, and Section 179

Refer to the data in Practice 4-19. Assume that the company elects to deduct $10,000 of the cost of the equipment immediately as a Section 179 expensing election. The remaining cost of $40,000 is deducted according to the MACRS schedule for 5-year property. The MACRS percentages (incorporating the half-year convention) are as follows:

Year 1	0.2000
Year 2	0.3200
Year 3	0.1920
Year 4	0.1152
Year 5	0.1152
Year 6	0.0576

Compute the net present value of the investment. As before, the tax rate is 30%, and the discount rate is 10%.

exercises

Note: Unless otherwise indicated, the exercises and problems assume that all payments are made or received at the end of the year.

Exercise 4-1

Present Values

Consider each part independently.

1. Super-Fix Company would like to move its auto repair shop to a downtown location in order to attract more customers. What is the maximum Super-Fix should pay to purchase a building at the new location, assuming that the company needs to earn 12%? The new building will last 40 years. Super-Fix estimates that moving to the new location will result in a $10,000 increase in annual income.
2. If Audrey Ostler buys a new small automobile that costs $14,000 and provides annual gasoline savings of $1,200, how long must she own the car before the savings justify its cost? Assume an 8% cost of capital.

Exercise 4-2

Time Value of Money

Your late, rich uncle left you $250,000. The executor of the estate has asked if you would rather receive the full amount now or $30,000 a year for the next 40 years.

Which of these options would you take, assuming that your desired rate of return is:

1. 10%?
2. 12%?

Exercise 4-3

Payback Method

The manager of Simple Company must choose between two investments. Project A costs $50,000 and promises cash savings of $10,000 a year over a useful life of 10 years. Project B costs $60,000, and the estimated cash savings are $11,000 per year over a useful life of 11 years. Using the payback method, determine which project the manager should choose.

Exercise 4-4

Unadjusted Rate of Return Method

Um Good, Inc., a candy maker, is thinking of purchasing a new machine. A marketing firm has estimated that the new machine could increase revenues by $30,000 a year for the next five years. The expenses directly relating to the machine total $60,000 ($12,000 $\times$ 5 years). The initial purchase cost would be $80,000. What is the unadjusted rate of return?

Exercise 4-5

Net Present Value Method

The Carroll Broom Company is thinking of purchasing a new automatic straw-binding machine. The company president, Joan Carroll, has determined that such a machine would save the company $10,000 per year in labor costs. The machine would cost $46,500 and would have a useful life of 10 years and a scrap value of $500. The machine would require servicing after five years at a cost of $1,000. Carroll uses a discount rate of 16%. Compute the net present value. From a quantitative standpoint, should the machine be purchased?

Exercise 4-6

Least-Cost Decision

The local fire department has determined the Sleep-Eazy Mattress Company is not in full compliance with local fire regulations. To comply, Sleep-Eazy has two alternatives: It may install an automatic sprinkler system, or it may hire a fire safety expert to make weekly fire safety checks. The automatic sprinkler system will cost $125,000, including installation charges, and will last for 10 years. It will have no salvage value. The entire system is virtually maintenance-free. The fire safety expert's fee is $14,000 per year. The cost of capital is 10%. Which alternative should Sleep-Eazy Mattress Company choose? Why?

Exercise 4-7

Internal Rate of Return
Juan Gonzales, the president of Nogalis Corporation, is trying to decide whether he should buy a new machine that will improve production efficiency. The machine will increase cash inflows $5,000 a year for five years. It will cost $18,000, and there will be no salvage value. What is the internal rate of return?

Exercise 4-8

Cost of Capital
Daphney Corporation has raised $200,000 in equity financing through the issuance of shares. Stockholders expect to earn an average of 20% per year on their equity investment in Daphney. In addition, the corporation has issued $100,000 of 10% bonds. The corporation has also accumulated $25,000 in earnings that have been retained in the company. Investors expect to earn about 16% on the earnings that are retained in the company. Using the weighting procedure discussed in the chapter, calculate Daphney Corporation's cost of capital. (Ignore taxes in calculating the cost of debt.)

Exercise 4-9

Net Present Value and Internal Rate of Return
A real estate investment requires an initial outlay of $150,000 in cash. The investment will return a single sum cash payment of $606,796 after 10 years. The rate of return required on projects as risky as this one is 18%.

1. What is the net present value of this real estate investment?
2. What is the internal rate of return of this real estate investment?
3. Is this an attractive investment?

Exercise 4-10

Net Present Value and Internal Rate of Return
A retired person has $700,000 in a retirement account. An insurance company is offering to give the retired person an annuity of $61,029 at the end of each year for the next 20 years in exchange for the $700,000. The retired person requires a rate of return of 8% on investments; this is the rate currently being earned in the retirement account.

1. What is the net present value of this exchange?
2. What is the internal rate of return implied in this exchange?
3. Should the retired person accept the exchange offered by the insurance company?

Exercise 4-11

Quality and Time Factors
Tucker Yard Service Company is contemplating purchasing a new riding lawnmower for its business. One particular model has special features that enhance the cutting and the collecting of the mowed grass, but that mower is quite expensive. Another model is more basic and costs $1,000 less. The payback period on the more expensive model is estimated to be 3.5 years and on the less expensive model 2.5 years. The "bumper-to-bumper" warranties are two years and one year, respectively. From these limited data, what factors should Tucker consider in making this decision?

Exercise 4-12

Qualitative Considerations
The Upscale Department Store has been plagued with shoplifting. The president, Hector Conrad, has suggested that the store hire a security force to "frisk" all customers as they leave the store. It is estimated that annual shoplifting losses are $100,000. Expenses associated with the security force are estimated to be $50,000 annually. Before Mr. Conrad makes his final decision, what other factors might he consider?

Problem 4-5

Spreadsheet

Payback, Net Present Value, and Internal Rate of Return Methods

Nucore Company is thinking of purchasing a new candy-wrapping machine at a cost of $370,000. The machine should save the company approximately $70,000 in operating costs per year over its estimated useful life of 10 years. The salvage value at the end of 10 years is expected to be $15,000. (Ignore income tax effects.)

Required:
1. What is the machine's payback period?
2. Compute the net present value of the machine if the cost of capital is 12%.
3. What is the expected internal rate of return for this machine?

Problem 4-6

Internal Rate of Return

The manager of Soft & Creamy Ice Cream is thinking of buying a new soft ice cream machine. The machine will cost $13,500 and will last 10 years. Soft ice cream sales are expected to generate $3,000 in income per year.

Required:
What is the internal rate of return on this project?

Problem 4-7

Choosing among Alternatives

Tom Thurlow wants to buy a boat but is short of cash. Two alternatives are available: Tom can accept $2,000 per year from his brother for partial ownership in the boat, or he can earn money by renting the boat to others. Rental income would be $2,500 per year. Under either alternative, the boat will last eight years. If Tom rents the boat out, he will have to pay $3,000 to overhaul the engine at the end of the fourth year.

Required:
Which alternative should Tom select, assuming that the cost of capital is 12% and that only quantitative considerations are involved?

Problem 4-8

Lease-or-Buy Decision

A small sales company is committed to supplying three sales representatives with new cars. The company has two alternatives. It can either buy the three cars and sell them after two years, or it can lease the cars for two years. The company uses a 16% discount rate. The information for each alternative is as follows:

Alternative 1: Buy

Cost	$36,000
Annual service costs	3,000
Anticipated repairs during the 1st year	700
Anticipated repairs during the 2nd year	1,500
Salvage value at the end of 2 years	10,000

Alternative 2: Lease
To lease the cars, the company would simply pay $20,000 a year for the two years.

Required:
Assuming the lease is paid at the end of each year, determine the better alternative.

Problem 4-9

Spreadsheet

Rent-or-Purchase Decision

As one aspect of its business, New Lawn Company currently rents a ditch-digging machine for an average of $48 per job. A used machine is available for $995 but would cost $498 to repair. The machine, if purchased, would cost $800 a year to maintain and in two years would need a new chain costing $394. The used digger has a useful life of four years with no salvage value.

(continued)

Required:
If the company averages 30 jobs a year and has a cost of capital of 10%, which alternative is more profitable?

Problem 4-10

Sell-or-Rent Decision
Clarence Gleason has inherited an apartment complex. He is now faced with the decision of whether to sell or to rent the property. A real estate adviser believes that Clarence should rent the property, because he could receive $65,000 per year for 10 years and then could sell the property for $400,000. A development company has offered Clarence $300,000 down and promises to pay $50,000 per year for the next 15 years. The land has a remaining mortgage of $130,000. If Clarence sells the complex, he will have to pay that sum now. If he rents the property, he will have to pay $20,000 per year for 10 years. The cost of capital is 16%.

Required:
1. Calculate the net present value of each alternative.
2. **Interpretive Question:** Discuss the qualitative factors that might affect the decision to sell or rent.

Problem 4-11

Unifying Concepts: Net Present Value and Internal Rate of Return Methods
Julie Kowalis, an investment analyst, wants to know if her investments during the past four years have earned at least a 12% return. Four years ago, she had the following investments:

a. She purchased a small building for $50,000 and rented space in it. She received rental income of $8,000 for each of the four years and then sold the building this year for $55,000.
b. She purchased a small refreshment stand near the city park for $25,000. Annual income from the stand was $5,000 for each of the four years. She sold the stand for $20,000 this year.
c. She purchased an antique car for $5,000 four years ago. She sold it this year to a collector for $7,000.

Required:
1. Using the net present value method, determine whether or not each investment earned at least 12%.
2. Did the investments as a whole earn at least 12%? Explain.

Problem 4-12

Sensitivity Analysis
Falcon Manufacturing is a leading manufacturer of airframe components for small aircraft. Heidi Saxton, Falcon's operations manager, has submitted a request for a new piece of production equipment. Using the new machine, the company will be able to reduce expenses for both maintenance and labor. Data on the project are as follows:

Initial investment	$80,000
Useful life	10 years
Salvage value of old machine	$1,500
Annual cash savings	$15,000
Salvage value of new machine	$10,000
Maintenance overhaul (Year 5)	$7,600
Cost of capital	12%

Assume all cash flows occur at the end of each year. (Ignore income tax effects.)

Required:
1. Using the above data, calculate the net present value of the investment. From a strictly quantitative standpoint, should the machine be purchased?
2. Suppose that Heidi receives another analysis that increases the cost of capital estimate to 14% and the new machine's salvage value to $17,000. Would the purchase still make sense?
3. Falcon's CEO, Kevin Davis, is responsible for approving all capital investment projects. Having spent his entire career dealing with one estimate after another, Kevin has asked you to consider two specific changes:
   a. Reduce annual cash inflows by 10%.
   b. Cut in half the estimated salvage value of new equipment.
   Using the original problem data, calculate the net present value using the CEO's two changes.

Problem 4-13

Net Present Value Used to Rank Alternatives

Taglioni's Pizza Company has to choose a new delivery car from among three alternatives. Assume that gasoline costs $1.30 per gallon and that the firm's cost of capital is 12%. The car will be driven 12,000 miles per year.

	Car 1	Car 2	Car 3
Cost	$12,000	$4,000	$8,000
Mileage per gallon	40	8	12
Useful life	5 years	5 years	5 years
Salvage value	$2,000	$500	$1,000

Required:
1. Which car should the company purchase?
2. How would your answer change if the price of gasoline increased to $2 per gallon?

Problem 4-14

Screening and Ranking Alternatives

Sunshine Corporation is considering several long-term investments. Management wants to accept the two best projects, given the following data:

	Project				
	A	**B**	**C**	**D**	**E**
Present value of net cash inflows	$24,000	$44,000	$15,000	$30,000	$50,000
Investment cost	20,000	40,000	16,000	24,000	41,000

Required:
1. Determine the net present value and the profitability index for each project.
2. Which projects are acceptable using the profitability index as a screening tool?
3. What would be the ranking of the acceptable projects according to the profitability indexes?
4. **Interpretive Question:** What additional information would be needed to screen and rank the projects using the internal rate of return method? What are the decision rules using the IRR method for screening and ranking capital budgeting projects?

Problem 4-15

Unifying Concepts: Comparing the Internal Rate of Return and the Net Present Value Methods

Get Rich Corporation has to choose between two investment opportunities. Investment A requires an immediate cash outlay of $100,000 and provides after-tax income of $20,000 per year for 10 years. Investment B requires an immediate cash outlay of $1,000 and generates after-tax income of $350 per year for five years.

(continued)

Required:

1. Using a cost of capital of 12%, calculate the net present value of each investment, and determine which one Get Rich should select.
2. Calculate the internal rate of return of each investment. On the basis of this method, which investment should Get Rich select?
3. **Interpretive Question:** How do you account for the difference in rankings? Under the circumstances, which method would you rely on for your decision?

Problem 4-16

Unifying Concepts: Payback and Internal Rate of Return

The management of Kitchen Shop is thinking of buying a new drill press to aid in adapting parts for different machines. The press is expected to save Kitchen Shop $8,000 per year in costs. However, Kitchen Shop has an old punch machine that isn't worth anything on the market and that will probably last indefinitely. The new press will last 12 years and will cost $41,595. (Ignore income tax effects.)

Required:

1. Compute the payback period of the new machine.
2. Compute the internal rate of return.
3. **Interpretive Question:** What uncertainties are involved in this decision? Discuss how they might be dealt with.

Problem 4-17

Unifying Concepts: Capital Rationing Using the Payback and Net Present Value Methods

Dino Corporation is trying to decide which of five investment opportunities it should undertake. The company's cost of capital is 16%. Owing to a cash shortage, the company has a policy that it will not undertake any investment unless it has a payback period of less than three years. The company is unwilling to undertake more than two investment projects. The following data apply to the alternatives:

Investment	Initial Cost	Expected Returns
A	$100,000	$30,000 per year for 5 years
B	50,000	25,000 per year for 6 years
C	30,000	8,000 per year for 10 years
D	20,000	7,000 per year for 6 years
E	10,000	3,500 per year for 3 years

Required:

1. Using the payback method, screen out any investment project that fails to meet the company's payback period requirement.
2. Using the net present value method, determine which of the remaining projects the company should undertake, keeping in mind the capital rationing constraint.
3. **Interpretive Question:** What advantages do you see in using the payback method together with other capital budgeting methods?

Problem 4-18

Income Tax Effects

Sylvania Manufacturing Company is considering the purchase of new equipment to perform operations currently being performed on less efficient equipment. The purchase price is $142,000 delivered and installed. The company elects to expense $10,000 of the purchase price in the first year. A company engineer estimates that the new equipment will save $28,000 in labor and other direct costs annually. The new equipment will have an estimated life of 10 years and zero salvage value at the end of the 10 years. The equipment will be depreciated over 10 years on the optional straight-line basis for income tax purposes, after taking the

$10,000 expense election in the first year. The existing equipment has a book value of $4,000, a remaining economic life of five years, and can be disposed of now for $4,000. The company's average tax rate is 40% (including federal, state, and local taxes), and its after-tax cost of capital is 12%.

Required:
1. Should the new equipment be purchased?
2. What would the decision be if the cost of capital were 10%?
3. **Interpretive Question:** Assuming that the net present value of an investment in new equipment is so small that you are indifferent about whether to make the purchase or keep the old equipment, what other factors would you consider in making the decision?

d iscussion cases

Case 4-1

Should We Purchase That New Copier?
Campus Print Shop is thinking of purchasing a new, modern copier that automatically collates pages. The machine would cost $22,000 cash. A service contract on the machine, considered a must because of its complexity, would be an additional $200 per month. The machine is expected to last eight years and have a resale value of $4,000. By purchasing the new machine, Campus would save $450 per month in labor costs and $100 per month in materials costs due to increased efficiency. Other operating costs are expected to remain the same. The old copier would be sold for its scrap value of $1,000. Campus requires a return of 14% on its capital investments.

1. As a consultant to Campus, compute:
   a. The payback period.
   b. The unadjusted rate of return.
   c. The net present value.
   d. The internal rate of return.
2. On the basis of these computations and any qualitative considerations, would you recommend that Campus purchase the new copier?

Case 4-2

Cost and Qualitative Factors in Capital Investment Decisions
Yoshika Landscaping is contemplating purchasing a new ditch-digging machine that promises savings of $5,600 per year for 10 years. The machine costs $21,970, and no salvage value is expected. The company's cost of capital is 12%. You have been asked to advise Yoshika relative to this capital investment decision. As part of your analysis, compute:

1. The payback period.
2. The unadjusted rate of return.
3. The net present value.
4. The internal rate of return.

What factors besides your quantitative analysis should be considered in making this decision?

j udgment calls

Judgment 4-1

You Decide: Which measurement is the most important when making a capital budgeting decision, net present value or improved customer satisfaction?
Your company is considering purchasing a server to host the company Web site, which customers use to place their orders.

When deciding on this new capital investment, you realize that the net present value of the purchase is negative, meaning the future cash flows associated with the server will not replace the initial investment. However, an important qualitative factor that should be considered with the purchase of a new server is the improved customer service and satisfaction that will be achieved as a result of the purchase. What should you do?

Judgment 4-2

You Decide: Should a project be accepted or rejected if the project has an internal rate of return that is less than the company's hurdle rate?

You are the CFO for an automobile manufacturer. The board of directors is considering expanding the current product line to include sports utility vehicles. As you look at the new product line's internal rate of return, it is 12% and the company's overall discount rate is 15%. Should the new line be added to the company's existing lines? The board wants your input before they make a decision. What factors should you consider?

Competency Enhancement Opportunities

▶ **Analyzing Real Company Information**
▶ **International Case**
▶ **Ethics Case**
▶ **Writing Assignment**

▶ **The Debate**
▶ **Internet Search**

The following additional assignments provide opportunities for students to develop critical thinking, ethical perspectives, oral and written communication skills, experience with electronic research, and teamwork through group and business activities.

▶ *Analyzing Real Company Information*

Analyzing 4-1 (Microsoft)

The 2002 Form 10-K for MICROSOFT is included in Appendix A. The section of the Form 10-K relating to management's discussion and analysis provides detail as to factors that might affect Microsoft's future and, as a result, the company's long-term decisions. Review the financial statements and the "Management Discussion and Analysis" section, and answer the following questions:

1. Microsoft has no long-term debt. Does that mean its cost of capital is zero? Explain.
2. Microsoft specifically states that the company "does not provide forecasts of future financial performance." If that is the case, how can it make any capital budgeting decisions?

Analyzing 4-2 (The Boeing Company)

As you probably know, BOEING builds airplanes. While most famous for the big 747, Boeing is continually developing newer models. Over the past several years, Boeing has been developing the 737 and 777 families of airplanes. In 1996, Boeing formed a joint venture with GENERAL ELECTRIC to develop planes that can fly over 6,000 miles without refueling.

1. What factors must Boeing consider when making the decision to produce a new family of airplanes like the 777? What would be the expected cash inflows, and what would be the expected cash outflows? Categorize the outflows into two types: one-time outflows and annual outflows.
2. The costs of developing a new family of airplanes are enormous. Why would Boeing agree to incur these costs when it is able to continue producing older model planes like the 747 and the 767? Frame this discussion in terms of a capital budgeting decision. That is, evaluate the opportunities in terms of cash inflows and cash outflows.

International

▶ *International Case*

DaimlerChrysler

DAIMLERCHRYSLER discloses the following information relating to its long-term debt in its 2002 annual report:

- 6.3% notes/bonds
- 2.6% commercial paper
- 5.3% liabilities to financial institutions

FORD MOTOR COMPANY also provides information relating to its debt in the notes to its annual report. That information is given below.

- Secured indebtedness, 7.6%
- Unsecured senior indebtedness—notes and bank debt, 4.8%
- Unsecured subordinated indebtedness—notes, 9.4%

1. Assume that each company's debt is distributed equally across the various categories. Compute an average cost interest rate for each company.
2. If your answer from part (1) represented each firm's cost of capital, what would it tell you about the kinds of projects that DaimlerChrysler can undertake as compared to Ford?

▶ *Ethics Case*

Wheeler, Nevada

The city council of Wheeler, Nevada, is faced with an important decision: whether or not to re-zone a parcel of property and allow ChemStor, Inc., to purchase the land and build a chemical waste storage facility on the property. Several factors enter into the decision.

a. The property is currently zoned for agricultural use and is surrounded by ranching operations in a rural community.
b. Several ranchers have joined together and offered to buy the property from the city over a 40-year period. In return for an agreed-upon interest rate of one point below prime, they will donate 20 acres of the land for a city park.
c. ChemStor has offered to pay cash for the land. Company management also points out that the facility will create about 25 new jobs for local residents and generate close to $100,000 a year in increased property taxes for the city.
d. ChemStor, a New Jersey-based company, learned of this property from its controller, who is a brother-in-law to one of the Wheeler City council members. ChemStor has offered a "finder's fee" for locating a waste storage site. The finder's fee would be split between the controller and the brother-in-law.

Identify the ethical and other issues involved in this capital investment decision.

▶ *Writing Assignment*

Lease versus Buy

You are fresh out of college, have your first real job, and just received your first big paycheck. You decide you need some wheels. Off you go to the car dealer. You carefully review the various makes and models of cars, determine the price range you can afford, and select "YOUR FIRST CAR." You thought that was the hard part. Now you need to decide on financing. The salesperson says you can either borrow money to purchase the vehicle or you can lease the car.

What factors should you consider in making this capital budgeting decision? Identify those factors that should enter into the lease versus buy decision. Prepare a short memo discussing the pros and cons of leasing versus buying and identifying the cash inflows and outflows associated with each option.

▷ *The Debate*

The Time Value of Money

The text discusses two general types of capital budgeting techniques: nondiscounted and discounted. The nondiscounted methods involve comparing the outflows of cash to the inflows. These methods do not take into account the time value of money. The discounted capital budgeting techniques factor in the evaluation of the time value of money.

Divide your group into two teams.

- Team 1 is to take the position that the nondiscounted methods provide the best means of evaluating capital budgeting alternatives. Prepare a short presentation that identifies the advantages of using the nondiscounted methods and discusses the disadvantages of the discounted capital budgeting techniques.
- Team 2 is to take the position that the discounted methods are preferred. Prepare a short presentation in support of the various methods that incorporate into their analysis the time value of money.

▷ *Internet Search*

Federal Express

We began this chapter with a look at FEDERAL EXPRESS. Let's continue our examination of this company using its Internet site. Access Federal Express's site at **http://www.fedex.com**. Sometimes Web addresses change, so if this address doesn't work, access the Web site for this book at **http://swain.swlearning.com** for an updated link to Federal Express.

Once you have gained access to the company's Web site, answer the following questions:

1. Find the portion of the Web site containing information about the early history of FedEx Express. Why was Memphis, Tennessee, chosen as the company headquarters?
2. Find the portion of the Web site containing "FedEx Express Facts." How many aircraft does FedEx have in its worldwide fleet?
3. Find FedEx's most recent annual report. Does the company lease any of its aircraft or equipment? (*Hint:* Look in the notes to the financial statements.) What factors would the company have considered when determining whether to lease or buy its aircraft and equipment?

Imagine that one of your parents has traveled across the country to visit you at college. As the two of you have dinner together at one of your favorite restaurants, the discussion turns to your accounting class. You begin describing some of the new ideas and techniques you have been learning lately. Suddenly, your parent wants to talk about the family business. As the discussion goes on, it becomes clear that your parent is expecting you to provide some specific ideas about how to improve the management process in the family business using current accounting methods. You certainly want to impress your parent with all the detailed knowledge that you have gained since beginning your course work in accounting. However, you are also concerned that you may describe something incorrectly or say something misleading. One day you expect to inherit the family business, and you would hate to say anything during dinner that might later cause problems in the company!

Required:

You need to respond to your parent using insights gained from the first four chapters of management accounting. Further, answering your parent's questions will require you to carefully construct your remarks in light of the exact nature of the family business. Hence, we will assume three separate types of businesses for your family:

1. Computer manufacturing plant
2. Neighborhood grocery store
3. Large architectural firm

Listed below are a number of topics from the first four chapters of management accounting. Briefly describe in three sentences or less how each topic may relate to the family business.

1. Direct materials costs
2. Direct labor costs
3. Overhead costs
4. Direct materials inventory
5. Work-in-process inventory
6. Finished goods inventory
7. Job order costing
8. Process costing*
9. Cost behavior
10. Break-even analysis
11. Capital budgeting
12. Net present value
13. Internal rate of return

*Relates to expanded material.

c h a p t e r

5

Operational Budgeting

After studying this chapter, you should be able to:

1 Describe the importance of personal budgeting.

2 Identify the purposes of budgeting for organizations.

3 Explain the budgeting process and its behavioral implications in organizations.

4 Construct an operating budget and its components for manufacturing firms.

5 Compare the operating budget for a manufacturing firm to that of a merchandising or service firm.

6 Create the cash budget.

7 Prepare pro-forma financial statements.

8 Distinguish between static and flexible budgets.

Every organization needs to budget. Budgets help allocate resources effectively so that the organization can accomplish its mission. Consider how the federal government budgets, for example. The arrival of the president's budget on Capitol Hill signals the beginning of the annual budget process in Congress—a process that can last more than eight months and require the passage of scores of bills and resolutions.[1] Congress drafts a budget resolution—a spending plan that defines in broad terms how much the government will take in through taxes and other receipts and spend on all government accounts during the coming fiscal year. The House and Senate Budget Committees each draft their own version, bring the drafts to their respective chambers for approval, iron out differences in conference, and return the resulting version to their chambers for adoption. Discretionary spending is allocated to the Appropriations Committees in both chambers. Throughout the budget process, Congress passes authorization bills that set the maximum amounts that may be spent in specific fiscal years for individual discretionary programs, as well as goals for those programs. The budget resolution serves as a blueprint for congressional spending decisions. It sets the total levels for budget authority, outlays, incoming revenues, direct-loan obligations, and loan guarantee commitments, as well as the public debt ceiling for the upcoming fiscal year.

For example, the 2004 federal budget is broken down as follows:

Spending Category	Amount*	Percentage of Total
Social Security	$ 478 billion	21.8%
Other human resources (training, health, etc.)	697	31.8
Defense	376	17.2
Medicare	245	11.2
Interest on debt	161	7.4
Other functions (science, justice, etc.)	118	5.4
Physical resources (energy, commerce, etc.)	115	5.3
Total	$2,190 billion	100.0%

*Amounts reflect estimates provided in fiscal year 2004. Available at **http://www.whitehouse.gov/omb/budget**.

As you can see, a significant portion of the budget goes to pay interest on the national debt. However, given that between $200 and $300 billion in budget deficits are predicted in each of the six years beginning with 2003 (see Exhibit 1 on the next page), you can probably expect this cost to grow.

Budgeting probably consumes more congressional time than any other single activity. Even though you may argue that Congress and the president have not been as fiscally responsible as they could have been, you should be comforted that the budgeting process instills some discipline in their spending habits and provides a sense of order for governmental expenditures and management of programs.

Exhibit 1 demonstrates the expectations of the 2003 administration. However, these numbers are only estimates, and many economic factors can influence the amount of taxes collected (i.e., receipts) by the government. It is important to point out that it is difficult to make changes to spending (i.e., outlays) on committed government programs like Social Security. On the other hand, economic downturns create smaller tax bases that *immediately* result in less revenue receipts for the federal government. It's not easy to maintain a balanced federal government budget!

1 Further information on the federal budget process can be obtained from **http://www.house.gov/rules/budget_pro.htm**.

Exhibit 1: U.S. Federal Government Estimated Annual Budget*

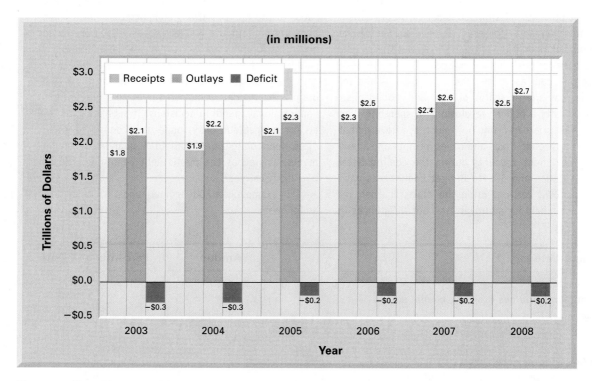

*Amounts reflect estimates provided in fiscal year 2004. Available at **http://www.whitehouse.gov/omb/budget**.

a budget is a quantitative expression of a plan of action that shows how a firm, an organization (such as the government in the opening scenario), or an individual will acquire and use resources over a specified period of time. For a firm, implicit in most budgets is management's expectation of earning sufficient profit to provide a reasonable return on investment. The budget identifies and allocates resources necessary to effectively and efficiently carry out the mission of the organization. Al-

though budgeting may sound to you like an unappealing activity (maybe you have tried budgeting your personal expenditures), successful budgeting is absolutely critical to the success of a business. In this chapter, we will briefly touch on personal budgeting and then cover budgeting for manufacturing, merchandising, and service firms.

budget A quantitative expression of a plan of action that shows how a firm or an organization will acquire and use resources over some specified period of time.

Purposes of Budgeting

▌ Describe the importance of personal budgeting.

Whether we're talking about an individual, a family, or a large organization, the overall purpose of a budget is to clearly establish a plan so that performance in relation to a goal can be carefully monitored. Thus, budgeting has a twofold purpose. The first purpose is to allow individuals or companies to develop a plan to meet a specified goal. The second purpose is to allow ongoing comparison between actual results and the plan in order to better control operations or activities. To illustrate, let us assume that Dick Cotton earns $3,600 a month (and takes home only $2,390 after taxes) and has prepared a budget of his income and expenses.

The budget in Exhibit 2 contains an important warning that spending is exceeding earnings. The commitment of $1,700 to fixed expenses leaves only $690 to cover all of Dick's necessary expenditures for utilities, food, clothing, and the like. Because Dick cannot cover these expenditures using his **disposable income** of $690 a month, he must revise his plans; perhaps he could ask for a raise, get a second job or a new job that pays more, or decrease his spending. This simple illustration shows that budgeting is extremely important. Unless Dick takes corrective action, he will soon join the growing number of individuals declaring bankruptcy.

In addition, someday Dick will want to retire. Currently, Dick's budget does not provide for any savings or investments. With all the planning tools available today, such as tax-sheltered retirement plans, investments, annuities, and so forth, an individual who plans and budgets well can prepare adequately for the future. Unfortunately, at his present rate, Dick will not be one of these individuals.

Indeed, the penalty for not budgeting is severe. Individuals who budget successfully typically find that they can purchase those things that they feel they really want to have. In fact, budgeting does not really limit spending. The only real difference between individuals who budget and those who don't is that those who budget will spend money how, where, and when they want to, and those who do not budget often feel like they never have enough money to purchase those things that they really need.

Are you wondering which category you fall into—those who successfully budget or those who don't? Review these characteristics of good personal budgeters and see how you compare.

- Understand debt and interest
- Disciplined
- Flexible
- Organized
- Good communicator (especially important if married)
- Proactive
- Goal-driven

disposable income Income left after withholdings and fixed expenses have been subtracted from gross salary; the amount left to cover variable expenditures.

FYI:

According to a MERRILL LYNCH survey, 65% of the nation's 76 million baby boomers will not have sufficient funds to retire at age 65. This means that 49 million people who will be turning 65 between 2011 and 2026 will have no choice but to keep working!

Exhibit 2: Monthly Budget for Dick Cotton

Gross salary		$ 3,600
Withholdings:		
Federal income taxes	$ 600	
State income taxes	180	
FICA taxes	270	
Other withholdings	160	(1,210)
Net take-home pay		$ 2,390
Fixed expenses:		
House mortgage	$1,100	
Car payment	350	
Insurance	250	(1,700)
Disposable income		$ 690
Utilities	$ 200	
Food	400	
Clothing	100	
Entertainment	100	
Miscellaneous	200	(1,000)
Net surplus (deficit)		$ (310)

> **TO SUMMARIZE:** It is just as important for in-
> dividuals to create and follow a budget as it is for organi-
> zations. Individuals who budget are able to plan their
> spending and are better prepared for the future. Those who
> budget typically are goal oriented, organized, proactive, and
> disciplined.

Types and Purposes of Budgeting

2 Identify the purposes of budgeting for organizations.

As you learned in the earlier chapter when we introduced management accounting, budgeting is part of the management planning process, a process that involves identifying problems or opportunities, identifying alternative solutions, evaluating those alternatives, then choosing and implementing the best alternatives. There are two basic types of planning: (1) long-run planning, which includes strategic planning and capital budgeting, and (2) short-run planning, which includes production and process prioritizing and operational budgeting or profit planning. Long-run planning involves making decisions where the effects will extend several years into the future. Long-run planning includes broad-based decisions about products, markets, productive facilities, and financial resources. This type of planning is often referred to as strategic planning. Strategic planning takes place at the executive level in an organization and involves identifying the organization's mission, the goals flowing from that mission, and the strategies and actions that will be taken to accomplish those goals. With strategic planning in place, the company can then plan for the purchase and use of major assets such as buildings or equipment to help the company meet its long-range goals. This type of planning, which you studied in the previous chapter, is called capital budgeting.

To further review, short-run planning is divided into two categories. Once the organization has made long-term commitments to capital structure (land, buildings, equipment, management personnel, etc.), then managers need to determine how to best use those committed resources to maximize the return on their capital investments—a process often referred to as production prioritizing. We'll discuss production prioritizing decisions in a later chapter on making decisions.

> **FYI:**
>
> While budgeting is very helpful for decision making, organizations are often required to prepare detailed budgets before bankers will loan money or before a company can issue stock or debt for sale to the public. When companies declare bankruptcy and are taken over by court-ordered trustees, one of the trustee's first steps is to prepare detailed budgets. These budgets help to determine whether the company should cease operations and liquidate (known as a Chapter 7 bankruptcy), or whether the trustee should ask the court to give the company time to work through its financial problems so that it can fully or partially repay its debts (known as a Chapter 11 bankruptcy).

Once the organization has determined what to produce or otherwise provide to the marketplace in order to maximize its goals, managers are ready to go to the next phase of short-run planning—operational budgeting. Sometimes known as profit plans, operational budgets are used by managers to establish and communicate daily, weekly, and monthly goals for the organization. Failure to carefully perform strategic planning, capital budgeting, or budgeting for operations can have adverse consequences for organizations, even to the point of causing bankruptcy. The list of companies that have failed in recent years as a result of poor planning and execution is getting longer each day. Casualties of poor planning include such common names as K-MART, ADELPHIA, US AIRWAYS, EXIDE TECHNOLOGIES (the world's largest maker of car batteries), POLAROID, CONVERSE, CONSECO, and UAL (the parent of UNITED AIRLINES). (Some of these companies were done under by unethical behavior as well.) In 2002, the 186 companies that filed for bankruptcy had combined total assets equal to $368 billion, over $100 billion greater than the 2001 mark of $259 billion.[2] In this chapter, our focus is on creating a "profit plan" in order to better control operations companies both large and small.

master budget A network of many separate schedules and budgets that together constitute the overall operating and financing plan for the coming period.

The **master budget** is the most detailed and most heavily used budget in an organization. As the name implies, this budget depicts the organization's goals and plans for revenues, pro-

---

2 "U.S. Bankruptcies Break Records," *BBC News*, December 30, 2002, **http://news.bbc.co.uk/1/hi/business/ 2616135.stm**.

duction, expenses, and cash for the next period. Essentially, the same advantages that individuals experience with personal budgeting also exist for organizations that follow a master budget. Specifically, there are six major reasons why a master budget is important to an organization's success. As you review this list, think about your own personal budget and how these budgeting objectives relate to you.

1. *Planning and setting objectives.* The preparation of a master budget forces managers to consider explicitly where the firm is going and how it is going to get there. By budgeting, an organization, such as the U.S. government as described in the opening scenario, will be better prepared to decide where its scarce resources will be spent.

2. *Communication and coordination.* Budgets improve communication between the various management levels of a business, helping managers plan activities that focus the organization on its strategy and goals, as well as enhance the smooth functioning of the enterprise in general. In both families and business organizations, it is usually not the lack of money that causes problems but the lack of communication about money. Couples and organizations that budget adequately find that their budgets are a great coordination tool when a critical resource (such as money) is in short supply!

3. *Authorization.* Once budgets are approved by top management, they provide authorization for investing, spending, ordering, producing, and borrowing by lower-level managers and employees. At most major companies, IBM for example, the budget becomes the law. If something is budgeted, it can be purchased. If not budgeted, the purchase cannot be made without careful consideration and approval from a high level of management. (This is one area where many personal budgets fail.)

4. *Motivation.* Budgets help motivate people. By providing a clear set of quantified objectives, budgets can help guide people to focus on important activities that need to be accomplished. The motivational aspect of budgets can be quite strong.

5. *Conflict resolution.* In most organizations, everyone usually wants additional resources. Budgeting forces up-front planning, which helps resolve conflicts over how limited resources will be allocated among an organization's various parts. (Remember the conflicting objectives of the government in the opening scenario?) Similarly, when a couple or a family prepares a budget together, the budget can help them resolve conflicting priorities by providing a way for them to plan when important purchases can be made (either now or sometime later in the future).

6. *Evaluation.* Budgets provide quantitative measures of expectations and objectives. These objectives later serve as performance measures (or benchmarks) against which the performance of managers and others in a firm can be evaluated.

In recent years, a number of concerns have been expressed about operational budgeting and the way firms budget. Some companies have found that their business environment is changing so rapidly that once the process is finally finished, the budget has little to do with the realities they face. In some companies, managers use budgets to analyze detailed spending without recognizing the bigger picture, such as the fact that the company is losing customers or that a new product is selling far below expectations. In other companies, traditional budgets have undermined the long-term growth potential of companies by motivating managers to focus exclusively on short-term financial numbers. The following are some of the problems with traditional budgeting that have led to revisions in the way companies budget:

- Departments and business units tend to create budgets based on how much they spent in previous years.
- Once budgets are set, resource allocations are too inflexible and are unable to adapt to change.
- In many companies, managers who have been evaluated and compensated according to how well they met their budget numbers feel powerless to act on new opportunities that are not already factored into the master budget.

- Often budgeting timelines do not match new product schedules, which makes it difficult to budget and measure performance on a long-term (e.g., three-year) development project using annual or quarterly budgets.
- Frequently, because of fast-paced business changes, a budget is outdated before it is even completed!

A high-level manager of a large company summed up the shortcomings of traditional budgets with this comment: "Trying to figure out how much fax paper you will need next November and what that will cost is like forecasting the weather." Recognizing such concerns but also realizing that a well-conceived strategy and supporting budgets are essential to effective growth, in recent years some organizations have spent large sums of money to make their budgeting more relevant and timely to what they do. Effective and timely budgets, aided by developments in technology, can help companies overcome the weaknesses in traditional budgeting. As noted earlier, however, the faster an industry moves, and the faster a company shifts its priorities, the more often plans must be adjusted and budgets changed.

Recent developments in software have made the budgeting process much more useful and relevant. Using enterprise-wide software systems, such as that developed by ORACLE, SAP, and PEOPLESOFT, companies can now integrate their budgeting process into their accounting systems, get immediate feedback about how they are doing, and use the feedback to make timely changes in their budgeting process. With developments in technology, companies can now measure results almost instantly. CISCO and DELL COMPUTER, for example, can receive immediate information about how they are doing (compared to processes that used to take several months) and can use these data to make real-time decisions on resource allocations and forecasts about profit margins and growth rates of different products. With such timely information, organizations can now both predict revenues and costs and measure them on a timely basis. Because companies can make real-time changes in their budgets, projections are much more accurate, and the budgeting process is much more meaningful. FUJITSU, for example, uses a monthly, rolling forecast, which is part of its enterprise planning software, that allows financial managers to make corrective budget changes on a timely basis.

TO SUMMARIZE: Budgeting in most organizations is based on that organization's strategic plan. Using the strategic plan to guide decisions, organizations perform two types of budgeting: capital budgeting and operations budgeting. The operating budget has several purposes: (1) assist in planning and setting objectives, (2) facilitate communication and coordinate activities, (3) authorize expenditures and actions, (4) motivate employees, (5) assist in resolving conflicts, and (6) provide a vehicle for performance measurement.

The Budgeting Process

3 Explain the budgeting process and its behavioral implications in organizations.

budget committee A management group responsible for establishing budgeting policy and for coordinating the preparation of budgets.

Budgeting is such an important activity that the top executives of most companies coordinate and participate in the process. Large firms usually establish a **budget committee**, which includes among its members the vice presidents for sales, production, purchasing, and finance and the controller or chief financial officer. These executives work to implement the organization's strategy by coordinating the preparation of a detailed budget in their areas of responsibility and then together oversee the integration of a comprehensive master budget for the firm. Two important issues faced by executives in the budgeting process are:

1. Behavioral considerations, and
2. Involvement in preparing the budget.

Behavioral Considerations

Research has shown that several behavioral factors determine how successful the budgeting process will be. First, the process must have the support of top management. Without a clear indication from top management that the budgeting process is important to the organization, managers will not be motivated to devote the time necessary to formulate an effective and efficient budget.

Second, managers and other employees are more motivated to achieve budget goals that they understand and helped design. For this process to work, managers must feel that their opinions are respected and given full consideration. In addition, this communication and participation process should remain open throughout the year. When internal or external circumstances change, all parties involved should discuss the necessary budget adjustments. Generally, the most effective (though not necessarily the most *efficient*) companies are those that involve employees in the decision-making process. However, as you'll see in the next section, involving a lot of employees adds significant time and cost to the budgeting process.

Third, deviations (also known as variances) from the budget must be addressed by managers in a positive and constructive manner. Identifying deviations from the plan is simply a way to focus management's attention on areas needing improvement. Unfortunately, some managers treat these deviations as an opportunity to find fault and assign blame to lower-level managers. The result is usually a loss of motivation, accompanied by such dysfunctional behavior as interdepartmental bickering, defensive attitudes, and overall unethical behavior. One output of such behavior is **budgetary slack** in the budget system; that is, intentionally creating an easy budget target that a manager is certain he or she can meet.

Obviously, all these behaviors waste an organization's resources and do not contribute to meeting its strategic and operational goals. A more useful reaction to deviations is to focus on the action to be taken. As one CEO stated, "I never made a dime for the company by assessing blame or firing a manager. If I can provide help to a manager to solve a problem, though, we can see the benefit." In administering the budget process, it is extremely important that top management not use the budget as a "club" or "whipping stick."

budgetary slack The process of inflating a department's budget request for resource inputs (e.g., materials, labor, time, etc.) or deflating the department's budget commitment to output (products, services, etc.) so that the department manager can more easily achieve the budget.

Involvement in Preparing the Budget: Top-Down versus Bottom-Up

A firm-wide operating budget could be prepared by top management, distributed to the major segments of the firm, and then further spread out to each lower-level segment manager. This is the top-down approach. Its proponents argue that only top management knows the strategic direction of the firm and is aware of all the external factors influencing its operations. Further, since top management involves only a few people who have risen to positions where they should no longer have special interests to protect, they are in the best position to *efficiently* coordinate the competing needs of the segments.

The alternative is the bottom-up approach, also known as **participative budgeting**. Essentially, each division manager in a bottom-up approach prepares a budget request for his or her segment. These requests are combined and reviewed as they move up the organization hierarchy, with adjustments being made to coordinate the needs and goals of individual units with the overall organization. Proponents of this approach contend that segment managers have the best information on the products or services they provide, the customers they serve, and the technology that is emerging; they are, therefore, in the best position to identify segment needs and to weigh alternative courses of action. More importantly, as mentioned earlier, managers who have a role in setting segment goals are more motivated to achieve these goals. It is also good training for managers to develop their planning skills in preparation for promotions to positions of greater authority. Naturally, the organization also benefits when its managers are proficient in planning. However, the bottom-up approach is very costly and time-intensive when compared to the top-down approach. In order to achieve personal goals, participants may also engage in political maneuvering that creates budgetary slack and other problems in the budgeting system.

participative budgeting A bottom-up approach to budgeting that involves the full cooperation and participation of managers at all levels of the organization.

Because both top-down and bottom-up are legitimate approaches, most organizations use some combination of the two. The budget committee members know the strategic direction of the firm and the important external factors that affect it, so they prepare a set of planning guidelines that are communicated to lower-level managers. These guidelines include such things as a forecast of key economic variables and their potential impact on the firm, plans for introducing and advertising new products, and some broad sales targets and resource allocations. With these guidelines in mind, lower-level managers prepare their individual budgets. These budgets are always reviewed to be sure they are consistent with the objectives of other segments and of the company as a whole. The budget committee understands that, from a behavioral point of view, any changes to a manager's budget should be made with great care. This is not to suggest that changes should not be made, only that reasons for those changes should be substantial and should be discussed with the managers involved.

The blending of these two approaches will vary among organizations. A smaller organization with few management levels will rely more on the top-down approach than a larger organization. Top management in smaller organizations tends to be more knowledgeable about and more involved in the operating details.

TO SUMMARIZE: The behavioral factors that contribute to the success of the budgeting process include the support of top management, the participation of all managers in the budgeting process, and the need to address deviations from the budget in a positive and constructive manner. With the top-down approach, top management prepares the entire budget. With bottom-up budgeting, each segment manager makes budget requests. Most firms use a combination of the two approaches.

The Master Budget

4 Construct an operating budget and its components for manufacturing firms.

The master budget is an integrated group of detailed budgets that together constitute the overall operating and financing plans for a specific time period. In a manufacturing firm, the master budget begins with a forecast of sales; is followed by detailed budgets for the production, selling, administrative, and financial activities; and culminates in a set of pro-forma (or budgeted) financial statements. The flow of the preparation of the individual budgets within this master budget network is shown in Exhibit 3. Notice that the budgeting process is based on the long-term strategic and short-term operational plans established by top management in the organization. Also note how the capital budgeting process fits into the master budget. The final items forming the financial budget include the capital expenditures budget (or the capital budget), the cash budget, and the budgeted or pro-forma financial statements. Preparing the cash budget and the pro-forma statements is discussed in the expanded material. (You have already studied capital budgeting in the previous chapter.)

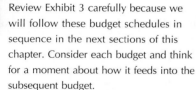

STOP & THINK

Review Exhibit 3 carefully because we will follow these budget schedules in sequence in the next sections of this chapter. Consider each budget and think for a moment about how it feeds into the subsequent budget.

To help explain these steps, we will illustrate the budgeting process in a manufacturing firm using an integrated example of budgets for the Sunbird Boat Company, a manufacturer of small fishing boats. Because it is important that you understand the budgeting process, you should work through the calculations of each budget schedule. Be sure to keep in mind that this formalized budgeting activity forces management to make many important decisions that guide a company toward its goals—decisions involving scheduling, pricing, borrowing, investing, and cost control.

Budgeting for Operations in a Manufacturing Firm

Our first illustration of the budgeting process is for Sunbird Boat Company, a manufacturing company that makes fishing boats. The boats are made of fiberglass and wood. To help us move

Exhibit 3: The Master Budget

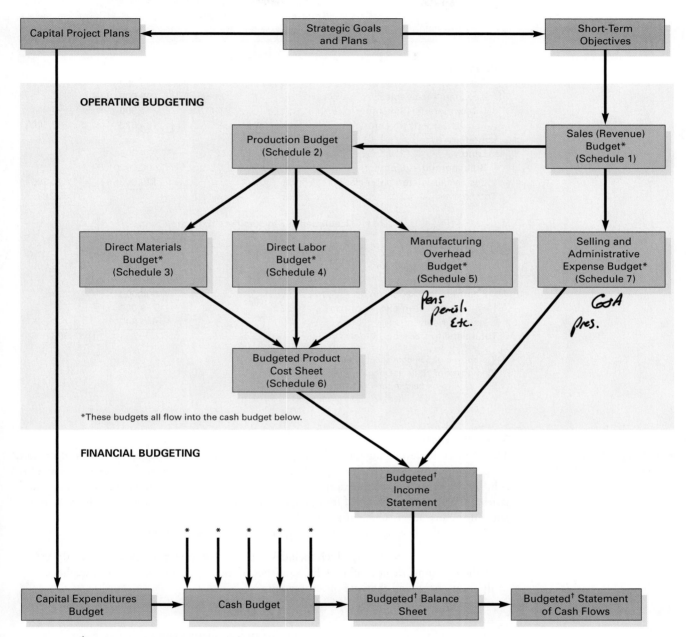

PLANNING PROCESS

OPERATING BUDGETING

*These budgets all flow into the cash budget below.

FINANCIAL BUDGETING

†Also known as pro-forma financial statements.

through this example more quickly, we will assume that Sunbird only makes one type of boat—a 15-foot fishing boat. Exhibit 4 contains Sunbird's actual balance sheet for 2005. This is our beginning point for creating Sunbird's 2006 operational budget. In explaining the budgeting for Sunbird Boat Company, we will begin with the sales budget and then discuss each budget identified in Exhibit 3.

Exhibit 4: Sunbird Boat Company 2005 Balance Sheet

Sunbird Boat Company
Balance Sheet (Actual)
December 31, 2005

Assets

Current assets:		
Cash	$ 135,000	
Accounts receivable	56,000	
Direct materials inventory[1]	7,980	
Finished goods inventory[2]	83,520	$ 282,500
Long-term assets:		
Land	$ 234,305	
Building and equipment	1,500,000	
Less accumulated depreciation	(120,000)	1,614,305
Total assets		$1,896,805

Liabilities & Stockholders' Equity

Current liabilities:		
Accounts payable[3]	$ 9,000	
Income taxes payable[3]	96,000	$ 105,000
Stockholders' equity:		
Common stock, $5 par	$1,000,000	
Paid-in capital in excess of par	250,000	
Retained earnings	541,805	1,791,805
Total liabilities & stockholders' equity		$1,896,805

[1]Composed of 588 board feet of lumber and 420 square feet of fiberglass.
[2]Composed of 18 finished boats.
[3]Expected to be paid in the first quarter of 2006.

Sales Budget

The first step in developing a master budget is to prepare a **sales budget**. As shown in Exhibit 3, all the other budgets are developed from this budget. Projecting accurate sales is very difficult, however, because sales are a function of both uncontrollable external variables (customer tastes and economic conditions, for example) and controllable internal variables (such as price, sales effort, and advertising expenditures).

Uncontrollable external factors driving sales include the following:

- The business environment, which includes current government policies and law, the status of the economy, demographics (characteristics of the population such as age, wealth, family status, etc.), and the state of technology.
- Customer needs and tastes with respect to the product or service being analyzed and other substitute products.
- Intensity of the competition and possible barriers to market entry (barriers can include technology copyrights, government contracts, reputation, or large sales volumes that provide economies of scale).
- Seasonal cycles creating abrupt changes in sales demand due to holidays or weather patterns.
- Unexpected events such as terrorist acts, droughts, hurricanes, and earthquakes.

Analysis of external variables is accomplished through research and sales forecasting techniques. These techniques may be as simple as having the sales staff ask major customers about their buying plans for the next year or as sophisticated as statistical market research techniques. Some firms use quantitative forecasting models—these range from simple growth rate trends derived from the past year's sales to complex forecasting models that attempt to measure the influence of many economic and industry variables. Data used to drive these analyses are obtained from a variety of sources.

FYI:

A number of commercial sales forecasting software programs are available that focus on specific industries. These software packages typically incorporate economic assumptions, company-specific marketing strategies, and standard price and cost relationships to build complex forecasts of sales and revenues.

Controllable internal variables include the following four factors (sometimes known as the "4 P's" of the marketing mix):

- Product design in order to establish its function and appeal to customers.
- Pricing of the product, which can be used to brand the product as a luxury or a common good.
- Promotion of the product in order to target the product to specific groups in the market.
- Placement of the product, which involves the logistics of how the product will be made available and distributed to customers.

The marketing research on uncontrollable external variables is complicated. However, analyzing the influence of controllable internal variables is also a very difficult management process because these variables affect and are affected by the external variables. In fact, many or all of these factors must be considered when performing cost-volume-profit (C-V-P) analysis—the subject of an earlier chapter on cost-volume-profit analysis.

For purposes of this illustration, we will not go further into the details about the development of data for the sales budget. This is an important topic for your coursework in marketing and strategy. At this point, let's assume that Sunbird Boat Company has projected 2006 sales to be 100 boats. The anticipated sales price for each boat is $10,000.

Most organizations divide their yearly sales budget into monthly, weekly, or even daily budgets in order to plan production schedules and cash flows more precisely. For our illustration, we will assume that Sunbird Boat Company projects its boat sales on a quarterly basis, as shown in Schedule 1. However, whether the budget is on a quarterly or a daily basis, the concepts we're going to talk about are the same.

Schedule 1

**Schedule 1
Sunbird Boat Company
2006 Sales Budget**

	Q1	Q2	Q3	Q4	Total
Sales volume	24 boats	28 boats	30 boats	18 boats	100 boats
Price	×$ 10,000	×$ 10,000	×$ 10,000	×$ 10,000	×$ 10,000
Revenue earned	$240,000	$280,000	$300,000	$180,000	$1,000,000
Received in current quarter	× 80%	× 80%	× 80%	× 80%	
Current revenue collected	$192,000	$224,000	$240,000	$144,000	$ 800,000
Prior revenue collected*	56,000	48,000	56,000	60,000	220,000
Collections from customers	$248,000	$272,000	$296,000	$204,000	$1,020,000

*Prior revenue collected in Q1 (Quarter 1) represents the accounts receivable balance from the 2005 balance sheet. Prior revenue collected in Q2 through Q4 represents the revenue not collected in the prior quarter (i.e., revenue earned in prior quarter times 20%).

As you can see in Schedule 1, the sales budget that we are creating for Sunbird is computing two important numbers. First, we can assume that the marketing department for Sunbird has effectively researched all the relevant variables in order to predict the number of boats that will be sold each quarter. These numbers are used to determine the budgeted sales revenue that Sunbird expects to recognize. However, remember that this revenue still needs to be collected because at least some boats are sold on account. Based on past experience, Sunbird is able to collect approximately 80% of revenue from customers in the quarter in which the sale took place, with the remaining 20% collected in the following quarter. Happily, in this example, Sunbird doesn't expect to have any uncollectible accounts. Using this information, Sunbird also budgets the level of cash collections from customers for each quarter. Take a moment to study Schedule 1 in order to understand exactly how Sunbird is computing cash collections.

production budget A schedule of production requirements for the budget period.

Production Budget

The second detailed budget (Schedule 2) covers production, the number of units to be produced during the period. Factors to be considered in preparing this **production budget** are projected sales volume for the period, the desired amount of ending inventory, and the amount of inventory already on hand in the beginning inventory.

Ending inventory is an important figure because management wants enough units on hand to meet customer demands, but not so many that unnecessary costs will be incurred because of excessive inventory. Inventory management is an important management process that we'll discuss in a later chapter. For our work in this chapter, the desired ending inventory for any period will be expressed as a percentage of the following period's expected sales volume. Let's assume that Sunbird Boat Company has determined that its desired ending inventory for each quarter should be approximately 50% of projected sales for the next quarter. The fourth quarter's ending inventory is 13 15-foot boats, which is 50% of the next quarter's (first quarter of 2007) expected sales.

The production budget (Schedule 2) supplies information needed for all manufacturing cost budgets. Only after production quantities are known can management determine the amount of direct materials, direct labor, and manufacturing overhead needed during the period. As you study Schedule 2, be sure to note how the expected inventory of boats leads to the result that budgeted production levels are different from the budgeted levels of sales volumes.

STOP & THINK

Sunbird plans to keep its inventory level of boats at 50% of next quarter's sales. That is a lot of inventory! Why do you think that Sunbird follows this kind of an inventory policy?

STOP & THINK

Some companies work very hard to reduce or remove inventory from their organization. You'll learn in a later chapter on activity-based costing that this management technique is called a just-in-time or JIT inventory method. Think carefully about Sunbird's production budget (Schedule 2). Would this budget be needed if Sunbird had a JIT inventory system?

Schedule 2

	Schedule 2 Sunbird Boat Company 2006 Production Budget				
	Q1	Q2	Q3	Q4	Total
Sales volume (Schedule 1)	24 boats	28 boats	30 boats	18 boats	100 boats
Desired ending inventory[1]	14 boats	15 boats	9 boats	13 boats	13 boats
Total boats needed	38 boats	43 boats	39 boats	31 boats	113 boats
Less beginning inventory[2]	(18 boats)	(14 boats)	(15 boats)	(9 boats)	(18 boats)
Total boats to produce	20 boats	29 boats	24 boats	22 boats	95 boats

[1]Sunbird desires to have ending boat inventory equal to 50% of the expected sales volume for the following quarter. Sunbird's marketing department forecasts sales of 26 boats during the first quarter of 2007.
[2]Sunbird's beginning finished goods inventory for 2006 is 18 boats. Beginning inventory for Q2 through Q4 is equal to the ending inventory for the prior quarter.

direct materials budget A schedule of direct materials to be used during the budget period and direct materials to be purchased during that period.

Caution

Note that the entries in the Total column do not always equal the sum of the four quarters. For example, the beginning inventory balance in Schedule 2 is the same for the year as it is for the first quarter. Similarly, the ending inventory balance is the same for the year as it is for the fourth quarter. Be sure to watch for similar patterns in subsequent budget schedules.

Direct Materials Budget

The next detailed budget to be prepared is the **direct materials budget** (Schedule 3). Based on the engineering department's estimates of the materials required to make a boat, this budget helps management schedule purchases from suppliers. Sunbird's engineers estimate that the amounts of wood and fiberglass needed per boat are as follows:

	15-Foot Boat
Direct materials requirements:	
Wood	70 board feet
Fiberglass	50 square feet

Sunbird's purchasing agent has been able to purchase wood at $10 per board foot and fiberglass at $5 per square foot. The purchasing agent expects that these prices will continue to be available to Sunbird through 2006.

Schedule 3

Schedule 3
Sunbird Boat Company
2006 Direct Materials Budget

Wood	Q1		Q2		Q3		Q4		Total	
Production volume (Schedule 2)		20 boats		29 boats		24 boats		22 boats		95 boats
Standard feet per boat	×	70 feet	×	70 feet	×	70 feet	×	70 feet	×	70 feet
Wood needed in production		1,400 feet		2,030 feet		1,680 feet		1,540 feet		6,650 feet
Desired ending inventory[1]		609 feet		504 feet		462 feet		546 feet		546 feet
Total wood needed		2,009 feet		2,534 feet		2,142 feet		2,086 feet		7,196 feet
Less beginning inventory[2]		(588) feet		(609) feet		(504) feet		(462) feet		(588) feet
Total wood to purchase		1,421 feet		1,925 feet		1,638 feet		1,624 feet		6,608 feet
Standard purchase price	×	$10	×	$10	×	$10	×	$10	×	$10
Wood purchases		$14,210		$19,250		$16,380		$16,240		$66,080

Fiberglass	Q1		Q2		Q3		Q4		Total	
Production volume (Schedule 2)		20 boats		29 boats		24 boats		22 boats		95 boats
Standard feet per boat	×	50 feet	×	50 feet	×	50 feet	×	50 feet	×	50 feet
Fiberglass needed in production		1,000 feet		1,450 feet		1,200 feet		1,100 feet		4,750 feet
Desired ending inventory[1]		435 feet		360 feet		330 feet		390 feet		390 feet
Total fiberglass needed		1,435 feet		1,810 feet		1,530 feet		1,490 feet		5,140 feet
Less beginning inventory[2]		(420) feet		(435) feet		(360) feet		(330) feet		(420) feet
Total fiberglass to purchase		1,015 feet		1,375 feet		1,170 feet		1,160 feet		4,720 feet
Standard purchase price	×	$5	×	$5	×	$5	×	$5	×	$5
Fiberglass purchases		$ 5,075		$ 6,875		$ 5,850		$ 5,800		$23,600
Total materials purchases		$19,285		$26,125		$22,230		$22,040		$89,680
Paid in current quarter	×	75%	×	75%	×	75%	×	75%	×	75%
Current purchase payments		$14,464		$19,594		$16,673		$16,530		$67,260
Prior purchase payments[3]		9,000		4,821		6,531		5,558		25,910
Payments to suppliers		$23,464		$24,415		$23,204		$22,088		$93,170

[1]Sunbird desires to have ending raw materials inventory equal to 30% of the materials needed to support production volume for the following quarter. Sunbird's production volume for the first quarter of 2007 is expected to be 26 boats.
[2]Sunbird's beginning raw materials inventory for 2006 is 588 board feet of wood and 420 square feet of fiberglass. Beginning inventory for Q2 through Q4 is equal to the ending inventory for the prior quarter.
[3]Prior purchase payments in Q1 represent the accounts payable balance from the 2005 balance sheet. Prior purchase payments in Q2 through Q4 represent the purchases not paid for in the prior quarter (i.e., total materials purchases in prior quarter times 25%).

Based on these requirements for materials, the direct materials budget for Sunbird Boat Company for 2006 is shown in Schedule 3. Note that the materials needed are based on expected quarterly production and on the desired quarterly ending inventories. Then, similar to the approach used in the production schedule, the materials needed are adjusted for the beginning inventory expected for each quarter. Like the production budget, the direct materials budget depends on the desired level of ending inventory. If management does not maintain sufficient materials inventory levels, costly work stoppages can occur; if inventories are excessive, inventory investment and storage costs may be unduly high. Based on how long it takes Sunbird to receive wood and fiberglass from its suppliers, Sunbird's management has decided to maintain a supply of about 30% of the next quarter's production requirements for wood and fiberglass.

Finally, as is typical in most supplier relationships, Sunbird does not pay for raw materials at the time of the purchase, which means that Sunbird maintains an accounts payable balance. Sunbird's policy is to pay for 75% of its raw materials purchases in the current quarter, and the remaining 25% in the subsequent quarter. This payment policy is used to adjust the total purchases in Schedule 3 to compute the cash payments made to suppliers in each quarter (similar to the approach used to compute cash payments received from customers in the sales budget in Schedule 1).

Direct Labor Budget

direct labor budget A schedule of direct labor requirements for the budget period.

The fourth budget in the master budget is the **direct labor budget** (Schedule 4). The direct labor budget for Sunbird Boat Company is based on an average hourly wage rate of $15 per hour for production workers and 80 labor hours to make a 15-foot boat. In our example, the $15 per-hour wage rate includes fringe benefits (i.e., the cost of sick leave, vacation pay, insurance, etc.) and payroll taxes.[3] We will assume in our example that Sunbird's budgeted labor costs for each quarter are all paid in that same quarter. Hence, there is no need to adjust the labor costs in order to budget for labor cash payments each quarter.

Schedule 4

Schedule 4 Sunbird Boat Company 2006 Direct Labor Budget					
	Q1	Q2	Q3	Q4	Total
Production volume (Schedule 2)	20 boats	29 boats	24 boats	22 boats	95 boats
Standard hours per boat	× 80 hours	× 80 hours	× 80 hours	× 80 hours	× 80 hours
Budgeted labor hours	1,600 hours	2,320 hours	1,920 hours	1,760 hours	7,600 hours
Standard wage rate per hour[1]	× $15	× $15	× $15	× $15	× $15
Direct labor cost[2]	$24,000	$34,800	$28,800	$26,400	$114,000

[1]Includes fringe benefits and payroll taxes.
[2]These costs are all paid in the quarter incurred.

© 2003 Getty Images

Banks have replaced many of their full-time customer representatives with part-time employees. From management's perspective, the use of part-time workers makes direct labor budgeting easier.

Management must plan so that sufficient (but not excessive) labor is always available.[4] Otherwise, the company is likely to suffer the high cost of frequent hiring, firing, layoffs, and overtime work. Probably even more important than the high cost of employee turnover, however, is the feeling of demoralization among employees that such events can cause. If employees lack job security, they usually behave in ways that maximize their own personal short-run benefits (e.g., they may slow down production, thus creating the need for more employment or overtime work).

The recent trend in many companies has been to keep a relatively small full-time staff and hire an increasing number of part-time or temporary employees. Not only are these employees much easier to hire and terminate, but the company does not have to pay retirement and other benefits for them. Banks, for example, have replaced many of their full-time customer representatives with part-time employees. As a result of

3 The inclusion of fringe benefits and payroll taxes into the standard wage rate per hour is a significant decision in the budgeting process. Companies may also choose to include in the standard wage rate some measure of expected overtime pay. Other companies do not include some or all of these costs into the standard wage rate, but add them to the overhead application rate. This has the effect of spreading these costs evenly across all production output. However, including these costs into overhead will enhance the impact of inventory changes on the income statement due to absorption costing (a topic that we'll discuss in a chapter on managing inventory).

4 Just how variable labor costs are has aroused significant controversy in the management accounting literature. Some researchers argue that employees cannot easily be hired or terminated and, therefore, labor should be a fixed cost. Other researchers argue that labor is constantly hired and terminated—just read business newspapers where announcements of employee layoffs are printed every day. One thing is certain, though—labor costs are a very large component of the product cost that management strives to be able to control.

the smaller full-time workforce, companies that provide temporary workers are increasing in both size and number. From management's perspective, both part-time and temporary workers increase workforce flexibility and make direct labor budgeting easier. Unfortunately, these same trends probably mean less stable and secure careers for more and more workers unless, of course, part-time employment agencies take over the role of providing job security, retirement, and other benefits.

Manufacturing Overhead Budget

manufacturing overhead budget A schedule of production costs other than those for direct labor and direct materials.

The **manufacturing overhead budget** (Schedule 5) includes all production costs other than those for direct materials and direct labor. As noted in earlier chapters, manufacturing overhead is a major element of total manufacturing costs in many organizations. Hence, organizations that are able to effectively plan and control these costs have a significant advantage in the marketplace.

Schedule 5

Schedule 5 Sunbird Boat Company 2006 Manufacturing Overhead (MOH) Budget						
Variable MOH costs		**Q1**	**Q2**	**Q3**	**Q4**	**Total**
Total labor hours (Schedule 4)		1,600 hours	2,320 hours	1,920 hours	1,760 hours	7,600 hours
Variable MOH rates per hour:						
Indirect materials	$ 1.50	$ 2,400	$ 3,480	$ 2,880	$ 2,640	$ 11,400
Indirect labor	5.50	8,800	12,760	10,560	9,680	41,800
Utilities	1.00	1,600	2,320	1,920	1,760	7,600
Total variable MOH costs	$ 8.00	$12,800	$18,560	$15,360	$14,080	$ 60,800
Fixed MOH costs per quarter						
Property taxes	$ 760	$ 760	$ 760	$ 760	$ 760	$ 3,040
Insurance	900	900	900	900	900	3,600
Depreciation—plant	16,500	16,500	16,500	16,500	16,500	66,000
Supervisors' salaries	22,500	22,500	22,500	22,500	22,500	90,000
Total fixed MOH costs	$40,660	$40,660	$40,660	$40,660	$40,660	$162,640
Total MOH costs		$53,460	$59,220	$56,020	$54,740	$223,440
Less depreciation		(16,500)	(16,500)	(16,500)	(16,500)	(66,000)
Total MOH payments*		$36,960	$42,720	$39,520	$38,240	$157,440

*Because depreciation does not represent a cash payment, these costs are removed to determine cash payments made each quarter for manufacturing overhead costs. All other manufacturing overhead costs are paid for in the quarter incurred.

In preparing this budget, Sunbird's accounting department first estimates the annual variable and fixed manufacturing overhead costs, as shown in the first column of Schedule 5. As you can see, the estimated variable manufacturing overhead costs are based on a cost per direct labor hour. In our example, we are assuming that volume of direct labor hours is a good predictor of variable manufacturing overhead costs for Sunbird, and that Sunbird uses direct labor hours to allocate these costs to each quarter. These variable cost rates per hour have been estimated previously by Sunbird's accountants. These rates are then multiplied by the number of direct labor hours estimated for each quarter (from Schedule 4) to figure the budgeted variable manufacturing overhead cost for boats for that quarter.[5] Total fixed costs are simply allocated evenly across the four quarters.

5 In an earlier chapter on product cost flows, we typically used direct labor hours to assign manufacturing overhead costs. This is actually a very simplistic approach to managing these important costs. The basic approach is for the total variable cost of each item to be allocated among the four quarters on the basis of some appropriate activity or cost driver. In a later chapter, we'll talk about an important technique called activity-based costing that is used by some organizations to carefully manage all overhead costs. We use direct labor hours here because using various cost drivers would unnecessarily complicate our examples.

Caution

Remember that the budgets being discussed in this chapter are for only one level of expected sales. If the level of sales changes, the budgeted variable costs will also change. This means that all the direct materials and direct labor budgets will change, as will some of the manufacturing overhead and selling and administrative expense budgets. This issue of changing levels of sales or operations is covered in the expanded material section of the chapter under the topic of flexible budgeting.

budgeted product cost sheet A schedule of all of the product costs (i.e., the costs of direct materials, direct labor, and manufacturing overhead) used to create a single product.

Schedule 6

To be sure that you understand how the variable manufacturing overhead cost rates are used to create Schedule 5, assume that total indirect materials costs for 2006 were estimated to be $11,400. Dividing that number by 7,600 direct labor hours (the total labor hours from Schedule 4) yields a rate of $1.50 per hour. Multiplying the $1.50 rate by 1,600 direct labor hours produces $2,400 to be assigned to the first quarter as the budgeted cost of indirect materials. With 2,320 direct labor hours in the second quarter, the cost for that quarter is $3,480. The calculation is the same for the remaining quarters, as well as for other variable overhead items.

The final computation on the manufacturing overhead budget is to determine the budgeted cash payments for these costs to be made each quarter. We assume that Sunbird stays current with these costs and makes payments as the costs are used in production. However, depreciation does not represent an actual cash outflow. Hence, these costs are removed from the budgeted manufacturing overhead costs to determine the payments expected to be made each quarter related to manufacturing overhead.

Budgeted Product Cost Sheet

The **budgeted product cost sheet** (Schedule 6) accumulates all the budgeted product costs (direct materials, direct labor, and manufacturing overhead) to estimate the total production cost of building each boat. The product cost sheet is useful to help us understand that the operational budget serves two different management purposes. First, by comparing actual sales and costs, the master budget data can be used as the basis for controlling costs and evaluating the performance of the managers responsible for those costs. (You'll clearly see how this control process works when we study variance analysis in the next chapter.)

		Total
Schedule 6		
Sunbird Boat Company		
2006 Budgeted Product Cost Sheet		
Direct materials cost per boat (Schedule 3):		
Wood (70 board feet @ $10 per foot)	$700	
Fiberglass (50 board feet @ $5 per foot)	250	$ 950
Direct labor cost per boat (Schedule 4): 80 hours x $15 per hour		1,200
Variable MOH cost per boat (Schedule 5): 80 hours x $8 per hour		640
Total variable cost per boat		$2,790
Total Fixed MOH (Schedule 5)	$162,640	
Divided by production volume (Schedule 2)	÷ 95 boats	
Fixed MOH cost allocated per boat*		1,712
Total production cost per boat		$4,502

*Note that the production costs per boat for Sunbird will actually vary from quarter to quarter because of the change in fixed MOH costs per boat due to changes in quarterly production volume. To avoid these artificial changes in quarterly budgeted boat production costs, Sunbird creates the budgeted product cost sheet on an annual basis only.

Second, these budgets are used in product costing. As you will recall from a previous chapter, the manufacturing overhead costs that flow through Work-in-Process Inventory to Finished Goods Inventory (and eventually to Cost of Goods Sold) are standardized costs that are *applied* based on predetermined overhead rates. Accountants then track the difference between actual overhead costs and applied overhead costs (the over- or underapplied manufacturing overhead amount you studied in the earlier chapter on product cost flows) in order to determine if overhead resources are being efficiently used.[6] In our example, this predetermined overhead rate

6 In fact, as you will learn in the next chapter on monitoring performance, we can use similar standardized costs of direct materials and direct labor to track and control how efficiently direct materials and direct labor are used to produce goods and services.

that Sunbird will use during the year to apply overhead costs to products being manufactured is calculated by dividing estimated annual direct labor hours (from Schedule 4) into estimated annual *total* manufacturing overhead (from Schedule 5). The rate is then computed as $223,440 ÷ 7,600 hours = $29.40 per hour.

Using the direct materials, direct labor, and manufacturing overhead budgets (the three elements of a product's cost), we are able to compute Sunbird's budgeted cost of making its 15-foot boats. As you can see in Schedule 6, these costs are largely based on data from the budgets we have been preparing. This information is then used to measure budgeted cost of goods sold for the pro-forma income statement that we will study in the expanded material section of this chapter.

Selling and Administrative Expense Budget

selling and administrative expense budget A schedule of all nonproduction spending expected to occur during the budget period.

The **selling and administrative expense budget** (Schedule 7) includes planned expenditures for all areas other than production. The costs of supplies used by the office staff, the salaries of the sales manager and company president, and the depreciation of administrative office buildings (*not* production facilities) all belong in this category. Because this budget covers several areas, it is usually quite large and may be supported by individual budgets for specific departments within the selling and administrative functions.

The selling and administrative expense budget for Sunbird is prepared in a manner similar to the manufacturing overhead budget. Total selling and administrative expenses are estimated for the year, with each expense then being distributed among the four quarters. As shown in Schedule 7, fixed expenses are assigned equally to each quarter, whereas variable expenses are allocated according to the number of boats to be sold. Variable delivery expenses, for example, are allocated to quarters by first determining the delivery expense rate [$50,000 estimated delivery expenses ÷ 100 boats expected to be sold during the year (from Schedule 1) = $500 per boat]. This rate is multiplied by the number of boats sold in a quarter to determine the delivery expenses allocated to that quarter. Because Sunbird expects to sell 24 boats in the first quarter at a rate of $500 per boat, the amount of delivery expense budgeted for that quarter is $12,000 ($500 × 24 boats). Sales commissions are allocated to each quarter in the same way.

Schedule 7

Schedule 7 Sunbird Boat Company 2006 Selling and Administrative (S&A) Expense Budget					
Variable S&A expenses		Q1	Q2	Q3	Q4	Total
Sales volume (Schedule 1)		24 boats	28 boats	30 boats	18 boats	100 boats
Variable expense per boat sold:						
Delivery expense	$ 500	$ 12,000	$ 14,000	$ 15,000	$ 9,000	$ 50,000
Sales commissions	1,600	38,400	44,800	48,000	28,800	160,000
Total variable S&A expenses	$ 2,100	$ 50,400	$ 58,800	$ 63,000	$ 37,800	$210,000
Fixed S&A expenses per quarter						
Executives' salaries	$35,000	$ 35,000	$ 35,000	$ 35,000	$ 35,000	$140,000
Depreciation expense	8,000	8,000	8,000	8,000	8,000	32,000
Advertising expense	20,000	20,000	20,000	20,000	20,000	80,000
Miscellaneous expenses	2,500	2,500	2,500	2,500	2,500	10,000
Total fixed S&A expenses	$65,500	$ 65,500	$ 65,500	$ 65,500	$ 65,500	$262,000
Total S&A expenses		$115,900	$124,300	$128,500	$103,300	$472,000
Less depreciation		(8,000)	(8,000)	(8,000)	(8,000)	(32,000)
Total S&A payments*		$107,900	$116,300	$120,500	$ 95,300	$440,000

*Because depreciation does not represent a cash payment, these expenses are removed to determine cash payments made each quarter for selling and administrative expenses. All other selling and administrative expenses are paid for in the quarter incurred.

Similar to our approach with the manufacturing overhead budget (Schedule 5), depreciation expense is eliminated from the budgeted selling and administrative expense to determine the expected quarterly cash payments for these expenses.

Although the selling and administrative expense budget in Schedule 7 looks reasonably simple, it is often more complex in actual practice than it appears here. Traditionally, these types of costs have not been a focus of management accounting control efforts. However, selling and administrative costs have become proportionately larger for many organizations and now receive substantial management attention. Hence, rather than classifying these costs based on their function (salaries, depreciation, etc.), we often see in practice that these budgets are divided into multiple categories that may emphasize how costs are related to important management emphases such as research and development (R&D), product or service design, marketing, distribution, and customer service.

Caution

Variable expenses in the sales and administrative expense budget are typically based on the volume of *sales*, not on the volume of production.

TO SUMMARIZE: The operating budget, an important part of the master budget, consists of detailed budgets for sales revenue, production costs, and selling and administrative expenses. The detailed schedules that make up the operating budget are prepared in a logical sequence, as shown in Exhibit 3. The sales budget is largely determined by marketing research. The production budget is based on the expected volume of sales for each period and the desired ending inventory of finished goods and is adjusted for the expected beginning inventory of finished goods. The direct materials budget is based on the expected volume of production for each period and the desired ending inventory of direct materials and is similarly adjusted for the expected beginning inventory of direct materials. The direct labor budget is also based on the expected volume of production. The manufacturing overhead budget is divided into its variable and fixed cost components, with the variable cost component based on some activity driver (such as direct labor hours), which is in turn based on production volume. Data from the direct materials, direct labor, and manufacturing overhead budgets are then used to create a budgeted product cost sheet. Finally, the selling and administrative expense budget, like the manufacturing overhead budget, is divided into its variable and fixed cost components, with the variable costs determined based on sales (not production) volume.

Budgeting in Merchandising and Service Firms

5 Compare the operating budget for a manufacturing firm to that of a merchandising or service firm.

We have worked through the operating budget process for a manufacturing firm, Sunbird Boat Company, a manufacturer of small fishing boats. We will now compare this integrated budget with budgets for merchandising firms (retail and wholesale) by describing the operating budget process for Wind River Boat Company, a company that buys its boats for resale from other manufacturers rather than making the boats itself. Then we will illustrate budgeting in service firms by illustrating the operating budget process for a small motel, the Boulder View Inn.

As we examine a merchandise company and a service company, you will see similarities in the budgeting process for manufacturing businesses. Basically, the budgeting process involves budgeting (or forecasting) revenues and cash that will be generated by those revenues and budgeting expenses that will be incurred and cash that will be expended. Managers are always interested in how much revenues and expenses they will have during each budgeted period and how much cash and other assets and liabilities they will have at the end of each budgeted period.

Budgeting for Operations in a Merchandising Firm

As we discussed previously in a chapter on product cost flows, organizations that purchase the products they resell are often referred to as merchandising companies; these include retailers that sell directly to consumers and wholesale distributors that buy products from manufacturers or other suppliers and sell to retailers. Well-known retail companies include WAL-MART, SEARS, and KMART. Retail companies such as Wal-Mart buy many of the products they sell directly from manufacturers (e.g., COCA-COLA, NABISCO, WRIGLEY, etc.); however, they also buy from wholesalers who either buy from domestic manufacturers or import their products from other countries.

STOP & THINK

In this chapter, the emphasis is on budgeting costs and revenues. Remember, though, that management is also interested in managing quality and timeliness. Do you think management performs any budgeting related to the quality or the delivery time of products or services to customers?

Because merchandising companies buy products (rather than make them), their budgeting process is less complicated than the budgeting done by manufacturing companies. For example, if Sunbird Boat Company were a merchandising firm rather than a manufacturing firm, the company would prepare a purchases budget, rather than a production budget, for boats. However, the format of the merchant's purchases budget would be *very* similar to the format of the manufacturer's production budget (see, for example, Schedule 2 for Sunbird Boat Company). By combining expected sales with desired ending inventory, and subtracting the beginning inventory expected to be on hand, the merchant will arrive at the number of boats to be purchased (rather than produced) for the period.

Exhibit 5 compares the master budgeting process for a merchandising firm with that for a manufacturing firm (from Exhibit 3).

Looking at Exhibit 5, you can see that in merchandising companies, the purchases budget replaces four budgets (production budget, direct materials budget, direct labor budget, and manufacturing overhead budget) used by manufacturing firms.

Because the sales budget and the selling and administrative expense budget are similar to those prepared for manufacturing firms, we will not discuss them again. To illustrate budgeting in a merchandising company, we will assume that Wind River Boat Company is a retail company that buys boats from manufacturers and sells them to consumers.

Purchases Budget

purchases budget A schedule of projected purchases over the budget period.

Assuming the same level of sales as we did for Sunbird, the **purchases budget** for Wind River Boat Company is shown in Schedule 8.

You can see from Schedule 8 that Wind River Boat Company pays its suppliers $8,000 for each 15-foot boat. (If you compare this cost with the total manufacturing cost for Sunbird Boat Company, you will see that it is higher. This is because manufacturing companies also need to make a profit.) In Schedule 8, we have assumed the same beginning and ending inventory policy we used in Schedule 2 for Sunbird, the manufacturing company.

Schedule 8

Schedule 8 **Wind River Boat Company** **2006 Purchases Budget**					
15-Foot Boats	**Q1**	**Q2**	**Q3**	**Q4**	**Total**
Sales volume (Schedule 1)	24 boats	28 boats	30 boats	18 boats	100 boats
Desired ending inventory[1]	14 boats	15 boats	9 boats	13 boats	13 boats
Total boats needed	38 boats	43 boats	39 boats	31 boats	113 boats
Less beginning inventory[2]	(18 boats)	(14 boats)	(15 boats)	(9 boats)	(18 boats)
Total boats to purchase	20 boats	29 boats	24 boats	22 boats	95 boats
Cost per boat	×$ 8,000	×$ 8,000	×$ 8,000	×$ 8,000	×$ 8,000
Boat purchases	$160,000	$232,000	$192,000	$176,000	$760,000
Paid in current quarter	× 75%	× 75%	× 75%	× 75%	× 75%
Current purchase payments	$120,000	$174,000	$144,000	$132,000	$570,000
Prior purchase payments[3]	9,000	40,000	58,000	48,000	155,000
Payments to suppliers	$129,000	$214,000	$202,000	$180,000	$725,000

[1]Wind River desires to have ending boat inventory equal to 50% of the expected sales volume for the following quarter. Wind River's marketing department forecasts sales of 26 boats during the first quarter of 2007.
[2]Wind River's beginning finished goods inventory for 2006 is 18 boats. Beginning inventory for Q2 through Q4 is equal to the ending inventory for the prior quarter.
[3]Prior purchase payments in Q1 represent the accounts payable balance from the 2005 balance sheet. Prior purchase payments in Q2 through Q4 represent the purchases not paid for in the prior quarter (i.e., total boat purchases in prior quarter times 25%).

Exhibit 5: A Comparison of the Master Budgets for a Manufacturing and a Merchandising Firm

MANUFACTURING FIRM

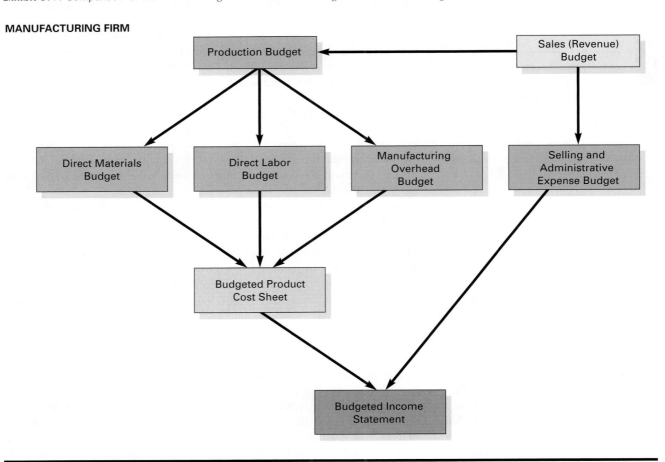

MERCHANDISING FIRM

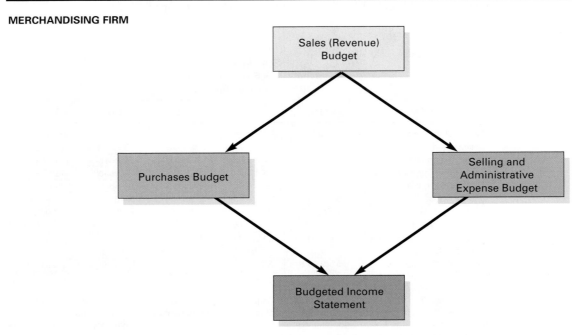

Budgeting for Operations in a Service Firm

Each year, a larger and larger percentage of businesses in the United States is service companies. Service companies differ from manufacturing and merchandising companies in that they provide services to customers instead of products. Examples of service organizations are law, accounting, and engineering firms; doctors and dentists; hotels and motels; hunting and fishing guide services; automotive, home, and appliance repair services; and Internet providers. Budgeting for service firms is similar to budgeting for manufacturing firms. As was the case with both manufacturing and merchandising companies, the budgeting process for service firms begins with a sales budget (sometimes called a revenue budget). Exhibit 6 compares the operating budgeting process for a service firm with a manufacturing firm. You can see that the service firm does not require a production budget. If you compare Schedule 1 and Schedule 2 for Sunbird Boat Company, you can see that the production budget starts with the sales volume and makes adjustments to it based on expected beginning and ending inventories of finished goods. Service firms sell intangible products (for example, physician appointments, car repairs, room rentals, monthly Internet access) that can't be inventoried. Therefore, the sales volume determined in the revenue budget is the "production" for the operating period.

Revenue Budget

To illustrate the budgeting process in service firms, we will use the example of Boulder View Inn, a small motel that has 12 rooms to rent each night. Boulder View Inn is located adjacent to a national park in southern Utah, and its business is highly seasonal, with April through December being busy (peak period) and January through March being very slow. Boulder View Inn rents its rooms for an average rate of $155 per night during the peak period and $85 per night during the slow period. Guests who stay at the hotel either pay cash or use credit cards, such as VISA, MASTERCARD, AMERICAN EXPRESS, or DISCOVER. The motel has a direct link with its bank that immediately deposits credit card receipts in Boulder View Inn's bank account after charging a 4 to 5% discount fee, which covers the bank's costs as well as fees charged by the credit card companies. Historically, Boulder View Inn has found that because most customers use credit cards to pay for their rooms, it pays an average of $4 per room per night to the credit card companies to cover the discount fee. Based on past experience, occupancy rates for the coming year are expected to be as follows:

January–March	25%
April–June	90%
July–September	80%
October–December	60%

revenue budget A service entity's budget that identifies how much revenue (and often cash) will be generated during a period.

Using these data, the **revenue budget** for Boulder View Inn is shown in Schedule 9.

Schedule 9

	Q1	Q2	Q3	Q4	Total
Schedule 9				
Boulder View Inn				
2006 Revenue Budget				
Number of rooms	12 rooms	12 rooms	12 rooms	12 rooms	
Number of days in quarter	× 90 days	× 91 days	× 92 days	× 92 days	
Potential rental volume	1,080 rentals	1,092 rentals	1,104 rentals	1,104 rentals	
Occupancy rate	× 25%	× 90%	× 80%	× 60%	
Rented rooms[1]	270 rentals	983 rentals	883 rentals	662 rentals	**2,798 rentals**
Room rate	× $85	× $155	× $155	× $155	
Revenue[2]	$22,950	$152,365	$136,865	$102,610	$414,790

[1]These calculations are rounded to the nearest whole unit.
[2]These revenues are all collected in the quarter earned.

Exhibit 6: A Comparison of the Master Budgets for a Manufacturing and a Service Firm

MANUFACTURING FIRM

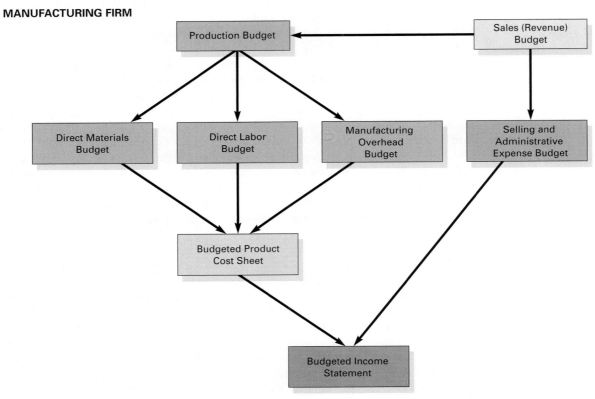

SERVICE FIRM

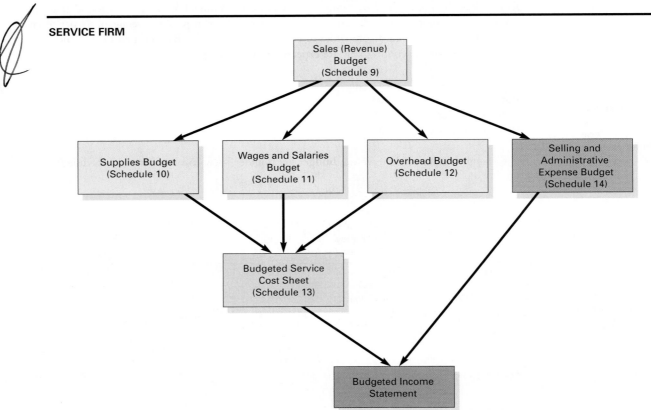

This budget shows that Boulder View Inn will generate gross revenues of $414,790 during the next year. Because Boulder View Inn collects cash or its equivalent (credit cards) from each guest, the revenue earned is expected to be collected each quarter. Remember that the revenue budget also establishes the expected "production," or number of rooms expected to be rented each quarter. Hence, you can see from the revenue budget that Boulder View Inn expects to rent 2,798 rooms next year. And as you can see in Exhibit 6, this volume will be used to determine the subsequent supplies, wages and salaries, overhead, and selling and administrative expense budgets.

The revenue budget for Boulder View Inn would be similar for other types of service firms, except that instead of a per-room revenue, the revenue would be based on per patient visit (for doctors and dentists), per contract (for engineers, accountants, and lawyers), or per subscription (for Internet providers). Service companies that do not collect cash, but rather bill clients on a periodic basis (such as lawyers and accountants), would also need to extend the revenue budget to determine when the cash generated from revenues will be collected.

Supplies Budget

supplies budget The budget, prepared by service entities, that identifies projected supplies expenses over the budget period.

Most service businesses need supplies to operate. For a restaurant, supplies include the food used in preparing meals, cleaning materials, and the paper goods needed for menus and customer invoices. For a medical doctor, supplies might include needles, tape, and bandages, as well as office supplies. For Boulder View Inn, supplies include soap and shampoo for the guest rooms, as well as doughnuts, cereal, juice, and milk for the continental breakfast. The **supplies budget** for Boulder View Inn is shown in Schedule 10.

Schedule 10

Schedule 10 Boulder View Inn 2006 Supplies Budget						
		Q1	Q2	Q3	Q4	Total
Total rental days (Schedule 9)		270 rooms	983 rooms	883 rooms	662 rooms	2,798 rooms
Supplies needed per room:						
Bathroom supplies cost	$1.20	$ 324.00	$1,179.60	$1,059.60	$ 794.40	$ 3,357.60
Laundry supplies cost	0.50	135.00	491.50	441.50	331.00	1,399.00
Breakfast supplies cost	7.50	2,025.00	7,372.50	6,622.50	4,965.00	20,985.00
Total supplies cost per room*	$9.20	$2,484.00	$9,043.60	$8,123.60	$6,090.40	$25,741.60

*Because the level of supplies is immaterial, the supplies cost each quarter is essentially paid in cash in each quarter.

Wages and Salaries Budget

wages and salaries budget The budget, prepared by service entities, that identifies projected labor costs involved directly in providing the service over the budget period.

The **wages and salaries budget** is reserved for labor costs involved directly in providing the service (similar to direct labor in a manufacturing firm). Administrative labor costs are not included in this budget; they are part of the selling and administrative expense budget. For a law firm, the wages and salaries budget would include salaries of lawyers; but not of paralegals, photocopy personnel, computer specialists, or office secretaries—these personnel costs would all be part of the selling and administrative expense budget. For Boulder View Inn, the only labor cost included in this budget is the $15 per room that is paid for cleaning the rooms. Schedule 11 is the wages and salaries budget for Boulder View Inn.

Overhead Budget

service overhead budget The budget, prepared by service entities, that identifies projected costs associated with providing the service.

As was the case with manufacturing firms, the **service overhead budget** includes all the costs associated with providing the product, or service, in this case. The overhead budget does not include selling and administrative costs not directly associated with providing the service. For Boulder View Inn, overhead includes utilities, depreciation, TV and telephone service, and

Schedule 11

Schedule 11 Boulder View Inn 2006 Wages and Salaries Budget					
	Q1	**Q2**	**Q3**	**Q4**	**Total**
Total rental days (Schedule 9)	270 rooms	983 rooms	883 rooms	662 rooms	2,798 rooms
Cleaning fee[1]	× $15	× $15	× $15	× $15	× $15
Total wages[2]	$4,050	$14,745	$13,245	$9,930	$41,970

[1]Includes fringe benefits and payroll taxes.
[2]These costs are all paid in the quarter incurred.

miscellaneous expenses. In the case of this particular service provider, all overhead costs are fixed. In other words, regardless of whether or not a room is rented, these overhead costs are incurred. Schedule 12 is the overhead budget for Boulder View Inn.

Schedule 12

Schedule 12 Boulder View Inn 2006 Overhead Budget					
	Q1	**Q2**	**Q3**	**Q4**	**Total**
Utilities	$3,000	$3,000	$3,000	$3,000	$12,000
Depreciation expense	5,000	5,000	5,000	5,000	20,000
TV and telephone	1,200	1,200	1,200	1,200	4,800
Miscellaneous costs	600	600	600	600	2,400
Total overhead costs	$9,800	$9,800	$9,800	$9,800	$39,200
Less depreciation	(5,000)	(5,000)	(5,000)	(5,000)	(20,000)
Total overhead payments*	$4,800	$4,800	$4,800	$4,800	$19,200

*Because depreciation does not represent a cash payment, these costs are removed to determine cash payments made each quarter for overhead costs. All other overhead costs are paid for in the quarter incurred.

The depreciation in Schedule 12 is calculated by dividing the motel cost of $500,000 by its 25-year life to arrive at $20,000 per year (and further divided into quarterly costs of $5,000). The utilities include heat, lights, sewer, and garbage removal.

Budgeted Service Cost Sheet

budgeted service cost sheet A schedule of all of the service costs (i.e., the costs of supplies, wages and salaries, and overhead) used to provide a single service event.

The **budgeted service cost sheet** (Schedule 13) is similar to the budgeted product cost sheet for manufacturing firms. This schedule accumulates all the budgeted service costs (supplies, wages and salaries, and overhead) to estimate the total service cost of providing a room to rent at Boulder View Inn. Based on the three service-related budgets (supplies, wages and salaries, and overhead), we know it costs Boulder View Inn approximately $24.20 in variable costs to provide the services needed to rent one room for one night. Because Boulder View Inn expects to rent 2,798 rooms during the year, the overhead cost assigned to each room rental (all of which is fixed) is $14.01 ($39,200 ÷ 2,798 rooms). The calculation of these service costs is shown in Schedule 13.

Selling and Administrative Expense Budget

As was the case for Sunbird Boat Company, the selling and administrative expense budget for Boulder View Inn includes planned expenditures for all selling and administrative expenses. As in manufacturing companies, the selling and administrative expense budget for a service firm

Schedule 13

	Schedule 13 Boulder View Inn 2006 Budgeted Service Cost Sheet	
		Total
Annual supplies cost (Schedule 10)	$25,741.60	
Annual wage cost (Schedule 11)	41,970.00	
Total annual variable service costs	$67,711.60	
Annual volume of rental rooms	÷ 2,798 rooms	
Total variable cost per rental		$24.20
Annual fixed overhead costs (Schedule 12)	$39,200.00	
Annual volume of rental rooms	÷ 2,798 rooms	
Fixed MOH cost allocated per rental*		14.01
Total service cost per room rental		$38.21

*Note that the service costs per room rental for Boulder View Inn will actually vary from quarter to quarter because of the change in fixed overhead costs per rental due to changes in occupancy rate each quarter.

can be quite large and is sometimes supported by individual budgets for specific elements included in this budget. The selling and administrative expense budget for Boulder View Inn would be as shown in Schedule 14.

Schedule 14

Schedule 14 Boulder View Inn 2006 Selling and Administrative (S&A) Expense Budget					
Variable S&A expenses	**Q1**	**Q2**	**Q3**	**Q4**	**Total**
Total rental days (Schedule 9)	270 rooms	983 rooms	883 rooms	662 rooms	2,798 rooms
Average credit card discount fee	× $4	× $4	× $4	× $4	× $4
Total variable S&A expenses	$ 1,080	$ 3,932	$ 3,532	$ 2,648	$11,192
Fixed S&A expenses per quarter					
Manager's salary	$ 7,500	$ 7,500	$ 7,500	$ 7,500	$30,000
Depreciation expense	1,200	1,200	1,200	1,200	4,800
Advertising expense	800	800	800	800	3,200
Miscellaneous expenses	500	500	500	500	2,000
Total fixed S&A expenses	$10,000	$10,000	$10,000	$10,000	$40,000
Total S&A expenses	$11,080	$13,932	×$13,532	×$12,648	×$51,192
Less depreciation	(1,200)	(1,200)	(1,200)	(1,200)	(4,800)
Total S&A payments*	$ 9,880	$12,732	$12,332	$11,448	$46,392

(handwritten annotation: "1 period cost" pointing to Total variable S&A expenses)

*Because depreciation does not represent a cash payment, these expenses are removed to determine cash payments made each quarter for selling and administrative expenses. All other selling and administrative expenses are paid for in the quarter incurred.

This selling and administration expense budget shows that Boulder View Inn's total selling and administrative expense for the year is budgeted to be $51,192. The selling and administrative expenses include credit card charges, the manager's salary, miscellaneous expenses around the office, and advertising expense (which includes yellow page directory advertisement and Internet listings). This budget also includes the depreciation expense on the cottage provided by Boulder View to the manager who must be available at the inn on a 24-hour, 7-days-a-week basis.

(handwritten notes at bottom of page:)
why open in Q1 - some contribution to fixed cost.
SET UP for The following year.
shut down/start up cost may not be beneficial

Wall Street Is Unforgiving of Companies Who Don't Hit Their Mark Not only must companies forecast their revenues and earnings as part of the budgeting process, but analysts and various investment institutions forecast companies' earnings as well. And, when a company's actual earnings fall short of analysts' expectations, the company's stock price usually falls.

Security analysts are often optimistic when making earnings forecasts—particularly forecasts made months in advance of the actual report date. Nevertheless, investors often punish companies that consistently fail to meet their early forecasts.

One research project analyzed companies in the S&P 500 and found eight companies that, over eight consecutive quarters from 2000 to 2002, rarely lived up to their consensus forecasts made 60 days prior to quarterly report dates. These eight stocks had an average price decline of 39%.

Over the same 2-year period, the S&P 500 was down 42%. In contrast, the 31 S&P stocks that met or beat their 60-day-out consensus numbers for eight straight quarters had an average gain of 40%.

One of the companies that consistently missed its consensus numbers during that time was pharmaceuticals giant BRISTOL-MYERS SQUIBB. The third quarter of 2002 was representative of what happened to this New York City-based firm. In early summer 2002, security analysts, as a group, initially thought that Bristol-Myers Squibb would earn $1.34 per share for the third quarter. Eventually, the 26 analysts reporting on Bristol-Myers Squibb revised their forecast to $1.20 per share (versus $2.41 in 2001—a 50% decline). Not surprisingly, shares of Bristol were off 59% in October 2002 compared to the previous year when they traded at their 52-week high of $59.95.

The table below lists the eight companies that consistently missed their 60-day prior estimates over eight quarters ending in 2002.

	Price	Price Change	Sales ($ in millions)	Estimated 2002 EPS	Actual 2002 EPS
ALCOA	$19.57	−35%	$20,920	$ 1.15	$ 1.06
AON	20.25	−47	8,158	1.64	0.74
BRISTOL-MYERS SQUIBB	24.55	−51	18,160	1.20	1.30
DELTA AIR LINES	10.06	−58	12,379	−7.59	−9.99
DOW CHEMICAL	27.64	−14	26,554	0.98	−0.46
FLEETBOSTON FINANCIAL	19.98	−42	11,668	1.52	0.84
J.P. MORGAN CHASE	18.64	−43	27,316	1.74	0.84
UNUMPROVIDENT	19.73	−17	9,389	2.54	2.41

Source: John J. Ray, "Companies Missing the Mark" *Forbes*, September 25, 2002. **http://www.forbes.com/2002/09/25/0925sf.html.**

TO SUMMARIZE: The operating budgeting process for merchandising organizations (both retail and wholesale companies) is similar, but significantly easier, than that for manufacturing firms. The major difference is that a merchandising firm's purchases budget replaces four of a manufacturing firm's budgets—the production, direct materials, direct labor, and manufacturing overhead budgets. Otherwise, the entire master budgeting process is the same.

The operating budgets for a service company are quite similar to the operating budgets in a manufacturing company. The major difference is that a production budget is generally not required. Because services cannot usually be inventoried, the sales volume for most service firms also represents the production (i.e., service) budgeted volume. As a result, six operating budgets are prepared: the revenue budget, the supplies budget, the wages and salaries budget, the overhead budget, the budgeted service cost sheet, and the selling and administrative expense budget. The revenue budget is usually based on the expected volume of service to be performed (e.g., rooms rented, services performed, patients seen, subscriptions delivered). The expected volume of service is then used to prepare the supplies, wages and salaries, and overhead budgets. The selling and administrative expense budget includes all costs not directly related to providing the service.

The budgeting process discussed to this point allows management to plan various operating activities within the firm, such as purchasing, hiring, and overall management of the production or service process. Armed with these budgets, management is now prepared to monitor the firm's performance and compare actual results to budgeted results. If corrective action is needed, management can identify deviations from the budget early and take the appropriate steps to remedy problems. In addition to preparing the detailed operating budgets, management can combine the various budgets to arrive at financial budgets, specifically, the cash budget and the pro-forma (or budgeted) financial statements. In this section, we use the operating budgets from the Sunbird Boat Company to prepare a cash budget, as well as a pro-forma income statement, balance sheet, and statement of cash flows. The section concludes with a discussion of static and flexible budgeting and illustrates the advantages of flexible budgeting.

Cash Budget — *Hire Accountant.*

6 Create the cash budget.

cash budget A schedule of expected cash receipts and disbursements during the budget period.

The **cash budget**, which shows expected cash receipts and disbursements during a period, summarizes much of the information discussed thus far. A detailed cash budget will point out when a company has excess cash to invest and when it has to borrow funds. This allows a firm to earn maximum interest on excess funds and to avoid the costs of unnecessary borrowing.

Typically, a cash budget is divided into four sections:

1. Cash receipts
2. Cash payments
3. Cash excess or deficiency
4. Financing

The cash receipts section summarizes all cash expected to flow into the business during the budget period. Because companies generally extend credit to their customers, most of their sales are originally recorded as accounts receivable. The collection of accounts receivable is thus a major source of cash, and its timing is an important consideration in preparing a cash budget.

As we worked through the operating budgeting process for Sunbird Boat Company, we determined the impact on cash flows of this company's management policies regarding its receivables and payables. In fact, you can see this effort illustrated clearly in Schedules 1, 3, 5, and 7.

As you can see in Schedule 1, an analysis of how Sunbird's customers pay on accounts receivable shows that total collections during 2006 are budgeted to be $1,020,000. In particular, you should note that based on Sunbird's expectation that the remaining 20% of accounts are collected in the subsequent quarter, we can assume that the entire beginning balance in

Caution

When preparing a cash budget, be careful not to include expenditures that do not require cash (e.g., depreciation expense from the manufacturing overhead and selling and administrative expense budgets).

accounts receivable is collected in the first quarter of 2006. Further, in the Sunbird example, we assumed that all proceeds from credit sales are eventually collected. Usually, however, some customers never pay, and these uncollectible accounts must be considered when analyzing estimated cash collections from accounts receivable. You should recognize that economic factors play a significant role in the timing of collections of accounts receivable. During recessionary periods, customers often drag out their payments much longer than they would in prosperous times.[7]

The cash budget for Sunbird is shown in Schedule 15. Cash receipts for Sunbird are composed solely of what the company collects from its customers, and the computation is reasonably straightforward. However, the cash payments section of this schedule is a bit more involved. You can see that the first four items come directly from the operating budgets for purchases of materials, payments for direct labor, and payments for manufacturing overhead and selling and administrative expense. In addition, there are four other payments that Sunbird has scheduled which take place outside of its day-to-day operations.

Schedule 15

Schedule 15 Sunbird Boat Company 2006 Cash Budget					
	Q1	Q2	Q3	Q4	Total
Beginning cash balance	$135,000	$140,000	$147,308	$201,284	$ 135,000
Collections from customers (Schedule 1)[1]	248,000	272,000	296,000	204,000	1,020,000
Cash available	$383,000	$412,000	$443,308	$405,284	$1,155,000
Payments:					
Direct materials (Schedule 3)[2]	$ 23,464	$ 24,415	$ 23,204	$ 22,088	$ 93,170
Direct labor (Schedule 4)	24,000	34,800	28,800	26,400	114,000
Manufacturing overhead (Schedule 5)[3]	36,960	42,720	39,520	38,240	157,440
Selling and admin. expense (Schedule 7)[3]	107,900	116,300	120,500	95,300	440,000
Income tax payment for 2005	96,000				96,000
Interest payments (10% annual rate)[4]		1,133			1,133
Dividends			30,000		30,000
Equipment purchase				100,000	100,000
Total payments	$288,324	$219,368	$242,024	$282,028	$1,031,743
Minimum cash balance desired[5]	140,000	140,000	140,000	140,000	140,000
Total cash needed	$428,324	$359,368	$382,024	$422,028	$1,171,743
Excess (deficiency)[6]	$ (45,324)	$ 52,632	$ 61,284	$ (16,743)	$ (16,743)
Financing:					
Borrowings	$ 45,324			$ 16,743	$ 62,067
Repayments of principle		$ (45,324)			(45,324)
Total financing inflows (outflows)	$ 45,324	$ (45,324)		$ 16,743	$ 16,743
Ending cash balance	$140,000	$147,308	$201,284	$140,000	$ 140,000

[1]Q1 = Beginning accounts receivable balance from balance sheet + 80% of Q1 revenue; Q2 thru Q4 = 80% of current quarter revenue + 20% of previous quarter revenue.

[2]Q1 = Beginning accounts payable balance from balance sheet + 75% of Q1 purchases; Q2 thru Q4 = 75% of current quarter purchases + 25% of previous quarter purchases.

[3]MOH and S&A depreciation is not included in the cash cost of these expenses.

[4]Interest expense for Q2 = $45,324 × 10% × 1/4 year = $1,133 (rounded).

[5]Ending cash balance for each quarter must be at least $140,000. Otherwise, the company must borrow on its line of credit at the bank (interest rate is 10% annual).

[6]Due to rounding of earlier numbers on the Direct Materials Budget (Schedule 3), the deficiency in Q4 appears to be in error by $1 (actually it's not an error).

- First, Sunbird accrued at the end of 2005 a $96,000 payable for income taxes (see Sunbird's 2005 balance sheet in Exhibit 4). This bill to the IRS is expected to be paid during the first quarter of 2006.

7 Although the reality that some customers never pay off their account does complicate the cash collection budget for accounts receivable, the use of a contra account such as "Allowance for Doubtful Accounts" establishes a net balance for accounts receivable on the balance sheet that represents what is realistically expected to be collected. The "net balance" accounting is very helpful when creating a budget for cash receipts.

- Second, at the end of the first quarter, Sunbird needs to borrow $45,324 from the bank in order to maintain its desired $140,000 cash balance. At the end of the second quarter, Sunbird has enough excess cash to repay this loan and pay the interest outstanding on this loan (the interest calculation is shown as a footnote in this schedule). This is perhaps the most complicated item on the cash budget. You should be sure to work through the calculation of the loan amount in the first quarter, as well as the interest calculation in the second quarter.
- Third, Sunbird plans to declare dividends in the first quarter of 2006, which it expects to pay in the third quarter.
- Fourth, based on its capital projects plan, Sunbird is planning to make a capital expenditure of $100,000 for equipment in the final quarter of 2006. You can see how this capital expenditure decision fits into the master budget by reviewing Exhibit 3.

By combining the expected cash payments with the desired ending cash balance, Sunbird can determine its total cash need for each quarter and compare that need with the total amount of cash it expects to have available during the quarter. The final section of this budget reports the cash excess or deficiency as the difference between budgeted cash availability and cash needs. With a prospective excess of cash, management may want to look for some attractive short-term investments. A deficiency obviously means that additional short-term funds will be needed.

In addition to the timing and amounts of all projected borrowings and repayments during the period, the financing section of the cash budget is also used to estimate the amount of interest to be paid on borrowed funds. By accurately projecting these amounts and events, firms can give banks and other lending institutions advance notice of their needs. Banks appreciate, and sometimes insist, that companies plan their cash needs in advance. Because money has a time value, management always walks a tightrope between having too much or too little cash on hand.

Exhibit 7 shows how a typical company's cash balance and requirements fluctuate constantly. Most of this fluctuation is due to the varying amounts of raw materials and finished goods that are needed in the different seasons of the year. A prosperous firm could, if it desired, maintain enough cash on hand so that short-term borrowing would never be necessary, but such a policy might not be cost-beneficial. Long-term investments in productive assets usually earn considerably more than short-term cash investments; firms are generally better off maintaining lower cash balances, keeping as much capital as possible "at work" in the company's productive assets, and borrowing from time to time for short periods. For this reason, most companies obtain a line of credit from banks. A **line of credit** is a prearranged agreement whereby an organization or individual can borrow money on demand, up to a specific amount at specific rates.

line of credit An arrangement whereby a bank agrees to loan an amount of money (up to a certain limit) on demand for short periods of time, usually less than a year.

Exhibit 7: A Typical Relationship between Cash Balance and Cash Needs

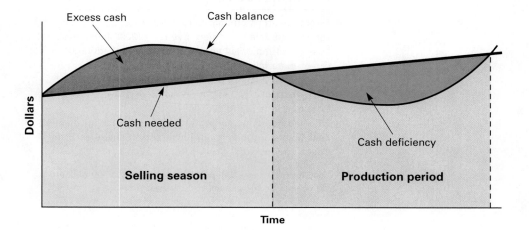

FYI:

Remember that having income does *not* mean that the organization will have cash. Revenues don't get collected immediately (which leads to accounts receivable). Expenses don't get paid immediately (which leads to accounts payable). And capital expenditures (which are not reflected on the income statement) use up a lot of cash.

With the cash budget, the company is now able to make planning decisions regarding financing. For example, Sunbird is now aware that although the cash balance will be sufficient at the end of the year, there will probably be a cash shortage in the second quarter of 2006. With this knowledge, the company can take steps to deal with the situation. One solution would be to negotiate with a bank to obtain a loan. The company might also obtain money by attempting to get customers to pay sooner, trying to negotiate with creditors for a longer repayment period, or simply reducing the desired ending cash balance (currently at $140,000). The point is, with knowledge of the coming cash shortfall, Sunbird is able to formulate a method of dealing with the problem now, rather than waiting until the company actually finds itself in a cash shortage crisis.

TO SUMMARIZE: The cash budget shows expected cash receipts and disbursements as the result of receipts from customers, payments for inventory, labor, and overhead. Cash budgets must also track expenditures for capital equipment, taxes, interest payments, and various other items. The budgets are important in that they signal when the company can expect a cash shortage, which requires outside financing using a line of credit or another similar finance tool, or a cash excess, which should be temporarily invested in income-producing assets.

Pro-Forma Financial Statements

7 Prepare pro-forma financial statements.

The pro-forma income statement (often called a budgeted income statement) projects income for the coming period and, therefore, is valuable to management in making key decisions. Such questions as how high a dividend to pay, whether to invest in a new plant, and how strenuously to bargain with unions are usually decided on the basis of projected and actual profits. Because budgeting for manufacturing firms is the most complicated, we will illustrate pro-forma financial statements using the Sunbird Boat Company example used throughout the chapter.

Perhaps the most challenging aspect of determining Sunbird's pro-forma income statement is computing cost of goods sold. To help you better understand this computation, we will carefully lay out the computation for cost of goods sold. This computation requires a careful assessment of changes in Sunbird's inventory balances. In making this computation, we will assume that Sunbird does not typically have significant work-in-process inventory at the end of a quarter. However, the company does have significant inventory in direct (or raw) materials and finished goods (as shown in Sunbird's balance sheet in Exhibit 4).

Cost of Goods Sold	2006
Direct materials purchases (Schedule 3)	$ 89,680
Direct materials beginning inventory (2005 balance sheet)	7,980
Less direct materials ending inventory (Schedule 3)[1]	(7,410)
Direct materials costs in production	$ 90,250
Direct labor costs in production (Schedule 4)	114,000
MOH costs in production (Schedule 5)	223,440
Cost of goods manufactured	$427,690
Finished goods beginning inventory (2005 balance sheet)	83,520
Less finished goods ending inventory (Schedules 2 and 6)[2]	(58,526)
Cost of goods sold	$452,684

[1](546 feet of wood × $10 purchase price) + (390 feet of fiberglass × $5 purchase price) = $7,410.
[2]13 boats × $4,502 product cost per boat = $58,526.

You will note that this computation is based on the standard calculation that we studied earlier in the chapter on product cost flows for cost of goods manufactured and cost of goods sold.

Now that we have computed the expected cost of goods sold for 2006, Sunbird is ready to compose its pro-forma income statement, which is shown in Schedule 16. In this income statement, we assume an income tax rate of 27% for Sunbird.

Schedule 16

After Budgeting over Pro formA Run Pro formA to see if it makes sense.

Schedule 16 Sunbird Boat Company Pro-Forma Income Statement For the Year Ended December 31, 2006		
Sales revenue (Schedule 1)		$1,000,000
Cost of goods sold:		
Finished goods beginning inventory	$ 83,520	
Cost of goods manufactured	427,690	
Cost of goods available for sale	$511,210	
Less finished goods ending inventory	(58,526)	(452,684)
Gross margin		547,316
Selling and administrative expense (Schedule 7)		(472,000)
Operating income		$ 75,316
Interest expense (Schedule 15)		(1,133)
Income taxes (27% average tax rate)		(20,335)
Net income		$ 53,848

The final two items to be projected are the balance sheet and the statement of cash flows. These statements are presented in Schedules 17 and 18. All of the calculations necessary to complete these pro-forma financial statements have been effectively developed all along as we have worked through previous budgets. Be sure to work through each line item in these pro-forma

Schedule 17

Schedule 17 Sunbird Boat Company Pro-Forma Balance Sheet December 31, 2006		
Assets		
Current assets:		
Cash (Schedule 15)	$ 140,000	
Accounts receivable (Schedule 1)[1]	36,000	
Direct materials inventory[2]	7,410	
Finished goods inventory[2]	58,526	$ 241,936
Long-term assets:		
Land	$ 234,305	
Building and equipment (Schedule 15)[3]	1,600,000	
Less accumulated depreciation (Schedules 5 and 7)[4]	(218,000)	1,616,305
Total assets		$1,858,241
Liabilities & Stockholders' Equity		
Current liabilities:		
Accounts payable (Schedule 3)[5]	$ 5,510	
Income taxes payable (Schedule 16)	20,335	
Short-term loan payable (Schedule 15)	16,743	$ 42,588
Stockholders' equity:		
Common stock, $5 par	$1,000,000	
Paid-in capital in excess of par	250,000	
Retained earnings (Schedules 15 and 16)[6]	565,653	$1,815,653
Total liabilities & stockholders' equity		$1,858,241

[1]Q4 revenue × 20%.
[2]See the calculation for cost of goods sold in chapter text.
[3]Original account balance ($1,500,000) + equipment purchase ($100,000).
[4]Original account balance ($120,000) + MOH depreciation ($66,000) + S&A depreciation ($32,000).
[5]Q4 purchases × 25%.
[6]Original account balance ($541,805) + income ($53,848) − dividends ($30,000).

Schedule 18

Schedule 18 Sunbird Boat Company Pro-Forma Statement of Cash Flows For the Year Ended December 31, 2006		
Cash flow from operating activities		
Net Income (Schedule 16)		$ 53,848
Adjustments:		
Depreciation (Schedules 5 and 7)	$ 98,000	
Accounts receivable decrease (Schedule 17)*	20,000	
Direct materials inventory decrease (Schedule 17)*	570	
Finished goods inventory decrease (Schedule 17)*	24,994	
Accounts payable decrease (Schedule 17)*	(3,490)	
Income taxes payable decrease (Schedule 16)*	(75,665)	64,409
Net cash provided by operating activities		$118,257
Cash flow from investing activities		
Purchase of Equipment (Schedule 15)	$(100,000)	
Net cash used in investing activities		(100,000)
Cash flow from financing activities		
Cash obtained from borrowing (Schedule 15)	$ 62,067	
Repayment of borrowed funds (Schedule 15)	(45,324)	
Payment of dividends (Schedule 15)	(30,000)	
Net cash used in financing activities		(13,257)
Net Increase in cash		$ 5,000
Beginning cash balance		135,000
Ending cash balance		$140,000

*Compare the relevant ending account balance on these schedules with the beginning account balance on Sunbird's 2005 balance sheet (Exhibit 4).

STOP & THINK

How would the three financial statements be different if we assumed Sunbird was a merchandising company instead of a manufacturing company?

statements to be sure you see which schedule is the source of the computation. (This is an excellent way to review everything you've studied in this chapter on computing budgets for manufacturing companies!)

The master budget is now complete. It is ready for use to communicate information, coordinate and authorize activities, motivate employees, and measure performance. The decisions to be made on the basis of this budget depend on the answers to such questions as:

1. Is the net income of approximately $53,848 adequate? If not, how can it be increased?
2. How does the expected financial position at the end of the year fit with long-range objectives and goals?
3. Is the projected increase in cash sufficient to meet the firm's goals?
4. Are there sufficient liquid assets to purchase needed assets?
5. How should management be rewarded if these budgets are met?
6. Who should be responsible for meeting the goals set for sales, production, and costs?

These are only a few of the questions that management needs to answer. However, these questions should give you a sense of the master budget's usefulness. In fact, it is hard to imagine how a company could be profitable in the long run without such planning.

TO SUMMARIZE: Following the preparation of the cash budget, which provides an indication of the financing activities of the business, pro-forma financial statements can be prepared. The pro-forma income statement, balance sheet, and statement of cash flows follow directly from the components of the master budget. The pro-forma balance sheet also relies heavily on beginning account balances. Once these pro-forma financial statements have been prepared, management can then determine if budgeted sales and production levels will allow the company to achieve its strategic goals. These pro-forma financial statements serve as a basis for key management decisions.

business environment (READ)

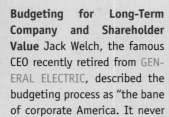

Budgeting for Long-Term Company and Shareholder Value Jack Welch, the famous CEO recently retired from GENERAL ELECTRIC, described the budgeting process as "the bane of corporate America. It never should have existed. A budget is this: if you make it, you generally get a pat on the back and a few bucks. If you miss it, you get a stick in the eye—or worse." Some reports state that managers spend up to 20% of their valuable time on planning and budgeting. If the time and effort apparently outweigh the benefit, why do corporations, governments, and (for that matter) individuals continue to budget? *Because budgeting is important.* However, focusing solely on the quarterly budget can be problematic, creating a budget trap.

A "traditional" budgeting process can motivate managers to:

- Lowball the budget target.
- Do whatever it takes to "make the numbers."
- Overestimate required resources.
- Use the budgeted funds ("use it or lose it!").

Possible results from these actions are:

- Negotiating superficial budget targets.
- "Cooking the books."
- Pushing to "book orders" at year-end, despite customers' true needs.
- Budget wasting.

The increase in the pace of change across most industries, combined with an increasingly harsh and punitive investment community, has forced many companies to become focused on short-term results at the expense of long-term value. The drive to focus on short-term results leads to decision making that is focused on the quarterly budget, rather than on long-term strategy. And while maintaining a reign on the quarterly budget ap-

pears to be in the interest of the organization's health, these short-term decisions in fact can and do cut off longer-term opportunities. Short-term decisions can stifle the potential for growth because they appear to be made in a vacuum independent of what the organization is trying to achieve over time.

The Keys to Success

There are five key principles that distinguish successful organizations that are able to forecast results and allocate resources efficiently while achieving their overall long-term strategy. These organizations do the following:

- Align operational planning and budgeting for strategy execution: Bring together the often disparate processes of operations planning and budgeting to ensure they are consistent, linked together, and reflective of each others' priorities.
- Increase adaptability to change through continuous planning: Adopt a rolling forecast approach.
- Manage strategic initiatives to achieve results: Focus the organization on the key strategic initiatives, while systematically and rigorously jettisoning those initiatives and activities that are not tied to strategic goals.
- Motivate people and actions through relative performance targets: Engage everyone in the long-term success of the organization by tying individual performance targets to strategic results.
- Increase planning efficiency by reducing detail and effort: Home in on the key strategic elements and activities to focus on doing and reporting on only those aspects of the business that drive the strategy, eliminating the effort and time required to track and plan elements of the business that derail this focus.

Sources: Marshall Loeb, "Jack Welch Lets Fly on Budgets, Bonuses, and Buddy Boards," *Fortune*, May 29, 1995; Horvath & Partners Database; IMA and Balanced Scorecard Collaborative, Inc., found on the site **http://www.smartpros.com/x38510.xml**.

Static versus Flexible Budgeting

8 Distinguish between static and flexible budgets.

static budget A quantified plan that projects revenues and costs for only one level of activity.

The budgets discussed thus far in this chapter are **static budgets**; that is, they are geared to only one level of sales activity. Although such budgets help in planning, they are not very useful for controlling costs and measuring performance because the actual level of activity may differ significantly from the planned level. In the next chapter, we will compare actual results to budgets in order to control and evaluate performance. However, before we can do this, we will need to adjust budgets to make them relevant to the actual results. To be specific, we will need to recompute the budgets based on the actual sales activity. This is the process of creating a flexible budget.

A **flexible budget** is much more useful for control and performance evaluation because it is not confined to one level of activity. Flexible budgets are dynamic; that is, they can be tailored to any level of activity within the relevant range. Using flexible budgeting, a manager can look at the actual level of activity attained and then determine what costs should have been at that level.

flexible budget A quantified plan that projects revenues and costs for varying levels of activity.

STOP & THINK

Suppose that a production department's budget is based on manufacturing and selling 10,000 widgets at a standard product cost of $10 per widget. The department actually produced 9,000 widgets and spent $95,000. Obviously, it didn't meet its sales goal. However, did it spend more or less than it should have? What if it had actually produced 11,000 widgets and spent $105,000?

Weaknesses in Static Budgeting

To illustrate why a static budget is inadequate for controlling operations, let's return once more to the Sunbird Boat Company example. In particular, let's look at its budgeted product cost sheet (Schedule 6). Based on the information from that schedule, Sunbird developed the following budgeted per-unit manufacturing costs for 15-foot boats:

Direct materials	$ 950
Direct labor	1,200
Variable manufacturing overhead	640
Fixed manufacturing overhead	1,712
Total	$4,502

As you consider these numbers, you need to be very careful with the fixed manufacturing overhead. The $1,712 represents the *average* fixed manufacturing overhead cost per boat for the year. However, fixed manufacturing overhead is expected to be $40,660 each quarter (for a total of $162,640 for the year, *regardless of the number of boats actually produced.* (You can review these numbers in Schedule 5.) And if you review Schedule 2, you'll see that Sunbird's expected production will vary from quarter to quarter. What this means is that we shouldn't multiply the $1,712 with the expected volume of production in order to determine the budgeted fixed manufacturing overhead for the quarter. Fixed manufacturing overhead is actually what it says—it is fixed! In other words, if you want to predict the level of total manufacturing costs each quarter for Sunbird, you won't multiply the expected production volume by $4,502. The better way to do this is to use the following formula:

Total budgeted manufacturing costs =
Total fixed manufacturing costs + (Variable manufacturing cost per unit × Production volume)

Extending this budget formula to establish a total budgeted amount for the first quarter of 2006, Sunbird Boat Company might then prepare a static budget as follows:

Sunbird Boat Company Budgeted Manufacturing Costs January–March 2006		
Budgeted production (boats)		20
Variable manufacturing costs per boat:		
Direct materials	$ 950	
Direct labor	1,200	
Variable manufacturing overhead	640	
Total variable manufacturing costs per boat	$2,790	
Total variable manufacturing costs ($2,790 × 20 boats)		$55,800
Total fixed manufacturing costs		40,660
Total budgeted manufacturing costs		$96,460

STOP & THINK

Consider the budget formula used to compute total budgeted manufacturing costs of $96,460 in the first quarter of 2006 for Sunbird Boat Company. Does this formula look familiar to you? If should look familiar if you studied how to analyze mixed costs using the least squares method in the earlier chapter on cost-volume-profit analysis!

This simple operating budget for the first quarter of 2006 can be quite useful to Sunbird *if* it actually produces 20 boats. Now, let's assume that Sunbird actually produced 23 boats in that first quarter. Sunbird's actual costs incurred were $63,350 for direct materials, direct labor, and variable manufacturing overhead, and $41,040 for fixed manufacturing overhead. Comparing actual results with the static budget information, the performance report for the quarter would be as follows:

Sunbird Boat Company
Static Budget Performance Report
January–March 2006

	Budgeted	Actual	Difference
Production (units)	20	23	3
Manufacturing costs:			
Variable manufacturing costs	$55,800	$ 63,350	$7,550
Fixed manufacturing overhead	40,660	41,040	380
Total actual and budgeted manufacturing costs	$96,460	$104,390	$7,930

According to this report, Sunbird has spent $7,930 more than it should have. However, something is wrong with this performance report. Producing more boats than budgeted (23 actual boats versus 20 budgeted boats) has led to more actual costs than were expected. But given the increase in production, Sunbird should have spent more in manufacturing costs (right?). The real question is, should management be punished for allowing actual costs to be $104,390 or rewarded for producing more units than budgeted? Using the static budget doesn't help us answer this question. The deficiencies of this static budget performance report can be explained as follows: A production manager is responsible for controlling two things—production (output) and costs (input); that is, he or she must try to meet budgeted production volume and control costs in the process. To measure a manager's performance, the production and cost control functions must be separated. It makes no sense to note that the total actual cost of producing 23 boats is more than the budgeted cost of producing 20 boats. It obviously should be. The manager in our example clearly has exceeded budgeted production volume, but to determine whether he or she has controlled costs adequately, we must be able to compare actual costs to budgeted costs at the same number of units of production. In other words, how much more costs *should have* been incurred given this higher level of production? Answering this question correctly *is* the process of using a flexible budget.

Using the Flexible Budget

Instead of providing budgeted costs for only a single level of production or sales activity that was predicted before the operating period began, the flexible budget effectively recomputes that static budget after the conclusion of the operation period based on the actual activity level. To make it possible to prepare budgeted costs at any possible activity level within the relevant range, per-unit variable costs and total fixed costs are budgeted at the beginning of the operating period and are then used at the end of the period to create a flexible budget that is useful in measuring and analyzing actual input and output performance. The steps in preparing a flexible operating budget are as follows:

1. Determine a relevant range over which production is expected to vary during the coming operating period.

2. Before the operating period begins, establish the budgeted per-unit variable manufacturing costs and total fixed manufacturing costs.
3. At the conclusion of the operating period, use the per-unit variable costs and total fixed costs to build a flexible budget based on actual output activity.

To illustrate the preparation of a flexible budget, let us assume that Sunbird's relevant range of production activity per quarter is between 20 and 30 boats. This is important because producing outside of this relevant range is likely to result in expected differences in per-unit variable and total fixed costs.[8] As noted earlier, the per-unit variable manufacturing costs are expected to be $2,790, while total fixed manufacturing costs are expected to be $40,660 per quarter. These budgeted costs can now be used at the conclusion of the first quarter of 2006 to prepare a flexible budget that is relevant to assess the actual costs of producing 23 boats. This performance report based on flexible budgeting for the 23 boats actually produced now makes much more sense.

Sunbird Boat Company
Flexible Budget Performance Report
January–March 2006

Actual production (units) 23
Budgeted production (units) 20
   Difference 3

	Budgeted Costs	Budgeted Costs for 23 Boats	Actual Costs Incurred for 23 Boats	Difference
Variable manufacturing costs	$ 2,790 per boat	$ 64,170	$ 63,350	$ 820
Fixed manufacturing costs	40,660 in total	40,660	41,040	380
Total costs		$104,830	$104,390	$ 440

Caution

Note that the "flex" in flexible budgeting really only relates to the variable costs. Fixed costs are expected to remain fixed!

Notice that the actual variable manufacturing costs are lower than the flexible budget, which is based on how much should have been spent to produce 23 boats. Only the actual fixed manufacturing costs have exceeded the flexible budget. We are now comparing apples with apples, or actual costs of producing 23 boats with budgeted costs of producing 23 boats. Using the same activity level has revealed that total manufacturing costs actually were less than budget by $440.

Flexible budgets provide management with useful information for investigating problem areas. This flexible budget performance report shows that actual production exceeded planned production, and that the costs incurred were less than those budgeted at the attained level of activity. Assuming that the company actually needed those 23 boats, the manager appears to be doing well with cost control. Having meaningful cost comparisons as a result of using flexible budgeting is very useful for evaluating performance. We'll spend a lot of time in the next chapter to more specifically analyze cost variances for Sunbird Boat Company.

TO SUMMARIZE: The master budget described in this chapter was a static budget. A static budget is a budget that is prepared for only one level of activity. Static budgets are useful for planning purposes, but flexible budgets are much more useful for control and performance evaluation. A flexible budget can be prepared over a range of actual activity levels by multiplying the variable costs per unit of output and then adding the total budgeted fixed cost amount. Flexible budgets allow budgeted and actual costs to be compared at the same level of activity.

8 See the earlier chapter on cost-volume-profit analysis if you need to review the concept of "relevant range."

review of learning objectives

1 **Describe the importance of personal budgeting.** A budget is a quantitative expression of a plan of action. Individuals who budget spend money how, where, and when they want. Those who do not budget often don't have enough money to purchase those things that they really need.

2 **Identify the purposes of budgeting for organizations.** The master budget identifies and allocates resources necessary to carry out the mission of the organization. Based on the strategic plan, the organization prepares a capital budget and a budget for operations. The operating budget provides quantitative estimates of sales and expected costs for each activity to be performed during a specified period of time (usually, one year). The budgeting process has several purposes. Budgeting encourages planning, enhances communication and coordination, provides authorization for actions (investing, spending, borrowing, producing), helps motivate employees to perform, assists in reducing conflicts, and provides quantitative measures of expectations and objectives.

3 **Explain the budgeting process and its behavioral implications in organizations.** Most organizations establish a budget committee composed of several vice presidents who coordinate the preparation of detailed budgets in their areas of responsibility and oversee the preparation of the overall budget. There are significant behavioral ramifications to consider in preparing an operating budget. For the process to be successful, top management must give its full support, all members of management must actively participate in the process, and deviations from the budget must be addressed in a constructive manner. If only the top management is involved in budget preparation, it is referred to as top-down budgeting. When each segment manager prepares a budget for that segment's operations, it is called bottom-up budgeting. Most budgeting processes incorporate both approaches to some degree.

4 **Construct an operating budget and its components for manufacturing firms.** The operating budget, an integral part of the master budget, is an integrated group of detailed budgets that together provide overall operating plans for a specific time period. The operating budget for a manufacturing firm starts with a sales forecast, which serves as the basis for the sales budget. The sales budget is followed in sequence with detailed budgets for production, direct materials usage and purchases, direct labor, manufacturing overhead, the product cost sheet, and selling and administrative expenses. These detailed budgets are usually prepared on a monthly or quarterly basis.

5 **Compare the operating budget for a manufacturing firm to that of a merchandising or service firm.** For operational budgeting in merchandising companies, a purchases budget replaces the production, direct materials, direct labor, and manufacturing overhead budgets used in manufacturing companies. Because service firms cannot effectively hold an inventory of finished services ready to deliver to customers, the revenue and production budgets in service firms are typically the same budget. Thereafter, operational budgeting in services firms is quite similar to that of manufacturing firms. Operational budgets provide management of manufacturing, merchandising, or service firms with a plan of action for the coming year.

eXpanded *Material*

6 **Create the cash budget.** The cash budget shows expected cash receipts and disbursements; it also signals when the company can expect a cash shortage requiring outside financing or excess cash that could be temporarily invested in income-producing assets.

7 **Prepare pro-forma financial statements.** Once a cash budget is prepared to project the firm's ending cash balances and borrowing and investing activities, pro-forma financial statements can be prepared. The pro-forma balance sheet relies heavily on the balances at the beginning of the period, along with components of the master budget. The pro-forma income statement and statement of cash flows are prepared primarily from the detailed budgets included in the master budget. With these pro-forma financial statements, management is able to determine if budgeted results are consistent with the firm's master plan.

8 **Distinguish between static and flexible budgets.** Static budgets project expected results at only one activity level. When the actual production level differs significantly from the budgeted level, it is difficult to know what costs should have been for the actual production level. Flexible budgets allow costs to be estimated for the actual activity level, which then allows actual costs to be compared to budgeted costs for the actual production level.

key terms & concepts

budget, 256
budget committee, 260
budgetary slack, 261
budgeted product cost sheet, 270
budgeted service cost sheet, 278
direct labor budget, 268
direct materials budget, 266
disposable income, 257
manufacturing overhead budget, 269
master budget, 258

participative budgeting, 261
production budget, 266
purchases budget, 273
revenue budget, 275
sales budget, 264
selling and administrative expense
  budget, 271
service overhead budget, 277
supplies budget, 277
wages and salaries budget, 277

cash budget, 281
flexible budget, 288
line of credit, 283
static budget, 287

review problem

Budgeting in a Manufacturing Firm

The following information is available for the Call Company:

Expected sales (units):

June	840
July	980
August	1,400
Selling price per unit	$15
Accounts receivable balance, June 1	$6,300
Accounts payable balance, June 1	$2,350
Desired finished goods inventory, August 31 (units)	250
Beginning finished goods inventory, June 1 (units)	270
Direct materials needed per unit	11 lbs.
Desired direct materials inventory, August 31	2,800 lbs.
Beginning direct materials inventory, June 1	2,700 lbs.
Total direct labor time per finished unit	3 hours
Direct materials cost per pound	$0.60
Direct labor cost per hour	$8

Additional information:

a. Seventy-five percent of a month's sales is collected by the month's end; the remaining 25% is collected in the following month.

b. Sixty percent of a month's purchases are paid by the month's end; the remaining 40% is paid in the following month.

c. The desired ending finished goods inventory every month is 25% of the next month's sales.

d. The desired ending direct materials inventory every month is 20% of the next month's production needs.

Required:

1. Prepare the sales budget, including cash collections, for June, July, and August (in dollars).
2. Prepare the production budget for June, July, and August (in units).
3. Prepare the direct materials budget, including cash payments, for June, July, and August (in dollars).
4. Prepare the direct labor budget for June, July, and August (in dollars).

Solution

1. Sales Budget

	June	July	August
Expected sales (units)	840	980	1,400
Selling price per unit	× $15	× $15	× $15
Revenue earned	**$12,600**	**$14,700**	**$21,000**
Percent received in current month	× 75%	× 75%	× 75%
Current revenue collected	$ 9,450	$11,025	$15,750
Prior revenue collected*	6,300	3,150	3,675
Collections from customers	**$15,750**	**$14,175**	**$19,425**

*Prior revenue collected in June represents the accounts receivable balance on June 1. Prior revenue collected in July and August represents the revenue *not* collected in the prior month (i.e., revenue earned in prior month times 25%).

2. Production Budget

	June	July	August
Expected sales (units)	840	980	1,400
Add desired ending inventory*	245	350	250
Total needed	1,085	1,330	1,650
Less beginning inventory**	(270)	(245)	(350)
Budgeted production (units)	**815**	**1,085**	**1,300**

*Desired ending inventory for June and July is equal to 25% of next month's sales. Desired ending inventory in August is given.
**Beginning inventory in June is given. Beginning inventory in July and August is based on the desired ending inventory for the previous month.

3. Direct Materials Budget

	June	July	August
Units to be produced	815	1,085	1,300
Direct materials needed per unit	× 11 lbs.	× 11 lbs.	× 11 lbs.
Total production needs	8,965 lbs.	11,935 lbs.	14,300 lbs.
Desired ending direct materials inventory* ...	2,387	2,860	2,800
Total pounds needed	11,352 lbs.	14,795 lbs.	17,100 lbs.
Less beginning inventory**	(2,700)	(2,387)	(2,860)
Materials to be purchased	**8,652 lbs.**	**12,408 lbs.**	**14,240 lbs.**
Standard cost per pound	× $0.60	× $0.60	× $0.60
Materials purchases (rounded)	**$ 5,191**	**$ 7,445**	**$ 8,544**
Paid in current month	× 60%	× 60%	× 60%
Current purchase payments (rounded)	$ 3,115	$ 4,467	$ 5,126
Prior purchase payments***	2,350	2,076	2,978
Payments to suppliers	**$ 5,465**	**$ 6,543**	**$ 8,104**

*Desired ending direct materials inventory for June and July is equal to 20% of next month's production needs. Desired ending direct materials inventory in August is given.
**Beginning direct materials inventory in June is given. Beginning direct materials inventory in July and August is based on the desired ending direct materials inventory for the previous month.
***Prior purchase payments in June represent the June 1 accounts payable balance. Prior purchase payments in July and August represent the purchases *not* paid for in the prior month (i.e., material purchases in prior month times 40%—rounded).

4. Direct Labor Budget

	June	July	August
Units to be produced	815	1,085	1,300
Direct labor hours per unit	× 3 hrs.	× 3 hrs.	× 3 hrs.
Total hours needed	2,445 hrs.	3,255 hrs.	3,900 hrs.
Cost per hour	× $8	× $8	× $8
Direct labor cost	**$19,560**	**$26,040**	**$31,200**

d iscussion questions

1. How are strategic planning, capital budgeting, and operations budgeting different?
2. What are the advantages of budgeting?
3. How does management use the operating budget?
4. Describe the advantages of the top-down approach and the bottom-up approach to budgeting.
5. Why are budgets usually prepared for one year?
6. Why does the accuracy of the entire master budget depend on a reliable sales forecast?
7. Identify the sequence of schedules used in preparing a master budget for a manufacturing firm.
8. How is the budgeting process for a merchandising firm different from the budgeting process for a manufacturing firm?

9. How is the budgeting process for a service firm similar to the budgeting process for a manufacturing firm? What are any differences?

10. Describe the four sections of a cash budget.
11. How does a cash budget differ from a pro-forma income statement?
12. How are flexible budgets useful in controlling costs?

p ractice exercises

Practice 5-1

Purposes of Budgeting
Which one of the following statements is *false*?

a. Budgeting facilitates communication in an organization.
b. Budgeting is best used as a management tool to punish departments that do not perform well.
c. Budgeting helps management coordinate activities of business segments.
d. Budgeting can help motivate managers and workers.
e. Budgeting can help resolve conflicts that arise regarding the use of limited resources.

Practice 5-2

Behavioral Considerations of Budgeting
Which one of the following is *not* a behavioral consideration of the budgeting process?

a. Top management must support the budgeting process.
b. All managers, and as many employees as possible, should participate in the budgeting process.
c. Deviations from the budget must be addressed by managers in a positive and constructive manner.
d. The budgeting process should remain impersonal in nature.

Practice 5-3

Top-Down versus Bottom-Up Budgeting
Which one of the following statements is *false*?

a.   An advantage of top-down budgeting is that upper management knows the strategic objectives of the company.
b.   An advantage of bottom-up budgeting is that segment managers have an excellent understanding of products, technology, and current customer needs.
c.   An advantage of top-down budgeting is universal acceptance of the final budget from line employees.
d.   An advantage of bottom-up budgeting is that lower managers who help prepare the budget are likely to support the final budget.

Practice 5-4

Master Budget
Which one of the following is *not* part of the master budget of a manufacturing firm?

a.   Depreciation budget
b.   Sales budget
c.   Production budget
d.   Direct labor budget
e.   Selling and administrative expense budget

Practice 5-5

Master Budget Information Flow
Place the following schedules in chronological order from start to finish in the master budgeting process.

a.   Cash budget
b.   Pro-forma income statement
c.   Production budget
d.   Sales budget
e.   Direct materials budget

Practice 5-6

Sales Budget
Is the following statement true or false?
   Since external variables (such as customer tastes and economic conditions) cannot be controlled by a company, those inputs are not used when computing a sales budget. Instead, the sales budget is generated using only historical sales data and internal cost information.

Practice 5-7

Production Budget
Using the following information, compute the number of units to be produced.

Desired ending inventory (in units)	3,600
Beginning inventory (in units)	3,400
Expected sales (in units)	24,150

Practice 5-8

Direct Materials Budget
Refer to the data in Practice 5-7. Using the following additional information, compute the cost of materials to be used in the coming period. (Assume no beginning nor ending direct materials inventory.)

Wood requirement per unit	10 board feet
Aluminum requirement per unit	7.5 square feet
Cost of wood (per board foot)	$4.60
Cost of aluminum (per square foot)	$5.75

Practice 5-9

Direct Labor Budget
Refer to the data in Practice 5-7. Using the following additional information, compute the direct labor cost.

Direct labor hours per unit	6
Rate per direct labor hour	$12

Practice 5-10

Manufacturing Overhead Budget
Using the following information, compute total manufacturing overhead.

Indirect labor rate	$4.00 per unit
Indirect materials rate	$2.50 per unit
Utilities rate	$1.25 per unit
Property tax expense	$29,000
Depreciation expense	$133,600
Insurance expense	$38,000
Supervisor salaries expense	$240,300
Expected production (in units)	21,000

Practice 5-11

Purchases Budget
Using the following information, compute the dollar amount of total purchases to be made in the coming period.

Beginning inventory (in units)	123
Expected sales (in units)	1,240
Desired ending inventory (in units)	128
Cost per unit	$685

Practice 5-12

Master Budget for Manufacturing Firms versus Service Firms
Which one of the following budgets do manufacturing firms and service firms have in common?

a. Direct labor budget
b. Supplies budget
c. Revenue budget
d. Production budget
e. Direct materials budget

Practice 5-13

Revenue Budget
The company performs tune-ups on standard diesel engines. Using the following information, compute the budgeted gross revenue for the period.

Gross revenue per tune-up	$180
Tune-up capacity per day	13
Number of working days in period	76
Historical occupancy rate*	65%

*This refers to the rate at which the companies' service bays are actually occupied compared to their total capacity. It is similar to the concept of hotel room occupancy rate.

Practice 5-14

Cash Budget
Using the following information, determine how much external funding will be necessary during the coming period (if any).

Collections from customers	$104,300
Minimum cash balance desired	25,000
Direct labor expense	24,350
Cash balance, beginning	32,000
Manufacturing overhead expense	22,750
Income tax expense	21,680
Selling and administrative expenses	54,140
Direct materials expense	43,200

Practice 5-15

Pro-Forma Financial Statements

Which one of the following statements regarding pro-forma financial statements is *false?*

a. Most companies do not create pro-forma financial statements because of the many assumptions required.
b. The pro-forma financial statements complete the master budget for a company.
c. Pro-forma financial statements help companies make decisions regarding dividends and management bonus opportunities for the coming year.
d. Pro-forma financial statements include an income statement, a balance sheet, and a statement of cash flows.

Practice 5-16

Flexible Budgets

Using the following manufacturing costs per unit, prepare a flexible budget for the company at levels of production of 550, 600, and 650 units.

Direct materials	$6.80
Direct labor	8.90
Manufacturing overhead	5.20

Practice 5-17

Flexible Budget Performance Report

Refer to the data in Practice 5-16. Using the flexible budget created in Practice 5-16 and the following actual data, prepare a flexible budget performance report.

Actual number of units produced	650
Actual direct materials costs	$4,200
Actual direct labor costs	$5,750
Actual manufacturing overhead costs	$3,430

 e xercises

Exercise 5-1

Spreadsheet

Personal Budgeting

Jennifer Swartz works as an interior decorator for Modern Fashion Corporation. Her annual salary is $36,500. Of that amount, 20% is withheld for federal income taxes, 7.15% for state taxes, 7.65% for FICA taxes, and 2% as a contribution to the United Way. Another 5% is deposited directly into a company credit union for savings. Jennifer has four monthly payments: $225 for her car, $80 for furniture, $410 for rent, and $100 to repay college loans. Jennifer's other monthly expenses are approximately:

Food expense	$250
Clothing expense	100
Entertainment expense	125
Utilities expense	80
Insurance expense	30
Gas and maintenance expenses on car	180
Miscellaneous expenses	200
Total	$965

(continued)

Prepare both a monthly budget and an annual budget for Jennifer that identifies gross salary, net take-home pay, net disposable income, and net surplus or deficit.

Exercise 5-2

Personal Budgeting

George Marcus, a recent college graduate, has been hired by Taylor Corporation at a salary of $54,000 per year. In anticipation of his salary, George purchased a $20,000 new ski boat and will pay for it at a rate of $425 per month, including interest, for five years. He also rented a condominium for $600 a month and bought a car on account for $350 a month. In addition, George figures that his other monthly expenses will be:

Food expense	$250
Clothing expense	125
Entertainment expense	250
Insurance expense	150
Gas and other car expenses	200
Utilities expense	130

1. On the assumption that George also pays income and FICA taxes of 25 and 7.65%, respectively, prepare his monthly budget.
2. George plans to save enough money for a down payment on a house. If a $20,000 down payment is needed, how long will it take him to save the needed amount? (For this exercise, ignore interest on savings, and assume that George does not have any savings at the present time.)

Exercise 5-3

Budgeting Sales Revenue and Collections

Frank's Frames mass produces and wholesales wooden picture frames at an average price of $7 per frame. Expected sales volumes over the first six months of 2006 are forecasted as follows.

January	7,900
February	8,500
March	8,200
April	9,000
May	8,800
June	8,000

Frank's Frames expects to collect 85% of its revenues in the month of the sale, with the remaining 15% collected in the following month.

1. Compute the expected balance in Accounts Receivable as of February 1, 2006. (*Hint:* It is based solely on sales in January 2006.)
2. Budget the expected monthly revenue and collections for the *five months* of February through June.

Exercise 5-4

Spreadsheet

Production Budgeting

Daytona Electric makes and sells two kinds of portable music players—a CD player and an MP3 player. The sales forecasts for these players for the next four quarters are as follows:

	CD Player	MP3 Player
First quarter	170	130
Second quarter	178	139
Third quarter	166	127
Fourth quarter	190	145
Totals	704	541

At the beginning of the first quarter, Daytona has 140 CD players and 120 MP3 players in stock. Experience has shown that Daytona must maintain an inventory equal to two-thirds of the next quarter's sales.

How many players of each type must be produced during each of the first three quarters to meet sales and inventory demands?

Exercise 5-5

Production Budgeting

James Seigel is the CEO of Seigel Monitor Company, a manufacturer of computer monitors. Seigel manufactures three types of flat panel LCD computer monitors: 15-inch, 17-inch, and 19-inch. The sales projections (in units) for 2006 and the first quarter of 2007 are:

	15-inch	17-inch	19-inch
First quarter, 2006	3,000	5,000	2,000
Second quarter, 2006	2,500	4,750	2,150
Third quarter, 2006	2,850	4,900	1,800
Fourth quarter, 2006	3,200	4,876	2,150
First quarter, 2007	2,900	5,100	2,200

Beginning inventory for 15-inch, 17-inch, and 19-inch monitors are 1,350, 1,500, and 1,275, respectively. Seigel requires that half of the next quarter's sales be maintained in inventory.

How many monitors must be manufactured for each quarter of 2006 to meet sales and inventory demand?

Exercise 5-6

Direct Materials Budgeting

Shaver Bicycle Shop assembles and sells tricycles and bicycles. The frames are purchased from one supplier and the wheels from another. The following materials are required:

Bicycles	Tricycles
One 22-inch frame, $35	One 12-inch frame, $15
Two 22-inch wheels, $10 each	Two 4-inch wheels, $10 each
	One 12-inch wheel, $7.50

Management anticipates that 150 bicycles and 160 tricycles will be assembled during the first quarter of 2006. On December 31, 2005, the following assembly parts are on hand:

22-inch frames	12
22-inch wheels	20
12-inch frames	8
4-inch wheels	24
12-inch wheels	10

Management also decides that, beginning in January, the inventory of parts on hand at the end of each month should be sufficient to make 10 bicycles and 10 tricycles.

Prepare a budget for direct materials purchases for the first quarter of 2006. (*Note:* You are not required to extend the budget to determine the budget for cash payments to suppliers.)

Exercise 5-7

Direct Materials Budgeting

Shanahan Corporation produces three types of videocassettes: VHS, S-VHS, and 8 millimeter. Shanahan purchases tape for the videocassettes from a firm in Mexico and purchases the cases from another supplier in Brazil. The following materials are required for production.

(continued)

	VHS	**S-VHS**	**8MM**
Tape	$1.75	$2.30	$3.05
Cases	2.50	2.50	2.00

Beginning inventory for Shanahan Corporation is 5,000, 7,000, and 3,500 tapes for VHS, S-VHS, and 8 MM, respectively. Management wants to have 5,000 VHS and 8 MM tapes and 2,500 S-VHS tapes in ending inventory. Projected sales for the first half of 2006 are 40,000 VHS tapes, 14,000 S-VHS tapes, and 21,000 8 MM tapes.

Shanahan's policy is to pay 80% of its accounts with suppliers by the end of each half year. The balance in accounts payable on January 1, 2006, is $55,000.

1. Prepare a budget for direct materials purchases for the first half of 2006.
2. Prepare a budget for payments to direct materials suppliers for the first half of 2006.

Exercise 5-8

Direct Labor Budgeting

Super Good Chocolate Company makes and sells two kinds of candy: chocolate peanut bars and caramel bars. The production budget for the next three months for each of the bars is as follows:

	Boxes of Chocolate Peanut Bars	**Boxes of Caramel Bars**
January	640	700
February	870	450
March	920	630

From experience, Super Good's management knows that it takes approximately 20 minutes to make a box of chocolate peanut bars and 30 minutes to make a box of caramel bars. Super Good pays its direct labor employees $8 per hour.

Prepare a direct labor budget for each of the two products in both hours and costs for January, February, and March.

Exercise 5-9

Direct Labor Budgeting

Sanford Shoe Company makes three shoe styles: loafers, work boots, and tennis shoes. The production budget for the next three months for each type of shoe is:

	Loafers	**Work Boots**	**Tennis Shoes**
January	2,900	5,400	3,160
February	3,100	6,000	5,400
March	2,750	6,600	4,300

From experience, Sanford's management knows that it takes 15 minutes of direct labor to make a pair of loafers, 20 minutes to make a pair of work boots, and 12 minutes to make a pair of tennis shoes. At Sanford, direct labor employees are paid $10 per hour.

Prepare a direct labor budget in both hours and costs for each of the three months.

Exercise 5-10

Production Overhead Cost Budget

Linden Nursery grows and sells potted perennial plants, as well as ornamental and fruit trees. The owner of Linden Nursery has determined that variable overhead costs are largely a function of direct labor hours spent growing and tending the plants and trees. Variable overhead costs include supervisory costs, indirect materials, and utilities (power and water) and are estimated to be $0.75, $0.40, and $0.55 per direct labor hour, respectively. Fixed overhead costs for property taxes, equipment depreciation, and night security are expected to be $1,500, $900, and $1,100, respectively, each quarter. Linden keeps a minimal staff during the winter season and then expands its workforce substantially during the gardening season. The direct labor hours budgeted for 2006 are as follows:

First quarter	1,000 hours
Second quarter	9,500
Third quarter	6,100
Fourth quarter	800

Prepare a production overhead budget for Linden Nursery.

Exercise 5-11

Budgeted Product Costs

Hard Hitting Bat Company makes two types of baseball bats: aluminum and wood. During the past several years, management has kept accurate records of costs and resource requirements and has determined that the following is needed to make the baseball bats:

Wood Bat	Production Requirements	Unit Cost
Wood	4 board feet	$ 5.50
Paint and protective finish	1 pint	8.50
Direct labor	3 hours	12.00
Manufacturing overhead	3 hours	6.75
Aluminum Bat		
Aluminum	6 pounds	$ 4.00
Paint and protective finish	1/2 pint	8.50
Direct labor	2 1/2 hours	12.00
Manufacturing overhead	2 1/2 hours	6.75

Compute the budgeted product costs for both the wood and aluminum baseball bats.

Exercise 5-12

Operational Budgeting (Service Company)

Dr. Dawn Gifford is a new dentist specializing in treating children under the age of 18. Dr. Gifford has two primary sources of revenues: (1) fees from regular dental work (checkups, cleanings, fillings, etc.) and (2) fees from specialized dental reconstructive surgery. Last year, Dr. Gifford earned an average of $75 per patient visit from regular customers and $800 per surgery. The following operating expenses were incurred last year in running the office:

Variable operating expenses:	
Dental supplies (per patient)	$ 10
Hospital surgery room rental (per surgery)	200
Annual fixed operating expenses:	
Office manager's salary	$18,000
Dental hygienist's salary	26,000
Utilities	3,600
Rental of office space	12,000
Depreciation expense on office equipment*	20,000
Liability insurance	48,000
Other expenses	9,600

*Total equipment cost, $200,000; depreciated over 10 years on a straight-line basis.

(continued)

Last year, Dr. Gifford treated an average of 200 patients per month and performed an average of eight surgeries per month. She expects to increase the number of patients serviced by 10% this coming year and the number of surgeries by two per month. She also expects the average patient fee to be $80 and the average surgical fee to be $850. Dr. Gifford expects the variable expenses to remain constant this year, but is expecting to raise the manager's salary by 5% and the hygienist's by 15%. She thinks the other expenses will stay about the same. All revenues are expected to be collected and all payable expenses are expected to be paid during the year.

Based on these data (and ignoring payroll and income taxes):

1. What was the operating profit (loss) for last year?
2. Prepare a revenue budget and an operating expense budget for this coming year.

Exercise 5-13

Cash Budgeting—Hospital

The management of West Valley Memorial Hospital needs to prepare a cash budget for July 2006. The following information is available:

a. The cash balance on July 1, 2006, is $236,000.
b. Actual services performed during May and June and projected services for July are:

	May	June	July
Cash services (bills paid by individuals as they leave the hospital)	$110,000	$ 90,000	$120,000
Credit services (bills paid by insurance companies and Medicare)	900,000	1,000,000	875,000

Credit sales are collected over a 2-month period, with 60% collected during the month the service is performed and 40% in the following month.

c. Hospital personnel plan to purchase $80,000 of supplies during July on account. Accounts payable are usually paid one-half in the month of purchase and one-half in the following month. The accounts payable balance on July 1, 2006, is $35,000.
d. Salaries and wages paid during July will be approximately $600,000. (Ignore income and other tax withholdings.)
e. Depreciation on the hospital and equipment for July will be $100,000.
f. A short-term bank loan of $80,000 (including interest) will be repaid in July.
g. All other cash expenses for July will total $56,000.

Prepare the hospital's July cash budget.

Exercise 5-14

Cash Budgeting

Medical Supplies, Inc., purchases first-aid items from large wholesalers. Medical Supplies then assembles and sells first-aid kits to businesses and contracts to maintain the first-aid kits. You have been asked to prepare a cash budget for January. The following information is provided:

a. Cash in the bank on January 1 is $33,000.
b. Actual sales for October, November, December, and projected sales for January are as follows:

	October	November	December	January
Cash	$12,000	$11,500	$ 8,200	$12,500
Credit	31,000	29,400	32,000	28,000

Payments on credit sales are received 50% in the month of sale, 31% in the month following the sale, and 15% and 4% in the second and third months, respectively, following the sale.

c. Total administrative and selling expenses (all cash) are $25,000.

d. Purchases are always paid 30 days after delivery. Purchases for October, November, and December were $28,000, $39,000, and $29,500, respectively.

e. Cash dividends of $22,000 are paid.

f. Any cash excess is used to purchase 30-day government securities, and any cash deficiency is compensated by short-term borrowing.

g. Management desires a minimum balance of $9,000 in the bank.

Prepare a cash budget for the month of January.

Exercise 5-15

*S*preadsheet

Cash Budgeting (Merchandising Company)

Whitlock, Inc., buys hardware parts from various manufacturers and sells them to retail stores. Management is currently trying to prepare a cash budget for August and has the following information available:

a. The cash balance on August 1 is $25,000.

b. Actual sales for June and July and projected sales for August are as follows:

	June	July	August
Cash sales	$ 30,000	$ 45,000	$ 50,000
Credit sales	100,000	120,000	130,000

Credit sales are collected 63% during the month of sale, 26% during the month following the sale, and 11% during the second month following the sale.

c. Whitlock's actual purchases for June and July and its projected purchases for August are as follows:

	June	July	August
Cash purchases	$10,000	$20,000	$25,000
Credit purchases	40,000	50,000	60,000

All accounts payable are paid in the month following the purchase.

d. Total administrative and selling expenses (including $14,000 depreciation) for August are expected to be $105,000.

e. Whitlock expects to pay a $26,000 dividend to stockholders and to purchase, for cash, a $25,000 piece of land during August.

f. Cash on hand should never drop below $25,000.

1. Prepare Whitlock's August cash budget, assuming that the company borrows any amounts needed to meet its minimum desired balance.

2. **Interpretive Question:** What types of expenses other than depreciation would be excluded from a cash budget?

Exercise 5-16

Pro-Forma Income Statement

Gold Manufacturing, Inc., is a manufacturer of electric pencil sharpeners. The following is information regarding Gold Manufacturing for the fiscal year-end, May 31, 2006:

Beginning finished goods inventory	$ 55,000
Ending finished goods inventory	42,000
Interest expense	28,000
Selling and administrative expenses	72,000
Sales revenue	425,000
Direct materials used	52,000
Direct labor	63,000
Manufacturing overhead	32,000

Assume a tax rate of 33%. Prepare a pro-forma income statement for the year ended May 31, 2006, for Gold Manufacturing, Inc. (Note that Gold Manufacturing does not have work-in-process inventory.)

Exercise 5-17

Pro-Forma Income Statement

Silver Company has asked you to prepare a pro-forma income statement for the coming year. The following information is available:

Expected sales revenue	$1,240,000
Manufacturing costs:	
Variable cost of goods sold	625,000
Fixed overhead	125,000
Selling expenses:	
Variable expenses	140,000
Fixed expenses	45,000
Administrative expenses:	
Variable expenses	45,000
Fixed expenses	160,000
Other:	
Interest expense	28,000
Income tax rate	35%

Prepare a pro-forma contribution margin income statement for Silver Company.

Exercise 5-18

Pro-Forma Statement of Cash Flows

The accountants at Karl's Fish Hatchery are currently preparing the pro-forma statement of cash flows for May. In getting ready to prepare the statement, they have the following information available:

Dividends to be paid in May	$ 1,500
Bonds to be issued in May	8,000
Equipment to be purchased in May	15,000
Repayment of short-term loans in May	3,000
Depreciation expense during May	2,500
Expected May net income	10,000
Expected changes in current assets and liabilities during May:	
Accounts receivable decrease	1,200
Accounts payable decrease	1,730
Increase in inventory	2,580
Increase in income taxes payable	2,550

Prepare Karl's pro-forma statement of cash flows (using the indirect method).

Exercise 5-19

Pro-Forma Income Statement and Balance Sheet (Service Industry)

Horrock's, Inc., is a small engineering corporation that surveys land for development. The company has grown rapidly over the past few years, and management has to decide whether to hire new engineers and open new offices. To assess future growth, the company's accountant has gathered budgeted information for the coming year, 2006:

Ending common stock balance	$ 48,000
Beginning retained earnings balance	34,000
Ending accounts payable balance	6,000
Ending equipment balance	159,000
Ending accumulated depreciation balance	24,000
Ending accounts receivable balance	19,500
Ending cash balance	18,000
Interest expense	3,000
Salary expense	105,000
Other expenses (including depreciation)	37,500
Service revenue	300,000
Income tax rate	33%

Income taxes due on the coming year's net income will be paid during 2007. Dividends of $70,000 are to be declared and paid during 2006.

1. Prepare a pro-forma income statement and balance sheet for 2006 from which the company president can make expansion decisions.
2. **Interpretive Question:** On the basis of this information, is the company very profitable? How should this level of profits affect its expansion plans?

Exercise 5-20

Static versus Flexible Budgeting—Performance Reports (Service Firm)

Flannery Muffler Shop has budgeted to repair 10,000 mufflers during 2006. Each repair job takes 1 1/2 hours, and employees are paid $12 per hour. During 2006, Flannery actually repaired 9,425 mufflers, and the salary expense amounted to $179,000.

1. Assuming a static budget, use the information to prepare a performance report for Flannery Muffler Shop for 2006.
2. Assuming a flexible budget, use the information to prepare a performance report for Flannery Muffler Shop for 2006.
3. **Interpretive Question:** The manager of the muffler shop believes he deserves a bonus because the actual wage expense ($179,000) was less than budgeted. Do you agree? Explain.

Exercise 5-21

Flexible Budgets (Service Firm)

Outdoors Unlimited operates a fishing lodge in northern Canada. The following cost information has been developed by the company's accountant:

Fixed costs:

Salaries	$68,000
Mortgage payments	24,000
Taxes	4,000
Other	3,000

Variable costs (per guest):

Fishing tackle	$20
Food	80
Other	16

(continued)

1. In planning for its 2006 summer season, Outdoors Unlimited does not know exactly how many guests to expect and, hence, how much to charge per guest. Prepare a flexible budget showing expected total costs at 200, 300, 400, and 500 guests.
2. Assume that Outdoors Unlimited conservatively estimates 300 guests for the year. If it wants to earn profits of $100,000 for the 300 guests, how much should it charge per guest?

problems

Problem 5-1

Personal Budgeting

Ben Fleming has just received a job offer of $35,000 salary per year plus overtime pay, which will amount to 10% of his salary. Ben estimates his living costs as follows:

Federal, state, and FICA taxes amount to	35% of income
Rent	$550/month
Car payment	$210/month
IRA	$1,500/year
Other savings	4% of net take-home pay
Utilities	$90/month
Gas and maintenance—automobile	$130/month
Insurance	$75/month
Food	$240/month
Entertainment	$170/month
Clothing	$80/month

Required:
1. Prepare a budget for the year. Assume Ben starts his job on January 1.
2. Is Ben's offer sufficient to meet his projected expenses?
3. Ben has always dreamed of going to Africa to photograph wildlife. The trip will cost $5,000. How long will it take Ben to save for the trip? (Ignore interest earnings, and assume that he has no savings at the present time.)

Problem 5-2

Personal Budgeting

Carol Baum is an advertising specialist for Success Advertising, Inc. Her annual salary is $37,500, of which 20% is withheld for federal income taxes, 7% for state income taxes, 7.65% for FICA taxes, and 5% for a tax-sheltered annuity. She estimates that her monthly expenses are approximately as follows:

Rent	$ 475
Automobile payment	250
Food	240
Automobile gasoline and maintenance	120
Utilities	70
Clothing	100
Entertainment	150
Miscellaneous	130
Total monthly expenses	$1,535

Required:
1. Prepare Carol's monthly budget, assuming that the car payments will continue for about three years.
2. Assume that Carol would like to accumulate savings of $12,000 in order to take an extended leave from her job. This will allow her to travel and take courses as a way of gener-

ating some fresh ideas she can use in creating new approaches to advertising. How long will it take her to save the needed amount? (Ignore interest earnings, and assume that she has no savings at the present time.)

3. **Interpretive Question:** If Carol asked you for advice on how she might reduce her expenses, what would you suggest?

Problem 5-3

Sales Revenue Budgeting (Service Firm)

Six-Peak Pools in Montana is open May through September. It has the capability of serving approximately 600 patrons each day. July is the peak month for Six-Peak Pools. With kids being in school, May and September are its slowest months. For the upcoming 2006 season, Six-Peak's management projects the following usage rates.

May	30%
June	80
July	90
August	75
September	20

The pool admission fees for Six-Peak are as follows.

Adults (12 years and up)	$5
Children (3 to 11 years)	$3
Babies (2 and under)	Free

On a typical day, 40% of the patrons are adults, 50% are children, and 10% are babies. Because Six-Peak only accepts cash and credit cards, its daily admission revenue and daily cash collections are the same.

Required:
Budget the expected monthly sales in admission fees for Six-Peak Pools.

Problem 5-4

Sales Collections

Rocky Peak Company plans on the following collection pattern on its sales:

Collected in month of sale	70%
Collected in the first month after sale	15
Collected in the second month after sale	10
Collected in the third month after sale	4
Uncollectible	1

Budgeted sales for the last six months of 2006 are shown below:

July	$ 60,000
August	70,000
September	80,000
October	90,000
November	100,000
December	85,000

Required:
1. What are the estimated total cash collections during October 2006?
2. How much of the third quarter sales (i.e., July, August, and September) are expected to be collected during the third quarter?
3. What is the expected 2006 ending balance in accounts receivable, net of allowance for doubtful accounts?

Problem 5-5

Production Budgeting

Nebo Company makes and sells two products: leather and vinyl briefcases. The sales forecasts for these briefcases for the next four quarters are as follows:

	Leather Briefcases	Vinyl Briefcases
First quarter	90	90
Second quarter	150	180
Third quarter	270	228
Fourth quarter	288	144
Total	798	642

On January 1, Nebo has a stock of 80 completed leather briefcases and 60 vinyl briefcases. Experience indicates that Nebo must maintain an inventory equal to one-half of the next quarter's sales.

Required:

1. How many leather and vinyl briefcases must be produced during each of the first three quarters to meet sales and inventory demands?
2. **Interpretive Question:** Assume Nebo is a wholesale merchandising company instead of a manufacturing company. How would the budget information provided in part (1) change?

Problem 5-6

Production and Direct Materials Budget

Chandler Manufacturing Company makes two products: widgets and gidgets. The following information is available on May 1:

a. Direct materials needed to make a widget: six units of X, three units of Y. Direct materials needed to make a gidget: two units of X, six units of Y.

b. Number of units available at beginning of May:

Direct material X	72 units
Direct material Y	43 units
Finished widgets	12
Finished gidgets	15

c. Expected sales during May:

Widgets	100
Gidgets	95

d. Desired levels of ending inventory:

Direct material X	70 units
Direct material Y	35 units
Widgets	11
Gidgets	13

e. Cost of direct materials:

Direct material X	$3 per unit
Direct material Y	$2 per unit

Chandler has a $1,300 balance in accounts payable on May 1 and expects to pay for half of its May purchases by the end of the month. All accounts are paid in full within 30 days.

Required:
Prepare a production budget and a direct materials budget for Chandler Company for the month of May.

Problem 5-7

Manufacturing Overhead Cost Budget

World-Wide Gym, Inc. makes weight lifting equipment. It designs and manufactures its own weight plates, as well as home gym sets such as workout towers, strength cages, and universal stations. Its variable manufacturing overhead (MOH) costs are determined as a result of either the pounds of weight plates or the number of gym sets manufactured. The variable MOH rates are as follows: $0.05 and $0.02 per pound of weight plates for materials handling and storage costs, respectively; and $45 and $12 per gym set for insurance and inspection work, respectively. The fixed MOH costs each month are $2,200 for property taxes, $3,200 for plant depreciation, $450 for utilities, and $17,000 for research and development.

The following monthly manufacturing volumes are expected for the second quarter of 2006:

	Pounds of Weight Plates	Number of Gym Sets
April	10,000	775
May	11,500	650
June	11,000	700
Total	32,500	2,125

Required:
Prepare a monthly manufacturing overhead budget for World-Wide Gym, Inc.

Problem 5-8

Budgeted Product Cost Sheet

Jersey Candy Company makes and sells two kinds of candy bars: chocolate almond and coconut. During the past several years, the company has kept accurate records of costs and resource requirements and has determined that the following are needed to make the candy bars:

One Box of 24 Chocolate Almond Bars	Cost
Chocolate (1½ pounds)	$3.00/pound
Almonds (1 pound)	$5.00/pound
Sugar (2 pounds)	$0.50/pound
Direct labor (20 minutes)	$9.00/hour
Manufacturing overhead (20 minutes)	$7.00/direct labor hour

One Box of 24 Coconut Bars	Cost
Chocolate (1 pound)	$3.00/pound
Coconut (1¼ pounds)	$2.00/pound
Sugar (1¾ pounds)	$0.50/pound
Direct labor (30 minutes)	$9.00/hour
Manufacturing overhead (30 minutes)	$7.00/direct labor hour

Required:
1. Establish the budgeted product cost sheet for each type of candy bar.
2. If management wants to mark up each box of candy 30% to cover other costs and earn a profit, how much should be charged for a box of each type of candy bar?

Problem 5-9

Unifying Concepts: Sales, Cash Collections, and Purchases Budgets
The following information is available for Laura Company, a wholesale company:

Expected sales volume:

October	6,400 units
November	6,000 units
December	7,000 units
Selling price per unit	$40
Accounts receivable balance, October 1	$50,000
Desired ending inventory, December 31	1,850 units
Beginning inventory, October 1	2,000 units

Additional information:

a. Each month 75% of sales is collected by month-end; the remaining 25% is collected in the following month.
b. The desired inventory every month is 30% of the next month's sales.

Required:
1. Prepare sales budgets for October, November, and December (in dollars).
2. Prepare cash collection budgets for October, November, and December (in dollars). Assume that all sales are on credit.
3. Prepare purchases budgets for October, November, and December (in units).

Problem 5-10

Spreadsheet

Unifying Concepts: Production, Direct Materials, Direct Labor, and Manufacturing Overhead Budgets; and Budgeted Product Cost Sheets
San Antonio Furniture Company makes two products: bookshelves and rocking chairs. The following information is available for September:

a. Production requirements:

	Bookshelves	**Rocking Chairs**
Materials needed:		
Wood	100 board feet at $0.90 per foot	90 board feet at $0.90 per foot
Stain	2 gallons at $9 per gallon	3 gallons at $9 per gallon
Bolts, nuts, etc.	1 dozen at $1.50 per dozen	1½ dozen at $1.50 per dozen
Direct labor	12 hours at $8.50 per hour	10 hours at $8.50 per hour
Variable manufacturing overhead	12 hours at $4 per direct labor hour	10 hours at $4 per direct labor hour
Fixed manufacturing overhead*	$1,521 per month	

*Fixed manufacturing overhead is assigned to products using direct labor hours.

b. Levels of inventories:

	Actual Beginning Inventory	**Desired Ending Inventory**
Wood	1,100 board feet	1,000 board feet
Stain	11 gallons	12 gallons
Bolts, nuts, etc.	15 dozen	9 dozen
Finished bookshelves	3	5
Finished rocking chairs	6	7

Required:
1. Prepare the production budget, assuming that the company expects to sell 40 bookshelves and 50 rocking chairs in September.
2. Based on the production budget and the desired ending inventory level, prepare the direct materials usage and purchases budget for September. (*Note:* Direct materials purchases are paid for at the time of the purchase.)
3. Based on the production budget, prepare the direct labor budget for September.
4. Based on the production budget, prepare the manufacturing overhead budget for September.
5. Based on the operating budgets prepared above, prepare the budgeted product cost sheets for bookshelves and rocking chairs for September.

Problem 5-11

Spreadsheet

Unifying Concepts: Sales, Cash Collections, Production, Direct Materials, and Direct Labor Budgets

The following information is available for Raleigh Company:

Expected sales volume:

April	1,600 units
May	1,500 units
June	1,750 units
Selling price per unit	$12
Accounts receivable balance, April 1	$6,000
Accounts payable balance, April 1	$796
Desired finished goods inventory, June 30	200 units
Beginning finished goods inventory, April 1	210 units
Direct materials needed per unit	5 pounds
Desired direct materials inventory, June 30	550 pounds
Beginning direct materials inventory, April 1	420 pounds
Total direct labor time per finished product	2 hours
Direct materials cost per pound	$0.50
Direct labor cost per hour	$8

Additional information:

a. Each month 70% of sales are collected by month-end; the remaining 30% are collected in the following month.
b. The desired finished goods inventory every month is 20% of the next month's sales.
c. The desired direct materials inventory every month is 10% of the next month's production needs.
d. Each month 80% of direct materials purchases are paid by month-end; the remaining 20% are paid in the following month.

Required:
1. Prepare sales budgets for April, May, and June (in dollars).
2. Prepare cash collection budgets for April, May, and June (in dollars). Assume that all sales are on credit.
3. Prepare production budgets for April, May, and June (in units).
4. Prepare direct materials budgets for April, May, and June (in dollars).
5. Prepare direct labor budgets for April, May, and June (in dollars).

Problem 5-12

Budgeting for a Service Company

Riverside Country Club has 435 members at the end of 2005 (including 25 new members who joined during the year). Each member has paid a $10,000 initiation fee and pays $100 a month in dues to remain an active member of the club (new members do not pay monthly dues during the first calendar year of their membership). The club offers golf, tennis, and food and beverage services. The club is essentially run on a cash basis. Operating data for 2005 are as follows:

(continued)

Riverside Country Club
Operating Data
For the Year 2005

Revenues:		
Dues[1]	$742,000	
Guest fees[2]	6,500	
Golf revenues	455,000	
Tennis revenues	145,000	
Food and beverage	325,000	
Miscellaneous	2,500	$ 1,676,000
Expenses:		
Golf course	$395,000	
Tennis courts	170,000	
Food and bar	272,000	
Administration and maintenance[3]	515,000	
Interest on debt[4]	50,000	
Miscellaneous	27,000	(1,429,000)
Net operating profit		$ 247,000

[1]Dues (410 × $1,200 = $492,000; 25 new members × $10,000 = $250,000).
[2]Guest fees (130 × $50 = $6,500).
[3]Maintenance includes $125,000 depreciation on facilities.
[4]Interest ($500,000 × 0.10 × 1 year).

Assume the following additional facts for the year 2006:

a. There are 435 members paying dues, as well as 10 additional new members.
b. Guest fees are 110% of 2005 fees.
c. Golf revenues are 125% of 2005 revenues.
d. Tennis revenues are 90% of 2005 revenues (due to courts being closed for one month).
e. Food and beverage revenues are the same as 2005.
f. Operating expenses (golf, tennis, and food and beverage) are up 5%.
g. Administration and maintenance will increase $40,000 due to expected repairs.
h. Principal payment of $50,000 during 2006 will reduce interest expense by 10% for 2006.
i. Miscellaneous revenues will stay the same; miscellaneous expenses are expected to be $25,000.

Required:
1. Prepare an annual budget for Riverside for the year 2006.
2. **Interpretive Question:** Is Riverside in better shape financially in 2006 as compared to 2005? What areas of concern do you see?

Problem 5-13

Cash Budgeting (Manufacturing Company)
Hare Manufacturing Company makes wax for automobiles. As part of overall planning, a cash budget is prepared quarterly each year. You have been asked to assist in preparing the cash budget for the fourth quarter of the company's fiscal year. The following information is available:

a. Sales:

Third quarter (actual)	$180,000
Fourth quarter (expected)	175,000

All sales are made on account, with 70% collected in the quarter in which the sales are made and 30% collected during the following quarter.

b. Materials purchases are scheduled as follows:

Third quarter (actual)	$90,000
Fourth quarter (expected)	80,000

Materials are purchased on account and paid for at the rate of 80% in the quarter of purchase and 20% in the following quarter.

c. Direct labor and manufacturing overhead costs (including $6,000 of depreciation) are expected to be $45,000 and $21,000, respectively, during the fourth quarter.

d. Selling and administrative expenses are expected to total $27,000 during the fourth quarter, including $2,000 of depreciation.

e. Plans have been made to purchase, for cash, $15,000 of equipment during the fourth quarter.

f. The cash balance at the beginning of the quarter is $16,000. The company can borrow money in $1,000 multiples at 12% interest from a local bank. The bank assesses interest for a full quarter, both for the quarter in which the money is borrowed and for the quarter in which it is repaid. All interest is paid at the time of note repayment. Hare ran short of cash during the third quarter and had to borrow $8,000 from the bank. Hare wishes to maintain a minimum cash balance of $16,000.

Required:
Prepare a schedule showing the cash budget and financing needs of Hare Manufacturing Company for the fourth quarter.

Problem 5-14

Cash Budgeting (Merchandising Company)

Jim Henry, owner of Henry's Retail, is negotiating a $100,000, 15%, four-month loan from the Garfield County Bank, effective October 1, 2006. The bank loan officer has requested that Henry's prepare a cash budget for each of the next four months as evidence of its ability to repay the loan. The following information is available as of September 30, 2006:

Cash on hand	$ 9,000
Accounts receivable	97,500
Inventory	64,000
Accounts payable	144,500

a. The accounts payable are for September merchandise purchases and operating expenses and will all be paid in October. Sales forecasts for the next few months are October, $220,000; November, $300,000; December, $400,000; January, $200,000; February, $140,000.

b. Collections on sales are usually made at the rate of 20% during the month of the sale, 60% during the month following the sale, and 15% during the second month after the sale. Five percent of accounts receivable are written off as uncollectible. Of the $97,500 of accounts receivable at September 30, $65,000 will be collected in October, and $32,500 will be collected in November. Cost of goods sold is 55% of sales, with all purchases paid for in the month following purchase. Ending inventory should always equal the cost of the goods that will be sold during the next month. Operating expenses are $18,000 a month plus 5% of sales, all paid in the month following their incurrence.

Required:
Prepare a cash budget showing receipts and disbursements for October, November, December, and January. Also prepare supporting schedules for cash collections, purchases, and operating expenses. Assume that the loan plus interest will be paid on January 31.

Problem 5-15

Cash Budgeting

Athlete World is a sporting goods store. The following data are for use in preparing its forecast of cash needs for June:

(continued)

a. Current assets (May 31):

Cash	$22,000
Inventory	17,500
Accounts receivable	29,400
Property, plant, and equipment	90,000
Accounts payable (merchandise purchases only)	13,100

Recent and estimated future sales:

May	49,000
June	57,000
July	52,000

b. Sales are made 60% on credit and 40% for cash. All credit sales are collected in the month following the sale.

c. Athlete World's June expenses are estimated to be:

Salaries and wages expense	20% of sales
Rent expense	4% of sales
All other cash expenses	6% of sales
Depreciation expense	$600
Gross margin	40% of sales

d. Athlete World buys all its inventory from companies on the West Coast and wants to maintain an inventory level equal to one-half of the next month's sales. Payments for merchandise are made 50% during the month of purchase and 50% in the next month.

e. Other cash expenditures planned for June are:
(1) The purchase of $8,000 of furniture.
(2) The payment of $5,000 of dividends.

f. Athlete World desires to maintain a minimum cash balance of $10,000. The store has an arrangement with a local bank whereby it can borrow money in multiples of $1,000. Interest is charged on all loans at an annual rate of 10% and is assessed for a full quarter both in the quarter in which the money is borrowed and in the quarter in which the money is repaid. Interest is paid when the loan is repaid.

Required:
Prepare Athlete World's cash budget for June.

Problem 5-16

Unifying Concepts: The Pro-Forma Income Statement, Balance Sheet, and Statement of Cash Flows

Pun Corporation makes construction cranes. During the past few days, the company's accountants have been preparing the master budget for 2006. To date, they have gathered the following projected data:

For the Year Ended December 31, 2006:

Sales revenue	$20,254,400
Variable selling expenses	896,000
Variable administrative expenses	1,344,000
Interest expense	134,400
Cost of goods sold (variable costs only)	11,200,000
Fixed manufacturing expenses	1,568,000
Fixed administrative expenses	984,000
Fixed selling expenses	672,000

Account Balances at December 31, 2006:

Cash	$ 896,000
Accounts receivable	336,000
Land	834,400
Buildings	1,008,000
Equipment	716,800
Accumulated depreciation—equipment	179,200
Accumulated depreciation—buildings	160,000
Direct materials inventory	212,800
Finished goods inventory	235,200
Accounts payable	90,480
Common stock	1,400,000
Retained earnings	?
Paid-in capital in excess of par	80,000
Income taxes payable	400,000

Other Information:

Dividends to be declared and paid during 2006	$1,303,680
Income tax rate	30%

In addition, last year's balance sheet was as follows:

Pun Corporation
Balance Sheet
December 31, 2005

Assets

Cash		$ 379,200
Accounts receivable		90,800
Direct materials inventory		180,000
Finished goods inventory		246,400
Land		672,000
Buildings	$ 896,000	
Less accumulated depreciation	(100,000)	796,000
Equipment	$ 649,600	
Less accumulated depreciation	(120,000)	529,600
Total assets		$2,894,000

Liabilities and Stockholders' Equity

Liabilities:

Accounts payable	$ 150,000	
Income taxes payable	450,000	
Total liabilities		$ 600,000

Stockholders' Equity:

Common stock	$1,400,000	
Paid-in capital in excess of par, common stock	80,000	
Retained earnings	814,000	
Total stockholders' equity		2,294,000
Total liabilities and stockholders' equity		$2,894,000

Required:

1. Prepare a pro-forma income statement for 2006 (contribution margin approach).
2. Prepare a pro-forma balance sheet as of December 31, 2006.
3. Prepare a pro-forma statement of cash flows for 2006 (indirect method).

Problem 5-17

Pro-Forma Income Statement and Balance Sheet

Style Right Company makes hair dryers. During the past few days, its accountants have been preparing the master budget for the coming year, 2006. To date, they have gathered the following projected data:

Sales revenue (at $20 per unit)	$281,750
Variable selling expenses	17,250
Variable administrative expenses	40,250
Interest expense (not included in selling and administrative expenses)	1,725
Cost of goods sold (includes only variable costs)	103,500
Ending cash balance	30,475
Ending accounts receivable balance	47,150
Ending land balance	24,150
Ending buildings balance	71,300
Ending equipment balance	24,150
Ending accumulated depreciation—buildings balance	47,150
Ending accumulated depreciation—equipment balance	9,200
Ending direct materials inventory balance	16,100
Ending finished goods inventory balance	25,300
Ending accounts payable balance	6,900
Ending common stock balance	32,200
Retained earnings balance, January 1	64,050
Balance in paid-in capital in excess of par account	23,000
Fixed selling expenses	23,000
Fixed administrative expenses	28,750
Fixed manufacturing overhead	11,150
Income tax rate	35%

Required:

1. Prepare a pro-forma income statement (contribution margin approach) and balance sheet for the coming year. Any income taxes owed on the coming year's net income will be paid the following year.
2. By approximately how much would Style Right's profits increase if another 3,000 units were produced and sold for $20 each?

Problem 5-18

Pro-Forma Statement of Cash Flows

The accountants at Toledo Department Store are preparing the pro-forma statement of cash flows for 2006. The following information is available:

Expected net income	$70,000
Dividends to be paid	22,000
Equipment to be purchased	34,000
Expected short-term borrowing	8,000
Expected long-term borrowing	24,000
Expected depreciation expense for 2006	15,000
Expected issuance of common stock	80,000
Expected purchase of a new plant	71,000

Expected changes in current assets and liabilities during 2006:

Increase in accounts receivable	$ 900
Increase in accounts payable	1,000
Increase in inventory	1,000
Decrease in income taxes payable	1,800

Required:

Prepare the pro-forma statement of cash flows for Toledo Department Store (indirect method).

Problem 5-19

Static versus Flexible Budgeting (Service Firm)

Wasatch Medical Clinic has three doctors on staff. The clinic's budget for 2006 is as follows:

Wasatch Medical Clinic
Budget for the Year Ended December 31, 2006

Expected number of patient visits		26,000
Average charge per patient		× $25
Total revenues		$650,000
Budgeted costs:		
Variable costs:		
Supplies for each patient ($2 × 26,000)		$ 52,000
Fixed costs:		
Utilities	$ 2,400	
Rent	9,600	
Nurses' salaries	90,000	
Malpractice insurance	150,000	
Equipment leases	25,000	
Other	30,000	
Total fixed costs		307,000
Total budgeted costs		$359,000
Expected income		$291,000
Number of doctors on staff		÷ 3
Expected income per doctor		$ 97,000

Required:

1. Is this a static or flexible budget?
2. Prepare a flexible budget showing expected income per doctor at 22,000, 26,000, 30,000, and 34,000 total patient visits.
3. **Interpretive Question:** Why does the expected income per doctor increase so dramatically as the number of patient visits increases?

Problem 5-20

Static versus Flexible Budgeting (Service Firm)

Peterson Management, Inc., is a small firm that sponsors time-management seminars in hotels throughout the country. It sponsors 20 two-day seminars during the year for a tuition fee of $200 per student. The following is a budget for a single seminar:

Peterson Management, Inc.
Budget per Seminar

Expected enrollment	40
Tuition per person	× $200
Revenue per seminar	$8,000
Variable costs:	
Catering ($25 per person)	$1,000
Books and handouts ($10 per person)	400
Fixed costs:	
Airfare	425
Hotel rental fee	600
Advertising	1,000
Other	300
Total costs	$3,725
Expected income	$4,275

(continued)

Required:

1. Bruce Peterson, owner of the company and the speaker at the seminars, would be pleased with an income of $4,275 per seminar. With 20 seminars per year, the company's annual income would be $85,500. He is concerned, however, that every seminar may not have 40 participants. Prepare a flexible budget, showing what annual income would be if 10, 20, 40, or 50 people enroll in each seminar.
2. What is the break-even point per seminar in number of participants?

d iscussion cases

Case 5-1

West Mountain Canning Company

West Mountain Canning Company produces several food items, including certain tomato-based products. For about nine months during the year, the company is able to purchase tomatoes from various parts of the country. The tomatoes are then processed and canned for sale in grocery stores.

The processing department employs three highly skilled workers, who are paid an average of $15 per hour. Between January and March, tomatoes are not available, and the processing and canning departments are shut down. Rather than lay off these three specialists, who have excellent alternative job opportunities, the company transfers them to the shipping department, at the same $15 pay rate. The shipping department manager is not happy, however, because his five regular employees are paid only $9 per hour. His unhappiness has become particularly acute since he was told he was $9,000 over budget for wages during the January-to-March quarter (budget was $36,000; actual was $45,000). Note that the actual amount includes 1,500 hours (3 employees × 500 hours) at $15 per hour, and that each employee works 2,000 hours in a year.

The shipping department manager feels that he is being unduly penalized for two reasons: (1) $15 is too much to pay even a good shipping clerk, and (2) the three skilled workers do not work as hard as his regular employees because they know they are needed for tomato processing and will not be fired. Therefore, he has suggested to his boss that the wages in excess of the $9 he normally pays be assigned elsewhere or that he be allowed to hire his own temporary employees (if needed) during this part of the year.

Answer the following questions:

1. Does the shipping department manager have a legitimate complaint? Explain.
2. Explain how management arrived at the budgeted figure of $36,000 for shipping wages.
3. How might the quarterly figures be reported to satisfy the shipping department manager?
4. How would you recommend that the problem be solved?

Case 5-2

Tip Top Company

Tip Top Company recently hired a new hot-shot CEO. Traditionally, the budgeting process at Tip Top has been pretty relaxed, with the executive vice president for sales providing "best-guess" sales projections and the controller providing "ballpark" cost estimates. Although the budget has been due each year 30 days prior to the new fiscal year, it generally is not finalized until two or three months into the new fiscal year. One of the first actions of the new CEO is to institute a formalized top-down budgeting process, complete with fairly sophisticated sales projections and cost data based on benchmark statistics from industry competitors.

Discuss the issues involved in the new budgeting process for Tip Top Company.

Case 5-3

New Age Budgeting

Manes.com is an Internet company that searches out job listings on corporate home pages, organizes them by type of job, and lists them so that individuals seeking jobs can see the kinds of jobs that are available. The Internet site is free to all users. Manes.com hopes that by providing a job-matching service, its site will attract substantial traffic, and advertisers will be willing to pay large sums of money to advertise. The company has a $20 million investment from a venture capitalist to get started but must provide budget projections to secure additional funding. Assume you are the controller for the company. How would you go about forecasting revenues and preparing budgets and profit projections to show potential investors?

Case 5-4

Disagreements over the Value of Budgets

Tueller Enterprises is a large manufacturer of airplane parts for commercial and military aircraft. In addition to making parts, it also serves as a distributor for other, smaller manufacturers. Traditionally, the company has spent large amounts of time preparing operational budgets, only to find that they are rarely useful and often outdated. Some managers have even argued that because they are evaluated on the basis of how well they meet the budget, they have been unable to react to changing markets and take advantage of new opportunities that have become available. The managers argue that the entire budgeting process is too constraining and should be scrapped. The new controller agrees that the traditional budgeting process has been flawed but argues that with the availability of new computer technology and up-to-date performance information, budgets can now be revised more frequently and will be much more useful than in the past. The company is trying to decide what to do. Should it scrap the entire budgeting process? Or, should it work to make the budgeting process more relevant and useful?

 j u d g m e n t   c a l l s

Judgment 5-1

You Decide: Is budgeting a necessary tool to help a fast-growing company plan and prepare for the future, or is budgeting too complicated and subjective for a growing company?

A budget is a good tool for a company to use to determine how it will secure the necessary finances to accomplish its business goals. However, a fast-growing company does not always know how its needs will grow or change over a short time frame. In addition, often a new company has no history to use in guiding budgets and, as a result, budgeting often involves substantial guesswork.

Judgment 5-2

You Decide: Should pro-forma financial statements be prepared in a manner consistent with **GAAP**, or do pro-forma statements provide enough useful information to investors in their current form?

Most financial statements prepared by companies and filed with the Securities and Exchange Commission are prepared using generally accepted accounting principles. However, pro-forma financial statements are often not prepared in accordance with these standards. Many of the numbers included by companies in these "pro-forma" statements are based on assumptions that are not recognized as appropriate for SEC filings. Sometimes, companies highlight positive information and leave out information about certain costs or charges, such as stock-based compensation, interest, and taxes. The real question is whether or not investors are being misled.

Competency **E**nhancement **O**pportunities

▶ **Analyzing Real Company Information**   ▶ **The Debate**
▶ **International Case**   ▶ **Internet Search**
▶ **Ethics Case**
▶ **Writing Assignment**

The following additional assignments provide opportunities for students to develop critical thinking, ethical perspectives, oral and written communication skills, experience with electronic research, and teamwork through group and business activities.

▶ *Analyzing Real Company Information*

Analyzing 5-1 (Microsoft)

Auditors are extremely reluctant to publish any projections of future financial performance for the companies they are auditing. DELOITTE & TOUCHE LLP obviously has made no such predictions in its audit of MICROSOFT's 2002 financial performance (see the Form 10-K in Appendix A). However, the Management's Discussion and Analysis of Results of Operations and Financial Condition, in the section titled "Issues and Uncertainties," provide some hints about what executives may expect to affect future revenues. Elsewhere in the management discussion are insights useful in predicting future operating expenses, interest income, and income taxes. These discussions can be extremely useful to investors who are trying to understand what Microsoft plans to do in 2003. Essentially, these investors need to put together their own pro-forma financial statements on Microsoft for use in planning, controlling, and evaluating their investment decisions in this company.

Consider the 2002 income statement below and use the information provided in Microsoft's Management Discussion of "Issues and Uncertainties," as well as any other comments in the management's discussion that you might find useful, to prepare your own pro-forma 2003 income statement for Microsoft. Be sure to read and consider each item in the management discussion relating to Microsoft's income statement in the Form 10-K in Appendix A. You may also want to consider the 2000 and 2001 revenue and cost trends from the income statement published in this same Form 10-K. For each line item (i.e., for each revenue and cost category), briefly defend the budget number you chose to use.

	2002
Revenue	$28,365
Operating expenses:	
Cost of revenue	$ 5,191
Research and development	4,307
Sales and marketing	5,407
General and administrative	1,550
Total operating expenses	$16,455
Operating income	$11,910
Losses on equity investees	(92)
Investment income	(305)
Income before income taxes	$11,513
Provision for income taxes	3,684
Net income	$ 7,829

Analyzing 5-2 (Participative Living, Inc.)

Participative Living, Inc. (a fictitious name) is an actual charitable organization in a medium-size community in Canada. It was organized by parents of disabled adults to provide accommodation and training for severely disabled adults in the community. With the help of the Ministry of Community and Social Services, the parents eventually organized six different homes, each with two to four residents. In addition to the six homes, Participative Living also had an employment and education program that provided training and assistance for residents seeking employment or educational opportunities. Overall, the organization had eight divisions composed of six homes, the employment and education program, and an administrative program. A supervisor who reports to the Participative Living executive team staffs each division. The executive team, in turn, reports to a volunteer board of directors composed of 12 people from the community.

Participative Living is a not-for-profit organization. Hence, while surpluses and deficits are occasionally expected, each division is expected to break even each operating period. Seven of the eight divisions are established as break-even operations, with responsibility for both revenues and expenses. The main revenue source is the Ontario government, through the Ministry of Community and Social Services, which provides all funding necessary to support each home as well as the employment and education program. All costs of Participative Living's administrative division in excess of any donations from the community are allocated to its other seven divisions. The Ministry follows a procedure of disbursing operating funds for all social service agencies under its direction based on annual operating budgets submitted to the Ministry. Generally, the Ministry is not concerned about whether an individual budget item was overspent as long as the overall spending is within the approved budget. As a result, it became a common practice among agencies to transfer expenses from one budget line to another and, in the case of Participative Living, to transfer expenses from one division to another depending on which division had excess budgeted funds. As with most government organizations, the Ministry's administrative process of reviewing and approving a new home for Participative Living is often quite slow. As long as the Ministry is holding up the establishment of a proposed new home, it provides significant interest payments to Participative Living. The Ministry was making large interest payments during the first few months of Participative Living's 2000 fiscal year (which ended on March 31, 2000) while the organization waited for government approval and funding of the sixth group home.

In November 1999, Mr. Brad Dunford, the executive director of Participative Living, Inc., was reviewing the financial statements for the first seven months of the 2000 fiscal year. He was puzzled about how the agency could suddenly be $50,000 over budget in salaries and benefits when just last month the statements indicated that spending was slightly under budget.

1. As you review operating results for the last seven months at Participative Living, Inc., what problems do you foresee?
2. Consider the style of management and management accounting for this not-for-profit organization, as well as its relationship with the Ministry of Community and Social Services. What aspects of the way business is conducted here do you think have led to the current situation?

(continued)

Participative Living, Inc.
Operating Results
For the Seven Months Ended October 31, 1999

YTD	Admin. Costs	Admin. Budget	Employ. and Edu. Costs	Employ. and Edu. Budget	Group Homes Costs	Group Homes Budget	Total Actual	Total Budget*	% of Budget
Revenues:									
Ministry**	$ —	$ —	$206,315	$297,675	$521,841	$476,714	$728,156	$774,389	94.0%
Interest	20,943	—	—	—	—	—	20,943	—	0%
Donations	1,567	—	—	—	—	—	1,567	—	0%
Total revenues	$ 22,510	$ —	$206,315	$297,675	$521,841	$476,714	$750,666	$774,389	96.9%
Expenses:									
Salaries	$ 59,029	$ 61,754	$141,034	$197,386	$434,014	$327,789	$634,077	$586,929	108.0%
Occupancy costs	10,392	12,264	39	2,205	61,598	68,761	72,029	83,230	86.5%
Services, supplies, and food	4,375	7,000	3,643	14,147	16,812	35,301	24,830	56,448	44.0%
Personal needs	—	—	3,077	—	35	26,327	3,112	26,327	11.8%
New furnishing and equip.	5	350	60	2,765	6,548	19,236	6,613	22,351	29.6%
Other expenses	1,176	4,669	197	7,707	15,681	7,868	17,054	20,244	84.2%
Travel and training	436	875	1,972	8,792	1,992	4,900	4,400	14,567	30.2%
Specific reimbursements	—	—	—	—	(32,119)	(35,707)	(32,119)	(35,707)	90.0%
Allocated admin. costs	(75,417)	(86,912)	56,293	64,673	19,123	22,239	(1)	—	0.0%
Total expenses	$ (4)	$ —	$206,315	$297,675	$523,684	$476,714	$729,995	$774,389	94.3%
Net surplus (deficit)	$ 22,514	$ —	$ —	$ —	$ (1,843)	$ —	$ 20,671	$ —	N/A

*Budget columns represent the total annual budget. Note that Participative Living is now seven months into its fiscal year.
**Ministry revenues are based on actual payments made by the Ministry. Total payments limited to maximum of total annual budget approved.

Source: Adapted from M. Heisz, "Participative Living, Inc.," *Journal of Accounting Case Research* 2(3), 1995, pp. 87–91. Permission to use has been granted by Captus Press, Inc. and the Accounting Education Resource Centre of The University of Lethbridge. [Journal Subscription: Captus Press Inc., York University Campus, 4700 Keele Street, North York, Ontario, M3J1P3, by calling (416) 736-5537, or by fax at (416) 736-5793, E-mail: info@captus.com, Internet: **http://www.captus.com**]

▶ *International Case*

International

It's Not Easy Being an Accountant in Poland

The late 1980s and early 1990s were a very significant time for Eastern Europe. Several national boundaries and political ideologies, as well as the names of a few countries, changed during this period. Poland, like its neighbors, experienced tremendous upheaval in its political and economic climate during this time. In 1989, Poland changed to a non-Communist government and a free market economy. Since the end of World War II in 1945, Poland had been a centrally planned economy with government-enforced economic rules based on Marxism-Leninism. A Polish accountant's professional life during the 1945–1989 period was not very exciting. Most university-trained accountants worked in a state-owned enterprise, earning a reasonable salary. The work was not complicated, generally entailing only basic bookkeeping. Performing the accounting work essentially required simple mathematical operations. In addition, the nature of Poland's history since the fifteenth century had generally created disdain for business and profiteering in general. These traditions, coupled with the social environment engendered by a Marxist government, resulted in a serious lack of respect (sometimes bordering on distrust) for accountants, economists, and business managers from 1945 to 1989.

The failure of the Communist system in 1989 was the beginning of a new career stage for most accountants in Poland. The accounting profession suddenly became prestigious. It also became very challenging. Past accounting knowledge and skills were simply inadequate for the new economic situation, particularly for accountants moving out of state-owned enterprises and into the private sector. Business terminology, performance measures, and goals changed. Before 1989, the Communist regime promoted a view that everything a "capitalist" did was wrong and everything a Communist did was right. After the change in the political system, a lot of people began to see things in an opposite way; they expected that life in a capitalist country would be completely just and everyone would be employed with plenty of money. Obviously, life in a capitalist country is not perfect. There are problems, including injustice and unemployment. Complicating this reality, many people also carried over into the 1990s some of the prevailing pre-1989 attitudes that accountants and for-profit businesses were not trustworthy. Today Poland is making steady progress, but the accounting profession continues to face a number of challenges as attitudes and business processes are still in transition.

Assume that you have just been transferred by your U.S.-based company to an accounting or management position in the company's Poland division. Your assignment is to implement a traditional budgeting system (similar to the budget systems described in this chapter) in a large-scale manufacturing plant. Based on your understanding of Polish history and attitudes, what specific challenges would you expect to encounter in this new assignment? Do you have any ideas on how to handle these challenges?

Source: Adapted from P. Stec, "Mr. Kowalski: A Man Against All Odds," *The Journal of Accounting Case Research* 2(3), 1995, pp. 52–54. Permission to use has been granted by Captus Press, Inc. and the Accounting Education Resource Centre of The University of Lethbridge. [Journal Subscription: Captus Press Inc., York University Campus, 4700 Keele Street, North York, Ontario, M3J 1P3, by calling (416) 736-5537, or by fax at (416) 736-5793, E-mail: info@captus.com, Internet: **http://www.captus.com**]

▶ *Ethics Case*

Skipper Enterprises

You are the management accountant for Skipper Enterprises, a manufacturer of screen doors. Recently, one of the commissioned salespersons (your close personal friend) confided in you that a problem with the budgets is hurting the company's profitability.

Your friend explained that salespersons are paid a straight commission of $15 for every screen door they sell. If a salesperson meets the budgeted sales of 3,000 screen doors per year, he or she is paid an annual bonus of $5,000. Your friend stated that it is actually quite easy to reach budgeted sales of 3,000 doors by October or early November. Because there is no financial incentive to sell additional doors once the 3,000 sales level is met and the $5,000 bonus is earned, salespersons only "line up" sales for next year during the last couple of months of each year. In other words, instead of selling additional doors during November and December, they commit customers to buy during January of next year. This way, the doors count as next year's sales, ensuring that the commissioned salespersons are well on their way to meeting the sales budget for next year.

You realize the current bonus plan is causing two problems. First, valuable sales are being deferred each year because there is less incentive to sell near the end of the year. Second, customers are receiving less than optimum service because it can take as long as two months for customers to get their desired doors.

You don't know what to do with your new information.

1. Should you inform management that the sales plan is hurting company profits, or should you keep the information confidential as your friend requested?

(continued)

2. If it becomes known that you had this information and didn't come forward, you could lose your job. On the other hand, you hate to lose a good friend. What should you do?

▶ *Writing Assignment*

Preparing a Personal Budget

Most people have the ability to spend more than they make. As a student, you probably fit in that category. This writing assignment requires you to prepare a personal budget for a one-month period. Forecast your income and expenses to determine what your cash position will be at the end of the month. If you forecast a cash shortage, what actions can you take to address the problem (e.g., increase income, reduce expenses, borrow money, etc.)? If you forecast a cash surplus, what are your options for the surplus?

▶ *The Debate*

The Hatchet Has Arrived!

Assume that your local hospital has just hired a new COO (chief operating officer). Everyone in the hospital understands that the new COO was essentially hired to save the hospital. During the last five years, cost overruns have created tremendous spending deficits in the organization. The hospital is clearly headed for insolvency within three to five years if something isn't done. The new COO has a reputation as a focused manager, who is able to make difficult decisions. She doesn't waste any time proving her reputation in the new job. At the first meeting with the chief medical staff and administrators, the COO rolls out the new budget goals with the following statement:

> Everyone here knows that this hospital is in serious financial trouble, and it's not hard to understand why. After carefully reviewing cost reports for the last several years, it's obvious that there has been very little discipline in controlling costs. There are no improvement goals for cost savings, and no one is required to take responsibility when cost overruns occur. Looking at next quarter's operating budget doesn't give me much hope for improvement in this mess. Well, folks, that party is over! It's time to get to work saving this hospital. We will reconvene in one week; I expect each department head to provide a new departmental operating budget that demonstrates a reduction in costs that is equal to 5% of department revenues. Thereafter, until we turn this situation around, each new quarterly budget will reflect an additional decrease in operating costs equal to 2% of department revenues. Any questions?

There were no questions. Everyone filed out of the meeting in shocked silence. Five percent of revenues is a big number!

Divide your group into two teams and prepare a two-minute defense of your team's assigned position.

- One team represents "Support the COO!" A difficult situation requires a tough response. Defend the COO's new budget proposal. What should be the positive results in the hospital if the COO's budget instructions are fully implemented?
- The other team represents "Out with the new budget proposal!" Overreacting to a difficult situation only worsens the problem. Criticize the COO's new budget proposal. What could be the negative results in the hospital if the COO's budget instructions are fully implemented?

▶ *Internet Search*

Using the Internet to Budget Personal Finances

There are a number of terrific tools on the Internet that can be very useful to you in managing your finances. For one example, go to **http://www.financenter.com**. Sometimes Web addresses change, so if this address does not work, access the Web site for this textbook (**http://swain .swlearning.com**) for an updated link. Once there, select the "Consumer Tools" tab, and then select "Calculators" from the drop down menu. Finally, scroll down to the Budget area and select "How much am I spending?" You will see here that you can enter your current income and expenditures, as well as your desired expenditures.

1. Complete the information on the input form, and then hit the "get your results" button. You should now learn whether your income is sufficient to handle your expenditures (actually, you probably already knew the answer to this question). You'll also learn about the importance of creating some excess in your budget to save for the future. Print out your budget.

2. Now go back to the input form and change the numbers in order to assess what might need to change in your future personal "operations." Put together a realistic budget. Try to create a little "extra" that can be used for investment. Note how the difference affects your long-term savings. When you're satisfied, print out your new budget.

3. Now that you have a better understanding of your cash budget, work through FinanCenter's budget calculators to identify and answer another important personal finance and budgeting question for yourself. Go back to the Calculators page and select an additional budgeting function to perform. When completed, list two important insights you learned about your personal budgeting process.

Part

3

Control

chapter

6

Monitoring Performance in Cost, Profit, and Investment Centers

Before Randy Curran was appointed CEO, ICG COMMUNICATIONS was losing $34 million a month. That was in September 2000. On November 14, 2000, ICG filed for Chapter 11 bankruptcy. Chapter 11 is a plan that allows the company some time to try to work out its financial matters. Many companies never successfully emerge from Chapter 11 bankruptcy. ICG, on the other hand, is currently a prosperous company. ICG's story is about how a company gone awry can be saved through fiscal responsibility and customer focus.[1]

ICG's intial strategy was to provide the systems—networks of switches, modem banks, and fiber-optic cable—that linked people at home via their local telephone company with the high-speed fiber-optic lines that carry Internet traffic. If the Internet is a superhighway, ICG would build the entry ramps that carried traffic from the local roads—i.e., local telephone lines—onto the Internet superhighway. Because more and more people wanted to get onto the Internet, the demand for the ramps was practically unlimited in the heyday of the Internet explosion in the late 1990s. Although its intent was to dominate the ramp business, ICG became the poster child for the failed "build it and they will come" business model. However, today the company's local network presence spans more than 30 metropolitan areas including Denver, Cleveland, Dallas, Los Angeles, San Francisco, Seattle, Atlanta, New York, Boston, and Washington, D.C. Randy Curran, as the current CEO, is largely responsible for this tremendous recovery.

Curran is a stark contrast to previous CEO J. Shelby Bryan. Until Bryan left his position with ICG in 2000, he seemed to be obsessed with the spotlight, not just in trade and business publications, but in the society pages as well. Although ICG is headquartered in Colorado, Bryan lived in Manhattan where he held fund-raising parties for President Clinton and Vice President Al Gore. This fact alone raised serious concerns with ICG's investors; in fact, it led one major investor to nix an earlier investment in 1999 due in part to worry that Bryan was not keeping a close eye on the company. During this time, ICG quickly burned through $2 billion raised through Wall Street investors. While some of the money was used to build Internet ramps, part of it was used to build ICG's striking new headquarters, a tower that the architect described as "the curve of a ship's prow looking toward the mountains." One staffer remarked, "when we show people the building, it becomes clear to them why we went bankrupt."

Randy Curran faced a difficult task in carefully controlling a turnaround of ICG's financial position. He also needed to restore ICG's image. Curran said, "The relationships with our customers were . . . awful. When you do these turnarounds, you have to have strengths that you can build off of. When you turn [a company] around, you strip it back to its core and then you go from there." Curran believes strongly that ICG's core strength is its $4 billion dollar Internet ramp system, but ICG also has employees with tremendous technical capabilities. Curran stated at the time he took over the company, "Our staff is young and energetic, so the talent here is fabulous. [And] even though the customer relationships are bad, they are still great customers." ICG's customer list has included such giants as MICROSOFT, ORACLE, NETZERO, EARTHLINK, and some of the nation's major universities.

When Curran looked at a high level view of the company, he found numerous problems that needed his immediate attention. He realized that a poor-performing network would kill the business, regardless of the reported value of the network assets. He identified a large number of unprofitable markets, products and services, and customers. The reorganization involved turning $2.5 billion of debt on the balance sheet into $200 million of equity.

ICG emerged from Chapter 11 protection on October 10, 2002, and is alive and well today, although its employee head count has dropped from 3,000 to 1,000. With the conclusion of its bankruptcy plan, ICG distributed about 8 million new shares of common stock to certain creditors to pay down some debt. Upon its emergence, ICG had $205 million in short- and long-term debt and $94 million in cash. If ICG continues to thrive, its management model might serve as an outline for other tech companies on how to control and grow a successful business in the post-Internet bubble era.

1 Paul M. Sherer and Gary McWilliams, "How a Brash Provider of Internet Services Became Unplugged," *The Wall Street Journal*, November 13, 2000, p. A1; Paul M. Sherer, "ICG Files for Protection from Creditors," *The Wall Street Journal*, November 15, 2000, p. A1; John Sullivan and Tom Cross, "A New Day at ICG," *Boardwatch Magazine*, April 2002, Vol. 16, Issue 4, pp. 42–44; "ICG out of Bankruptcy," *Denver Business Journal*, October 10, 2002, **http://denver.bizjournals.com**, accessed September 5, 2003; Client Interview with ICG, **http://www.gapinter.com/ClientProfiles**, accessed September 5, 2003.

Setting the Stage

i n the previous chapter, we created the master budget, which is a major planning tool for management. In this chapter, we will examine how managers and executives create and maintain an effective system of control within their organizations. Traditional control systems are initially based on using the standard cost and revenue data created in the master budget. These data are used to assess business processes throughout the year in order to identify performance in various organizational units that require management attention.

In the process of establishing effective management control within an organization, it is critical to clearly define each division's and each person's specific responsibility within the organization. Since it is often difficult to separate the performance of a unit from the performance of its managers, managers are most often evaluated on how well their units perform. If managers are responsible for costs only, they are usually evaluated on how well they control costs. If they are responsible for revenues and costs, they are usually evaluated on the profitability of their units. And, if they are responsible for costs, revenues, and investments, managers are most frequently evaluated on the return their division investments generate. In the case of ICG, past CEO J. Shelby Bryan was responsible for costs, revenues, and investments. Since the company initially lost large sums of money, one may fairly question the effectiveness of cost, revenue, and asset controls at ICG prior to 2000. On the other hand, ICG's turnaround since 2000 is largely attributable to new CEO Randy Curran's fiscal responsibility and his efforts to bring ICG's operations into control.

Management Control of Personnel and Divisions

I Explain why control is such an important activity in the management process.

Today, we live in a new and different economy. At least three major developments have dramatically changed the environment in which businesses operate. First, new technology has made information inexpensive. Low-cost, high-speed digital and cable video and data transmission hardware produces information quickly and easily, and the constant churn of new software makes preparation, data, and communication tools available to individuals who previously did not have access to needed information. As technology continues to develop, constraints on acquiring the information you will want in your business career will continue to be reduced, or even be eliminated.

A second major development that has significantly affected business has been globalization. Faster methods of transportation, together with nearly instantaneous information, have allowed the world to become one giant marketplace. Consumers can now buy products from foreign firms as easily as from a local store. Organizations such as GENERAL MOTORS have to worry not only about what CHRYSLER and FORD are doing, but also about what TOYOTA, VOLKSWAGEN, and BMW are doing as well. In fact, Chrysler is not just "Chrysler" anymore. It is now a conglomeration of European, North American, and Asian manufacturers known as DAIMLERCHRYSLER. Instead of having only two major American competitors, General Motors and all other business organizations now have to compete with similar companies throughout the world. In addition, with the increased availability of inexpensive information, more is known about these competitors and about General Motors than ever before. If a GM product has deficiencies, for example, the world knows about and can act on those problems instantly. If GM or one of its units is not performing well, investors will be reluctant to invest money and GM's management may direct its resources to other operating units.

A third major change is the concentration of power in certain market investors, primarily large mutual and pension funds. Mutual funds such as FIDELITY and VANGUARD and pension funds such as CALPERS and TIAA-CREF, for example, now hold major stock positions in many companies. The influence of these major market players is so significant that if they are displeased, corporate executives will find that their positions within the company are in jeopardy. Armed with easily available and inexpensive information about investees and their competitors, large institutional investors raise the competitive bar very high and shorten the periods over which success is measured. The influence of these institutional investors, combined with the power of readily-accessible information and the intensity of global competition, means that only organizations that are truly the best will be able to survive and remain successful.

A number of business developments have occurred because of these changes. Some of the most obvious are:

- An increased pace of change in the business world
- Shorter product life cycles and shorter competitive advantages
- Demand for better, quicker, and more decisive actions by management
- The emergence of new companies, new industries, and new professional services
- Outsourcing of many company processes to specialty organizations
- Increased uncertainty that requires careful and explicit management of risk
- Increasingly complex business transactions
- Increased focus on customer service and satisfaction

To be able to react to fast-paced business changes, managers and investors must have good control of and/or good insight on business units and their managements. They must know as early as possible whether a unit's profit or market share is decreasing. They must be able to assess trends and changes in performance quickly. They must know when new competitors are getting stronger and encroaching on the business's success. They must know when supervisors and staff are performing in ways that are resulting in the organization losing ground to competitors. Only if they have accurate information about how well personnel and various organizational units are performing can managers effectively plan, control, and evaluate personnel, processes, and resources. As we have stated previously, good planning leads to good control, which leads to good evaluation. If management does not carefully plan for and control the operations in their organization, then they cannot accurately evaluate how they are doing, what needs to be improved, and where resources must be placed and withdrawn. As a result, their organizations will most likely be unsuccessful in the future. The result of faster-paced changes in today's economy must be better planning and control of fast-paced organizations. We described the planning process in the two previous chapters on capital budgeting and operational budgeting. This chapter focuses on traditional methods of establishing an effective system of management control.

> **TO SUMMARIZE:** The business world is changing faster than ever before. These fast-paced changes require that decision makers (managers and investors) have better information and perform more timely evaluations of organizational units and the individuals responsible for the organizations. Good evaluation leads to better planning and control decisions and the better allocation of resources.

Control of Divisions and Personnel in Different Types of Operating Units

2 Describe the responsibility accounting concept and identify the three types of organizational control units.

segments Parts of an organization requiring separate reports for evaluation by management.

Most companies are made up of a number of relatively independent **segments** or subunits, sometimes called groups, divisions, or subsidiaries. As an example, Exhibit 1 shows an organizational chart for a hypothetical company that we will call International Manufacturing Corporation (IMC). IMC has three operating (subsidiary) companies: Acme Computer, Edison Automobile, and Jennifer Cosmetics. Although each of these companies has several divisions and other subsegments, only a few of those for Edison Automobile are shown. Edison has three geographic bases: the United States, the Far East, and Europe. The making and selling of automobiles in the Far East division is further broken down into the Japanese and Korean units.

Exhibit 1: An Organizational Chart

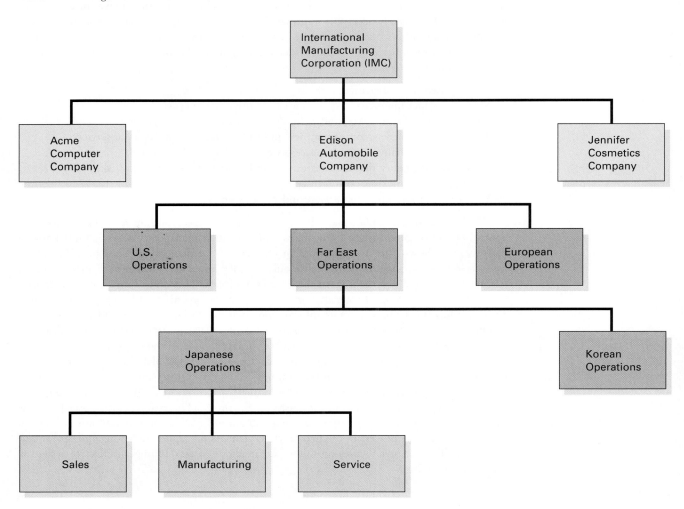

The Japanese unit is separated into its sales, manufacturing, and service functions. Edison Automobile's other geographic divisions have similar subsegments.

You will notice that IMC uses different criteria to define its segments at each level. At the highest level, product group (computers, autos, cosmetics) is used, probably because there is a significant difference in the business knowledge needed to produce and sell these products. At the middle level, segments are defined geographically because of the unique needs of each market and the distances involved. At the lowest level, each country unit is subdivided by function—sales, manufacturing, and service.

Given the organizational chart in Exhibit 1, how much autonomy should the executives of each division be granted by corporate management? If each company (Acme, Edison, and Jennifer) has its own president, vice presidents, and other officers, should these executives be allowed to operate independently of one another? If Acme, for example, is the most profitable company, should it be given more operating capital than Edison and Jennifer, or less? Should a decision for Acme to expand into hand-held computers be made by Acme's executives or by IMC's corporate officers? Within Edison Automobile, how much autonomy should each of the geographic offices have? Should a decision to double the advertising budget or offer consumer rebates in the Far East operations be made by the manager of that division, by the president of Edison Automobile, or by the CEO of IMC?

decentralized company An organization in which managers at all levels have the authority to make decisions concerning the operations for which they are responsible.

Questions such as these are difficult to answer. In fact, it would probably be difficult to find two companies that would answer them the same way. Assuming that IMC is basically a **decentralized company**, managers at all levels will have the authority to make decisions concerning the operations for which they are directly responsible. Regarding the question of rebates in the Far East, for example, the operating manager of that geographic division should probably decide whether to offer them. Likewise, the manager of the Japanese Manufacturing division should decide where to buy engine parts, and the manager of the Service division should have primary responsibility for setting the price to charge for repairing a muffler in Japan. These managers would also be held responsible for the consequences of their decisions.

business environment (READ)

Berkshire Hathaway As an example of how businesses are divided into segments, consider BERKSHIRE HATHAWAY, INC., which is primarily owned by Warren E. Buffett, one of the richest individuals in the United States. In a 2002 SEC filing, Berkshire stated that its most important business is the property and casualty insurance business, which includes GEICO, the sixth largest auto insurer in the United States, GENERAL RE, one of the four largest reinsurers in the world, and the BERKSHIRE HATHAWAY REINSURANCE GROUP. In addition, it identified several other types of businesses, including the publication of a daily and Sunday newspaper in western New York (BUFFALO NEWS); the manufacture and sale of boxed chocolates and other confectionery products (SEE'S CANDIES); diversified manufacturing and distribution; the retail sale of home furnishings (NEBRASKA FURNITURE MART, R.C. WILLEY HOME FURNISHINGS, STAR FURNITURE COMPANY, and JORDAN'S, INC.); the manufacture, import, and distribution of footwear (H.H. BROWN SHOE COMPANY, LOWELL SHOE, INC., DEXTER SHOE COMPANY, and JUSTIN BRANDS); the retail sale of fine jewelry; the providing of training to operators of aircraft and ships throughout the world; the providing of fractional ownership programs for general aviation aircraft; the licensing and servicing of almost 6,000 DAIRY QUEEN stores; the rental of furniture and accessories; the PAMPERED CHEF, the largest direct seller of houseware products in the United States; and the manufacturing and production of face brick and concrete masonry products (ACME BUILDING BRANDS).

In addition to its own business segments, Berkshire Hathaway also owns large segments of AMERICAN EXPRESS COMPANY, THE COCA-COLA COMPANY, FEDERAL HOME LOAN MORTGAGE CORPORATION, THE GILLETTE COMPANY, THE WASHINGTON POST COMPANY, and WELLS FARGO COMPANY.

As you consider all of these different businesses that are owned or controlled by Berkshire Hathaway, can you see what they all have in common? It's difficult to see the relationship, isn't it? Actually, the one thing they have in common is that they are all considered to be good investments by Warren Buffett, who is generally believed to be one of the most astute investors in the United States. As he states in his annual report, "We are eager to hear from principals or their representatives about businesses that meet all of the following criteria:

1. Large purchases (at least $50 million of before-tax earnings),
2. Demonstrated consistent earning power (future projections are of no interest to us, nor are "turnaround" situations),
3. Businesses earning good returns on equity while employing little or no debt,
4. Management in place (we can't supply it),
5. Simple businesses (if there's lots of technology, we won't understand it),
6. An offering price (we don't want to waste our time or that of the seller by talking, even preliminarily, about a transaction when price is unknown).

Source: Berkshire Hathaway, 2002 Annual Report.

"*The Buffett way*"

Benefits and Problems of Decentralization

To what degree should a company decentralize? BERKSHIRE HATHAWAY, for example, is very decentralized, allowing managers of its various business units to operate nearly autonomously. Clearly, a large company employing thousands of people in different geographic areas could not remain completely centralized, with top management making all the decisions. The president of IMC would not know enough about the costs and varieties of paint in Japan, for example, or have enough time to make all the operating decisions for the manufacturing subsegment of the Japanese operations of Edison Automobile. Though such decisions would never be made by the president of a large international company, they would be made at a higher level in a **centralized company** than in a decentralized one.

Currently, the trend in most companies is to decentralize. The reasons often cited for making decisions at the lowest possible level in an organization are:

1. Segment managers usually have more information about matters within their area of responsibility than do managers at higher levels.
2. Segment managers are in a better position to see current problems and to react quickly to local situations.
3. Higher-level management can spend more time on broader policy and strategic issues because the burden of daily decision making is distributed.
4. Segment managers have a greater incentive to perform well because they receive the credit (or blame) for performance resulting from their decisions.
5. Employees have greater incentives and motivation to perform well because there are more opportunities for advancement into leadership positions when a company is decentralized.
6. Managers and officers can be evaluated more easily because their responsibilities are more clearly defined.

Decentralization has its drawbacks as well. Decisions made by managers of decentralized units are sometimes not consistent with the overall objectives of the firm. For example, Edison Automobile might find it less expensive to buy computer parts for its automobiles from an outside source than from Acme Computer, or the Service division of Japanese operations may find it cheaper to buy repair parts from outsiders rather than from the Manufacturing division. Such decisions would allow the buying divisions to report lower costs, but the decisions might decrease the company's overall profitability (depending on the costs in the selling divisions that can actually be avoided).

There are two ways to prevent such problems. First, certain decisions should be centralized. For example, all decisions related to insurance coverage, which benefits the entire company, should probably be made at the corporate level. Second, a system of responsibility accounting should be established so that a manager's decisions will benefit not only the segment but also the firm as a whole. This **goal congruence**, whereby the goals of the company and all its segments are in harmony, can be achieved only if the responsibility accounting system is well designed.

Responsibility Accounting

Responsibility accounting is a system in which managers are assigned and held accountable for certain costs, revenues, and/or assets. There are two important behavioral considerations in assigning responsibilities to managers.

- First, the responsible manager should be involved in developing the plan for the unit over which the manager has control. Current research indicates that people are more motivated to achieve a goal (budget or standard) if they participate in setting it. Such participation assures that the goals will be reasonable and, more importantly, that they will be *perceived* to be reasonable by the managers.

centralized company An organization in which top management makes most of the major decisions for the entire company rather than delegating decisions to managers at lower levels.

goal congruence The selection of goals for responsibility centers that are consistent, or congruent, with those of the company as a whole.

responsibility accounting A system of evaluating performance; managers are held accountable for the costs, revenues, assets, or other elements over which they have control.

- Second, a manager should be held accountable only for those costs, revenues, or assets over which the manager has substantial control. Some costs may be generated within a segment, but control over them lies outside that unit. The manager of the Japanese Manufacturing division, for example, may be responsible for labor costs, but employee wages may be determined by a union scale controlled elsewhere. Admittedly, determining "substantial control" requires a judgment based on the circumstances, but if all relevant factors are considered, careful and fair judgments can be made.

Responsibility Accounting Reports

Regardless of the degree of autonomy given to managers at various operating levels, performance reports based on responsibility accounting are needed at all levels of the organization. At the lowest levels, these reports tell managers where corrective action must be taken to control their segments' operations. At top levels, these reports keep management informed of the activities of all segments. The reports are then used to reward past performance and set incentives for future performance.

Exhibit 2 illustrates the kind of responsibility accounting reports a company might use. Note that reporting begins at the bottom and "rolls" upward, with each manager receiving information on the operations for which that manager is responsible, as well as summary information on the performance of lower-level managers. Note also that these reports are **exception reports**, meaning that variances from, or exceptions to, the budget are highlighted. In the report, unfavorable variances are labeled "U" while favorable variances are labeled "F." Such reports direct management immediately to the areas requiring their attention. Note that Exhibit 2 reports only on cost management. In this chapter, we'll also discuss reporting performance on revenue and asset management.

Responsibility Centers

In our example, the president of IMC is responsible for the entire organization and should be held accountable for the company's overall successes and failures. At lower levels, the president of Edison Automobile Company, the manager of Edison's operations in the Far East, the manager in charge of Japanese operations in Edison's Far East operations, and the manager of the Japanese Manufacturing division, for example, would be held responsible for operations within their respective units.

Each unit is referred to as a **responsibility center**, and, depending on the operation, it may be a cost, profit, or investment center. As the name implies, a **cost center** is any organizational unit in which the manager of that unit has control only over the costs incurred. The manager of a cost center has no responsibility for revenues or assets, either because revenues are not generated in the center or because revenues and assets are under the control of someone else. The manufacturing unit of Japanese operations of IMC, for example, could be designated a cost center. A **profit center** manager, however, has responsibility for both costs and revenues. Profit centers are usually found at higher levels in an organization than are cost centers. The geographic regions (United States, Far East, and Europe, as well as various country operations within the Far East region) of Edison Automobile would probably be profit centers.

In an **investment center**, the manager is responsible for costs, revenues, and assets. This means that the manager is responsible not only for operating costs and revenues, but also for determining the amount of funds to be invested in the center's plant and equipment and for the rate of return earned on those investments. Investment centers are usually found at relatively high levels in organizations. The different companies in IMC (Acme Computer, Edison Automobile, and Jennifer Cosmetics) would probably be investment centers.

exception reports Reports that highlight variances from, or exceptions to, the budget.

responsibility center An organizational unit in which a manager has control over and is held accountable for performance.

cost center An organizational unit in which a manager has control over and is held accountable for cost performance.

profit center An organizational unit in which a manager has control over and is held accountable for both cost and revenue performance.

investment center An organizational unit in which a manager has control over and is held accountable for cost, revenue, and asset performance.

TO SUMMARIZE: Most companies are divided into segments with specific responsibilities assigned to each segment manager. In a centralized organization, top management makes most of the operating decisions; in a decentralized organization, decision-making authority is delegated down the corporate ladder to the managers most immediately responsible. It is very important in a decentralized company that the goals of the company and all its segments are in harmony. This concept is referred to as goal congruence. Regardless of the degree of decentralization, almost all companies use performance reports that show variances from budgeted amounts for each division, department, and unit. These reports pass upward through an organization so that supervisors and managers at all levels can assess the performance of the units serving under them. Decentralized companies are divided into fairly independent responsibility centers. There are three types of responsibility centers: cost, profit, and investment. Managers of responsibility centers usually have control over, and are held accountable for, the performance of the center.

Exhibit 2: Responsibility Accounting Reports for Edison Automobile Company of IMC

President, Edison Automobile	Responsibility Centers	Budgeted Costs	Actual Costs	Variance*
The president receives from each geographic area of operations a report summarizing its performance. The president can see where corrective action needs to be made by tracing the differences between budget and actual downward to their sources.	General Administration	x	x	x
	United States	x	x	x
	Far East	$58,000	$65,000	$7,000 U
	Europe	x	x	x

Far East Operations	Responsibility Centers	Budgeted Costs	Actual Costs	Variance
The manager of Far East operations receives a report from each country segment's head. These reports are then summarized and passed on to the president of Edison Automobile.	Japanese Operations	$21,000	$23,000	$2,000 U
	Korean Operations	x	x	x
	Total costs	$58,000	$65,000	$7,000 U

Japanese Operations	Responsibility Centers	Budgeted Costs	Actual Costs	Variance
The manager of Japanese operations receives from each unit a report summarizing its performance. These reports are combined and sent up to the next level, the manager of Far East operations.	Sales	x	x	x
	Manufacturing	$ 9,000	$10,200	$1,200 U
	Service	x	x	x
	Total costs	$21,000	$23,000	$2,000 U

Japanese Manufacturing Division	Variable Costs of Manufacturing	Budgeted Costs	Actual Costs	Variance
The Manufacturing division supervisor receives a performance report on the supervisor's center of responsibility. The totals from these reports are then communicated to the manager of Japanese operations, the next level of responsibility.	Direct materials	$ 2,000	$ 2,500	$ 500 U
	Direct labor	6,000	6,400	400 U
	Manufacturing overhead	1,000	1,300	300 U
	Total costs	$ 9,000	$10,200	$1,200 U

*U means unfavorable.

Standard Cost Systems

3 Describe standard costing and the basic variance analysis model.

standard cost system A cost-accumulation system in which standard costs are used as product costs instead of actual costs. The standard costs are then adjusted to actual costs when financial reports are created. This adjustment creates variances that are reported to management.

If managers are to be held responsible for the costs incurred in their centers, they must have control over those costs, have relevant information about those costs, and have a system that focuses on and supports effective cost controls. Traditionally, companies have used a *standard costing* system that isolates differences between actual and standard (or budgeted) costs to determine whether costs are too high or too low, as well as whether costs are improving (decreasing) or getting worse (increasing). This is critical information if the organization expects to be competitive. In a standard costing management system, standard costs are compared to actual costs, and variances are computed.

Service, merchandising, and manufacturing firms that use standard costing design their accounting systems to incorporate standard costs and variances. This type of system, called a **standard cost system**, is a cost-accumulation process based on costs that *should have been* incurred rather than costs that *were actually* incurred. The steps in establishing and operating a standard cost system are:

standard cost cards An itemization of the components of a product's standard cost.

These steps describe a typical standard cost system. You are likely to find an extensive standard cost system in most manufacturing firms, which usually have standard costs for direct materials, direct labor, and manufacturing overhead. However, many service and merchandising firms also use a standard cost system to effectively manage critical costs in their organizations. Standard costs usually are reported on **standard cost cards**, often stored in a computer. In the previous chapter on operational budgeting, we created an operating budget for Sunbird Boat Company. A critical part of creating this budget was establishing the standard costs to produce a 15-foot fishing boat. These costs are reported in the previous chapter, although they are spread across a number of budget schedules that we created in that chapter. The management team and accountants at Sunbird Boat Company can compile all of these standard cost data into a standard cost card for 15-foot fishing boats. The standard cost card for Sunbird Boat Company is shown in Exhibit 3. We will use the data in Exhibit 3 to illustrate how variances are calculated and analyzed.

> ⚠ **Caution**
>
> All of the cost variances we compute in this chapter are based on Sunbird's standard cost card. Be sure to return to Exhibit 3 to review these standards as you work through the remainder of this chapter.

Determining Standard Costs and Identifying Variances

In a manufacturing firm, standard costs are determined on the basis of careful analysis and the experience of many people, including accountants, industrial engineers, purchasing agents, and the managers of the departments to be judged. Accountants play an important role in developing standard costs because they have the data needed to determine how costs have changed in the past in relation to levels of activity. This is not an easy task. Changes in methods of production, technology, worker efficiency, and plant layout, for example, can affect the behavior of costs. Before using standard costs to create the annual budget, past costs often have to be adjusted to take changes in operating conditions into account. These changes sometimes occur gradually and may not be easily noticeable, making it difficult for accountants to identify cost characteristics that will be useful in setting standards for the future.

Engineers are often involved in setting standard costs because of their knowledge of the most efficient way of performing each task in relation to the existing technology of the operation.

Exhibit 3: Standard Cost Card

	(1) Standard Quantity	(2) Standard Price or Rate	(3) Standard Cost (1) × (2)
Sunbird Boat Company			
Standard Cost Card—15-Foot Fishing Boats			
Inputs:			
Direct materials:			
Wood	70 feet	$10.00	$ 700.00
Fiberglass	50 feet	5.00	250.00
Direct labor	80 hours	15.00	1,200.00
Manufacturing overhead:			
Variable	80 hours	8.00	640.00
Fixed	80 hours	21.40	1,712.00
Total standard cost per boat			$4,502.00

Managers who will be judged by the standard costs should be involved in the standard-setting process; they are more likely to be motivated to meet standards if they have participated in setting the standards and have accepted them. In addition, managers' experience and judgment can be quite valuable in establishing appropriate cost standards.

Once management has established a standard price for each resource (direct materials, direct labor, and manufacturing overhead) and has determined the standard input quantity allowed, the standard price is multiplied by the standard quantity to arrive at a standard dollar cost for the product or service. Actual costs are then compared with these standards to calculate the **variance**, the amount by which the actual cost differs from the standard. This variance, if significant, is a signal to management that costs may be "out of control" and that corrective action should be taken to eliminate the variance. This process of using variances from a standard to isolate problem areas is called **management by exception**. It is the basis of the control function.

Let's review Exhibit 3 again. You can see in the third column that the standard costs to produce boats at Sunbird Boat Company are composed of both a price (or rate) and a quantity (or usage). Hence, comparing actual costs with standard costs results in two variances: a price (or rate) variance and a quantity (or usage) variance. These variances are usually computed for direct materials, direct labor, and variable manufacturing overhead.

Exhibit 4 is a general model for calculating variances for direct materials, direct labor, and variable manufacturing overhead. (It is *not* the model used to calculate variances for fixed manufacturing overhead.) Let's first consider column (1) and column (2). These two columns are used to compute the price (rate) variance, which is the difference between the actual quantity of inputs times the actual price and the actual quantity of inputs times the standard price. Another way of mathematically saying the same thing is the price variance is the difference between the actual price and the standard price, times the actual quantity. Now before you start to memorize either of these equations, think about what a price variance is signaling—that the actual price is different than the standard or expected price.[2] Essentially, if the actual price is more than the expected price, then we have an unfavorable variance. And if the actual price is

variance Any deviation from standard.

management by exception The strategy of focusing attention on significant deviations from a standard.

STOP & THINK

Is it possible for a company to have positive variances (actual costs are less than standard costs) and still have problems? Can you think of an example?

2 In this discussion, the terms *standard* and *expected* are often used interchangeably. Some people refer to prices and quantities as standard; others refer to them as expected because they aren't under the complete control of the company.

Exhibit 4: General Model for Variance Analysis

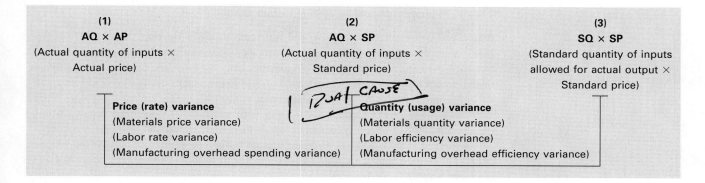

less than the expected price, then the variance is favorable. It then makes sense to multiply the difference between these two prices by the actual quantity in order to know the total financial impact on the organization of paying a price or rate that was more or less than was expected.

Now let's consider how column (2) and column (3) are used to compute the quantity (or usage) variance. This variance is essentially an input-output analysis. It compares the actual quantity of inputs to the standard quantity of inputs allowed for actual output. The concept *quantity allowed for actual output* is important here. This concept essentially refers to the quantity that should have been used to produce the actual output and relates back to the principle of flexible budgeting that we discussed in the expanded material section of the previous chapter on operational budgeting. Unless actual production output equals budgeted production output, management can't really know how much material, labor, and overhead input should have been used during the period. Hence, at the end of the operating period, the accountant will multiply the standard quantity per unit of product by the actual volume of units produced to determine the *standard quantity allowed*. This number is then compared to the actual quantity used to determine if there is a favorable or unfavorable quantity (usage) variance. Then, in order to be able to account for this variance in the organization's accounting system (which we will discuss in the next section), we multiply this difference by the standard price per unit of input. The standard price is used so that the quantity variances will not be influenced by price changes. Hence, the quantity variance is the difference between the actual quantity and the standard quantity allowed, times the standard price.

STOP & THINK

When computing the quantity (usage) variance, do you understand why it is important to compare actual quantity of inputs to the standard quantity of inputs allowed for actual output? Is the standard quantity budgeted (determined at the beginning of the operating period) different from the standard quantity allowed for actual output (determined at the end of the operating period)? If so, what is the difference?

Evaluation of Standard Costing

Standard cost systems, such as those discussed in this chapter, have many advantages and disadvantages. The advantages include the following:

1. Standard costs are very important to the budgeting process.
2. A standard cost system is simpler to operate than a system using actual costs because the cost flows are recorded at standard.
3. The setting of standard costs requires a careful analysis of operations. Such an analysis can lead to improvements in costs and efficiencies even before the standard cost system is fully operative.
4. A standard cost system helps identify and control problem areas, which leads to increased production efficiency.
5. Standard costs provide a basis for measuring performance by assigning variances to the responsible manager.

6. A standard cost system is compatible with the principle of management by exception, which contributes to the effective utilization of management's time and effort.

The disadvantages of standard costing include the following:

1. A standard cost system is expensive and time consuming to develop.
2. It is easy to misinterpret the causes of a variance because so many factors are involved.
3. Standard costs must be changed as conditions change (e.g., as the product, the materials, or the production methods change). Sometimes these changes occur so quickly that standards become out of date before management realizes it.
4. Workers tend to view measures of efficiency with mistrust. Responsibility for significant variances may be erroneously assigned, which then leads to morale problems.
5. The setting of standards is not an exact science. Although standards are reported as specific figures, smart managers realize that these numbers should sometimes be treated as ranges of acceptable performance.
6. Random fluctuations in the differences between standards and actual results are to be expected but often are hard to distinguish from situations requiring action.
7. Standard costs are based on the simplistic cost model in which every cost has to be treated as either fixed or variable. In the real world, however, many costs do not behave according to these idealized models, which means that managers can always legitimately point to shortcomings in the variance analysis and standard costing.

Although the disadvantages noted here are real and should not be minimized, standard cost systems have generally been cost beneficial and are widely used across manufacturing, service, and even merchandising organizations. Manufacturing firms use standards and budgets for their nonmanufacturing activities, as do merchandising and service businesses. In essence, the concepts of standards and cost systems apply to all types of organizations in varying degrees.

TO SUMMARIZE: Standard cost systems are used to accumulate costs based on standards rather than actual costs. Standard costs are predetermined or budgeted costs that serve as benchmarks for judging what actual costs should be. Standard costs are usually expressed as the per-unit cost of materials, labor, and manufacturing overhead and are used by managers for planning, implementing, and controlling decisions. The total variance between actual and standard costs is made up of price (or rate) and quantity (or efficiency) variances. Standard costs are based on careful analysis by many people, including accountants, engineers, and managers. Standard costs are compared with actual costs incurred to determine variances, the amounts by which actual costs differ from standards. Significant variances alert management to specific problem areas that may require corrective action. The strategy of focusing on significant variances, called management by exception, is essential to the controlling function.

Overall, standard costs can be used in nonmanufacturing firms, as well as manufacturing firms. Standard cost systems have both advantages and disadvantages. Most advantages center on achieving greater accuracy and efficiency. Most disadvantages center on the challenges involved in setting standards and the inability to establish exact standards in a changing environment.

Controlling Performance in Cost Centers

4 Use materials and labor cost variance analysis to explain how performance is controlled in cost centers.

As we stated earlier, managers of cost centers are responsible for costs incurred. Most cost centers usually have one type of cost that is more significant than any other. In service organizations, salaries are generally the major cost. In wholesale and retail businesses, the cost of merchandise purchased for resale is often the most significant cost. In manufacturing firms, costs incurred to make products (direct materials, direct labor, and manufacturing overhead) are usually most significant. The standard cost system described in the previous section is an effective method of controlling these kinds of costs.

Direct Materials Variances

Variance analysis is an essential part of an effective standard cost system. We will first explain how direct materials variances are computed and analyzed. Then, we will explain the computation and analysis of direct labor variances. The more complex variances for manufacturing overhead will be discussed and illustrated in the expanded material section of this chapter.

To illustrate the computation of the price and quantity variances for direct materials, we will assume the following actual results for the year on the 90 fishing boats made by Sunbird Boat Company:

Direct materials purchased	
Wood	6,900 feet at $9.20 per foot
Fiberglass	4,800 feet at $5.20 per foot
Direct materials used	
Wood	6,435.0 feet
Fiberglass	4,432.5 feet
Boats produced	90

Keep in mind throughout the following discussion that the standard cost card (Exhibit 3) specifies that wood materials should cost $10 per foot, fiberglass materials should cost $5 per foot, and each boat produced should require 70 feet of wood and 50 feet of fiberglass. (Obviously, many different kinds of raw materials are required to make boats. To keep the example simple, we are assuming only two materials are used.)

Materials Price Variance

materials price variance
The extent to which the actual price varies from the standard price for the quantity of materials purchased or used; computed by multiplying the difference between the actual and standard prices by the quantity purchased or used.

The **materials price variance** reflects the extent to which the actual price varies from the standard price for the actual quantity of materials purchased or used. Although the price variance can be calculated either when materials are purchased or when they are used, it is generally best to isolate the variance at purchase and report the variance to the purchasing manager who has responsibility for controlling the purchase price. If management waits until the materials are used before calculating variances, the information needed by the purchasing managers to take corrective action is delayed.

In calculating the materials price variance, the standard price per unit of materials should reflect the final, delivered cost of materials, net of any discounts taken. For example, Sunbird Boat Company may have determined its standard materials price per foot of wood as follows:

Purchase price	$ 9.84
Freight	0.17
Handling costs	0.04
Less purchase discounts	(0.05)
Standard wood materials cost per foot	$10.00

The standard cost above assumes that the materials were purchased in certain lot sizes (for example, 100-foot quantities) and delivered a certain way (by rail, for example). Handling costs and purchase discounts have also been included.

Assume that variances are determined when materials are purchased. Based on the fact given above that 6,900 feet of wood are purchased by Sunbird during the year, the price variance for wood is computed as follows:

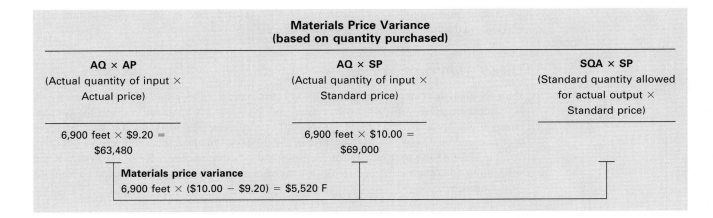

Materials Price Variance
(based on quantity purchased)

AQ × AP	AQ × SP	SQA × SP
(Actual quantity of input × Actual price)	(Actual quantity of input × Standard price)	(Standard quantity allowed for actual output × Standard price)
6,900 feet × $9.20 = $63,480	6,900 feet × $10.00 = $69,000	

Materials price variance
6,900 feet × ($10.00 − $9.20) = $5,520 F

Caution

As you can see in the illustration on this page, when the actual quantity used is the basis for the materials price variance, the materials price variance and the materials quantity variance share some of the same computations, making these calculations somewhat easier. However, remember that basing the materials price variance on the actual quantity used will delay the recognition of price problems from the time that the materials are purchased until the time they are transferred to production.

This variance indicates that the company spent $5,520 less than the total standard cost for the wood purchased. Because less money was spent than the standard cost, the variance is labeled "F," meaning "favorable." If the amount expended had been more than the standard cost, the variance would have been "unfavorable," designated with a "U."

Isolating materials price variances at the time of purchase has the advantage of providing immediate information on purchasing decisions. This also allows companies to carry inventory in the accounting records at the standard cost. Some companies, however, prefer to compute materials price variances at the time the materials are transferred to Work-in-Process Inventory (i.e., when these materials are actually used in production). The facts stated above indicate that 6,435 feet were used in production. If materials price variances are computed when materials are transferred to Work-in-Process, the 6,435 feet would be used in the calculation rather than the 6,900 feet purchased. In this case, a favorable price variance of $5,148 would result, as shown below.

Materials Price Variance and Materials Quantity Variance
(based on quantity used in production)

AQ × AP	AQ × SP	SQA × SP
(Actual quantity of input × Actual price)	(Actual quantity of input × Standard price)	(Standard quantity allowed for actual output × Standard price)
6,435 feet × $9.20 = $59,202	6,435 feet × $10.00 = $64,350	6,300 feet × $10.00 = $63,000

Materials price variance
6,435 feet × ($10.00 − $9.20) = $5,148 F

Materials quantity variance
$10.00 × (6,435 feet − 6,300 feet) = $1,350 U

materials quantity variance The extent to which the actual quantity of materials varies from the standard quantity; computed by multiplying the difference between the actual quantity of materials used and the standard quantity of materials allowed by the standard price.

Materials Quantity Variance

The standard quantity of materials should reflect the amount needed for each completed unit of product but should allow for normal waste, spoilage, and other unavoidable inefficiencies. The standard cost card indicates that 70 feet of wood is allowed for each 15-foot fishing boat produced. Because Sunbird Boat Company produced 90 of these boats last year, the standard quantity of wood allowed is 6,300 feet (70 feet × 90 boats). As already reported above, actual use of wood amounted to 6,435 feet. The computation of the **materials quantity variance** for wood is shown in the illustration above. As you can see, the company used 135 more feet of wood than expected, resulting in an unfavorable quantity variance of $1,350 (135 feet $\times$ $10 per foot).

Controlling Materials Variances

Materials price variances are usually under the control of the purchasing department. The purchasing function involves getting a variety of price quotations, buying in economic lot sizes to take advantage of quantity discounts, buying and paying on a timely basis to obtain cash discounts, and paying attention to alternative forms of delivery to minimize shipping costs. Some of these factors will be less important when there are few suppliers or when purchase contracts with suppliers are for long periods. In any case, the existence of unfavorable price variances may suggest a problem that needs correcting.

The buyer responsible for these purchases should be able to explain the variance even though the buyer may not be able to control its occurrence. This may be the case, for example, when market prices change after the standard is set, which could be the explanation for the favorable price variance. Or materials may be damaged, requiring the reorder of a small quantity on a rush basis; this usually raises the price of the materials as well as the cost of shipping, causing an unfavorable price variance. The point is that the cause of any significant variance (whether favorable or unfavorable) must be explained and steps taken to avoid such variances in the future. The purpose of variance analysis is not to browbeat employees for failing to meet impossible expectations, but rather to provide information that will help management identify ways of improving the production process.

Materials quantity variances may be caused by quality defects, poor workmanship, poor choice of materials, inexperienced workers, machines that need repair, or an inaccurate materials quantity standard. Just as the purchasing manager must explain significant price variances, generally the production manager must analyze significant quantity variances to determine their cause. If the material is of inferior quality, the purchasing manager, rather than the production manager, may be responsible for the variance. Again, the point is that the cause of the variance must be determined; only then can it be decided what action, if any, to take to prevent its recurrence. Further, production managers should constantly receive reports on these variances in order to maintain good control of costs and usage. If this is done, production managers can then take quick corrective action before many problems become significant in size. Corrective action, for example, may involve being careful to return excess materials to the storeroom rather than being careless about control in the production area, which could lead to waste or theft.

Accounting for Materials Variances

The journal entries for recording the purchase and use of materials, as well as the materials price variance (isolated at purchase) and the quantity variance (isolated when materials are used), are:

Materials Price Variance:

Direct Materials Inventory ($10.00 $\times$ 6,900 feet)	69,000	
Materials Price Variance [($10.00 − $9.20) $\times$ 6,900 feet]		5,520
Cash (or Accounts Payable) ($9.20 $\times$ 6,900 feet)		63,480
Purchased 6,900 feet of wood at $9.20 per foot and entered the		
materials in inventory at the standard price of $10.00 per foot.		

Materials Quantity Variance:

Work-in-Process Inventory (6,300 feet $\times$ $10.00)	63,000	
Materials Quantity Variance [(6,435 feet − 6,300 feet) $\times$ $10.00]	1,350	
Direct Materials Inventory (6,435 feet $\times$ $10.00)		64,350
Transferred 6,435 feet of wood out of inventory and recorded		
standard usage of 6,300 feet of wood to produce 90 boats.		

Note that the $63,000 debit to Work-in-Process Inventory is based on the standard amount of wood allowed for 90 boats actually produced, which is 6,300 feet (90 boats $\times$ 70 standard feet per boat).

As you can see, Materials Price Variance and Materials Quantity Variance are debited when the variances are unfavorable; they are credited when the variances are favorable. A good way to remember that unfavorable variances are debited is to think of an unfavorable variance as an expense, which is also debited. Conversely, a favorable variance, which is credited, can be considered an expense reduction or savings. The actual cost deviations from the standard costs are now recorded in variance accounts. Similar to the approach used to close over- or underapplied manufacturing overhead (discussed previously in the chapter on product cost flows), the variance accounts are usually closed and the amounts transferred to Cost of Goods Sold at the end of the period. Thus, Cost of Goods Sold as reported on the income statement is based on actual costs, while inventory accounts on the balance sheet include only the standard costs of materials. Alternatively, when variances are significant in amount, variance account balances at the end of a period should be allocated among Cost of Goods Sold, Raw Materials Inventory, Work-in-Process Inventory, and Finished Goods Inventory instead of simply transferred entirely to Cost of Goods Sold.

Now that we've worked through the accounting for variances on Sunbird's wood materials, see if you can correctly compute and account for the variances on Sunbird's fiberglass materials (base the price variance on the amount purchased). As you make the variance computations, try to understand the *meaning* of each calculation. To help you, consider the following three-step conceptual approach to variance analysis.

1. First, determine whether the variance is favorable or unfavorable.

    In the case of the wood price variance, the fact that the actual price ($9.20) is less than the standard price ($10.00) is obviously a favorable situation. And the fact that the actual quantity of wood used (6,435 feet) is more than the standard quantity allowed (6,300 feet) is clearly an unfavorable situation.

2. Next, compute the underlying difference that actually determines the variance calculation.

    What we mean here is that the "real" price variance is $0.80 (the difference between $9.20 and $10.00) and the "real" quantity variance is 135 feet (the difference between 6,435 feet and 6,300 feet).

3. Finally, calculate the financial impact of the underlying difference on the company. This is the variance that must be accounted for in the company's accounting system.

    Given a "real" price variance of $0.80 per foot that is favorable, the impact of this difference on Sunbird is a function of the number of board feet actually purchased; that is, $0.80 favorable × 6,900 feet = $5,520 F. Similarly, the financial impact on Sunbird of a "real" quantity variance of 135 feet that is unfavorable is a function of the standard price of $10 per foot; that is, 135 feet unfavorable × $10 = $1,350 U.

The correct computations and journal entries for Sunbird's fiberglass variances are provided in the footnote below.[3]

---

3 The actual fiberglass price was $5.20 and the standard price is $5.00. Hence, the price variance is unfavorable based on an underlying difference of $0.20. Because 4,800 feet of fiberglass were actually purchased, the total financial impact of the underlying unfavorable price difference is a price variance of $960 U ($0.20 × 4,800 feet).

Now turning to the quantity variance, the actual fiberglass used was 4,432.5 feet and the standard quantity allowed is 4,500 feet (50 standard feet per boat × 90 boats actually produced). Hence, the quantity variance is favorable based on the underlying difference of 67.5 feet (4,500 feet − 4,432.5 feet). Using a standard price per foot of $5, the total financial impact of the underlying favorable quantity difference is a quantity variance of $337.50 F (67.5 feet × $5).

The journal entries to account for the price and quantity variances, respectively, are:

Direct Materials Inventory ($5.00 × 4,800 feet)	24,000	
Materials Price Variance [($5.20 − $5.00) × 4,800 feet]	960	
Cash (or Accounts Payable) ($5.20 × 4,800 feet)		24,960
Work-in-Process Inventory (4,500 feet × $5.00)	22,500	
Materials Quantity Variance [(4,500 feet − 4,432.5 feet) × $5.00]		337.50
Direct Materials Inventory (4,432.5 feet × $5.00)		22,162.50

Direct Labor Variances

Typically when a standard cost system is being used in a manufacturing or service firm, a direct labor rate variance and a direct labor efficiency variance are determined for personnel directly involved in the creation of the organization's product or service. These variances are computed in a manner similar to the materials price and quantity variances.

Labor Rate Variance

labor rate variance The extent to which the actual labor rate varies from the standard rate for the quantity of labor used; computed by multiplying the difference between the actual rate and the standard rate by the quantity of labor used.

A **labor rate variance** is a price variance; it shows the difference between actual and standard wage rates. Unfavorable labor rate variances may occur when skilled workers with high hourly pay rates are placed in jobs intended for less skilled or lower-wage-rate employees. Unfavorable labor rate variances may also occur when employees work overtime at premium pay (time and a half or double time). Conversely, favorable labor rate variances occur when less skilled or lower-wage-rate employees perform duties intended for higher-paid workers.

For Sunbird Boat Company, the standard cost card (Exhibit 3) indicates that the standard direct labor rate per boat is 80 hours at $15 per hour. Actual labor used during the year to make 90 boats was 7,092 hours at an average rate of $14.50 per hour. The labor rate variance is thus $3,546 favorable, computed as follows:

Labor Rate Variance and Labor Efficiency Variance		
AH × AR (Actual hours of input × Actual rate)	**AH × SR** (Actual hours of input × Standard rate)	**SHA × SR** (Standard hours allowed for actual output × Standard rate)
7,092 hours × $14.50 = $102,834	7,092 hours × $15.00 = $106,380	7,200 hours × $15.00 = $108,000
Labor rate variance 7,092 hours × ($15.00 − $14.50) = $3,546 F	**Labor efficiency variance** $15.00 × (7,200 hours − 7,092 hours) = $1,620 F	

As this variance indicates, the $0.50 difference between the standard wage rate and actual average wage rate results in $3,546 less spent than expected for the actual number of direct labor hours used. Sunbird's management now needs to determine whether the variance should be investigated. Depending on the company's hiring policies, and the degree of authority given to the operating manager in setting wage rates and assigning workers to particular jobs, the operating manager may or may not be responsible for this labor rate variance. In general, labor rates are the responsibility of the manager who makes hiring and staffing decisions.

Labor Efficiency Variance

labor efficiency variance The extent to which the actual labor used varies from the standard quantity; computed by multiplying the difference between the actual quantity of labor used and the standard quantity of labor allowed by the standard rate.

The **labor efficiency variance** is a quantity variance. It measures the cost (or benefit) of using labor for more (or fewer) hours than prescribed by the standard. Computed in the same manner as the materials quantity variance, the labor efficiency variance computation is also illustrated in the schedule above for Sunbird Boat Company. Note that total standard hours are computed by multiplying the standard hours per boat by the actual number of boats produced (80 hours × 90 boats = 7,200 standard hours allowed). The manufacturing division used 108 less direct labor hours than the standard allowed for actual production output, which generates a favorable efficiency variance of $1,620 (108 hours × $15).

The labor efficiency variance shows how efficiently the workers performed, which is an important measure of the productivity of the department. The variances might be unfavorable for a variety of reasons, including poorly trained employees, poor-quality materials that require extra processing time, old or faulty equipment, and improper supervision of employees. Note

FYI:

Employee compensation is a much more involved management process than simply determining salaries and wages. Many managers think of employee compensation as involving the following four elements: base salary, bonus incentives, benefits, and noncash compensation. Employees generally receive semiannual or annual reviews to determine changes to salary. Bonus incentives that are linked to the organization's goals give employees a stake in the success of the business. Benefits include such items as retirement packages, health and life insurance, paid vacations, and tuition reimbursements. Organizations build benefits packages that satisfy their employees' expectations. However, money is not the ultimate motivator for employee productivity. The best motivator can be feedback—both positive and negative. A total compensation approach that intelligently combines base pay, bonuses, benefits, and effective feedback enables organizations to retain their best staff and motivate superior job performance.

Source: Kirk J. Hulett, "The Price Is Right: Your staff compensation plan should address four elements: base pay, bonus incentives, benefits and non-cash compensation. Here's how." *Financial Planning*, September 1, 2001, p. 1.

Caution

When computing variances, be careful not to confuse actual and standard hours and actual and standard rates. The rate variance is always the difference between the standard and actual rate multiplied by the actual hours. (To multiply it by standard hours would not tell you how much the rate increase actually cost or saved the company in total.) On the other hand, the efficiency variance is a time-based variance; therefore, it is the difference between the standard hours allowed and actual hours multiplied by the standard rate.

that the labor efficiency variance is probably the most important and closely watched manufacturing variance. It has become even more important in recent years as U.S. industries have tried to increase the efficiency of their production to match that of Japan, Korea, and other countries.

Controlling Labor Variances

Labor rate variances are normally the responsibility of either the production manager who is responsible for employees' work assignments or the individuals responsible for hiring employees. As indicated, rate variances are likely to be due to (1) certain tasks being performed by workers with different pay rates or (2) working overtime at rates higher than the normal wage rate. These variances may be manageable if care is taken in assigning workers to jobs that are consistent with their skills and pay scales. Deviations may be necessary in certain situations because of vacations, sickness, or absences of other employees. If the variances are caused by factors beyond the manager's control, he or she should not be held responsible for the unfavorable variance.

In a labor-intensive company, the labor efficiency variance is much more important than in a company that has low labor costs. Depending on the intensity of management attention on labor costs, the related variances can be separated into categories by causes so that judgments can be made about what corrective action should be taken. Some typical causes of labor inefficiency variances are absenteeism, machinery breakdowns, poor-quality materials, poor work environment, inadequate machinery, lack of employee skills on a given job, poor employee attitudes, lazy employees, and inaccurate standards. The sooner these causes can be identified, the more opportunity exists for management to effectively take corrective action. However, if management waits until labor efficiency variances are computed before taking action, the data necessary to take action may not be available until the end of each pay period when accounting reports are issued.

Accounting for Labor Variances

Because the labor rate and labor efficiency variances are both computed for a given period of time or for a given amount of production, the labor costs and variances for Sunbird Boat Company can be accounted for in a single journal entry.

Work-in-Process Inventory (7,200 hours × $15.00)	108,000	
Labor Rate Variance		
[($15.00 − $14.50) × 7,092 hours]		3,546
Labor Efficiency Variance		
[(7,200 hours − 7,092 hours) × $15.00]		1,620
Wages Payable (7,092 hours × $14.50)		102,834

To charge Work-in-Process Inventory for standard labor hours at the standard wage rate to produce 90 boats; to set up favorable labor rate and efficiency variances to reflect the use of 108 hours below standard at an average wage rate that was $0.50 below standard.

As with all production variances, labor variances are closed to Cost of Goods Sold at the end of the period or allocated among Cost of Goods Sold and the inventory accounts on the balance sheet. By closing variances into Cost of Goods Sold, actual cost of goods sold will be reported on the income statement, and Work-in-Process Inventory and Finished Goods Inventory will include only the standard costs of labor.

Satisfied Employees Are More Productive For many companies, labor costs are the highest cost. This is certainly true for service firms and may even be true for manufacturing firms. Labor rate and labor efficiency variances provide information about whether labor rates are higher than expected or standard and whether workers are performing as efficiently as expected or standard. However, there are important labor costs that are difficult to report and control using traditional labor variances. Take employee turnover, for example. Common estimates are that employee turnover costs range from $10,000 to $40,000 per person, depending on the position, while employee retention actually increases revenues. In addition, it has been estimated that a 5% increase in employee retention can result in a 10% decrease in labor costs and lead to productivity increases ranging from 25 to 65%.

Because of the high costs of employee turnover, most companies work hard to increase employee retention. The most common approach is to "buy" employee satisfaction with increased pay and benefits. However, a 1998 survey of 206 medium-to-large companies conducted by WILLIAM M. MERCER, INC., found that in organizations with high turnover, compensation was the most common reason for dissatisfaction. In companies with very low turnover, 40% of the respondents said that emotional factors (work satisfaction, good relationships with managers and other employees) were the sole reasons for their retention; only 21% attributed their retention to financial factors (satisfaction with compensation and benefits).

If these data seem conflicting, then consider the following management theory of employee motivation. Certain aspects of our job create dissatisfaction, but do not generate satisfaction. Other factors can lead to strong feelings of satisfaction with our job, but do not necessarily create dissatisfaction if the factor is absent. In other words, employees are generally unsatisfied with their jobs if the compensation is unacceptable, regardless of any other positive aspects of the job. On the other hand, if the compensation is acceptable, most employees are not necessarily satisfied. At this point, their attention turns to other factors such as feedback, recognition, opportunities for growth, etc. Evidence suggests that creating a workplace where employees feel better about themselves is extremely important. If a work environment constantly raises employees' self-esteem to a higher level than they experience elsewhere, they will want to spend more time at work and will enjoy very high job satisfaction.

Source: "Increasing Employee Satisfaction," **http://www.performance-unlimited.com/satisfy.htm**.

TO SUMMARIZE: The difference between actual and standard costs of materials for a given production level can be separated into a materials price variance and a materials quantity variance. The materials price variance can be computed when the materials are purchased or when they are used in production. The managers responsible for the variances must determine their causes and, if the variances are outside an acceptable range, take corrective action. The materials variances (price and quantity) are recorded in individual accounts when materials are acquired and used. The accounts for materials variances are generally closed into Cost of Goods Sold in order to adjust this account to actual costs; inventory accounts on the balance sheet include only standard materials costs.

The labor rate variance is the difference between the actual and the standard labor rates multiplied by the actual hours worked. The labor efficiency variance is the difference between actual and standard hours multiplied by the standard wage rate. Labor variances are usually controllable by manufacturing division managers. The labor variances (rate and efficiency) are recorded in individual accounts when labor costs are incurred. Like materials variances, labor variances are typically closed in their entirety to Cost of Goods Sold so that the work-in-process inventory and finished goods inventory accounts include only standard labor costs.

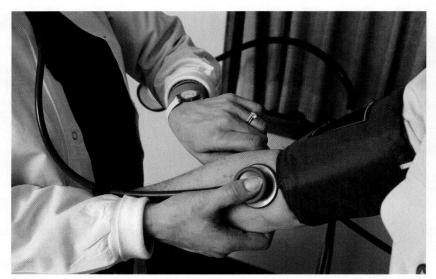

© 2003 Getty Images

A nonmanufacturing organization sometimes expresses standards in quantitative terms. For example, a hospital might have standard times for activities such as taking blood pressure readings.

Controlling Performance in Profit Centers

5 Use revenue variance analysis to explain how performance is controlled in profit centers.

As defined earlier, a profit center is an organizational unit (segment) in which a manager has responsibility for both costs and revenues. Profit centers both produce and market goods or services. For example, the U.S., Far East, and European operations of the Edison Automobile Company of IMC, illustrated in Exhibit 1 on page 332, might be profit centers.

The Segment-Margin Income Statement

segment-margin income statement An income statement that identifies costs directly chargeable to a segment and further divides them into variable and fixed cost behavior patterns.

direct costs Costs that are specifically traceable to a unit of business or segment being analyzed.

indirect costs Costs normally incurred for the benefit of several segments or activities; sometimes called common costs or joint costs.

To evaluate the performance of profit centers and to decide how limited resources will be divided among profit centers, management needs a report that compares the revenues and costs of the profit centers being evaluated. One report that is often used is the **segment-margin income statement**, such as the one presented in Exhibit 5 for IMC on pages 350–351.

To keep Exhibit 5 reasonably simple, we have limited the report to only two divisions for IMC: Acme Computer and Edison Automobile. Further, we have included only the regions of Edison Automobile. You will note that it includes three geographic regions; the Far East Region has operations in two countries—Japan and Korea. As you read across, note that the segment focus becomes narrower: from divisions to geographic regions to countries within geographic regions.

Before reviewing specific aspects of this segment-margin income statement, we want to remind you of that very important management accounting principle called *responsibility accounting*. Following this principle, segment managers should be evaluated on only the items they can control or influence. As was the case with cost centers, in evaluating profit centers it is important that managers be held responsible only for the controllable costs; the costs over which they have control are usually called **direct costs**. In Exhibit 5, we apply responsibility accounting to IMC by including in each segment report only the revenues and costs controlled by that segment manager. This implies that some costs, **indirect costs**, will not be assigned to a particular segment because the manager cannot control them. As you can observe in Exhibit 5, when we break IMC down into smaller and smaller segments, more and more costs are considered to be indirect or common. For example, the $1.5 million indirect costs listed in the IMC column are not assigned to the Acme Computer and Edison Automobile segments. These costs might include the IMC president's salary and interest on company-wide debt. As you can imagine, these costs are not controlled by Acme Computer and Edison Automobile. Therefore, these costs are not assigned to these segments.

> **Caution**
>
> Many students confuse the terms *variable* and *fixed costs*, *controllable* and *noncontrollable costs*, and *direct* and *indirect costs*. Costs are variable if they fluctuate with activity. If they don't fluctuate with activity, costs are fixed. Costs are controllable if they can be changed by the activity manager. If they can't be changed by the activity manager, costs are noncontrollable. Costs are direct if removing the activity results in the costs being eliminated. Costs that remain after an activity is eliminated are indirect.

Similarly, when Edison Automobile is broken down into smaller segments for analysis, we see an additional $200,000 of indirect costs that are not assigned to Edison Automobile's three regions. Costs such as the division manager's salary and advertising for all regions are not controlled by the region manager and so are not allocated to the regions. You will note that as we move down the organizational hierarchy, from divisions to geographic regions to countries, indirect costs increase in total; managers at the lower levels have the narrowest range of responsibility and the fewest costs to control. The manager of manufacturing in Japan, for example, will be responsible for the items ordered for that unit but not for setting the salary of the manager of Far East operations; this is the responsibility of the manager of Edison Automobile. The salary of the manager of Far East operations is thus a direct and controllable cost of Edison Automobile and is an indirect and noncontrollable cost to Japanese operations.

Interpreting Profit Center Performance Results

segment margins The difference between segment revenue and direct segment costs; a measure of the segment's contribution to cover indirect fixed costs and provide profits.

Given that the segment-margin income statement in Exhibit 5 was prepared in light of the principles of controllable and direct costs, how does management use the information it contains? First, the net income figure provides management with concrete information for evaluating the performance of the company as a whole. Second, the **segment margins** enable management to analyze company results by evaluating the performance of each segment.

We are now ready to examine the operations of IMC segments in detail. In absolute terms, Edison Automobile has a larger segment margin than Acme Computer ($2 million versus $1.8 million). U.S. operations has earned more than the Far East and European operations; the Japanese operations has a larger segment margin than the Korean operations. Absolute profits, however, often favor those segments with a larger asset base—with larger manufacturing facilities, for example. A larger facility with more manufacturing capacity should naturally have higher production and higher sales and, hence, a higher segment margin and higher income. A more equitable way to assess performance is to compare **segment-margin ratios** (segment margin divided by net sales), because ratios focus on relationships rather than absolute dollar amounts. For example, though the segment margin of European operations is larger than that of Far East operations, the latter has a higher segment-margin ratio (25% versus 18.3%).

segment-margin ratios The segment margin divided by the segment's net sales revenue; a measure of the efficiency of the segment's operating performance and, therefore, of its profitability.

In using segment-margin income statements to evaluate profit centers, it is important to review performance over several periods or months. A single period or month may not be typical of overall performance. In our example, September might have been an unusually bad profitability month for the Korean unit of Far East operations because of a slump in the Korean economy or a labor strike. In fact, the performance can be evaluated only by looking at cost and profit trends over several periods, and by comparing the results of these units with those of other similar units.

Managing Revenues in Profit Centers

Profit center managers manage their costs the same way cost center managers evaluate and manage costs. That is, they use the standard costing concepts that we have already discussed. Unlike cost center managers, however, profit center managers are also responsible for managing revenues because the segment profit they are evaluated on is a function of both costs and revenues. In the next section, we examine how variance analysis is used to manage revenues.

Exhibit 5: A Segment-Margin Income Statement

International Manufacturing Corporation (IMC)
Segment-Margin Income Statement
September 2006
(in thousands of dollars)

		Segments	
	IMC	**Acme Computers**	**Edison Automobile**
Net sales revenue	$ 25,000	$ 15,000	$10,000
Variable costs:			
Cost of goods sold	$(16,000)	$(10,000)	$ (6,000)
Selling and administrative costs	(3,300)	(2,000)	(1,300)
Total variable costs	$(19,300)	$(12,000)	$ (7,300)
Contribution margin	$ 5,700	$ 3,000	$ 2,700
Less fixed costs controllable by segment manager	(1,900)	(1,200)	(700)
Segment margin	$ 3,800	$ 1,800	$ 2,000
Less indirect costs to segments (common costs)	(1,500)		
Net income	$ 2,300		
Segment-margin ratio	9.2%	12.0%	20.0%

Managing Revenues and Revenue Variances

A segment's actual and expected revenues may differ for several reasons including the following:

- Sales prices were higher or lower than expected → a sales price variance.
- Sales volume was higher or lower than expected → a sales volume variance.
- The company's market share was higher or lower than expected → a market share variance.
- The industry, as a whole, sold fewer products than expected → an industry volume variance.
- The mix of products sold was different than expected → a sales mix variance.[4]

Because management is interested in knowing which of these factors contributed to differences between actual and expected or standard[5] revenues, variances that help isolate these factors are calculated. To illustrate how revenue variances are calculated, let's return to our Sunbird Boat Company example. Market share, industry volume, and sales data for Sunbird's 15-foot boat line are as follows:

	Expected (Standard) Sales Data			
	Sales Price	**Boat Sales**	**Total Market**	**Percent of Market**
15-foot boats	$10,000	100	625 boats	16.00%

	Actual Sales Data			
	Sales Price	**Boat Sales**	**Total Market**	**Percent of Market**
15-foot boats	$10,500	90	480 boats	18.75%

4 Sales mix variance is a complex topic that we'll reserve for more advanced textbooks.
5 Again remember that the terms *standard* and *expected* are being used interchangeably in this analysis work.

International Manufacturing Corporation (IMC)
Segment-Margin Income Statement
September 2006
(in thousands of dollars)

	Segments				Segments	
Edison Automobile	U.S. Operations	Far East Operations	European Operations	Far East Operations	Japanese Operations	Korean Operations
$10,000	$ 5,000	$ 2,000	$ 3,000	$ 2,000	$1,200	$ 800
$ (6,000)	$(2,900)	$(1,100)	$(2,000)	$(1,100)	$ (700)	$(400)
(1,300)	(700)	(300)	(300)	(300)	(170)	(130)
$ (7,300)	$(3,600)	$(1,400)	$(2,300)	$(1,400)	$ (870)	$(530)
$ 2,700	$ 1,400	$ 600	$ 700	$ 600	$ 330	$ 270
(500)	(250)	(100)	(150)	(70)	(60)	(10)
$ 2,200	$ 1,150	$ 500	$ 550	$ 530	$ 270	$ 260
(200)				(30)		
$ 2,000				$ 500		
20.0%	23.0%	25.0%	18.3%	25.0%	22.5%	32.5%

Now take a moment and study these data. In terms of Sunbird's revenue performance, what do you see? You should see both positive (favorable) and negative (unfavorable) results on sales-related issues. For instance, the sales price is higher than expected. If Sunbird can sell the same volume of boats at a higher sales price, then revenue is going to increase. This would mean that Sunbird had a favorable sales price variance. On the other hand, Sunbird actually sold fewer boats than expected, which means that it had an unfavorable sales volume variance. This sales volume variance could be explained in part due to the fact that the overall industry is selling fewer boats. This fact means that there was an unfavorable industry volume variance. However, Sunbird would have had even fewer sales but it was able to increase its share of the overall boat market (from 16% to 18.75%). Hence, Sunbird's unfavorable sales volume variance was offset by a favorable market share variance. Does this discussion of Sunbird's revenue performance make sense to you? If so, then you're getting a good feel for how variances are computed and what they signal to management. All that we need to do now is determine the total dollar value (i.e., size) of these revenue variances. The calculations for these four revenue variances are shown below.

sales price variance The difference between the actual price and the expected or standard price multiplied by the actual quantity sold; measures that part of the variance between expected and actual sales revenue that is due to differences between expected and actual prices of goods.

sales volume variance The difference between the actual quantity and the expected quantity sold multiplied by the expected or standard price; measures that part of the variance between expected and actual sales revenue that is due to the difference between expected and actual volume of goods sold.

Sales Price Variance. The **sales price variance** indicates the impact of a different price than expected on the organization's revenues. Hence, the sales price variance is a function of the difference between the actual sales price and the expected (or standard) sales price. This difference is then multiplied by the actual quantity of goods or services sold in order to determine the financial impact of this variance on the company. Therefore, Sunbird's favorable price variance of $500 ($10,500 − $10,000) is multiplied by the 90 boats actually sold to determine a total sales price variance of $45,000 F.

Sales Volume Variance. As the organization sells more or less than what was expected, this results in a **sales volume variance** that has an important and immediate effect on the organization's revenues. Sunbird has an unfavorable sales volume variance of ten boats. What is the economic impact on Sunbird of selling ten fewer boats? We need to be careful here. If you understand economics, then you understand one important factor that determines the volume of sales is the sales price (e.g., higher prices typically result in lower volumes and vice-versa).

However, there are other factors that affect the volume of sales (effort, advertising, competitors, technology, etc.). Nevertheless, in variance analysis it is important to isolate the effect of sales volume on revenues from the effect of sale prices on revenues. Therefore, similar to the approach used with materials quantity and labor efficiency variances, we multiply the underlying "real" volume variance of ten boats by the expected (or standard) sales price to calculate the financial impact on Sunbird of selling fewer boats; in other words, 10 boats × $10,000 = $100,000 U.

You can see how the calculations of the sales price variance and the sales volume variance are related in the illustration below.

Sales Price Variance and Sales Volume Variance

Actual quantity × Actual price	Actual quantity × Standard price	Expected quantity × Standard price
90 boats × $10,500 = $945,000	90 boats × $10,000 = $900,000	100 boats × $10,000 = $1,000,000

Sales price variance = $45,000 F   Sales volume variance = $100,000 U

As you work through these calculations, be sure to keep in mind that you already know which variances are favorable and unfavorable even before you make the calculations. As we discussed previously with cost variances, it's usually best to determine the nature of the variance (favorable versus unfavorable) before you calculate the actual size of the variance.

market share variance The part of the sales volume variance that accounts for the difference between the actual market share of each product sold and the expected market share of each product sold.

Market Share Variance. The sales volume variance can be further analyzed by breaking it down into two underlying variances, one of which is the **market share variance**. One of the reasons that an organization has lower sales is because its share of the overall market for the goods and services it sells has declined. This probably seems like an obvious point to you, but sometimes an organization has an unfavorable sales volume even though its share of the overall market has increased! This happens when the overall market is shrinking. It is one thing to compete for sales in a growing market, and it is entirely another thing to compete in a shrinking market. The market share variance, coupled with the industry volume variance, helps the organization understand both of these important revenue performance issues. You can see in the illustration on the following page how the calculation is done for the market share variance. You can also see the underlying cause of this variance: the difference between the actual and expected market share.

industry volume variance The part of the sales volume variance that accounts for the impact on sales revenue of an actual total market size that is different from the expected size.

Industry Volume Variance. To a large extent, the organization can't individually control the size of the overall industry in which it competes for customers' business. For example, as consumer tastes change, the overall industry (or market) will shift in size. Alternative and complimentary products and services also impact the size of the market. And, these market changes generally have a very direct impact on the sales volume for each merchant in the market. The **industry volume variance** isolates the effect of the changing size of the industry from changes in the merchant's individual share of the industry's total sales. You can see from the original data for Sunbird that the overall industry has reduced in total size from 625 annual boat sales to 480. Holding all else equal (that is, Sunbird's expected market share and standard selling price), we can calculate the financial impact of the change in the industry. As you review the calculation for this variance in the illustration on the next page, you should note that we isolate the impact of industry volume on Sunbird's revenues by multiplying the change in industry volume (145 boats) by the expected market share (16%) and by the standard price ($10,000).

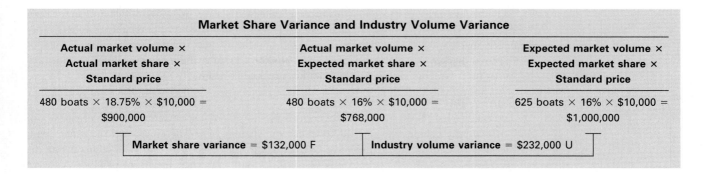

There is one more thing to note before we finish the calculations for the market share and industry volume variances. If you inspect carefully the calculations in the earlier illustrations for the sales volume variance, market share variance, and industry volume variance, you may see that these calculations are very closely related. In fact, once you've calculated the sales volume variance, you only need to compute one more number to compute both the market share and industry volume variances. This is illustrated below.

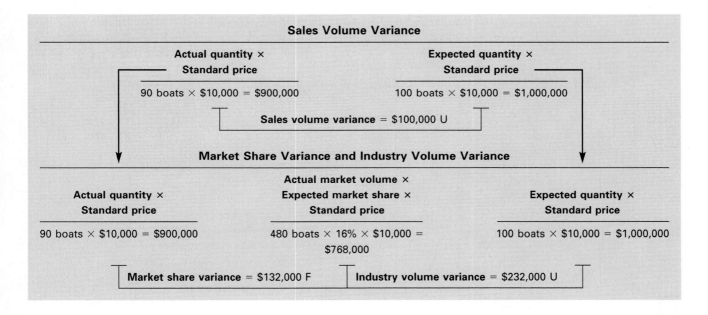

Summarizing these variances, we see that the revenue variances for Sunbird's 15-foot boats are as follows:

Variances	Sales Price	Sales Volume	Total
15-foot boats	$ 45,000 F	$100,000 U	$ 55,000 U

Breakdown of Sales Volume Variance			
	Market Share	Total Industry	Total
15-foot boats	$132,000 F	$232,000 U	$100,000 U

The sales price variance informs users whether actual sales prices were higher or lower than expected. The sales volume variance informs users whether the number of units sold was more or less than expected. The market share variance informs users whether the company's share of the total market was higher or lower than expected. Finally, the industry volume variance informs users whether the actual total market was higher or lower than expected.

Controlling Revenue Variances

Typically, sales prices are under the control of the marketing executives in the organization. These are the people who carefully establish the strategy of setting prices. On the other hand, the sales volume is largely under the control of the sales executives and sales teams in the organization. These are the people who work closely with customers to sell the product. As we've discussed above, several factors impact sales volume, including price (which is under the control of marketing) and the size of the total industry (which is very difficult to control at all).

Accounting for Revenue Variances

The nature of the sales volume variance makes accounting for revenue variances in the general ledger more challenging than the accounting for materials and labor variances. While the organization can recognize and record sales price variances throughout the reporting period, it really doesn't know if there is a sales volume variance until the end of the period. To handle this difficulty, some organizations set up a revenue control account at the beginning of the period and use it to immediately record revenues at the expected level. The control account is then used throughout the period to record actual revenue. Any remaining balance in the control account at the end of the period is equal to the difference between expected and actual revenue. This difference is used in the process of recording the revenue variances in a single entry at the end of the period as shown.

Caution

Remember that the industry volume variance and the market share variance combine to make up the sales volume variance. In other words, you either make a single accounting entry for the sales volume variance or you can make two separate entries for the industry volume variance and the market share variance. Managers who want more rather than less information for revenue management decisions will generally choose to report the two separate variances.

Industry Volume Variance		
(145 boats × 16% × $10,000)	232,000	
Market Share Variance		
(480 boats × 2.75% × $10,000)		132,000
Sales Price Variance (90 boats × $500)		45,000
Revenue Control		55,000

Use the revenue control account to establish the unfavorable industry volume variance to reflect an overall market decline of 145 boat sales; to establish the favorable market share variance to reflect a 2.75% increase; to establish the favorable sales price variance to reflect a $500 price increase.

Once the revenue variances have been established, they are immediately closed to Revenue. By closing these variances to Revenue, the expected revenues will be adjusted to actual revenues which are then reported on the income statement.

STOP & THINK

Is it possible that a manager could be doing a poor job of managing revenues and revenue growth even though revenues were increasing from period to period?

TO SUMMARIZE: Profit center managers are usually evaluated on both costs and revenues. The most common profit center measurement tool is the segment-margin income statement. This statement identifies both direct and indirect costs and charges only the direct costs to segments. Segment-margin income statements subdivide direct costs into their variable and fixed cost components. Costs in profit centers are analyzed and managed the same way they are in cost centers—using standard costing. Because profit center managers are also held responsible for revenues, a revenue variance analysis procedure is used that breaks down differences between actual and expected revenues into sales price variances and sales volume variances. Sales volume variances can be further broken down into market share variances and industry volume variances.

Evaluating Performance in Investment Centers

6 Use ROI and residual income analysis to explain how performance is controlled in investment centers.

An investment center was defined earlier as an organizational unit in which a manager has responsibility for costs, revenues, and assets. Overall, companies would be considered investment centers, as would some independent segments of decentralized companies. For example, the Acme Computer and Edison Automobile subsidiaries of IMC (see Exhibit 1) would probably both be investment centers. Officers of such segments are responsible for acquiring and managing the assets required to manufacture and market their products, as well as for managing the revenues and costs related to those products. The assets include inventory, accounts receivable, and long-term operating assets such as equipment and delivery trucks. On the other hand, Edison's Japanese operation could be considered a profit center if all asset management decisions are handled by Far East operations. Further, the Manufacturing center for Japanese operations is likely a cost center since it doesn't control sales.

In business, the distinction between profit and investment centers often becomes blurred or even nonexistent. Many companies refer to segments as profit centers when they are really investment centers. Nevertheless, because the distinction between profit and investment centers is important for defining responsibilities and determining how performance will be evaluated, we discuss them separately.

There are several methods of evaluating the performance of an investment center. When a segment operates almost as a separate company, the rate of return on invested assets and the residual income are usually measured.

Return on Investment (ROI)

return on investment (ROI) A measure of operating performance and efficiency in utilizing assets; computed in its simplest form by dividing net income by total assets.

As you will recall, we introduced management accounting in an earlier chapter by describing how the management team at DUPONT used **return on investment (ROI)** (sometimes called return on total assets[6]) to manage their company to success in the early 1900s. ROI is a measure of how much has been earned on the assets of a company; it is equal to net income divided by total assets. For example, if a company earned $1,000 on $10,000 of assets for one year, its ROI would be $1,000 ÷ $10,000, or 10%.

Because an investment center operates as if it were an independent company, its performance can also be evaluated using ROI. In calculating the ROI for an investment center, however, management must be sure to consider only the assets, revenues, and costs controlled by that center. In other words, assets used and costs incurred for the benefit of several investment centers should not be included in the calculation. To stress this concept, we will restate the basic ROI formula as:

$$\text{Investment center ROI} = \frac{\text{Investment center income}}{\text{Investment center average assets}}$$

Generally, when an investment center's ROI is analyzed, this formula is divided into its components—the operations performance (sometimes called profit margin) and asset turnover ratios—as follows:

$$\text{Profit margin} \times \text{Asset turnover} = \text{ROI}$$

$$\frac{\text{Net income}}{\text{Revenue}} \times \frac{\text{Revenue}}{\text{Average total assets}} = \frac{\text{Net income}}{\text{Average total assets}}$$

Net income, which is a function of costs or expenses and revenues, and revenues were considered in profit centers. The ROI formula expands the use of cost and revenue measures to

---

6 In this chapter, we will use the term *ROI* instead of *return on total assets* because it is more commonly used in management decision making. To be consistent with how we've calculated ROI in other chapters, we will use average total assets instead of ending total assets (although in actual practice, management teams in some organizations may choose to use ending total assets). Average total assets is generally computed by adding the assets balances at the beginning and end of the year, and then dividing the sum in half.

also include measures of assets. Thus, when combined with cost and revenue variance analysis, ROI is an effective tool in evaluating investment centers where management has responsibility for assets as well as profits. It is this ROI calculation that investors commonly use to evaluate companies in which they are considering investing.

Clearly, in the above calculations, we could have eliminated the two revenue figures because they cancel each other out, making ROI equal to net income divided by average total assets. However, including revenue draws attention to the important concept that ROI is a function of both operating performance and asset turnover.

The expanded formula shown above helps us identify the three ways an investment center can improve its ROI: (1) it can decrease costs to increase its **profit margin (operating performance) ratio** (net income divided by revenue), (2) it can decrease assets to increase its **asset turnover ratio** (revenue divided by average total assets), or (3) it can increase revenue with a corresponding increase in net income. An investment center requiring a major investment in assets (such as a steel mill) will necessarily have a low asset turnover and will therefore have to rely primarily on a higher operating performance to increase its return. An investment center with few operating assets (such as a grocery store) has a more rapid asset turnover and can sustain a lower profit margin ratio while still earning an attractive ROI. For example, a grocery store might make only 2 cents profit per dollar of product sold, but its asset turnover of 12 times a year makes its ROI 24%. A steel mill with an asset turnover of 2 times a year would have to earn 12 cents per dollar of sales to produce an ROI of 24%.

To illustrate the three ways of increasing ROI, we will assume that Acme Computer has revenue of $10,000,000, profit (segment) margin of $1,000,000, and average total assets of $5,000,000. The ROI is:

$$\text{Profit margin} \times \text{Asset turnover} = \text{ROI}$$

$$\frac{\$1,000,000}{\$10,000,000} \times \frac{\$10,000,000}{\$5,000,000} = \text{ROI}$$

$$10\% \times 2 = 20\%$$

The following examples show how each of the three alternatives increases ROI:

1. Increase ROI by reducing expenses by $400,000, providing a profit margin of $1,400,000:

$$\frac{\$1,400,000}{\$10,000,000} \times \frac{\$10,000,000}{\$5,000,000} = \text{ROI}$$

$$14\% \times 2 = 28\%$$

2. Increase ROI by reducing average total assets to $4,000,000:

$$\frac{\$1,000,000}{\$10,000,000} \times \frac{\$10,000,000}{\$4,000,000} = \text{ROI}$$

$$10\% \times 2.5 = 25\%$$

3. Increase ROI by increasing revenue to $12,000,000 (assume that profits increase proportionately):[7]

$$\frac{\$1,200,000}{\$12,000,000} \times \frac{\$12,000,000}{\$5,000,000} = \text{ROI}$$

$$10\% \times 2.4 = 24\%$$

---

7 As discussed earlier in the cost-volume-profit chapter, because of the concept of operating leverage, profits are likely to increase more than proportionately when revenue rises. When revenue increases 10%, fixed costs may remain the same. The result is that both the operating performance and asset turnover ratios are likely to increase when revenue goes up. We are ignoring these C-V-P considerations in order to keep the example simple.

profit margin (operating performance) ratio An overall measure of the profitability of operations during a period; computed by dividing net income by revenue.

asset turnover ratio An overall measure of how effectively assets are used during a period; computed by dividing revenue by average total assets.

Reduce Cost
Decrease of Assets needed to produce
Comply Intelligently.
ex. OSHA. Benefit effectiveness)
Analysis.

Although ROI is an effective way of evaluating managers of investment centers, it has certain drawbacks. For example, assume that an investment center currently has an ROI of 22%, but the company has an overall ROI of only 16%. If a new project or investment that promises a return of 19% becomes available to the investment center manager, it might be rejected because the center's ROI would be reduced, even though the company's overall ROI would be increased.

Residual Income

residual income The amount of net income earned above a specified minimum rate of return on assets; used to evaluate investment centers.

Although ROI is widely used to evaluate investment centers, because of its drawbacks, some companies use a closely related measure called **residual income**, which is the amount of net income an investment center is able to earn above a certain minimum rate of return on assets. The formula for residual income is as follows:

Net income − (Minimum required rate of return × Average total assets) = Residual income

To illustrate, let's return to Acme Computer and calculate its residual income. Assuming that the specified minimum rate of return on assets at IMC is 15%, Acme Computer needs to earn at least $750,000 (15% × $5,000,000 average total assets) before it can report any residual income. We then compute Acme Computer's residual income as follows:

$1,000,000 segment margin − $750,000 minimum return on assets = $250,000 residual income

To further illustrate why many companies prefer to use residual income over ROI for evaluating investment center performance, assume that Acme Computer has an opportunity to invest $1,200,000 in a new project that will generate a return of 16% ($192,000 per year). If Acme Computer's manager is being evaluated on ROI, she would probably reject this investment opportunity because, as the following analysis shows, it would reduce the division's overall ROI from 20% to 19.2%.

	Without the New Investment	The New Investment	With the New Investment
Total assets	$5,000,000	$1,200,000	$6,200,000
Segment margin	$1,000,000	$ 192,000	$1,192,000
ROI	20%	16%	19.2%

On the other hand, if the manager is being evaluated on residual income (with a minimum rate of return of 15%), she would probably be more positive about the project because it increases residual income from $250,000 to $262,000.

	Without the New Investment	The New Investment	With the New Investment
Total assets	$5,000,000	$1,200,000	$6,200,000
Segment margin	$1,000,000	$ 192,000	$1,192,000
Less the minimum rate of return ...	750,000*	180,000**	930,000
Residual income	$ 250,000	$ 12,000	$ 262,000

*$5,000,000 × 15% = $750,000
**$1,200,000 × 15% = $180,000

Whether or not the investment should actually be made also depends on several other factors, including what other alternatives are or will be available. The advantage of residual income is that it encourages managers to make as much profit as possible rather than merely achieving a certain ROI; this means making investments that benefit not only their centers but also the company as a whole.

> **TO SUMMARIZE:** Managers of investment centers are usually held responsible for costs, revenues, and assets. The most common performance measures used in investment centers are ROI and residual income. ROI is a function of both operating performance and asset turnover.
>
> Residual income is the amount of income left over after a certain minimum rate of return has been earned on assets. Both ROI and residual income must be used with care because they can encourage managers to maximize short-run profits at the expense of long-term profitability.

Earlier in the chapter, you were introduced to standard costing as a way to evaluate performance in cost centers and were shown how standard costing can be used to compute variances for materials and labor. Information relating to these material and labor variances can be used by decision makers to evaluate the acquisition and use of these important resources. In this expanded material section, we introduce you to the variances associated with manufacturing overhead costs. While several of the computations associated with overhead variances are similar to those used for materials and labor, they are generally more complicated. As a result, interpreting the results and assigning responsibility must be done with caution.

Variable Manufacturing Overhead Variances in Cost Centers

7 Compute and interpret variable overhead cost variances.

Manufacturing overhead is the third type of product cost that must be controlled and accounted for. In this section we will cover variable overhead. Fixed overhead will be covered in the next section.

Measuring and Controlling Variable Manufacturing Overhead Costs

Variable manufacturing overhead includes such costs as indirect materials, indirect labor, utilities, and repairs and maintenance. Like direct materials and direct labor, variable manufacturing overhead is measured and controlled by establishing standard costs, measuring actual costs, analyzing variances from standard, and reporting the variances to managers so they can take necessary corrective action.

Identifying Variable Overhead Elements, Cost Drivers, and Per-Unit Costs

The first step in controlling variable manufacturing overhead is to study the behavior of each overhead cost to determine whether it is fixed, variable, or mixed. (You will recall that we analyzed cost behavior previously in the cost-volume-profit chapter.) The second step is to develop a cost driver for each variable manufacturing overhead element that relates the variable manufacturing overhead cost to specific activities or volume changes. In a later chapter, we will introduce you to new product costing methods, including activity-based costing, where multiple cost drivers are used. For simplicity in illustrating variable overhead variances, we will assume that variable manufacturing overhead costs vary with direct labor hours. However, you should be aware that, where possible, costs are assigned to activities based on cost drivers that reflect the actual usage of costs for each activity. Thus, instead of using one cost driver, such as direct labor hours, a company might identify different cost drivers for each type of variable overhead cost.

To illustrate the calculation of variable manufacturing cost variances using direct labor hours as the cost driver, we will return again to our Sunbird Boat Company example. Assume that, for Sunbird, direct labor hours worked fluctuate between 6,500 and 8,500 hours each month. At the beginning of the year, Sunbird's management team and accountants analyzed the company's cost behavior patterns over this relevant range to create an annual budget. Based on their sales budget, they also established a production budget to produce 95 15-foot boats.[8] As you recall from its standard cost card (Exhibit 3 on page 338), Sunbird allows 80 standard direct labor hours for each 15-foot boat produced. This means that 7,600 direct labor hours (95 boats × 80 standard hours) were originally estimated to be used in the current year. These data were then used to establish standard variable manufacturing overhead rates as shown below:

	Annual Budgeted Costs		Divided by the Total Standard Direct Labor Hours Allowed		Variable Manufacturing Overhead Rate
Indirect materials	$11,400	÷	7,600 hours	=	$1.50 per hour
Indirect labor	41,800	÷	7,600 hours	=	5.50 per hour
Utilities	7,600	÷	7,600 hours	=	1.00 per hour
Variable manufacturing overhead . . .	$60,800				$8.00 per hour

Caution

Be sure you understand that in our Sunbird example overhead costs are applied on the basis of *standard direct labor hours allowed*, and not on the actual direct labor hours used. Hence, regardless of how many hours are actually used to produce a boat, variable manufacturing overhead of $640 is applied ($8.00 × 80 hours). This is the approach used by most companies that follow a standard cost accounting system.

As you can see, by summing these amounts, Sunbird developed a total standard variable manufacturing overhead rate of $8.00 per direct labor hour. Since Sunbird allows 80 standard direct labor hours for each 15-foot boat produced, it applies $640.00 to each boat produced ($8.00 × 80 hours).

Variable Manufacturing Overhead Variances

Let's now illustrate how variances are calculated for variable manufacturing overhead costs. You'll recall from our work with direct labor variances that the Sunbird Boat Company actually used 7,092 direct labor hours to produce 90 15-foot boats during the year. Given that only 90 boats were actually produced (rather than the 95 boats originally budgeted to be produced), Sunbird Boat Company should have used 7,200 direct labor hours (as calculated in the table below). Sunbird's end-of-year results, including the total variable manufacturing overhead costs actually incurred, are summarized as follows:

Caution

The 7,600 direct labor hours *budgeted* at the beginning of the year are not to be confused with the 7,200 hours *allowed for actual production* by the end of the year. Similarly, do not confuse the $60,800 variable manufacturing overhead costs *budgeted* at the beginning of the year with the $57,600 variable manufacturing overhead costs *allowed for actual production* by the end of the year.

Boats produced	90
Direct labor hours used	7,092
Standard direct labor hours for boats produced (80 hours × 90 boats)	7,200
Standard variable manufacturing overhead for boats produced (7,200 hours × $8)	$57,600
Actual variable manufacturing overhead costs incurred:	
Indirect materials	$ 9,373
Indirect labor	42,710
Utilities	8,199
Total variable manufacturing overhead costs	$60,282

8 These are the same production and sales numbers we created in the previous chapter on operational budgeting. In fact, all standard costs and budgets used in the Sunbird Boat Company example in this chapter are based on data established in the operational budgeting chapter. You're encouraged to review the previous chapter if needed to better understand these standard (or budgeted) costs.

As you can see in the table on the previous page, on the basis of 7,200 standard direct labor hours allowed to produce an actual output of 90 boats, the standard cost allowed for variable manufacturing overhead is $57,600 (7,200 hours × $8.00 per hour). The difference between the $60,282 actually incurred and the $57,600 standard cost allowed is the amount of over- or underapplied variable overhead. In this example, variable manufacturing overhead has been underapplied by $2,682 ($60,282 − $57,600). As with direct materials and direct labor, the total variable manufacturing overhead variance is separated into two major variances: spending and efficiency. The spending and efficiency variances are computed as follows:

Variable Manufacturing Overhead Variances

Actual amount spent	AH × SR Actual hours of input × Standard rate	SHA × SR Standard hours allowed for actual output × Standard rate
$60,282	7,092 hours × $8.00 = $56,736	7,200 hours × $8.00 = $57,600

Variable overhead spending variance
$60,282 − $56,736 = $3,546 U

Variable overhead efficiency variance
$8.00 × (7,200 hours − 7,092 hours) = $864 F

---

variable manufacturing overhead spending variance The difference between actual variable manufacturing overhead incurred and the amount that should have been incurred based on the actual activity used to assign overhead costs to production.

Variable Manufacturing Overhead Spending Variance. The **variable manufacturing overhead spending variance** ($3,546 U) is the difference between the actual variable manufacturing overhead costs incurred ($60,282) and the amount that should have been incurred at the actual activity level, $56,736 (7,092 direct labor hours × $8.00 standard rate).

Because manufacturing overhead contains several different cost items, it is possible to compute a spending variance for each variable overhead item. This analysis helps managers determine which costs are largely responsible for creating the variances. For Sunbird Boat Company, the analysis would be as follows:

	Actual Costs	Actual Hours of Input × Standard Rate	Spending Variance
Indirect materials	$ 9,373	7,092 hours × $1.50 = $10,638	$1,265 F
Indirect labor	42,710	7,092 hours × $5.50 = 39,006	3,704 U
Utilities	8,199	7,092 hours × $1.00 = 7,092	1,107 U
	$60,282	$56,736	$3,546 U

variable manufacturing overhead efficiency variance The difference between the standard variable manufacturing overhead for the actual activity level and standard variable manufacturing overhead for the standard activity level allowed. This variance effectively measures the efficiency of the underlying activity used to assign variable manufacturing overhead costs; it does not measure the efficiency of how variable manufacturing overhead costs are used.

Looking at the spending variance column, we see a $1,265 favorable variance for indirect materials, a $3,704 unfavorable variance for indirect labor, and a $1,107 unfavorable variance for utilities. The favorable variance for indirect materials means that less was spent than was expected for the actual hours worked, indicating either that spending is in control or that the standards are too high. The unfavorable variances indicate that spending exceeded the standard and that there may be a problem. In both cases, managers and others responsible for any significant variances (favorable or unfavorable) should be asked to explain the reasons for their existence. Of course, this example assumes that variable overhead is a function of direct labor hours. If direct labor hours is not a good cost driver of (i.e., does not influence) variable overhead costs, the variances are highly suspect.

Variable Manufacturing Overhead Efficiency Variance. The $864 favorable **variable manufacturing overhead efficiency variance** is the standard variable overhead rate times the difference between the standard and actual activity levels [$8.00 × (7,200 standard direct labor hours allowed − 7,092 actual direct labor hours)]. When direct labor hours are used as the basis for assigning manufacturing overhead, the efficiency variance simply indicates whether the standard number of hours allowed for production are more (favorable) or less (unfavorable) than the actual hours used for production. As you will recall, the same relationship was used on page 345 in computing the direct labor efficiency variance. Hence, since Sunbird's direct labor efficiency variance is favorable ($1,620), the variable manufacturing overhead efficiency variance is also favorable ($864). Conversely, of course, an unfavorable direct labor efficiency variance would have produced an unfavorable variable manufacturing overhead efficiency variance. The only difference between the value for the direct labor efficiency variance and the variable manufacturing overhead efficiency variance is the rate used in computing each variance. What this means is that the variable manufacturing overhead efficiency variance really doesn't describe the efficiency of using variable manufacturing overhead; rather, it reports the efficiency of how the manufacturing allocation basis is being used. Since Sunbird is using direct labor hours to assign manufacturing overhead, the variable manufacturing overhead variance doesn't really provide any additional information for management beyond that already provided by the direct labor efficiency variance. As a result, the manager responsible for the control of direct labor hours should be credited for Sunbird's favorable manufacturing overhead efficiency variance because the variance is a measure of the efficiency with which direct labor is used. (Again, it is important to note that we are assuming that direct labor hours is an appropriate cost driver at Sunbird Boat Company for variable manufacturing overhead costs.)

The only reason for computing the variable manufacturing overhead efficiency variance at Sunbird Boat Company is to be able to account for over- or underapplied manufacturing overhead and close the amount to Cost of Goods Sold. We'll talk more about over- or underapplied manufacturing overhead in the next section.

TO SUMMARIZE: Cost drivers that relate to individual overhead items are used to relate overhead costs to activities. Standard overhead costs are then computed for each variable overhead item to determine a standard variable rate that is used in applying variable manufacturing overhead to each unit of product. This rate is also used in the process of analyzing variable manufacturing overhead variances. The total variable manufacturing overhead variance can be segregated into two variances: spending and efficiency. The variable manufacturing overhead spending variance measures the difference between the costs actually incurred and the amount that should have been incurred at the actual activity level. The variable manufacturing overhead efficiency variance is the difference between variable manufacturing overhead costs at the actual and standard activity levels. Because the spending variance highlights the differences between actual costs incurred and standard amounts for individual manufacturing overhead items, it is generally the more useful overhead variance to analyze for control purposes. The variable manufacturing overhead efficiency variance doesn't really report on the efficiency of variable manufacturing overhead costs, but on the efficiency of the *activity used to allocate* variable manufacturing overhead costs.

Fixed Manufacturing Overhead Variances in Cost Centers

8 Compute and interpret fixed overhead cost variances.

The final product cost to account for is fixed manufacturing overhead. Fixed manufacturing overhead includes such costs as rent, insurance, depreciation, staff and supervisor salaries, and taxes. This cost is unique among the product costs. Since direct materials and direct labor are generally characterized as variable costs similar to variable manufacturing overhead, the process of "controlling" fixed manufacturing overhead is different from the other costs we've studied in this chapter. Nevertheless, fixed manufacturing overhead is a very significant cost in most organizations that requires careful management attention.

Measuring and Controlling Fixed Manufacturing Overhead Costs

Reporting on how well fixed manufacturing overhead costs are controlled is actually a fairly straightforward process. Because these costs are fixed in total, measuring variances around these costs is simply a matter of comparing the original budget with the total fixed overhead costs that were actually spent. To demonstrate, let's return once more to our Sunbird Boat Company example. Similar to the variable manufacturing overhead budget established at the beginning of the year, Sunbird's management team and accountants also created a fixed manufacturing overhead budget. Then, in order to subsequently allocate these costs to boats as they are produced during the year, Sunbird created standard fixed manufacturing overhead rates using an approach similar to that used to create standard variable manufacturing overhead rates. This process is shown below:

	Annual Budgeted Costs	Divided by the Total Standard Direct Labor Hours Allowed	Fixed Manufacturing Overhead Rate
Property taxes	$ 3,040 ÷	7,600 hours	= $ 0.40 per hour
Insurance	3,600 ÷	7,600 hours	= 0.47 per hour
Depreciation on the plant	66,000 ÷	7,600 hours	= 8.68 per hour
Supervisors' salaries	90,000 ÷	7,600 hours	= 11.84 per hour
Fixed manufacturing overhead ...	$162,640		$21.40 per hour*

*Rounded.

As you compare this chart to the similar chart we created earlier for variable manufacturing overhead, be sure to bear in mind that we're dealing with fixed costs here. Similar to the $8.00 variable manufacturing overhead rate created earlier, the $21.40 fixed manufacturing overhead rate above will be used by Sunbird's accountants to allocate manufacturing overhead to production (again, remember that we discussed the overhead allocation process previously in an earlier chapter on product cost flows). Hence, Sunbird applies $1,712 ($21.40 × 80 hours) in fixed manufacturing overhead costs to each 15-foot boat produced. In addition, you'll remember from the previous section on variable manufacturing overhead that Sunbird uses the variable manufacturing overhead rate of $8.00 to apply $640 ($8.00 × 80 hours) to each boat produced. Sunbird also uses the $8.00 rate to measure expected variable manufacturing overhead costs based on actual production. On the other hand, Sunbird's accountants don't use the $21.40 rate to measure expected fixed manufacturing overhead costs. These costs are fixed and are expected to be $162,640, regardless of the level of boats actually produced.

Fixed Manufacturing Overhead Variances

During the year, Sunbird incurred the following costs:

Actual fixed manufacturing overhead costs incurred:

Property taxes	$ 4,015
Insurance	2,986
Depreciation on the plant	65,533
Supervisors' salaries	83,490
Total actual fixed manufacturing overhead costs	$156,024

These costs, combined with Sunbird's fixed manufacturing overhead budget and the standard fixed manufacturing overhead rate (also known as the predetermined manufacturing overhead rate), are used by Sunbird's accountants to create the two variances in this illustration:

Fixed Manufacturing Overhead Variances

Actual amount spent	Budgeted amount (used to establish the predetermined allocation rate)	SHA × SR Standard hours allowed for actual output × Standard rate
$156,024	$162,640; $162,640 ÷ 7,600 hours = $21.40 per hour	7,200 hours × $21.40 = $154,080

Fixed overhead budget variance
$162,640 − $156,024 = $6,616 F

Volume variance
$21.40 × (7,600 hours − 7,200 hours) = $8,560 U

---

fixed manufacturing overhead budget variance The difference between actual fixed manufacturing overhead incurred and the standard (or budgeted) fixed manufacturing overhead established at the beginning of the reporting period.

Fixed Manufacturing Overhead Budget Variance. The $6,616 favorable **fixed manufacturing overhead budget variance** is the difference between what was actually spent and the original budget. Hence, it is a simple matter to create a detailed budget variance report for each fixed overhead item. This analysis helps managers determine which costs have the biggest impact on the budget variance. For Sunbird Boat Company, the analysis would be as follows:

	Actual Costs	Budgeted Costs	Budget Variance
Property taxes	$ 4,015	$ 3,040	$ 975 U
Insurance	2,986	3,600	614 F
Depreciation on the plant	65,533	66,000	467 F
Supervisors' salaries	83,490	90,000	6,510 F
	$156,024	$162,640	$6,616 F

A quick review of the table above reveals that supervisors' salaries are the largest source of the favorable fixed manufacturing overhead budget variance. Generally, one would expect little change in fixed costs unless a decision is made by management to make a direct change to a cost item. For example, buying or selling property, changing the insurance contract, or adjusting the depreciation schedule will affect the actual fixed costs incurred. Apparently, Sunbird's management team made little change to these items. However, there was apparently a big adjustment in the salaries, perhaps due to a shift in personnel serving in management roles.

volume variance The difference between actual production output and the expected (or budgeted) production output established at the beginning of the reporting period. This difference is then converted into a dollar number by multiplying it by the standard fixed manufacturing overhead costs per unit.

Volume Variance. The $8,560 unfavorable **volume variance** shown in the illustration above is a variance unlike any other we've studied in this chapter. Every variance studied thus far has been an *input* variance; that is, it has been either a variance on how much was spent on the input (materials price, labor rate, variable overhead spending, fixed overhead budget) or a variance on how much of the input was used (materials quantity, labor efficiency, variable overhead efficiency). The volume variance is an *output* variance and measures the difference between expected and actual production volumes.

In the case of Sunbird Boat Company, you will recall that at the beginning of the year management expected to produce 95 15-foot boats. However, at the end of the year the company had only produced 90 boats. This is an unfavorable volume variance, and the amount of that variance is five boats. The problem in a standard costing system is that you can't debit or credit "five boats" into the accounting system. To record this variance requires that the difference between expected and actual output volume be changed into a dollar amount. This is done

Caution

Remember that overhead costs are applied on the basis of *standard direct labor hours allowed*, and not on the actual direct labor hours used. Sunbird will apply $1,712 in fixed manufacturing overhead to each boat produced *regardless* of how many hours are actually used to produce the boat.

FYI:

Managers who understand how to use the volume variance as a performance measure know that this dollar figure doesn't really indicate the volume of costs flowing into or out of their organization. They know that if they divide this number by the predetermined fixed manufacturing overhead rate, they can then see exactly how many units were actually produced above or below the expected level of production.

using the fixed manufacturing overhead rate of $21.40 per direct labor hour. Using the production standards set in its standard cost card, Sunbird allocates $1,712 (80 standard direct labor hours allowed × $21.40 per direct labor hour) in fixed manufacturing overhead to each boat produced. (Remember that Sunbird established the $21.40 rate based on an expectation of producing 95 boats and uses the rate to allocate the budgeted fixed costs of $162,640.) Because Sunbird only produced 90 boats, it only allocated $154,080 ($1,712 × 90 boats). In other words, Sunbird underapplied its fixed manufacturing overhead costs by $8,560 ($162,640 − $154,080), which results in an unfavorable volume variance of $8,560. Another way of calculating this volume variance would be to simply multiply the volume difference of five boats by the $1,712 per-boat application rate.

Accounting for Manufacturing Overhead Variances. The four manufacturing overhead variances we've described in the expanded materials section of this chapter all combine together to form the total over- or underapplied manufacturing overhead in the organization. At the end of the current year, Sunbird's manufacturing overhead account appears as shown below:

Manufacturing Overhead

(Actual costs)		(Applied costs)	
Indirect materials	9,373	57,600	applied variable costs
Indirect labor	42,710	154,080	applied fixed costs
Utilities	8,199		
Property taxes	4,015		
Insurance	2,986		
Depreciation—plant	65,533		
Supervisors' salaries	83,490		
	216,306	211,680	
Balance (underapplied)	4,626		

In a normal cost system, we would close out the underapplied overhead directly to Cost of Goods Sold with the following journal entry:

Cost of Goods Sold	4,626	
Manufacturing Overhead		4,626
To close the balance in Manufacturing Overhead and adjust		
the balance in Cost of Goods Sold up to the actual amount.		

However, since Sunbird uses a standard cost system, it recognizes variances in its accounting system and then uses those variances to adjust standard costs and revenues to actual costs and revenues for the income statement. Consistent with the accounting for variances we've done in this chapter, Sunbird will use the underapplied overhead to recognize the four manufacturing overhead variances as shown below:

Variable Overhead Spending Variance	3,546	
Volume Variance	8,560	
Variable Overhead Efficiency Variance		864
Fixed Overhead Budget Variance		6,616
Manufacturing Overhead		4,626
To close the balance in Manufacturing Overhead and recognize		
the manufacturing overhead variances.		

These overhead variances are subsequently closed to Cost of Goods Sold, which will result in an adjustment that increases Cost of Goods Sold by $4,626.

STOP & THINK

As you have worked through the accounting for manufacturing overhead variances, do you see that applied manufacturing overhead is the same number as standard overhead allowed for actual output? A rule of thumb to use in accounting for overhead variances is that when overhead is underapplied, the total of the four overhead variances will be unfavorable (and vice versa). What kind of adjustment to Cost of Goods Sold is required when manufacturing overhead is underapplied? When manufacturing overhead is overapplied? Do you see why managers and accountants think of underapplied overhead as unfavorable and overapplied overhead as favorable?

TO SUMMARIZE: The process of reporting and controlling fixed manufacturing overhead costs is unique among product costs due to the fact that the other product costs are considered to be variable. As a result, the fixed manufacturing overhead budget variance is a fairly straightforward calculation that is essentially measuring the difference between the original budget amount and what was actually spent for fixed manufacturing overhead. Like the variable manufacturing overhead spending variance, the fixed manufacturing overhead budget variance can be further scrutinized by breaking it down into its individual cost components. On the other hand, the volume variance, which is associated with fixed manufacturing overhead, doesn't really report at all on how fixed manufacturing overhead costs are being used. Instead, the volume variance is an output measure that reports on the difference between expected production volume and actual production volume. The standard (predetermined) fixed overhead rate is used to translate the difference in production output units into a dollar number that can be entered into the standard cost accounting system. The volume variance can then be combined with the fixed manufacturing overhead budget variance and the variable manufacturing overhead spending and efficiency variances to account for over- or underapplied overhead.

review of learning objectives

1 **Explain why control is such an important activity in the management process.** Today, information about how efficiently and effectively an organization is operating is easily accessible worldwide. For a company to survive in this information age, it must deliver the highest-quality products to its customers at the least possible price in the shortest amount of time. The only way an organization can continue to improve on these dimensions is to control well its performance on key processes and products and to identify areas for improvement. This need for continuous improvement makes management control more important than ever before.

2 **Describe the responsibility accounting concept and identify the three types of organizational control units.** Most companies are divided into segments with responsibilities assigned to segment managers. These segments may be defined in terms of product line, geographic area, or function, for example. In a centralized organization, top management makes most of the important operating decisions; in a decentralized organization, decision-making authority is delegated to lower-level managers as well. The current trend

is toward decentralization because it usually results in better, more informed decisions.

With responsibility accounting, managers are held accountable for the costs, revenues, or assets over which they have control. The three types of responsibility centers are cost, profit, and investment. Cost centers are usually found at relatively low levels in the organization, and the managers are held accountable for the costs they incur. Profit and investment centers are found at higher levels, and the managers are held accountable for the profits or the return on investments in assets they generate.

3 **Describe standard costing and the basic variance analysis model.** Traditionally, performance has been evaluated in cost centers using standard costs. A standard cost system involves setting standard (predetermined) costs that serve as a benchmark for judging what actual costs should be. Standard costs are usually expressed as the per-unit cost of materials, labor, and manufacturing overhead and are used by managers for planning, implementing, and controlling decisions. Standard costs are developed on the basis of careful analysis using the experience of many types of staff, including engineers, supervisors, accountants, purchasing agents, and others. Standard costs have a price component and a quantity component. A comparison of actual and standard costs usually results in two variances: a price (rate) variance and a quantity (usage) variance. In a process referred to as management by exception, significant variances alert management to specific problem areas that require corrective action.

A standard cost system is designed to accumulate actual costs, to compare actual and standard costs to identify variances, and to report operating results (including variances) to management for review and for corrective action when significant variances occur. Manufacturing firms make extensive use of standard costing systems, although these kinds of accounting systems are being increasingly used by service and merchandising organizations as well. While standard cost systems have specific advantages and disadvantages, many organizations have found that the control and insight provided by these systems are worth the effort and investment.

4 **Use materials and labor cost variance analysis to explain how performance is controlled in cost centers.** Materials variances are usually called price variances and quantity variances. The materials price variance reflects the extent to which the actual price varies from the standard price for the actual quantity of materials purchased or used. The materials quantity variance measures the extent to which the quantity of materials used varies from the standard quantity allowed for the achieved level of production. Labor variances are called rate variances and efficiency variances. The labor rate variance is the difference between the actual and the standard labor rates multiplied by the actual hours worked. The labor efficiency variance is the difference between actual and standard hours multiplied by the standard wage rate. Unfavorable variances are recorded in the standard cost system with debit accounting entries, while favorable variances are recorded with credit accounting entries.

5 **Use revenue variance analysis to explain how performance is controlled in profit centers.** Profit center managers are responsible for revenues as well as costs. The best measure of performance in a profit center is a segment-margin income statement, which distinguishes between indirect and direct costs and reports a segment margin that is controllable by segment managers. In profit centers, costs are analyzed in the same way they are in cost centers. Revenues are analyzed by calculating sales price and sales volume variances. The sales volume variance is further broken down into market share and industry volume variances.

6 **Use ROI and residual income analysis to explain how performance is controlled in investment centers.** Investment centers are usually found at higher levels in an organization than profit centers. The managers of investment centers are responsible for costs, revenues, and assets. Commonly used measures of investment center performance are return on investment (ROI) and residual income. ROI is calculated by dividing net income by total assets. An investment center can improve its ROI by (1) decreasing its costs to increase its operating performance ratio, (2) decreasing its assets to increase its asset turnover ratio, or (3) increasing revenue with a corresponding increase in income or segment margin. Residual income is the amount of segment margin an investment center is able to earn above a certain minimum rate of return on assets. The problem with both ROI and residual income is that they tend to encourage managers to make decisions that increase short-run profits but may diminish profits in the long run.

eXpanded *Material*

7 **Compute and interpret variable overhead cost variances.** Using an appropriate cost driver, standard costs are computed for each variable overhead item to determine a standard variable overhead rate that is used in applying variable manufacturing overhead to each unit of product. The variable overhead variances may be divided into spending and efficiency variances. The spending variance measures the difference between the costs actually incurred and the amount that should have been incurred at the attained level of activity. The efficiency variance, however, doesn't report on how variable overhead costs were used; rather, this variance reports on the efficient or inefficient use of the underlying activity basis. Hence, if direct labor hours are used to apply variable manufacturing overhead, then the variable manufacturing overhead efficiency variance effectively provides the same information as the direct labor efficiency variance.

8 **Compute and interpret fixed overhead cost variances.** The variances related to fixed manufacturing overhead can be divided into a budget variance and a volume variance. Because fixed manufacturing overhead represents the fixed production costs in the organization, the variance analysis process is different from the variance analysis done for direct materials, direct labor, and variable manufacturing overhead. The fixed manufacturing overhead budget variance is simply the difference between budgeted fixed costs and actual fixed costs. On the other hand, the volume variance is a measure of the difference between expected and actual production output. The number of production units that represent this difference is multiplied by the standard fixed manufacturing overhead per unit to compute the volume variance. By converting the volume variance into a dollar-measured number, this variance can then be combined with the other three overhead variances to account for over- or underapplied manufacturing overhead.

key terms & concepts

asset turnover ratio, 356
centralized company, 334
cost center, 335
decentralized company, 333
direct costs, 348
exception reports, 335
goal congruence, 334
indirect costs, 348
industry volume variance, 352
investment center, 335
labor efficiency variance, 345
labor rate variance, 345
management by exception, 338
market share variance, 352
materials price variance, 341

materials quantity variance, 342
profit center, 335
profit margin (operating performance)
    ratio, 356
residual income, 357
responsibility accounting, 334
responsibility center, 335
return on investment (ROI), 355
sales price variance, 351
sales volume variance, 351
segment margins, 349
segment-margin income statement,
    348
segment-margin ratios, 349
segments, 331

standard cost cards, 337
standard cost system, 337
variance, 338

fixed manufacturing overhead budget
    variance, 363
variable manufacturing overhead
    efficiency variance, 360
variable manufacturing overhead
    spending variance, 360
volume variance, 363

review problems

Materials, Labor, and Revenue Variances

The standard cost sheet for Kendra Box Company shows the following unit costs for direct materials and direct labor for each box made:

Direct materials (4 board feet of lumber @ $2)	$ 8
Direct labor (2 standard hours @ $6)	12
Total standard materials and labor costs per box	$20

During the month of October, 83,000 board feet of lumber were used to produce 20,000 boxes, and the following actual costs were incurred:

Lumber purchased (100,000 board feet @ $2.20)	$220,000
Direct labor (39,600 hours @ $6.05)	239,580

The standard selling price per box is $52. The overall market for the box industry is expected to be 420,000 boxes per month. Kendra's expected share of this market is 12%. Actual revenue results for October are as follows:

Actual revenue (47,355 boxes sold at $53 per box)	$2,509,815
Total boxes sold in the box industry during October	430,500 boxes

Required:
Compute the materials, labor, and revenue variances.

Solution
Materials Variances
The price variance is computed when the lumber is purchased, and the quantity variance is computed when the lumber is used.

(continued)

Materials price variance:

Purchase price per board foot for 100,000 feet	$ 2.20	
Standard price per board foot	(2.00)	
Difference	$ 0.20	U
Feet of lumber purchased	×100,000	
Total price variance	$ 20,000	U

Materials quantity variance:

Actual lumber used	83,000	feet
Standard lumber required (20,000 boxes × 4 feet)	(80,000)	feet
Difference	3,000	feet U
Standard cost per board foot	× $2.00	
Total quantity variance	$ 6,000	U

Labor Variances

The labor rate and labor efficiency variances are both based on direct labor hours used; thus, they are computed at the same point in time.

Labor rate variance:

Actual rate	$ 6.05	
Standard rate	(6.00)	
Difference	$ 0.05	U
Actual direct labor hours used	×39,600	
Total labor rate variance	$ 1,980	U

Labor efficiency variance:

Actual direct labor hours	39,600	
Standard direct labor hours	40,000	
Difference	400	F
Standard direct labor rate	× $6.00	
Total labor efficiency variance	$ 2,400	F

Revenue Variances

Sales price variance:

Actual price	$ 53.00	
Standard price	(52.00)	
Difference	$ 1.00	F
Actual quantity of boxes sold	× 47,355	
Total sales price variance	$ 47,355	F

Sales volume variance:

Actual quantity of boxes sold	47,355	boxes
Expected (budgeted) quantity*	50,400	boxes
Difference	3,045	boxes U
Standard price	× $52.00	
Total sales volume variance	$158,340	U

*Expected quantity = Expected total market × Expected market share

Market share variance:

Total actual market × actual market share × standard price (430,500 × 11% × $52)**	$2,462,460	
Total actual market × expected market share × standard price (430,500 × 12% × $52)	2,686,320	
Total market share variance	$ 223,860	U

**Alternative calculation: Actual quantity sold × Standard price

Industry volume variance:

Total actual market × expected market share × standard price (430,500 × 12% × $52)	$2,686,320	
Total expected market × expected market share × standard price (420,000 × 12% × $52)***	2,620,800	
Total industry volume variance	$ 65,520	F

***Alternative calculation: Expected quantity sold × Standard price

Variable and Fixed Manufacturing Overhead Variances

Use the information given in the previous problem, plus the following information, to address issues associated with Kendra Box Company's manufacturing overhead variances.

The company's budget shows the following monthly variable manufacturing overhead costs at several production levels:

	Percent of Standard Capacity		
	80%	90%	100%
Expected number of boxes	20,000	22,500	25,000
Expected direct labor hours	40,000	45,000	50,000
Variable manufacturing overhead costs	$80,000	$90,000	$100,000
Fixed manufacturing overhead costs	$125,000	$125,000	$125,000

The company normally produces at 100% of capacity and uses this production level to establish its predetermined manufacturing overhead rates. The following actual information for October is available:

Variable manufacturing overhead	$83,000
Fixed manufacturing overhead	$133,000
Production	20,000 boxes

Required:

1. Compute the variable manufacturing overhead cost rate (a) per box and (b) per direct labor hour assuming Kendra Box Company produces at normal capacity.
2. Compute the variable manufacturing overhead spending and efficiency variances for October assuming that Kendra produces at normal capacity and that variable manufacturing overhead costs vary with direct labor hours.
3. Compute the fixed manufacturing overhead cost rate (a) per box and (b) per direct labor hour.
4. Compute the fixed manufacturing overhead budget and volume variances for October using direct labor hours to establish the predetermined overhead rate.

Solution
1. Variable Manufacturing Overhead Cost Rates

		Rate per Box	Rate per Hour
Flexible budget at normal capacity:			
Boxes produced per month	25,000		
Labor hours per month	50,000		
Variable manufacturing overhead costs	$100,000	$4	$2

2. Variable Manufacturing Overhead Variances

The following diagram shows the computation of the variable overhead spending and efficiency variances:

(continued)

	AH × SR	SHA × SR
Actual amount spent	Actual hours of input × Standard rate	Standard hours allowed for actual output × Standard rate
$83,000	39,600 hours × $2.00 = $79,200	40,000 hours × $2.00 = $80,000

Variable overhead spending variance
$83,000 − $79,200 = $3,800 U

Variable overhead efficiency variance*
$2.00 × (40,000 hours − 39,000 hours) = $800 F

*Be sure to compare this calculation to the labor efficiency variance calculated earlier for Kendra Box Company. Do you see how similar these calculations are? Both are based on the efficiency in labor hour usage.

3. Fixed Manufacturing Overhead Cost Rates

		Rate per Box	Rate per Hour
Flexible budget at normal capacity:			
Boxes produced per month	25,000		
Labor hours per month	50,000		
Fixed manufacturing overhead costs	$125,000	$5	$2.50

4. Fixed Manufacturing Overhead Variances

The following diagram shows the computation of the fixed overhead budget and volume variances:

		SHA × SR
Actual amount spent	Budgeted amount (used to establish the predetermined allocation rate)	Standard hours allowed for actual output × Standard rate
$133,000	$125,000; $125,000 ÷ 50,000 hours = $2.50 per hour	40,000 hours × $2.50 = $100,000

Fixed overhead budget variance
$133,000 − $125,000 = $8,000 U

Volume variance**
$2.50 × (50,000 hours − 40,000 hours) = $25,000 U

**Alternative calculation: Rate per box × (Expected production − Actual production) or $5 × (25,000 boxes − 20,000 boxes) = $25,000 U

d iscussion questions

1. Why is evaluating personnel and divisions so important to a business, especially in today's economy?
2. Why is it practically impossible for a large firm to be completely centralized, that is, to have top management making all operating decisions?
3. Why is a system of responsibility accounting necessary in most businesses?
4. What are some important behavioral factors that must be considered when responsibilities are assigned to managers?
5. Why are most performance reports called exception reports?
6. What is the difference between a cost center and a profit center? Between a profit center and an investment center?
7. What is a standard cost?

8. What is the purpose of a standard cost system?
9. Who is responsible for the development of the standards to be used in a standard cost system?
10. What is a variance from standard?
11. What is the relationship of a standard cost system to the principle of management by exception?
12. What are the steps in establishing and operating a standard cost system?
13. Why are two variances, rather than one, used to measure and control materials and labor costs?
14. Who is usually responsible for each of the following variances?
    a. Direct materials price variance
    b. Direct materials quantity variance
    c. Direct labor rate variance
    d. Direct labor efficiency variance
15. What are the major advantages and disadvantages of a standard cost system?
16. If a profit center has a net loss, does that always mean it is not making a contribution to the company as a whole?
17. What are the variances used to analyze revenues in profit and investment centers?
18. What is the major disadvantage of using ROI to evaluate the performance of investment centers?

19. What is the major advantage of using residual income to evaluate the performance of investment centers?

20. What are the two steps in developing a management system for use in controlling variable manufacturing overhead?
21. What is a variable manufacturing overhead spending variance, and what does it indicate about variable manufacturing overhead costs?
22. What is a variable manufacturing overhead efficiency variance, and how does it relate to the labor efficiency variance?
23. What does the fixed manufacturing overhead budget variance measure?
24. What does the volume variance measure, and how is this variance different from the other cost variances studied in this chapter?

p ractice exercises

Practice 6-1

Changes in the Business Environment
Which one of the following statements is *incorrect*?

a. Globalization has greatly affected business over the past few years.
b. Certain market investors have gained a large amount of power in determining what happens at the companies in which they invest.
c. New technology has made information more expensive.
d. The fast pace of business requires managers to have better information and perform more timely evaluations of personnel and divisions.

Practice 6-2

Centralization versus Decentralization
Which one of the following statements is *not* an advantage of decentralization?

a. Segment managers usually have more information regarding matters within their segments than do managers at higher levels.
b. Segment managers' decisions are always consistent with the overall objectives of the firm.
c. Managers can be evaluated more easily because their responsibilities are more clearly defined.
d. Higher-level management has more time to consider strategic goals when daily decision making is distributed throughout the organization.
e. Segment managers can spot problems and react more quickly than can managers at higher levels.

Practice 6-3

Responsibility Accounting
The company is producing an exception report. One division had $45,000 in budgeted costs, but it actually spent $47,500. How would this variance appear on the exception report?

Practice 6-4

Responsibility Centers
Which one of the following is *not* an example of a responsibility center in an organization?

a.   Profit center
b.   Asset center
c.   Cost center
d.   Investment center

Practice 6-5

Standard Cost Card
Using the following standard quantities and standard rates, prepare a standard cost card to determine the total standard cost per unit.

	Standard Quantity	Standard Price or Rate
Direct materials	4 pounds	$ 1.25
Direct labor	2.5 hours	15.00
Variable manufacturing overhead	2.5 hours	1.70
Fixed manufacturing overhead	2.5 hours	0.50

Practice 6-6

Materials Price Variance
The company purchased 4,000 pounds of raw materials at $3.75 per pound. The company's standard cost per pound is $3.60. Calculate the materials price variance for this purchase.

Practice 6-7

Accounting for Materials Price Variances
Refer to the data in Practice 6-6. Make the necessary journal entry to record the cash purchase of the raw materials inventory at standard cost.

Practice 6-8

Materials Quantity Variance
The company used 5,500 board feet of raw materials with a standard cost of $6.00 per board foot to make 400 tables. The company's standard is 14 board feet per table. Calculate the company's materials quantity variance.

Practice 6-9

Accounting for Materials Quantity Variance
Refer to the data in Practice 6-8. Make the necessary journal entry to record the transfer of these raw materials into work-in-process inventory.

Practice 6-10

Labor Rate Variance
Using the following information, compute the labor rate variance.

Number of nightstands produced	150
Actual hours used to produce nightstands	720
Actual labor rate per hour	$15.30
Standard labor rate per hour	$15.00
Standard labor hours per nightstand	5

Practice 6-11

Labor Efficiency Variance
Refer to the data in Practice 6-10. Compute the labor efficiency variance.

Practice 6-12

Accounting for Labor Variances
Refer to the data in Practices 6-10 and 6-11. Make the necessary journal entry to record direct labor at the standard rates.

Practice 6-13

Segment-Margin Income Statement

The company reports the following costs and revenues for one of its segments:

Net sales revenue	$910,000
Cost of goods sold	520,000
Selling and administrative costs	130,000
Advertising cost	94,000
Insurance cost	78,000

Of these costs, cost of goods sold and selling and administrative costs are variable, advertising is a direct fixed cost, and insurance is an indirect fixed cost. Using this information, prepare a segment-margin income statement for this segment.

Practice 6-14

Segment-Margin Ratio

Refer to the data in Practice 6-13. Compute the segment-margin ratio.

Practice 6-15

Revenue Variances

Which one of the following is *not* an example of a revenue variance?

a. Sales price variance
b. Spending variance
c. Industry volume variance
d. Market share variance
e. Sales volume variance

Practice 6-16

Computing Revenue Variances

The company sells one product, which is called Product A. Actual and expected sales data for the most recent year are as follows:

	Company Sales	Sales Price	Total Market	Percent of Market
Actual	500 units	$15	2,500 units	20.0%
Expected	600	13	2,400	25.0

Using these data, compute the following:

1. Sales price variance
2. Sales volume variance
3. Market share variance
4. Industry volume variance

Practice 6-17

Accounting for Revenue Variances

Refer to the data in Practice 6-16. Use the revenue control account to make the single necessary journal entry to record the revenue variances for the period.

Practice 6-18

Return on Investment

The company's profit margin is 8%, and its asset turnover is 4.2. Compute the company's return on investment (ROI).

Practice 6-19

Residual Income

The company had $360,000 in total assets and $94,000 in net income this year, and the company requires at least a 12% return on assets. Compute the company's residual income.

Practice 6-20

Variable Manufacturing Overhead Spending Variance
Using the following data, compute the variable manufacturing overhead spending variance.

Number of nightstands produced	150
Actual hours used to produce nightstands	720
Total actual variable overhead costs incurred	$8,352
Standard variable overhead rate per direct labor hour	$11.00
Standard labor hours per nightstand	5

Practice 6-21

Variable Manufacturing Overhead Efficiency Variance
Refer to the data in Practice 6-20. Compute the variable manufacturing overhead efficiency variance.

Practice 6-22

Fixed Manufacturing Overhead Budget and Volume Variances
The company spent $60,000 on fixed manufacturing overhead during the year. As of the beginning of the year, the company had budgeted to spend $57,000 on fixed manufacturing overhead and to work 1,000 direct labor hours (based on the production of 500 units at two direct labor hours per unit). The actual number of units produced during the year was 400. Fixed manufacturing overhead is applied to production based on direct labor hours. Compute (1) the fixed manufacturing overhead budget variance, (2) the fixed manufacturing overhead volume variance, and (3) the total amount of under- or overapplied fixed manufacturing overhead.

Practice 6-23

Accounting for Manufacturing Overhead Variances
The company has the following manufacturing overhead variances.

Variable manufacturing overhead spending variance	$ 300 F
Variable manufacturing overhead efficiency variance	425 U
Fixed manufacturing overhead budget variance	1,000 U
Fixed manufacturing overhead volume variance	740 F

Make the journal entry necessary to recognize these variances.

e x e r c i s e s

Exercise 6-1

Responsibility Accounting Reports
Lorlily Company is an agricultural supply firm. The management of the company is decentralized, with division managers heading the two operating divisions: Machinery and Seed/Fertilizer. Within each division, the sales are split between the two states of Indiana and Illinois.

The following data are applicable to revenue in 2006:

	Budget	Actual
Machinery—Indiana	$800,000	$750,000
Seed/Fertilizer—Illinois	500,000	580,000
Seed/Fertilizer—Indiana	400,000	530,000
Machinery—Illinois	350,000	250,000

1. Prepare a responsibility accounting report for the head of the Machinery division. For each of the two geographic areas (Indiana and Illinois), show whether the variance between budgeted and actual machinery revenue is favorable or unfavorable.
2. Prepare a responsibility accounting report for the head of the entire company. The company head wants to see only the overall results for each of the two operating divisions (Machinery and Seed/Fertilizer); a detailed breakdown by geographic area is not requested.

Exercise 6-2

Materials Price Variance

Hogan Manufacturing Company has just adopted a standard cost system. You have been asked to analyze the materials purchases and usage for the month of August to determine the materials price variance to be recorded at the end of the month. During August, 5,000 gallons of a chemical were purchased at $3.20 per gallon. Only 4,200 gallons were put into production. The standard price per gallon is $3.15. Compute the following variances:

1. The materials price variance if the chemical is carried in inventory at standard price (i.e., the price variance is accounted for at the time of purchase).
2. The materials price variance if the chemical is carried in inventory at actual price and is charged to Work-in-Process Inventory at the standard price (i.e., the price variance is accounted for at the time of use in production).

Exercise 6-3

Materials Price and Quantity Variances—Journal Entries

Genesis Enterprises produces one product—MX4. The following information relating to raw materials is available for the month of March:

Beginning direct materials inventory	1,500 pounds @ $3.10 per unit
Purchases made during the month	11,000 pounds @ $3.10 per unit
Direct materials placed in production	11,750 pounds

The standard materials usage for one unit of MX4 is 2 pounds with a standard price per pound of $3. Genesis produced 6,000 units of Product MX4 during the month.

1. Compute the materials price and quantity variances for Genesis assuming the materials price variance is computed at the time of purchase.
2. Provide the journal entries required to record:
   a. The purchase of direct materials and the materials price variance.
   b. Placing the direct materials in production and the materials quantity variance.

Exercise 6-4

Direct Materials Purchased and Used

Mary Clarke is concerned about her performance as a recently employed purchasing agent. The accounting department has provided her with the following data for the month of August:

Units produced	2,000
Materials used	1,078 tons
Materials purchased	1,400 tons at $43 per ton

The standard materials usage set by management for one unit of product is half a ton of materials per unit, at $45 per ton. Her performance report shows the following variances:

Used (1,078 tons − 1,000 tons standard) × $45 per ton	$3,510 U
Purchased ($45 per ton standard − $43 per ton actual) × 1,400 tons	2,800 F

If you were Mary Clarke, how would you explain this report?

Exercise 6-5

Analyzing Materials Cost

Mr. Rogers, the production manager, has received a report showing a $16,500 unfavorable total materials variance (materials price variance plus materials quantity variance). He knows that production used 10,000 pounds less than the budgeted amount of direct materials allowed for actual output. Mr. Rogers also knows that the standard price for direct materials was determined to be 80 cents per pound.

What was the actual cost of direct materials used during the period if the budgeted amount allowed was estimated to be 500,000 pounds?

Exercise 6-6

Materials Price and Quantity Variances

Daniel Smith, production manager, has just received a report stating that the total materials variance (materials price variance plus materials quantity variance) for last month was $6,710 unfavorable. However, he is not certain whether the production foremen are overdrawing from inventory or the purchasing department has been unable to acquire materials at reasonable prices. The information he needs is contained in the following report:

Standard production	125,000 units
Actual production	122,000 units
Standard materials per unit	1.5 pounds
Materials used in March	193,000 pounds
Standard price for materials	$1.25 per pound
Actual price for materials	$1.22 per pound

1. Compute the materials price and quantity variances for the month. (*Note:* Mr. Smith's company computes the materials price variance at the time that materials are issued to production.)
2. **Interpretive Question:** What was the cause of the unfavorable variance, and what recommendation would you make to Mr. Smith?

Exercise 6-7

Materials Price and Quantity Variances—Journal Entries

Starship Enterprises produces and sells calibrators. The company began the period with the following inventory of raw material:

200 units at $5.50 per unit (the materials price variance is taken at the time of purchase)

A standard of four units of material for each calibrator produced has been established. During the period, Starship purchased an additional 1,500 units of material at a total cost of $8,220. The dollar amount of materials transferred to Work-in-Process Inventory during the period was $8,800. At the end of the period, Starship had an ending materials inventory of 50 units.

1. Provide the journal entry required to record the materials price variance.
2. Provide the journal entry required to record the materials quantity variance.

Exercise 6-8

Labor Rate and Efficiency Variances

To produce one unit of Product CD requires eight hours of labor at a standard cost per hour of $11.00. During the month of September, 5,000 units were produced. Actual hours and costs for the month are as follows:

Actual direct labor hours	38,400
Actual direct labor costs	$428,160

1. Compute the actual cost per hour of direct labor for the month of September.
2. Compute the labor rate variance.
3. Compute the labor efficiency variance.

Exercise 6-9

Responsibility for Labor Costs

Raymond Stone, a recent business school graduate, has taken a job with Farben Corporation as production manager. His job is to see that production is efficient. After his first month, he is given this memo.

Performance Report

Raymond Stone: $32,000 Unfavorable

The following data are also known for Raymond Stone's first month:

Units produced .... 750 units
Direct labor used .... 7,600 hours at $20
Standard direct labor hours per unit .... 10 hours at $16

1. What justification would you give if you were in Raymond Stone's position, keeping in mind that he is not responsible for hiring, firing, and wage rates? These decisions are handled by the personnel department.
2. What might be theoretically wrong with a conclusion that Raymond Stone is not at all responsible for labor rates?

Exercise 6-10

Labor Variances

During the year, Thompson Plastics was in negotiation with the local union over wages. A settlement was finally reached, and the average wage per hour was increased to $32.80. Production fell to 145,000 units, and 220,000 hours were incurred. Standard production has been set at 150,000 units; 1.5 hours of labor were expected to produce one unit at a standard labor cost of $48.75 per unit. Actual labor cost for the period was $7,216,000.

1. Calculate the labor variances at Thompson Plastics.
2. Prepare the journal entry to enter labor costs in Work-in-Process Inventory and set up the rate and efficiency variances for labor.
3. **Interpretive Question:** Are these variances significant in light of the new wage agreement?

Exercise 6-11

Employee Morale and Production Efficiency

Crest Fabrics is a nonunion textile firm. Employee morale and production efficiency have dropped in the last few weeks, causing management some concern. Further, quality control problems have resulted in a 10% increase in rejects in the last two weeks. The following information may help management identify the causes of current problems:

Employee Production Efficiency Report
(in percentages)

Employee	Wk 14	Wk 15	Wk 16	Wk 17	Wk 18	Wk 19	Wk 20
Baker	96	100	86	93	91	89	85
Johnson	101	97	89	90	93	91	87
Becker	105	109	93	96	95	92	90
Howard	99	98	88	93	97	94	88
Kettle	92	93	81	85	90	91	90

Additional information:

a. Standards for measuring worker efficiency were raised at the start of week 16.
b. Crest Fabrics changed its source of supply of materials in week 15.

1. From the production efficiency report, can you identify trends in the efficiency of individual workers? Which employees might have low morale?
2. **Interpretive Question:** What clues to the causes of the diminishing efficiency and quality can you draw from the information given?

Exercise 6-12

Labor Variances
Compute the missing amounts.

Total labor variance (efficiency plus rate variances)	$ 47,500 U
Labor efficiency variance	42,000 U
Actual labor hours incurred	110,000
Units produced	50,000
Standard hours allowed per unit	2
Total actual labor costs	$467,500
Standard labor hours allowed for output	(a)
Actual labor cost per hour	(b)
Actual labor cost per unit	(c)
Standard labor cost per hour	(d)
Labor rate variance	(e)
Standard labor cost per unit	(f)

Exercise 6-13

Segment-Margin Income Statements
Professional Management, Inc., is a company that sponsors seminars for executives. It has two profit centers, or divisions: a time-management group and a money-management group. Financial information for the two divisions for the year just ended follows:

	Time Management	Money Management
Revenue	$842,000	$965,000
Mailing costs	48,000	102,000
Printing costs	146,000	98,000
Hotel rental costs	425,000	501,000
Travel expenses	72,000	60,000
Advertising costs	108,000	106,000

Of these costs, printing and advertising are direct fixed costs, whereas mailing, hotel rental, and travel are variable costs. Using this information, prepare segment-margin income statements for the two divisions. Include in your statements the computation for contribution margin.

Exercise 6-14

Spreadsheet

Evaluating Performance with Segment and Contribution Margins
Sunshine Center's three profit centers had the following operating data during 2006:

	South	North	East
Revenue (at $21.50 per unit)	$322,500	$215,000	$430,000
Fixed costs:			
Costs unique to the division	131,150	64,500	150,500
Costs allocated by corporate headquarters	45,150	30,100	60,200
Variable costs per unit	13	14	10

Sunshine's management is concerned because the company is losing money. They ask you to:

1. Calculate each profit center's contribution and segment margins, and overall company profits.
2. Determine, on the basis of these calculations, which center(s), if any, should be discontinued. (Assume that the 2006 performance is indicative of all future years. Ignore all nonfinancial factors.)

Exercise 6-15

Measuring Performance Using Segment and Contribution Margins

El Pico Company has two divisions: Maya and Aztec. During 2006, they had the following operating data:

	Maya Division	Aztec Division
Revenue	$100,000	$120,000
Fixed costs:		
Costs unique to the division	50,000	45,000
Costs allocated by corporate headquarters	11,000	10,000
Variable costs per unit	4	4
Unit sales price of division's product	10	8

1. Compute each division's contribution and segment margins, and the contribution each makes to overall company profits.
2. **Interpretive Question:** Based on only the financial information given, should either division be discontinued? Why?

Exercise 6-16

Spreadsheet

Revenue Variances

Fabulous Fragrances makes two products: lotion and shampoo. Actual and expected revenue data for the two products are as follows:

	Actual Data		
	Units Sold	Sales Price	Total Actual Market
Lotion	2,400 bottles	$12.00	30,000 bottles
Shampoo	4,800 bottles	7.50	50,000 bottles

	Expected Data		
	Units Sold	Sales Price	Expected Market Share
Lotion	3,000 bottles	$11.00	12%
Shampoo	5,600 bottles	8.00	10%

1. Using the above data, compute the sales price and sales volume variances for lotion and shampoo for Fabulous Fragrances.
2. Using the above data, compute the market share and industry volume variances for both lotion and shampoo.

Exercise 6-17

Revenue Variances

Telling Time is a watch retailer. It sells two types of watches: digital and analog. The results for the third quarter for Telling Time are as follows:

	Digital	Analog
Expected sales in units	400	500
Expected sales price	$50	$75
Expected percent of market	12.5%	12.5%
Actual sales in units	375	530
Actual total sales revenue	$19,500	$38,955
Actual total market volume	2,500	5,000

(continued)

1. Calculate the sales price variance, the sales volume variance, the market share variance, and the industry volume variance for digital watches.
2. Calculate the sales price variance, the sales volume variance, the market share variance, and the industry volume variance for analog watches.

Exercise 6-18

Return on Investment

Compute the missing data, items (a) through (i), in the following table:

	Division X	Division Y	Division Z
Revenue	$600,000	$500,000	(g)
Net income	$30,000	$25,000	(h)
Total assets	(a)	$100,000	$200,000
Operating performance ratio	(b)	(d)	10%
Asset turnover ratio	(c)	(e)	4 times
ROI	12%	(f)	(i)

Exercise 6-19

Return on Investment

During 2006, the East and West divisions of Granger Company reported the following:

	East Division	West Division
ROI	12%	24%
Operating performance ratio	3%	4%
Revenue	$72,000	$90,000
Total assets	$18,000	$15,000

1. What was each division's asset turnover ratio in 2006?
2. What operating performance ratio would each division need in order to generate an ROI of 25%?

Exercise 6-20

Measuring Performance: Residual Income and ROI

McCormick Corporation measures the performance of its divisions by using the residual income approach, with a minimum accepted rate of return of 16%. In 2006, the printing division, which has total assets of $250,000, generated a net income of $55,000, or 8% of sales. The operating results are expected to be the same in 2007. In early 2007, the printing division receives a proposal for a $50,000 investment that would generate an additional $10,000 of income per year.

1. Should the manager of the printing division make the investment?
2. Would your answer to part (1) be different if McCormick Corporation used the ROI approach to evaluate the performance of its various divisions? Why or why not?

Exercise 6-21

Measuring Performance: Residual Income and ROI

An investment center of Southwick Corporation made three investment proposals. Details of the proposals follow.

	Proposals		
	1	2	3
Required investment	$80,000	$50,000	$65,000
Annual return	13,000	9,000	9,500

Southwick Corporation uses the residual income method to evaluate all investment proposals. Its minimum rate of return is 15%.

1. As president of Southwick Corporation, which of the investments, if any, would you make? Why?
2. Assuming that Southwick Corporation uses the ROI approach to evaluate investment proposals, which investments, if any, would you make? (Southwick Corporation's current return on assets is 20%.)

Exercise 6-22

Variable and Fixed Manufacturing Overhead Variances

Lauder Company manufactures one product. The standard capacity is 20,000 units per month. Manufacturing overhead costs are budgeted and applied on the basis of two machine hours per unit. At standard capacity, the monthly variable overhead budget is $500,000 and the monthly fixed overhead budget is $900,000. During February, 18,000 units of product were actually manufactured, $460,000 of variable manufacturing overhead was incurred, and $975,000 of fixed manufacturing overhead was incurred. Actual machine hours were 35,000.

1. Compute the variable manufacturing overhead spending and efficiency variances.
2. Compute the fixed manufacturing budget and volume variances.

Exercise 6-23

Manufacturing Overhead Variances

Rollins Manufacturing Company estimates variable manufacturing overhead for the month of November to be $80,000. Fixed manufacturing overhead is estimated to be $195,000. All manufacturing overhead is estimated and applied on the basis of 10,000 direct labor hours. At standard production output capacity, each unit of finished product requires two direct labor hours to complete. During November, 4,900 units of finished product were produced. Actual variable and fixed manufacturing overhead costs incurred were $77,500 and $203,000, respectively. Actual direct labor hours during the month were 9,850.

1. Compute the total amount of manufacturing overhead applied during November.
2. Compute the amount of under- or overapplied overhead for the month.
3. Compute the variable manufacturing overhead spending and efficiency variances.
4. Compute the fixed manufacturing budget and volume variances.

 problems

Problem 6-1

Responsibility Accounting Reports

Ryhan Company is a multinational computer services firm. The management of the company is decentralized, with division managers heading the following three divisions: Europe, Asia, and the Americas. Within each division, the three sources of revenue are software sales, service contracts, and consulting fees.

The following data are applicable to revenue in 2006:

(continued)

	Budget	Actual
Europe—software sales	$200,000	$230,000
Asia—software sales	200,000	130,000
Americas—software sales	350,000	420,000
Europe—service contracts	120,000	90,000
Asia—service contracts	70,000	80,000
Americas—service contracts	250,000	190,000
Europe—consulting fees	40,000	90,000
Asia—consulting fees	50,000	35,000
Americas—consulting fees	100,000	60,000

Required:

1. Prepare a responsibility accounting report for the head of the Europe division. For each of the three revenue sources (software sales, service contracts, and consulting fees), show whether the variance between budget and actual is favorable or unfavorable.
2. Prepare a responsibility accounting report for the head of the entire company. The company head wants to see only the overall results for each of the three geographic divisions (budget versus actual); a detailed breakdown by revenue source is not requested.

Problem 6-2

Spreadsheet

Materials and Labor Variances

The standard cost data for Madison Machinery Company show the following costs for producing one of its machines:

Direct materials	400 pounds at $8 = $3,200
Direct labor	150 hours at $15 = $2,250

During April, four machines were built, with actual total costs as follows:

Materials purchased	2,000 pounds at $8.20 = $16,400
Materials used	1,700 pounds
Direct labor incurred	625 hours at $14.80 = $9,250

Required:

1. Compute the following variances:
   a. Materials price variance (raw materials inventory is carried at standard cost)
   b. Materials quantity variance
   c. Labor rate variance
   d. Labor efficiency variance
2. Record the standard materials and labor costs in Work-in-Process Inventory, and enter the variances in appropriate journal entries.

Problem 6-3

Materials and Labor Variances

Mayhem Manufacturing provides the following standard cost data for one of its products:

Direct materials	12 feet at $2.50 per foot
Direct labor	3 hours at $9.50 per hour

During the month of February, the following actual cost data were accumulated:

Materials purchased	94,000 feet at $2.40 per foot
Materials used	92,650 feet
Direct labor incurred	21,750 hours at a total cost of $215,500
Units produced	7,530 units

Required:
Compute the following variances:

1. Materials price variance (this variance is computed at the time of purchase)
2. Materials quantity variance
3. Labor rate variance
4. Labor efficiency variance

Problem 6-4

Materials and Labor Variances

Actual materials	2,000 tons
Actual hours used	1,500 hours
Standard materials for output (tons)	(a)
Standard hours for output	(b)
Actual cost per ton of material	(c)
Standard cost per ton of material	$ 4
Actual cost per direct labor hour	$ 4
Standard cost per direct labor hour	(d)
Total direct labor variance*	$1,625 U
Total direct materials variance**	$ 400 F
Direct materials price variance	(e)
Direct materials quantity variance	$ 0
Direct labor rate variance	$ 750 U
Direct labor efficiency variance	(f)

*Total direct labor variance = Labor rate variance + Labor efficiency variance

**Total direct materials variance = Materials price variance + Materials usage variance (Materials price variance is computed at the time of use in production.)

Required:
Compute the missing amounts.

Problem 6-5

Materials and Labor Variances

Sports Manufacturing, Inc., produces and sells footballs. The standard cost for materials and labor for one regulation-size football is as follows:

Direct materials	2 feet of leather at $5.50 per foot
Direct labor	1/2 hour at $9.00 per hour

During the period, Sports Manufacturing recorded a materials price variance of $100 U and a materials quantity variance of $380 F. In addition, the company recorded a labor rate variance and a labor efficiency variance of $1,200 U and $450 U, respectively. Seven thousand footballs were produced during the period, and the materials inventory did not change during the period.

Required:
1. Compute the actual costs for materials and labor during the period.
2. Provide the journal entries to record the materials price and quantity variances. (*Hint:* The amount of materials purchased and used is the same.)
3. Provide the journal entries to record the labor rate and efficiency variances.

Problem 6-6

Materials and Labor Variances

The following information was taken from the records of Liberty Manufacturing Company for the month of July:

(continued)

Materials (actual):

Purchases of material A:	1,300 pounds × $5.25
Purchases of material B:	750 pounds × $2.50
Used 900 pounds of material A	
Used 525 pounds of material B	

Direct labor (actual):

Manufacturing Division:	1,050 hours × $8.90
Assembly Division:	450 hours × $4.50

Standard cost per unit:

Material A: 2 pounds × $5.20 per pound	$10.40
Material B: 1 pound × $2.60 per pound	2.60
Direct labor—manufacturing: 2 hours × $8.50	17.00
Direct labor—assembly: 1 hour × $4.60	4.60
Standard cost per unit	$34.60

Units produced: 500

Required:

1. Calculate the materials price and quantity variances, assuming that the materials price variance is recognized at the time of purchase.
2. Calculate the labor rate and labor efficiency variances.
3. **Interpretive Question:** What is the advantage, if any, of calculating the materials price variance at the time of purchase rather than at the time of use in production?

Problem 6-7

Materials and Labor Variance Analysis

Cooke Manufacturing Company produces high-quality men's pajamas for several large retail stores. The standard cost card for each dozen pairs of pajamas is as follows:

Direct materials, 30 yards at $0.80	$24
Direct labor, 4 hours at $5.00	20
Manufacturing overhead:	
Variable cost: 4 direct labor hours at $2.00	8
Fixed cost: 30% of direct labor cost	6
Total product cost per dozen pairs	$58

During the month of September, the company filled three orders of pajamas at the following costs:

Order	Number of Dozens	Yards Used	Labor Hours
8	400	12,200	1,500
9	900	26,750	3,750
10	500	15,450	2,140
	1,800	54,400	7,390

The following additional information involving materials and labor was supplied by the accounting department:

a. Purchases of materials during the month amounted to 60,000 yards at $0.82 per yard.
b. Total direct labor cost for the month was $37,689.

Required:

1. Compute the materials price variance for September. (Materials are carried in Direct Materials Inventory at standard.)
2. Compute the materials quantity variance for September.
3. Compute the labor rate and labor efficiency variances for September.

Problem 6-8

Determining How Variances Are Computed

Helon Company uses a standard cost system in its accounting for the manufacturing costs of its only product. The standard cost information for materials and labor is as follows:

Direct materials: 5 pounds at $7	$35
Direct labor: 3 hours at $8	24

During April of its first year of operation, the company completed 2,300 units and had the following materials and labor variances:

Materials price variance	$1,400 F
Materials quantity variance	2,100 F
Labor rate variance	2,115 U
Labor efficiency variance	1,200 U

There was no Work-in-Process Inventory at the beginning or end of April.

Required:
Compute the following amounts:

1. The amount of materials and labor debited to Work-in-Process Inventory during April.
2. The pounds of materials used in production.
3. The actual hours of labor used in production.
4. The actual labor rate per hour.

Problem 6-9

Evaluation of Profit Centers—Segment Margin

Della Brown is the manager of one of the stores in the nationwide EatRite supermarket chain. The following information has been gathered about the performance of Della's store in the most recent quarter:

Operating Departments	Revenue	Contribution-Margin Ratio
Groceries	$600,000	20%
Fresh produce	200,000	40%
Dry goods	500,000	35%
Fixed costs controllable by:		
Manager of grocery department	$ 50,000	
Manager of fresh produce department	70,000	
Manager of dry goods department	80,000	
Store manager	100,000	
Corporate headquarters	100,000	
Total	$400,000	

Required:
Prepare a segment-margin income statement for corporate headquarters' use in evaluating the store manager, Della Brown, and which Della can use to evaluate the managers of the three departments within the store.

Problem 6-10

Evaluation of Profit Centers—Segment Margin

Derrald Pearl Company has two divisions, Computer Consulting and Construction. During the most recent year, the two divisions had the following operating data:

(continued)

Spreadsheet

	Computer Consulting	Construction
Revenue	$600,000	$250,000
Contribution-margin percentage	45%	15%
Fixed costs controllable by division managers	$200,000	$30,000
Fixed costs allocated by corporate headquarters	$100,000	$100,000

Required:

1. Prepare a segment-margin income statement for Derrald Pearl Company. Include three columns—one for the company total and one for each of the two divisions.
2. Based on the segment-margin income statement prepared in part (1), what would happen to overall company profits if the Construction Division were to be discontinued?
3. Should either of the divisions be discontinued? Explain.

Problem 6-11

Revenue Variances

Menendez Company is a merchandiser that sells three products: Product X, Product Y, and Product Z. The following are the actual and expected (standard) data for the three products:

	Actual Data		
	Units	**Sales Price**	**Total Actual Market**
Product X	530	$5.00	2,500 units
Product Y	760	4.00	10,000
Product Z	660	7.00	2,500

	Standard Data		
	Units	**Sales Price**	**Total Market Share**
Product X	500	$6.00	25%
Product Y	900	3.00	10
Product Z	600	5.00	20

Required:

1. Compute the sales price variance, the sales volume variance, the market share variance, and the industry volume variance for Product X.
2. Compute the sales price variance, the sales volume variance, the market share variance, and the industry volume variance for Product Y.
3. Compute the sales price variance, the sales volume variance, the market share variance, and the industry volume variance for Product Z.

Problem 6-12

Revenue Variances

Family Friendly Photography has just finished its first year of business. It specializes in group portraits, though the company also handles individual portraits. Revenue is determined per photo shooting. Family Friendly Photography has divided prices into three different groups: groups of 15 or more, groups of 2 to 15, and individuals. The following information is for its first year of operation:

	Number of Photo Shoots	Price per Photo Shoot	Total Actual Market
Groups of 15+	330	$280.00	1,875 shoots
Groups of 2–15	475	180.00	2,500
Individuals	175	105.00	3,125

At the first of the year, Family Friendly Photography created a budget of expectations for the first year of business. Following are the expectations for the first year of business:

	Number of Photo Shoots	Price per Photo Shoot	Total Market Share
Groups of 15+	300	$275.00	20%
Groups of 2–15	450	200.00	15
Individuals	200	115.00	8

Required:
1. Compute the sales price variance and the sales volume variance for each of the three groups listed above.
2. Compute the market share variance and the industry volume variance for each of the three groups listed above.

Problem 6-13

ROI and Contribution-Margin Analysis

Macro Data Corporation's three divisions had the following operating data during 2006:

	Fax Machine	Calculator	Computer
Revenue	$100,000	$150,000	$200,000
Variable costs	50,000	90,000	135,000
Fixed costs	45,000	56,000	53,000
Total assets	50,000	38,000	120,000

Required:
1. Compute the contribution margin for each division.
2. Compute the segment margin for each division (assume that all fixed costs are direct to each division).
3. Compute the ROI for each division.
4. Which division had the highest operating performance ratio?
5. **Interpretive Question:** Which division had the best performance in 2006? Why?

Problem 6-14

ROI

Frank's Fixtures has two divisions: the Plumbing Division and the Electrical Division. Following are their operating data for 2006:

	Plumbing Division	Electrical Division
Revenue	$150,000	$180,000
Net income	15,000	16,200
Total assets	75,000	72,000
Stockholders' equity	36,000	20,800
Long-term debt	34,500	26,000

(continued)

Required:
1. Calculate the ROI for each division.
2. **Interpretive Question:** On the basis of this return, which division appears to have the better performance? Why?

Problem 6-15

ROI

The following information for 2006 applies to the two sales divisions of Ward Enterprises:

	Division A	Division B
Total inventory	$33,333	$37,500
Operating performance ratio	12%	16%
Net income	$12,000	$10,000

Required:
1. Calculate each division's revenue.
2. Calculate each division's asset turnover ratio assuming that controllable assets include inventory only.
3. **Interpretive Question:** Which division had the better performance for the period? Why?

Problem 6-16

ROI and Residual Income

Pacific Corporation has a number of autonomous divisions. Its real estate division has recently reviewed a number of investment proposals.

a. A new office building would cost $450,000 and would generate yearly net income of $80,000.
b. A computer system would cost $350,000 and would reduce bookkeeping and clerical costs by $50,000 annually.
c. A new apartment house would cost $900,000 and would generate yearly net income of $150,000.

The real estate division currently has total assets of $1.8 million and net income of $350,000.

Required:
1. Assuming that the performance of the manager of the real estate division is evaluated on the basis of the division's ROI, evaluate each of the independent proposals, and determine whether it should be accepted or rejected.
2. Assuming that the manager's performance is evaluated on a residual income basis, determine whether each of the proposals should be accepted or rejected. (The division's minimum accepted rate of return is 15%.)

Problem 6-17

ROI and Residual Income

Albertson Furniture Company is a retailer of home furnishings. It currently has stores in three cities—San Francisco, Los Angeles, and Phoenix. Operating data for the three stores in 2006 were as follows:

	San Francisco	Los Angeles	Phoenix
Revenue	$1,500,000	$1,900,000	$1,800,000
Variable costs	900,000	1,200,000	1,200,000
Fixed costs	300,000	350,000	250,000
Total assets	1,800,000	2,500,000	1,300,000

Required:
1. Compute the segment margin for each store.
2. Compute the operating performance ratio for each store.
3. Compute the asset turnover for each store.
4. Compute the ROI for each store.
5. Compute the residual income for each store. (The minimum rates of return for the stores are San Francisco, 15%; Los Angeles, 13%; and Phoenix, 18%.)

Problem 6-18

ROI and Residual Income

	Division W	Division X	Division Y	Division Z
Revenue	$180,000	$750,000	$ (i)	$950,000
Net income	$ (a)	$175,000	$ (j)	$ (m)
Total assets	$153,000	$ (e)	$400,000	$ (n)
Operating performance ratio	17%	(f)	9%	(o)
Asset turnover ratio	(b)	0.75 time	(k)	3.0 times
ROI	(c)	(g)	(l)	18%
Minimum accepted rate of return	15%	(h)	16%	14%
Residual income	$ (d)	$ 15,000	$ 16,000	$ (p)

Required:
Compute the missing data, labeled (a) through (p).

Problem 6-19

Measuring Performance: Residual Income and ROI
The gaming division of Nevada Corporation had income of $550,000 and total assets of $3 million in 2006. The figures are expected to be similar in 2007. The manager of the gaming division has an opportunity to purchase some new gambling machines for $250,000. He concludes that the new machines would increase annual net income by $44,000.

Required:
1. Calculate the current ROI and the expected return on the proposed investment.
2. Calculate the gaming division's current residual income and the expected residual income on the proposed investment. (Assume that the division's minimum accepted rate of return is 17%.)
3. Should the new machines be purchased:
   a. If the division uses the ROI method?
   b. If the division uses the residual income method?

Problem 6-20

ROI and Residual Income
The manager of the manufacturing division of Minolta Company is evaluated on a residual income basis. He is in the process of evaluating three investment proposals.

a. Pay $500,000 for a new machine that will increase production substantially. This will result in an increased income of $80,000 annually.
b. Pay $350,000 for a new machine that will reduce labor costs by $70,000 annually.
c. Pay $800,000 for a new machine that will increase annual net income by $115,000.

The manufacturing division currently has total assets of $1.2 million and net income of $200,000. Its minimum accepted rate of return is 15%.

Required:
1. Evaluate the three investment proposals independently, and determine which should be accepted.
2. Assuming that the division manager is evaluated on the basis of the division's ROI, determine whether each of the proposals should be accepted or rejected.

Problem 6-21

Manufacturing Overhead Variances

Engraph Manufacturing Company uses standard direct labor hours as a basis for charging manufacturing overhead to Work-in-Process Inventory. The following data were taken from the records:

Data for August:

Actual variable manufacturing overhead	$217,000
Actual fixed manufacturing overhead	$265,700
Actual units produced	8,000
Actual direct labor hours	33,000

Annual budget data:

Budgeted fixed manufacturing overhead	$3,304,800
Budgeted variable manufacturing overhead cost	$2,611,200
Budgeted direct labor hours	408,000
Budgeted units of production	102,000

Required:
1. Compute the annual variable manufacturing overhead rate and annual fixed manufacturing overhead rate to be used to apply overhead to Work-in-Process Inventory.
2. Determine the variable overhead spending variance and the variable overhead efficiency variance for August.
3. Determine the fixed overhead budget variance and the volume variance for August.
4. Prepare the journal entry to transfer standard variable and fixed overhead costs to Work-in-Process Inventory.

Problem 6-22

Variable Manufacturing Overhead Variances

Grover Glove Company attempts to control manufacturing overhead costs through the use of a flexible budget. Standards are set by studying historical overhead cost data, which are shown here. Actual total overhead costs for each month of the second quarter are also shown.

Standard variable overhead: $2.20 per direct labor hour

Months	Actual Direct Labor Hours	Actual Variable Overhead Costs	Standard Hours Allowed
April	76,000	$155,500	74,500
May	57,750	130,000	55,000
June	63,500	150,000	65,000

Required:
1. Compute the variable overhead spending variance and the variable overhead efficiency variance for each month.
2. **Interpretive Question:** Give several reasons why the variable overhead spending variances might be unfavorable.

Problem 6-23

Fixed Manufacturing Overhead Variances

Standard and actual cost data for Willey Corporation for the first three quarters of the year are shown below:

Standards:

Machine hours per unit produced	5.0 machine hours
Units produced per quarter	25,000 units
Fixed manufacturing overhead per quarter	$325,000

	Actual Direct Machine Hours	Actual Fixed Overhead Costs	Actual Number of Units Produced
First quarter	126,000	$321,000	25,500
Second quarter	120,000	330,000	23,000
Third quarter	124,000	324,500	26,500

Required:
1. Compute the fixed overhead budget variance for each quarter.
2. Compute the volume variance for each quarter.
3. **Interpretive Question:** At the end of the third quarter, the production manager at Willey Corporation believes that favorable volume variance in the third quarter means that he has more money to spend in production. Explain to the production manager what the volume variance represents and why it does not indicate that there is more money to spend in production.

Problem 6-24

Variable Manufacturing Overhead Spending and Efficiency Variances
The following production information is available for Porter Corporation:

Budgeted production	150,000 units
Actual production	145,000 units
Actual variable manufacturing overhead	$175,000
Variable manufacturing overhead applied	$0.80 per machine hour
Actual fixed manufacturing overhead	$88,500
Budgeted fixed manufacturing overhead	$90,000
Actual machine hours	220,000 hours
Standard machine hours per unit produced	1.5 machine hours

Required:
1. Calculate the following variances for Porter Corporation:
   a. Variable manufacturing overhead spending variance
   b. Variable manufacturing overhead efficiency variance
   c. Fixed manufacturing overhead budget variance
   d. Volume variance
2. **Interpretive Question:** Explain how the spending variance and the efficiency variance are used to control overhead costs.
3. Identify cost drivers other than machine hours that might be better measures of spending and efficient use of variable manufacturing overhead costs.
4. Can machine hours be considered a good cost driver for fixed manufacturing overhead costs?

 iscussion cases

Case 6-1

Continuous Improvement Needed

One evening after a strenuous day at the office, Janis Walker, president of Western Mills, Inc., a leading textile manufacturing firm, was out jogging to help relieve the tensions of that day's work. While jogging, she focused her thinking on the firm's commercial carpeting division. The major customers of the division are companies that are building new office buildings, hotels, and motels and need quality carpet in their buildings. The carpet division is doing quite well, but Walker has a nagging feeling that the division could be doing better. She decided to discuss the performance of the division with the division manager. When she arrived home after jogging, Walker called the division manager and arranged a meeting for the next day.

(continued)

At the meeting, Walker asked the division manager how long it took to deliver an order to the building site after production started. The manager's answer was 17 days. Walker then asked what the industry average was for delivery. The answer was 15 days. Walker wanted to know why Western Mills took longer than competitors to meet order requirements. The manager answered that its product was of a higher quality, so customers were willing to wait longer for the order to be filled. With this information in hand and without hesitation, Walker said, "I will give you six months to reduce the delivery time to 10 days! You study the problem and tell me what resources you need to meet this 10-day delivery goal. I want a report from you as soon as possible."

1. Assuming that the division already has a standard cost system, what limitations of that system resulted in two more days of delivery time than its competitors?
2. Assuming this company has a standard cost system, what changes is the division manager likely to make in order to meet the president's 10-day delivery mandate?

Case 6-2

What Are My Costs Anyway?

You have recently been promoted to be the manager of the camera division of a large corporation. Your most profitable product is an instant camera that takes pictures and then develops them immediately. Historically, the pictures taken by the camera were of a poor quality, but due to large investments in research and new breakthroughs in technology, the instantly developed pictures are of increasingly higher quality. You have just received your segment financial statements for the period, which report the following:

Revenue	$81,000,000
Cost of products sold	40,000,000
Gross margin	$41,000,000

On the basis of this performance you are due to receive a $300,000 bonus. The top executives of the company are ecstatic about your performance because you have increased quality, reduced defects, and dramatically increased the productivity of your segment. Having studied management accounting, however, you know that the manufacturing costs are not the only ones that add value to your products. In fact, in your heart, you believe that were it not for the fact that you've pushed very hard this last year for more research and development, aggressive marketing, and good customer service subsequent to sales, your segment would not be nearly so profitable. Yet, these costs are tracked in other departments and are not your responsibility.

As a manager who is benefiting from traditional performance evaluation methods, you wonder whether you should inform management that they are actually giving you a bonus that is too high. Apparently, you are the only one in your company that is aware that these other value-adding costs should be included in your performance evaluation. What should you do? Do you let well enough alone, or should you go to management and let them know that you are probably being overpaid?

judgment calls

Judgment 6-1

You Decide: Which is more conducive to a successful organization: a centralized or decentralized company?

With the improvements in technology and communication, many companies are able to decentralize their operations and still work effectively. Many segment managers have been given the responsibility to make decisions and react quickly to problems for their respective department without consulting upper management. Although the trend has been towards decentralization for some time, is this the best solution for today's companies? Many people believe that by decentralizing operations, the overall goals and objectives of the company are forgotten. What one segment manager does for his or her department may not be in the best interest of the company as a whole.

Judgment 6-2

You Decide: Can a company make a conscious decision and set the prices of its products, or does the supply and demand of the market automatically dictate the price?

You were talking to your good friend in the economics department about companies and their pricing strategies. You mentioned a number of models used in accounting, such as variance analysis and ROI, and how these accounting models are helping companies accurately price their products, leading to better financial results. However, your friend disagreed. He believes that all the analysis in the world won't help a company price its products because that is left to the consumer. He said, "The consumer dictates what prices you will charge. It is the law of supply and demand. If you have a product that people want but it is priced too high, they won't buy it!"

Competency Enhancement Opportunities

▶ Analyzing Real Company Information

▶ International Case

▶ Ethics Case

▶ Writing Assignment

▶ The Debate

▶ Internet Search

The following additional assignments provide opportunities for students to develop critical thinking, ethical perspectives, oral and written communication skills, experience with electronic research, and teamwork through group and business activities.

▶ *Analyzing Real Company Information*

Analyzing 6-1 (Microsoft)

In the 2002 Form 10-K for MICROSOFT, you will find Segment Information in Note #20 in the Notes to the Financial Statements. That note is shown below:

	Desktop and Enterprise Software and Services	Consumer Software, Services, and Devices	Consumer Commerce Investments	Other	Reconciling Amounts	Consolidated
Notes to Financial Statements continued (in millions) Segment Information Year Ended June 30						
2000						
Revenue	$20,410	$ 1,654	$ 182	$691	$ 19	$22,956
Operating income (loss)	13,210	(1,090)	(60)	86	(1,140)	11,006
2001						
Revenue	$22,720	$ 1,961	$ 522	$652	$ (652)	$25,203
Operating income (loss)	14,261	(1,666)	(222)	97	(750)	11,720
2002						
Revenue	$23,786	$ 3,531	$ 245	$537	$ 266	$28,365
Operating income (loss)	14,671	(1,778)	23	59	(1,065)	11,910

1. As you can see, Microsoft has four different segments: Desktop and Enterprise Software and Services; Consumer Software, Services, and Devices; Consumer Commerce Investments; and Other (that is, all other segments combined). How do you think Microsoft primarily evaluates these segments—as cost centers, as profit centers, or as investment centers?

2. Compute the margin (operating income/revenue) for the four divisions for 2000, 2001, and 2002. Which segment is the most profitable? Which is growing the fastest in terms of revenues?

Analyzing 6-2 (Petersen Pottery)

Just outside Elkins, West Virginia, Clive Petersen has been making ceramic bathroom fixtures (sinks, toilets, and bathtubs) since 1960. Petersen's fixtures had become known over the years for their distinctive customer features, their high quality, and their long life. PETERSEN POTTERY started out as a two-man operation. By 1980 it had grown to 20 master potters. By this time, Clive Petersen felt that he had expanded to a point that he needed to institute a formal accounting control system. The insistence of his banker that he get a "real" management accounting system in place was also compelling. As a result, Petersen hired a formally trained management accountant who began working with his most experienced master potters to design cost standards. After some research, Petersen's accountant arrived at the following cost standards for a toilet (note that manufacturing overhead is allocated based on direct labor hours):

Direct materials:
Raw clay	25 lbs. × $0.95 per lb. = $23.75
Glazing mix	5 lbs. × $0.75 per lb. = 3.75

Direct labor:
Molding	1.0 hr. × $15.00 per hour = 15.00
Glazing	0.5 hr. × $15.00 per hour = 7.50
Variable manufacturing overhead	1.5 hrs. × $3.00 per hour = 4.50
Fixed manufacturing overhead*	2.0 hrs. × $4.00 per hour = 8.00
Total per fixture	$62.50

*Based on budgeted production of 1,200 toilets.

After six months of operations, Petersen was disturbed over the lack of attention paid to the standards by his potters. He felt that the potters were just too set in their ways to adhere to the new system. Many of the potters told Petersen that the new system was "confusing" and didn't help them in their work. In reviewing the June production results, the following actual costs were noted in connection with manufacturing 1,145 toilets:

Materials used:
Raw clay	28,900 lbs. @ $0.92 per lb.
Glazing mix	5,900 lbs. @ $0.78 per lb.

Direct labor:
Molding	1,200 hrs. @ $15.25 per hour (average)
Glazing	600 hrs. @ $15.00 per hour (average)
Actual variable manufacturing overhead	$5,120
Actual fixed manufacturing overhead	$9,700

1. Compute all cost variances for the month of June.
2. What suggestions do you have for Mr. Petersen regarding his new standard cost system?

Source: Adapted from J. K. Shank, "Petersen Pottery" case, *Cases in Cost Management: A Strategic Emphasis* (Cincinnati: South-Western, 1996).

▷ *International Case*

International

Target Costing in Japan

Japan is always a good place for useful insight on innovative management accounting practice and technique. From early on, the Japanese recognized that the most efficient way to keep costs down was to *design* them out of their products, not to reduce them after the products entered production. This realization reflects a fundamental reality of cost management in Japan; the majority of a product's costs (as much as 90 to 95% according to some experts) are "designed in." Consequently, effective cost control programs in a Japanese business typically focus heavily on the design process for a particular product. This is done primarily using a concept known as target costing, as well as value engineering (VE). Target costing is used to determine what the market is willing to pay for a product. Using the target market price (i.e., the price required to win the customer's business), the manager then subtracts the target profit to arrive at the target cost. After the target cost is determined, VE then is used to design the product in order to achieve the prespecified targeted level of costs. Thus, target costing manages costs by effectively designing into the products and processes the required costs in order to achieve the desired profit.

What do you think is the effect of target costing and VE on the use of variances? Specifically, will materials usage variances and labor efficiency variances be more or less important to a firm that strictly uses target costing and VE versus a traditional firm that is more focused on controlling daily production processes?

▶ *Ethics Case*

Cool Air, Inc.

Jack Lear, an internal auditor for Cool Air, Inc., met with Paul Marsh, the manager of the cost accounting department, to discuss a concern about a possible "glitch" in the standard cost system. Jack explained that he had been reviewing the employee time cards in the company division where air-conditioning units and refrigerators were assembled. The time cards reflected how much employee time was devoted to the assembly of air-conditioning units and how much time applied to refrigerators. Jack's concern was that the hours actually charged for each of these operations always seemed to be right on target with the standard labor times for each air-conditioning unit and each refrigerator unit assembled; yet Jack had been told a number of times by employees in the assembly department that the standard hours for assembling air-conditioning units were too low. The employees felt that they could not meet these standards without "fudging" their time cards or sacrificing some quality work in the assembly process. Since company policy emphasized product quality, Jack suspected that time sheets were being modified by shifting hours worked on air-conditioning units to the time sheets for assembling refrigerators.

Paul Marsh, the cost manager, thought for a minute about what Jack was telling him and then made an interesting observation. He said that he had been concerned about the fact that the company's prices for its air-conditioning units were generally lower than its competitors' prices for the same size and quality of units, whereas its prices for refrigerators were generally higher than those of its competitors. He wondered if the company's pricing structure, which was tied to its standard costs, was out of line with competition. This position was reinforced when Paul and Jack looked at the company's sales of each of these products. Over the past year or so, the company had gained market share in air-conditioner sales and had lost market share in refrigerators! Based on this information, Paul asked Jack to do some "detective" work on the time cards in the assembly division and report back his findings.

A few days later, Jack reported that he had found convincing evidence that the foremen in the assembly division had been in collusion to "doctor" employee time sheets in order to more closely meet the time standards for both air-conditioner and refrigerator assembly.

1. Who are the stakeholders affected by the "doctoring" of time sheets?
2. What are the ethical issues in this situation?
3. What should Paul do?

▶ *Writing Assignment*

Qualitative Variance Analysis

With the push for continuous improvement, stable standards may become a thing of the past. As companies strive for and achieve zero defects and no waste, variances quantifiable in terms of dollars become more and more difficult to obtain. To determine variances from a standard, firms are now turning their attention to qualitative measures such as the number of customer complaints or the number of machine setups. In a one- to two-page paper, identify three standards that might be used in a manufacturing environment and three standards that might be used in a service environment that cannot be readily quantifiable in dollars. Discuss how each of those standards would be measured, as well as how variances from those standards would be measured.

▷ *The Debate*

When Might a Favorable Variance Turn "Bad"?

Consider the labor efficiency variance. As you now understand after working through this chapter, a labor efficiency variance occurs when the hours actually used are more or less than the standard hours allowed based on actual production output. Assume that a team of internal auditors was able to complete a particular auditing project in one of the company's divisions in fewer hours than originally expected. Does this team have a favorable labor efficiency variance? More importantly, assuming there is a favorable labor efficiency variance, is this a good or a bad thing?

Divide your group into two teams and prepare a two-minute defense of your team's assigned position.

- One team represents "Favorable labor efficiency variance—GOOD!" Answer the following questions in your discussion. (1) Is measuring the difference between auditing hours *originally* budgeted and the actual hours used the proper way to measure a labor efficiency variance? (2) Your team should take the position that favorable labor efficiencies are a *good* result in this operation. What positive aspects concerning the audit team's work are indicated by a favorable labor efficiency variance?
- The other team represents "Favorable labor efficiency variance—BAD!" Answer the following in your discussion. (1) Respond to Team 1's report on whether measuring the difference between auditing hours *originally* budgeted and the actual hours used is the proper way to measure a labor efficiency variance. If you disagree, provide a correct response. (2) Your team should take the position that favorable labor efficiencies may *not* be a good result in this operation. What negative aspects concerning the audit team's work could be indicated by a favorable labor efficiency variance?

▷ *Internet Search*

Motivating Employees to Be More Productive

In addition to evaluating employees, as was discussed in this chapter, it is also important to motivate employees and managers by providing appropriate incentives. Many companies provide consulting services to organizations to help them create winning incentives for their employees. For an example of the kinds of services that are offered and some examples of incentives that seemed to work, go to **http://www.goalmanager.com**. Sometimes Web addresses change, so if this address does not work, access the Web site for this textbook (**http://swain.swlearning .com**) for an updated link. Once you've gained access to the site, look over some of the success stories and answer the following questions:

1. Describe one employee motivation success story described at this Web site.
2. What was the key to motivating employees in that organization?

Gonzales Company makes compact discs, which it sells to music companies. The following data are available for the company:

Expected sales in units:

January	1,200 discs
February	1,400 discs
March	1,800 discs
Selling price	$10.00 per disc
Beginning accounts receivable balance, January 1	$4,000.00
Desired finished goods inventory, March 31	380 discs
Beginning finished goods inventory, January 1	300 discs*
Beginning direct materials inventory, January 1	400 ounces*
Desired direct materials inventory, March 31	600 ounces
Standard direct materials needed per disc	4 ounces
Standard direct labor time per finished product	10 minutes
Standard direct materials cost per ounce	$0.50
Standard direct labor cost per hour	$18.00

*The beginning inventory numbers for January were based on the best estimate of January sales in December. The expectations changed in January, and the new expected sales numbers should be used to estimate beginning inventory on hand for February and March.

Additional information:

- Of a month's sales, 60% is collected by month-end; the remaining 40% is collected the following month.
- The desired finished goods inventory each month is 20% of the next month's sales.
- The desired direct materials inventory every month is 10% of next month's production needs.

Required:
1. Using the standard costs for making the discs, prepare the following:
   a. Sales forecasts for January, February, and March (in dollars).
   b. Cash collections budgets for January, February, and March (in dollars). Assume that all sales are on credit.
   c. Production budgets for January, February, and March (in units).
   d. Direct materials usage budgets for January, February, and March (in ounces).
   e. Direct materials purchases budgets for January, February, and March (in ounces).
   f. Direct labor budgets for January, February, and March (in dollars).
2. Assume that actual usage of direct materials to make the discs was $4^{1}/_{2}$ ounces at a cost of $0.60 per ounce. Compute the materials price and quantity variances for each month.
3. Assume that actual labor costs to make the discs were 12 minutes of labor at a cost of $19 per hour. Compute labor rate and efficiency variances for each month.
4. Assuming again that Gonzales is able to make the discs at the standard costs, how much will profits increase if it raises its price to $12 per disc in January, February, and March? Assume total fixed costs of $5,000 per month.
5. Assuming again that Gonzales is able to make the discs at its standard costs, if sales decrease by 300 discs during the three months at the increased price of $12 per disc, should Gonzales raise its price?

chapter

7

Managing Inventory and Service Costs

After studying this chapter, you should be able to:

Learning Objectives

1 Identify the different types of inventory in manufacturing, service, and merchandising organizations and understand how these inventory costs are reflected on the income statement and balance sheet.

2 Analyze the levels of raw materials, work-in-process, and finished goods inventories in a manufacturing organization.

3 Understand how merchants manage inventory in their organizations.

4 Measure profitability and personnel utilization in a service organization.

5 Describe how the concept of just-in-time (JIT) inventory systems is used to improve cost, quality, and timely performance in organizations.

eXpanded *Material*

6 Calculate and interpret holding costs in merchandising and service businesses.

7 Use classic quantitative tools in inventory management (economic order quantity, reorder point, and safety stock).

Sam Walton didn't invent discount retailing, but the company he founded, WAL-MART, is now the undisputed giant in the field.[1] Sam Walton started his career in retailing at a J.C. PENNEY store in Des Moines, Iowa. Sam was a good salesperson, though he disliked the bookkeeping that went along with the job: "[I] couldn't stand to leave a new customer waiting while I fiddled with paperwork on a sale I'd already made."

After World War II, Sam borrowed $20,000 from his father-in-law and bought a variety store in Newport, Arkansas. By 1962, Sam Walton had built a chain of 16 variety stores located in Missouri, Arkansas, and Kansas. By this time, however, Walton had become convinced that there were big opportunities in opening discount retail locations in the smaller U.S. towns and cities that were being overlooked by the traditional retailers such as SEARS. Walton pitched his idea to a couple of retail chains, but he couldn't generate any interest. He finally had to fund the start-up of his first discount store with his own money, putting up 95% of the financing, with another 3% coming from his skeptical brother Bud and 2% from the person he hired to manage the store. On July 2, 1962, this first Wal-Mart opened its doors. Today, Wal-Mart Stores, Inc. is the world's largest retailer ($218 billion in sales in 2002), employing approximately 1.3 million people in more than 4,300 stores. Each week, more than 100 million customers visit Wal-Mart stores worldwide.

FYI:

Two other well-known discount retailers also began operations in 1962: KMART and TARGET.

Providing the management accounting information necessary to effectively control this massive merchandising organization is no easy task. Providing merchandise at the right time, to the right place, and at the right price is how a retailer "wins" customers. Sound simple? Consider that at any given moment, a typical Wal-Mart discount store has more than 70,000 different items of inventory in stock. Every one of these items must be identified, ordered, inventoried, and replenished—all the while keeping an eye on costs. (Inventory costs at a typical Supercenter are even tougher to manage because these stores also carry more than 20,000 grocery items, many of them perishable.) The crucial idea behind discount retailing is that lower prices will lead to a large enough increase in sales volume to make up for the fact that a smaller profit is made on each inventory item. As the discount retailing industry has expanded and become more competitive, Wal-Mart has had to be ever more aggressive in cutting its profit margins in order to keep its prices low. To illustrate, in 1980 Wal-Mart's gross profit percentage was 27%; in 2003, the percentage had dropped to 22%. For a company wrestling with tightening margins, inventory control is a crucial part of operations. Wal-Mart leased its first computer, an IBM 360, in 1969 in order to track the inventory flow at its new distribution center in Bentonville, Arkansas. Ever since, Wal-Mart has been a leader in using information technology to monitor and manage its inventory.

Today, Wal-Mart is a leader in implementing electronic data interchange (EDI), which involves the electronic transfer of invoices, purchase orders, and shipping notices, thus speeding up the communication between Wal-Mart and its suppliers. One important tool in Wal-Mart's EDI system is small handheld computers that link by radio frequency to in-store terminals. The next time you're in a Wal-Mart store, watch to see if you can spot an employee using one of these handheld computers to manage inventory on the shelves. These devices provide the critical link between Wal-Mart's suppliers and customers. With this technology, Wal-Mart management is able to get faster and more accurate information to plan, control, and evaluate every aspect of inventory management. This leads to better cost control and better merchandise and service.

In addition to the use of handheld computers, Wal-Mart's "Retail Link" system now gives vendors access to Wal-Mart's own store-by-store sales information and inventory levels in real time, so that the vendors themselves can know when to make additional product shipments to specific Wal-Mart locations. The information partnership between Wal-Mart and PROCTER & GAMBLE, dating back to 1987, is legendary as an example of a buyer and a seller exchanging detailed transaction data in order to improve the operating efficiency of both companies. As a result of its leadership in technology, Wal-Mart is able to generate management accounting information that provides truly competitive cost, quality, and time information.

FYI:

In its 2003 financial statements, Procter & Gamble (P&G) disclosed that Wal-Mart is its single largest customer, accounting for 18% of P&G's sales in 2003.

---

1 Information from Sandra S. Vance and Roy V. Scott, *Wal-Mart: A History of Sam Walton's Retail Phenomenon* (New York: Twayne Publishers, 1994); Sam Walton and John Huey, *Sam Walton: Made in America* (New York: Doubleday, 1992); Wal-Mart Stores, Inc., **http://www.walmart.com**, accessed September 25, 2003.

ome companies, such as COCA-COLA and NIKE, have become successful through convincing potential customers that their soft drinks or sports shoes are superior to all others. Hence, we talk of the marketing genius of Coca-Cola and Nike, not their cost management techniques. In contrast, WAL-MART does not offer unique products; to a large extent, Wal-Mart sells the same products sold by every other discount retailer in the world. Wal-Mart attracts us with its low prices, and consistent low prices are possible only in an organization that meticulously and relentlessly controls its inventory costs. In this chapter, we will introduce techniques used to manage inventory in manufacturing organizations, service organizations, and merchandising organizations (like Wal-Mart).

Inventory in Organizations

1 Identify the different types of inventory in manufacturing, service, and merchandising organizations and understand how these inventory costs are reflected in the income statement and balance sheet.

In an earlier chapter on product cost flows, we discussed the ways in which costs flow from one activity to the next in manufacturing, merchandising, and service organizations. These cost flow patterns are summarized in Exhibit 1. You can see in this exhibit that product costs first appear on the balance sheet in the form of inventory, and then flow onto the income statement as cost of goods or services sold (an expense account). Recall that the extended production process characteristic of both manufacturing and service firms means that those organizations have significant levels of work-in-process inventory—goods or services that have not yet been completed but have already resulted in work being done and costs being incurred. In addition, note that both manufacturing and merchandising firms maintain significant inventories of goods that are ready for sale (finished goods or merchandise inventory). On the other hand, it is typically not in the nature of a service business to have finished goods inventory. As soon as the service (e.g., the accountant's audit, the doctor's office visit, the trucking company's transportation contract) has been completed and moves out of the work-in-process services account

Exhibit 1: Cost Flows in Manufacturing, Service, and Merchandising Organizations

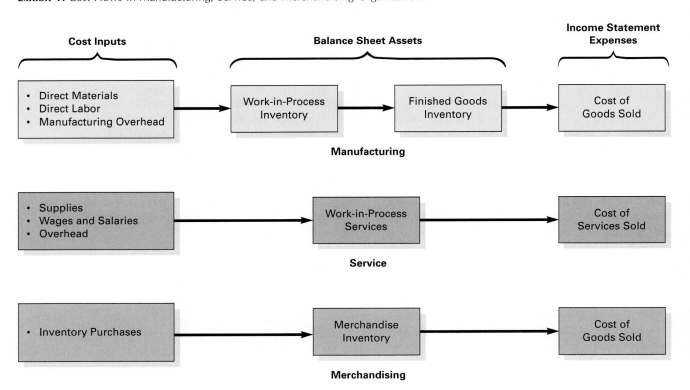

(sometimes known as the unbilled services account), it is delivered to the final customer, and the product cost[2] is transferred to the cost of services sold expense account.

Exhibit 2 compares the income statements for three fictitious firms. The exhibit also presents selected balance sheet accounts. Carefully examine this exhibit to be sure you understand how the activities and inventories of manufacturing, service, and merchandising organizations are reported in the financial statements.

Exhibit 2: Financial Statement Comparison: Manufacturing, Service, and Merchandising Firms

Income Statements for Different Types of Firms
For the Year Ended December 31, 2006

	Manufacturing Firm	Service Firm	Merchandising Firm
	Mason Tool Company	Brown Engineering, Inc.	Smith Office Supply, Inc.
Sales revenue	$4,000,000	$5,000,000	$2,500,000
Cost of goods sold/Cost of services:			
Cost of goods manufactured/Cost of services:			
Beginning raw materials/supplies inventory	$ 24,000	$ 230	
+ Purchases of materials/supplies	1,153,000	11,400	
Total raw materials/supplies available	$1,177,000	$ 11,630	
− Ending raw materials/supplies inventory	(25,000)	(180)	
Raw materials/supplies used in production	$1,152,000	$ 11,450	
+ Direct labor	445,000	1,890,000	
+ Applied manufacturing/service overhead	1,003,000	798,000	
Total manufacturing/service costs	$2,600,000	$2,699,450	
+ Beginning work-in-process inventory/services	24,000	75,000	
− Ending work-in-process inventory/services	(19,000)	(83,000)	
Cost of goods manufactured/Cost of services	$2,605,000	$2,691,450	
Merchandise purchases			$1,713,000
+ Beginning finished goods/merchandise inventory	24,000		37,000
− Ending finished goods/merchandise inventory	(47,000)		(36,000)
Cost of goods sold/Cost of services	$2,582,000		$1,714,000
+Underapplied manufacturing/service overhead	307,000	22,100	
Adjusted cost of goods sold/Cost of services	$2,889,000	$2,713,550	
Gross margin	$1,111,000	$2,286,450	$ 786,000
Selling and administrative expenses:			
Selling expenses	$ 256,000	$ 367,000	$ 406,000
Administrative expenses	474,000	1,003,000	188,000
Total selling and administrative expenses	$ 730,000	$1,370,000	$ 594,000
Operating income	$ 381,000	$ 916,450	$ 192,000

Selected Balance Sheet Information
December 31, 2006

Accounts receivable	$74,000	$63,000	$ 3,900
Raw materials inventory	25,000		
Work-in-process inventory/services	19,000	83,000	
Finished goods/Merchandise inventory	47,000		36,000
Supplies inventory	750	180	450
Accounts payable	28,000	16,000	48,000

---

2 We use the term "product cost" to refer to both the cost of goods in manufacturing and merchandising organizations and to the cost of services in service organizations.

As you can see, each income statement in Exhibit 2 follows a typical income statement format:

Sales revenue	$XXX,XXX
Costs of goods sold	(XX,XXX)
Gross margin	$XXX,XXX
Selling and administrative expenses	(X,XXX)
Operating income	$XXX,XXX

Remember that the calculation for cost of goods sold for a manufacturing company (and for a service company) comes from the cost of goods manufactured schedule.[3] This schedule is also included in Exhibit 2 and follows the format below:

Beginning raw materials inventory	$ XXX	
Add: Raw materials purchased	X,XXX	
Total raw materials available	$X,XXX	
Less: Ending raw materials inventory	(XXX)	
Raw materials used in production		$ X,XXX
Direct labor		X,XXX
Applied manufacturing overhead		X,XXX
Total manufacturing costs		$XX,XXX
Add: Beginning work-in-process inventory		XXX
Less: Ending work-in-process inventory		(XXX)
Cost of goods manufactured		$XX,XXX

You should note two important items in Mason Tool's cost of goods manufacturing calculation versus the similar calculation for Brown Engineering. First of all, notice that Brown is using a rather insignificant amount of supplies ($11,450) to create its service product, especially when compared with Mason Tool, which is using a very significant amount of raw materials ($1,152,000) to create its tools. This difference underscores the fact that some supplies are often used in the process of creating and delivering a service product, but these costs are typically not a significant component of cost of services. Secondly, when calculating cost of services (analogous to cost of goods sold), note that Brown Engineering does not hold finished service products for later sale to its customers. Again, the very nature of a service business determines that a completed service is delivered to the customer almost instantly. In contrast, Brown Engineering does have significant work-in-process "inventory," representing the costs of engineering contracts that have not yet been completed.

Smith Office Supply does not create the products it sells. As a result, Smith has no work-in-process inventory, and the cost of goods sold calculation only requires that Smith adjust the total amount of merchandise it purchased in 2006 by the change in its merchandise inventory account.

Balance sheet information for the three companies is presented at the bottom of Exhibit 2. As you can see, all three firms have accounts receivable, supplies inventory, and accounts payable accounts. Because Brown uses supplies directly in providing engineering services to its clients, this account is used in the calculation of cost of services. On the other hand, cost of supplies for Mason Tool and Smith Office Supply is included in the overhead and administrative expenses accounts. In addition, you can see that Mason Tool has three inventory accounts; Smith Office Supply has one inventory account to record the costs of goods until the goods are sold to customers. Brown does not have a raw materials inventory, finished goods inventory, or merchandise inventory account (though supplies inventory is analogous to raw materials inventory for many service firms). However, its work-in-process services account acts much like Mason Tool's work-in-process inventory account and is similarly used to adjust the cost of services account in Brown's income statement.

---

3 If necessary, be sure to review the earlier chapter on product cost flows, particularly Exhibit 3 on page 125 and Exhibit 5 on page 134.

Exhibit 1 reviews how product costs and inventory flow through manufacturing, merchandising, and service organizations, and Exhibit 2 illustrates how these different types of inventory are reflected in the income statement and the balance sheet. In the remainder of this chapter, we will discuss how companies can use this information to manage inventory. The extended production process of a manufacturing or service firm requires careful scrutiny of costs at each important stage of the process. For a merchandising company, cost management focuses on acquiring the right amount of inventory for the right price.

> **TO SUMMARIZE:** Both manufacturing and service organizations must manage substantial production processes; an important managerial accounting function in these organizations is tracing the flow of costs through the various stages of production. Both manufacturing and merchandising organizations traditionally maintain significant levels of inventory ready for sale to customers. These differences among manufacturing, merchandising, and service organizations are reflected in differences in their income statements and balance sheets.

Analyzing Inventory Levels

2 Analyze the levels of raw materials, work-in-process, and finished goods inventories in a manufacturing organization.

In the income statement and balance sheet figures reported in Exhibit 2 for Mason Tool Company, cost of goods sold was determined to be $2,889,000 (after the adjustment for underapplied manufacturing overhead). This is a summary number that is used in the financial statements and is the number that the company's auditors will work hard to attest for the company's published financial statements. However, because it is a summary number, it is not useful for detailed internal decision making. To be useful, management may want to analyze product costs on a product-by-product basis, a period-by-period basis, and a department-by-department basis. By breaking costs down by product, period, and department, management can determine which departments and products are performing well and which are performing poorly. Further, because product costs are used to measure inventory values on the balance sheet, these costs can be used to determine how effectively Mason Tool Company manages its investments in inventory. Exhibit 3 reports the monthly ending balances for the three inventories necessary to produce its products: raw materials, work-in-process, and finished goods. These inventories represent significant investments necessary to support Mason Tool Company's production processes.[4]

Mason maintains a raw materials inventory in order to ensure that there are materials always available for use in production. This flow of materials is represented by the cost of materials used (i.e., the materials transferred onto the factory floor). The work-in-process inventory is important to maintaining a constant flow of production through the factory and into the finished goods warehouse. This "flow" is represented by the cost of goods manufactured (i.e., the completed goods transferred off of the factory floor). Finally, the finished goods inventory is necessary to be sure that products are always available for sale to customers. The flow of product costs to customers is represented by the cost of goods sold.

The top panel of Exhibit 3 reports product cost and inventory ending balance data for table saws at Mason Tool Company (we'll assume that table saws are this company's only product). These data are listed by month, and the total values for the year tie back to the income statement data in Exhibit 2. As you review these data, try to put yourself in the shoes of the Mason Tool Company production manager. Ask yourself this question: how effectively is the company using inventory to support its purchasing, production, and sales processes? It is difficult to answer this question based solely on the data reported in the top panel of Exhibit 3.

---

4 The need to maintain inventory in order to support key business processes such as production and sales is challenged by an important new management concept known as just-in-time inventory systems or JIT. We discuss JIT later in this chapter.

Exhibit 3: Mason Tool Company Inventory Report

Monthly Table Saw Inventory and Cost Data
(numbers are reported in thousands)

	Jan.	Feb.	March	April	May	June	July	Aug.	Sept.	Oct.	Nov.	Dec.	Balance
Raw materials inventory	$ 25	$ 20	$ 28	$ 24	$ 24	$ 22	$ 20	$ 21	$ 22	$ 23	$ 27	$ 25	$ 25
Work-in-process inventory	19	20	18	17	21	20	21	23	18	19	21	19	19
Finished goods inventory	48	46	48	46	42	40	41	47	46	48	49	47	47

	Jan.	Feb.	March	April	May	June	July	Aug.	Sept.	Oct.	Nov.	Dec.	Total
Cost of raw materials used	$ 77	$ 86	$ 86	$ 92	$102	$119	$116	$113	$ 94	$ 87	$ 80	$100	$1,152
Cost of goods manufactured	196	195	201	215	226	245	248	234	222	211	207	205	2,605
Cost of goods sold*	195	190	212	223	230	227	247	236	221	198	208	195	2,582

*Because cost of goods sold is usually adjusted only once per year (at the end of the year), these monthly cost of goods sold numbers are unadjusted for over- or underapplied overhead.

Monthly Table Saw Inventory Performance Measures

	Feb.	March	April	May	June	July	Aug.	Sept.	Oct.	Nov.	Dec.
Raw materials inventory turnover	3.8	3.6	3.5	4.3	5.2	5.5	5.5	4.4	3.9	3.2	3.8
Work-in-process inventory turnover	10.0	10.6	12.3	11.9	12.0	12.1	10.6	10.8	11.4	10.4	10.3
Finished goods inventory turnover	4.0	4.5	4.7	5.2	5.5	6.1	5.4	4.8	4.2	4.3	4.1

	Feb.	March	April	May	June	July	Aug.	Sept.	Oct.	Nov.	Dec.
Days in raw materials inventory	7.8	8.4	8.5	7.1	5.8	5.4	5.4	6.9	7.8	9.4	7.8
Days in work-in-process inventory	3.0	2.8	2.4	2.5	2.5	2.5	2.8	2.8	2.6	2.9	2.9
Days in finished goods inventory	7.4	6.7	6.3	5.7	5.4	4.9	5.6	6.3	7.1	7.0	7.4

inventory turnover The number of times the inventory in the organization "turns over" during a period of time. It is often easier to think of inventory turnover as the number of times a dollar invested in inventory generates output. Output for raw materials inventory is measured by the cost of raw materials used in production. Output for work-in-process inventory is measured by cost of goods manufactured. Output for finished goods (or merchandise) inventory is measured by cost of goods sold. Inventory turnover is computed as total output for the period divided by average inventory level.

days in inventory Average number of days of use provided by the level of inventory maintained by the organization. This definition is closely related to the "inventory turnover" concept. Days in inventory is computed as number of days in the period being assessed divided by the inventory turnover. (See related definition and computation for inventory turnover.)

By combining inventory data with its related cost flow data, management is able to create a report that helps it control how effectively raw materials, work-in-process, and finished goods inventories are being used. Two measures used to evaluate a company's inventory management practices are **inventory turnover** and **days in inventory**. Exhibit 4 illustrates the computations of inventory turnover and days in inventory in February for table saws at Mason Tool Company.

The inventory turnover measure is based on the following formula:

$$\frac{\text{Cost flow for the period}}{\text{Average inventory level*}} = \text{Inventory turnover}$$

*where the average inventory level is generally measured as:

$$\frac{\text{Beginning inventory} + \text{Ending inventory}}{2} = \text{Average inventory level}$$

This turnover measure indicates how many times during the period the organization completely replenished or replaced the inventory, given the rate at which costs are flowing through the production process. For example, Exhibit 3 reports that Mason's cost of raw materials used during February was $86,000. As shown in Exhibit 4, Mason's average raw materials inventory level for February was approximately $22,500 [($25,000 + $20,000) ÷ 2], which means that its raw materials inventory "turned over" or was replaced 3.8 times during the month. Inventory turnover measures the intensity with which Mason is managing its raw materials inventory—low inventory turnover indicates lots of idle

Caution

Days in inventory is a function of the time period used to compute the production costs used in the related inventory turnover measure. Therefore, if the cost of raw materials used (or cost of goods manufactured or cost of goods sold) is for a six-month period, then the days in raw materials inventory (or days in work-in-process inventory or days in finished goods inventory) should be computed using the numbers of days in a six-month period. The organization generally sets a policy on numbers of days to use. For example, it may choose to consistently use 30 days in a month, 90 days in a quarter, 180 days in a half year, and 360 days in a year.

inventory lying around the raw materials warehouse whereas high inventory turnover indicates extremely active management with little excess inventory.

The days in inventory measure provides an alternative measure of the inventory turnover concept. The computation of this measure is as follows:

$$\frac{\text{Number of days in the reporting period}}{\text{Inventory turnover}} = \text{Days in inventory}$$

For example, Exhibit 3 reports that Mason's cost of goods manufactured (which "flows" out of the work-in-process inventory account) during February was $195,000. Using the inventory turnover formula shown above, Mason's work-in-process inventory turnover for the month is 10.0, meaning that inventory was replaced 10 times in February. If we assume that on average there are 30 days in a month,[5] then Mason maintained approximately three days' worth of work-in-process inventory in February to support the production process. The fewer numbers of days in work-in-process inventory, the more streamlined the production process; a long, complex manufacturing process (such as the construction of a ship) could have more than a year's worth of production costs tied up in unfinished inventory.

Mason Tool Company's performance in terms of how well it efficiently uses finished goods inventory is indicated by the fact that this inventory turned over

---

Exhibit 4: Analysis of the Levels of Raw Materials, Work-in-Process, and Finished Goods Inventories

Raw Materials Inventory—February

Cost of raw materials used during February	$86,000
Beginning raw materials inventory in February*	$25,000
Ending raw materials inventory in February	$20,000
Average inventory balance during the month	$22,500
Raw materials inventory turnover (cost flow ÷ average inventory)	3.8
Days in raw materials inventory (30 days ÷ inventory turnover)[†]	7.8 days

Work-in-Process Inventory—February

Cost of goods manufactured during February	$195,000
Beginning work-in-process inventory in February*	$19,000
Ending work-in-process inventory in February	$20,000
Average inventory balance during the month	$19,500
Work-in-process inventory turnover (cost flow ÷ average inventory)	10.0
Days in work-in-process inventory (30 days ÷ inventory turnover)[†]	3.0 days

Finished Goods Inventory—February

Cost of goods sold during February	$190,000
Beginning finished goods inventory in February*	$48,000
Ending finished goods inventory in February	$46,000
Average inventory balance during the month	$47,000
Finished goods inventory turnover (cost flow ÷ average inventory)	4.0
Days in finished goods inventory (30 days ÷ inventory turnover)[†]	7.4 days

*Equal to the ending inventory level in January.
[†]<u>Don't</u> round the turnover ratio when computing days in inventory.

---

5 Although there are 28 (occasionally 29) days in the month of February, we use an average of 30 days per month in this textbook for all monthly days in inventory calculations. This is a standard number of days per month used by many organizations for similar calculations.

4.0 times during February. Alternatively, Mason reports 7.4 days in finished goods inventory for February. This means that Mason is able to sell its entire inventory of table saws to customers approximately every 7.4 days.

Mason Tool Company's inventory turnover and days in inventory computations for the remainder of 2006 are reported in the bottom panel of Exhibit 3. Take a moment to scan these numbers. Do you see any patterns across time in the way that Mason Tool Company is able

business environment

That's a Lot of Inventory! During your last trip to the grocery store, did you count the number of types of product on the shelves? How many different stock keeping units (SKUs) or product items would you estimate your local grocery store uses to monitor its inventory activity? 1,000? 10,000? 100,000? Keeping track of the catalog and inventory of SKUs is made easier by technology. Managers need detailed information to help keep the shelves fully stocked without having too much invested in inventory.

In 1883, when Arthur and Howard Hannaford opened their fruit and vegetable stand in Portland, Maine, life was just a bit slower. Now HANNAFORD BROS. is a supermarket chain operating 116 supermarkets and three distribution centers located throughout Maine, New Hampshire, Vermont, New York, and Massachusetts under the names of SHOP 'N SAVE and HANNAFORD FOOD AND DRUG SUPERSTORES with an average store size of about 48,000 square feet per store. Just like every business, the grocery business is competitive; traditionally thin margins make every penny count. Store managers are under a lot of pressure to control inventory and costs and generate as much revenue as possible.

The company's information philosophy is expressed by Bill Homa, chief information officer of Hannaford, "If we can provide managers with the information they need to reduce their out-of-stocks, we can help them increase their sales." The company used to distribute daily printed merchandising reports to its stores via FEDERAL EXPRESS. Given the number of stores involved, this procedure cost Hannaford several hundred thousand dollars each year.

In order to provide managers with the inventory information they need to effectively operate their stores, Hannaford and

CISCO developed an inventory SKU system to manage its perishable dated products to reduce costs and increase sales. This system alerts managers to early indications of inventory problems, improving their ability to make strategic merchandising and buying decisions. The system also hosts merchandising reports that are updated daily and centralizes decision-support information for corporate planners and store managers.

The Hannaford inventory SKU system eliminates the need for daily printed merchandising reports, which were costing the company hundreds of thousands of dollars in annual express delivery charges. It also gives managers Web-based access to daily merchandising reports and affords them the means to examine sales by item or by category. Thanks to the system, they are able to control "shrink" (the loss associated with products that are outdated, damaged, or stolen), look at weekly variances in sales and labor, and centralize all of this information so that corporate planners can make timely decisions based on updated knowledge of chain-wide trends.

"In the past, we printed new reports every day and shipped them out to the stores. Now store and department managers can use Web browsers to search the online reports and immediately pull off the information they need. And by eliminating paper reports, we're also saving several hundred thousand dollars in annual FedEx charges."

—Bill Homa, chief information officer, Hannaford Bros.

In 1999, Hannaford announced its merger with DELHAIZE AMERICA; allowing Hannaford Bros. Co. to operate as a separate business while being part of a $14 billion company with 1,400 stores from Maine to Florida.

Sources: http://www.cisco.com, "Hannaford Bros. Enables Managers;" http://www.hannaford.com, "About Us" content page, accessed August 18, 2003.

to manage its three types of inventory? Look closely at the days in inventory numbers. You should see that Mason is able to reduce its days in finished goods inventory during the summer months by approximately two days (from more than seven days to a little more than five days). This suggests that Mason is experiencing more sales of its table saws in the summer.

STOP & THINK

It appears in Exhibit 3 that the inventory performance measures are missing for January. Is it possible to compute these measures using the data provided? What data would you need to analyze how well Mason Tool Company managed its three inventory levels during January?

While Mason may or may not be able to control this seasonal cycle, it does need to anticipate these surges in market demand and plan its production process accordingly. The fact that Mason is basically holding its days in work-in-process inventory consistent at between approximately 2.5 and 3 days indicates that it is working hard to adjust its production outflow to the market demand for its table saws. One inventory problem that Mason likely needs to address is the way it controls its raw materials inventory. This inventory level fluctuates from about 5.5 days in the summer to about 8 days during the winter. Perhaps Mason needs to more aggressively tailor its volume of raw material purchases to coincide with production and sales.

As we finish this section on managing inventory levels, it is important to point out that comparing performance across periods of time is only one way that these two measures can be used to control inventory. Management may also want to compare the inventory levels of different products across the organization, or may want to "benchmark" the performance of its products with those of other companies. Further, in addition to assessing production cost and inventory levels, managers are just as interested in indicators of product and production quality. We'll address some of these quality issues in the next chapter.

TO SUMMARIZE: Cost of goods sold is a summary number that is audited and used in the financial statements, but it is not very useful for managers to use when assessing how well the company controls inventory costs and inventory levels. Two management accounting tools can be used to support good management control of levels of raw materials, work-in-process, and finished goods inventories. These two measures are inventory turnover and days in inventory. Inventory turnover is a measure of the intensity with which the organization is using its inventory. Higher turnover numbers indicate a more efficient use of inventory. The days sales in inventory measure reports the average number of days of inventory use. A lower number of days indicates a more efficient use of inventory.

Managing Cost Information

3 Understand how merchants manage inventory in their organizations.

As discussed in the preceding section, cost data can be used in a manufacturing firm to evaluate the appropriateness of the levels of raw materials, work-in-process, and finished goods inventories. Merchants, or managers of merchandising organizations, are particularly conscious of inventory levels currently in the retail store or in the distribution center. Managing this inventory takes careful and detailed planning. The detail in these plans results from merchants having *many* different types of inventory items, each with its own particular supplier source and targeted customer. Merchants must also be very careful in planning their inventory levels because having either too little or too much inventory can involve critical issues. These issues are listed in Exhibit 5. If accountants are aware of these issues, they can help their organizations avoid a variety of unnecessary out-of-pocket costs or opportunity costs.

Carrying Too Much Inventory

Having inventory is certainly necessary for most merchants if they expect to do business with their customers. However, accumulating as much inventory as possible is *not* the purpose of merchandising (or manufacturing) companies. Good business management entails having the right assets at the right place in the right time and in the right quantity (always a challenging

Exhibit 5: Inventory Management Issues

Carrying Too Much Inventory	Carrying Too Little Inventory
• Increased overhead costs	• Increased risk of lost sales
• Increased financial holding costs	• Increased ordering costs
• Increased risk of loss of market value	• Increased risk of supplier price increases
• Decreased inventory flexibility	• Increased exposure to nondelivery
• Increased inventory shrinkage	• Decreased bulk order discounts

holding costs The financial opportunity costs that result from investing money in an asset such as inventory. Whatever income the money could generate in an alternative investment is the holding cost of the current investment.

inventory shrinkage The disorder, spoilage, and theft that result when a company chooses to maintain inventory on site, resulting in additional out-of-pocket costs to replace inventory.

FYI:

In 1999, FRUIT OF THE LOOM reported that it experienced inventory shrinkage totaling $70.4 million. This represented a 25% increase in shrinkage compared to the prior year. Fruit of the Loom attributed the shrinkage increase to expansion of its network of contractors (factories where its clothing items are produced).

FYI:

How important is the Christmas buying season for a toy merchant? The 2002 annual report for TOYS "R" US, INC., reports that approximately 43% of its sales occur in the months of November, December, and January.

endeavor!). Later in this chapter, we'll introduce you to the concept of just-in-time (JIT) inventory management, which emphasizes the fact that too much inventory creates a lot of management problems. Managers of merchandising organizations are particularly sensitive to this fact. First of all, clearly many out-of-pocket costs are involved in having inventory on site, including costs of storage, security, and record keeping. What may not be as clear is the financial opportunity cost (sometimes called the **holding cost**) of the inventory investment. Every dollar that is invested in inventory cannot be used in alternative business investments, such as expanding another part of the business or simply investing in the stock market or in a bank savings account. Whatever money we *could* make by investing the money elsewhere is the holding cost of the current inventory investment. Accountants measure and report holding costs all the time. We will demonstrate the calculation of holding costs in the expanded material section of this chapter.

Increased overhead costs and holding costs are not the only issues involved in carrying too much inventory. The more inventory a merchant elects to carry, the more risk the merchant faces that the inventory will decrease in market value before it can be sold (of course, inventory may unexpectedly increase in market value as well). In addition, when a merchant invests in a lot of one type of inventory, it becomes difficult to shift to another inventory type that customers may suddenly want to buy. Finally, every merchant understands the tough reality that inventories "shrink" over time. **Inventory shrinkage** happens in a lot of ways. The type of shrinkage we hear about most often is theft (either by customers or employees). However, when inventory is being moved, stacked, stored, retrieved, and rotated, things get broken, parts get lost, and items become mislabeled. Liquid and gas stocks spill or evaporate. Cloth material becomes soiled. Grocery items spoil or become stale. As inventory is piled up around the store or distribution center, this disorder, spoilage, and theft are revealed every time the company takes an annual inventory count, resulting in additional out-of-pockets costs to replace the inventory.

Carrying Too Little Inventory

Clearly, having too much inventory is a poor use of resources. However, poor planning that results in not having enough inventory on hand can also be a source of trouble. It is obvious to most managers and owners that potential sales are lost when customers are turned away because of a lack of inventory. Accountants can support good inventory management when they are able to quantify these opportunity costs for decision makers. As can be seen in Exhibit 5, however, an organization that has inadequate inventory levels also incurs other costs. For example, initiating an order with a wholesaler or manufacturer for the delivery of goods often requires a number of business processes, including counting inventory, preparing purchase orders, receiving and inspecting shipments of goods, and initiating payments for purchases. Most merchants have to initiate and pay for each of these steps every time they purchase inventory. Merchants that maintain low inventory levels by buying in smaller quantities will generally have to make more purchases, and pay for additional employee time, to replenish their stock.

Prices for most types of inventory increase with time. Some items are particularly susceptible to sudden price increases. Have you ever awakened to hear the morning newscast report that automobile gasoline prices have suddenly surged? When you go out to your car and discover the gas tank nearly empty, don't you wish you had filled the tank yesterday? One reason some merchants purchase large amounts of inventory is to temporarily protect themselves from sudden increases in prices. Companies without similar foresight will experience greater out-of-pocket expenses if prices do increase. Companies that keep very low levels of inventory are most likely to have to pay for every price increase. In addition, these same companies are much more dependent on their suppliers to *always* meet their delivery commitments. If a supplier is late in making promised shipments or delivers inventory that is damaged or of the wrong type, the merchant may miss making sales to some customers. Finally, merchants that regularly purchase large levels of inventory often enjoy price discounts from their suppliers. Merchants making smaller purchases should be aware of the opportunity cost related to missing these potential bulk purchase discounts.

Example of Inventory Management Costs

We'll use the fictitious example of two large retailers of children's toys, Kids N Toys, Inc., and Child's Delight, Inc., to explore the issues and costs involved in inventory management for merchandising organizations. As you might expect, the Christmas buying season is a big deal for a toy retailer. Management and buyers for these companies study trend reports and catalogs all year in order to properly plan their investments for December. Both companies have limited resources that can be invested in inventory for the holiday season. Given the necessary **lead time**, as well as the size of the investment, these decisions are absolutely critical to both companies. Once December has arrived, it becomes very difficult to make many adjustments to preplanned inventory types and levels.

A wholesaler of children's dolls has announced the availability of a new doll for Christmas this year, the Burzee Doll. Based on the manufacturer's reputation, as well as the fact that the manufacturer of the doll intends to do a lot of promotional advertising, the wholesaler is confident that the Burzee Doll will sell very well this year. To help make planning decisions, each retailer has its management accountants prepare some forecasts on potential revenues and costs related to the issues listed in Exhibit 5. Based on the projections of its accountants, Kids N Toys, Inc., decides to invest very heavily in the Burzee Doll and orders 50,000 dolls for delivery on November 1. Because of the size of its order, the wholesaler offers Kids N Toys a discount of $2 per doll. On the other hand, the accountants' projections of revenues and costs at Child's Delight, Inc., are not as optimistic. As a result, Child's Delight orders only 5,000 dolls and pays the full wholesale price of $12 per doll. Both retailers follow the manufacturer's recommendation to set the customer price at $30 per doll.

Exhibit 6 outlines all the Burzee Doll events that take place during the holiday season, as well as the resulting revenues and costs for the two companies. As it turns out, the Burzee Dolls are a real hit during the holiday buying season. Child's Delight keeps running out of inventory and must reorder dolls three times during the season. As you can see in Exhibit 6, each time Child's Delight reorders dolls, it is not hard for the accountants to note the amount of inventory shrinkage. Occasionally, dolls are stolen, misplaced, or destroyed in the process of moving, sorting, and stacking. On the other hand, Kids N Toys has lots of dolls spread out all over the store, making it difficult to know much about shrinkage without taking a very expensive inventory count. The accountants at Kids N Toys elect to wait until all the inventory is sold before measuring inventory shrinkage.

network exercises

Toys "R" Us

TOYS "R" US is the largest toy retailer in the United States. With its toysrus.com Web site (in partnership with AMAZON.COM), it has also sought to expand its success to the Internet. As discussed in the chapter, effective management of a merchandising company requires information about both profitability and inventory management. Go to the investor relations page at the corporate Web site for Toys "R" Us at **http://www.toysrusinc.com** and find the company's earnings news release for August 18, 2003.

Net Work:

In addition to discussing the company's profitability, what does this news release say about the company's inventory management?

lead time Generally, the time interval between initiating a request and finally fulfilling the request.

STOP & THINK

These two companies begin the holiday season with very different levels of inventory in Burzee Dolls. With its very large inventory investment, what additional inventory costs are now a factor for Kids N Toys? What additional inventory costs is Child's Delight susceptible to with its relatively small inventory investment?

Exhibit 6: Management Events in the Burzee Doll Inventory

Date	Event	Kids N Toys, Inc.	Child's Delight, Inc.
Nov. 1	Retailers establish the Burzee Doll inventory.	Company buys 50,000 dolls at $10 per doll. Customer price is set at $30.	Company buys 5,000 dolls at $12 per doll. Customer price is set at $30.
30	Sales on the doll start increasing.	Company has sold 7,500 dolls.	Company has sold 4,950 dolls and is out of stock. Reorders another 5,000 dolls at $12 per doll.
Dec. 10	Sales on the doll are really strong.	Company has sold another 12,000 dolls.	Company has sold another 4,970 dolls and is out of stock again. Reorders another 5,000 dolls at $15 per doll (supplier has increased price).
20	Sales on the doll continue to be very strong.	Company has sold another 15,000 dolls.	Company has sold another 4,990 dolls and is out of stock again. Reorders another 5,000 dolls at $15 per doll.
31	Sales have nearly halted in the last few days.	Company has sold another 7,000 dolls.	Company has sold another 4,940 dolls and is out of stock again. Chooses not to reorder.
Jan. 15	Sales are nearly nonexistent.	Company has sold another 500 dolls and now puts dolls on sale at cost ($10).	Out of Burzee Doll business.
30	Sales pick up a little.	Company has sold another 2,000 dolls and now sells the remaining 4,400 usable dolls to a small merchant for $3 per doll.	Out of Burzee Doll business.
31	Evaluate inventory shrinkage.	Sold a total of 48,400 units indicating that 1,600 units were lost due to shrinkage.	Sold a total of 19,850 units indicating that 150 units were lost due to shrinkage.

By the end of December, Child's Delight has sold all of its dolls and elects not to place a fifth order. On the other hand, Kids N Toys still has a large number of dolls remaining. Since the buying craze for Burzee Dolls appears to be finished, Kids N Toys puts the dolls on sale at cost ($10 per doll) in mid-January. At the end of January, the store liquidates the remaining 4,400 dolls to another retailer at $3 per doll.

The Gross Margin Report

When all Burzee Doll sales are totaled, Kids N Toys sold 48,400 dolls (indicating inventory shrinkage over the last three months of 1,600 dolls); Child's Delight sold 19,850 dolls (indicating inventory shrinkage of 150 dolls). Which of the two retailers did better with the Burzee Dolls? Exhibit 7 provides a gross margin report based on what each company spent on inventory purchases and received in inventory sales. When you look at the gross margin of $793,200 for Kids N Toys, it appears that this company did a much better job selling Burzee Dolls than its competitor, Child's Delight, based on its gross margin of only $325,500.

Return on Inventory Investment

The gross margin numbers presented in Exhibit 7 suggest that Kids N Toys outperformed Child's Delight. However, if you had money to invest in these companies, you might actually like Child's Delight's retail work on Burzee Dolls better than the work done by Kids N Toys.

Exhibit 7: Gross Margin Report on the Burzee Doll Inventory

	Kids N Toys, Inc.		Child's Delight, Inc.	
	42,000 units × $30	$1,260,000		
	2,000 units × $10	20,000		
	4,400 units × $3	13,200		
Sales revenue		$1,293,200	19,850 units × $30	$ 595,500
			10,000 units × $12	
Cost of purchases	50,000 units × $10	(500,000)	10,000 units × $15	(270,000)
Gross margin		$ 793,200		$ 325,500

STOP & THINK

Is there anything wrong with using the gross margin analysis presented in Exhibit 7 to evaluate management performance in these two companies? What costs may be missing?

Think about the average size of the inventory investment that each company maintained. Kids N Toys initially spent $500,000 to acquire 50,000 dolls. By the end of January, this inventory had been fully liquidated back into cash. Hence, Kids N Toys had quite a bit of cash tied up in Burzee Doll inventory! On average, how much cash did it have invested in this inventory during its selling period? On November 1, Kids N Toys had $500,000 in Burzee Doll inventory. On January 30, it had no Burzee Doll inventory. On average, Kids N Toys had about a $250,000 investment in inventory during its three-month selling period ($500,000 ÷ 2).[6]

How does Kids N Toys' average inventory investment compare to its competitor's investment? Rather than one large inventory purchase at the beginning of November, Child's Delight made four smaller investments as needed during November and December. The average inventory purchase amount was $67,500 [($60,000 + $60,000 + $75,000 + $75,000) ÷ 4]. On December 31, it had no Burzee Doll inventory. On average, then, Child's Delight had only about a $33,750 investment in inventory during its two-month selling period ($67,500 ÷ 2).

Obviously, the difference between the two companies' gross margins reported in Exhibit 7 is dramatic. However, the difference in Kids N Toys' average inventory investment of $250,000 versus the $33,750 average inventory investment at Child's Delight is also impressive. Remember from the introductory chapter that the executives in the early days at DUPONT COMPANY recognized that it is just as important to manage the money outflow for asset investment as it is to manage the money inflow from profits. This is the logic underlying Pierre du Pont and Donaldson Brown's ROI (return on investment) formula. Remember that the ROI formula has two parts (if you need a review, see the previous chapter on monitoring performance in cost, profit, and investment centers):

$$\frac{\text{Profit margin}}{\text{(Profit ÷ Revenue)}} \times \frac{\text{Asset turnover}}{\text{(Revenue ÷ Total assets)}} = \text{ROI}$$

Based on ROI, which of these two companies has created the most revenue for each dollar invested in its Burzee Doll inventory asset? Answering this question is really a function of the "asset turnover" section of the ROI formula. Notice, however, that rather than *total* revenue and *total* assets, we are focusing only on Burzee Doll revenue and the value of the Burzee Doll

---

6 Be careful with this calculation! The fact that Kids N Toys held its doll inventory for three months (or two months, or four months) does not change the fact that average inventory for the company is $250,000. The formal calculation here is (Beginning balance + Ending balance) ÷ 2. Instead of having no inventory, what if Kids N Toys still had $50,000 worth of Burzee Dolls on January 31? The average inventory investment would then be $275,000 [($500,000 + $50,000) ÷ 2]. You might also note that a more accurate measure of average inventory for Kids N Toys could involve assessing inventory levels on a month-by-month basis (we use an approach similar to this when we compute average inventory for Child's Delight, Inc.). However, unless otherwise indicated, this text-book will use the traditional (Beg+End)/2 formula to calculate average inventory.

inventory asset. This fact really doesn't present a problem. Rather than measuring how much total revenue is generated per dollar of total assets, we will simply measure *how much specific revenue is generated per dollar of a specific inventory item*. Hence, how many sales dollars does Kids N Toys generate for each dollar invested in its Burzee Doll inventory compared to Child's Delight?

$$\text{Kids N Toys: Revenue} \div \text{Average inventory}$$
$$\$1,293,200 \div \$250,000 = \$5.17$$

$$\text{Child's Delight: Revenue} \div \text{Average inventory}$$
$$\$595,500 \div \$33,750 = \$17.64$$

Note that organizations have a limited amount of resources to invest. Using the ROI formula, DuPont Company was able to wisely manage the task of maximizing the value of its investments by knowing where in the massive organization to invest its resources. Looking at the calculations above, you can see that Child's Delight made the better use of limited purchasing dollars to manage the Burzee Doll inventory in order to create sales revenue.[7]

Combining the gross margin per sales dollar with the number of sales dollars generated per dollar of inventory yields the following return on inventory investment calculations for Kids N Toys and Child's Delight:

$$(\text{Gross margin} \div \text{Revenue}) \times (\text{Revenue} \div \text{Inventory}) = \text{Return on inventory investment}$$

$$\text{Kids N Toys: } (\$793,200 \div \$1,293,200) \times (\$1,293,200 \div \$250,000) = 317\%$$

$$\text{Child's Delight: } (\$325,500 \div \$595,500) \times (\$595,500 \div \$33,750) = 964\%$$

These numbers suggest that although Child's Delight generated a lower gross margin, it actually performed better than Kids N Toys because of superior inventory management. By the way, these numbers (317% and 964%) probably seem high to you. Don't confuse these numbers with the classic ROI results you'd expect to see in most companies. (We've been careful to not refer to these calculations as ROI calculations.) These numbers *are* high because we have focused on the utilization of just one asset—inventory. In order to sell Burzee Dolls, each merchandiser must also invest in buildings, store shelving and displays, cash registers, and so forth. When we add all of these assets to the inventory, *then* we can calculate the traditional ROI measure. However, these calculations on Burzee Doll inventory usage give a strong indication that, regardless of what the overall ROI of each company is, it appears that Child's Delight has been more effective at managing its acquisition and sales of Burzee Dolls.

The day-to-day effort to manage the Burzee Doll inventory involves many other important issues (as listed in Exhibit 5). Even the inventory measures above do not provide Kids N Toys and Child's Delight management with the data necessary to address all issues as they *plan* for future inventory investments and *control* and *evaluate* the current inventory acquisition and selling process. This is where good management accounting can provide real value in management's effort to improve a merchandising operation. Exhibit 8 provides a management accounting view of the two companies' retail work with the Burzee Doll line of operations. Study both Exhibit 8 and Exhibit 5 for a moment. What information in Exhibit 8 could help a manager trying to work with some of the issues described in Exhibit 5?

---

7 As you can see, we're essentially adjusting the inventory turnover measure here by dividing the retail value of revenue by the wholesale value (or purchase cost) of inventory, and we're very careful to label this new calculation "inventory turnover." As illustrated in the preceding section, inventory turnover is traditionally measured using cost of goods sold rather than sales or revenue. Conceptually, comparing a wholesale number (inventory) to a wholesale number (cost of goods sold) makes more sense than comparing a wholesale number to a retail (sales revenue) number. However, as long as a consistent approach is used, the insights gained are the same. Further, the "revenue ÷ average inventory" calculation allows us to combine inventory turnover and profit margin in our analysis of these two retailers. As you can see, management accounting sometimes must adjust in order to suit the needs of the current decision-making situation.

Exhibit 8: Management Accounting Report on the Burzee Doll Inventory

In addition to cost of purchases, note the following additional inventory costs:

- Average inventory overhead costs are $1.10 per unit per month.
- Average costs to initiate and receive a purchase order are $1,250 per event.

	Kids N Toys, Inc.		Child's Delight, Inc.	
Expected revenue	50,000 units × $30 standard price	$1,500,000	20,000 units × $30 standard price	$600,000
Shrinkage loss	1,600 units × $30	(48,000)	150 units × $30	(4,500)
Market loss	2,000 units × ($30 − $10) +			
	4,400 units × ($30 − $3)	(158,800)		(0)
Actual revenue		$1,293,200		$595,500
Purchase costs	50,000 units × $10 standard cost	(500,000)	20,000 units × $10 standard cost	(200,000)
Lost discount		(0)	20,000 units × $2 lost discount	(40,000)
Price increase		(0)	10,000 units × $3 price increase	(30,000)
Gross margin		$ 793,200		$325,500
Overhead costs	50,000 units ÷ 2 = 25,000 average		5,000 units ÷ 2 = 2,500 average	
	inventory level × $1.10 × 3 months	(82,500)	inventory level × $1.10 × 2 months	(5,500)
Order costs	1 order × $1,250	(1,250)	4 orders × $1,250	(5,000)
Net operating profit		$ 709,450		$315,000

The Management Accounting Report on Kids N Toys' Net Operating Profit

As you can see in Exhibit 8, we are identifying some additional out-of-pocket costs on the Burzee Doll operation for each company. Note that the gross margin for each company is the same as that calculated in the gross margin report in Exhibit 7. However, we're approaching the calculation of gross margin differently, as well as identifying some other relevant costs to calculate **net operating profit** for each company. Net operating profit is useful in measuring the performance of these operations. Much more important, though, are the insights gained in the management accounting numbers used to calculate gross margin and net operating profit. These numbers, presented in Exhibit 8, are extremely useful for planning, controlling, and evaluating the Burzee Doll retail operations.

Let's work with Kids N Toys first. This company originally purchased 50,000 units with the intent of selling all of them for $30. Why didn't it then have $1.5 million in revenue? This question cannot be answered using the gross margin report in Exhibit 7, but the answer is obvious in the management accounting report in Exhibit 8. Somehow, 1,600 dolls that Kids N Toys planned to sell were broken, misplaced, or stolen. Based on an intended $30 selling price, this cost the company $48,000 in lost revenue. In addition, the market demand changed while Kids N Toys still had dolls to sell. As a result, the store had to sell some dolls for prices lower than the planned $30. Specifically, Kids N Toys reduced expected revenue by $40,000 when it sold 2,000 dolls for $10, and reduced expected revenue by another $118,800 when it sold 4,400 dolls for $3. This loss of market value is a risk that Kids N Toys management should consider when planning for next year's purchases. Further, management should also evaluate the information on inventory shrinkage to better control the inventory operation.

We mentioned briefly the concept of activity-based costing (ABC) in an earlier chapter on product cost flows. We'll spend a lot of time on the ABC concept in the next chapter. Briefly, ABC is an approach to tracking the relationship between activities and costs that is generally used to better allocate manufacturing overhead costs to products. This concept can also be used to analyze overhead costs in merchandising organizations. Managing the Burzee Doll inventory

net operating profit The difference between normal business sales and normal business expenses.

Caution

Note that shrinkage loss and market loss are based on expected selling prices, not purchase costs.

STOP & THINK

Both Kids N Toys and Child's Delight are investment centers. If you studied the previous chapter on monitoring performance in cost, profit, and investment centers, you should realize that Exhibit 8 is providing a report on *variances*. Think carefully about some of the items being reported in Exhibit 8 and see if you can identify which variances are being described here.

requires some overhead costs. In this example, let's assume an ABC analysis reveals that the cost for storage, security, and other supervisory activities works out to be about $1.10 per doll per month. In addition, the effort to count inventory and prepare the purchase order, as well as to receive and pay for the inventory, requires about $1,250 in administrative costs each time inventory is purchased. In a standard income statement, only the direct cost of inventory purchases would be used to measure gross margin. Those overhead and purchasing costs related to managing the Burzee Doll inventory are typically combined with all other administrative costs to form Selling and Administrative Expenses on the income statement. However, the management accounting report in Exhibit 8 has specifically identified and related these costs to the Burzee Doll inventory line (this is the goal of the ABC concept). This information allows management to see exactly how the Burzee Doll product line is contributing to Kids N Toys' overall net operating profit. Further, management can evaluate how having a lot of inventory leads to higher overhead costs. On the other hand, though, purchasing all these dolls at once saved Kids N Toys additional purchasing costs.

The Management Accounting Report on Child's Delight's Net Operating Profit

Now let's evaluate operations at Child's Delight using the management accounting report in Exhibit 8. During November and December, Child's Delight purchased a total of 20,000 units with the intent of selling all of them for $30. Similar to Kids N Toys, the difference between expected revenue and actual revenue is explained by the inventory shrinkage of 150 units. Compared to Kids N Toys, why does Child's Delight have a much lower percentage of dolls being broken, misplaced, or stolen? It seems reasonable to expect that Child's Delight found it much easier to maintain and keep track of its much smaller level of inventory. Can this shrinkage be further reduced? Child's Delight should carefully consider this question as it plans for the next buying season.

As noted in Exhibit 5, keeping the inventory levels low helps protect the organization against certain types of costs and risks. However, this can be a challenging balance because other costs occur as a result of low inventory levels; Child's Delight incurred three of these costs. First, because Child's Delight made small inventory purchases, bulk discounts were unavailable to the company. The effect of losing these discounts, $40,000, was to pay $2 more per doll (20,000 dolls × $2). Second, each time Child's Delight ran out of inventory and had to reorder, it had to pay the current market rate. Given the high popularity of Burzee Dolls during the holiday buying spree, it is not surprising that the manufacturer raised the price. This cost was passed through the distributor to Child's Delight, which had to pay an additional $3 per doll for its last two shipments. Overall, this resulted in an additional $30,000 in cost (10,000 dolls × $3). Finally, each purchase event at Child's Delight adds to the management activities that must take place. If we assume that both companies have similar inventory acquisition activities, then Child's Delight must have $5,000 in purchase order costs (4 purchases × $1,250 activity costs). Again, though, low inventory levels have their advantage. Because Child's Delight orders only 5,000 dolls at a time, its inventory will range from 0 to 5,000 dolls. On average, it will generally have 2,500 dolls on hand. Based on an average monthly overhead cost of $1.10 per doll, selling Burzee Dolls led to relatively low overhead costs of $5,500 (again, assuming similar ABC costs for storage, security, and other supervisory activities for Child's Delight and Kids N Toys). Clearly, Child's Delight management should pay attention to all these numbers as it evaluates this year's operations and make plans for next year.

STOP & THINK

What other major costs might Child's Delight have had that are not being considered in this anaylsis?

Remember that the format and content of *financial accounting* reports are standardized in order to allow external users to compare reports from many different companies. In contrast, the format and content of internal *management accounting* reports differ across organizations because each organization customizes the reports to fit specific needs. Hence, the format of the management accounting report in Exhibit 8 is not regulated by anyone! The accountants for one particular retailer will customize the report to best support their own management processes of planning, controlling, and evaluating. The cost calculations displayed in Exhibit 8 are used by many, but not all, organizations in the merchandising industry. In this case, we saw that a simple comparison of gross margins does not necessarily indicate which company (Kids N Toys with a gross margin of $793,200 or Child's Delight with a gross margin of $325,500) made better decisions. By including information on inventory management, we concluded that Child's Delight had more successfully combined the activities of profitable sales with efficient use of its inventory assets. The more detailed profit analysis contained in Exhibit 8 enabled us to look more closely at the specific factors affecting the net operating profit of Kids N Toys and Child's Delight.

TO SUMMARIZE: Because wholesalers and retailers generally do not have to deal with raw materials or work in process, the process of accounting for inventory in a merchandising business is not nearly as complicated as it is in a manufacturing business. However, *managing* inventory costs is both complicated and critical for a merchant. Having too much inventory creates unnecessary overhead costs, financial holding costs, costs due to loss of market value, and costs due to inventory shrinkage. Not having enough inventory may result in unnecessary ordering costs and loss of bulk order discounts, as well as opportunity costs due to lost sales and increased supplier prices. While measuring some of these costs presents a challenge to accountants, the information is very important to the processes of planning, controlling, and evaluating gross margins and net operating profits for individual product lines.

Managing Service Organizations

4 Measure profitability and personnel utilization in a service organization.

As discussed earlier in the chapter on product cost flows, service organizations have many characteristics in common with manufacturing organizations. Both types of organizations engage in a substantial production process before delivering the final product to the customer. In a manufacturing organization, this production process involves people assembling materials using equipment located in factories. In a service organization, materials are of much smaller importance, and the production process focuses on people delivering a service within an infrastructure of tangible assets (hotels, delivery trucks, barbershops, doctors' offices, etc.). In some service organizations, such as airline service, the focus is on the tangible asset infrastructure—while the pilots, flight attendants, and ticket agents are important, most of our interest centers around the reliability of the planes and the baggage handling equipment. In other service organizations, such as legal services, the focus is on person-to-person delivery of customized service—we don't really care how nice the attorney's office is, as long as the attorney gives us good legal counsel. In this section, controlling product costs will be discussed in the context of a service organization.

Characteristics of a Service Organization

Service organizations can be broadly categorized into three basic types: professional services, service shops, and mass services.[8] A professional services organization is associated with people providing a highly customized service process. For example, a good family doctor tailors the treatment to the specific patient, after developing a personal rapport with the patient and carefully extracting a thorough case history. At the other end of the continuum, a mass service organization provides a standardized product with little emphasis on the person delivering the product. For example, MCDONALD'S has developed its fast-food business around the delivery of standard-quality food in a predictable atmosphere; we are pleased when the person serving us is competent and cheerful, but we are primarily interested in the taste of the food and

8 See Lin Fitzgerald, Robert Johnson, Stan Brignall, Rhian Silvestro, and Christopher Voss, *Performance Measurement in Service Businesses* (London: CIMA, 1991).

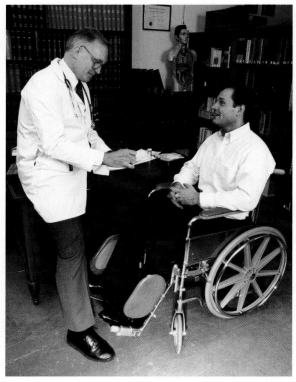

© 2003 Getty Images

A family doctor clinic is categorized as a professional services organization because the doctor provides a highly customized service—treatment is tailored to individual patients.

the cleanliness of the restrooms. A service shop is somewhere between a professional service and a mass service. For example, in a large-scale laser eye surgery clinic, there is more emphasis on standardization and on the equipment itself than one finds in a family doctor clinic. Also, in a high-end sit-down restaurant, the taste of the food is still important, but the quality of the personal service is at least as important.

The different characteristics of professional services, service shops, and mass services are summarized in Exhibit 9. Professional services are those services that emphasize person-to-person delivery, that focus on the process of service delivery rather than the creation of some final, tangible product, and that are highly customized. Mass services are those services that rely on equipment more than people in delivering the service, that result in the customer taking away a tangible product, and that do little, if any, tailoring to individual customer needs. Service shops provide a mixture of the three dimensions of people/equipment, process/product, and high/low customization.

Cost Management in a Service Organization

As we saw earlier in the chapter in our discussion of cost management in manufacturing and merchandising organizations, it is important for an organization to evaluate the magnitude of its costs and the degree to which it is efficiently utilizing its resources. We looked at cost and profitability measures, as well as at indicators of inventory management (such as inventory turnover). The same two concepts—evaluation of profitability and efficiency—will be used in developing cost management tools for service organizations.

For a manufacturing organization, key resources used in the production process are raw materials, machine hours, factory space, and labor. For a merchandising organization, the management of the level of inventory is crucial to the efficient use of the organization's resources. For a service organization, the management of materials inventories, building space, and equipment usage is also important. However, to emphasize the importance of people in service organizations, our illustration in this chapter will focus on how a service organization can measure the degree to which it is efficiently using its people.

Exhibit 9: Characteristics of Service Organizations

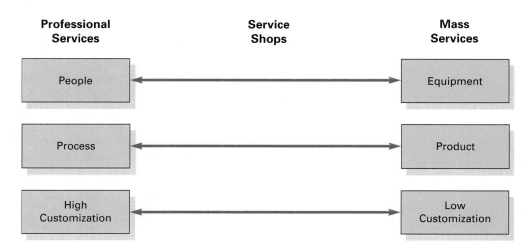

Illustration: Cost Management in an Audit Firm

A large audit firm is a good example of a professional services organization. An "audit" firm is composed of CPA (certified public accountant) professionals who provide specialized accounting, tax, and information systems consulting; and conduct audits of financial statements. The illustration in this section is for the hypothetical audit firm of LeviForrester. This illustration will center on the audit services offered in one large regional office of the firm. The office employs approximately 200 professionals and another 100 support staff. We will examine the costs associated with the professionals in the office. The costs of the support staff, as well as the training, recruiting, marketing, and technical analysis costs charged to the regional office by the national headquarters of LeviForrester, are also very important to the overall profitability of the regional office. However, assigning these support costs and national charges to specific jobs is quite difficult. The task of identifying cost drivers, common costs, and other concepts important to the proper treatment of these indirect support costs will be undertaken in the next chapter where we discuss activity-based costing. For the example in this chapter, we will restrict our attention to personnel costs that can be directly traced to specific client engagements.

The regional office of LeviForrester employs five types of professionals, as listed below.

	Average Years of Service with the Firm	Number of Professionals in the Office
Partner	More than 12 years	10
Senior manager	9 to 12 years	15
Manager	6 to 8 years	20
Senior	3 to 5 years	50
Staff	1 to 2 years	100

The partners exercise overall oversight of the audit practice. They review and approve the supporting documents (in electronic form) for each audit. They also seek to build the business by finding new clients. One of the 10 partners is designated the "managing partner" and is responsible for running the office and setting the strategic direction for the practice in that area. The senior managers and the managers are the professionals who are the primary interface between the audit firm and the clients. These managers keep the client informed about the progress of the audit and also supervise the other members of the audit team (the seniors and staff). The seniors spend much of their time at the clients' offices supervising and performing the actual work of the audit. The staff accountants do the bulk of the routine work of the audit.

Partners are expected to spend about half of their time working on specific client jobs during the year. This works out to be 1,000 hours out of the potential 2,000 working hours (50 weeks × 40 hours per week) during the year. At other times, partners are cultivating new client relationships and making proposals in order to get new client engagements. Senior managers and managers are expected to spend 75% of their time working on specific client engagements; seniors and staff are expected to spend all of their time working on specific client engagements. In fact, an important responsibility within the audit firm is the planning of the demands of various audit engagements to make sure that all of the seniors and the staff are always scheduled for specific engagements and are not sitting around the main office because of "unassigned" time.

These expectations about how much of a professional's time is to be spent in serving specific clients are used to develop billing rates and job cost charges. The computation of these billing rates that are used for job cost charges is shown in Exhibit 10. The job cost charges are

Exhibit 10: Billing Rates and Job Cost Charges for LeviForrester

	Annual Compensation	Expected Billable Hours	Compensation Cost per Billable Hour	Client Billing Rate per Billable Hour
Partner	$400,000	1,000	$400	$500
Senior manager	130,000	1,500	87	300
Manager	100,000	1,500	67	225
Senior	50,000	2,000	25	150
Staff	40,000	2,000	20	100

computed as a professional's total annual compensation divided by the number of client hours to be worked (i.e., billable hours) during a year. For example, the average annual compensation of partners at LeviForrester is $400,000, and each partner is expected to work on specific client engagements for 1,000 hours during a year. Thus, the partner compensation cost assigned to a job is $400 per hour ($400,000 ÷ 1,000 hours). These job cost charges are used by LeviForrester to compute the professional labor cost associated with each audit engagement.

The billing rates are used in computing how much is to be charged to a client for an audit engagement. The billing rate for professional services should be large enough to cover both the professional's compensation and general administrative costs such as secretarial support, computers, supplies, travel, and so forth. As you can imagine, the determination of the billing rates in Exhibit 10 is an extremely important element in LeviForrester's success. Billing rates that are too high will drive away potential customers, whereas billing rates that are too low will lead to low profitability and, perhaps, the inability to appropriately compensate the professionals.

On October 5, the managing partner for the regional office of LeviForrester received the profitability report contained in Exhibit 11. The report is generated in early October because LeviForrester's fiscal year ends on September 30. (It is impossible for LeviForrester to analyze its own business operations at the end of the normal calendar year because January is the busiest month of the year for audit firms as they perform audit work for their clients with December 31 year-ends.) The managing partner used the data in the profitability report to compute profit percentage from personnel (PPP), which is the fundamental measure of profitability used by LeviForrester. The overall PPP for this regional office is computed as follows:

$$PPP = (Revenue - Personnel\ compensation\ cost) \div Revenue$$
$$= (\$60,975,000 - \$14,450,000) \div \$60,975,000$$
$$= 76.3\%$$

Exhibit 11: Profitability Report for LeviForrester Regional Office

	Number of Professionals	Actual Billable Hours	Billing Rate	Total Revenue	Total Compensation Cost
Partners	10	8,200	$500	$ 4,100,000	$ 4,000,000
Senior managers	15	20,000	300	6,000,000	1,950,000
Managers	20	35,000	225	7,875,000	2,000,000
Seniors	50	120,000	150	18,000,000	2,500,000
Staff	100	250,000	100	25,000,000	4,000,000
Total				$60,975,000	$14,450,000

The managing partner is quite pleased with this report because the firm-wide goal for PPP is just 73.0%. As the various regional offices within LeviForrester are evaluated, each region's PPP is used to allocate a firm-wide bonus pool—the employees in regions with PPP in excess of 73.0% can expect to receive higher-than-average year-end bonuses.

The managing partner also received the personnel utilization report contained in Exhibit 12. The report contains personnel utilization rates (PUR) for each category of professionals within the firm. The contents of this report are somewhat disturbing. The managing partner sees that the partners in the office spent only 82.0% of the time that they should have on specific client engagements. Senior managers are also working with clients at less than desirable levels (88.9%). On the other hand, the hours billed by other managers, as well as seniors and staff accountants, were well in excess of 100% of the expected amount. This personnel utilization pattern suggests at least two potential future problems. First, existing clients may become concerned that the LeviForrester partners and senior managers are not spending as much time with them as they had anticipated. The clients may feel that the LeviForrester partners are now spending too much time finding new clients and not enough time attending to the needs of the existing clients. Second, the high utilization rates for the managers, seniors, and staff are a warning sign that these key professionals may be working too many hours. Hiring and training new professionals is an expensive process, and LeviForrester does not want to overwork its young professionals, resulting in abnormally high employee turnover.

The two specific measures—PPP and PUR—used to describe service process management at LeviForrester are intended only as illustrations; measures with these specific names are not in use in any real professional services firm. However, measures similar to these are very commonly used in service organizations. These two measures are representative of a broad class of measures that indicate the performance of service organizations on two important dimensions—profitability and personnel utilization. These two performance indicators connect directly with similar concepts used to manage inventory assets in manufacturing and merchandising organizations.

Exhibit 12: Personnel Utilization Report for LeviForrester

	Actual Billable	Budgeted Billable	Utilization Rate
Partners	8,200	10,000	82.0%
Senior managers	20,000	22,500	88.9%
Managers	35,000	30,000	116.7%
Seniors	120,000	100,000	120.0%
Staff	250,000	200,000	125.0%

TO SUMMARIZE: Three broad types of service organizations are professional services, service shops, and mass services. The dimensions on which these types of organizations differ are people/equipment, process/product, and high/low customization. As with manufacturing and merchandising organizations, it is important to measure both profitability and resource utilization in a service organization. In a professional services firm, profitability is measured by comparing the service revenues with the compensation costs associated with the professionals. It is also important to monitor the degree to which the professionals are appropriately utilized within the firm.

Just-in-Time

5 Describe how the concept of just-in-time (JIT) inventory systems is used to improve cost, quality, and timely performance in organizations.

Remember in the introductory management chapter that we described briefly the history of management accounting, and that management accounting has evolved as a result of competition. When one company or industry (or, in the new global economy, country) develops a better management accounting technique or measure, it then competes more strongly in the marketplace. Eventually, the success of the innovator puts pressure on other organizations to adopt the same or a similar approach to their own management accounting systems. This was exactly the situation when U.S. companies began adjusting their management teams and management accounting systems to focus on quality and timeliness. In the 1980s, American manufacturers faced an assault from Japanese companies such as TOYOTA and NEC. These Japanese companies had mastered quality and inventory control, as well as speedier ways to get products to market. Western CEOs studied the competition, deconstructed what made it so good, adopted the better features of their rivals, and changed their management systems. Since then, this new management focus on controlling the cost, quality, and timeliness of inventory has had an impact on management accounting and has spread into U.S. merchandising and service industries, as well as into industries in other countries around the world.

JIT Inventory Systems

just-in-time (JIT) A management philosophy that emphasizes removing all waste of effort, time, and inventory costs from the organization. One obvious result of JIT is the reduction or removal of needless inventory in a production system.

The effort of management to compete on measures of time and to make improvements involving time is captured in the concept of **just-in-time (JIT)** management processes. To understand JIT, you need to first understand how JIT is used to manage inventory, including raw materials inventory, work-in-process inventory, and finished goods inventory. Let's talk for a moment about inventory. What is the purpose of inventory in a manufacturing plant? This may seem obvious. In the past, manufacturers stockpiled inventories in order to avoid shutdowns or slowdowns and to meet customer needs if suppliers were late or if production or delivery was slow. Occasionally (sometimes more than occasionally!), suppliers deliver raw materials that contain some defects, or the production process ruins some work-in-process, or a customer returns an unacceptable product. How do we deal with these unexpected surprises? Again the answer has been to "have a little extra on hand" so that bad parts or products can be replaced without having to interrupt the manufacturing process. Not surprisingly, production managers can get a little nervous when inventory levels get too low.

Because of concerns about risks due to scheduling and quality problems, companies establish policies to keep inventory levels at or above some minimal level. This minimum level of inventory is usually called a "safety stock" (which we will discuss later in the expanded material section of this chapter). However, several years ago some cagey accountants and business owners in Japan created a new competitive view of inventory management. They (like everyone else) realized that maintaining these inventories can be very expensive because of warehousing costs, interest costs incurred to finance inventory, and the opportunity cost of money tied up in stockpiled inventory. The real insight these Japanese business professionals had was that inventories are really only "buffers" that mask inefficient operations or product quality problems. Eliminate these timing and quality problems, and you no longer need the inventory buffers. By concentrating on improving product quality and timely deliveries, many Japanese companies became much more efficient and profitable at the same time that inventories were kept to a minimum or even eliminated. The emerging inventory systems that allow for the elimination of inventory stockpiles, inefficiency, and waste are referred to as just-in-time inventory systems. The competitive value of these new management systems eventually caught on and came to America.

JIT began as a management tool for manufacturing. So, when first learning about JIT, it's probably best to think of it in this context. In a manufacturing setting, JIT is a process by which only enough materials to satisfy immediate production are shipped to the job site. When JIT is functioning perfectly, companies take delivery from suppliers only as raw materials are needed

The Japanese Focus on Inventory Henry Ford, the famous automotive production industrialist, lifted the FORD MOTOR COMPANY to great success during the early and mid-1900s by achieving tremendous cost efficiencies in producing cars. He believed in long production runs where low-skilled workers could build the same car part over and over again. As a result, high manufacturing costs per automobile plummeted, and he was able to offer cars to the public at extremely competitive prices. However, this production approach required high levels of raw materials, work-in-process, and finished goods inventories.

Meanwhile, across the ocean in Japan, Taiichi Ohno, an industrial scientist, and Eliji Toyoda, an executive vice president at TOYOTA MOTOR CORPORATION (and the son of the founder of Toyota), were experimenting with a different approach to large-scale production. While other Toyota executives thought that Toyoda's ideas were impractical, in 1949, in a machine shop in Koromo, Eliji Toyoda began experimenting with a new production control approach using the concepts of a just-in-time (JIT) inventory system. By 1953, the Koromo machine shop had a fully implemented *Kanban* system, which was based on the concept that supplies should be "pulled" through the production process as they are needed. (*Kanban* is essentially a signaling system that pulls parts forward through the production system.) Interestingly, Toyoda copied this idea from the sales methods of U.S. supermarkets. He was able to demonstrate that *Kanban* eliminated waste due to the overproduction of parts, reduced or eliminated the need for buffer inventories in the plant, and dramatically reduced production defects. In 1963, top management decided on the full application of *Kanban* as a means of transforming the production control system. Cost accountants were charged with developing and maintaining performance measures that tracked defects, excess inventory, and throughput time. Eliji Toyoda became chairman of Toyota in 1983. The rest, as they say, is history.

Source: M. Udagawa, "The Development of Production Management at the Toyota Motor Corporation," *Business History*, 1995, pp. 107–120.

for production and complete all inventory started during the day. In addition, inventory is completed only as it is ordered by customers and can be shipped immediately. As the name implies, materials are delivered "just in time" for production, and goods are manufactured "just in time" to meet customers' needs. As described earlier, JIT inventory systems started in Japan and have now been adopted successfully by a number of U.S. organizations. The results of JIT implementation are often dramatic. For example, one AT&T shop realized 54% improvement in quality yield, a 12-fold decrease in manufacturing time, an 88% reduction in scrap and rework, and a 95% increase in on-time deliveries.[9]

JIT and Value-Added Activities

Benefits such as those experienced by AT&T occur because companies that have adopted JIT have been able to avoid buildups of parts and materials and still ensure a smooth and orderly flow of goods to customers. JIT-based environments manage the flow of goods using a "pull" process. Essentially, this means that the final assembly stage for a product sends a signal (a *Kanban*; see the Business Environment on The Japanese Focus on Inventory) to the preceding workstation indicating what parts and materials will be needed during the next few hours.

9 F. B. Green, F. Amenkhienan, and G. Johnson, "Performance Measures and JIT," *Management Accounting*, February 1991, pp. 50–54.

value-added activities Necessary activities in a production or service process that customers identify as valuable and for which they are willing to pay.

non-value-added activities Unnecessary activities in a production or service process that customers typically do not see or care about and for which they are unwilling to pay.

The preceding workstation then sends similar signals all the way back through the manufacturing cycle, ensuring an orderly flow of products. Thus, the demand at the final assembly stage "pulls" the inventory through the production process only as it is needed. Using this system, nothing is produced unless customers demand it. At all stages, inventories are eliminated or reduced to the lowest possible level. Obviously, then, progress toward successful implementation of JIT is inventory-related. Inventory reduction is not the primary purpose of JIT, but it generally is a consequence of JIT efforts to eliminate waste. The goal is to add value to the product or service and reduce or eliminate activities that do not. To be specific, **value-added activities** are essentially defined as those activities for which the customer is willing to pay. On the other hand, **non-value-added activities** are those for which the customer is not willing to pay. For example, clients in a law office are not interested in paying for the time spent running the payroll, organizing the file room, or computing billable hours. These are non-value-added activities. However, these clients should be willing to pay for court time and consultation time. These are clearly value-added activities that the law firm should emphasize. Under JIT, waste is considered to be anything other than the minimum amount of equipment, materials, parts, space, and workers' time that is essential to add desired value to a product. This results in careful management of time spent on value-added activities such as machining and assembly operations (for a manufacturer) and customer service and contact activities (for a service firm). More importantly, the JIT focus on eliminating waste emphasizes removing as much as possible the time spent on non-value-added activities such as setup work, materials handling, and inspection.

JIT and Time

It is important to understand that JIT encourages accountants to emphasize providing time-based performance measures to management. Critical success factors for many JIT manufacturing, service, and merchandising firms include improving timeliness of customer delivery and increasing the product or service provider's flexibility in handling customers' needs. Exhibit 13 provides a sample of appropriate performance measures that support these factors of success, which are particularly important in today's dynamic, customer-oriented environment.

TO SUMMARIZE: Fundamentally, just-in-time (JIT) is an inventory management method that focuses on removing all waste from a production or service process. Originally a Japanese management system, JIT has made a significant impact on the way manufacturing, service, and merchandising companies in the United States and other nations are managed. JIT has a strong emphasis on costs and quality. However, JIT adds an important third dimension to the management process—management of timeliness and flexibility. In a manufacturing setting, demand at the final assembly stage "pulls" the inventory through the production process only as it is needed. Using this system, nothing is produced until customers demand it.

The main goal of JIT is to add value to the product or service and to reduce or eliminate activities that do not. By focusing on removing non-value-added activities and managing time spent on value-added activities, inventories and costs are reduced, while quality and timeliness are improved. Timeliness issues include emphasis on reducing customer delivery times and increasing flexibility within the production, service, or merchandising process.

Exhibit 13: Time-Based Performance Measures in a JIT Firm

Customer Delivery Success Factor (On-time delivery to customers can be affected by suppliers, product design time, and the production process and distribution time.)		Provider Flexibility Success Factor (Manufacturing, service, and merchandising flexibility includes the ability to respond quickly to changes in customer demand and product design changes.)	
Measure	**Computation Method**	**Measure**	**Computation Method**
Customer on-time delivery	Number of on-time deliveries divided by total deliveries. Goal: higher	Lead time for new product introduction	Amount of time from idea to readiness for sale. Goal: lower
Supplier on-time delivery	Number of on-time deliveries divided by total deliveries. Goal: higher	Parts and product availability	Number of times a part or product is unavailable when requested. Goal: lower
Design cycle time	Amount of time from initial idea to readied plans. Goal: lower	Number of common parts	Number of parts in a product design common to other products. Goal: higher
Number of contract changes	Number of times a contract is changed. Goal: lower	Inventory level	Average level of inventory. Goal: lower
Schedule attainment	Number of unchanged schedules divided by total schedules. Goal: lower	Capacity utilization	Percentage of process capacity used in current operations. Goal: higher
Lead time	Amount of time from customer's initial request to final product or service delivery. Goal: lower	Downtime	Amount of time a manufacturing or service process was unavailable. Goal: lower
Setup time*	Amount of time required to set up a production run. Goal: lower	Setup time*	Amount of time required to set up a production run. Goal: lower
Throughput time*	Amount of time from beginning of production or service process until process conclusion. Goal: lower	Throughput time*	Amount of time from beginning of production or service process until process conclusion. Goal: lower

*Note that some performance measures are important to both customer delivery and flexibility success factors.

Source: Adapted from J. A. Hendricks, "Performance Measures for a JIT Manufacturer," *Management Accounting*, January 1994, pp. 26–30.

As mentioned earlier in the chapter, an important element of cost management is the evaluation of whether an organization is utilizing its resources efficiently. In the expanded material section of this chapter, you will learn further details about inventory management. In particular, the expanded material discusses ways to determine the appropriate level of inventory that should be maintained by an organization.

Opportunity Costs in Managing Inventory and Work-in-Process Services

6 Calculate and interpret holding costs in merchandising and service businesses.

Let's return to our Burzee Doll example to discuss opportunity costs involved in managing inventory. As discussed in the introductory management chapter, there are many types of costs involved in managing an organization. All the costs that we discussed in the management accounting report for Kids N Toys and Child's Delight involved out-of-pocket costs (see Exhibit 8). However, there are several cost issues listed in Exhibit 5 that we did not include in the earlier analysis for these two companies. For example, inventory flexibility involves potential opportunity costs related to investing in a lot of inventory. Kids N Toys tied up a lot of money in securing 50,000 Burzee Dolls for the Christmas season—a shopping season that is particularly critical for retailers in the United States. Kids N Toys may have been fortunate that the Burzee Doll line sold as well as it did. If fickle shopper tastes had turned instead to another toy, it would have been difficult for Kids N Toys to shift this part of its inventory investment out of Burzee Dolls and into an alternative item in time to take advantage of the Christmas shopping rush. Kids N Toys may not have had any real problems in this area, but it needs to pay attention to this issue in planning for next year.

Child's Delight was also exposed to some opportunity costs. For example, because it kept its inventory of Burzee Dolls much lower than its competitor, Child's Delight was much more at risk of losing sales due to problems with supplier delivery and other logistics beyond its control. We'll assume in this case that all its deliveries were on time and without problems. However, another opportunity cost that Child's Delight was clearly not so fortunate in avoiding was lost sales due to lack of inventory. During the same period of time that Child's Delight sold its 19,850 dolls, Kids N Toys sold 41,500 dolls (see Exhibit 6 on page 410). If these retailers were at all similar in terms of competitive factors such as location and advertising, then it appears certain that Child's Delight could have sold more dolls *if* it had had more dolls! How many more dolls could have been sold? Frankly, this is a very difficult number to measure—even for a good accountant. You won't see it measured on any of the management accounting reports in this chapter. That does not at all imply that this number is less important than the others. There is a lot of discussion (and disagreement) on how to measure this number. The important thing is to somehow make decision makers aware of this cost. However, there is so much disagreement in practice as to how to specifically calculate this number that it is best in a textbook such as this to simply make you aware of this particular opportunity cost issue.

Holding Costs and Economic Profit in Merchandising Organizations

Another opportunity cost that both companies in our example experienced is financial holding costs. Financial holding costs are very well defined in practice. We'll use this cost to calculate for these two merchants a third income number called **economic profit**. As we calculated before, during the three-month period of November, December, and January, Kids N Toys had an average of $250,000 invested in Burzee Doll inventory. (See page 411 if you need help remembering how to calculate average inventory levels.) This money could alternatively have been earning money in a financial investment, or it could have been used to pay off loans or retire stock that Kids N Toys currently has outstanding. Every business has a **cost of capital** that relates to its cost of using money. In fact, you likely have your own individual cost of capital. Do you have any loans? What is the average interest rate on those loans? Let's assume it is 15%. Hopefully, you understand that as long as you have loans, every dollar you use for anything besides paying down your loan(s) costs you 15%. This 15% rate is your cost of capital. To be specific, for every dollar you spend buying a new stereo system, your loan(s) will increase by $0.15 at the end of the year. Hence, buying the stereo had better be worth this implicit financial holding cost. Even if you don't have any loans, you probably (hopefully!) have a savings account. Your cost of capital would then be the interest rate on your investment in the savings account. Let's assume you get a 4% return on your account. In this case, for every dollar you delay putting into the account (such as money spent on your new stereo), at the end of the year, your account will be $0.04 less than it could have been. Obviously, this cost information is important to all decisions involving the investment of limited resources. The formula to calculate a financial holding cost is the same approach traditionally used to calculate interest costs. We'll assume that the cost of capital for both Kids N Toys and Child's Delight is 20%. The financial holding cost of the average Burzee Doll inventory investment for Kids N Toys can be calculated in the following manner:

economic profit The difference between net operating profit and holding costs of inventory and other asset investments. Note that generally accepted accounting principles (GAAP) do not formally recognize opportunity costs such as holding costs.

cost of capital The weighted-average cost of a firm's debt and equity capital equals the rate of return that a company must earn in order to satisfy the demands of its owners and creditors.

Financial holding cost = Average investment × Annual rate × Number of years
$250,000 × 20% × 3/12 year = $12,500

The financial holding cost for Child's Delight can also be calculated. Remember, we calculated earlier that Child's Delight had a much lower average investment in inventory. In addition, this company's investment in Burzee Dolls lasted for only two months—November and December. As a result, its financial holding cost was much lower than Kids N Toys and is calculated as follows:

$33,750 × 20% × 2/12 year = $1,125

The financial holding cost is as much a cost of being in the business of selling Burzee Dolls as any other cost we calculated and listed earlier in Exhibit 8. Most accountants recognize that measuring financial holding costs is important to managing the economic well-being of the organization. Hence, in Exhibit 14 we have expanded the original management accounting report on the Burzee Doll inventory to include financial holding costs in order to calculate the organization's economic profit.

Before we leave this example and move on to discuss holding costs in service organizations, take one more opportunity to compare the gross margin report in Exhibit 7 and the management accounting report in Exhibit 14. These two merchandising reports would look basically the same regardless of whether Child's Delight and Kids N Toys were retailers or wholesalers of toys. You should now have a pretty clear understanding of how dramatically management

Exhibit 14: Expanded Management Accounting Report on the Burzee Doll Inventory

In addition to cost of purchases, note the following additional inventory costs:

- Average inventory overhead costs are $1.10 per unit per month.
- Average costs to initiate and receive a purchase order are $1,250 per event.
- Average costs of capital are 20%.

	Kids N Toys, Inc.		**Child's Delight, Inc.**	
Expected revenue	50,000 units × $30 standard price	$1,500,000	20,000 units × $30 standard price	$ 600,000
Shrinkage loss	1,600 units × $30	(48,000)	150 units × $30	(4,500)
Market loss	2,000 units × ($30 − $10) +			
	4,400 units × ($30 − $3)	(158,800)		(0)
Actual revenue		$1,293,200		$ 595,500
Purchase costs	50,000 units × $10 standard cost	(500,000)	20,000 units × $10 standard cost	(200,000)
Lost discount		(0)	20,000 units × $2 lost discount	(40,000)
Price increase		(0)	10,000 units × $3 price increase	(30,000)
Gross margin		$ 793,200		$ 325,500
Overhead costs	50,000 units ÷ 2 = 25,000 average		5,000 units ÷ 2 = 2,500 average	
	inventory level × $1.10 × 3 months	(82,500)	inventory level × $1.10 × 2 months	(5,500)
Order costs	1 order × $1,250	(1,250)	4 orders × $1,250	(5,000)
Net operating profit		$ 709,450		$ 315,000
Holding costs	$500,000 in purchases ÷ 2 =		($60,000 + $60,000 + $75,000 +	
	$250,000 average inventory		$75,000) ÷ 4 = $67,500 average	
	investment × 20% × 3/12 year	(12,500)	purchase ÷ 2 = $33,750	
			average inventory investment ×	
			20% × 2/12 year	(1,125)
Economic profit		$ 696,950		$ 313,875

segment Any part of an organization requiring separate reports for evaluation by management.

Economic Value Added (EVA™) A commercialized performance measurement system that emphasizes the incremental profits an organization creates over and above the profit required to cover the costs of capital.

accounting can differ from financial accounting in analyzing results of merchandising organizations. It is also important to point out that the reports in Exhibits 7 and 14 are both **segment** reports that are specific to inventory lines in these companies. A complete net operating profit analysis of all operations at either company should obviously include revenues and costs that are specific to all other inventory lines and overhead costs that are common across the organization (for example, the salaries for company executives). A complete economic profit analysis (sometimes called an **Economic Value Added** or **EVA™** analysis) would include a "holding cost" on all assets belonging to the company (cash, investments, equipment, buildings, land, etc.).

Service Organizations and Holding Costs

Something you should realize about GAAP and the service industry is that there typically has not been nearly as much emphasis on measuring and reporting work-in-process costs as compared to the manufacturing industry. However, it is important that the accountants support the management process by reporting on the costs and processes involved in work-in-process services. Think about the economic facts of work-in-process services for a moment. What do these costs represent? They represent significant investments in services provided to a client that typically have yet to provide any kind of a return in terms of cash receipts. Work in process is obviously necessary in many service companies. However, service companies cannot allow work-in-process services to build up in their organizations without restraint. Otherwise, resources are tied up that could otherwise be used to provide additional salable services. These opportunity costs eventually reduce profits in the company. Doesn't this sound a lot like the same risk of holding costs we described for merchandising companies earlier in this section? Accountants can and should measure holding costs on large service projects. Such measures provide decision makers with the insight to assess the effects of not properly planning and controlling large service projects. For example, consider a large accounting firm that is planning an audit which is expected to take three months to complete. Suppose that by the end of the three months, this large accounting firm has invested $400,000 in supplies, labor, and overhead for the audit project. Because most service companies have outstanding debts that are accruing interest costs or investment opportunities that have a measurable rate of return, these companies will incur a cost of capital just like merchants and manufacturers. If the accounting firm's cost of capital is 20%, the holding costs on this project are:

Average investment during the three-month period—($0 + $400,000) ÷ 2 = $200,000
Holding cost—$200,000 × 20% × 3/12 month = $10,000

What if the accounting firm has not completed the audit at the end of three months? At this point, it appears that the audit will require another month and another $40,000 in costs to complete. What are the additional holding costs of this extra month?

Average investment during the fourth month—($400,000 + $440,000) ÷ 2 = $420,000
Additional holding cost—$420,000 × 20% × 1/12 month = $7,000[10]

Computing and understanding these cost data provide a lot of incentive for the audit manager to complete the job and collect fees as quickly as possible. In providing these data, the accountant is supporting good planning and control of work in process in the audit service process.

---

10 Note that ($440,000 ÷ 2) × 20% × (4/12) < $10,000 + $7,000. This is because the costs on this audit contract are building much faster in the first three months ($400,000 in three months) than in the last month ($40,000 in one month). Similarly, using $400,000 ÷ 2 assumes that the $400,000 in costs is growing evenly over the three-month period ($133,333 per month). A more accurate method of computing the total holding costs for the four-month period would involve calculating and summing the holding costs for each individual month.

TO SUMMARIZE: Both merchandising and service firms often experience several types of opportunity costs, such as lost sales due to not having enough inventory or delays in completing work in process for customers. These costs are extremely difficult to measure. One important category of opportunity costs that accountants can measure is financial holding costs, which is a measure of the costs of having money tied up in inventory (for merchants) or in work-in-process services (for service companies). Measuring holding costs requires that the company's cost of capital first be identified. The holding cost formula is Average investment in inventory or Work-in-process services × Annual rate × Number of years. Financial holding costs can be deducted from net operating profit to measure economic profit for a particular product line.

Quantitative Inventory Management Methods

7 Use classic quantitative tools in inventory management (economic order quantity, reorder point, and safety stock).

We have spent a lot of time in this chapter discussing the many types of costs involved in managing inventory for merchants (once again, refer to Exhibit 5 to see a list of these issues). Generally, service companies do not carry significant levels of inventory and do not need to pay as much attention to inventory management costs. However, many manufacturing companies carry significant inventory levels of raw materials, work in process, and finished goods. These companies need to pay attention to issues involved in managing costs of carrying too much versus too little inventory. The primary question here is, "How much inventory should a company have?" This section will describe some quantitative methods that can be useful to accountants working to answer this question. We will use the example of a merchandising company to illustrate these methods; however, these inventory management calculations are equally applicable to manufacturing companies.

economic order quantity (EOQ) A specific calculation used to determine the most cost-effective size of a purchase order. The EOQ balances the costs of placing an order against the costs of carrying inventory in the organization.

Economic Order Quantity

It is a significant challenge to balance the costs of carrying too much inventory against the costs of carrying too little inventory. Determining how much inventory a company should have involves two important issues: (1) knowing *how much* inventory to order and (2) knowing *when* to place the inventory order. One well-known method used to handle the first issue is the **economic order quantity (EOQ)**. In calculating the optimal size of an inventory order, the EOQ attempts to balance the costs of carrying inventory (e.g., overhead costs, holding costs, risk of lost market values, shrinkage, etc.) against the costs involved in purchasing inventory.

> ⚠ **Caution**
>
> It is important that you understand that the purchase costs used to calculate the EOQ are *not* the inventory purchase prices, but the overhead costs involved in handling a purchase order (e.g., preparing purchase orders, receiving and inspecting shipments, initiating payment for purchases, etc.).

We'll return once more to the Burzee Doll example to demonstrate how to balance carrying costs and purchasing costs to calculate EOQ. First, we need to determine a cost per doll that includes all the costs of carrying Burzee Dolls during the two-month holiday buying season (November and December). Look back at Exhibit 14. Carrying costs should include the cost due to shrinkage loss, cost due to market loss, overhead costs, and holding costs. You should realize that combining all these carrying costs into a single cost per unit requires a great deal of analysis and intuition on the part of the accountant. However, let's assume that carrying costs are approximately $5 per doll. In addition, purchase order costs are $1,250 per order. Finally, we'll assume that a merchant can sell as many as 40,000 dolls during the holiday buying season. Exhibit 15 demonstrates one method of calculating EOQ using a cost schedule approach. As you can see, as the order quantity gets higher, the average inventory level in the store increases, and total carrying costs increase; in addition, the total purchase orders for the buying season are reduced, resulting in lower total ordering costs. By calculating the total of both carrying and ordering costs, the accountant can get a general idea of the optimal (i.e., economic) order quantity. According to the numbers in Exhibit 15, it appears that the store should request approximately 4,500 dolls for each of its nine orders during the buying season.

Exhibit 15: Calculating EOQ Using a Cost Schedule

Base data:

- Total market demand for dolls for the period: 40,000 dolls
- Average carrying cost per doll for the period: $5
- Average overhead costs per purchase order: $1,250

Order Quantity	1,500	2,250	3,000	3,750	4,500	5,250	6,000	6,750
	÷ 2	÷ 2	÷ 2	÷ 2	÷ 2	÷ 2	÷ 2	÷ 2
Average inventory level	750	1,125	1,500	1,875	2,250	2,625	3,000	3,375
× Carrying cost	$ 5	$ 5	$ 5	$ 5	$ 5	$ 5	$ 5	$ 5
Total Carrying Costs	**$ 3,750**	**$ 5,625**	**$ 7,500**	**$ 9,375**	**$11,250**	**$13,125**	**$15,000**	**$16,875**
Total demand	40,000	40,000	40,000	40,000	40,000	40,000	40,000	40,000
÷ Order quantity	1,500	2,250	3,000	3,750	4,500	5,250	6,000	6,750
Number of orders (rounded up)	27	18	14	11	9	8	7	6
× Costs per order	$ 1,250	$ 1,250	$ 1,250	$ 1,250	$ 1,250	$ 1,250	$ 1,250	$ 1,250
Total Ordering Costs	**$33,750**	**$22,500**	**$17,500**	**$13,750**	**$11,250**	**$10,000**	**$ 8,750**	**$ 7,500**
Total Costs	**$37,500**	**$28,125**	**$25,000**	**$23,125**	**$22,500**	**$23,125**	**$23,750**	**$24,375**

STOP & THINK

Think about EOQ and the relationship between the costs of carrying inventory versus the costs involved in purchasing inventory. As costs of carrying inventory increase, should the organization increase or decrease the size of its purchase orders? As costs of purchasing inventory increase, should the organization increase or decrease the size of its purchase orders?

There is an alternative, and more precise, approach to calculating the EOQ using a formula (derived by calculus). Without working through the calculus derivation, the EOQ formula is:

$$EOQ = \sqrt{\frac{2QP}{C}}$$

Q = The market demand in units for the period
P = The overhead cost of placing one order
C = The total carrying cost for one unit for the period

By inserting our Burzee Doll data into the EOQ formula, we can calculate the precise EOQ as follows:

$$EOQ = \sqrt{\frac{2(40,000)(\$1,250)}{\$5}} = \sqrt{\frac{\$100,000,000}{\$5}} = \sqrt{20,000,000} = 4,472 \text{ dolls}$$

Now that we have the EOQ, we can calculate the following exact costs:

Total carrying costs = 4,472 ÷ 2 = 2,236 average inventory × $5 = $11,180
Total ordering costs = 40,000 ÷ 4,472 = 9 orders × $1,250 = $11,250
Total inventory management costs = $11,180 + $11,250 = $22,430

Using the EOQ formula is much faster and more precise than working through an EOQ cost schedule. With the EOQ, we can resolve the first of two important issues involved in determining how much inventory a company should have—knowing *how much* inventory to order. Now we will turn our attention to the second issue—knowing *when* to place the inventory order.

Reorder Point and Safety Stock

Knowing *when* to place the inventory order involves the reorder point and the desired safety stock. Assume for a moment that you are the manager of the Kids N Toys store. Now that you have calculated the EOQ, you need to know exactly when to place your order. You don't want to reorder Burzee Dolls too soon, or you'll end up with more inventory on hand than you need.

reorder point The point at which the inventory level in the organization drops low enough to trigger a new purchase order.

This will result in unnecessary overhead costs, holding costs, and possibly increased inventory shrinkage. On the other hand, if you wait until you're nearly out of dolls before you place the order, you'll probably run out of inventory before the next shipment arrives. This will result in lost sales—a serious opportunity cost. Walking through your store, you watch the levels of dolls on your shelves and in your storeroom decline as customers make purchases. In terms of level of Burzee Doll inventory, at what point do you place your next order? Essentially, you need to calculate a **reorder point**. The calculation is quite simple:

Reorder point = Average lead time in days × Average daily sales

Lead time, in this case, is the time between when store management initiates a purchase order and when the inventory is finally delivered and ready for sale. Lead time for Burzee Dolls would include the time it takes for Kids N Toys to process any necessary paperwork to initiate the purchase order, for the distributor to process the purchase order and deliver the goods, and for Kids N Toys to receive and prepare the dolls for aisle display. Let's assume that lead time for the Burzee Doll is three days. Further, Kids N Toys sells, on average, 800 dolls per day. The reorder point calculation is:

Reorder point = 3 days × 800 dolls = 2,400 dolls

When the inventory falls to 2,400 dolls, you need to initiate a new purchase order. By the time the order arrives, the store should be selling its last doll.

At this point, a couple of things about this reorder point number may be bothering you. One possible problem is that the reorder point calculation is assuming a perfect world. In other words, the reorder point calculation shown assumes that sales are *always* 800 dolls per day and that the lead time is *always* three days. A sudden surge in customer demand or any problems in order processing or shipping could result in empty shelves. As manager for Kids N Toys, you may think you should build a little cushion into your reorder point calculation to allow for any unexpected problems. This is the purpose of **safety stock**. The calculation of the amount of safety stock has two parts: (1) to handle possible problems in the reorder process and (2) to handle an unexpected spike in sales demand. Let's assume that problems in the reorder process could result in a maximum lead time of four days. Further, as many as 875 dolls could sell in one day. The safety stock calculation would be as follows:

safety stock The minimal level of inventory required to insure against the organization running out of inventory in the case of unforeseen problems in receiving its next purchase order.

Maximum lead time	4 days	
Average lead time in days	3 days	
Surplus	1 day	
Average expected sales per day	× 800 dolls	
Safety stock for reorder problem		800 dolls
Maximum expected sales per day	875 dolls	
Average expected sales per day	800 dolls	
Surplus	75 dolls	
Maximum lead time	× 4 days	
Safety stock for demand changes		300 dolls
Total safety stock		1,100 dolls

Based on these numbers, Kids N Toys will always want to keep at least 1,100 dolls on hand to handle unexpected situations involving either its suppliers or its customers. Hence, this safety stock number should be added to the original reorder point calculation, resulting in a new reorder point calculation that includes a cushion for safety stock:

Reorder point with safety stock = (Average lead time in days × Average daily sales)
+ Safety stock
= (3 days × 800 dolls) + 1,100 dolls = 3,500 dolls

Caution

Perhaps you've heard of the saying "Garbage in, garbage out!" The quality of these three quantitative inventory management models (like all decision models and systems in business) is only as good as the quality of the information that is used in the calculations. Before using the EOQ, reorder point, or safety stock calculations, the accountant needs to be sure that all costs and risks of carrying and ordering inventory are understood. Current JIT thinking suggests that accountants in the past may have severely understated the costs of carrying inventory, resulting in unnecessarily large inventory orders and high levels of inventory in the organization.

You've likely noticed that the reorder point calculation that includes safety stock can be directly calculated as:

Reorder point with safety stock = Maximum lead time in days
$$\times \text{ Maximum daily sales}$$
$$= 4 \text{ days} \times 875 \text{ dolls}$$
$$= 3,500 \text{ dolls}$$

Combining these two calculations into one simple calculation is acceptable, assuming that management is not interested in knowing the specific level for safety stock. Usually, though, store management wants to know when sales are eating into the safety stock. Such a situation signals that special attention is needed to ensure that the store does not run out of stock and miss some customer sales. Exhibit 16 graphically depicts these relationships.

TO SUMMARIZE: Balancing costs of carrying too much inventory against the costs of carrying too little inventory is a significant challenge for accountants in both merchandising and manufacturing organizations. The economic order quantity, reorder point, and safety stock calculations can help. Exhibit 16 graphically summarizes the relationship between EOQ, reorder points, and safety stock inventory levels. Consider Exhibit 16 in light of the inventory management issues in Exhibit 5. The EOQ model is a useful tool for managing carrying costs (e.g., overhead costs, holding costs, losses due to decreased market value, and the cost of inventory shrinkage). The EOQ model balances these carrying costs against ordering costs. In addition, the EOQ should be combined with intelligent calculations of reorder points and safety stock in order to guard against excessive risk of lost sales due to delivery problems and fluctuating market demand.

Exhibit 16: Graphical Display of EOQ, Reorder Points, and Safety Stock Inventory Levels

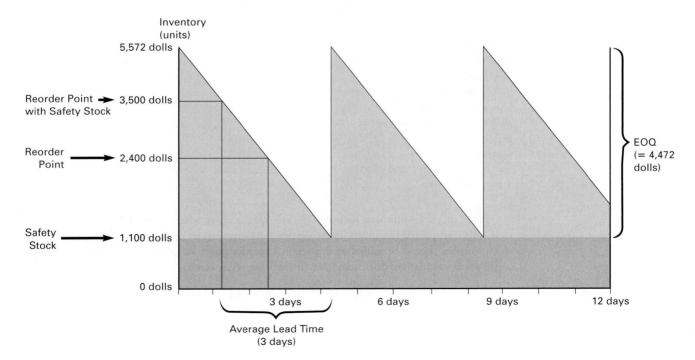

r e v i e w   o f   l e a r n i n g   o b j e c t i v e s

1 Identify the different types of inventory in manufacturing, service, and merchandising organizations and understand how these inventory costs are reflected in the income statement and balance sheet. Both manufacturing and service organizations maintain substantial production processes. As a result, both types of organizations report work-in-process inventory in the balance sheet. In addition, the computation of cost of goods sold can be quite complex for these types of organizations because the computation involves combining information about materials, labor, and overhead costs. The computation of cost of goods sold in a merchandising organization is relatively simple because inventory is purchased in its final form and substantial additional costs are generally not incurred in getting it ready to sell. Both manufacturing and merchandising organizations maintain significant levels of ending inventory that are reported in the balance sheet.

2 Analyze the levels of raw materials, work-in-process, and finished goods inventories in a manufacturing organization. Inventory turnover measures can be used to evaluate effective use of raw materials, work-in-process, and finished goods inventories. The average level of raw materials inventory is used to support the cost of materials used during the period. Work-in-process inventory is used to support the cost of goods manufactured. Finished goods inventory is used to support the cost of goods sold during the period. Two measures of inventory management performance are used to report on and control inventory levels: inventory turnover and days in inventory.

3 Understand how merchants manage inventory in their organizations. Because merchants basically purchase inventory in a finished state, the process of accounting for inventory in a merchandising business is not nearly as complicated as it is in a manufacturing business. However, there are a number of important issues associated with managing the inventory in order to maximize sales and minimize a variety of inventory costs. For example, having too much inventory creates unnecessary overhead costs, financial holding costs, costs due to loss of market value, and costs due to inventory shrinkage. Not having enough inventory may result in unnecessary ordering costs and loss of bulk order discounts, as well as opportunity costs due to lost sales and increased supplier prices. Measuring these costs allows management accountants to prepare detailed cost reports that support effective management of gross margins and net operating profits for individual product lines.

4 Measure profitability and personnel utilization in a service organization. Like a manufacturing organization, a service organization involves a substantial process before delivering a final product to the customer. Three types of service organizations are professional services, service shops, and mass services. Professional service firms emphasize people-to-people service over automation, the delivery of a process rather than a final tangible product, and high customization. A mass service organization emphasizes the standardized, automated delivery of a tangible product. Service organizations, similar to manufacturing and merchandising organizations, must measure profitability and resource utilization. A professional services firm uses profitability measures based on a comparison of revenues to the compensation cost of the professionals. This textbook reports this performance using a measure called profit percentage from personnel (PPP). Personnel utilization can be measured by comparing the number of billable hours actually worked to the number that was expected. This measure is referred to in this textbook as personnel utilization rates (PUR).

5 Describe how the concept of just-in-time (JIT) inventory systems is used to improve cost, quality, and timely performance in organizations. Just-in-time (JIT) has become an important tool for managing manufacturing, service, and merchandising companies across the world. In a manufacturing setting, demand at the final assembly stage "pulls" the inventory through the production process only as it is needed. Using this system, nothing is produced until customers demand it. JIT puts a strong emphasis on costs and quality. However, JIT also focuses on management of timeliness and flexibility. The main goal of JIT is to add value to the product or service and reduce or eliminate activities that do not. By focusing on removing non-value-added activities and reducing time spent on value-added activities, inventories and other costs are reduced, while quality and timeliness are improved.

6 Calculate and interpret holding costs in merchandising and service businesses. Although opportunity costs can be extremely difficult to measure, one important type of opportunity cost that accountants can measure is financial holding costs. Financial holding costs measure the costs of having money tied up in inventory (for merchants) or tied up in work-in-process services (for service companies). Measuring holding costs requires that the company's cost of capital first be identified. The holding cost formula is Average investment in inventory or work-in-process services × Annual rate × Number of years. Financial holding costs can be deducted from net operating profit to measure economic profit for a particular product line. Measuring economic profit for an entire company is sometimes called Economic Value Added (EVA™).

7 **Use classic quantitative tools in inventory management (economic order quantity, reorder point, and safety stock).** Both merchandising and manufacturing orga-

nizations have significant investments in inventory costs. Accountants can balance the costs of carrying too much inventory against the costs of carrying too little inventory by calculating the economic order quantity (EOQ), reorder point, and safety stock. The EOQ model is a useful tool for managing carrying costs (e.g., overhead costs, holding costs, losses due to decreased market value, and the costs of inventory shrinkage). The EOQ model balances these carrying costs against ordering costs. The EOQ is combined with reorder point and safety stock calculations in order to guard against excessive risk of lost sales due to delivery problems and fluctuating market demand.

k ey terms & concepts

days in inventory, 404
holding costs, 408
inventory shrinkage, 408
inventory turnover, 404
just-in-time (JIT), 420
lead time, 409
net operating profit, 413
non-value-added activities, 422

value-added activities, 422

cost of capital, 424
economic order quantity (EOQ), 427

economic profit, 424
Economic Value Added (EVA™), 426
reorder point, 429
safety stock, 429
segment, 426

r eview problem

Inventory Performance Measures
Part 1
Sparky Manufacturing, Inc. manufactures cell phones. A comprehensive income statement and a partial balance sheet for Sparky Manufacturing, Inc. follow:

Income Statement	
Sales revenues	$2,640,000
Cost of goods sold/Cost of goods manufactured:	
Cost of goods manufactured:	
Beginning raw materials	$ 23,300
+ Purchases of materials	950,000
Total raw materials available	$ 973,300
− Ending raw materials	(20,000)
Raw materials used	$ 953,300
+ Direct labor	380,000
+ Applied manufacturing overhead	120,000
Total manufacturing costs	$1,453,300

Total manufacturing costs	$1,453,300
+ Beginning work-in-process inventory	12,400
− Ending work-in-process inventory	(15,200)
Cost of goods manufactured	$1,450,500
+ Beginning finished goods inventory	40,700
− Ending finished goods inventory	(37,600)
Cost of goods sold	$1,453,600
− Overapplied manufacturing overhead	(12,000)
Adjusted cost of goods sold	$1,441,600
Gross margin	$1,198,400
Selling and general administrative expenses:	
Selling expenses	$ 128,000
Administrative expenses	237,000
Total selling and general administrative expenses	$ 365,000
Net operating income	$ 833,400

Selected Balance Sheet Information

Accounts receivable	$59,200
Raw materials inventory	20,000
Work-in-process inventory	15,200
Finished goods inventory	37,600
Supplies inventory	600
Accounts payable	22,400

Required:

Use Sparky Manufacturing, Inc.'s income statement and partial balance sheet to answer the following question.

1. Compute the turnover ratio and days in inventory ratio for all three inventories (use 365 days in a year).

Part 2

Toadstool Wireless is a cell phone retailer that purchases its cell phones from Sparky Manufacturing, Inc. To support sales in the months April through June, Toadstool Wireless bought 890 phones in one order that were received in multiple shipments. Of those 890 phones, 815 were sold at the suggested retail price of $250. The other 75 cell phones were lost due to poor controls in the shipping process. The average cost to initiate and receive each purchase order was $550 per order. Toadstool Wireless expected to pay $110 per phone but due to unexpected tariffs that affected some of Sparky's competitors, the cost per phone was raised to $125. Overhead costs for the three months were initially expected to be $60,000, but were actually only $49,000.

Required:

2. Create a management accounting report that helps management to understand the impact of these changes on net operating profit.
3. Compute the return on inventory investment for Toadstool Wireless.
4. Assume that the company's cost of capital is 12%. Compute the holding costs and economic profit for the company.

Solution
Part 1

1. **Raw materials inventory turnover:**
    $953,300 ÷ [($23,300 + $20,000) ÷ 2] = 44.0$ times
    Raw materials days in inventory: $365 ÷ 44.0 = 8.3$ days
    Work-in-process inventory turnover:
    $1,450,500 ÷ [($12,400 + $15,200) ÷ 2] = 105.1$ times
    Work-in-process days in inventory: 365 days $÷ 105.1 = 3.5$ days
    Finished goods inventory turnover:
    $1,441,600 ÷ [($40,700 + $37,600) ÷ 2] = 36.8$ times
    Finished goods days in inventory: 365 days $÷ 36.8 = 9.9$ days

Part 2

2.

Expected revenue	$250 × 890 units	$222,500
Shrinkage loss	$250 × 75 units	(18,750)
Actual revenue		$203,750
Expected product costs	$110 × 890 units	(97,900)
Cost increase	$15 × 890 units	(13,350)
Gross margin		$ 92,500
Expected overhead costs		(60,000)
Decrease in overhead costs	$60,000 − $49,000	11,000
Order costs	$550 × 3 orders	(1,650)
Net operating profit		$ 41,850

3. **Return on inventory investment:**
    ($97,900 + $13,350) ÷ 2 = $55,625 average inventory level
    $92,500 ÷ $55,625 = 166.3%

4. **Holding costs:** $55,625 × 12% × 3/12 = $1,669*
    Economic profit: $23,100 − $1,669 = $21,431

    *Rounded.

d iscussion questions

1. What similarities are there in the inventories of a manufacturing and a merchandising organization? What are the differences?
2. What similarities are there in the inventories of a manufacturing and a service organization? What are the differences?
3. How does the work-in-process inventory in a manufacturing organization differ from that in a service organization?
4. What is represented by total cost of goods manufactured?
5. Why is the total cost of goods sold number of limited usefulness for detailed internal decision making?
6. What amount is compared to the level of raw materials inventory in computing a useful measure of raw materials inventory turnover? Of work-in-process inventory turnover? Of finished goods inventory turnover?
7. Name three problems associated with carrying too much inventory.
8. Name three problems associated with carrying too little inventory.
9. What is inventory shrinkage? Name three things that can cause inventory shrinkage.
10. What can a company do to evaluate the management of its inventory investment?
11. What are the three basic types of service organizations?
12. The different types of service organizations vary in the emphasis they place on three dimensions. What are these three dimensions?
13. The same two concepts that underlie cost management in manufacturing and merchandising organizations are also used in developing cost management tools for service organizations. What are these two concepts?

14. How did the concept of just-in-time (JIT) change most companies' view that maintaining a minimum level of inventory was desirable? Use the measures of cost, quality, and time as you prepare your answer.

15. "The purpose of just-in-time (JIT) is to reduce inventory." Do you agree or disagree? Explain.

16. What causes holding costs to exist? How is it that holding costs exist in the service industry, which typically does not have inventories?

17. What are the advantages of purchasing inventory in large quantities? What are the advantages of purchasing it in small quantities?

18. What are carrying costs in the denominator of the economic order quantity (EOQ) formula? How do large carrying costs affect the economic order quantity?

19. Explain the reasoning behind the reorder point formula, Reorder point = Lead time × Average daily sales. How does safety stock fit into the reorder point concept?

practice exercises

Practice 7-1

Inventory Turnover

Using the following *annual* information, calculate inventory turnover for (1) raw materials inventory, (2) work-in-process inventory, and (3) finished goods inventory.

Cost of raw materials used	$100,000
Ending raw materials inventory	20,000
Ending work-in-process inventory	50,000
Cost of goods sold	250,000
Beginning finished goods inventory	60,000
Cost of goods manufactured	200,000
Beginning work-in-process inventory	40,000
Beginning raw materials inventory	15,000
Ending finished goods inventory	70,000

Practice 7-2

Days in Inventory

Refer to the data in Practice 7-1. Compute the number of days in inventory for (1) raw materials inventory, (2) work-in-process inventory, and (3) finished goods inventory. (Assume 365 days in the year.)

Practice 7-3

Carrying Too Much Inventory versus Carrying Too Little Inventory

Which one of the following statements is *false*?

a. Companies that carry too much inventory face increased overhead costs.
b. Companies that carry too little inventory face increased bulk order discounts.
c. Companies that carry too little inventory face increased exposure of suppliers not delivering inventory on time.
d. Companies that carry too much inventory face increased inventory shrinkage.
e. Companies that carry too much inventory face increased financial holding costs.

Practice 7-4

Gross Margin Comparison

Which of the following companies performed better during the period based on gross margin alone?

(continued)

	Company A	Company B
Beginning total assets	$ 183,000	$ 92,000
Ending total assets	192,000	95,000
Cost of goods sold	1,360,000	420,000
Revenue	1,840,000	870,000

Practice 7-5

Return on Investment Comparison

Refer to the data in Practice 7-4. Based on DuPont's return on investment (ROI) formula, which company performed better during the period?

Practice 7-6

Reports and Decision Making

Which one of the following reports provides management with the most valuable information related to sales of products?

a. Master budget
b. Management accounting report
c. Gross margin report
d. Balance sheet

Practice 7-7

Cost Management in Service Organizations

Which one of the following statements is *false*?

a. Service firms place no emphasis on the cost of materials.
b. Cost management in service organizations measures how efficiently the company uses its people.
c. Professional service organizations implement a high degree of customization.
d. Mass service firms place more emphasis on equipment than on people.

Practice 7-8

Measuring Profitability in Service Organizations

The company is a service organization and has the following numbers of professionals:

	Number of Individuals	Client Billable Hours Expected to Be Worked per Year	Billing Rate per Hour
Class A	5	1,500	$200
Class B	10	2,000	100
Class C	20	2,000	60

During the most recent year, the class A professionals billed a total of 7,000 hours, the class B professionals billed a total of 17,000 hours, and the class C professionals billed a total of 30,000 hours. The 5 class A professionals were paid a total of $1,000,000, the 10 class B professionals were paid a total of $1,500,000, and the 20 class C professionals were paid a total of $1,000,000. The company measures its profitability with the following ratio:

(Revenue − Personnel compensation cost) ÷ Revenue

Given the data above, compute the value of this ratio (known as the profit percentage from personnel, or PPP).

Practice 7-9

Measuring Personnel Utilization in Service Organizations

Refer to the data in Practice 7-8. For each class of professional, compute the total actual billable hours during the year as a percentage of total expected billable hours.

Practice 7-10

Just-in-Time Inventory
Which one of the following statements is *false*?

a. Carrying large amounts of inventory can be very costly for a company.
b. JIT environments are usually "push" systems.
c. JIT inventory systems started in Japan.
d. JIT emphasizes reduction of non-value-added activities.
e. Under a JIT system, accountants are encouraged to provide time-based performance measures to management.

Practice 7-11

Opportunity Costs
Which one of the following statements is *false*?

a. Economic profit is less than or equal to net operating profit.
b. A company that has a high quantity of one type of inventory may incur opportunity costs related to other inventory items in lower quantity.
c. Both service and manufacturing firms often experience opportunity costs.
d. Opportunity costs include a number of out-of-pocket costs.
e. Opportunity costs are difficult to measure.

Practice 7-12

Financial Holding Costs
The company had an average of $160,000 worth of a certain product in inventory from September 1 to December 31. If the company's cost of capital is 16%, what is the financial holding cost of this inventory?

Practice 7-13

Economic Order Quantity
Using the following data, compute the company's economic order quantity.

Total units demanded annually	150,000
Cost to place one order	$3,200
Total carrying cost for one unit for the year	$4

Practice 7-14

Reorder Point
The company sells 130 units daily; each time the company orders more units, it takes the supplier four days to deliver the inventory. What is the company's reorder point (in number of units)?

Practice 7-15

Safety Stock
Refer to the data in Practice 7-14. The supplier may take five days to deliver the inventory if any unexpected event occurs, and the daily demand for inventory may also spike to 160 units. Compute the amount of safety stock the company should keep on hand in case both of these events should happen.

Practice 7-16

Reorder Point and Safety Stock
Refer to the data in Practice 7-14. If the company never wants inventory to drop below 200 units, what is the company's reorder point (in number of units)?

e x e r c i s e s

Exercise 7-1

Spreadsheet

Inventory Turnover in a Manufacturing Company

The following information is the end of year data for Pecos Yo Company:

Raw materials purchased during the year	$203,000
Beginning raw materials inventory	20,000
Ending raw materials inventory	25,000
Applied manufacturing overhead	350,000
Direct labor costs	100,000
Beginning work-in-process inventory	64,000
Ending work-in-process inventory	60,000
Beginning finished goods inventory	37,000
Ending finished goods inventory	40,000

Compute the following:

1. Inventory turnover for raw materials inventory.
2. Days in raw materials inventory. Assume 360 days in a year.
3. Inventory turnover for work-in-process inventory.
4. Days in work-in-process inventory. Assume 360 days in a year.
5. Inventory turnover for finished goods inventory.
6. Days in finished goods inventory. Assume 360 days in a year.

Exercise 7-2

Inventory Turnover in a Merchandising Company

Beanie Company is a merchandising company. Beanie had the following financial data for the years 2005 and 2006:

	2006	2005
Revenues	$200,000	$180,000
Cost of goods sold	110,000	109,000
Gross margin	$ 90,000	$ 71,000
Inventory	$ 40,000	$ 50,000

1. Calculate Beanie Company's turnover for inventory for 2006 and explain what it means.
2. Calculate Beanie Company's days in inventory for 2006, assuming 365 days in a year, and explain what it means.

Exercise 7-3

Inventory Turnover in a Merchandising Company

Both Dave and Kelly own auto parts stores. The following information is available for 2005 and 2006:

	Dave	Kelly
Cost of goods sold:		
2005	$150,000	$300,000
2006	130,000	350,000
Ending inventory:		
2005	75,000	225,000
2006	55,000	255,000

1. Calculate each company's turnover for inventory for 2006.
2. Calculate each company's days in inventory for 2006 (assume 365 days in a year).
2. Which owner manages inventory better? Explain your answer.

Exercise 7-4

Analyzing a Management Accounting Report

You have just finished preparing the management accounting report for your division. You show the following report to your division president, Karen, and tell her that you are very pleased with the performance of your division.

Division Management Accounting Report

Expected revenue	$1,200,000
Shrinkage loss	(38,400)
Market loss	(127,040)
Actual revenue	$1,034,560
Expected purchase costs	(400,000)
Lost discount	(38,000)
Gross margin	$ 596,560
Overhead costs	(66,000)
Order costs	(1,000)
Net operating profit	$ 529,560

After reviewing the report, Karen does not understand what some of the costs are and why they are in the report. Respond to her questions listed below.

1. What does the $38,400 shrinkage signify?
2. What does it mean to have a $127,040 market loss?
3. Just because we didn't take advantage of a discount on a purchase, why is this a cost when there was no outflow of dollars directly related to the discount?

Exercise 7-5

Analysis of Return on Inventory Investment

Plaids & Stripes and Audrey's Apparel are clothes retailers. August and September are busy months for these two stores because many people are buying new clothes for the start of school. This year these stores expect the largest demand to be in children's clothing. The following information has been given for both stores' children's departments during the months of August and September:

	Plaids & Stripes	Audrey's Apparel
Revenue	$565,000	$1,115,000
Gross margin	296,100	527,300
Average investment in inventory	29,000	165,000

Using the above information, answer the following questions about Plaids & Stripes and Audrey's Apparel.

1. Using the information given, which store generated the most total profit from inventory sales?
2. Calculate the return on inventory investment for both stores' children's departments. (Use both the profit margin and inventory turnover ratios.)
3. Using the calculations from part (2), which store actually manages its inventory more effectively? Explain your answer.

Exercise 7-6

Profitability in a Service Organization

Lorien Company is an engineering firm composed of five engineers. It is expected that each engineer will work 2,000 hours during a year on client jobs. The following additional information has been given for each of the five engineers:

(continued)

	Annual Compensation	Billing Rate per Engineering Hour	Actual Billable Hours
Penny	$270,000	$300	1,900
Jacob	250,000	250	1,900
Mandy	230,000	225	1,800
Edwin	200,000	200	1,800
Jackie	180,000	175	1,800

1. Calculate each engineer's profit percentage from personnel (PPP).
2. Calculate the profit percentage from personnel (PPP) for the entire firm.
3. Which engineer is bringing the most value to the company?

Exercise 7-7

Spreadsheet

Personnel Utilization in a Service Organization

Magily Company is a mathematical model consulting firm. Magily's services are sought by oil exploration companies for interpreting seismic data, by NASA for deciphering signals from deep space probes, and by Wall Street derivatives speculators who want to predict the weather in order to know whether to buy or sell soybean futures. Magily maintains the following mathematician staff:

	Number of Individuals	Client Billable Hours Expected to Be Worked per Year
Full mathematician consultants	5	700
Associate mathematician consultants	10	2,100
Assistant mathematician consultants	40	2,600

During the most recent year, full mathematician consultants worked a total of 3,000 hours; associate mathematician consultants worked a total of 25,000 hours; and assistant mathematician consultants worked a total of 140,000 hours. Compute personnel utilization ratios for each class of mathematician.

Exercise 7-8

Value-Added and Non-Value-Added Activities

Below is a list of activities performed by the Ibapah Bijou, a movie theater. Indicate whether each activity is a value-added activity (VA) or a non-value-added activity (NVA).

a. Redesigning the staff uniforms.
b. Cooking popcorn.
c. Counting the ticket stubs at night to make sure no one got in free.
d. Servicing the quadraphonic speaker system.
e. Paying for the rights to show the next movie starring Julia Roberts.
f. Paying a management fee for the employee pension fund.
g. Renting a storage facility to store the excess inventory of candy, uncooked popcorn, and soft drinks.
h. Paying the accounts payable.
i. Cleaning the white movie screens.
j. Scrubbing the theater floor to remove the sticky residue of spilled soft drinks.

eXpanded *Material*

Exercise 7-9

Financial Holding Costs

On January 1, 2006, Owen Corporation has $350,000 in inventory. On May 1, 2006, Owen's inventory is at $400,000. Owen's cost of capital is 13%. What were Owen's financial holding costs for January through April?

Exercise 7-10

Financial Holding Costs

Brady Company sells imported goods made in India. One product it sells is a wooden music box. The music boxes cost Brady $65, and Brady charges its customers a price of $250. Brady's cost of capital is 12%. On average, an entire year elapses between the time Brady pays for a music box and the time Brady collects the cash from the sale of the music box. What are Brady's annual financial holding costs per unit for the wooden music boxes?

Exercise 7-11

Economic Order Quantity

Pace Retailers' best-selling item is its reinforced bicycle tires. Pace sells 4,745 of these tires each year. It costs approximately $200 for Pace to place a purchase order, and it costs on average about $2.50 per tire per year for inventory overhead costs. The retail price of the tires is $12.50. What is the economic order quantity of tires Pace should order at one time?

Exercise 7-12

Reorder Point

Refer to Exercise 7-11. Suppose the lead time to receive a purchase order of reinforced bicycle tires is 13 days. To ensure adequate inventories at all times, Pace maintains a safety stock of 80 tires. Assuming Pace sells the 4,745 bicycle tires uniformly over the 365 days of the year, what is Pace's reorder point?

Exercise 7-13

Spreadsheet

Economic Order Quantity

For the past three years, Hawkeye Army Surplus Store has had excessive inventory holding costs. Management believes the excessive costs are due to the large inventory purchase orders the company places. The company hires a consultant, Brad Miles, to analyze the problem and suggest a solution. Information about two products, combat boots and backpacks, is as follows:

	Combat Boots	Backpacks
Annual market demand	20,000 pairs	5,000 packs
Cost per unit	$20	$55
Annual carrying cost per unit	$7	$16
Ordering cost	$500	$500

In order to balance the cost of placing a purchase order against the overhead cost of controlling inventory, how many pairs of combat boots should Brad suggest Hawkeye purchase at a time? How many backpacks?

Exercise 7-14

Reorder Point

Avery Grocery Store is the only grocery store in Rayville, a small town populated mostly by college students. Students have been complaining lately because Avery always runs out of macaroni and cheese, the students' favorite food. Avery management decides it needs to calculate a more suitable reorder point. Information about the macaroni and cheese is as follows:

(continued)

Average daily sales	500 boxes
Average lead time to receive an order	5 days
Avery's cost per unit	$0.30
Price charged to customers	$0.75

1. What should be the reorder point if Avery does not want to maintain any safety stock?
2. What should be the reorder point if Avery wants to maintain a safety stock of 1,000 boxes of macaroni and cheese?

p roblems

Problem 7-1

Inventory Turnover in a Manufacturing Company

The following information is for Bun MaScare Company:

Beginning raw materials inventory	$ 25,000
Raw materials purchased	110,000
Ending raw materials inventory	15,000
Manufacturing overhead (actual)	300,000
Beginning work-in-process inventory	50,000
Ending work-in-process inventory	40,000
Direct labor costs	90,000
Beginning finished goods inventory	200,000
Ending finished goods inventory	270,000
Overapplied manufacturing overhead	15,000

Required:

Compute the following (assume 365 days in a year):

1. Inventory turnover for raw materials inventory.
2. Days' supply of raw materials inventory.
3. Inventory turnover for work-in-process inventory.
4. Days of manufacturing represented by work-in-process inventory.
5. Inventory turnover for finished goods inventory.
6. Days' sales in finished goods inventory.
7. **Interpretive Question:** What conclusions can you draw from your inventory turnover calculations?

Problem 7-2

Spreadsheet

Management Accounting Reports in a Merchandising Company

Ride EZ and Happy Trails are mountain bike retailers. This season a new bike, the Coaster, was introduced in the market. It was believed that the Coaster would be the most popular mountain bike sold during the season. Both companies sold the bike at the suggested retail price. At the end of each month during the season (May through September), store managers made notes of how many bikes were sold or purchased during the month. The following is a list of these notes:

Date	Ride EZ	Happy Trails
May 1	30 bikes purchased	150 bikes purchased
May 31	27 bikes sold, out of stock; 30 more bikes are purchased	30 bikes sold

June 30	29 bikes sold, out of stock; 30 more bikes are purchased	35 bikes sold
July 31	28 bikes sold, out of stock; 30 more bikes are purchased	37 bikes sold
Aug. 31	24 bikes sold	24 bikes sold
Sept. 30	4 bikes sold at cost; out of stock, no bikes purchased	13 bikes sold at cost; out of stock, no bikes purchased

The following information is also known:

- Suggested retail price is $600.
- The manufacturer sells the Coaster for a normal price of $275.
- Discounts of $25 off the normal price are given on purchases of 100 bikes or more.
- Average overhead costs used to purchase and initiate a purchase order for both retailers are $450 per event.
- Purchases are always made on the last day of the month.
- On June 15, the manufacturer raised the price of the Coaster to $290.
- Average inventory overhead costs for both retailers are $15 per unit per month.
- Both Ride EZ and Happy Trails account for inventory using FIFO.

Required:
Prepare a management accounting report for both Ride EZ and Happy Trails using the information given in the problem.

Problem 7-3

Personnel Utilization in a Service Business
Columbus & Hercules offers the following annual estimates (based on a 50-week work year) regarding the salaries and estimated hours associated with the professionals employed by the firm:

Position	Total Estimated Salaries	Total Estimated Billable Hours
Partners (2 × $100,000)	$200,000	4,400
Managers (3 × $70,000)	210,000	6,600
Seniors (6 × $50,000)	300,000	13,200
Staff accountants (10 × $25,000)	250,000	22,000

During February, Managers 1 and 2 were assigned three staff accountants each; Manager 3 was assigned four staff accountants. At the end of February, the following staff utilization report was generated:

Staff Working for:	Budgeted Billable Hours	Actual Billable Hours
Manager 1	528	690
Manager 2	528	530
Manager 3	704	630
Total	1,760	1,850

Required:
Use the staff utilization numbers to evaluate the staff usage practices by the three managers.

Problem 7-4

Profitability and Personnel Utilization in a Service Company

Diggy Company specializes in caring for the pets of the rich and famous. Diggy gives personal care to each and every pet, and its professional animal "consultants" are on call 24 hours per day. Some details about Diggy's business are given below.

	Number of Individuals	Client Billable Hours Expected to Be Worked per Year	Annual Compensation	Billing Rate
Partners	5	500	$500,000	$400
Consultants	40	2,500	35,000	250

During the most recent year, the five partners billed a total of 3,000 hours, and the 40 consultants billed a total of 56,000 hours.

Required:
1. Compute personnel utilization ratios for each of the two classes of professionals within the firm.
2. Compute the firm's profit percentage from personnel (PPP).
3. Compute the PPP for each of the two classes of professionals within the firm.
4. **Interpretive Question:** Speculate on why the 40 consultants worked the number of billable hours that they did.

Problem 7-5

JIT Inventory

The president of Penman Corporation, John Burton, has asked you, the company's controller, to advise him on whether Penman should develop a just-in-time (JIT) inventory system. Your research concludes that there is a high cost associated with inventory storage facilities; that inventories use a large portion of the company's cash flow; and that because of the nature of the inventory, there is a significant amount of shrinkage. Research also shows that neither of Penman's two competitors uses a JIT inventory system. Most of Penman's employees are trained to do only one job and belong to a local union. The union is strong and, in the past, has opposed major production changes. The union believes major changes will result in the loss of union employees' jobs. Your research indicates that Penman's major production item (a fairly new product in the market) should continue to have strong sales growth.

Required:
1. Using the information provided, advise John Burton to either continue the present system or work to develop a JIT inventory system.
2. Assume John decides to develop an inventory management system. He plans to evaluate the system after one year. List at least four possible performance measures John could use to evaluate the effectiveness of the system. Describe what information these measures would provide John.

Problem 7-6

Economic Profit

Larsen Company has two divisions. The following is information about these two divisions over the past six months:

	Division L	Division M
Net operating profit	$390,000	$400,000
Average investment	$35,000	$200,000
Annual cost of capital	12%	18%

Required:

1. Use the above information to calculate the economic profit for the two divisions.
2. **Interpretive Question:** The division manager for Division M asks you why it is appropriate to include holding costs in the calculation of economic profit. Since holding costs are not included in the audited income statements that are reported by the company to its shareholders, then why would it be appropriate to use this cost in the internal reports that are used to evaluate managers and divisions? How would you respond?

Problem 7-7

Inventory Management

Watersports, Inc., sells high-performance water skis. Because its sales are seasonal, Watersports calculates and uses different reorder points for summer and winter months. The following information is available:

	April–October	November–March
Lead time (days)	3	7
Total customer demand for the period	1,600	400

The water skis cost $150 each, and Watersports sells them to its customers for $300. Watersports' supplier charges $500 for each order placed. Watersports incurs an *annual* carrying cost of $17 per set of skis. Watersports has noticed in the past that sometimes the deliveries can be up to two days later than average and that the customer demand can be as much as 1,800 skis during April through October and 500 skis during the rest of the year.

Required:

1. Calculate the appropriate economic order quantities for the two seasons.
2. Calculate the safety stock for the two seasons that are necessary to accommodate potential delays in inventory deliveries and potential spikes in sales demand.
3. Calculate reorder point (with safety stock) for the two seasons.
4. **Interpretive Question:** What are the value and the cost of having safety stock?

discussion cases

Case 7-1

Buying Inventory for the Holiday Selling Season

Ryan Baird owns a small retail shop. Historically, her annual sales have been about $250,000, with 60% of that coming in the holiday selling season of November and December. This year on a buying trip to southern China, Ryan discovered an item that she is certain will be in huge demand. The item is a mechanical cricket powered by a photovoltaic cell—the cricket automatically silences at night when it gets dark and then starts chirping in the morning when the sun's rays hit it. Ryan can buy the crickets from her Guangdong supplier for $1.00 each; she plans to sell them for $9.95 each.

Ryan is trying to decide how many of the crickets she should order. If she orders 30,000 or more, she can get a volume discount and pay just $0.80 each. However, she does not have room to store that many crickets, and she will have to rent storage space for $3,000 per month (three-month minimum). Also, the Guangdong supplier will only accept cash, and, because Ryan does not have very good credit, she will have to pay 17% annual interest on any money she borrows. She expects any loan to be outstanding for about two months.

Ryan has come to you for advice about whether she should buy a large quantity of crickets or play it safe and order just 10,000. What advice would you give her?

Case 7-2

Financial Holding Costs

You work in the accounting department of Cox Company. You are having a debate with one of your co-workers about holding costs. Your co-worker insists that holding costs should not be considered in making decisions because they do not involve any cash flows. He believes that cash flows are all that the business really cares about. How do you respond to him?

judgment calls

Judgment 7-1

You Decide: Can inventory management tools, such as turnover and days in inventory, be used in a service company that doesn't have significant levels of tangible inventory? Why is it important to manage costs in a service organization?

You have just been hired as an accountant for a large law firm. Your first project is to look at some financial information and determine why net income is declining. The senior partner tells you that total revenues for the company have increased each of the last five years. As a result, a proposal to substantially increase salaries for senior associates is being strongly considered. "A number of partners are preparing to retire, and we need to retain our best associates for future partnership," he said. "No one else in the company has done any research as to why net income has gone down, so we are excited to see what you come up with!" How should you perform the analysis?

Judgment 7-2

You Decide: Can a just-in-time inventory system help companies minimize inventory costs, or is JIT too expensive and cumbersome to implement?

Lately, you have heard a lot of talk about just-in-time inventory systems and how they help companies, like WAL-MART, keep track of inventory. You know that a JIT system can help track and keep inventory costs at a minimum, but is JIT really a viable option for all companies? For example, your neighbor works at a local automobile repair shop and he is always complaining about not having the right parts on hand, which causes him to get behind on his work. He can frequently be heard saying, "We always seem to run out of parts at the wrong time. Jan does a good job at trying to keep inventory in stock, but sometimes that job can get too big. Something else needs to be done or we are going to start losing customers!" How large does a company have to be and how much inventory must it have before JIT makes sense?

Competency Enhancement Opportunities

▶ **Analyzing Real Company Information**   ▶ **The Debate**
▶ **International Case**   ▶ **Internet Search**
▶ **Ethics Case**
▶ **Writing Assignment**

The following additional assignments provide opportunities for students to develop critical thinking, ethical perspectives, oral and written communication skills, experience with electronic research, and teamwork through group and business activities.

▶ Analyzing Real Company Information

Analyzing 7-1 (Microsoft)

1. For the year ended June 30, 2002, MICROSOFT's total cost of revenue was $5.191 billion. Can you compute Microsoft's total manufacturing costs for the year? Cost of goods manufactured for the year? Explain.

2. As of June 30, 2002, Microsoft reported the following about the number of its employees:

Employees engaged in research and development	20,800
Employees in sales and marketing	23,500
Employees in administration	4,000
Other employees	2,200
Total	50,500

Refer to Microsoft's income statement in Appendix A and compute the following:

a. Total revenue per employee.
b. Total R&D cost per R&D employee.
c. Total sales and marketing cost per sales and marketing employee.
d. Total administrative cost per administrative employee.

Analyzing 7-2 (Wal-Mart)

1. Through its Retail Link™ system, WAL-MART gives its suppliers access to detailed sales information "store by store, item by item, day by day." What advantages are there to Wal-Mart in sharing this kind of detailed data with suppliers? What disadvantages?

2. Wal-Mart reports (in its 2003 10-K report filed with the Securities and Exchange Commission) that 83% of the goods sold in Wal-Mart stores and Supercenters are first shipped to one of Wal-Mart's 84 regional distribution centers and then shipped to the individual stores. On the other hand, SAM'S CLUBS receive 63% of their goods directly from the supplier. Why is there a difference in the distribution procedure for these two groups of stores?

3. In recent years, SAM'S Clubs sales, as a percentage of total Wal-Mart sales, have decreased, from 15% of sales in fiscal 2000 to 13% of sales in fiscal 2003. What impact do you think this change in sales mix has had on Wal-Mart's overall gross margin percentage? Explain.

▶ *International Case*

International

Deloitte & Touche

DELOITTE & TOUCHE is one of the largest professional services firms in the world. In 2003, the company reported revenues of $15.1 billion generated from its various business units—accounting, assurance and advisory, tax, legal, and management, financial and human capital consulting. Deloitte & Touche has 698 offices in 144 countries, and it employs almost 120,000 people.

1. What does Deloitte & Touche sell?
2. Deloitte & Touche has an office in Quito, Ecuador. What type of company operating in Ecuador would hire Deloitte & Touche instead of a local Ecuadorian professional services firm?
3. Review the chapter discussion of cost information for service companies. What costs would be important to Deloitte & Touche in deciding how much to bid on a consulting contract for a potential new client?

▶ *Ethics Case*

Performance Evaluation: The Illusion of Objectivity?

You are a store manager for a large, regional department store chain. You have been asked by company headquarters to submit an evaluation of the performance of two of your assistant managers. The company is considering promoting one of them to be the manager of another store in the chain.

One of the assistant managers heads the Electronics Department in your store. She is a long-time friend of yours and you would like her to get the promotion. The other candidate heads the Home and Garden Department; she is a good assistant manager but you just don't know her well. You decide to recommend your friend, the head of the Electronics Department, for the promotion.

In order to support your recommendation with objective evidence, you include the following departmental profit numbers for the most recent year:

	Electronics	**Home and Garden**
Sales	$500,000	$300,000
Net profit	$100,000	$40,000
Profit percentage	20%	13%

On this basis, arguing that the Electronics Department has generated higher sales, higher net profit, and a higher profit margin percentage, you recommend that the promotion be given to your friend. However, you are a little troubled by the following two additional pieces of information:

1. The average value of inventory held in the Electronics Department at any given time is $1.2 million. The comparable number for the Home and Garden Department is $250,000.
2. The profit percentage in the Electronics Department has been fairly stable over the last five years. On the other hand, the profit percentage in the Home and Garden Department is at a 10-year high; the increase coincides with the hiring of the current head of the Home and Garden Department.

Is it ethical for you to recommend the promotion for your friend, the head of the Electronics Department? How should you use the numerical evidence in support of your recommendation?

▶ *Writing Assignment*

Consultant's Report for a Small-Town Supermarket
You have been hired as a financial consultant by a small-town supermarket. The supermarket is considering building a new, larger store and requests your expertise in evaluating the feasibility of the project. You know that the construction of the store will cost $3 million. You also know that the average gross margin percentage in supermarkets is 27%.

Draft a one-page memo to the owner of the supermarket requesting additional cost information to be used in your analysis. The store owner is a clever businessperson but has no experience in using quantitative data in making decisions. Therefore, your memo must be very specific in identifying the information that you will need to perform a useful analysis.

▶ *The Debate*

Overutilization of Young Professionals
As seen in this chapter, an important dimension of performance for a manufacturing, merchandising, or service organization is the efficient utilization of resources. The more intensively resources are used, the greater a company's return on investment. However, when talking about a service organization, this "resource" is often the time of young professionals who are just starting their careers. Competitive pressures on companies can translate into 70- and 80-hour work weeks for college graduates in the first few years of their careers. These work pressures make it difficult for young professionals to develop their lives outside work.

Divide your group into two teams and prepare a two-minute oral presentation supporting the following views.

- One team supports "Work/Life Balance." This group believes that young professionals should not be viewed as "resources" to be utilized but as human beings to be respected.
- The other team supports "Survival of the Fittest." This group believes that it is a dog-eat-dog world out there, and that those young professionals who can't stand the long hours should get out of the way of those who can.

▶ *Internet Search*

Toyota Motor Corporation
Go to TOYOTA's North America Web site at **http://www.toyota.com**. Sometimes Web addresses change, so if this Toyota address doesn't work, access the Web site for this textbook (**http://swain.swlearning.com**) for an updated link to Toyota. Once you have gained access to Toyota's Web site, answer the following questions:

1. Access Toyota's Operations section (you can find it within the "About Toyota" menu selection). Find the timeline for Toyota's sales and service. When did Toyota begin selling in North America? When did Toyota begin manufacturing cars in North America?
2. Next, move to Toyota's corporate Web site in Japan at **http://www.toyota.co.jp** and learn about how the just-in-time (JIT) concept works at Toyota. You can do this by finding a news release dated October 9, 2003, titled "The Essence of TPS (the Toyota Production System)." In this article, Teruyuki Minoura, former CEO of Toyota Motor Manufacturing North America, talks about his experiences with TPS, which represents how his company implements a JIT management system. Minoura describes nine concepts that capture the concept of JIT. What are these concepts? (*Hint:* They're listed as subtopic headings in his presentation.)

c h a p t e r

8

Activity-Based Costing and Quality Management

Learning Objectives

After studying this chapter, you should be able to:

1 Explain the fundamentals of activity-based costing (ABC) and activity-based management (ABM).

2 Describe total quality management (TQM) and costs of quality (COQ).

3 Compute the opportunity cost of lost sales.

You most likely wouldn't want to be in Harry Stonecipher's shoes anytime in the next few years; then again, maybe you would.[1] Stonecipher is the recently named President and CEO of BOEING COMPANY, the largest manufacturer of commercial airplanes in the world. If you have ever flown on a commercial jet, odds are you were in one of Stonecipher's (or one of his predecessor's) products. In fact, a Boeing airplane is taking off somewhere in the world every 3.5 seconds. And in the next 24 hours, three million passengers will board 42,300 flights on Boeing jetliners, which will carry them to nearly every country on earth! With its $16.3 billion merger with MCDONNELL DOUGLAS in 2000, Boeing commanded approximately two-thirds of the $65 billion global market for commercial planes with 100 seats or more. Further, just prior to the McDonnell Douglas merger, Boeing completed a $3.1 billion acquisition of the defense and space operations of ROCKWELL INTERNATIONAL, making Boeing the largest builder of military aircraft in the world, as well as the number one supplier of goods and services to both the Pentagon and NASA. Boeing is basically sitting in the catbird seat. So, why might you hesitate to take Condit's job right now if it were offered to you?

Recent world events have walloped the airline industry. Terrorism, regional conflict, the SARS epidemic, and a sluggish economy have taken their toll on the airlines with a number of airlines filing for bankruptcy protection in the past few years. However, behind the turmoil, Boeing is facing an even more dangerous force: AIRBUS INDUSTRIE is emerging as the world's leading maker of commercial airplanes. The recent economic downturn has forced Boeing's customers to be more cost-conscious, leading to major pricing battles with Boeing's last remaining major competitor.

Airbus, based in Toulouse, France, has been successful against Boeing. By mid-June 2003, Airbus had won 64% of 2003's airplane orders—161 versus 92 for Boeing, including firm orders and memoranda of understanding. But in total value, where it counts the most, Airbus' share is 76% of 2003's orders, with list prices totaling about $26.7 billion versus only $8.2 billion for Boeing. If this lead holds up, it would be the third year in a row Airbus won not only more orders but also more of the lucrative widebody aircraft products. Airbus CEO Noel Forgeard says, "Airbus is taking the lead in a market [that] was considered the home ground of our competitor [that is, Boeing]." Airbus enjoys several key

advantages in widebodied aircraft. Its intermediate-size A330 has essentially killed off the Boeing 767 with its greater fuel efficiency and longer flying range. Another plus is Airbus' uniform cockpit design, which gives airlines greater scheduling flexibility as pilots shift easily from one plane model to another.

So, how will Boeing compete? Boeing is counting on successful development of the 7E7. This superefficient plane, which could enter service in 2008, is critical to Boeing's future. "This is a big deal for us," says Michael Bair, a Boeing vice president who oversees the 7E7 program. "If we don't get it right, it influences our future in the business."

At first glance, it seems a good time for Boeing to launch a fuel-sipping jet. Carriers, battered by the falloff in travel, are desperate to cut costs. Boeing believes it could sell 2,500 7E7s in the next 20 years. However, to build the plane, Boeing must reengineer its production. It needs to overcome technical hurdles, including building a plane designed for both short and long hauls that can carry between 220 and 250 passengers while consuming significantly less fuel than planes of similar size now flying. The 7E7 would also be the first commercial aircraft built mostly of composites—carbon-reinforced materials stronger and lighter than the aluminum used in most jetliners. In addition, Boeing aims to assemble each 7E7 in three days, compared with the 20 or so it takes to weld and rivet a 767. Boeing would do so by relying on key suppliers to deliver completed plane sections, meaning fewer workers would be required to actually assemble the 7E7. None of this will come cheap. Development costs could reach $8 billion over five years.

Building this plane requires a radical departure from Boeing's current production practices. Yet the company's history on making such shifts isn't reassuring. In 1997, in another effort to cut costs, Boeing ramped up production too quickly based on unrealistic assumptions. As a result, it lost control of the entire production system, forcing the shutdown of two assembly lines for 30 days. Boeing missed hundreds of airplane deliveries, and the fiasco cost the company more than $2 billion during the biggest boom in commercial airplane history. If you were to take a walking tour of Boeing's 747, 767, and 777 plant in Everett, Washington, you would understand how important (and how difficult) it is for Boeing to control its production process. The cavernous plant in Everett is monstrous, able to house 74 football fields. Planes are

1 Information from "Boeing Is Choking On Airbus' Fumes," *Business Week*, June 30, 2003, p. 50; Boeing Company's home page at **http://www.boeing.com**; "Will this Idea Really Fly?" *Business Week*, June 30, 2003, p. 34.

everywhere in various stages of completion, and *a lot* of mechanics are running around with nothing more complicated than a set of hand tools turning out four massive jets per month, each priced at about $170 million. Each jet is tailor-made to the desires of each customer. The company has always prided itself on giving customers *exactly* what they want. This customization doesn't end with engine specifications and landing systems. It includes choice of paint colors (e.g., if you want white, Boeing offers nearly 110 shades to choose from) and location in the cockpit where the pilot's clipboard will be placed. These are not simple adjustments. Every alteration, even a seemingly minor one such as moving the location of an emergency flashlight holder, consumes thousands of hours of engineering time, requires hundreds of pages of detailed drawings, and costs hundreds of thousands, if not millions, of dollars to execute. Boeing is constantly evaluating and reengineering processes, information systems, and management procedures involved in the manufacturing of its products. It works to better manage costs by reducing and streamlining activities in the production process, as well as reducing parts and work-in-process inventories in order to significantly increase stockturns. It is focused on correcting problems with receiving shipments of parts on time from suppliers and getting completed planes out the door on time to customers. And all these changes must be accomplished without diminishing the absolute quality that is expected of aircraft technology that carries satellites into space, carries military weapons into

Good statement.

battle, and (most importantly) carries three million people daily—a number that exceeds the world's population over a six-year period!

Introducing the 7E7 into the Boeing production system will not be easy. John Leahy, Airbus' chief of global sales, said this about the 7E7, "Dreamliner—a salesman's dream and an engineer's nightmare." Boeing will be working hard to prove Airbus wrong. Success would bring restored credibility and renewed market leadership. Some analysts view the battle between Boeing and Airbus as the "dogfight of the century." So the future certainly does look very exciting, as well as uncertain, for Harry Stonecipher. What do you think? Still want to trade places with him?

Caution

Just because the science of product costing was first developed over 100 years ago, don't assume that there are no new issues today. Business is now more complicated and competitive than ever before. Management accounting systems are expected today to provide cost and performance measures that are more accurate, more relevant, and more strategically focused than ever before!

f there is one thing that is constant in the history of business (and, for that matter, history at large), it is change. A hundred years ago, the executives and management accountants of successful companies such as CARNEGIE STEEL and DUPONT created cost accounting and performance measurement systems that were so new and unique at the time that the decision makers in these companies were able to plan, control, and evaluate critical business processes better than most of their competition. However, these management accounting practices are now well understood and serve as a minimum expectation of most organizations desiring to remain competitive and viable in today's business environment. New management accounting theories and techniques are being developed constantly and tested in the laboratory of the current international market economy. Some of these

new ideas are gaining a lot of attention, and you need to be aware of them. This chapter will introduce two important topics that have had a significant impact in the last 10 or 20 years on the types of information that many management accounting systems are now providing to the management process in an effort to keep organizations competitive. These topics are activity-based costing (ABC) and costs of quality (COQ). In the last chapter of this book where we discuss continuous improvement in management accounting we will introduce a new model of strategic performance measurement that has come into the spotlight in just the last six or seven years. This new innovation, called the balanced scorecard, is getting a lot of attention and may be the next significant step in the innovation of management accounting.

Activity-Based Costing

▌ Explain the fundamentals of activity-based costing (ABC) and activity-based management (ABM).

In the late 1800s, Andrew Carnegie competed very strongly in the steel market with an almost fanatical emphasis on product cost information. Since then, product costing has been a primary purpose of management accounting. Manufacturing processes of today don't look at all like the manufacturing processes of the late 1800s, however. Advances in technology, combined with increasingly intense global competition, have resulted in manufacturing systems that are very complex compared to their predecessors. Because the companies that best understand their costs generally compete well in the economy, product costing has also undergone some important changes that we will consider in this chapter. It is important, though, to remember that the economy has shifted dramatically since the days of Andrew Carnegie. Service companies, such as transportation, consulting, and financial institutions, are the dominant force in today's economy. As you know from your study of the chapter on product cost flows, the service provided by these companies to their clients is a "product" that requires a product costing system very similar to that of manufacturing companies. In fact, service companies are some of the heaviest users of the management accounting techniques discussed in this chapter.

One major development in product costing is **activity-based costing** (**ABC**). Basically, ABC identifies and uses a number of critical activities within the organization to measure product costs. For many types of manufacturing and service companies, ABC is a more accurate product costing system than the traditional product costing systems introduced in the product cost flows chapter. However, ABC requires more time and expense to administer than traditional costing systems.

activity-based costing (ABC) A method of attributing costs to products based on first assigning costs of resources to activities and then costs of activities to products.

Product Costing Review

Consider, for example, a small ice cream shop that is owned and managed by one person. Lucas, the owner, hires college students to run the daily operations of preparing and selling his various ice cream desserts. Lucas must decide how to properly price his ice cream desserts. One of his employees, Sally, who just completed her first economics class, tells him to simply "charge whatever the market will bear." Yet this advice provides Lucas only with a price ceiling. Obviously, he cannot charge more than his customers will pay. However, in response to important matters of profitability such as competition and market share, Lucas wonders about his price floor—how low can he go? The obvious answer is that he cannot price below cost (except on occasion). But this begs the elemental question: What does it cost Lucas to make each of his ice cream desserts? Frankly, despite being in the ice cream business for several years, Lucas is not sure.

In relatively "simple" operations like Lucas's ice cream shop, as well as in complex operations such as an airplane manufacturer or a large law firm, product costing is a critical management issue. Today, cost accountants are paid rather well to answer the question, "What does it cost to make a product and prepare it to sell?" In working with Lucas and his ice cream shop, the classic approach to this question is to apply the traditional product cost models that we studied in the chapter on product cost flows. Essentially, for a manufacturing organization, this model states that:

Cost of product = Direct materials + Direct labor + Manufacturing overhead

conversion costs The costs of converting raw materials to finished products; include direct labor and manufacturing overhead costs.

prime costs The direct costs that are "primarily seen" in the product (i.e., direct materials and direct labor).

To calculate the direct materials cost of a banana split, for example, Lucas needs simply to determine the cost of materials directly involved in making a banana split; in other words, the cost of ingredients. The process of converting these "raw" materials into a banana split (the conversion process) requires direct labor and overhead costs, known together as **conversion costs**. Direct labor is simply the hourly wage Lucas pays his employees to physically assemble the ingredients of each dessert sold. Clearly, because each type of dessert requires different ingredients and different amounts of time to create, each will have a different set of direct materials and direct labor costs. Direct materials and direct labor, the **prime costs**, are obvious components in the ice cream dessert production process. Prime costs are easily understood and, typically, can be directly traced and assigned to each type of product produced.

The second cost of the conversion process, overhead, is a little more difficult to understand and directly trace to the dessert production operation. Typically, in a "manufacturing" company like Lucas's shop, manufacturing overhead costs are thought of as "manufacturing support costs." In order to produce banana splits and other desserts, Lucas must have several other components in place besides ice cream and an ice cream scooper. Lights, heat, and other utilities must be present in the kitchen area. Equipment, such as blenders and freezers, must be purchased and maintained. Indirect materials, such as cleaning supplies and light bulbs, must be provided. Likely, Lucas will have other personnel on the payroll besides the counter help. A shop manager and a nightly cleanup crew add additional production costs in the form of indirect labor. All these costs are necessary for Lucas to produce his wares; hence, all are included in manufacturing overhead. As you understand after studying previous chapters, manufacturing overhead is, in essence, a catchall category. In other words, the total cost of a product or service is the cost of everything necessary to produce the product or service. In the case of a manufacturing company, after identifying direct materials and direct labor costs, any remaining product costs are manufacturing overhead costs.

Direct materials, direct labor, and manufacturing overhead do not comprise the total set of costs in Lucas's ice cream shop. Traditionally, product costs are defined as only those costs necessary to actually produce the product. There are other nonproduction costs in Lucas's ice cream shop. These include selling costs, such as costs of advertising the shop and maintaining an area for customers to enjoy their ice cream. Administrative expenses, such as office expenses and Lucas's own salary, are also costs that must be planned and controlled. Because these selling and general administrative costs are not directly connected to any aspect of the production process, they are typically not included in the product cost category. Nonetheless, these are still essential costs. If Lucas does not invest in selling and administrative activities, soon there will be no production. Costs related to selling and administration come under the heading of "period costs." In contrast to product costs, which are incurred as products are produced, period costs seem to be strictly related to the passage of "periods" of time.

Hence, we can summarize all these costs (originally defined in the chapter where we introduced management accounting) as follows:

- *Direct materials:* The cost of the materials that actually become part of the product.
- *Direct labor:* Wages paid to those who physically work to assemble direct materials into the finished product.
- *Manufacturing overhead:* All costs required to produce a product *other than* direct materials and direct labor.
- *Product costs:* Direct materials + Direct labor + Manufacturing overhead.
- *Period costs:* All costs in the company *other than* the product costs; usually include selling and administrative costs.

Hopefully, this quick discussion of Lucas's ice cream shop is simply a review of what you already understand about product costing. At this point, you may feel that it should be a simple task to track the total costs Lucas spends on direct materials, direct labor, and manufacturing overhead in order to answer his question, "What does it cost to make a dessert?" Frankly, tracking Lucas's *total* product costs in his shop is a fairly simple task. However, the key issue for Lucas (and all other product and service managers) is to break those total product costs down for *each type* of product being created. For an ice cream shop that makes and sells many types of desserts, the product cost question becomes much more difficult to answer. It is precisely this question that accountants and managers have been struggling to answer for the last several decades.

SeatJoy, Inc., Is in Trouble!

Consumers are better informed and more demanding than ever before. In addition, competition is increasing as industries are deregulated, technology improves, and national barriers to worldwide competition are removed. The bottom line in this business environment is that margins on goods and services are becoming increasingly tighter. In terms of the ROI model, because most companies cannot sell their goods and services for more money, they need to sell more of their products faster (i.e., increase turnover) in order to remain profitable. What does this mean to an organization that sells a large variety of goods or services? Basically, it means that the organization could be losing money on some of its products and not even realize what is happening. In addition, it may choose to stop providing a particular product based on the false assumption that the product is a money loser. We can better demonstrate this point with an example that we will use for the remainder of this section.

Exhibit 1 displays the 2005 operating results for SeatJoy, Inc. (a fictitious company in the business of making high-quality leather desk chairs). As you can see, SeatJoy has three lines of reclining desk chairs. The Cushman model is its "bread and butter" product. This is the original chair that SeatJoy introduced in 1992 when the company started business. Shortly thereafter, SeatJoy introduced a similar chair that included a swing-out leg rest when the chair reclined. SeatJoy called this chair the Cushman II. More recently (2003), SeatJoy came out with

Exhibit 1: SeatJoy, Inc.: 2005 Operating Results

Manufacturing Overhead Cost Analysis

Annual manufacturing overhead	$18,240,000
Total annual direct labor hours	÷ 456,000
Manufacturing overhead rate per direct labor hour	$40

Labor Cost Analysis

	Cushman	Cushman II	Luxor	Total
Direct labor hours per product	10.0 hours	15.0 hours	12.5 hours	
Annual sales volume	× 18,000 chairs	× 14,400 chairs	× 4,800 chairs	
Total annual direct labor hours	180,000 hours	216,000 hours	60,000 hours	456,000 hours
Wage rate per hour	× $20	× $20	× $20	× $20
Total annual direct labor costs	$3,600,000	$4,320,000	$1,200,000	$9,120,000

Individual Unit Analysis

	Cushman	Cushman II	Luxor
Sales price	$1,000	$ 1,500	$ 3,000
Direct materials per product	$ (335)	$ (650)	$(1,395)
Direct labor per product	(200)	(300)	(250)
Manufacturing overhead per product	(400)	(600)	(500)
Total cost per product	$ (935)	$(1,550)	$(2,145)
Margin per product	$ 65	$ (50)	$ 855
Margin percent	6.5%	(3.3)%	28.5%

Total Annual Results

	Cushman	Cushman II	Luxor	Total
Sales revenue	$ 18,000,000	$ 21,600,000	$ 14,400,000	$ 54,000,000
Total direct materials	$ (6,030,000)	$ (9,360,000)	$ (6,696,000)	$(22,086,000)
Total direct labor	(3,600,000)	(4,320,000)	(1,200,000)	(9,120,000)
Total manufacturing overhead	(7,200,000)	(8,640,000)	(2,400,000)	(18,240,000)
Total product costs	$(16,830,000)	$(22,320,000)	$(10,296,000)	$(49,446,000)
Total margin	$ 1,170,000	$ (720,000)	$ 4,104,000	$ 4,554,000
Selling and administrative expenses				(4,000,000)
Operating profit				$ 554,000

a premium chair made from exotic leathers called the Luxor. Compared to the Cushman lines, the Luxor production process requires closer supervision, as well as more specialized production equipment.

SeatJoy follows a traditional approach of applying manufacturing overhead to products using an overhead application rate based on direct labor hours. The computation of the 2005 overhead rate is shown first in Exhibit 1. Now take a moment to look through all the numbers in SeatJoy's 2005 operating results. Based on an analysis of 2005 results, it appears that the Cushman II line is dragging down company profits. After evaluating these numbers, the management team decides to drop the Cushman II product line. As a result, some suppliers are notified that SeatJoy will be reducing or canceling orders for certain raw materials. Further, one supervisor and the entire Cushman II labor crew are laid off. These are difficult decisions, but management feels strongly that SeatJoy should not absorb in 2006 another $720,000 reduction in operating profit (the total loss on the Cushman II line in 2005). SeatJoy is now in a position to realize a significant jump in operating profit in 2006. Or is it?

As the accountant prepares and provides the first few monthly profit reports in 2006, it is obvious that there are problems in the operations of the remaining two product lines, particularly in the Cushman line. By the end of the year, when the annual operating results are put together (Exhibit 2), the debacle is confirmed. SeatJoy is in serious trouble! What happened? Sales of both the Cushman and the Luxor product did not change from 2005 results. Further, labor and materials costs per product stayed consistent with 2005 costs, and total manufacturing overhead decreased in 2006. Why didn't company profits improve as management expected after making the decision to drop the Cushman II product line? It looks as if SeatJoy should now consider dropping the Cushman product line in order to save the company.

Comparing the operations reports for 2005 and 2006 should reveal a significant problem. Take a second look at the manufacturing overhead numbers at the top of each exhibit, particularly the overhead rate per direct labor hour. Yes, manufacturing overhead costs did decrease in 2006, as expected since some costs were saved by dropping the Cushman II product. However, these costs did not drop nearly as much as the direct labor hours, resulting in a sharp increase in the overhead application rate per direct labor hour ($40 in 2005 versus nearly $50 in 2006). When the management team decided to drop the Cushman II line, why didn't manufacturing overhead costs decrease as much as expected? Obviously, the current manufacturing overhead application system based on direct labor hours does not provide very accurate insight on cost behavior, particularly in decision-making situations that have strategic implications like adding or dropping a major product line. When management made the decision to drop the Cushman II line, it failed to consider two very important issues:

- First, if the allocation system based on direct labor hours is improper, then it is possible that the Cushman II product line was actually subsidizing some manufacturing overhead costs that should have been assigned to one or both of the other products (a problem called product cost **cross-subsidization**). When a poor cost accounting system allows cross-subsidization of product costs, then the management process of planning, controlling, and evaluating is severely compromised.
- Second, some manufacturing overhead costs (known as **common costs**) simply do not relate directly to any particular product line. Examples of these common costs include executive salaries, rent or property taxes on administrative buildings, and general liability insurance. Common costs cannot be allocated meaningfully to products without potentially creating confusion as the organization works to manage its costs effectively.

ABC-based accounting systems are designed to avoid problems related to cross-subsidization effects and common costs allocations by categorizing and assigning manufacturing overhead costs based on the Hierarchical Product Cost Model. Essentially, the **Hierarchical Product Cost Model** provides management accountants with a method for categorizing costs according to the types of activities those costs support. One important benefit of ABC and the Hierarchical Product Cost Model is the way these tools affect our view of variable and fixed costs (more on this in the next section of this chapter).

STOP & THINK

What do you think is the source of the problem with operations at SeatJoy, Inc.? Should SeatJoy now drop the Cushman product line? Why or why not?

cross-subsidization A distortion of costs that occurs when costs of one product are erroneously assigned to another product.

common costs Manufacturing overhead costs, such as executive salaries or property taxes, that cannot be attributed to products. Costs of facility support activities are common costs.

Hierarchical Product Cost Model A method of categorizing costs based on types of activities. Activity types include unit-level activities, batch-level activities, product line activities, and facility support activities.

Exhibit 2: SeatJoy, Inc.: 2006 Operating Results

Manufacturing Overhead Cost Analysis

Annual manufacturing overhead	$11,920,000
Total annual direct labor hours	÷ 240,000
Manufacturing overhead rate per direct labor hour	$49.67 (rounded) (*Note:* All computations below are based on rounding the overhead rate to the nearest penny.)

Labor Cost Analysis

	Cushman	Luxor	Total
Direct labor hours per product	10.0 hours	12.5 hours	
Annual sales volume	× 18,000 chairs	× 4,800 chairs	
Total annual direct labor hours	180,000 hours	60,000 hours	240,000 hours
Wage rate per hour	× $20	× $20	× $20
Total annual direct labor costs	$3,600,000	$1,200,000	$4,800,000

Individual Unit Analysis

	Cushman	Luxor
Sales price	$ 1,000.00	$ 3,000.00
Direct materials per product	$ (335.00)	$(1,395.00)
Direct labor per product	(200.00)	(250.00)
Manufacturing overhead per product	(496.70)	(620.88)
Total cost per product	$(1,031.70)	$(2,265.88)
Margin per product	$ (31.70)	$ 734.12
Margin percent	(3.2)%	24.5%

Total Annual Results

	Cushman	Luxor	Total
Sales revenue	$ 18,000,000	$ 14,400,000	$ 32,400,000
Total direct materials	$ (6,030,000)	$ (6,696,000)	$(12,726,000)
Total direct labor	(3,600,000)	(1,200,000)	(4,800,000)
Total manufacturing overhead	(8,940,600)	(2,980,224)	(11,920,824)
Total product costs	$(18,570,600)	$(10,876,224)	$(29,446,824)
Total margin	$ (570,600)	$ 3,523,776	$ 2,953,176
Selling and administrative expenses			(4,000,000)
Operating loss			$ (1,046,824)

The ABC Hierarchical Product Cost Model

In the first chapter where we introduced management accounting, we provided some very simple definitions of fixed and variable costs. Later in the cost-volume-profit chapter, we spent considerable time describing how much variety there actually is in fixed and variable costs. The important thing to understand in this chapter is that, in practice, very few costs can be definitely categorized as fixed or variable with respect to a single type of activity in the organization, such as direct labor hours, machine hours, or units produced. In fact, every organization has many different kinds of activities, each of which directly affects certain costs. Stated differently, *given enough time and with respect to a particular activity, most costs in the organization can be considered variable.* This is really quite an important concept in the theory of ABC. Before you can predict a cost behavior (which is necessary before you can begin managing the cost), you need to identify the activity that actually drives the cost in question.

Let's return to the situation at SeatJoy, Inc. As you now know, the traditional approach SeatJoy is using to assign manufacturing overhead costs to its products appears to be causing problems. This approach is demonstrated in Exhibit 3. As you can see, SeatJoy simply sums together all manufacturing overhead costs within the organization and assigns those costs to products based on a single activity, direct labor hours. However, consider the variety of costs that are being combined into a single pool of costs. The purpose of a manufacturing overhead allocation rate (in this case, based on direct labor hours) is to *meaningfully* allocate costs to products in a manner that relates to the behavior of the costs. Think about property taxes on the production facility for a moment. Do these costs adjust at all based on changes in total direct labor hours within the organization? Of course not! Neither do the costs of insuring these facilities against damage and liability claims. Perhaps engineering costs and supervision costs, as well as costs to set up a production run and perform quality checks on the output, are related to direct labor hours, but the relationship is not very strong. There likely are other activities in the SeatJoy organization that relate more closely to increases and decreases in these costs than direct labor hours. Identifying these activities is the intent of the Hierarchical Product Cost Model.

Look back at Exhibit 1 for a moment. How does SeatJoy determine how many direct labor hours are used in the plant? As you can see in the second table (labeled "Labor Cost Analysis"), annual labor hours for each product line are really just a function of how many chairs SeatJoy intends to produce and sell. Allocating manufacturing overhead on the basis of the number of direct labor hours per chair is essentially the same thing as allocating manufacturing overhead on the basis of the number of chairs produced. How much of manufacturing overhead costs will be assigned to the Luxor product line? Well, that really depends on how many units SeatJoy will produce in this product line (which then determines how many direct labor hours will be

Exhibit 3: Traditional (Unit-Based) Costing at SeatJoy, Inc.

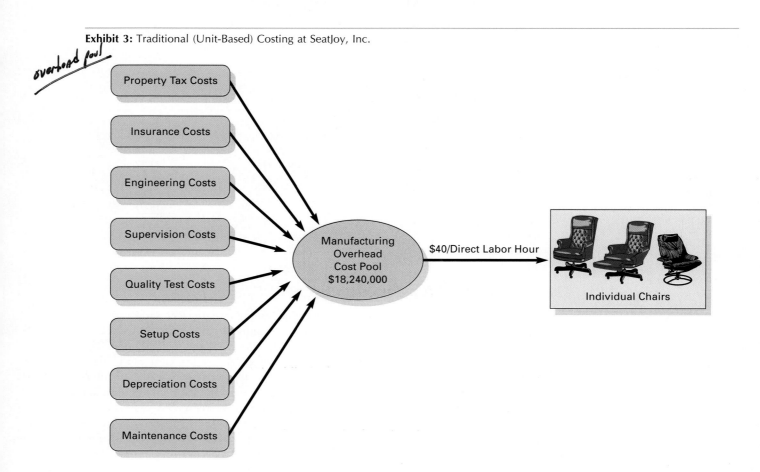

unit-based costing (UBC)
The traditional method of allocating manufacturing overhead using an approach that is essentially based on the number of units produced.

STOP & THINK

We have stated that the overhead allocation rate per direct labor hour for SeatJoy is really just a rate per chair (i.e., unit). Hence, we call this a UBC allocation system. Look at Exhibit 1. What is the manufacturing overhead allocation rate per chair (i.e., per unit)?

⚠ Caution

Don't get the idea from the SeatJoy example that UBC is always a "bad" cost allocation method. On the contrary, UBC is a very good cost allocation method for manufacturing and service organizations with overhead that essentially does change based on the number of units of goods and services produced. Further, compared to ABC, UBC is typically easier and less costly. However, if UBC is causing reported product costs to be distorted, then the management process in the organization can be seriously affected.

cost driver A factor that determines an activity cost. An activity can have more than one cost driver.

used). Because the allocated manufacturing overhead is really a function of the number of units produced, we call this method of allocating manufacturing overhead costs **unit-based costing (UBC)**. Think back to the chapter on product cost flows. Isn't this the basic approach we used in that chapter to allocate overhead in both manufacturing and service companies? UBC is a very traditional cost accounting method used in many types of organizations, and it is the cost allocation approach currently used by the SeatJoy organization in this example. UBC is a good method of cost allocation *in the right context.* However, a UBC approach usually creates problems in an organization with multiple products and services. Cost distortions can develop that make both strategic and short-term planning decisions difficult. The distortions are the result of using an oversimplified information system to represent the complex realities of modern business processes.

You have probably noticed by now that allocating manufacturing overhead costs to products is a two-stage process. First, we gather all the manufacturing overhead costs into a common pool of costs. Second, we allocate these costs to products based on an (hopefully) appropriate allocation rate. This rather simple UBC two-stage allocation process is characterized by the following relationship:

Costs ➔ **Production Department(s)** ➔ Products

You can see this relationship demonstrated in Exhibit 3. All the support costs related to the production department at SeatJoy are gathered into a single cost pool. The costs are then allocated to individual chairs using a UBC rate based on direct labor hours.

The two-stage UBC relationship seems to say that products consume costs in production departments. However, that is not true. Costs are consumed by activities. And activities are necessary to create and deliver products and services. Based on this fact, the activity-based costing (ABC) method of allocating manufacturing overhead costs (which is also accomplished in two stages) makes a rather subtle change to the UBC relationship. The ABC two-stage allocation process is characterized by the following relationship:

Costs ➔ **Activities** ➔ Products

In the ABC relationship, costs are first attributed to activities. Then, each activity is studied to determine its relationship to the product, and product costs are determined based on these activities. Using this relationship allows the management accountant to refine the categorization of costs as either variable or fixed. The UBC approach, with its focus on production units, strictly defines variable costs as those that proportionally shift when an additional unit is produced. This approach probably works well with direct labor, direct materials, and *some* overhead costs. All other remaining costs are then considered fixed and allocated to units using a unit-based driver such as direct labor hours.

However, in today's complex manufacturing and service environments, production costs are determined by many types of activities, not by the production of single units. An activity that affects a particular cost is called a **cost driver** for that cost. Given the right cost drivers and enough time, most costs are variable. For instance, many costs in a manufacturing organization are variable based on the number of and type of *batches* produced or the number of and the characteristics of *product lines* within the company's product mix. Conversely, these costs are fixed based on the number of units produced. Nearly every cost has at least one cost driver (an activity). Effectively managing costs of providing a product means that *activities, not products, must be managed.* The bottom line is that the traditional management accounting approach to product costs, which states that

Individual cost of product = Direct materials + Direct labor + Manufacturing overhead,

may not be the best perspective of production costs when making planning decisions such as the one facing SeatJoy. Notice, though, that this is the approach used by SeatJoy's management

© 2003 Michael Rosenfeld/Getty Images

accountants to analyze individual unit costs and total annual operating results in Exhibit 1. ABC recommends a different view of production costs based on production activities. Using the Hierarchical Product Cost Model, we can see that production costs are a function of many types of activities. As shown in Exhibit 4, there are four categories of activities that result in production costs. Rather than focusing on the cost for an individual product, the Hierarchical Product Cost Model recognizes that an organization's total production costs are a function of these four categories of activities. As a result, these categories need to be well understood in order to manage the costs related to production. We need to spend some time discussing these four types of activities in order to better assess the situation at SeatJoy, Inc. We'll start at the top with unit-level activities and work our way down.

An activity that affects a particular production cost is called a cost driver. Given the right cost drivers, most costs are variable. Many costs in a manufacturing organization, such as a pharmaceutical factory, are variable based on the number of and type of batches produced.

unit-level activities Activities that take place each time a unit of product is produced.

Unit-Level Activities

In the Hierarchical Product Cost Model, activities that are performed each time a unit of a product or service is produced are classified together and called **unit-level activities**. Think about the SeatJoy production setting. Obviously, direct materials are released and direct labor is used each time a chair is produced. Perhaps many of the production processes are automated, minimizing the amount of direct labor involved in the production of a single chair. Nevertheless, each chair produced increases the amount of operating time on the machinery. Operating SeatJoy's assembly, sewing, and packing equipment generates machine maintenance activities. If SeatJoy uses the unit-based depreciation method on its machinery, then depreciation charges occur as chairs are produced. Energy costs required to run the production machinery are also directly tied to the number of hours the machines are operated. Costs related to all these activities are categorized as unit-based costs. Note that in the traditional UBC approach, all costs are treated as if they took place at the unit level. Direct materials and direct labor are attributed to each unit produced. Additionally, all manufacturing overhead is allocated to each unit produced. In the ABC approach, direct materials, direct labor, and *some types* of manufactur-

---

Exhibit 4: Hierarchical Product Cost Model

Total Production Costs

Costs of Products

Unit-Level Activities

Batch-Level Activities

Product Line Activities

Common Costs

Facility Support Activities

ing overhead are handled at the unit level. Traditionally, these costs are considered to be the variable costs of production. The remaining manufacturing overhead costs are traditionally considered fixed. In ABC, however, these fixed manufacturing costs are related to batch-level, product line, or facility support activities. It is really this categorization, illustrated in Exhibit 5, that makes ABC quite different from UBC.

Let's assume that the accountants at SeatJoy determine that $3,420,000 of the $18,240,000 in annual manufacturing overhead costs is related to unit-level activities. SeatJoy can continue to use direct labor hours to allocate these costs to chairs. Based on 456,000 annual direct labor hours, this works out to $7.50 per direct labor hour ($3,420,000 ÷ 456,000 hours). As a result, a Cushman II chair is allocated $112.50 in manufacturing overhead for unit-level activities (based on 15 direct labor hours per Cushman II chair).

As you can see in Exhibit 5, ABC takes a hard look at manufacturing overhead costs historically considered fixed. Remember that ABC is based on the premise that, once the proper cost driver is identified, most costs can be managed as variable costs. In terms of both the traditional UBC approach and the more modern ABC approach, unit-level costs are variable. As a product unit is produced or a service is performed, unit-level costs increase. Traditional management accounting using UBC then maintains that all other costs are fixed. Frankly, if we're talking about using individual units of the product as a cost driver, then these costs are fixed. However, the ABC Hierarchical Product Cost Model looks for other activities, required by the production process, that make many (though not all) fixed costs act variable. The result is the categorization of batch-level and product line activities and their related costs.

Batch-Level Activities

Let's consider batch costs. Many production runs flow in batches. An automotive production line builds a particular line of cars until market orders are met. Then the current production line is changed over to produce a different car. A steel mill or a flour mill mixes different components into customized batches, then packages the output to meet customer specifications. These attempts to individually satisfy customer demands result in the need for batch setups on the production line. During setup, production must pause while employees recalibrate or install different machines. The new batch often requires a different mix of raw materials. Ordering, paying for, and moving raw materials into production position entail time and expense. Often some inspection takes place, such as testing the first item of the batch run, to ensure that

Exhibit 5: Relationship between Unit-Based Costs and Activity-Based Costs in a Manufacturing Organization

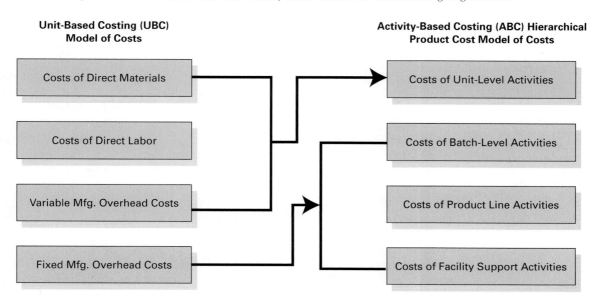

batch-level activities Activities that take place in order to support a batch or production run, regardless of the size.

the configuration and quality of the product are acceptable. These activities that are necessary each time products or services are processed as a batch are known as **batch-level activities**.

Batch-level activities are more common in service firms where there is a lot of customization of the product for customers. A public accounting firm undertakes a lot of setup activities before work can begin on an audit, tax, or consulting job. A trucking company must perform many activities related to setting up a contract and organizing pickup and delivery details before transportation work can begin for a customer. A radio station that sells advertising often does a lot of design work before it can begin running a customer's advertising spot.

Regardless of the size of the batch (1 or 10,000 units, miles, or broadcasts), batch activities must take place, and batch-related costs must be spent. Each organization must evaluate its production operation to determine if and what activities take place to support a batch run. Then, the individual costs of each of these activities are determined. In line with the two-stage cost attribution process of ABC, once costs are assigned to activity cost pools, then batches that require a particular activity are assigned the attending costs. Examples of batch activities at a manufacturing company like SeatJoy include:

- number of setups,
- setup hours,
- movements of materials,
- orders for nonstocked items,
- purchase orders,
- number of inspections, and
- inspection hours.

By tracking batch costs in this manner, much product cost cross-subsidization is avoided. Batch costs can then be averaged across the number of units in the batch (if desired). Units in small batches will then be required to carry a larger burden of these costs. Units in larger batches will experience favorable economies of scale. The cost information system begins reflecting what most managers and supervisors already know: poor scheduling leading to unnecessary production setups results in wasted resources. With this information available, managers can make better-informed decisions concerning the trade-off of large, cost-efficient batches versus production flexibility and low inventory levels that accompany smaller batch runs. Later we will work through some calculations that demonstrate the negative impact that product cost cross-subsidization can have on decisions.

Product Line Activities

product line activities Activities that take place in order to support a product line, regardless of the number of batches or individual units actually produced. Costs of product line activities are also known as capability costs.

Henry Ford infamously said that his customers were welcome to have their Model T car in any color they wanted, so long as it was black! That position has obviously changed at FORD MOTOR COMPANY, as well as at many other companies. Products, including the huge airplanes produced at BOEING, are often customized to satisfy rather small pockets of customers. This leads to the third level of activities in the Hierarchical Product Cost Model—product line activities. **Product line activities** are required to supply a particular product type to the market. These activities are constant regardless of the number of units or batches produced. The number of product line activities is tied to the diversity of the company's product mix and the individual complexity of each product, both of which are important issues in the organization's strategy. Most organizations want to produce more than one or two types of products or services. Otherwise, they are at risk of going out of business should the demand for their particular product or service suddenly drop. Hence, to diversify the risk of market fluctuations and satisfy a myriad of demanding and informed customers, companies must develop and provide a diverse set of products. Organizations with many types of goods or services will require many more product line activities than organizations that produce only a few types of goods or services. This results in increased overhead costs related to product line activities.

Management must be constantly aware of the costs of activities necessary to support an expanding product mix. As with batch activities, management must intelligently trade off the value of a large product mix against the cost of providing a variety of products. There are great opportunities for product cost savings through evaluating the inefficient use of resources by both batch-level and product line activities. Product lines that experience such cost savings should then be able to compete in the market at reduced prices. Sources of product line activities in a manufacturing firm like SeatJoy might include:

- engineering departments where product design changes in a product or production process take place,
- warehouses where materials necessary to each product line are stored and managed,
- supervisors who are dedicated to managing a particular product line,
- purchasing departments that initiate purchase orders, and
- receiving and shipping docks that receive raw materials and ship finished products.

In service organizations like a public accounting firm, a transportation company, or a bank, product line activities might include:

- in-house training resources required to provide specific audit, tax, or consulting services,
- safety specialists who manage transportation of hazardous material, and
- loan officers dedicated to home mortgages versus commercial lending.

Only when the organization decides to permanently eliminate the product from its product mix can product line activities and their related costs be removed. Costs of product line activities are also referred to as **capability costs**—costs necessary to the capability of providing a particular product or service to the market.

Facility Support Activities

Up to this point we have discussed the top three layers of activities in the Hierarchical Product Cost Model: unit-level, batch-level, and product line (see Exhibit 4). The final level of activities in the Hierarchical Product Cost Model is facility support activities. Essentially, **facility support activities** are those activities that must be in place before development and production of any product or service can begin. Most of these activities are administrative in nature. Facility support activities are the source of the true common costs in the production facility. No single product or product line is responsible for the creation of these costs. Facility support activities are necessary for a business to create any products or services. Examples of facility support costs for a company like SeatJoy include:

- property taxes,
- plant security,
- landscaping,
- accounting, and
- salaries of the general administration (e.g., the vice president of manufacturing) and support staff.

The extent of facility support activities is unrelated to production volume or diversity. Therefore, it is impossible to sensibly relate these costs to the production of any particular product or product line. In the ABC model, there is no intervening activity that can connect costs of facility-sustaining activities to the products. Any assignment of these costs to products is doomed to be arbitrary. Therefore, the ABC approach is to *not* allocate these costs to products.[2] Allocating these costs simply distorts management's view of the relevant costs to be considered when strategically managing a product or product line.

Costs of facility support activities should be pooled together and kept separate from the other product costs. Only the costs of activities at the unit, batch, and product line levels are

capability costs Costs necessary to have the capability to produce a particular product or to provide a particular service. Capability costs are also known as the costs of product line activities.

facility support activities Activities necessary to have a facility in place in order to participate in the development and production of products or services. However, these activities are not related to any particular line of products or services. Costs of facility support activities are often called common costs.

---

2 Actually, the idea that allocating common costs cannot be done sensibly does not belong solely to ABC theory. The traditional theory of responsibility accounting also supports not allocating the costs of facility support activities to products.

relevant to the production and management of a particular product line. For this reason, costs of facility support activities are part of the total production costs, but they should not be included in the costs and analysis of any specific line of products. Separating the costs of facility support activities from specific product costs is illustrated in the Hierarchical Product Cost Model in Exhibit 4.

Exhibit 6 illustrates how the two-stage ABC model is blended with the Hierarchical Product Cost Model. As you can see, the total manufacturing overhead costs shown in Exhibit 3 have been split into four separate cost pools based on how the costs relate to types of activities. The manufacturing overhead allocation rates per direct labor hour, per batch run, and per product line are discussed in the next section.

Resolving Cost Distortions

Poor management accounting can create tremendous problems within an organization, particularly when the competition starts driving down market prices. As profit margins are reduced in a competitive market, it becomes increasingly more important for a manufacturing, merchandising, or service firm to accurately identify its product costs. The Boeing Company situation described at the beginning of this chapter is a classic example of an organization that produces many types of complex products in an environment with lots of batch-level and product line activities. Competition is pressuring Boeing to reduce its prices, requiring that Harry Stonecipher and the other executives and managers at Boeing fully understand all production

Exhibit 6: Activity-Based Costing at SeatJoy, Inc.*

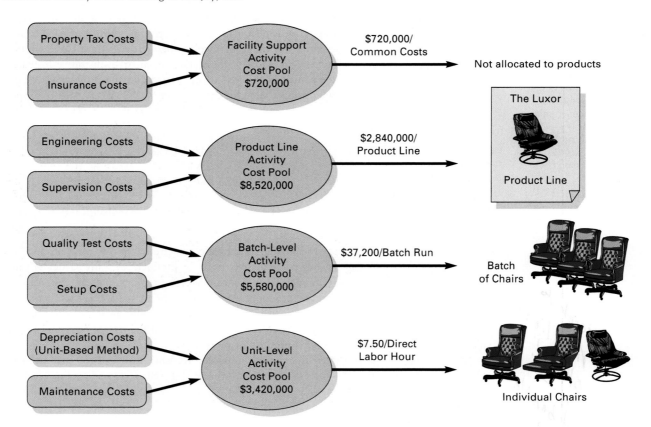

*Calculation of ABC allocation rates is demonstrated in Exhibit 7.

costs *and* how these costs relate to the aircraft they are manufacturing. There is little room for error. To the extent that management accountants provide poor data because of inappropriate cost allocation methods, Boeing will be susceptible to cost distortions such as cross-subsidization and inappropriate allocation of common costs. Each of these cost distortions can lead to decisions that reduce, rather than enhance, the organization's competitive strength.

Product Cost Cross-Subsidization

Let's return to SeatJoy, Inc. The production supervisors at SeatJoy have organized the production process by producing one batch run of each product each week. Typically, production workers spend Monday mornings setting up equipment to produce Cushman chairs. Once everything is set, some chairs are produced and evaluated for quality assurance. With the inspectors' OK, the production process begins, and company employees work until enough chairs are produced to fill all orders placed that week. Sometime Tuesday afternoon or Wednesday morning, they switch to producing Cushman II chairs, and all the setup and quality assurance activities again take place. Hopefully, by Friday morning SeatJoy can begin setting up the production equipment to make Luxor chairs. As you can see in Exhibit 3, SeatJoy has specific costs related to performing setup and quality test activities. Currently, SeatJoy combines these costs with all other manufacturing costs in order to establish its manufacturing overhead allocation rate. However, because the weekly batch run of Luxor chairs is much smaller than the weekly batch run of either Cushman or Cushman II chairs, some of the batch costs related to producing Luxor chairs are being subsidized by the other two products.

With a little additional data, we can compute the size of the product cost cross-subsidization taking place at SeatJoy. Of the $18,240,000 in 2005 manufacturing overhead costs, SeatJoy's cost accountant determines that $5,580,000 is related to batch-level activities. SeatJoy works 50 weeks a year and produces one batch of each product weekly, which works out to 150 total batches each year (50 weeks × 1 batch per week × 3 product lines). As a result, SeatJoy should establish a manufacturing overhead allocation rate of $37,200 *per batch* ($5,580,000 ÷ 150 batches). The average cost *per chair* for batch-level activities at SeatJoy is computed as follows.[3]

Manufacturing Overhead Allocation Using Batch-Level Activities

$5,580,000 ÷ 150 batches = $37,200 Manufacturing Overhead Costs per Batch

	Cushman	Cushman II	Luxor
Annual sales volume in chairs	18,000	14,400	4,800
Annual number of batches	÷ 50	÷ 50	÷ 50
Average batch size in chairs	360	288	96
Overhead costs per batch	$37,200	$37,200	$37,200
Average batch size in chairs	÷ 360	÷ 288	÷ 96
Average batch costs per chair	$103.33	$129.17	$387.50

How do these costs per chair compare when we allocate the $5,580,000 based on direct labor hours? Total direct labor hours for 2005, as well as the average number of direct labor hours per chair, are provided in Exhibit 1. The UBC allocation is computed on the next page.

---

3 It is critical to remember that we are computing *average* costs per chair here. Hence, because these are batch-level activities, SeatJoy *cannot* change these costs by changing the number of chairs produced. The cost driver for these costs is batches, not units (i.e., individual chairs).

Manufacturing Overhead Allocation Using Unit-Level Activities

$5,580,000 ÷ 456,000 hours = $12.24 Manufacturing Overhead Costs per Direct Labor Hour (rounded)

	Cushman	Cushman II	Luxor
Manufacturing overhead costs per direct labor hour	$ 12.24	$ 12.24	$ 12.24
Direct labor hours per product	× 10.0	× 15.0	× 12.5
Average batch costs per chair	$122.40	$183.60	$153.00

Caution

Be sure to bear in mind that the $5,580,000 in manufacturing overhead costs that we're analyzing here are SeatJoy's 2005 overhead costs related to batch-level activities. We've already determined that $3,420,000 of SeatJoy's overhead costs are related to unit-level activities. The remaining $9,240,000 in overhead costs ($18,240,000 − $3,420,000 − $5,580,000) are related either to product-line activities or to facility support activities.

Look carefully at the difference in the calculations when using batches versus direct labor hours as the cost driver. If these manufacturing overhead costs are truly consumed by batch-level activities, then the first set of calculations is more accurate than the second set. However, in Exhibits 1 and 2, SeatJoy is allocating manufacturing overhead costs using direct labor hours. As a result, Luxor chairs are receiving only *some* of the $387.50 average batch-level overhead costs per chair that this product is actually creating. The rest of these costs are being inappropriately allocated to the Cushman and Cushman II products. In other words, Luxor's batch-level product costs are being *cross-subsidized* by the Cushman and Cushman II product lines. The result of this product cost cross-subsidization is that Cushman and Cushman II products will look less profitable than they really are; and conversely, Luxor chairs will look more profitable than they should.

Just like the product cost cross-subsidization that resulted from using direct labor hours to allocate costs of batch-level activities, SeatJoy is also likely cross-subsidizing costs of product line activities. Of the $18,240,000 in 2005 manufacturing overhead costs at SeatJoy, it is determined that $8,520,000 is related to product line activities. Assuming that each product line consumes about the same level of product line activities (e.g., engineering support, purchasing effort, safety training, etc.), each product line should receive $2,840,000 of these costs ($8,520,000 ÷ 3 product lines).[4] The average cost per chair for these manufacturing overhead costs is computed as follows:

Product Line Manufacturing Overhead Allocation Using Product Line Activities

$8,520,000 ÷ 3 lines = $2,840,000 Manufacturing Overhead Costs per Product Line

	Cushman	Cushman II	Luxor
Manufacturing overhead costs per product line	$2,840,000	$2,840,000	$2,840,000
Annual sales volume in chairs	÷ 18,000	÷ 14,400	÷ 4,800
Average product line costs per chair	$ 157.78	$ 197.22	$ 591.67

How do these costs per chair compare when we allocate the $8,520,000 based on direct labor hours? Again, total direct labor hours for 2005, as well as the average number of direct labor hours per chair, are provided in Exhibit 1. The UBC allocation is computed on the next page.

4 To simply divide the costs of product line activities evenly across the three product lines is a relatively straightforward approach to assigning these overhead costs. You'll recall that we used essentially this same approach when assigning the costs of batch-level activities in SeatJoy's ABC system. Another approach is to determine the total costs of each product line activity (as well as each unit- and batch-level activity) and then assign those costs based on how much of that activity is consumed by each product line. Many of the exercises and problems at the end of this chapter use that approach.

Product Line Manufacturing Overhead Allocation Using Unit-Level Activities

$8,520,000 ÷ 456,000 hours = $18.68 Manufacturing Overhead Costs per Direct Labor Hour (rounded)

	Cushman	Cushman II	Luxor
Manufacturing overhead costs per direct labor hour	$ 18.68	$ 18.68	$ 18.68
Direct labor hours per product	× 10.0	× 15.0	× 12.5
Average product line costs per chair	$186.80	$280.20	$233.50

business environment

ABC Provides Legal Defense for Major Chain of Retail Gasoline Service Centers*
State and federal laws have been enacted against predatory pricing, which is the selling of products below cost as a deliberate action to drive out the competition. Alternatively, a product may *appear* to be priced below cost because of the use of unrealistic, unit-based traditional costing systems, which results in the appearance of predatory pricing where it does not exist. This occurred in a case brought under the Motor Fuel Marketing Practices Act of Florida.

The lawsuit was brought against a major chain of retail gasoline service centers, alleging that the chain was selling regular-grade gasoline below cost, as defined under state statutes. The plaintiff's expert witness used a unit-based approach to assign the gasoline service center's average monthly costs to the three grades of gasoline: regular (87 octane), plus (89 octane), and premium (91 octane). When these monthly costs were added to the purchase costs of the gasoline, this approach supported the allegation.

The defendant's original expert witness used a simple average-cost approach to assign the average monthly gasoline service center costs equally to the three grades of gasoline, which supported the defendant's position. The judge in the case made a preliminary ruling that rejected the defendant's analy-

sis and accepted the plaintiff's. The judge issued an injunction prohibiting the defendant from selling regular gasoline below cost as determined in the plaintiff's analysis.

The defendant then engaged an accounting professor as an additional expert witness to review the cost assignment process and make his own recommendation. The expert witness used activity-based costing (ABC) as a third approach to cost assignment. The professor prepared activity cost pools based on labor, kiosk, and gas dispensing to better distribute the costs to the activities performed by the gasoline service centers.

Based on the ABC analysis, the cost per gallon sold actually fell in between the amounts derived from the plaintiff's unit-based approach and the defendant's equal split of labor and overhead costs. In essence, the ABC approach split the difference between the costs per gallon sold obtained from the two extreme approaches. In addition, the ABC analysis better reflected the activities driving the cost of business for the gasoline service centers. After this analysis, the case was settled, and the injunction against the gasoline retailer was lifted.

*The name of the gasoline chain is not disclosed.

Source: Thomas L. Barton and John B. MacArthur, "Activity-Based Costing and Predatory Pricing: The Case of the Petroleum Retail Industry," *Management Accounting Quarterly*, Spring 2003.

As you can see, there is a significant difference in the average costs per chair based on allocating these manufacturing overhead costs using product lines rather than direct labor hours. If these manufacturing overhead costs are truly determined by product line activities, then the first set of calculations is more accurate than the second set. However, since SeatJoy is allocating manufacturing overhead costs using direct labor hours, Luxor chairs are receiving only *some* of the $591.67 product line manufacturing overhead costs. Just like the previous situation involving batch-level activities, some of the product line manufacturing overhead costs belonging to Luxor products are being inappropriately allocated to the Cushman and Cushman II products. Luxor product costs are being *cross-subsidized* by the Cushman and Cushman II product lines in the case of manufacturing overhead costs related to both batch-level and product line activities.

By understanding that batch and product line activities act as cost drivers, costs previously considered to be fixed (which are then allocated using a simple measure like direct labor hours) are actually variable with respect to these types of activities. Products that require these activities should be assigned the burden of these costs. As you can see, product cost cross-subsidization occurs when unit-level cost drivers such as direct labor costs are used to allocate costs of batch-level and product line activities.

Allocating Common Costs and the Death Spiral

Suppose, for example, that it is a company's practice to allocate a share of the cost of property taxes to each product. Neither the product manager nor the production line supervisor has any control over this cost (other than to argue vehemently in management meetings for a smaller share of this cost). When the company is trying to manage the cost effectiveness and customer satisfaction of product lines, this cost allocation only makes the management process more unclear. The product line is not responsible for creating activities that lead to property taxes, so these costs should not be combined with costs of unit-level, batch-level, and product line activities in determining product costs.

Some individuals argue that allocating facility support costs is useful because these activities result in very real costs and must be "covered" by product revenues if the company is to be profitable. It is true that these costs are real. Management needs to be constantly aware of these costs and should be constantly working to ensure that all facility support activities are cost effective. However, consider a simple example. Suppose that a company's annual property taxes are $100,000 and are allocated evenly across four products (Products A, B, C, and D). The product cost information system indicates that the Product D line is generating a $10,000 loss. After several unsuccessful attempts to make the product more profitable, it is discontinued. However, property taxes remain unchanged and are now allocated evenly over the remaining three product lines. Thus, where the three remaining product lines were each previously receiving $25,000 in allocated common costs ($100,000 ÷ 4 product lines), now each receives $33,333 ($100,000 ÷ 3 product lines). Suppose that, with the new allocation, Product C turns unprofitable. Should management now consider discontinuing Product C?

It is doubtful that anyone would be fooled into making the mistake of discontinuing Product C in the simple example above. Hopefully, few would have originally discontinued Product D either. Such imprudent decisions result in a classic case of "death spiral." Essentially, a **death spiral** begins when a company does not fully understand its costs and then attempts to reduce costs by cutting products or other business segments that in fact do not create the costs in question. This results in the remaining costs being reallocated over fewer product lines. So, although the Product D line may be displaying a $10,000 loss, once the unavoidable $25,000 allocation is removed, it is clear that the Product D line is actually contributing $15,000 to help "cover" the $100,000 tax cost and provide overall profit for the company. Removing this product from the company only results in other products having to carry an even larger burden of facility support costs. Continuing to drop products in such a manner will leave the company with $100,000 in property taxes and no revenue-generating products.

Given this simple example, you might expect few to fall into a death spiral trap. However, most large-scale organizations are much more complex than this example. For example, the situation at Boeing Company involves many activities and much cost complexity. It would be

death spiral A series of management decisions based on bad information that results in reducing or removing activities or segments from the organization that are actually profitable.

quite easy to become confused about cost relationships in such a setting. There are several cases of companies falling into this trap and seriously damaging their competitive position before realizing what was happening.

The situation at SeatJoy certainly looks like the beginning of a death spiral. As demonstrated earlier, the accountants are allocating costs of batch-level and product line activities to the Cushman and Cushman II product lines that should belong to the Luxor product line. When SeatJoy management elects to drop the Cushman II product line, the Luxor manufacturing overhead costs being subsidized by the Cushman II line are reallocated to the remaining products. The result is that the Cushman product now looks as if it is unprofitable. Remember, though, that the Cushman line is subsidizing some Luxor costs. In addition, some common costs (i.e., costs of facility support activities) are being allocated to all three products. As demonstrated in Exhibit 6, property tax and insurance costs are facility support costs that really shouldn't be allocated to any of the products. Dropping the Cushman II product line results only in a reallocation of these common costs. This reallocation also contributes to the Cushman product becoming unprofitable in 2006 as shown in Exhibit 2. Of the $18,240,000 in manufacturing overhead at SeatJoy, $720,000 is facility support costs. The average facility support cost per chair as allocated by the traditional manufacturing overhead allocation system is computed below.

Facility Support Manufacturing Overhead Allocation Using Unit-Level Activities

$720,000 ÷ 456,000 hours = $1.58 Manufacturing Overhead Costs per Direct Labor Hour (rounded)

	Cushman	Cushman II	Luxor
Manufacturing overhead costs per direct labor hour	$ 1.58	$ 1.58	$ 1.58
Direct labor hours per product	× 10.0	× 15.0	× 12.5
Average facility support costs per chair	$15.80	$23.70	$19.75

As you can see, the UBC allocation approach assigns $23.70 per chair in common costs to the Cushman II product line. These costs, if removed from the 2005 operating results in Exhibit 1, would go a long way toward reversing what appears to be a loss in this product line. In fact, as you might suspect, once we have corrected accounting problems related to product cost cross-subsidization, removing these common costs should demonstrate that the Cushman II is not an unprofitable product line. Exhibit 7 combines all the ABC allocations we've discussed into a new view of the 2005 operating results. With this information, SeatJoy management should clearly see that dropping the Cushman II product line is not a good decision and will drive overall SeatJoy operations into a loss situation in the year 2006. With the information shown in Exhibit 7, managers at SeatJoy can understand that to improve profits, they must focus on better controlling existing costs rather than making plans to drop any specific line of products.

Activity-Based Management (ABM)

By identifying and classifying activities according to the Hierarchical Product Cost Model, we have seen how SeatJoy is then able to intelligently assign activity costs to products. This is the ABC (activity-based costing) process and is an important tool in managing the costs and quality of *products*. Managers can also use these data to begin the process of improving the costs and quality of *activities*. Remember that ABC is basically a two-stage process. The first stage of ABC involves tracing the flow of resources (and their costs) to activities. The result of the first stage of ABC is activity cost pools. Exhibit 6 illustrates activity cost pools for SeatJoy, Inc. It looks like a simple process to establish activity cost pools for an organization, right? Actually, this work can be both difficult and time-consuming. Allocating costs using UBC can often be done simply by using available records (such as payroll sheets or production reports)

(handwritten margin notes: "Correct way to process", "setup? cost.", "Maintain Line Cost", "Start the unit level - unit level / Exclude. Facility support", "GOH Could be Problem if tried to spread most of unit levels.")

Exhibit 7: SeatJoy, Inc.: ABC Analysis of 2005 Operating Results

	Unit-Level	Batch-Level	Product Line	Facility-Support
Activity cost pools	$3,420,000	$5,580,000	$8,520,000	$720,000
Cushman activity units	180,000 hours	50 batches	1 product line	
Cushman II activity units	216,000 hours	50 batches	1 product line	
Luxor activity units	60,000 hours	50 batches	1 product line	
Total activity units	456,000 hours	150 batches	3 product lines	1 facility
Cost per activity (cost pools ÷ total activity)	$7.50	$37,200	$2,840,000	$720,000
	per direct labor hour	per batch	per product line	in common costs

Labor Cost Analysis

	Cushman	Cushman II	Luxor	Total
Labor hours per product	10.0 hours	15.0 hours	12.5 hours	
Annual sales volume	× 18,000 chairs	× 14,400 chairs	× 4,800 chairs	
Total annual direct labor hours	180,000 hours	216,000 hours	60,000 hours	456,000 hours
Wage rate per hour	× $20	× $20	× $20	× $20
Total annual direct labor costs	$3,600,000	$4,320,000	$1,200,000	$9,120,000

Total Annual Results

	Cushman	Cushman II	Luxor	Total
Sales revenue	$ 18,000,000	$ 21,600,000	$ 14,400,000	$ 54,000,000
Total direct materials	$ (6,030,000)	$ (9,360,000)	$ (6,696,000)	$(22,086,000)
Total direct labor	(3,600,000)	(4,320,000)	(1,200,000)	(9,120,000)
Unit-level overhead	(1,350,000)	(1,620,000)	(450,000)	(3,420,000)
Batch-level overhead	(1,860,000)	(1,860,000)	(1,860,000)	(5,580,000)
Product line overhead	(2,840,000)	(2,840,000)	(2,840,000)	(8,520,000)
Total product-related costs	$(15,680,000)	$(20,000,000)	$(13,046,000)	$(48,726,000)
Total product margin	$ 2,320,000	$ 1,600,000	$ 1,354,000	$ 5,274,000
Facility support overhead				(720,000)
Selling and administrative expenses				(4,000,000)
Operating profit				$ 554,000

Individual Unit Analysis

	Cushman	Cushman II	Luxor
Sales price	$1,000.00	$ 1,500.00	$ 3,000.00
Direct materials per product	$ (335.00)	$ (650.00)	$(1,395.00)
Direct labor per product	(200.00)	(300.00)	(250.00)
Average unit-level OH per product	(75.00)	(112.50)	(93.75)
Average batch-level OH per product	(103.33)	(129.17)	(387.50)
Average product line OH per product	(157.78)	(197.22)	(591.67)
Total cost per product	$ (871.11)	$(1,388.89)	$(2,717.92)
Margin per product	$ 128.89	$ 111.11	$ 282.08
Margin percent	12.9%	7.4%	9.4%

to identify the number of direct labor hours or number of chairs produced. All manufacturing overhead costs are then averaged across the total number of hours or units. On the other hand, to find out how costs *really* flow (i.e., to trace costs to activities), the accountant must leave the office and go out on the production floor or into the service area. Interacting with those involved (department managers, line supervisors, etc.) is the only way to gather accurate insight about how activities affect costs.

The second stage of ABC is assigning to products the costs now pooled (or organized) by activities. In the work of tracing resources to activity cost pools, much of the insight necessary to establish the second ABC stage is also developed. Typically, a budgeted cost is established for each activity. The expected use of the activity is also determined (e.g., number of direct labor hours for unit-level activities, number of batches for batch-level activities, number of product lines for product line activities). Similar to the traditional manufacturing overhead allocation rate, an activity cost allocation rate is established and used to transfer costs as an activity is actually employed.

For example, think of the activity "purchasing" for a merchandising company. The accountants and managers using ABC must determine what costs are required to purchase inventory for the company. The total cost of purchasing activities, as well as the number of expected purchase orders, is budgeted for the year. Using this information, costs per purchase order are set. Then, each time a purchase order is initiated, the costs are assigned to the product requiring a purchase order. Most merchants purchase inventory in large lots, or batches. If this is the case, then costs of purchase orders are related to batch-level activities. Hence, using ABC, the accountants and managers may be able to demonstrate and understand clearly that it is batches of products that must carry (and cover) the costs of purchasing. If the company wants to know the average purchasing costs of a particular inventory item, this is simply a function of the number of product units in each batch of products purchased.

ABC does not provide all the information a company needs to *manage* the costs of purchasing, however. Other things besides number of purchase orders requested may be driving the costs of purchasing activities. Further, the merchant also needs to manage the performance (i.e., the quality and timeliness) of its purchasing activities. With ABC, our focus is on activities. However, effectively tracing costs to products is a separate issue from managing the activity process. In order for the accountant to provide useful information for managing activities within the organization, we need to expand our ABC model as shown below.

Assume that for our purchasing activity example, the ABC team finds that the number of line items in the purchase order and the amount of lead time provided for the purchase order are important drivers of the costs of this activity. In managing costs, it is important that this set of cost drivers be related to the purchasing activity. To better control costs, management needs to concentrate on controlling needlessly high levels of the cost drivers.[5]

In addition, activity *performance* measures should be established. The drive to improve the overall company so that it can better compete within its market means that every critical activity in the organization, not just those directly affecting customers, must be continuously improved. Every activity has a customer—either inside or outside the company. Performance measures used to evaluate the quality of purchasing might include the amount of time required to complete an order (i.e., lead time) and the level of errors in filling an order. The effort to become a world-class merchandiser (or manufacturer or service provider) requires a company

---

5 Often the measure used to assign activity costs to products is also included in the total set of activity cost drivers used to evaluate and control activity costs. However, an activity pool's set of cost drivers and the allocation rate used to assign its cost to products do not have to be the same.

activity-based management (ABM) The identification and use of cost drivers and performance measures to manage the costs, quality, and timeliness of activities.

to clearly identify its strategy and then intelligently build performance measures that support achieving its strategic goals.

Identifying and using multiple cost drivers and performance measures to manage an activity is called **activity-based management (ABM)**. As you can see in the previous diagram, ABM expands the basic ABC model by separating the task of product costing using activity-based relationships (Costs → Activities → Products) from the task of directly managing activities in order to achieve cost efficiencies and to enhance quality in business processes (Activity Cost Drivers → Activities ← Performance Measures). Using ABM, opportunities for cost efficiencies are created by separately tracking multiple cost drivers for each critical activity. Using these performance measures to manage important activities contributes to the effort to continuously improve the organization. As you can see, managing activity cost drivers and performance measures for a particular activity is a management task that is actually exclusive of the processes of tracking a single cost driver that allocates the activity's costs to products. Exhibit 8 illustrates the application of ABM for two activities at SeatJoy.

Exhibit 8: Activity-Based Management at SeatJoy, Inc.

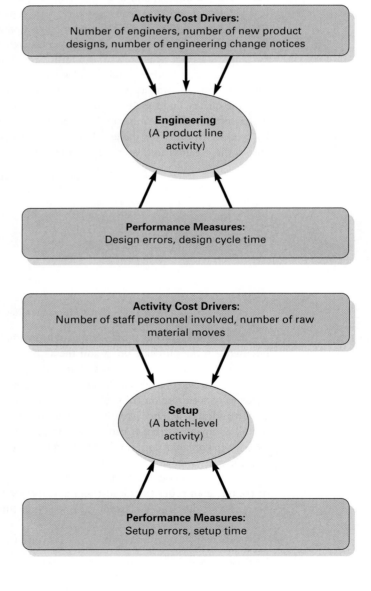

TO SUMMARIZE: Traditional product cost models generally focus on allocating overhead costs based on some measure that is a function of the number of products being produced or the amount of service being provided in the organization. This approach, called unit-based costing (UBC), works well in fairly simple settings with little diversity in the types of products or services offered to customers. In contrast, activity-based costing (ABC) recognizes that activities are the causes of costs. By understanding how activities relate to products, a company with a diverse set of products and processes, such as Boeing Company, can more intelligently allocate manufacturing overhead costs to products.

Activities can be categorized across four levels: unit-level activities, batch-level activities, product line activities, and facility support activities. Generally, variable manufacturing overhead, such as machine maintenance or energy costs to run production equipment, is a function of the number of units produced. Setup costs, materials purchase orders, and route planning are examples of costs traditionally considered fixed that actually are variable in relation to the number of batch runs within the organization. Overhead costs that are a function of product line activities are generally related to engineering, supervision, and warehousing. In contrast to unit-level, batch-level, and product line activities, costs of facility support activities cannot sensibly be connected to any particular product line. Examples of these activities include property taxes, plant security, landscaping, accounting, and executive administration.

Once costs have been pooled together according to the proper activity level (the first stage of ABC), new overhead allocation rates can then be created to separately allocate costs of unit-level, batch-level, and product line activities to product lines (the second stage of ABC). Costs of facility support activities are classified as common costs and should *not* be allocated to individual product lines; otherwise, product costs are distorted. If costs of batch-level and product line activities are allocated using UBC, then cost distortions called product cost cross-subsidization can also take place as one product is erroneously allocated another product's cost in the accounting system. Product cost distortions can lead to a series of management decisions called a death spiral. Managers inadvertently involved in a death spiral will make a decision to drop what is actually a profitable product or service line based on UBC data that erroneously suggest this product or service is unprofitable. Once one product line is dropped, the reallocation of overhead to the remaining products may result in another product looking unprofitable, thereby continuing the spiral.

Once the organization has developed an accurate ABC system, it can turn its attention toward improving activities that support its competitive strategy. The crucial information to be developed for important activities in the organization includes the following:

- A set of activity cost drivers that provides the greatest influence on the activity cost pool. These cost drivers become the focus of effort in controlling the activity cost pool.
- A set of performance measures used to evaluate the quality and timeliness of the activity.

This information is used to expand the ABC model in order to perform activity-based management (ABM).

Total Quality Management

2 Describe total quality management (TQM) and costs of quality (COQ).

We ended the last section on ABC by introducing the important concept that tracking and effectively allocating activity costs is not sufficient for managing activities. In today's highly competitive global markets, managing both the cost *and the performance* of activities is critical to the success of most organizations. This fact supports the importance of ABM to the management process of planning, controlling, and evaluating activities within the organization. Since

total quality management (TQM) A management philosophy focused on increasing profitability by improving the quality of products and processes and increasing customer satisfaction, while promoting the well-being and growth of employees.

the early 1980s, an important management model known as **total quality management (TQM)** has had significant impacts on modern management accounting. TQM is a management philosophy focused on increasing profitability by improving the quality of products and processes and increasing customer satisfaction while promoting the well-being and growth of the employees of the organization. Most managers, if asked, would say that their company seeks to improve quality, increase customer satisfaction, and take care of its employees. Implementing TQM, however, requires more than just endorsing the importance of quality in the company. An organization that has truly implemented TQM exhibits two defining characteristics. First, quality and continuous improvement are emphasized above all else within the organization. The premise here is one of priority. A company focused on TQM manages itself with the assumption that if product quality is high, customers will be satisfied and employees will be happy, and *then* profits can be expected. This contrasts with the assumption that the company cannot focus on quality until it is performing well financially. Second, TQM in the organization is the result of continuously planning, controlling, and evaluating improvement using specific measures. It is in this second assumption that accounting systems built to perform ABM can interface well with TQM. By tracking costs and performance related to TQM activities, accounting can be used to support this critical trend in business management.

TQM Comes to the United States

W. Edward Deming is widely credited with leading the quality revolution in Japan that started in the 1950s. Ironically, Deming received little attention as a consultant to U.S. companies prior to 1950. In contrast, at this same time Japan began to heed his advice on controlling processes, improving systems, and empowering workers. Soon, Deming moved to Japan where he remained for approximately 30 years. In honor of his work, Japan established the national Deming Prize to annually honor companies making significant improvements in the TQM process.

During the 1980s, concerns about American competitiveness spurred many U.S. companies to take a new interest in quality. Several companies invited Deming, then in his eighties, back to the United States to challenge the "old way" of thinking about costs and quality. A hundred years ago Andrew Carnegie essentially built an empire in the steel industry with the following motto: "Watch the costs and the profits will take care of themselves." Deming essentially revised this phrase to "Watch the *quality* and the profits will take care of themselves." The effect he and his colleagues have had on the way organizations work and compete is profound. Deming passed away in December 1993 at the age of 93.

TQM and Management Accounting

statistical process control (SPC) A statistical technique for identifying and measuring the quality status of a process by evaluating its output to determine if serious problems exist in the process.

Perhaps you've heard the term *statistical process control*. **Statistical process control (SPC)** is a technical tool that provides users with the ability to study, control, and improve processes of all types. Using statistical probability analysis, SPC provides management with the ability to know whether the errors in a production or service process are a signal that a serious problem exists in the process. Deming refined this early engineering tool and placed it squarely in the center of his TQM theory of management. Basically, Deming recognized that variation is a regular fact of life. No matter how carefully the fry cook at your local MCDONALD'S prepares a set of hamburgers, each one will be slightly different from the others. This is a natural fact of variation. Frankly, it's probably not very important to you as a consumer that every McDonald's hamburger you purchase is *exactly* like every other hamburger made that day in that store. However, if you're in the business of manufacturing or purchasing baseballs to be used in major league games throughout the summer, you're probably quite interested in consistent product quality. If you're in the business of manufacturing or purchasing surgical scalpels, computer chips, or rocket boosters for the U.S. Space Shuttle Program, then consistent product quality may be even more important.

Health Care Recognized for Quality Since 1988, the president and secretary of commerce annually have presented U.S. organizations with the Malcolm Baldrige National Quality Award, the nation's premier award for performance excellence and quality achievement. The Malcolm Baldrige National Quality Award was established in 1988 to recognize U.S. manufacturing, service, small business, and starting in 1999, education and health care companies that excel in quality management. The award's threefold purpose is to promote awareness of quality as an important competitive element, recognize quality achievements of U.S. companies, and publicize successful quality strategies. The award can be presented to a maximum of three companies per category each year that exemplify these characteristics. Due to the award's strict criteria, however, the Baldrige Award has *never* been given to more than five companies in one year.

Since 1999, a total of 61 applications have been submitted in the health care category, including 19 in 2003. In 2002, SSM HEALTH CARE (SSMHC) was the first winner to be named in the health care category. "Being the first health care organization to win the Baldrige is an extraordinary achievement made possible by extraordinary people," said Sr. Mary Jean Ryan, president/CEO of SSM Health Care. She adds, "In a world where people's worth is often measured in monetary terms, we see each of our patients as a unique person of worth who is in need of healing. And in our sisters' tradition, we continue to view health care as a service to people in need. As we continue to improve ourselves, we want to inspire other to join us in raising health care to a new standard for people of this country. The people of this nation deserve no less."

Sponsored by the Franciscan Sisters of Mary and based in St. Louis, Missouri, SSMHC is one of the largest Catholic systems in the country. The system owns, manages, and is affiliated with 21 acute care hospitals and three nursing homes in four states: Missouri, Illinois, Wisconsin, and Oklahoma. Nearly 5,000 affiliated physicians and 23,200 employees work together to provide a wide range of services that are compassionate, holistic, and of high quality. SSMHC's health-related businesses include information systems, home care management, and support services such as material management and clinical engineering.

SSM Health Care won the award in large part due to its work on its "clinical collaborative" process whereby physicians work with other caregivers, administrators, and staff to make rapid improvements in clinical outcomes. SSMHC undertook six collaboratives, involving 85 teams in 2002, up from 14 teams in 1999. The results for SSMHC's clinical collaboratives for patients with congestive heart failure and ischemic heart disease demonstrated levels that approached or exceeded national benchmarks.

Sources: The Baldrige National Quality Program, **http://www.quality.nist.gov**; SSM Health Care home page, **http://www.ssmhc.com**.

SPC is having a large effect on management accounting in many organizations today. An accountant usually doesn't need to perform statistical analysis and probability procedures in order to participate in the TQM effort. SPC work is typically the responsibility of engineers and statisticians. Nevertheless, using SPC to support TQM in a company involves a lot of cost management issues. It costs money to create low-variation, high-quality products and services. It costs money to inspect and measure processes in order to know when problems exist. On the other hand, Deming and others have taught us that it costs a great deal of money to allow high-variation, low-quality products and services to exist in our organizations. Tracking and managing these costs is an important part of the TQM effort and is often the responsibility of accountants.

Costs of Quality (COQ)

Let's use baseball manufacturing to help understand exactly how management accounting works with SPC to measure and report quality costs. You may be interested to learn that, although

National Institute of Standards and Technology (NIST)

The NATIONAL INSTITUTE OF STANDARDS AND TECHNOLOGY (NIST) sponsors a site for the Malcolm Baldrige National Quality Award program at **http://www.quality.nist.gov**. This site will keep you up to date on the latest quality award winners, quality programs for students, presidential speeches on "Baldrige" quality, and descriptive portfolios of the award winners. Check out this site to answer these fundamental questions.

Net Work:

1. Who was Malcolm Baldrige?
2. Why is the award named after him?

FYI:

A Rawlings baseball doesn't last long in a major league game (average life is about six game minutes), but it has to be as perfect as possible. When a professional pitcher throws a ball toward home plate at nearly 100 miles per hour, the slightest blemish in stitching, size, or weight can be the difference between a strike and a home run, the difference between winning a pennant and having a disappointing season.

costs of quality (COQ)
Costs spent to achieve high quality of products and services, as well as costs spent when products fail to have high quality. The four types of costs of quality are prevention costs, appraisal costs, internal failure costs, and external failure costs.

China produces 80% of the world's baseballs, every single baseball pitched in the major leagues is made in a Costa Rican factory owned by RAWLINGS SPORTING GOODS COMPANY. A Rawlings baseball begins life as a "pill," a small sphere of cork and rubber enclosed in a rubber shell. The pill is tightly wound with three different layers of wool yarn, and then finished with a winding of cotton/polyester yarn. This "core" is then coated with a latex adhesive. Over this gooey, hard lump, must be sewn an extremely tight-fitting jacket of leather using exactly 216 raised stitches. Sewing on the cover is a major effort. No one has been able to successfully create a machine that can automatically stitch the cover on a professional baseball. Hence, Rawlings employs about 1,000 baseball sewing experts. In its factory, top sewing pros can sew four to six baseballs an hour, achieving perfect string tension by feel. A wooden press rolls the seams flat, and finished balls are stored in a dehumidifying room that shrinks the covers tight and protects the balls from tropical humidity that might make them bloat illegally. Baseballs are carefully inspected at the Rawlings plant before being packed for shipping. A baseball that turns out too skinny, too hefty, or otherwise off-spec is "blemmed." It's stamped "blem" for blemish and sold as a practice ball.[6]

To be used in the major leagues, a Rawlings baseball should weigh approximately 5.12 ounces and be 9.12 inches in circumference. As we pointed out, however, regardless of how hard the Rawlings Sporting Goods Company works to make sure its sewers are consistently producing baseballs of the perfect weight and size, variation occurs.[7] For the Rawlings plant, the important thing is to distinguish simple random variations in baseball weight and size that occasionally occur in a well-controlled production environment from systematic variations that occur more often when a poorly trained sewer is working or when low-quality leather is being used. Consider the following hypothetical example. Rawlings has determined upper and lower control limits for a baseball. Specifically, baseballs must weigh between 5 and 5.25 ounces and have a circumference between 9 and 9.25 inches. Exhibit 9 shows an SPC chart of measurements of daily baseball weights at Rawlings. As you can see, some of these measurements are outside the control limits, indicating that there are potentially serious quality problems in the factory. Although getting the production process back in control will require some management effort, the problem cannot go on unchecked. Blemmed baseballs cost Rawlings money because the balls cannot be sold at game prices. Worse, though, is the cost to Rawlings' reputation. If Major League Baseball switches to another supplier because of inconsistent quality at Rawlings, the long-term opportunity costs to Rawlings could be devastating.

Before Rawlings' production managers can begin working on a potential quality problem on the production floor, the management accountants need to answer a couple of important questions: "What is it costing Rawlings when it produces blemmed baseballs? What will it cost to get the production process back within control limits?" These questions are the initial step in identifying an important set of costs called "costs of quality." **Costs of quality (COQ)** are costs spent to achieve TQM, as well as costs spent when products and processes fail to have high quality. Once activities that relate to quality in the organization have been identified, the accountant must be able to track the costs of those activities in order to measure COQ. Joseph M. Juran, another American quality guru who, like Deming, was enormously influential in the Japanese quality movement, originally identified COQ as an important accounting concept. Eventually, Juran also returned from Japan to the United States with his COQ theories to guide notable companies such as TEXAS INSTRUMENTS, DUPONT, and XEROX.

---

6 Hannah Holmes, "The Skinny on Sewing Up Baseballs," at **http://www.discovery.com**.
7 *Note:* This example uses fictitious production standards and results in the setting of an actual company. Data used to illustrate quality concepts in this text should not be construed as actual production standards and results for the Rawlings Sporting Goods Company.

Exhibit 9: Rawlings Baseball Production: Statistical Process Control (SPC) Chart of Daily Operating Results

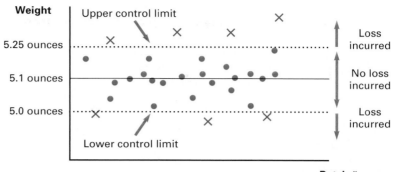

● = Ball weight within control limits with some random variation (no correction required).
✕ = Ball weight outside control limits (correction to production system required).

He understood that organizations need to balance costs of achieving quality against the costs of poor quality. Most importantly, he specifically defined four types of quality costs that form the COQ model: prevention costs, appraisal costs, internal failure costs, and external failure costs.

Prevention Costs

prevention costs Costs of quality that specifically relate to the effort to ensure that processes are performed correctly the first time and that products and services meet customers' expectations.

Prevention costs are costs incurred to ensure that tasks are performed correctly the first time and that the product or service meets customer requirements. Examples of prevention costs include costs of process or product design, employee training, education of suppliers, preventive maintenance, and other quality improvement meetings and projects. In the case of Rawlings Sporting Goods, the quality of its baseballs is highly dependent on the quality of its raw materials and on the expertise of those who stitch on the leather covers. This company will likely spend a lot of money working with its suppliers and training its employees to build a quality product.

Appraisal Costs

appraisal costs Costs of quality that specifically relate to the effort of inspecting, testing, and sampling activities performed in order to identify and remove low-quality products and services from the system.

Appraisal costs are the amounts spent on inspection, testing, and sampling of raw materials, work in process, and finished goods and services. They include overhead expenses for quality inspectors, costs to adjust measuring and test equipment, and costs of associated supplies and materials. Rawlings performs extensive inspections to gather data similar to that shown in Exhibit 9. These inspections require individuals to invest time using special equipment to evaluate each ball for size, weight, color, stitching, etc. Both appraisal and prevention costs can be viewed as investments in the process of providing quality baseballs to Major League Baseball.

FYI:

Rawlings baseballs are selected at random from each shipment to Major League Baseball and shot from an air cannon at a speed of 85 feet per second at a wall made of northern white ash (the wood used to make bats). Each tested ball must bounce back at between 0.514 and 0.578 of its original speed to be suitably lively for Major League Baseball.

Internal Failure Costs

Juran categorizes all the scrap and rework costs that are incurred to dispose of or fix defective products *before* they are shipped to the customer as **internal failure costs**. Costs of downtime or reduced yield due to production of defective parts or services are also included in this cost category. For example, if a Rawlings employee spends 10 minutes sewing a baseball, only to have the cover suddenly rip

internal failure costs Costs of quality that specifically relate to the expenses that occur when low-quality products and services fail before production and delivery to customers.

because of poor-quality leather, the company has lost money due to both the scrapped leather and the wages paid for 10 minutes of sewing a useless ball. In addition, all the materials and labor time spent previously winding, coating, and fitting the ball before the stitching work started are lost and become part of the internal failure costs. Clearly, Rawlings wants to be able to reduce scrap and sell more baseballs. Investments in prevention and appraisal work should reduce internal failure costs in the organization.

external failure costs Costs of quality that specifically relate to the costs that occur when low-quality products and services fail after production and delivery to customers.

FYI:

Most experts agree that losses on gross sales due to poor quality range from 20% to 30%. However, most executives underestimate these losses because they consider only the most obvious costs, such as scrap and rework, to be the costs of low quality.

Source: K. G. Rust, "Measuring the Costs of Quality," *Management Accounting*, August 1995, pp. 33–37.

External Failure Costs

Internal failure costs are very expensive. Nevertheless, Rawlings would *much* rather experience an internal failure than an external failure (defined as failure after the product has been delivered to the customers). **External failure costs** are generally the highest costs of a poor-quality process. Some examples are the costs of processing complaints, customer returns, warranty claims, product recalls, field service, and product liability. The most serious type of external failure cost likely results from unhappy customers; because bad news travels fast, defects found by a customer can cause the firm to lose both market share and future profits. In fact, a FORD MOTOR COMPANY survey indicates that a dissatisfied customer tells, on average, six other people. Sometimes the bad news can travel even faster. If a cover of a Rawlings baseball is pulled loose by a pitcher in the act of throwing a knuckleball during a game, the ball is immediately removed from the game. Obviously, more than six people instantly know about the product failure. Worse, though, is when product failure leads to news announcements and discussion in the media. In the last few years, you may recall some famous examples of publicized product failure involving software with bugs, unsafe tires on vehicles, and medicine or medical procedures with unexpected side effects.

Juran originally related all four of these COQ categories back to Deming's SPC model. He taught that if companies really understood the extent of failure costs, they would be willing to invest more in appraisal and prevention costs to keep more of their products performing within established control limits. Accountants should track these costs so that they can better manage the important relationship between costs of low-quality products and costs required to create high-quality products. This is an important relationship to manage. Obviously, high quality saves the company a lot of money as both internal and external product failures are reduced. On the other hand, high quality likely requires large investments in appraisal and prevention costs. Even though TQM requires that managers focus first on quality and then on profits, managers still need to understand how their commitment to TQM affects the company's bottom line (i.e., its profits). The dollar amounts involved in COQ are often quite large. Accountants add important competitive value to the organization when they are able to provide this important cost information. Hence, the ABC/ABM accounting system should identify appraisal and prevention activities, track the cost drivers of these activities, and establish performance measures that relate to reductions in failure costs and activities as a result of appraisal and prevention activities.

COQ Example

Let's return to our example involving the production of baseballs at Rawlings Sporting Goods Company. Rawlings has invested expensive time and equipment to inspect all baseballs represented on the graph in Exhibit 9. As you can see, there are a few baseballs whose individual weights are outside the control limits. Balls failing the test are marked "blems" and sold very cheaply as practice balls. Other balls are not even usable as practice balls and must be scrapped. (Remember that weight is not the only quality criterion at Rawlings. The company is inspecting and scrapping balls for size, stitching, and color problems as well.) In addition to the balls failing the SPC tests, as displayed in Exhibit 9, Rawlings may also occasionally deal with complaints from merchants, athletes, and other organizations involving balls that fail in "the field." Because of the company's high commitment to customer satisfaction, it incurs significant costs in handling these calls, providing replacement balls, and investigating the cause of the product failure back at the factory. To counter these problems, Rawlings is considering making a large investment in its inspection equipment and in better training for its factory workers. Additionally, it is considering a new supplier for some of its raw materials (there are significant costs involved in establishing the new supplier relationship). Rawlings has a difficult planning decision to make that will likely require an intelligent evaluation of the trade-offs across all its quality costs. Rawlings will invest in an increasing level of appraisal and prevention costs in order to increase the percentage of baseballs that conform to all control limits. As the quality of baseballs increases, failure costs decrease dramatically. However, achieving perfect quality requires higher and higher prevention and appraisal costs. Balancing the decreasing costs of product failure with the increasing costs of high quality requires combining *all* costs in order to compute total COQ. The idea is to find the quality level where total COQ is minimized. As an example, look at the fictitious cost numbers in the following table. As the percentage of baseballs that comply with all control limits (color, weight, diameter, etc.) increases, total appraisal and prevention costs increase. On the other hand, as the percentage of baseballs that comply with all control limits decreases, total failure costs increase. Rawlings needs to balance these costs by focusing on the appropriate level of quality in its production process. As you can see by inspecting the numbers presented, all quality costs are minimized in this example at 94% conformance where total COQ equals $2,237,155.

% of balls within all control limits	84%	86%	88%	90%	92%	94%	96%	98%	100%
Total appraisal & prevention costs	$ 100,037	$ 122,554	$ 156,347	$ 211,347	$ 311,850	$ 530,663	$1,164,270	$4,214,198	$44,172,984
Total failure costs	52,100,456	7,927,472	3,713,274	2,549,005	2,018,342	1,706,492	1,495,145	1,338,798	1,216,244
Total costs of quality (COQ)	$52,200,493	$8,050,026	$3,869,621	$2,760,352	$2,330,192	$2,237,155	$2,659,415	$5,552,996	$45,389,228

Locating COQ in the Accounting Records

It is important to see that tracking COQ within traditional accounting records can be challenging. Essentially, if the accountant desires to provide COQ data, most of these data are generally buried in the accounting records. As we discussed in previous chapters, many organizations traditionally categorize product costs as direct materials, direct labor, and overhead; and they categorize period costs as selling or general administrative. Quality costs used in the COQ model are typically spread throughout these traditional categories as shown below.

Prevention Costs		Appraisal Costs		Internal Failure Costs		External Failure Costs	
Cost Type	**Where Found**	**Cost Type**	**Where Found**	**Cost Type**	**Where Found**	**Cost Type**	**Where Found**
Process or product design	General administrative	Quality inspectors	Overhead	Scrap	Direct materials	Processing complaints & returns	Selling
Employee training	Overhead	Purchasing test equipment	Overhead (depreciation)	Rework	Direct labor	Product recalls	Selling or general administrative
Educating suppliers	General administrative	Adjusting test equipment	Overhead	Downtime	Direct labor and overhead or general administrative	Product liability	General administrative
Preventive maintenance	Overhead	Special supplies and materials	Overhead	Reduced yield	Direct materials and direct labor	Lost sales	Not found in the accounting system

Companies using a traditional cost accounting system may have some difficulty separating quality costs from other costs. However, companies using an ABC system should have already identified activities related to many of these quality processes. Often, it is much easier to implement a COQ accounting system in an organization that uses ABC. Note that lost sales (one type of failure costs) are *not* found in the accounting system. Lost sales are an opportunity cost, and opportunity costs are typically not tracked within most accounting systems. Nevertheless, these are extremely important costs for the accountant to measure and provide to decision makers trying to plan, control, and evaluate the quality process in the organization. Lately, there has been some progress in the effort to track these important opportunity costs. Measuring the costs of lost sales is discussed in the expanded material section of this chapter.

TO SUMMARIZE: W. Edward Deming was extremely influential in helping companies understand that quality is an important competitive necessity in business. One of the main TQM (total quality management) tools he prescribed was SPC (statistical process control). Companies use SPC to identify an acceptable range of variation in their products and services. When the variation in the product or service exceeds the control limits established by the firm, then managers begin working to increase the quality of the production process.

A contemporary of Deming, Joseph M. Juran, developed a new categorization of costs called COQ (costs of quality) that can be used to manage decision making based on SPC. Keeping products or services in conformance with control limits requires investing in two types of quality costs: prevention costs (such as good product design and employee training) and appraisal costs (such as inspection and testing). When the production process starts creating variation outside the control limits, two types of quality costs result: internal failure costs (such as scrap and employee downtime) and external failure costs (such as handling complaints and product recalls). Perhaps the most important external failure costs are the opportunity costs of lost sales.

The COQ information that accountants provide managers should illustrate how decreasing failure costs may be offset by increasing prevention and appraisal costs. The level of quality conformance in a production process should be at the point where total quality costs are minimized. Identifying quality costs can be a challenge because these costs are generally intermingled across all the product and period costs within many organizations' accounting systems. Of all the quality costs identified in the COQ model (i.e., appraisal, prevention, internal failure, and external failure costs), the external failure costs are most difficult to measure because these costs include the opportunity costs of lost sales due to customer dissatisfaction.

The focus of this chapter is to introduce you to some of the "cutting-edge" issues in management accounting today. The topics in this chapter are organized around the strategic imperatives of costs (e.g., activity-based costing or ABC) and quality (e.g., total quality management or TQM). Remember that management accounting is not dictated by some regulatory agency. Management accounting practice is determined by competition and the strategic needs of each organization. Accounting tools such as ABC and COQ essentially focus on new ways of measuring and reporting costs. These costs are often recorded somehow in the traditional accounting system. In this expanded section, we will explore a *very* new way of thinking about and reporting the opportunity costs of lost sales. The interesting thing about measuring the costs of lost sales is that this is a measure of costs that is rarely recorded anywhere within the traditional accounting system.

Measuring Costs of Lost Sales

3 Compute the opportunity cost of lost sales.

Want to set a manager's teeth on edge? If you're in manufacturing, show the manager a pile of scrapped work-in-process inventory due to low-quality materials or mistakes made in the production process. If you're in merchandising, show the manager a pile of merchandise that can't be sold due to low-quality materials, poor design, or damage during shipping. These piles represent wasted costs and opportunities and translate into lost profits. The accountant using COQ in a manufacturing or merchandising organization will report these costs as internal failure costs. However, identifying internal failure costs within service companies is more challenging. Where are the piles of scrapped inventory in a service company? Actually, there is often no distinction between internal failures and external failures for a service company such as an airline, a law firm, or a bank. Baggage is misplaced, a client's phone calls are not returned, or deposits are recorded in the wrong account. Internal processes have failed at these service companies, and external customers are *immediately* affected. Instead of scrapped inventory that can't be sold, service companies identify their own kind of scrap heap: customers who will not come back. Frankly, all three types of companies (service firms, merchants, and manufacturers) experience lost opportunities due to disgruntled customers. Perhaps the most significant impact of the TQM revolution across businesses is an increasing determination to make sure the customers' experience with the company is exemplary. (Hopefully, you've personally had a positive experience with a company determined to "delight the customer.")

As we discussed earlier, disappointed customers can lead to a number of external failure costs, including costs of processing complaints, customer returns, warranty claims, product recalls, field service, and product liability. Many of these costs don't apply to service companies. As a result, these companies naturally focus on the effect of losing the goodwill of their customers, which in turn leads to loss of future sales. However, the risk to manufacturers and merchants is that they will focus too much on external failure costs that are easy to measure and will fail to fully appreciate the opportunity cost of lost sales (which is more the focus of service companies).

Robust Quality

If the accountant is somehow able to identify and measure the cost of lost sales, then managers can use this information in better planning, controlling, and evaluating the process of delivering the products that customers want. What kinds of products do customers want? Let's return to our earlier discussion about baseball manufacturing. Think about Randy Johnson pitching for the Arizona Diamondbacks. Does he care if a RAWLINGS baseball appropriately weighs between 5 and 5.25 ounces and has a circumference between 9 and 9.25 inches? Actually, no. What Randy Johnson cares about is that the baseball, when pitched, will perform as he intends—that it will have the desired curve, fade, slide, drop, or heat. Referring back to the SPC chart in Exhibit 9, a ball that weighs between 5 and 5.25 ounces and has a circumference between 9 and 9.25 inches is determined to have no defects because it is within MLB (Major League Baseball) limits. However, one-tenth of an ounce is pretty important to a professional baseball pitcher trying to throw a split-fingered fastball. Hence, we might expect that Randy Johnson's pitching performance will improve and be more consistent as Rawlings works to reduce variation in the weight and size of baseballs—even if the variation is within the limits imposed by Major League Baseball.

robust quality The capability of a product to perform according to customer expectations regardless of surroundings and circumstances.

The effort to reduce all variation is related to the concept of robust quality. **Robust quality** essentially means that the product will perform for the customer under all kinds of circumstances. In other words, you and I really don't care if the stereo, shirt, or sports car we buy was manufactured within some set of control limits or specifications. For us, the proof of a product's quality is in its performance when it is rapped, overloaded, stretched, or soaked. We all prefer stereos that continue to power up (even after a lightning storm has sent electrical surges throughout our neighborhood); we all prefer clothes that don't tear (even when a small child yanks on the sleeve to get our attention); we all prefer cars designed to steer safely and predictably (even on roads that are wet or full of potholes). We say these products are robust. They gain steadfast customer loyalty.

In the mid-1980s, FORD MOTOR COMPANY had a valuable experience with the importance of robust quality.[8] At that time, Ford owned 25% of MAZDA and asked the Japanese company to help build some of the transmissions for a car Ford was selling in the United States. Both Ford and Mazda built their transmissions using the same specifications. Yet, after the cars with Ford-built transmissions had been on the road for a while, they began developing much higher warranty costs and more customer complaints about noise than the cars with Mazda-built transmissions. As a result, Ford engineers disassembled and inspected transmissions made by both companies. They were astounded at the comparison. The Ford transmissions were all built within the range of engineering specifications, but the Mazda transmissions displayed absolutely no variability from the target measures. The Ford transmissions that were breaking down were those shipped with components built quite close to (but still within) the manufacturing control limits. Because the Mazda plant was working hard to reduce all variance—even variance within the acceptable control limits—its transmissions had lower production, scrap, rework, and warranty costs.

Taguchi's Quality Loss Function

> **Taguchi quality loss function** A method developed by Genichi Taguchi for estimating the actual size of all external failure costs, particularly the opportunity costs of lost customer sales that result from dissatisfied customers.

Genichi Taguchi is a very famous Japanese quality expert who made an important adaptation to SPC charts that allows management accountants to actually measure the external failure costs of lost customers. Since its introduction in the 1980s, many U.S. companies have used Taguchi's famous quality loss function. Essentially, the **Taguchi quality loss function** is a method of relating the amount of variation in a product to external failure costs due to dissatisfied customers. Managers and accountants who use the Taguchi quality loss function recognize that shipping a product that barely satisfies the corporate standard gains you virtually nothing over shipping a product that fails. Translation: There is a lot more difference between baseballs that weigh 5.12 ounces versus 5.24 ounces (both balls are within MLB tolerance specifications) than there is between baseballs weighing 5.24 ounces versus 5.26 ounces (only one ball is within tolerance specifications). Nevertheless, using the upper and lower limit controls displayed in Exhibit 9 would have Rawlings feeling just as confident shipping a baseball to the National League weighing 5.24 ounces as shipping a baseball weighing 5.12 ounces. Can you see why this might create a performance problem for Rawlings' customers? The Taguchi motto is: "Don't just try to stay within specifications, get on target!" Every time Rawlings ships a baseball that is more or less than the perfect size and weight, robust quality is reduced, and the likelihood increases that the ball will not perform in the field as expected. The result of being off target is dissatisfied customers, and dissatisfied customers talk to other customers, which can significantly reduce future sales.

The quality loss, as defined by Taguchi, is all the costs of external failure (including costs of lost customer sales). A simple formulation of Taguchi's loss function looks a bit like Einstein's theory of relativity formula (remember $E = MC^2$?). Using Taguchi's formula, the cost of external failures is computed as follows:

$$L = CD^2$$

where L = total external quality loss due to external failures
  C = internal costs required to fix the problem and get the product back on target
  D = distance from the target measured in standard units

8 G. Taguchi and D. Clausing, "Robust Quality," *Harvard Business Review*, January–February 1990, pp. 65–75.

If your geometry skills are reasonably fresh, you might note that this formula is a quadratic function (because of the D^2 term). If it has been a while since your last geometry class, you just need to note that quality loss increases very quickly as the distance between the product and the target increases. The implication here is that if management decides not to incur the voluntary expenses of reducing variation, it involuntarily incurs several times that amount in the form of warranty costs, lost sales due to customer ill will, and so forth. One important idea behind Taguchi's quality loss function is that it disagrees with the traditional notion of quality control limits. Look back at the SPC chart in Exhibit 9. This chart indicates that there is no loss as long as baseballs weigh between 5.0 and 5.25 ounces. Since the SPC chart is reporting that very few balls being shipped to the major leagues are outside the weight specifications, the data suggest that probably little loss is being incurred. But how much is Rawlings potentially losing in external failure costs, and how much could be saved if Rawlings reduced weight variation in baseballs? This is difficult to know precisely. Remember that Rawlings is trying to manufacture baseballs that weigh exactly 5.12 ounces. Let's assume that it would cost $10,000 in prevention and appraisal costs to reduce average variation at Rawlings by each 0.01 ounce. Therefore, if baseballs varied on average only 0.01 ounce from the target of 5.12 ounces (i.e., from 5.11 to 5.13), then it would require only $10,000 to correct the problem and get the production system exactly on the 5.12 ounce target. According to the Taguchi quality loss function, Rawlings would then save approximately $10,000 in external failure costs by making this reduction. It looks like an even trade-off between costs and cost savings, doesn't it? Remember, though, that Rawlings would also save some internal failure costs as well (waste, scrap, downtime, etc.). Now look at the chart of numbers below. As you can see, it will cost Rawlings more to get the baseball weight on target as the distance between the target weight and the actual weights increases. However, the opportunity loss (i.e., external failure costs) is much larger as the variation (i.e., the distance from target) increases. Hence, the Taguchi quality loss function really emphasizes the importance of reducing variation in order to increase robust quality within products and services.

Cost per 0.01 ounce unit to correct	$10,000	$10,000	$10,000	$10,000	$10,000	$10,000
Average distance from target	×1 unit	×2 units	×3 units	×4 units	×5 units	×6 units
Total cost to correct	$10,000	$20,000	$30,000	$40,000	$50,000	$60,000
Cost per 0.01 ounce unit to correct (C)	$10,000	$10,000	$10,000	$10,000	$10,000	$10,000
Distance squared (D^2)	×1 unit	×4 units	×9 units	×16 units	×25 units	×36 units
Total quality loss (L)	$10,000	$40,000	$90,000	$160,000	$250,000	$360,000

FYI:

In 1989, Genichi Taguchi received the Ministry of International Trade and Industry (MITI) Purple Ribbon Award from the emperor of Japan for his contribution to Japanese industrial standards.

Obviously, Taguchi's quality loss measures are not very precise and objective. He is making general *approximations* about how quality problems affect all companies. Some companies may experience more or less loss due to quality problems than Taguchi suggests. Nevertheless, the importance of the quality loss function is to use the management accounting system to provide a valuable *signal* to managers about the importance of continuously improving the quality of their goods and services. Measuring deviations from specifications has always been the job of engineers. However, by taking those deviations and translating them into costs, the accountant is able to draw a lot of attention to the problem.

Is Quality Free?

Before we finish our discussion on quality, you need to know that there is some disagreement in the profession on how to measure quality costs. In fact, you may have even noticed a discrepancy in the section you just read. Remember that in a previous section in this chapter we discussed the importance of identifying the proper level of quality in the organization by offsetting prevention and appraisal costs against internal and external failure costs in order to minimize total costs of quality (COQ). It appears, therefore, that COQ trade-offs will typically justify a level of quality that is less than 100% conformance to all control limits. On the other hand, our discussion in this section of measuring the costs of lost sales using the Taguchi quality loss function seems to indicate that "quality is free!" In other words, when one understands the *full extent* of external failure costs, the minimal quality cost trade-off point is very close to or exceeds 100% conformance. Hence, using the Taguchi quality loss function, companies should spend whatever it takes to have absolute quality and customer satisfaction. Remember that this is the essence of TQM—that quality is emphasized above all else, including costs. Not everyone feels this strongly about TQM. Some managers and accountants disagree with a "field of dreams" approach to managing quality costs (i.e., "if you build *perfect* quality, profits will come"). You should pay attention to this current debate, as there is good logic on both sides. The real test of this concept is in the competitive marketplace. In any event, management accounting systems should be structured to measure COQ, including the cost of lost sales, in order to add competitive value to the organization's TQM efforts.

> **TO SUMMARIZE:** The Taguchi quality loss function attempts to measure external failure costs using a formula where L (quality loss) = C (cost to correct) $\times$ D^2 (distance from target). The quality loss function is not a precise measure of external failure costs, but it provides an approximate signal of the significant opportunity costs organizations experience when less-than-perfect goods and services are provided to customers. Using the quality loss function, accountants can provide important insight to help their companies better compete in the marketplace. Some TQM advocates suggest that organizations should strive for 100% quality conformance. These individuals defend this position by suggesting that most organizations underestimate failure costs as a product or service process moves away from 100% quality conformance. Nevertheless, there is currently an active debate on the issue of whether perfect quality is too costly to achieve.

review of learning objectives

Explain the fundamentals of activity-based costing (ABC) and activity-based management (ABM). Unit-based costing (UBC) systems generally allocate all manufacturing overhead costs based on some measure related to the number of products being produced or the amount of service being provided in the organization (e.g., direct labor hours). In settings with little diversity in the types of products or services offered to customers, UBC may be an appropriate tool. On the other hand, activity-based costing (ABC) recognizes that activities are the causes of costs. Activities can be categorized across four levels: unit-level activities, batch-level activities, product line activities, and facility support activities. Generally, variable overhead such as machine maintenance or energy costs to run production equipment is a function of the number of units produced. Setup costs, materials purchase orders, and route planning are examples of costs traditionally considered fixed that actually are variable in relation to the number of batch runs within the organization. Overhead costs that are a function of product line activities are generally related to engineering, supervision, and warehousing. Once activity cost pools have been created, costs of unit-level, batch-level, and product line activities can be assigned to

products. If costs of batch-level and product line activities are allocated using UBC, then some products may be inappropriately assigned costs that actually belong to another product. This particular cost distortion is referred to as product cost cross-subsidization.

Costs of facility support activities (e.g., property taxes, plant security, landscaping, accounting, and executive administration) cannot be sensibly connected to any particular product line. These costs (also known as common costs) should *not* be allocated to individual product lines. Otherwise, product costs are distorted, which can lead to a series of management decisions called a death spiral. Managers inadvertently involved in a death spiral will make a decision to drop a product or service line based on UBC data that erroneously suggest that these products or services are unprofitable.

The point of ABC is to appropriately *assign* costs to products. However, ABC does not really provide useful information for managing activities. To *manage* costs of activities, a set of activity cost drivers that provides the greatest influence on the activity cost pool is identified. To manage activity performance, a set of quality- and time-based measures is also created and related to each critical activity in the organization. The process of managing activities using cost drivers and performance measures is called activity-based management (ABM). ABC and ABM combine to form the following model of activities:

Activity Cost Drivers

↓

Costs → **Activities** → Products

↑

Performance Measures

2 **Describe total quality management (TQM) and costs of quality (COQ).** Total quality management (TQM) is a philosophy in which (1) product and process quality is emphasized over profits and (2) quality must be measured in order to be realized. Using SPC (statistical process control), W. Edward Deming became one of the pioneers of TQM in both Japan and America. SPC establishes control limits. When the variation in the product or service exceeds the control limits established by the firm, then managers begin work to increase the quality of the production process. Joseph M. Juran expanded the process of SPC in order to manage four specific types of costs of quality (COQ). Prevention and appraisal costs are viewed as investments in the process of keeping products and services within established control limits. When the production process starts creating variation outside the control limits, internal failure costs (such as scrap and employee downtime) and external failure costs (such as handling complaints and product recalls) occur. If increasing preven-

tion and appraisal costs offset decreasing failure costs, then management accountants should help companies understand how to minimize total quality costs. Identifying quality costs can be a challenge, however, because these costs are generally intermingled across both product and period costs within most organizations' accounting systems. Costs of lost sales due to customer dissatisfaction are important opportunity costs, yet they are particularly difficult to measure.

3 **Compute the opportunity cost of lost sales.** The Taguchi quality loss function provides a means of approximately measuring the impact of *all* external failure costs on the company's costs—including the opportunity costs of lost sales due to customer dissatisfaction. The Taguchi quality loss function measures these costs using a formula where L (quality loss) = C (cost to correct) $\times$ D^2 (distance from target). Using this formula, accountants can provide an important signal of the significant opportunity costs organizations experience when less-than-perfect goods and services are provided to customers. Currently, in light of the likely size of cost of external failure, there is some debate on whether prevention and appraisal costs can ever increase enough to justify having less-than-perfect conformance to control limits (i.e., perfect quality).

k ey terms & concepts

r eview problem

ABC versus Conventional Product Costing

Willett Company makes two types of products: Product A and Product B. The company's management accountants accumulated the following production cost information for 2006:

	Product A	Product B	Total
Production volume (units)	1,000	500	
Number of engineering changes per			
product line	4	8	
Total cost of engineering changes			$12,000
Direct labor hours per unit	3	2	
Direct materials cost per unit	$5	$7	
Direct labor cost per hour	$6	$12	

Required:

Assume Product A sells for $42 each and Product B sells for $50 each. Assume also that engineering changes are the only manufacturing overhead cost Willett Company incurs. If all products are sold, what is the gross margin of each product assuming the following:

1. Engineering change costs are allocated on the basis of direct labor hours.
2. Engineering change costs are allocated on the basis of the number of engineering changes made.

Solution

1. Allocation on the Basis of Direct Labor Hours

	Product A (1,000 units)	Product B (500 units)
Sales	$42,000 (1,000 × $42)	$25,000 (500 × $50)
Cost of goods sold:		
Direct materials	$ 5,000 (1,000 × $5)	$ 3,500 (500 × $7)
Direct labor	18,000 (1,000 × 3 hrs. × $6)	12,000 (500 × 2 hrs. × $12)
Manufacturing overhead . .	9,000 (1,000 × 3 hrs. × $3*)	3,000 (500 × 2 hrs. × $3*)
Total cost of goods sold . . .	$32,000	$18,500
Gross margin	$10,000	$ 6,500

*Overhead allocation per direct labor hour:

$$\frac{\$12,000 \text{ total costs}}{4,000 \text{ total direct labor hours}} = \$3 \text{ per direct labor hour}$$

Product A (1,000 × 3 hrs.) = 3,000
Product B   (500 × 2 hrs.) = 1,000
    Total   4,000 direct labor hours

2. Allocation on the Basis of Engineering Changes

Sales	$42,000	$25,000
Cost of goods sold:		
Direct materials	$ 5,000	$ 3,500
Direct labor	18,000	12,000
Manufacturing overhead	4,000*	8,000*
Total cost of goods sold	$27,000	$23,500
Gross margin	$15,000	$ 1,500

*Overhead allocation per engineering change:

Cost per change: $\frac{\$12,000}{12} = \$1,000$ per change

Overhead allocations per product:
    Product A: 4 changes × $1,000 per change = $ 4,000
    Product B: 8 changes × $1,000 per change =   8,000
        Total $12,000

d iscussion questions

1. What is the lowest price that a company should charge its customers?
2. What is the difference between a product cost and a period cost?
3. Traditionally, what basis has been used to allocate manufacturing overhead costs to products?
4. What type of incorrect decision can be made if a cost accounting system allows cross-subsidization of product costs?
5. "Given enough time, every cost is fixed." Do you agree or disagree? Explain.
6. In what context does a unit-based costing (UBC) system cause problems?
7. Under a Hierarchical Product Cost Model, what are the four classifications of production costs?
8. Give three examples of batch-level activities.
9. In general, which type of fast-food outlet would have higher overhead costs: an outlet selling hamburgers, pizza, and chicken or an outlet selling only hamburgers? Explain.
10. Give three examples of facility support costs.
11. How can the allocation of common costs potentially cause a death spiral?

12. ABC (activity-based costing) uses activity allocation rates in product costing. How are activity cost drivers used in ABM (activity-based management)?
13. In what way do Edward Deming's ideas of total quality management (TQM) change Andrew Carnegie's slogan, "Watch the costs and the profits will take care of themselves"?
14. Briefly describe the four types of costs in costs of quality (COQ).

15. Why are external failure costs generally the highest of the costs of quality (COQ)?
16. Describe the concept of robust quality.
17. According to the Taguchi quality loss function, what happens to the total loss due to external failure as a product's quality gets further from target specifications?

p ractice exercises

Practice 8-1

Product Costing Terminology
Which one of the following statements is *false*?

a. Conversion costs include direct labor and manufacturing overhead costs.
b. Prime costs include direct materials and direct labor.
c. Period costs are all costs other than the product costs.
d. The production supervisor's salary is included in direct labor costs.
e. Product costs include direct labor, direct material, and manufacturing overhead.

Practice 8-2

Overhead Allocation Problem in the SeatJoy Example
Which one of the following statements is *true* with respect to the SeatJoy example described in the text of this chapter?

a. The original process costing system ignored the impact of spoiled goods on the calculation of equivalent units.
b. The original materials warehouse requisition system did include adequate controls to ensure separation of duties.
c. The original manufacturing overhead application system based on direct labor hours did not provide accurate insight on cost behavior.
d. The original prime cost application system overstated cost of goods sold during times of inflation.

Practice 8-3

Overhead Allocation Problems

Which one of the following statements is *false*?

a. Common manufacturing costs should *not* be allocated over each division.
b. Common manufacturing costs include direct labor and direct materials.
c. Cross-subsidization results from incorrect application of manufacturing overhead costs.
d. Cross-subsidization effects are addressed by ABC accounting systems.

Practice 8-4

Characteristics of Traditional Unit-Based Costing

Which one of the following statements is *false* with respect to traditional unit-based costing?

a. Unit-based costing is a good method of cost allocation in the right context.
b. Unit-based costing is widely used by many companies.
c. Unit-based costing essentially allocates overhead costs based on the number of units produced.
d. Unit-based costing usually works well in a company with multiple products and services.

Practice 8-5

Difference between Unit-Based Costing and Activity-Based Costing

Which one of the following statements best summarizes the difference between unit-based costing (UBC) and activity-based costing (ABC)?

a. With UBC, costs are first allocated to departments; with ABC, costs are first allocated to activities.
b. With UBC, costs are first allocated to activities; with ABC, costs are first allocated to departments.
c. With UBC, costs are first allocated to departments; with ABC, costs are first allocated to products.
d. With UBC, costs are first allocated to products; with ABC, costs are first allocated to departments.

Practice 8-6

ABC Hierarchical Product Cost Model

Which one of the following is *not* one of the types of activities in the Hierarchical Product Cost Model?

a. Facility support activities
b. Batch-level activities
c. Unit-level activities
d. Product line activities
e. Manufacturing application activities

Practice 8-7

Unit-Based Costing

The company expects to produce 500,000 units of its only product. Using the unit-based costing approach and the following manufacturing overhead costs for the year, compute the manufacturing overhead allocation rate.

Electricity	$ 48,000
Depreciation	140,000
Engineering	60,000
Quality testing	173,000
Property tax	53,000
Supervisors' salaries	210,000
Maintenance	110,000

Practice 8-8

Unit-Level Activities

The company has determined that $1,029,600 of its total manufacturing overhead costs related to unit-level activities such as electricity costs for running the manufacturing equipment and equipment maintenance costs. The company allocates these costs over the individual units of production based on machine hours. Using the following expected machine hours for the company's three divisions that all make the same product, (1) determine the manufacturing overhead rate per machine hour and (2) allocate the manufacturing overhead to each division.

Division A . . . .   20,000 hours
Division B   40,000
Division C   50,000

Practice 8-9

Batch-Level Activities

Which one of the following would *not* be an example of a batch activity for a manufacturing firm?

a.   Purchase orders
b.   Production manager's salary
c.   Number of setups
d.   Number of inspections

Practice 8-10

Product Line Activities

Which one of the following is *not* an example of a product line activity?

a.   Orders for nonstocked items
b.   Costs related to specialized materials warehouses
c.   Production process design activities
d.   Training activities for specific types of consulting services

Practice 8-11

Facility Support Activities

Which one of the following is *not* an example of a facility support activity?

a.   Manufacturing vice president's salary
b.   Property taxes
c.   Accounting
d.   Production supervisor's salary
e.   Plant security

Practice 8-12

Resolving Cost Distortions

Which one of the following statements is *false*?

a.   Cross-subsidization can cause a manager to evaluate products incorrectly.
b.   Cross-subsidization is a common problem caused by activity-based costing.
c.   The death spiral begins when a company cuts products that do not create the costs in question.
d.   Allocating common costs can begin the death spiral.

Practice 8-13

Overhead Costs and Dropping a Product Line

The company manufactures three products. Profit computations for these three products for the most recent year are as follows:

	Product X	Product Y	Product Z	Total
Sales	$ 300,000	$ 700,000	$ 800,000	$ 1,800,000
Direct materials	(70,000)	(150,000)	(200,000)	(420,000)
Direct labor	(50,000)	(200,000)	(250,000)	(500,000)
Manufacturing overhead	(100,000)	(400,000)	(500,000)	(1,000,000)
Profit	$ 80,000	$ (50,000)	$(150,000)	$ (120,000)

(continued)

The company traditionally allocates manufacturing overhead based on the level of direct labor cost—$2 of manufacturing overhead are allocated for each $1 of direct labor cost. However, of the company's $1,000,000 in manufacturing overhead costs, $700,000 is directly related to the number of product batches produced during the year. The number of batches of the three products for the year was as follows: Product X, 20 batches; Product Y, 30 batches; Product Z, 50 batches. The remaining $300,000 in overhead is for facility support (property taxes, security costs, general administration, and so forth).

As you can see, the total company loss is $120,000. In an effort to reduce or eliminate this loss, the company has decided to drop Product Z. What would total company profit (or loss) have been in the most recent year if Product Z had been dropped at the beginning of the year?

Practice 8-14

Unit-Level, Batch-Level, Product Line, and Facility Support Costs

The company has determined that its total manufacturing overhead cost of $900,000 is a mixture of unit-level, batch-level, product line, and facility support costs. The company has assembled the following information concerning the manufacturing overhead costs, the annual number of units produced, production batches, and number of product lines in each division.

	Total Overhead Costs	Division A	Division B
Unit-level overhead	$210,000	7,500 units	13,500 units
Batch-level overhead	280,000	50 batches	90 batches
Product line overhead	210,000	10 lines	18 lines
Facility support overhead	200,000	—	—
Total	$900,000		

Compute how much total overhead cost would remain if Division A were eliminated.

Practice 8-15

Activity-Based Management

Which one of the following is a correct flow of information in activity-based management?

a. Activities → Costs → Products
b. Activity Cost Drivers → Performance Measures → Activities
c. Activity Cost Drivers → Activities → Performance Measures
d. Activity Cost Drivers → Activities → Performance Measures
e. Products → Activities → Costs

Practice 8-16

Total Quality Management

Which one of the following statements is *false*?

a. Total quality management is simply a general endorsement of quality in a company.
b. W. Edward Deming led the quality revolution in Japan during the 1950s.
c. Total quality management shifted some of the companies' focus from costs to quality.
d. Statistical process control can help management know whether a process has serious problems.

Practice 8-17

Costs of Quality

Which one of the following is *not* a type of costs of quality?

a. Appraisal costs
b. Adaptive costs
c. Internal failure costs
d. Prevention costs
e. External failure costs

Practice 8-18

Taguchi's Quality Loss Function
The cost required to fix a product defect and get that product on target would cost the company $500. Currently, the product is three standard units from the target specifications. Using Taguchi's quality loss function, compute the total quality loss due to external failures.

exercises

Exercise 8-1

Product Costing Review
Mad Dog Enterprises manufactures computer game control devices such as joysticks and steering wheels. Following is a list of the costs incurred by Mad Dog in 2006:

Wages paid to assembly workers	$100,000
Cost of plastic used in making devices	25,000
Insurance on factory building	12,000
Salary of factory supervisor	57,000
Interest on money borrowed to finance operations	34,000
Wages paid to factory maintenance workers	61,000
Cost of computer/controller boards installed in devices	38,000
Advertising costs	127,000
Cost of electricity used in factory	46,000

Compute the total cost for each of the following categories:

1. Direct materials
2. Direct labor
3. Manufacturing overhead
4. Period costs

Exercise 8-2

Importance of Manufacturing Overhead Allocation
The percentages of product costs comprised by direct materials, direct labor, and manufacturing overhead for three companies are as follows:

	Company A	Company B	Company C
Direct materials	7%	21%	42%
Direct labor	13	42	49
Manufacturing overhead	80	37	9
	100%	100%	100%

Based on this information, which of these three companies would probably improve its product costing accuracy most by converting to activity-based costing (ABC)? Explain your answer.

Exercise 8-3

Product Cost Hierarchy
For the following list of costs, indicate by the appropriate letter which category of activities each cost applies to: unit level (U), batch level (B), product line (P), or facility support (F):

(continued)

a. Machine fine-tuning adjustment cost (required after the production of each unit)
b. Salary of vice president of finance
c. Machine inspection cost (required after the completion of each day's production)
d. Cost of the external audit firm
e. Direct labor
f. Product testing cost (performed at the start of each day's production)
g. Direct materials
h. Factory security cost
i. Machine straight-line depreciation cost (Generally, machines are dedicated to producing a particular type of product.)
j. Warehousing cost (Each type of product has its own warehouse.)
k. Employee training cost (Training is generally specific to different types of products.)

Exercise 8-4

Spreadsheet

Identifying Cross-Subsidization

Cottrell Company manufactures three products. Gross margin computations for these three products for 2006 are given below.

	Product A	**Product B**	**Product C**
Sales	$ 300,000	$ 500,000	$ 600,000
Direct materials	(50,000)	(250,000)	(200,000)
Direct labor	(150,000)	(50,000)	(100,000)
Manufacturing overhead*	(225,000)	(75,000)	(150,000)
Gross margin	$(125,000)	$ 125,000	$ 150,000

*Manufacturing overhead is allocated to production based on the amount of direct labor cost.

Cottrell has reexamined the factors that cause its manufacturing overhead costs and has discovered that the annual amount of manufacturing overhead is more closely related to the number of product batches produced during the year than it is to direct labor costs. The number of batches of the three products for 2006 was as follows: Product A, 10 batches; Product B, 60 batches; Product C, 30 batches.

1. Prepare gross margin calculations for Cottrell's three products assuming that manufacturing overhead is allocated based on the number of batches.
2. Under the direct labor cost method of manufacturing overhead allocation, one of Cottrell's products received a cross-subsidization from the others. Which product received the subsidization, and what was the amount of the subsidization?

Exercise 8-5

Identifying Cross-Subsidization

Halsey, Inc. manufactures two types of baby car seats: standard and deluxe. Information for the year 2006 has been given as follows.

	Standard	**Deluxe**
Sales price	$50	$80
Units produced and sold	23,400	9,750
Direct materials cost	$195,000	$130,000
Direct labor cost per hour	$10	$10
Direct labor hours	35,100	42,900
Purchase orders	100	25

Manufacturing overhead for the year totals $650,000. Halsey allocates manufacturing overhead by direct labor hour.

1. Prepare gross margin calculations for each product line using direct labor hours as an allocation base.
2. Management has determined that a more correct method of allocating manufacturing overhead is by the number of purchase orders. Prepare new gross margin calculations for management using purchase orders as the allocation base.
3. Assuming that allocating manufacturing overhead by purchase orders is more correct, did one of the product lines receive a cross-subsidization? If so, how much was the cross-subsidization?

Exercise 8-6

Spreadsheet

Allocating Batch-Level and Product Line Manufacturing Overhead Costs

Giles Company has two divisions. Gross margin computations for these two divisions for 2006 are as follows:

	Standard Products	Custom Products
Sales	$1,200,000	$1,800,000
Direct materials	(200,000)	(300,000)
Direct labor	(600,000)	(600,000)
Manufacturing overhead*	(500,000)	(500,000)
Gross margin	$ (100,000)	$ 400,000

*Manufacturing overhead is allocated to production based on the amount of direct labor cost.

Giles has determined that its total manufacturing overhead cost of $1,000,000 is a mixture of batch-level costs and product line costs. Giles has assembled the following information concerning the manufacturing overhead costs, the annual number of production batches in each division, and the number of product lines in each division:

	Total Mfg. Overhead Costs	Standard Products	Custom Products
Batch-level manufacturing overhead	$ 600,000	15 batches	60 batches
Product line manufacturing overhead	400,000	10 lines	30 lines
	$1,000,000		

1. Prepare gross margin calculations for Giles' two divisions assuming that manufacturing overhead is allocated based on the number of batches and number of product lines.
2. Under the direct labor cost method of manufacturing overhead allocation, which division received a cross-subsidization, and what was the amount of the cross-subsidization?

Exercise 8-7

Allocating Batch-Level and Product Line Manufacturing Overhead Costs

Sundance Skis Company is preparing its end-of-year gross margin computations. Sundance Skis manufactures three types of products: skis, snowboards, and snow skates. The following information, as of the end of the year, is available for these products.

(continued)

	Skis	Snowboards	Snow Skates
Total sales revenue	$1,250,000	$1,500,000	$750,000
Units produced	4,500	3,750	6,750
Direct materials	$(625,000)	$(500,000)	$(125,000)
Direct labor	$(125,000)	$(250,000)	$(375,000)
Number of setups	9	18	3
Number of product styles	5	7	3

Total manufacturing overhead is $1,125,000, with $506,250 related to batch-level activities and $618,750 related to product line activities.

1. In the past, Sundance Skis has allocated manufacturing overhead based on the number of units produced. Prepare gross margin calculations for Sundance Skis' three divisions allocating manufacturing overhead according to the number of units produced.
2. After investigation, management at Sundance Skis determined that a more accurate allocation of manufacturing overhead would be to assign these costs using batch-level and product line activities. Prepare gross margin calculations for Sundance Skis' three divisions by assigning manufacturing overhead using batch-level and product line activities. Assume that the number of setups is the activity allocation basis for assigning costs of batch-level activities and that the number of product styles is the allocation base for assigning costs of product line activities.

Exercise 8-8

Common Costs and the Death Spiral

Blaine Avenue Company manufactures three products. Gross margin computations for these three products for 2006 are as follows:

	Product X	Product Y	Product Z
Sales	$800,000	$ 700,000	$ 600,000
Direct materials	(50,000)	(150,000)	(200,000)
Direct labor	(50,000)	(200,000)	(250,000)
Manufacturing overhead*	(80,000)	(320,000)	(400,000)
Gross margin	$620,000	$ 30,000	$(250,000)

*Manufacturing overhead is allocated to production based on the amount of direct labor cost.

Blaine Avenue has reexamined the activities that relate to its manufacturing overhead costs and has discovered that $500,000 of the annual amount of manufacturing overhead is directly related to the number of product batches produced during the year. The number of batches of the three products for 2006 was as follows: Product X, 100 batches; Product Y, 100 batches; Product Z, 50 batches. The remaining $300,000 in overhead is for facility support (property taxes, security costs, general administration, etc.) and does not vary at all with the level of activity.

1. Prepare gross margin calculations for Blaine Avenue's three products assuming that manufacturing overhead is allocated based on the number of batches. Also, show a "total" column. Facility support costs are not to be allocated to any of the products, but are to be subtracted in the "total" column in the computation of total company operating profit.
2. Using the gross margin numbers prepared under the direct labor cost method of manufacturing overhead allocation, Blaine Avenue's board of directors has tentatively decided to discontinue the Z product line. Assume that this was done at the beginning of 2006. What would have happened to total company operating profit for the year? Explain.

Exercise 8-9

Common Costs and the Death Spiral

Wilken Sandwich Shop maintains three separate menus for breakfast, lunch, and dinner. Gross margin computations for the three menu lines for 2006 are as follows:

	Breakfast	Lunch	Dinner
Sales	$ 880,000	$1,015,000	$ 720,000
Direct materials	(260,000)	(217,500)	(175,000)
Direct labor	(325,000)	(290,000)	(155,000)
Overhead*	(528,000)	(264,000)	(264,000)
Gross margin	$(233,000)	$ 243,500	$ 126,000

*Overhead is allocated to the menu lines based on the number of customers served each day. In 2006, 4,000 breakfast customers, 2,000 lunch customers, and 2,000 dinner customers were served.

Management at Wilken has tentatively decided to stop serving breakfast in its restaurants because of poor financial performance. Before doing so, they have reexamined the costs of all three menu lines in order to verify that they are correct. Management determined that direct materials and direct labor costs are correct. However, using an activity-based costing approach, they discovered that $408,000 of overhead costs are related to facility support activities and the rest of the overhead ($648,000) is related to the kitchen setup activities required to prepare the menu line each day (a batch-level activity). They determined that a good cost allocation base for batch-level kitchen activities is number of setups per business day. Wilken was open for business 360 days in 2006. The number of daily setup activities for each menu line is as follows:

Breakfast	10
Lunch	15
Dinner	5

1. Since management has tentatively decided to stop serving breakfast, they have asked to see gross margin calculations for the lunch and dinner menus. Assuming the breakfast menu was dropped at the beginning of 2006, prepare gross margin calculations for the lunch and dinner menu lines assuming overhead is allocated based on the number of customers served. Be sure to show a "total" column.
2. Prepare gross margin calculations for Wilken's three menu lines assuming that overhead is assigned using activity-based costing. Facility support costs are not to be allocated to any of the menu lines, but are to be subtracted in the "total" column in the computation of total company operating profit.
3. Using the gross margin numbers prepared in parts (1) and (2), what would have happened to total company operating profit for the year 2006 if Wilken would have dropped its breakfast menu at the beginning of the year? Explain.

Exercise 8-10

Costs of Quality

Some of the costs in the list below are costs of quality. For each cost, indicate by the appropriate letter what type of cost it is: prevention cost (P), appraisal cost (A), internal failure cost (I), external failure cost (E), or not a cost of quality (N/A).

a. Cost of raw materials used in discarded, defective products
b. Salary of the president of the company
c. Cost to purchase product testing equipment
d. Lawsuit costs stemming from the sale of defective products
e. Cost to repair defective products before shipment

(continued)

f. Employee quality training costs
g. Employee downtime caused by production halts to repair defective products
h. Cost of sampling raw materials to ensure quality
i. Customer warranty costs
j. Property taxes
k. Cost of lost reputation (i.e., lost sales)
l. Cost to help suppliers improve their product shipping procedures
m. Interest cost on short-term loans
n. Production process design costs

Exercise 8-11

Costs of Quality

Sara's Stylish Suppers prepares food for wholesale to gourmet restaurants. Quality is very important to consumers of gourmet food. Following is a list of costs that Sara incurred during 2006:

Wages paid during downtime to fix machinery	$ 50,000
Cost of spoiled raw materials (cheese, meat, etc.)	85,000
Training cost for new food handlers	12,000
Wages paid to food samplers	15,000
Lawsuits for severe food poisoning	134,000
Cost of refrigerator used to keep food fresh	75,000
Wages paid to quality inspectors	21,000
Wages paid to chefs who create new gourmet dishes	97,000
Wages paid for redoing poor quality food (found before delivery)	46,000

In addition, Sara's accountants estimated approximately $100,000 in lost sales due to restaurant managers who are unhappy with Sara's products and service.

Compute the total cost for each of the following categories:

1. Prevention costs
2. Appraisal costs
3. Internal failure costs
4. External failure costs

Exercise 8-12

Optimal Level of Costs of Quality

Beki Browne is planning to open her own homebuilding company. Beki is trying to decide whether to provide low-quality homes, average-quality homes, or high-quality homes. Beki has analyzed the costs of quality related to building homes and has developed the following analysis of the costs of quality:

*   *Prevention costs:* The best way to ensure the quality of a home is to hire good subcontractors and use quality materials. Of course, high-quality subcontractors and materials cost more.
*   *Appraisal costs:* To improve the quality of the homes, Beki can hire independent verifiers to determine whether the home is adequately livable and "up to code."
*   *Internal failure costs:* Sometimes a defect in the home is found just before the home is to be sold. In such a case, Beki must require the subcontractors to spend extra time fixing the home.
*   *External failure costs:* If a home containing lots of defects is sold, the bad reputation created will hurt potential future sales. To counteract this effect, Beki must spend more on advertising.

Beki has gathered the following numerical information about the costs of quality in relation to building homes:

	Low Quality	Average Quality	High Quality
Prevention costs:			
Hours spent building home	1,400 hours	1,600 hours	1,800 hours
Subcontractor salary rate	$35/hour	$45/hour	$55/hour
Materials cost per home	$50,000	$60,000	$70,000
Appraisal costs:			
Verifier hours spent on home	4 hours	10 hours	20 hours
Verifier salary rate	$20/hour	$20/hour	$20/hour
Internal failure costs:			
Hours spent fixing home	350 hours	175 hours	15 hours
Subcontractor salary rate	$35/hour	$45/hour	$55/hour
Materials cost for repairs	$10,000	$7,000	$3,000
External failure costs:			
Cost of advertising	$40,000	$10,000	$2,000

Which type of home—low-, average-, or high-quality—should Beki build in order to minimize her total costs of quality? Show your calculations.

Exercise 8-13

Spreadsheet

Taguchi Quality Loss Function

Cooley Lane Company manufactures computer disk drives. Occasionally, a defective disk drive (one that spins at the wrong revolutions per minute) is shipped to a customer. Cooley Lane's policy is to fix the drive for free when it is returned by a complaining customer. Cooley Lane has a standardized statistical defect measure whereby each defective drive is given a score of 0 through 5 to indicate how bad it is, with 5 being the worst. A perfect drive receives a score of 0. The direct material and direct labor cost to fix a defective drive is only $25.

The manager in charge of product quality has recently been reading about the Taguchi quality loss function, and she thinks that Cooley Lane is underestimating the external failure costs associated with a defective disk drive. She thinks that Cooley Lane should consider increasing the amount it spends on prevention and appraisal in order to reduce the number of defective drives returned by customers. In the past month, 15 drives have been returned by customers. The drives had the following standardized defect scores:

Standardized Defect Score	Number of Defective Drives
1	2
2	1
3	1
4	4
5	7

Using the Taguchi quality loss function, estimate the dollar value of the quality loss associated with the external failure of these defective drives.

Exercise 8-14

Taguchi Quality Loss Function

Tenille's Toyshack is an online toy store. Customers can log on to the Internet to see Tenille's selection of toys and to make purchases. Tenille's shipping policy is that it will ship any order within 24 hours after the purchase is made. After a purchase has been made, Tenille prepares the purchase order and sends an email notification to all customers as soon as the purchase has been shipped. Tenille provides a $20 store credit if the purchase is not shipped within 24 hours after purchase. Following is information on the purchases that were not shipped within 24 hours of being purchased during the past quarter, listed in order of the number of days the order was actually late.

Number of Purchases Not Shipped in 24 Hours	Number of Days Late
4	6
8	5
15	4
9	3
22	2
31	1
89	

Using the above information and the Taguchi quality loss function, estimate the dollar value of the quality loss associated with the external failure of Tenille's shipping methods.

p roblems

Problem 8-1

Identifying Cross-Subsidization

Rockwell Company has three operating divisions. Gross margin computations for these three divisions for 2006 are given below.

	Division M	Division N	Division O
Sales	$ 600,000	$ 400,000	$ 300,000
Direct materials	(100,000)	(200,000)	(80,000)
Direct labor	(300,000)	(60,000)	(140,000)
Manufacturing overhead*	(210,000)	(42,000)	(98,000)
Gross margin	$ (10,000)	$ 98,000	$ (18,000)

*Manufacturing overhead is allocated to production based on the amount of direct labor cost.

Rockwell has determined that its total manufacturing overhead cost of $350,000 is a mixture of batch-level costs and product line costs. Rockwell has assembled the following information concerning the overhead costs, the annual number of production batches in each division, and the number of product lines in each division:

	Total Mfg. Overhead Costs	Division M	Division N	Division O
Batch-level overhead	$200,000	20 batches	80 batches	100 batches
Product line overhead	150,000	10 lines	30 lines	40 lines
	$350,000			

Required:

1. Prepare gross margin calculations for Rockwell's three divisions assuming that manufacturing overhead is allocated based on the number of batches and the number of product lines.
2. Under the direct labor cost method of manufacturing overhead allocation, one or more of Rockwell's divisions received a cross-subsidization from one or more of the others. Which division(s) received subsidizations, and what was the amount of the subsidizations?
3. After preparing the gross margin calculations in part (1), what advice do you have for Rockwell concerning whether it should shut down any of its three divisions? Is this the same advice that would come from looking at the original gross margin calculations using manufacturing overhead allocated according to direct labor cost? Why is there a difference?

Problem 8-2

Allocating Unit-Level, Batch-Level, and Product Line Manufacturing Overhead Costs

Solar Salt Company has two divisions. Gross margin computations for these two divisions for 2006 are given below.

	Agricultural Products	Retail Products
Sales	$1,600,000	$ 900,000
Direct materials	(100,000)	(50,000)
Direct labor	(900,000)	(500,000)
Manufacturing overhead*	(450,000)	(250,000)
Gross margin	$ 150,000	$ 100,000

*Manufacturing overhead is allocated to production based on the amount of direct labor cost.

Solar Salt has determined that its total manufacturing overhead cost of $700,000 is a mixture of unit-level costs, batch-level costs, and product line costs. Solar Salt has assembled the following information concerning the manufacturing overhead costs, the annual number of units produced, production batches, and number of product lines in each division:

	Total Mfg. Overhead Costs	Agricultural Products	Retail Products
Unit-level overhead	$210,000	13,500 units	7,500 units
Batch-level overhead	280,000	90 batches	50 batches
Product line overhead	210,000	18 lines	10 lines
	$700,000		

(continued)

Required:

1. Prepare gross margin calculations for Solar Salt's two divisions assuming that manufacturing overhead is allocated based on the number of units, number of batches, and number of product lines.
2. Comment on the comparison between the original overhead allocation done using direct labor cost and the manufacturing overhead allocation done in part (1).
3. Repeat part (1), assuming the following information concerning the number of units, batches, and product lines in each division.

	Total Mfg. Overhead Costs	Agricultural Products	Retail Products
Unit-level overhead	$210,000	13,500 units	7,500 units
Batch-level overhead	280,000	50 batches	90 batches
Product line overhead	210,000	10 lines	18 lines
	$700,000		

Problem 8-3

Spreadsheet

Identifying and Using Volume-Based and Activity-Based Cost Allocation Rates

Rane Company produces electronic fish finders. It makes two different fish finders: the standard model, which is produced in bulk and sells for $150, and the deluxe model, which comes in various configurations and sells for $300. Rane's engineering and design overhead cost for 2006 is $60,000. The following information relates to production in 2006:

Number of different machine setups needed for a standard model production run	4
Number of different machine setups needed for a deluxe model production run	11
Number of standard fish finders produced	22,000
Number of deluxe fish finders produced	8,000
Number of engineering design changes needed on the standard model	6
Number of engineering design changes needed on the deluxe model	2
Average batch size per production run for standard model	400
Average batch size per production run for deluxe model	200

Required:

1. Determine the engineering and design costs to be assigned to standard and deluxe fish finders using the following allocation methods:
   a. Number of units produced
   b. Number of setups required
   c. Number of engineering design changes needed
2. Which allocation method do you believe is more equitable?

Problem 8-4

Common Costs and the Death Spiral

Ashlyn Company manufactures three products. Gross margin computations for these three products for 2006 are as follows:

	Widgets	Gidgets	Zidgets
Sales	$ 600,000	$ 525,000	$ 450,000
Direct materials	(112,500)	(37,500)	(150,000)
Direct labor	(37,500)	(150,000)	(187,500)
Manufacturing overhead*	(60,000)	(240,000)	(300,000)
Gross margin	$ 390,000	$ 97,500	$(187,500)

*Manufacturing overhead is allocated to production based on the amount of direct labor cost.

Ashlyn has reexamined the factors that cause its manufacturing overhead costs and has discovered that $225,000 of the annual amount of manufacturing overhead is directly related to the number of product batches produced during the year. The number of batches of the three products for 2006 was as follows: Widgets, 225 batches; Gidgets, 150 batches; Zidgets, 75 batches. The remaining $375,000 in manufacturing overhead is for facility support (property taxes, security costs, general administration, etc.) and does not vary at all with levels of manufacturing activity in the company.

Required:
1. Assume that the Zidget product was eliminated at the start of the year. Estimate what the gross margin for the remaining two products would have been. Use the direct labor cost method of overhead allocation.
2. Now, assume that both the Gidget and Zidget products were eliminated at the start of the year. Estimate what the gross margin for the remaining product, Widgets, would have been. (Note that no manufacturing overhead allocation computation is needed because there is only one product.)
3. In light of your answers in parts (1) and (2), what problems can arise when facility support manufacturing overhead costs are allocated?
4. Prepare gross margin calculations for Ashlyn's three products assuming that manufacturing overhead is allocated based on the number of batches. Also, show a "total" column. Facility support costs are not to be allocated to any of the products, but are to be subtracted in the "total" column in the computation of total company operating profit.

Problem 8-5

Manufacturing Overhead Allocation Using Activity-Based Costing
The following information is given for Greenbaum Manufacturing Company:

	Product A	Product B	Product C	Product D
Units produced	3,000	3,450	2,875	2,400
Direct materials cost	$135,000	$169,050	$149,500	$103,200
Direct labor cost	$75,000	$124,200	$117,875	$93,600

Manufacturing Overhead	Mfg. Overhead Costs	Relevant Activities
Engineering	$209,950	Engineering changes
Quality control	129,500	Number of setups
Maintenance	41,065	Maintenance hours worked in each area of production
Manufacturing support	93,800	Production volume (units produced)

(continued)

Activities	Product A	Product B	Product C	Product D
Engineering changes	300	150	275	125
Number of setups	12	5	9	11
Maintenance hours worked in each area of production . . .	45	49	56	41
Production volume	3,000	3,450	2,875	2,400

Required:
1. Determine the ABC allocation rate for each activity (i.e., each manufacturing overhead cost pool).
2. Determine the manufacturing overhead cost for each product.
3. If Products A, B, C, and D sell for $130, $125, $156, and $166, respectively, determine the gross margin for Greenbaum's four products. Assume all units are sold.

Problem 8-6

Manufacturing Overhead Allocation Using Activity-Based Costing

Rick's Crane Company manufactures three different crane engines with 50 horsepower (hp), 60 horsepower, and 70 horsepower engines, respectively. Relevant information for each engine is provided as follows:

	50 hp Total	50 hp Per Unit	60 hp Total	60 hp Per Unit	70 hp Total	70 hp Per Unit
Units produced	2,500		2,000		1,500	
Direct materials cost	$425,000	$170	$370,000	$185	$360,000	$240
Direct labor cost	$595,000	$238	$510,000	$255	$472,500	$315
Sales price		$450		$540		$630
Purchases per year	44		52		54	
Number of machine setups per year . .	60		68		80	
Engineering change orders per year . .	72		84		100	

Total manufacturing overhead cost pools:

Engineering	$102,400
Quality control	88,400
Purchasing costs	49,200
Machine maintenance costs	81,000
Total costs	$321,000

Required:
1. Determine the gross margin for each product allocating manufacturing overhead costs on the basis of production volume (units produced).
2. Identify appropriate allocation bases for each of the four pools of manufacturing overhead costs.
3. Determine the ABC allocation rates for each of the four cost pools suggested in part (2).
4. Using the allocation bases suggested in part (2), determine manufacturing overhead costs per product.
5. a. Determine the gross margin per product using the manufacturing overhead costs determined in part (4).
   b. **Interpretive Question:** Which of the methods (unit-based costing or activity-based costing) is the better method to allocate the manufacturing overhead costs?

Problem 8-7

Manufacturing Overhead Allocation with Multiple Products

Schmidt Electronics produces two products: CD105 and HD210. Relevant costing information for each product is as follows:

Per Unit	CD105	HD210
Direct materials	$10.50	$17.25
Direct labor	$10.00	$15.00
Direct labor hours per unit	1	2
Total number of machine setups	400	200
Units produced	6,000	7,000

Manufacturing overhead costs and associated ABC allocation bases are as follows:

	Mfg. Overhead Costs	Allocation Bases
Product inspection	$30,000	Units produced
Materials management	48,000	Number of machine setups
Manufacturing support	16,000	Product lines

Required:
1. If manufacturing overhead is allocated on the basis of direct labor hours, compute the cost per unit for CD105 and HD210.
2. Determine the allocation rate per activity for each ABC allocation basis.
3. Determine the manufacturing overhead cost for each product using your answer to part (2).
4. Using your answer to part (3), compute the cost per unit for CD105 and HD210.
5. Compare your answers to part (1) and part (4). Why the difference in costs?

Problem 8-8

Activity-Based Costing and Gross Margin Calculations

Stafford Manufacturing, Inc., produces two different products. Product 1 sells for $950 each, and Product 2 sells for $700 each. Estimated annual production and sales for Product 1 and Product 2 are 2,100 units and 2,900 units, respectively. Direct materials are $350 for Product 1 and $200 for Product 2. Direct labor costs are $300 for Product 1 and $310 for Product 2. Stafford purchases materials for Product 1 every month and for Product 2 every two months. On average, Stafford performs 10 setups each month for Product 1 production and 8 setups each month for Product 2 production. The following are manufacturing overhead costs incurred by Stafford Manufacturing:

Quality control	$150,000
Purchasing costs	74,880
Miscellaneous manufacturing overhead	62,640

Required:
1. Assuming that the allocation bases for the three manufacturing overhead costs are production volume for quality control, number of purchases for purchasing costs, and number of setups for miscellaneous manufacturing overhead, calculate the cost per unit of each allocation basis.
2. Determine total manufacturing overhead costs for each product.
3. Determine the gross margin percent for Stafford Manufacturing for each product it produces.

Problem 8-9

Allocation of Manufacturing Overhead with Multiple Products

Geddy, Inc., is a manufacturing firm that manufactures two types of boat engines. The Type A engine is designed for a specific type of cruise ship. Because of a long-term commitment with

(continued)

a cruise company, Type A engines need no modifications. Type B engines are designed for slightly smaller cruise ships. Because the Type B engine is designed for several different models of cruise ships and the mounting hardware is different for each, retooling is regularly required. Costs for the two types of engines are presented here:

	Type A Engine (200 Units Produced)		Type B Engine (90 Units Produced)	
	Total	Per Unit	Total	Per Unit
Direct materials cost	$176,000,000	$880,000	$70,200,000	$780,000
Direct labor cost	147,000,000	735,000	60,300,000	670,000
Manufacturing overhead costs:				
Engineering costs			$144,000,000	
Quality control			38,880,000	
Utilities and maintenance			1,305,000	

Required:

1. Determine the amount of manufacturing overhead to be assigned to each unit of activity assuming the following ABC information:

   Manufacturing Overhead Cost
   - Engineering costs
   - Quality control
   - Utilities and maintenance

   Type A Engines
   - 0 engineering change orders per unit
   - 9 machine setups per unit
   - 200 units produced

   Allocation Bases
   - Engineering change orders per unit
   - Machine setups per unit
   - Production volume

   Type B Engines
   - 8 engineering change orders per unit
   - 16 machine setups per unit
   - 90 units produced

2. Determine the amount of manufacturing overhead to be assigned to each type of engine.
3. Compute the gross margin on Type A and Type B engines assuming selling prices of $2,000,000 and $2,300,000, respectively.

Problem 8-10

Allocation of Manufacturing Overhead with Multiple Products

Macey Sprinkling Company produces two types of pipe: (1) lawn sprinkler pipe and (2) building sprinkler pipe. Relevant information for the production of the two types of pipe for 2006 is as follows:

	Lawn Sprinkler Pipe	Building Sprinkler Pipe
Feet produced	325,000	150,000
Prime costs	$243,750	$123,000
Manufacturing overhead costs:		
Utilities	$ 75,000	$ 40,000
Support staff	63,000	35,750
Quality control	8,000	4,060
Purchasing	19,200	10,250

Macey allocates utilities and support staff costs on the basis of production volume, quality control costs on the basis of number of machine setups required, and purchasing department costs on the basis of number of purchase orders. During 2006, volume of these various activities per *product line* was:

	Lawn Sprinkler Pipe	Building Sprinkler Pipe
Production volume	325,000 feet	150,000 feet
Machine setups	12	24
Purchase orders	1	30

Required:

1. Determine the cost per unit for each cost driver.
2. Determine the amount of manufacturing overhead to be assigned to the two types of sprinkler pipe.
3. Determine the total cost for each type of pipe produced for the year.

Problem 8-11

Costs of Quality

DeeAnn Martinez is preparing to open her own CPA firm. DeeAnn is a smart businessperson and wants to maximize her profits. She has not yet decided whether to run a low-quality CPA firm (basically offering to sign the financial statements of anyone who will pay her fee), an average CPA firm, or a premium-quality CPA firm (competing head-to-head with the large international accounting firms such as PRICEWATERHOUSE COOPERS).

DeeAnn has analyzed the costs of quality related to operating a CPA firm and has developed the following analysis:

- *Prevention costs:* The best way to ensure the quality of the audit is to increase the quality of the staff hired and to increase the time that the staff spends on each audit. DeeAnn realizes that hiring higher-quality staff will cost more.
- *Appraisal costs:* DeeAnn plans to inspect the work of the staff auditors by having audit managers review the work. The average salary rate for an audit manager (including all fringe benefits) is $50 per hour.
- *Internal failure costs:* Sometimes the audit team will do such a poor job that one of DeeAnn's audit partners will have to personally supervise the completion of the audit work. The average salary rate for an audit partner is $100 per hour.
- *External failure costs:* If investors or creditors rely on financial statements that later prove to be false, the audit firm that approved those financial statements will probably be sued. Of course, the frequency of being sued, and the cost of each lawsuit, will be higher if DeeAnn decides to provide low-quality audits.

DeeAnn has gathered the following numerical information about the costs of quality in relation to operating a CPA firm:

	Low Quality	Average Quality	Premium Quality
Prevention costs:			
Staff hours spent on audit	10 hours	30 hours	100 hours
Staff salary rate	$20/hour	$25/hour	$35/hour
Appraisal costs:			
Manager review of audit work	1 hour	5 hours	20 hours
Internal failure costs:			
Frequency of bad audits	1 in 3	1 in 10	1 in 50
Partner time to fix bad audit	10 hours	5 hours	3 hours
External failure costs:			
Frequency of lawsuits	1 in 5	1 in 40	1 in 100
Expected loss on each lawsuit	$200,000	$100,000	$100,000

(continued)

Required:
1. Assume that the revenue from each audit is the same no matter what the quality of the audit. Therefore, in order to maximize her profits, DeeAnn must minimize the expected cost of each audit. Which type of audit firm—low quality, average quality, or premium quality—should DeeAnn operate in order to maximize her expected profit per audit? Show your calculations.
2. Comment on whether the assumption about revenue made in part (1) seems appropriate.

Problem 8-12

Taguchi Quality Loss Function

TAC Computers is a nationwide distributor of personal computers for home and business use. Its main sales channels are the Internet and telephone sales. Customers either call in to TAC's customer sales center or log on to TAC's Web site to place orders for custom-made computers. One of TAC's distinguishing marketing strategies is its three-year 24 × 7 customer support call center. All TAC customers have the ability to call the customer support center 24 hours a day, seven days a week to receive technical assistance with their machine. TAC prides itself on the high quality of service in this call center. Every customer call is immediately followed with either an e-mail or a postcard survey that asks the customer to provide feedback on the experience and answer the following questions:

1. Was your concern or question thoroughly resolved by the TAC technician?
2. Did the TAC technician handle your call with courtesy and professionalism?

Technicians' performance on the first question is referred to as the "error rate." Performance on the second question is referred to as the "care rate." The customer support call center management team uses performance on the error rate and care rate to manage operations and determine additional training needed by individual call center technicians. Performance on these two measures has been quite good for TAC. The TAC standard for each technician is to have no more than 1% complaints per month on the first question and no more than 0.5% complaints per month on the second question (a full-time technician handles 600 calls per month on average). Management feels that 99% quality on error and 99.5% quality on care is an excellent performance level for this industry.

   Currently, few technicians need additional training each month. However, if a technician's error rate exceeds 1% of any month's call volume, that technician goes through a skills verification test to identify areas of weakness in handling specific technical issues, then undergoes some customized training. The cost of running a technician through this analysis and training process is estimated to be about $600. In the event that a technician's care rate exceeds 0.5% of a month's call volume, a manager is assigned to observe the technician in order to identify specific problems in working with customers. Then the technician works through a specialized training program based on the manager's assessment. The average cost of running a technician through this process is about $900.

   As the controller for TAC Computers, you've been reading lately about the opportunity costs of low quality, and you're concerned that management of the customer support call center may not recognize the significant cost of lost sales that result when the company's reputation is hurt by technician error or lack of care for the customer.

Required:
1. Assuming that the Taguchi quality loss function is approximately accurate in measuring TAC's quality loss due to the external failure of handling customer calls, calculate the opportunity cost of lost sales when a technician's error rate hits 1%. Calculate the opportunity cost of lost sales when a technician's care rate hits 0.5%.

2. Explain to the management team of the customer support call center how they should interpret and use these Taguchi calculations to improve the operations in their center.

Problem 8-13

Taguchi Quality Loss Function

NorseLabs is a manufacturer of helium-neon (HeNe) lasers used in research. In order to have the maximum amount of energy produced, HeNe lasers must have certain proportions of helium and neon gases. The combination should be 15% helium and 85% neon. There can be an error of $\pm 0.5\%$ of either gas without noticeable energy loss. HeNe lasers must perform within this specification range before they can be approved for delivery to customers.

Each HeNe laser is sold for $600. NorseLabs offers a limited warranty on each HeNe laser sold. If a laser is not performing properly, NorseLabs exchanges the malfunctioning laser for a new laser at a cost to the consumer of 40% of the new laser. The old laser is then refurbished and re-sold. Refurbishing a laser costs NorseLabs $350. A refurbished laser can be resold for $450.

In the past month, NorseLabs has had to exchange and replace 15 lasers. NorseLabs' engineers estimate that these 15 lasers had the average error of approximately $\pm 0.3\%$ from the 15% target ratio in helium and 85% target ratio for neon, which is within the company's established control limits. The controller at NorseLabs, Ronda, has been learning about the high costs of external failure and the Taguchi quality loss function. She is concerned that NorseLabs is underestimating the cost of replacing defective lasers.

Required:

1. Use the Taguchi quality loss function to approximate NorseLabs' quality loss due to external failure of the 15 defective lasers during the past month. Assume that error distance in the gas ratio is measured in 0.01% units. Hence, the 15 returned lasers are measuring 30 units (0.3% ÷ 0.01%) from the targeted gas combination ratio.

2. Help Ronda explain to management at NorseLabs how they should interpret and use the Taguchi calculations [from part (1)] to improve the operations at NorseLabs.

3. Assume management at NorseLabs has decided to improve the process in which gas is measured in its lasers before being sold to a consumer. Management wants to reach a balance between prevention costs, appraisal costs, internal failure costs, and external failure costs. Management determines that this balance should be reached if the Taguchi calculation each month does not exceed $104,000. Assume that NorseLabs sells 100 lasers on average each month. Using the Taguchi quality loss function, determine the maximum average distance from its gas combination target that NorseLabs can have and still remain below a $104,000 external failure cost.

iscussion cases

Case 8-1

Stott Knife Company

Stott Knife Company produces three models of kitchen knives: Dicer, Slicer, and CutsAll. Sales and costing information for the three models are as follows:

	Dicer	Slicer	CutsAll
Selling price per unit . .	$35	$65	$80
Units produced	26,000	16,000	12,000
Direct materials cost . . .	$410,000	$215,000	$125,000
Direct labor cost	$110,000	$45,000	$35,000

In the past, manufacturing overhead has been allocated based on number of units produced. Manufacturing overhead for the period is $810,000, and the predetermined overhead rate is $15 per unit produced.

Based on this information, management has determined that the Dicer is barely breaking even. Because the market for knives is quite competitive, the price for each model is set by the market—not by management. Thus, increasing the price charged for products is not an option. As a result, management is considering discontinuing the Dicer. Before making a final decision, management has come to you for advice. You collect the following information regarding manufacturing overhead:

(continued)

Manufacturing Overhead	Manufacturing Overhead Costs	Allocation Bases
Engineering	$125,000	Engineering changes
Quality control	375,000	Number of units produced
Manufacturing support	310,000	Number of setups
Total overhead	$810,000	

Allocation Bases	Dicer	Slicer	CutsAll
Engineering changes	2	7	6
Number of units produced . .	26,000	16,000	12,000
Number of setups	28	77	65

Determine the gross profit for each model under the current manufacturing overhead allocation scheme. Determine the manufacturing overhead cost for each model using the information relating to activities. Determine the gross profit for each model using the ABC allocated manufacturing overhead. What recommendation would you make to management regarding its decision to discontinue the Dicer?

Case 8-2

Costs of Quality (Starving Sailor Restaurant)

You are the leader of a group of investors that is planning to open a nationwide chain of seafood restaurants that you will call "Starving Sailor Restaurant." You are preparing for a strategy meeting that will be held tomorrow. The investor group is considering two strategies for how the restaurant chain will be operated. One strategy, which you have titled "Classy," proposes to market the restaurant chain as the quality leader among seafood restaurants. The restaurants will be located in good neighborhoods, will offer choice seafood selections, and will have an excellent cleanup crew. Each restaurant will also have a trained manager on site during business hours to handle customer complaints in addition to a national troubleshooting team that will promptly fly to any location to investigate consistent patterns in customer complaints received via a toll-free complaint hotline.

You have titled the other strategy "Tight Budget." The restaurants will be located wherever cheap real estate can be found, will be staffed with the lowest-cost labor possible, and will focus on offering low-cost food. There will be no mechanism for receiving customer complaints, and the store manager will not be trained in customer satisfaction.

A significant portion of the investor group advocates the "Tight Budget" strategy, arguing that it offers the lowest operating costs and, therefore, the highest profit. You are worried that these investors may not have thought carefully about all the costs associated with this strategy. Using the costs of quality (COQ) categories, outline some of the major costs that will differ between these two restaurant strategies.

judgment calls

Judgment 8-1

You Decide: Does cost information provide help in running a business, or is it only useful within the bounds of an accounting system?

Your friends in the MBA program at your university seem to think that cost information in a company is helpful but that it is rarely used in the decision-making process within a company. One friend said, "You have to know how to work with people and manage what they do on a day-to-day basis. Cost information has its place and time, but is often not relevant. The executives in upper management have more important things to consider in running a business than the cost of products and services!" Do you agree or disagree?

Judgment 8-2

You Decide: Does total quality management help a company revamp and improve its business operations, or is it too much of an administrative burden that takes away from the company's primary goals?

Over the last 20 years, there have been many new developments in the area of total quality management. Companies strive to increase profitability by improving their products and processes. However, you are still a bit skeptical. At your current place of employment, your boss has heard about TQM and tries to meet at least every six weeks to talk about what is being done in implementing TQM and what could be improved. You don't see any benefits from the meetings. Nothing that is brought up in the meetings is ever implemented. It just seems to be an opportunity to meet with your friends and have a free lunch. Are you wasting your time?

▶ **Analyzing Real Company Information**
▶ **International Case**
▶ **Ethics Case**
▶ **Writing Assignment**

▶ **The Debate**
▶ **Internet Search**

The following additional assignments provide opportunities for students to develop critical thinking, ethical perspectives, oral and written communication skills, experience with electronic research, and teamwork through group and business activities.

▷ *Analyzing Real Company Information*

Analyzing 8-1 (Microsoft)

MICROSOFT, like most other companies, is continually striving to appropriately allocate costs and to increase the quality of its products. We have studied Microsoft's financial statements in past chapters. Now it is time to think beyond the numbers and examine other factors that might affect a firm's performance. Use your knowledge of Microsoft and your understanding of the computer software industry to answer the following questions:

1. What types of overhead costs might Microsoft incur that would be associated with its software products? Identify several cost drivers that Microsoft might consider in allocating overhead using the ABC method of overhead allocation.
2. What sort of product quality issues might Microsoft face associated with its software? List the various costs of quality associated with a faulty software product.

Analyzing 8-2 (Deluxe Corporation)

DELUXE CORPORATION (DELUXE) is the world's largest printer of checks as well as a provider of electronic products and services to financial institutions and retail companies. The company produces more of the nearly 42.5 billion checks written by American consumers and businesses annually than any other check printer. In fact, Deluxe printed enough checks in 2001 that if lined up end to end would stretch to the moon and back. The company serves nearly 1.8 million small businesses annually and provides 2 million products—each with personalized information, most within two days of receiving the order, with 98% order accuracy. Revenues in 2002 were $1.28 billion, with operating income of $214 million. Deluxe was recently ranked by *Fortune* magazine as the 936th largest U.S. company.

Although Deluxe has been profitable in all but one year since it was founded in 1915, market shifts in 1997 from paper-based to electronic transactions were causing margins to erode and revenues to decline in Deluxe's core checkprinting business. These competitive pressures brought about many changes at Deluxe in regards to management and strategy. The centerpiece of all these changes to its management process was a new measure called Deluxe value added (DVA). DVA measures the incremental profits of customers and customer segments after the costs of capital assets required to support these customers are covered. This focus on the profitability of customers was a significant change in view from the company's previous focus on the profitability of its check products.

Measurement of DVA at Deluxe requires accurate cost information. However, at the time that Deluxe adopted DVA, Deluxe's costing system was used primarily to value its check inventory for financial statement purposes. Hence, in 1997 the company decided to implement an activity-based costing (ABC) system to measure the costs of specific customers. A comprehensive project structure was put into place in order to design and implement the new ABC system. An executive sponsor provided focus, resources, and leadership and reviewed performance. A steering committee approved the project plan, established priorities, and approved ongoing progress and results. Two project managers were responsible for quality control, problem resolution, leadership, and training. Field teams consisting of full- and part-time members were responsible for executing the work plan.

A multi-phased project was initiated with a timeline of six months. The plan included forming project teams, analyzing activities and linking costs to customers, analyzing customer profitability, and building a sustainable ABC information system that could be updated on a regular basis as activities and customers changed.

Answer the following questions:

1. Deluxe implemented ABC over a time period of six months. Does this time period seem too short, too long, or just right? Explain your answer.
2. Upon implementing ABC, Deluxe involved teams and groups from various departments within the company. Why do you think it was important for Deluxe to involve so many employees in its implementation of ABC?
3. Is Deluxe's approach to implementation likely to increase or decrease management's use of ABC information for decision making? Explain your answer.

Source: Adapted from P. B. B. Turney, "Deluxe Corporation: Activity-Based Costing," University of Virginia Darden School Foundation (1999).

International Case

International

Deming in Japan

As noted in this chapter, the ideas of W. Edward Deming received little attention in the United States in the late 1940s and early 1950s. Deming then moved to Japan where his ideas were accepted and implemented almost immediately. The result was that industries in Japan, such as automobile production, quickly developed a reputation for producing quality products. In the 1980s, the United States found itself trying to catch up to the Japanese in the race for quality products. Can you speculate as to why Deming's ideas were not readily accepted in the United States, yet were quickly adopted in Japan? To answer this question, you may need to recall your world history during the 1940s.

Ethics Case

Minuteman Enterprises

You are the controller for Minuteman Enterprises, a manufacturer of rocket booster engines and various aerospace products. Though there are many commercial customers for most of the company's products, the federal government is the only buyer of your rocket booster engines. Because you are the only provider for the engines, the government has agreed to buy these engines at a price equal to your cost plus a 10% markup.

As the controller, you have recently been studying the accuracy of your product costs. Traditionally, manufacturing overhead has been allocated on the basis of direct labor hours. Using this method, rocket boosters have borne a high percentage of manufacturing overhead because they take many more direct labor hours than do the other products.

You have just been presented an analysis by one of your staff members that shows that direct labor hours is not a very relevant base for allocating manufacturing overhead costs.

Rather, she has made a very convincing case that manufacturing overhead should be allocated using activity-based costing with multiple cost drivers. Using her suggested approach, however, you discover that the rocket boosters bear a much smaller portion of manufacturing overhead costs, and therefore, the total cost of the boosters is considerably less than the amount you had been using to determine the price charged to the government.

You know that her calculations using ABC are likely more accurate than the current cost allocation method and that the commercial products should bear a larger amount of manufacturing overhead costs. Yet, you also know that by using ABC and the more accurate cost drivers, your profits from both the boosters and the commercial products will be reduced.

1. What should you do?
2. Is it ethical to continue to allocate manufacturing overhead costs on the basis of direct labor hours?
3. Would it be ethical to use direct labor hours if that were the basis used by other government contractors?
4. If you decide to switch to ABC, should you inform the government that you have over-charged it and return the excess profits?

▷ *Writing Assignment*

Advantages and Disadvantages of ABC

Your boss recently attended a conference where activity-based costing was discussed. She is intrigued by the ABC concept and wonders if the company is appropriately costing its products. Your company produces and sells four different styles of briefcases. The production process differs for each briefcase, as different features require different equipment. She returns from the conference and asks you to summarize the advantages and disadvantages of ABC. Your assignment is to write a two-page memo addressing these issues.

▷ *The Debate*

ABC or Bust!

As the text indicates, activity-based costing has received much attention from businesses around the world. Yet some firms still resist adopting an ABC system, and others have adopted ABC and then reverted to their more traditional costing systems. Divide your group into two teams and prepare five-minute presentations defending the following positions:

• Team One is "In Support of ABC." Your team's task is to identify the benefits of using an activity-based product costing system. Briefly explain the advantages that a company will realize if it adopts ABC.

• Team Two is "In Support of Tradition." Your team's task is to identify the benefits of using a more traditional product costing system based on, for example, direct labor hours. Explain the advantages of a traditional system that cause many firms to still choose it over ABC.

▷ *Internet Search*

The W. Edwards Deming Institute

The home page for the W. EDWARDS DEMING INSTITUTE can be found at **http://www.deming .org.** Go to this Web site to learn more about the Deming Institute and the Deming Prize and answer the following questions. Sometimes Web addresses change, so if this address does not work, access the Web site for this textbook (**http://swain.swlearning.com**) for an updated link.

1. When was the Deming Institute founded, where is it headquartered, and what is its purpose?
2. What is the history of the Deming Prize?
3. What organization won the 2002 Deming Quality Control Award for Operations Business Units?

Part

4

Evaluation

9 Making Decisions Using Relevant
   Information

10 Continuous Improvement in
    Management Accounting

Making Decisions Using Relevant Information

Learning Objectives

After studying this chapter, you should be able to:

1   Explain how evaluation leads to planning and why products and processes must be continuously evaluated.

2   Understand why benchmarking is so important and how it is conducted.

3   Understand the concepts of sunk costs and differential costs and revenues, and be able to identify those costs and revenues that are relevant to making product and process decisions.

4   Identify several examples of product and process evaluation decisions, and be able to analyze and select the best alternative for each example.

eXpanded *Material*

5   Understand the theory of constraints and how focusing on scarce resources can direct activities in manufacturing companies.

Consider the following three scenarios:

- You are the general manager of a professional basketball team. You have decided to keep a player on your team who has a multi-year, multi-million dollar salary contract even though the player is not playing well. To make room for this fading star, you cut a young, promising, inexpensive player. You make this decision because of the high committed cost of the veteran player who will have to be paid whether or not he is cut. You also instruct the coach to give the veteran player more time on the court to justify the high salary he is being paid.
- You and your companion have driven halfway to a mountain resort. Responding to a reduced-rate advertisement, you have previously made a nonrefundable $100 deposit to spend the weekend at the resort, which is at an elevation of 10,000 feet. Both you and your companion are starting to get headaches and are feeling nauseous; you suspect this is because of mild altitude sickness. Your companion says it's too bad that you have already paid for the room because you both would much rather spend the time at home; however, you can't afford to waste $100. You agree.
- You are a theater aficionado and have traveled to New York City for the express purpose of watching as

many Broadway plays as possible. On your first night in town, you realize upon arrival at the theater that you've lost your ticket which cost $100. You check in your wallet, and you do have another $100 with which you can replace the ticket. Instead, you decide to go back to your hotel and watch TV because you believe that while the play is worth seeing for $100, it is not worth seeing for $200.

In each of these cases, you are making irrational decisions because you are not recognizing past costs as sunk costs. No matter how much a player is being paid, it is the future performance you should be interested in as long as you can afford to pay the young, promising player. The past contract that was signed with the veteran player is irrelevant. Similarly, the $100 you and your companion spent to reserve the weekend at the resort is irrelevant. The $100 is a sunk cost, and you should do what will benefit you the most in the future. Similarly, in the Broadway play example, the lost ticket and the $100 you paid for it are irrelevant. The new cost of seeing the play is $100, not $200, and to sit around in your hotel room watching TV because you bought and lost a ticket is irrational.

t was Kenny Rogers who sang, "You gotta know when to hold 'em and know when to fold 'em..." A singing accountant would add, "Once you fold 'em, forget 'em." In each of the three opening scenarios, you should have "folded" or "forgotten" the past costs and not considered them in the decision process. When individuals don't understand the relevance or irrelevance of various costs in decision making, they make bad decisions. It doesn't matter whether you are an individual making a decision to spend the weekend in a resort, or a business making a major, multi-million dollar decision.

In this chapter, we will consider several types of business decisions that are routinely made by business managers. If you become skilled in differentiating between differential costs, sunk costs, opportunity costs, and costs that don't change as a result of future actions, you will be a much better business decision maker.

Evaluating Products and Processes

▌ Explain how evaluation leads to planning and why products and processes must be continuously evaluated.

Before we discuss decision making, it is important that we review the three functions of planning, controlling, and evaluating. It is these three functions that lead to decision making of the type we will be discussing in this chapter. Thus far in this book, we have discussed the planning and controlling functions. You have learned that planning involves long-run planning, including strategic planning and capital budgeting, and short-run planning, including production prioritizing and operational budgeting. You have learned that controlling involves tracking actual performance in terms of costs, quality, and timeliness measures. These tracked measures (costs, quality, and timeliness) are then used in the evaluating process to compare against budgets previously prepared. Evaluating involves analyzing results, providing feedback to managers and other employees, rewarding performance, and identifying problems. One specific type of evaluation focuses on products and processes. As you learned in the introductory chapter on management accounting, managers need to assess the performance of their products or services, as well as the processes that are in place to create those products or services. In this chapter, we focus on evaluating and making decisions to improve products, services, and processes.

Evaluation brings us back to the point where we started—planning. Information gained through the evaluation process is used for planning during the following period. When managers are evaluating last period's performance, they are also probably making planning decisions that will affect, and hopefully improve, performance in the next period. This planning, controlling, and evaluating cycle is diagrammed below.

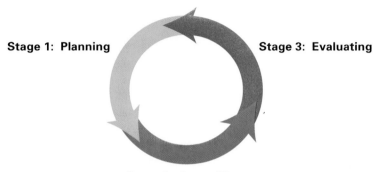

Stage 1: Planning

Stage 3: Evaluating

Stage 2: Controlling

The evaluation of products, services, and processes leads to decisions that will affect future operations, including whether to enter or exit a market for a particular service or product, whether to make or buy a component, whether to sell a product before or after additional processing, and what prices to charge for services and products.

The evaluation decisions we will discuss in this chapter can have a significant impact on the profitability, quality, and timeliness of the products of an organization for several periods and so must be considered very carefully. In a manufacturing company, for example, evaluation can help a company decide whether to accept a special order, whether to make or buy manufacturing components, whether to build or sell plants, and how to best use limited raw materials in the manufacturing process. In a merchandising company, evaluation can lead to decisions about how to use limited store shelves and whether to open a new store. In a service company, evaluation can help the company decide whether to hire a particular specialist or contract that service to another firm, how to use scarce labor resources, and whether to merge with another company. In a governmental unit, evaluation can affect decisions about whether to collect garbage at the curb or at the house site, whether to hire an in-house lawyer or contract out all legal services, and whether to develop a water system or buy water from a nearby community. In a dot.com company, evaluation could lead to decisions about how to price banner ads, whether to charge an access or user fee, or whether to add or drop existing lines.

At the evaluation stage, companies can make decisions to help them improve their competitive positions. After evaluating its employee health costs, JOHNSON & JOHNSON, the company that makes healthcare, hygiene and pharmaceutical products you are so familiar with, initiated an employee wellness (preventative) program that has saved the company an average of $8.5 million per year since it was put in place. (See the Business Environment on the Web.)

Why Evaluation Is So Important

Today, we live in an age when information is transmitted worldwide almost instantaneously, and change is occurring faster than ever before. With accurate and timely information so readily available, it is absolutely critical that companies produce the highest-quality products at the lowest possible price and faster than anyone else. If a U.S. automobile manufacturer produces a car that is more expensive or of lower quality than cars made in Japan or Germany, for example, U.S. consumers will buy foreign automobiles because information about the Japanese and German cars is readily available to U.S. car buyers. Likewise, if a U.S. automobile company can buy higher-quality tires at a lower price from a Korean tire manufacturer than it can from a U.S. tire manufacturer, it will buy Korean tires because information about the foreign tires is easily accessible.

This increased availability of up-to-date information and the ease with which products and services can be acquired internationally have made it critically important for companies to operate as efficiently and effectively as possible. Because it is so important to be a high-performing, or "world-class," company, organizations are placing more and more emphasis on evaluating their performance and continuously improving. Managers recognize that, in this information age, it is "survival of the fittest" and that only the best-performing companies will be able to compete in the long run.

Companies can be poor performers for several reasons. Some companies do not perform well because they fail to develop appropriate corporate strategies or goals or because they lack vision (planning). Some companies do not perform well because their evaluation methods are poor or do not fit their organizational structures and, therefore, fail to accurately assess how well they are doing. Perhaps most commonly, some companies do not perform well because they fail to execute their strategies and planned actions.

In this chapter, we will discuss several ways companies organize and set goals and then evaluate their performance against those goals. As was the case with product cost determination discussed in the chapter on cost-volume-profit analysis, performance evaluation has been the subject of considerable research in the past few years and has undergone significant changes. Much emphasis has been placed on developing evaluation systems that align performance evaluation with an organization's strategic plan and objectives and that focus on customer and employee needs. Historically, many performance measures have been backward looking and have tended to report results too late to allow corrective action to be taken. New evaluation systems link daily activities with measures that help organizations guide decisions and actions.

Obviously, to effectively evaluate performance, organizations must have goals, objectives, or benchmarks against which to assess their performance. Most organizations establish these goals and benchmarks through a process called strategic planning, which we have already discussed.

Quality and Time Standards

In evaluating performance, it is important to focus on both monetary and nonmonetary measures. For example, one well-known fast-food chain's managers are evaluated not only on the profitability of their unit, but also on such quality standards as cleanliness and the kind of service provided to customers. In another company, some managers receive more points for developing new technologies and making innovations than for keeping costs in line. At another company, production employees are rewarded on how much they can reduce the delivery time of products to customers. Other nonmonetary measures of performance include creating good employee morale and maintaining equipment in good running order.

For an evaluation system to be successful, the criteria by which products and processes are evaluated should be well defined, objective, and measurable. Usually, qualitative criteria are

© 2003 Getty Images

Fast-food managers can be evaluated on the kind of service provided to customers. Thus, it is important that employees offer fast service with a smile.

much harder to evaluate than objective cost measures and resulting variances, but that does not diminish their importance. In fact, quality and time standards are often as important to a firm's success as financial results. Those companies that can deliver the highest-quality products quickest and at the most competitive price will usually be the most successful. Some companies have even developed "best supplier" awards to recognize those suppliers that deliver products at the lowest price, with the highest quality and with the fewest late orders. Criteria used in making these awards usually include such elements as cost reductions, delivery improvement (frequency as well as timeliness), and percentage of defects.

In evaluating quality and time considerations, quality is usually defined as the total features and characteristics of a product or service that bear on its ability to satisfy stated or implied needs. Generally, as a final measure, quality must be viewed from a customer perspective as determined by acceptance in the marketplace. One writer has suggested that quality includes the following eight dimensions:[1]

1. *Performance*—a product's primary operating characteristic. Examples are automobile acceleration and a television set's picture clarity.
2. *Features*—supplements to a product's basic functioning characteristics, such as power windows on a car.
3. *Reliability*—a probability of not malfunctioning during a specified period.
4. *Conformance*—the degree to which a product's design and operating characteristics meet established standards.
5. *Durability*—a measure of product life.
6. *Serviceability*—the speed and ease of repair.
7. *Aesthetics*—how a product looks, feels, tastes, and smells.
8. *Perceived quality*—as seen by a customer.

As an example of how management might apply these quality components to a specific product, consider an automobile tire. Its quality may be measured by tread-wear rate, handling, traction, impact on gas mileage, noise levels, resistance to punctures, and appearance. As another example, the tax service of a CPA may be measured by timely completion of tax returns, tax savings, number of audits or letters from the IRS, suggestions made for future investment opportunities, fees charged, and personal attention given.

This discussion of quality suggests that performance evaluation must be viewed more broadly and from a different perspective than it has been in the past. Controlling costs is still essential, but the emphasis should also be on quality and improvement in processes, products, and services. As we discussed previously, some people argue that the competitive advantage of some Japanese companies is the direct result of acceptance of this quality philosophy, attributed to W. Edwards Deming. The Deming chain reaction is depicted in Exhibit 1.

STOP & THINK

What do you think researchers mean when they say that current evaluation methods do not give enough consideration to intangible capabilities and focus too much on financial returns?

With a broader perspective, managers can seek ways to measure all aspects of company performance. The emphasis should be on the critical activities of the company. The goal is to identify and concentrate on those activities that add the most value to products or services.

In addition to quality, performance evaluation now often considers the time it takes to get a product to the marketplace. By using technology and re-engineering processes, most companies today can deliver goods to customers faster than ever before.

The challenge is to integrate cost, quality, and speed considerations into evaluation systems effectively. The objectives of zero defects, continuous improvement, decreasing manufacturing and delivery time, and meeting customer expectations of quality are admirable. Developing and effectively implementing performance measures that help achieve these objectives is not an easy task, but it is certainly worthy of management's effort. In the end, those organizations that develop the most appropriate performance measures and provide the necessary encouragement and motivation for employees to achieve the organization's objectives will be the most successful.

1 David A. Garvin, "Competing on the Eight Dimensions of Quality," *Harvard Business Review* 65 (November–December 1987): pp. 101–109.

Exhibit 1: Deming Chain Reaction

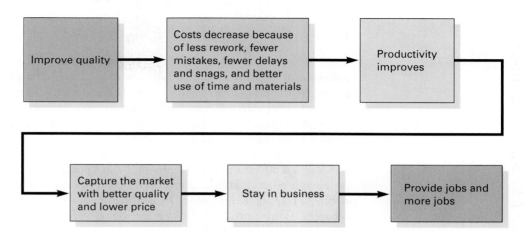

TO SUMMARIZE: In an age when information is inexpensive and readily available, it is important that companies offer the highest-quality products at the lowest possible price and faster than their competitors. Because quality, speed, and price are so important, it is critical that organizations establish good evaluation methods and continuously improve. A company cannot improve its performance until it knows how it is doing. Evaluation helps an organization plan better and control its operations more effectively. In addition to cost considerations, nonmonetary measures should be used in evaluating performance. To be effective, these criteria must be well defined, objective, and measurable. New approaches to performance evaluation include quality and time considerations. The new approaches are required because all aspects of a company's performance need to be monitored. In the final analysis, those organizations that can deliver the highest-quality products to their customers at the lowest prices and in the shortest amount of time will be the most successful. Significant challenges exist in implementing new performance evaluation approaches.

Benchmarking

2 Understand why benchmarking is so important and how it is conducted.

benchmarking A performance evaluation process used by companies to target areas for improvement by comparing the company's financial and operating performance against the performance of other companies or by comparing the performance of internal departments against each other.

In recent years, there has been an evaluation revolution. Several new evaluation methods have been developed. In this chapter, we will describe only one—benchmarking. One other (the balanced scorecard) will be discussed in the next chapter.

Benchmarking involves comparing a company's financial and operating performance against a competitor's performance or comparing the performance of various internal departments against each other. The benchmarking process usually consists of four steps. Step 1 is to analyze the company's practices, procedures, and performance in a given process and to set forth goals and objectives for improving them. Analysis of the company's practices and procedures is crucial because the practices of other firms will not prove very revealing unless a company has determined its own strengths and weaknesses.

Step 2 involves the selection of a benchmark (or benchmarks). These benchmarks can be departments within a company or competing companies that optimally perform the process under analysis. This step is critical because selection of the wrong benchmarks can result in identifying inappropriate procedures and unrealistic goals for a firm.

In step 3, detailed information on the benchmarks' practices and procedures for that process is collected and shared. Although collecting such data on competing companies may prove difficult, various sources offer benchmark data, and companies are often willing to share information with each other.

In step 4, a company must carefully analyze the data collected in step 3 to determine which of the policies and procedures used by benchmarked companies can best be employed.

Internal versus External Comparisons

The standards of comparison used for benchmarking can be based on the performance of departments or divisions within the same company or appropriate departments from other companies. When using internal units as benchmarks, a company can begin by identifying its best-performing units and then analyze their strategies and practices for performance. Once the approaches have been determined and quantified, less effective departments are encouraged to adopt the practices of the more successful units.

A drawback to internal comparisons alone, however, is that they may foster complacency and may not afford a realistic picture of a unit's potential within the industry. Internal comparisons are often of limited value because a company may be unable to recognize its own shortcomings and faults. Also, although one department within a company may outperform other departments substantially, that fact is not indicative of its performance relative to the industry as a whole. In essence, the department may be outperforming other units within the company, but still be falling short of the performance yields found in other similar companies. For example, it is easy to assume that a growth rate of 4% a year is satisfactory; yet, if outside competitors are realizing growth rates of 8%, there is clearly great room for improvement.

A second approach to benchmarking is to compare a company against top competitors. Most experts believe that this approach is the most relevant point of comparison for both services and products. As mentioned above, a major stumbling block is that obtaining the necessary data for an effective comparison may be difficult. Nevertheless, this type of analysis, peer group benchmarking, is beneficial because it not only allows a company to compare itself to another company with a similar set of attributes, but it may also afford a more invigorating view of what is possible within the industry. Thus, to the extent that key result measurement ratios of individual companies can be compared with averages of a select group of companies with generally similar attributes, peer group examinations can be quite revealing.

A third form of benchmarking is to compare a company with the "best-in-class." This approach entails comparing a company with top-performing firms sharing comparable functions or philosophies, although they may not be in the same industry. The advantage of this type of cross-industry comparison is that practices and procedures followed in other industries may prove very beneficial, even though they have not been used previously in the same industry. Best-in-class comparisons can bring new ideas, new thoughts, and even new concepts. On the downside, however, the introduction of new concepts is somewhat speculative. There is risk whenever a company adapts a new concept or procedure. Because a process performs well in one industry does not necessarily mean it can be carried over effectively to a different industry. This limitation has to be considered before implementing any new ideas.

Benchmarking can yield great benefits in the education of executives and the realized performance improvements of operations. In addition, benchmarking can be used to determine strategic areas of opportunity. In general, it is the application of what is learned in benchmarking that delivers the impressive results so often noted.

The benefits of benchmarking are realized when companies employ recommendations and embark on a change process leading to marked improvements in productivity, costs, and revenues. The following are examples of how companies improved their results through benchmarking:

- GLAXO WELLCOME (now part of GLAXOSMITHKLINE) had over 80 toll-free telephone numbers, over half of which failed to ring anywhere. By eliminating all but one telephone number, Glaxo greatly reduced customer frustration and confusion.
- IBM CANADA suffered a substantial drop in customer satisfaction. In response, the company measured itself against various models to come up with the "Best of the Breed" (BoB) competitors in each of its market segments. Eleven basic processes were reevaluated. The company set some performance improvement targets as high as 200%. Two levels of

authority were dropped, and the corporate culture was redirected toward taking risks and being responsive to customers.
- NORWEST (now part of WELLS FARGO) embarked on a benchmarking campaign and was able to quantify the following benefits:
  - Sales brochure consolidation: $430,000 in savings.
  - Customer and direct mail consolidation: $1 million in savings.
  - Opportunity lending: $20 million in added growth.
  - Teller referrals: up 15%, 33% of which results in additional sales.
  - Use of sales road maps: sales increase up to 102%.
  - Use of partner letters: 150% increase in commercial sales.
  - Performance coaching: 5.08 products per new customer.
- MARRIOTT improved its guest check-in service process 500% by benchmarking the patient admittance process used by hospital emergency rooms.
- SOUTHWEST AIRLINES saved millions of dollars a year and was able to put more aircraft in the air while reducing the number on the ground by benchmarking Indy 500 pit crews.
- XEROX dramatically improved its warehouse order-picking process by benchmarking L.L. BEAN, a catalog order company.
- KPMG borrowed the concept of a supermarket's express checkout to start an express line in its word-processing pools. The change enabled teams with minor document changes to go through an expedited process, which was of great value to the word-processing department and solved a long-standing problem of work assignments.[2]

TO SUMMARIZE: Several new performance measures have been developed in recent years. In this chapter, we discuss one—benchmarking. Benchmarking is the process of comparing a unit's performance with other units either within or outside the company. Benchmarking can result in marked improvements in productivity, costs, and revenue.

Differential Costs, Sunk Costs, and Decision Making

3 Understand the concepts of sunk costs and differential costs and revenues, and be able to identify those costs and revenues that are relevant to making product and process decisions.

sunk costs Costs, such as depreciation, that are past costs and do not change as the result of a future decision.

differential costs Future costs that change as a result of a decision.

opportunity cost The maximum available contribution to profit foregone (or passed up) by using limited resources for a particular purpose.

One of the major reasons companies benchmark and evaluate products and processes is so they can make informed decisions about future actions. In order to make good decisions, however, organizations must understand the nature of their costs and how those costs will change in the future based on actions taken. Earlier in this text and in the opening scenario to this chapter, you were introduced to cost concepts that are critical for making future decisions. To help you remember these cost concepts, consider the following definitions of three cost terms:

- **Sunk cost:** A cost that has already been incurred and that cannot be avoided, regardless of what a manager decides to do. These costs are always the same, no matter what alternatives are being considered and are, therefore, always irrelevant to a decision.
- **Differential cost:** A cost that differs between alternatives. These costs are sometimes referred to as avoidable or incremental costs. Because differential costs differ between alternatives, they are always relevant for decision making. Differential costs can be eliminated in whole or in part by choosing one alternative over another.
- **Opportunity cost:** The maximum available contribution to profit foregone (or passed up) by using limited resources for a particular purpose.

2 These examples were taken from "Benefits and Values of Benchmarking," Best Practices, LLC, 6320 Quadrangle Drive, Suite 200, Chapel Hill, NC 27514.

Evaluation of products and processes usually leads to consideration of alternative courses of action. For example, the evaluation of a particular product may lead a company to believe that it must expand capacity, outsource production, or even drop the product in favor of an alternative product. It may also result in the company deciding to buy a competitor. In the rest of this chapter, we provide examples of how products and processes are evaluated to make better decisions. These concepts are probably best understood by examining examples of decisions to change, add, or drop products or processes. Before you can understand how evaluation can lead to better product and process decisions, however, a framework is necessary. In building a framework, we will focus mostly on costs and revenues. Do not forget, however, that the evaluation of timeliness and quality must be considered as well. In making decisions about products and processes, the costs and revenues that are different for, and hence relevant to, various alternative courses of action must be identified. You must be able to distinguish among sunk costs, opportunity costs, future costs that don't change, and differential costs.

To illustrate, assume that you own Speedy Print Shop. A customer wants you to print 500 copies of a one-page flyer immediately. To price the job, you need to know what it will cost. Exhibit 2 includes both an incorrect and a correct analysis of the available cost data. The left column (the incorrect analysis) includes all costs; the right column (the correct analysis) includes only the differential costs. We will explain each cost and how to determine whether the cost is relevant to the pricing decision.

network exercises

Kinko's

The activities of Speedy Print Shop in this illustration mirror the real-life business of KINKO'S. Kinko's started in 1970 with one copy machine near a U.S. college campus and now has over 900 branches in at least nine different countries. Access Kinko's Web site at **http://www.kinkos.com**.

Net Work:

1. Near which college campus was Kinko's first opened?

2. In which countries does Kinko's now operate?

1. *Paper.* The cost of the paper for the printing job is differential because it is a future expenditure that must be made as a result of the decision to accept the order. In a sense, therefore, it is a cost that changes as a result of the decision. If we do not accept the order, we do not need to purchase the paper. Note also that paper is a variable cost—its total cost increases proportionately to the size of the order.

2. *Printing labor.* Accepting the order will require a future expenditure for additional labor to operate the press. This again obviously represents a change from the existing situation—without the order, we would not incur the cost of labor. Also, this example illustrates another important point about measuring future costs. Since this rush order will have to be printed during overtime hours, the appropriate labor rate is time and a half. (Given a normal hourly rate of $16, the labor rate for this job would be $24.) It is easy to overlook this and assume that the normal labor cost per hour ($16) applies. The differential cost of $24 per hour that will be incurred as a result of the decision, however, is the appropriate cost to use. Like paper, printing labor is a variable cost that increases in total proportionately to the size of the order.

Exhibit 2: Speedy Print Shop Rush Order Analysis

	Incorrect Analysis (all costs)	Correct Analysis (differential costs)
Variable costs:		
Paper (500 at 10¢)	$ 50	$ 50
Printing labor (5 hours at $16; 5 hours at $24) . . .	80	120
Fixed costs:		
Printing plates	100	100
Printing press depreciation (5 hours at $10)	50	
Manager's salary (5 hours at $20)	100	
Totals	$380	$270

Caution

In this particular case, the issue of whether or not the depreciation is a differential cost is a subtle one. If an asset, such as a building, wears out over time, independent of the level of its use, then its depreciation is irrelevant to a decision of whether or not to use the building. However, if an asset, such as a machine, wears out with the level of its use, then perhaps its depreciation is a differential cost when deciding whether to use the machine or not.

3. *Printing plates.* New printing plates must be prepared for this order, so it is a future expenditure that changes as a result of the decision to accept the order. The important point here is that printing plates are a fixed cost (you can print as many copies as you want from the same set of plates), but the cost is still differential because it is an additional expenditure for this order. A common but incorrect assumption is that only variable costs are relevant and that fixed costs do not have to be taken into account. This is not the case. All future costs that change as a result of accepting the order, whether fixed or variable, are differential.

4. *Printing press depreciation.* This is not a differential cost because it is not a future cost (depreciation is an allocation of a past cost), and it does not change as a result of the decision to accept the order. Costs such as depreciation, which are past costs and do not change, are sunk costs. No decision can change past, or sunk, costs; they are never relevant to a decision.

5. *Manager's salary.* Although the manager's salary is a future cost (we will be paying for future services), it will be paid whether or not the order is accepted. Consequently, the manager's salary is not a differential cost; it does not change as a result of the decision to accept this order. The manager's salary is not a sunk cost because it will be paid in the future, but it is a cost that will not change as a result of whether or not the printing job is accepted.

The differential costs for this rush order total $270. This means that in pricing the job, Speedy Print Shop will be losing money unless it charges at least this much. Similarly, if Speedy Print Shop declines the job at an offered price of $300 because that price is less than the incorrectly calculated differential cost of $380, the company will experience an opportunity cost (loss) of $30 ($300 − $270).

Speaking of opportunity costs, Speedy Print Shop must also carefully consider any other opportunity costs associated with accepting this order. If Speedy Print Shop accepts this order, it may not be able to accept another order that already exists or one that might arrive tomorrow. The lost contribution to profit from not being able to accept alternative jobs is an opportunity cost that must be considered. Obviously, if there is plenty of printing capacity available to accept all jobs that are received, opportunity costs are zero.

To further illustrate the role of differential and sunk costs in making a product or process decision, we assume that Dixon Wholesale Company is thinking of purchasing a delivery truck with an estimated useful life of five years. Following are the costs of acquiring and operating a truck:

Original cost		$20,000
Variable costs per mile:		
Gasoline and oil	$ 0.50	
Repairs and maintenance	0.06	
Tires	0.04	
Total variable costs per mile		$ 0.60
Fixed costs per year:		
Insurance	$1,000	
Licenses	220	
Depreciation expense ($20,000 ÷ 5 years)	4,000	
Total fixed costs per year		$ 5,220

These variable and fixed operating costs are incurred each year the truck is used. However, they are not all differential costs; they are not all relevant to every decision made about the truck. For the following decisions, we identify the differential costs, the sunk costs, and the reason for the classifications.

Decision 1

Should the truck be purchased? Whether to purchase the truck is really a capital budgeting decision, a topic we discussed in the chapter on capital investment decisions. But the decision is based on differential (future) costs to be incurred if the truck is purchased.

- **Differential costs:** All variable costs (60 cents per mile driven); all fixed costs except depreciation (which is already included in the purchase cost); and the purchase cost ($20,000).
- **Sunk costs:** None.
- **Comment:** All costs except depreciation are differential costs because the truck has not yet been purchased; all costs can be avoided by an alternative decision.

Decision 2

Let's now jump forward in time two years. The truck has now been owned and used for two years, but it has not been licensed or insured for the current (third) year. Should it be licensed and insured, or should some other means of transportation be used? (Assume for now that the truck will not be sold, even if not used.)

- **Differential costs:** All variable costs (60 cents per mile driven) and some fixed costs (insurance, $1,000; licenses, $220).
- **Sunk costs:** Remaining book value of the truck ($12,000 at the beginning of the year).
- **Comment:** As soon as the truck is purchased, its cost becomes a sunk cost. During its estimated life, its remaining book value is a sunk cost if we assume, for simplicity, that the truck has no resale value. The company must absorb the cost of the truck either by using the truck (and depreciating its cost each year) or by writing off the entire cost. All costs except depreciation and the remaining book value are, therefore, differential costs.

Decision 3

The truck has been owned and used for two years and has been licensed and insured for the current (third) year. Should the truck be used for transporting inventory this year? Should other means be arranged?

- **Differential costs:** All variable costs (60 cents per mile driven) and no fixed costs.
- **Sunk costs:** Insurance ($1,000); licenses ($220); remaining book value ($12,000 at the beginning of the year).
- **Comment:** If insurance and license fees are not refundable, these are sunk costs, as is the remaining book value.

Analysis of the costs that are relevant in making these three decisions should help you understand how differential costs are determined. As you can see, variable costs are *usually* differential; fixed costs are *sometimes* differential; and past costs are *never* differential.

Total Costs versus Differential Costs

In trying to improve performance, managers usually prefer to use the differential-cost approach; that is, they disregard sunk costs and other costs that are the same for each alternative being considered. This approach highlights costs that make a difference, takes less time, and reduces the chance of error in the calculation (fewer numbers reduce the chances for mistakes). In some cases, however, a manager may want to review the **total cost** to ensure that some relevant costs are not overlooked.

total cost The total variable and fixed costs incurred in making a product or providing a service.

To illustrate this total-cost approach, we will assume that Dixon Wholesale Company has another decision to make about its truck.

Decision 4

The truck has been owned for four years, but it has not yet been licensed or insured for the current (fifth) year. Should the truck be used for the last year of its economic life, or should it be traded for a new truck that will be driven five years?

Pertinent information is presented in the following table:

	Old Truck	New Truck
Original cost	$20,000	$25,000
Current book value	4,000	
Current resale value	3,400	
Resale value at end of year	0	20,000
Variable operating costs	$0.60 per mile	$0.54 per mile
Annual fixed costs:		
Insurance	$ 1,000	$ 1,100
Licenses	220	220
Depreciation expense	4,000	5,000
Estimated mileage per year	50,000 miles	50,000 miles

On the basis of this information, the total cost of operating the old truck and the total cost of operating a new truck are shown in Exhibit 3.

Note that the total cost of operating the old truck includes the yearly $4,000 depreciation expense. If the new truck is bought, the $4,000 book value of the old truck must still be written off. Thus, the $4,000 is a sunk cost and is the same under both alternatives, so it is not relevant to the decision at hand. The current resale value of the old truck, however, is a reduction in cost that will occur only if the new truck is purchased.

Two observations should be made about the total-cost approach to analyzing alternatives. First, it highlights the more attractive alternative in terms of cost only. In our example, the data appear to favor buying a new truck. However, this requires an investment of additional funds, which forces consideration of other factors. Because these factors were covered in the chapter on capital investment decisions, we have tried to keep our example simple by assuming a fair market value of $20,000 for the new truck at the end of one year. This means that the new truck's annual depreciation expense of $5,000 is equal to the difference between its original cost and its resale value after one year. Had the drop in value been greater than the depreciation expense, the excess would have been an additional cost of using the new truck during its first year.

Second, the total-cost approach is time-consuming because it involves differential costs as well as costs that are the same for all alternatives under consideration. With the differential-cost

Exhibit 3: Total-Cost Analysis for the Current Year: Keeping the Old Truck versus Selling It and Buying a New Truck*

Total Costs	Old Truck	Difference	New Truck
Variable costs:			
$0.60 × 50,000 miles	$30,000		
$0.54 × 50,000 miles			$27,000
Fixed costs:			
Insurance	1,000		1,100
Licenses	220		220
Depreciation expense	4,000		5,000
Book value of old truck to be written off			4,000
Resale value of old truck	0		(3,400)
Total cost	$35,220		$33,920
Difference		$1,300	

*Be aware that in order to emphasize the total-cost and differential-cost approaches, this analysis ignores the time value of money and related income tax effects, which we discussed in the chapter on capital investment decisions.

approach, only costs that are different need to be accumulated and analyzed. Thus, the costs of licensing both trucks and the $4,000 book value of the old truck to be depreciated or written off would not be considered. Exhibit 4 provides a list of the differential costs taken from Exhibit 3.

Although the differential-cost approach accumulates comparative costs and revenues that are different from those of the total-cost approach, it does not alter the relative attractiveness of the alternatives. Both the total and the differential analyses show a savings of $1,300 if the new truck is purchased. Thus, the acquisition of the new truck should bring future benefits to the company.

It should be noted that in both the total analysis and the differential analysis, the resale value of the old truck was treated as a negative cost. Instead, it could have been treated as a differential revenue from which the differential costs had been subtracted. It should also be noted that since both methods of analysis provide the same answer, it is likely that a firm will use the differential analysis method to save time in the collection and analysis of data. The total-cost method will likely be used only when there is considerable uncertainty about whether all differential costs and revenues have been accounted for in the differential-cost approach.

Qualitative Considerations

As has been the case with all management accounting decisions discussed in this book, the effect of product or process decisions on the time and quality with which products or services can be delivered must be considered. In deciding whether to accept the rush print job, for example, Speedy Print Shop must consider the possibility that while accepting the job might lead to additional business, it could affect the quality of printing services to other customers. Likewise, if accepting the rush print job will slow down service to other customers, accepting the job may not be a good decision, no matter how financially attractive it seems to be.

In making a final decision, the cost and qualitative factors may lead you to the same conclusion. If they do not, you must decide what to do to enhance your company's overall profitability in the future. You might decide, for example, to accept the rush print job for an amount near or even below your differential cost to ensure that you get the order and establish a relationship with the customer.

Exhibit 4: Differential-Cost and Revenue Analysis for the Current Year: Operating the Old Truck versus Selling It and Buying a New Truck

Differential Costs and Revenues	Old Truck	New Truck	Difference
Variable costs	$30,000	$27,000	$ 3,000
Insurance	1,000	1,100	(100)
Depreciation expense		5,000	(5,000)
Resale value of old truck	0	(3,400)	3,400
Total differential costs and revenues	$31,000	$29,700	$ 1,300

TO SUMMARIZE: Differential costs are the future costs that change as a result of a decision. Differential costs and revenues are those costs and revenues that are relevant to decisions. Sunk costs are never relevant because they are past costs that cannot be changed. Care must be exercised when estimating future costs because past cost relationships may not continue into the future. Some future costs may not be differential because they do not change as a result of a decision. Both variable and fixed costs may be differential.

There are two approaches to analyzing alternatives: total cost and differential cost. With the total-cost approach, all costs (including sunk costs) are accumulated. The differential-cost approach excludes sunk costs and all common costs, dealing only with costs that are different for the alternatives being considered. Once the quantitative analysis has been completed, qualitative factors must be considered.

Examples of Product and Process Evaluation Decisions

4 Identify several examples of product and process evaluation decisions, and be able to analyze and select the best alternative for each example.

The concepts of differential, sunk, and opportunity costs apply to all evaluation decisions covered in this and the next chapter. In the remainder of this chapter, we will apply differential costing to several examples of short-term product and process evaluation decisions. We will consider five separate examples: (1) accepting or rejecting special orders, (2) making or buying products, (3) exiting or entering a market, (4) determining at what stage of production to sell products, and (5) selecting the best use of a scarce resource. We will also consider the impact of differential, opportunity, and sunk costs on setting selling prices for products.

STOP & THINK

In addition to the specific examples covered in this chapter, identify two other types of decisions that organizations make that would involve evaluating products and/or processes.

special order An order that may be priced below the normal selling price in order to utilize excess capacity and thereby contribute to company profits.

Accepting or Rejecting Special Orders

A **special order** is an order that may be priced below the normal price in order to utilize excess capacity, thus contributing to company profits. We will look at special orders from the perspective of the seller. (A special order from the perspective of the buyer is really a make or buy decision that will be covered later in this chapter.) PRICELINE.COM is a company that specializes in "special orders." That is, this online service specializes in matching customers who insist on paying less than standard market prices with companies that have excess capacity to sell. In a sense, Priceline.com is a special order matchmaker.

Special orders can involve products or services. For example, in manufacturing companies, the special order might involve buying or selling parts on a one-time basis to or from other companies because of a sudden surge in demand. Another example is the one-time outsourcing of the preparation of quarterly payroll tax reports to a local CPA firm. When parts are involved, both the buying and selling companies are manufacturing firms. When a service (such as payroll accounting) is involved, the buyer may be a manufacturing, merchandising, or service company, but the provider is always a service company.

Special Orders—The Seller's Decision

If a seller can sell its products or services profitably at market prices, the decision is an easy one—provide the product or the service. After all, that is the purpose of being in business. Where the difficulty comes is in deciding whether to reduce the normal price of a product or service in order to obtain a special order. Typical situations involving a possible price reduction when idle capacity exists are as follows:

1. A manufacturer sells products under its own brand name, as well as to retail chain stores for sale under the chain's in-store generic brand name.
2. A firm, such as a building contractor or an equipment manufacturer, sells its products or services in a competitive bidding situation.
3. A firm sells a product under distress conditions, for instance, when there has been a sharp decline in demand for its products because of a new product offered by a competitor.
4. A product has significant sales potential with a foreign distributor, whose market demands lower prices than those in the United States.
5. A provider of a product or service has extra capacity and has the opportunity to sign a large contract, at a lower-than-normal price, that would consume the excess capacity.

In each of these situations, we assume that a firm has available capacity that can be utilized to fill the special order. The relevant costs for this decision are the additional, or incremental, costs necessary to produce and deliver the special order. Management must therefore know the incremental costs. This information will indicate the lowest price at which the special order will begin to contribute to the firm's profits.

To illustrate, we will assume that Kent Electronics, which usually sells business calculators for a wholesale price of $29, receives an order from a large department store chain for 10,000 calculators at a price of $23 each. The requested calculators are to be sold under the store's brand name. Kent currently has excess capacity that could be used in producing enough calculators to fill the order. Should the company accept the order?

The answer to this question does not, of course, depend on cost and price factors alone. An obvious consideration, for example, would be whether the order would result in a significant loss of sales of the company's own brand of calculators. Let's assume that this is not a problem.

If the accounting department presents the data on a total-cost basis, the manager might erroneously reject the order. It appears from the schedule on the following page that the firm would have a loss if it accepted the special order:

business environment

Priceline.com: The Special Order Matchmaker What began as an outlet to "name-your-price" for airline travel has exploded to include car rentals and purchases, hotel bookings, grocery sales, mortgages, and yard sales. PRICELINE.COM's best sellers are airline tickets. In a recent week, for example, Priceline sold about 80,000 airline tickets. The reason Priceline is so successful is that it offers a tremendous twofold value proposition to its customers. The buyer is able to buy things at a substantial discount below the retail price (or below the price line, hence the name of the company). Savings motivate buyers. Sellers, however, are equally motivated in the Priceline system. The reason for this is that sellers can generate incremental sales of their products by selling below retail prices (special orders) without staining their brand name with a "discount" image. In a sense, Priceline shields the sellers' brands so that the sellers can continue to capture more of the market below their own retail prices. Because of the value Priceline offers to both buyers and sellers, in its first 20 months, the company grew 5% a week.

As an example, consider the travel services Priceline offers. The airline tickets offered by Priceline are strictly for leisure travelers. "Fly any time of the day on any airline" is not the company's business proposition and never was. Instead, Priceline offers cheap air tickets to leisure travelers with flexibility in their travel plans. Priceline's attraction is that instead of driving or staying at home, consumers can now afford to fly. Because airlines have a lot of empty seats, it is a win-win situation for both buyers and sellers.

In essence, Priceline has allowed companies in the travel industry to utilize their excess capacity. Priceline allows an airline, a hotel, or a rental car company to capture incremental sales without publicly discounting its product. If a company publicly discounts its product on the Internet, all buyers see the discounted price and customers who paid the regular price become disgruntled. Priceline solves a very big problem by allowing the seller to privately discount its product and dynamically set prices as a way to clear excess capacity. Is Priceline's model good for selling all products? Probably not. However, any market with excess capacity that attracts buyers who are willing to be flexible on some critical dimension is ideal for the Priceline system.

Source: Information obtained from **http://www.priceline.com/pricelineASPOurCompany/html/presssayings.htm** (Accessed on November 29, 2003).

Special Order for Calculators—Total-Cost Approach

Sales price		$ 23
Manufacturing costs:		
Direct materials	$ 8	
Direct labor	4	
Manufacturing overhead	14	
Total manufacturing costs		26
Loss per unit		$ (3)
Number of units in order		×10,000
Expected loss exclusive of selling and administrative expenses		$(30,000)

It is not unusual for managers to base decisions on total-cost information because the data are readily available, having been collected in order to prepare financial statements and income tax returns. Unfortunately, such information may lead management to the wrong conclusion—in this case, to reject the order.

The only differential costs, however, are those future costs that change if the order is accepted. These include the variable product costs as well as the direct fixed costs. Fixed costs that are incurred regardless of whether the order is accepted should not be considered. The following analysis, prepared on a differential-cost basis, shows that Kent Electronics should accept the order.

Special Order for Calculators—Differential-Cost Approach

Sales price		$ 23
Variable and differential fixed costs:		
Direct materials	$8	
Direct labor	4	
Variable manufacturing overhead costs	5	
Differential fixed overhead costs	3	
Variable selling and administrative expenses	1	
Total variable and differential fixed costs		21
Remaining margin to cover fixed costs and provide a profit		$ 2
Number of units in order		×10,000
Expected contribution to fixed costs and profit		$ 20,000

These data assume that additional fixed costs of $3 per unit will be incurred if the order is accepted. If no additional fixed costs would be incurred, the margin would increase to $5. The analysis clearly suggests that, from a financial point of view, management should accept the order. This approach identifies not only the differential costs but also a price floor (the total variable and differential fixed costs of $21) below which management should probably not accept an order. As long as the price exceeds total variable and differential fixed costs, the firm will increase its profits by accepting the order. This analysis assumes that the company has no better alternative uses for its excess capacity and that special sales by the chain will have no adverse effect on Kent's normal sales. But what if regular customers hear about this special order and insist on lower prices, thus disrupting the normal pricing structure? Or, what if filling the special order will have an adverse effect on the quality of current products or the speed with which products can be offered to regular customers? These and other qualitative factors must also be considered.

A manager must also consider whether acceptance of such an order would be a violation of the Robinson-Patman Act. This legislation, enacted in 1936, prohibits firms from quoting different prices to competing customers for the same goods unless differences in price can be attributed to differences in cost. In the case of Kent Electronics, the sale is probably legal because the calculators are to be sold under the store's brand name, and the department store will assume all advertising costs.

The differential-cost approach to pricing can also be used in explaining why theater tickets are less expensive for matinees than for evening performances and why it is cheaper to make telephone calls at night and on weekends than on weekdays. If there is excess capacity that can be used to provide a service or make a product that will generate more revenue than the differential cost of providing the service or making the product, the firm will increase its profits by the amount of the margin remaining after deducting differential costs. As explained in a Business Environment included earlier in the chapter, this is exactly the rationale for the existence of PRICELINE.COM.

A few words of caution are in order when making these special order decisions. First, in some situations, there may also be some additional fixed costs that are relevant to the pricing decision. Second, a company must not accept too many orders that barely cover variable costs, or it will not be able to cover all its fixed costs. Third, using all extra capacity to fill a special order at a lower-than-normal price may prevent a company from being able to accept additional work at higher prices in the future; this is an example of an opportunity cost. Fourth, accepting a special order may force a company to cut corners with normal customers, resulting in lower-quality products or services to those customers or decreasing the speed at which other customers are served.

Making or Buying Products

In the previous section, we looked at special orders from the perspective of the seller. Whenever there is a special order, there is also a buyer. Many times, when a buyer has placed a special order, that buyer has made a decision to purchase rather than make the purchased product or service. Other times, the buyer may be a company that does not have the capacity to make the product or service and is placing the special order in the belief that the product or service can be purchased at less than market prices because the seller has excess capacity. If a buyer cannot make the product or service, the only decision is whether or not to buy. Differential-cost analysis doesn't help in making that decision. Rather, questions such as "can we afford to make the purchase," "do we need to make the purchase," and "where should we make the purchase" drive the purchase decision. Where differential-cost analysis makes a difference is when companies are making tradeoffs between making or buying products or services.

Many companies outsource virtually everything. For example, a food packaging plant might outsource to an employment agency the task of hiring, firing, training, and paying its production line employees. The plant might also outsource its custodial and bookkeeping services to local providers of those services. The plant might even outsource key management tasks by asking a consulting or professional services firm to provide a top-level manager to run the plant. As another example, many Internet businesses are "virtual outsourcers." They take orders from customers and relay those orders to manufacturers, which, in turn, ship the products directly to the customers. In contrast, other organizations make or provide most of their products and services internally. In the following section, we describe the factors companies must consider when deciding whether to buy products and services from outsiders or to produce these products and services themselves.

Making or Buying Manufactured Parts

Companies, such as automobile manufacturers, must decide which products and services they will produce and offer internally and which ones they will outsource or buy from outsiders. With respect to manufactured products, if a product consists of a number of parts, management must decide for each component whether to produce it or purchase it from an outside supplier. Over time, and based on a consideration of the relevant quantitative and qualitative

Automobile Manufacturers: Make or Buy? As an example of a make or buy decision, consider the case of automobile manufacturers. More than most firms, automobile manufacturers have to decide whether to make or buy component parts for their cars.

For a number of years, in-house production has been in steady decline and outsourcing has been on the rise, for both U.S. domestic and foreign manufacturers. Among U.S. car makers, GENERAL MOTORS continues to manufacture a high percentage of components internally, while DAIMLERCHRYSLER outsources more than any other firm. VOLKSWAGEN produces on average less than 50% of its automotive components in Germany. Indeed, in terms of country of origin, Volkswagen is as much a Mexican product as it is a German one. And, as international trade arrangements such as NAFTA and the European Union continue to gain favor and provide regional comparative advantages, international outsourcing will accelerate.

Source: Information obtained from **http://www .toyota.co.jp/Rueb/special.rep/pdf/toyotaphilosophy .pdf**

factors, management develops a long-term policy regarding the use of its facilities to produce components for its products.

The fact that a long-term policy about make versus buy has been established by a particular company does not mean that the issue is permanently closed. In fact, management should always be reconsidering its decisions and looking for new ways to save money, improve quality, or speed up manufacturing and delivery processes. If a firm has idle facilities, for example, management may wish to find a use for those facilities. One possibility is to manufacture components that are normally purchased. Whether this decision is wise depends not only on cost considerations but also on a number of qualitative factors, such as the likely effect on the regular source of supply, the company's ability to produce a high-quality component, speed of delivery, and management's interest in keeping workers on the payroll. Thus, even though a firm has a long-term policy of purchasing some components and producing others, certain situations may require decisions that alter that policy.

Assuming that the qualitative factors favor the use of idle facilities to produce the part, what costs are relevant to a make-or-buy decision? In general, the purchase cost and all other costs that can be avoided if the part is manufactured are differential costs. Any cost that will be incurred regardless of whether the part is purchased or manufactured is not a differential cost and is irrelevant.

To illustrate how the differential costs in such a decision are identified, assume that Ritter Manufacturing Company has excess capacity that could be used in producing wheel bearings. The accounting department has compiled the following projected total-cost figures for producing the bearings.

	Cost per Unit	Costs for 1,000 Units
Direct materials	$ 3.00	$ 3,000
Direct labor	8.00	8,000
Variable manufacturing overhead	4.00	4,000
Fixed manufacturing overhead, direct	2.50	2,500
Fixed manufacturing overhead, indirect	5.00	5,000*
Total costs	$22.50	$22,500

*Total indirect fixed costs are the same under both alternatives.

The company has been buying this bearing from a regular supplier in 1,000-unit quantities at a price of $19 per unit. Should Ritter continue to buy or start making the bearings? To answer this question, management must identify the differential costs of each alternative, taking into account any additional resources that may be needed, as well as alternative uses for the currently idle facilities. Two possible situations are presented here.

Situation 1

The currently idle facilities have no alternative uses. If the idle facilities do not have any practical alternative use, the opportunity cost is zero. With no opportunity cost, the differential costs would be the costs strictly associated with manufacturing (direct labor, direct materials, and so on).

The costs of the two alternatives can be presented on a total-cost or a differential-cost basis, as shown in Exhibit 5. Although each analysis produces different total costs, both demonstrate that the firm would save $1,500 per 1,000 units ($1.50 per unit) by making the component rather than buying it. The company's final decision would depend, of course, on whether there were negative qualitative factors that would, in the opinion of management, more than offset the $1.50 unit-cost advantage of making the part.

Situation 2

The idle facilities can be rented for $4,000 if they are not used to manufacture bearings. Management estimates that, if the facilities are used for manufacturing, 1,000 wheel bearings could be manufactured during this time.

In this case, the opportunity cost of producing the bearings is $4,000, or an average cost of $4 per unit ($4,000 ÷ 1,000 units). This opportunity cost is an important consideration in the firm's decision whether to buy or make the part, as shown in Exhibit 6. When the opportunity cost is considered, the cost of producing the part is $2,500 more than the cost of buying it. Unless there are quality, time, or other qualitative factors that override this cost, Ritter should buy the bearing and rent the idle facilities. Remember, the essence of the make-or-buy problem is management's desire to achieve the best utilization of existing facilities in the short term.

Because opportunity costs do not represent actual transactions, they are not recorded in the accounts. Yet they are always significant in the decision-making process because each situation has at least two alternatives. Thus, opportunity costs provide a good illustration of why a manager cannot rely solely on the data collected for external financial reports.

FYI:

To see exactly how significant opportunity costs are, consider the following question: What is the largest cost borne by New York City in maintaining Central Park? The answer is not the cost of maintenance employees or equipment. Instead, the largest cost is the opportunity cost of the tens of billions of dollars the city could get by selling the land to real estate developers.

Exhibit 5: Analyses of the Costs of Using Idle Facilities (Situation 1)

	Total-Cost Analysis (per 1,000 Units)		Differential-Cost Analysis (per 1,000 Units)	
	Buy	**Make**	**Buy**	**Make**
Purchase cost	$19,000		$19,000	
Direct materials		$ 3,000		$ 3,000
Direct labor		8,000		8,000
Variable manufacturing overhead		4,000		4,000
Fixed manufacturing overhead:				
Direct		2,500		2,500
Indirect	5,000	5,000		
Total cost	$24,000	$22,500	$19,000	$17,500
Difference		$1,500		$1,500

Exhibit 6: The Effect of an Opportunity Cost on Analyses (Situation 2)

	Total-Cost Analysis (per 1,000 Units)		Differential-Cost Analysis (per 1,000 Units)	
	Buy	**Make**	**Buy**	**Make**
Purchase cost	$19,000		$19,000	
Direct materials		$ 3,000		$ 3,000
Direct labor		8,000		8,000
Variable manufacturing overhead		4,000		4,000
Fixed manufacturing overhead:				
Direct		2,500		2,500
Indirect	5,000	5,000		
Opportunity cost, rental		4,000		4,000
Total cost	$24,000	$26,500	$19,000	$21,500
Difference		$2,500		$2,500

Purchasing Services or Providing Them Internally

In recent years, companies have not only outsourced product parts, but more and more they are also outsourcing services such as cafeteria service, garbage removal, payroll accounting, legal services, and even basic accounting. In deciding whether to acquire services or provide them internally, companies go through the same kind of analysis as if they were buying products. That is, they consider the differential costs of each alternative, as well as qualitative factors, such as the quality of the service, whether space exists to house the service, whether services can be delivered on a timely basis, and management's interest in keeping workers on the payroll. Assuming management believes it can acquire high-quality services both within and outside the company, what costs are relevant to the purchase-or-provide decisions? Costs that will be incurred regardless of whether the service is purchased or provided internally are not differential costs and are irrelevant to the decision.

To illustrate how the differential costs are identified, assume that Ritter Manufacturing Company is considering outsourcing its payroll function. The following annual cost information relating to payroll accounting is available.

Costs of Payroll Accounting Department

Salaries of payroll accounting employees	$2,600,000
Training costs	100,000
Depreciation on payroll accounting offices	50,000
Utilities for payroll accounting offices	40,000
Computers, software, and supplies	150,000
Other variable costs	75,000
Total costs of payroll accounting	$3,015,000

A CPA firm has offered to perform the payroll accounting services for $3,100,000 per year. You have determined that if payroll accounting services were contracted out to the CPA firm, the space currently used by the payroll department could be used by the purchasing department, which is currently occupying rented space in a nearby city. The rent paid for offices used by the purchasing department is $10,000 per month.

FYI:

In the 1990s and early 2000s, major CPA firms became professional service firms that offered all kinds of new services. One of the fasting-growing services that was offered by CPA firms was internal audit services for major corporations. However, with the plethora of financial statement frauds in companies such as ENRON and WORLD-COM, Congress passed the Sarbanes-Oxley Act that, among other things, prohibited CPA firms from being both the external auditor and the internal auditor. ARTHUR ANDERSEN, which went out of business after the Enron debacle, for example, was both the internal and external auditor for Enron. However, CPA firms can still perform internal audit services as long as they are not the external auditor of the same company.

Should Ritter continue to have its own payroll department, or should it outsource its payroll accounting function to a CPA firm? From a strictly financial point of view, Ritter should not outsource, as shown below.

Cost of outsourcing:

CPA firm cost		$3,100,000
Rent saved by relocating purchasing department		
($10,000 per month × 12 months)		(120,000)
Net cost of outsourcing		$2,980,000

Cost of maintaining payroll department:

Total cost of payroll department		$3,015,000
Less: Nondifferential costs (incurred under either alternative)		
Depreciation expense	$50,000	
Utilities	40,000	
Total nondifferential costs		(90,000)
Differential cost of maintaining payroll department		$2,925,000
Excess cost incurred by outsourcing payroll accounting		$ 55,000

Of course, the one-year cost analysis is really an incomplete analysis. In making the decision, management must determine what the future costs of each alternative will be. If, for example, management can lock into a five-year commitment of $3,100,000 annually and it believes costs of keeping the payroll department will rise $100,000 per year, from a cost perspective, the company may want to outsource even though the cost is higher in the current year.

In addition to costs, management must consider many other factors. For example, will the CPA firm provide payroll services of the same or higher quality as those provided by the internal accountants? Quality of services is very important in an area like payroll accounting, where it is difficult for management to judge whether the company is getting value for its money. Management would also want to consider other factors: (1) Will the CPA firm be able to provide the services in the long run? (2) Can the company use the displaced payroll accounting employees in other positions, or is the company willing to lay off employees? (3) Will outsourcing the payroll accounting services affect the cost of other services received by the company? (4) If payroll accounting was used as an accounting trainee development area (as it is in many companies), are there other efficient and effective ways to train future company accountants?

Caution

Be careful to consider all differential costs and revenues in making evaluation decisions and to exclude the nondifferential costs. For example, in this payroll accounting example, if depreciation and utilities (which will be incurred whether or not payroll accounting services are outsourced) are considered, an incorrect decision will be made.

TO SUMMARIZE: Managers must often decide whether a special order should be accepted (from the seller's perspective) or placed (from the buyer's perspective). A special order is a one-time order that is not considered part of the company's normal ongoing business. Considering finances only, from the seller's perspective, the special order should be accepted if the seller has excess capacity and if the differential costs of providing the special order are less than the differential revenues that will be generated from the special order.

Differential-cost analysis is only helpful in considering special orders from the buyer's perspective when the buyer has an option to either make or buy the product or service. In choosing whether to make or buy a component or service, management must compare the differential costs of making the part or providing the service (including the opportunity costs of alternative uses of the facilities) with the cost of purchasing (outsourcing) the part or service. Qualitative factors must also be considered in special order decisions because they may be significant enough to reverse a decision based only on quantitative considerations.

Exiting or Entering a Market

The decision of whether to exit or enter a market is usually based on careful evaluation, although companies seem to be buying and selling businesses quite often these days. We will first consider the decision of whether to exit a market and then the decision of whether to enter a market.

Exiting a Market

When a segment (product or line of products) is losing money, management must decide whether to drop it. In the Web support material to this textbook, we provide an example of Philips, a company that decided to exit the semiconductor business. Such decisions are particularly difficult because the differential costs are not easy to identify, and this can lead to analyses based on invalid assumptions, as the following example demonstrates.

To illustrate, assume that Augusta Retail Company is thinking of closing one of its stores. The question of the store's continuing viability arose because of the July financial results for the company's three stores (amounts are in thousands):

	Store 1	Store 2	Store 3	Total
Sales revenue	$250,000	$90,000	$60,000	$400,000
Cost of goods sold	170,000	40,000	30,000	240,000
Gross margin	$ 80,000	$50,000	$30,000	$160,000
Operating expenses	55,000	30,000	35,000	120,000
Net income (or loss)	$ 25,000	$20,000	$ (5,000)	$ 40,000

If Store 3 is closed, it would seem reasonable to assume that Augusta Retail Company's profits will increase by $5 million, as shown here.

	Store 1	Store 2	Total
Sales revenue	$250,000	$90,000	$340,000
Cost of goods sold	170,000	40,000	210,000
Gross margin	$ 80,000	$50,000	$130,000
Operating expenses	55,000	30,000	85,000
Net income	$ 25,000	$20,000	$ 45,000

This analysis is based on three assumptions:

1. That all costs shown are differential and therefore relevant to the decision. In other words, there are no joint costs (costs that are common to two or more stores).
2. That the sales of the other stores will not be affected by dropping Store 3.
3. That no qualitative factors have a bearing on the decision.

Before closing Store 3, the company's general manager should check the validity of these assumptions. For simplicity, suppose that the second and third assumptions are valid, and that only the first assumption needs verification. First, the accounting department must separate the total costs of each store into variable costs, direct fixed costs, and indirect (or unavoidable) fixed costs. With this new information, the accounting department might prepare the following modified report for July (amounts are in thousands).

	Store 1	Store 2	Store 3	Total
Sales revenue	$250,000	$90,000	$60,000	$400,000
Variable costs	190,000	50,000	40,000	280,000
Contribution margin	$ 60,000	$40,000	$20,000	$120,000
Direct fixed costs	20,000	15,000	18,000	53,000
Segment margin	$ 40,000	$25,000	$ 2,000	$ 67,000
Indirect fixed costs (not allocated)				27,000
Net income				$ 40,000

The manager can use this modified report to determine whether Store 3 made a positive contribution toward covering the indirect (unavoidable) fixed costs. In looking at this modified report, the manager would immediately see that the segment margin for Store 3 is a positive $2 million. This means that Store 3 is contributing $2 million to the company's overall profit. Thus, if Store 3 is dropped, profits will decrease by $2 million unless another store with greater profit potential is added or Store 3 can be sold to another company. To illustrate the potential decline in profits if Store 3 is dropped, the manager might ask the accounting department to prepare a report to indicate what the company's July financial results would show without Store 3. This pro-forma report would show the following information (amounts are in thousands):

	Store 1	Store 2	Total
Sales revenue	$250,000	$90,000	$340,000
Variable costs	190,000	50,000	240,000
Contribution margin	$ 60,000	$40,000	$100,000
Direct fixed costs	20,000	15,000	35,000
Segment margin	$ 40,000	$25,000	$ 65,000
Indirect fixed costs (not allocated)			27,000
Net income			$ 38,000

Although the original report suggested that profits would increase by $5 million if Store 3 were dropped, total profits would actually decrease by $2 million ($40 million − $38 million). The reason is that Store 3 is generating revenues that are $2 million greater than differential costs (variable costs and avoidable fixed costs). This analysis suggests that Store 3 should not be dropped, unless it can be replaced by another store or business that will contribute more than $2 million to cover unavoidable indirect fixed costs. (Obviously, we have not considered any sales price Augusta could receive from selling Store 3. Any money received from selling Store 3 would need to be weighed against the $2 million annual contribution Store 3 is making toward covering indirect costs.)

Entering a Market

The considerations involved in deciding whether to enter a market are quite similar to those when deciding whether or not to exit a market. From a financial perspective, if adding a product line (segment) will contribute to the income of a firm, it is generally a good decision. The contribution can come in several forms. First, entering a new market can reduce the current cost of doing business. For example, assume that Augusta is considering purchasing a wholesale distribution company that will allow the company to buy directly from manufacturers, rather than from other wholesalers, when acquiring merchandise for its stores. Even if the new wholesale company is not profitable on its own, if it could reduce Augusta's costs enough so that overall profits are higher, the decision to buy might be a good one. Buying a new company or entering a new market could increase overall company profits by having the new segment cover some of the indirect fixed costs now being borne entirely by existing businesses. From a financial perspective, the important point to consider is whether total profits will be higher or lower after the purchase.

In addition to the financial considerations, organizations consider the effects on quality and time to deliver products to customers when deciding whether to enter a market. For example, suppose a small company has superior-quality products, manufacturing knowledge, or other attributes that could enhance the quality of the organization's products. Would it be wise to buy this smaller company even if the purchase doesn't increase overall short-term profits? Probably so. Or, what if a company occupies a strategic location for serving an organization's customers and buying the company would allow the organization to deliver its products more quickly to customers? Would buying the strategically located company be a good decision even if short-term overall profits aren't increased? Again, probably so. Both purchases would allow the organization to serve its customers better by increasing quality and decreasing delivery time. Hopefully, the result of both purchases would be a larger market share and higher profits in the long run. Unfortunately, it is hard to quantify by how much quality and/or delivery time must improve before a purchase is a good one. Because quality and time decisions are subjective, we will focus on the short-term financial considerations in deciding whether to enter a market. You should realize, however, that quality and time considerations are very important, and in considering some purchases, they may be the overriding factors that outweigh short-term financial considerations.

To illustrate entering a new market, assume that Augusta Retail Company now has only two stores. Further, assume that it is considering purchasing the wholesale company just discussed. The following data are available for Augusta Retail Company prior to making the purchase (amounts are in thousands):

	Store 1	Store 2	Total
Sales revenue	$250,000	$90,000	$340,000
Cost of goods sold	170,000	40,000	210,000
Other variable costs	20,000	10,000	30,000
Contribution margin	$ 60,000	$40,000	$100,000
Direct fixed costs	20,000	15,000	35,000
Segment margin	$ 40,000	$25,000	$ 65,000
Indirect fixed costs (not allocated)			27,000
Net income			$ 38,000

As these data show, Augusta currently makes a net income of $38 million. Now, assume that Augusta can purchase a wholesale company that will allow Augusta to buy directly from manufacturers, thus decreasing its cost of goods sold by 30%. However, the wholesale company is currently losing $10 million per year. Should Augusta buy the wholesale company? The following analysis shows that, from a financial perspective, buying the wholesale company would be a good decision (again, amounts are in thousands).

Effect on Current Stores

	Store 1 Before	Store 1 After	Store 2 Before	Store 2 After	Total (before and after purchase) Before	Total (before and after purchase) After	Wholesale Company	Total (including wholesale company)
Sales revenue	$250,000	$250,000	$90,000	$90,000	$340,000	$340,000	$110,000	$450,000
Cost of goods sold	170,000	119,000[1]	40,000	28,000[2]	210,000	147,000	70,000	217,000
Other variable costs	20,000	20,000	10,000	10,000	30,000	30,000	15,000	45,000
Contribution margin	$ 60,000	$111,000	$40,000	$52,000	$100,000	$163,000	$ 25,000	$188,000
Direct fixed costs	20,000	20,000	15,000	15,000	35,000	35,000	35,000	70,000
Segment margin	$ 40,000	$ 91,000	$25,000	$37,000	$ 65,000	$128,000	$ (10,000)	$118,000
Indirect fixed costs (not allocated)					27,000	27,000	—	27,000
Net income					$ 38,000	$101,000	$ (10,000)	$ 91,000

[1]$170,000 − (0.3 × $170,000) = $119,000.
[2]$40,000 − (0.3 × $40,000) = $28,000.

This analysis shows that even though the wholesale company is losing $10 million per year, purchasing the wholesale company will increase overall company profits by $53 million ($91 million − $38 million). Of course, this elaborate analysis really wasn't necessary since many costs (other variable costs, direct fixed costs, and indirect fixed costs) stayed the same. In fact, the only differential costs were the decrease in cost of goods sold (facilitated by being able to buy directly from manufacturers instead of wholesalers) and the $10 million loss the wholesale company incurs. Focusing only on the differential costs, you can see that the net income of the company would be increased by $53 million upon buying the wholesale company (numbers are in thousands).

Differential Costs of Deciding to Enter a Market

Decrease in cost of goods sold of Store 1	$ 51,000
Decrease in cost of goods sold of Store 2	12,000
Loss incurred by wholesaler	(10,000)
Increase in income from buying wholesaler	$ 53,000

This analysis suggests that, from a financial perspective, the wholesale company should be purchased. The decreases in cost of goods sold that will result in Store 1 and Store 2 more than compensate for the losses currently being incurred by the wholesaler.

TO SUMMARIZE: In deciding whether to exit or enter a market, the effect on profits, quality, and speed of delivery should be considered. When focusing on the financial aspects of exiting or entering a market, only the differential costs and revenues need be considered. A product or line of products should not be dropped unless it does not make a contribution toward covering indirect fixed costs. An alternative product or line of products can be added that will contribute more toward covering unavoidable indirect fixed costs. A segment should be added if it increases overall company profits. The increase in overall company profits can come from reduced costs in existing segments or from the profitable margin of the acquired segment.

Determining at What Stage of Production to Sell Products

joint manufacturing process When one material input is used to produce more than one product.

In some companies, all the products evolve out of a **joint manufacturing process**, meaning that one material input is used to produce more than one product. Gasoline, oil, and kerosene, for example, are all produced from refining crude oil; various cuts of beef are provided from butchering a steer; and different qualities and types of lumber are available from processing timber. In all these cases, the products are produced simultaneously and are not individually identifiable until the split-off point in the process. When this is the case, management must decide whether a particular product from the joint manufacturing process should be sold as is at the split-off point, or processed further at additional cost, with the expectation of obtaining a higher price.

In choosing the best time to stop processing a product, management basically compares the additional costs that would be incurred from further processing with the additional revenues. If the incremental revenues are greater than the incremental costs, net income is increased, and additional processing is worthwhile (unless qualitative factors dictate otherwise). If the incremental revenues are less than the incremental costs, the product should probably be sold without further processing. The costs that a firm incurs before the point at which the different products are separated for further processing or immediate sale are called **joint product costs**. These costs are incurred whether the separate products are sold at the point of separation or after further processing. Thus, they are not relevant to a choice between the two alternatives.

joint product costs The costs that a firm incurs before the point at which the different products are separated for further processing or immediate sale.

To illustrate the decision-making process related to further processing, we will assume that Armaco Oil Company derives two products, jet fuel and reformate, from crude oil. Although crude oil cannot be sold independently, both jet fuel and reformate can be, either at the point of separation or after further processing. Further processing jet fuel results in a petrochemical product called xylene, while further processing of reformate results in a petrochemical called tolulene. The cost of refining 375,000 gallons of crude oil up to the point of separation is $300,000. Crude oil is then separated into 200,000 gallons of jet fuel and 150,000 gallons of reformate. The remaining 25,000 gallons are lost in the process of refining. The selling prices of jet fuel and reformate at the point of separation, the costs of processing further, and the selling prices after this further processing are estimated by the accounting department to be as follows:

	Gallons	Net Selling Price per Gallon at Separation	Additional Processing Costs	Net Selling Price of Xylene and Tolulene per Gallon After Processing
Jet fuel	200,000	$1.20	$80,000	$1.70 (xylene)
Reformate	150,000	1.00	90,000	1.50 (tolulene)

To help management decide whether to sell jet fuel or reformate at the point of separation or to process them further, the following analysis can be prepared.

Product: Jet Fuel/Xylene

Sales revenue after further processing (200,000 gallons @ $1.70)	$340,000
Sales revenue at point of separation (200,000 gallons @ $1.20)	240,000
Additional revenue from further processing	$100,000
Additional processing costs	80,000
Additional profit from further processing	$ 20,000

Product: Reformate/Tolulene

Sales revenue after further processing (150,000 gallons @ $1.50)	$225,000
Sales revenue at point of separation (150,000 gallons @ $1.00)	150,000
Additional revenue from further processing	$ 75,000
Additional processing costs	90,000
Additional loss from further processing	$ (15,000)

This analysis shows that further processing of jet fuel into xylene will contribute an additional $20,000 to net income because the additional revenues generated exceed the additional processing costs by $20,000. On the other hand, further processing of reformate into tolulene will reduce net income by $15,000 because the additional processing costs are greater than the additional revenues by that amount. Therefore, reformate should be sold at the point of separation.

A total-cost approach to analyzing this decision is shown in Exhibit 7. Selling both products after further processing increases net income by $5,000, but the best choice is to sell reformate at the point of separation and to process jet fuel into xylene before it is sold. The worst choice is to sell jet fuel at the point of separation and further process reformate, resulting in only $75,000 of profit. Note that the joint processing costs were not considered in the earlier analysis of the individual products since they are not differential costs but are the same for each alternative. In the later analysis of the alternative treatments of jet fuel and reformate, however, the joint costs are included simply to illustrate the total-cost approach. But they are not really necessary because the difference in net income is the same whether or not the $300,000 of joint costs are included.

In deciding whether to sell products at the point of separation or after further processing, management must also consider qualitative factors. For example, management will need to consider quality and time issues, as well as the hiring or firing of employees and customers' demands for particular products.

Exhibit 7: A Comparison of Alternatives: Selling at Point of Separation or After Further Processing

	Sell Both Products at Separation	Sell Both Products After Further Processing	Sell Reformate at Separation and Process Jet Fuel Further	Sell Jet Fuel at Separation and Process Reformate Further
Sales revenue:				
Jet fuel/Xylene	$240,000	$340,000	$340,000	$240,000
Reformate/Tolulene	150,000	225,000	150,000	225,000
Total sales revenue	$390,000	$565,000	$490,000	$465,000
Joint product costs	$300,000	$300,000	$300,000	$300,000
Further processing costs	0	170,000	80,000	90,000
Total costs	$300,000	$470,000	$380,000	$390,000
Net income	$ 90,000	$ 95,000	$110,000	$ 75,000

TO SUMMARIZE: In some industries, a number of end products are produced from a single raw material input. Two or more products that are produced from a common input are known as joint products. Joint costs are the costs that are incurred up to the point where the products can be sold as separate products. Differential-cost analysis can help determine whether joint products should be sold at the point where they become recognized as separate products or processed further. It will always be profitable to continue processing a joint product after the split-off point as long as the incremental revenue from the extra processing exceeds the incremental processing costs incurred after the split-off point. Joint costs that have been incurred up to the point of split-off are always irrelevant to the additional processing decision.

Selecting the Best Use of a Scarce Resource

Organizations are often faced with the decision of how to best use scarce resources. In a manufacturing company, the scarce resource might be limited raw materials or limited production capacity. For a retail merchandising firm, such as WAL-MART, the scarce resource might be limited shelf space. For a service firm, the scarce resource might be the limited expertise of the trained professionals. We will illustrate the concept of scarce resources using limited shelf space for a retail merchandising firm.

When a retail merchandising firm sells more than one product and store shelves are inadequate to display all products equally, management has to decide to which products the store should allocate shelf space and how much space should be allocated to each product. With limited shelf space, stocking one product means that another product cannot be stocked or will have to be stocked on a more limited basis. In deciding which products to stock, management needs to know which products and how much of each product to stock in order to maximize net income. A retail store will normally maximize net income by stocking those products that contribute the most toward covering fixed costs and providing profit in relation to the "critical resource factor," in this case, shelf space. The **critical resource factor** is the resource that limits operating capacity by its availability. For example, in a manufacturing company, if machine hours are the most critical resource, a company should concentrate on the product for which revenues exceed variable costs by the highest margin per machine hour. Other critical resources in manufacturing companies might include labor hours, floor space, or special raw materials. Because shelf space is the critical resource factor for our retail store example, from a financial point of view, management should stock those products for which revenues exceed variable costs by the highest margin per square foot of shelf space.

To illustrate, we assume that Bolten Retail Company stocks potato chips and cookies. Let's further assume that its capacity, at least in the short term, is limited by the availability of only 20 square feet of shelf space for these two products. The revenue and cost data for one package each of potato chips and cookies are:

	Potato Chips	Cookies
Selling price	$3.10	$3.50
Variable costs	2.48	3.15
Contribution margin per unit	$0.62	$0.35
Percentage contribution margin (contribution margin ÷ selling price)	20%	10%

On the basis of this limited information, it would appear that potato chips are more profitable than cookies. The sale of one bag of potato chips will contribute $0.62 toward fixed costs, whereas the sale of one package of cookies will contribute only $0.35.

Before Bolten can decide whether or not to emphasize potato chips, however, management must consider the extent to which each product uses the critical resource, limited shelf space. If a bag of potato chips takes up twice as much space as a package of cookies (two bags of potato chips occupy one square foot of shelf space, while four packages of cookies can occupy the same one square foot of shelf space), the sale of cookies will make a greater total contribution to profits than the sale of potato chips, as shown by the following calculations:[3]

	Potato Chips	Cookies
Contribution margin per unit	$0.62	$0.35
Packages per square foot	× 2	× 4
Contribution margin per square foot of shelf space	$1.24	$1.40

3 We are assuming that the company can sell all the potato chips and cookies it stocks. If it can't, or if one product sells faster than the other, rate of turnover must be considered.

critical resource factor The resource that limits operating capacity by its availability.

Even though potato chips have a higher contribution margin per unit of product ($0.62 versus $0.35), cookies have a higher contribution margin per square foot of shelf space ($1.40 versus $1.24), which is the critical resource. The management of Bolten Retail Company should stock cookies rather than potato chips, assuming that the company's only critical resource is shelf space.

STOP & THINK

Why do you think that most grocery stores allocate more space to breakfast cereals than to most other products?

However, if the demand for cookies is limited and Bolten never has potato chips for sale, will customers start shopping at other stores? In that case, Bolten should stock as many cookies as it can sell and use the balance of the critical resource for stocking potato chips. To illustrate, we assume that the market demand for cookies is 1,800 packages per month or an average of 60 per day. Because it takes only 15 square feet of shelf space (60 packages ÷ 4 packages per square foot) to store one day's worth of cookies, 5 square feet of shelf space are available to stock potato chips. This means that 10 bags of potato chips can be stocked. Assuming all 10 bags are sold during each day, the combined sales of cookies and potato chips will contribute $27.20 to cover fixed costs and provide a profit, as shown below.

	Daily Contribution Margin
Packages sold:	
Potato chips (10 bags × $0.62 per bag)	$ 6.20
Cookies (60 packages × $0.35 per package)	21.00
Total	$27.20

This analysis shows that from a financial perspective, the best use of the 20 square feet of shelf space is to use 15 square feet for cookies and 5 square feet for potato chips. Because demand for cookies is limited, only a $21 daily contribution margin can be earned by selling cookies. The other 5 feet of shelf space should be used to stock potato chips. Obviously, nonfinancial factors, such as customer satisfaction, would also have to be considered in making the final decision of how much of each product to stock.

Caution

It is essential to carefully and accurately identify the scarce resource and the quantity of the scarce resource consumed by each product. For example, in the store shelf space decision, if you don't carefully calculate the amount of space needed for cookies and potato chips and instead look only at the contribution margin per unit, an incorrect decision will be made. It is only when you consider the contribution margin per square foot of shelf space that the correct decision is made.

The foregoing analysis dealt with only two constraints: store shelf space and product demand. If a firm is further limited by other factors (such as the ability to buy certain amounts of particular products), management generally has to use the quantitative techniques of linear programming or simulation to help decide how many of each product to produce and/or sell. You can learn about this technique in advanced accounting or business management courses. Regardless of the number of constraints, though, the essence of the decision is to achieve the best short-term utilization of available resources.

In the expanded material section of this chapter, you will find a discussion of the theory of constraints, a philosophical approach to focusing on "constraints" as a way to allocate limited resources and improve management processes.

TO SUMMARIZE: In deciding how to make the best use of critical resource factors, management should choose the item that provides the greatest contribution margin per unit of the most critical resource.

Setting Selling Prices

Some people argue that a discussion of setting prices in a book such as this is a waste of time because the market sets the price and there is nothing management can do to affect prices. Others argue that, especially in some markets, management does set prices or at least influence prices. In this section, we assume that management can influence prices and discuss those factors management should consider.

Pricing a product is partly a matter of guesswork because managers rarely know with any precision how price affects demand (e.g., how many more units could be sold if the price were to be lowered by a certain amount). In addition, other factors, such as advertising and packaging, affect the sale of a product.

The pricing process is further complicated by the fact that there are several broad categories of pricing decisions and the same cost information is not appropriate for all of them. Earlier, we considered the pricing of special orders. In this section, we cover the pricing of normal products. Other pricing categories, including the pricing of new products, are covered in advanced accounting and marketing texts.

Normal Pricing of Products

In deciding whether to accept special orders, we stated that the price must be high enough to cover variable and incremental fixed costs. The price normally charged for a product or service, however, must be high enough to cover all costs (including production, selling, and administrative costs) and still provide a reasonable return on the owners' investments. Therefore, all costs (variable, as well as a fair share of fixed costs) are relevant to the pricing decision. In some cases, however, the final price may be set somewhat above or below the price suggested by total cost plus a reasonable return. This occurs when pricing decisions are based primarily on supply and demand, competition, and other market factors. For example, textbook prices are strictly competitive. Whether it costs $250,000 or $500,000 to produce a textbook, the price of the book has to be close to that of the nearest competitors.

In supplying cost data to aid management in normal pricing decisions, accountants may use a functional approach, summarizing costs by function (manufacturing, selling, or administrative), or a contribution approach, classifying costs by behavior (fixed or variable). To illustrate the two approaches, we assume that Kent Electronics (from the calculator example earlier in the chapter) is pricing a desk calculator. The relevant costs for each approach are as follows:

Functional Cost Approach

Direct materials	$ 6
Direct labor	8
Manufacturing overhead (200% × direct labor cost)	16
Total manufacturing cost	$30
Markup to cover selling and administrative expenses and provide a reasonable return on investment (0.40 × selling price)	20
Estimated normal selling price	$50

Contribution Approach

Direct materials	$ 6
Direct labor	8
Variable manufacturing overhead	7
Variable selling and administrative overhead expenses	4
Total variable costs	$25
Markup to cover fixed costs and provide a reasonable return on investment (0.50 × selling price)	25
Estimated normal selling price	$50

The markups calculated here are based on the selling price because marketing people generally use this approach. How do we calculate the markup as a percentage of the selling price before that price is known? If the markup is to be 40% of the selling price, as in our first example, the total manufacturing cost must be 60% of the selling price. So we simply divide the manufacturing cost by 60% to get the selling price ($30 ÷ 0.60 = $50). Then, the selling price minus the manufacturing cost is the markup ($50 − $30 = $20).

If a functional cost approach is used, the markup must be large enough to cover all selling and administrative costs and provide a reasonable return on investment. If a contribution approach is used, the markup must be large enough to cover all fixed costs and generate a reasonable return on investment.

> **TO SUMMARIZE:** For normal pricing of products, management should consider all costs, not just differential costs (as was the case with pricing special orders). The markups applied must be high enough to cover all costs and expenses and provide a reasonable return on investment.

Thus far in this chapter, we have discussed how and why organizations evaluate products and processes, including the concepts of benchmarking and differential costs and revenues. We have also provided several examples of evaluation decisions, such as whether to accept special orders, whether to outsource or provide services and products internally, whether to continue or discontinue existing product lines or expand into new product lines or geographic regions, whether to sell or continue processing products developed from joint manufacturing processes, how best to use critical resources, and how to set selling prices. We have also explained how to make product and process evaluation decisions by focusing on differential costs and revenues. In this expanded section, we discuss another approach to making product and process evaluation decisions—the theory of constraints. This approach or philosophy, which has gained in popularity in recent years, was developed during the 1980s and involves making production decisions by focusing on bottleneck resources. The theory of constraints advocates that only constraint resources should operate at full capacity.

Theory of Constraints

5 Understand the theory of constraints and how focusing on scarce resources can direct activities in manufacturing companies.

theory of constraints (TOC) A management philosophy that focuses on constraint resources and holds that they should operate at full capacity.

To compete against global rivals in the early 1980s, managers from a variety of industries worked hard to revitalize their manufacturing practices. During this period, a manufacturing philosophy called the **theory of constraints (TOC)** or optimized production technology (OPT) received considerable attention. TOC was popularized by Eliyahu Goldratt, an Israeli physicist, in his book *The Goal*. Goldratt claimed that by scheduling production by focusing on bottleneck resources, a firm could develop and maintain a manufacturing-based competitive advantage over other firms. The premise of TOC is that only constraint resources should operate at full capacity. That is, a facility can produce a finished product no faster than the constraint resource can process the materials that go into the product. The constraint resource acts as the "drum," setting the production pace for the entire operation. Once material has been processed on the constraint resource, it should not sit idle but should be kept moving until shipped to the customer. By following a few basic rules, each of which focuses management's attention on the firm's constraint resource, managers can use TOC to maximize the throughput (amount of product produced in available facilities) of their production facility. The result is that the firm is better able to meet its customers' needs.

Constraint management can improve a company's competitive position by helping it better schedule and utilize its productive resources. When the constraint resource becomes the focal point, nonconstraint operations will operate below capacity, facilitating several positive outcomes. For example, nonconstraint resources no longer produce excess work-in-process (WIP) inventory; shop floor clutter and confusion are thereby reduced, production quality is improved, preventive maintenance activities are enhanced, and more time is available for employee training. By identifying the constraint resource and using it as the reference point for decision making, management can alter the very nature of key assumptions regarding product costing, performance measurement, product and process design, and make-versus-buy decisions. In general, the theory holds that more accurate assumptions lead to better decisions and enhanced competitiveness.

Employing TOC requires five basic steps:

1. *Understand the system's constraints.* The constraint may be a manufacturing process, a delivery process, or any other aspect of the process from taking delivery of raw materials to making sure finished products are sold and delivered.
2. *Decide how to exploit the system's constraints.* Production and pricing decisions should be based on the throughput yield per unit of constraint resource.
3. *Subordinate everything else to keeping the constraint resource operating at optimal capacity.* All nonconstraint activities should be coordinated with the constraint resource. This often requires a dramatic shift in managerial mindset, including allowing workers and machinery to sit idle or perform other, unrelated activities when not needed.
4. *Elevate the constraint.* By focusing on the constraint, it may be possible to offload some work to nonbottlenecks by acquiring more equipment or outsourcing some bottleneck work.
5. *If a constraint has been broken, go back to step 1.* Do not allow nonaction or inertia to cause a system constraint. Bottlenecks can, and will, shift around within an organization. Not properly identifying the relevant and current constraint can lead to a return of process inefficiencies and confused management policies.

Examples of companies that have adopted TOC are plentiful in the literature. For example, before employing TOC, a privately held metal tool manufacturing company used the ratio of indirect to direct labor hours as its key performance measure. Focusing on this measure caused the company to develop a "keep the workers busy at all costs" attitude, resulting in piles of excess WIP inventory, production inefficiencies, and a poorly focused pricing strategy. Under TOC, nonconstrained resources are allowed to sit idle, and the company uses this idle time to cross-train employees. As another example, a packing company struggled for a period of time with employees at nonbottlenecks who tried to stay busy by releasing WIP too early to the bottleneck operation. By implementing new, TOC-consistent performance measures, the company was able to eliminate buildups of WIP inventory and become more efficient.

As a simple example of the TOC, assume that Wilton Company requires five processes to make treadmills. The first process involves purchasing materials such as metal, rubber, and electronic components. There is no constraint on the amount of any of these materials that can be purchased. The second process involves manufacturing the various components of the treadmills. The equipment and personnel available to manufacture the components can produce parts for 20 treadmills per hour. The third process involves painting the various components. Painting equipment and personnel can process 18 treadmills per hour. The fourth process involves assembling the finished parts into completed treadmills. Assembly requires specially manufactured equipment that can process only 15 treadmills per hour. Finally, the fifth process, testing, has unlimited capacity because it involves labor only and additional workers can be hired. The following diagram shows the manufacturing processes and their capacities.

eXpanded *Material*

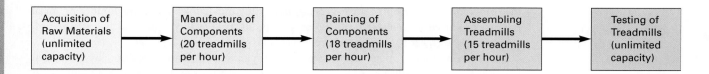

| Acquisition of Raw Materials (unlimited capacity) | → | Manufacture of Components (20 treadmills per hour) | → | Painting of Components (18 treadmills per hour) | → | Assembling Treadmills (15 treadmills per hour) | → | Testing of Treadmills (unlimited capacity) |

As you can see, if each process operated at full capacity, every hour the components for two treadmills would be produced that painting couldn't process, and three treadmills would be painted that couldn't be assembled. WIP inventory would accumulate in both the third and fourth processes, making production less efficient.

By focusing on the constraint resource—assembling in this case—the company might choose to purchase another specialized assembly machine, outsource some assembly, use the extra time in manufacturing components and painting to complete other jobs or cross-train, or even have some of the idle employees help out in testing treadmills. By focusing on constraint resources, management will know exactly where the bottlenecks are and can take action to fix the problem. Of course, if the constraint resource—assembly—is allowing the company to meet customer demands for treadmills, management may choose to undertake promotional campaigns or add additional products that can be made using excess capacity in component manufacturing and painting.

TO SUMMARIZE: TOC is a management philosophy that focuses management's attention on the bottlenecks or constraint resources. Other measures can result in excess WIP inventory or other inefficiencies. TOC helps management understand the kinds of decisions that will make the firm more productive.

review of learning objectives

1 Explain how evaluation leads to planning and why products and processes must be continuously evaluated. Evaluation is designed to improve the efficiency and cost-effectiveness of existing operations related to products and operating processes. Such decisions usually are in the form of corrective actions regarding machinery efficiency, reduction of waste, efficient task performance, and overcoming bottlenecks. Evaluation takes place regularly, often daily, weekly, or monthly. Sometimes evaluation leads to strategic decisions that deal with changes in the product or the processes. These decisions might be related to the type or quality of the company's products, fundamental changes in the production process, changing suppliers or types of raw materials, or changing the product distribution system.

2 Understand why benchmarking is so important and how it is conducted. Benchmarking involves comparing a company's financial and operating performance against a competitor's performance or comparing the performance of various internal departments against each other. It consists of four steps: (1) analyzing the company's practices, procedures, and performance in a given process; (2) selecting a benchmark

or benchmarks; (3) gathering information on the benchmark's practices and procedures; and (4) analyzing the data collected in step 3 to determine which policies and procedures used by the benchmarked companies can best be employed.

3 Understand the concept of differential costs and revenues, and be able to identify those costs and revenues that are relevant to making product and process decisions. Making product and process decisions involves a consideration of sunk costs, opportunity costs, and differential costs and revenues. Differential costs are future costs that will change as a result of the decision and therefore are the relevant costs in determining whether the decision to change should be made. Differential costs may be variable, fixed, or both. Past costs that do not change as a result of a decision are not relevant to the decision and are called sunk costs.

4 Identify several examples of product and process evaluation decisions, and be able to analyze and select the best alternative for each example. Examples of product and process decisions are (1) accepting or rejecting special orders, (2) making or buying products, (3) exiting or entering a market, (4) determining at what stage of production to sell products, and (5) selecting the best use of a scarce resource. In choosing whether to make or buy a component or service, management must compare the differential costs of making the part or providing the service (including the opportunity cost of alternative uses of the facilities or labor) with the cost of purchasing the part or service. In deciding whether or not to accept a special order in situations where there is excess capacity, the price should be high enough to provide a positive contribution toward covering normal fixed costs and increasing profit. A product or product line should not be dropped or a market exited unless that unit does not make a positive contribution toward covering indirect fixed costs. An alternative product or line of products can be added that will contribute more toward covering unavoidable indirect costs. A market should be entered only if it contributes to the overall profitability of the firm. It will always be profitable to continue processing a joint product after the split-off point as long as the incremental revenue from the extra processing exceeds the incremental processing costs incurred after the split-off point. Joint costs that have been incurred up to the point of split-off are always irrelevant to the decision. In deciding

how to use a scarce resource, management should choose the item that provides the greatest contribution margin per unit of the most critical resource. A product should be processed further if the additional revenues from further processing will exceed the additional costs of further processing. For normal pricing, management should consider all costs, not just differential costs.

5 **Understand the theory of constraints and how focusing on scarce resources can direct activities in manufacturing companies.** The theory of constraints (TOC) suggests that management should focus on the few "constraints" that are found in any management setting. The premise of TOC is that only constraint resources should operate at full capacity and that a facility can produce a finished product no faster than the constraint resource can process the materials that go into the product.

k ey terms & concepts

benchmarking, 519
critical resource factor, 541
differential costs, 521
joint manufacturing process, 539
joint product costs, 539

opportunity cost, 521
special order, 527
sunk costs, 521
total cost, 524

theory of constraints (TOC), 544

r eview problem

Whether to Make or Buy a Part

Schill Manufacturing Company makes lawn mowers. It has been buying a component from a regular supplier for $11.50 per unit. Because Schill recently has been operating at less than full capacity, the president is considering whether to make the part rather than purchase it. The estimated total cost of making the part under the company's costing system is $14.40, computed as follows:

Direct materials	$ 3.20
Direct labor	5.60
Manufacturing overhead (100% of direct labor cost)	5.60
Estimated total cost to make	$14.40

Variable manufacturing overhead costs are estimated to be 40% of direct labor cost. Fixed manufacturing costs that are not differential are 60% of direct labor cost.

Required:
Decide whether Schill should make or buy the component.

Solution

Differential-Cost Analysis

	Cost to Make	Cost to Buy
Purchase price		$11.50
Direct materials	$ 3.20	
Direct labor	5.60	
Variable manufacturing overhead (40% of direct labor cost)	2.24	
Differential cost to make the part	$11.04	
Differential cost to buy the part		$11.50
Cost savings by making the part	$ 0.46	

Total-Cost Analysis

	Cost to Make	Cost to Buy
Purchase price		$11.50
Direct materials	$ 3.20	
Direct labor	5.60	
Variable manufacturing overhead (40% of direct labor cost)	2.24	
Fixed manufacturing overhead	3.36	3.36
Total cost to make	$14.40	
Total cost to buy		$14.86
Cost savings by making the part	$ 0.46	

Calculations:
$5.60 × 0.40 = $2.24 variable manufacturing overhead
$5.60 × 0.60 = $3.36 fixed manufacturing overhead

Unless qualitative factors override the cost estimate, Schill should make the part rather than purchase it. The decision will be the same whether the calculation is based on differential costs only or on total costs. Note that the fixed manufacturing overhead cost applies to both making and buying the part under the total-cost analysis because these costs will be incurred whichever alternative is selected.

d iscussion questions

1. Why is it so important to continuously evaluate products and processes?
2. Many accounting systems are designed to collect financial information for the purpose of preparing financial statements. What problem does this create for an accountant who is asked to compile relevant data for use by managers to make product and process decisions? Explain.
3. What is a differential cost? Give an example of how differential costs are used by managers making product and process decisions.

4. Distinguish between variable costs and differential costs. Why is the distinction important?
5. Can a fixed cost be relevant to a decision? Explain.
6. What is a sunk cost? Why are sunk costs irrelevant in product and process decision making?
7. In deciding whether to replace an old asset with a new one, which of the following are differential revenues and costs?
   a. Cost of the new equipment
   b. Resale value of the old equipment
   c. Resale value of the new equipment
   d. Book value of the old equipment
   e. Operating costs of the new equipment
8. Distinguish between the total-cost approach and the differential-cost approach to analyzing data for product and process decisions.
9. What is the major limitation in using the total-cost approach to analyze data for product and process decisions?
10. Why must business decisions be based on qualitative as well as quantitative information? Explain.
11. Explain what costs are generally relevant to make-or-buy decisions.
12. Explain why opportunity costs are not included in the accounting records.
13. What is the significance of idle capacity in determining the price of a special order?
14. If total manufacturing costs, including fixed manufacturing overhead, are larger than the price offered by a purchaser for a special order, the order should not be accepted because the profits of the company will be adversely affected. Do you agree? Explain. (Ignore qualitative factors.)
15. In deciding whether to exit or enter a market, what factors should be considered?
16. When should a segment (product, product line, division, etc.) be dropped? When should a segment be added?
17. Why is the contribution margin per unit of a critical resource more important than the contribution margin per unit of product in deciding which products to produce and sell?
18. What determines whether a product should be sold at the point of separation from a joint process or after further processing? (Assume that a decision is to be based solely on quantitative information.)

19. Why does employing the TOC in manufacturing processes lead to less WIP inventory?
20. Proponents argue that the TOC helps management make better use of production resources and better decisions about whether or not to outsource and how to use employees effectively. Explain why this is so.

practice exercises

Practice 9-1

Evaluating Products and Processes
Which one of the following statements is *true*?

a. A company should be careful to completely separate the planning and evaluating functions.
b. Globalization has reduced the need for companies to operate efficiently and effectively.
c. Some companies do not perform well because they fail to develop appropriate corporate strategies.
d. Most methods of performance evaluation are the same now as they were 40 years ago.

Practice 9-2

Quality Dimensions
Which of the following is *not* one of the dimensions of quality mentioned in the chapter?

a. Reliability
b. Changeability
c. Serviceability
d. Durability
e. Perceived quality

Practice 9-3

Benchmarking
Which one of the following is *not* an example of effective benchmarking?

a. Comparing the company to other companies in the industry that have recently declared bankruptcy

(continued)

b. Comparing less effective departments against the best-performing departments within the same organization
c. Comparing the company against top competitors
d. Comparing the company against the "best-in-class" both from within and outside of the company's industry

Practice 9-4

Differential Costs, Sunk Costs, and Opportunity Costs
Which one of the following statements is *false?*

a. A sunk cost is one that has already been incurred.
b. Differential costs can be eliminated in whole or in part by choosing one alternative over another.
c. Opportunity cost is the amount of profit given up by choosing one alternative over another.
d. A differential cost is one that cannot be avoided.

Practice 9-5

Sunk Costs
Which one of the following would be considered a sunk cost?

a. Variable cost of materials to build a new product
b. Additional insurance for a new product line
c. The total amount paid to purchase investment securities last year; the securities have recently declined in value by 50%
d. Expected annual maintenance costs for new equipment

Practice 9-6

Differential Costs and Decision Making
Using the following cost data, decide which alternative the company should pursue with respect to buying and operating a new piece of equipment. Use the differential-cost approach.

	Alternative A	Alternative B
Cost of new equipment	$23,300	$25,000
Licensing fee to operate equipment	1,200	800
Resale value of old equipment	500	500
Expected fixed operating costs	400	120
Original cost of old equipment	20,000	20,000

Practice 9-7

Total-Cost Approach
Refer to the data in Practice 9-6. Repeat your analysis using the total-cost approach.

Practice 9-8

Special Order Pricing
The company is deciding whether to accept a special order. The company's costs for the most recent year were as follows:

Total variable costs	$3,200,000
Total fixed costs	1,300,000

The company produced 100,000 units in the most recent year. What is the minimum price per unit at which the company should accept the special order (ignoring any qualitative factors)?

Practice 9-9

Special Orders—The Seller's Decision
At the end of a very mild winter, the company has enough raw materials to produce 1,000 coats, and the materials can be used only for coats. The material is very sensitive and will not be usable if it is not used immediately. The company does not expect to be able to receive the full sales price of $120 per coat, and the company needs production storage space to make room

for the raw materials for its summer clothes inventory production. The company has received a special order from one of its customers for 1,000 coats at $70 per coat. The cost of making one coat (assuming a production run of 1,000 coats) is as follows:

Direct materials	$25 per coat
Direct labor	$40 per coat
Manufacturing overhead	$20 per coat

For the manufacturing overhead, $15 per coat relates to fixed overhead, primarily wages paid to special technicians who repair the equipment used to make the coats. These technicians are hired from an outside company and will not be hired if the coats are not made. Should the company accept the special order?

Practice 9-10

Making or Buying Manufactured Parts

The company currently makes a part used in the production of its best-selling product. The company has the option to buy this same part from a supplier for $34 per part. The company uses 750 of these parts each period and has the following cost data for producing these 750 parts:

	Cost per Unit
Direct labor	$12
Direct materials	7
Variable manufacturing overhead	8
Fixed manufacturing overhead, direct*	4
Fixed manufacturing overhead, indirect*	6

*Based on 750 units per period. If the parts are purchased from the supplier, the direct fixed manufacturing overhead costs can be avoided.

Should the company buy the 750 parts per period from the supplier or continue to make them?

Practice 9-11

Exiting a Market

Using the following information, decide whether the company should close any of its stores:

	Store 1	Store 2	Store 3
Sales revenue	$1,000,000	$1,200,000	$800,000
Variable costs	550,000	610,000	450,000
Direct fixed costs	200,000	310,000	305,000
Indirect fixed costs	70,000	70,000	70,000

Practice 9-12

Entering a Market

Refer to the data in Practice 9-11. The company's main customer is considering whether to merge with the company (and its three stores). If the merger takes place, the efficiencies associated with combining the stores with their main customer will cause variable costs at each of the three stores to decline by 25%. However, the merger will increase overall fixed costs by $300,000. Should the merger take place?

Practice 9-13

Additional Processing

Panaca Pork Products produces and sells ham, bacon, and sausage. For years, Panaca has sold only one version of its three products. However, Panaca is now considering selling "premium" versions of each of its products. The following information is available:

(continued)

	Number of Pounds Produced	Selling Price per Pound for Regular Product	Additional Processing Costs	Selling Price per Pound for Premium Product
Ham	1,000,000	$1.00	$120,000	$1.20
Bacon	400,000	0.90	90,000	1.10
Sausage	600,000	1.10	200,000	1.40

Before any additional processing costs, the total production cost for the 2,000,000 combined pounds of ham, bacon, and sausage is $1,400,000. Which, if any, of the three products (ham, bacon, and sausage) should Panaca sell as a premium product?

Practice 9-14

Contribution Margin Percentage
Using the following information, compute the contribution margin percentage for each product.

	Product A	Product B
Selling price	$380	$140
Variable costs	235	75

Practice 9-15

Critical Resource Factor
Refer to the data in Practice 9-14. Product A requires three units of the company's critical resource, while Product B requires only two units. Compute the contribution margin per unit of critical resource to determine which product the company should emphasize in its marketing campaign.

Practice 9-16

Setting Selling Prices: Contribution Approach
The company prices its products using a 40% markup on total variable cost to cover fixed costs and to provide a reasonable return on investment. Using the following data and the contribution approach to pricing products, estimate the normal selling price. *Note:* The markup will end up being 40% of the selling price.

	Cost per Unit
Direct materials	$10
Direct labor	17
Variable manufacturing overhead	13
Variable selling and administrative expenses	8

Fixed manufacturing overhead totals $80,000 per year. Fixed selling and administrative expenses are $55,000 per year. The average number of units sold per year is 5,000.

Practice 9-17

Setting Selling Prices: Functional Cost Approach
Refer to Practice 9-16. Assume that the company prices its products using a 30% markup on total manufacturing cost to cover selling and administrative expenses and to provide a reasonable return on investment. Using the following data and the functional cost approach to pricing products, estimate the normal selling price. *Note:* The markup will end up being 30% of the selling price.

Practice 9-18

Theory of Constraints

Which one of the following statements is *false*?

a. The process that is the company's constraint will always remain the company's constraint.
b. The constrained resource of an organization sets the pace for the whole operation.
c. Eliyahu Goldratt popularized the theory of constraints in his book, *The Goal.*
d. A company should focus much of its production efforts on exploiting the system's constraint.

Practice 9-19

Identifying the Constraint

The following chain of events represents the production process of the company. Which process is the constraint?

a. Acquisition of raw materials—200 units per hour
b. Cutting—35 units per hour
c. Shaping—65 units per hour
d. Sanding—50 units per hour
e. Assembling—30 units per hour
f. Delivering—150 units per hour

e x e r c i s e s

Exercise 9-1

Classifying Decisions

Indicate whether each of the following activities appears to be mostly related to planning, controlling, or evaluating:

1. Operational budgeting
2. Production prioritizing
3. Providing feedback to managers
4. Tracking performance
5. Strategic planning
6. Rewarding performance
7. Capital budgeting
8. Comparing costs, quality, and timeliness against previously prepared budgets
9. Analyzing results
10. Identification of problems

Exercise 9-2

Relevant Costs

Gilliland Company provides maid services for local hotels. Last year the firm acquired a cleaning machine for $50,000. The firm expected to use the machine for five years. However, this year a new, more efficient machine has been introduced on the market. The accountant for Gilliland has determined that the annual total operating costs for the old machine are $120,000. The annual operating costs for the new machine would be $100,000, and the purchase price is $65,000. The president of Gilliland feels the company should not buy the new machine. He points out that the operating costs of $100,000 and the purchase price of $65,000 for the new machine, plus the original cost of the old machine of $50,000, are greater than the operating costs of the old machine.

1. Do you agree with the president?
2. What type of cost is the $50,000 purchase price of the old machine?

Exercise 9-3

Qualitative Factors

Sturdy Chair Company manufactures wooden chairs. In producing the chairs, a great deal of scrap wood is created. The company currently uses the wood as fuel in a factory furnace. However, it has the opportunity to send the scrap wood to a subcontractor, who would turn it into pressed board to be used to produce small end tables as a new product of Sturdy Chair.

Identify any qualitative factors that Sturdy Chair Company might want to consider in deciding how to use the scrap wood.

Exercise 9-4

Special Order Pricing

You are the controller for Tippets Watch Company. The company has excess watches, which it has not been able to market through its own distribution outlets. To utilize the excess capacity, the president is negotiating with a large department store chain to sell Tippets watches. He has asked you to estimate the minimum selling price below which Tippets should not accept an order from the retail chain. Cost information per watch is:

Direct materials	$16
Direct labor	10
Manufacturing overhead:	
Variable	6
Fixed	4
Selling and administrative expenses:	
Variable	2
Fixed	6

The fixed costs are the same whether or not the order is accepted.

1. What is the minimum selling price the company should accept based solely on cost information (not considering qualitative factors)?
2. Assume that the president agrees to sell 20,000 watches at a price of $38 per watch. What would be the expected increase in profit?

Exercise 9-5

Make-or-Buy Decisions

Nelson Car Audio needs 500 amplifiers to complete this month's car stereo shipment. If Nelson Car Audio buys rather than makes the amplifiers, some of the facilities still cannot be used in another manufacturing activity. Twenty-five percent of the fixed manufacturing overhead costs are indirect and will still be incurred regardless of which decision is made. The per-unit costs of making and buying the amplifiers are:

Cost to make the amplifier:	
Direct materials	$ 25
Direct labor	50
Variable manufacturing overhead	35
Fixed manufacturing overhead	40
	$150
Cost to buy the amplifier from another company	$144

Identify the differential costs of making the amplifier as a basis for deciding whether to make or buy it.

Exercise 9-6

Spreadsheet

Make-or-Buy Decisions

Miller Manufacturing builds and markets personal computers for home and small business use. The company has been approached by an outside supplier offering to provide monitors to the company for $65 each. The company's marketing director negotiated the deal personally and is thrilled about how much cheaper it will be to purchase the monitors from outside. Producing the following cost data, the manager proudly proclaims, "Look, a $9 per-unit savings!"

	Per Unit	15,000 Units per Year
Direct materials	$28	$ 420,000
Direct labor	10	150,000
Variable manufacturing overhead	3	45,000
Fixed manufacturing overhead, direct	6	90,000
Fixed manufacturing overhead, indirect	27	405,000
Total cost	$74	$1,110,000

1. Assuming zero opportunity costs, should the company accept the outside offer?
2. If the monitors are purchased from outside, Miller can produce an alternative product that will contribute $250,000 per year toward covering indirect fixed overhead. Will this affect your decision in part (1)?

Exercise 9-7

Make-or-Buy Decisions

Tricia Company has been manufacturing 9,000 units of part Y for its products. The unit cost for the part is as follows:

Direct materials	$ 9
Direct labor	24
Variable manufacturing overhead	12
Fixed manufacturing overhead	18
Total	$63

A supplier has offered to sell 9,000 units of part Y to Tricia for $54 each. If the part is purchased, Tricia can use its facilities to manufacture another product, which would generate a contribution margin of $12,000. Seventy-five percent of the fixed manufacturing overhead costs are indirect and will still be incurred even if the part is purchased.

Compute the net differential cost in deciding whether to make or buy the part.

Exercise 9-8

Purchasing Services from Outside

Dr. Anderson, a local dentist, is considering reducing his office staff and outsourcing the management of his accounts receivable. Currently, he has an office manager and two part-time workers on his staff. One part-time employee spends almost 100% of her time sending out billing notices and following up on collections. Even then, Dr. Anderson is able to collect on only about 80% of the receivables. A collection agency wants Dr. Anderson's business. It will handle all billing and collection details for a monthly fee of $1,500. The agency believes it can deliver a 90% collection of receivables. Another firm, We Collect, Inc., has approached Anderson with a proposal that would shift all accounts receivable risk to We Collect, Inc. Anderson would receive 85% of all receivables automatically. Additional information follows:

Anderson's average yearly accounts receivable	$400,000
Anderson's average annual bad debt expense	80,000
Part-time accounts receivable employee salary	12,000

Which of the following alternatives should Anderson pursue concerning his accounts receivable?

1. Maintain status quo (part-time employee handling accounts receivable).
2. Outsource to collection agency.
3. Outsource to We Collect, Inc.

Exercise 9-9

Joint Costs and Further Processing

Pure Paint Company has been known for years for its two excellent interior wall paints: Nice & Smooth and Rich & Thick. The company has discovered that by processing Rich & Thick further it could produce a slightly different paint.

Nice & Smooth and Rich & Thick are produced jointly at a cost of $160,000, which is allocated equally between them. If Rich & Thick were processed further, its selling price would increase by $2.25 per unit, and the additional cost per unit would be $1.80.

1. On the basis of the information given (and disregarding qualitative factors), should the company process Rich & Thick further? Do you have enough information to make a recommendation? Explain.
2. **Interpretive Question:** Is the joint cost of $160,000 relevant to this discussion? Why or why not?

Exercise 9-10

Sell Now or Process Further

Colorado Company uses a joint process to manufacture Products R, S, and T. Each product can be sold at the point of separation, or it can be processed further. All additional processing costs are directly traceable to each product that is processed further. Joint production costs for the year are $140,000 and are allocated to Products R, S, and T on the basis of their sales values at the point of separation. The pertinent data accumulated by the accounting department for these products are:

Product	Units	Sales Value at Separation	Allocation of Joint Costs	Sales Value and Additional Costs of Processing Further	
				Sales Value	Additional Costs
R	18,000	$150,000	$70,000	$190,000	$24,000
S	20,000	120,000	56,000	150,000	40,000
T	10,000	30,000	14,000	60,000	25,000

1. Which products should Colorado Company process further (after separation) in order to maximize its profits? Show computations.
2. Explain why you did or did not use the allocated joint costs in deciding which of the products to process further.

Exercise 9-11

Spreadsheet

Discontinuing a Product Line

Swanton Company currently sells three products: desk calendars, pen sets, and paper-clip holders. The company is thinking of discontinuing the production and sales of paper-clip holders. However, because many customers buy the products as a set, Swanton estimates that the sales of the other two products will decrease by 20% if the paper-clip holders are discontinued.

Current data on each of the three products are provided below.

	Desk Calendars	Pen Sets	Paper-Clip Holders	Total
Units	40,000	20,000	12,000	
Sales revenue	$280,000	$240,000	$24,000	$544,000
Variable costs	160,000	160,000	26,000	346,000
Direct fixed costs	40,000	20,000	5,000	65,000
Indirect fixed costs	30,000	40,000	6,000	76,000

1. What is the segment margin of the paper-clip holders?

2. **Interpretive Question:** Would you recommend dropping the paper-clip holder product line? Why or why not?

Exercise 9-12

Adding a New Product

Cuda, Inc. is thinking about adding a new product line. Marketing surveys indicate that sales of the new product would be 100,000 units. Each unit sells for $8. Direct variable costs would be $5.60 per unit, direct fixed costs would be $60,000, and $45,000 represents the company's indirect fixed costs. The company does not expect the new product to affect the sales of its other products.

Should Cuda, Inc. add the new product? Why or why not?

Exercise 9-13

Contribution Margin per Unit of a Critical Resource

Haws Electronics produces two products, CD players and clock radios. Both products are extremely popular, and the company can sell as many of either product as it can produce. Haws Electronics can produce only a limited number of products, however, because only 12,000 direct labor hours are available due to the isolated location of the community. It takes four hours of direct labor to produce a CD player and three hours to produce a clock radio. The selling price of a CD player is $68, and the variable costs are $40. The selling price of a clock radio is $52, with variable costs of $28.

Which product should Haws Electronics produce if its direct labor hours are limited?

Exercise 9-14

Critical Resource Constraints

Whiz Kids manufactures two computer games. Far Out is a quiz game about astronomy, and Dynamite is a mystery game. The company has a limited supply of skilled labor and has been able to obtain only a limited number of "chips," a necessary part in the production process.

Information on each product is as follows:

	Far Out	Dynamite
Contribution margin per unit	$ 4	$ 3
Units produced per hour	2	3
Units produced per 100 chips	80	60

Anticipated sales exceed capacity for both products.
Total labor hours available: 9,000 hours
Total chips available: 30,000 chips

1. Identify the critical resource constraint under which Whiz Kids must operate.
2. Which product should be produced?

Exercise 9-15

Pricing Regular Products

Medical Care, Inc., is considering what price to charge for Sparkle, a toothpaste that is sold in its leased store at a hospital. The accountant has been asked to prepare an estimated normal selling price based on the costs that Medical Care incurs in making the product in a factory it operates. Costs of producing one tube of Sparkle are 20 cents for direct materials, 10 cents for direct labor, 20 cents for variable manufacturing overhead, and 10 cents for variable selling and administrative costs. Total direct fixed costs are $10,000. The company estimates that a markup of 40% of the selling price is necessary to cover the fixed costs and provide a reasonable return on investment.

1. Calculate the estimated normal selling price.
2. Would you recommend that the company obtain any other information before establishing a sales price?

Exercise 9-16

Theory of Constraints

Rudyard Company makes replacement engines for jet aircraft. Making the engines involves four processes: (1) purchasing materials, (2) assembling the engines, (3) testing the engines, and (4) delivering the completed engines to customers. Although each of these processes is critical, delivery to customers is very difficult because of the weight of the engine, the sensitivity of the calibration, and the stabilization required for shipment. Rudyard has no problem purchasing component parts for the engines. Upon order, suppliers can deliver needed parts in any quantity within one day. Assembling engines, however, requires highly skilled employees. The company has three employees who can each assemble one engine every three days. Testing also requires highly skilled engineers who use simulators made to the company's specifications. Right now, Rudyard has two simulators, each of which can test one engine every four days. Currently, there is only one trucking company that can deliver the engines to customers and ensure that they will be treated with the necessary care. The trucking company can haul three engines per truck, but given the location of customers, it can deliver only 15 engines per month.

1. What is the constraint resource in this company?
2. How many engines should Rudyard be making per month?
3. How much excess time is available in the other processes?
4. How would you suggest the company use its excess resources?

p roblems

Problem 9-1

Special Order Pricing

Midwest Company manufactures portable radios. Shop Smart, a large retail merchandiser, wants to buy 200,000 radios from Midwest Company for $12 each. The radio would carry Shop Smart's name and would be sold in its stores.

Midwest Company normally sells 420,000 radios per year at $16 each; its production capacity is 540,000 units per year. Cost information for the radios is as follows:

Production costs:	
Variable production costs	$7
Fixed manufacturing overhead ($2,100,000 ÷ 420,000 units)	5
Selling and administrative expenses:	
Variable	1
Fixed ($420,000 ÷ 420,000 units)	1

The $1 variable selling and administrative expenses would not be applicable to the radios ordered by Shop Smart because that is a single large order. Shop Smart has indicated that the company is not interested in signing a contract for less than 200,000 radios. Total fixed costs will not change regardless of whether the Shop Smart order is accepted.

Required:
1. Identify any opportunity costs that Midwest Company should consider when making the decision.
2. Determine whether Midwest Company should accept Shop Smart's offer.
3. **Interpretive Question:** What qualitative factors might be relevant to this decision?

Problem 9-2

Make-or-Buy Decisions

Logan Company manufactures several toy products. One is a large plastic truck, which requires a plastic truck body, two metal axles, and four rubber wheels. Logan currently manufactures and assembles all the parts.

Another toy company has offered to sell the parts to Logan at $1.70 per truck if 20,000 or more parts are purchased each year, and at $2 per truck if less than 20,000 parts are purchased. Logan is considering this offer. The space used in producing the parts could be used for a new toy, which is scheduled to begin production next year. If Logan continues to produce the parts for the plastic truck, the company will have to lease space from another company in an adjacent building to produce the new toy. The rent would be $8,000 per year.

Other information related to the truck is:

	Produce Parts	Assemble Truck	Total
Direct materials	$1.10	$0.20	$1.30
Direct labor	0.30	0.20	0.50
Variable manufacturing overhead	0.20	0.15	0.35
Fixed manufacturing overhead	0.20	0.40	0.60
Total manufacturing costs	$1.80	$0.95	$2.75

The marketing department has estimated that sales for the plastic truck will be approximately 16,000 units per year for the next three years. The fixed manufacturing overhead is indirect and will still be incurred regardless of which decision is made.

Required:
1. Describe Logan Company's two alternatives for this decision.
2. What costs are relevant to the decision?
3. Which alternative should Logan Company select?
4. What would be the best decision had Logan not planned to produce the new toy?
5. **Interpretive Question:** What are some of the qualitative factors that Logan Company might consider in making the decision?

Problem 9-3

Choosing between Two Machines

Bruce's Bakery is thinking of making its own Danishes. Two machines, A and B, are being considered for purchase. The company now purchases the Danishes from an outside supplier for 20 cents each. The cost information for producing the Danishes would be:

	Machine A	Machine B
Variable costs per Danish	$0.16	$0.14
Annual fixed costs	$3,500	$5,000
Initial cost of machine	$10,000	$24,000
Salvage value at end of five years	$0	$8,000
Estimated life of machine	5 years	5 years

Required:
1. At a sales volume of 275,000 Danishes per year, which of these alternatives is best—buying the Danishes, using machine A, or using machine B? (Ignore the time value of money, and assume straight-line depreciation.)
2. At what level of production would you be indifferent between machine A and machine B? Which machine is preferable if production exceeds this volume?

Problem 9-4

Purchasing Services from Outside

Northeast Reinsurance Company is growing rapidly. As it has grown, it has added legal staff to provide for its legal services. One of the principals of the company is an attorney who has provided oversight over the growing legal department. However, she is now too busy to continue this "legal counsel" role. She suggests that the senior company attorney become an officer of the company and be given the title "legal counsel and secretary." Another of the principals is good friends with an attorney at a prestigious regional law firm. That law firm has offered to provide Northeast with legal services for an annual retainer of $500,000 plus an average billing rate of $100 per hour for all work done over 5,000 hours per year. It is expected that legal work, whether done inside or outside the company, will require about 6,000 hours this coming year and will probably increase by 10% a year thereafter. The current company legal staff may be able to handle the work load for two years before it will have to hire another attorney (at an expected salary and benefit package of $100,000). Other variable costs are expected to increase by 5% a year.

Additional information follows:

	Current Costs of Internal Legal Department
Salaries and benefits of legal staff	$350,000
Travel costs	80,000
Required continuing education costs	10,000
Legal support costs (library, computers, software, supplies, etc.)	100,000
Other variable costs	25,000
Allocated office overhead (depreciation, utilities, etc.)	40,000
Total costs of legal department	$605,000

Required:

1. What are the relevant costs for Northeast to consider in making this decision?
2. From a financial standpoint, should Northeast continue to use its own legal department for legal services or outsource this function to the regional law firm?
3. What other factors might Northeast consider in making this decision?

Problem 9-5

Spreadsheet

Unifying Concepts: Make-or-Buy Decisions (Differential Costs and Opportunity Costs)

Snow Corporation manufactures freezers for residential use. The company is planning to produce a new freezer suitable for apartments. These smaller freezers require a component that Snow Corporation can either make or buy from a subcontractor. The subcontractor will sell the part for $46. The costs for making 12,000 units of the part are as follows:

Direct materials	$20 per unit
Direct labor	$15 per unit
Variable manufacturing overhead	$10 per unit
Fixed manufacturing overhead	$40,000*

*The $40,000 fixed manufacturing overhead includes $24,000 of indirect fixed costs allocated to the part and $16,000 for a production manager.

If the part is produced, Snow Corporation will use an idle machine it already owns. If the part is bought, the company plans to rent the machine and the factory space to another company for $8,000 and $14,000 a year, respectively.

Snow expects that, if the part is produced, the company will be able to schedule production so that no warehouse space will be needed. However, if the part is bought, Snow will need to use warehouse space, for which it will have to pay $2,000 a year in rent.

Required:
1. Identify any opportunity costs relevant to the decision to make or buy the component.
2. Determine the differential costs of making the product.
3. Determine the differential costs of buying the product.
4. **Interpretive Question:** Would you recommend that Snow make or buy the component? Why?

Problem 9-6

Processing Past the Point of Separation

Style Company manufactures three items, S1, S2, and S3, which are used in the production of fabrics. Each item can be sold at the point that all three are separated from the joint production process, or they can be processed further. Presently, S1 and S2 are processed past the point of separation. The joint cost of producing the three items to the point of separation is $450,000. The costs past the point of separation are variable and can be traced to each product. The $450,000 joint costs are allocated to each product equally.

The following information is available:

	Number of Units Produced	Selling Price per Unit at Point of Separation	Additional Processing Costs	Selling Price per Unit After Processing
S1	100,000	$10	$120,000	$12
S2	40,000	9	90,000	11
S3	60,000	11	?	13

Required:
1. Should S1 and S2 be processed after the separation point?
2. What maximum additional processing costs could be incurred to process S3 further and still leave a profit?

Problem 9-7

Dropping a Product Line

Bryce Baseballs manufactures baseballs, baseball bats, and baseball gloves. The company is thinking of dropping baseball gloves as a product line. The following report was prepared by the accounting department:

	Baseballs	Baseball Bats	Baseball Gloves	Total
Sales revenues	$ 240,000	$105,000	$ 25,000	$ 370,000
Variable costs	(185,000)	(70,000)	(12,000)	(267,000)
Contribution margin	$ 55,000	$ 35,000	$ 13,000	$ 103,000
Direct fixed costs	(20,000)	(10,000)	(13,500)	(43,500)
Segment margin	$ 35,000	$ 25,000	$ (500)	$ 59,500
Indirect fixed costs	(17,500)	(10,000)	(2,500)	(30,000)
Net income	$ 17,500	$ 15,000	$ (3,000)	$ 29,500

Required:
1. Should the baseball glove line be dropped? Why or why not?
2. **Interpretive Question:** What qualitative factors should be considered in deciding whether to drop the baseball glove line?

Problem 9-8

Adding and Dropping Product Lines

Park Manufacturing Company has been producing three products: W, X, and Y. Now that the plant has been shifted to an assembly-line operation, a fourth product, Z, has been added. Each product has its own assembly-line operation, producing 10,000 units. Total indirect fixed costs of $48,000 are divided proportionately, based on the space allocated to each assembly line. Other pertinent information is given below.

	W	X	Y	Z
Selling price per unit	$6.00	$5.00	$5.40	$3.00
Variable cost per unit	$4.00	$3.60	$3.60	$2.60
Number of square feet	1,600	1,200	1,100	900

Required:
1. Prepare a schedule that shows net income for each product line.
2. Would total company income increase if product Z were dropped? Why or why not?
3. **Interpretive Question:** If you could double the production of W, X, or Y in place of having Z, which would you choose? Why?

Problem 9-9

Shutting Down or Continuing Operations

End Trail Campground is open year-round. However, 80% of its revenues are generated from May through October. Because only 20% of the revenues are generated from November to April, the campground is considering closing during those months. The yearly revenues and cost information expected by End Trail for next year if the campground does not close are:

Camping fees	$1,800,000
Variable costs	990,000
Fixed costs ($40,000 per month)	480,000

The cost to close the campground at the end of October would be $20,000, and the cost to reopen in May would be $50,000. If the campground is closed, the total fixed costs are only $25,000 per month, rather than the $40,000 per month when the campground is open.

Required:
Determine whether End Trail Campground should close from November to April or remain open for the entire year.

Problem 9-10

Determining Production with a Critical Resource Limitation

Clarity Corporation produces three sizes of television sets: 10-inch screen, 19-inch screen, and 24-inch screen. The revenues and costs per unit for each size are as follows:

	Screen Size		
	10-inch	**19-inch**	**24-inch**
Selling price	$195	$325	$450
Variable costs:			
Direct materials	$ 55	$100	$126
Direct labor	80	120	180
Variable manufacturing overhead	40	60	90
Total variable costs	$175	$280	$396
Contribution margin	$ 20	$ 45	$ 54
Units ordered for next week	200	150	75

The company has a constraint on the amount of skilled labor available to produce television sets. Direct labor employees are paid $8 per hour. The total amount of labor time available for next week's production is 2,700 hours.

Required:
Given the units ordered for next week, which size or sizes of television sets should be produced and sold to maximize the company's profit?

Problem 9-11

Determining Production with a Critical Resource Limitation
A company is examining two of its products, X-121 and Y-707. The following information is being reviewed:

	X-121	Y-707
Unit selling price	$28.50	$21.00
Materials required per unit	$3.00	$1.50
Direct labor required per unit	$2.50	$1.25
Variable manufacturing overhead per unit	$0.50	$1.00
Production time per unit (in hours)	1.5	1

Required:
1. Which item should the company manufacture if there is no constraint on hours of production?
2. If full production capacity is 1,500 hours, and if the company can sell all the units it makes, which item should it manufacture? Why?

Problem 9-12

𝒮preadsheet

Contribution Margin per Unit of a Critical Resource
Dresser, Inc., manufactures three super-sports-hero dolls: Super Dunk, Pete Tulip, and Zonk. Production, however, is limited by the skilled labor necessary to produce these unique dolls. Data on each of the dolls are as follows:

	Super Dunk	Pete Tulip	Zonk
Contribution margin per doll	$6	$4	$5
Dolls produced per hour	20	28	25
Expected total market volume (units)	20,000	9,000	100,000

Total skilled labor hours available: 4,500 hours.

Required:
Assuming that there are no relevant qualitative factors, how many dolls of each type should Dresser produce?

Problem 9-13

Unifying Concepts: Production and Advertising
Cole Company manufactures only two products—a battery charger and a testing machine for automobile engines. An average of 30,000 chargers and 50,000 testers are sold each year. This year, the company can afford only $60,000 for advertising the products, which is just enough to advertise one product effectively. The marketing manager expects that the sales of chargers will increase by 20% if they are advertised and that the sales of testers will increase by 10% if they are advertised.

The following information about the two products has been provided by the accountant:

(continued)

	Charger	Tester
Selling price per unit	$70	$90
Variable cost per unit	$30	$40
Fixed cost per unit	$30	$40
Production time per unit (in hours)	2	4

Required:
1. If Cole had an unlimited number of labor hours, would you recommend that it advertise either of its products? If yes, which one and why?
2. Assume that Cole has a capacity of 260,000 labor hours. Should Cole still advertise? If so, which product should it advertise?

Problem 9-14

Normal Selling Price

Chojna Lighting Supply manufactures desktop and ceiling-mounted light fixtures. The company is seeking to come up with a reasonable price for its desktop executive model. Production costs for each unit follow:

Direct materials	$7 per unit
Direct labor	1.5 hour per unit
Direct labor rate	$4 per hour
Variable manufacturing overhead	$3 per labor hour
Variable selling and administrative costs	$2 per unit
Fixed overhead (direct)	$3 per unit
Markup of selling price to cover indirect overhead and expected profit	40%

Required:
Calculate the estimated normal selling price.

Problem 9-15

Theory of Constraints

Dalton Enterprises makes several products, including microwave ovens, dishwashers, and vacuum cleaners. Each manufacturing process requires several production processes. Right now, the company has large amounts of money tied up in work-in-process inventory at various locations throughout the company. Although Dalton has tried to eliminate this inventory, each month the inventory seems to increase. In addition, the company has a salary incentive system that pays production employees bonuses if they meet budgeted production quotas. The bonuses pay increasingly higher amounts for each unit that is produced in excess of the quota. In recent years, employees have been receiving large production bonuses under the incentive plan, so management knows that the employees are working hard and being productive. These higher bonuses, combined with the money tied up in work-in-process inventory, are creating a cash flow problem for the company.

You have been hired to help the company fix its cash flow problems. You have just attended a conference on the theory of constraints.

Required:
Explain how you could apply what you have learned to help the company with its problems.

d iscussion cases

Case 9-1

Buying from Inside or Outside the Company

E & B Company has two divisions, processing and finishing. The Finishing Division has been purchasing certain products from the Processing Division at a price of $80 per unit. (A unit consists of 100 yards of material.) The Processing Division has announced that, starting next month, it will raise its price to $100 per unit. As the manager of the Finishing Division, you object to this price and have indicated that you are planning to purchase these units of material from outside suppliers at a price of $85 per unit. You have asked the accounting department to furnish cost data to help you understand why the Processing Division's price has to be raised to $100 per unit. Following is the information supplied about the Processing Division's operations:

Units produced for Finishing Division	2,000
Variable production costs per unit	$60
Indirect fixed costs allocated to the	
Processing Division	$50,000
Normal profit per unit in Processing Division	$15

If the Finishing Division buys from outside suppliers, the facilities used by the Processing Division to manufacture these units for the Finishing Division will remain idle.

Answer the following questions:

1. If the Processing Division is successful in imposing the $100 price and the Finishing Division elects to buy from outside suppliers, what impact does this action have on the overall profit of E & B Company?
2. Explain why the variable production costs, the fixed costs, and the normal profit are, or are not, each relevant to this decision. (You are not being asked to discuss whether the $100 price is an appropriate price or whether the division managers should be allowed to maintain an autonomous posture in this decision.)
3. What additional factors should E & B Company's top management consider in resolving this matter?

Case 9-2

Sunk Costs

Sam Love owns and manages a small but growing service business. In fact, this year has been so good that Sam is moving his office to a larger, more centrally located site. In an effort to save on moving costs, Sam employs his brother Dan (who owns a large truck) to haul his office furniture and equipment. Unfortunately, Dan doesn't properly secure the rear door of the truck, and one of Sam's two copy machines winds up in a million pieces in the middle of the highway. As the two brothers survey the damage, Sam's office manager approaches and says, "Well, look on the bright side, the machine was half depreciated."

Should Sam take comfort from this statement? Explain your answer.

Case 9-3

Why Most Companies Want to Benchmark

Everyone wants to benchmark these days. Assume you are the dean of a business school with a highly successful MBA program. You have enjoyed increasing numbers of highly qualified applicants, recruiters love your students, and both *Business Week* and *U.S. News and World Report* have ranked you in the top 10 business schools in the United States. You have just been contacted by the deans of two other business schools, whose MBA programs rank well below yours. They would like to spend a couple of days at your school benchmarking against your admissions, advising, placement, and other services, as well as studying your curriculum, faculty development processes, and other ingredients of your success. You would like to help them but are not sure you want to reveal why you have been so successful. If you don't expose your secrets of success, however, their visits would largely be a waste of time. What should you do? Should you welcome your competitors with open arms, or should you refuse to allow them to benchmark against you? Or, should you allow them to come but hide your best secrets from them?

j u d g m e n t   c a l l s

Judgment 9-1

You Decide: Should a company benchmark its financial performance against competitors, or does such benchmarking create tunnel vision with respect to a company's growth and achievement of goals?

Over the years, it has become very common for companies to benchmark or compare themselves to others in the same industry or market. Are companies similar enough that benchmarking is useful, or is it a waste of time? In addition, do you really believe that competitors will share confidential information with each other?

Judgment 9-2

You Decide: Which is more important to a company's overall success and profitability: quantitative or qualitative factors?

Often a company is judged based on the strength of financial indicators, such as sales revenue, net income, or earnings per share. However, many of these measures fail to incorporate intangible items, such as delivery time, quality control, and customer service. In a management accounting field setting, which factors are most important?

C o m p e t e n c y   E n h a n c e m e n t   O p p o r t u n i t i e s

- ▶ **Analyzing Real Company Information**
- ▶ **International Case**
- ▶ **Ethics Case**
- ▶ **Writing Assignment**

- ▶ **The Debate**
- ▶ **Internet Search**

The following additional assignments provide opportunities for students to develop critical thinking, ethical perspectives, oral and written communication skills, experience with electronic research, and teamwork through group and business activities.

▶ ## Analyzing Real Company Information

Analyzing 9-1 (Microsoft)

Go to the Form 10-K for MICROSOFT provided in Appendix A at the back of this textbook. Read through the report to determine how many segments of business exist within Microsoft. What approach does Microsoft appear to use in identifying operating segments within the company at large?

Analyzing 9-2 (Main Line Pictures, Inc. versus Kim Basinger)

Hollywood produces a lot of entertainment, including accounting entertainment! In early 1993, the Superior Court of the State of California (Los Angeles County) heard a litigation suit filed by MAIN LINE PICTURES, INC., against the actress Kim Basinger for breach of contract. At issue was Basinger's decision to withdraw from a film project after making a verbal commitment to appear in it. The film, released in September 1993, was *Boxing Helena*. Didn't see it? That was the point of Main Line's lawsuit: the studio claimed a lot of people didn't see *Boxing Helena* because the actress who replaced Basinger (Sherilyn Fenn) did not have nearly the same box office appeal.

Main Line claimed damages due to an incremental difference in revenues and costs, which led to actual profits being less than expected, all due to not having Basinger in the film. An expert economist and an expert in film finance were called to testify regarding the appropriate size of the incremental revenue and cost differences. Hence, the case essentially became an accounting argument.

Main Line's lawyers argued that their client lost between $5.1 million and $9.7 million as a result of Basinger's withdrawal. The $5.1 million loss calculation is shown below (all amounts are in millions).

Minimum Damages, Plaintiff			
	With Basinger	**Without Basinger**	**Difference**
Foreign presales	$ 7.60	$ 2.70	$ 4.90
Domestic presales	3.00		3.00
Total revenue	$10.60	$ 2.70	$ 7.90
Production costs	(7.60)	(4.80)	(2.80)
Profit (loss)	$ 3.00	$(2.10)	$ 5.10

To understand the numbers above, you need to know a couple of things about revenues and costs in the movie business and this film in particular.

- It is extremely difficult to predict what a film will actually earn when released. There are *plenty* of examples of big budget films that did poorly at the box office, as well as inexpensive, independent films that have done very well. Hence, presale revenue (guaranteed minimum payments by a film distributor to the film producer) is the only sure revenue the producer can bank on when budgeting costs of making the film. If the film does well, then the distributor and producer share in the profits.
- After Basinger dropped out of the film, one of Main Line's partners loaned $1.7 million to the project, to be repaid out of domestic revenues.
- Often the producer will contract to share profits from presales, as well as incremental profits, with key actors. Basinger was to be paid a guaranteed $1 million to star in the film. In addition, she, her proposed co-star Ed Harris, and writer/director Jennifer Lynch were to be paid a total of 20.5% of the producer's net profits. On the other hand, Sherilyn Fenn and her co-star, Julian Sands, each received only a $100,000 guaranteed salary.
- After Basinger dropped from the film project, the producer made some changes to scale back production costs by $1.9 million.
- Often a movie project has many investing partners. Main Line had a partnership with Philippe Caland, who was, essentially, to receive 50% of net profits (after participation payments to the actors and writer), up to a maximum of $2 million.
- After withdrawing from *Boxing Helena*, Basinger received $3 million from a separate producer to star in *Final Analysis*.

Do you agree with the numbers presented above by the plaintiff? Consider all the information provided above and adjust the incremental profit analysis if needed. Be sure to defend your decision to use or not use each piece of information provided.

Source: Adapted from T. L. Barton, W. G. Shenkir, and B. C. Marinas, "Main Line vs. Basinger: A Case in Relevant Costs and Incremental Analysis," *Issues in Accounting Education*, Spring 1996, pp. 163–174.

International Case

International

Ameripill Company

Located in Bartow, Alabama, the Pharmaceutical Division of AMERIPILL COMPANY ranks among the top 15 drug companies in the world. The European Unit of the Pharmaceutical Division is divided into three markets: United Kingdom (U.K.), Germany, and France. Actual and budgeted operating reports for two recent years are presented below for these three markets.

	United Kingdom		Germany		France	
	Year 2 Budget	Year 1 Actual	Year 2 Budget	Year 1 Actual	Year 2 Budget	Year 1 Actual
Sales	$49,960	$48,080	$156,840	$137,440	$108,720	$102,560
Cost of sales	(21,982)	(21,155)	(65,872)	(57,995)	(53,414)	(50,254)
Direct expenses	(14,658)	(14,512)	(50,286)	(46,603)	(31,529)	(29,742)
Other income/expenses	(1,499)	(1,155)	(300)	(210)	(946)	(1,026)
Responsibility earnings	$11,821	$11,258	$ 40,382	$ 32,632	$ 22,831	$ 21,538
Interest income/expense*	(358)	(241)	(1,312)	(939)	(1,033)	(1,047)
Exchange gain/loss**	(142)	(338)	(150)	(210)	(272)	(286)
Division charges***	(1,629)	(1,640)	(4,700)	(4,123)	(3,262)	(3,077)
Earnings before taxes	$ 9,692	$ 9,039	$ 34,220	$ 27,360	$ 18,264	$ 17,128
Segment assets	$84,500	$88,860	$ 73,760	$ 72,900	$ 74,220	$ 73,460
Earnings before taxes	19.4%	18.8%	21.8%	19.9%	16.8%	16.7%
Return on assets	11.5%	10.2%	46.4%	37.5%	24.6%	23.3%

*Based on locally incurred debt.

**Based on the average Year 1 exchange rate with the United States.

***Fixed charge negotiated annually between the Bartow Division and the market subsidiary.

1. Analyze these reports carefully. Assuming that Ameripill requires a minimum ROA of 12%, should the company consider dropping the U.K. market?
2. Ameripill currently has a problem with one of the drugs sold in France. In the French market, Saincoeur is a highly successful treatment for heart-attack victims. (It is also sold under other names in all of Ameripill's markets.) Because of regulatory pressure in France, Saincoeur is being sold at a much lower price in France than in Germany or the United Kingdom. Despite the price ceiling, Saincoeur is a profitable product (barely) in France. However, word of the lower price is creating a lot of pressure in the neighboring markets to reduce the prices to a level similar to that of the French market. Saincoeur is a very profitable product in both Germany and the United Kingdom. How do these facts affect your previous decision regarding the U.K. market in part (1)?

Source: Adapted from S. F. Haka, B. A. Lamberton, and H. M. Sollenberger, "International Subsidiary Performance Evaluation: The Case of the Ameripill Company," *Issues in Accounting Education,* Spring 1994, pp. 168–190.

Ethics Case

Play World, Inc.

Roger Smith, the controller of Play World, Inc., a toy company, has just completed an analysis of a make-or-buy decision with respect to a particular part for one of the new toys the company is planning to manufacture. The result of the analysis clearly shows that the company should buy the part from one of the three available suppliers (based on written price quotations received from those suppliers within the past few weeks). Based on this analysis, Smith and the division manager, Kate Pfirman, agreed to proceed with placing an order. They issued instructions to the purchasing department indicating that the order should be placed for a price not higher than $3.40 per part. A few days later, Smith received a phone call from the purchasing department indicating that all three suppliers had raised their price to $4.00 per unit. It was a normal business practice to raise prices after written quotations had been issued.

It was immediately clear to Smith that it would be disadvantageous to his company to buy the part at the higher price. He discussed the new information with Pfirman, and they agreed to proceed with manufacturing plans to make the part internally. Smith thought it was rather strange that all three suppliers had raised their price to the same amount, but felt there was nothing he could do about it.

A few days later, Smith's secretary, Lynn Berry, asked if she could have a private conversation with him. Berry was obviously upset, so Smith asked her to come into his office and shut the door. Berry told him she was good friends with the secretary for the president of one of the suppliers from which Play World had planned to buy the part for the new toy. Berry's friend had casually mentioned that her boss had been on the phone with the other suppliers and they had agreed to raise the price for certain parts they were manufacturing to specified dollar amounts. Berry said she was reluctant to tell Smith because she didn't want her friend to get in trouble for revealing confidential information outside her company. For Smith, this information was the missing piece that explained why the price for the part had been raised to $4.00 by all three companies. Smith thanked Berry for the information and told her not to worry; he would keep the information to himself but would give some thought to what he would eventually do with what she had told him.

1. Who are the parties that are affected by this bid-rigging scheme?
2. What should Smith do with the information he received from Berry (keep in mind his responsibilities to the accounting profession, to his company, and to Berry)?

▶ *Writing Assignment*

Airline Ticket Prices

If you have ever shopped for airline tickets, you are aware of the tremendous diversity in ticket prices for the same flight, even for those who sit in the same section (first-class, coach, etc.). Much of the difference is based on two factors: (1) when you bought your ticket and (2) whether you plan to stay over a Saturday night.

Write a one- to two-page paper describing why airline companies have so many different ticket prices. Also, why do you think it is important to the airline that clients fly back from their business trips on Sunday instead of Saturday?

▶ *The Debate*

Total Costs versus Differential Costs

As discussed in this chapter, a management accountant can choose whether to present information using total costs or differential (e.g., incremental) costs. Divide your group into two teams. Each group will defend cost analysis for relevant decision making using either total costs or differential costs.

- One team represents "Total Costs." Present the advantages of using total costs for decision making. What are the disadvantages of using differential costs?

(continued)

• The other team represents "Differential Costs." Present the advantages of using differential costs for decision making. What are the disadvantages of using total costs?

▶ *Internet Search*

Benchmarking in Europe

Early in the chapter, we discussed the concept of benchmarking, a new evaluation method that has been used extensively in recent years. We discussed benchmarking in the context of one company comparing its financial and operating performance against a competitor's performance or comparing the performance of various internal departments against each other. However, benchmarking is a concept that can be used in any type of organization or even for yourself. Take the EUROPEAN COMMISSION, for example. Since the mid-1990s, the commission has undertaken a number of benchmarking initiatives so that member countries can compare best practices at three levels: country and business environment, company or enterprise, and industry or sector. The European Commission discusses its benchmark initiatives at the following Web site: **http://www.benchmarking-in-europe.com**. (Sometimes Web addresses change, so if this address does not work, access the Web site for this textbook, **http://swain.swlearning.com**, for an updated link.) Go to this site and answer the following questions:

1. List the four basic steps in benchmarking it identifies.
2. Identify the objective of enterprise policy benchmarking.
3. What method has been used to benchmark in the area of enterprise policy?

c h a p t e r

10

Continuous Improvement in Management Accounting

After studying this chapter, you should be able to:

1 Explain the fundamentals of building a balanced scorecard.

2 Anticipate that both management accounting and financial accounting are poised for important changes.

© 2003 Getty Images

It has been said, "knowledge is power!" The ability to compete effectively in the economy has always been a function of the knowledge and abilities that a company can pull together and emphasize in the process of creating new products, making good decisions, and implementing effective processes. Throughout this text, we have generally classified organizations as manufacturers, merchandisers, or service providers. However, in this new age, more and more successful companies really can't be classified into *one* of these three categories. We've often used MICROSOFT as an example company in this textbook. What kind of company is Microsoft? Does this company manufacture products? Does it distribute merchandise? Does it sell services? Actually, Microsoft does all three things, but that still doesn't adequately describe this company. Microsoft is one of the key citizens in what might be called a "New Economy" that runs more on intangible assets, such as intellectual property, than tangibles such as plants, equipment, and distribution channels. A lot of these New Economy companies have comparatively few tangible assets, and yet they are obviously considered to be very valuable by the stock market. What this tells you is that traditional accounting models aren't capturing the value. Accounting, in other words, may no longer deliver accountability for many organizations.

For example, Bill Gates and Microsoft are continually hiring many of the world's smartest scientists and creating a giant research laboratory. Their goal is to determine the future of computing. As this effort goes forward, the value of Microsoft as a company rises and falls based on progress and problems in its research and development processes. To support Microsoft's quest to develop new products and technologies, 20,800 of its 50,500 full-time employees work in product development and research. One very interesting process to watch at Microsoft is the internal conflict regarding its flagship Windows product and a rising new software called ".Net"—a platform for XML Web services that allows applications to communicate and to share data over the Internet, regardless of operating system or programming language. Putting an accurate value on the Windows technology at Microsoft is difficult, but no one can question that much of the market value of Microsoft, one of the most important companies in the world today, is based on Windows—a proprietary technology that Microsoft guards very carefully.

However, .Net technology may be the biggest threat to the future of Windows that Microsoft has ever seen. It's ironic, then, that .Net is Microsoft's own technology. When the .Net strategy was launched, Chairman and Chief Software Architect Bill Gates said .Net was a "bet-the-company thing." Initially, Gates committed half of Microsoft's $4 billion budget to .Net breakthroughs. June 2003 marked the third anniversary of the unveiling of .Net and although Microsoft is committed to the vision of .Net, its success has been guarded. Neil Charney, director of Microsoft's Platform Strategy Group, said this about .Net, "If you look back from where we were three years ago, it's been incredible progress. But is there more work to do? Absolutely."

In the midst of all this effort and diverging opinions, the economic value of Microsoft is changing, though traditional accounting has no effective way of measuring or helping to manage these very real changes in the company's critical intangible assets. Only the future will reveal how Microsoft's bottom line will be affected by the efforts of its research teams and the strategic decisions of its executives. One thing is certain, however, traditional performance evaluation systems will struggle very hard to place a value on these kinds of changes.

Sources: A. Webber, "New Math for a New Economy," *Fast Company* (January–February 2000); J. Greene, "Microsoft's Big Bet," *Business Week* (October 30, 2000); Microsoft 2002 Annual Report; P. Galli, ".Net: 3 Years of the 'Vision' Thing," *eWeek* (July 7, 2003), Vol. 20, Issue 27, pp. 26–27.

ompetitive pressures in the marketplace require that companies continually look for ways to improve their information systems in order to obtain better insights into how to operate their businesses more effectively and more efficiently. Management accounting, being at the core of business information systems, is always evolving. Managers want management accounting information that supports the strategy of the company. They do not want the information limited to financial measures of performance only. Quality and time measures of performance in customer service (e.g., timely deliveries), internal business processes (e.g., production defects), and growth in the organization (e.g., employee education levels) are becoming more important all the time. As a result, we are at the intersection of new directions in accounting. It's time we take a brief look at the future of management accounting.

You are now in the last chapter of this textbook. You've spent a lot of time studying many details concerning the process of creating and using accounting to add value to an organization. We've established that the management process involves planning, controlling, and evaluating business activities in order to compete well on issues involving cost, quality, and time. We've also discussed managing these concerns across three different types of firms: manufacturing, merchandising, and service. We understand that the accountant must customize a great variety of information sources to fit the specific strategic and operating needs of decision makers. The effort to "manage" this management accounting process may cause you to feel a bit overwhelmed. Of all the information that is possible (and we've presented in this text only a subset of a growing list of possibilities), what information is best for a particular company? Does a model exist that helps accountants and managers identify specific performance measures critical to surviving and thriving in the fast-paced, highly competitive, worldwide economy of the twenty-first century? More importantly, how does management accounting continue to improve performance measures in pace with innovations in products and processes and changes in markets and competition? Actually, there's been a lot of discussion recently among managers and management accountants on this very question. One approach to answering this question is gaining attention in many companies. The approach is called the "Balanced Scorecard," and no education on management accounting is really complete without some awareness of this approach. We'll spend most of this chapter illustrating this new performance measurement model and how it could affect the nature of both management accounting and financial accounting.[1]

The Value of Intangible Assets

The beginning of this chapter discussed the challenges that Microsoft faces in managing a very large organization that is focused essentially on building and selling "knowledge." In other words, the value of Microsoft is not its buildings or inventory, but the capability of its people; and the value of its products is not the software package that you buy, but in the capability of that software to solve problems. These intangible "knowledge" assets are very expensive both to acquire and to develop. And they're extremely difficult to manage. When a drug passes its clinical tests, huge value is created—but there's no transaction. Nothing changes hands. Nobody buys anything, and nobody sells anything. As a result, accounting, by tradition, does not measure or report this kind of information to managers (or investors). When software passes a beta-test, it suddenly becomes valuable—but there's no transaction, so there's no reporting. Or think about how value is destroyed: when a large, older company is late in figuring out how to enter the world of e-commerce, huge value is destroyed—but there's no transaction, and the company continues to be reported by accountants to its managers as doing well. Traditional measures of performance may ignore intangible corporate capabilities that can often lead to higher long-term returns than plant and equipment assets. In short, technology has created far more data than ever before. But what we all need—and what accounting now needs to work on—is the transformation of data into valuable information and knowledge that applies to the unique needs of specific organizations.

---

1 The Balanced Scorecard Model was first presented in a series of articles in the *Harvard Business Review* by Robert S. Kaplan and David P. Norton: "The Balanced Scorecard—Measures That Drive Performance" (January–February 1992); "Putting the Balanced Scorecard to Work" (September–October 1993); "Using the Balanced Scorecard as a Strategic Management System" (January–February 1996). The most complete discussion on this theory is found in Kaplan and Norton's *The Balanced Scorecard: Translating Strategy into Action* (Boston, MA: Harvard Business School Press, 1996) and *The Strategy-Focused Organization: How Balanced Scorecard Companies Thrive in the New Business Environment* (Boston, MA: Harvard Business School Press, 2001).

Let's Take a Flight!

Imagine that a friend of yours is getting her airplane pilot's license and has invited you to sit in the passenger seat of the airplane during her next pilot's lesson. Your friend has not been taking flying lessons very long. However, as you listen to her enthusiastic description of past lessons as the two of you drive out to the airfield the next afternoon, you begin to really look forward to the experience. After parking the car and walking to the Cessna plane that waits on the tarmac, your friend introduces you to the flight instructor, and the three of you climb into the plane. Soon after you take your seat and buckle the seatbelt, your friend revs the engine and the small plane surges forward. The instructor is sitting next to your friend, providing advice and guidance as the plane taxis down the runway gathering speed for takeoff. Suddenly, as you peer over the shoulders of the instructor and your friend in front of you, you notice with some concern that the small plane's instrument panel is noticeably bare of the assortment of instruments, dials, gauges, and controls that are typically part of an airplane's cockpit. In fact, there appears to be only one gauge on the whole panel. Trying to make your question sound casual, you ask about the barren panel and the sole gauge. The instructor looks back over his shoulder to tell you that the gauge measures airspeed. The plane is nearing the end of the runway and is just about to lift off. After swallowing once or twice, you brave more questions about direction, altitude, fuel, temperature, and thrust. Aren't these items also important in flying a plane? Don't most planes have gauges to provide feedback to the pilot on details other than simply airspeed? The instructor agrees but indicates that your friend is currently concentrating on airspeed in her flying lessons. Once she excels at managing airspeed, perhaps the airspeed gauge will be switched for an altimeter, and she can then concentrate on managing altitude. The instructor tells you that he feels it's important to not make the pilot concentrate on too many things at the same time. You notice that your friend is concentrating very hard on the airspeed gauge as the plane noses up and lifts off from the ground. You swallow hard and tighten your seatbelt until it is very snug around your waist. For some reason, you're suddenly imagining about a hundred others places you'd rather be than sitting in this plane.

Flying an airplane is a complicated process. To do it successfully requires that the pilot process a lot of information about various performance aspects of both the equipment and the environment. Managing a company is certainly no less complicated. A lot has to happen at once in order for a company to perform well in its competitive environment as the demands of products, customers, and regulatory agencies change constantly. One of a management accountant's most important functions is to identify and implement **performance measures** that are focused on key strategic and operating plans established by management. These performance measures then become the primary means of controlling and evaluating business processes in the organization. What is the best performance measure for an accountant to provide for an organization? Frankly, there is no one best performance measure.

performance measures A general term used to describe all measures designed to capture information about performance related to a particular activity or process.

The Balanced Scorecard

Explain the fundamentals of building a balanced scorecard.

Balanced Scorecard A new management model designed to link together performance measures for financial, customer, internal process, and learning/growth perspectives that are unique to an organization's particular strategy.

Previous chapters and sections in this textbook have typically focused on subsets of management accounting issues such as merchandising, cost measurement, or the evaluating process. However, in this chapter we are not going to focus the discussion on any particular type of firm, strategic imperative, or management process. Instead, we present a *framework* that a management accountant can use to work with any of these issues. That framework is the Balanced Scorecard.

The **Balanced Scorecard** is a process to manage a set of performance measures that support directly the unique strategy an organization is trying to establish and follow. Exhibit 1 presents the framework of the Balanced Scorecard. The strategic performance measures that a company develops for itself are largely determined by how the organization answers the four basic questions listed in Exhibit 1. The answers to these questions then determine the man-

Exhibit 1: The Balanced Scorecard Framework

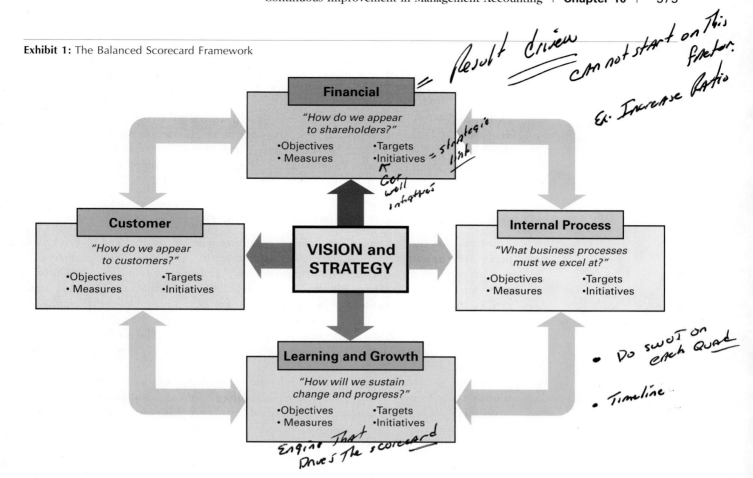

agement *objectives* for the organization, the *measures* that support those objectives, the immediate and long-term *targets* or goals for those measures, and what *initiatives* need to be put into place to begin working toward the targets. The entire balanced scorecard process is driven by the organization's overall vision or strategy.

At first glance, the Balanced Scorecard may not seem to be a very new idea. Shouldn't all performance measures support the organization's strategy? Hasn't management accounting always been focused on supporting the objectives of managers and executives to create a profitable company? Actually, although the purpose of management accounting is to establish performance measures that add value to the organization, too often these measures have been limited to periodic reports composed solely of financial measures. Advances in computer systems technology today allow more information, more variety in information, and more timely information to be created and reported than ever before. The existence of better information capabilities provides an opportunity for accountants, working in conjunction with system technologists and organization executives, to significantly expand the definition of management accounting. As you study this chapter, you need to understand that the Balanced Scorecard is really a guiding theory of management, rather than an exact formula or blueprint that can be automatically implemented in any organization to improve its management processes. Once created, each organization's own balanced scorecard is a direct view of its strategy, its plans, and its management processes. The idea that a balanced scorecard is extremely personal for each organization is captured in the following comment made by an executive as his division completed work on its first balanced scorecard:

> In the past, if you had lost my strategic planning document on an airplane and a competitor found it, I would have been angry, but I would have gotten over it. In reality, it wouldn't have been that big a loss. Or if I had left my monthly operating review somewhere and a competitor obtained a copy,

I would have been upset, but, again, it wouldn't have been that big a deal. This balanced scorecard, however, communicates my strategy so well that a competitor seeing this would be able to block the strategy and cause it to become ineffective.[2]

Hence, there is no such thing as a *standard* balanced scorecard that any organization can use to operate successfully in its environment. Therefore, as we use example performance measures throughout the chapter to describe the Balanced Scorecard theory, you should remember that each organization must design its own performance measures that support its own particular strategy.

Adding Value with Performance Measures

Think back on the last nine chapters involving management accounting and all the various performance measures we've studied involving cost, quality, and time. Frankly, there are a number of problems associated with the performance evaluation methods currently used in many organizations. Some individuals argue that current performance measurement systems even encourage waste, inefficiency, and poor quality. For example, a measure that emphasizes purchase price may encourage the purchasing department to increase the purchase quantity to get a lower price but might ignore quality and speed of delivery. The results may be excess inventory, increased storage and other carrying costs, and failure to use suppliers with the best quality and service.

Another example may be allocating overhead costs based on direct labor hours. Direct labor is often a cost that is small in relation to manufacturing overhead items, which are becoming more significant for many companies. The result of any overemphasis on direct labor as a mechanism for managing overhead costs may be missed opportunities for cost control since major overhead activities are not *directly* planned, controlled, and evaluated by management.

If machine utilization is the performance measure being emphasized, a supervisor may run a machine in excess of daily production requirements to maximize the performance measure. This may result in excess inventory or production that is not needed. Similarly, if the performance measure is focused solely on the number of units produced, poor-quality goods or inventory that is not desired by customers may be produced. A specific example from the former Soviet Union illustrates this point. Oil drillers, in competition with one another, received recognition and compensation based on the number of meters drilled. The award-winning team recognized by *Pravda* (Russia's leading newspaper) drilled meter upon meter but never struck oil. It seems that the first 100 meters of drilling do not require as much effort and expense as the second, third, fourth, and so on. The winning team drilled dry hole after dry hole. And the depth of these wells never exceeded 100 meters.

Some prominent researchers believe that performance evaluation systems used in the United States are quite ineffective and have contributed to a decline in America's competitiveness. One major problem that these researchers identify with traditional performance evaluation methods is the limited focus of these methods. To be specific, they argue that current evaluation methods, which mostly focus on financial returns, are not designed to cope with such intangible corporate capabilities as an excellent workforce, research and development, and knowledge assets. They argue that we have moved from a manufacturing society to an information society and that performance evaluation systems have not kept pace. This argument certainly seems to have merit when considering the competitive position of MICROSOFT described at the beginning of this chapter. Are Microsoft's real assets appropriately displayed on a balance sheet that focuses on inventory, equipment, and buildings? Does it make sense to evaluate performance at Microsoft based on controlling costs of materials, labor, and manufacturing overhead? Microsoft, like many other companies, needs a performance measurement system that is customized to fit its particular strategy.

2 R. S. Kaplan and D. P. Norton, *The Balanced Scorecard: Translating Strategy into Action* (Boston, MA: Harvard Business School Press, 1996), p. 148.

Every company ultimately must perform well financially in order to survive. Even not-for-profit organizations must be able to consistently pay their bills, including payrolls and loans, in order to survive over time. Other companies must consistently show profits, build equity, and provide a return to stockholders. The DUPONT COMPANY made a lot of money by carefully tracking financial measures that contributed to consistent ROI and ROE performance. Remember, however, that successful management accounting methods are eventually copied by other organizations. Hence, strictly using ROI to manage an organization does not provide a competitive edge in today's economy. Organizations must continuously improve their management information processes in order to continue to compete. Traditional financial measures are now being vigorously supplemented in three new areas: customer service, internal process improvement, and learning and growth throughout the organization.

FYI:

In harmony with the idea of an instrument panel on an airplane, some companies prefer to refer to their strategic measurement systems as dashboards rather than scoreboards.

Customers

The first key to strong financial performance is customer satisfaction. When companies understand what their customers value and what services and products they are willing to pay for, then these companies can design customer-focused performance measures that lead to growth in market share, increased revenues, and long-term profits. There are two types of customer performance measures: leading measures and outcome measures. **Leading measures** focus on fulfilling customer expectations regarding cost, quality, and time factors. **Outcome measures** determine if the improvements in leading measures result in more satisfied, loyal customers. Therefore, it is important that there be a clear link between the company's efforts to provide low-cost, high-quality, timely products and services and customer response to these efforts as demonstrated by increased market share and customer profitability (i.e., the company is able to earn sufficient profits by serving its customers). Exhibit 2 provides measures of customer-focused performance.

leading measures Measures that, if successfully implemented, will support desired performance in other business activities. Note that some leading measures can also serve as outcome measures.

outcome measures Measures of desired outcome performance in activities critical to an organization's strategic goals. Note that some outcome measures are also leading measures to support desired performance in other business activities.

Leading Measures of Customer Satisfaction

We have discussed cost, quality, and time measures throughout the last nine chapters of this textbook. Naturally, most customers desire low-cost products and services. However, customer satisfaction is the result of the right combination of cost, quality, and time. As customers, we are willing to balance our demands for these three objectives. For example, when you mail a

Exhibit 2: Performance Measures of Customer Satisfaction

#3   *Good Treatment of scorecard*

Ⓐ Leading Performance Measures

Cost *payroll*	Quality	Time	
		Reliable Delivery	**Fastest Delivery**
• Purchase cost to customer	• Returns by customers	• Percentage of on-time deliveries	• Average response time for service call
• Delivery cost to customer	• Quality rankings by other agencies	• Number of production interruptions	• Time to complete contract
• Setup cost to customer	• Customer survey response		• Production cycle time
• Maintenance and repair cost to customer			

Ⓑ Outcome Performance Measures

Customer Retention	Customer Acquisition	Market Share
• Retention rates	• Acquisition rates	• Percent of total number of customers
• Number of defecting customers	• Number of new customers	• Percent of total dollars spent by customers
• Costs to retain customers	• Costs to recruit customers	• Percent of total units sold to customers

Types of customers
loyal
Repeat

Balanced Scorecard and the Government The DEFENSE LOGISTICS AGENCY (DLA) was founded in 1961 to provide worldwide logistics support to U.S. Armed Forces. Logistics support includes fuels, food, clothing, medical and industrial supplies, land weapons systems support, and aviation supplies. The DLA has annual sales of over $29 billion and employs 28,000 people in all 50 states and in 27 countries.

The DLA is run like a business—its services and material are purchased by the Armed Forces. However, it was at one time an enterprise without a "management plan." The DLA was reactive in its approach to customer requests, divided into silos by product, and very decentralized. The DLA at that time was about "filling an order, not about supporting the customer," according to retired Admiral Ray Archer, vice commander of the DLA. At the same time, customers were not obligated to buy from the DLA and would use external vendors if items were out of stock or unavailable—making customer support an important issue.

The DLA and its leadership needed to restructure for change. The DLA was inwardly focused. The organization lacked a common vision and had no management process to guide it through the strategic transformation into an enterprise that was customer focused. In the effort to make this significant change, a balanced scorecard was adopted in the spring of 2000. The DLA believed this was the right tool to address the transformation. The new DLA balanced scorecard provided the strategies and initiatives that supported a corporate vision and allowed the DLA to:

- describe the enterprise,
- define its customers and stakeholders,
- define the value it provided to them,
- identify its internal strengths and weaknesses, and
- put a plan in place for change.

The DLA used its balanced scorecard to define its strategy, restructure the organization, and focus on customers as well as target the internal capabilities (processes and people) needed to deliver its promise—"Right Item, Right Time, Right Place, Right Price, Every Time . . . Best Value Solution for America's Warfighter."

The bottom line results are beginning to come in. In 2002, the DLA achieved $130 million in savings while processing $2.2 billion more in requisitions for its customers.

Source: Taken from the site **http://www.bscol.com/training/success/dla**, accessed August 15, 2003.

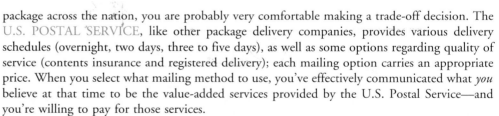

package across the nation, you are probably very comfortable making a trade-off decision. The U.S. POSTAL SERVICE, like other package delivery companies, provides various delivery schedules (overnight, two days, three to five days), as well as some options regarding quality of service (contents insurance and registered delivery); each mailing option carries an appropriate price. When you select what mailing method to use, you've effectively communicated what *you* believe at that time to be the value-added services provided by the U.S. Postal Service—and you're willing to pay for those services.

Most companies have spent a great deal of effort understanding how their customers perceive value in terms of timeliness, quality, and price. For many companies, customers are more concerned with reliability than with the fastest delivery. This is particularly true in a JIT environment. TOYOTA demands deliveries from its suppliers to assembly plants within a one-hour time window. Early arrivals of parts are as unacceptable as late deliveries. Hence, observers have sometimes witnessed delivery trucks driving around and around a Toyota assembly plant until it is time to deliver their goods. If you think about it, this is not really strange behavior. Have you ever scheduled a telephone repairperson to come to your home during the day? Your definition of "on time" is probably not sometime between 9:00 A.M. and 3:00 P.M., is it? Further, given a 1:00 P.M. appointment, you probably would not be particularly pleased at the repairperson's effort to "delight the customer" by arriving two hours early. Performance measures regarding reliability versus fastest delivery of goods or services depend on both the strategy of the company and the demands of its customers. A few examples of these types of measures are

© 2003 Getty Images

When you buy a car, the purchase price represents only part of the total cost of car ownership. You must also consider such costs as maintenance, repairs, and gas. In an effort to account for all costs incurred throughout the entire life of a product, some companies use life cycle costing.

life cycle costing The process of measuring all costs involved in creating, producing, and using a product or service. Life cycle costing is not limited to costs incurred by the organization measuring these costs but also includes all costs incurred by the suppliers and the customers of the product or service.

market share The percentage share one company receives of the total sales revenue in the economy for a particular product or service.

 Caution

Research indicates that adequate scores on customer satisfaction surveys are not sufficient to create the kind of loyalty that results in high customer retention rates. Companies that cannot consistently *delight* their customers on the most valued performance factors will lose business.

Source: M. C. H. Yeung, L. C. Ging, and C. T. Ennew, "Customer Satisfaction and Profitability: A Reappraisal of the Nature of the Relationship," *Journal of Targeting, Measurement and Analysis for Marketing*, 2002 (Vol. 11, Issue 1), pp. 24–33.

provided in Exhibit 2. You can look back at Exhibit 13 on page 423 in the chapter on managing inventory for more examples of time-based performance measures.

As you remember from the chapter on activity-based costing, total quality management (TQM) has been firmly rooted in the United States since the 1980s. Commitment to quality is now generally assumed for most products and services—it is a competitive necessity. Companies not committed to the total quality effort will typically struggle to survive. Hence, organizations must pay careful attention to what quality factors are important to their customers and then build measures that accurately track performance of these quality factors.

As mentioned earlier, customers compare timeliness and quality factors with price to evaluate the real value of a product or service. Many companies realize, however, that the purchase price of their product often does not represent the total cost to their customer. If you own a car, you may be painfully aware of this fact. The purchase price of your car is only part of its total cost. Maintenance, repairs, gas mileage, and insurance also combine with the original purchase price to determine the total cost of owning your car. Perhaps you wish you had spent a little more (or less) when purchasing your car in order to better balance the subsequent costs of owning your car. In an effort to account for costs that are an essential part of the total value of a product, some firms are turning to a concept known as life cycle costing. Essentially, **life cycle costing** is a method of costing that focuses on all costs that will be incurred throughout the entire life of a product. The life cycle approach to costing helps to ensure that no costs are omitted when evaluating performance and value. Hence, when evaluating customer satisfaction, an organization also needs to measure performance of its product or service in terms of *all* its costs for its customers. These cost measures are listed as leading performance measures in Exhibit 2.

Outcome Measures of Customer Satisfaction

An organization's focus on customers must be twofold. First, the company works to measure up to customer expectations regarding cost, quality, and time. Then the company must determine if its efforts are being rewarded with increased market share and customer profitability. **Market share** is the proportion of industry sales of a particular product or service that is controlled by a specific firm. Companies increase their market share in two ways: retaining current customers and acquiring new customers. Clearly, companies that cannot service their current customers better than competitors will be hard-pressed to maintain market share. Absolute customer satisfaction is key in this regard. Interestingly, when management accountants ignore expected future cash flows over a customer's life, they miss reporting the real cost (the opportunity cost) of losing customers. Exhibit 3 reports a past study showing how much profit a customer generates over time in four different industries. The implication of this study continues to be true today. As you can see, customer profitability over time really takes off *if* the company can retain its customers' loyalty. This increased profitability over time is the result of increased purchases or higher account balances, reduced operating costs, and profits from referrals. Hence, customer retention rates are very important outcome measures that result from good performance of leading measures related to customers' overall costs, quality of product, and timeliness of delivery.

Once the company has established leading measures that result in high customer retention, it can turn its attention to acquiring new customers in order to grow its market share. Obviously, there is a strong relationship between loyal customers who speak enthusiastically about the company's product and the company's ability to win new customers. As a result, many companies identify customer loyalty as the best way to acquire new customers. In addition, companies also spend a great deal of effort and resources recruiting new customers. Hence, tracking performance in customer acquisition is a strategy of growth in market

Exhibit 3: How Much Profit an Average Customer Generates over Time

Industry	Year 1	Year 2	Year 3	Year 4	Year 5
Credit cards	$ 30	$ 42	$ 44	$ 49	$ 55
Industrial laundry	144	166	192	222	256
Industrial distribution	45	99	121	144	168
Auto servicing	25	35	70	88	88

Source: Adapted from F. F. Reichheld and W. E. Sasser, "Zero Defections: Quality Comes to Services," Harvard Business Review (September–October 1990), pp. 105–112.

FYI:

The cost to acquire new customers in the wireless industry is significant. In 2002, AT&T WIRELESS spent $377 on average to acquire each new subscriber to its service, which was an increase from $334 the previous year. On the other hand, average monthly revenue per user was $60.20, down from $62.60 the previous year. In other words, it takes AT&T more than six months of customer loyalty just to recoup the cost of getting the customer to subscribe in the first place! With the constant churn of customers affecting companies' bottom lines, customer satisfaction is becoming more and more important to companies.

Source: AT&T Wireless, 2002 Annual Report, p. 24.

share. It is important to understand that there are many ways to successfully maintain and increase market share through customer retention and acquisition. However, retaining and recruiting customers *profitably* is important to strong financial performance. Hence, companies must track the costs spent recruiting new customers, as well as the costs spent retaining current customers. Using activity-based costing (ABC) to track the costs of activities necessary to recruit and retain customers can provide a company with the necessary information to identify desirable customers and to make important decisions to drop certain unprofitable customers. Management accountants who provide outcome measures of their companies' efforts to profitably grow market share can add competitive value to the management process. These customer outcome measures are listed in Exhibit 2.

Internal Processes

Effective management accounting that is built around the Balanced Scorecard can help organizations better understand how satisfying customers (using leading performance measures) relates to growth in customer profitability (using outcome measures). The next issue to be resolved is what processes within the organization must take place in order to satisfy the customer completely? Most of your work in the last nine chapters has focused on building performance measures to support the manager's efforts to plan, control, and evaluate processes within the company. However, building performance measures that effectively support the goal of customer satisfaction requires that the management accountant first understand that there are three types of processes that must be in place in order to take care of the customer: innovation processes, operations processes, and service-after-sale processes. Examples of performance measures for management of internal processes are provided in Exhibit 4.

Innovation Process Measures

We've talked very little in this textbook about planning, controlling, and evaluating the *innovation process*, which involves identifying new products and services, and then creating and bringing those products to market. The reason for this is that most of the management accounting effort has historically been focused on the operations process, which involves building goods or providing services that already exist. For example, accountants spend a great deal of effort developing budgets of operations, then measuring variances from standard costs of direct materials, direct labor, and manufacturing overhead. We focused on this particular management process in earlier chapters on operational budgeting and monitoring performance. However, the innovation process of identifying and creating new products is where much of a company's competitive edge is created. This is why Microsoft spends so much money hiring some of the best minds in the software industry—to ensure that it will continue to create new products that

Exhibit 4: Performance Measures of Internal Processes

	Innovation Processes	Operations Processes	Service-after-Sale Processes
Cost measures	• R&D costs per new product • Payback on R&D costs	• Unit-level costs • Batch-level costs • Product line costs	• Costs per service incidence • Costs of replacement parts
Quality measures	• Number of modifications required per design • Percentage of sales from new products	• Defects-per-million opportunities (six sigma) • Errors in customer service	• Customer requests handled on first call • Satisfaction survey responses
Time measures	• Lead time (from idea to working model) • Design cycle time	• Lead time (from order to delivery) • Production cycle time	• Lead time (from request to fulfillment) • Repair cycle time

network **exercises**

J.D. Power and Associates

retain and recruit customers. As we move further into the new century, many businesses are spending more in their research, design, and development processes than they do to support their production and operating processes. Microsoft is a great example of this trend. If you look at its income statements for 2000 through 2002, you will see that this company often spends more money on research and development of new products than it spends providing current goods and services to its current customers. These data are provided below.

	2000	2001	2002
Cost of revenue	$3,002 million	$3,455 million	$5,191 million
Research and development	$3,772 million	$4,379 million	$4,307 million

Admittedly, many companies do not spend the kind of money on the innovation process that Microsoft does. Nevertheless, the resources invested in the innovation process for most companies are significant. It's important to the ultimate financial success of the organization that the critical effort to identify and develop new products and services is effectively managed. At some point, the money invested in the research and development (R&D) effort must provide financial returns. However, an R&D project can require a very long payback period. Many organizations begin significant R&D projects expecting that financial returns will not be realized for many years. Sometimes basic research is done in organizations with no clear idea of what profitable product or service may eventually result. Occasionally, some of our society's most useful innovations have resulted from these kinds of R&D investments. On the other hand, with this strategy it is possible that a lot of resources and energy will be needlessly spent in the innovation process, which means that the strategic imperatives of cost, quality, and time still apply here. Given the size of the investments made, it is important that organizations develop measures to evaluate the costs of their innovation processes. In addition, organizations should assess the effectiveness (e.g., the quality) of innovation work.

Finally, without proper controls, R&D work is at risk of simply taking too long. You're likely familiar with the old adage that "time is money." Clearly, any project that requires time extensions will cost more to complete. You'll remember from the activity-based costing chapter that additional costs due to time overruns will also include increased holding costs. However, in the case of R&D, "time is opportunity!" The market is always moving. Organizations that take longer than their competitors to complete the research and development of new products or services may quickly find themselves seriously disadvantaged in the marketplace. Hence, organizations that manage well their innovation processes will compete well in the marketplace. Performance measures that support the management of the innovation process will typically be custom-built for each organization based on its strategic intent and on the particular nature of its R&D work. Exhibit 4 provides examples of cost, quality, and time-based measures for the innovation process.

business environment

The Balanced Scorecard— Code Red! The job of managing a hospital is extremely difficult! On the one end, you must deal with doctors who oppose any monetary label on patient care, and on the other end you must make financial decisions that will keep the hospital operational. Some of these decisions can be agonizing, leaving you to wonder where you draw the line. For example, do you make the questionably unethical decision of turning away needy patients because of money? These were the very problems facing Dr. Jon Meliones, chief medical director of DUKE CHILDREN'S HOSPITAL in Durham, North Carolina, in the mid-1990s.

The hospital was $11 million in the red. Critical programs were being canceled, the number of patient beds was being reduced, and the quality of patient care was in a miserable state. Dr. Meliones, faced with the disastrous state of the hospital, came across the Balanced Scorecard strategy and instantly decided that applying the principles from the Balanced Scorecard was the solution. Upon learning that the Balanced Scorecard dealt with finance, customer service, learning and growth, and internal processes, Dr. Meliones saw this model as a perfect fit for his hospital. Not only did it deal with the financial administration of running a hospital, but it also took into consideration the very real needs of the patients and doctors who receive and provide the care.

"We wanted everyone—from accountants to physicians to therapists—focusing on a common goal, not individual goals," explained Meliones. "We needed to become a strategy-focused organization if our balanced scorecard was to succeed and, in turn, if the hospital was to succeed." The balanced scorecard effort at Duke Children's Hospital involved distributing daily "re-port cards" to all hospital employees to ensure they understood where they stood within the strategic goals of the hospital. These report cards empowered the hospital staff to find creative ways to reduce costs, increase the quality of patient care, and help hospital administrators see more than just the bottom line. For example, physicians received information pertaining to their own patient loads, such as average length of stay and average cost per patient. They could then evaluate the results themselves and determine where to cut costs rather than having to follow a mandate issued by someone in management who doesn't understand the medical issues involved in these kinds of decisions.

Not only did these report cards allow doctors and other medical staff to evaluate where they could cut costs, but it also empowered them to look for other ways to improve quality of care. For example, a chief complaint of patients' parents was not being able to identify their child's primary caregiver. So a secretary decided that as patients were admitted, labels with the names of each one's primary doctor and nurse would be placed on their doors. "Prior to this simple solution, only 42% of parents could identify their child's doctor," said Meliones. "But as soon as we began labeling, that number rose to 99%. The balanced scorecard began turning everyone into a chief strategy officer of some sort."

As a result of the cooperative effort between management and medical staff to implement a balanced scorecard, Duke Children's Hospital has gone from $11 million in the red to $4 million in the black, an incredible turnaround!

Source: SAS Institute, Inc., News and Events, "Life in the Balance: Duke Children's Hospital," **http://www.sas.com/news/success/dukehosp.html**, accessed March 5, 2001.

Operations Process Measures

Operations processes involve all of the activities directly related to the sale of goods or services to customers, including receipt of customer orders, creation of products, and delivery of products. Ever since Francis Cabot Lowell established his cotton mill in Waltham, Massachusetts, in 1814 and created the "Waltham system" of accounting to track manufacturing costs, accountants have focused on adding value to the operations processes by measuring cost, quality, and time performance. In the effort to support operations processes, many valuable accounting methods have been developed. As a result, several of the previous chapters have focused on helping you understand these methods. Though management accounting for operations processes has been in place for a long time, new methods continue to evolve in an effort to create information that has competitive value.

The concepts of activity-based costing (ABC) and the Hierarchical Production Model (discussed in the activity-based costing chapter) represent some of the important cost measures created recently to fulfill competitive needs for organizations. An example of a quality measure for manufacturing processes that strongly impacts performance in the marketplace is "six sigma quality." One of the famous measures of quality, six sigma quality is now becoming an important operations management tool for many types of merchandising and service firms. Sigma[3] is a statistical measure of variation in a product or process and is used in statistical process control (SPC) charts to evaluate upper and lower control limits (see the ABC chapter for a review of SPC charts). Sigma measures also provide insight about probabilities. Specifically, when the incidence of a single error in the product or service process occurs at a distance of six sigma from the target value, then the probability that the process itself has quality problems is very low. To be precise (without getting into all the statistics involved), an operation process is said to have **six sigma quality** when defects in the process are occurring at the low rate of 3.4 defects per million opportunities—now that's a high-quality process! Other measures of cost, quality, and time that have competitive value continue to be developed and refined. Exhibit 4 provides some measures that exemplify the continuous improvements we now see in cost, quality, and time measures to support operations processes.

six sigma quality A measure of quality based on statistical analysis. Products or services with six sigma quality have no more than 3.4 defects per million opportunities (e.g., parts or events).

FYI:

LANDS' END is a garment mail-order merchant that exemplifies the growing trend of excellent service-after-sale to customers. Despite being a very large company (during peak seasons, close to 1,100 phone lines handle over 100,000 calls per day), it has established a strong reputation for customer service. Lands' End offers one of the simplest guarantees in the industry—"GUARANTEED. PERIOD.®" This means letting the customer return the product at any time, for any reason. As an example of the extent of its guarantee, customers who need additional buttons, have lost a belt, or need a piece of luggage repaired can receive all these services at any time after purchase, free of charge. Even if a child loses a mitten from Lands' End during the same season it was purchased, the "Lost Mitten Club" will replace it at half the price of a pair, and Lands' End will pick up the costs of shipping.

Service-after-Sale Process Measures

Service-after-sale processes are of two types. One type of service-after-sale process involves the billing and collection of payments from customers. The other type involves the organization's commitment to warranty its product, including efforts to repair or replace products and provide post-sale support and guidance in the use of the product. If you've ever purchased a personal computer, you have likely had some experience with technical support to help you resolve a computer problem or simply to figure out how to better use your new computer. Depending on your experience with your computer merchant's technical support (or, for that matter, the post-sale support of any other product or service you've purchased), you probably have strong positive or negative feelings about the quality and timeliness of the support you received, and about the company itself! Do organizations create a competitive edge when they provide quality, timely post-sale support while controlling the costs of that support? You bet! Is it important to effectively control the process of billing and collecting payments from customers? If you remember our extensive discussion of holding costs in an earlier chapter on managing inventory, you know that companies can spend a lot of time and resources creating customer invoices and then following up to ensure prompt collection. Poor management of service-after-sale processes can result in many opportunity costs. Hence, management accountants also pay attention to management of these processes using effective performance measures, some examples of which are provided in Exhibit 4.

---

3 Sigma is the name of the Latin symbol σ and is used to represent a statistical measure more commonly known as "standard deviation."

Learning and Growth

Perhaps the most interesting example of continuous improvement in management accounting is found in the very recent trend for accountants to help management teams better understand the process of building learning and growth within the organization. In order to survive and thrive in this competitive economy, an organization must continue to learn and grow. Or, to be more specific, the organization's employees, system, and structure must learn, grow, and change in order to continuously build and improve internal processes and satisfy customers. Certainly, the demand of customers today is well described by the question, "What have you done for me lately?" Without learning and growth, internal processes stop improving, customers grow restless and defect, and financial performance stagnates. However, many might react rather strongly to the trend to create performance measures on learning and growth by challenging whether this kind of work is really management accounting at all! How does one measure learning and growth? Frankly, it's not a well-developed accounting discipline. However, because development in this area is rather slight, there is much opportunity for management accountants to create significant competitive value for their organizations by working to build good measures. Don't forget the lesson learned from Donaldson Brown and the DuPont ROI formula in the first chapter where we introduced management accounting. Accountants who are able to provide information useful to plan, control, and evaluate critical business processes, regardless of the initial difficulty of the effort, will add the most value to their organization. By dividing this effort into leading measures and outcome measures (somewhat similar to the effort of managing an organization's work with its customers), the Balanced Scorecard Model suggests some interesting possibilities for measuring performance in the learning and growth effort. Exhibit 5 illustrates some example measures that can be used for managing learning and growth performance.

Leading Measures of Learning and Growth

The ultimate result of building learning and growth in the organization is based on developing employee productivity. Employee productivity then leads to internal process improvements. Related to employee productivity is employee retention and employee satisfaction. These three issues form the desired outcome measures of learning and growth. Therefore, the organization should track performance in the productivity, retention rates, and satisfaction of its employees. However, managing improvements in these important outcome measures requires that management accountants identify the factors that result in high employee productivity, retention, and satisfaction. These factors form *leading* measures in learning and growth: employee capabilities, information system capabilities, and organizational structure capabilities.

Improvements in employee capabilities should lead to improvements in employee productivity. However, improving employee productivity does not necessarily mean that employees are satisfied with their work situation and are committed to staying with the company. If investments in employee capabilities are expected to result in higher satisfaction and retention rates among employees, then companies should also expect to see positive improvements in internal processes, customer care, and financial performance. Measures here can focus on the level of qualifications and certifications among employees, as well as investments made by the company in employee training and education.

In this information age, the strength of a company's information system structure is critical to employee productivity. To build an excellent organization, employees need relevant, accurate, and timely information on the effects of their efforts to improve processes, satisfy customers, and strengthen financial performance within the organization. In addition to information systems, modern technology continues to provide significant opportunities for directly improving

network **exercises**

Metrus Group

Balanced scorecards are often implemented with the help of an outside consultant. METRUS GROUP is an organization whose employees are experts in balanced scorecards and performance measurement strategies. Access the Web site at **http://www .metrus.com**. Then select the "Products and Services" tab, and then "Strategic Performance Measurement." In the first sentence of this Web page, Metrus indicates the importance of focusing attention on the critical few *performance measures* that drive success.

Net Work:

1. According to Metrus, what are the key measures that drive company success?

2. What is the key to creating successful balanced scorecards?

⚠ Caution

Remember that management accounting is not a precisely defined discipline. Individual companies adapt good management accounting principles to fit specific information needs to plan, control, and evaluate their unique organizations. Nowhere is this more true than with the Balanced Scorecard, particularly when it comes to measures of an organization's performance on learning and growth. Every organization will have a *very* specific view of what it means for that organization to learn and grow. Therefore, remember that Exhibit 5, as well as other exhibits in this chapter listing balanced scorecard measures, is an example of what some companies might choose to measure when developing an effective balanced scorecard. No two companies' scorecards are alike!

Excellent

#1

measures that move you.
fix leading measures
Executives should look down at outcome perf. measures.

Exhibit 5: Performance Measures of Learning and Growth

	Leading Performance Measures		
	Employee Capabilities	**Information Systems Capabilities**	**Organizational Structure Capabilities**
Cost measures	• On-site training expense per employee • Off-site education expense per employee	• Total costs invested in computer systems within the organization • Systems R&D expense per total systems expense	• Costs invested in assessing and building new communication structures • Costs invested in activities to align goals within the company
Quality measures	• Number of new certifications or degrees • Percentage of employees participating in education activities	• System capability compared to competitor systems • Percentage of employees with access to personal computer	• Assessment of effective communication • Assessment of effective teamwork • Assessment of goal alignment
Time measures	• Average yearly training or education hours per employee • Time required to complete a training module	• Average life cycle time of personal computers (e.g., how often are machines upgraded?) • Time required to complete a system upgrade	• Amount of time spent in teamwork versus individual work • Average time to disseminate information or to receive employee feedback

	Outcome Performance Measures	
Employee Retention	**Employee Satisfaction**	**Employee Productivity**
• Employee turnover rate • Average employee years with company • Number of female managers • Average age of employees	• Survey of employee satisfaction • Percentage of employees having leadership opportunities • Management positions filled by inside versus outside recruits	• Output per employee • Billable hours per consultant • New ideas or patents per employee • Recognition of employees by customers

various business processes in all kinds of organizations. Performance measures on information systems and other types of technologies can focus on the quality of systems, accessibility to systems, and investments in systems.

Poorly run organizations can quickly damage employee satisfaction, as well as create confusion that limits employee productivity. Factors that define a well-run organization include effective communication; alignment of goals (i.e., everyone understands and is working toward the same goals); integration of team efforts across departments; and clearly defined planning, controlling, and evaluating processes. Measuring performance and capability in organizational structures is likely the most undefined and challenging "next step" for management accountants today. Nevertheless, this is important work. Organizations usually work very hard to create effective communication channels, to obtain buy-in from employees on company goals, to form an environment where people will work together, and to establish good management processes. Surveys of employees' perspectives are one good way to measure performance on the drive to create good organizational structure.

Outcome Measures of Learning and Growth

Examples of leading and outcome measures of learning and growth are provided in Exhibit 5. As accountants track these measures, it is critical that good performance in employee capabilities, information system capabilities, and organizational structure capabilities results in improvements in employee satisfaction, retention, and productivity. Obviously, then, management

STOP & THINK

Market value for a company is computed as the number of shares of stock outstanding multiplied by the average price per share. Essentially, market value measures how much money stockholders believe the company is worth. MICROSOFT's stock price as of June 30, 2002, was $54.70 per share. Based on 5,359,000,000 common shares outstanding at the end of its 2002 fiscal year (ending June 30), this works out to a market value of over $293 billion! However, if you look at Microsoft's 2002 balance sheet (again, dated June 30), you'll see that its net assets (total assets minus total liabilities) are valued at just over $52 billion. Why the huge difference?

accountants can (and should) test the relationship between leading measures and outcome measures by evaluating satisfaction of employees using surveys; reporting on resignation trends within the company; and measuring employees' productivity in terms of volume, quality, and timeliness of output. When investments in employee education programs or improvements in information systems fail to improve employee outcome measures, then management accountants should provide useful information to better manage these critical processes. Otherwise, there is likely to be little improvement in internal processes, customer satisfaction, and (finally) financial performance. Are you getting the sense that linking together all performance measures within the organization may be a critical aspect of developing a balanced scorecard? If so, then you are on track with the final concept that we discuss in the next section.

Linking It All Together

So far in this chapter, and, for that matter, throughout this entire textbook, we have been discussing *a lot* of different performance measures! Do management accountants really need to track *all* these data in order to effectively support the management processes within their companies? Clearly, the answer is no. Too much information is often as harmful as too little. Managers and organizations can become overloaded with information. The key is to clearly identify the vision and strategy a company chooses to pursue, and then establish a set of performance measures that supports progress toward specific company goals. Thus far in this chapter, we have learned that a balanced scorecard approach recognizes that management of a company requires information on financial, customer, internal process, and learning and growth activities. Further, performance measures of these activities are not limited to financial measures, but should include nonfinancial measures as well (e.g., quality and time-based measures). Perhaps the most important aspect of a balanced scorecard approach is that all measures must *link together* to eventually support the ultimate financial goals of a company.[4] Good performances on activities that do not directly or indirectly contribute to the ultimate goals the organization has established are obviously a waste of resources. Nevertheless, pointless investments in non-value-added activities probably occur in many organizations. Distinguishing non-value-added activities from value-added activities and identifying which performance measures successfully contribute to helping the company accomplish its strategic goals are the ideas behind linkages within a balanced scorecard.

To illustrate the importance of clearly linking performance measures in a balanced scorecard, look at Exhibit 6. It should be clear that the ability to achieve target financial goals such as a positive ROI (return on investment) or ROE (return on equity) is closely linked to success on customer outcome measures (customer retention, customer acquisition, and market share). However, a company can increase its market share and still experience declining ROI because the type of customers it is serving, or the way it is serving its customers, does not lead to positive profits for the company. This is the concept of leading versus lagging indicators. **Leading indicators** are measures of performance that, if accomplished, should lead to a desired result. Measures of performance on the desired results are the **lagging indicators**. A company may desire positive ROI. However, the company does not really "manage" ROI directly; instead, it manages performance that *leads* to positive ROI. Hence, it is important that the company has clearly determined that there is a strong relationship between its leading and lagging indicators. In other words, a company may determine that high rates of customer acquisition should lead to improvements in its overall ROI. Nevertheless, if the company actually does acquire a lot of new customers but does not experience improved ROI performance, it likely needs to spend some time better identifying exactly what the real leading indicators are for improved profits in its industry.

leading indicators Measures that indicate the potential success of future business activities. Leading indicators are related to the concept "leading measures."

lagging indicators Measures that indicate the success of past business activities. Lagging indicators are related to the concept "outcome measures."

4 The ultimate goals of an organization do not need to be financial profits in order to apply the Balanced Scorecard Model. For example, not-for-profit organizations (such as governments or charities) will likely emphasize service to constituents or clients as their ultimate strategic goals.

Exhibit 6: Performance Measurement Linkages in a Balanced Scorecard

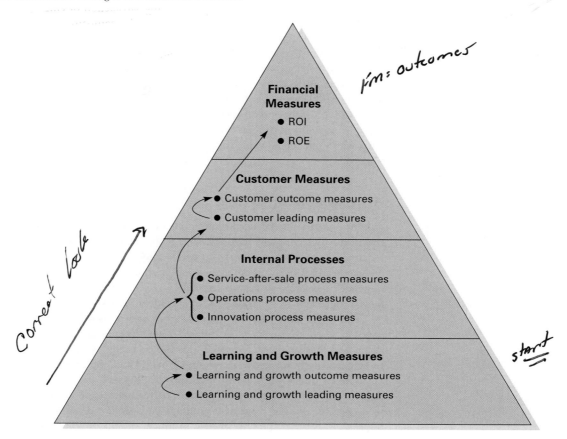

As you can see in Exhibit 6, cause-and-effect relationships between leading and lagging indicators should exist throughout a company's balanced scorecard. Customer outcome measures are leading indicators for financial measures. If the company identifies the cost, quality, and time factors that customers care about, then improved performance in these activities will lead to good outcomes in customer retention, acquisition, and market share. Similarly, effective innovation, operations, and service-after-sale processes should lead to improved performance in customer leading measures. Continuous improvements in these internal processes are then linked to learning and growth outcome measures (i.e., employee retention, satisfaction, and productivity), which are linked to investments in leading measures of employee, information systems, and organizational structure capabilities. Exhibit 6 illustrates that most performance measures serve as both leading and lagging indicators. When an accountant builds a performance measurement system based on this perspective, it should be clear that financial performance is no more important than performance related to internal processes or learning and growth effort. This is the concept of "balance" in a balanced scorecard.

To illustrate this idea of linkages, suppose that a company has identified that repeat and expanded sales to current customers (e.g., the result of customer retention) is the most important factor leading to improved ROI. Next, customer loyalty is assured by continuous improvement in product design, coupled with short lead times on customer orders. Finally, improving the process of product design and delivery requires committed and well-educated employees working with state-of-the-art computer systems in an organization with clear communication channels. These cause-and-effect relationships form the company's strategy. By building a balanced scorecard that focuses on this particular set of performance measures, a management accountant is able to clearly support the company strategy. Accountants do not *traditionally* perform this kind of work. However, according to a survey, eighty percent of large American companies want to change their performance measurement systems to better support competitive company strategies.[5] Traditional financial measures such as net income or ROI are really "after the fact." The fact that a company is reporting either positive or negative profits is the result of *past* performance with customers, internal processes, and learning and growth efforts. Can an ROI measure be used to predict future performance? As illustrated in Exhibit 6, financial measures are the ultimate lagging indicators of a successful strategy. Managing an organization's strategy requires insight on leading performance measures. What we see from this reality is that the Balanced Scorecard is really a management system. Management accountants who want to add value to the organization must build and support effective management systems.

An Example Scorecard

Exhibit 7 shows the balanced scorecard for a small company (between 100 and 1,000 employees) in the biotechnology industry. This scorecard is in an ever-constant state of evaluation and redesign as the company works to better understand the right strategy and the right performance measures to use in implementing its strategy to succeed in its particular market. Take a moment to examine this scorecard. Can you recognize the objectives this company has identified as important to its strategy? Can you identify linkages between its performance measures?

You might note that the financial goals and measures for this firm are rather basic. The majority of companies in most industries are working to build return on equity, earnings per share, and market share. However, this biotechnology company has determined that it needs to be particularly aggressive in revenue growth in its top line (i.e., best selling) products.

The customer goals are divided into leading and outcome measures. The company has linked early customer payment, product performance, and customer satisfaction as important to its percent of sales from new products and percent of sales taking place early in the buying season. Further, growth in new products should provide future top line products. Getting customers to buy early in the season also seems to be important to building market share and profitability.

Innovation is likely the most important factor in internal processes for a research-intensive firm. This is especially so in the biotechnology industry. Accordingly, you can see that there are a number of measures encouraging successful efforts in innovation processes, which should support customer and financial goals for this company. Additionally, this firm also emphasizes keeping product costs and inventory levels low in order to further support the effort to improve return on equity and earnings per share. Finally, providing accurate invoices should encourage customers to pay early.

At the foundation of this company's business are its investments in learning and growth. It is making substantial investments in training and desires to continually train as many employees as possible. In addition, it is also focusing on teamwork efforts. The expectation is that these leading measures of learning and growth will link to improved employee retention and satisfaction, as well as support internal processes and customer service.

As you consider this scorecard, you may feel that some measures and linkages among measures may be missing. You are probably right! Nevertheless, in contrast to being solely focused on short-term financial performance, the management accountants in this company are on their way to creating a performance measurement system that truly incorporates the entire strategy of their company. Studying this scorecard should make it clear to you that good performance measures can capture a unique strategy for a specific firm.

FYI:

No company would actually track as many measures as are being listed in Exhibits 2, 4, and 5. Like the example company in Exhibit 7, most organizations will limit their balanced scorecard to between three and six measures in each of the four categories of financial, customer satisfaction, internal processes, and learning and growth.

5 B. Birchard, "Making It Count," *CFO* (October 1995), pp. 42–48.

Exhibit 7: Sample Balanced Scorecard

Scorecard for a Biotechnology Firm

Strategic Objectives	Performance Measures
Financial Perspective ①	
• Growth	• Percent increase in revenue of top line products
• Profitability	• Return on equity; earnings per share
• Industry leadership	• Market share
Customer Perspective Outcome: ②	
• New products	• Percent of sales from new products
• Early purchase of seasonal products	• Percent of sales recorded by early purchase date
Leading:	
• Early payment	• Percent of customers who pay early
• Product quality	• Product performance vs. industry quality standards
• Customer satisfaction	• Customer satisfaction surveys
Internal Processes Perspective ③	
Service-after-Sale:	
• Accurate invoices	• Percent of error-free invoices
Operations:	
• Low-cost producer	• Unit cost vs. competitors
• Reduce inventory	• Inventory as percent of sales
Innovation:	
• New products	• Number of actual introductions vs. target
• New active ingredients	• Number of new ingredients identified by research program
• Proprietary positions	• Number of patents that create exclusive marketing rights
Learning and Growth Perspective ④	
Outcome:	
• Employee retention	• Average employee years with company
• Employee satisfaction	• Employee satisfaction surveys
Leading:	
• Employee capabilities	• Training costs invested per employee; percent of employees participating annually in training
• Organizational structure capabilities	• Average weekly hours in teamwork settings; survey of effective teamwork

Source: Adapted from C. W. Chow, K. M. Haddad, and J. E. Williamson, "Applying the Balanced Scorecard to Small Companies," *Management Accounting* (August 1997), Institute of Management Accountants, Montvale, NJ, pp. 21–27.

There Is No "Quick Approach"

The Balanced Scorecard approach to performance measurement recognizes that every organization is unique. This is not the only tool available for organizations that desire to better manage strategy, information, and performance; but it is currently one of the most well-known. Hopefully, as you conclude your work with this textbook, it is clear that a manufacturing company will not manage itself the same as a merchandising or service company. Further, even companies competing within the same industry will each have different sets of goals, objectives, and strategies to attain a specific mission. The process of building a balanced scorecard takes time and effort. The management accountant must have a clear knowledge of both financial and management accounting concepts. Then the organization's specific strategy must be clearly

The **Malcolm Baldrige National Quality Award** (described earlier in the activity-based costing chapter) is given to companies that have demonstrated excellence in quality management. Since 1988, fifty-one companies have received the Baldrige Award. However, high quality has not always translated into strong financial performance. Many early winners of the Baldrige Award struggled financially after winning the award. For example, FEDEX lost $1.5 billion on its European operation, the WALLACE COMPANY declared bankruptcy, and many RITZ-CARLTON hotels have lost money or become insolvent since winning the award. Furthermore, GM, IBM, KODAK, and WESTINGHOUSE each had Baldrige Award-winning divisions, yet each sustained substantial overall corporate losses that led to the replacement of their chairmen.

On the other hand, the Baldrige Award winners as a group have generally performed quite well in the stock market. The NIST (National Institute of Standards and Technology), the sponsoring agency for the Baldrige Award, has tracked a fictitious stock fund made up of publicly-traded U.S. companies that received the Malcolm Baldrige National Quality Award be-

tween 1992 and 2001. The NIST hypothetically "invests" $1,000 into each of the Baldrige company winners and tracks the performance of this stock fund against the Standard & Poor's (S&P) 500 stock index. (The S&P 500 index is generally regarded as an indicator of the overall performance of the entire stock market.) In nearly every year since 1995 when the NIST began the research project, the Baldrige Index has outperformed the S&P 500 by a significant margin. Only in 2003 did the Baldrige Index return a value less than the S&P 500.

Overall, Baldrige winners seem to be financially successful companies. Yet some individual winners of this quality award subsequently fail to deliver award-winning financial results. One possible explanation for the failure can be explained by an important underlying principle of the Balanced Scorecard—the importance of linking performance in strategic focus of a company to financial performance. It may be that failure to invest in quality measures that translate (i.e., *link*) to desired performance financial measures is the reason that some Baldrige Award companies have struggled financially.

Sources: D. Benson and M. Swain, "A Study of the Impact of TQM on the Financial Performance of Firms," *Academy of Accounting and Financial Studies Journal* (Vol. 3, No. 1, 1999), pp. 145–159; Baldrige Stock Studies at **http://baldrige.nist.gov/Stock_Studies.htm**, accessed September 1, 2003.

and specifically defined in terms of cause-and-effect relationships (i.e., linkages) for its particular industry. What cost, quality, and time issues are important to compete successfully within a particular market? An organization cannot expect to be financially rewarded for world-class performance in response time to customer repair requests unless that type of response time is truly valued by its customers. Finally, measures must be developed, tested, and implemented into clear reporting systems that support effective planning, controlling, and evaluating procedures.

Management accountants can easily build elegant looking but irrelevant performance measurement systems. There are examples of this in far too many organizations. The best example of this bad situation is when accounting is determined to be a non-value-added activity in an organization, and managers simply ignore accounting data as they work on their own to build the company. One of the authors of this textbook is reminded of an experience of having dinner with a plant manager who had established his plant as the most successful division within the company. When asked how the plant controller's work figured into the division's successful implementation of cutting-edge management principles such as JIT and TQM, the plant manager smiled grimly and indicated that the controller really had only two jobs in the organization. First, the controller was responsible for handling all requests from the external auditors. Second, the controller was simply to "stay out of his way!" He felt that the controller (the chief accountant in the organization) provided no information useful to him in his efforts to implement and execute strategy. Clearly, both the controller and the plant manager were missing important opportunities. The division was making significant investments in its accounting system without receiving any competitive benefits. The controller's reports were irrelevant to the core activities of the organization. How long would it be before one of the competitors in this division's market could effectively use management accounting to better implement its own strategy and seize the market?

Good management accounting requires that both managers and accountants work together to create information systems and performance measures that add value—that support the organization's unique strategy. This kind of work is not easy, nor is it done quickly. Management accountants must clearly understand the nature of critical business processes in the organization, as well as how managers and executives intend to strategically plan, control, and evaluate those processes. Linkages between activities must be tested. If performance in one activity does not lead to desired outcomes in customer service or financial performance, then relationships need to be reexamined. This is exciting work! The history of business in America has clearly

business environment

Wendy's Balanced Scorecard

WENDY'S INTERNATIONAL, INC., one of the leading fast-food chains in the world with over 8,400 restaurants worldwide, realizes the importance of using nonfinancial performance measures in a balanced scorecard. After adopting a balanced scorecard in 2000, Wendy's was recently inducted into the Hall of Fame of the Balanced Scorecard Collaborative.

When the company began using the scorecard approach, its market capitalization was $2.3 billion; now it is $4 billion. John Barker, vice president over investor relations and financial communications for Wendy's and part of Wendy's strategic planning team, says, "Our stock has been up 73% since we started the balanced scorecard approach in our strategic planning process."

The company's balanced scorecard includes performance measures that track intangibles, such as employee turnover and customer satisfaction. Since implementing its balanced scorecard, Wendy's has reduced employee turnover to 140% per year, while the fast-food industry's employee turnover remains at 230% per year. With lower employee turnover, the company has enjoyed increased profitability and efficiency. To measure customer satisfaction, Wendy's surveys its customers across the nation on certain characteristics of the fast-food industry to find

out how Wendy's ranks among its competitors. Recently, customers rated Wendy's as number 1 in 46 of the 58 characteristics of quality.

"We look at the measures quarterly, annually, and then every three years. You can't move the needle in a quarter or even in half a year," says Barker. "We set goals for three years and then track them. At the beginning of the process, people were skeptical and didn't believe in it. Now we believe in it and live by it every single day." Barker continues, "If you only look at financial measures, what's happening is that you are waiting until you are off course to find out that you have to do something to get back on course. Intangible measures are predictors of the future and will help you see those things to prevent you from getting off course."

Wendy's focus on nonfinancial performance measures has helped the company realize financial targets as well. Since adopting its balanced scorecard in 2000, the company has experienced a 29% growth in profitability; and from March 2000 to August 2003, the company's stock price almost doubled. Wendy's will continue to see long-term growth, as long as it continues to achieve its balanced scorecard objectives.

Sources: "How Wendy's Tracks Value of Intangibles in Its Balanced Scorecard Menu," *Financial Analysis, Planning & Reporting* (August 2002), pp. 1 and 13–14; Balanced Scorecard Collaborative, **http://www.bscol .com/bscol/hof/members/**, accessed August 23, 2003.

demonstrated that successful organizations are willing to spend the necessary creative energy to really understand how the work they do adds value to the marketplace. The spirit of continuous improvement that is now prevalent throughout our economy requires that management accounting continue to identify and support opportunities to improve the cost, quality, and timeliness of the information it provides.

TO SUMMARIZE: The Balanced Scorecard is an important management tool that explicitly supports strategy by integrating performance measures of financial, customer, internal process, and learning and growth activities within an organization. Both financial and nonfinancial measures are used throughout this new management model. A balanced scorecard, once created, is unique to each organization. The process of building a balanced scorecard requires that management accountants work closely with managers, executives, and information technologists in order to clearly understand how measures link together to eventually support successful financial results for the company. This idea of linkages across performance measures is critical to a successful balanced scorecard. Financial performance is linked to customer outcome measures of customer retention, customer acquisition, and market share.

These customer outcome measures in turn are linked to leading measures on customer service involving cost, quality, and time. Supporting customer service are the internal processes that take place within an organization. These internal processes include innovation processes (identifying and creating new products), operations processes (obtaining customer orders and producing and delivering products), and service-after-sale processes (handling warranties and providing support to customers). In order to continually improve its internal processes, an organization must emphasize its employees by measuring outcome performance on employee retention, satisfaction, and productivity. Finally, these employee outcome measures are linked to important investments in the capabilities of employees, information systems, and organizational structure.

Accounting for Tomorrow

2 Anticipate that both management accounting and financial accounting are poised for important changes.

"There is a bulldozer of change coming. You can either be part of the bulldozer, or you can be part of the road."[6] The Balanced Scorecard is one important example of continuous improvement that is characteristic of a competitive world economy that is always growing and changing. Managers and accountants in many organizations are creating new performance measurement systems that support dramatic improvements in products, processes, and people. These professionals understand that measures should focus on monitoring *all* critical activities in an organization in order to anticipate and prepare for future decisions, rather than simply report the financial effects of past decisions.

In this atmosphere of healthy competition and change, you can expect that new models and methods of management accounting will continue to be developed. Financial accounting is moving in this direction as well. Investors, creditors, and regulators are putting a lot of pressure on companies to make public more relevant and more timely information than is now contained in annual reports prepared using the financial accounting model first developed by Italian merchants in the 1300–1400s. The American Institute of Certified Public Accountants (AICPA) has commissioned special committees to study these demands for additional public data about companies and to propose new models of financial accounting. Robert Elliott, chairman of the AICPA in 2000/2001, is one of many leaders in industry who believe that accounting will continue to grow and mature as the global economy and technology grow. He describes the professional practice of a "new finance" that "encompasses hard-core management accounting topics such as cost management, discount rates, and capacity management; manufacturing issues including just-in-time production, distribution channel management, and competitive intelligence; and softer topics like benchmarking, performance measurement, and managing change."

6 Frank Ogden, "Navigating in Cyberspace," MacFarland, Walter, and Ross, 1995.

He says the new finance is "less about accounting and more about becoming strategic advisors and decision makers in our companies."[7]

Exhibit 8 illustrates one way to view the current direction of change that is necessary for accounting in today's marketplace. As you can see, the pressure on accounting to change is threefold. First, financial accounting is being pressured to provide *nonfinancial* data in public reports. Second, preparation of financial accounting reports has always focused on making reports objective, consistent, and reliable. However, users of financial accounting reports want these reports to emphasize more the *relevance* of information to important investing, lending, and regulatory decisions for individual companies. Finally, in an age when the Internet allows users to access and analyze huge amounts of data almost instantaneously, there is increased demand by decision makers trying to evaluate a company based on financial accounting to be able to access information *systems* throughout the year, rather than having to wait one to three months after the year-end for the company to release an annual report document; or, in the case of internal management accounting reports, having to wait days or weeks for cost, quality, and time analysis reports to be completed and delivered to management. It's difficult to predict how these demands will eventually affect the financial accounting reports provided by thousands of companies like Microsoft. However, it's not difficult to predict that changes are coming. This is a very exciting time to be preparing to enter the world of business. Regardless of whether you intend to actually work as an accountant, it is clear that accounting will dramatically impact the way you work. By understanding the concepts of financial and management accounting, as well as the great potential for continuous improvement in these areas, you will be better prepared to use accounting to personally add value to your organization.

Exhibit 8: The Future of Financial Accounting in Public Reports

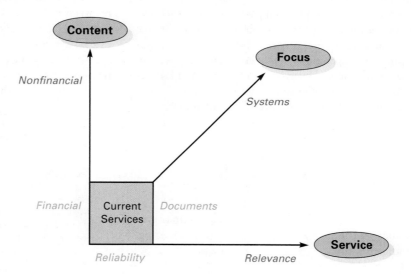

Source: From a 1996 presentation by Robert K. Elliott, Chairperson of the AICPA Special Committee on Assurance Services.

7 P. Fleming, "Steering a Course for the Future," *Journal of Accountancy* (November 1999), pp. 35–38.

review of learning objectives

1 Explain the fundamentals of building a balanced scorecard. Competition requires that companies continually improve their performance measures in order to add value to the products and services they provide within their industries. Nonfinancial measures are growing in importance in today's marketplace as companies work to build better management systems. The Balanced Scorecard is being heralded as an important new management model that explicitly supports a successful strategy by integrating performance measures of financial, customer, internal process, and learning and growth activities within an organization. Management accountants must work closely with managers, executives, and information technologists in order to build a balanced scorecard that is unique to their own organization. One of the most important aspects of a successful scorecard is *linking* all performance measures either directly or indirectly to desired financial performance. The Balanced Scorecard approach to these linkages is to connect financial performance directly to customer outcome measures of customer retention, customer acquisition, and market share. These customer outcome measures in turn are linked to leading measures on customer service involving cost, quality, and time. Internal processes taking place within an organization that support value-added services expected by customers are then identified. These internal processes include innovation processes (identifying and creating new products), operations processes (obtaining customer orders and producing and delivering products), and service-after-sale processes (handling warranties and providing support to customers). Positive employee outcome performance

in terms of employee retention, satisfaction, and productivity is necessary in order to support continual improvement of internal processes. Employee outcome measures on retention, satisfaction, and productivity are linked to important investments in the capabilities of employees, information systems, and organizational structure.

2 Anticipate that both management accounting and financial accounting are poised for important changes. This textbook has covered a lot of territory in an effort to introduce you to the world of accounting. You should understand that management accounting has always been a function of competitive need. In other words, the desire to compete well in the marketplace drives companies to develop better methods of management accounting. Hence, as you would expect, today's competitive markets continue to put pressure on both management and financial accounting to make some fundamental changes. The AICPA (American Institute of Certified Public Accountants) has commissioned special committees to investigate these trends. The pressure on accounting to grow and change involves three essential areas: (1) the need to include nonfinancial measures in public accounting reports; (2) the need to better emphasize relevant, rather than just reliable, data; and (3) the need to allow continual access to data systems rather than periodic report documents. Accountants, as well as other business professionals, who can anticipate these needs will be best positioned to add value to their organizations throughout the future.

key terms & concepts

review problem

Applying the Balanced Scorecard to a School District
Knowlton School District is currently developing a balanced scorecard to be used by all the schools in the district (K-12). At a meeting with all of the principals in the Knowlton School District, the following objectives were created for each of the five categories shown on the next page. (Note that balanced scorecard categories can and should be adjusted to suit the specific needs of the organization.)

1. *Student Achievement*
   Objectives:
   - Student mastery of curriculum
   - Nationally competitive students
2. *Customer Satisfaction*
   Objectives:
   - Safe and enriching school environment
   - Parent satisfaction
   - Community involvement
3. *Instructional and Administrative Processes*
   Objectives:
   - Effective instruction
   - Safe and efficient transportation
   - Well-maintained facilities
4. *Staff Learning and Growth*
   Objectives:
   - Competent staff
   - Staff satisfaction
5. *Financial Performance*
   Objective:
   - Sound fiscal management

Required:
For each of these objectives, provide one measure of performance that the school district could use.

Solution*
There are many different measures that could be used. Here are some possible measures.

Goal Area	Objective	Measure
1. Student Achievement	Student mastery of curriculum	• Proficiency tests in various subjects • Retention rates • Drop-out rates
	Nationally competitive students	• SAT scores • AP Exam scores • Enrollments in college-credit courses
2. Customer Satisfaction	Safe and enriching school environment	• Absenteeism and tardy rates • Participation in extracurricular activities • Perception of safety (student surveys)
	Parent satisfaction	• Scores on parent surveys • Number of parent complaints
	Community involvement	• Total volunteer hours • Dollars donated • Number of business partners
3. Instructional and Administrative Processes	Effective instruction	• Percent of students in summer school • Percent of teachers certified in special programs • Percent of teachers using technology
	Safe and efficient transportation	• Accidents per million miles • On-time bus delivery
	Well-maintained facilities	• Accidents per student days • Scores on inspection reports • Level of backlogged maintenance reports

(continued)

	Goal Area	Objective	Measure
4.	Staff Learning and Growth	Competent staff	• Percentage of teachers with 7+ years of experience • Percentage of teachers with advanced degrees • Percentage of board-certified teachers
		Staff satisfaction	• Absenteeism rates • Percentage of teachers retiring early • Scores on teacher surveys
5.	Financial Performance	Sound fiscal management	• Revenue variances of actual to budget • Expense variances of actual to budget • Fund balances

*This balanced scorecard is adapted from the actual balanced scorecard for the Fulton County School System in Georgia and can be viewed at **http://www.fulton.k12.ga.us/bsc200203.pdf**, accessed September 1, 2003.

d iscussion questions

1. Why is it unwise for a company to focus on only one performance measure while ignoring other performance measures?
2. Why do you think performance measures vary from company to company?
3. Why do you think there has been such a revolution in the way companies think about and measure their performance in recent years?
4. What is one way that traditional performance measurement systems, which have historically been tied to financial reporting, may be dysfunctional?
5. Why do you think some researchers argue that traditional performance measures are partly responsible for a decline in America's competitiveness?
6. Describe the two classifications of customer performance measures.
7. What are the key ingredients of customer satisfaction?
8. Why doesn't the purchase price of a product equal the product's total cost to customers?
9. What are the two issues involved in managing a company's market share of its products?
10. What are the three types of processes that should be in place to effectively support customer satisfaction?
11. How can companies plan, control, and evaluate their innovation processes?
12. Is it possible for a company to spend more money on the innovation process than on providing goods and services to current customers?
13. What are the three leading measures of learning and growth in an organization?
14. What are some of the factors of effective organizational structures discussed in this chapter?
15. Why do you think the market value of many companies (as measured by per-share stock price times the number of shares outstanding) is greater than the book value of the net assets (as measured by total assets minus total liabilities) listed on the balance sheets of those companies?
16. How do companies go about managing directly their return on investment (ROI)?
17. Pressure to provide better information to support the competitive needs of today's marketplace is resulting in fundamental changes in the accounting information that is being provided to managers, investors, and creditors. Identify the three primary areas of change.

p ractice exercises

Practice 10-1

The Balanced Scorecard

Which one of the following statements is *false*?

a. Companies that use the Balanced Scorecard do not need to focus on financial performance.
b. The Balanced Scorecard is not an exact formula that can be automatically implemented in any organization.
c. Companies using the Balanced Scorecard should implement performance measures that support the organization's goals.
d. Lower-level managers tend to pattern their efforts after the performance measures that upper-level management has implemented.

Practice 10-2

Customer Satisfaction

Which one of the following statements is *false*?

a. Leading measures focus on fulfilling customer expectations.
b. Outcome measures focus on whether improvements in leading measures result in more satisfied customers.
c. A decreasing market share is a good indication of high customer satisfaction.
d. Companies that are not committed to quality products usually do not last long.

Practice 10-3

Internal Processes

Which one of the following statements is *false*?

a. One type of operations process is the organization's commitment to warranty its product.
b. Research and development projects can require a very long payback period.
c. An operation process that has six sigma quality allows for only 3.4 defects per million opportunities.
d. One type of service-after-sale process is billing and collection of payments from customers.

Practice 10-4

Learning and Growth

Which one of the following statements is *false*?

a. The ultimate result of building learning and growth in an organization is based on developing employee productivity.
b. Poorly run organizations often have low employee morale.
c. Outcome performance measures, such as output per employee, can be used to estimate how well the leading performance measures, such as training hours per employee, add value to the organization.
d. Learning and growth measurement is a well-developed accounting discipline.

Practice 10-5

Linking It All Together

Which one of the following statements is *false*?

a. All measures of the Balanced Scorecard must link together to eventually support the ultimate financial goals of a company.
b. No company will use every single performance measure available.
c. Lagging measures indicate the potential success of future business activities.
d. Too much information is often as harmful as too little information.

Practice 10-6

Performance Measurement Linkages

Which one of the following represents the correct cause-and-effect sequence of leading and lagging measures in an organization?

(continued)

a. Learning and Growth → Internal Processes → Customer → Financial
b. Financial → Learning and Growth → Internal Processes → Customer
c. Customer → Internal Processes → Learning and Growth → Financial
d. Internal Processes → Financial → Learning and Growth → Customer

Practice 10-7

Implementing a Balanced Scorecard
Which one of the following statements is *true*?

a. The same Balanced Scorecard can be implemented at all organizations for maximum success.
b. Management accountants may build performance measurement systems that are irrelevant to the needs of the business.
c. A correctly implemented Balanced Scorecard usually fails to add value to the organization.
d. Two companies that have different performance measures will not be able to compete against each other.

Practice 10-8

Accounting for Tomorrow
The accounting industry is currently facing pressure in each of the following areas *except*:

a. The need to better emphasize relevant, rather than just reliable, data.
b. The need to include nonfinancial measures in public accounting reports.
c. The need to grow at a faster rate than the other industries to keep up with business demands.
d. The need to allow continual access to data systems rather than periodic report documents.

exercises

Exercise 10-1

Customer Satisfaction Performance Measures
The following are possible performance measures of customer satisfaction:

1. Purchase cost to customer
2. Customer defection rate
3. Returns by customers
4. Number of new customers
5. Time to complete contract
6. Percent of total units sold
7. Customer survey response
8. Costs to recruit customers

Identify which of these measures are most likely to be considered leading measures and which are outcome performance measures. Also, if they are leading performance measures, identify whether they relate to cost, quality, or time. If they are outcome performance measures, identify whether they relate to customer retention, customer acquisition, or market share.

Exercise 10-2

Internal Processes Performance Measures
The following are possible performance measures of internal processes:

1. Cost of replacement parts
2. Lead time (order to delivery)
3. Lead time (idea to working model)
4. Payback on R&D costs
5. Percentage of sales from new products
6. Unit-level costs
7. Defects per million
8. Repair cycle time

Identify the type of performance measure (cost, quality, or time) and the related process (innovation, operations, or service-after-sale) for each of these measures.

Exercise 10-3

Performance Measures of Learning and Growth

The following are performance measures of learning and growth:

1. Number of new certifications or degrees
2. Average life cycle time of personal computers
3. Assessment of effective communication
4. Employee turnover rate
5. Output per employee
6. Average yearly training or education hours per employee
7. Survey of employee satisfaction
8. Amount of time spent in teamwork versus individual work

Identify which of these learning and growth measures are leading performance measures and which are outcome performance measures. Also, if they are leading performance measures, identify whether they would be classified as cost, quality, or time measures and whether they relate to employee, information system, or organizational structure capabilities. If they are outcome performance measures, identify whether they relate to employee retention, employee satisfaction, or employee productivity.

Exercise 10-4

Balanced Scorecard Linkages

The following are examples of performance measures in a balanced scorecard:

1. ROI
2. Percentage of employees having leadership opportunities
3. Repair cycle time
4. Quality rankings by other agencies
5. ROE
6. Design cycle time
7. Six sigma
8. Systems R&D expense per total systems expense

Classify each of the above performance measures using the categories in Exhibit 6. For each measure, identify the type of lagging measure to which it links.

Exercise 10-5

Classifying Balanced Scorecard Elements

Listed below are a number of scorecard measures for a manufacturing company:

a. Number of new customers
b. Percentage of customers who place multiple orders
c. Percentage of on-time deliveries
d. Number of worker accidents
e. Number of customer complaints about products
f. Number of employees who attend training seminars
g. Percentage of product defects
h. Percentage of back-ordered products
i. Customer satisfaction, as measured through periodic surveys
j. Unit product cost
k. Percentage of revenues from new products
l. Earnings per share
m. Gross margin on products
n. Employee turnover
o. Costs to retain customers
p. Amount of time spent in teamwork

(continued)

Classify each performance measure according to the following:

1. *Perspective:* financial, customer, internal processes, or learning and growth
2. *Focus:* cost, quality, time, or overall financial (*Note:* Some measures may have more than one focus.)
3. *Relationship:* leading or outcome (*Note:* As the measure relates to other measures within its own perspective.)

Exercise 10-6

Balanced Scorecard and Incentives

Recall from the chapter the discussion of the oil drillers from the former Soviet Union who won a production competition based on the number of meters drilled. Those drillers determined that the first 100 meters of drilling were the easiest, so they simply drilled dry wells that never exceeded 100 meters in depth. Naturally, management would be upset when the drillers' tactics were exposed. After all, management's objective was to drill wells and find oil.

1. Can you suggest to management an incentive system that would have prevented such behavior and would instead encourage the desired behavior?
2. Do you consider what the drillers did to be wrong or smart?

Exercise 10-7

Thinking about the Balanced Scorecard

Albert Einstein once commented that "sometimes what can be counted doesn't count, and what can't be counted is what really counts." A business executive stated, "The first indication we don't know what we are doing is a preoccupation with numbers." How do you think these two statements relate to the Balanced Scorecard approach to performance measurement?

Exercise 10-8

Applying the Balanced Scorecard to a Bank*

You have just been hired as the CFO of Bridger Bank, a small community bank in your town. Management is currently in the process of creating a balanced scorecard management system. You have been given the following list of performance measures.

a. Return on equity
b. Sales calls to potential customers
c. Thank you calls or cards to existing customers
d. Lending income
e. Number of new customers
f. Referrals (a referral is when one employee suggests that a customer see another employee for more information about a bank product)
g. Cross-sells (selling multiple products to one customer when the customer comes in for only one product)
h. Employee training hours
i. Nonlending income
j. Employee turnover
k. Customer satisfaction
l. New products introduced
m. Employee satisfaction
n. Customer retention

1. Classify these measures as learning and growth measures, internal processes, customer measures, and financial measures by grouping the measures in a column for each respective category.
2. After classifying the measures in columns, draw arrows from the leading measures to the lagging measures. (*Hint:* Some measures may be both a leading and lagging measure, and some measures may be a leading or a lagging measure for more than one other measure.)

*This exercise is adapted from T. Albright, S. Davis, and A. Hibbets, "Tri-Cities Community Bank: A Balanced Scorecard Case," *Strategic Finance* (October 2001), pp. 54–59.

problems

Problem 10-1

Applying the Balanced Scorecard to Manufacturing

Martin, Inc., manufactures pleasure and fishing boats. Management's goals and objectives for the company are:

1. *Goal:* To maintain strong financial health.
   Objectives:
   - Maintain sufficient cash balances to assure liquidity and solvency
   - Achieve continued growth in sales and profits
   - Provide a good return to investors
   - Increase market share
2. *Goal:* To provide excellent customer service.
   Objectives:
   - Provide boats that meet customer needs
   - Meet customer needs on a timely basis
   - Exceed customer quality standards
3. *Goal:* To be the industry leader in product innovations.
   Objectives:
   - Bring new boats and features to the market before competitors
   - Increase efficiency and productivity faster than competitors

Required:
For each of these objectives, provide one measure of performance the company could use.

Problem 10-2

Applying the Balanced Scorecard to a Small Business

You are an optometrist with your own practice. For the past 20 years, you have focused almost exclusively on profitability of your practice as your sole performance measure. In fact, you have been quite profitable. However, during the past two years, a number of new, low-cost, commercial optometric offices including LENSCRAFTERS, WAL-MART, SHOPKO, and even KMART have opened in your practice area. As a result, your profitability has decreased to the point where you are barely breaking even. Because of your concern for your practice, you have asked a business consultant what you should do.

She has told you that your single-minded focus on profitability is no different than that of your new commercial competitors and has convinced you that these competitors will be more successful than you in making profits because they have lower cost structures than you do. She has suggested that you read her recently published book on the Balanced Scorecard measurement system and respond to the following questions:

Required:
1. Are your current success measures mostly financial, internal processes, learning and growth, or customer focused?
2. Has your focus been on financial, quality, or time measures, or on an appropriate balance of the three?
3. Thinking about your performance perspective (financial, customer, internal processes, and learning and growth), how could you distinguish yourself from the commercial optometrists and create value for your customers?
4. Are there ways you should change your focus regarding cost, quality, and time measures?

Problem 10-3

Applying the Balanced Scorecard to an Internet Company

OnRamp, Inc., is a technology company that provides connections for Internet service providers (ISPs) to the information highway. If U.S. WEST and other long-distance companies that own fiber optic cable are the information highway, OnRamp, Inc., views itself as the on- and off-ramps that provide access to the highway for ISPs, such as EARTHLINK, INC., and their customers. Two years ago, OnRamp, Inc., had an initial public offering (IPO) where it raised $500 million in operating capital. With that money, it built a new office building and developed much of the infrastructure needed to serve as the on- and off-ramp market leader. The company gets its revenue from charging ISPs a small user fee for each customer connected to the information highway. In its prospectus for the IPO, OnRamp, Inc., stated that its only critical performance measure of success was the number of users that it served. It stated that if, in two years, it serviced 2 million individual users, then it would consider itself to be successful. Now, two years later, there are 5 million individual customer accounts within OnRamp's system. Unfortunately, however, OnRamp, Inc., is still losing considerable amounts of money and is experiencing serious complaints about delayed Internet access and server problems.

Required:
1. What do you think about OnRamp, Inc.'s "number of ISP customers" performance measure?
2. If, in fact, OnRamp, Inc., measures its success solely on the basis of number of individual ISP customers, what important performance measures is it ignoring?

Problem 10-4

Applying the Balanced Scorecard to a University
The dean of your business school has determined that there are four major drivers of success for her business school. Those success drivers are having outstanding (1) faculty, (2) students, (3) curricula, and (4) alumni and recruiter support.

Required:
Based on these drivers of success, develop a balanced scorecard performance system that the dean could use to evaluate the operations of her school. Be specific and indicate the purpose of each measure. Make sure that you clearly include both leading and outcome measures in your balanced scorecard.

Problem 10-5

Applying the Balanced Scorecard to a Church
As an accountant and active member of a local church, you have been asked by your pastor to help him develop a balanced scorecard measurement system for the church. He is seriously interested in continuous improvement and believes that by identifying and monitoring the right performance measurements, the church will be more successful. In discussions with the pastor, you have determined that the scorecard should focus on the following four areas:

- Increase in learning and commitment of members
- Size of congregation and membership
- Respect in the community
- Amount of financial contributions

Required:
Develop a performance measurement system for these four areas that includes both leading and outcome measures that could be used by the pastor and his church to grow and measure the success of his ecumenical efforts.

discussion cases

Case 10-1

Strategy for Developing a Balanced Scorecard

A company is interested in developing a balanced scorecard approach to evaluating and enhancing its performance. It is looking at two ways of accomplishing the task. The first is for top management to develop the scorecard approach and impose it on managers throughout the organization. The second is to involve managers, customers, and other stakeholders in a grass-roots approach to determine what cost, quality, and time factors should be measured. Which of the two approaches would you recommend to the company?

Case 10-2

How Soon Can You Make Us a Balanced Scorecard?

You are currently the controller for a large manufacturing company. The president of the company calls you to his office and states the following: "I just went to a round-table discussion with presidents of other companies, and they told me that the most important development they had made in their companies was to implement balanced scorecards. I want you to drop whatever you are doing this week and develop a balanced scorecard for our company." You are vaguely aware of the concept of Balanced Scorecards from your reading, but you aren't too sure what they are all about. As you begin to think about your upcoming task, you discover that your com-

pany does not have a strategic plan or mission statement. Is the task given you by the president one that can be accomplished in a week or accomplished at all? What is the effect of not having a strategic plan or mission statement on the development of a balanced scorecard for the company?

Case 10-3

Get Those Business School Ratings Up!

You are the dean of the business school at North Central University. You have recently gone through a strategic planning process involving representatives from all your stakeholder groups (students, staff, faculty, recruiters, alumni, administration, etc.). The result is a newly refined strategic plan, including a mission statement, underlying values, specific objectives and strategies, and assessment outcomes (performance measurements). One of your objectives is to increase the ranking of your business school by *Business News*, a magazine that annually ranks business programs in your region. Given your understanding of the Balanced Scorecard approach and the material covered in this textbook, answer the following questions.

1. Even though it takes longer, is it wise to involve various stakeholders in developing your strategic plan? Why or why not?
2. What are some likely strategies that might be implemented to increase your business school ranking? Explain.

judgment calls

Judgment 10-1

You Decide: By encouraging employees to work harder and to increase quality, are companies lowering overall costs, or are they increasing waste and inefficiency of materials?

You have just been hired to work as a part-time accountant for a small, local flower shop. Jim, the manager, feels the costs of doing business (purchasing flowers, vases, etc.) are getting too high, and he has asked you to find a solution to this problem. The shop employs two full-time workers and one part-time worker. Jim's philosophy is if you use the highest quality, you will increase business through customer loyalty. However, you have found out that Jim has given the employees permission to use whatever means necessary to ensure the

flower arrangements and bouquets are made of the highest quality, even if it means wasting a lot of materials to create the best flower products possible.

Judgment 10-2

You Decide: Should the Balanced Scorecard concept be a "one-size fits all," or is the Balanced Scorecard more effective when it is catered to and created with an individual company in mind?

You have been introduced to the idea of a balanced scorecard through your classes in business school. At a recent family gathering, you began talking to your Uncle Richard about what you have learned. He has been president of a regional furniture store for the last 10 years and has tried to implement the Balanced Scorecard in his company, but with no success. Your uncle says, "I had a college buddy e-mail me his company's scorecard as an example. He works in the real estate industry and said that it has changed the way they do business. We tried to implement his scorecard in our business, but it just didn't make sense. It might work for some companies, but it sure doesn't work for mine!"

Competency Enhancement Opportunities

▶ **Analyzing Real Company Information**
▶ **International Case**
▶ **Ethics Case**
▶ **Writing Assignment**

▶ **The Debate**
▶ **Internet Search**

The following additional assignments provide opportunities for students to develop critical thinking, ethical perspectives, oral and written communication skills, experience with electronic research, and teamwork through group and business activities.

▶ *Analyzing Real Company Information*

Analyzing 10-1 (Futura Industries)

Remember the last time you walked through a grocery store? Did you notice all of the shelves holding the food? If you are like most people, you probably did not pay much attention to the shelves except to take the food off of them. The aluminum parts that make up the shelves in a grocery store (and other stores) are part of a product family known as aluminum extrusions. Many aluminum extrusions are manufactured by a company in Clearfield, Utah, called FUTURA INDUSTRIES. While Futura's products are not very exciting, they are pretty important. Hence, the management process at Futura is as important as it is at any other type of company, and Futura Industries has a very interesting balanced scorecard. Futura Industries began in the 1930s producing a product called colfonite. During the late 1940s, it started producing aluminum extrusions. By 1979, the Seattle, Washington-based company had moved its entire company to Clearfield, Utah. Futura's current president, Susan Johnson, has chosen to pursue her company's mission (Extraordinary Value through Extrusions) by careful alignment of the company's measures and tactics. She and the rest of the management staff at Futura have developed a balanced scorecard that has proven to be very successful in helping the company to grow.

Strategy of Futura:

> Futura strives to insure financial growth and prosperity by developing customer intimacy, providing flawless new products, and identifying new opportunities in products and processes. In addition, it emphasizes speed and quality in operations, planning and delivery accuracy, and continual reduction of costs. Futura is also focused on working to improve its competencies, providing a safe, challenging, and enjoyable workforce, and hiring people who have its same values.

The following is an alphabetical list of Futura's balanced scorecard measures along with a definition of each measure.

Balanced Scorecard Measure	Definition
Accuracy of price quotes	Number of correct price quotes ÷ total price quotes issued
Average job certification levels	Total sum of job certification levels ÷ total employees
Birthday review	Score based on yearly review on date of employee's birthday
Cash return on total assets	Cash flow ÷ total assets
Cost of plant scrap	Dollar value of scrapped material
Cost of rework	Dollar value of rework before sale
Customer complaints	Number of complaints ÷ total number of customers
Customer satisfaction	Periodic customer surveys
Dollar value of products packaged per person	Total dollar value of product packed ÷ number of employees working
Employees with one year or more turnover ratio	Number of employees employed for one year or more ÷ total number of employees
Income growth	(Current year's income − previous year's income) ÷ previous year's income
Leadership survey	Yearly survey score of employees
Leadership turnover	Number of new employees in leadership positions ÷ total number of employees in leadership positions
Margins on new products and standard products	Gross profit margin on new products and on standard products
On-time deliveries	Number of on-time deliveries ÷ total deliveries
Percent of market in commercial retailing	Number of commercial retail customers ÷ total number of customers
Percent of market in original equipment manufacturers (OEM)	Number of OEM customers ÷ total number of OEM customers
Percent of sales from new products	Sales revenue from new products ÷ total sales revenue
Pounds of products packaged per person	Number of pounds packed ÷ number of employees working
Product returns	Number of items returned
Total company employee turnover	Number of new employees ÷ total number of employees
Total finished goods turnover	Total cost of finished goods sold during year ÷ average finished goods inventory
Total inventory turnover	Total cost of goods sold during the year ÷ average inventory
Total production cost per direct labor hour	Total cost of production ÷ total direct labor hours

Classify Futura's balanced scorecard measures into the four Balanced Scorecard categories: financial measures, customer measures, internal process measures, and learning and growth measures. Use Futura's strategy to help you determine how to classify each measure.

International

▶ *International Case*

A Balanced Scorecard in Russia

This chapter has discussed the need for companies to focus on more than just the numbers. Additional factors must be considered in addition to financial results. Thus, the concept of the Balanced Scorecard. Consider the case of a country where the economy is not as sophisticated as in the United States—Russia. Inflation runs rampant, shortages prevail, organized crime rules. How could a balanced scorecard approach help a company that finds itself in this situation? Or could it? Can you suggest areas from the balanced scorecard perspective that a company in Russia might emphasize?

▶ *Ethics Case*

"Family" Business

Martin Beemer is the purchasing manager for the police department in a large metropolitan city. The city has 13,000 police officers. The city currently purchases police uniforms from three different manufacturers, one of which is SunKing, International (a Korean company). Martin recently agreed (in private) with SunKing's vice president to give SunKing increased business if SunKing would hire his daughter as a "ghost" salesperson in the United States at a salary of $350,000 per year.

1. Do you believe the actions of Martin and SunKing are unethical? Fraudulent?
2. What internal process performance measures could the city have had in place in the purchasing department that could have revealed the kickback arrangement?

▶ *Writing Assignment*

More Than Just the Numbers

You have found in your study of accounting that accountants generally focus on the numbers. Their job is to summarize financial results and provide information for decision makers. In this chapter, you have read about additional measures that are critical to a company's success: items like customer loyalty and satisfaction and employee productivity. Your assignment is to prepare a one- to two-page memo summarizing the following points:

1. Select an internal process measure, like research and development, and map out how the careful monitoring of that process will eventually show up in a financial measure like ROI.
2. Are accountants the best people to collect information on items such as customer satisfaction and customer loyalty? If not, who in a business would be best suited to collect this type of information?

▶ *The Debate*

Quantitative vs. Qualitative

The concept of the Balanced Scorecard suggests that instead of focusing on the financial aspects of business decisions, a company should manage such items as customer satisfaction, employee growth, and total quality, and the profits will follow. Divide your group into two teams. Each team should prepare a five-minute presentation addressing the following issues:

- One team supports "quantitative" measures. Defend the position that a company should manage by the numbers. The DuPonts and the Carnegies achieved the success they did because they focused on costs and profits. Provide reasons in support of your assigned position.

- The other team supports "qualitative" measures. Defend the position that a company's management should examine more than just the financial statement numbers. Other important information must be managed if a company is to be successful. In your presentation, identify some of that "other important information."

▶ *Internet Search*

Balanced Scorecard Collaborative

The home page for the Balanced Scorecard Collaborative (BSCol) can be found at **http://www .bscol.com**. Go to this Web site to learn more about the Balanced Scorecard Collaborative and answer the questions below. Sometimes Web addresses change, so if this address does not work, access the Web site for this textbook (**http://swain.swlearning.com**) for an updated link.

1. What is the purpose or mission of the Balanced Scorecard Collaborative?
2. The BSCol recognizes companies that have successfully implemented the Balanced Scorecard in its Hall of Fame. What are the nomination/selection criteria to be recognized as a BSC Hall of Fame member?

Microsoft Corporation

FORM 10-K

For The Fiscal Year Ended June 30, 2002

INDEX

Access the Microsoft Annual Report at **http://www.microsoft.com**.

United States Securities and Exchange Commission
Washington, D.C. 20549

FORM 10-K

☒ ANNUAL REPORT PURSUANT TO SECTION 13 OR 15(d) OF THE SECURITIES EXCHANGE ACT OF 1934
FOR THE FISCAL YEAR ENDED JUNE 30, 2002

☐ TRANSITION REPORT PURSUANT TO SECTION 13 OR 15(d) OF THE SECURITIES EXCHANGE ACT OF 1934
FOR THE TRANSITION PERIOD FROM _____ TO _____

COMMISSION FILE NUMBER 0-14278

MICROSOFT CORPORATION

WASHINGTON	91-1144442
(STATE OF INCORPORATION)	(I.R.S. ID)

ONE MICROSOFT WAY, REDMOND, WASHINGTON 98052-6399

(425) 882-8080

Securities registered pursuant to Section 12(b) of the Act:
NONE

Securities registered pursuant to Section 12(g) of the Act:
COMMON STOCK

Indicate by check mark whether the registrant (1) has filed all reports required to be filed by Section 13 or 15(d) of the Securities Exchange Act of 1934 during the preceding 12 months (or for such shorter period that the registrant was required to file such reports), and (2) has been subject to such filing requirements for the past 90 days. YES ☒ NO ☐

Indicate by check mark if disclosure of delinquent filers pursuant to Item 405 of Regulation S-K is not contained herein, and will not be contained, to the best of registrant's knowledge, in definitive proxy or information statements incorporated by reference in Part III of this Form 10-K or any amendment to this Form 10-K. ☐

The aggregate market value of common stock held by non-affiliates of the registrant as of July 31, 2002 was $215,553,343,213.

The number of shares outstanding of the registrant's common stock as of July 31, 2002 was 5,378,746,853.

DOCUMENTS INCORPORATED BY REFERENCE

Portions of the definitive Proxy Statement to be delivered to shareholders in connection with the Annual Meeting of Shareholders to be held November 5, 2002 are incorporated by reference into Part III.

PART I

ITEM 1. BUSINESS

GENERAL

Microsoft Corporation (the "Company" or "Microsoft") was founded as a partnership in 1975 and incorporated in 1981. Microsoft's mission is to enable people and businesses throughout the world to realize their full potential, and the Company's vision is empowering people through great software—any time, any place, and on any device. Microsoft develops, manufactures, licenses, and supports a wide range of software products for a multitude of computing devices. Microsoft software products include scalable operating systems for servers, personal computers (PCs), and intelligent devices; server applications for client/server environments; information worker productivity applications; business solutions applications; and software development tools. During fiscal 2002, Microsoft launched Xbox, the Company's next-generation video game system. The Company's online efforts include the MSN network of Internet products and services and alliances with companies involved with broadband access and various forms of digital interactivity. Microsoft licenses consumer software programs; sells hardware devices; provides consulting services; and trains and certifies system integrators and developers.

Microsoft also researches and develops advanced technologies for future software products. A significant portion of the Company's focus is on Microsoft's .NET architecture. Using common industry standards based on XML, a universal language for describing and exchanging data, the Company's goal is to enable seamless sharing of information across many platforms and programming languages, and over the Internet, with XML Web services. In addition, Microsoft has embarked on a long-term initiative called Trustworthy Computing, which aims to bring an enhanced level of security, privacy, reliability, and business integrity to computer systems.

PRODUCTS

During fiscal 2002, Microsoft had four operating segments based on its product and service offerings: Desktop and Enterprise Software and Services; Consumer Software, Services, and Devices; Consumer Commerce Investments; and Other. See Note 20 of the Notes to Financial Statements for financial information regarding segment reporting.

DESKTOP AND ENTERPRISE SOFTWARE AND SERVICES

Desktop and Enterprise Software and Services includes Desktop Applications; Desktop Platforms; and Enterprise Software and Services. For segment reporting purposes, Desktop Applications includes revenue from Microsoft Office; Microsoft Project; Visio; client access licenses (CALs) for Windows NT Server and Windows 2000 Server, Exchange, and BackOffice; Microsoft Great Plains; and bCentral. Desktop Platforms includes revenue from Windows XP Professional and Home; Windows 2000 Professional; Windows NT Workstation; Windows Millennium Edition; Windows 98; and other desktop operating systems. Enterprise Software and Services includes Server Platforms; Server Applications; Developer Tools and Services; and Enterprise Services.

DESKTOP APPLICATIONS

Microsoft Office. Microsoft Office is a software product featuring commonly used desktop functionality. The product is based upon a document-centric concept, with common commands and extensive use of cross-application capabilities. Microsoft Office is available in several versions for the Windows and Macintosh operating systems. Microsoft Office XP, the latest Microsoft Office release, helps users complete common business tasks, including word processing, electronic mail (e-mail), presentations, and data management, with features like smart tags, task panes, integrated e-mail, document recovery, and send for review. The various versions of Microsoft Office include the word processor Microsoft Word, Microsoft Excel spreadsheet, Microsoft Outlook personal information management and e-mail communication client, Microsoft PowerPoint presentation graphics program, and may include Microsoft Access database management application, Microsoft FrontPage Web site creation and management tool, and Microsoft Publisher business desktop publishing program. Most of these applications are also licensed separately.

Other Desktop Application Products. The Company also offers other stand-alone desktop application products. Microsoft Project is a project management program for scheduling, organizing, and analyzing tasks, deadlines, and resources. Visio is a diagramming program that helps people visualize and communicate ideas, information, and systems.

Client Access Licenses. A client access license gives its holder the legal right to access a computer running a Microsoft server product and the services supported by the server using a client computer.

Microsoft Great Plains. Microsoft Great Plains offers a range of integrated business and accounting products, including Dynamics, Solomon, and eEnterprise. Dynamics provides Internet-ready accounting and business management capabilities for small- to mid-sized companies. Solomon offers a full range of e-business and accounting applications for small- to mid-sized companies. eEnterprise supports mid-sized to larger companies by providing a collaborative environment for information management and sharing.

bCentral. Microsoft's small businesses portal, bCentral, includes Site Manager, a Web site management and hosting service which empowers small businesses to easily create and manage their own Web sites, while allowing for higher-end editing in Microsoft FrontPage, and LinkExchange, which provides services to small businesses and Web site owners to increase their online traffic and sales with free advertising banner ads on their site in exchange for placing ads on other network sites.

DESKTOP PLATFORMS

Windows XP. Microsoft launched Windows XP in October 2001. Windows XP extends the personal computing experience by uniting PCs, devices, and services, while enhancing reliability, security, and performance. Windows XP Home Edition is designed for individuals or families and includes experiences for digital photo, music, video, home networking, and communications. Windows XP Professional includes all the features of Home Edition, plus remote access, security, performance, manageability, and multilingual features to help users improve productivity and connectivity.

Windows 2000 Professional. The successor to Windows NT Workstation, Windows 2000 Professional operating system combines features to create a mainstream operating system for desktop and notebook computing in all organizations. Windows 2000 Professional contains the enhanced business features of Windows 98 such as Plug and Play, easy-to-use user interface, and power management and integrates the strengths of Windows NT Workstation including standards-based security, manageability, and reliability.

Windows NT Workstation. A fully integrated, multitasking 32-bit PC operating system, Windows NT Workstation provides improved security features, robustness, and portability. Windows NT Workstation combines the Windows 98 operating system interface and usability features with the reliability and security of Windows NT for the business environment.

Windows Millennium Edition. Windows Millennium Edition (Me) operating system is designed specifically for home users, including capabilities to manage digital photos and music, work with video, create a home network, and communicate with other consumers.

Windows 98. The successor to Windows 95, Windows 98 is a personal computer operating system that provides a Web-oriented user interface and better system performance along with easier system diagnostics and maintenance. Windows 98 supports graphics, sound, and multimedia technologies and provides the ability to easily add and remove peripheral devices and support for Universal Serial Bus (USB).

ENTERPRISE SOFTWARE AND SERVICES

Windows 2000 Server, Advanced Server, and Datacenter Server. Windows 2000 Server is a multipurpose network operating system for businesses of all sizes. Windows 2000 Advanced Server operating system is ideal for e-commerce and line-of-business applications and provides enhanced performance and scalability through symmetric multiprocessing (SMP) and extended memory support. Windows Datacenter Server operating system is built for large-scale line-of-business and enterprise backend usage and supports server consolidation and enhanced scalability.

Microsoft .NET Enterprise Servers. Microsoft .NET Enterprise Servers include Microsoft SQL Server, Exchange Server, Application Center, BizTalk Server, Commerce Server, Content Management Server, Host Integration Server, Internet Security and Acceleration Server, Microsoft Operations Manager, Mobile Information Server, and SharePoint Portal Server.

SQL Server is a comprehensive data management and analysis platform that enables rapid delivery, dependable performance and secure operation of connected applications.

Exchange Server is a messaging and collaboration server that provides e-mail, group scheduling, task management, contact management and document routing capabilities.

Application Center is Microsoft's deployment and management tool for high-availability Web applications built on the Microsoft Windows 2000 operating system.

BizTalk Server enables companies to rapidly build and deploy integrated business processes within their organizations and with partners.

Commerce Server provides a comprehensive set of features for building scalable, user-centric, business-to-consumer, and business-to-business e-commerce sites.

Content Management Server is the enterprise Web content management system that enables companies to quickly and efficiently build, deploy, and maintain highly dynamic Internet, intranet, and extranet Web sites.

Host Integration Server extends Microsoft Windows applications to other systems by providing application, data, and network integration.

Internet Security and Acceleration Server provides secure, fast, and manageable Internet connectivity. It integrates an extensible, multilayer enterprise firewall and a scalable high-performance Web cache.

Microsoft Operations Manager delivers enterprise-class solutions for operations management of Windows 2000, the Microsoft Active Directory service, and other component services in Windows 2000, as well as other Microsoft .NET Enterprise Server applications such as Exchange and SQL Server.

Mobile Information Server mobile-enables the enterprise, extending the reach of Microsoft .NET Enterprise applications, enterprise data, and intranet content to the mobile user.

SharePoint Portal Server extends the capabilities of Microsoft Windows and Microsoft Office by offering information workers a powerful new way to easily organize, find, and share information. It combines the ability to easily create corporate Web portals with document management, content searching, and team collaboration features.

Other Servers. Small Business Server is the flexible network solution designed to help businesses with up to 50 computers. Systems Management Server helps centrally manage the distributed environment with integrated features, including hardware inventory, software inventory and metering, software distribution and installation, and remote troubleshooting tools.

Developer Tools and Services. Software development tools and computer languages allow software developers to write programs in a particular computer language and translate programs into a binary machine-readable set of commands that activate and instruct various hardware devices. The Company develops and markets a number of software development environments and language compilers. In February 2002, Microsoft launched Visual Studio .NET, a comprehensive tool for rapidly building and deploying XML Web services and applications. Visual Studio .NET provides software developers with powerful tools to rapidly design broad-reach Web applications for any device and any platform, and to build powerful Windows applications. Microsoft Visual C++ is the Company's development system for Windows-based application development. Microsoft Visual C# offers beginning and intermediate developers with C++ or Java experience a modern language and robust development environment for creating XML Web services and Microsoft .NET-based applications for Windows and the Web. The Microsoft Visual Basic development system provides easy access to a wide variety of data sources by integrating the Microsoft Access database engine and the ability to take advantage of investments in commercial applications. The Microsoft Visual InterDev development system includes integrated, team-based development tools for building Web-based applications based on HTML, Script, and components written in any language. Developers can subscribe to the Microsoft Developer Network (MSDN) information service and receive periodic updates via CD-ROMs, magazines, and several online information services. In addition, Microsoft receives certification fees through the Microsoft Certified Professional (MCP) program, a program that provides credentials for those who have demonstrated in-depth knowledge of at least one Microsoft product.

Enterprise Services. Microsoft Enterprise Services assist organizations with every stage of technology planning, building, deployment, and support. Specializing in IT solutions for the enterprise, Microsoft offers a full range of consulting services for advance technology requirements, including custom solutions services, enterprise application planning, architecture and design services, and proof-of-concept services. The Company provides product support services aligned to customer segments, partner segments, and communities.

CONSUMER SOFTWARE, SERVICES, AND DEVICES

Consumer Software, Services, and Devices includes Xbox video game system, MSN Internet Access, MSN Network Services, PC and Online Games, Learning and Productivity Software, Mobility, and Embedded Systems.

Xbox. Microsoft Xbox, released in fiscal 2002, is Microsoft's next-generation video game console system that delivers high quality graphics and audio gameplay experiences. For information on Xbox manufacturing, see "Manufacturing" below. Games for the Xbox are developed by Microsoft Game Studios, such as Halo and Project Gotham Racing, and by third-party game development partners, such as Tecmo's Dead or Alive 3. Xbox Live, an online service available to owners of Xbox systems, is expected to be launched in the second quarter of fiscal 2003 and will allow online game play among users of online-enabled Xbox games.

MSN Internet Access. MSN Internet access is Microsoft's service for accessing the Web and experiencing a wide range of rich online services and content. MSN Internet access subscribers can access their account from multiple sources, including a computer, television, Internet appliances, and Personal Data Assistants.

MSN Network Services. The MSN network provides services, content and advertising on the Internet, encompassing MSN Search, Messenger, eShop, Hotmail, Money, and Music, as well as other services and content. MSN Search makes Web searches more useful by providing users with the most relevant results for the most popular search queries on the Web. MSN Messenger is a free Internet messaging service that enables users to see when others are online and exchange instant messages with them. MSN eShop is a one-stop online shopping resource. MSN Hotmail is the world's leading free Web-based e-mail service. MSN Money is a complete online personal financial service that combines finance tools and content from Microsoft with exclusive investment news and analysis from CNBC. MSN Music provides consumers with one place online to find old favorites, as well as discover new music, and delivers a high quality listening experience.

PC and Online Games. The Company offers a line of entertainment products from classic software games to online games, simulations, sport products, and strategy games. Microsoft Flight Simulator is a popular aircraft flight simulation product. Other games include Age of Empires, Dungeon Siege, MechWarrior, Microsoft Links, Train Simulator, Zoo Tycoon, and other action and sports titles. Zone.com is a gaming community on the Internet allowing multiplayer gaming competitions of Microsoft's popular CD-ROM games and classic card, board, and puzzle games.

Learning and Productivity Software. Learning titles include Microsoft Encarta Reference Library, a complete research and reference source with a multimedia encyclopedia database with interactive information, an interactive world atlas with three-dimensional maps, a world English dictionary, Encarta Africana, Researcher, and an online version with monthly updates. Titles for children include a series of products based on the popular children's book and television series, Scholastic's The Magic School Bus. Microsoft's productivity offerings include Microsoft Works, an integrated software program that contains basic word processing, spreadsheet, and database capabilities that allows the easy exchange of information from one tool to another. Microsoft Picture It! brand of products includes Picture It! Photo, with photo editing tools and wizards to easily capture, correct and create photos, and Picture It! Publishing, used to create greeting cards and other print and Web based products. Microsoft Money offers leading tools and resources to conduct a wide range of financial activities. The

Works Suite provides a comprehensive collection of software, including Microsoft Works, Microsoft Word, Microsoft Money, Microsoft Encarta encyclopedia, Microsoft Picture It! Photo, and Microsoft Streets & Trips.

Mobility and Embedded Systems. Microsoft develops a number of software platforms for mobile computing. Products such as Pocket PC, Pocket PC Phone Edition, and Microsoft Windows Powered Smartphone are designed to enable a variety of mobile scenarios. Microsoft's embedded offerings include two embedded operating systems, Microsoft Windows CE and Microsoft Windows NT Embedded, as well as device specific solutions. Microsoft Windows CE, a robust real-time embedded operating system, is targeted at mobile 32-bit devices. Microsoft Windows NT Embedded, based on the desktop and server versions of Microsoft's operating systems, is targeted at higher-end embedded products and devices. Both embedded operating systems offer integrated tool sets to enable embedded system developers to quickly create sophisticated embedded device and application solutions. Microsoft Mobile Information Server is a scalable and reliable mobile applications server that provides enterprise customers and mobile operators with a rich platform for extending .NET Enterprise application and securely delivering real-time, wireless data to mobile devices.

CONSUMER COMMERCE INVESTMENTS

Consumer Commerce Investments include the HomeAdvisor online real estate service and the CarPoint online automotive service.

HomeAdvisor online real estate service. The HomeAdvisor online real estate service is a complete guide to the home-buying process and provides comprehensive tools for finding homes and loans on the Internet. The service includes customized search features, worksheets and calculators, and editorial content and home-buying advice.

CarPoint online automotive service. The CarPoint online automotive service is the leading online automotive marketplace, visited by more than 7 million consumers each month. With details on more than 10,000 car models and 100,000 used vehicles, users can research and compare cars of virtually every make and model, identify local dealers, and receive instructions for post-purchase service and maintenance.

Expedia, Inc. Expedia was included in the Consumer Commerce Investments segment until Microsoft sold its interest in Expedia to USA Networks, Inc. in February 2002. Expedia, Inc. operates Expedia.com, a leading online travel service. Expedia.com provides air, car, and hotel booking, vacation package and cruise offerings, destination information, and mapping.

OTHER

Hardware. The Hardware Group develops and markets several PC accessories including the Microsoft IntelliMouse family of hand-held pointing devices using the IntelliEye optical technology. Hardware also markets several types of keyboards including the Microsoft Natural Keyboard, an ergonomically designed keyboard, the Internet Keyboard featuring two USB ports and Internet hot keys, and a new Wireless Desktop product including wireless keyboard and mouse. Also included in the Hardware Group's portfolio of devices are SideWinder game controllers and force feedback joysticks with realistic performance technology to use with PC games.

Microsoft Press. Microsoft Press offers comprehensive learning and training resources to help new users, power users, and professionals get the most from Microsoft technology through books, CDs, self-paced training kits, and videos that are created to accommodate different learning styles and preferences. Microsoft Press books are authored by professional and technical writers, both by Microsoft employees and independent authors.

SEGMENT REPORTING

In fiscal 2003, the Company will begin reporting the following operating segments: Client; Information Worker; MSN; Home and Entertainment; CE Mobility; Server and Tools; and Business Solutions. These changes are designed to provide a comprehensive end-to-end financial view of Microsoft's key businesses; promote better alignment of strategies and objectives between development, sales, marketing, and services organizations; provide for more timely and rational allocation of development, sales, and marketing resources within businesses; and focus strategic planning efforts on key objectives and initiatives and give business owners more autonomy in detailed planning.

EQUITY METHOD INVESTMENTS

The Company has entered into joint venture arrangements to take advantage of creative talent and content from other organizations. For example, Microsoft owns 50 percent of MSNBC Cable L.L.C., a 24-hour cable news and information channel, and 50 percent of MSNBC Interactive News L.L.C., an interactive online news service. National Broadcasting Company (NBC) owns the remaining 50 percent of these two joint ventures.

PRODUCT DEVELOPMENT

During fiscal years 2000, 2001, and 2002, research and development expense was $3.77 billion, $4.38 billion, and $4.31 billion, respectively. Those amounts represented 16.4%, 17.3%, and 15.2%, respectively, of revenue in each of those years. In accordance with Statement of Financial Accounting Standards (SFAS) 142, *Goodwill and Other Intangible Assets,* the amortization of goodwill was discontinued in fiscal 2002. The amount of goodwill amortization included in research and development expense in fiscal years 2000 and 2001 was $232 million and $272 million, respectively. The Company plans to continue significant expenditures for research and product development.

Most of the Company's software products are developed internally. The Company also purchases technology, licenses intellectual property rights, and oversees third-party development and localization of certain products. Internal development allows Microsoft to maintain closer technical control over its products and gives the Company the freedom to designate which modifications and enhancements are most important and when they should be implemented. Microsoft works on devising innovative solutions to computer science problems, such as making computers easier to use, designing software for the next generation of hardware, improving the software design process, and investigating the mathematical underpinnings of computer science. The Company has created a substantial body of proprietary development tools and has evolved development methodologies for creating and enhancing its products. These tools and methodologies are also designed to simplify a product's portability among different operating systems, microprocessors, or computing devices. Product documentation is generally created internally. The Company strives to become informed at the earliest possible time about changing usage patterns and hardware advances that may affect software design. Before releasing new software platforms, Microsoft provides to software vendors a range of development, training, testing resources, and guidelines for developing applications.

The software industry is characterized by rapid technological change, which requires constant attention to computing technology trends, shifting consumer demand, and rapid product innovation. The pace of change is accelerating as the computing needs of our customers move beyond the PC toward intelligent devices and appliances, such as the Tablet PC. Tablet PCs extend the power of laptop computers running Windows XP with enhanced capabilities such as handwriting and speech input.

The Company believes that making its products trustworthy is critical to their success and has launched a company-wide effort called Trustworthy Computing. Trustworthy Computing has four pillars: reliability, security, privacy, and business integrity. Reliability means that a computer system is dependable, is available when needed, and performs as expected and at appropriate levels. Security means that a system is resilient to attack, and that the confidentiality, integrity and availability of both the system and its data are protected. Privacy means that individuals have the ability to control data about themselves and that those using such data faithfully adhere to fair information principles. Business integrity, in this context, is about being responsible to customers and helping them find appropriate solutions for their business issues, addressing problems with products or services, and being open in interactions with customers. While the Company is continuing to invest significantly in delivering new capabilities that customers ask for, Microsoft is making security improvements a high priority.

Microsoft .NET is Microsoft's platform for XML Web services. XML Web services allow applications to communicate and share data over the Internet or an intranet, regardless of operating system or programming language. The Microsoft .NET platform includes a comprehensive family of products, built on XML and other Internet industry standards, which provide for each aspect of developing, managing, using, and experiencing XML Web services. There are five areas where Microsoft is building the .NET platform today: Tools, Servers, XML Web Services, Clients, and .NET Experiences. In the Tools area, Visual Studio .NET and the Microsoft .NET framework supply a complete solution for developers to build, deploy, and run XML Web services. They maximize the performance, reliability, and security of XML Web services. The .NET Enterprise Servers, including the Windows 2000 Server family, make up Microsoft .NET's server infrastructure for deploying, managing, and orchestrating XML Web services. Designed with mission-critical performance in mind, they provide enterprises with the agility they need to integrate their systems, applications, and partners through XML Web services, and the flexibility to adapt to changing business requirements. Clients are PCs, laptops, workstations, phones, handheld computers, Tablet PCs, game consoles, and other smart devices. These smart devices use software that supports XML Web services, which enable users to access their data regardless of the location, type, and number of clients used. Smart clients and devices leverage XML Web services to create .NET experiences that allow users to access information across the Internet and from stand-alone applications in an integrated way.

To best serve the needs of users around the world, Microsoft "localizes" many of its products to reflect local languages and conventions and to improve the quality and usability of the product in international markets. Localizing a product might require modifying the user interface, altering dialog boxes, and translating text. In Japanese versions, for example, all user messages and documentation are in Japanese with monetary references in the Japanese yen. Various Microsoft products have been localized into more than 30 languages.

MANUFACTURING

Microsoft contracts out most of its manufacturing activities to third parties. Outside manufacturers produce the Xbox, various retail software packaged products, and hardware. There are other custom manufacturers Microsoft could use in the event outsourced manufacturing becomes unavailable from current vendors. The Company generally has multiple sources for raw materials, supplies, and components and is often able to acquire component parts and materials on a volume discount basis. The graphics processing unit (GPU) for the Xbox was custom designed and is produced by NVIDIA Corporation. Quality control tests are performed on purchased parts, CD-ROMs, and other products.

Part I
Item 1

OPERATIONS

The Company has regional operations centers in Ireland, Singapore, and the Greater Seattle area. The regional centers support all operations, including information processing, vendor management and logistics by geographical regions. The regional center in Dublin, Ireland supports the European, African, and Middle East regions, the center in Singapore supports the Asia Pacific region, and the center in the Greater Seattle area supports North and South America. Microsoft Licensing, Inc. (MSLI), a wholly-owned subsidiary in Reno, Nevada, manages the Company's original equipment manufacturer (OEM) and certain organizational licensing operations.

DISTRIBUTION, SALES AND MARKETING

Microsoft distributes its products primarily through the following channels: OEM; volume licensing; online services and products; and distributors and retailers. In fiscal 2002, Microsoft had three major geographic sales and marketing regions: the South Pacific and Americas Region; the Europe, Middle East, and Africa Region; and the Asia Region. Beginning with fiscal 2003, the Company's geographic sales and marketing organization was modified to remove the South Pacific region from the Americas organization, and combine it with Asia. Sales of volume licenses and packaged software products via these channels are primarily to distributors and resellers.

OEM. Microsoft operating systems are licensed primarily to OEMs under agreements that grant the OEMs the right to distribute copies of the Company's products with their computing devices, principally PCs. The Company also markets and licenses certain server operating systems, desktop applications, hardware devices, and consumer software programs to OEMs under similar arrangements. In almost all cases, the products are distributed under Microsoft trademarks. The Company has OEM agreements covering one or more of its products with virtually all of the major PC OEMs, including Acer, Actebis, Dell, eMachines, Fujitsu, Fujitsu Siemens Computers, Gateway, HP, IBM, NEC, Samsung, Sony, and Toshiba. A substantial amount of OEM business is also conducted with system builders, which are low-volume customized PC vendors.

Volume Licensing. The Microsoft Enterprise Agreement program is a licensing program designed to provide a flexible licensing and service solution tailored to customers making a long-term licensing commitment. The agreements are designed to simplify license administration, payment terms, and the contract process. The Microsoft Select program offers flexible software acquisition, licensing, and maintenance options specially customized to meet the needs of large multinational organizations. Marketing efforts and fulfillment are generally coordinated with large account resellers. The Microsoft Open program is a licensing program that is targeted for small- and medium-sized organizations. It is available through the reseller channel and offers discounts based on initial purchase volumes. The Microsoft Enterprise Agreement and Software Assurance under the Select and Open programs provide customers the right to install any new release of products covered in the licensing agreement during the term of their coverage.

Network Service Providers. Microsoft Network Service Providers (NSP) work with a variety of companies worldwide to help them develop and deploy end-to-end network solutions based on Microsoft platforms. NSPs focus on key network service industries including telecommunications and wireless companies and hosts.

Online Services and Products. Microsoft distributes online content and services through MSN Access, MSN Network Services, bCentral small business portal, and other online services. MSN Access delivers simple, personalized Internet access, useful content, services and tools using MSN Internet Explorer. MSN Network Services delivers advertising and other services including online search, shopping, and messaging capabilities to Internet users. bCentral provides the tools and expertise for small-business owners to build, market and manage their businesses online. Other services delivered online include MSDN subscription content and updates, periodic product updates, and online technical and practice readiness resources to support Microsoft partners in developing and selling Microsoft products and solutions.

Distributors and Resellers. The Company distributes products in the finished goods channels primarily to independent non-exclusive distributors and resellers. Distributors and resellers include Ingram Micro, Tech Data, Level 3 Communications, SOFTBANK, Software House International, ASAP Software Express, and Happinet Corporation. Microsoft has a network of field sales representatives and field support personnel who solicit orders from distributors and resellers and provide product training and sales support.

CUSTOMERS

The Company's customers include individual consumers, small- and medium-sized organizations, enterprises, educational institutions, Internet Service Providers (ISPs), application developers, and OEMs. Consumers and organizations obtain Microsoft products primarily through resellers and OEMs, which include certain Microsoft products with their computing devices. No single customer accounted for 10% or more of revenue in 2000, 2001, or 2002.

Part I
Item 1

COMPETITION

The software business is intensely competitive and subject to rapid technological change. As the company pursues its largest strategic initiative, Microsoft .NET, the Company could experience more intense competition during the transition from the traditional core businesses to its new products based on the .NET architecture. The Company continues to face movement from PC-based applications to server-based applications or Web-based application hosting services, from proprietary software to open source software such as the Linux operating system, and from PCs to Internet-based devices. A number of Microsoft's most significant competitors, including IBM, Sun Microsystems, Oracle, and AOL-Time Warner, are collaborating with one another on various initiatives directed at competing with Microsoft. These initiatives relate in part to efforts to move software from individual PCs to centrally managed servers, which would present significant challenges to the Company's historical business model. Other competitive collaborative efforts include the development of new platform technologies that are intended to replicate much of the value of Microsoft Windows operating systems. New computing form factors, including non-PC information devices, are gaining popularity and competing with PCs running Microsoft's software products.

Microsoft faces formidable competition in these new areas and in all areas of its current business activities. The rapid pace of technological change, particularly in the area of Internet platforms and services, continually creates new opportunities for existing competitors and start-ups and can quickly render existing technologies less valuable. Global software piracy—the unlawful copying and distribution of Microsoft's copyrighted software products—deprives the Company of large amounts of revenue on an annual basis.

The Company's competitive position may be adversely affected in the future by one or more of the factors described in this section, particularly in view of the fast pace of technological change in the computing industry.

DESKTOP AND ENTERPRISE SOFTWARE AND SERVICES

The Company's competitors include many software application vendors, such as IBM, Oracle, Apple, Sun Microsystems, Corel, Qualcomm, and local application developers in Europe and Asia. IBM and Corel have large installed bases with their spreadsheet and word processor products, respectively, and both have aggressive pricing strategies. Also, IBM and Apple preinstall certain of their application software products on various models of their PCs, competing directly with Microsoft's desktop application software. Sun Microsystems' Star Office is aggressively priced. Additionally, Web-based application hosting services provide an alternative to PC-based applications such as Microsoft Office.

Microsoft's PC and server operating system products face substantial competition from a wide variety of companies. Competitors such as IBM, Apple Computer, Sun Microsystems, and others are vertically integrated in both software development and hardware manufacturing and have developed operating systems that they preinstall on their own computers. Many of these operating system software products are also licensed to third-party OEMs for preinstallation on their computers. Microsoft's operating system products compete with UNIX-based operating systems from a wide range of companies, including IBM, Hewlett-Packard, Sun Microsystems, and others. Variants of UNIX run on a wide variety of computer platforms and have gained increasing acceptance as desktop operating systems. The Linux open source operating system has gained increasing acceptance as well. Several computer manufacturers preinstall Linux on PC servers and many leading software developers have written applications that run on Linux. Microsoft Windows operating systems also face competition from alternative platforms such as those based on Internet browsing software and Java technology promoted by AOL-Time Warner and Sun Microsystems.

The Company competes in the business of providing enterprise-wide computing solutions with several competitors who enjoy a larger share of sales and larger installed bases. Many companies offer operating system software for mainframes and midrange computers, including IBM, HP, and Sun Microsystems. Since legacy business systems are typically support-intensive, these competitors also offer substantial support services. Software developers that provide competing server applications for PC-based distributed client/server environments include Oracle, IBM, Computer Associates, Sybase, and Informix. There are also several software vendors who offer connectivity servers. As mentioned above, there are numerous companies and organizations that offer Internet and intranet server software, which compete against the Company's business systems. Additionally, IBM has a large installed base of Lotus Notes and cc:Mail, both of which compete with the Company's collaboration and e-mail products.

The Company's developer products compete against offerings from BEA Systems, Borland, IBM, Macromedia, Oracle, Sun Microsystems, Sybase, and other companies.

CONSUMER SOFTWARE, SERVICES, AND DEVICES

Microsoft's online services network, MSN, faces formidable competition from AOL-Time Warner, Yahoo!, and a vast array of Web sites and portals that offer content of all types and e-mail, instant messaging, calendaring, chat, and search and shopping services, among other things.

Xbox competes head-to-head against game systems from Nintendo and Sony, both of which have a large established base of game system users. Game developers like Activision, Capcom, Electronic Arts, Sega, Tecmo, and THQ, to name a few, are both partners and competitors.

Microsoft faces many competitors in the mobile devices space, including Palm, Symbian, Nokia, and Openwave. The embedded operating system market is highly fragmented with many competitive offerings. Key competitors include Wind River and versions of embeddable Linux from commercial Linux vendors such as Red Hat, Lineo, and MontaVista.

CONSUMER COMMERCE INVESTMENTS

Microsoft faces many competitors in the online real estate and online automotive service spaces, including Homestore, AOL's House and Home channel, Autobytel, AOL autos, and Yahoo! autos.

OTHER

PC input devices face substantial competition from computer manufacturers, since computers are typically sold with a keyboard and mouse, and other manufacturers of these devices. Microsoft Press competes in the retail book and eLearning markets with publishers that also create content on Microsoft technologies. A few of the retail competitors are Pearson, WROX, Sybex, and Wiley. The major eLearning competitors are Smartforce and NetG.

EMPLOYEES

As of June 30, 2002, the Company employed approximately 50,500 people on a full-time basis, 34,600 in the United States and 15,900 internationally. Of the total, 20,800 were in product research and development, 23,500 in sales, marketing, and support, 2,200 in manufacturing and distribution, and 4,000 in finance and administration. Microsoft's success is highly dependent on its ability to attract and retain qualified employees. Competition for employees is intense in the software industry. To date, the Company believes it has been successful in its efforts to recruit qualified employees, but there is no assurance that it will continue to be as successful in the future. None of the Company's employees are subject to collective bargaining agreements. The Company believes relations with its employees are excellent.

ITEM 2.   PROPERTIES

The Company's corporate offices consist of approximately 8.4 million square feet of office building space located in King County, Washington, of which 5.7 million square feet of corporate campus space situated on slightly more than 300 acres of land is owned and approximately 2.7 million square feet is leased. The Company is constructing three buildings with approximately 392,000 square feet of space that will be occupied in the Fall of 2003. To accommodate expansion needs the Company purchased approximately 38 acres, and has an option to purchase approximately 112 additional acres, of land in Issaquah, Washington, which can accommodate 2.95 million square feet of additional office space. The Company leases many sites domestically totaling approximately 3.0 million square feet of office building space.

The Company leases many sites internationally totaling approximately 4.1 million square feet, including the Company's European Operations Center and localization division which leases a 382,000 square-foot campus in Dublin, Ireland, a 45,000 square-foot disk duplication facility in Humacao, Puerto Rico and a 36,000 square-foot facility in Singapore for the Company's Asia Pacific Operations Center. Leased office building space includes the following locations: Tokyo, Japan 343,000 square feet; Unterschleissheim, Germany 253,000 square feet; United Kingdom campus 242,000 square feet; Les Ulis, France 229,000 square feet; and Beijing, China 115,000 square feet.

The Company's facilities are fully used for current operations of all segments and suitable additional space is available to accommodate expansion needs.

ITEM 3.   LEGAL PROCEEDINGS

See Note 19—Contingencies of the Notes to Financial Statements (Item 8) for information regarding legal proceedings.

ITEM 4.   SUBMISSION OF MATTERS TO A VOTE OF SECURITY HOLDERS

No matters were submitted to a vote of security holders during the fourth quarter of fiscal 2002.

EXECUTIVE OFFICERS OF THE REGISTRANT

The executive officers of Microsoft as of July 31, 2002 were as follows:

Name	Age	Position with the Company
William H. Gates, III	46	Chairman of the Board; Chief Software Architect
Steven A. Ballmer	46	Chief Executive Officer
James E. Allchin	50	Group Vice President, Platforms Group
Orlando Ayala	46	Group Vice President, Worldwide Sales, Marketing, and Services Group
Robert J. (Robbie) Bach	40	Senior Vice President, Games Division
Douglas J. Burgum	46	Senior Vice President, Business Solutions
David W. Cole	40	Senior Vice President, MSN and Personal Services Group
John G. Connors	43	Senior Vice President; Chief Financial Officer
Jean-Philippe Courtois	41	Senior Vice President; President, Microsoft Europe, Middle East, and Africa
Jon Stephan DeVaan	41	Senior Vice President, TV Division
Richard P. Emerson	40	Senior Vice President, Corporate Development and Strategy
Paul Flessner	43	Senior Vice President, .NET Enterprise Servers
Kevin R. Johnson	41	Senior Vice President, Microsoft Americas
Robert L. Muglia	42	Senior Vice President, Enterprise Storage Division
Craig J. Mundie	53	Senior Vice President; Chief Technical Officer, Advanced Strategies and Policy
Jeffrey S. Raikes	44	Group Vice President, Productivity and Business Services
Richard F. Rashid	50	Senior Vice President, Research
Eric D. Rudder	35	Senior Vice President, Developer and Platform Evangelism
Steven J. Sinofsky	36	Senior Vice President, Office
Bradford L. Smith	43	Senior Vice President and General Counsel
Brian Valentine	42	Senior Vice President, Windows
David Vaskevitch	49	Senior Vice President; Chief Technical Officer, Business Platform
Deborah N. Willingham	46	Senior Vice President, Human Resources

Mr. Gates co-founded Microsoft in 1975 and served as its Chief Executive Officer from the time the original partnership was incorporated in 1981 until January 2000, when he resigned as Chief Executive Officer and assumed the position of Chief Software Architect. Mr. Gates has served as Chairman of the Board since the Company's incorporation.

Mr. Ballmer was named Chief Executive Officer and a director of the Company in January 2000. He served as President from July 1998 to February 2001. Previously, he had served as Executive Vice President, Sales and Support since February 1992. He joined Microsoft in 1980.

Mr. Allchin was named Group Vice President, Platforms Group in December 1999. He had been Senior Vice President, Platforms since March 1999. He was previously Senior Vice President, Personal and Business Systems since February 1996. Mr. Allchin joined Microsoft in 1990.

Mr. Ayala was named Group Vice President, Worldwide Sales, Marketing, and Services Group in August 2000. He had been Senior Vice President, South Pacific and Americas since February 1998, and before holding that position, was Vice President of the developing markets of Africa, India, the Mediterranean and Middle East, Latin America, Southeast Asia and the South Pacific. He joined Microsoft in 1991 as Senior Director of the Latin America Region.

Mr. Bach was named Senior Vice President, Games Division in March 2000. He had been Vice President, Home and Retail since March 1999. Before holding that position, he had been Vice President, Learning, Entertainment and Productivity since 1996. Mr. Bach joined Microsoft in 1988.

Mr. Burgum joined the Company upon Microsoft's acquisition of Great Plains Software, Inc. in April 2001. Mr. Burgum became Great Plains' first outside investor in March 1983. He was named President of Great Plains in 1984 and subsequently named Chairman and Chief Executive Officer.

Mr. Cole was named Senior Vice President, MSN and Personal Services Group in November 2001. Before holding that position, he had been Senior Vice President, Services Platform Division since August 2000. He had been Senior Vice President, Consumer Services since December 1999 and Vice President, Consumer Windows since March 1999. Previously, he was Vice President, Web Client and Consumer Experience and Vice President, Internet Client and Collaboration. Mr. Cole joined Microsoft in 1986.

Mr. Connors was named Senior Vice President and Chief Financial Officer in December 1999. He had been Vice President, Enterprise since March 1999. Mr. Connors had been Vice President, Information Technology, and Chief Information Officer since July 1996. He joined Microsoft in 1989.

Mr. Courtois was named Senior Vice President and President, Microsoft Europe, Middle East, and Africa in July 2000. He had been Vice President, Customer Marketing since July 1998. Before holding that position, he had been Vice President of Microsoft Europe since 1997 and General Manager for Microsoft France since 1994. Mr. Courtois joined Microsoft in 1984.

Mr. DeVaan was named Senior Vice President, TV Division in December 1999. He had been Senior Vice President, Consumer and Commerce since September 1999. Mr. DeVaan had been Vice President, Consumer and Commerce since March 1999. He had been Vice President, Desktop Applications since 1995. Mr. DeVaan joined Microsoft in 1985.

Mr. Emerson joined Microsoft in November 2000 as Senior Vice President, Corporate Development and Strategy. Prior to joining Microsoft, he was Managing Director and co-head of Technology and Telecommunications Advisory Services at international investment bank Lazard Freres & Co. LLC. He spent 12 years in San Francisco and New York with Lazard and Morgan Stanley, specializing in advising clients in the technology and telecommunications sectors on mergers, acquisitions, and strategic partnerships.

Mr. Flessner was named Senior Vice President, .NET Enterprise Servers in December 1999. He had been Vice President, Database and Data Access. Since joining the Company, Mr. Flessner's primary responsibilities have been the development of Microsoft's database business. He joined Microsoft in 1994.

Mr. Johnson was named Senior Vice President, Microsoft Americas in February 2002. He had been Senior Vice President, U.S. Sales, Marketing, and Services since August 2001, and before that, Vice President, U.S. Sales, Marketing and Services. Mr. Johnson was named Vice President, Product Support Services in July 1998. He joined Microsoft in 1992.

Mr. Muglia was named Senior Vice President, Enterprise Storage Division in November 2001. Before holding that position, he had been Group Vice President, Personal Services Group since August 2000. He had been Group Vice President, Business Productivity since December 1999. He was named Senior Vice President, Business Productivity in March 1999 and was named Senior Vice President, Applications and Tools in February 1998. He had been Vice President, Server Applications since 1997. He joined Microsoft in 1988.

Mr. Mundie was named Senior Vice President and Chief Technical Officer, Advanced Strategies and Policy in August 2001. He was named Senior Vice President, Consumer Platforms in February 1996. He joined Microsoft as General Manager, Advanced Consumer Technology in 1992.

Mr. Raikes was named Group Vice President, Productivity and Business Services in August 2000. He had been Group Vice President, Sales and Support since July 1998. Before holding that position, he had been Group Vice President, Sales and Marketing since July 1996. Mr. Raikes joined Microsoft in 1981.

Mr. Rashid was named Senior Vice President, Research in May 2000. He had been Vice President, Research since July 1994. He joined Microsoft in 1991.

Mr. Rudder was named Senior Vice President, Developer and Platform Evangelism in October 2001. He had been Vice President, Technical Strategy. Mr. Rudder joined Microsoft in 1988 and has worked in several areas, including networking, operating systems and developer tools, where he previously served as General Manager for the Visual Studio development system.

Mr. Sinofsky was named Senior Vice President, Office in December 1999. He had been Vice President, Office since December 1998. Mr. Sinofsky joined the Office team in 1994, increasing his responsibility with each subsequent release of the desktop suite. He joined Microsoft in 1989.

Mr. Smith was named Senior Vice President and General Counsel in November 2001. He had been Deputy General Counsel for Worldwide Sales and previously was responsible for managing the Company's European Law and Corporate Affairs Group, based in Paris. He joined Microsoft in 1993.

Mr. Valentine was named Senior Vice President, Windows in December 1999. He had been Vice President, Business and Enterprise since March 1999. He had been Vice President, Windows since December 1998. Before managing the Windows group, Mr. Valentine managed the server applications division and had been responsible for the Exchange product unit. He joined Microsoft in 1987.

Mr. Vaskevitch was named Senior Vice President and Chief Technical Officer, Business Platform in August 2001. He was named Senior Vice President, Business Applications in March 2000. He had been Senior Vice President, Developer since December 1999. Before holding that position, he had been Vice President, Distributed Applications Platform. He joined Microsoft in 1986.

Ms. Willingham was named Senior Vice President, Human Resources in February 2001. She had been Vice President, Human Resources since April 2000. Ms. Willingham had been Vice President, Business and Enterprise Division Marketing and was responsible for Windows operating system client and server marketing strategy and training, as well as for providing centralized marketing services for the Consumer Windows Marketing and Streaming Media Marketing teams. She joined Microsoft in 1993.

PART II

ITEM 5.   MARKET FOR REGISTRANT'S COMMON STOCK AND RELATED STOCKHOLDER MATTERS

The Company's common stock is traded on The Nasdaq Stock Market under the symbol MSFT. On June 30, 2002, there were 117,730 registered holders of record of the Company's common stock. The Company has not paid cash dividends on its common stock. The high and low common stock prices per share were as follows:

Quarter Ended	Sept. 30	Dec. 31	Mar. 31	June 30	Year
Fiscal 2001					
Common stock price per share:					
High	$ 82.00	$ 70.88	$ 64.69	$ 73.68	$ 82.00
Low	60.31	41.50	43.38	51.94	41.50
Fiscal 2002					
Common stock price per share:					
High	$ 72.57	$ 69.49	$ 69.86	$ 60.38	$ 72.57
Low	49.71	51.79	57.99	48.62	48.62

ITEM 6.   SELECTED FINANCIAL DATA

FINANCIAL HIGHLIGHTS

In millions, except earnings per share

Year Ended June 30	1998	1999	2000	2001[1]	2002[2]
Revenue	$ 15,262	$ 19,747	$ 22,956	$ 25,296	$ 28,365
Operating income	6,585	10,010	11,006	11,720	11,910
Income before accounting change	4,490	7,785	9,421	7,721	7,829
Net income	4,490	7,785	9,421	7,346	7,829
Diluted earnings per share before accounting change	0.84	1.42	1.70	1.38	1.41
Diluted earnings per share	0.84	1.42	1.70	1.32	1.41
Cash and short-term investments	13,927	17,236	23,798	31,600	38,652
Total assets	22,357	38,321	51,694	58,830	67,646
Stockholders' equity	16,627	28,438	41,368	47,289	52,180

(1) Fiscal year 2001 includes an unfavorable cumulative effect of accounting change of $375 million or $0.06 per diluted share, reflecting the adoption of SFAS No. 133, and $4.80 billion (pre-tax) in impairments of certain investments, primarily cable and telecommunication investments.

(2) Fiscal year 2002 includes $4.32 billion (pre-tax) in impairments of certain investments, primarily related to the Company's AT&T investment and further declines in the fair values of European cable and telecommunications holdings, and a $1.25 billion (pre-tax) gain on the sale of Expedia, Inc.

ITEM 7. MANAGEMENT'S DISCUSSION AND ANALYSIS OF RESULTS OF OPERATIONS AND FINANCIAL CONDITION·

RESULTS OF OPERATIONS FOR 2000, 2001, AND 2002

Management's Discussion and Analysis contains statements that are forward-looking. These statements are based on current expectations and assumptions that are subject to risks and uncertainties. Actual results could differ materially because of factors discussed in "Issues and Uncertainties."

REVENUE

The Company's revenue growth rate was 16% in fiscal 2000, 10% in fiscal 2001, and 12% in fiscal 2002. Revenue growth in fiscal 2002 was led by the addition of Xbox video game system revenue and the strong penetration of Microsoft Windows XP Professional and Home operating systems. Revenue growth in fiscal 2001 was driven primarily by licensing of Microsoft Windows 2000 Professional, Microsoft SQL Server, and the other .NET Enterprise Servers. Revenue growth in fiscal 2000 was driven by strong licensing of Microsoft Windows NT Workstation, Windows 2000 Professional, Windows NT Server, Windows 2000 Server, Microsoft Office 2000, and SQL Server.

Microsoft continued to see a mix shift to volume licensing programs. On October 1, 2001, Microsoft launched Licensing 6.0 to simplify and improve its volume licensing programs, including a simplified approach to software upgrades. One feature of Licensing 6.0 is Software Assurance which gives customers the right to install any new release of products covered in the licensing agreement during the term of their coverage. The success of Microsoft's new volume licensing programs will continue to affect the mix of multi-year licensing agreements with a resulting impact on the timing of revenue recognition. In addition, the timing and extent of a recovery in consumer and corporate spending on PCs and information technology (IT) will be factors affecting revenue growth.

PRODUCT REVENUE

In fiscal 2002, Microsoft had four segments: Desktop and Enterprise Software and Services; Consumer Software, Services, and Devices; Consumer Commerce Investments; and Other. The revenue figures in this Management's Discussion and Analysis (MD&A) differ from those reported in the Company's Segment Information appearing in Note 20 of the Notes to Financial Statements. The revenue figures in the Segment Information represent amounts reported internally for management reporting, while the revenue figures in the MD&A reflect revenue recognized in accordance with generally accepted accounting principles. On July 1, 2002, Microsoft revised its product segments and will begin reporting the new segments in fiscal 2003.

Desktop and Enterprise Software and Services. Desktop and Enterprise Software and Services revenue was $20.40 billion, $22.41 billion, and $24.01 billion in 2000, 2001, and 2002. Desktop and Enterprise Software and Services includes Desktop Applications; Desktop Platforms; and Enterprise Software and Services.

Desktop Applications revenue was $9.30 billion, $9.54 billion, and $9.60 billion in 2000, 2001, and 2002. Desktop Applications includes revenue from Microsoft Office; Microsoft Project; Visio; client access licenses (CALs) for Windows NT Server and Windows 2000 Server, Exchange, and BackOffice; Microsoft Great Plains; and bCentral. In fiscal 2002, Office licensing revenue declined during the year due to a strong mix shift to multi-year annuity licensing agreements, which deferred revenue recognition to future years, and a decrease in consumer purchases in the Asia region, most notably Japan, partially offset by strong OEM licensing. Revenue from client access licenses grew 3% in fiscal 2002 and revenue from Great Plains contributed to the growth in Desktop Applications. In fiscal 2001, revenue from client access licenses increased 14% reflecting strong licensing growth of Windows NT Server and Windows 2000 Server CALs. Office revenue growth was flat during fiscal 2001. In fiscal 2000, revenue growth from Microsoft Office integrated suites, including the Premium, Professional, Small Business, and Standard Editions was very solid.

Desktop Platforms revenue was $7.02 billion, $8.04 billion, and $9.30 billion in 2000, 2001, and 2002. Desktop Platforms includes revenue from Windows XP Professional and Home, Windows 2000 Professional, Windows NT Workstation, Windows Me, Windows 98, and other desktop operating systems. In fiscal 2002, the growth in Desktop Platforms revenue reflected strong multi-year licensing revenue growth and a continued mix shift to the higher priced Windows 2000 and Windows XP Professional operating system through OEMs, despite a decline in reported OEM unit shipments. Fiscal 2001 revenue growth reflected the strong adoption of Windows 2000 Professional, partially offset by flat revenue growth from Windows Me and Windows 98 operating systems, reflecting the slowdown in consumer PC shipments and a higher mix of Windows 2000 Professional and Windows NT Workstation. In fiscal 2000, Desktop Platforms revenue growth was modest due to soft demand for business PCs during most of the year; a slowdown in shipments in anticipation of the post mid-year availability of Windows 2000 operating systems; and, as expected, a longer business migration cycle for the newest Windows operating system offerings. The rate of growth in PC shipments and the mix of Windows 2000 and Windows XP Professional as a percentage of all 32-bit operating systems will continue to impact revenue growth in the future.

Enterprise Software and Services revenue was $4.08 billion, $4.83 billion, and $5.11 billion in 2000, 2001, and 2002. Enterprise Software and Services includes Server Platforms, Server Applications, Developer Tools and Services, and Enterprise Services. In fiscal 2002, Server Applications, including Microsoft SQL Server and .NET Enterprise Servers, increased 10% compared to fiscal 2001. Server Platform revenue, which includes Windows 2000 Server and Windows NT Server operating systems, increased 10% versus fiscal 2001 driven by a modest overall increase in Windows-based server shipments and increased deployment of Windows 2000 Server. Enterprise Services revenue, representing consulting and product support services, was up 17% compared to fiscal 2001, while revenue from Developer Tools and Services was down 19% from fiscal 2001. In fiscal 2001, Server Applications revenue increased 31% versus the prior year as a result of the continued adoption of Microsoft's .NET Enterprise Server offerings. Enterprise Services revenue in fiscal 2001, was up 34% compared to fiscal 2000 and Server Platforms increased 10% while revenue from Developer Tools and Services was flat. In fiscal 2000, Server Platforms revenue growth was particularly strong led by increased adoption by customers of Windows NT Server and Windows 2000 Server. Revenue from Server Applications grew strongly in fiscal 2000, largely due to the strong success of SQL Server 7.0, while Software Developer Tools and Services revenue declined, due to increased suite licensing versus stand-alone licenses, and the lack of a release upgrade of the Visual Studio development system.

Consumer Software, Services, and Devices. Consumer Software, Services, and Devices revenue was $1.63 billion, $1.95 billion, and $3.59 billion in 2000, 2001, and 2002. Consumer Software, Services, and Devices includes the Xbox video game system; MSN Internet access; MSN network service; PC and online games; learning and productivity software; mobility; and embedded systems. The majority of the revenue growth from fiscal 2001 stemmed from sales of the Xbox video game system released in fiscal 2002. MSN Internet access revenue increased as a result of both a higher subscriber base and higher average revenue per subscriber due to a reduction in promotional subscriber programs. Revenue from MSN network services increased despite a declining Internet advertising market. Revenue from embedded systems in fiscal 2002 grew nicely, however learning and productivity software revenue and PC and online games declined compared to fiscal 2001. In fiscal 2001, revenue from MSN network services grew strongly despite a decline in the online advertising market. MSN Internet access revenue also grew solidly from fiscal 2000 as a result of an increased subscriber base, partially offset by a decline in the average revenue per subscriber due to a larger mix of subscribers contracted under rebate programs. Revenue from embedded systems grew strongly from the prior year, while learning and productivity software revenue and PC and online games revenue declined, reflecting softness in the overall consumer market. In fiscal 2000, online revenue growth was very strong and reflected higher subscriber totals, offset by lower net prices for Internet access subscriptions compared to the prior year. Additionally, strong sales of entertainment software in fiscal 2000 produced robust revenue growth in PC and online games.

Consumer Commerce Investments. Consumer Commerce Investments revenue was $182 million, $299 million, and $242 million in 2000, 2001, and 2002. Consumer Commerce Investments include Expedia, Inc., the HomeAdvisor online real estate service, and the CarPoint online automotive service. The decline in revenue compared to fiscal 2001 reflects the sale of Microsoft's majority ownership of Expedia, Inc. to USA Networks, Inc. on February 4, 2002. Acquisitions of Travelscape.com and VacationSpot.com by Expedia, Inc., and increased product offerings from Expedia led to the strong revenue growth in fiscal 2001. The increased overall reach of all properties led to the strong revenue growth in fiscal 2000.

Other. Other revenue, which primarily includes Hardware and Microsoft Press, was $754 million, $630 million, and $530 million in 2000, 2001, and 2002. In fiscal 2002, continued declines in the IT book and consumer market led to a decline in Microsoft Press and Hardware sales. Lower sales of gaming devices and other hardware peripherals as a result of weakness in the consumer market caused the decline in revenue in fiscal 2001. Continued success of the Company's new hardware device offerings led to revenue growth in fiscal 2000.

DISTRIBUTION CHANNELS

Microsoft distributes its products primarily through the following channels: OEM; volume licensing; online services and products; and distributors and retailers. OEM channel revenue represents license fees from original equipment manufacturers who preinstall Microsoft products, primarily on PCs. Microsoft has three major geographic sales and marketing regions: the South Pacific and Americas Region; the Europe, Middle East, and Africa Region; and the Asia Region. Sales of volume licenses and packaged software products via these channels are primarily to distributors and resellers.

OEM revenue was $7.01 billion in 2000, $7.86 billion in 2001, and $9.00 billion in 2002. In fiscal 2002, reported licenses declined compared to fiscal 2001. However, a strong increase in the mix of the higher priced Windows 2000 and Windows XP Professional licenses, and healthy growth in direct and system builder OEMs licenses, led to higher average revenue per license and contributed to the overall OEM revenue growth over fiscal 2001. In fiscal 2001, while total licenses were also impacted by a slowdown in PC shipments, the mix of the higher priced Windows 2000 Professional and Windows NT Workstation increased substantially resulting in higher average revenue per license. A relatively low growth rate in fiscal 2000 was due to lower business PC shipment growth combined with post mid-year availability of Windows 2000 Professional. Average earned revenue per license also declined in fiscal 2000 compared to the prior year, due in part to a mix shift to the lower-priced Windows 98 operating system reflecting the softness in demand for business PCs and lower prices on operating systems licensed through certain OEM channel sectors.

South Pacific and Americas Region revenue was $8.33 billion, $9.52 billion, and $11.41 billion in 2000, 2001, and 2002. In fiscal 2002, the majority of the revenue growth was driven by sales of the Xbox video game system released during the year, as well as strong Windows XP Professional licensing, MSN subscription revenue, and revenue from Microsoft Great Plains. In fiscal 2001, revenue growth was led by strong licensing of Windows 2000 Professional and the family of .NET Enterprise Servers, particularly SQL Server 2000 and Exchange 2000 Server. Revenue from Enterprise services and MSN subscription and services also grew strongly in fiscal 2001. In fiscal 2000, Office 2000 integrated suites, Windows 2000 Server, online revenue, and SQL Server sales were the primary drivers of the revenue growth. Strong retail sales of hardware devices and consumer software also contributed to the growth over the prior year.

Europe, Middle East, and Africa Region revenue was $5.02 billion, $4.86 billion, and $5.13 billion in 2000, 2001, and 2002. In fiscal 2002, the majority of the growth was a result of strong multi-year licensing revenue of Windows XP Home and Professional operating systems and Enterprise Software, as well as the addition of Xbox video game system revenue in the second half of the year. In fiscal 2001, weakening local currencies negatively impacted translated revenue compared to the prior year, while revenue from Windows 2000 Professional and the .NET Enterprise Server family of products was very healthy. In fiscal 2000, retail sales of Windows operating systems and

Office licensing produced moderate growth in the region. Growth from SQL Server licensing, new hardware device offerings, and entertainment software was especially strong.

Asia Region revenue was $2.60 billion in 2000, $3.06 billion in 2001, and $2.83 billion in 2002. In fiscal 2002, Asia region revenue declined most notably due to lower consumer PC shipments, which hampered revenue from localized versions of Microsoft Office 2000 and Microsoft Office XP, especially the Office Personal Edition. Xbox video game system sales partially offset the decline in Office revenue. In fiscal 2001, the region's growth rate reflected strong revenue from localized versions of Microsoft Office 2000 and Microsoft Office XP, especially the Office Personal Edition. This growth was also attributable to Windows 2000 Professional and .NET Server applications licensing. In fiscal 2000, the region's growth rate reflected strong performance resulting from improved local economic conditions. Revenue growth was also influenced by robust growth of localized versions of Microsoft Office 2000, especially the Office Personal Edition sold in Japan, Windows platform and server licensing, and strong adoption of SQL Server.

The Company's operating results are affected by foreign exchange rates. Approximately 30%, 27%, and 25% of the Company's revenue was collected in foreign currencies during 2000, 2001, and 2002. Since a portion of local currency revenue is hedged and much of the Company's international manufacturing costs and operating expenses are also incurred in local currencies, the impact of exchange rates is partially mitigated.

OPERATING EXPENSES

Cost of Revenue. Cost of revenue as a percent of revenue was 13.1% in 2000, 13.7% in 2001, and 18.3% in 2002. Cost of revenue in fiscal 2002 increased primarily due to costs related to Xbox. In fiscal 2001, higher support and service costs associated with the MSN Internet access and MSN network services were partially offset by the lower relative costs associated with organizational licensing and the drop in the mix of packaged product versus the prior year. Cost of revenue in fiscal 2000 reflected lower costs associated with WebTV Networks' operations, partially offset by the growth in hardware peripherals costs.

Research and Development. The discontinuation of goodwill amortization in fiscal 2002 in accordance with Statement of Financial Accounting Standards (SFAS) 142, *Goodwill and Other Intangible Assets,* offset the growth in headcount and development costs. In fiscal 2001, the increase in R&D expense was the result of higher headcount-related costs and investments in new product initiatives. The increase in fiscal 2000 was driven primarily by higher headcount-related costs. Prospectively, increased headcount and increased spending in Server Platforms, Home & Entertainment, Business Solutions and CE are currently expected to be significant factors affecting future research and development expense growth.

Sales and Marketing. Sales and marketing expense as a percentage of revenue was 18.0% in 2000, 19.3% in 2001, and 19.1% in 2002. In fiscal 2002, sales and marketing expense as a percentage of revenue decreased due to lower relative MSN customer acquisition marketing and the large relative increase associated with the onset of Xbox video game system revenue. In fiscal 2001, sales and marketing expenses as a percentage of revenue increased due to higher relative headcount-related costs, higher marketing and sales expenses associated with MSN, the Microsoft Agility advertising campaign, and other new sales initiatives. In fiscal 2000, sales and marketing expenses as a percentage of revenue increased due to higher relative marketing costs associated with new product releases and online marketing. Microsoft expects that it will increase spending on Information Worker, Server Platforms, and Business Solutions sales forces and Windows Client, MSN and Home & Entertainment marketing.

General and Administrative. General and administrative expenses in fiscal 2002 increased due to a charge of approximately $660 million for estimated expenses related to the Company's consumer class action lawsuits and higher legal fees. In fiscal 2001, general and administrative costs decreased due to a charge related to the settlement of the lawsuit with Caldera, Inc. recorded in fiscal 2000. Excluding this charge in fiscal 2000, general and administrative expenses in fiscal 2001 increased from the prior year due to higher headcount-related costs and legal fees. For fiscal 2000, besides the settlement of the lawsuit, general and administrative expenses also reflected increased legal fees and certain employee stock option-related expenses.

NON-OPERATING ITEMS, INVESTMENT INCOME/(LOSS), AND INCOME TAXES

Losses on equity investees and other consists of Microsoft's share of income or loss from investments accounted for using the equity method, and income or loss attributable to minority interests. The decrease in losses on equity investees and other in fiscal 2002 was attributed to the divestiture of certain equity investments in fiscal 2002. The increase in losses on equity investees and other in fiscal 2001 reflects an increase in the number of such investments during the year. In fiscal 2000 losses on equity investees and other decreased reflecting smaller losses from the MSNBC entities.

The Company recorded net investment income/(loss) in each year as follows:

In millions

Year Ended June 30		2000		2001		2002
Dividends	$	363	$	377	$	357
Interest		1,231		1,808		1,762
Net recognized gains/(losses) on investments:						
Net gains on the sales of investments		1,780		3,175		2,379
Other-than-temporary impairments		(29)		(4,804)		(4,323)
Net unrealized losses attributable to derivative instruments		(19)		(592)		(480)
Net recognized gains/(losses) on investments		1,732		(2,221)		(2,424)
Investment income/(loss)	$	3,326	$	(36)	$	(305)

In fiscal 2002, other-than-temporary impairments primarily related to the Company's investment in AT&T and other cable and tele-communication investments. Net gains on the sales of investments included a $1.25 billion gain on the sale of the Company's share of Expedia. Interest and dividend income decreased $66 million from fiscal 2001 as a result of lower interest rates and dividend income.

In fiscal 2001, other-than-temporary impairments primarily related to cable and telecommunication investments. Net gains from the sales of investments in fiscal 2001 included a gain from Microsoft's investment in Titus Communications (which was merged with Jupiter Telecommunications) and the closing of the sale of Transpoint to CheckFree Holdings Corp. Interest and dividend income increased $591 million from fiscal 2000, reflecting a larger investment portfolio. In fiscal year 2000, investment income increased primarily as a result of a larger investment portfolio generated by cash from operations coupled with realized gains from the sale of securities.

At June 30, 2002, unrealized losses on Equity and Other Investments of $623 million were deemed to be temporary in nature. The following, among other factors, could result in some investments being deemed other-than-temporarily impaired in future periods: changes in the duration and extent to which the fair value is less than cost; the financial health of and business outlook for the investee, including industry and sector performance, changes in technology, and operational and financing cash flow factors; and the Company's intent and ability to hold the investment.

In connection with the definitive agreement to combine AT&T Broadband with Comcast in a new company to be called AT&T Comcast Corporation, Microsoft has agreed to exchange its AT&T 5% convertible preferred debt securities for approximately 115 million shares of AT&T Comcast Corporation. It is expected that the transaction will close by December 31, 2002. While it is possible that Microsoft could incur a loss on this exchange transaction up to the carrying value of the AT&T debt securities, management believes that the ultimate loss, if any, will be significantly less. As management is unable to predict whether there will be a gain or loss on the exchange, no loss has been recorded related to this contingent exchange transaction as of June 30, 2002.

The Company's effective tax rate for fiscal 2002 was 32%. The effective tax rate for fiscal 2001 and fiscal 2000 was 33% and 34%, respectively. The decrease in the effective tax rate is due primarily to lower taxes on foreign earnings.

ACCOUNTING CHANGES

Effective July 1, 2001, Microsoft adopted SFAS 141, *Business Combinations,* and SFAS 142, *Goodwill and Other Intangible Assets.* SFAS 141 requires business combinations to be accounted for using the purchase method of accounting. It also specifies the types of acquired intangible assets that are required to be recognized and reported separate from goodwill. SFAS 142 requires that goodwill and certain in-tangibles no longer be amortized, but instead tested for impairment at least annually. There was no impairment of goodwill upon adoption of SFAS 142. Goodwill amortization (on a pre-tax basis) was $234 million in fiscal 2000 and $311 million in fiscal 2001.

Effective July 1, 2000, Microsoft adopted SFAS 133, *Accounting for Derivative Instruments and Hedging Activities,* which establishes accounting and reporting standards for derivative instruments, including certain derivative instruments embedded in other contracts and for hedging activities. The adoption of SFAS 133 resulted in a cumulative pre-tax reduction to income of $560 million ($375 million after-tax) and a cumulative pre-tax reduction to other comprehensive income (OCI) of $112 million ($75 million after-tax). The reduction to income was mostly attributable to a loss of approximately $300 million reclassified from OCI for the time value of options and a loss of approx-imately $250 million reclassified from OCI for derivatives not designated as hedging instruments. The reduction to OCI was mostly attribut-able to losses of approximately $670 million on cash flow hedges offset by the reclassifications out of OCI of the approximately $300 million loss for the time value of options and the approximately $250 million loss for derivative instruments not designated as hedging in-struments.

FINANCIAL CONDITION

The Company's cash and short-term investment portfolio totaled $38.65 billion at June 30, 2002. The portfolio consists primarily of fixed-income securities, diversified among industries and individual issuers. Microsoft's investments are generally liquid and investment grade. The portfolio is invested predominantly in U.S. dollar denominated securities, but also includes foreign currency positions in order to diversify financial risk. The portfolio is primarily invested in short-term securities to minimize interest rate risk and facilitate rapid deploy-ment for immediate cash needs.

Cash flow from operations was $14.51 billion for fiscal 2002, an increase of $1.09 billion from fiscal 2001. The increase reflects strong growth in unearned revenue. Cash used for financing was $4.57 billion in fiscal 2002, a decrease of $1.01 billion from the prior year. The decrease reflects the repurchase of put warrants in the prior year. The Company repurchased 122.8 million shares of common stock under its share repurchase program in fiscal 2002, compared to 89.0 million shares repurchased in the prior year. In addition, 5.1 million shares of common stock were acquired in fiscal 2002 under a structured stock repurchase transaction. The Company entered into the structured stock repurchase transaction in fiscal 2001, giving it the right to acquire 5.1 million of its shares in exchange for an up-front net payment of $264 million. Cash used for investing was $10.85 billion in fiscal 2002, an increase of $2.11 billion from fiscal 2001.

Cash flow from operations was $13.42 billion in fiscal 2001, an increase of $2.00 billion from the prior year. The increase was primarily attributable to the growth in revenue and other changes in working capital, partially offset by the decrease in the stock option income tax benefit, reflecting decreased stock option exercises by employees. Cash used for financing was $5.59 billion in fiscal 2001, an increase of $3.39 billion from the prior year. The increase primarily reflects the repurchase of put warrants in fiscal 2001, compared to the sale of put warrants in the prior fiscal year, as well as an increase in common stock repurchased. All outstanding put warrants were either retired or exercised during fiscal 2001. During fiscal 2001, the Company repurchased 89.0 million shares. Cash used for investing was $8.73 billion in fiscal 2001, a decrease of $658 million from the prior year. In fiscal 2000, cash flow from operations was $11.43 billion, a decrease of $720 million from the prior year, reflecting working capital changes partially offset by the increase in the stock option income tax benefit. Cash used for financing was $2.19 billion in fiscal 2000, an increase of $1.33 billion from the prior year, reflecting an increase in common stock repurchased versus the prior year. During fiscal 2000, the Company repurchased 55.2 million shares. Cash used for investing was $9.39 billion in fiscal 2000, a decrease of $808 million from the prior year.

Microsoft has no material long-term debt. Stockholders' equity at June 30, 2002 was $52.18 billion. Microsoft will continue to invest in sales, marketing, and product support infrastructure. Additionally, research and development activities will include investments in existing and advanced areas of technology, including using cash to acquire technology. Additions to property and equipment will continue, including new facilities and computer systems for R&D, sales and marketing, support, and administrative staff. Commitments for constructing new buildings were $111 million on June 30, 2002. The Company has not engaged in any transactions or arrangements with unconsolidated entities or other persons that are reasonably likely to affect materially liquidity or the availability of or requirements for capital resources. Since fiscal 1990, Microsoft has repurchased 982 million common shares while 2.23 billion shares were issued under the Company's employee stock option and purchase plans. The Company's convertible preferred stock matured on December 15, 1999. Each preferred share was converted into 1.1273 common shares.

Management believes existing cash and short-term investments together with funds generated from operations should be sufficient to meet operating requirements. The Company's cash and short-term investments are available for strategic investments, mergers and acquisitions, other potential large-scale needs and to fund the share repurchase program. Microsoft has not paid cash dividends on its common stock.

SUBSEQUENT EVENT

On July 11, 2002, Microsoft acquired Navision a/s as a result of the successful close of a tender offer. Microsoft purchased Navision's shares for approximately $1.45 billion in stock and cash. Navision is a provider of integrated business software solutions for small and medium-sized companies.

APPLICATION OF CRITICAL ACCOUNTING POLICIES

Microsoft's financial statements and accompanying notes are prepared in accordance with generally accepted accounting principles in the United States. Preparing financial statements requires management to make estimates and assumptions that affect the reported amounts of assets, liabilities, revenue, and expenses. These estimates and assumptions are affected by management's application of accounting policies. Critical accounting policies for Microsoft include revenue recognition, impairment of investment securities, accounting for research and development costs, accounting for legal contingencies, and accounting for income taxes.

Microsoft accounts for the licensing of software in accordance with American Institute of Certified Public Accountants (AICPA) Statement of Position (SOP) 97-2, *Software Revenue Recognition.* The application of SOP 97-2 requires judgment, including whether a software arrangement includes multiple elements, and if so, whether vendor-specific objective evidence (VSOE) of fair value exists for those elements. End users receive certain elements of the Company's products over a period of time. These elements include browser technologies updates and technical support, the fair value of which is recognized over the product's estimated life cycle. Changes to the elements in a software arrangement, the ability to identify VSOE for those elements, the fair value of the respective elements, and changes to a product's estimated life cycle could materially impact the amount of earned and unearned revenue. Judgment is also required to assess whether future releases of certain software represent new products or upgrades and enhancements to existing products.

SFAS 115, *Accounting for Certain Investments in Debt and Equity Securities,* and Securities and Exchange Commission (SEC) Staff Accounting Bulletin (SAB) 59, *Accounting for Noncurrent Marketable Equity Securities,* provide guidance on determining when an investment is other-than-temporarily impaired, which also requires judgment. In making this judgment, Microsoft evaluates, among other factors, the duration and extent to which the fair value of an investment is less than its cost; the financial health of and business outlook for the investee, including factors such as industry and sector performance, changes in technology, and operational and financing cash flow; and the Company's intent and ability to hold the investment.

Microsoft accounts for research and development costs in accordance with several accounting pronouncements, including SFAS 2, *Accounting for Research and Development Costs,* and SFAS 86, *Accounting for the Costs of Computer Software to be Sold, Leased, or Other-*

wise Marketed. SFAS 86 specifies that costs incurred internally in creating a computer software product should be charged to expense when incurred as research and development until technological feasibility has been established for the product. Once technological feasibility is established, all software costs should be capitalized until the product is available for general release to customers. Judgment is required in determining when the technological feasibility of a product is established. Microsoft has determined that technological feasibility for its products is reached shortly before the products are released to manufacturing. Costs incurred after technological feasibility is established are not material, and accordingly, the Company expenses all research and development costs when incurred.

Microsoft is subject to various legal proceedings and claims, the outcomes of which are subject to significant uncertainty. SFAS 5, *Accounting for Contingencies,* requires that an estimated loss from a loss contingency should be accrued by a charge to income if it is probable that an asset has been impaired or a liability has been incurred and the amount of the loss can be reasonably estimated. Disclosure of a contingency is required if there is at least a reasonable possibility that a loss has been incurred. The Company evaluates, among other factors, the degree of probability of an unfavorable outcome and the ability to make a reasonable estimate of the amount of loss. Changes in these factors could materially impact the Company's financial position or its results of operations.

SFAS 109, *Accounting for Income Taxes,* establishes financial accounting and reporting standards for the effect of income taxes. The objectives of accounting for income taxes are to recognize the amount of taxes payable or refundable for the current year and deferred tax liabilities and assets for the future tax consequences of events that have been recognized in an entity's financial statements or tax returns. Judgment is required in assessing the future tax consequences of events that have been recognized in the Company's financial statements or tax returns. Fluctuations in the actual outcome of these future tax consequences could materially impact the Company's financial position or its results of operations.

ISSUES AND UNCERTAINTIES

The following issues and uncertainties, among others, should be considered in evaluating the Company's financial outlook.

Challenges to the Company's Business Model. Since its inception, the Company's business model has been based upon customers agreeing to pay a fee to license software developed and distributed by Microsoft. Under this commercial software development ("CSD") model, software developers bear the costs of converting original ideas into software products through investments in research and development, offsetting these costs with the revenues received from the distribution of their products. The Company believes that the CSD model has had substantial benefits for users of software, allowing them to rely on the expertise of the Company and other software developers that have powerful incentives to develop innovative software that is useful, reliable and compatible with other software and hardware. In recent years, there has been a growing challenge to the CSD model, often referred to as the Open Source movement. Under the Open Source model, software is produced by global "communities" of programmers, and the resulting software and the intellectual property contained therein is licensed to end users at little or no cost. The Company believes that there are significant problems with the Open Source model, the principal drawback being that no single entity is responsible for the Open Source software, and thus users have no recourse if a product does not work properly or at all. Further, without the market incentives associated with the CSD model, the Company believes that the vigorous innovation and growth of the software industry over the last 25 years would not have occurred. Nonetheless, the popularization of the Open Source movement continues to pose a significant challenge to the Company's business model, including recent efforts by proponents of the Open Source model to convince governments worldwide to mandate the use of Open Source software in their purchase and deployment of software products. To the extent the Open Source model gains increasing market acceptance, sales of the Company's products may decline, the Company may have to reduce the prices it charges for its products, and revenues and operating margins may consequently decline.

New Products and Services. The Company has made significant investments in research and development for new products, services and technologies, including Microsoft .NET, Xbox, business applications, MSN, mobile and wireless technologies, and television. Significant revenue from these investments may not be achieved for a number of years, if at all. Moreover, these products and services may never be profitable, and even if they are profitable, operating margins for these businesses are not expected to be as high as the margins historically experienced in our Desktop and Enterprise Software and Services businesses.

Declines in Demand for Software. If overall market demand for PCs, servers and other computing devices declines significantly, and consumer and corporate spending for such products declines, Microsoft's revenue growth will be adversely affected. Additionally, the Company's revenues would be unfavorably impacted if customers reduce their purchases of new software products or upgrades to existing products if such new offerings are not perceived to add significant new functionality or other value to prospective purchasers.

Product Development Schedule. The development of software products is a complex and time-consuming process. New products and enhancements to existing products can require long development and testing periods. Significant delays in new product releases or significant problems in creating new products could negatively impact the Company's revenues.

International Operations. Microsoft develops and sells products throughout the world. The prices of the Company's products in countries outside of the United States are generally higher than the Company's prices in the United States because of the cost incurred in localizing software for non-U.S. markets. The costs of producing and selling the Company's products in these countries also are higher. Pressure to globalize Microsoft's pricing structure might require that the Company reduce the sales price of its software in other countries, even though the costs of the software continue to be higher than in the United States. Unfavorable changes in trade protection laws, policies and measures, and other regulatory requirements affecting trade and investment; unexpected changes in regulatory requirements for software; social, political, labor, or economic conditions in a specific country or region, including foreign exchange rates; difficulties in staffing and managing foreign operations; and potential adverse foreign tax consequences, among other factors, could also have a negative effect on the Company's business and results of operations outside of the United States.

Intellectual Property Rights. Microsoft diligently defends its intellectual property rights, but unlicensed copying and use of software represents a loss of revenue to the Company. While this adversely affects U.S. revenue, revenue loss is even more significant outside the United States, particularly in countries where laws are less protective of intellectual property rights. Throughout the world, Microsoft actively educates consumers on the benefits of licensing genuine products and educates lawmakers on the advantages of a business climate where intellectual property rights are protected. However, continued efforts may not affect revenue positively and further deterioration in compliance with existing legal protections or reductions in the legal protection for intellectual property rights of software developers could adversely affect revenue.

Taxation of Extraterritorial Income. In August 2001, a World Trade Organization ("WTO") dispute panel determined that the extraterritorial tax ("ETI") provisions of the FSC Repeal and Extraterritorial Income Exclusion Act of 2000 constitute an export subsidy prohibited by the WTO Agreement on Subsidies and Countervailing Measures Agreement. The U.S. government appealed the panel's decision and lost its appeal. On January 29, 2002, the WTO Dispute Settlement Body adopted the Appellate Body report. President Bush has stated the U.S. will bring its tax laws into compliance with the WTO ruling, but the Administration and Congress have not decided on a solution for this issue. In July 2002, Representative Bill Thomas, Chairman of the House Ways and Means Committee, introduced the American Competitiveness and Corporate Accountability Act of 2002. If enacted, that bill would repeal the ETI regime and introduce broad-based international reform. The proposed reforms would not materially affect the Company. On August 30, 2002, a WTO arbitration panel determined that the European Union may impose up to $4.04 billion per year in countermeasures if the U.S. rules are not brought into compliance. The WTO decision does not repeal the ETI tax benefit and it does not require the European Union to impose trade sanctions, so it is not possible to predict what impact the WTO decision will have on future results pending final resolution of these matters. If the ETI exclusion is repealed and replacement legislation is not enacted, the loss of tax benefit to the Company could be significant.

Litigation. As discussed in Note 19—Contingencies of the Notes to Financial Statements, the Company is subject to a variety of claims and lawsuits. While the Company believes that none of the litigation matters in which the Company is currently involved will have a material adverse impact on the Company's financial position or results of operations, it is possible that one or more of these matters could be resolved in a manner that would ultimately have a material adverse impact on the business of the Company, and could negatively impact its revenues and operating margins.

ITEM 7A. QUANTITATIVE AND QUALITATIVE DISCLOSURES ABOUT MARKET RISK

The Company is exposed to foreign currency, interest rate, and equity price risks. A portion of these risks is hedged, but fluctuations could impact the Company's results of operations and financial position. The Company hedges the exposure of accounts receivable and a portion of anticipated revenue to foreign currency fluctuations, primarily with option contracts. The Company monitors its foreign currency exposures daily to maximize the overall effectiveness of its foreign currency hedge positions. Principal currencies hedged include the Euro, Japanese yen, British pound, and Canadian dollar. Fixed income securities are subject to interest rate risk. The portfolio is diversified and consists primarily of investment grade securities to minimize credit risk. The Company routinely uses options to hedge its exposure to interest rate risk in the event of a catastrophic increase in interest rates. Many securities held in the Company's equity and other investments portfolio are subject to price risk. The Company uses options to hedge its price risk on certain highly volatile equity securities.

The Company uses a value-at-risk (VAR) model to estimate and quantify its market risks. VAR is the expected loss, for a given confidence level, in fair value of the Company's portfolio due to adverse market movements over a defined time horizon. The VAR model is not intended to represent actual losses in fair value, but is used as a risk estimation and management tool. The model used for currencies and equities is geometric Brownian motion, which allow incorporation of optionality of these exposures. For interest rates, the mean reverting geometric Brownian motion is used to reflect the principle that fixed-income securities prices over time revert to maturity value.

Value-at-risk is calculated by, first, simulating 10,000 market price paths over 20 days for equities, interest rates and foreign exchange rates, taking into account historical correlations among the different rates and prices. Each resulting unique set of equities prices, interest rates, and foreign exchange rates is applied to substantially all individual holdings to re-price each holding. The 250th worst performance (out of 10,000) represents the value-at-risk over 20 days at the 97.5th percentile. Several risk factors are not captured in the model, including liquidity risk, operational risk, credit risk, and legal risk.

A substantial amount of the Company's equity portfolio is held for strategic purposes. The Company attempts to hedge the value of these securities through the use of derivative contracts such as collars. The Company has incurred substantial impairment charges related to certain of these securities in fiscal 2002 and fiscal 2001. Such impairment charges have been incurred primarily for strategic equity holdings that the Company has not been able to hedge. The VAR amounts disclosed below are not necessarily reflective of potential accounting losses, as they are used as a risk management tool and reflect an estimate of potential reductions in fair value of the Company's portfolio. Losses in fair value over a 20-day holding period can exceed the reported VAR by significant amounts and can also accumulate over a longer time horizon than the 20-day holding period used in the VAR analysis.

The VAR numbers are shown separately for interest rate, currency, and equity risks. These VAR numbers include the underlying portfolio positions and related hedges. Historical data is used to estimate VAR. Given reliance on historical data, VAR is most effective in estimating risk exposures in markets in which there are no fundamental changes or shifts in market conditions. An inherent limitation in VAR is that the distribution of past changes in market risk factors may not produce accurate predictions of future market risk.

Part II
Item 7A, 8

The following table sets forth the VAR calculations for substantially all of the Company's positions:

In millions

Risk Categories	As of June 30,		Year ended June 30, 2002		
	2001	2002	Average	High	Low
Interest rates	$ 363	$ 472	$ 435	$ 535	$ 333
Currency rates	58	310	162	310	58
Equity prices	520	602	584	757	488

The total VAR for the combined risk categories is $908 million at June 30, 2002 and $759 million at June 30, 2001. The total VAR is 34% less at June 30, 2002 and 19% less at June, 30 2001 than the sum of the separate risk categories for each of those years in the above table, due to the diversification benefit of the combination of risks. The reasons for the change in risk in portfolios include: larger investment portfolio size, higher foreign exchange exposure due to stronger non-U.S. currencies, and asset allocation shifts.

ITEM 8.   FINANCIAL STATEMENTS AND SUPPLEMENTARY DATA

INCOME STATEMENTS

In millions, except earnings per share

Year Ended June 30	2000	2001	2002
Revenue	$ 22,956	$ 25,296	$ 28,365
Operating expenses:			
Cost of revenue	3,002	3,455	5,191
Research and development	3,772	4,379	4,307
Sales and marketing	4,126	4,885	5,407
General and administrative	1,050	857	1,550
Total operating expenses	11,950	13,576	16,455
Operating income	11,006	11,720	11,910
Losses on equity investees and other	(57)	(159)	(92)
Investment income/(loss)	3,326	(36)	(305)
Income before income taxes	14,275	11,525	11,513
Provision for income taxes	4,854	3,804	3,684
Income before accounting change	9,421	7,721	7,829
Cumulative effect of accounting change (net of income taxes of $185)	–	(375)	–
Net income	$ 9,421	$ 7,346	$ 7,829
Basic earnings per share:			
Before accounting change	$ 1.81	$ 1.45	$ 1.45
Cumulative effect of accounting change	–	(0.07)	–
	$ 1.81	$ 1.38	$ 1.45
Diluted earnings per share:			
Before accounting change	$ 1.70	$ 1.38	$ 1.41
Cumulative effect of accounting change	–	(0.06)	–
	$ 1.70	$ 1.32	$ 1.41
Weighted average shares outstanding:			
Basic	5,189	5,341	5,406
Diluted	5,536	5,574	5,553

See accompanying notes.

BALANCE SHEETS

In millions

June 30		2001		2002
Assets				
Current assets:				
Cash and equivalents	$	3,922	$	3,016
Short-term investments		27,678		35,636
Total cash and short-term investments		31,600		38,652
Accounts receivable, net		3,671		5,129
Inventories		83		673
Deferred income taxes		1,522		2,112
Other		2,334		2,010
Total current assets		39,210		48,576
Property and equipment, net		2,309		2,268
Equity and other investments		14,361		14,191
Goodwill		1,511		1,426
Intangible assets, net		401		243
Other long-term assets		1,038		942
Total assets	$	58,830	$	67,646
Liabilities and stockholders' equity				
Current liabilities:				
Accounts payable	$	1,188	$	1,208
Accrued compensation		742		1,145
Income taxes		1,468		2,022
Short-term unearned revenue		4,395		5,920
Other		1,461		2,449
Total current liabilities		9,254		12,744
Long-term unearned revenue		1,219		1,823
Deferred income taxes		409		398
Other long-term liabilities		659		501
Commitments and contingencies				
Stockholders' equity:				
Common stock and paid-in capital—shares authorized 12,000;				
Shares issued and outstanding 5,383 and 5,359		28,390		31,647
Retained earnings, including accumulated other comprehensive income of $587 and $583		18,899		20,533
Total stockholders' equity		47,289		52,180
Total liabilities and stockholders' equity	$	58,830	$	67,646

See accompanying notes.

CASH FLOWS STATEMENTS

In millions

Year Ended June 30		2000		2001		2002
Operations						
Net income	$	9,421	$	7,346	$	7,829
Cumulative effect of accounting change, net of tax		–		375		–
Depreciation, amortization, and other noncash items		1,250		1,536		1,084
Net recognized (gains)/losses on investments		(1,732)		2,221		2,424
Stock option income tax benefits		5,535		2,066		1,596
Deferred income taxes		(425)		(420)		(416)
Unearned revenue		6,177		6,970		11,152
Recognition of unearned revenue		(5,600)		(6,369)		(8,929)
Accounts receivable		(944)		(418)		(1,623)
Other current assets		(775)		(482)		(264)
Other long-term assets		(864)		(330)		(9)
Other current liabilities		(992)		774		1,449
Other long-term liabilities		375		153		216
Net cash from operations		11,426		13,422		14,509
Financing						
Common stock issued		2,245		1,620		1,497
Common stock repurchased		(4,896)		(6,074)		(6,069)
Sales/(repurchases) of put warrants		472		(1,367)		–
Preferred stock dividends		(13)		–		–
Other, net		–		235		–
Net cash used for financing		(2,192)		(5,586)		(4,572)
Investing						
Additions to property and equipment		(879)		(1,103)		(770)
Purchases of investments		(42,290)		(66,346)		(89,386)
Maturities of investments		4,025		5,867		8,654
Sales of investments		29,752		52,848		70,657
Net cash used for investing		(9,392)		(8,734)		(10,845)
Net change in cash and equivalents		(158)		(898)		(908)
Effect of exchange rates on cash and equivalents		29		(26)		2
Cash and equivalents, beginning of year		4,975		4,846		3,922
Cash and equivalents, end of year	$	4,846	$	3,922	$	3,016

See accompanying notes.

STOCKHOLDERS' EQUITY STATEMENTS

In millions

Year Ended June 30	2000	2001	2002
Convertible preferred stock			
Balance, beginning of year	$ 980	$ –	$ –
Conversion of preferred to common stock	(980)	–	–
Balance, end of year	–	–	–
Common stock and paid-in capital			
Balance, beginning of year	13,844	23,195	**28,390**
Common stock issued	3,554	5,154	**1,801**
Common stock repurchased	(210)	(394)	**(676)**
Sales/(repurchases) of put warrants	472	(1,367)	**–**
Stock option income tax benefits	5,535	2,066	**1,596**
Other, net	–	(264)	**536**
Balance, end of year	23,195	28,390	**31,647**
Retained earnings			
Balance, beginning of year	13,614	18,173	**18,899**
Net income	9,421	7,346	**7,829**
Other comprehensive income:			
Cumulative effect of accounting change	–	(75)	**–**
Net gains/(losses) on derivative instruments	–	634	**(91)**
Net unrealized investment gains/(losses)	(283)	(1,460)	**5**
Translation adjustments and other	23	(39)	**82**
Comprehensive income	9,161	6,406	**7,825**
Preferred stock dividends	(13)	–	**–**
Immaterial pooling of interests	97	–	**–**
Common stock repurchased	(4,686)	(5,680)	**(6,191)**
Balance, end of year	18,173	18,899	**20,533**
Total stockholders' equity	$ 41,368	$ 47,289	$ **52,180**

See accompanying notes.

NOTES TO FINANCIAL STATEMENTS

NOTE 1   ACCOUNTING POLICIES

ACCOUNTING PRINCIPLES

The financial statements and accompanying notes are prepared in accordance with accounting principles generally accepted in the United States of America.

PRINCIPLES OF CONSOLIDATION

The financial statements include the accounts of Microsoft Corporation and its subsidiaries (Microsoft). Intercompany transactions and balances have been eliminated. Equity investments in which Microsoft owns at least 20% of the voting securities are accounted for using the equity method, except for investments in which the Company is not able to exercise significant influence over the investee, in which case, the cost method of accounting is used. Issuances of shares by a subsidiary are accounted for as capital transactions.

ESTIMATES AND ASSUMPTIONS

Preparing financial statements requires management to make estimates and assumptions that affect the reported amounts of assets, liabilities, revenue, and expenses. Examples include estimates of loss contingencies and product life cycles, and assumptions such as the elements comprising a software arrangement, including the distinction between upgrades/enhancements and new products; when the Company reaches technological feasibility for its products; the potential outcome of the future tax consequences of events that have been recognized in the Company's financial statements or tax returns; and determining when investment impairments are other-than-temporary. Actual results and outcomes may differ from these estimates and assumptions.

FOREIGN CURRENCIES

Assets and liabilities recorded in foreign currencies are translated at the exchange rate on the balance sheet date. Translation adjustments resulting from this process are charged or credited to other comprehensive income (OCI). Revenue and expenses are translated at average rates of exchange prevailing during the year.

REVENUE RECOGNITION

Microsoft accounts for the licensing of software in accordance with American Institute of Certified Public Accountants (AICPA) Statement of Position (SOP) 97-2, *Software Revenue Recognition.* The Company recognizes revenue when (i) persuasive evidence of an arrangement exists; (ii) delivery has occurred or services have been rendered; (iii) the sales price is fixed or determinable; and (iv) collectibility is reasonably assured. For software arrangements with multiple elements, revenue is recognized dependent upon whether vendor-specific objective evidence (VSOE) of fair value exists for each of the elements. When VSOE does not exist for all the elements of a software arrangement and the only undelivered element is postcontract customer support (PCS), the entire licensing fee is recognized ratably over the contract period. Revenue attributable to undelivered elements, including technical support and Internet browser technologies, is based on the average sales price of those elements when sold separately, and is recognized ratably on a straight-line basis over the product's life cycle. PCS and subscription revenue is recognized ratably over the contract period.

Revenue from products licensed to original equipment manufacturers (OEMs) is based on the licensing agreement with an OEM and has historically been recognized when OEMs ship licensed products to their customers. Licensing provisions were modified with the introduction of Windows XP in 2002 and revenue for certain products is recorded upon shipment of the product to OEMs. The effect of this change in licensing provisions was not material. Revenue from packaged product sales to distributors and resellers is usually recorded when related products are shipped. However, when the revenue recognition criteria required for distributor and reseller arrangements are not met, revenue is recognized as payments are received. Revenue related to the Company's Xbox game console is recognized upon shipment of the product to retailers. Online advertising revenue is recognized as advertisements are displayed. Costs related to insignificant obligations, which include telephone support for certain products, are accrued. Provisions are recorded for estimated returns, concessions, and bad debts.

COST OF REVENUE

Cost of revenue includes direct costs to manufacture and distribute product and direct costs to provide online services, consulting, product support, and training and certification of system integrators.

RESEARCH AND DEVELOPMENT

Technological feasibility for Microsoft's software products is reached shortly before the products are released to manufacturing. Costs incurred after technological feasibility is established are not material, and accordingly, the Company expenses all research and development costs when incurred.

ADVERTISING COSTS

Advertising costs are expensed as incurred. Advertising expense was $1.23 billion in 2000, $1.36 billion in 2001, and $1.27 billion in 2002.

INCOME TAXES

Income tax expense includes U.S. and international income taxes, plus the provision for U.S. taxes on undistributed earnings of international subsidiaries not deemed to be permanently invested. Certain items of income and expense are not reported in tax returns and financial statements in the same year. The tax effect of this difference is reported as deferred income taxes.

FINANCIAL INSTRUMENTS

The Company considers all liquid interest-earning investments with a maturity of three months or less at the date of purchase to be cash equivalents. Short-term investments generally mature between three months and six years from the purchase date. Investments with maturities beyond one year may be classified as short-term based on their highly liquid nature and because such marketable securities represent the investment of cash that is available for current operations. All cash and short-term investments are classified as available for sale and are recorded at market value using the specific identification method; unrealized gains and losses are reflected in OCI.

Equity and other investments include debt and equity instruments. Debt securities and publicly traded equity securities are classified as available for sale and are recorded at market using the specific identification method. Unrealized gains and losses (excluding other-than-temporary impairments) are reflected in OCI. All other investments, excluding those accounted for using the equity method, are recorded at cost.

Microsoft lends certain fixed income and equity securities to enhance investment income. Collateral and/or security interest is determined based upon the underlying security and the creditworthiness of the borrower. The fair value of collateral that Microsoft is permitted to sell or repledge was $499 million at both June 30, 2001 and 2002.

Investments are considered to be impaired when a decline in fair value is judged to be other-than-temporary. The Company employs a systematic methodology that considers available evidence in evaluating potential impairment of its investments. In the event that the cost of an investment exceeds its fair value, the Company evaluates, among other factors, the duration and extent to which the fair value is less than cost; the financial health of and business outlook for the investee, including industry and sector performance, changes in technology, and operational and financing cash flow factors; and the Company's intent and ability to hold the investment. Once a decline in fair value is determined to be other-than-temporary, an impairment charge is recorded and a new cost basis in the investment is established. In 2001, the Company recognized $4.80 billion in impairments of certain investments, primarily in the cable and telecommunication industries. In 2002, Microsoft recognized $4.32 billion in impairments of certain investments, primarily related to further declines in the fair values of U.S. and European cable and telecommunications holdings.

The Company uses derivative instruments to manage exposures to foreign currency, security price, and interest rate risks. The Company's objectives for holding derivatives are to minimize these risks using the most effective methods to eliminate or reduce the impact of these exposures.

Foreign Currency Risk. Certain forecasted transactions and assets are exposed to foreign currency risk. The Company monitors its foreign currency exposures daily to maximize the overall effectiveness of its foreign currency hedge positions. Principal currencies hedged include the Euro, Japanese yen, British pound, and Canadian dollar. Options used to hedge a portion of forecasted international revenue for up to three years in the future are designated as cash flow hedging instruments. Options and forwards not designated as hedging instruments under SFAS 133 are also used to hedge the impact of the variability in exchange rates on accounts receivable and collections denominated in certain foreign currencies.

Securities Price Risk. Strategic equity investments are subject to market price risk. From time to time, the Company uses and designates options to hedge fair values and cash flows on certain equity securities. The security, or forecasted sale thereof, selected for hedging is determined by market conditions, up-front costs, and other relevant factors. Once established, the hedges are not dynamically managed or traded, and are generally not removed until maturity.

Interest Rate Risk. Fixed-income securities are subject to interest rate risk. The fixed-income portfolio is diversified and consists primarily of investment grade securities to minimize credit risk. The Company routinely uses options, not designated as hedging instruments, to hedge its exposure to interest rate risk in the event of a catastrophic increase in interest rates.

Other Derivatives. In addition, the Company may invest in warrants to purchase securities of other companies as a strategic investment. Warrants that can be net share settled are deemed derivative financial instruments and are not designated as hedging instruments.

For options designated either as fair value or cash flow hedges, changes in the time value are excluded from the assessment of hedge effectiveness.

ALLOWANCE FOR DOUBTFUL ACCOUNTS

The allowance for doubtful accounts reflects management's best estimate of probable losses inherent in the account receivable balance. Management determines the allowance based on known troubled accounts, historical experience, and other currently available evidence. Activity in the allowance for doubtful accounts is as follows:

In millions

Year Ended June 30	Balance at Beginning of Period		Charged to Costs and Expenses		Write-offs and Other		Balance at End of Period	
2002	$	174	$	192	$	157	$	209
2001		186		157		169		174
2000		204		77		95		186

INVENTORIES

Inventories are stated at the lower of cost or market, using the average cost method. Cost includes materials, labor, and manufacturing overhead related to the purchase and production of inventories.

PROPERTY AND EQUIPMENT

Property and equipment is stated at cost and depreciated using the straight-line method over the shorter of the estimated life of the asset or the lease term, ranging from one to 15 years. Computer software developed or obtained for internal use is depreciated using the straight-line method over the estimated useful life of the software, generally not in excess of three years.

GOODWILL

Beginning in fiscal 2002 with the adoption of SFAS 142, *Goodwill and Other Intangible Assets,* goodwill is no longer amortized, but instead tested for impairment at least annually. Prior to fiscal 2002, goodwill was amortized using the straight-line method over its estimated period of benefit.

INTANGIBLE ASSETS

Intangible assets are amortized using the straight-line method over their estimated period of benefit, ranging from three to seven years. The Company periodically evaluates the recoverability of intangible assets and takes into account events or circumstances that warrant revised estimates of useful lives or that indicate that an impairment exists. All of Microsoft's intangible assets are subject to amortization.

RECLASSIFICATIONS

Certain reclassifications have been made for consistent presentation.

NOTE 2 ACCOUNTING CHANGES

Effective July 1, 2000, the Company adopted SFAS 133, *Accounting for Derivative Instruments and Hedging Activities,* which establishes accounting and reporting standards for derivative instruments, including certain derivative instruments embedded in other contracts and for hedging activities. The adoption of SFAS 133 on July 1, 2000, resulted in a cumulative pre-tax reduction to income of $560 million ($375 million after-tax) and a cumulative pre-tax reduction to OCI of $112 million ($75 million after-tax). The reduction to income was mostly attributable to a loss of approximately $300 million reclassified from OCI for the time value of options and a loss of approximately $250 million reclassified from OCI for derivatives not designated as hedging instruments. The reduction to OCI was mostly attributable to losses of approximately $670 million on cash flow hedges offset by reclassifications out of OCI of the approximately $300 million loss for the time value of options and the approximately $250 million loss for derivative instruments not designated as hedging instruments. The net derivative losses included in OCI as of July 1, 2000 were reclassified into earnings during the twelve months ended June 30, 2001. The change in accounting from the adoption of SFAS 133 did not materially affect net income in 2001.

Effective July 1, 2001, Microsoft adopted SFAS 141, *Business Combinations,* and SFAS 142, *Goodwill and Other Intangible Assets.* SFAS 141 requires business combinations initiated after June 30, 2001 to be accounted for using the purchase method of accounting. It also specifies the types of acquired intangible assets that are required to be recognized and reported separate from goodwill. SFAS 142 requires that goodwill and certain intangibles no longer be amortized, but instead tested for impairment at least annually. There was no impairment of goodwill upon adoption of SFAS 142.

Net income and earnings per share for fiscal 2000 and fiscal 2001 adjusted to exclude amortization expense (net of taxes) is as follows:

In millions, except earnings per share

Year Ended June 30		2000		2001
Net income:				
Reported net income	$	9,421	$	7,346
Goodwill amortization		203		252
Equity method goodwill amortization		1		26
Adjusted net income	$	9,625	$	7,624
Basic earnings per share:				
Reported basic earnings per share	$	1.81	$	1.38
Goodwill amortization		0.04		0.05
Equity method goodwill amortization		–		–
Adjusted basic earnings per share	$	1.85	$	1.43
Diluted earnings per share:				
Reported diluted earnings per share	$	1.70	$	1.32
Goodwill amortization		0.04		0.05
Equity method goodwill amortization		–		–
Adjusted diluted earnings per share	$	1.74	$	1.37

NOTE 3   UNEARNED REVENUE

A portion of Microsoft's revenue under volume licensing programs is earned ratably over the period of the license agreement. Also, revenue attributable to undelivered elements, including technical support and Internet browser technologies, is based on the average sales price of those elements when sold separately, and is recognized ratably on a straight-line basis over the product's life cycle. The percentage of revenue recognized ratably for undelivered elements ranges from approximately 20% to 25% for Windows XP Home, approximately 10% to 15% for Windows XP Professional, and approximately 10% to 15% for desktop applications, depending on the terms and conditions of the license and prices of the elements. Product life cycles are currently estimated at three years for Windows operating systems and 18 months for desktop applications.

The components of unearned revenue were as follows:

In millions

June 30		2001		2002
Volume licensing programs	$	1,922	$	**4,158**
Undelivered elements		2,818		**2,830**
Other		874		**755**
Unearned revenue	$	5,614	$	**7,743**

Unearned revenue by product was as follows:

In millions

June 30		2001		2002
Desktop Applications	$	2,189	$	**3,489**
Desktop Platforms		2,586		**3,198**
Enterprise Software and Services		391		**791**
Desktop and Enterprise Software and Services		5,166		**7,478**
Consumer Software, Services, and Devices, and Other		448		**265**
Unearned revenue	$	5,614	$	**7,743**

Of the $7.74 billion of unearned revenue at June 30, 2002, $2.28 billion is expected to be recognized in the first quarter of fiscal 2003, $1.64 billion in the second quarter of fiscal 2003, $1.18 billion in the third quarter of fiscal 2003, $817 million in the fourth quarter of fiscal 2003, and $1.82 billion thereafter.

NOTE 4   CASH AND SHORT-TERM INVESTMENTS

In millions

June 30, 2001	Cost Basis		Unrealized Gains		Unrealized Losses		Recorded Basis	
Cash and equivalents:								
Cash	$	1,145	$	–	$	–	$	1,145
Commercial paper		894		–		–		894
Certificates of deposit		286		–		–		286
U.S. government and agency securities		400		–		–		400
Corporate notes and bonds		1,130		–		–		1,130
Municipal securities		67		–		–		67
Cash and equivalents		3,922		–		–		3,922
Short-term investments:								
Commercial paper		635		3		–		638
U.S. government and agency securities		7,355		9		(42)		7,322
Corporate notes and bonds		17,256		214		(149)		17,321
Municipal securities		1,662		41		–		1,703
Certificates of deposit		694		–		–		694
Short-term investments		27,602		267		(191)		27,678
Cash and short-term investments	$	31,524	$	267	$	(191)	$	31,600

In millions

June 30, 2002	Cost Basis		Unrealized Gains		Unrealized Losses		Recorded Basis	
Cash and equivalents:								
Cash	$	1,114	$	–	$	–	$	1,114
Commercial paper		260		–		–		260
Certificates of deposit		31		–		–		31
Money market mutual funds		714		–		–		714
Corporate notes and bonds		560		–		–		560
Municipal securities		337		–		–		337
Cash and equivalents		3,016		–		–		3,016
Short-term investments:								
Commercial paper		552		–		–		552
U.S. government and agency securities		10,726		114		(13)		10,827
Corporate notes and bonds		18,822		255		(241)		18,836
Municipal securities		4,462		86		–		4,548
Certificates of deposit		873		–		–		873
Short-term investments		35,435		455		(254)		35,636
Cash and short-term investments	$	38,451	$	455	$	(254)	$	38,652

Realized gains and (losses) from cash and short-term investments were $80 million and $(226) million in 2000, $541 million and $(369) million in 2001, and $816 million and $(558) million in 2002.

NOTE 5   INVENTORIES

In millions

June 30	2001	2002
Finished goods	$ 78	$ 505
Raw materials and work in process	5	168
Inventories	$ 83	$ 673

NOTE 6   PROPERTY AND EQUIPMENT

In millions

June 30	2001	2002
Land	$ 185	$ 197
Buildings	1,584	1,701
Computer equipment and software	2,292	2,621
Other	1,214	1,372
Property and equipment – at cost	5,275	5,891
Accumulated depreciation	(2,966)	(3,623)
Property and equipment – net	$ 2,309	$ 2,268

During 2000, 2001, and 2002, depreciation expense, of which the majority related to computer equipment, was $668 million, $764 million, and $820 million.

NOTE 7   EQUITY AND OTHER INVESTMENTS

In millions

June 30, 2001	Cost Basis	Unrealized Gains	Unrealized Losses	Recorded Basis
Debt securities recorded at market, maturing:				
Within one year	$ 500	$ –	$ –	$ 500
Between 2 and 10 years	643	12	(3)	652
Between 10 and 15 years	513	–	(9)	504
Beyond 15 years	4,754	–	(829)	3,925
Debt securities recorded at market	6,410	12	(841)	5,581
Common stock and warrants	5,555	2,030	(285)	7,300
Preferred stock	881	–	–	881
Other investments	599	–	–	599
Equity and other investments	$ 13,445	$ 2,042	$ (1,126)	$ 14,361

Part II
Item 8

In millions

June 30, 2002	Cost Basis	Unrealized Gains	Unrealized Losses	Recorded Basis
Debt securities recorded at market, maturing:				
Within one year	$ 485	$ 26	$ –	$ 511
Between 2 and 10 years	893	46	(4)	935
Between 10 and 15 years	541	19	(2)	558
Beyond 15 years	3,036	–	–	3,036
Debt securities recorded at market	4,955	91	(6)	5,040
Common stock and warrants	6,930	1,287	(617)	7,600
Preferred stock	1,382	–	–	1,382
Other investments	169	–	–	169
Equity and other investments	$ 13,436	$ 1,378	$ (623)	$ 14,191

Debt securities include corporate and government notes and bonds and derivative securities. Debt securities maturing beyond 15 years are composed entirely of AT&T 5% convertible preferred debt with a contractual maturity of 30 years. The debt is convertible at the Company's option into AT&T common stock on or after December 1, 2000, or may be redeemed by AT&T upon satisfaction of certain conditions on or after June 1, 2002. In connection with the definitive agreement to combine AT&T Broadband with Comcast in a new company to be called AT&T Comcast Corporation, Microsoft has agreed to exchange its AT&T 5% convertible preferred debt securities for approximately 115 million shares of AT&T Comcast Corporation. It is expected that the transaction will close by December 31, 2002. While it is possible that Microsoft could incur a loss on this exchange transaction up to the carrying value of the AT&T debt securities, management believes that the ultimate loss, if any, will be significantly less. As management is unable to predict whether there will be a gain or loss on the exchange, no loss has been recorded related to this contingent exchange transaction as of June 30, 2002.

Equity securities that are restricted for more than one year or not publicly traded are recorded at cost. At June 30, 2001 the estimated fair value of these investments in excess of their recorded basis was $161 million. At June 30, 2002 the recorded basis of these investments in excess of their estimated fair value was $34 million. This excess of cost over estimated fair value was deemed temporary in nature. The estimate of fair value is based on publicly available market information or other estimates determined by management. Realized gains and (losses) from equity and other investments (excluding impairments discussed previously) were $1.94 billion and $(10) million in 2000, $3.03 billion and $(23) million in 2001, and $2.24 billion and $(121) million in 2002.

NOTE 8   GOODWILL

During fiscal 2002, goodwill was reduced by $85 million, principally in connection with Microsoft's exchange of all of its 33.7 million shares and warrants of Expedia, Inc. to USA Networks, Inc. No goodwill was acquired or impaired during fiscal 2002. As of June 30, 2002, Desktop and Enterprise Software and Services goodwill was $1.1 billion, Consumer Software, Services, and Devices goodwill was $258 million, and Consumer Commerce Investments goodwill was $72 million.

NOTE 9   INTANGIBLE ASSETS

During fiscal 2002, changes in intangible assets primarily relates to the Company's acquisition of $25 million in patents and licenses and $27 million in existing technology, which will be amortized over approximately 3 years. No significant residual value is estimated for these intangible assets. Intangible assets amortization expense was $202 million for fiscal 2001 and $194 million for fiscal 2002. The components of intangible assets were as follows:

In millions

June 30	2001		2002	
	Gross Carrying Amount	Accumulated Amortization	Gross Carrying Amount	Accumulated Amortization
Patents and licenses	$ 407	$ (177)	$ 421	$ (290)
Existing technology	157	(27)	172	(71)
Trademarks, tradenames and other	83	(42)	15	(4)
Intangible assets	$ 647	$ (246)	$ 608	$ (365)

Amortization expense for the net carrying amount of intangible assets at June 30, 2002 is estimated to be $115 million in fiscal 2003, $90 million in fiscal 2004, $36 million in fiscal 2005, and $2 million in fiscal 2006.

NOTE 10   DERIVATIVES

For fiscal 2001, investment income included a net unrealized loss of $592 million, comprised of a $214 million gain for changes in the time value of options for fair value hedges, $211 million loss for changes in the time value of options for cash flow hedges, and $595 million loss for changes in the fair value of derivative instruments not designated as hedging instruments. For fiscal 2002, investment income included a net unrealized loss of $480 million, comprised of a $30 million gain for changes in the time value of options for fair value hedges, $331 million loss for changes in the time value of options for cash flow hedges, and $179 million net loss for changes in the fair value of derivative instruments not designated as hedging instruments.

Derivative gains and losses included in OCI are reclassified into earnings at the time forecasted revenue or the sale of an equity investment is recognized. During fiscal 2001, $214 million of derivative gains were reclassified to revenue and $416 million of derivative losses were reclassified to investment income/(loss). During fiscal 2002, $234 million of derivative gains were reclassified to revenue and $10 million of derivative losses were reclassified to investment income/(loss). The derivative losses reclassified to investment income/(loss) were offset by gains on the item being hedged. The Company estimates that $63 million of net derivative gains included in other comprehensive income will be reclassified into earnings within the next twelve months.

For instruments designated as hedges, hedge ineffectiveness, determined in accordance with SFAS 133, had no impact on earnings for the fiscal 2001 and 2002. No fair value hedges or cash flow hedges were derecognized or discontinued for fiscal 2001 and 2002.

NOTE 11   INVESTMENT INCOME/(LOSS)

The components of investment income/(loss) are as follows:

In millions

Year Ended June 30	2000	2001	2002
Dividends	$ 363	$ 377	$ 357
Interest	1,231	1,808	1,762
Net recognized gains/(losses) on investments:			
Net gains on the sales of investments	1,780	3,175	2,379
Other-than-temporary impairments	(29)	(4,804)	(4,323)
Net unrealized losses attributable to derivative instruments	(19)	(592)	(480)
Net recognized gains/(losses) on investments	1,732	(2,221)	(2,424)
Investment income/(loss)	$ 3,326	$ (36)	$ (305)

NOTE 12   INCOME TAXES

The provision for income taxes consisted of:

In millions

Year Ended June 30	2000	2001	2002
Current taxes:			
U.S. and state	$ 4,744	$ 3,243	$ 3,644
International	535	514	575
Current taxes	5,279	3,757	4,219
Deferred taxes	(425)	47	(535)
Provision for income taxes	$ 4,854	$ 3,804	$ 3,684

U.S. and international components of income before income taxes were:

In millions

Year Ended June 30	2000	2001	2002
U.S.	$ 11,860	$ 9,189	$ 8,920
International	2,415	2,336	2,593
Income before income taxes	$ 14,275	$ 11,525	$ 11,513

In 2000, the effective tax rate was 34.0%, and included the effect of a 2.5% reduction from the U.S. statutory rate for tax credits and a 1.5% increase for other items. In 2001, the effective tax rate was 33.0%, and included the effect of a 3.1% reduction from the U.S. statutory rate for tax credits and a 1.1% increase for other items. The effective tax rate in 2002 was 32.0%, and included the effect of a 2.4% reduction from the U.S. statutory rate for the extraterritorial income exclusion tax benefit and a 0.6% reduction for other items.

Deferred income taxes were:

In millions

June 30	2001	2002
Deferred income tax assets:		
Revenue items	$ 1,469	$ 2,261
Expense items	691	945
Impaired investments	1,070	2,016
Deferred income tax assets	$ 3,230	$ 5,222
Deferred income tax liabilities:		
Unrealized gain on investments	$ (395)	$ (887)
International earnings	(1,667)	(1,818)
Other	(55)	(803)
Deferred income tax liabilities	$ (2,117)	$ (3,508)

Microsoft has not provided for U.S. deferred income taxes or foreign withholding taxes on $780 million of its undistributed earnings for certain non-U.S. subsidiaries, all of which relate to fiscal 2002 earnings, since these earnings are intended to be reinvested indefinitely.

On September 15, 2000, the U.S. Tax Court issued an adverse ruling with respect to Microsoft's claim that the Internal Revenue Service (IRS) incorrectly assessed taxes for 1990 and 1991. The Company has filed an appeal with the Ninth Circuit Court of Appeals on this matter. Income taxes, except for items related to the 1990 and 1991 assessments, have been settled with the IRS for all years through 1996. The IRS is examining the Company's 1997 through 1999 U.S. income tax returns. Management believes any adjustments which may be required will not be material to the financial statements. Income taxes paid were $800 million in 2000, $1.3 billion in 2001, and $1.9 billion in 2002.

NOTE 13   STOCKHOLDERS' EQUITY

Shares of common stock outstanding were as follows:

In millions

Year Ended June 30	2000	2001	2002
Balance, beginning of year	5,109	5,283	5,383
Issued	229	189	104
Repurchased	(55)	(89)	(128)
Balance, end of year	5,283	5,383	5,359

The Company repurchases its common shares in the open market to provide shares for issuance to employees under stock option and stock purchase plans. In 2002, the Company acquired 5.1 million of its shares as a result of a structured stock repurchase transaction entered into in 2001, which gave it the right to acquire such shares in exchange for an up-front net payment of $264 million. To enhance its stock repurchase program, Microsoft has sold put warrants to independent third parties. These put warrants entitled the holders to sell shares of Microsoft common stock to the Company on certain dates at specified prices. In the third quarter of fiscal 2001, the Company issued 2.8 million shares to settle a portion of the outstanding put warrants. At June 30, 2001 and 2002, there were no outstanding put warrants.

During 1996, Microsoft issued 12.5 million shares of 2.75% convertible exchangeable principal-protected preferred stock. The Company's convertible preferred stock matured on December 15, 1999. Each preferred share was converted into 1.1273 common shares.

NOTE 14   OTHER COMPREHENSIVE INCOME

In millions

Year Ended June 30	2000	2001	2002
Cumulative effect of accounting change, net of tax effect of $(37)	$ –	$ (75)	$ –
Net gains/(losses) on derivative instruments:			
Unrealized gains, net of tax effect of $246 in 2001 and $30 in 2002	–	499	55
Reclassification adjustment for (gains)/losses included in net income, net of tax effect of $67 in 2001 and $(79) in 2002	–	135	(146)
Net gains/(losses) on derivative instruments	–	634	(91)
Net unrealized investment gains/(losses):			
Unrealized holding gains/(losses), net of tax effect of $248 in 2000, $(351) in 2001, and $(955) in 2002	531	(1,200)	(1,774)
Reclassification adjustment for (gains)/losses included in net income, net of tax effect of $(420) in 2000, $(128) in 2001, and $958 in 2002	(814)	(260)	1,779
Net unrealized investment gains/(losses)	(283)	(1,460)	5
Translation adjustments and other	23	(39)	82
Other comprehensive income/(loss)	$ (260)	$ (940)	$ (4)

The components of accumulated other comprehensive income were:

In millions

June 30	2001	2002
Net gains on derivative instruments	$ 177	$ 86
Net unrealized investment gains	598	603
Translation adjustments and other	(188)	(106)
Accumulated other comprehensive income	$ 587	$ 583

NOTE 15   EMPLOYEE STOCK AND SAVINGS PLANS

EMPLOYEE STOCK PURCHASE PLAN

The Company has an employee stock purchase plan for all eligible employees. Under the plan, shares of the Company's common stock may be purchased at six-month intervals at 85% of the lower of the fair market value on the first or the last day of each six-month period. Employees may purchase shares having a value not exceeding 15% of their gross compensation during an offering period. During 2000, 2001, and 2002, employees purchased 2.5 million, 5.7 million, and 5.4 million shares at average prices of $72.38, $36.87, and $50.52 per share. At June 30, 2002, 56.8 million shares were reserved for future issuance.

SAVINGS PLAN

The Company has a savings plan, which qualifies under Section 401(k) of the Internal Revenue Code. Participating employees may contribute up to 25% of their pretax salary, but not more than statutory limits. The Company contributes fifty cents for each dollar a participant contributes, with a maximum contribution of 3% of a participant's earnings. Matching contributions were $47 million, $63 million, and $77 million in 2000, 2001, and 2002.

STOCK OPTION PLANS

The Company has stock option plans for directors, officers, and employees, which provide for nonqualified and incentive stock options. Options granted prior to 1995 generally vest over four and one-half years and expire 10 years from the date of grant. Options granted between 1995 and 2001 generally vest over four and one-half years and expire seven years from the date of grant, while certain options vest either over four and one-half years or over seven and one-half years and expire after 10 years. Options granted during 2002 vest over four and one-half years and expire 10 years from the date of grant. At June 30, 2002, options for 371 million shares were vested and 543 million shares were available for future grants under the plans.

Stock options outstanding were as follows:

In millions, except per share amounts

	Shares	Price per Share Range	Weighted Average
Balance, June 30, 1999	766	$ 0.56 – $ 83.28	$ 23.87
Granted	304	65.56 – 119.13	79.87
Exercised	(198)	0.56 – 82.94	9.54
Canceled	(40)	4.63 – 116.56	36.50
Balance, June 30, 2000	832	0.56 – 119.13	41.23
Granted	224	41.50 – 80.00	60.84
Exercised	(123)	0.59 – 85.81	11.13
Canceled	(35)	13.83 – 119.13	63.57
Balance, June 30, 2001	898	0.56 – 119.13	49.54
Granted	41	48.62 – 72.57	62.50
Exercised	(99)	1.02 – 69.81	12.82
Canceled	(38)	1.15 – 116.56	68.67
Balance, June 30, 2002	802	0.79 – 119.13	53.75

For various price ranges, weighted average characteristics of outstanding stock options at June 30, 2002 were as follows:

In millions, except per share amounts

Range of Exercise Prices	Outstanding Options Shares	Remaining Life (Years)	Weighted Average Price	Exercisable Options Shares	Weighted Average Price
$ 0.79 – $ 5.97	36	1.6	$ 4.83	35	$ 4.82
5.98 – 13.62	44	0.5	11.19	42	11.18
13.63 – 29.80	90	2.0	15.02	84	14.97
29.81 – 43.62	73	2.7	32.19	66	32.09
43.63 – 60.00	191	6.9	55.81	41	54.03
60.01 – 69.50	146	6.4	66.24	35	66.53
69.51 – 83.28	80	5.1	71.17	21	71.84
83.29 – 119.13	142	4.2	89.87	47	89.29

The Company follows Accounting Principles Board Opinion 25, *Accounting for Stock Issued to Employees,* to account for stock option and employee stock purchase plans. An alternative method of accounting for stock options is SFAS 123, *Accounting for Stock-Based Compensation.* Employee stock options are valued at grant date using the Black-Scholes valuation model, and this compensation cost is recognized ratably over the vesting period.

Had compensation cost for the Company's stock option and employee stock purchase plans been determined as prescribed by SFAS 123, pro forma income statements for 2000, 2001, and 2002 would have been as follows:

In millions, except per share amounts

Year Ended June 30	2000		2001		2002	
	Reported	Pro Forma	Reported	Pro Forma	Reported	Pro Forma
Revenue	$ 22,956	$ 22,956	$ 25,296	$ 25,296	$ 28,365	$ 28,365
Operating expenses:						
Cost of revenue	3,002	3,277	3,455	3,775	5,191	5,699
Research and development	3,772	4,814	4,379	6,106	4,307	6,299
Sales and marketing	4,126	4,468	4,885	5,888	5,407	6,252
General and administrative	1,050	1,284	857	1,184	1,550	1,843
Total operating expenses	11,950	13,843	13,576	16,953	16,455	20,093
Operating income	11,006	9,113	11,720	8,343	11,910	8,272
Losses on equity investees and other	(57)	(57)	(159)	(159)	(92)	(92)
Investment income/(loss)	3,326	3,326	(36)	(36)	(305)	(305)
Income before income taxes	14,275	12,382	11,525	8,148	11,513	7,875
Provision for income taxes	4,854	4,210	3,804	2,689	3,684	2,520
Income before accounting change	9,421	8,172	7,721	5,459	7,829	5,355
Cumulative effect of accounting change	–	–	(375)	(375)	–	–
Net income	$ 9,421	$ 8,172	$ 7,346	$ 5,084	$ 7,829	$ 5,355
Basic earnings per share	$ 1.81	$ 1.57	$ 1.38	$ 0.95	$ 1.45	$ 0.99
Diluted earnings per share	$ 1.70	$ 1.48	$ 1.32	$ 0.91	$ 1.41	$ 0.98

The weighted average Black-Scholes value of options granted under the stock option plans during 2000, 2001, and 2002 was $36.67, $29.31, and $31.57. Value was estimated using a weighted average expected life of 6.2 years in 2000, 6.4 years in 2001, and 7.0 years in 2002, no dividends, volatility of .33 in 2000, .39 in 2001, and .39 in 2002, and risk-free interest rates of 6.2%, 5.3%, and 5.4% in 2000, 2001, and 2002.

NOTE 16   EARNINGS PER SHARE

Basic earnings per share is computed on the basis of the weighted average number of common shares outstanding. Diluted earnings per share is computed on the basis of the weighted average number of common shares outstanding plus the effect of outstanding preferred shares using the "if-converted" method, outstanding put warrants using the "reverse treasury stock" method, and outstanding stock options using the "treasury stock" method.

The components of basic and diluted earnings per share were as follows:

In millions, except per share amounts

Year Ended June 30		2000		2001		2002
Income before accounting change	$	9,421	$	7,721	$	7,829
Preferred stock dividends		13		–		–
Net income available for common shareholders	$	9,408	$	7,721	$	7,829
Weighted average outstanding shares of common stock		5,189		5,341		5,406
Dilutive effect of:						
Put warrants		2		21		–
Preferred stock		7		–		–
Employee stock options		338		212		147
Common stock and common stock equivalents		5,536		5,574		5,553
Earnings per share before accounting change:						
Basic	$	1.81	$	1.45	$	1.45
Diluted	$	1.70	$	1.38	$	1.41

For the years ended June 30, 2000, 2001 and 2002, 45 million, 351 million, and 373 million shares attributable to outstanding stock options were excluded from the calculation of diluted earnings per share because the effect was antidilutive.

NOTE 17   OPERATIONAL TRANSACTIONS

In January 2000, the Company acquired Visio Corporation in a transaction that was accounted for as a pooling of interests. Microsoft issued 14 million shares valued at approximately $1.5 billion in the exchange for the outstanding stock of Visio. Visio's assets and liabilities, which were nominal, are included with those of Microsoft as of the merger. Operating results for Visio from periods prior to the merger were not material to the combined results of the two companies. Accordingly, the financial statements for such periods have not been restated.

In April 2001, the Company acquired Great Plains Software, Inc. for approximately $1.1 billion in stock. Great Plains is a leading supplier of mid-market business applications. The acquisition was accounted for by the purchase method and operating results for Great Plains subsequent to the date of acquisition are included with those of Microsoft. The pro forma impact of Great Plains' operating results prior to the date of acquisition was not material.

NOTE 18   COMMITMENTS

The Company has operating leases for most U.S. and international sales and support offices and certain equipment. Rental expense for operating leases was $201 million, $281 million, and $318 million in 2000, 2001, and 2002. Future minimum rental commitments under noncancellable leases, in millions of dollars, are: 2003, $260; 2004, $219; 2005, $197; 2006, $170; 2007, $135; and thereafter, $302. Microsoft has committed $111 million for constructing new buildings. In addition, the Company has guaranteed $536 million in debt of its equity investees.

NOTE 19   CONTINGENCIES

The Company is a defendant in *U.S. v. Microsoft*, a lawsuit filed by the Antitrust Division of the U.S. Department of Justice (DOJ) and a group of eighteen state Attorneys General alleging violations of the Sherman Act and various state antitrust laws. After the trial, the District Court entered Findings of Fact and Conclusions of Law stating that Microsoft had violated Sections 1 and 2 of the Sherman Act and various state antitrust laws. A Judgment was entered on June 7, 2000 ordering, among other things, the breakup of Microsoft into two companies.

The Judgment was stayed pending an appeal. On June 28, 2001, the U.S. Court of Appeals for the District of Columbia Circuit affirmed in part, reversed in part, and vacated the Judgment in its entirety and remanded the case to the District Court for a new trial on one Section 1 claim and for entry of a new judgment consistent with its ruling. In its ruling, the Court of Appeals substantially narrowed the bases of liability found by the District Court, but affirmed some of the District Court's conclusions that Microsoft had violated Section 2. On October 12, 2001, the trial court held a status conference and entered orders requiring the parties to engage in settlement discussions until November 2, 2001. Microsoft entered into a settlement with the United States on November 2, 2001. Nine states (New York, Ohio, Illinois, Kentucky, Louisiana, Maryland, Michigan, North Carolina and Wisconsin) agreed to settle on substantially the same terms on November 6, 2001. A hearing on the settlement was held by the Court on March 6, 2002. The Court will now decide whether to approve the settlement as being in the public interest. Nine states and the District of Columbia continue to litigate the remedies phase of *U.S. v. Microsoft*. The non-settling states are seeking imposition of a remedy that would impose much broader restrictions on Microsoft's business than the proposed settlement with the DOJ and nine other states. The Court conducted an evidentiary hearing related to the non-settling states' proposed remedies from March 18 to June 19, 2002. A decision is anticipated later in calendar 2002.

In other ongoing investigations, the DOJ and several state Attorneys General have requested information from Microsoft concerning various issues. In addition, the European Commission has instituted proceedings in which it alleges that Microsoft has failed to disclose information that Microsoft competitors claim they need to interoperate fully with Windows 2000 clients and servers and has engaged in discriminatory licensing of such technology, as well as improper bundling of multimedia playback technology in the Windows operating system. The remedies sought, though not fully defined, include mandatory disclosure of Microsoft Windows operating system technology and imposition of fines. Microsoft denies the European Commission's allegations and intends to contest the proceedings vigorously.

A large number of overcharge class action lawsuits have been initiated against Microsoft in various state and Federal courts. These cases allege that Microsoft has competed unfairly and unlawfully monopolized alleged markets for operating systems and certain software applications and seek to recover alleged overcharges that the complaints contend Microsoft charged for these products. Microsoft believes the claims are without merit and is vigorously defending the cases. To date, Microsoft has won dismissals of all claims for damages by indirect purchasers under Federal law and in 17 separate state court proceedings, of which seven have been affirmed and one has been reversed. Claims on behalf of foreign purchasers have also been dismissed. Appeals of several of these rulings are still pending. No trials or other proceedings have been held concerning any liability issues. Courts in several states have ruled that these cases may proceed as class actions, while two courts have denied class certification status to the claims in that state proceeding and another has ruled that no class action is available for claims in that state. In fiscal 2002, the Company recorded a contingent liability of approximately $660 million representing management's estimate of the costs of resolving the contingency. Management's contingent liability estimate is based upon a proposed settlement between Microsoft and lead counsel for the Federal plaintiffs. While the proposed settlement was not approved by the District Court, management believes that the proposal represents the best estimate of the costs of resolving the contingency based on currently available information. The Company intends to continue vigorously defending these lawsuits.

Netscape Communications Inc., a subsidiary of AOL-Time Warner Inc., filed suit against Microsoft on January 22, 2002 in Federal court in the District of Columbia, alleging violations of antitrust and unfair competition laws and other tort claims relating to Netscape and its Navigator browser. The complaint includes claims of unlawful monopolization or attempted monopolization of alleged markets for operating systems and Web browsers, illegal tying of operating systems and browsers, and tortuous interference with Netscape's business relations. Netscape seeks injunctive relief, unquantified treble damages and its fees and costs. Microsoft denies these allegations and will vigorously defend this action. The case has been transferred for pretrial purposes to the District Court in Baltimore, Maryland and is being coordinated with the overcharge class actions described above.

Be Incorporated, a former software development company whose assets were acquired by Palm Incorporated in August 2001, filed suit against Microsoft on February 18, 2002 in Federal court in San Francisco, alleging violations of Federal and state antitrust and unfair competition laws and other tort claims. Be alleges that Microsoft's license agreements with computer manufacturers, pricing policies, and business practices interfered with Be's relationships with computer manufacturers and discouraged them from adopting Be's own operating system for their products. Be is seeking unquantified treble and punitive damages for its alleged injuries along with its fees and costs. Microsoft denies these allegations and will vigorously defend this action. The case has been transferred for pretrial purposes to the District Court in Baltimore, Maryland and is being coordinated with the overcharge class actions described above.

On March 8, 2002, Sun Microsystems, Inc. filed suit against Microsoft alleging violations of Federal and state antitrust and unfair competition laws as well as claims under the Federal Copyright Act. Sun seeks injunctive relief and unspecified treble damages along with its fees and costs. Microsoft denies these allegations and will vigorously defend this action. The case has been transferred for pretrial purposes to the District Court in Baltimore, Maryland and is being coordinated with the overcharge class actions described above.

On June 3, 2002, Microsoft and the Securities and Exchange Commission entered into an administrative settlement resolving a non-public investigation of certain of Microsoft's accounting and record keeping practices during fiscal years 1995 through 1998 (SEC File No. 3-10789). The settlement provides that Microsoft will not violate securities regulations that require companies to make accurate filings and maintain sufficient records and controls. The settlement has no impact on the Company's financial results.

The Company is also subject to a variety of other claims and suits that arise from time to time in the ordinary course of its business.

Management currently believes that resolving all of these matters will not have a material adverse impact on the Company's financial position or its results of operations.

Part II
Item 8

NOTE 20   SEGMENT INFORMATION

In millions

Year Ended June 30	Desktop and Enterprise Software and Services	Consumer Software, Services, and Devices	Consumer Commerce Investments	Other	Reconciling Amounts	Consolidated
2000						
Revenue	$ 20,410	$ 1,654	$ 182	$ 691	$ 19	$ 22,956
Operating income/(loss)	13,210	(1,090)	(60)	86	(1,140)	11,006
2001						
Revenue	$ 22,720	$ 1,961	$ 522	$ 652	$ (559)	$ 25,296
Operating income/(loss)	14,261	(1,666)	(222)	97	(750)	11,720
2002						
Revenue	$ 23,786	$ 3,531	$ 245	$ 537	$ 266	$ 28,365
Operating income/(loss)	14,671	(1,778)	23	59	(1,065)	11,910

Desktop and Enterprise Software and Services Revenue:

In millions

Year Ended June 30	2000	2001	2002
Desktop Applications	$ 9,013	$ 9,580	$ 9,327
Desktop Platforms	7,383	8,265	9,276
Desktop Software	16,396	17,845	18,603
Enterprise Software and Services	4,014	4,875	5,183
Total Desktop and Enterprise Software and Services	$ 20,410	$ 22,720	$ 23,786

In fiscal 2002, Microsoft had four segments: Desktop and Enterprise Software and Services; Consumer Software, Services, and Devices; Consumer Commerce Investments; and Other. Desktop and Enterprise Software and Services operating segment includes Desktop Applications, Desktop Platforms, and Enterprise Software and Services. Desktop Applications include Microsoft Office; Microsoft Project; Visio; client access licenses for Windows NT Server and Windows 2000 Server, Exchange, and BackOffice; Microsoft Great Plains; and bCentral. Desktop Platforms include Windows XP Professional and Home, Windows 2000 Professional, Windows NT Workstation, Windows Millennium Edition (Windows Me), Windows 98, and other desktop operating systems. Enterprise Software and Services includes Server Platforms; Server Applications; developer tools and services; and Enterprise services. Consumer Software, Services, and Devices operating segment includes Xbox video game system, MSN Internet access, MSN network services, PC and online games, learning and productivity software, mobility, and embedded systems. Consumer Commerce Investments operating segment includes Expedia, Inc., the HomeAdvisor online real estate service, and the CarPoint online automotive service. Other primarily includes Hardware and Microsoft Press.

Segment information is presented in accordance with SFAS 131, *Disclosures about Segments of an Enterprise and Related Information.* This standard is based on a management approach, which requires segmentation based upon the Company's internal organization and disclosure of revenue and operating income based upon internal accounting methods. The Company's financial reporting systems present various data for management to run the business, including internal profit and loss statements (P&Ls) prepared on a basis not consistent with U.S. generally accepted accounting principles. Assets are not allocated to segments for internal reporting presentations.

Reconciling items for revenue include certain elements of unearned revenue and the treatment of certain channel inventory amounts and estimates. In addition to the reconciling items for revenue, reconciling items for operating income/(loss) include general and administrative expenses ($1.05 billion in 2000, $857 million in 2001, and $1.55 billion in 2002), certain research expenses ($141 million in 2000, $154 million in 2001, and $166 million in 2002), and other corporate level adjustments. The internal P&Ls use accelerated methods of depreciation and amortization. Additionally, losses on equity investees and minority interests are classified in operating income for internal reporting presentations.

Revenue attributable to U.S. operations includes shipments to customers in the United States, licensing to OEMs and certain multinational organizations, and exports of finished goods, primarily to Asia, Latin America, and Canada. Revenue from U.S. operations totaled $15.7 billion, $17.8 billion, and $20.9 billion in 2000, 2001, and 2002. Revenue from outside the United States, excluding licensing to OEMs and certain multinational organizations and U.S. exports, totaled $7.3 billion, $7.5 billion, and $7.5 billion in 2000, 2001, and 2002. No single customer accounted for 10% or more of revenue in 2000, 2001, or 2002.

Long-lived assets (principally property and equipment) totaled $2.2 billion and $2.0 billion in the United States in 2001 and 2002 and $154 million and $220 million in other countries in 2001 and 2002.

NOTE 21   SUBSEQUENT EVENT

On July 11, 2002, Microsoft acquired Navision a/s as a result of the successful close of a tender offer. Microsoft purchased Navision's shares for approximately $1.45 billion in stock and cash. Navision is a provider of integrated business software solutions for small and medium-sized companies. The purchase price allocation is currently being developed for this acquisition.

QUARTERLY INFORMATION

In millions, except per share amounts (unaudited)

Quarter Ended	Sept. 30	Dec. 31	Mar. 31	June 30	Year
Fiscal 2000					
Revenue	$ 5,384	$ 6,112	$ 5,656	$ 5,804	$ 22,956
Gross profit	4,672	5,356	4,904	5,022	19,954
Net income	2,191	2,436	2,385	2,409	9,421
Basic earnings per share	0.43	0.47	0.46	0.46	1.81
Diluted earnings per share	0.40	0.44	0.43	0.44	1.70
Fiscal 2001					
Revenue	$ 5,766	$ 6,550	$ 6,403	$ 6,577	$ 25,296
Gross profit	4,941	5,686	5,504	5,710	21,841
Net income	2,206[1]	2,624	2,451	65[2]	7,346
Basic earnings per share	0.42[1]	0.49	0.46	0.01	1.38
Diluted earnings per share	0.40[1]	0.47	0.44	0.01	1.32
Fiscal 2002					
Revenue	$ 6,126	$ 7,741	$ 7,245	$ 7,253	$ 28,365
Gross profit	5,242	6,197	5,850	5,885	23,174
Net income	1,283[3]	2,283	2,738[4]	1,525[5]	7,829
Basic earnings per share	0.24	0.42	0.51	0.28	1.45
Diluted earnings per share	0.23	0.41	0.49	0.28	1.41

(1) Includes an unfavorable cumulative effect of accounting change of $375 million or $0.07 per basic share and $0.06 per diluted share, reflecting the adoption of SFAS No. 133.

(2) Includes $3.92 billion (pre-tax) in impairments of certain investments.

(3) Includes $1.82 billion (pre-tax) in impairments of certain investments.

(4) Includes $1.25 billion (pre-tax) gain on the sale of Expedia, Inc. and $1.19 billion (pre-tax) in impairments of certain investments.

(5) Includes $1.19 billion (pre-tax) in impairments of certain investments.

INDEPENDENT AUDITORS' REPORT

To the Board of Directors and Stockholders of Microsoft Corporation:

We have audited the accompanying consolidated balance sheets of Microsoft Corporation and subsidiaries (the Company) as of June 30, 2001 and 2002, and the related consolidated statements of income, cash flows, and stockholders' equity for each of the three years in the period ended June 30, 2002. These financial statements are the responsibility of the Company's management. Our responsibility is to express an opinion on these financial statements based on our audits.

We conducted our audits in accordance with auditing standards generally accepted in the United States of America. Those standards require that we plan and perform the audit to obtain reasonable assurance about whether the financial statements are free of material misstatement. An audit includes examining, on a test basis, evidence supporting the amounts and disclosures in the financial statements. An audit also includes assessing the accounting principles used and significant estimates made by management, as well as evaluating the overall financial statement presentation. We believe that our audits provide a reasonable basis for our opinion.

In our opinion, such consolidated financial statements present fairly, in all material respects, the financial position of Microsoft Corporation and subsidiaries as of June 30, 2001 and 2002, and the results of their operations and their cash flows for each of the three years in the period ended June 30, 2002 in conformity with accounting principles generally accepted in the United States of America.

As described in Note 2 to the financial statements, the Company adopted Statement of Financial Accounting Standards No. 133, *Accounting for Derivative Instruments and Hedging Activities*, effective July 1, 2000, and Statement of Financial Accounting Standards No. 142, *Goodwill and Other Intangible Assets*, effective July 1, 2001.

/s/ DELOITTE & TOUCHE LLP

Deloitte & Touche LLP
Seattle, Washington
July 18, 2002

ITEM 9.   CHANGES IN AND DISAGREEMENTS WITH ACCOUNTANTS
ON ACCOUNTING AND FINANCIAL DISCLOSURES

None.

PART III

ITEM 10. DIRECTORS OF THE REGISTRANT

Information with respect to Directors may be found under the caption "Election of Directors and Management Information" of the Company's Proxy Statement for the Annual Meeting of Shareholders to be held November 5, 2002 (the "Proxy Statement"). Such information is incorporated herein by reference.

ITEM 11. EXECUTIVE COMPENSATION

The information in the Proxy Statement set forth under the captions "Information Regarding Executive Officer Compensation" and "Information Regarding the Board and its Committees" is incorporated herein by reference.

ITEM 12. SECURITY OWNERSHIP OF CERTAIN BENEFICIAL OWNERS AND MANAGEMENT AND RELATED STOCKHOLDER MATTERS

EQUITY COMPENSATION PLAN INFORMATION

In millions, except per share amounts

June 30, 2002 Plan category	(a) Number of securities to be issued upon exercise of outstanding options, warrants and rights	(b) Weighted-average exercise price of outstanding options, warrants and rights	(c) Number of securities remaining available for future issuance under equity compensation plans (excluding securities reflected in column (a))
Equity compensation plans approved by security holders	802	$ 53.75	600
Equity compensation plans not approved by security holders	–	–	–
Total	802	$ 53.75	600

The information set forth under the caption "Information Regarding Beneficial Ownership of Principal Shareholders, Directors, and Management" of the Proxy Statement is incorporated herein by reference.

ITEM 13. CERTAIN RELATIONSHIPS AND RELATED TRANSACTIONS

The information set forth under the captions "Certain Relationships and Related Transactions" of the Proxy Statement is incorporated herein by reference.

PART IV

ITEM 14.   EXHIBITS, FINANCIAL STATEMENT SCHEDULES, AND REPORTS ON FORM 8-K

(a) Financial Statements and Schedules

The financial statements are set forth under Item 8 of this report on Form 10-K. Financial statement schedules have been omitted since they are either not required, not applicable, or the information is otherwise included.

(b) Reports on Form 8-K

The Company filed no reports on Form 8-K during the quarter ended June 30, 2002.

(c) Exhibit Listing

Exhibit Number	Description
3.1	Restated Articles of Incorporation of Microsoft Corporation (1)
3.2	Bylaws of Microsoft Corporation
10.1	Microsoft Corporation 2001 Stock Plan (2)
10.2	Microsoft Corporation 1991 Stock Option Plan (3)
10.3	Microsoft Corporation 1981 Stock Option Plan (4)
10.4	Microsoft Corporation 1999 Stock Option Plan for Non-Employee Directors (5)
10.5	Microsoft Corporation Stock Option Plan for Consultants and Advisors
10.6	Microsoft Corporation 1997 Employee Stock Purchase Plan (6)
10.7	Microsoft Corporation Savings Plus Plan (7)
10.8	Trust Agreement dated June 1, 1993 between Microsoft Corporation and First Interstate Bank of Washington
10.9	Form of Indemnification Agreement
10.10	Resignation Agreement between Richard Belluzzo and Microsoft Corporation
21.	Subsidiaries of Registrant
23.	Independent Auditors' Consent
99.1	Certification Pursuant to 18 U.S.C. Section 1350, as Adopted Pursuant to Section 906 of the Sarbanes-Oxley Act of 2002
99.2	Certification Pursuant to 18 U.S.C. Section 1350, as Adopted Pursuant to Section 906 of the Sarbanes-Oxley Act of 2002

(1) Incorporated by reference to Annual Report on Form 10-K For The Fiscal Year Ended June 30, 1999.

(2) Incorporated by reference to Registration Statement 333-52-852 on Form S-8.

(3) Incorporated by reference to Annual Report on Form 10-K For The Fiscal Year Ended June 30, 1997.

(4) Incorporated by reference to Registration Statement 33-37623 on Form S-8.

(5) Incorporated by reference to Registration Statement 333-91755 on Form S-8.

(6) Incorporated by reference to Annual Report on Form 10-K For The Fiscal Year Ended June 30, 2001.

(7) Incorporated by reference to Annual Report on Form 10-K For The Fiscal Year Ended June 30, 2000.

SIGNATURES

Pursuant to the requirements of Section 13 or 15(d) of the Securities Exchange Act of 1934, the Registrant has duly caused this report to be signed on its behalf by the undersigned; thereunto duly authorized, in the City of Redmond, State of Washington, on September 5, 2002.

MICROSOFT CORPORATION

By /s/ JOHN G. CONNORS
_____
John G. Connors
Senior Vice President; Chief Financial Officer

Pursuant to the requirements of the Securities Exchange Act of 1934, this report has been signed below by the following persons on behalf of Registrant and in the capacities indicated on September 5, 2002.

Signature	Title
/s/ WILLIAM H. GATES, III William H. Gates, III	Chairman of the Board of Directors and Chief Software Architect
/s/ STEVEN A. BALLMER Steven A. Ballmer	Chief Executive Officer
/s/ JAMES I. CASH, JR. James I. Cash, Jr.	Director
/s/ RAYMOND V. GILMARTIN Raymond V. Gilmartin	Director
/s/ ANN MCLAUGHLIN KOROLOGOS Ann McLaughlin Korologos	Director
/s/ DAVID F. MARQUARDT David F. Marquardt	Director
/s/ WM. G. REED, JR. Wm. G. Reed, Jr.	Director
/s/ JON A. SHIRLEY Jon A. Shirley	Director
/s/ JOHN G. CONNORS John G. Connors	Senior Vice President; Chief Financial Officer (Principal Financial and Accounting Officer)

CERTIFICATIONS

I, Steven A. Ballmer, certify that:

1. I have reviewed this annual report on Form 10-K of Microsoft Corporation;

2. Based on my knowledge, this annual report does not contain any untrue statement of a material fact or omit to state a material fact necessary to make the statements made, in light of the circumstances under which such statements were made, not misleading with respect to the period covered by this annual report; and

3. Based on my knowledge, the financial statements, and other financial information included in this annual report, fairly present in all material respects the financial condition, results of operations and cash flows of the registrant as of, and for, the periods presented in this annual report.

Date: September 5, 2002

/s/ STEVEN A. BALLMER
_____
Steven A. Ballmer
Chief Executive Officer

I, John G. Connors, certify that:

1. I have reviewed this annual report on Form 10-K of Microsoft Corporation;

2. Based on my knowledge, this annual report does not contain any untrue statement of a material fact or omit to state a material fact necessary to make the statements made, in light of the circumstances under which such statements were made, not misleading with respect to the period covered by this annual report; and

3. Based on my knowledge, the financial statements, and other financial information included in this annual report, fairly present in all material respects the financial condition, results of operations and cash flows of the registrant as of, and for, the periods presented in this annual report.

Date: September 5, 2002

/s/ JOHN G. CONNORS
_____
John G. Connors
Chief Financial Officer

WORLDWIDE MARKETING LOCATIONS*

WWW.MICROSOFT.COM/WORLDWIDE/

Argentina	www.microsoft.com/argentina/	Lebanon	www.microsoft.com/middleeast/
Australia	www.microsoft.com/australia/	Luxembourg	www.microsoft.com/Belux/
Austria	www.microsoft.at/	Malaysia	www.microsoft.com/malaysia/
Belgium	www.microsoft.com/Belux/	Mauritius	www.microsoft.com/africa/ioi/
Bolivia	www.microsoft.com/bolivia/	Mexico	www.microsoft.com/mexico/
Brazil	www.microsoft.com/brasil/	Morocco	www.microsoft.com/northafrica/Morocco/
Bulgaria	www.microsoft.com/bulgaria/	Namibia	www.microsoft.com/africa/southern/
Canada	www.microsoft.com/canada/	Netherlands	www.microsoft.com/netherlands/
Chile	www.microsoft.com/chile/	New Zealand	www.microsoft.com/nz/
China	www.microsoft.com/china/	Nigeria	www.microsoft.com/africa/nigeria/
Colombia	www.microsoft.com/colombia/	Norway	www.microsoft.com/norge/
Costa Rica	www.microsoft.com/costarica/	Pakistan	www.microsoft.com/asia/asiapacific/
Cote d'Ivoire	www.microsoft.com/africa/	Panama	www.microsoft.com/panama/
Croatia	www.microsoft.com/Croatia/	Peru	www.microsoft.com/peru/
Czech Republic	www.microsoft.com/cze/	Philippines	www.microsoft.com/philippines/
Denmark	www.microsoft.com/danmark/	Poland	www.microsoft.com/poland/
Dominican Republic	www.microsoft.com/dominicana/	Portugal	www.microsoft.com/portugal/
Ecuador	www.microsoft.com/ecuador/	Puerto Rico	www.microsoft.com/puertorico/
Egypt	www.microsoft.com/egypt/	Romania	www.microsoft.com/romania/
El Salvador	www.microsoft.com/elsalvador/	Russia	www.microsoft.com/rus/
Finland	www.microsoft.com/finland/	Saudi Arabia	www.microsoft.com/saudi/
France	www.microsoft.com/France/	Singapore	www.microsoft.com/singapore/
Germany	www.microsoft.com/germany/	Slovakia	www.microsoft.com/slovakia/
Greece	www.microsoft.com/hellas/	Slovenia	www.microsoft.com/slovenija/
Guatemala	www.microsoft.com/guatemala/	South Africa	www.microsoft.com/southafrica/
Hong Kong	www.microsoft.com/hk/	Spain	www.microsoft.com/spain/
Hungary	www.microsoft.com/hun/	Sweden	www.microsoft.com/sverige/
India	www.microsoft.com/india/	Switzerland	www.microsoft.com/switzerland/
Indonesia	www.microsoft.com/indonesia/	Taiwan	www.microsoft.com/taiwan/
Ireland	www.microsoft.com/ireland/	Thailand	www.microsoft.com/thailand/
Israel	www.microsoft.com/israel/	Tunisia	www.microsoft.com/northafrica/tunisia/
Italy	www.microsoft.com/italy/	Turkey	www.microsoft.com/turkiye/
Jamaica	www.microsoft.com/westindies/jamaica/	Ukraine	www.microsoft.com/rus/
Japan	www.microsoft.com/japan/	United Arab Emirates	www.microsoft.com/middleeast/
Jordan	www.microsoft.com/middleeast/	United Kingdom	www.microsoft.com/uk/
Kenya	www.microsoft.com/africa/east/	Uruguay	www.microsoft.com/uruguay/
Korea	www.microsoft.com/korea/	Venezuela	www.microsoft.com/venezuela/
Kuwait	www.microsoft.com/middleeast/	Vietnam	www.microsoft.com/vietnam/
Latvia	www.microsoft.com/latvija/		

* For a complete list of subsidiaries, joint ventures, and other legal entities, See the Exhibits to the Company's Form 10-K as Filed with the Securities and Exchange Commission

DIRECTORS AND OFFICERS OF MICROSOFT CORPORATION

DIRECTORS

William H. Gates, III
Chairman;
Chief Software Architect,
Microsoft Corporation

Steven A. Ballmer
Chief Executive Officer,
Microsoft Corporation

James I. Cash Jr.
James E. Robison Professor,
Harvard Business School;
Chairman, Harvard Business
School Publishing

Raymond V. Gilmartin
Chairman; President;
Chief Executive Officer,
Merck & Co., Inc.

Ann McLaughlin Korologos
Chairman Emeritus,
The Aspen Institute;
Senior Advisor, Benedetto,
Gartland & Co., Inc.

David F. Marquardt
General Partner,
August Capital

Wm. G. Reed Jr.
Chairman (retired),
Simpson Investment
Company

Jon A. Shirley
President;
Chief Operating
Officer (retired),
Microsoft Corporation

EXECUTIVE OFFICERS

William H. Gates, III
Chairman of the Board;
Chief Software Architect

Steven A. Ballmer
Chief Executive Officer

James E. Allchin
Group Vice President,
Platforms Group

Orlando Ayala
Group Vice President,
Worldwide Sales, Marketing,
and Services Group

Robert J. (Robbie) Bach
Senior Vice President,
Games Division

Douglas J. Burgum
Senior Vice President,
Business Solutions

David W. Cole
Senior Vice President,
MSN and Personal Services

John G. Connors
Senior Vice President;
Chief Financial Officer

Jean-Philippe Courtois
President, Europe,
Middle East & Africa

Jon Stephan DeVaan
Senior Vice President;
TV Division

Richard P. Emerson
Senior Vice President,
Corporate Development
and Strategy

Paul Flessner
Senior Vice President,
.NET Enterprise Servers

Robert J. (Bob) Herbold
Executive Vice President,
Chief Operating Officer
(Retired)

Kevin R. Johnson
Senior Vice President,
Microsoft Americas

Robert L. Muglia
Senior Vice President,
Enterprise Storage Division

Craig J. Mundie
Senior Vice President and
Chief Technology Officer,
Advanced Strategies
and Policy

Jeffrey S. Raikes
Group Vice President,
Productivity and
Business Services

Richard F. Rashid
Senior Vice President,
Research

Eric D. Rudder
Senior Vice President,
Developer and Platform
Evangelism

Steven J. Sinofsky
Senior Vice President,
Office

Bradford L. Smith
Senior Vice President
and General Counsel

Brian Valentine
Senior Vice President,
Windows

David Vaskevitch
Senior Vice President;
Chief Technical Officer,
Business Platforms

Deborah N. Willingham
Senior Vice President,
Human Resources

DIRECTORS AND OFFICERS OF MICROSOFT CORPORATION

OFFICERS

Brian E. Arbogast
Corporate Vice President,
.NET Core Services
Platform

Deborah A. Black
Corporate Vice President,
Platforms

Scott M. Boggs
Corporate Vice President,
Corporate Controller

Richard I. (Dick) Brass
Corporate Vice President,
Technology Development

Lisa E. Brummel
Corporate Vice President,
Home and Entertainment
Division

Thomas L. (Tom) Button
Corporate Vice President,
Developer Marketing and
Enterprise Tools

Brent Callinicos
Corporate Vice President,
Treasurer

Juha C. Christensen
Corporate Vice President,
Mobility Marketing

Rodrigo Costa
Corporate Vice President,
Original Equipment
Manufacturers

Kurt D. DelBene
Corporate Vice President,
Authoring & Collaborative
Services

Richard R. (Rick) Devenuti
Corporate Vice President,
Chief Information Officer

Gerri T. Elliott
Corporate Vice President,
Industry Solutions Group

Joseph E. Eschbach
Corporate Vice President,
Information Worker, Product
Mgmt Group

Edward (Ed) Fries
Corporate Vice President,
Game Content

Susumu (Sam) Furukawa
Vice President,
Advanced Strategy
& Policy, Japan

Grant N. W. George
Corporate Vice President,
Office Test and Operations

Ralf Harteneck
Corporate Vice President,
Communications and
Meeting Services

Kathleen C. Hebert
Corporate Vice President

Blake J. Irving
Corporate Vice President,
MSN Communications

Bruce A. Jaffe
Corporate Vice President,
MSN Business
Development

Theodore C. (Ted) Johnson
Corporate Vice President,
Business Tools

**Christopher R.
(Chris) Jones**
Corporate Vice President,
Windows Client

Norman B. Judah
Corporate Vice President,
Business Development

Richard J. (Rich) Kaplan
Corporate Vice President,
Content Delivery and
Development Group

Jawad Khaki
Corporate Vice President,
Windows Networking and
Communications

Pieter C. Knook
Corporate Vice President,
Network Service Providers
& Mobility Devices

Mitch L. Koch
Corporate Vice President,
Worldwide Retail Sales
& Marketing, Home &
Entertainment Division

**Theodore G. (Ted)
Kummert**
Corporate Vice President,
Subscription Software

Michel Lacombe
Chairman, Europe,
Middle East & Africa

Bruce A. Leak
Corporate Vice President

Kai-Fu Lee
Corporate Vice President,
Natural Interactive
Services Division

Andrew P. Lees
Corporate Vice President,
US Marketing & Sales

Lewis Levin
Corporate Vice President,
Business Intelligence
Applications

Dan'l Lewin
Corporate Vice President,
.NET Business
Development

Moshe Lichtman
Corporate Vice President,
MSTV

Dr. Daniel T. Ling
Corporate Vice President,
Research

Alexandra W. Loeb
Corporate Vice President,
Tablet PC

Gordon J. Mangione
Corporate Vice President,
SQL Server

**Michelle J. (Mich)
Mathews**
Corporate Vice President,
Marketing

Richard J. McAniff
Corporate Vice President,
Data and Developer
Services

Yusuf I. Mehdi
Corporate Vice President,
MSN

Lori J. Moore Ross
Corporate Vice President,
Product Support Services

Satya Nadella
Corporate Vice President,
Business Solutions
Applications

Michael L. (Mike) Nash
Corporate Vice President,
Security

Yuval Neeman
Corporate Vice President,
Enterprise Storage Division

William C. (Bill) Norman
Corporate Vice President,
Worldwide Operations

Umberto Paolucci
Corporate Vice President,
Europe, Middle East &
Africa, Corporate and
Government Strategy

Sanjay Parthasarathy
Corporate Vice President,
.NET Strategy

Peter D. Pathe
Corporate Vice President,
Structured Document
Services

William (Will) Poole
Corporate Vice President,
New Media Platforms
Division

Michael C. Rawding
Corporate Vice President,
Asia Pacific & Japan

Tami Reller
Corporate Vice President,
Business Solution

Peter Rinearson
Corporate Vice President,
Information Worker New
Markets

Stephen A. (Steve) Schiro
Corporate Vice President,
Retail Sales, South Pacific
& Americas Region,
Home & Entertainment
Division

Robert T. Short
Corporate Vice President,
Windows Core Technology

Michael J. (Mike) Sinneck
Corporate Vice President,
Worldwide Service

Rex C. Smith
Corporate Vice President,
MSN Operations

Mary E. Snapp
Vice President,
Deputy General Counsel,
Product Development
and Marketing

S. Somasegar
Corporate Vice President,
Windows Engineering
Solutions and Services

Lindsay Sparks
Corporate Vice President,
Worldwide Small &
Medium Business Group

Charles G. V. Stevens
Corporate Vice President,
Enterprise Storage Division

Kirill Tatarinov
Corporate Vice President,
Windows Systems
Management

David M. Thompson
Corporate Vice President,
Windows Server
Product Group

Michael J. Toutonghi
Corporate Vice President,
eHome

Jodi A. Uecker-Rust
Corporate Vice President,
Business Solutions Sales,
Marketing, and Services

William L. (Bill) Veghte
Corporate Vice President,
Windows Server Group

Bernard Vergnes
Chairman Emeritus,
Europe, Middle East
& Africa

Hank P. Vigil
Corporate Vice President,
Consumer Strategy and
Partnerships

Ben Waldman
Corporate Vice President

Rogers A. Weed
Corporate Vice President,
Windows Product
Management

accretive Any investment that provides a positive return (increases net income and EPS).

activity-based costing (ABC) A method of attributing costs to products based on first assigning costs of resources to activities and then costs of activities to products or other cost objects.

activity-based management (ABM) The identification and use of costs drivers and performance measures to manage the costs, quality, and timeliness of activities.

appraisal costs Costs of quality that specifically relate to the effort of inspecting, testing, and sampling activities performed in order to identify and remove low-quality products and services from the system.

asset turnover ratio An overall measure of how effectively assets are used during a period; computed by dividing revenue by average total assets.

Balanced Scorecard A new management model designed to link together performance measurers for financial, customer, internal process, and learning/growth perspectives that are unique to an organization's particular strategy.

batch-level activities Activities that take place in order to support a batch or production run, regardless of the size.

benchmarking A performance evaluation process used by companies to target areas for improvement by comparing the company's financial and operating performance against the performance of other companies or by comparing the performance of internal departments against each other.

break-even point The amount of sales at which total costs of the number of units sold equal total revenues; the point at which there is no profit or loss.

budget A quantitative expression of a plan of action that shows how a firm or an organization will acquire and use resources over some specified period of time.

budget committee A management group responsible for establishing budgeting policy and for coordinating the preparation of budgets.

budgetary slack The process of inflating a department's budget request for resource inputs (e.g.,

materials, labor, time, etc.) or deflating the department's budget commitment to output (products, services, etc.) so that the department manager can more easily achieve the budget.

budgeted product cost sheet A schedule of all of the product costs (i.e., the costs of direct materials, direct labor, and manufacturing overhead) used to create a single product.

budgeted service cost sheet A schedule of all of the service costs (i.e., the costs of supplies, wages and salaries, and overhead) used to provide a single service event.

capability costs Costs necessary to have the capability to produce a particular product or to provide a particular service. Capability costs are also known as the costs of product line activities.

capital The total amount of money or other resources owned or used to acquire future income or benefits.

capital budgeting Systematic planning for long-term investments in operating assets.

capital rationing Allocating limited resources among ranked acceptable investments.

cash budget A schedule of expected cash receipts and disbursements during the budget period.

cash inflows Any current or expected revenues or savings directly associated with an investment.

cash outflows The initial cost and other expected outlays associated with an investment.

centralized company An organization in which top management makes most of the major decisions for the entire company rather than delegating decisions to managers at lower levels.

channel The distribution line that a product travels from the original manufacturer to the eventual end-user customer. The channel is typically composed of a manufacturer, a wholesaler, a retailer, and the end-user customer.

common costs Manufacturing overhead costs, such as executive salaries or property taxes, that cannot be attributed to products. Costs of facility support activities are common costs.

contribution margin The difference between total sales and variable costs; the portion of sales revenue available to cover fixed costs and provide a profit.

contribution margin ratio The percentage of net sales revenue left after variable costs are deducted; the contribution margin divided by net sales revenue.

controlling Implementing management plans and identifying how plans compare with actual performance.

conversion costs The costs of converting raw materials to finished products; include direct labor and manufacturing overhead costs.

cost behavior The way a cost is affected by changes in activity levels.

cost center An organizational unit in which a manager has control over and is held accountable for cost performance.

cost driver A factor that determines an activity cost. An activity can have more than one cost driver.

cost of capital The average cost of a firm's debt and equity capital; equals the rate of return that a company must earn in order to satisfy the demands of its owners and creditors.

Cost of Goods Manufactured schedule A schedule supporting the income statement that summarizes the total cost of goods manufactured and transferred out of the work-in-process inventory account during a period. These costs include direct materials, direct labor, and applied manufacturing overhead.

costs of quality (COQ) Costs spent to achieve high quality of products and services, as well as costs spent when products fail to have high quality. The four types of costs of quality are prevention costs, appraisal costs, internal failure costs, and external failure costs.

cost-volume-profit (C-V-P) analysis Techniques for determining how changes in revenues, costs, and level of activity affect the profitability of an organization.

critical resource factor The resource that limits operating capacity by its availability.

cross-subsidization A distortion of costs that occurs when costs of one product are erroneously assigned to another product.

curvilinear costs Variable costs that do not vary in direct proportion to changes in activity level but vary at decreasing or increasing rates due to economies of scale, productivity changes, and so on.

cycle time The total time a product spends moving through a particular process or cycle within the organization, such as the product design cycle, the production cycle, or the order and delivery cycle.

days in inventory Average number of days of use provided by the level of inventory maintained by the organization. This definition is closely related to the "inventory turnover" concept. Days in inventory is computed as number of days in the period being assessed divided by the inventory turnover. (See related definition and computation for *inventory turnover*.)

death spiral A series of management decisions based on bad information that results in reducing or removing activities or segments from the organization that are actually profitable.

decentralized company An organization in which managers at all levels have the authority to make decisions concerning the operations for which they are responsible.

differential costs Future costs that change as a result of a decision; also called incremental or relevant costs.

direct costs Costs that are specifically traceable to a unit of business or segment being analyzed.

direct labor Wages that are paid to those who physically work on direct materials to transform them into a finished product and are traceable to specific products.

direct labor budget A schedule of direct labor requirements for the budget period.

direct materials Materials that become part of the product and are traceable to it.

direct materials budget A schedule of direct materials to be used during the budget period and direct materials to be purchased during that period.

discounted cash flow methods Capital budgeting techniques that take into account the time value of money by comparing discounted cash flows.

disposable income Income left after withholdings and fixed expenses have been subtracted from gross salary; the amount left to cover variable expenditures.

economic order quantity (EOQ) A specific calculation used to determine the most cost-effective size of a purchase order. The EOQ balances the cost of placing an order against the costs of carrying inventory in the organization.

economic profit The difference between net operating profit and holding costs of inventory and other asset investments. Note that generally accepted accounting principles (GAAP) do not formally recognize opportunity costs such as holding costs.

Economic Value Analysis (EVA™) A commercialized performance measurement system that emphasizes the incremental profits an organization creates over and above the profit required to cover the costs of capital.

equivalent units of production A method used in a process costing system to measure the production output during a period. Equivalent units of production essentially measures the "work done" by the center or department in terms of units of output.

estimated manufacturing overhead Budgeted manufacturing overhead costs that are used to establish the predetermined overhead rate.

evaluating Analyzing results, rewarding performance, and identifying problems.

exception reports Reports that highlight variances from, or exceptions to, the budget.

external failure costs Costs of quality that specifically relate to the costs that occur when low-quality products and services fail after production and delivery to customers.

facility support activities Activities necessary to have a facility in place in order to participate in the development and production of products or services. However, these activities are not related to any particular line of products or services. Costs of facility support activities are often called common costs.

finished goods inventory Inventory that has completed the production process and is ready for sale to customers.

fixed costs Costs that remain constant in total, regardless of activity level, at least over a certain range of activity.

fixed manufacturing overhead budget variance The difference between actual fixed manufacturing overhead incurred and the standard (or budgeted) fixed manufacturing overhead established at the beginning of the reporting period.

flexible budget A quantified plan that projects revenues and costs for varying levels of activity.

goal congruence The selection of goals for responsibility centers that are consistent, or congruent, with those of the company as a whole.

Hierarchical Product Cost Model A method of categorizing costs based on types of activities. Activity types include unit-level activities, batch-level activities, product line activities, and facility support activities.

high-low method A method of segregating the fixed and variable components of a mixed cost by analyzing the costs at the highest and the lowest activity levels within a relevant range.

holding costs The financial opportunity costs that result from investing money in an asset such as inventory. Whatever income the money could generate in an alternative investment is the holding costs of the current investment.

hurdle rate The minimum rate of return that an investment must provide in order to be acceptable.

indirect costs Costs normally incurred for the benefit of several segments within the organization; sometimes called common costs or joint costs.

indirect labor Labor that is necessary to a manufacturing or service business but is not directly related to the actual production of the manufactured or service product.

indirect materials Materials that are necessary to a manufacturing or service business but are not directly included in or are not a significant part of the actual product.

industry volume variance The part of the sales volume variance that accounts for the impact on sales revenue of an actual total market size that is different from the expected size.

interest The payment (cost) for the use of money.

internal failure costs Costs of quality that specifically relate to the expenses that occur when low-quality products and services fail before production and delivery to customers.

internal rate of return The "true" discount rate that will produce a net present value of zero when applied to the cash flows of investment inventory goods held for resale.

internal rate of return method A capital budgeting technique that uses discounted cash flows to find the "true" discount rate of an investment; this true rate produces a net present value of zero.

interpolation A method of determining the internal rate of return when the factor for that rate lies between the factors given in the present value table.

inventory shrinkage The disorder, spoilage, and theft that result when a company chooses to maintain inventory on site, resulting in additional out-of-pocket costs to replace inventory.

inventory turnover The number of times the inventory in the organization "turns over" duing a period of time. It is also often easier to think of inventory turnover as the number of times a dollar invested in inventory generates output. Output for raw materials inventory is measured by the cost of raw materials used in production. Output for work-in-process inventory is measured by cost of goods manufactured. Output for finished goods (or merchandise) inventory is measured by cost or goods sold. Inventory turnover is computed as total output for the period divided by average inventory value.

inventory turnover (stockturns) The number of times the inventory in an organization "turns over" during a period of time. It is often easier to think of inventory turnover as the number of times a dollar invested in inventory is sold during a period of time. Inventory turnover is computed as cost of goods sold divided by average inventory value.

investment center An organizational unit in which a manager has control over and is held accountable for cost, revenue, and asset performance.

job order costing A method of product costing whereby each job, product, or batch of products is costed separately.

joint manufacturing process When one material input is used to produce more than one product.

joint product costs The costs that a firm incurs before the point at which the different products are separated for further processing or immediate sale.

just-in-time (JIT) A management philosophy that emphasizes removing all waste of effort, time, and inventory costs from the organization. One obvious result of JIT is the reduction or removal of needless inventory in a production process.

labor efficiency variance The extent to which the actual labor used varies from the standard quantity; computed by multiplying the difference between the actual quantity of labor used and the standard quantity of labor allowed by the standard rate.

labor rate variance The extent to which the actual labor rate varies from the standard rate for the quantity of labor used; computed by multiplying the difference between the actual rate and the standard rate by the quantity of labor used.

lagging indicators Measures that indicate the success of past business activities. Lagging indicators are related to the concept "outcome measures."

lead time Generally, the time interval between initiating a request and finally fulfilling the request.

leading indicators Measures that indicate the potential success of future business activities. Leading indicators are related to the concept "leading measures."

leading measures Measures that, if successfully implemented, will support desired performance in other business activities. Note that some leading measures can also serve as outcome measures.

least squares method A method of segregating the fixed and variable portions of a mixed cost; the regression line, a line of averages, is statistically fitted through all cost points.

least-cost decision A decision to undertake the project with the smallest negative net present value.

life cycle costing The process of measuring all costs involved in creating, producing, and using a product or service. Life cycle costing is not limited to costs incurred by the organization measuring these costs but also includes all costs incurred by the suppliers and the customers of the product or service.

line of credit An arrangement whereby a bank agrees to loan an amount of money (up to a certain limit) on demand for short periods of time, usually less than a year.

logistics The management process involved in obtaining, managing, and transporting inventory and other assets in organizations.

management by exception The strategy of focusing attention on significant deviations from a standard.

manufacturing organizations Organizations that focus on using labor and/or machinery to convert raw materials into marketable products.

manufacturing overhead All costs incurred in the manufacturing process other than direct materials and direct labor.

manufacturing overhead budget A schedule of production costs other than those for direct labor and direct materials.

manufacturing overhead rate The rate at which manufacturing overhead is assigned to products; equals estimated manufacturing overhead for the period divided by the number of units of the activity base being used.

market share The percentage share one company receives of the total sales revenue in the economy for a particular product or service.

market share variance The part of the sales volume variance that accounts for the difference between the actual market share of each product sold and the expected market share of each product sold.

master budget A network of many separate schedules and budgets that together constitute the overall operating and financing plan for the coming period.

materials price variance The extent to which the actual price varies from the standard price for the quantity of materials purchased or used; computed by multiplying the difference between the actual and standard prices by the quantity purchased or used.

materials quantity variance The extent to which the actual quantity of materials varies from the standard quantity; computed by multiplying the difference between the actual quantity of materials used and the standard quantity of materials allowed by the standard price.

merchandising organizations Organizations that focus on procuring tangible products, then distributing them to customers. These customers may include individuals or other business organizations such as manufacturing organizations.

mixed costs Costs that contain both variable and fixed cost components.

net operating profit The difference between normal business sales and normal business expenses.

net present value The difference between the present values of an investment's expected cash inflows and outflows.

net present value method A capital budgeting technique that uses discounted cash flows to compare the present values of an investment's expected cash inflows and outflows.

non-value-added activities Unnecessary activities in a production or service process that customers typically do not see or care about and for which they are unwilling to pay.

operating leverage The extent to which fixed costs are part of a company's cost structure; the higher the proportion of fixed costs to variable costs, the faster income increases or decreases with changes in sales volume.

operational budgeting Managerial planning decisions regarding current operations and those of the immediate future (typically one year or less) that are characterized by regularity and frequency.

opportunity costs The benefits lost or forfeited as a result of selecting one alternative course of action over another.

outcome measures Measures of desired outcome performance in activities critical to an organization's strategic goals. Note that some outcome measures are also leading measures to support desired performance in other business activities.

out-of-pocket costs Costs that require an outlay of cash or other resources.

overapplied manufacturing overhead The excess of applied manufacturing overhead (based on a predetermined application rate) over the actual manufacturing overhead costs for a period.

participative budgeting A bottom-up approach to budgeting where each division manager prepares a budget request for his or her segment.

payback method A capital budgeting technique that determines the amount of time it takes the net cash inflows of an investment to repay the investment cost.

performance measures A general term used to describe all measures designed to capture information about performance related to a particular activity or process.

period costs Costs not directly related to a product, service, or asset. These costs are charged as expenses to the income statement in the period in which they are incurred.

per-unit contribution margin The excess of the sales price of one unit over its variable costs.

planning Outlining the activities that need to be performed for an organization to achieve its objectives.

predetermined overhead rate A rate at which estimated manufacturing overhead costs are assigned to products throughout the year; equals total estimated manufacturing overhead costs divided by a suitable allocation base, such as number of units produced, direct labor hours, direct materials used, or direct labor costs.

prevention costs Costs of quality that specifically relate to the effort to ensure that processes are performed correctly the first time and that products and services meet customers' expectations.

prime costs The direct costs that are "primarily seen" in the product (i.e., direct materials and direct labor).

process costing A method of product costing whereby costs are accumulated by process or work centers and averaged over all products manufactured in a center or department during a particular production period. There are two methods of process costing: The FIFO method separately tracks the costs of beginning work-in-process units and the costs of units started in the current production period. The weighted-average method (not discussed in this text) averages together the costs of beginning work-in-process units and the costs of units started in the current production period.

product costs Costs associated with products or services offered.

product line activities Activities that take place in order to support a product line, regardless of the number of batches or individual units actually produced. Costs of product line activities are also known as capability costs.

production budget A schedule of production requirements for the budget period.

production cost report A document that compiles all the costs of a manufacturing center for a particular production period. The information on this report is used to control and evaluate production costs, as well as transfer costs and units of output from one manufacturing center to another.

production prioritizing Management's continual evaluation of the profitability of the various product lines and divisions within an organization so that products or divisions that are performing below expectations can be analyzed to identify problems and potential solutions.

profit center An organizational unit in which a manager has control over and is held accountable for both cost and revenue performance.

profit graph A graph that shows how profits vary with changes in volume.

profit margin (operating performance) ratio An overall measure of the profitability of operations during a period; computed by dividing net income by revenue.

profitability index The present value of net cash inflows divided by the cost of an investment.

purchases budget A schedule of projected purchases over the budget period.

ranking The ordering of acceptable investment alternatives from most to least desirable.

raw materials inventory The inventory of raw materials that have not yet begun the production process.

regression line On a scattergraph, the straight line that most closely expresses the relationship between the variables.

relevant range The range of operating level, or volume of activity, over which the relationship between total costs (variable plus fixed) and activity level is approximately linear.

reorder point The point at which the inventory level in the organization drops low enough to trigger a new purchase order.

residual income The amount of net income earned above a specified minimum rate of return on assets; used to evaluate investment centers.

responsibility accounting A system of evaluating performance; managers are held accountable for the costs, revenues, assets, or other elements over which they have control.

responsibility center An organizational unit in which a manager has control over and is held accountable for performance.

retailers Second-tier merchants who typically purchase products from wholesalers to distribute to end-user customers. Many large retailers, however, often bypass wholesalers to purchase products directly from the original manufacturers.

return on investment (ROI) A measure of operating performance and efficiency in utilizing assets; computed in its simplest form by dividing net income by average total assets. This measure is also known as ROA (return on assets).

return on sales revenue A measure of operating performance; computed by dividing net income by total sales revenue. Similar to profit margin.

revenue budget A service entity's budget that identifies how much revenue (and often cash) will be generated during a period.

robust quality The capability of a product to perform according to customer expectations regardless of surroundings and circumstances.

safety stock The minimal level of inventory required to ensure against the organization running out of inventory in the case of unforeseen problems in receiving its next purchase order.

sales budget A schedule of projected sales over the budget period.

sales mix The relative proportion of total units sold (or total sales dollars) that is represented by each of a company's products.

sales price variance The difference between the actual price and expected or standard price multiplied by the actual quantity sold; measures that part of the variance between expected and actual sales revenue that is due to differences between expected and actual prices of goods.

sales volume variance The difference between the actual quantity and the expected quantity sold multiplied by the expected or standard price; mea-

sures that part of the variance between expected and actual sales revenue that is due to the difference between expected and actual volume of goods sold.

scattergraph (visual-fit) method A method of segregating the fixed and variable components of a mixed cost by plotting on a graph total costs at several activity levels and drawing a regression line through the points.

screening Determining whether a capital investment meets a minimum standard of financial acceptability.

segment Any part of an organization requiring separate reports for evaluation by management.

segment margins The difference between segment revenue and direct segment costs; a measure of the segment's contribution to cover indirect fixed costs and provide profits.

segment-margin income statement An income statement that identifies costs directly chargeable to a segment and further divides them into variable and fixed cost behavior patterns.

segment-margin ratios The segment margin divided by the segment's net sales revenue; a measure of the efficiency of the segment's operating performance and, therefore, of its profitability.

selling and administrative expense budget A schedule of all nonproduction spending expected to occur during the budget period.

sensitivity analysis A method of assessing the reasonableness of a decision that was based upon estimates; involves calculating how far reality can differ from an estimate without invalidating the decision.

service organizations Organizations that focus on delivery of marketable services, such as legal advice or education, to individuals or other organizations.

service overhead budget The budget, prepared by service entities, that identifies projected costs associated with providing the service.

six sigma quality A measure of quality based on statistical analysis. Products or services with six sigma quality have no more than 3.4 defects per million opportunities (e.g., parts or events).

special order An order that may be priced below the normal selling price in order to utilize excess capacity and thereby contribute to company profits.

standard cost cards An itemization of the components of a product's standard cost.

standard cost system A cost-accumulation system in which standard costs are used as product costs instead of actual costs. The standard costs are then adjusted to actual costs when financial reports are created. This adjustment creates variances that are reported to management.

static budget A quantified plan that projects revenues and costs for only one level of activity.

statistical process control (SPC) A statistical technique for identifying and measuring the quality status of a process by evaluating its output to determine if serious problems exist in the process.

stepped costs Costs that change in total in a stair-step fashion (in large amounts) with changes in volume of activity.

strategic planning Broad, long-range planning usually conducted by top management.

sunk costs Costs, such as depreciation, that are past costs and do not change as a result of a future decision.

supplies budget The budget, prepared by service entities, that identifies projected supplies expenses over the budget period.

Taguchi quality loss function A method developed by Genichi Taguchi for estimating the actual size of all external failure costs, particularly the opportunity costs of lost customer sales that result from dissatisfied customers.

target income A profit level desired by management.

theory of constraints (TOC) A management philosophy that focuses on constraint resources and holds that they should operate at full capacity.

total cost The total variable and fixed costs incurred in making a product or providing a service.

total quality management (TQM) A management philosophy focused on increasing profitability by improving the quality of products and processes and increasing customer satisfaction, while promoting the well-being and growth of employees.

unadjusted rate of return method A capital budgeting technique in which a rate of return is calculated by dividing the increase in the average annual net income a project will generate by the initial investment cost.

underapplied manufacturing overhead The excess of actual manufacturing overhead costs over the applied overhead costs for a period (based on a predetermined application rate).

unit-based costing (UBC) The traditional method of allocating manufacturing overhead using an approach that is essentially based on the number of units produced.

unit-level activities Activities that take place each time a unit of product is produced.

value-added activities Necessary activities in a production or service process that customers identify as valuable and for which they are willing to pay.

variable cost rate The change in cost divided by the change in activity; the slope of the regression line.

variable costs Costs that change in total in direct proportion to changes in activity level.

variable manufacturing overhead efficiency variance The difference between the standard variable manufacturing overhead for the actual activity level and standard variable manufacturing overhead for the standard activity level allowed. This variance effectively measures the efficiency of the underlying activity used to assign variable manufacturing overhead costs; it does not measure the efficiency of how variable manufacturing overhead costs are used.

variable manufacturing overhead spending variance The difference between actual variable manufacturing overhead incurred and the amount that should have been incurred based on the actual activity used to assign overhead costs to production.

variance Any deviation from standard.

volume variance The difference between actual production output and the expected (or budgeted) production output established at the beginning of the reporting period. This difference is then converted into a dollar number by multiplying it by the standard fixed manufacturing overhead costs per unit.

wages and salaries budget The budget, prepared by service entities, that identifies projected labor costs involved directly in providing the service over the budget period.

wholesalers Top-tier merchants who typically deal directly with the original manufacturers to distribute products to retailers.

work-in-process inventory Inventory that is partly completed in the production process, but not yet ready for sale to customers.

CHAPTER I

Exercises

1-2   N/A
1-4   N/A
1-6   N/A
1-8   N/A
1-10   200 baby chairs
1-12   (1) 113,696 gallons (rounded up)
1-14   (1) Variable costs = $11.80 per bat
1-16   (1) Segment profit for RX-5 = $18,840
1-18   (1) Segment profit = $4,350,000

CHAPTER 2

Exercises

2-2   (1) $2,000 per boat
2-4   (2) $2.50 per unit
2-6   (1) Total variable costs = $22,500 at 750,000 copies
2-8   (1) Profit = $17
2-10   (1) Contribution margin = $360,000
2-12   (1) (b) 15,000 units
2-14   (3) Approximate answers (based on graph) fixed costs $15,000; variable costs $12,000; profits $3,000
2-16   N/A
2-18   (2) Profit = $267,000
2-20   (1) Variable cost per unit = $1.39
2-22   (1) Break-even point in units = 20,000

Problems

2-2   (1) Variable cost = $4 per unit
2-4   (1) Profit = $36,900
2-6   (3) 7,560 units
2-8   (1) Contribution margin ratio = 25%
2-10   (1) (e) Total variable costs per unit = $12.50
2-12   (2) Break-even sales = $93,771
2-14   (1) Profit = $310,000
2-16   Fixed cost = $70,966.36
2-18   (1) Break-even point in sales dollars = $432,000

CHAPTER 3

Exercises

3-2   (1) Predetermined manufacturing overhead rate = $5
3-4   (1) (c) Predetermined overhead rate = $1.30/hr for 2005 and $1.29/hr for 2006
3-6   N/A

3-8   (2) Overhead is underapplied by $2,750
3-10   (2) Total manufacturing overhead in Job #402X = $5,654
3-12   (1) Total manufacturing costs = $193,000
3-14   (1) Overhead rate = $81.82 per direct labor hour
3-16   (1) (b) 2005: $3,000 per moving job; 2006: $3,871 per moving job (rounded)
3-18   (1) Overhead rate = $41.33 per consulting hour
3-20   (1) Equivalent units of production: 610 for materials costs; 582 for conversion costs

Problems

3-2   N/A
3-4   (1) Predetermined overhead rate = $4 per direct labor hour
3-6   (2) Manufacturing overhead charged to Job #29 = $7,191
3-8   (1) (c) Total cost per chair = $190.10
3-10   Total manufacturing costs = $594,500
3-12   (1) (b) Cost of goods manufactured = $700,000
3-14   N/A
3-16   N/A
3-18   (3) Total costs transferred out = $108,760
3-20   Cost of ending work-in-process = $19,180

CHAPTER 4

Exercises

4-2   (1) Present value = $293,372 (rounded)
4-4   Unadjusted rate of return = 22.5%
4-6   Net present value of fire safety expert = $86,024 (rounded)
4-8   Cost of capital = 16.7%
4-10   (1) Present value of future cash inflow (20 years) = $599,189 (rounded)
4-12   N/A
4-14   N/A
4-16   Investment A's profitability index = 1.05

Problems

4-2   Net present value = $12,060 (rounded)
4-4   (1) Internal rate of return = 10.55% (rounded)
4-6   Internal rate of return is approximately 18%
4-8   Net present value of Alternative A (Buy) = $(35,102) (rounded)
4-10   (1) Net present value to rent = $308,174 (rounded)
4-12   (2) Net present value = $380

*Note: Check figures are provided for even-numbered exercises and problems, where applicable.

4-14   (1) Net present value and profitability index of Project A: $4,000 and 1.20
4-16   (1) Payback period = 5.2 years
4-18   (1) Net present value at 12% cost of capital = $(7,523)

CHAPTER 5

Exercises

5-2   (1) Salary available for savings = $551
5-4   First quarter budgeted production: CD player = 149; MP3 player = 103
5-6   Total cost of materials used = $15,050
5-8   Total direct labor cost in February = $4,120
5-10   Q1 payments for production overhead = $4,300
5-12   (2) Total revenue = $313,200
5-14   Required financing = $10,430
5-16   Net income = $110,550
5-18   Net increase in cash = $440
5-20   (2) Budgeted wage expense = $169,650

Problems

5-2   (2) 34 months (rounded)
5-4   (2) Third Quarter Collections = $172,500
5-6   Total direct materials purchase = $4,028
5-8   (1) Chocolate almond bars total unit cost = $15.83
5-10   (4) Total MOH costs = $5,577
5-12   (1) Total revenue = $1,655,900
5-14   December excess cash = $87,000
5-16   (2) Total assets = $3,900,000
5-18   Net cash provided by operating activities = $82,300
5-20   (1) Expected annual income for 20 enrollees = $19,500

CHAPTER 6

Exercises

6-2   (1) Materials price variance = $250 U
6-4   N/A
6-6   (1) Materials quantity variance = $12,500 U
6-8   (2) Labor rate variance = $5,760 U
6-10   (1) Labor efficiency variance = $81,250 U
6-12   (d) Standard labor cost per hour = $4.20
6-14   (1) North segment margin = $10,500
6-16   (2) Shampoo industry volume variance = $4,800 U
6-18   (f) 25%
6-20   (1) Residual income of new investment = $2,000
6-22   (2) Volume variance = $90,000 U

Problems

6-2   (1) (c) Labor rate variance = $125 F
6-4   (e) $400 F
6-6   (1) Material B quantity variance = $65 U
6-8   (2) Pounds of material actually used = 11,200 lbs.
6-10   (1) Total net loss = $(122,500)
6-12   (2) Individuals market share variance = $8,625 U
6-14   (1) Electrical division ROI = 22.5%
6-16   (2) Total residual income with the new investment = $95,000
6-18   (p) $12,667
6-20   (2) Total ROI with the new investment = 15.8%
6-22   (1) June variable overhead efficiency variance = $3,300 F
6-24   (1) (a) Variable overhead spending variance = $1,000 F

CHAPTER 7

Exercises

7-2   (1) Inventory turnover = 2.44
7-4   N/A
7-6   (1) Penny's PPP = 52.6%
7-8   N/A
7-10   Annual financial holding costs = $7.80 per unit per year
7-12   Reorder point = 249 tires
7-14   (1) Reorder point = 2,500 boxes

Problems

7-2   Ride EZ net operation profit = $29,135
7-4   (2) Profitability percentage = 74.3%
7-6   (1) Division L economic profit = $387,900

CHAPTER 8

Exercises

8-2   N/A
8-4   (1) Product B gross margin = $(70,000)
8-6   (1) Standard gross margin = $180,000
8-8   (1) Product Z gross margin = $50,000
8-10   N/A
8-12   High Quality: Total expected cost of quality = $175,225
8-14   Total external failure quality loss = $15,700

Problems

8-2   (1) Agriculture gross margin = $150,000

8-4   (2) Gross margin = $(37,500)

8-6   (4) Total manufacturing overhead costs allocated to 70 hp engines = $111,962

8-8   (3) Product 1 gross margin percent = 24.2%

8-10   (3) Total manufacturing overhead costs allocated to Building Pipe = $227,040

8-12   (1) Total external failure quality loss = $21,600

CHAPTER 9

Exercises

9-2   (1) Total relevant costs of the new machine = $465,000

9-4   (1) Total variable costs = $34

9-6   (1) Cost difference between making or buying = $270,000

9-8   Expected benefit of Alternative 2 = $342,000

9-10   (1) Loss of S is processed further = $(10,000)

9-12   Product line contribution = $180,000

9-14   (2) Maximum production of Dynamite = 18,000 units

9-16   (2) Rudyard should produce 10 engines per month

Problems

9-2   (3) The total cost to buy is $1,600 lower than the total cost to make

9-4   (2) Total relevant costs to keep the internal legal department = $565,000

9-6   (1) Advantage of further processing S1 = $80,000

9-8   (2) Total net income without Product Z = $4,000

9-10   Contribution margin per direct labor hour for 24-inch screens = $2.40 per hour

9-12   Hours spent to produce Super Dunks = 500

9-14   Markup = $15.00

CHAPTER 10

Not Applicable

ABC. *See* Activity-based costing
ABM. *See* Activity-based management
Accounting
    and the "Shaq impact", 19
    for labor variances, 346
    for manufacturing overhead variances, 364
    for materials variances, 343
    for overhead, 130
    for revenue variances, 354
    for tomorrow, 592
    records, locating COQ in, 479
    management and financial, 4, 6
    responsibility, 334
    role of ethics in management, 23
Activities
    batch-level, 461, 462
    facility support, 463
    measuring level of, 46
    non-value-added, 422
    product line, 462
    unit-level, 460
    value-added, 422
Activity-based and unit-based costs in a manufacturing organization, relationship between, illus., 461
Activity-based costing (ABC)
    analysis of operating results, illus., 470
    def., 120, 453
    hierarchical product cost model, 457
    illus., 464
    provides legal defense, 467
Activity-based management (ABM), 469
    def., 472
    illus., 472
Administrative expense budget, selling and, 278
American Institute of Certified Public Accountants (AICPA), 592
Amount of $1 due in n periods (Table III), 233
Amount of an annuity of $1 per number of payments (Table IV), 234
Analytical Perspectives, 201
Annuity of $1 per number of payments
    amount of, (Table IV), 234
    present value of, (Table II), 232
Annuity, present value of, 227
Appraisal costs, def., 477
Asset turnover ratio, def., 356
Audit firm, cost management in, 417
Automobile manufacturers: make or buy, 531

Balance sheet, illus, 264
Balanced scorecard, 588
    and the government, 578
    code red, 582
    def., 574
    framework, illus., 575
    illus., 589
    performance measurement linkages in, illus., 587
    Wendy's, 591
Batch-level activities, 461
    def., 462
Behavioral considerations, 261
Benchmarking, 73
    def., 519
Billing rates and job cost charges, illus., 418
Break-even point, def., 61
Budget
    cash, 281
    committee, def., 260
    def., 256
    direct labor, 268
    direct materials, 266
    flexible, 288
    manufacturing overhead, 269
    master, 258, 262
        illus., 263
    (monthly), illus., 257
    production, 266
    purchases, 273
    revenue, 275
    sales, 264
    selling and administrative expense, 271, 278
    service overhead, 277
    static, 287
    supplies, 277
    top-down versus bottom-up, 261
    U.S. federal government estimated annual, illus., 256
    using flexible, 289
    wages and salaries, 277
Budgetary slack, def., 261
Budgeted product cost sheet, def., 270
Budgeted service cost sheet, def., 278
Budgeting
    capital, 7, 199
    conceptual basis of capital, 200
    for long-term company and shareholder value, 287
    in merchandising and service firms, 272
    operational, 9

    participative, 261
    process, 260
    purposes of, 256
    static versus flexible, 287
    types and purposes of, 258
    weaknesses in static, 288
Budgeting for operations
    manufacturing firm, 262
    merchandising firm, 272
    service firm, 275
Business, steely-eyed tycoon, 13
Business-to-business (B2B), 148
Business-to-consumer (B2C), 147

Capability costs, def., 463
Capital
    cost of, 207, 424
    def., 200
Capital budgeting
    conceptual basis of, 200
    decision rules, illus., 221
    decisions, income tax considerations in, 221
    def., 7., 199
    income tax effects of, illus., 223
    uses of, 201
Capital budgeting techniques
    comparative example of, 214
    discounted, 207
    nondiscounted, 204
Capital investment decisions
    dealing with uncertainty in, 217
    ethics in, 216
    in planning, 200
    qualitative factors in strategic and, 215
Capital rationing, def., 219
Cash balance and cash needs, typical relationship between, illus., 283
Cash budget, def., 281
Cash flow methods, discounted, 204
Cash flows
    discounting, 202
    if expected are uncertain, 218
    problem of uneven, 213
Cash inflows, def., 204
Cash outflows, def., 203
Centers
    controlling performance in profit, 340
    cost, 335
    investment, 335
    profit, 335
    responsibility, 335

p

Pampered Chef, 333
Paper Company, The, 111–112
Peoplesoft, 260
Petersen Pottery, 393–394
Polaroid, 258
Priceline.com, 527, 528, 530
PricewaterhouseCoopers, 505
Procter & Gamble, 399
Prodigy, 119

r

R. C. Willey Home Furnishings, 333
R. H. Macy & Company, Inc., 115
Rawlings Sporting Goods Company, 476, 481
Ritz-Carlton, 590
Rockwell International, 451

s

Safeway, 537
Sam's Clubs, 447
Sap, 260
Schwab, 537
Sears, Roebuck & Company, 13, 115, 272
SEE's Candies, 333
Shop 'N Save, 406
Shopko, 601
Southwest Airlines, 149, 521
SSM Health Care (SSMHC), 475
Star Furniture Company, 333

t

Target, 399
Texas Instruments, 476
3Com, 537
TIAA-CREF, 330
Toyota Motor Corporation, 38–39, 116, 330, 420, 421, 449, 578
Toyota Spinning and Weaving Company, 38

Toys "R" Us, Inc., 408, 409
TWA, 57

u

U.S. Air Force, 189
U.S. Postal Service, 578
U.S. West, 601
UAL, 258
Union Pacific Railroad, 13, 115
United Airlines, 57, 189, 258
United States Steel Corporation, 13
Unumprovident, 280
US Airways, 57, 258
USA Interactive, 537

v

Vanguard, 330
Visa, 275
Volkswagen, 330, 531

w

W. Edwards Deming Institute, 511
Wallace Company, 590
Wal-Mart, 115, 136, 149, 195, 200, 272, 399, 400, 446, 447, 601
WalMart.com, 147
Washington Post Company, The, 333.
Wells Fargo Company, 333, 521
Wendy's International, Inc., 591
Westinghouse, 590
William M. Mercer, Inc., 347
Winchell's, 45
Worldcom, 533
Wrigley, 273

x

Xerox, 476, 521